ENCYCLOPEDIA OF
ANTHROPOLOGY

# ENCYCLOPEDIA OF ANTHROPOLOGY

Edited by

**David E. Hunter**

*Southern Connecticut
State College*

**Phillip Whitten**

*Harvard University*

**Harper & Row, Publishers**

New York    Hagerstown
San Francisco    London

ENCYCLOPEDIA OF ANTHROPOLOGY

Library of Congress Cataloging in Publication Data

Main entry under title:

Encyclopedia of anthropology.

    1. Anthropology—Dictionaries.   I. Hunter, David E.   II. Whitten, Phillip.
GN11.E52       301.2'03       75—41386
ISBN 0–06–047094–1

**Produced by Ken Burke & Associates**
Text and cover designer: Christy Butterfield
Copyeditor: Don Yoder
Illustrator: Barbara Hack
Photo researcher: Audrey Ross
Compositor: Typothetae
Printer: Kingsport Press

## CREDITS

**Photographs**

Cover  Martin Etter, Anthro-Photo
1  Dimitri Kessel, Time-Life Picture Agency, © Time Inc.
2  Edward O. Henry
6  New Zealand Information Service
7  Richard Graber
8  Irven DeVore and William James, Anthro-Photo
10, 11  Wide World Photos
14  General Services Administration F. W., Black Star
15  Top: Wide World Photos   Bottom: G. D. Plage, Bruce Coleman, Inc.
18  Top: United Press International Photo   Bottom: Audrey Ross
19  Top: Toni Schneiders, Bruce Coleman, Inc. Bottom: Ken Heyman
20  Top: Louise and Walter Arensberg Collection, Philadelphia Museum of Art   Bottom: The Fine Arts Museums of San Francisco
21  Top: Lowie Museum of Anthropology, University of California, Berkeley Bottom: Asian Art Museum of San Francisco, The Avery Brundage Collection

22, 23   The Fine Arts Museums of San Francisco
24   Top: Audrey Ross   Bottom: The Fine Arts Museums of San Francisco
26   Top and bottom left: Philip J. C. Dark   Bottom right: The Fine Arts Museums of San Francisco
27   Top and bottom left: Lowie Museum of Anthropology, University of California, Berkeley   Bottom right: Asian Art Museum of San Francisco, The Avery Brundage Collection
28   (Both): Asian Art Museum of San Francisco, The Avery Brundage Collection
29, 30   (All), 31 Top: Photographs courtesy of Museum of the American Indian, Heye Foundation
31   Bottom, 33: The Fine Arts Museums of San Francisco
34, 35   (Both): Photographs courtesy of Museum of the American Indian, Heye Foundation
36, 37   Asian Art Museum of San Francisco, The Avery Brundage Collection
38   Top: Lowie Museum of Anthropology, University of California, Berkeley   Bottom (both): Asian Art Museum of San Francisco, The Avery Brundage Collection
39   (Both), 40, 41 (all), 42 (all): Photographs courtesy of Museum of the American Indian, Heye Foundation
43   Top: Portland Art Association   Bottom (both): Photographs courtesy of Museum of the American Indian, Heye Foundation
44   Photograph courtesy of Museum of the American Indian, Heye Foundation
45   New Zealand Information Service
46   Courtesy of The Museum of Primitive Art, New York
48   Courtesy of The American Museum of Natural History
52   Buddy Mays, Black Star
53   Courtesy of Peabody Museum of Salem, Massachusetts
54, 55   Photographs courtesy of Museum of the American Indian, Heye Foundation
56   Mel Konner, Anthro-Photo
57   Wide World Photos
62   The Bettmann Archive
63   Napoleon Chagnon, Anthro-Photo
65   Photograph courtesy of Museum of the American Indian, Heye Foundation
66   The Bettmann Archive
68   Top: J. M. Bishop, Bruce Coleman, Inc.   Bottom: Bruce Coleman, Inc.
69   Laurence Wylie, Anthro-Photo
71   Dr. Helmut Albrecht, Bruce Coleman, Inc.
72   Top: Courtesy of The American Museum of Natural History   Bottom: Tourist Information Center of Mexico
73   Elliott Erwitt, Magnum Photos, Inc.
75   Marc and Evelyne Bernheim, Woodfin Camp & Associates
76   Mike Youse, BBM Associates
78   George Rodger, Magnum Photos, Inc.
79   Courtesy of National Trust of Scotland
80   Anthony Leeds, Anthro-Photo
82   Rene Burri, Magnum Photos, Inc.
89   Catherine Noren, Magnum Photos, Inc.
92   The Australian News and Information Bureau
94   Courtesy of The American Museum of Natural History, restoration by Dr. J. H. McGregor
98   Richard B. Lee, Anthro-Photo
112   Top: Cornell Capa, Magnum Photos, Inc.   Bottom: The University Museum, Philadelphia
113   Napoleon Chagnon, Anthro-Photo
114   Richard B. Lee, Anthro-Photo
115   The Bettmann Archive
118   Ken Heyman
125   Wide World Photos
126   Photograph courtesy of Museum of the American Indian, Heye Foundation
127   David Maybury-Lewis, Anthro-Photo
128   Martie and Stewart Guthrie
133   (Both): Edward O. Henry
134   Edward O. Henry
135   Napoleon Chagnon, Anthro-Photo
136   The Bettmann Archive
138   Anthony Leeds
141   Martie and Stewart Guthrie
143   Press Information Bureau, Government of India
144   The Bettmann Archive
145   United Press International Photo
151   Yves De Braine, Black Star
160   The Society of Antiquaries of London
163   Richard Harrington, Camera Press Ltd., London
164   Top: Library of Congress   Bottom: Irven DeVore, Anthro-Photo
168   Colin Turnbull
169, 170   Napoleon Chagnon, Anthro-Photo
171   Irven DeVore, Anthro-Photo
172   John R. Brownlie, Photo Researchers, Inc.
179   The Bettmann Archive
180   Culver Pictures
183   David Maybury-Lewis, Anthro-Photo
191   Austin Post, U.S. Geological Service
196   Leanne T. NASH
199   Leopold Pospisil
201   Hirmer Fotoarchiv München
207   Service Info Sénégal and La Documentation Française, Paris
208   (Both), 208 Left: Anthony Leeds
209   Right: Marc Riboud, Magnum Photos, Inc.
210   Ken Heyman
213   Hirmer Fotoarchiv München
215   Sergio Larrain, Magnum Photos, Inc.
216   United Press International Photo
220   Richard W. Franke
221   (Both): Photographs courtesy of Museum of the American Indian, Heye Foundation
224   E. Hosking, Bruce Coleman, Inc.
225   Leonard Freed, Magnum Photos, Inc.
231   Wide World Photos
245   Top: The Bettmann Archive   Bottom: Tony Howarth, Woodfin Camp & Associates
246   Henri Cartier-Bresson, Magnum Photos, Inc.
251   Wide World Photos
253   The Bettmann Archive
256   Irven DeVore, Anthro-Photo
257   Top: Edward C. Green   Bottom: Edward O. Henry
258   Culver Pictures
260   (Both): Photographs courtesy of Museum of the American Indian, Heye Foundation
261   Edward O. Henry
262   Peter Menzel, Stock, Boston
263   Culver Pictures
265   Ken Heyman
267   Photograph courtesy of Museum of the American Indian, Heye Foundation
270   National Museums of Canada
272   Marc and Evelyne Bernheim, Woodfin Camp & Associates
276   Photograph courtesy of Museum of the American Indian, Heye Foundation
277   George Peter Murdock
278   Top: Irven DeVore, Anthro-Photo   Bottom: Edward O. Henry
280   The Bettmann Archive
282   Top: Ralph S. Solecki   Bottom: Wide World Photos
290   United Press International Photo
295   Irven DeVore, Anthro-Photo
296   Bill Owens
297   Laurence Wylie, Anthro-Photo
306   Laurence Wylie, Anthro-Photo
307   Richard B. Lee, Anthro-Photo
310   Irven DeVore, Anthro-Photo
311   National Museums of Canada
312   Top: Photograph courtesy of Museum of the American Indian, Heye Foundation   Bottom left: Field Museum of Natural History, Maude Wahlman   Bottom right: Wide World Photos
313   Rosemarie Greiner
314   Photograph courtesy of Museum of the American Indian, Heye Foundation
315   Top: Photograph courtesy of Museum of the American Indian, Heye Foundation   Bottom: Steve Gaulin, Anthro-Photo
317   Edward O. Henry
319   Russell A. Mittermeier, Anthro-Photo

324   Laurence Wylie, Anthro-Photo
331   United Press International Photo
336   Top: Burk Uzzle, Magnum Photos, Inc. Bottom left: David-Maybury Lewis, Anthro-Photo Bottom right: Fritz Goro, Time-Life Picture Agency, © Time, Inc.
337   Top: Martin Etter, Anthro-Photo Bottom: Emil Schultess, Black Star
338   Culver Pictures
339   Top: Ian Berry, Magnum Photos, Inc. Bottom: Pitt Rivers Museum, University of Oxford
341   Dennis Stock, Magnum Photos, Inc.
344   Constantine Manos, Magnum Photos, Inc.
346   Bill Owens
347   Left: Anthony Leeds Right: Edward O. Henry
348   Top: Richard B. Lee, Anthro-Photo Bottom: Colin Turnbull
349   Leanne T. Nash
350   Ruth and Hassoldt Davis, Rapho/Photo Researchers, Inc.
351   Irven DeVore, Anthro-Photo
352   Irven DeVore, Anthro-Photo
353   Top: Laurence Wylie, Anthro-Photo Bottom: Anthony Leeds
355   Top: Photograph courtesy of Museum of the American Indian, Heye Foundation Bottom: United Press International Photo
364   The Bettmann Archive
365   Photograph courtesy of the Museum of the American Indian, Heye Foundation
370   Rod Allin, Bruce Coleman, Inc.
371   Charles Gatewood, Magnum Photos, Inc.
374   Leanne T. Nash
377   David Maybury-Lewis, Anthro-Photo
378   Edward O. Henry
381   Cornell Capa, Magnum Photos, Inc.
384   Jan Lukas, Black Star
385   Edward O. Henry
388   Constantine Manos, Magnum Photo, Inc.
390   Top: Photograph courtesy of Museum of the American Indian, Heye Foundation Bottom left: Charles May, Black Star Bottom right: Audrey Ross
391   Rosemarie Greiner
392   Marjorie Shostak, Anthro-Photo
394   Photograph courtesy of Museum of the American Indian, Heye Foundation
399   Naturhistorisches Museum, Vienna
402   Top: Rosemarie Greiner Bottom: Library of Congress
403   Russell Mittermeier, Anthro-Photo
404   Library of Congress
406   Courtesy of The American Museum of Natural History
407   Cary Wolinsky, Stock, Boston
410   Hiroshi Hanaya, Magnum Photos, Inc.
411   Wide World Photos

**Line Drawings**

9   From Jack R. Harlan, "Agricultural Origins: Centers and Noncenters," *Science*, Vol. 174, October 29, 1971, p. 472. Reprinted by permission.
49   Reprinted by permission of Bernard C. Campbell, *Human Evolution* (Chicago: Aldine Publishing Company); copyright © 1966, 1974 by Bernard C. Campbell.
60   Modified from Dr. A. L. Zihlman's drawing, 1967. Used with permission of Dr. A. L. Zihlman.
71   Reprinted by permission from H. L. Movius, "The Lower Paleolithic Cultures of Southern and Eastern Asia," *Transactions of the American Philosophical Society*, Vol. 38, Pt. 4 (1948).
120   Adapted from F. E. Zeuner, *Dating the Past* (London: Methuen and Company, Ltd.), 1950, p. 10.
129   Reprinted with permission of the publisher, from "Sex Differences and Cultural Institutions," by Ray D'Andrade, in *The Development of Sex Differences*, edited by Eleanor Maccoby (Stanford University Press, 1966), Tables 1 and 2, pp. 177–178. Adapted from G. P. Murdock's "Comparative Data on the Division of Labor by Sex," *Social Forces*, Vol. 15, pp. 551–553, 1937.
131   From Marvin Harris, *Culture, People, Nature*, 2nd edition, 1975. Copyright © 1975 by Dun-Donnelley Publishing Corp. Reprinted by permission.
185   From *Introduction to Anthropology* by Roger Pearson. Copyright © 1974 by Holt, Rinehart, and Winston. All rights reserved.
192   From *Glacial and Quaternary Geology* by Richard Foster Flint. Copyright © 1971 by John Wiley & Sons, Inc. Reprinted by permission of John Wiley & Sons, Inc.
198   From *The Hunting Peoples* by Carleton S. Coon. Copyright © 1971 by Carleton S. Coon. Reprinted by permission of Little, Brown and Company.
232   From *An Introduction to Social and Cultural Anthropology* by Peter B. Hammond. Copyright © 1971 by Macmillan Publishing Co. Reprinted by permission of the publisher.
236   From "The Origins of Speech" by Charles F. Hockett in *Scientific American*, copyright © 1960 by Scientific American, Inc. All rights reserved. Reprinted by permission of W. H. Freeman and Company for Scientific American, Inc.
239   Compiled by Dr. Sidney S. Culbert, University of Washington. Reprinted by permission of *The World Almanac*, 1975. Copyright © 1974 by Newspaper Enterprise Association.

240–241   From *Atlas for Anthropology* by Robert F. Spencer and Elden Johnson. Copyright © 1960 by Robert F. Spencer and Elden Johnson. Reprinted with permission.
248   A revision and expansion of Figure 1 in Chad Gordon's "Role and Value Development Across the Life Cycle," in John Jackson (ed.), *Sociological Studies, IV: Role*. London: Cambridge University Press, 1971, pp. 65–105. Reprinted by permission of Chad Gordon.
293   From "Radiocarbon Dating by Edward S. Deevey, Jr.," *Scientific American*, February 1952. Copyright © 1952 by Scientific American, Inc. All rights reserved. Reprinted by permission of W. H. Freeman and Company for Scientific American, Inc.
295   From *Introduction to Anthropology* by Roger Pearson. Copyright © 1974 by Holt, Rinehart, and Winston. All rights reserved.
301   From *On the Origins of Language* by Philip Lieberman. Copyright © 1975 by Macmillan Publishing Co., Inc. Reprinted by permission.
308   From *Glacial and Quaternary Geology* by Richard Foster Flint. Copyright © 1971 by John Wiley & Sons, Inc. Reprinted by permission of John Wiley & Sons, Inc.
327   From Stanley Garn, *Human Races*, 1962. Courtesy of Charles C. Thomas, publisher, Springfield, Illinois.
329   From "New Configurations in Old World Archaeology," *World Archaeology*, Vol. 2, No. 2, p. 200. Reprinted by permission of Colin Renfrew.
330   From *Proceedings of the National Academy of Sciences*.
333   From *Religion: An Anthropological View* by Anthony F. C. Wallace. Copyright 1966 by Random House, Inc. Reprinted by permission of Random House, Inc.
372   From *Man the Tool Maker* by Kenneth Page Oakley, 1963. Reprinted by permission of British Museum (Natural History).
383   From *Culture, People, Nature* by Marvin Harris. Copyright © 1971, 1975 by Thomas Y. Crowell Co., Inc. Reprinted with permission from the publisher.
396   Photo and drawing courtesy of Alexander Marshack.
408–409   From "The Sumerians" by Samuel Noah Kramer, *Scientific American*, October 1957. Copyright © 1957 by Scientific American, Inc. All rights reserved. Reprinted by permission of W. H. Freeman and Company for Scientific American, Inc.

**To Gayle**

*with love and appreciation*

# PREFACE

There is, perhaps, no academic discipline of more inherent interest to people than anthropology. Anthropology is, after all, the study of humanity—its physical evolution, its varied cultures, its languages.

Much of what anthropologists study is familiar to most people, and much of the language used to describe what is studied is familiar. But, in order to permit accurate, unambiguous communication, anthropologists not only have devised a number of technical terms and names to describe artifacts and phenomena, but also have invested common words with precise anthropological meanings. In studying anthropology, therefore, it is important to have clear and precise definitions of terms—to understand the language of anthropology.

The *Encyclopedia of Anthropology* is an attempt to fill an important need—the need for a compact, comprehensive, accessible reference work devoted to the field of anthropology. The book deals not only with the concepts and language of anthropology, but with its theories and leading figures (both historical and contemporary) as well. In addition there are several hundred articles covering theories, concepts, research findings, and personalities in related fields such as linguistics, psychology, and sociology.

The *Encyclopedia of Anthropology* is arranged alphabetically and contains approximately 1,400 articles ranging in length from 25 to 3,000 words. The articles are integrated with each other with a comprehensive system of two kinds of cross references: *See* references—which appear in alphabetical sequence as individual entries and which direct you to the information you need; and *See also* references—which direct you to other related articles. In addition, at the end of all but the shortest articles, is a bibliography listing important books and articles on the subject.

The *Encyclopedia of Anthropology* was written by almost one hundred contributors—anthropologists as well as sociologists, psychologists, biologists, and population geneticists—each writing in his or her own speciality. Many of the contributors are well-known authorities who have made important professional contributions in their areas of expertise.

In addition, four academic advisors—James Clifton, Philip J. C. Dark, MaryAnn B. Foley, and Anthony Leeds—helped us in preparing and reviewing the list of entries for the book. The book is immeasurably better because of their participation, for which we are profoundly grateful.

The encyclopedia could not have been completed without the help of some very fine typists—George Beck, Ronna Greif, Bev Hower, Wendy Isaacson, Barbie Morin, and Renée Rausch. Leslie Palmer deserves special mention, not only for her typing but for her very competent assistance in handling the thousand-and-one administrative details that were a necessary part of producing this book.

Finally, there are two people to whom we owe a very special debt of gratitude: Gayle Johnson, whose technical expertise helped us avoid numerous problems and potential pitfalls; and Bill Eastman, editorial director at Harper & Row and our editor on this project, who was as encouraging and helpful as it is humanly possible to be.

*David E. Hunter*
*Phillip Whitten*

## READERS' RESPONSE

This encyclopedia is an attempt to provide accurate, useful information to students and instructors of anthropology. We view the task as a constant one—one that has only begun. Indeed, plans for the revision of the book are already under way. One source of information that will help us in making future editions of this book even more accurate and useful is *you*. We would like to know your opinion of the book: what you liked and didn't like, what was missing in the book, and what might be done in the next edition to improve it. Please take a few minutes to fill out the "Reader Evaluation Questionnaire" at the end of the book and drop it in the mail to us. Thank you.

## Editors

David E. Hunter, Southern Connecticut State College
Phillip Whitten, Harvard University

## Academic Advisors

James A. Clifton, University of Wisconsin, Green Bay
Philip J. C. Dark, Southern Illinois University
MaryAnn B. Foley, Southern Connecticut State College
Anthony Leeds, Boston University

## Contributors

Dean E. Arnold, Wheaton College
Don Bahr, Arizona State University
Richard Barrett, University of New Mexico
James M. Bellis, University of Oregon
Daniel P. Biebuyck, University of Delaware
Beatrice A. Bigony, University of Wisconsin, Stout
Maurice Bloch, London School of Economics
Stanley H. Brandes, University of California, Berkeley
Elizabeth A. Brandt, Arizona State University
Roland A. Brooks, University of California, Berkeley
Patricia Eyring Brown, Arizona State University
Geoffrey A. Clark, Arizona State University
James A. Clifton, University of Wisconsin, Green Bay
John R. Cole, Hartwick College
Linda S. Cordell, University of New Mexico
Justine M. Cordwell, Chicago City Colleges/Malcolm X
Philip J. C. Dark, Southern Illinois University
Frederick J. Dockstader, Director, Museum of the American Indian
Alan Dundes, University of California, Berkeley
Art Einhorn, Jefferson Community College
Edwin E. Erickson, University of Virginia
Pell Fender
Shirley Fiske, University of Southern California
MaryAnn B. Foley, Southern Connecticut State College
Roland W. Force, Director, Bernice P. Bishop Museum
William H. Gilbert, United States Library of Congress (ret.)
Nelson H. H. Graburn, University of California, Berkeley
Edward C. Green, University of Kentucky

Suzanne Reber Griffin, Catholic University
Stewart E. Guthrie, University of Rhode Island
Charles B. Heiser, Indiana University
Jeanne Henderson, Cornell University
John S. Henderson, Cornell University
Edward O. Henry, San Diego State University
Regina E. Holloman, Roosevelt University
James Howe, Massachusetts Institute of Technology
David E. Hunter, Southern Connecticut State College
Judith T. Irvine, Brandeis University
Shien-Min Jen, California State University, Fresno
Adrienne L. Kaeppler, Bernice P. Bishop Museum
Phillip S. Katz, State University of New York, Brockport
Michael Kenny, University of Mexico
Evelyn S. Kessler, University of South Florida
Klaus-Friedrich Koch, University of Virginia
Anthony Kroch, Temple University
Anthony Leeds, Boston University
John R. Lombardi, Boston University
George R. Mead, Eastern Oregon State College
James Metress, University of Toledo
Mary Jane Moore, San Diego State University
Thomas P. Myers, University of Nebraska
Leanne T. Nash, Arizona State University
Martin K. Nickels, Illinois State University
Michael D. Olien, University of Georgia
Bruno Pajaczkowski, Cambridge University
William L. Partridge, University of Southern California
Lilah Pengra, Kenyon College
Barbara Pillsbury, San Diego State University
Amos Rapoport, University of Wisconsin, Milwaukee
Catherine E. Read-Martin, California State University, Los Angeles
Stanley Rhine, University of New Mexico
Ian Robertson, Cambridge University
Bettina H. Rosenberg, Arizona State University
Roy Rosenblatt, University of Massachusetts
Ino Rossi, St. John's University
Joseph S. Roucek, City University of New York (ret.)
Eugene E. Ruyle, University of Virginia
Frank Salamone, St. John's University
Emily J. Sano, Vassar College
Seth Schindler, Southern Illinois University
Henry F. Schwarz, Ohio State University
M. Nazif Shahrani, University of Washington
Charles T. Snow, California State University, Chico
Ralph S. Solecki, Columbia University
John D. Speth, Hunter College
Richard L. Stone, California State University, Los Angeles
Alan C. Swedlund, University of Massachusetts
Maude Wahlman, Field Museum of Natural History
R. Linda Wheeler, Arizona State University
Norman E. Whitten, Jr., University of Illinois
Phillip Whitten, Harvard University
Stanley Wilk, Lycoming College
J. Raymond Williams, University of South Florida
Paul C. Winther, Eastern Kentucky University
Cathie J. Witty, University of Washington
Daniel Wolfman, Arkansas Archaeological Survey
Marianne Wolfman

# ENCYCLOPEDIA OF ANTHROPOLOGY

**Abbevillian Culture.** *See* Chellean culture.

**Aberle, David Friend** (b. 1918). Cultural anthropologist known for his work on nativistic movements, especially peyotism, and on social structure. Aberle's ethnographic interests have focused primarily on the Navajo.

**Abnormality.** *See* Deviance; Normality.

**Abortion.** *See* Contraception and abortion.

**Absolute Dating.** *See* Dating, absolute.

**Acculturation.** This term is defined as one kind of cultural change, specifically the processes and events which come from the conjunction of two or more formerly separate and autonomous cultures. The terms *culture contact* and *transculturation* are synonyms for acculturation. Transculturation was coined to stress the now accepted fact that acculturation is a two-way process: all cultures involved are affected. Generally, anthropologists have elected to study only the impact of acculturation on the smaller, less powerful, or subordinate participants in the contact situation. Yet the growth of a colonial nation is partly the result of specific contacts with other cultures. The development of New France in the 17th century, for ex-

*Acculturation: Arabs take up the great American pastime.*

ample, was substantially dependent on acculturative contacts with American Indian tribes.

*Conjunctive relations* has a special meaning with reference to the nature of the contact situation. There may or may not be direct, face-to-face contact between the people involved. Mutual language learning may or may not occur. A third language may be used, or a new trade jargon developed. But such direct contacts may be few, brief, or even absent. One culture may influence another through a middle group, for example.

Similarly, *autonomy* has a special meaning. This term refers to the absence of prior contact between cultures. Obviously, autonomy is a relative matter, especially so in an increasingly interdependent world.

To understand the processes and results of culture contacts, the first important task is to characterize the cultures as they were before the contact. This baseline description is essential for two reasons. First, it eliminates the error of confusing a practice which existed prior to contact with one which is a result of the contact. Second, some charac-

*This "English band"—derived from the British military band—is entertaining at a Muslim wedding in a village in northern India near Varanasi. Bands such as this one play* ragas *(Hindustani classical music), Western folk and popular songs, and Indian folk and film songs.*

teristics of a sociocultural system are especially influential in determining the outcome of a contact situation. For example, some cultures are relatively flexible and open to new cultural elements, while others maintain rigid boundaries which control and limit the flow of new ideas. Religious enclaves such as Hutterite communities, for instance, can only persist by limiting and controlling the flow of new practices into a community. On the other hand, the rigid controls exercised by some Pueblo Indian communities seem to have developed as a consequence of contact with Spanish and other societies.

Similarly, some cultures are much more integrated and balanced than others, and this may affect what happens in the contact situation. Great rigidity combined with a high order of integration may spell disaster for some societies in acculturation situations. For example, the Huron Indian tribes

on the Ontario peninsula collapsed in a very few years under the pressure of invasions from the Iroquois of New York State. Here a whole cultural system disintegrated, and nearly the entire population disappeared.

To understand the processes of acculturation it is also important to know the nature of the contact situation proper. In this connection, the ecological adaptations of the cultures in contact are crucial variables; two cultures may have quite different adaptations to the same environment (e. g., agricultural versus hunting). Also important in the contact situation are the exact demographic characteristics of the populations in contact. Rarely does the whole population in one society come into contact with that of another. Sometimes only a few contact agents are involved—missionaries or traders, for example. Sometimes only one sex is involved, as in the instance of the traders and trappers from New France who lived with the tribes in the interior of North America.

Once the representatives of the cultures come into contact, a specialized intercultural role network becomes established. This role network then influences the amount, kind, direction, and impact of the communications which flow between the cultures.

The results of such intercultural communication are of several kinds. One basic process is diffusion, the transfer of cultural elements from one society to another. Some degree of reinterpretation and change in the elements invariably accompanies such diffusion. Moreover, the contact situation generally stimulates the innovation of new ideas, practices, techniques, and roles. In this fashion, acculturation may involve an active, creative, culture-building process. Such creative reinterpretation and combination are sometimes known as syncretisms. Often, however, the acquisition of new cultural elements has dysfunctional or disintegrative consequences. This is particularly true in situations of directed or forced acculturation, where one group exercises dominion over another, and forcibly changes the ways of the subordinate culture in directions thought desirable by the dominant group. In such circumstances, when the members of a subordinate group perceive that the contact situation is a threat to the persistence of their culture, they may attempt to withdraw from the contact or erect social barriers to slow down change.

Long and continued acculturation may involve the fusion of two formerly autonomous cultures—particularly when both occupy one ecological zone. The result in this case is the development of an entirely new cultural system. Sometimes several cultures work out a mutual accommodation in one area, perhaps in an asymmetric, symbiotic relationship which allows each to persist in its distinctive ways. Such an outcome is known as stabilized *pluralism*. Sometimes the representatives of one culture may come to identify themselves with another system, with extensive change in their internal values and world views. If they are fully accepted into the other culture, the outcome is assimilation. Anthropologists and sociologists have often confused acculturation with assimilation, or assumed that assimilation is the sole consequence of culture contact. It is now recognized that the two are quite different processes and that other consequences such as pluralism and fusion often result from acculturation.

*See also* Assimilation; Cultural change; Innovation; Syncretism

Consult: Teske, R. H. C., Jr., and Nelson, B. H., "Acculturation and Assimilation: A Clarification," *American Ethnologist* I: 351–368, 1974.

—James Clifton, University of Wisconsin, Green Bay

**Acephalous Social Organizations.** In the classification of societies on an evolutionary basis, this term applies to bands and tribes, groups characterized by a decentralized or polycentric political organization.

*See also* Band; Tribe

**Acheulean Culture.** This group of Lower Paleolithic assemblages is characterized by bifacial hand axes (type site St. Acheul in NW France) dated from 1 million to ca. 60,000 years old. The Acheulean culture is derived from the Oldowan culture of E. Africa and is associated with *Homo erectus* fossil remains there. It is best known in E and NW Africa, but is found also in S Africa, W Europe, the Near East, W India, and Pakistan. The lower stage is sometimes called Abbevillian. This stage, along with the middle and upper stages, is defined on subjective morphological criteria and crude temporal order, using such data as faunal and floral spectra and fossil beach lines. Sites are mainly open rather than in caves—e.g., Olduvai, Olorgesailie, Kalambo Falls (E Africa); Torralba/Ambrona (EC Spain); Terra Amata (SC France). They are often found on

ACHEULIAN TOOLKIT

*Acheulian tools from Kalambo Falls, Zambia, front and side views (one-third actual size). This represents the second stage of the hand ax tradition, which evolved out of the first stage around 400,000 BP.*

river terraces (especially in the Somme, Manzanares, and Thames valleys). The people lived as unspecialized hunter/gatherers, probably organized into extended family bands. However, evidence suggests occasional larger (probably temporary) social aggregates (e.g., Torralba/Ambrona). Some functionally specific sites (kill/butchering sites, workshops, base camps) have been found, and regional artifacts appear for the first time (especially Upper Acheulean).

*See also* Chellean culture

**Achieved Roles.** *See* Role.

**Action Anthropology.** *See* Applied anthropology.

**Adams, Robert McCormick** (b. 1926). Archaeologist best known for his comparative research on the process of urbanization in SW Asia and Middle America.

**Adaptation.** *See* Adaptation, biological; Adaptation, cultural; Cultural ecology.

**Adaptation, Biological.** The concept of adaptation has been fundamental to explanations of the biology and evolution of organisms, populations, and species since Darwin's *On the Origin of Species by Means of Natural Selection* (1859). Basic to the concept is the assumption that populations change over time in a manner controlled by natural selection. The most fit organisms in a population will survive best and pass on relatively more of their genes to the next generation. Each generation is thus better adapted in terms of a given environmental setting and life-style than the preceding one. Changes in the environment will result in alterations of selective pressures in accordance with new demands.

While some authorities believe that all biological traits have evolved in response to selective forces, others claim that there are characteristics with "neutral" fitness value. Attempts to trace the history of races through the use of easily distinguishable "marker" traits have been based on the assumption that these attributes do not change over time. Increasingly, however, such traits as skin color, hair form, and nose shape are considered to be the result of specific adaptations to environment and climate.

Another area of disagreement concerns survivals—traits no longer useful in terms of their original functions. Although it is argued that these traits will disappear with time, the difficulty lies in attributing their elimination to natural selection. If the traits become detrimental, adaptation will result in their reduction. For those characteristics, if any, which are neutral, explanations must take a different form. Brace's *probable mutation effect* contends that mutations occurring at random will result in metabolic blockages and the ultimate disappearance of a trait for which there is no selective advantage. Another hypothesis concerns the conservation of energy, whereby a negative selective pressure is set up by the metabolic energy drained unnecessarily by structural features with no positive adaptive value.

Still another problem involves the distinction between levels at which adaptation occurs. Natural selection operates through the relative reproductive advantages of some organisms over others, but some authorities believe that selection can also favor traits, such as altruism, that are not beneficial for individual organisms but useful to the population as a whole.

The extent to which populations are at any given time maximally or optimally adapted to their environments is difficult to measure. The fact that a population exists

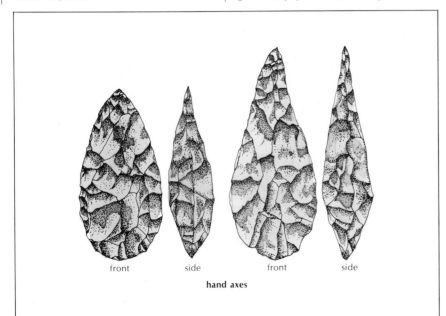

front    side    front    side

**hand axes**

and reproduces itself is taken as evidence that its characteristics are adaptive. Yet most species evolved on earth are now extinct. Since adaptation must be to the total environment—including all living and nonliving substances articulating with a population—the number of variables is great and calculations are highly complex. For human groups, such cultural factors as birth control and infanticide interact with biological ones to influence the relative numbers of offspring contributed by different populations.

Natural selection and adaptation are today taken as the major long-term processes affecting populations. Other evolutionary forces may also have been important, however, in the development of the hominids. Mutation provides new genetic material. Gene flow results in new trait combinations. Preferential mating systems affect patterns of gene transmission. Finally, genetic drift—the statistical effect of random fluctuations in gene frequencies in small populations due to sampling inadequacies—may have had a major effect when populations were smaller and more isolated. In fact, genetic drift may have operated in a manner directly opposed to adaptation, causing some populations to become extinct and others eventually to evolve to higher adaptive levels which natural selection could not have brought about.

See also Evolution, genetic mechanisms of; Selection, natural

Consult: Bajema, C. J. (ed.), *Natural Selection in Human Populations* (New York: Wiley, 1971); Brace, C. L., "Structural Reduction in Evolution," *American Naturalist* 97:39–49, 1963; Hardin, G., *Nature and Man's Fate* (New York: Holt, 1959); Klopfer, P. H., *Habitats and Territories* (New York: Basic Books, 1969).

—Catherine E. Read-Martin, *California State University, Los Angeles*

**Adaptation, Cultural.** Culture is the most important means for adaptation among all human groups. It is a dynamic invention for solving the problems of human existence. Human society is primarily distinguished from nonhuman society by its capacity to adapt culturally to changing environmental circumstances. Thus, while *Homo sapiens* can and does adapt genetically to changing conditions, most anthropologists agree that the primary mode of adaptation has been cultural. Rather than changing genetic composition to adapt to cold, for example, arctic

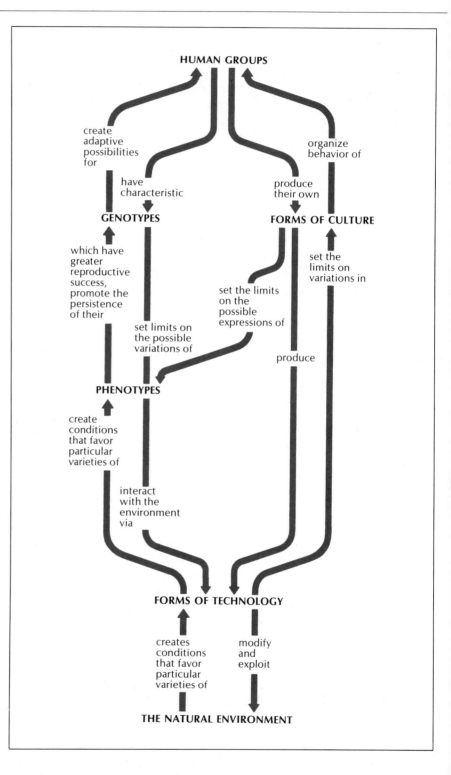

BIOLOGICAL AND CULTURAL ADAPTATION

*This model is intended to illustrate how forms of technology act as an adaptive buffer between human groups and their natural environment—but with both biological and cultural consequences. Changes in any of the elements can affect the other elements either directly or indirectly.*

*Read any capitalized label; then follow an arrow leaving that label and read the text along the arrow; finally, read the capitalized label to which that arrow leads. Each time you do this you will find a sentence that expresses one of the relationships or processes operating in the interactions between human groups and their environment.*

groups dress in skins and build shelters to keep warm.

**Adaptation and Evolution.** Evolution is best viewed as the interaction between the cultural institutions of groups and their environment. The term *environment* needs to be carefully understood. To anthropologists it means the physical, social, and cultural reality to which groups must adapt. For it is groups or populations (rather than the individual) that are the anthropologist's primary concern (as they are the biologist's). It is the group that adapts—that is, makes a stable adjustment to the environment.

The physical environment to which a group adapts is best understood as a specific ecological niche rather than the total environment. When studying cultural adaptation, the anthropologist is careful to specify exactly which segment of the environment is being studied at what time.

The concept of environment becomes clearer when its social dimension is considered. A group is rarely found in isolation from other groups. The patterns of interaction it has with other groups form part of its system of adaptation. Frequently, the larger physical environment is divided into a number of smaller niches exploited in different ways by each group in the area. Thus one group may be pastoral nomads, another farmers, and a third merchants. Further, each group may even use the same piece of land but at different seasons. Frederick Barth has used the biological concept of symbiosis to describe this phenomenon.

Culture may be viewed as an energy system. The institutions of a society related to the harnessing of energy (technology) are sometimes called *core* institutions. These institutions form a basis for cross-cultural comparison. Thus it is important to know not only what a group's neighbors do for a living, or where they live, or how many of them there are, but also what their technology is vis-à-vis the group. Chicago, for example, is still located on the Plains. However, the use made of it by its current inhabitants is qualitatively different from that made by mounted nomadic hunters—just as their use was different from that made by Indians before the arrival of the horse.

Cultural evolution is seen as a result of adaptations that increasingly harness energy and make it more readily serviceable to the group. The more effectively a group uses energy (e.g., by substituting animal for human power), the more efficiently its institutions can be run. As energy is harnessed and produced for efficient societal use, both the core and other institutions become more complex. This, in Julian Steward's terminology, is the process of sociocultural evolution.

**Methods of Studying Cultural Adaptation.** All adaptation involves change. Change can be viewed in specific or in general terms. Specific changes of particular cultures can be studied in their environmental contexts; or general trends of cultural change that result in increased ability to harness energy and become more adaptable in all environments can be emphasized. As more microstudies using the former approach are completed, our macrostudy of human cultural evolution will improve.

*See also* Ecological niches
Consult: Bennett, John W., *Northern Plainsmen: Adaptive Strategy and Agrarian Life* (Chicago: Aldine, 1969); Cohen, Yehudi (ed.), *Man in Adaptation,* 2nd ed. (Chicago: Aldine, 1974).
—*Frank A. Salamone, St. John's University*

**Adaptation, Reactive.** *See* Acculturation.

**Adaptive Strategy.** The concept of adaptive strategy is fundamental to cultural ecological and cultural adaptational theory. An adaptive strategy is a generalization constructed on the basis of analyzed individual, group, or aggregate plans of action known to have been carried out over a specified time period in relation to external or internal exigencies or constraints. Adaptive strategies may be conscious or unconscious, explicit or implicit. Recent attempts to clarify the conceptual basis of adaptive strategy analysis can be found in Carneiro (1968), Bennett (1969), and Whitten and Whitten (1972).

*See also* Adaptation, cultural; Cultural ecology
Consult: Bennett, John W., *Northern Plainsmen: Adaptive Strategy and Agrarian Life* (Chicago: Aldine, 1969); Carneiro, Robert, "Cultural Adaptation," in *International Encyclopedia of the Social Sciences* (New York: Free Press, 1968); Whitten, Norman E., Jr., and Whitten, Dorothea S., "Social Strategies and Social Relationships," *Annual Review of Anthropology,* 1:247–270, 1972.

**Adolescence.** The stage in human development called adolescence falls between puberty and the attainment of physical and emotional maturity in adulthood. This stage of life is as much a product of cultural definitions as of biological maturation; many cultures scarcely recognize adolescence or its equivalent at all, and even where the period is recognized, its content and duration differ widely from culture to culture. The concept of adolescence is in fact of very recent origin in our own culture; the term was used for the first time at the turn of the 20th century, when prolongation of education was leading to the emergence of a "new" stage in the life cycle between childhood and adulthood.

Although Americans tend to think of adolescence as a time of turmoil, anthropological research by Margaret Mead and others has shown that this is by no means universally the case. Preliterate societies usually offer clearly defined roles for those who are entering puberty. In many cases, formal initiation rites confer a new and sometimes adult identity on the young person, and the highly structured role into which the initiate moves leaves little room for the uncertainty and confusion that characterize adolescence in the modern world.

*See also* Initiation; Life cycle; Rites of passage
—*Ian Robertson, Cambridge University*

**Adornment.** The study of personal decoration is properly part of the study of the social context of art. Literally, personal adornment simply refers to the ways in which members of a group decorate their bodies. It comprises such seemingly diverse practices as tattooing, hair decoration, scarification, styles of clothing, and various other means of self-decoration, such as the wearing of ornaments.

Adornment is symbolic activity. Every society has its own set of meanings attached to modes of dress and its views on what is appropriate adornment for each sex, age, and status. Anthropologists have long appreciated the fact that changes in style indicate deeper sociocultural changes. Styles help define the social situation and, consequently, changes in fashions of adornment often are indicators of changes in social relationships.

Adornment is related to a number of other sociocultural factors: aesthetics, modesty, age, marital condition, status, and sex, among others.

**Adultery.** This term signifies a sexual relationship with a person other than one's legal spouse; it is to be distinguished from *fornication*, which refers to sexual intercourse between two unmarried people.

**Functional Perspective** (social anthropology). Social attitudes toward extramarital intercourse vary widely in time and place, but they are generally supposed to be negative. The more highly the individual is placed in society, the stronger become the sanctions against such behavior. By threatening illegitimacy of potential offspring, adultery undermines both social and legal rules concerning the inheritance of power and property. Bohannan (1963) considers it a "flagrant violation" of the consort role which helps to define the status and identity of an individual. Exclusivity of sexual rights with respect to the legal spouse, especially the wife, is a common expectation in marriage.

**Psychological Perspective** (psychological anthropology). It is likely that in every culture a genuine emotional relationship between legal spouses is expected or anticipated, whatever the definition of the proper emotions may be. Members of a society may learn to be overwhelmed with fondness when a spouse is kind and considerate, and so may regret the loss of this feeling when it is no longer forthcoming. Expecting a spouse's exclusive sexual attention, a person may become jealously angered that the spouse is now devoting this attention to someone else. The person may fear a loss in economic security or personal freedom resulting from the absence of the partner. Such feelings are not lost on observers who

*Facial tattooing is a right restricted to men of noble descent in Polynesia. In this painting by Gottfried Lindaver, a Maori chieftain exhibits these traditionally prescribed designs, which are gouged into the skin in a lengthy and painful process.*

can all too easily identify with such deprivations. It is not surprising, therefore, that social sanctions of many kinds—legal, religious, moral, emotional, even torture and death—are brought to bear against adultery and those who are tempted by it.

*See also* Marriage

Consult: Bohannan, Paul, *Social Anthropology* (New York: Holt, 1963).

—Mary Ann Foley, Southern Connecticut State College

**Adulthood.** This period in the human life cycle is reached by living long enough and learning everything necessary to assume the rights, privileges, duties, and responsibilities intrinsic to reproductive, economic, ritual, and other essential social functions.

In large and technologically complex societies, adulthood tends to be deferred until formal education is completed and people can support themselves independently. In such societies adulthood also lasts longer before declining into senescence because people live longer in good health so that the aging process·is slowed. Old age brings a decline in status and power.

In small and technologically simple societies the life cycle tends to be compressed into a shorter period of time, so that adulthood begins and ends sooner. Everyone's economic and personal contributions from an early age are more necessary to the survival of the society. A person must be able to complete all necessary functions before a shorter life expectancy takes its toll.

*See also* Life cycle; Maturity; Role; Role recruitment criteria; Status

**Aegyptopithecus.** This Oligocene fossil series was discovered in the Fayum Depression in Egypt. Before 1960, only seven jaw fragments had been unearthed, but between 1960 and 1967, under the supervision of Elwyn Simons of Yale University, the discovery of five partial jaws and a nearly intact skull revealed that *Aegyptopithecus* ("Egyptian Ape"), with primitive snout, apelike dentition, and a cranial capacity smaller than any living monkey, was an arboreal vegetarian. *Aegyptopithecus*, whose estimated antiquity is 33–36 million years, was definitely ancestral to modern higher apes, and evidence suggests that it is probably the long-sought ancestor of both apes and humans.

*See also* Fayum culture; Hominoids; Pongids; Primates, evolutionary features of

**Aesthetic Appreciation.** For the anthropologist, aesthetic appreciation refers to the way in which cultures classify something as beautiful. Usually studies are made in a specific society, although some anthropologists are interested in the cross-cultural study of beauty. It is very difficult to discuss aesthetic appreciation apart from art and society. However, the latter usually refers to the place of art and its creators in a specific social context, whereas aesthetic appreciation, although related, usually refers to the evaluation of the beauty of a piece of art.

Anthropologists differ from philosophers of art and most art critics in holding that there are no universal standards of beauty. In other words, though there may well be a category of reality labeled beauty in every society, there is no evidence to suggest a universal standard that is valid for all societies.

Aestheticians, those dedicated to the study of the human response to what is perceived as beautiful, have a number of theories at their disposal. There is as yet no single accepted theory to explain how and why humans respond to beauty. These theories can be grouped under the following categories: hedonistic, gestalt, Kantian, contextual, organistic, formistic, linguistic.

The *hedonistic* approach to aesthetic appreciation examines the pleasure that a given experience excites in an individual. The reasons for the pleasure can be many, but hedonism insists on the inherent importance of pleasure to humans in explaining the appreciation of beauty.

*Gestalt* (pattern) is a theory that stresses the need to examine the whole work of art beyond its constituent parts in understanding the way in which it produces pleasure. It is not necessarily antagonistic to a hedonistic theory of art appreciation.

*Adulthood is a matter of cultural definition rather than simply a biological state of maturation. In the* bar mitzvah *ritual, Jews celebrate the transition of a boy to the status of manhood at age 13.*

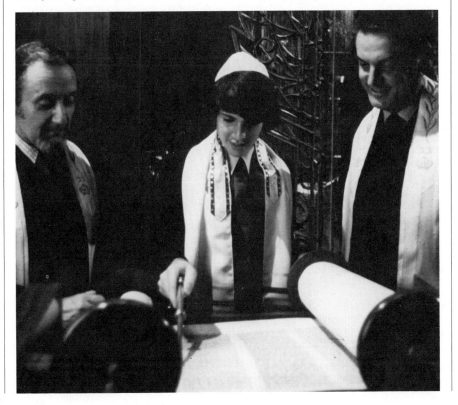

*Immanuel Kant* (1724–1804) argued that the appreciation and classification of beauty is a universal category of the mind, producing a purely mental pleasure. He saw mind imposing reality on objects, thus arguing a sort of mentalistic hedonism.

*Contextualism* in its purest form contends that intuition is the key component in art appreciation. Scientific analysis and prediction are foreign to an appreciation of the quality of an art product.

*Organicism* is the approach to aesthetic appreciation that stresses the value of art as an integrating mechanism. Art appreciation is directly related to the manner in which an artistic experience of any kind integrates the viewer's experiences.

*Formism*, a development of both Platonic and Aristotelian philosophy, is the theory which states that the true artist is one who depicts the "essence" of reality rather than imitating a particular manifestation of it.

Among the other approaches to the study of aesthetic appreciation, one has been strongly influenced by anthropology's early stress on relativism—the *linguistic* theory of art appreciation. In brief, this theory states that no universal aesthetic values can be posited: one can only ask open-ended questions of people when attempting to study their appreciation of beauty and art. The proponents of this view, like all relativists, have probably overstated their case. They have served, however, to sensitize aestheticians to sociocultural factors in art appreciation.

See also Art and society

Consult: Beardsley, Monroe C., *Aesthetics: Problems in the Philosophy of Criticism* (New York: Harcourt Brace Jovanovich, 1958); Goodman, Nelson, *Languages of Art* (Indianapolis: Bobbs-Merrill, l968).

—Frank A. Salamone, St. John's University

**Affinity.** This term refers to a kin relationship involving one marriage link—e.g., a man is related by affinity to his wife and her consanguineals. Two persons related by affinity are *affines.*

See also Kinship

**Age-Area Hypothesis.** This concept was developed by Clark Wissler to determine the relative age of a cultural trait from its spatial distribution. Traits tend to diffuse outward in all directions from their center of origin. Thus traits found at the edge of an area would be the oldest and furthest from their center of origin. The analogy is similar to that of ripples spreading outward from a stone thrown into water.

This assumption is no longer accepted, for it ignores the kinds of contact between groups that may result in diffusion and does not account for differing acceptance, rejection, or modification of traits by receiving groups.

See also Diffusion; Wissler, Clark

**Age Grades.** Also known as *age classes,* age grades are specialized hierarchical associations based on age. Youths—more commonly males than females—enter and pass through a series of age-graded associations which stratify the population by seniority. Members of a specific age grade are bound together by obligatory cooperation and mutual aid, as well as by symbols of common status and special responsibilities. The primary functions of age grades are cultural transmission and promotion of larger, tribal solidarity.

*See also* Associations; Solidarity

**Aggression.** The term *aggression* is a very loose one that is often popularly used to cover a wide range of hostile, threatening, competitive, or even predatory acts. Social scientists, however, generally use the term in a narrow sense to refer to acts—or threats of acts—designed to cause injury between members of the same species. This aggression is frequently manifested in the context of territorial defense.

In most species, intraspecific aggression is readily inhibited by ritualized gestures or other signals of submission on the part of the vanquished animal. Under normal conditions, it is extremely rare for one animal to

*Adult male savannah baboon in Nairobi Park, Kenya, makes a threatening gesture, exhibiting his large canines and his light-colored eyelids.*

kill another of the same species. Humans, however, appear to lack such inhibiting mechanisms, and in advanced societies they have the capacity to kill members of their species under impersonal conditions and over great distances.

Three main theories have been forward to account for human aggression. Some ethologists contend that humanity is innately aggressive; the species is said to have an aggressive drive that requires periodic expression. This view is strongly rejected by most anthropologists, who believe that the argument is based on faulty evidence and false analogies. A second theory explains aggression as a response to frustration of various kinds; this view has won some support from research evidence, but it is doubtful whether the theory provides a comprehensive account of human aggression. A third theory claims that aggressive behavior is learned and that its frequency and the contexts in which it appears therefore vary from individual to individual and from culture to culture, depending on the distinctive learning experiences offered in each case. This is the view most widely accepted by contemporary social scientists.

*See also* Conflict; Warfare

Consult: Lorenz, Konrad, *On Aggression* (London: Methuen, 1966); Montagu, Ashley (ed.), *Man and Aggression,* 2nd ed. (London: Oxford University Press, 1973).

—*Ian Robertson, Cambridge University*

**Agriculture.** Farming and husbandry involve the tillage of soil for the production of crops and the raising of livestock for food. With the introduction of agriculture, food producing gradually replaced a hunting/gathering economy, and with it came increases in population and the birth of civilization. The origin of agriculture in the Near East occurred nearly 10,000 years ago (with the domestication of wheat and barley). In the Americas, agriculture had its origin some 2,000 or more years later in Mexico and Peru (with the domestication of maize). Animal (sheep, goats, and eventually cattle) and plant domestication apparently developed nearly simultaneously in the Old World. In the New World animal husbandry never became as important as in the Old World, and apparently came later than plant cultivation. Some would limit the term *agriculture* to field-scale cultivation of crops with draft animals (or machinery) and plows

to till the soil. If this definition is accepted, the earliest raising of plants is better called horticulture (or garden cultivation), which involved use of the hoe or digging stick. The invention of the plow and the use of animals (probably cattle) for tillage probably took place in the Near East, perhaps over 5,000 years ago. It was the Spanish who introduced the use of draft animals for tillage into the New World.

*See also* Agriculture, origins of; Domestication of plants and animals; Food and food crops

—*Charles B. Heiser, Jr., Indiana University*

**Agriculture, Origins of.** The invention of agriculture was one of the most significant events in human social evolution. Our early ancestors subsisted by hunting and foraging for vegetable foods. By the time of *Homo erectus* they had developed both the technology and the forms of social organization necessary to be very successful big game hunters, a pattern that continued among groups of modern *Homo sapiens* until about 22,000 years ago. At that time, at least in the Middle East, a shift in subsistence strategy took place, from a narrow spectrum of food resources to a much broader one (Flannery 1968). Archaeological data indicate that plant domestication was caused by population pressures in marginal areas to which people had migrated from the more favorable, crowded ones. The data also suggest that the innovation was taken up by populations in the more favorable areas.

Agriculture was invented at least three times in three different areas of the world: in the Middle East, in SE Asia, and in the New World.

**Middle East.** The Middle East is the area in which the food tradition we associate with European society originated some 10,000 years ago. Its center included the arc described by the mountain flanks from Iran through SE Turkey to the southern highlands of Jordan (Harlan 1971). Plants domesticated in this area include wheat, barley, rye, peas, lentils, flax, and chickpeas; animals domesticated include sheep, goats, pigs, dogs, and, somewhat later, cattle.

**SE Asia.** Currently archaeologists are debating the location of the SE Asian center. Harlan (1971) argues that the center was in China about 4000 BC. Solheim (1972) holds that it is to be found in Thailand. He concludes that the evidence suggests a food tradition in Thailand as early as 9000 BC that was

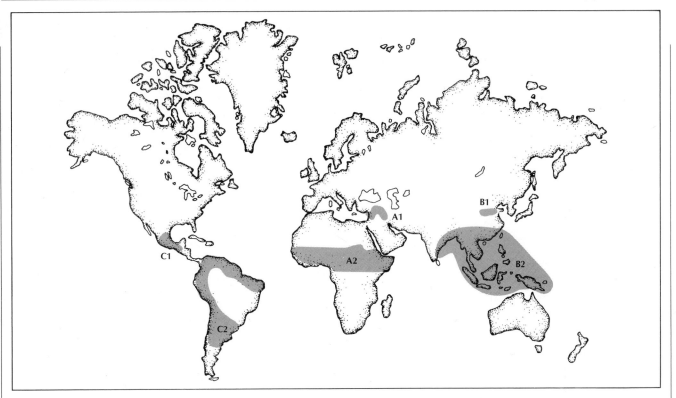

*Shown on this map are the centers and non-centers of agricultural origins: A1, Near East center; A2, African noncenter; B1, North Chinese center; B2, Southeast Asian and South Pacific noncenter; C1, Mesoamerican Center; C2, South American noncenter.*

based on rice and included chiles, beans, soybeans, peas, cucumbers, chickens, cattle, and water buffalo.

**New World.** The center of the New World food tradition appears to have been in Mesoamerica, where the dominant crop was maize (corn). Maize was domesticated in the Mexican highlands between 7000 and 4000 BC (Meggers 1968). Other domesticates include the bean, cassava, lima bean, avocado, peanut, and sweet potato. Tobacco was also domesticated in this region.

Why and how people developed agriculture remains a mystery. Childe (1951, 1952) advanced the so-called Oasis Hypothesis for the Middle East: the increasingly arid environment at the end of the Pleistocene forced human and animal populations to concentrate around sources of water, where a symbiotic interdependence developed. Humans harvested wild grains, especially wheat; wild sheep and goats came to depend on the stubble as a food source; humans began to make systematic use of these wild herds and also attempted to perpetuate what previously had been a wild harvest.

Sauer (1952) contends that agriculture was invented only once—in SE Asia—and that it subsequently diffused to all other centers. This radical diffusionist position is not accepted by most scholars.

Robert J. Braidwood, one of America's foremost archaeologists, argues that the climatic changes at the end of the Pleistocene had in fact occurred several times previously during late Pleistocene interglacial periods without an agricultural revolution resulting as an adaptive response to the environmental changes. Braidwood (1960) sees the development of agriculture as a natural consequence of the broad evolutionary processes by which human society was becoming increasingly differentiated.

Perhaps the most sophisticated theories about the origins of agriculture are those of Kent Flannery. Flannery (1965, 1968) argues that the shift to agriculture was part of a slow process by which hunting/gathering populations gradually reduced the number of their subsistence resources. These people began to concentrate their foraging into decreasing ranges, and they adapted to the use of a few selected plants and animals. In Mesoamerica, people came to depend more and more on the wild ancestors of maize and beans. Gradually this concentration on the harvesting of wild maize and beans led to the deliberate sowing of seeds; the genetic changes in the plants that led to their full domestication was only a matter of time and selection. In the Middle East, people concentrated on the large stands of wild grasses that were ancestral to modern wheat and barley. The resulting life-style, Flannery contends, was so successful that people began to concentrate into relatively permanent settlements by around 7000 BC. The population began to rise, forcing people to migrate into marginal areas where they attempted to recreate the abundant environments they had left behind by sowing the cereal grains they had carried with them—and the invention of agriculture was under way.

Although we do not yet know the exact causes of the domestication of plants and animals, we do know that this adaptive strategy was very successful. It spread across the ancient world and became the material basis for the development of all civilizations.

*See also* Agriculture; Cities, development of; Civilization, origins of; Domestication of plants and animals; Economics and subsistence

Consult: Braidwood, Robert J., "The Agricultural Revolution," *Scientific American* 203: 130–148, 1960; Childe, V. Gordon, *Man Makes Himself* (New York: Mentor, 1951); Childe, V. Gordon, *New Light on the Most Ancient East,* 4th ed. (London: Routledge, 1952); Darlington, C. D., "The Origins of Agriculture," in *Anthropology: Contemporary Perspectives,* ed. David E. Hunter and Phillip Whitten (Boston: Little, Brown, 1975); Flannery, Kent V., "The Ecology of Early Food Production in Mesopotamia," *Science* 147:1247–1256, 1965; Flannery, Kent V., "Archaeological Systems Theory and Early Mesopotamia," in Meggers (1968); Harlan, Jack R., "Agricultural Origins: Center and Noncenter," *Science* 174:468–474, 1971; Meggers, Betty J. (ed.), *Anthropological Archaeology in the Americas* (Washington, D.C.: Anthropological Society of Washington, 1968); Sauer, Carl O., *Agricultural Origins and Dispersals* (New York: American Geographical Society, 1952); Solheim, Wilhelm G., "An Earlier Agricultural Revolution," *Scientific American* 226:34–51, April 1972.

—*David E. Hunter, Southern Connecticut State College*

—*Phillip Whitten, Harvard University*

## Albinism.
This condition—the lack of pigmentation (melanin in primates) in external body tissues and hair—is believed to be a genetic mutation that appears in about 1 of every 20,000 human births. It makes people very susceptible to sunburn.

## Alienation.
In the social sciences the concept of alienation refers to the process of being estranged from a group. This use of the concept does not deny that people can become estranged from themselves. In fact, the two understandings are interrelated. Thus the fact that one gets one's identity from a group means that loss of connection with that group would lead to one's questioning of one's identity—i.e., alienation from oneself. The concept is related to mar-

ginality, and one can speak of a group's being alienated from the larger society. The concept is central in studies of deviance, for alienated groups are by definition liable to behave in a deviant manner.

*See also* Anomie; Deviance

## Alland, Alexander
(b. 1931). Medical anthropologist at Columbia University, associated with the application of evolutionary theory to the analysis of modern biosocial problems.

## Allele.
One of the variant forms of a single gene.

*See also* Gene; Genetics

## Alliance.
This term refers to a bond or relationship between social groups (e.g., families, lineages, associations, nations) involving reciprocal rights and duties. In anthropology, special consideration is given to the study of alliances formed by affinal ties between kin groups, partly because the majority of societies studied by anthropologists are kin-based, but also because alliance theory, the explanatory hypothesis concerning alliances between kin groups, involves the interrelations among marriage rules, kinship terminologies, descent rules, and postmarital residence rules.

**Symmetric Alliance.** Sister exchange (man A marries the sister of man B and man B marries the sister of man A) is the basis of symmetric alliance. If the offspring of the two marriages also practice sister exchange, the marriages will be between bilateral cross cousins. When the members of two kin groups practice sister exchange with each other, the result is called *dual organization.*

**Asymmetric Alliance.** When more than two kin groups are linked by affinal ties, with each group receiving wives from one group and giving wives to another group, the alliances are asymmetric and the resulting organization is called a *circulating* connubium.

*See also* Affinity; Descent; Kinship; Kinship and alliance; Kinship and descent
—*Lilah Pengra, Kenyon College*

## Allomorphs.
All the different-sounding versions of the same morpheme.

*See also* Morphemes

*Albinism occurs among all human populations. Shown here is a native of the Trobriand Archipelago Coral Islands. Fellow villagers take great care of their "white" relatives, who can hardly see in the glare of the tropical sun.*

## Allophones.
All the different-sounding variants of a single phoneme.

*See also* Complementary distribution; Phoneme

## Alphabet.
This writing system seems to have developed in the Middle East around 10,000 years ago. Other writing systems may use a symbol to represent a whole word or part of a word (logographic) or a sequence of consonant plus vowel (syllabic), but an alphabetic system in its pure form uses one symbol or one letter for each significant sound (phoneme) in the language. This makes it possible to represent any word or part of a word with a small number of symbols which can be used over and over in different combinations. The advantage that an alphabetic system has over a logographic or syllabic one can be illustrated by Mandarin Chinese. Since the syllables of Mandarin number slightly over 1,300, a syllabic system would need 1,300 different characters—and the logographic system in actual use requires 1,500 basic characters. The English alphabet can represent the major sounds of English with only 26 basic letters. Acquiring literacy is much easier in an alphabetic system.

Most alphabetic systems do not actually achieve the one sound to one symbol principle but do represent most of the sound system of the language. Sometimes different symbols represent allophones (the *o* in *women* is the same phoneme as the *i* in *pin*), and sometimes the same symbol is used to represent two different sounds (the letter *c* may represent both the /s/ sound in *face* and the /k/ sound in case).

See also Phoneme; Syllabary; Symbol; Writing
—Elizabeth A. Brandt, Arizona State University

**Alpha State.** Through biofeedback mind control, hypnosis, or the skills of Zen monks and other adepts, alpha brain waves (which run 8–13 cycles per second) can be generated for a sustained period. This relaxed yet alert state of mind is associated with transcendental consciousness and heightened psychic (and even physical) abilities.

See also Altered states of consciousness

**Altered States of Consciousness.** Human consciousness may take many different forms—dreamless sleep, dreaming, coma, intoxication, trance, various forms of psychosis, deep meditation, visionary episodes, or psychedelic experiences. The physiological basis of these states of consciousness, their relationship to one another, and their adaptive significance (if any) are all imperfectly understood at present.

Altered states of consciousness may arise spontaneously, or they may be induced by a variety of factors, including hypnosis, fatigue, drugs, sensory deprivation, sensory overload, organic brain injury, fasting, biofeedback, psychological stress, or communal fervor.

All cultures tend to define some of these altered states of consciousness as valuable and desirable and others as negative and undesirable. Western cultures, which are committed to a rational-scientific view of reality, tend to deny the validity of altered states of consciousness. In our culture, those who deliberately seek such experiences are generally believed to do so for frivolous or hedonistic motives and are considered social deviants; indeed, their interest in these states of consciousness is often seen as a symptom of psychological maladjustment. In many non-Western cultures, however, altered states of consciousness are often highly regarded as valid and meaningful. Certain altered states of consciousness may be legitimated by the local religious belief system and may thus be located in a universe of meaning and regarded with reverence.

See also Dreams, psychological functions of; Drugs; Medication; Religion; Trance

Consult: Huxley, Aldous, *The Doors of Perception* (New York: Harper & Row, 1954).
—Ian Robertson, Cambridge University

**Ambilineal Descent.** Descent reckoned through both males and females (also called *cognatic descent*).

See also Descent

**Ambilocality.** Postmarital residence pattern in which a married couple may reside either with the husband's or with the wife's domiciliary group.

See also Marriage

**Analogy, Ethnographic.** See Ethnographic analogy.

**Anal Stage.** In Freudian psychoanalytic theory, this is the second psychosexual stage, following the oral stage, through which a person progresses. During this stage, which occurs at roughly the second year, a child's concerns are said to center around the anus and the process of defecation. Compulsivity and orderliness are the psychological themes attached to this stage.

See also Freud, Sigmund; Psychosexual stages of development

**Anarchism.** See Socialism.

**Ancestor Worship.** This widely distributed religious practice involves worship of the spirits of dead family and lineage members. From the folk perspective, this practice may ensure security and confidence during present life. From the analytic perspective, anthropologists regard ancestor worship as an expression of the importance of lineage in a society's social organization.

See also Religion

**Anima-Animus.** This term denotes, respectively, the feminine aspect of the male psyche and the masculine aspect of the female psyche in the analytic psychology of C. G. Jung. These unconscious psychological components are derived from innate psy-

chological predisposition (archetypes) and from experiences in the social and cultural milieu which shape ideas of the opposite sex and define characteristics of one's own sex. The contents of the anima or animus are frequently projected on others; they may also appear as powerfully charged figures in dreams and myths. Being archetypes, they are never experienced directly, only via symbolic representations such as the syzygy (divine couple) and idealized female and male figures.

See also Archetype; Jung, Carl Gustav
Consult: Jung, C. G., "Concerning the Archetypes, with Special Reference to the Anima Concept," in *The Archetypes and the Collective Unconscious*, Collected Works, 2nd ed., vol. 9 (Princeton: Princeton University Press, 1954).

**Animal Domestication.** See Agriculture.

**Animatism.** Belief in an impersonal, divisible, supernatural force or forces, such as mana, which may reside in both living and nonliving things.

See also Animism; Religion

*In many parts of the world, dead ancestors continue to play meaningful roles in the social lives of people. This New Guinea tribesman sleeps on the skull of his ancestor.*

**Animism.** In anthropology, this term refers to religious beliefs involving the attribution of life or divinity to such natural phenomena as trees, thunder, or celestial bodies. E. B. Tylor argued that animism was the first step in the evolution of religion. In developmental psychology, the term refers to the universal tendency of young children to attribute life, motives, and emotions to natural objects.

*See also* Religion; Soul

**Anomie.** Initially coined by Emile Durkheim to explain the cause of suicide, anomie is a state of deregulation or normlessness, a point where traditional rules have lost their meaning for one or more individuals. The latter consequently lack interpersonal ties by virtue of their marginal integration in society. Hence the collective order is disturbed or disrupted.

Today anomie is often an explanatory device in etiological studies of alienation, marginality, deviance, criminality, rebellion, violence, conflict, social disorganization, and similar phenomena. Statements such as "Life has no meaning, life is absurd" may indicate the presence of anomie. Literary expression of this state is found in Albert Camus' *The Stranger* and other existentialist writings.

*See also* Alienation; Durkheim, Emile; Suicide
Consult: Durkheim, Emile, *Suicide: A Study in Sociology* (New York: Free Press, 1951).

**Anthropoids.** This common name refers to those primates classified within the taxonomic suborder Anthropoidea (all living and extinct monkeys, apes, and humans). European scholars frequently use the term Simiae for this suborder. This is one of the two basic divisions of the order Primates, the other being the suborder Prosimii (prosimians). In contrast to the prosimians, anthropoids are characterized by eyes which are fully rotated around to the front of the skull and are completely enclosed within a bony eye socket. This development has resulted in overlapping fields of vision which in turn provide a crucial depth perception for these arboreal animals. This increased visual acuity counterbalances a decreased efficiency of the olfactory sense of anthropoids. In the great majority of anthropoids, manual dexterity is enhanced by the complete replacement of claws with nails and the sensitive digital

pads they protect and strengthen. More important, perhaps, is the generally larger and more complex anthropoid brain in relation to the overall body size of these primates. Vertical trunk posture is quite common in anthropoids when they are resting.

The Anthropoidea are often divided into three superfamilies: Ceboidea (New World monkeys), Cercopithecoidea (Old World monkeys), and Hominoidea (apes and humans). The living Ceboidea are found in Central and South America and are represented by some sixty-five species. Their main distinguishing features include nostrils that are more widely spaced and flatter than the Old World anthropoid's narrowly situated nostrils. This very basic distinction between the nostrils of the New World and Old World anthropoids is sometimes reflected in the former being referred to as platyrrhines ("flat-nosed") and the latter as catarrhines ("sharp-nosed"). (These names, in turn, are sometimes formalized into the taxonomic infraorder designations Platyrrhini and Catarrhini.) New World monkeys also differ from Old World anthropoids in that they have one more premolar in each dental quadrant, giving them a dental formula of 2:1:3:3 instead of the Old World 2:1:2:3. Some New World monkeys possess prehensile or gripping tails which provide them with an additional grasp on their arboreal environment. Further, they have tympanic bullae (balloonlike expansions of the walls of their middle ear cavities); Old World anthropoids lack such bony chambers.

The living Old World anthropoids (catarrhines) are represented by about seventy monkey species as well as by the apes and humans. The Cercopithecoidea differ from their New World counterparts in several interesting respects. For instance, some of them possess ischial callosities (skin calluses on their hind areas which permit these monkeys to remain sitting for extended periods of time) and cheek pouches which expand to provide temporary storage for foodstuffs. The females of some Old World monkey species also undergo swelling of the perineal skin during the peak of their estrous cycle, whereas such swelling is not found in the Ceboidea. There is also greater sexual dimorphism among the Cercopithecoidea and, unlike the Ceboidea, some have successfully adapted to living on the ground (e. g., baboons).

The Cercopithecoidea are frequently subdivided into two taxonomic subfamilies

on a principally dietary basis: the leaf-eating Colobinae and the more omnivorous Cercopithecinae. The Colobinae generally have very long (but not prehensile) tails, well-separated ischial callosities, and a specialized digestive system consisting of enlarged salivary glands and sacculated (pouched) stomachs which provide more efficient digestion of the cellulose that is common in their diets. The Colobinae are principally arboreal and generally lack both the cheek pouches and the sexual swelling common in the Cercopithecinae.

The evolutionary history of the anthropoids certainly extends as far back as the Oligocene and may even reach into the earlier Eocene in the form of the Omomyidae and possibly even *Amphipithecus* and *Pondaungia* from Burma.

*See also* Ceboidea; Ceropithecoidea; Primates, behavior of; Primates, evolutionary features of
Consult: Napier, J. R., and Napier, P. H., *A Handbook of Living Primates* (New York: Academic Press, 1967); Rosen, S. I., *Introduction to the Primates* (Englewood Cliffs, N.J.: Prentice-Hall, 1974); Schultz, Adolph H., *The Life of Primates* (New York: Universe Books, 1969).
—*Martin K. Nickels, Illinois State University*

**Anthropological Linguistics.** See Linguistics, anthropological.

**Anthropology.** This discipline may be defined as the systematic study of the nature of human beings. The term derives from two Greek words: *anthropos* (man) and *logia* (study).

**History.** The origins of anthropology can be traced back to the classical civilizations of Europe and the Middle East. Early travelers and philosophers noticed that social forms differed from one place to another, as did customs, rituals, religious beliefs, military techniques, languages, and the sizes, shapes, and colors of the human body. These observations led to speculations about human origins and about the nature and development of human society and culture—concerns which have become formalized into the modern academic discipline of anthropology in the 20th century.

Perhaps the earliest statement of the anthropological perspective was that of Xenophanes (ca. 570–475 BC), a Greek who traveled widely and is credited with being the first philosopher to emphasize that society is created by human beings themselves. Rejecting the literal interpretation of mythical tales, Xenophanes even argued that gods are created in human images and that religion is a social product.

The best-known early traveler and recorder of different social customs is Herodotus (ca. 484–425 BC), whose writings describe the life-styles of some fifty different peoples he visited. Although his methods of description and analysis were crude, his perspective was broad enough to satisfy modern standards: he systematically described the environment in which a people lived, their physical characteristics, language, institutions, customs, laws, political organization, military practices, and religious beliefs. Although Herodotus himself believed that the Greek way of life was superior to all those he encountered, he nevertheless recognized that every society believes its own way of life to be best—and thus he explicitly stated one of anthropology's fundamental propositions: all human groups are *ethnocentric*, preferring their own way of life to all others and judging other life-styles (usually negatively) in terms of their own value system.

The nature of human society continued to be a subject of concern throughout classical times, but anthropology as an identifiable social science was not to develop for many centuries. Medieval Europe had its eyes fixed on heaven, not earth, and Christian Europe was for the most part cut off from the social and philosophical speculations of classical scholars for some 800 years from the fall of the Western Roman Empire until the 12th century AD.

Although the major intellectual thrust of medieval Europe was away from social contemplation, there nevertheless developed an interest in the diverse peoples being described with increasing frequency by adventurous merchants, explorers, and Christian missionaries, as these emissaries of European civilization penetrated ever farther afield. Perhaps best exemplifying such writings are the works of Marco Polo (ca. 1254–1323) who served seventeen years in the court of the Kublai Khan and described in remarkable detail Asian customs, practices, and social institutions.

The Renaissance saw the widening of European horizons as monarchs came to appreciate the possibilities of world trade and subsidized exploratory expeditions. Ac-counts of these voyages were eagerly read for their descriptions of the ways of life practiced by strange and remote peoples. The information contained in these (often wildly incorrect and distorted) reports was used by social theorists to compare and contrast "primitive" society with that of Europe in order to gain understanding of basic social processes.

The science of anthropology really did not begin to emerge until the Enlightenment, however. This period was marked by the intellectual and political confrontation between the (liberal) followers of John Locke (1632–1704) and the pessimistic (monarchist) followers of Thomas Hobbes (1588–1679).

Locke, in his remarkable *Essay Concerning Human Understanding* (1690), formulated many of the concepts and ideas that 20th-century students of human behavior still use in their work: among other things, that human beings are born with blank or empty minds and learn all they know through their enculturation into groups. Human knowledge is thus culturally relative—as are political institutions. The human potential was conceived to be vast and noble, requiring democratic institutions for its flowering. Hobbes' followers, on the other hand, viewed human beings as innately selfish, and they argued for the retaining of despotic rule by monarchies—without which social life would be "nasty, brutish, and short." In somewhat different form, this debate still rages: some modern ethologists such as Konrad Lorenz advance the Hobbesian position with vigor; they are opposed by many cultural and physical anthropologists.

Many scholars trace the emergence of modern social science to the writings of Claude Henri Saint-Simon (1760–1825) and his collaborator Auguste Comte (1798–1857); they set out to develop a "science of man" in which "social physics" would lead to the discovery of underlying, unifying principles—comparable to the principle of gravity which had explained so much in the natural sciences.

With the dramatic emergence of Charles Darwin's fully developed theory of biological evolution on the European intellectual scene in 1859, interest in the "primitive" peoples of the world increased as the possibility of applying evolutionary concepts to the realm of cultural and social materials was eagerly explored. Anthropology, as a separate professional and academic field of study, came wholly into its own in the second half of the 19th century as scholars sought reliable information about isolated and technologically less developed peoples. An era of ambitious comparative studies commenced, covering areas such as jurisprudence (e.g., Sir Henry Maine's *Ancient Law*, 1861), kinship systems (e.g., Lewis Henry Morgan's *Systems of Consanguinity and Affinity of the Human Family*, 1870), and religion and other elements of culture (e.g., E. G. Tylor's *Primitive Culture: Researches into the Development of Mythology, Philosophy, Religion, Art, and Custom*, 1871).

Bridging the turn of the century was Emile Durkheim (1858–1917), the French social scientist who investigated the ways in which societies maintain themselves, the manner of their functioning. Both modern sociology and modern anthropology trace their intellectual roots to his writings, which dealt with a whole range of theoretical issues including primitive religion, problems of social organization and group cohesion, and the difficulties that modern society poses for the individual who is struggling to find a meaningful identity.

**Major subdisciplines.** Since the turn of the 20th century, anthropology has developed into an increasingly complex and segmented academic discipline. There are four subdisciplines which constitute the major areas of concern and research among contemporary anthropologists.

1. *Physical anthropology* is the study of human biology across space and time. It is divided into two subareas: *paleontology*, the study of the fossil evidence of primate (including human) evolution; and *neontology*, the study of the comparative biology of the living primates, including population and molecular genetics, ecological pressures, body shapes (morphology), and the extent to which behavior is biologically programmed.

2. *Archaeology* is the systematic retrieval and interpretation of the physical remains left behind by human beings, including their cultural and their skeletal remains. Archaeology is concerned with classical civilizations and with prehistoric groups, including those of our prehuman ancestors.

3. *Linguistics* is the study of language across space and time. *Historical linguistics* attempts to trace the tree of linguistic evolution and to reconstruct ancestral language forms. *Comparative* (or structural) *linguis-*

*tics* attempts formally to describe the basic elements of languages and the rules by which they are ordered into intelligible speech.

4. *Cultural anthropology* includes many different specialized subfields but is primarily concerned with describing the forms of social organization and the cultural systems of human groups. *Ethnography* is the description of the sociocultural system of one selected group; *ethnology* is the comparison of such descriptions for the ultimate purpose of generalizing about the nature of human groups.

> See also Archaeology; Cultural anthropology; Ethnocentrism; Ethnography; Ethnology; Linguistics; Linguistics, anthropological; Physical anthropology
> Consult: Harris, Marvin, *The Rise of Anthropological Theory* (New York: Crowell, 1968); Hunter, David E., and Whitten, Phillip, *The Study of Anthropology* (New York: Harper & Row, 1976); Malefijt, Annemarie deWaal, *Images of Man* (New York: Knopf, 1974).
> —David E. Hunter, Southern Connecticut State College

**Anthropology, Applied.** *See* Applied anthropology.

**Anthropology, Cultural.** *See* Cultural anthropology.

**Anthropology, Economic.** *See* Economic anthropology.

**Anthropology, Linguistic.** *See* Linguistics, anthropological.

**Anthropology of Law.** *See* Legal systems.

**Anthropology, Physical.** *See* Physical anthropology.

**Anthropology, Political.** *See* Political anthropology.

**Anthropology, Psychological.** *See* Culture and personality.

**Anthropology, Social.** *See* Social anthropology.

**Anthropology, Urban.** *See* Urban anthropology.

**Anthropometry.** A subdivision of physical anthropology that measures and statistically considers the human body.

> See also Physical anthropology

**Anthropomorphism.** This term refers to the ascription of human characteristics to objects not human, especially a deity. Expressions such as the "hand of God" and the "wrath of God" illustrate this phenomenon.

In the wider sense of the word, anthropomorphism may be illustrated by any analogical transfer of human qualities to animals, as when referring to their reasoning

*A scene from one of the many Nazi concentration camps of World War II. The atrocities committed in these camps perhaps more than any other phenomena have awakened in people an awareness of the ultimate consequences of prejudice.*

power or ascribing to them such psychological traits as courage or cowardice. The word may even be applied to descriptions of inanimate levels of reality in metaphors taken from human experience (as in speaking of the "anger of the storm").

> See also Animism; Religion
> Consult: Tax, Sol (ed.), *Horizons of Anthropology* (Chicago: Aldine, 1964).

**Anthropophagy.** *See* Cannibalism.

**Anti-Semitism.** Although this term literally refers to prejudice against all Semitic-speakers, it is commonly applied to anti-Jewish prejudice, historically a frequent feature of Christianity. Anti-Semitism was manifested in its most virulent form in Nazi Germany.

> See also Ethnocentrism

**Antler.** *See* Bone.

**Apartheid.** This system of racial segregation is practiced in the Republic of South Africa, where a minority of 4 million whites exercises total dominance over some 20 mil-

*Police in Johannesburg stopping a group of blacks to inspect their required passbooks. Those found without passbooks were held. Black opposition to these regulations resulted in numerous violent incidents in the early 1960s.*

lion blacks, Asiatics, and half-castes. The races are segregated by law in virtually every area of life, from residential accommodation to sexual relationships, and only whites may vote in national elections.

Effective control of the society is in the hands of the Afrikaners, the Calvinist descendants of early Dutch settlers who now comprise two-thirds of the white population and who generally regard the maintenance of apartheid as a divine imperative.

*See also* Racism

**Apes.** This common term refers to any one of the five distinct varieties of primates belonging to the hominoid families Pongidae or Hylobatidae. The Pongidae, generally known as the great apes, include the orangutan (Pongo) of the SE Asian archipelago, the gorilla (Gorilla), and the chimpanzee (Pan) of W, C, and E Africa. The Hylobatidae include the gibbon (Hylobates) and the closely related siamang (Symphalangus), the lesser apes of the Far East.

The apes probably originated in the late Oligocene period some 30 to 25 million years ago. They are well represented in the fossil record by such forms as *Aegyptopithecus, Aeolopithecus, Propliopithecus, Pliopithe-cus, Dryopithecus,* and others. In evolutionary terms they are the primates most closely related to *Homo sapiens.* The three great apes probably shared a common ancestor with the hominids, although the approximate time of separation and the physical nature of the ancestral lineage are still the subject of much scholarly debate.

As a group, the apes are quite variable, ranging in size from the relatively small gibbon with little sexual dimorphism to the huge gorilla (males 400 pounds average) with great sexual dimorphism. Their social structure ranges from the territorial, closed groups of the gibbon to the free-ranging, open groups of the chimpanzee. All are for the most part vegetarians, but the chimpanzee has been observed hunting and consuming meat.

A convenient way to get an overview of the ape grade of evolution is to consider the common evolutionary trends characteristic of the group. Some of the major trends of this sort are (1) upright orientation (brachiation, semibrachiation); (2) the ability to assume a fairly erect biped posture; (3) a large head and brain relative to body size; (4) absence of an external tail; (5) relatively longer necks and arms; (6) relatively wide shoulders, chest, and pelvis; (7) longer periods of pregnancy; (8) longer periods of growth to adult size and status.

As a group, the apes have been the subject of much mythology and many misconceptions, perhaps because of their rather humanlike appearance. Their behavior has been anthropomorphized by scientists observing them as well as by the public at large.

But with the accumulation of more and more field studies by researchers like Schaller, Reynolds, Sugiyama, Itani, and others, many of the old myths and misconceptions are being dismissed for what they are.

A serious problem facing some of the great apes is that of extinction in their native habitats. The orangutan will probably eventually survive only as a zoo animal and the gorilla is seriously threatened. This situation is due to hunting for zoo specimens in the past and destruction of habitats by the encroachment of people today. Although the chimpanzee and the gibbon appear relatively safe for now, their increasing use in medical research could change all that.

*See also* Primates, behavior of; Primates, evolutionary features of

Consult: Jolly, A., *Evolution of Primate Behavior* (New York: Macmillan, 1972); LeGros Clark, W. E., *Antecedants of Man* (Chicago: University of Chicago Press, 1971); Napier, J., and Napier, P., *Handbook of Living Primates* (New York: Academic Press, 1968); Reynolds, V., *The Apes* (New York: Dutton, 1967); Simons, E., *Primate Evolution* (New York: Macmillan, 1972).

—*James F. Metress, University of Toledo*

*A young female orangutan, in Sumatra.*

**Applied Anthropology.** In the broadest sense, this term refers to the use of anthropological concepts, methods, theories, and findings for a specific purpose. In this sense, a trained anthropologist need not be personally or directly involved in the actual application of the science or its conclusions. Some years after publication of his doctoral dissertation on the peyote religion, Weston La Barre discovered that converts were using his findings as a text to aid their learning of the rituals and practices of their Native American religion. Similarly, in later years his book was used in court cases which overturned state laws prohibiting the practice of the peyote religion. Whether or not a professional anthropologist is actively engaged, once the approaches and knowledge created by the science become publicly known they are subject to diffusion and use by others.

But applied anthropology is also defined in a narrower and more conventional fashion, one that requires the employment of an anthropologist by someone or some organization which is attempting to bring about technological, cultural, economic, or social changes. Generally such employment places the anthropologist—at least temporarily—outside the usual academic setting of the science.

**Beginnings.** However applied anthropology is defined, all subfields of the science have been used for various purposes. During World War II, for example, anthropological linguists were responsible for developing methods and materials for improved, intensive instruction in a large number of exotic languages. Similarly, today numerous linguists are involved in developing instructional programs which aim at teaching Native American children their tribal languages. Indeed, much of what is published as basic linguistic research has been funded by missionary societies which need knowledge of native languages to facilitate instruction in Christian dogma.

In like fashion, physical anthropologists are regularly employed in applied tasks of various kinds. These range from forensic medicine (where the physical anthropologist uses his skills to identify human remains for legal purposes) to specialized anthropometric studies involving improved design for man-machine relationships (e. g., cockpit design for the aerospace industry). And archaeologists are often involved in a variety of applied tasks—museum work, for example, or the reconstruction of historic sites for state and federal commissions interested in developing tourist facilities with educational functions.

However, it is social anthropology and cultural anthropology that are most deeply involved in direct applications. The potential applications of cultural anthropology were fully recognized by such founders of the science as E. B. Tylor and Sir John Lubbock. Moreover, the earliest anthropological organizations in Great Britain and the United States evolved directly out of antislavery and other reform groups. At that time the major field of potential application was the administration of native peoples. The basic concept was that anthropologists, with their special knowledge and involvement with native peoples, might be able to influence the development of social policy; or, once policy was established, they might be able to affect its execution. Thus some early 19th-century anthropologists sought the elimination of human slavery, the amelioration of poverty in urban areas, and the creation of development programs for defeated and colonized peoples. As it turned out, anthropologists had negligible impact on the formulation of new social policy. Their applications were confined largely to improving the execution of policies formed by others.

**Basic versus Applied.** By the opening years of the 20th century a new doctrine had emerged which firmly contrasted basic (or pure) anthropological research with applied work. Basic research became (and today remains) identified as the most valuable and prestigious variety. Applied anthropology was thereafter subject to invidious comparison. Supposedly this distinction was based on the ideal model of scientific inquiry—pure research proceeding unhampered by policy matters, practical issues, or similar involvement with the real world of affairs. Basic research, it was believed, was also a necessary precondition to application. Pure science had to generate sound theory before technological applications could be attempted. This doctrine, which is basically a rationalization for disengagement, does not, however, correspond to the facts of the history of science. There we find practical applications preceding (and often prompting) scientific inquiry. Steam engines were built well before there was a sound thermodynamic theory. And anthropological theorizing about the impact of inequality of opportunity and reward on the functioning of societies or the dynamics of personality came centuries after the adoption of slavery or the evolution of caste systems.

**Roles and Varieties.** The potential uses of anthropology have appealed to a wide variety of public and private organizations. Because anthropological research is expensive, generally the employing agencies have been highly placed and amply funded. Whether working for a colonial office with an interest in improving techniques of native administration, or an international organization assessing cultural factors in population control, or a private foundation seeking an independent judgment of the human impact of an established policy, most applied anthropologists have been the servants of those in power. It is not the anthropologist who decides that there should be a Peace Corps program: most anthropologists do not even have much influence upon those who make such decisions. Instead, once a Peace Corps is created, applied anthropologists become involved in training Peace Corps members to be more effective in their work. Or, using their research skills, they analyze the ongoing operations of specific Peace Corps programs. Thus the basic relationship of applied anthropologists has been unilateral. They are employed by, work under the direction of, and report to an agency which is external to the people whose culture they study. In recent years, such relationships have caused grave conflict and stress within the profession, turning on issues of ethics and responsibility to the cultures anthropologists have traditionally investigated.

Applied anthropologists have not, however, been proscribed from publishing their findings. Indeed, a great deal of what is published as basic anthropological research has in fact been funded by agencies with vested interests in the utility of the knowledge generated. This applied to most of the classic tribal studies of African and Pacific Island peoples, and it applies today to many sophisticated research programs carried out, for example, under the sponsorship of the National Institutes of Mental Health. Generally, such relationships create a variety of tensions. The funding source wants clear evidence of useful applications. It wants these results quickly. And it wants the anthropologist to assume some responsibility for the consequences of application. The anthropologist in turn wants maximum freedom of operation. Analysis and writing require large amounts of time. The language used is appropriate for a professional audience, not for administrators or legislators. And the issue of accepting administrative responsibility is seen as irrelevant, since the anthropologist is generally only on temporary leave from a university post. The administrator speaks of "involvement," the anthropologist of "objectivity," and often they part on less than agreeable terms.

Nearly all professional anthropologists earn their livelihoods as teachers-researchers in colleges and universities. Only a few have ever engaged themselves full time for long periods in directly applied roles. These roles are as varied as the agencies served. Anthropologists have taught in foreign service institutes and similar training programs for overseas personnel: thus they have participated in the training of colonial officials, native administrators, corporate executives, Peace Corps members, and others. Often they have served as cultural interpreters, explaining the workings of alien cultural ways to those who carry out policy. They have served in regional and country research institutes, generally overtly, as in time of war. As go-betweens in conflict situations, they have attempted to improve communications and relationships between opposed communities. They have served as expert witnesses before state and local courts, where they explain the history and culture of a society in order to produce equitable legal decisions. A few have assumed high administrative positions, perhaps in a federal bureau or a South American hacienda, where they attempt to improve administrative practice.

**Contemporary.** With the decline in the academic job market in the United States and with large numbers of highly trained anthropologists pouring out of the graduate schools, it is likely that professional anthropologists will be seeking careers in other than academic positions. Simultaneously, there has been increasing concern among anthropologists for a new work ethic, one that binds them more effectively and responsibly to the subjects of their research. These two trends may well result in a breakdown in the traditional pattern of unilateral relations with administrative or funding agencies. Henceforth, anthropologists are likely to serve the powerless outside of traditional academic contexts.

*See also* Acculturation; Cultural change
Consult: Clifton, J. A. (ed.), *Applied Anthro-*

*pology: Readings in the Uses of the Science of Man* (Boston: Houghton Mifflin, 1970); Foster, G. M., *Applied Anthropology* (Boston: Little, Brown, 1969).
—*James Clifton, University of Wisconsin, Green Bay*

**Appollonian-Dionysian.** Ruth Benedict believed there were two opposed types of North American Indian cultures. Taking her cue from Nietzsche's ideas about Greek tragedy, she attempted to find the basic values and themes in whole cultural systems. In her view, Appollonian versus Dionysian represented actively opposite ways of fixing the values and directions of human existence.

Benedict saw the Pueblo (town-dwelling) Indians of the Southwest as examples of culturally imposed moderation, restraint, cooperation, and control, whereas other North American tribes celebrated excess. Of the several Pueblo communities, the Zuni were exemplars of the Appollonian avoidance of excess—especially unusual psychological states—in day-to-day living. All the other tribes, particularly those of the Plains and the Northwest Coast, Benedict saw as Dionysian—their lives were intense emotional dramas involving pursuit of ecstatic experiences and personal vision states. Dionysian existence was charged with great competition and rivalry.

Benedict's broad characterizations of whole cultures as Appollonian or Dionysian have not been validated. Her approach has been regarded as too personal, her results as faulty generalizations. The Kwakiutl were not wholly Dionysian: they had an amiable, cooperative side to them. Nor were the Zuni wholly Appollonian: their lives exhibited much tension, strain, and conflict as well.

*See also* Configurationalism; Themes, cultural
Consult: Benedict, Ruth, *Patterns of Culture* (Boston: Houghton Mifflin, 1961).
—*James Clifton, University of Wisconsin, Green Bay*

**Arch.** There are two means of spanning large open spaces in buildings without use of horizontal beams or lintels. The *corbeled* or *false arch* achieves this by successive projections of blocks the ends of which are counterweighted. This simple device was known throughout the ancient world, being independently invented in numerous places. The *true arch*, however, spans open spaces

without the use of counterweights. The tapered, wedge-shaped blocks of the true arch are self-sustaining; they are held in place by friction and their own weight, locked together by the last stone (the keystone). The true arch was invented in the Near East more than 5,000 years ago and diffused widely thereafter.

*See also* Architecture

**Archaeology.** A dictionary defines this word as "the scientific study of the material remains of past human life and human activities, such as fossil human relics, artifacts, implements, inscriptions, interments, etc., especially from prehistoric or ancient or (less frequently) medieval times." Opposed to this bare approach is the observation that the primary objective of this social science is the study of human cultures. The ultimate appeal of archaeology is that we are dealing with human beings in the past.

Archaeology may be divided into two parts, classical and prehistoric. Classical archaeologists in the Old World deal with the periods of early history having writing. Since there is no ancient written language known in the New World, students of New World archaeology simply call themselves archaeologists. Classical archaeology (and all later history) includes roughly the most recent 5,000 years; prehistoric archaeology includes about 99.998 percent of our existence on earth, accepting the African dates for our ancestors of about 3 million years. In the United States, classical archaeology is generally studied in departments of art history and archaeology in universities and colleges, whereas prehistoric archaeology is traditionally studied in anthropology departments (where it is taught along with cultural anthropology, linguistics, and physical anthropology). A number of other branches of archaeology have arisen in the last two decades, among them historical archaeology, industrial archaeology, and nautical archaeology.

Chronology—the establishing of relative and absolute time sequences—is the foundation of archaeology. Climatology, botany, zoology, geology, chemistry, biology, and other sciences are drawn upon to elucidate the study.

In some countries, notably the totalitarian states, archaeology has been subverted to validate claims to territories and peoples and to support ideologies.

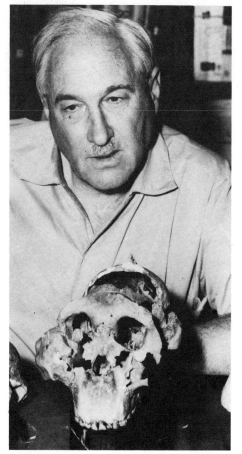

*Louis S. B. Leakey*

Some countries complain that their heritage is being drained overseas, reminding us that the great museums of the world are filled with archaeological treasures at the expense of the places of their origin. Insatiable demand by art collectors and museums for antiquities has contributed to the exploitation of archaeological sites by illicit excavators and to the wholesale manufacture of forgeries, posing a number of nettling problems. Behind all this is the realization that there is a finite number of archaeological sites in the world.

Since World War II, there has been an increased use of quantification in archaeology, with the application of computers and other sophisticated mathematical innovations. Attempts are being made to put archaeo-

logical studies through a systems analysis in order to extract new information from both old and new data. Such an approach promises greater understanding of the life and times of prehistoric people. To a similar end, some archaeologists are emphasizing cultural change, or what they call *processual archaeology*, in an effort to explore the causes and manifestations of cultural change.

See also Classical archaeology; Prehistoric archaeology; Prehistory

Consult: Daniel, Glyn E., *The Origins and Growth of Archaeology* (Baltimore: Penguin, 1970); Dunnell, Robert C., *Systematics in Prehistory* (New York: Free Press, 1971); Leone, Mark P. (ed.), *Contemporary Archaeology* (Carbondale: Southern Illinois University Press, 1972); Rouse, Irving, *Introduction to Prehistory: A Systematic Approach* (New York: McGraw-Hill, 1972); Woodall, J. Ned, *An Introduction to Modern Archaeology* (Cambridge, Mass.: Schenkman, 1972).

—Ralph S. Solecki, Columbia University

**Archaeology, Classical.** See Classical archaeology.

**Archaeomagnetism.** See Paleomagnetism and archaeomagnetism.

**Archetype.** C. G. Jung believed that under the unconscious symbolizations of individuals lay deposited the experience of the human race. This collective unconscious, according to Jung, consists of powerful resi-

*Digging site of a Stone Age camp in Olorgesailie Gorge, Kenya. It was in this gorge that Dr. Mary Leakey discovered the earliest hand axes.*

dues of ancestral experience with the critical problems of human existence. These unconscious archetypes are *structures* expressed as natural symbolizations which are distinguishable from the personal unconsciousness of individuals. Archetypes do not find expression in normal thinking or living. They are expressed only in the most profoundly human experiences, religious thought, great literature, or the thinking of psychotics whose egosystems have been overwhelmed by the archetypes of the collective unconscious.

See also Anima-animus; Collective unconscious; Jung, Carl Gustav; Symbol

**Architecture.** There are four architectural principles which have been employed in most of the buildings of history: the arch, the post and lintel, solid walls, and the tripod. In pole dwellings, the *arch* is an eminently simple construct. All it takes is a pole with one end set in the ground, then bent toward the center of the structure to meet a pole bent from the opposite direction. For early humans, post and lintel construction may have been quite a technological feat since it requires rigid timbers which can support considerable weight. Cutting such timbers with stone tools is a severe problem which some contemporary groups simplify by transporting the weight-bearing timbers from an old house site to a new one. Solid walls of stone, brick, or wood are also widely used. Occasionally a tripod principle is employed as in the tepee of the Plains Indian.

The economic system of a people places severe constraints upon the kind of structure they build. Mobile hunters and gatherers usually favored dwellings that could be erected quickly and easily from materials that came readily to hand. Pastoralists or horse nomads such as the Plains Indians could carry their building materials from place to place. Only people who expected to stay in one location for a number of years (or to return frequently) could afford the investment in time and materials which led to the construction of large, permanent dwellings.

Through history, many materials have been used for building and house coverings. The range of materials depends on the environment, but the choice of materials depends on human culture.

**Stone.** Although the use of stone is of great archaeological interest, stone is rarely

*Above, the Acropolis in Athens; below, a modern high-rise apartment building in New York City.*

employed for an entire structure. Sometimes it is laid in courses to create solid walls supporting a roof of wood or grass. Sometimes stone is piled up almost haphazardly and held together with mud. Occasionally, as in the Mediterranean and Africa, stone is used for both walls and roof. For the roof, often the stones are overlapped slightly until the open space is bridged with a *corbeled arch.* The *true arch* was not known until the Early Dynastic period at Ur (ca. 2900–2450 BC).

**Mud.** Mud was the favored building material among many peoples—often in conjunction with stone foundations, since mud melts if exposed to the wet for a long period of time. Sun-dried *mud bricks* could be laid in courses to build up walls in the same way stone or fired bricks could be used. Moreover, *wet mud* could be built up in courses and then allowed to dry in place. Frequently, mud is also used as plaster over walls made of stone or sticks.

**Reeds.** Reeds or grasses tied into bundles could substitute for poles or logs if the latter materials were not available. Grasses are also commonly used as a roofing material or to fill the spaces between the logs or poles which are the structural supports.

**Wood.** Wood is the most versatile building material. It is easily obtained, easily shaped, and adaptable. The simplest wooden structures are made with a framework of light poles bent over to meet in the middle *(arched poles).* The space between the poles may be covered with grass, mats, branches, skins, or bark. The most common form of wooden house consists of a series of upright posts connected by horizontal poles at the top (post and lintel). The space between the poles may be filled or left open, depending on the climate and local preference. The roof can be supported by a center pole or by a ridge pole. *Log cabins* made with notched logs belong to the Eurasian tradition, particularly in areas where tall, straight trees are available.

See also Arch; Housing and shelter; Stonework; Wood

Consult: Cranstone, B. A. L., "Environment and Choice in Dwelling and Settlement: An Ethnographical Survey," in *Man, Settlement and Urbanism,* ed. Peter J. Ucko, Ruth Tringham, and G. W. Dimbleby (London: Duckworth, 1972); Driver, H. E., *Indians of North America* (Chicago: University of Chicago Press, 1961); Piggott, Stuart, *Ancient Europe* (Chicago: Aldine, 1965).

—*Thomas P. Myers, University of Nebraska*

**Ardrey, Robert** (b. 1908). American playwright, amateur anthropologist and ethologist, who argues in his books, written for the lay person, that *Homo sapiens* is innately territorial and aggressive. Most social scientists are critical of Ardrey's evidence and conclusions.

See also Aggression; Territoriality

Consult: Ardrey, Robert, *The Territorial Imperative* (New York: Atheneum, 1966).

**Area Studies.** See Culture areas of the world.

**Arensberg, Conrad M.** (b. 1910). This anthropologist gained eminence through participation in Warner's Yankee City studies, industrial investigation, major Irish ethnographies, research on India, economic anthropology (with Polanyi), functionalism, and operationalism (with Chapple).

**Aristocracy.** In ancient Greece, aristocracy meant a system of government under control of a hereditary class considered superior to the masses because of its social prominence. Historically the term has been applied to such groups as the ruling nobility of prerevolutionary France and the nobility of pre-20th-century Great Britain. In contemporary usage, the term designates the privileged classes without narrow reference to political rule.

See also Class

**Army.** This term may be defined as an organized fighting force which generally represents a group in combat against another similarly organized unit. Disagreement exists regarding at what level a fighting force may be termed an army. Indeed, there is substantial disagreement regarding at what level of conflict the term *war* may be used. Otterbein (1973) has demonstrated that the relationship between warfare and level of sociocultural evolution is not a clear one.

Even simple societies may carry on efficient warfare, in which case their fighting forces may be considered true armies. Some, however, wish to reserve the term for permanently organized fighting forces representing the interests of politically organized states.

See also Social stratification; Warfare

Consult: Otterbein, Keith, "The Anthropology

of War," in *Handbook of Social and Cultural Anthropology*, ed. John Honigman (Chicago: Rand McNally, 1973).

**Art.** The arts and the canons of taste by which they are judged (aesthetics) arise out of cultural conditioning and are specific to a particular cultural tradition. Thus a conceptual groundwork must be laid before *art* and *aesthetics* can be defined. An anthropological definition of art must be broad enough to be used cross-culturally for comparison, but must also take indigenous categories of art and aesthetics into consideration. To understand (rather than just appreciate) art as human behavior, art styles, or aesthetic systems, it is essential to comprehend the principles on which such conceptualizations are based as perceived by the social group which holds them. This underlying organization or metastructure is as important for understanding art in society as an analysis of the content of the item itself. Only if we understand the principles of organization can we decide whether a creation conforms to the standards recognized by the society in which it was made. Such standards cannot be used cross-culturally, for members of different cultures simply do not react in the same ways to the same stimuli. This is well recognized in most social and cultural domains, but art is still too often regarded as a "universal language."

Artists in the West, especially the cubists, surrealists, and practitioners of other artistic movements of the 20th century, have used the arts of other societies as inspiration for their own work. They have transformed creations of other cultures into "primitive art" and treated them as part of the Western tradition and thus subject to Western standards of structure, function, and aesthetics. This is most apparent in the graphic and plastic arts, but it is also found in music (the influence of Indonesian gamelan music on Debussy), literature (the influence of Japanese No drama on Ezra Pound), and dance (the influence of folk dance movements on modern dance). Although metamorphosing the creations of other cultures into the mainstream of Western art is certainly valid, it must be recognized that the Western artist is bringing his or her own aesthetics to bear on non-Western art. The result can tell us little about non-Western art and little that is anthropologically significant. However, Western art is simply one of the artistic traditions of the

Marcel Duchamp's Nude Descending a Staircase, No. 2 *(1912).*

world, and thus such syncretisms are anthropologically interesting.

With this perspective in mind, art may be defined as cultural forms that result from creative processes which manipulate movement, sound, words, or materials. Aesthetics may be defined as ways of thinking about such forms. It is likely that these forms are thought of in a special way by the society that makes and uses them, but few anthropologists have investigated this problem. An anthropologist cannot be said to understand the art of another culture unless he or she can comprehend how that art is regarded by the society in question.

From the perspective of material culture, the arts are integral to all three levels of culture—that is, they are involved with the production of goods, social networks of interaction, and ideational expressions. Thus art must be studied with techniques appropriate to the investigation of technology, sociology, and aesthetics, as well as with tech-

niques that will illuminate history and change. Anthropological analyses of cultural forms usually attempt to elucidate function and structure, and art is no exception. In recent years structural relationships among the arts and society have been increasingly expressed in terms of *homology*—that is, as consistency of relationships between various cultural manifestations and the underlying structures they express. Techniques of analysis are often similar to those used in linguistics—such as the attempts of transformational grammar to present instructions on how to produce cultural forms or the etic/emic distinctions derived from phonology. These are not, however, strictly "linguistic methods." Rather, they can be used to analyze various cultural phenomena, including linguistics and art.

The proposition that the relationship between the arts and society is basically one of consistency with each other and the underlying structure need not be antagonistic to the idea that art may express avant-gardism or the protests of minority groups. Nor is it antagonistic to the idea that art may express official political philosophy. On the con-

*Ibeji, from the Yoruba tribe in Nigeria.*

*Attic red-figure skyphos. Monead with Thyrsos (5th century BC), from near Athens.*

ate" activity is basically ethnocentric, as it is a product of highly differentiated societies such as our own where artists exist as specialists. In many simpler societies the arts are embedded in other institutions and in everyday life, and it is we—the analysts—who tease them out for admiration or examination.

In all the manifestations of the arts—visual and plastic, temporal and spatial—there exists a performer or artist who produces a formal product which is experienced by an audience. The formal entity is the personal, and at the same time cultural and human, expression of the artist and contains

*Bronze statue of the god Siva, from southern India (14th-15th century).*

trary, such possibilities help to lay bare the complex underlying structures of societies and the functions of art within them.

Metaphorical analogies of art with language usually propose that art is a semiotic system in which aspects of art refer to ideas or things other than themselves. But it is by no means clear how such images and symbols come to acquire these meanings or how their messages are transmitted. Indeed, for some artistic media, such as music or painting in nonrealistic modes, it is often difficult to see the relevance of semiotic analysis. Yet for other artistic media, semiotic analysis may lead to a deep awareness of symbolic systems and meaning.

In short, the anthropological study of art is essentially an analysis of cultural forms and the social processes which produce them according to the aesthetic precepts of a specific group of people at a specific point in time. Discovering the structure and content of such forms, processes, and philosophies from the indigenous point of view is preeminently an ethnographic task. With empirical studies in hand, cross-cultural re-

search of real significance on the nature and universality of artistic and aesthetic systems becomes a possibility.

*See also* Art and anthropology; Art and society; Art of Africa; Art of India and Southeast Asia; Art of Mexico, Central America, and the West Indies; Art of Oceania; Art of the Eskimo; Art of the Far East; Art of the Middle East; Art of the North American Indian; Art of the Northwest Coast of North America; Art of the South American Indian; Art, primitive; Emics; Etics Consult: D'Azevedo, Warren L., "A Structural Approach to Esthetics: Toward a Definition of Art in Anthropology," *American Anthropologist* 60(4):702–714, 1958; Kaeppler, Adrienne L., "Aesthetics of Tongan Dance," *Ethnomusicology* 15:175–185, 1971; Maquet, Jacques, *Introduction to Aesthetic Anthropology* (Cambridge, Mass.: Addison-Wesley, 1971).
—Adrienne L. Kaeppler, Bishop Museum

**Art and Anthropology.** Art is a branch of what anthropologists call expressive (as opposed to instrumental) culture; it comprises those activities and products judged primarily by aesthetic experience. Both art and aesthetics are cultural universals, but satisfactory cross-cultural definitions have yet to be achieved. Our concept of art as a "separ-

many levels of representation in overt or symbolic guise. The audience (which for present purposes does not include the artist) derives aesthetic appreciation and intellectual understanding from the art form in terms of a set of values which may or may not be shared with the artist. It is the examination of these elements, taken separately and together, which forms the subject matter of the anthropology of art.

Early comparative studies of art concentrated on the forms, attempting to classify the arts and to place them in chronological, geographical, and stylistic schemes. Thus there were attempts to show evolution from naturalistic to geometric (and vice versa) and to reconstruct the paths by which various styles and features had diffused over time and between cultures. Sometimes the arts of primitives, children, neurotics, and early peoples were grouped together on the basis of formal divergences from European male academic arts. Such theories ignored the content and context of non-Western art, which required field investigation.

More sophisticated attention to style (permanence of formal features over time and space) and to iconography (the analysis of representation of subject matter) has shown that though originality is not a major goal and individualism is not highly valued in non-Western art, change does take place and personal styles and signs are almost universally recognizable. Materials, techniques, and available media also influence or limit style. Though all art has to do with symmetry, rhythm, and elements of form, arguments still rage as to whether there are any universals of aesthetics or beauty. Furthermore, for the anthropologist there is even the problem that what we call art in other peoples' culture may not be seen as an aesthetic experience by them and we may miss what is to them the highest form of aesthetic activity. We may assert, however, that all art is an attempt to manage one's aesthetic environment.

The content of art—from the simplest representations to the most abstruse modern music—is examined in terms of the signs and symbols transmitted and the context of production and consumption. Meanings conveyed may be at the level of personal symbols, deriving from the artist's own experience or from dreams and fantasy and therefore shared by few; or the symbols may be culturally specific, known to all members of the group but subject to different read-

*Twentieth-century fetish figure from the Congo.*

ings by outsiders. Some authorities, such as Freud and Jung and their followers, claim that there are universal human symbols common to all art traditions.

The psychocultural approach has also been applied to the characteristics and conditions of creativity—that special quality for insight and revelation, and the tolerance for ambiguities, which vex neater minds. Creativity in the arts is the ability to express in form in such a way as to emotionally arouse the audience. And the audience will respond in a culturally specific way, according to conscious expectations and traditions and unconscious features of enculturation.

Attempts have been made to explain art styles in terms of the social and cultural fea-

tures of the societies where they are found. Romanticism has been correlated with reform and classicism with entrenched authority; complex curvilinear forms have been correlated with harsh societies and empty spaces with egalitarian societies—but the task has just begun. An extension of this kind of association is the notion that art styles not only reflect society but are even ahead of general trends; thus art styles change with the vanguard of social change and artists are said to be leaders of trends.

The functions of art are manifold. One function is to provide aesthetic satisfaction, but only in the case of "art for art's sake" in highly stratified civilizations could this be taken as the main function. For the artist, art activity expresses and releases some inner urge or fantasy, often by sublimation. For the society, art often provides a safety valve for expressing, in a ritualized manner, dangerous or taboo thoughts. Art may function within (or function against) the religious and political order: it has been said that art expresses messages that words cannot convey. Thus most forms of art promote the religious beliefs and social order of the society. The culturally shared symbols are understood consciously or unconsciously and promote solidarity, internal order, ethnic identity, or social processes. The fact that these value statements are made in an art form which is ritual or entertainment makes them all the more unquestionable in the minds of the majority. At the conscious level, artists or authorities may attempt to use the power of the arts to promote their own ends or to arouse social protest: Picasso depicted the horrors of war in his *Guernica;* the government of Mexico has employed famous muralists to express the values of the revolution and the uniqueness of Mexican nationhood.

Artist, audience, and critic—and the latter is always a member of the former two categories—are in a dialectic whereby art is never stagnant. Artists are self-recruited or they are recruited and sustained by their ability to perform for their audience. They must follow the traditions of their culture; yet, at the same time, they must shape and lead them. Art is a mediator between scientific knowledge and mythical thought, between structure and event.

See also Art; Art and society; Art, primitive; Tourist art

Consult: Biebuyck, D. (ed.), *Tradition and Creativity in Tribal Art* (Berkeley: University of

California Press, 1969); Forge, A. (ed.), *Primitive Art and Society* (London: Oxford University Press, 1973); Gerbrands, A. A., *Art as an Element of Culture, Especially in Negro Africa* (Leiden: Rijksmuseum foor Volkenkunde, 1957); Helm, J. (ed.), "Essays in the Verbal and Visual Arts," *Proceedings of the 1966 Meetings of the American Ethnological Society* (1967); Jopling, C. F. (ed.), *Art and Aesthetics in Primitive Societies* (New York: Dutton, 1971); Otten, C. M. (ed.), *Anthropology and Art* (New York: Natural History Press, 1971).
　　*—Nelson H. H. Graburn, University of California, Berkeley*

## Art and Society.

The anthropological study of art, sometimes called "primitive art," focuses on the contextual setting in which art is produced and used. The anthropologist, as anthropologist, is not an art critic. His or her concern is with the meaning of art, a frozen bit of culture, in its proper socio-cultural setting. To discern the meaning of an item of art, it is necessary to know its relationships with other art items and the local social and cultural settings as well. By art is meant all the imaginative expressions of the human mind—painting, sculpture, music, folklore, and the like.

**Social Factors and Art.** Because anthropological science began with the study of rather small, homogeneous societies, an approach to cultural products (including art) developed which stressed the entire situation (holism). These small societies tended to be isolated, nonliterate, and lacking in full-time specialists. The audiences for art products tended to know each other and to share values. "They knew what they liked" and were quick to make their judgments known to the artist. Indeed such audiences have been observed to criticize works as they were being produced—thus giving the artist instant feedback. In simple societies most art has a use beyond the aesthetic. It is made for a practical purpose—to be part of a ritual, to be used as a drinking vessel, and so forth. There is no art produced for museums, though a lot of art consists of decorated structures (such as housebeams) and utensils.

This experience with small societies has influenced the way anthropologists view art in larger ones. They still look for social factors in interpreting its meaning. Thus, while

an American writer differs in social position from a storyteller among the Ibo of Nigeria, an understanding of both their social positions and functions is necessary to an understanding of their cultural products. In fact, there is still room for a good deal of ethnographic research on the role of the artist in various sociocultural contexts. More work such as that of Roger Abrahams and Charles Keil is needed. These two men have followed a tradition pioneered by Ruth Bunzel in her study of a Zuni potter. All three have looked at the role of creation. The importance of the artist's social position, motivation, attitude, training, use of his or her creation—all are given careful attention. Furthermore, the indigenous standards of excellence are examined. Abrahams calls this attention to the interaction between artist and audience the rhetorical approach to folklore. The object of creation has an especially important, sometimes supernatural, position in homogeneous societies—even those found within larger societies.

**Anthropology and Art Criticism.** Anthropologists have, since the days of Franz Boas, opposed the application of universal standards of judgment on art products. The total misunderstanding of African art has provided an object lesson. Ceremonial objects were interpreted in a Western frame of reference by critics who had no knowledge of the original context in which these objects were used. Various theories of "primitive prelogical mentality" were put forth to explain African and other primitive art.

The anthropological stress on understanding the total context has led to some changes in art criticism in our own society. Even specialists, after all, belong to some community, and a contextual approach, or Abrahams' rhetorical approach, can illuminate the interaction between artists and their audiences in the most industrialized countries. Eventually such an approach should produce truly valuable comparative studies of art and society.

*See also* Aesthetic appreciation; Art; Art, primitive

Consult: Abrahams, Roger D., "Introductory Remarks to a Rhetorical Theory of Folklore," *Journal of American Folklore* (81)320:1–16, 1968; Boas, Franz, *Primitive Art* (New York: Dover, 1927); Bunzel, Ruth, *The Pueblo Potter* (New York: Columbia University Press, 1929); Keil, Charles, *Urban Blues* (Chicago: University of Chicago Press, 1966).
　　*—Frank A. Salamone, St. John's University*

## Art of Africa: Central Africa.

The peoples of the Zaire Republic and neighboring areas have produced an immense variety of sculptures. Depending on diverse ethnic groups and stylistic areas, they range from human and animal figurines to masks, staffs, scepters, neckrests, stools, cups, boxes, slit-drums, bells, posts, and plankboards, and include delicately carved spear shafts and handles of axes, adzes, and knives. These sculptures are made in many different media. Preference is given to specified types of wood; but ivory, bone, iron, copper, stone, clay, and resin are also used. Masks are often intricate constructions made of a combination of wood, cloth, fibers, hide, resin, and metal. Some sculptures are richly adorned with decorative designs, beads, shells, exuviae, metal, or other materials; others excel by their unadorned simplicity. Colors

*Wood and cloth fetish figure, from the Byaka tribe, the Congo.*

(mostly red, white, black) may be applied to the entire sculpture or to parts of it. Some objects are darkened by means of fire, smoke, hot irons, or treatment with saps or mud; others are beautifully patinated through intensive usage and oiling. Oil, blood, or resin may be added to the surfaces in the course of consecration and usage.

The greatest diversity of sculpture occurs in the southern half of the Zaire Republic, overlapping into the Congo (Brazzaville), N Angola, and W Zambia. Among the better known art-producing groups we encounter, from west to east, the Kongo, Teke, Yaka, Suku, Mbala, Pende, Cokwe, Kuba, Ndengese, Luluwa, Lunda, Kanyok, Songye, Luba, and Tabwa. Many of these peoples have matrilineal and centralized political institutions, but there are several exceptions. All are Bantu-speakers, and many of the entities have close linguistic and historical connections. Among these entities are numerous smaller and larger groups—such as Dzing, Yans, Holo, Lwalwa, Mbagani, and Salampasu—where outstanding artistic traditions have flourished.

In the northern half of the Zaire Republic, overlapping into the Congo (Brazzaville), the Central African Republic, and the Sudan, the sculptural traditions have developed on a somewhat lesser scale throughout the rain

*Wood and leather chief's chair, from the Tokwe of Central Africa.*

forest and into the northern savannas, among such Bantu-speaking peoples as the Mongo, Ngala, Tetela, Mitoko, Lengola, Pere, Komo, Yela, Bali, and Lega, and among such non-Bantu peoples as the Ngbaka, Ngbandi, Mono, Furu, Zande, Mangbetu, and Bari. In many parts of this vast region, the relative scarcity of sculpture is amply compensated by rich smithing traditions, culminating in a great diversity of knives, swords, spears, arrowheads and spearheads, anklets, bracelets, and neckrings.

The first exhaustive attempts at a systematic classification of the various art styles in Central Africa were made by Olbrechts and Maesen. Detailed studies on specific groups or areas by Bastin, Biebuyck, Burssens, de Sousberghe, Timmermans, Volavkova, and others have added considerable refinement to these classifications, but definitive grouping and interpretation have yet to be produced.

No easy generalizations can be made about the usages, functions, and meanings of these sculptures, since various ethnic groups, and art-using institutions within and across them, have developed highly specific ideas about them. Many sculptures are directly linked with different forms of ancestral cult (heroic, royal, lineage, family, and personal ancestors). Others are intimately associated with beliefs about the survival of the soul and the life force, and are used in conjunction with burial ceremonies and grave sites. A few sculptures form an intrinsic part of healing, hunting, protective and aggressive magic, and divination. In widely scattered areas, sculptures are linked with initiation systems (circumcision and puberty ceremonies; membership in voluntary associations and cult groups). In addition to their ritual, social control, and status functions, they have an important didactic content. Sculptures as insignia and paraphernalia of rank and status, and as power and prestige symbols, also occur in many groups.

In any given group, numerous categories of artworks, with different functions and forms, may be present. A particular artwork can also carry multiple, more or less complementary, meanings and functions, depending to some extent on the context of usage.

In general, little is known regarding the artists, their method of working, their training, their motivations and creative freedom. Our ignorance is due partly to the rapid breakdown of the great artistic traditions in Central Africa under the impact of colonial

*Sisal vessel of the Boran tribe, Kenya.*

rule. Artists do not belong to exclusive castes, but operate within the framework of lineages, families, and courts. The users and patrons of the arts are overwhelmingly male, but in certain areas women have a special relationship with the arts. Many of the artworks are individually owned by chiefs, village headmen, lineage heads, cult leaders, or common members of the group; some are placed under the control of a collectivity (a lineage, a village, a chiefdom, a ritual community).

*See also* Art; Art, primitive; Art and society
Consult: Bastin, Marie-Louise, *Art decoratif Tshokwe*, 2 vols. (Lisbon: Publicacões Culturais, 1961); Biebuyck, Daniel, *Lega Culture: Art, Initiation, and Moral Philosophy among a Central African People* (Berkeley: University of California Press, 1973); Burssens, Herman, *Yanda-Beelden en Mani-Sekte bij de Azande*, 2 vols. (Tervuren: Musée Royal de l'Afrique Centrale, 1962); Cornet, J., *Art de l'Afrique noire au pays du fleuve Zaïre* (Brussels: Beaux-Arts, 1972); De Sousberghe, L., *L'Art pende* (Brussels: Beaux-Arts, 1958); Maesen, Albert, *Arte del Congo* (Rome: De Luca, 1959); Maesen, Albert, *Art of the Congo* (Minneapolis: Walker Art Center, 1967); Olbrechts, Frans M., *Plastiek van Kongo* (Antwerp: De Standaard-Boekhandel, 1946).
—*Daniel P. Biebuyck, University of Delaware*

**Art of Africa: West Africa.** West Africa is one of the great art-producing regions of the world. The geographical area stretches from the Atlantic coast in Senegal eastward to the Camerouns. The southern boundary is the Guinea coast. Northward, successively, through tropical forest, orchard scrub, and savannas, the area reaches into the desert scrub of the Sahara. The Sahara was not always a desert, for it has yielded evidence, notably the Tassili frescoes, of an extensive rock art practiced by hunters (6000 BC) followed by herders (4000 BC), who inhabited a fertile land. The peoples of the southern Camerouns are related to those to their south. Consideration of the art of West Africa should embrace the Fang and also the Pangwe and Kota in Gabon and Congo.

**Art.** The art of West Africa has a long history. Styles have come and gone, traditions have persisted but changed in expression. Much of the fame of African art rests on objects which found their way to museums and collections in the West, in the last century and in this one, but there they were enjoyed in a non-African context, their meaning gone with their separation from the role they played in the lives of the people who made them. Thus many of the great works of African art should be thought of as specimens for the study of the history of African art, although often their context is neither recorded nor understood.

Styles may have died. Some masks and figures may no longer be carved, and the brass smiths may no longer cast furnishings for shrines. Festivals and rituals and masquerades perhaps have changed. Nevertheless, the fame of West African art must not be thought of as resting solely with the work of artists now dead. West African art should be regarded in terms of the dynamic role it played in society. Sculpture functioned as a vital element in the role ancestors were believed to have in the lives of the living. Carved masks were agents for spirits and the benefits they could bring to the living, but they were art when the masqueraders appeared in full costume to cavort before an audience, to stress the need for social discipline at initiation rites, to chase away witches upsetting people's lives, or simply to add excitement to recreation. It is the dynamic quality of West African art which continues even if its forms of expression have been modified and it has been made to function in new ways.

Because great plastic art has been produced by so many peoples in West Africa, only a few cultures may be mentioned here even though others not mentioned may be of equal fame. Western scholars tend to give attention to carving and metalwork, but the use of a wide variety of materials for costume should also be noted. Moreover, fine weaving is practiced on vertical looms by women and on horizontal ones by men; pottery for utilitarian and ritual needs is made by women and sometimes by men; and architecture is present, particularly elaborate work in mud in the more arid areas. Nor may we dismiss the important role of music and song in ceremony and festival and the use of proverbs and poetry as forms of aesthetic expression.

**Historic Art.** The glories of past kingdoms that waxed and waned in the Sudan from AD 700 on, as they dominated the centuries-old trade across the Sahara, are hinted at in early Arab accounts. More knowledge of the past

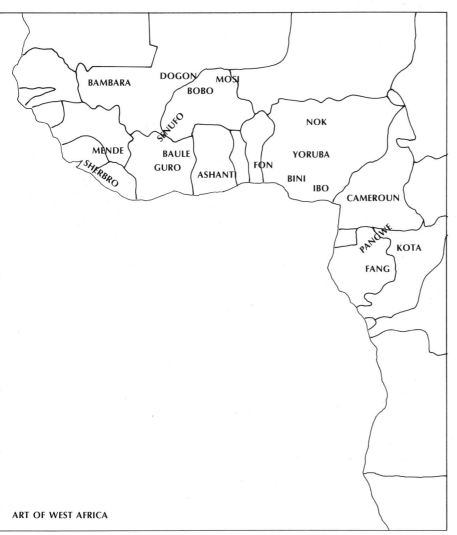

ART OF WEST AFRICA

**Recent Art.** Representative of art traditions of strength and history but also adaptive to the press of modern times are the following: (1) Dogon—ancestor figures (*tellem*) and masks with various extensions, some of giant extent (15 feet), and similar productions from neighbors such as the Mosi and Bobo. (2) Bambara—carved antelope headdresses. (3) Senufo—carved figures and many masks for secret societies. (4) Dan—masks for similar contexts, also found among neighbors to the west, such as the Mende. (5) Baule—carved figures and secret society masks of great repose, also found among neighbors such as the Guro. (6) Ashanti—brass weights and work in gold; carved stools as emblems of clan ancestors; small wooden fertility dolls (*akuaba*). (7) Fon—small genre figures in brass and silverwork. (8) Yoruba—tremendous range of artistic expression in wood and metal for shrines, masked societies, innumerable deities; small wooden effigies in memory of twins (*ibeji*). (9) Ibo and neighbors—carvings for ancestors and a vari-

*Above, ancestor shrines to Oka Eweka II (foreground) and Oka Obowanwe, the present king's father and grandfather, Benin City. Brass memorial heads support carved ivory tusks. Below, Fon brass figure, cast in 1954 in Ebomey.*

survives to us from the chronicles of European contacts with the Guinea coast which began in the 15th century. With evidence from such sources and from modern inquiry into archaeology, ethnology, and art history, it is possible to surmise the existence of a sculptural tradition in terra cotta going back to before the time of Christ—at Nok, in Nigeria; continuing at Ife with its richly varied but lifelike forms (? 10th century AD) and with additional manifestations there in bronze; and at Igbo Ukwu (9th century AD) and Benin (ca. AD 1325 onward). Knowledge of casting bronze at Benin came from Ife and resulted in six centuries of one of the world's great bronze traditions. Casting continues at Benin but it was in the 16th, 17th, and mid-18th centuries that the finest works, including ivory carvings, were produced. European contact in the 15th century led to a fine tourist art in ivory emanating from Benin and from the Sherbro of Sierra Leone. But it was not until the 19th century and increasing contact with people of the interior that the world really began to learn of the numerous art-producing cultures, many with long-established traditions of fine sculpture in wood (e.g., Dogon, Yoruba, Benin) and elaborate court arts supported by a variety of artisans, many engaged full time in their crafts (e.g., Fon, Ashanti, Cameroun grasslands people).

*Stone figure of the Yoruba tribe in Nigeria.*

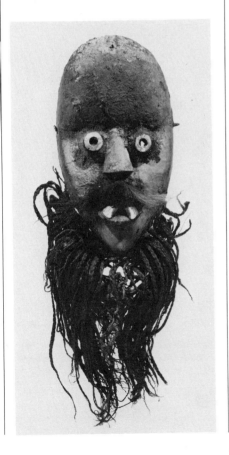

*Above, carved wood figure of the Senufo tribe of Mali. Below, wood face mask with braided hair fringe and eyes outlined in metal, from the Kono tribe of the Ivory Coast.*

ety of masks to various spirits for different cults. (10) Cameroons grasslands—wide variety of forms in wood: carved ancestor figures, masks, architectural decoration, furniture, utensils; tobacco pipes in clay and brass; elaborate use of bead decoration. (11) Pangwe and Fang—secret society masks and naturalistic grave guardian figures which become abstract reliquaries among the Kota.

Contemporary West African art shows great adaptability to the impact of the modern world and the social changes being wrought. Western forms of literature and the theater have been modified and charged with local expression, mainly in the large urban settings. Craftsmen have been quick to adapt their skills to the demand for tourist art, ranging from bric-a-brac and trinkets to carvings representative of traditional forms for the airport connoisseur. In the countryside, traditional needs continue even if the repertoire of forms and styles has changed.

See also Art and society; Tourist art
Consult: Willett, Frank, *African Art: An Introduction* (New York: Praeger, 1971).

—Philip J. C. Dark, Southern Illinois University

**Art of Asia.** See Art of India and Southeast Asia; Art of the Far East.

## Art of India and Southeast Asia.

### INDIA

The arts of India are essentially religious. They developed irregularly, changed slowly, and touched vast areas of the Asian continent. Aryan invaders from the Iranian plateau entered the Indus valley in ca. 1500 BC bringing civilization, the Sanskrit language, and the Vedic religion to India. Brahmanism, which unified Vedic beliefs in personified, natural phenomena into an abstract religion, became the dominant religious force in India and also gave structure to Indian society. However, the Jain and Buddhist faiths developed in the 6th century BC as a reaction to the inflexible Brahmanic caste. Buddhism, because it grew to develop two distinctive forms (Theravada, "the Lesser Vehicle"; Mahayana, "the Greater Vehicle") and incorporated the Brahmanic pantheon, had the most influence on art.

Archaeologists have uncovered ancient cities and a variety of objects and tools made from stone, metal, ivory, and pottery, but not until the establishment of the first pan-Indian empire of the Mauryas (ca. 4th century BC) was monumental art produced in durable materials. Notably, the Buddhist King Asoka, who reigned in the 3rd century BC, erected Persian-style commemorative columns that had a dual imperial and religious function.

**Architecture.** The earliest Indian architectural forms date to the period after the breakup of the Mauryan empire, from the 3rd century BC to the early years of the Christian era. The simple *stupa* (a dome-shaped structure designed to contain holy relics), *chaitya* halls, sanctuaries carved from rock in a basilica plan with barrel vault, and square monasteries and chapels—these are the basic structures in an architectural tradition that was to become increasingly complex. Significant advances are visible in structures made during the post-Gupta period (6th to 8th centuries AD), especially in the south where the style of cave sanctuaries like Ajanta, and

*Bronze statue of Kāliya Krishna, from Tanjavur District in southern India, 15th century.*

monolithic, free-standing rock structures like Ellura and Mamallapurum, is characterized by the repetition of certain ornamental forms into decorative motifs and by the development of layered, pyramid-shaped roofs.

In the medieval period (9th to 16th centuries) construction in brick and stone permitted greater complexity in architectural form. An array of niches, foliated cusps, pilasters, and ornamental sculpture disguised the strongly angular shape of temples to the point that square buildings took on a circular appearance. The pyramidal roof became taller and took the shape of a dome with smaller domes arranged in decreasing scale on each side. Every region of India elaborated endlessly on these basic principles and developed distinctive variations; probably the most original are the *gopuras* in SE India, which are rectangular towers topped with a barrel-shaped roof.

The final architectural contribution to India was made from the 13th to the 17th centuries by Muslim rulers who built numerous magnificent mosques, tombs, and palaces. By combining the Indian tradition with an architectural style created in Persia, they produced buildings that have a simplicity and elegance foreign to Indian architecture.

**Sculpture.** Early Indian sculpture, robust figures of male and female divinities and flat narrative reliefs, decorated post-Mauryan architectural monuments in stylized forms that, nevertheless, betray a spontaneous observation of nature. Although largely Buddhist in intent, the figure of the Buddha himself was never depicted in the sculpture of this period. The simultaneous appearance of the Buddha image in two different regions coincided with the reign of the Kushan ruler, Kaniska, in the 2nd century AD. The image from Gandhara, with wavy hair and heavy robes, is of Greco-Roman inspiration, whereas the Mathura image, with smooth head, smiling expression, and light robes that cling to the body, developed directly from the Indian sculptural context. Brahmanic sculpture, which also appeared, is important for the development of new Hindu iconographic themes. Moreover, the expression of a unified aesthetic paved the way for the full flowering of sculpture in the 5th century when, under the dynasty of the Guptas, an extreme refinement and a perfectly idealized human form were achieved.

In the post-Gupta period Buddhist sculpture declined, surviving until the 12th

*Above, head of a Dhyáni Buddha, carved from lava, Borobudur, Java (c. 800 AD). Below, balustre vase in stoneware with brown glaze, Thailand or Cambodia (c. 13th–14th century).*

century only in Bengal, but Hindu sculpture remained vital, and the grand Brahmanic temples of the medieval period are covered with an intensity of sculpture never before seen. The proliferation of *mithuna* (loving couples) and erotic groups, as well as south Indian bronze figures that balance poised movement with gracious form, are conspicuous to the late production of sculpture in India.

**Painting.** Because of the fragility of materials Indian painting has not survived well, but it did exist from ancient times on walls, cloth, wood, and palm leaves. The major extant examples are fresco illustrations of Buddhist gods and legends found in temples like Ajanta, where beautifully delineated figures appear in large compositions with several vanishing points; they display rich color and graceful, sensuous movement. Muslim rulers are responsible for the second major painting development: book and manuscript illustration in courtly styles that are a mixture of Persian styles and subject matter with traditional themes.

### SOUTHEAST ASIA

The countries now collectively called Southeast Asia experienced successive waves of cultural influences (Indian, Muslim, Chinese) that have left their mark on the contemporary ethnic and religious character of these various peoples. Aside from minor arts such as ceramics, textiles, and various native crafts, the major artistic monuments that have survived in these areas are related to Indian Brahmanism and Buddhism in both philosophy and style. However, since local labor was used in these efforts, the Indian influence in architecture, sculpture, and painting was assimilated, and native creativity asserted itself in each region, giving these forms a distinctive local character.

The most impressive structures in Southeast Asia are those built in the royal Khmer city of Angkor in Cambodia—especially Angkor Wat (12th century), a complex enclosed by double walls that symbolizes the Brahmanic idea of a cosmic temple-mountain, and Bayon (13th century), a Buddhist temple with fifty-four towers. Borobudur, a huge five-story pyramid crowned with a central *stupa*, was built in the 8th century on the island of Java in Indonesia: it is exceptional as an expression of the Mahayana Buddhist concept of an esoteric *mandala* (cosmic diagram) in an architectural form. A third important site is the Burmese city of Pagan, where numerous large *stupa*-temples devoted to Theravada Buddhism were built in the 11th century.

Some temples, such as those in Vietnam and Thailand, were built in styles not directly inspired by India, but filtered through neighboring areas. Furthermore, sculpture was produced throughout the area in the round and in relief, naturalistically depicting gods and great epics. Facial features, postures, and decorative motifs differ, but like architecture, the original inspiration remained Indian.

*See also* Art; Art of the Far East
Consult: Lee, Sherman E., *A History of Far Eastern Art* (New York: Abrams, 1964); Rowland, Benjamin, *The Art and Architecture of India* (Baltimore: Penguin, 1967); Basham, A. L., *The Wonder That Was India* (London: Methuen, 1954); Zimmer, Heinrich, *Myths and Symbols in Indian Art and Civilization* (New York: Harper & Row, 1946).
—Emily Sano, Vassar College

## Art of Mexico, Central America, and the West Indies.

### MEXICO

Although geographically part of North America, Mexico is so different in aesthetics it is often considered separately when art or culture is discussed. Accordingly, the several regions of Mexico are discussed here both in their prehistoric setting and in the later, strongly Hispanicized, forms active today. This is not to say that there are no "Indian" arts surviving; but it is true that there are few expressions in the Middle American region that do not reveal a greater or lesser degree of European influence in their form, design, or function.

The earliest identifiable art form in Mexico is that of the Olmec, a mysterious group which flourished from ca. 2000 BC until about AD 1 from Guerrero to Veracruz and south into Guatemala and Honduras. The colossal heads of stone, the lovely carved jades, the fine ceramics, the occasional shell or bone forms employing the famed were-jaguar motif—all have become characteristic of this period. Closely associated with the Olmec, although slightly later, were the occupants of Tlatilco and Chupicuaro, in central Mexico; these were the creators of the prolific "pretty ladies" and the finely worked clay sculptures. In western Mexico from 750 BC to AD 500, primarily in Nayarit, Jalisco, and

*Carved greenstone mask of the classic type from Teotihuacán, Mexico (c. 250–600 AD).*

Michoacan, but more particularly in the small state of Colima, clay modelers produced figurines, effigies, bowls, and redware *techichi,* the dogs raised for food. This profusion of figurines remains a mystery, but it betokens a tremendously active population whose total output staggers the imagination.

From about 250 BC until AD 750, a group in central Mexico built the tremendous pyramid complex of Teotihuacán, the greatest aggregate of such structures in the world. Their typical art form was a face mask, or panel. Not only was this a remarkable cultural representation, but it came out of one of the largest cities in the world of its time and certainly one which had a widespread influence throughout Middle America.

Other groups came and went: the Toltec; the Huastec in Veracruz, related to the Maya; the Mixtec and the Zapotec in present-day Oaxaca; and numerous lesser-known but equally significant peoples. In time, these gave way to the Aztec, about whom most is known, due to the early Spanish accounts. Of these, perhaps the most gifted were the Mixtec, whose technical craftsmanship, particularly in gold, was perhaps unrivaled in the pre-Columbian world.

In the Maya region, a quite different cultural complex became evident. Extending from Mexico into Guatemala and Honduras, even as far south as Costa Rica, this was undoubtedly the most aesthetically impressive people in Middle America. Their work in stone, particularly jade and serpentine, had few rivals. In pottery, Mayan polychrome has become synonymous with brilliance and colorful detail; a further vital technique was the carving of clay before (and occasionally after) firing. Yet surprisingly almost no gold or silver work is found in the Mayan area,

*Zapotec funeral urn representing a standing human figure, from Oaxaca, Mexico.*

*Painted cylindrical polychrome vessel from Campeche, Mexico. The design is of a seated Mayan noble in an elaborately decorated costume.*

and only limited amounts of copper (primarily bells and jewelry). Painting was an important art form, but little has survived except on pottery.

The great Mayan achievement was writing, and their glyph designs, carved in stone, wood, or clay, remain one of the great mysteries of prehistoric Middle America, as well as representing one of its aesthetic glories. By AD 900, the Mayan world fell into a decline from which it never recovered. While there are Mayan-speaking people throughout Middle America, their culture, except perhaps for textile weaving, has retained little of the magnificence of their ancestors.

## CENTRAL AMERICA

Farther south, in Nicaragua, Costa Rica, and Panama, influences from South America make themselves apparent. Although the Maya and the Aztec cultures were known, their impact on local tradition seems never to have equalled that of more southerly peoples. Superb polychrome pottery was produced, and stone carving became a major art expression; but it was in gold that the greatest technological and aesthetic qualities were manifest. It is probable that a larger

quantity in sheer bulk of gold was worked in this region than in any other area of America.

Unfortunately, we know far too little about these people. That they developed as early as ca. 250 BC is known. But we know little of their architecture, artistry in wood and textiles, or other facets of their daily life. Some large stone sculptures in Panama have survived, hinting at more important architectural accomplishments, but the later use of the cut stones by Spanish and Indian builders destroyed much of this evidence. Indeed, the eradication of native cultures in Central America by AD 1550 was so thorough that little has been preserved to indicate the artistic development that must have been in existence.

### WEST INDIES

The Caribbean region included several language groups, primarily the tribal groupings known as the Arawak, Ciboney, Carib, and Lucayan. These people inhabited the islands from the Bahamas and Puerto Rico to Cuba, Jamaica, and Santo Domingo. The Taino, a subgroup of the Arawak, seem to have been the most artistically talented; their cultural expressions, which were well elaborated by AD 1000 and reached their height at the time of the arrival of the Spanish explorers, made great use of stone, wood, shell, and bone, producing deeply carved effigies, bizarre forms, and (to us) weird designs hinting at a preoccupation with death. A few wood carvings are known, but they are rare; no textiles to speak of have survived. Yet these tantalizing hints indicate the wealth of artistry that must have been present at one time.

*Carved stone metate, formed in the shape of an elaborated jaguar and used for the ceremonial grinding of maize, Ometepe Island, Nicaragua (c. 1000–1500 AD).*

*Taino Indian modeled clay effigy, hollow and decorated with incised linear designs (Santo Domingo).*

The sophisticated, powerful forms found in the *zemi*, the many effigies, and the ubiquitous death heads indicate a powerful art form in the Caribbean. Stone pestles, the strange tri-point stone, and the stone collars so similar to the Mexican *yugo* hint at relationships still poorly understood. The "comma stones" and related odd forms of stone sculpture indicate a great feeling for stone. Pottery was a major art, but the poor clay prevented true ceramic success; instead, the Taino worked lumps of clay into grotesque *adornos*—ornate modeled heads and bodies attached to clay vessels in remarkable ways.

This is a tragic area of the New World, for it has undoubtedly lost more of its aboriginal character than any other region, and under particularly brutal circumstances. Within one generation after the arrival of the Spanish explorers, forced slavery, sheer cruelty, and disease had reduced the population from several million people to a few hundred thousand, and destroyed any significant continuation of the traditional cultures.

— Frederick Dockstader, *Museum of the American Indian*

**Art of Oceania: Melanesia.** The area known as Melanesia includes the large island of New Guinea and its offshore islands, the islands of the Bismarck Archipelago (Admiralty Islands, New Ireland, New Britain), the Solomon Islands, New Hebrides, and New Caledonia. Fijian art is characteristically Polynesian.

**Knowledge of Melanesian Art.** The first knowledge of Melanesian art stems from the 19th century, when the work of exploration and colonization by Europeans really began. Previous contact was ineffectual until the middle of the 19th century in style provinces 19 to 23 (see below). Contact came later in provinces 1, 2, and 6–18 (from 1884 on) and still later in provinces 3 to 5. Important collections of New Guinea art were made which are now in German and British museums, in Budapest, and in Chicago. At first only the coast and offshore islands were explored, and the lower waters of the Sepik River. Between the world wars and after, penetrations of the interior were made.

**Style Provinces.** Various attempts to distinguish art styles in Melanesia have been made (e.g., Linton and Wingert 1946), but lack of knowledge has prevented a clear view being projected until recently. The style provinces noted below are related to the geographical divisions of the area, but the student of the art of Melanesia should be cautious of making purely geographical distinctions, for trade in particular has caused styles to spread to several islands or parts of them. The history of the movements of peoples in Melanesia, though often only a matter of speculation, provides the reasons for a sudden change from one style to another as the area is scanned.

**Irian Jaya**

1. *Geelvink Bay:* carving of *korwar* figures for ancestor cult

2. *Humboldt Bay and Lake Sentani:* carving of canoe prows (which are painted and attached to the hull), paddles, posts and filials for men's houses, lime spatulas and containers

3. *Mimika:* carving of planks, poles to the dead, large female ancestor figures; masks

4. *Asmat:* one of the great carving cultures; many forms, particularly *bis* or ancestor poles, figures, canoes, shields, drums, masks, horns; art in the context of head-hunting; limited color

*Wooden ancestor figure from New Guinea.*

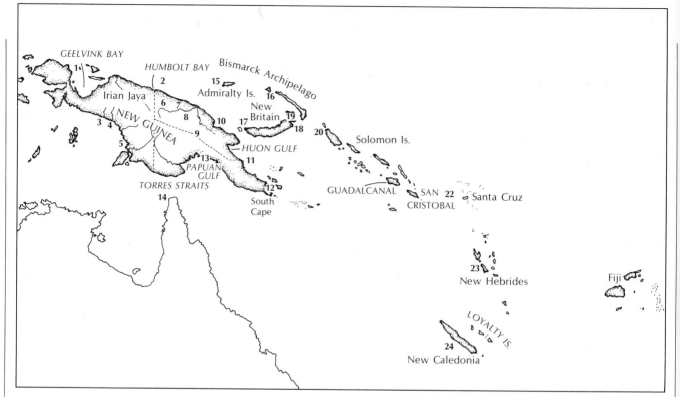

5. *Marind-Anim:* figures of mythical heroes used in ancestor cult; elaborate ceremonies and headhunting context

**Eastern New Guinea**

6. *Sepik River (upper, middle, lower):* one of the outstanding art areas of the world; tremendous range of carved forms, ceremonial and utilitarian, polychrome painting, very elaborate personal ornamentation, fine architecture in form of men's houses, pottery in Middle Sepik; headhunting and elaborate ceremonies

7. *Abelam:* similar in range to province 6; splendidly painted facades to 60-foot-high men's houses; elaborate cycle of initiation related to carved and painted figures and fantastic personal ornamentation and headdresses

8. *Highlands:* fine elaboration of personal ornamentation and attention to weapons, though no carving and painting

9. *Astrolabe Bay:* finely carved masks, houseposts, and figures (limited painting) in context of men's houses and cults; decoration of utilitarian objects, but ceasing before 1900; pottery still made

10. *Huon Gulf:* finely carved masks, houseposts, figures, canoes, utilitarian objects, particularly bowls, with limited painting; painted frame masks in context of men's houses and cults; centered on the Tami Islands, ceasing before 1914, with widespread influence, continuing in part in the Siassi Islands

11. *Massim:* includes the Trobriand Islands; an area of fine carving of everyday objects, such as canoe prow boards, lime spatulas, dance paddles; limited painting; pottery

12. *Papuan Gulf:* carving and painting limited to ancestral boards; constructed masks, fantastic and huge, made for elaborate, lengthy ceremonial cycles concerning sea and bush spirits; very high men's houses; considerable variation between east and west; pottery in the east traded widely

13. *Torres Straits:* some wooden masks and masks of turtle shell

**Bismarck Archipelago**

14. *Admiralty Islands:* carved figures, painted red; beds and wooden bowls; obsidian-bladed daggers and spears

15. *New Hanover and New Ireland:* very fine polychrome carvings in the round with elaborate low relief and cut-out forms for memorial ceremonies (*malanggan*); also masks and, centrally, cult figures *(uli);* in the south, chalk figures

16. *West New Britain:* carving tradition of masks and utilitarian objects, from Tami, for men's initiation cult; painted, conical masks, bark cloth on frame, for men's cult; painted canoes; giant constructed fanlike masks of feathers; elaborate dancing ceremonies with fine costume

17. *Eastern New Britain and Gazelle Peninsula:* elaborate polychrome, constructed masks (e.g., Sulka); skulls modeled in clay; conical, constructed masks for men's cults

18. *Baining:* elaborate, bark-covered, constructed masks, some of huge size used in celebrative contexts

**Solomon Islands**

19. *Western Solomon Islands:* carved ancestral figures, initiation figures, paddles with limited coloring

20. *Central Solomon Islands:* small carved guardian figures and heads for canoes; finely carved bowls with mother-of-pearl decorative inlays; cut-out shell ornaments

21. *Eastern Solomon Islands:* carvings of houseposts for canoe houses; large shell-

inlaid bowls and caskets for dead; canoe prow stems and shell ornaments

22. *New Hebrides:* elaborate carved and polychrome art in wood, tree fern, and clay modeling, in the form of masks, drums, figures, and headdresses serving funerary cults, secret societies, and graded associations (*suque*)

23. *New Caledonia:* carved door jambs, lintels, sills, posts, and spires to houses; ancestor figures; large masks; bird-head clubs and ceremonial axes with circular jade blades

**Areas and History.** Some style provinces can be combined into larger art areas (e.g., provinces 9, 10, 16) having certain basic forms and cultural traits in common, though each culture suits these forms and traits to its particular identity. Some provinces (12, for example) could be further subdivided. But it must be stressed that these provinces probably have only moderate validity as a distinguishing device of style for the period 1860–1960. Some provinces ceased to produce traditional art soon after coming into contact with Europeans (e.g., provinces 9, 10, 13); others survived in a traditional manner

*Ceremonial adze, done in jadeite, wood and shell, New Caledonia.*

until quite recently (provinces 4, 16, 18, 21) and still continue, if in a changed direction. Their recent histories depend on the time of contact and its intensity. Missionary activity in provinces 19–23 began in the first half of the 19th century with varying effects: in New Caledonia traditional art (province 23) had an early demise; that of the New Hebrides (province 22) persisted as parts of the area remained isolated. But in quite a number of the provinces craftsmen have been producing tourist and airport art, some for the last twenty years or more, no longer requiring traditional forms for a way of life that is no longer traditional.

*See also* Art and society; Tourist art
Consult: Cranstone, B. A. L., *Melanesia, A Short Ethnography* (London: Trustees of the British Museum, 1961); Guiart, Jean, *The Arts of the South Pacific* (London: Thames and Hudson, 1963); Linton, Ralph, and Wingert, Paul S., *Arts of the South Seas* (New York: Museum of Modern Art, 1946).
—*Philip J. C. Dark, Southern Illinois University*

## Art of Oceania: Polynesia and Micronesia.

### POLYNESIA

Although the arts of Polynesia have been known and admired by the Western world since the late-18th-century voyages of Captain Cook and others, few anthropologically significant studies of these arts have been carried out. The diverse forms of art in Polynesia parallel most of those found in the Western world, including graphic and plastic arts, music, dance, and oral literature.

Three-dimensional sculpture had an uneven distribution within Polynesia, being virtually absent in many of the low islands as well as in Samoa. Stone sculptures included huge Easter Island heads, medium-sized Marquesan temple figures, and small Necker Island (Hawaii) images. A similar range in size was found in wood sculpture: large Hawaiian temple images; medium-sized, free-standing images from Tonga, New Zealand, Mangareva, Cook Islands, Tahiti, and Easter Island; and small stick images from Hawaii. But sculpture in the round was also made from wicker and feathers in Hawaii, from ivory in Tongan pendants and food hooks, and even from sea urchin spines in Hawaii. Sculpture in relief was particularly characteristic of New Zealand, especially in carved wooden house panels and feather

*Wooden container from Samoa.*

boxes but also in nephrite *heitiki* neck pendants. Incised wood and ivory inlay were highly developed in Tonga. Two-dimensional graphic arts ranged from rock painting and rafter painting in New Zealand to mats with plaited designs of Hawaiian *makaloa* (sedge), New Zealand flax, or varieties of pandanus. New Zealand house panels were plaited from reeds, while decorated Tongan baskets were made from sennit of two colors interwoven with beads of seashell and coconut shell.

Clothing and ornament ranged from decorated bark-cloth skirts to "finger woven" flax cloaks (the loom was unknown in Polynesia); from feather headdresses, necklaces, and cloaks to aprons made of slips of seashell, carved coconut shell, plaited sennit, or flower petals; from human hair wigs, necklaces, and belts to ear, neck arm, and leg ornaments made of carved ivory elements, dog teeth, pig tusks, turtle shell, and sea and land snails. Tattooing was important in the Marquesas and New Zealand and, to a lesser extent, in Samoa, Tonga, and Hawaii. Pottery was made in prehistoric times, mainly in W Polynesia, decorated in Lapita style. Houses and furnishings, though usually simple, incorporated sculptural or decorative elements, especially those used by high-ranking chiefs. Rafters of Samoan and Tongan houses were decorated with complex designs formed by lashing with sennit of two colors. Tongan neckrests were made in a variety of forms. Wooden serving bowls had incised designs in the Marquesas Islands and carved human figures in Hawaii. Gourd containers from New Zealand and Hawaii were shaped (while growing) and decorated.

Oral literature, music, and dance were universal in Polynesia. Besides proverbs, prayers, genealogical recitations, and historical and legendary accounts that were rendered in poetry or prose, oral literature was also the basis of Polynesian music and dance. Poetic texts were often delivered with a small number of pitches and in a narrow melodic range. Except for Hawaii and New Zealand, polyphony was widespread—usually in the form of bourdon, but occasionally with as many as six parts. Dance was a stylized visual accompaniment to poetry: the performers told a story by alluding to selected words of the text with movements of the hands and arms, while the legs and body were used mainly for rhythm and keeping time.

### MICRONESIA

The art of Micronesia is irregularly known. Our meager knowledge of the pre-European Chamorro culture of the Marianas is based mainly on archaeological evidence whereas the cultures of the Carolines, Gilberts, and Marshalls have been documented by ethnographers. The most dramatic remnants of ancient Marianas culture are massive coral-stone houseposts called *latte*. Pottery was made in the Marianas, Yap, and Palau. In addition, Palauan women made ceramic lamps which burned coconut oil and sometimes featured three-dimensional human representations.

Wood carving was a widespread art in Micronesia. The shell-bladed adze was the principal tool used to make weapons, food bowls, boxes for fishing gear, and combs, as well as beautifully formed outrigger canoes, dwellings, shrines, community houses, and clubhouses. In Palau the latter were decorated with painted and incised designs. Canoes were painted too. Pigments were derived from earth, plants, and burnt coral. Wooden images were produced in Palau, both as free-standing carvings and as architectural components. A stylized mask of painted wood was made in the Mortlock Islands. Distinctive god images were carved on Nukuoro, a Polynesian outlier south of Ponape.

Stone sculpture was produced in Palau, and the stone money disks of Yap are unique. On Ponape at Nan Matol the basalt prisms used in construction were not worked.

Seashells provided raw material not only for adze blades but also for knives, signal trumpets, shell inlay for bowls and canoes (Palau), belts (Central Carolines), and money (Yap).

Loom weaving using backstrap looms was practiced in the Carolines. The weavers of Ponape and Kusaie were considered the most skilled. Banana and hibiscus fibers were employed to fashion *lavalavas* and belts. Finger weaving of mats was widespread, those of the Marshalls being recognized for their quality. Fans, baskets, and sometimes hats were made of pandanus and coconut leaves.

Bark-cloth manufacture was generally absent in Micronesia, but in ancient times Palauans did produce undecorated men's loincloths. Coconut-husk fiber (sennit) was widely used for fishing line and for lashing canoes and ornamental houses. In the Gilberts the tough cord was knotted into suits of armor worn by warriors to protect them from injury by long clubs or other weapons studded with shark teeth. Human hair was woven into cuirasses to make designs.

Turtle shell was widely used for ornaments such as belts, earrings, and bracelets. In Palau lime spatulas and women's money were made of this material.

Tattooing was practiced from the Marshalls to the Palaus—abundantly by the atoll people of the Carolines. Social and age distinctions were made manifest by tattooing. In addition, body painting with turmeric was common in ceremonial events, and tooth blackening as personal adornment was found in Yap and Palau. Modest cicatrization has been noted in Ponape.

Musical instruments were not numerous in Micronesia; dancing was often accompanied by chanting and clapping. The flute and jaw harp were known in Palau. Dancers often brandished dance wands or paddles as in Ponape. Chants were rich in historical and legendary references and in figurative expressions.

Consult: Dodd, E., *Polynesian Art* (New York: Dodd, Mead, 1967); Kramer, A., "Palau," in *Ergebnisse der Südsee—Expedition 1908–1910*, 11 Etnographie: B. Mikronesien, Band 3, ed. C. Thilenius (Hamburg: L. Friedlichsen & Co., 1913); Linton, R., *Ethnology of Polynesia and Micronesia* (Chicago: Field Museum of Natural History, 1926); Matsumura, A., "Contributions to the Ethnography of Micronesia," *Journal of the College of Science,* Imperial University of Tokyo, vol. 40, art. 7, 1918; Osborne, D., *The Archaeology of Palau,* Bulletin 230, Bernice P. Bishop Museum, 1966.
—Adrienne L. Kaeppler and Roland P. Force, Bishop Museum

**Art of the Eskimo.** The Eskimos, known also as Inuit and Yuit, have inhabited the coasts and hinterlands from Siberia to Greenland for more than 2,000 years, depending almost entirely on hunting and fishing for their subsistence. Their arts, of which the most famous are the recent sculptures and prints, also include engraved ivories, decorated utensils and clothing, and (more transitory but equally important) tattooing, dancing, singing, drumming, and oratory.

Only the plastic arts remain from archaeological times. The earliest, from the Bering Sea area, are small ivory figurines, developing over time into the more elaborate and stylized Ipiutak tradition (Bandi 1969). As the pre-Inuit Dorset culture spread eastward to Greenland, it left widespread remains of small, roughly carved, often incised figurines, perhaps associated with shamanism. About AD 1000 the Dorset people were replaced by the wave of Thule people—direct ancestors of the modern Inuit—who left small naturalistic ivories and incised ivory implements.

The traditional arts at the time of early contact exhibited regional differentiation. In W Alaska the Yuit were known for their wood and feather ceremonial masks, but bone, ivory, and wood carvings and decorated utensils were also found. The Alaskan, Canadian, and Greenlandic Inuit—the post-Thule Eskimos—continued the traditions of small tooth-ivory models used for charms, gambling dice, and toys. They also made human-like cairns which dotted the landscape like rough but imposing sculptures. The arts of appliqué skin clothing were valued especially in Greenland.

Since incorporation into the economic and national systems of the USSR, USA, Can-

*Carved ivory pipe, made from a walrus tusk and decorated with incised designs.*

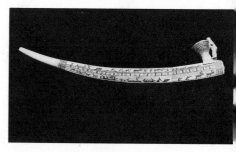

*Above, three carved ivory charms: from left to right, deer effigy, man riding a caribou, whale effigy; below, carved ivory doll with inlaid copper eyes, Point Barrow, Alaska.*

ada, and Denmark, the Eskimos have produced a variety of commercial arts reflecting partly their indigenous crafts and partly the tastes of the white newcomers. Siberian engraved mammoth ivories resemble Russian folk scenes and European art. Alaskan Eskimos learned scrimshaw ivory engraving from the whalers (Ray 1961) and incised an increasingly pictorial series of styles on tusks and developed a naturalistic genre of ivory model animals. Canadian Inuit made incised ivory cribbage boards and souvenir models until recently. Since 1950 they have made human and animal figures in soapstone and serpentine; these creations are naturalistic, but are often bold and simplified to the point of near abstraction. This successful venture has encouraged greatly increased size of sculptures and, more recently, carving in whalebone and even metalworking and pottery. Cape Dorset and other Inuit have also started lithographic and copper printmaking with great artistic and commercial success.

In Greenland, where formal education came earlier, many Eskimos have become artists in the European tradition, but at the more isolated Angmassalik on the eastern coast there flourished a style of souvenir models in wood and ivory, including the well-known *tupilak* "starvation figures."

Lesser-known artistic traditions of song, humor, and instrumental music still flourish as a means of intraethnic communication and expression. As in Greenland, however, education and occupational assimilation will in all Eskimo areas lead to the eventual dominance of Inuit–(Yuit)–ethnic expressions within mainly Western traditions and art and literature.

Consult: Bandi, H. G., *Eskimo Prehistory* (Fairbanks: University of Alaska Press, 1969); Burling, C., *Eskimo Art* (London: Hamlyn, 1973); Ray, D. J., *Artists of Tundra and Sea* (Seattle: University of Washington Press, 1961); Ray, D. J., *Eskimo Masks in Art and Ceremony* (Seattle: University of Washington Press, 1967); Swinton, G., *Sculpture of the Inuit* (Greenwich, Conn.: New York Graphic Society, 1972).

—Nelson H. H. Graburn, University of California, Berkeley

**Art of the Far East.** The arts of China, Korea, and Japan are closely related in form and content, but very different in spirit. Dec-

orated tombs, Buddhist art and architecture, calligraphy, painting, ceramics and lacquerwares are common to each country, yet each of these forms developed distinctions that are attributable to differences in technical competence, aesthetic values, and indigenous requirements. Generally speaking the Chinese have displayed more creative genius, the Korean peninsula was a conduit for the transmission of culture from China to Japan, and the Japanese remodeled the lofty aesthetics of Chinese art into forms that are more gentle, direct, and sensual.

**Prehistoric and Funerary Arts.** Artifacts from both China and Japan give evidence of prehistoric cultures dating to approximately the 8th century BC. Chinese sites have yielded handsome pottery wares such as red clay vessels painted with geometric designs and a thin, black burnished ware that appears to have been wheel made. Prehistoric Japanese pottery displays impressed corded decoration and sculptured curvilinear relief decoration. The most impressive prehistoric artifacts of East Asia are the Chinese bronze ritual vessels dating to the Shang period (ca. 1550–1030 BC). These vessels, decorated with zoomorphic and geometric designs in relief, are indicative of a highly sophisticated piece-mold casting technique. Bronze vessels continued to be made during the succeeding Chou (ca. 1030–256 BC) and Han (202 BC–AD 220) periods, but the early awe-inspiring motifs dissolved into meaningless decorative meanders and designs of inlaid gold and silver.

A conspicuous richness of materials characterizes Chinese grave goods from Chou and Han period tombs, and the recent excavations, which have uncovered beautifully preserved lacquerwares, pottery figurines, and suits of jade to clothe the body of the deceased, have contributed a great deal toward reconstructing China's ancient culture. Han period tombs are especially notable because they represent a significant shift in Chinese art away from the dominance of geometric motifs toward motifs of a pictorial nature. Han tomb mural decoration consists of low-relief carvings and paintings which illustrate legends, Confucian morals, and mourning rites. Korean and Japanese tombs are similar in structure and content to Chinese models, but those built during the Kofun period (AD 250–552) in Japan also had cylinders of clay, called *haniwa*, placed around and over the tomb. These cylinders were often decorated with sculptured hu-

*Container in the shape of an ancient bronze vessel of the Li-Ting type, done in jade in the Ming-Ch'inq period, c. 17th century, China.*

man and animal forms, but their intended function remains unknown.

**Buddhist Art.** Indian Buddhism began to filter into China during the Han period following the Silk Route from Central Asia. However, the religion was not firmly established in China until the Six Dynasties period (AD 256–581) when the Topa Tartars, who conquered northern China, supported the carving of large Buddhist sanctuaries in rock. The remains of some half dozen of the cave temples, as well as scattered pieces of sculpture in bronze, document the development of Buddhist sculpture in China. Early Chinese sculptors emphasized heavy, flat, linear drapery for artistic effect, but they gradually learned to handle the body in the round and by the early T'ang period (AD 618–906) managed to produce sculpture with the same sensuous fleshiness of form that is distinctive to Indian sculpture.

The introduction of Buddhism to Japan in the 6th century signals the first great wave of Chinese influence in that country when, together with religion, the Japanese undertook a wholescale importation of Chinese culture. Since most of the Buddhist art in China has not survived, it is fortunate that Japan remains a repository of Chinese style and technique in temple architecture, religious sculpture, and painting. By the 10th century the Japanese had absorbed these manifold influences, and began to integrate them into a unified style that responded to a native sensibility. Differences in religious dogma, rather than artistic style, provided variety in form, and by the end of the late Heian period (AD 897–1185) the religious arts had achieved a look of Japanized refinement.

**Painting.** Painting with brush and ink is known to have existed in China as early as the late Chou period, but not until the T'ang period did painting rise above a mere illustrative function. Figure painting reached a high point during T'ang, and as problems in rendering recession in space were solved, landscape painting became a major category of art. The Sung period (AD 960–1279), however, was the greatest age of painting in China. The monumental landscapes of the Northern Sung were followed in the Southern Sung by a more intimate style that emphasized large areas of empty space and asymmetrical compositions. Flower and bird painting in rich polychrome were not merely decorative, but the plants and animals were associated with human characteristics. Moreover, the seemingly careless, rapidly brushed paintings by Ch'an (Zen) priests in monochrome ink are expressive of the nonverbal, antiliterary bias of Zen teaching.

The achievements of Sung painters provided a context of style and a standard of technical excellence that were to challenge Chinese painters for generations. But the motivating impulse to later artists of the Yuan (AD 1260–1368), Ming (1368–1644), and Ch'ing (1644–1912) periods was the enduring dominance of the *wenjen,* or literati philosophy. In particular, an appreciation for the nonacademic, antiprofessional image of the artist as a man who paints as an avocation was the primary influence on the development of a free and individualistic expression that characterizes the work of the many artists of the late Ming and Ch'ing periods.

Secular painting reached an early height in Japan during the late Heian period when native taste asserted itself over the past dominance of Chinese culture. The patronage of the court was responsible for a rich production of art, especially of handscrolls that illustrate legends, romances, and the biographies of celebrated priests. Ink paintings by Zen priests dominated the late Ka-

*Pair of six-fold screens, done in ink, color and gold, on paper, Japan, 16th century.*

- makura (AD 1185–1392) and Muromachi (1393–1568) periods, but Japanese painters tended to emphasize the linear and decorative potential of ink brushwork. Strong ink outlines and the Japanese love of color and gold formed the basis of a decorative style that was perfect for the large screen and wall painting that brightened the castles of generalissimos during the Momoyama period (AD 1568–1615). Supported first by the court

and then by the warlords who ruled Japan, painting during the long Edo period (AD 1615–1868) saw the development of numerous schools maintained by a wealthy merchant class. Genre painting and a school of decorative painting flourished. Painters who used Western techniques, those who emulated the style of the Chinese literati, those who depicted the gay quarters, and those who worked in styles too personal to be classified as other than "eccentric" all contributed to the eclectic nature of Edo period painting.

See also Art; Art and society
Consult: Lee, Sherman E., *A History of Far Eastern Art* (New York: Abrams, 1964); Sullivan, Michael, *The Arts of China* (Berkeley: University of California Press, 1973); Sickman, L., and Soper, A., *The Art and Architecture of China* (Baltimore: Penguin, 1971); Noma, Seiroku, *The Arts of Japan* (Palo Alto, Calif.: Kodansha International, 1968).
—Emily J. Sano, Vassar College

**Art of the Middle East.** Middle Eastern art is diverse in form and style. This is because of the rich diversity of native ethnic groupings, the flow of conquerors and invaders who have swept over the area, and the number of different art forms which have flourished and developed during various periods of history.

**Language.** Probably the most longstanding art form in Middle Eastern society is language. Although linguistic styles have gone through periods of change in Arabic philosophy and literature, early evidence of an expressive art form is found in the few remaining poems of the pre-Islamic period (before AD 622). The form and cadence of the oral tradition were combined with a clarity of the sounds of Arabic to create images, allusions, fantasy, and mirage. The different peoples of all parts of the Middle East still appreciate an individual of vocal skill, artistry, emotion, and wit.

**Architecture.** A large part of Middle Eastern architecture is religious. The Islamic tradition has given preeminence to the mosque, but the spread of Islam throughout Persia, the Fertile Crescent, and North Africa has generated many local variations in Arab building styles: the grand mosque in Cordova is a good example of such blending in southern Spain.

The form of a mosque is generally characterized by a tower for the call to prayer (the minaret), a large rectangular courtyard often fringed with arches and columns, and rooms around the courtyard for religious classes. These classes are often held in the courtyard in the open air and can be observed in religious and educational centers such as Al-Azhar in Cairo. The mosques of Samarra and Ibn Tulun in Cairo, both prototypes for later stylistic developments, offer early examples of spherical minarets and the massive, unornamented walls which protect the mosque and its courtyard from the outside world.

The serenity provided by the courtyard is carried over into the architecture of private homes as well: "Because the sky is for the Arab at once the home of the holy and the most soothing face of Nature, he naturally wants to bring it into his own dwelling" (Fathy 1969: 77). So in desert countries people try to bring down the serenity and holiness of the sky into the house. The means of doing this is the courtyard.

**Calligraphy.** Symbolic elements are common to Arab art in many localities. Architectural embellishments are characteristically simple, but elegant. Calligraphy—decoration through the use of elaborate and abstracted script—became an accepted art form in the decoration of mosques throughout Arab

*Above, Prince Nepemnofret's funerary stela lists names and titles of the owner as well as all the goods he would need in the afterlife, from Ginza, IV Dynasty.*

*Below, earthenware bowl with an overglaze painting, 12th–13th century, Iran.*

*Three pottery figures from Amlash, Iran, 10th–8th century BC.*

lands and has developed a number of distinctive styles over the centuries.

**Other Art Forms.** From early prehistoric times to the present, the Middle East has been continuously inhabited, and in each area and period people have produced distinctive artifacts—which have, at different times, included rugs, pottery, figurines, stone monuments, pictographs, fabric, carving, and architecture. Because the Middle East has served as an economic crossroad between Europe and Asia, the mixture of internal and external influences on the various art forms has been extensive. Such diversity has given strength and creativity to an artistic production which continues to develop and spread to other parts of the world.

See also Architecture

Consult: Grabar, Oleg, *The Formation of Islamic Art* (New Haven: Yale University Press, 1973); Fathy, Hassan, *Gourna: A Tale of Two Villages* (Cairo: Dar al-Katab al-Arabi Press, 1969); Wooley, Leonard, *The Art of the Middle East* (New York: Crown, 1961).

—*Cathie J. Witty, University of Washington*

**Art of the North American Indian.** The qualities that distinguish North American native art include the use made of the rich variety of natural materials found in the environment, the particular talents which expressed that response, and the technical skills employed to achieve the desired results. These, of course, varied throughout the continent, just as did the forms and designs.

The *Eskimo* found their greatest success in the carving of ivory, obtained from the walrus, seal, and killer whale, the use of driftwood, and the occasional use of bone or stone. With these materials were created dance masks that reflected the sense of humor and surrealistic design forms so exciting in this region; small carvings of animals, either in outline or incised on the surfaces of smooth materials; or skillfully designed mechanical forms testifying to the ability of the Eskimo to make things fit. Perhaps the most characteristic features of Eskimo art are a remarkably vital and humorous quality and a fantasy form often accompanied by bizarre anthropomorphic or zoomorphic outlines.

Along the *Northwest Coast,* the great forests of tall cedar and spruce enabled the people, primarily the Tlingit, Niska, Kwakiutl, Haida, and Tsimshian, to achieve perhaps the most outstanding sculptural arts on the continent. The wooden masks, totem poles, houseposts, and carved wooden ornaments so rich in this region made it one of the major art-producing areas of the New World. Much of this sculpture was highlighted by the addition of haliotis shell inlay and paint. The wooden masks, furthermore, were frequently enhanced by the provision of movable features; these "transformation" masks were altered by the wearer, who pulled strings attached to mechanical parts—the masks opened out, revealing an inner design, often representing the spirit of the outer form. Many of these masks were quite large, measuring as much as 3 or 4 feet in length and width.

Copper was found naturally on the earth's surface, and was hammered into sheets for ornaments, weapons, and overlay needs. Ivory, again, was an important resource, as were antler, bone, and animal hides. Perhaps the most unusual material was the wool of the mountain goat and mountain sheep, from which the impressive Chilkat robes were woven in a unique technique.

This art was used primarily to impress the viewer, to enhance the prestige of the owner, to gain an advantage over a political or social rival (e.g., via the famous *potlatch),* and to increase the wealth of the village leaders. It was a remarkably adaptive art, since it employed every variety and form and quickly adopted new materials immediately upon exposure to them.

Farther south, the *California* tribes excelled in basketry. The Pomo, Hupa, Karok, and Yurok, all of which developed individual styles, produced work with a technical skill that surpassed anything produced elsewhere in the Western Hemisphere. Their baskets, some of which incorporated the feathers of birds into the weave, ranged in size from miniature creations measuring less than 1/16 inch to large storage containers 4 and 5 feet in diameter. The Chumash, in central California, not only made remarkable baskets but were also noted for carvings of local animals, often inlaid with shell beads, made from the common steatite found along the coast. Southern California tribes included the Dieguño and related peoples, whose basketry was excellent.

Inland, the *Basin-Plateau* tribes were artistically dominated by the Nez Perce, Bannock, Shoshoni, Ute, and Paiute, each of which developed an individual style. All were influenced to a greater or lesser degree by the Plains Indians to the east, and also by the Northwest Coast people to the west. They became well known for their costume

*Zuni vase.*

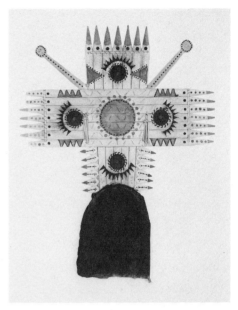

*Apache headdress mask for the Devil Dance.*

arts, at which the Nez Perce excelled; Shoshoni beadwork designs often duplicated those of the neighboring Crow, and the Ute incorporated elements of both Plains and Pueblo art.

The *Southwestern* Indians are divided into three major art groupings: (1) the Pueblo people, including the Hopi, Zuni, and Rio Grande Pueblos; (2) the Navajo and related Athapascan-speaking Apache, both of which were latecomers to the region; and (3) the more southerly tribes, such as the Pima, Papago, Maricopa, Yuma, and Mohave. Each of these developed an individual style and, with the exception of the Navajo-Apache, followed earlier ancestral peoples who had moved into the region many hundreds of years earlier.

The Pueblo tribes show strong linear patterns in their art, expressed on clay or wood, with dominant color patterns utilizing vegetal or mineral pigments. Taking advantage of the strong sunlight in their environments, their work achieves a crisp, easily recognizable quality similar to the black-on-white designs of the Anasazi, an ancestral group which settled in the Southwest. Near the

Pueblo were the Mogollon and Hohokam peoples, each of which had unusual artistic qualities. Perhaps the most remarkable artists were the Mimbreno of SW New Mexico, whose short-lived culture (AD 900–1100) gave birth to some of the most outstanding clay art of North America. Rich in humor, these charming black-on-white designs were executed in sharp line sketches on a poor quality clay.

Navajo art is at its best in textile weaving, in such items as the blankets and rugs for which these people have become famous. Yet, along with silversmithing, this is a late art. While the Navajo may have brought the art of weaving with them into the Southwest, they learned much from their Pueblo neighbors and soon surpassed their teachers. Similarly, the silversmithing arts, which were introduced only ca. 1853, rapidly gained importance in Navajo esteem. Today they are the artistic hallmark of the tribe.

Sculpture was never an important Southwest Indian art. Basketry was important to the Hopi, but none of the other Pueblos produced much beyond utilitarian containers; only the Apache, Pima, and some of the Colorado River tribes excelled in this art to any marked degree.

It is pottery for which the Pueblo are perhaps best known today, and this art has steadily improved in quality as well as value. From the early Anasazi craftsmen to the work of such artists as Julian and Maria Martinez, Pueblo ceramics have become widely known. Equally fine clay work is also produced by the neighboring Pueblos of Santa Clara, Hopi, Acoma, and Zia. In recent years pottery has been produced more for sale to tourists than for home use. As a result, aesthetic appearance and size differences have become more important than earlier functional forms.

The most common stone used for the ancient art of jewelry making is turquoise, followed by coral, jet (or lignite), and shell. Turquoise was widely traded throughout the area, and shells were occasionally brought in from as far away as the Pacific coast.

One unique art form is sand painting, practiced most notably by the Navajo, although it is also a well-known art among the Pueblo and desert tribes. These latter peoples no longer utilize sand painting to the degree now practiced by the Navajo, and their designs are not only less well known but far simpler in form.

*Huron moccasins made of black buckskin.*

The Plains Indians vary considerably from tribe to tribe in their artwork, each having its own particular skill. In the Northern Plains, the Crow, Cheyenne, and Sioux are certainly the most active artistically, exhibiting excellent abilities in beadwork on buckskin, superb quillwork, and an occasional use of wood. The Central Plains peoples, such as the Pawnee, Osage, Oto, and Iowa, are known today for their fine beadwork and interesting wood forms, which utilized a distinct and easily recognized design. The Southern Plains tribes, such as the Kiowa, Comanche, Wichita, and Caddo, are noted for intricate designs as well as for graceful costume forms. Little has survived from earlier times by which to judge the design elements and techniques of these people, and we must content ourselves with the arts of the historic period.

Porcupine quilling, the one art unique to America, was used widely throughout the Plains and the eastern part of the continent, wherever the animal ranged. In time this art gave way to the colorful glass beads introduced by European traders, but the designs and techniques were continued from the older practice.

It is often not realized the degree to which the Plains Indians decorated their bodies; indeed, more attention was paid by these people to self-beautification than perhaps by any other tribal group. Adornment not only included garments made from hides painted and decorated with extreme care, but extended to a variety of jewelry made from shell, bone, wood, metal, and even feathers. The same attention was devoted to the adornment of horses, and beautifully worked gear was produced for special occasions.

Painted hides and skins were of extreme importance. Shields involved physical and religious protection in their design, and buffalo hides not only provided protection from weather but also served as a canvas upon which to paint historical, decorative, or narrative designs.

In the *Midwest*, the Indians around the Great Lakes—such as the Chippewa, Potawatomi, Menomini, and Winnebago—attained great skills in the use of wood, shell, and stone. Some textiles were known in prehistoric times, but little of this art has survived the moist climate; this is true also of basketry. Pottery was never important in the region, but copper, occurring naturally, was used widely, both for manufacturing objects and as a trading material.

To the south and southeast are the Caddoan, Muskhogean, and related peoples

(Creek, Koasati, Alibamu, Cherokee), whose artistry dates from the time of the Spiro Mound people and extends to present-day weavers of baskets, such as the Chitimacha. A great profusion of stone sculpture was produced throughout this region, including effigy pipes, statues, stone bowls, implements, and a fantastic array of pottery forms. Wood was used widely, but as with textiles, has survived only in exceptional cases. Designs are linear, for the most part, and are often extremely complex. Shell gorgets, pendants, and inlays were incised or engraved with designs which frequently tell us a great deal about the lives of the people who used them. With the arrival of Europeans, new materials were introduced, particularly glass trade beads, trade cloth, and a variety of ribbon and cotton goods. All of these played a major role in fashioning a culture complex now regarded as traditional. Today the Seminole, Creek, and Cherokee people along the Atlantic coast have developed a quite different art style: stone sculpture has disappeared almost entirely; pottery has none of the vitality that once made it so exciting; but cotton cloth has become for the Seminole, in particular, a resource by which they have become identified.

The *Eastern Woodland* tribes, especially the Iroquois, Coastal Algonquin, and neigh-

*A Mimbres (New Mexico) black on white ware bowl. The painted decoration represents a man and a woman under a blanket.*

boring groups, are noted for the manufacture of *wampum* in the New York region, carved wooden False Face Society masks, and cornhusk weaving. Most of these art techniques have survived to the present time. Bark was fashioned into containers and the surface was scraped away to produce a contrasting design. Quillwork was commonplace, colored with vegetable dyes and deer and moose hair. The carving of wood into implements and objects was important, as was the use of shell and stone. Again, pottery was a secondary art, never achieving the significance it enjoyed in the Southeast.

North American Indian art has retained much of its technical skill and a great deal of the vitality it earlier expressed. It enjoys a wide audience, largely non-Indian, which has forced changes of function and form. Paintings are now applied to a rectangular paper or canvas surface rather than the earlier irregular-outline buffalo hide. Sculpture is largely in stone or wood and follows European concepts. Basketry is almost wholly a lost art: only a few tribes continue to follow their traditional ways.

Perhaps the most interesting phenomenon has been the increase in interest *via* the marketplace. With higher prices being realized for art products, an increased respect for the producer has developed—perhaps the most important result in the end.

—*Frederick Dockstader, Museum of the American Indian*

## Art of the Northwest Coast of North America.
Cedar and salmon formed the foundations of Northwest Coast culture. All along the richly convoluted coastline from Yakutat Bay to about the mouth of the Columbia River, the collision of land and sea spawned the bountiful resources from which Indians of diverse languages built a common culture. A bold and complicated yet refined art was already flourishing when the earliest explorers arrived during the final quarter of the 18th century. The remarkable carved houseposts and entrance poles noted at this time increased in number and size, developing into the "totem pole complex," which reached a peak in some areas at the beginning of the 20th century.

Their two-dimensional art is governed by a rigorous set of principles that apply equally to a painted house-front or a silver bracelet. The curvilinear designs seen on boxes and Chilkat blankets are distorted, simplified, and bisected to fill the given space. Here the art becomes its most abstract and difficult to interpret. A limited number of features have become conventions or symbols for representing animals, humans, and mythical beings. Thus a beaver is known by his broad cross-hatched tail and two large incisors; a killer whale by a single dorsal fin; and a woman by a labret in the lower lip. The artist typically used three colors: black from lignite or charcoal, red from ochre or cinnabar,

*Kwakiutl wooden mask, representing the spirit of the octopus.*

*Crow Indian painted shield cover, made of buckskin, depicting a vision seen by Pretty Bear (c. 1860).*

shian area, gave little freedom to express tribal variations—it was the totem poles and masks that gave the greatest rein to the imagination. In art historical terms, Tsimshian sculpture is "classical"; Haida is "classical to baroque"; Tlingit is "rococo"; and Kwakiutl exhibits a vigorous "eclecticism" (Wingert 1951:93). The masks of the Bella Coola were full and roundly carved; the Nootka used flatter, simpler shapes; and Salish carving was stark to plain. It should not be overlooked that differences between individual artists were greater, at times, than those between tribes.

The remarkable output of art in this area was closely tied to the social structure. Status was expressed through theatrical, musical, carved, and painted creations based on myths claimed by lineages, clans, and house groups. Where the ceremonies of the potlatch have endured, as among the Kwakiutl, the time-honored manner of training fine craftsmen has continued unbroken.

See also Art and society

Consult: Boas, Franz, *Primitive Art* (New York: Dover, 1955); Hawthorn, Audrey, *Art of the Kwakiutl Indians* (Seattle: University of Wash-

*Tlingit ceremonial mask and headdress.*

ington Press, 1967); Holm, Bill, *Northwest Coast Indian Art: An Analysis of Form* (Seattle: University of Washington Press, 1965); Inverarity, Robert, *Art of the Northwest Coast Indians* (Berkeley: University of California Press, 1950); Wingert, Paul, *Tsimshian Sculpture: The Tsimshian Indians and Their Arts,* part 2 (Seattle: University of Washington Press, 1951).

—Ronald A. Brooks, University of California, Berkeley

*Kitksan wooden rattle with a beaver motif.*

and blue-green from copper minerals. White and yellow had special applications.

The principles governing form have been recently worked out by Holm (1965). These apply to a wide range of Northwest Coast art but are followed most closely in the two-dimensional art of the northern coast, in the classic center of the Haida and Tsimshian. Three classes of design elements correspond to the three standard colors: black, red, and blue-green. Primary formlines are in black and can be traced in an unbroken path around and within the design field. They swell and then diminish as they meet other formlines. Secondary formlines are red and enclosed within the primary formlines. The tertiary elements are blue-green or left unpainted. In low-relief carving, primary and secondary elements are painted on the surface plane and then the tertiary units are carved out.

The conventions of box and blanket designs, said to have their origin in the Tsim-

*Tlingit woven "Chilkat" blanket, made of mountain-goat hair and twisted cedar bark. The design represents the killer whale.*

## Ceramics.

Ceramics provided the third avenue of aesthetic success, and here there is less argument, for the Chavin, and their successors the Mochica, went far beyond the artistic skills of most of the neighboring areas. All these peoples produced pottery in great profusion. The earliest pottery yet discovered was produced by the Valdivia people, who were working as early as 3200 BC in Ecuador. However, including even the Inca, whose wares impressed the Spanish, no South American pottery has the aesthetic impact of the Chavin, who were working some 1,000 to 1,500 years BC.

Although the entire continent had been penetrated, some areas were more heavily populated than others, and the climate is such that in some areas we still do not know whether, or to what degree, settlement was established. But wherever people settled, aesthetic forms developed. Brazil yields remarkable clay work in the Ilha Marajo region; Venezuela has slightly different but equally exciting clay ware, as well as sculpture in stone; the lowlands, however, seem never to have equalled the highlands in artistic productivity.

**Peru.** Much of the interest in the prehistory of South America, and more particularly

*Above, a wooden carved and painted Tsimshian Indian storage chest. The carving represents Gonak Ade't, a water monster. Below, Niska wooden mask of an old woman with a large labret, inlaid with haliotis shell.*

**Art of the South American Indian.** South America is perhaps the least-known region, as far as general knowledge of the aesthetics of Native American peoples is concerned. Only in the past fifty years or so has there been any major activity in the field of Indian art in the Southern Hemisphere; and in this instance, interest was by and large limited to the Inca.

**Weaving.** One of the three great arts has always been weaving, and it is here that the ancient Peruvians excelled. Indeed, probably no other ancient culture accomplished as much in as wide a range of techniques, styles, and designs as did the Andean people. Fortunately, many examples of Peruvian weaving have been preserved in the dry desert tableland of Peru.

**Metalworking.** A second major art was metalsmithing, particularly in gold. This skill was not limited to Peru, for there were equal if not superior talents to be found among the artists of Colombia and Ecuador. It is invidious to compare, for the matter of personal taste has much to do with the preference of one over the other; but certainly Tairona, Quimbaya, or Sinu goldwork can compare in beauty with that of the Chavin, Nazca, or Chimu goldsmiths. All these cultures had gifted artists capable of turning out masterpieces of embossed, repoussé, or cast-gold ornaments, some weighing as much as 15 pounds.

*Polychrome trio from Bahia de Manta, Manabi, Ecuador.*

that of Peru, stems from the great architectural monuments. The ruins of Machu Picchu, Tiahuanaco, and Sacsahuaman attest to the achievement of highly skilled artists. Pottery found in Peru is not as early as that of Colombia or Ecuador; the earliest yet excavated dates approximately from 1200 BC.

The ruins around Chavin de Huantar have given the name Chavin to one of the earliest and most remarkable civilizations of ancient South America. A wide variety of stone, clay, textile, and metal work all bear witness to this magnificent era. To the south, the Paracas peninsula has produced pottery, textiles, and related arts with sophisticated designs. The Paracas people, who gave way to the Nazca, produced superb robes, capes, and ponchos in an incredible profusion of designs and techniques.

The Mochica in N Peru, whose civilization lasted from ca. 250 BC to about AD 750, developed a genre art form which produced some of the finest sculpture in prehistoric America. The interest of the potters in daily life around them has left us with an incredibly rich mirror of the times. It was also this civilization which featured the greatest amount of erotic art in the New World. Why this civilization should have devoted so much attention to sexual aesthetics is not clear; while erotica is not absent from other Indian groups, it seems to have been far more commonplace and graphically elaborated here than elsewhere.

Succeeding the Mochica in Peru were the Chimu, whose great capital at Chan Chan remains one of the great wonders of prehistoric South America. The amount of gold, textiles, clay work, and sculpture which has been discovered testifies to a remarkable vitality from about AD 1000 to 1450.

**Tiahuanaco.** In neighboring Bolivia, another major civilization, known as Tiahuanaco, developed between AD 250 and 750. Its origins are not clearly understood, nor do we fully understand where the people went after the decline of the center near Lake Titicaca. Tiahuanaco art is relatively formal, stiff, and stark—yet the architectural ruins as well as the textiles give the impression of a remarkably rich and colorful civilization.

**Inca.** It is the Inca who have become best known to us today, largely because of the Spanish records. Surprisingly this cultural group, while late, is also less impressive in aesthetic content than other, earlier people. From its beginning around AD 1200, through the founding of the empire in 1438 and its

Polychrome urn of the Huari-Tiahuanaco culture, unearthed in Nazca, Peru.

destruction in 1532, the Inca civilization had extended its imperial boundaries from Ecuador in the north to Argentina and Chile in the south. It left major influences wherever it touched. Unfortunately, this widespread civilization included the seeds of its own dissolution, for rivalries, enmities, and factionalism weakened it to a point where its centralized autocracy was easily overthrown by the Spanish conquistadores.

Metalsmithing was well known to the Inca, and the great quantities of gold looted by the Spaniards emphasize this skill: because of this looting, little Inca gold survives today. Silver and copper were equally prevalent—indeed it is sometimes difficult to separate Chimu metalwork from Inca.

Farther south, the early cultural manifestations found in Chile and Argentina—the Diaguita, Calchaqui, and Atacameno—all developed highly sophisticated art forms. Copper was cast, often in remarkable quan-

tities and forms; textiles were woven in well-developed techniques; stone carving was well known. Pottery was made in great amounts, but not on the same aesthetic level as is found in Peru or Ecuador.

Indian groups in South America today have lost much of their earlier artistic vitality. After the Spanish conquest, decimation and annihilation erased most of the remnants of once-great civilizations; the Europeans saw little to save from pagan cultures, and after diligently searching out the treasures of the tribe, they departed, leaving behind only death, destruction, some settlers, and a wholly disorganized aboriginal culture.

Only the interior forest tribes, who had been able to hide from the Spaniards, seem to have retained much of their integrity. The Tapirape, the Karaja, the Piro—to name only a few—still follow some of the lifeways of their ancestors, and much of their artwork retains a flavor of earlier pre-Spanish forms. Beyond this, the European tradition has superimposed itself almost completely upon native life.

—Frederick Dockstader, Museum of the American Indian

**Art, Primitive.** Primitive art refers to the arts of the people of nonliterate societies; these arts are also referred to as tribal, exotic, traditional, preliterate, or even non-European arts (Gerbrands 1957:9–24). Defined this way, primitive art is not to be confused with European folk art, Western "primitive" (i.e., naive) arts, or archaeological and cave arts. The term *primitive* refers to the small scale of the society producing the arts rather than to the form of the arts, and these arts are to be found among the societies of the Americas, Africa, Oceania, and much of Asia.

Primitive art therefore covers or exceeds the range of activities found in Western art—it includes sculpture, painting, basketry, weaving, clothing, masks, body decoration, architecture, song, dance, instrumental music, and poetry. In spite of these parallels primitive arts are characterized by some unique factors (Lewis 1961), though it is difficult to generalize. In most cases these arts are produced by nonspecialists and part-time artists for their friends and neighbors, and they often show a vigor and spontaneity rare in Western academic arts. Though the architecture and building of ritual houses such as the *tamberans* of the Sepik River area require large cooperative efforts, most primitive arts are made by one or a few people using locally or easily traded materials; but the performances and rituals in which they are used may show great complexity and involve most of the community. Primitive arts follow local traditions and are not set apart from life. In this sense they are static or even backward-looking rather than part of a consciously changing stylistic endeavor; they are more embedded in the fabric of society than the "art for art's sake" characteristic of the highly specialized civilizations of the Eastern and Western worlds.

In the absence of literacy these arts bear religious and spiritual messages and are major forms of communication promoting conformity, identity, and solidarity. Often the arts themselves are thought to have magic and protective powers, and the production and use of an object is subject to ritual and secrecy (as when the sacred *churinga* totem is brought by Australian aborigine men to increase their ceremonies). Masks, dolls, paintings, and the verbal arts are often specifically didactic devices that are used in ritual and secular circumstances to train the young in the traditions and values of the tribe (in ways appropriate to books, sacred and secular, in literate societies).

In small-scale societies the artist is an ordinary or respected person, rather than a marginal. Whether a specialist or a part-time artist, he or she is a key person in the education and religious and social life of the people. These artists are not, however, individualists: they try to produce not what is new to society, but what is expected and typical. They are not anonymous, but neither are they motivated by striking originality. Usually they are unaware of alternative traditions within their society, or of previous styles or novelty and "progress." They receive the approbation of their public in the form of admiration for having done the right

*Maori wood carving. A Maori master carver in New Zealand instructs youths in this ancient skill. Aboriginal peoples most famous for the elaboration of wood carving styles and techniques include the Maori of New Zealand, West Africans, Northwest Coast Indians, and the Sepik River, New Guinea, lowlanders.*

thing; their recompense is mutual services and support rather than cash and adulation. Under conditions of acculturation and change, primitive art may still be produced—but for sale to outsiders for whom it is fashionable or decorative to collect. It may thus become simplified and repetitive, as with the souvenir arts, or individualized and fast changing, approaching the genres and characteristics of Western arts. Some may even become dual-purpose arts like the Arnhem Land bark in paintings used for instruction or the Cuna Indian *mola* textiles worn as blouses, both of which are sold to outsiders after use.

*See also* Art; Art and society; Art of the Eskimo; Expressive systems; Tourist art

Consult: Boas, F., *Primitive Art* (New York: Dover, 1955); Forge, A. (ed.), *Primitive Art and Society* (London: Oxford University Press, 1973); Gerbrands, A. A., *Art as an Element of Culture* (Leiden: Rijksmuseum foor Volkenkunde, 1957); Lewis, P. H., "A Definition of Primitive Art," *Fieldiana Anthropology* 36:221–241, 1961.

—*Nelson H. H. Graburn, University of California, Berkeley*

*A cast bronze plaque from Benin, West Africa (c. 16th century), depicting a warrior and his attendant.*

**Articulation, Features of.** See Phonetics.

**Artifact.** Any object manufactured, modified, or used by human beings as an expression of their cultural values and norms.

**Artisans.** See Skills and work.

**Artists.** See Skills and work.

**Ascribed Roles.** See Role.

**Assemblage.** This archaeological term denotes all the industries at one prehistoric site considered together. An assemblage consists of a set of artifacts: several similar assemblages at different sites are considered a prehistoric culture.

See also Archaeology; Excavation of a site

**Assimilation.** First and foremost, assimilation constitutes a specific kind of social policy. It involves one of the ways a host community may decide to deal with individuals and groups which are in cultural, linguistic, and social ways alien. An assimilation policy may be followed when alien individuals and groups migrate into or are brought within the social-territorial boundaries of a host society. But there are other policies for dealing with aliens: they may be driven away, settled in separate cultural enclaves, subject to a policy of forced acculturation but never fully assimilated, enslaved, or otherwise cast into an inferior status.

By 1649 the several tribes of the Huron confederacy in the Ontario peninsula had been destroyed as viable societies by Iroquois invasions from New York. Some of the few survivors migrated into upper New York, where they petitioned for admission into one or another of the tribes of the Iroquois confederacy. They were accepted, and within a few decades had disappeared as an identifiable group in Iroquois society.

Some years later, in 1667, a northern Wisconsin tribe asked the French authorities in Montreal to send a Frenchman to live among them. The next year Nicolas Perrot arrived. Perrot spent many years living with the Great Lakes tribes: he learned their languages, dressed as they did, acquired many of their skills for living in the woods, and served as an intermediary between the tribe and the French authorities, who regularly paid him for his services. In his later years, Perrot retired in Montreal.

A few years later, in 1685, a young Frenchman deserted Robert LaSalle's exploring party in West Texas. Half starved, he stumbled into a camp of the Cenis tribe, which fed and cared for him. Thereafter, he learned the native language, was adopted into a family, and assumed the dress and habits of his hosts. Soon he married and had children. Several years later, when another group of LaSalle's men found him, he refused to abandon the Cenis to accompany them.

About 1819 Captain Billy Caldwell of the British Indian Service in Canada immigrated to Chicago. He was the son of an Irish colonel in the British Army and an Ottawa Indian woman. Educated in the best schools available (he wrote English, French, and Latin), he was a military officer and a British civil servant for many years. In Canada he was listed in census reports as "An Officer and Gentleman." In Chicago, he first dabbled in real estate, then became a justice of the peace, and finally moved among the Potawatomi Indian tribe, where he married, became adopted, and was finally identified as a tribal chief. Although Caldwell was universally accepted and respected by the Potawatomi, Americans had mixed reactions to him. Some thought him a cosmopolitan gentleman, some a fine specimen of an Indian chief; others were highly suspicious, believing him to be a British secret agent.

In the last decades of the 19th century a retired sergeant of the 9th U.S. Cavalry settled in a Ute Indian community in southern Colorado. There he took several Ute women as wives and had many children and grandchildren. By 1960 he had more than seventy living descendants in this community; together they formed an identifiable and cohesive extended family unit which functioned in economic and political affairs within the tribal community. Collectively, the sergeant's descendants were sometimes called the Black Ute, for the sergeant had been an emancipated black slave from the South. Yet they enjoyed all the rights and privileges and carried out the responsibilities which were theirs as Ute Indians, and individually they identified themselves as such.

These few cases illustrate many of the characteristic features and dimensions of the complex process known as assimilation. The deserter from LaSalle's party, the descendants of the black cavalry sergeant, and the Huron migrant group all constitute clear examples of full-scale assimilation of individuals and groups from one society into another. The instance of Perrot, however, involved considerable acculturation of an individual, but not assimilation. And the brief biography of Captain Billy illustrates a complicated set of life experiences which is not easily classified in any fashion.

These cases were selected to make a point that is generally ignored. Assimilation is too often thought of as a policy characteristic only of large, complex nation-states, specifically those which are rapidly expanding their size in an undeveloped region of low population density. On the contrary, assimilation is a policy which is frequently adopted by many societies irrespective of their size, political complexity, or type of economy.

On the other hand, from the point of view of the theoretical interests of anthropology and other social sciences, these few cases exemplify all the features of assimilation which distinguish it from similar sociocultural processes such as acculturation, socialization, and enculturation.

First, assimilation is a dynamic process which necessarily involves a certain amount of acculturative contact between members of different cultures; yet culture contact is not itself sufficient to cause the assimilation of an alien group. East European Jewish communities and other religious enclaves such as the Hutterites may reside in a host community for centuries without being assimilated.

Second, like acculturation, assimilation may involve individuals, groups, or both. The Mexican-American subculture of the American Southwest regularly loses many individual members who assimilate into Anglo life; yet it is just as regularly replenished by new migrants from Mexico.

Third, quite unlike acculturation, assimilation operates in one direction only: a part or all of one community is incorporated into another. Situations where representatives from different societies come together to form an entirely new and separate third community are better understood as examples of ethnogenesis, as with the mixed French-Indian populations who developed what is known as the Metis culture.

Fourth, changes in important features of the internal, subjective views of the migrants are required. That is, the migrants must alter their basic values and eventually transform their personal identities to become assimilated.

Fifth, the host community must willingly accept or adopt the migrant individual or group.

Sixth, all these characteristics are best thought of as dimensions with considerable variation in quality, degree, or amount. Assimilation is not an all or nothing, either-or phenomenon, but a set of distinctive, variable processes. Generally these processes involve the resocialization and reculturation of individuals and groups originally socialized in one society, who thereby alter their status and transform their social identities sufficiently to be accepted fully as members of a new, host community.

*See also* Acculturation; Enculturation; Socialization

Consult: Teske, R. H. C., and Nelson, B. H., "Acculturation and Assimilation: A Clarifi-

cation," *American Ethnologist* 1:351–368, 1974.
—*James Clifton, University of Wisconsin, Green Bay*

**Associations.** This term refers to two domains of social life. Sometimes it specifies the relations a person has regularly with non-kin others (a person's "associates") in terms of some shared goals. More often, it specifies social groups organized to pursue definite ends. Since the first usage can be specified adequately by terms such as *relationship, cooperation,* and *collusion* (which are, in any case, more precise) whereas the second usage is not adequately covered by another term, the latter seems more important for social science.

The term points to the social importance of the fact that a number of persons join (or are made to join) together for a purpose. That is, associations involve (1) a group in the strict sense of that term; (2) its charter—i.e., its statement, written or unwritten, rigorous or loose—of group membership criteria, recruitment and extrusion procedures, group property, and the group's explicit aims; (3) property (e.g., money); (4) more or less standardized operating procedures such as meetings; (5) possibly an executive body all of whom may or may not be members; (6) action toward ends.

Within this set of attributes, associational organization varies widely, which sometimes makes it difficult to classify associations. For example, associations are classified as voluntary (like a country club) or involuntary (like a conscripted army); as formal (with an explicit, "public," often legally registered charter like the Chamber of Commerce) or informal (like a discussion group); as restricted (like the Ku Klux Klan) or open (like a museum—if you can pay); and so on. Classification is not very useful, however, because it adds no new information for understanding the social situation. On the contrary, classification has led to much fruitless argumentation as to whether, for example, government agencies are associations or organizations (an ambiguous term because it blurs varied modes of ordering persons into groups and is confused with *organization,* which refers generically to personal, categorical, network, and group linkages).

Solutions to such problems lie not in deciding on their essences for classification but rather in seeing that there are numerous devices for organizing and many attributes

of organization which can vary independently of each other. Thus families look like associations with respect to their actions toward certain ends, but they do not look like associations in terms of how they are initiated. With this approach, one may more clearly understand social processes of transition from networks to associations, formalizations of informal associations, conversions of associations into agencies, and the emergence of networks inside or cutting across associations or bureaucracies.

Clearly associations, varying vastly in scale, are not coterminous with a society. Most associations are relatively small and localized groups within a society, although some may relate to parts of the population spread across its entire territory and through many of its segments (the National Education Association, the American Medical Association, various federal agencies, many industrial and banking corporations). Still others are international in scope (the multinational corporations, the United Nations, the International Anthropological Union, the Catholic Church).

Associations satisfy human needs and wants by creating special organizations when other organizations, such as families, cannot do the tasks required. Associations are extraordinarily adaptable modes of social organization, in part because most of them can be readily extinguished when no longer useful. They are very rare in simple societies, but are perhaps the major organizational mode in more evolved ones.

*See also* Network, social

Consult: MacIver, Robert M., and Page, Charles H., *Society: An Introductory Analysis* (New York: Rinehart, 1949).
—*Anthony Leeds, Boston University*

**Assumed Roles.** *See* Role.

**Astronomy, Primitive.** Astronomy—along with other exact sciences—has often been emphasized as a feature of civilizations. V. Gordon Childe, for example, believed that the economic changes associated with the beginnings of civilization and urban life necessitated the emergence of sophisticated astronomy. It is certainly true that astronomy and calendrics were important in early civilizations. A precise solar calendar, which reflects seasonal changes, is extremely useful in scheduling agricultural activities, particularly when the state is involved in the organization of agricultural operations.

**Navigation.** Astronomy may also function in many other contexts, however. One of the most obvious is navigation, as in ancient Greece. Polynesian seafarers maintained and transmitted an elaborate body of astronomical knowledge entirely by oral tradition. Sophisticated astronomy and elaborate calendars occur in stateless societies as well as in civilizations; in some areas the beginnings of systematic observation and recording of celestial phenomena apparently predate the emergence of civilization, and even of agriculture, by many thousands of years. Anthropologists have been slow to recognize the quantity, precision, and level of systematization of the knowledge "primitive" groups have of all aspects of their environments. Few ethnographers have collected information about native traditions of astronomy; fewer still have investigated them as systematic bodies of knowledge. Even less information is available on prehistoric astronomy.

**Religion and Cosmology.** In most societies, astronomical observation and knowledge are intimately associated with cosmological thought and belief systems involving the supernatural; nonetheless, coherent and systematic bodies of knowledge are often involved, and they cannot be dismissed as mere astrology. In pre-Columbian Mesoamerica, astronomy and calendrics were particularly elaborate, and they are relatively well understood because contemporary descriptions of the Spanish conquerors are available in addition to native sources. The 365-day solar calendar used to schedule agricultural activities was only one of a great many calendrical cycles, not all of which were based upon astronomical phenomena. Astronomical observation and knowledge were accurate and detailed, especially among the Maya, who were able to predict solar eclipses and who recognized and tabulated the cycle of appearance and disappearance of Venus as morning and evening star. At the same time, astronomy was inseparable from religion and cosmology. All the celestial bodies were deities. Astronomical cycles, like all cycles and units of time, had a host of ritual and symbolic associations, and astronomy functioned as much in the context of astrology and divination as in the prediction of celestial events.

**Reconstructing Astronomical Knowledge.** It is extremely difficult to reconstruct

the astronomical knowledge of cultures of the past from strictly archaeological evidence, although it may be reflected in such features as building orientations and settlement plans. The existence of such knowledge becomes a great deal more evident with the appearance of writing and other systems of graphic notation, reinforcing the apparent association of astronomy with civilization. Interest in the history of astronomical knowledge has intensified since 1960, leading to the development of new techniques for recovering such information from archaeological evidence and even to the emergence of a subdiscipline called archaeoastronomy or astro-archaeology. Renewed interest since 1965 in the possible astronomical functions of European megalithic structures of the third and second millennia BC illustrates some of the problems involved. Gerald Hawkins and others have recently expanded older suggestions of astronomical associations at Stonehenge, on the Salisbury Plain in southern England. Hawkins argues that stone alignments at Stonehenge mark dozens of rise and set positions of the sun and moon and that the site was used as a "computer" to predict solar and lunar eclipses. Stonehenge certainly had some astronomical associations: for example, its main axis is oriented approximately to midsummer sunrise. Other features at Stonehenge may indeed reflect sophisticated astronomical knowledge, but there is little agreement on the proper methods for demonstrating the intentions of the builders and the actual functions of the site.

Recent discoveries also suggest that the systematic observation and recording of celestial events have a much greater antiquity than had previously been suspected. Alexander Marshack has shown through microscopic analysis that many apparently meaningless random markings of portable objects of the Upper Paleolithic period in Europe are actually highly patterned and constitute systematic notations of lunar cycles. This complex and systematic observation, and the use of symbols, have extremely important implications for the reconstruction of the intellectual and cognitive abilities of Paleolithic people.

See also Calendar, development of; Stonehenge; Upper Paleolithic art; Writing
Consult: Baity, Elizabeth Chesley, "Archaeoastronomy and Ethnoastronomy So Far," *Current Anthropology* 14(4):389–449, 1973; Hawkins, Gerald S., *Beyond Stonehenge* (New

York: Harper & Row, 1973); Satterthwaite, Linton, "Calendrics of the Maya Lowlands," in *Handbook of Middle American Indians*, ed. Robert Wauchope, vol. 3 (Austin: University of Texas Press, 1965); Thompson, J. Eric S., *Maya Hieroglyphic Writing: An Introduction*, 2nd ed. (Norman: University of Oklahoma Press, 1960).
—John S. Henderson, Cornell University

**Atlatl.** The atlatl or spear-thrower is a handheld implement which augments the propulsive force of the arm in casting a missile. Archaeological evidence suggests that the spear-thrower was developed in Europe during the middle to late Upper Paleolithic, at least 15,000 years ago. In recent times, it has been used by the indigenous peoples of Australia and New Guinea and by various groups in the New World from the arctic to the equator.

See also Hunting; Spear; Weapons

**Aurignacian Culture.** This Upper Paleolithic assemblage is represented by type sites at La Ferrassie and Laugerie-Haute (SW France). This culture, a lamellar industry with characteristic scalar retouch, was originally defined by D. Peyrony (Laugerie-Haute) using Breuil's "Middle Aurignacian" as a base. The Aurignacian culture is coex-

*Australian Aborigine hunter poised to hurl his spear with the help of an atlatl—a lever device that increases the spear's velocity but limits its accuracy to within a range of about 100 feet.*

tensive geographically and temporally with the Perigordian culture of W Europe, dating from 32,000 to 20,000 years BP. It is divided into five stages on the basis of an antler point typology: I—split-based points, strangled blades, du Four bladelets (e.g., Caminade). II, III—single, double-ended, oval-sectioned points; busked burins; Font-Yves points (e.g., Font-Yves). IV—biconical, circular-sectioned points; high incidence of simple-blade, carinate endscrapers (e.g., La Ferrassie). V—beveled-base point (e.g., Laugerie-Haute). This assemblage is best documented in S and SW France and in N Spain; it is also documented in N France, Belgium, Germany, Austria, and N Italy; similar industries have been found in E Europe. The term, however, is extended to refer to post-Mousterian assemblages in the Mediterranean basin (especially the E Mediterranean littoral).

*See also* Perigordian culture

**Australopithecines.** Australopithecines are a grade in hominid evolution usually accorded subfamily status (Australopithecinae, within Hominidae). The original type specimen was discovered in 1924 at Taung, Cape Province, South Africa, and was described by Raymond Dart, who coined the term *Australopithecus africanus.*

**Characteristics.** General morphological characteristics of the genus *Australopithecus* include a mean cranial capacity of 500 cc, with a range of 435–700 cc. Brow ridges are variably developed. A sagittal crest, developed to reinforce areas of muscle attachment on the parietals due to heavy use of the masticatory apparatus, is present in some robust specimens. Massive mandibles and posterior dentition are characteristic (esp. robust form), as are small incisors (esp. robust), parabolic dental arcades, reduced canines with no maxillary diastema, and a postcranial skeleton which is hominid in total morphology (i.e., functionally related to habitually erect posture, bipedal mode of locomotion) but which differs in detail from that of genus *Homo* (esp. some pelvic bones, proximal end of femur, some ankle and foot bones). Australopithecine mean stature varied from 4 feet 9 inches (gracile form) to 5 feet 4 inches (robust form); the estimated weight at maturity varied from 50–70 pounds (gracile) to 90–130 pounds (robust). They lived during the Upper Pliocene (e.g., Kanapoi, Lothagam Hill, Kenya), dated at 4.5 to 5.0 million years ago, until the Lower/Middle

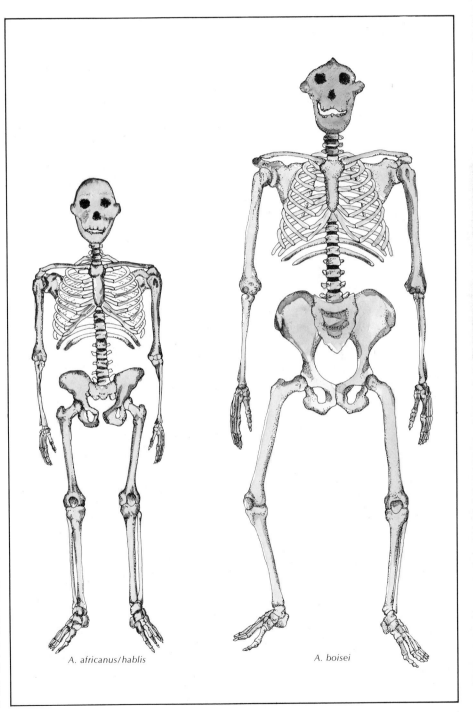

*A. africanus/hablis*

*A. boisei*

Pleistocene boundary (e.g., Peninj, Tanzania), dated at less than 1.5 million years ago. Geographical distribution is limited to EC Africa, S Africa, and possibly W Africa. Some claim that fossil remains from China and Java are australopithecines, but this view is contested.

**Distribution.** Two kinds of australopithecines (gracile and robust) are usually distinguished on hotly debated chronological, morphological, and paleoenvironmental criteria. Commonly included in the gracile group (called *Australopithecus africanus, A. habilis,* and *H. habilis* among others) are the following: the immature (and therefore taxonomically worthless) type specimen (Taung) and fossils from Makapan (Limeworks Cave, thirty individuals) and Sterkfontein (forty individuals) in S Africa; Garusi (one individual), Olduvai (six individuals, taxonomic status debated), Lothagam (one individual), Baringo (two or three individuals), E Rudolf (Koobi Fora, five or six individuals, taxonomic status debated), and Omo (ten individuals and many more unassigned, taxonomic status debated) in EC Africa; and Tchad (one individual) in W Africa. Usually included in the robust group (called *Australopithecus robustus, A. boisei,* and *Paranthropus robustus* among others) are the following: fossils from Kromdraai (six individuals) and Swartkrans (sixty individuals, taxonomic status of three to five individuals contested) in S Africa; Olduvai (three individuals and unassigned specimens), Baringo (one individual), Peninj (Lake Natron, one individual), E Rudolf (Koobi Fora, Ileret, more than twenty-five individuals and unassigned), Chesowanja (one individual), and Omo (more than five individuals and many unassigned) in EC Africa; and two individuals of debated taxonomic status from the Djetis beds in SC Java.

**Taxonomic Problems.** The taxonomic status of many australopithecine fossils, and their consequent placement in hominid phylogenetic schemes, is vigorously contested. Six alternative phylogenetic trees are presented here; each has its adherents, although D, E, and F are currently favored by most British and American hominid paleontologists. The taxonomic controversy turns on two complex and related issues: (1) whether or not the gracile/robust dichotomy can or should be maintained; and (2) whether or not a hominid more "advanced" (i.e., more *H. erectus*-like) than the australopithecines, and consequently a better candidate for the line leading to modern humans, is also present in deposits of Basal Pleistocene age in S and E Africa.

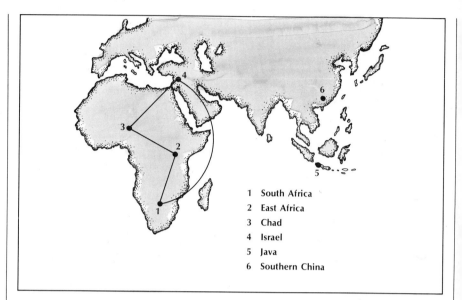

*Australopithecine fossil remains are concentrated in southern, central, and eastern Africa. However, these hominids apparently did exist outside the continent of Africa; specimens have been found in Israel and possibly in China and Java as well (although the taxonomic status of these eastern fossils is not clear).*

1   South Africa
2   East Africa
3   Chad
4   Israel
5   Java
6   Southern China

Advocates of the first position (e.g., Wolpoff and Brace) reject the gracile/robust dichotomy and assert that the criteria used to differentiate the two groups are related to variation in body size—variation which does not exceed that found among extant hominid populations. They regard all (contemporaneous) australopithecines, and fossils assigned by others to Basal Pleistocene genus *Homo,* as samples of a single, highly variable, sexually dimorphic, polytypic group (perhaps even a single species at any given point in time). Areal, intrasite, and temporal differences are attributed to a complex set of factors, the individual contributions of which cannot yet be isolated. Among these factors are sampling error (fossil finds inadequately reflect the original populations), sexual dimorphism, intergroup (?subspecific) variability (geographical races), and variation

through time (lineal or time-successive species). Advocates of this position tend to regard the australopithecines as a developmental "grade" in a unilineal scheme of hominid evolution, preceded by a ramapithecine grade and succeeded by pithecanthropines. They reject arguments for differentiation based on supposed differences in diet, culture, and adaptation.

Advocates of the second position (e.g., Howell, Clarke, Leakey, Tobias) either consider the differences among the australopithecines to be so great as to warrant the gracile/robust dichotomy or else they regard the australopithecines as a group to be distinctive enough vis-à-vis other Basal Pleistocene fossils assigned to genus *Homo* of indeterminate species to exclude the former entirely from the line leading to modern *Homo sapiens.*

The two positions cannot be reconciled. In part, the difficulty lies in evaluating variability in small samples of hominid skeletal material widely distributed in space and time. Students of fossil populations have yet to agree upon a large number of functionally based, morphological criteria which can be used in conjunction with multivariate statistics to differentiate groups and assign specimens of unknown affinity to them.

**Adaptation.** Taxonomic problems aside, a good deal is known of the paleoenvironmental circumstances in which the australopithecines lived and to which they adapted. Faunal and geomorphological studies permit reconstruction of local habitats, which seem to have been open woodland/savanna mosaics, with dense arboreal vegetation scarce and confined to watercourse margins (lake and river banks). Although the moisture regime appears to have varied across space and through time, there are no indications that the australopithecines occupied niches markedly different from those in which their remains are found today. This is a significant discovery because it has tended to undermine Robinson's (1963) dietary hypothesis, which prevailed in the United States during the late 1960s. Robinson, who

*Some alternative interpretations of the phylogenetic (evolutionary) relationships among the australopithecine fossil forms. The major author representing each interpretation is shown.*

maintains the gracile/robust distinction on the generic level, has argued that the massive molar and especially the premolar dentition of the robust australopithecines developed as a response to a strictly vegetarian diet, whereas the gracile form, with smaller premolars, was supposed to have been a savanna-adapted omnivore. These morphological differences were thought to correlate with differences in moisture regime at the gracile (supposedly more savannalike) and robust (supposedly wetter, with more arboreal vegetation) sites in E Africa and especially S Africa.

**Culture.** It is difficult to generalize about the nature of australopithecine sites. Some (e.g., Olduvai) are clearly living surfaces of short duration; others (e.g., Swartkrans and Sterkfontein) are long-term accumulations of bone, sediments, and artifactual debris due in part to geological agencies and nonhuman predation. Australopithecine skele-

tal material occurs in association with the remains of numerous animals, large and small, solitary and gregarious, some of which were probably prey elements in the australopithecine diet. The high incidence of small game (rodents, amphibians, reptiles) and immature or aged individuals of the large species (especially ungulates) suggests that if hunting were regularly practiced (as has been argued), it was a mode of subsistence supplemental and secondary to gathering and scavenging. If hunting can be documented, however, it has a number of important implications for hominid social development. It can imply, among other things, intragroup cooperation, food sharing, a probable minimal group size on the order of five active adults, sexual division of labor, pair bonding, intimate knowledge of (perhaps cyclical movement through) a recognized territory, and the concept of a home base.

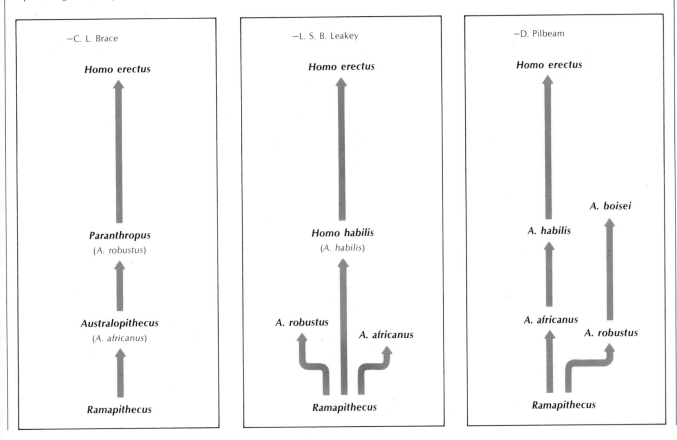

The eruption cycle of australopithecine dentition is known from the recovery of immature specimens: it implies a period of dependency equivalent to that of humans (i.e., much extended over that characteristic of pongids). Prolonged dependency would have facilitated enculturation and the acquisition of learned behavior in general. It is perhaps not coincidental, then, that artifacts assigned to the earliest recognized tool-making tradition, the Oldowan, occur with australopithecine material at Olduvai, Sterkfontein, and other hominid-bearing sites in S and E Africa. In the absence of compelling evidence to the contrary, it is assumed that the australopithecines themselves manufactured these crude but indubitable cobble and flake implements. The capacity to make standardized tools is dependent upon learning, and it is in this sense that the australopithecines are often described as the earliest "culture-bearing" hominids. Once tool-making became established, the australopithecines had started down the road to technological development, a characteristic unique to humans and one which has made us the dominant form of life on this planet.

See also Evolution, human; Fossil sequence of human evolution

Consult: Buettner-Janusch, J., *Physical Anthropology: A Perspective* (New York: Wiley, 1973); Le Gros Clark, W. E., *The Fossil Evidence for Human Evolution*, 2nd ed. (Chicago: University of Chicago Press, 1964); Pilbeam, D., *The Ascent of Man* (New York: Macmillan, 1962); Robinson, J., "Australopithecines, Culture and Phylogeny," *American Journal of Physical Anthropology* 21:595–605, 1963; Wolpoff, M., "The Evidence for Two Australopithecine Lineages in South Africa," *Yearbook of Physical Anthropology*, series 17, pp. 113–139, American Association of Physical Anthropologists, Washington, 1973.

—Geoffrey A. Clark, Arizona State University

**Australopithecus Africanus.** See Australopithecines.

**Australopithecus Boisei.** See Australopithecines.

**Australopithecus Habilis.** (*Homo Habilis*). See Australopithecines.

**Australopithecus Robustus.** See Australopithecines.

**Authority.** See Power; Social control.

**Autism.** A condition in which a child has withdrawn totally into itself, usually because reality has proved too painful or overwhelming to deal with.

**Autobiographies.** See Life history approach.

**Avoidance Behavior.** There are many socially standardized ways of controlling interactions between persons of different status. Persons may be avoided because they are considered ritually dangerous or polluting (as menstruating women) or potentially degrading to one's status (as in caste systems). Avoidance is also a means of eliminating role conflicts or conflicting claims on one person, as in affinal kin (in-law) relationships. Similarly, structured avoidance prevents improper relationships from developing, as in sibling avoidance directed at prevention of sexual relationships. By isolating categories of individuals in order to prevent conflict, rigorously enforced avoidance promotes social equilibrium and reinforces social structure. Ritualized avoidance involving things and behaviors, taboos, prohibitions, and the like is a broad class of cultural events. Such avoidance behaviors may have specific adaptive functions, as in mother-in-law avoidance, or they may simply reflect one expression of cultural values, symbolic of some ideal in its own right.

See also Ritual

—James Clifton, University of Wisconsin, Green Bay

**Ax.** See Hand ax.

**Aztecs.** This ancient empire of pre-Columbian central Mexico originated in the first half of the 14th century AD with the founding of the Aztec capital Tenochtitlán. The Aztec empire was dominated by three centers, Tenochtitlán, Texcoco, and Tlacopán, which were bound together by an alliance formed in 1428 and lasting until the conquest of Mexico by Cortes in 1521. Although Tenochtitlán was the dominant city at the time of Spanish conquest during Montezuma II's reign (1503–1520), Texcoco was often of

*These are modern Aztec dancers from Mexico.*

equal importance and was a larger center, especially during the reign of the great ruler Nezahualcoyotl (1402–1472). The Aztec empire formed the largest polity of pre-Columbian Mesoamerica—a population of about 6 million and a territory of about 80,000 square miles. The most important deity of the Aztecs was Huitzilopochtli, who demanded blood sacrifice.

Originally the organization of Aztec society was based in tribal kin residence groups called *calpulli*. Eventually a stratified society emerged, dominated by a group of nobles, the *pipiltin*, who controlled the bureaucracy, priesthood, and army and were the major landholders. As the Aztec rose to power, the commoners, *macehualtin*, lost most of the privileges they enjoyed when the society was kin-based.

See also Civilization, origins of

Consult: Brundage, Burr C., *A Rain of Darts: The Mexica Aztecs* (Austin: University of Texas Press, 1972); Madsen, William, *The Virgin's Children: Life in an Aztec Village Today* (Austin: University of Texas Press; 1960).

—Michael D. Olien, University of Georgia

**Baboon Social Organization.** The typical baboon troop—called a multimale group—consists of several adults of both sexes with associated immature animals. Membership is fairly stable through time, but some animals, particularly subadult males, may transfer between troops. Consequently, the core of the troop is a stable group of females. New data suggest that maternal genealogies probably play an important role in structuring social relationships (as in rhesus and Japanese macaques). Maternal kin associate, groom, and support one another in agonistic situations more than unrelated animals do.

Male-male social relations are also characterized by a complex ranking system. Certain males generally appear more dominant in aggressive situations, but may not be the most successful copulators. Other roles, such as policing the troop, watching for danger, and defending the troop may or may not be correlated with aggressive rank. Alliances between males further complicate ranking relationships. Alliances which are stable over long periods have been termed *central hierarchies;* however, alliances may also be of only a few moments' duration. Available data suggest that such alliances may be more stable in the savanna than in more favorable (less crowded, less exposed) forest or forest-fringe habitats.

See also Chimpanzee, social organization and behavior of; Primates, behavior of Consult: Hall, K. R. L., and DeVore, I., "Baboon Social Behavior," in *Primate Behavior: Field Studies of Monkeys and Apes,* ed. I. DeVore (New York: Holt, 1965); Ransom, T. W., and Rowell, T. E., "Early Social Development of Feral Baboons," in *Primate Socialization,* ed. F. E. Poirier (New York: Random House, 1972); Rowell, T. E., "Forest Living Baboons in Uganda," *Journal of Zoology* (London) 149: 344–364, 1966.
—Leanne T. Nash, Arizona State University

## Bachofen, Johann Jacob (1815–1887).
Bachofen, a Swiss jurist, was primarily interested in primitive peoples, primitive law, and primitive religion. From his studies he wrote eight major works, the most famous being *Das Mutterrecht* in which he was the first seriously to challenge the long-held conviction that the monogamous patriarchal family was the basis of society.

See also Mutterrecht, das

## Balanced Polymorphism. Polymorphism
is the presence in a population or species of two or more forms of a trait in frequencies higher than can be accounted for by mutation alone. A polymorphism is balanced if the relative proportions of the forms are in stable equilibrium. This term is most commonly used to refer to genotypes where the heterozygote has a selective advantage over the homozygotes.

Natural selection is thought to be responsible for the polymorphisms of many human blood groups, enzymes, and particularly for the abnormal hemoglobins, such as sickle-cell trait and thalassemia, both of which confer resistance to malaria.

See also Evolution, genetic mechanisms of; Genetics; Selection, natural; Sickle-cell anemia; Thalassemia

## Bamboo. There are many varieties of this
tropical plant. Bamboo has been intensively utilized by Asians since the Paleolithic period: bamboo spearheads and arrowheads have been found with other Paleolithic articles in China. The Shang people of ancient China wrote on bamboo slips and made bamboo musical instruments. For thousands

*Hawaiian bark cloth (tapa), considered to be the best. It was decorated by using small bamboo stamps to produce polychrome designs.*

of years, bamboo has been used to make utensils such as baskets, containers, knives, and gongs, as well as structural members for buildings and bridges. Cooked bamboo shoots are one of the favorite vegetable foods for various Asian groups.

## Band. The simplest level of social organiza-
tion is the band. It is marked by very little political organization and consists of small (50 to 300 persons) groups of families. Cohesion comes through charismatic leadership, marriage alliances with members of other bands, and family organization.

See also Chiefdom; Social organization; Tribe

## Bark Cloth. The use of bark cloth, made of
the inner bark of certain trees, is widespread in the non-Western world. It is particularly important where the loom is not known or where fibers suitable for spinning and weaving are not cultivated, but it is also known in areas such as Japan and Madagascar, where weaving traditions are well developed. In some areas the raw materials and processes are related to papermaking—for example, in Japan the making of paper and bark cloth can be considered different stages of the same process.

In some areas of New Guinea and Malaysia the first beating of the inner bark would

take place while it was still attached to the stem of the tree, but the more usual process is to remove the bark from the tree before pounding it. The outer bark is invariably removed and the inner bark soaked in water to soften it and occasionally to remove a poisonous sap characteristic of some trees. After soaking, the inner bark is beaten, usually with a wooden beater on a wooden anvil but occasionally with tools of stone. The inner bark pieces may be felted, pasted, and/or sewn together to form large pieces. At this stage the cloth often becomes a medium for artistic expression. Decorating the cloth requires another series of tools, as well as dyes and perfumes.

Before it was replaced by European cloth and blankets, bark cloth was used chiefly for clothing and bedding, but it was also used in ceremonial gift giving, for the making of kites, and as decoration for humans and for images of gods. The use of bark cloth is recorded for parts of Africa, Madagascar, Malaysia, East Asia, Indonesia, New Guinea, Melanesia, Micronesia, Polynesia, and South America. Its most varied and richest expression, however, was found in Polynesia and it is by the Polynesian name *tapa* that bark cloth is most often known. The finest bark cloth is made of the inner bark of the paper mulberry *(Broussonetia papyrifera)*, which is usually cultivated specifically for the purpose. Other trees used include *Artocarpus* (breadfruit), *Ficus* (fig), *Pipturus, Boehmeria,* and *Hibiscus.*

The earliest descriptions of the manufacture of bark cloth in Polynesia come from the 18th-century voyages of Captain Cook. As described in Tahiti, the cleaned and soaked strips of inner bark were laid out in two or three layers, with the longitudinal fibers laid lengthwise to form a collage a foot wide and 12 yards long. After lying overnight, much of the water evaporated and the fibers began to adhere together. The collage was then beaten with a four-sided wooden beater, each face carved with straight lines or furrows of different widths. By this process the layers were felted together to form one large piece, which might then be folded several times and again beaten to make a very soft and thin cloth. By a different process, more characteristic of W Polynesia, each piece of inner bark was beaten separately and then several were pasted together with a paste made from a vegetable such as arrowroot.

Although in many areas the making of bark cloth is no longer practiced, it is still universally made in Tonga, where it is a necessary ritual gift for rites of passage. In Tonga it has also become an economic commodity, sometimes sold to tourists in small pieces or as ladies' handbags and sometimes exported to various parts of the world for use as decoration in hotels or restaurants with "South Seas" decor.

Consult: Brigham, William T., *Ka Hana Kapa,* Memoirs of the Bernice P. Bishop Museum, vol. 3, Honolulu, 1911; Kooijman, Simon, *Tapa in Polynesia,* Bernice P. Bishop Museum, Bulletin 234, Honolulu, 1972.

**Barnett, Homer G.** (b. 1906). Barnett is best known for his study of innovation as the basis for culture change. Most of his writings are concerned with applications of anthropological research.

*See also* Cultural change; Innovation

**Barth, Fredrik** (b. 1928). Barth is best known for his structural studies of Middle Eastern groups, sedentary as well as nomadic, especially their kinship and political structures. His theoretical contributions include works on ethnicity, the boundary-maintaining mechanisms of various ethnic groups, and models of social organization, economic anthropology, and social change.

**Basic Personality.** As defined by A. Kardiner, this term refers to the adaptive psychological skills shared by all or most members of a society. Since basic personality structure is a product induced in a society's members by the specific institutional forms in each society, the form, content, style, and means of coping with the problems of living consequently vary widely from culture to culture; they also vary over time in any one culture as the primary institutions change. Kardiner, a neo-Freudian who emphasized both the formative influence of childhood experience and the importance of cultural determinants, claimed that primary institutions were a key influence on basic personality. Once formed, basic personality was then influential in molding secondary institutions—i.e., mythology, belief systems, folklore.

*See also* Primary institutions; Secondary institutions

**Basketry.** This form of textile art had developed by the early Neolithic. Basket making is a distinctive feature of the arts and crafts of many preindustrial societies. Where it is developed extensively, in contrast to the production of utilitarian ware, it is often women's work. Basket-making techniques were probably the forerunner of true weaving. The materials used are the bark, roots, and vines of various decorative shrubs and trees.

As an art form, basketry is a difficult technique, for the artist must construct both design and space simultaneously. Designs are produced by varying the nature of the materials used in successive weaves, by dyeing some of the materials, and by weaving in a variety of decorative pieces of shell, bird feathers, or other contrastive elements.

The West Coast of North America, from California to the Alaskan panhandle, was an area noted for its elaboration of basketry. There basketry was a favored and highly developed art form. All adults understood the basic techniques, but it was women who generally were the masters of the art. Three

*Apache storage basket, decorated with a fret design in bands around the top, center, and bottom. The decoration represents human and animal figures.*

tribes are noted for their unusually fine basketry: the Pomo, Karok, and Yurok. Among these, basketry achieved its greatest development and refinement. Pomo women, for example, would test their skill by weaving tiny baskets only a half inch wide, complete with design, whose stitches were so small they could only be seen under a magnifying glass.

Basketry techniques are used for making a wide variety of utilitarian as well as artistic items: hats, armor, bird and fish traps, carrying cases for medicines and valued goods, water containers, storage baskets, and many others.

*See also* Textiles

Consult: Boas, F., *Primitive Art* (New York: Dover, 1927); O'Neale, Lila, *Yurok-Karok Basket Weavers,* University of California Publications in American Archaeology and Ethnology, Berkeley, 1932.

## Bastian, Adolph (1826–1905).

Bastian, a German M.D. and world traveler, believed that uniform laws of growth and the physical unity of the human species were responsible for certain elementary ideas held by all individuals. These few elementary ideas are the primary units of which the *Völkergedanken* (folk ideas) are composed. These folk ideas, under the influence of their environment (physical surroundings) and historical events, develop differently from region to region. Hence, according to Bastian, cultures vary from place to place in spite of the physical unity of mankind.

## Bateson, Gregory (b. 1904).

Bateson has pioneered in a number of areas of anthropological research. A constant theme in his research has been the relationship between the individual and culture. His work has progressed from early studies of culture and personality to penetrating studies of cultural factors involved in schizophrenia, using a communications model for analysis. His most famous fieldwork was done with Margaret Mead in New Guinea.

One of the earliest of Bateson's concepts, and perhaps one of his more enduring ones, is that of schizmogenesis—the process through which a group splits into two or more factions due to the development of different ways of interpreting the world or simply as a result of trying to communicate.

*Wampum belt made of shell wampum beads, given to William Penn at the Treaty of Shakamaxon (1673) by Leni Lanape Indians.*

The term for an emotional, or affective, way of perceiving the world is *ethos,* and Bateson did much to popularize the use of this term in anthropology.

Bateson pioneered in the use of modern photographic techniques in fieldwork and anticipated the development of kinesic and proxemic studies. He was concerned about the need to standardize ethnographic methodology so that theories based on ethnography would prove valid.

More recently, Bateson has begun to work on an approach he calls "the ecology of mind." He views each person's mind as a system in interaction with many other systems—all of which must be described and analyzed. His studies have proved stimulating and have placed an anthropological viewpoint in an area where it has been traditionally neglected.

*See also* Culture and personality; Ethos; Film, ethnographic research and report; Photography as a research tool; Schizmogenesis; Schizophrenia

Consult: Bateson, G., *Naven,* 2nd ed.(Palo Alto, Calif.: Stanford University Press, 1958); Bateson, G., *Steps to an Ecology of Mind* (New York: Ballantine, 1972).

—*Frank A. Salamone, St. John's University*

## Beads and Beadwork.

Various materials have long been popular for body and costume ornamentation in almost all areas of the New World. In prehistoric times, favorite materials were bone, stone, shell, wood, and less frequently metal (primarily copper, gold, silver); even clay beads were popular. In more recent times, glass beads, obtained via European traders, have become a basic object for artwork. Beads seem always to have been valuable, regardless of the material—due probably to the amount of labor involved in their manufacture—and when they were formed from such materials as gold or shells, they became currency of sorts. Early trade beads were obtained from European colonists, primarily French or British, who in turn got their supplies from Italy and Central Europe. American traders followed this pattern in late colonial days, and on the West Coast trade beads came into the Northwest from Russia. The only example of Native American glass bead making seems to have been practiced by the historic Arikara Indians.

The uses of beads are not confined to jewelry making; these extend to costume ornamentation, and some garments are known to be completely composed of beads. A great variety of techniques are used in such work—not only the common appliqué, in which beads are sewn with sinew or fiber to the surface of a material, but also loom weaving, rope braiding, and netting. It is difficult to assess the aesthetic skills of Indian beadworkers, since the individual often surpasses the general artistic level of his or her cultural group; but certainly the most prolific seem to be found among the Northern Plains tribes. While largely a matter of personal taste and judgment, one would rate the artistry of Crow designs and technique as remarkable, seconded by the Blackfoot, Cheyenne, and Sioux. Yet there

*!Kung San woman making ostrich-egg-shell beads.*

are many skillful artists to be found in the Great Lakes area, and the delicacy of technique mastered by the Iroquois or the surprising effectiveness of Plateau solid beading designs are also representative of the best in the art. The weight of beadwork is a significant factor when one realizes that a woman wearing a heavily beaded buckskin garment from the Plains may be supporting the equivalent of 10 to 15 pounds of solid glass.

Beads are not only decorative: they also serve as indicators of aesthetic taste and wealth; and when used in realistic designs, they may serve a narrative function. With wampum, as among the Iroquois, a historic or quasi-religious purpose was served, as in the making of the shell-bead wampum belts. The size of beads varied tremendously; the early trade beads, commonly termed *pony beads,* were introduced around 1800; other styles were the minute seed beads and the so-called real beads which supplanted them. Each had its period of dominance, and this can be regarded as helpful in judging the date of manufacture of the object. The use of metal, particularly copper, gold, or silver, was more common in Central and South America than in the North, although some gold beads have been found in Florida and copper was commonly employed for making beads in the Midwest and East. Perhaps the most remarkable gold bead manufacture is to be found in the prehistoric areas of Colombia and Ecuador, where tiny cast-gold beads in granulation form were extremely common and of superb craftsmanship.

Bead decoration is also known in Mexico and Panama, where the Huichol have developed a woven bead technique; the Guamí of Panama make a loose-netted woven beadwork collar which is the pride of the menfolk. But these cases are somewhat exceptional, for beadwork is not one of the common craft techniques of Mesoamerica.

Seeds and related natural materials are frequently found in South America. Whether these materials can be regarded as beads or not is debatable; they are used in the same manner as formed beads, yet the natural quality may rule out their classification in this category.

*See also* Adornment

Consult: Bushnell, David I., "Origins of Wampum," *Journal of the Royal Anthropological Institute* 36:172–177, 1906; Ewers, John C., and Wildschut, William, "Crow Indian Beadwork," *Contributions from the Museum of the American Indian*, vol. 16, 1959; Hunt, B., and Burshear, J. F., *American Indian Beadwork* (New York: Macmillan, 1951); Orchard, William C., "Beads and Beadwork of the American Indians," *Contributions from the Museum of the American Indian*, vol. 11, 1929.

—*Frederick J. Dockstader, Museum of the American Indian*

## Beattie, John Hugh Marshall (b. 1915).
Social anthropologist interested in philosophy, methodology, and the ethnography of E Africa. Most of his research has focused on the Nyoro of W Uganda.

## Behaviorist School of Psychology.
This 20th-century psychological tradition insists that the proper subject matter of psychology is observable human behavior, rather than hypothetical intrapsychic events. Behaviorism arose in the United States early in this century, largely as a reaction to Freudian theory: behaviorists charged that psychology could never become a genuine science as long as it continued to focus on such hypothetical constructs as the unconscious, the superego, the ego, and the id.

Behaviorism is based on the view that all human behavior is learned through a process of *conditioning*. Behaviorist learning theory is based on the classical conditioning theories of Ivan Pavlov (1849–1936) and the more recent operant conditioning theories of the leading behaviorist, B. F. Skinner (b. 1904). Conditioning is said to take place through a process of positive or negative reinforcements (that is, rewards and punishments) which are associated with particular stimuli or responses. Behaviorists explain virtually all human cognitive and affective development as elaborations of this basic and essentially passive process.

Behaviorism has enjoyed an unchallenged dominance in American psychology until very recently, but it is now under strong attack. Critics, many of them adherents of the newer cognitive developmental school, have charged that behaviorism is mechanistic and antihumanistic in its approach, does not take adequate account of the self as the active constructor of meanings, and cannot provide an adequate account of many psychological phenomena (such as language acquisition).

See also Conditioning; Developmental school of psychology; Piaget, Jean; Psychoanalytic school of psychology; Reinforcement; Skinner, B. F.

Consult: Skinner, B. F., *Beyond Freedom and Dignity* (New York: Random House, 1973); Skinner, B. F., *About Behaviorism* (New York: Knopf, 1974).

—*Ian Robertson, Cambridge University*

## Behavior Pattern. *See* Pattern, behavior.

## Bellah, Robert Neeley (b. 1927).
Bellah specializes in the sociology of religion and comparative institutional structures. His writings include work on Apache kinship systems and religion and society in Tokugawa Japan.

## Bellows. *See* Metalworking.

## Benedict, Ruth (1887–1948).
This American cultural anthropologist was a leading member of the Culture and Personality movement that dominated much of the anthropological thought of the 1930s and 1940s. She was professor of anthropology at Columbia at the time of her death in 1948.

Benedict's most important and controversial contribution was her *configurationalist* approach to the study of entire cultures. Each culture, she believed, is patterned in a unique fashion. Although individual members in that culture may differ in their personalities, the cultural system tends to push them toward an ideal type of personality. Those whose personalities are most compatible with the cultural ideal should be the happiest and best adjusted. Configurationalism had as its objective the identification of fundamental ethos in each culture: for example, Benedict identified the Pueblo Indians as extrovert and Appollonian, and the Plains Indians as introvert and Dionysian. Such psychological characterizations have been strongly criticized on the grounds that they are merely stereotypes, abstracted from a very limited range of cultural roles.

Benedict was an early proponent of the concept of cultural relativism, but World War II led her to rethink some of the impli-

*Ruth Benedict.*

cations of this stance; she was reluctant to grant that the Nazi value system could not, in principle, be judged by other value systems. Her solution to this dilemma was the concept of *synergy*: any society that is compatible with human advancement is a good one, but a society that works against basic human goals is antihuman and evil, and can be judged as such.

See also Appollonian-Dionysian; Configurationalism; Configurations of culture; Cultural relativism; Culture and personality

Consult: Benedict, Ruth, *Patterns of Culture* (Boston: Houghton Mifflin, 1934); Mead, Margaret, *An Anthropologist at Work: Writings of Ruth Benedict* (Boston: Houghton Mifflin, 1959).

—*Phillip Whitten, Harvard University*

## Bennett, Wendell C. (1905–1953).
A Central Andean archaeologist, Bennett formulated the concept of co-tradition—a culture area which has a long tradition of intracultural interaction.

See also Culture area; Traditions

## Berdache.
French term for North American Indian transvestites, regarded as sacred, who

lived with other men and whose cultural roles included curing and organizing social events.

**Bergmann's Rule.** Based on the observation that (within a species) the colder the climate, the larger the animal, Bergmann's rule states that in mammals body size increases as environmental temperature decreases. The phenomenon is based on the relationship of body volume to skin area. Since heat loss occurs at the body surface and the ratio of surface to volume decreases with increased body size, the relatively smaller surface area of a large body dissipates less heat than a small one and hence is better adapted to cold climates. Conversely, a small body is better adapted to hot climates. Among human populations, the rule is generally applicable although factors such as nutrition affect body size.
*See also* Balanced polymorphism; Physical anthropology

**Berlin, Brent** (b. 1936). Berlin, an anthropologist interested in ethnoscience, has made important contributions to the study of Mayan folk biology and the evolution of color categories.

**Berreman, Gerald** (b. 1930). Berreman's special contributions include work on symbolic interaction, humanistic-existential approaches to research, cross-cultural studies of inequality (caste, racism, stratification), the ethnology of N India, and active concern with social responsibility in anthropology. He has had noted success in treating autistic children.

**Bettelheim, Bruno** (b. 1903). Known especially for his work in child psychoanalysis and educational psychology, Bettelheim has also dealt with the nature of prejudice and with puberty rites involving male genital mutilation.

**Bidney, David** (b. 1908). Bidney, a cultural anthropologist, is known primarily for his contributions to the history of anthropology, cultural theory, and comparative ethics. His best-known work is *Theoretical Anthropology* (1953).

**Biebuyck, Daniel P.** (b. 1925). Social anthropologist and ethnologist working in the areas of African art, ethnology, systems of thought, and oral tradition.

**Bifaces.** *See* Hand ax.

**Bifurcation.** Contrast among kin types based on the distinction between the mother's kinfolk and the father's kinfolk.
*See also* Descent; Kinship and descent

**Bilateral Descent.** The reckoning of descent through *both* male and female (mother's and father's) lines—typically found in Europe, USA, SE Asia.
*See also* Descent

**Bilocality.** Marriage residence pattern that locates a married couple with the husband's kin group part of the time and with the wife's kin group part of the time.
*See also* Marriage

**Binford, Lewis Roberts** (b. 1930). An archaeologist and a leading figure in the "new archaeology," Binford has urged greater use of evolutionary theory and systems analysis in archaeology.

**Binford, Sally R.** (b. 1924). An archaeologist who specializes in human ecology during the Pleistocene, Binford is primarily interested in the biological and cultural evolution of early *Homo sapiens*.

**Biological Adaptation.** *See* Adaptation, biological.

**Biological Anthropology.** *See* Physical anthropology.

**Biological Basis of Language.** Human language is a complex system of symbolic communication based on vocal-auditory transmission. Each language has a characteristic set of recognized sounds (phonemes) combined into units of meaning (morphemes) which in turn make up longer utterances according to underlying rules of grammar. Communication systems of other animals may be highly varied and complex, but human language exhibits a number of key properties—such as arbitrariness of the symbol in relation to the environmental referent and the ability to produce new utterances and to refer to events removed in time and space. In addition, language is transmitted by learning and is intimately bound not only to human cultural and technological developments but also to the capacity for thought, abstraction, and conceptualization.

While some authorities regard human speech as a highly evolved call system comparable to those of other primates, others claim that biological changes were a necessary prerequisite for language. Although speech may have developed from call systems by a process of blending for communication or communion, or from the lip-smacking prevalent in the grooming and greeting of other higher primates, at some point in human evolution important changes occurred in the structure of the brain and the speech apparatus—probably as a result of the feedback relationship involving the use of tools, language, and social behavior. A brain size threshold of 750 cc may be essential, but hemispheric asymmetry, whereby one hemisphere of the brain dominates the other and carries out different functions, is considered especially important. The left hemisphere contains several parts of the cerebral cortex crucial to speech: Broca's area, located toward the front and responsible for setting the speech apparatus in operation; Wernicke's area, further back and vital to comprehension; and the angular gyrus, serving to connect signals from the various senses. Compared to other primates, *Homo sapiens* has a smaller oral cavity, a thicker tongue which bends at a sharper angle in the throat, a proportionately larger pharynx (allowing for better modification of the sounds made by the vocal cords), and a larynx located further down in the throat. Adult humans vary the shape of the pharynx by use of their tongue and throat muscles and can shut off the nasal cavity completely, so that the air passes through the mouth and is affected by movements of the tongue and lips.

The relationship between the vocal apparatus for human speech and the linguistic abilities of extinct hominids has been investigated by the linguist Philip Lieberman and the anatomist Edmund Crelin. They determined that although the Steinheim fossil may have resembled modern *Homo sapiens*

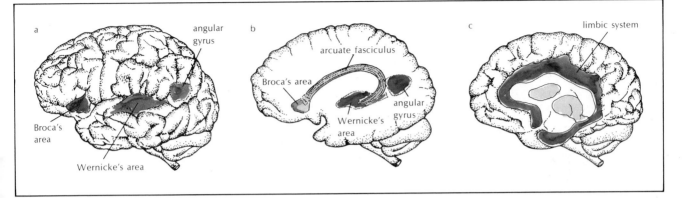

SPECIAL AREAS OF THE HUMAN BRAIN

(a) Brain speech areas are on the surface on one side (see inset). (b) A subsurface nerve bundle loops to connect Broca's and Wernicke's areas. (c) The limbic system for nonverbal communication is in both brain halves.

in the structure of his speech apparatus, the later Neanderthals did not. They also claim that early hominids could not have made the vowel sounds a, i, and u crucial to all languages today; nor could sounds have been connected with the great rapidity necessary for modern speech. Speech must have been slower and the utterance less varied.

Recently, chimpanzees have been taught to use nonverbal symbols and grammar in a way characteristic of human languages. Sarah can form sentences and answer questions with colored plastic symbols; Washoe and other chimpanzees have become quite adept at using sign language, even to the point of communicating among themselves in this manner. However, primates in the wild have not been observed to use such symbolic communication systems: they must be taught to do so. Barring extreme deprivation or deafness, humans automatically learn language. Chimpanzees, on the other hand, cannot acquire speech. It has thus been claimed that spoken language is a uniquely human adaptation; unless language is so broadly defined that it loses its usefulness as an analytic category.

See also Call systems; Capacity for language; Language; Morpheme; Phoneme
Consult: Lancaster, J. B., "Primate Communication Systems and the Emergence of Human Language," in Primates: Studies in Adaptation and Variability, ed. P. Jay (New York: Holt, 1968); Lenneberg, E., Biological Foundations of Language (New York: Wiley, 1967); Lieberman, P., "Primate Vocalizations and Human Linguistic Ability," Journal of the Acoustical Society of America 44:1574–1584, 1968; Linden, E., Apes, Men, and Language (New York: Dutton, 1974).
—Catherine E. Read-Martin, California State University, Los Angeles

**Biological Evolution.** See Evolution, biological

**Biological Parents.** In contrast to sociological parents, biological parents are those who conceive and give birth to a child, rather than those who are responsible for the child's care and education.

See also Sociological parents

**Biological Traits.** See Genotype.

**Bipedalism.** The ability to walk consistently on two legs—bipedalism—is a prime adaptation which distinguishes the human species from other animals. It occurs as a result of several modifications: feet have become differentiated from hands, the heel bone is longer and stronger, all foot bones are larger and less mobile than hand bones, the large toe has become strengthened, and the other toes have lost size and mobility. Further, the legs of humans are normally longer than their arms, the spinal column is held perpendicular to the ground by large extensor muscles (the buttocks), and the weight of the spine and internal organs rests on the pelvis—the shape of which has become tilted, shortened, and constricted to allow for the broadening of the pelvic shelf. The result of this latter distortion is the narrowing of the birth canal. Human infants are both small and immature compared to other animals. Such immaturity would be disastrous in any other animal, but the same erect posture which constricts the size of the birth canal also frees the hands so that human infants can be carried and cared for. This immaturity allows a longer period for enculturation. Freeing the hands also enabled tool use, invention, and innovation. (See art on next page.)

Consult: Birsell, J. B., Human Evolution (Chicago: Rand McNally, 1972); Buettner-Janusch, John, Origins of Man (New York: Wiley, 1966); Hulse, Frederick, The Human Species (New York: Random House, 1963).
—Evelyn Kessler, University of South Florida

**Birdwhistell, Ray Lee** (b. 1918). A major figure in the development of the science of kinesics, which extends the theory and methodology of linguistic analysis to the body movements and gestures that accompany or substitute for speech. Birdwhistell is the author of Kinesics and Behavior (1970).
See also Communication, nonverbal; Kinesics

**Black Muslim Movement.** The official title of this black nationalist and religious organization is the Nation of Islam. Members believe they are descendants of a lost Muslim tribe and adhere to many traditional tenets of Muslim faith. The movement was founded in the United States in 1930, but under radical leaders such as Malcolm X, it attracted national attention and a greatly in-

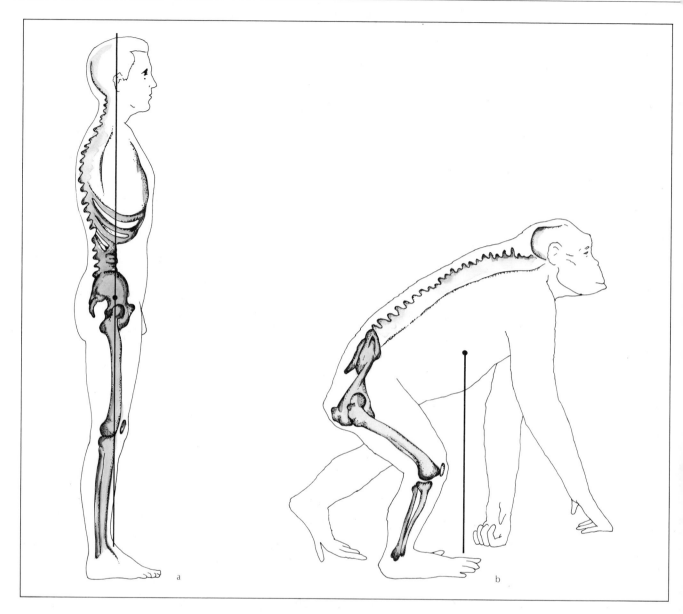

a

b

creased membership in the 1960s. Elijah Muhammed, its prophet and leader, died in 1975 and was succeeded in office by one of his sons.

**Black Power Movement.** This political movement of black Americans developed in the late 1960s and early 1970s. The slogan "Black Power" was coined by black leader Stokely Carmichael in 1966, and the ideology of the movement represented a break with the earlier integrationist objectives of American blacks. Instead, blacks were to develop a strong sense of group pride and identity, and seek self-determination.

**Blade Tools.** A blade is a long and narrow stone flake. Although a blade occasionally is produced in any flake tool industry, a spe-cialized technique is required to produce blades consistently. Projectile points, knives, and burins made from blades are called blade tools. Although they are found in sites as early as the European Acheulean, blade tool industries are primarily characteristic of the Upper Paleolithic of Europe and the Classic Period of Mesoamerica. Tiny blades (bladelets or microliths) are characteristic of some Mesolithic cultures of the Middle East,

## BIPEDALISM VERSUS KNUCKLE WALKING: A HUMAN EVOLUTIONARY DEVELOPMENT

a. *Human bipedal posture. The center of gravity of the body lies just behind the midpoint of the hip joint and in front of the knee joint, so that both hip and knee are extended when standing, thus conserving energy.*

b. *A knuckle-walking chimpanzee. The body's center of gravity lies in the middle of the area bounded by the legs and arms. When the ape walks bipedally, its center of gravity moves from side to side and up and down. The human center of gravity is displaced much less, making walking much more efficient. (After Zihlman.)*

## UPPER PALEOLITHIC STONE TOOLS

*Burins and scrapers, made from blades, are typical artifacts of all stages of Upper Paleolithic times. Burins were used for grooving wood, bone, and particularly antlers, which were made into spears and harpoon points. The chisel ends of burins were formed by taking an oblique or longitudinal flake off the end of a blade. Arrows indicate the chisel ends. Burins were also used to engrave figures. End scrapers were employed on bone and wood. Scraping edges are indicated by arrows.*

N Africa, and Europe, where they were sometimes set into wooden or bone handles to make sickles, knives, projectile points.

*See also Stonework*

**Blank State View** (Tabula Rasa). *See* Mind.

**Blood Groups.** Blood is composed of red blood cells (erythrocytes), white blood cells (leucocytes), and platelets, all suspended in plasma. If the clotting agent, fibrinogen, is removed from the plasma, the result is serum. The red blood cells carry the blood group antigens or agglutinogens characteristic of the various blood group types; the serum contains the antibodies which may react with antigens, causing agglutination or clumping.

People were first classified on the basis of blood type with the discovery by Landsteiner in 1901 of the ABO blood group system. Persons differed with respect to both their antigens and their serum. The antigens of a person of type A react with anti-A in the serum of an individual of types B or O; type B reacts with anti-B from types A and O; AB

with serum from types A, B, and O; and type O with neither anti-A nor anti-B antibodies. Individuals do not normally have antibodies to their own systems. Type O, the universal donor, can give red blood cells to persons of any ABO type; AB, the universal recipient, can receive erythrocytes from anyone.

"Public" antigens, those of populational importance, include the ABO, Auberger, Diego, Duffy, Kell, Kidd, Lutheran, MNSs, P, Rh, and Xg systems. Almost every person has antigens within each of these systems. The most famous are the ABO, MN, and Rh systems.

The ABO system is inherited by three different genes or alleles at a single genetic locus on the chromosome—$I_A$, $I_B$, and $I_O$. Alleles $I_A$ and $I_B$ are codominant to each other, and both are dominant over $I_O$. Allele $I_O$ is by far the most common: the frequency of the recessive homozygote O is 50 percent or more in most populations. Homozygote B, generally the rarest type, is most frequent in C Asia, where values of $I_B$ reach 25 to 30 percent. Allele $I_A$ is particularly prevalent among the North American Blackfeet and Blood Indians, perhaps as a result of genetic drift. Selective pressures maintaining these alleles in a genetic polymorphism are unknown, but correlations are claimed with certain diseases. Any ABO incompatibilities between husband and wife may result in selection against the sperm or the fertilized egg, preventing pregnancy or causing early termination.

The MN system, reported by Landsteiner and Levine in 1927, was the only blood group system discovered experimentally. The MN now appears to be linked to the Ss system. There are two codominant alleles and three blood types—M, MN, and N. The heterozygous MN person, for some unknown reason, appears to be favored by natural selection over either homozygote.

Inheritance of the Rhesus system is more complex and at present uncertain. People can most generally be divided into Rh positive and Rh negative types. Although Rh positive is characteristic of most individuals in the world, populations of European ancestry are approximately 15 percent Rh negative. Since the Basques have a very high Rh negative frequency, some claim that early European populations were principally Rh negative, with later immigrants contributing Rh positive alleles. Rhesus system incompatibilities between mother and fetus are important in hemolytic disease of the new-

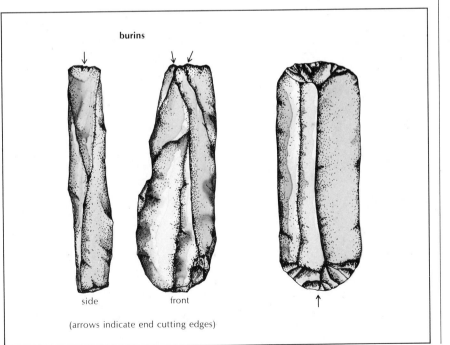

**burins**

side     front

(arrows indicate end cutting edges)

born, erythroblastosis fetalis. Difficulties may occur only when the mother is of Rh negative and the child of Rh positive blood types.

Blood groups have been highly significant for genetic studies—the mode of inheritance is known for a number of systems, testing is simple, and variations occur within and among populations. Other primates besides humans are also polymorphic for blood group systems. Besides their medical uses, practical applications include evidence in paternity suits.

See also Balanced polymorphism; Gene distributions

Consult: Race, R. R., and Sanger, R., *Blood Groups in Man* (Philadelphia: Davis, 1968); Snyder, L. H., *Blood Groups* (Minneapolis: Burgess, 1973).

—Catherine E. Read-Martin, California State University, Los Angeles

**Blood Groups, Distribution of.** See Gene distributions.

**Bloomfield, Leonard** (1887–1949). Often called the Father of American Linguistics, Leonard Bloomfield made linguistics a science and founded structural (or descriptive) linguistics. His major work, *Language* (1933), developed the phonemic and morphemic principles and became the framework for the descriptive study of language. This classic text, which applied behaviorist principles to the study of language, was used to train a whole generation of American linguists. Bloomfield also made important contributions to historical and comparative linguistics by successfully applying methods developed for written languages to unwritten American Indian languages, especially the Algonquian languages.

See also Descriptive linguistics

**Blowgun.** See Weapons.

**Boas, Franz** (1858–1942). Born in Westphalia, Germany, the Father of American Anthropology received both the Ph.D. and the M.D. in 1881 from the University of Kiel for his studies in the natural sciences. He began his studies in North America in 1883 in Baffin Land. In 1896 he joined the staffs of the American Museum of Natural History and

*Franz Boas*

Columbia University, where he remained after retirement (emeritus, 1937) until his death. World-renowned, he was the recipient of many awards and honors.

Boas' name, work, philosophy, and personality dominated American anthropology during the first two decades of the 20th century, only to be replaced in the next three decades by the dozens of his students who became illustrious scholars in the field. To them he was mentor and friend, paterfamilias and colleague.

He insisted upon the development of research methodology which conformed to rigorous scientific method—a notable lack in behavioral science at that time. Unsatisfied with sweeping theoretical generalizations about behavior that increasingly failed to account for more sophisticated observations of cultural variability, Boas all but declared a moratorium upon such constructs until such a time as the issues themselves became clearer. As a moralist and humanist, he deplored the ethic of applying anthropological skills and insights to political ends to the detriment of peoples anywhere.

Boas' lengthy bibliography ranges across the entire field of anthropological purview.

A sampling: *The Central Eskimo* (1888); *The Growth of Children* (1896); *The Kwakiutl of Vancouver Island* (1909); *Changes in Form of Body of Descendants of Immigrants* (1911); *The Mind of Primitive Man* (1911); *Dakota Grammar* (with E. Ella Deloria) (1911); *Primitive Art* (1927); *Race, Language and Culture* (1940).

**Boats.** See Watercraft.

**Body Language.** See Kinesics.

**Bohannan, Paul** (b. 1920). Bohannan's major early contributions include theoretical considerations of the study of legal processes cross-culturally, the development of analytic models for legal ethnography, and economic anthropology. His recent work involves issues of marriage, divorce, and the family. Bohannan's area of specialty is Africa, with emphasis on the Tiv of N Nigeria.

**Bone.** This highly complex tissue consists of specialized cells (osteocytes) within a matrix of both organic and inorganic substances. The composition of bone is approximately 25 percent water, 45 percent inorganic material, and 30 percent organic material. The hardness of bone is due principally to the high content (about 85 percent of its inorganic composition) of crystalline calcium phosphates ("bone salt"). About 95 percent of the organic material of bone is collagen, a fibrous protein. Together, the calcium salts and the collagen make bone strong enough to provide the necessary support for muscular movements and also to protect the internal body organs, while still being elastic enough to resist tension and pressure.

Bone is very much a living tissue. It undergoes continual internal remodeling as some osteocytes (osteoblasts) manufacture new bone and others (osteoclasts) break down older bone. Some bones contain marrow, which is important as a source for both red and white blood cells. Bone also serves as a storage site for phosphorus and calcium —minerals vital to other metabolic activities of the body. The majority of bones of the human body form from cartilaginous models which are transformed into bone through a process known as ossification.

Consult: McLean, Franklin C., and Urist, Marshall R., *Bone* (Chicago: University of Chicago Press, 1968); Weinmann, J. P., and Sicher, H., *Bone and Bones* (St. Louis: Mosby, 1955).
—*Martin K. Nickels, Illinois State University*

**Bordes, Francois** (b. 1919). A professor at the University of Bordeaux, Bordes has conducted his major research on the European Paleolithic, especially in SW France. His major theoretical contribution has been to focus on living floors rather than geological strata in excavation. Bordes' skill as a "Paleolithic" flint-knapper helped to refine tool typologies.

**Bott, Elizabeth** (b. 1924). One of the social anthropologists who introduced social network analysis into social and cultural anthropology as a result of her research on urban families.
*See also* Network study

**Bow and Arrow.** For preindustrial societies, the bow and arrow has served as both

*A Yanomamö archer standing on a sandbank in the middle of the Mavaca River in the Orinoco River region*

a formidable weapon of warfare and an important subsistence tool. Developed approximately 10,000 years ago, the bow was the first means of concentrating muscular energy for the propulsion of a missile. Use of the bow and arrow spread throughout most of the aboriginal world, with the exception of Australia and Tasmania and among groups who use alternative implements such as the blowgun. The bow and arrow is still indispensable to the few remaining African hunting/gathering groups, such as the !Kung San, and continues to be employed to supplement the diet of many simple horticulturalists of South America and Melanesia.
*See also* Fishing; Hunting; Weapons
Consult: Rogers, Spencer L., "The Aboriginal Bow and Arrow of North America and Asia," *American Anthropologist* 42:255–269, 1940.

**Brace, C. Loring** (b. 1930). Physical anthropologist at the University of Michigan, well known for his revival of the lineal theory of human evolution and his nonracial approach to the study of human diversity.

**Bracero Program.** The Mexican Contract Labor (Bracero) program, passed in 1951, was a temporary emergency measure designed to import Mexican field laborers into the U.S. in order to cope with reputed shortages of farm labor due to the Korean War. It has been renewed periodically.
Consult: Heller, Celia S., *Mexican American Youth: Forgotten Youth at the Crossroads* (New York: Random House, 1966).

**Brachiation.** This characteristic mode of locomotion of gibbons involves swinging by alternate arms under a support (e.g., a branch). The animal's full weight is carried by the arms.

**Braidwood, Robert John** (b. 1907). An archaeologist who has pioneered research on the origin of agriculture in the Near East, Braidwood developed the "hilly flanks" theory of plant domestication.

**Brain Size.** Mammals have the largest brains of any class in the animal kingdom, and the brains of primates are among the

largest of the mammals. The brain of *Homo sapiens* averages 1,350–1,450 cc in volume. Along with a considerable increase in the volume of the cerebral hemispheres, primate brains have evolved to accommodate stereoscopic color vision, the use of hands (and often feet) as manipulative organs, a reduction in the apparatus of smell, and other changes. The size of the brain can be a useful guide to the general intelligence of a species, but since an increase in size also increases variability, comparisons of brain size within a species are not considered a useful guide to intelligence.

Since brain material decomposes too rapidly for fossilization, cranial capacities must be used in comparing extinct and extant forms. The cranial capacity is larger than the brain itself because the cranial cavity (braincase) contains membranes and cerebrospinal fluid in addition to the brain. Cranial capacities are commonly used as one means of distinguishing among various fossil hominids. It may also be possible to derive information about the proportions and features of the brain from a study of the endocranium (the inside of the skull).
*See also* Evolution, human; Fossil sequence of human evolution
Consult: Tobias, Phillip V., *The Brain in Hominid Evolution* (New York: Columbia University Press, 1971).
—*Stanley Rhine, University of New Mexico*

**Breeding Populations.** *See* Populations, breeding.

**Breuil, Abbé Henri Edouard Prosper** (1877–1961). French archaeologist and specialist in the Paleolithic cultures of Europe, particularly Upper Paleoloithic cave art of France and Spain.
*See also* Upper Paleolithic art

**Bridewealth.** Valuables given by a man's kin group to his wife's kin group to legitimate their marriage, to compensate her kin for losing her presence and labor, and to give him rights regarding her children.
*See also* Marriage

**British Social Anthropology.** This intellectual discipline developed in Britain during the 1920s. The founders of the tradition were A. R. Radcliffe-Brown, E. E. Evans-Pritchard, and B. Malinowski. Students trained in those early years in Britain are now located throughout the world, so that the theoretical contributions of British social anthropology are no longer geographically centralized in the British academic community.

Radcliffe-Brown and his associates developed a precise definition of social structure and a method of analysis which has subsequently been labeled the *structural approach*. Radcliffe-Brown declared that his theory of social phenomena was derived from such earlier writers as Montesquieu, Comte, Spencer, and Durkheim and could be presented by means of three fundamental and connected concepts—structure, function, and process. Structure and function are complementarily related through his use of the organic analogy; process refers to the fact that concrete social reality is not an entity, but "consists of an immense multitude of actions and interactions of human beings" from which the structure may be inferred.

Whereas Radcliffe-Brown insisted that social phenomena must be explained at the social level, Malinowski emphasized the satisfying of biological needs. During long periods of field research among the Trobriand Islanders of Melanesia, Malinowski developed what has come to be called functional anthropology. This perspective stresses the utility and consequences of all behavior and insists on establishing the hidden as well as the obvious connections between all manifestations of social behavior. Especially emphasized is the task of finding how the organization of such behavior into institutions meets basic (primary) and culturally derived needs.

The concept of *social structure* is certainly the most influential aspect of early theory in British social anthropology. This term denotes the complex network of social relations that link human beings together. From this definition comes a methodology which entails direct observation of actual relationships—an endeavor which Malinowski first put into extended and intensive practice. The structure which persists in a social group is the structure of a particular geographic locality.

Raymond Firth later used the term *social organization* to account for the fact that individuals attempting to further their own interest may act in ways not in accordance with normative rules, thus causing a change in the overall structure (short term or long term). Social organization is behavior systematically regulated by acts of decision and choice; it is an individual's or group's use of structural principles and normative values to order social resources (time, alliances, etc.) to their best advantage. Firth did much to lay the foundation along which the processual school, and later network analysis, developed, by making explicit the distinction between form and process. The early British structuralists had failed to distinguish one from the other because their focus was on the study of rules and obligations with the concomitant emphasis on the group.

See also French structuralism; Functionalism; Network study; Structuralism
Consult: Kuper, Adam, *Anthropologists and Anthropology: The British School 1922–1972* (London: Allen Lane, 1973); Radcliffe-Brown, A. R., *Structure and Function in Primitive Society* (New York: Free Press, 1952).
—*Cathie J. Witty, University of Washington*

**British Structuralism.** *See* British social anthropology; Social anthropology.

**Bronze.** *See* Metalworking.

**Bronze Age.** Basically this term refers to a phase in the transition from the Neolithic to the age of large-scale use of metal tools and weapons. However, neither bronze nor technology is the best indicator of developments in this era. Bronze itself was very rare, difficult to produce, too expensive to find wide use. The important developments were social and cultural: increased population size, development of large towns, trade, communications, and government. In the process, Mediterranean Neolithic communities were transformed via extensive trade with distant cultures. The Bronze Age of early Crete and Greece (ca. 3000 BC) preceded that of N Europe by a thousand years.
*See also* Prehistory

**Brother-Sister Exchange.** This term refers to a form of marriage in which two men each marry the other's sister. Also known as sister-exchange, it is often applied as a shorthand label for systems in which men exchange women who are sometimes their own sisters or daughters and sometimes more distant relatives. In some societies men may arrange brother-sister exchanges to avoid paying bridewealth. In others such marriages are a preferred form within a wider system of prescriptive cross-cousin marriage.
*See also* Marriage; Matrilateral prescriptive cross-cousin marriage; Patrilateral cross-cousin marriage; Women, exchange of

**Brown, Roger** (b. 1925). This Harvard University social psychologist has contributed research on psycholinguistics and social psychology. Two of his published works are *Words and Things* (1958) and *A First Language* (1973).

**Bruner, Jerome** (b. 1915). An American psychologist (currently professor of psychology at Oxford University) whose interests have focused primarily on the area of cognitive development.

**Buck, Sir Peter** (Te Rangi Hiroa) (1880–1951). Part-Maori ethnologist, M.D., and director of the Bishop Museum (1936–1951), Buck contributed numerous publications on the arts and crafts of the Pacific (Hawaii, Samoa, Cooks, New Zealand, Kapingamarangi).
*See also* Art of Oceania: Polynesia and Micronesia

**Buddhism.** *See* Religions of the world.

**Buettner-Janusch, John** (b. 1924). A physical anthropologist now at New York University, Buettner-Janusch is known for his work on lemurs and blood groups.

**Bunzel, Ruth** (b. 1898). Bunzel is one of the many students of Franz Boas who has influenced the development of American anthropology. Most of her fieldwork has focused on Zuni ceremonialism. In World War II she worked for the Office of War Information and later conducted studies on American and Chinese national character.
*See also* Ceremony; National character

**Bureaucracy.** This term refers to a formal organization with a hierarchic authority structure and explicit procedural rules. Since the bureaucratic form provides an efficient means of coordinating the activities of large numbers of people in terms of explicit, impersonal goals, large-scale organizations almost inevitably are bureaucratic. Bureaucratic procedures are designed for general cases, however, and the indiscriminate application of rules and regulations to specific or changing circumstances may result in injustice or inefficiency in individual cases.

*See also* Social organization

**Burial.** The earliest evidence of ritual interment of the dead in a specially prepared grave is attributed to Neanderthaloid people (over 50,000 years ago), some of whom placed flowers and other artifacts within the grave and sprinkled the corpse with ground red earth. These finds have resulted in a reassessment of Neanderthal intellectual capabilities, since they suggest the presence of religious beliefs. Proper disposition of the soul of the deceased so that it may be guided into the spirit world and not haunt the living is often the explanation given for the burial ritual.

Many variations on the simple theme of placing a dead body in the earth have been recorded. Some of the most elaborate burials ever discovered have been royal graves excavated in Egypt and China, dating from thousands of years ago. Embalming the corpse with chemicals before interment, either for temporary or for long-term preservation, is a common practice in wealthy societies. The platform burial of the Plains Indians was not a burial at all. The body was placed on a pole platform high enough to be safe from ground predators. Predators from the sky, however, and the high-desert climate soon cleaned the bones, whereupon they were gathered into a woven or leather bag and stored in a safe place. *Secondary burial* involves burying a corpse until the flesh has rotted off the bones, then reburying the clean skeleton in a special place.

*See also* Religion; Rites of passage, Ritual
—*MaryAnn Foley, Southern Connecticut State College*

**Burling, Robbins** (b. 1918). Anthropological linguist interested in applying linguistic techniques and principles to the study of ethnography. His fieldwork has been in Burma.

*See also* Linguistics, anthropological

*Although the term burial refers to the placing of a deceased's remains under the ground, the particular nature of the grave, the container of the remains, and even the condition of the deceased, are very variable. Shown here is a burial urn from Marajó, Brazil, designed to contain the cremated ashes of a deceased person.*

**Butzer, Karl Wilhelm** (b. 1934). Pleistocene geologist whose primary research deals with the interrelationships between prehistoric environments and early humans. He has done fieldwork in E and S Africa, Egypt, and the Sudan.

**Calabashes and Gourds.** True gourds are *Lagenaria* spp., although other tough-rind fruits, such as squashes (Cucurbitae), melons, and coconuts are sometimes called gourds also. Gourds and calabashes are among the earliest domesticated plants (perhaps 9000 BC in Mexico), and wild forms were doubtlessly used even earlier. They serve as bottles, cups, dippers, dishes, bowls, decorations, rattles, pipes, and net floats, especially in nonceramic cultures. Often they are decorated with engraving, painting, and pyroengraving. Endemic to Africa, they are the only major Old World domesticate found in the pre-Columbian New World. They probably floated naturally across the Atlantic, but transatlantic or transpacific human transport remains a controversial possibility.

**Caldwell, Joseph R.** (1916–1973). Archaeologist who made important theoretical contributions to the prehistory of SE United States and SW Asia, including the introduction of the concept of interaction sphere. Promoted the "new archaeology" which emphasizes the study of cultural dynamics over mere taxonomic categorization.

**Calendar, Development of.** Early calendar systems were varied in the ways in which they divided time. Many societies counted, and continue to count, days from daybreak to daybreak and figure yearly seasons by the agricultural necessities of rainfall, harvest, and planting. The Egyptians were the first to devise a calendar which reckoned time in regular chronological divisions, and they began dating periods and events by this method. This principle was developed into the Julian calendar during the Roman period; improvements led to the Gregorian calendar, which has been used throughout the Western world ever since. The seven-day week probably originated through astronomical observation of the seven-day phases of the moon, as well as the early Babylonian belief in the magical properties of the number seven.

Different religious systems continue to reckon time originating from particular historical events, so that there coexist with the modern Gregorian calendar Hebrew, Muslim, Hindu, and Chinese variations as well. Many other calendars, such as the Roman Republican, French Republican, Sumero-Babylonian, Hittite, Egyptian, and Mesoamerican, have become extinct or fallen into disuse due to a variety of historical circumstances.

*See also* Numbering, systems of
—*Cathie J. Witty, University of Washington*

**Call Systems.** These systems of communication of nonhuman primates consist of a limited number of calls. Each call has a distinct and discrete meaning. For example, if a species has a call for danger and one for the presence of food, a species member cannot combine the two calls when both food and danger are present. Each call is tied to a specific environmental context or stimulus. The calls can, however, be varied in intensity, duration, and repetition. This variation can increase the number of messages conveyed through a call system.

Anthropologists are interested in call systems as clues to understanding the origin of human language. Obviously, it is impossible to find direct evidence of the language of our immediate ancestors. However, careful comparison of call systems with true language does suggest the kinds of developments necessary for the evolution of true language. For example, somewhere the evolution of language involved the combination of calls to convey complex messages. Furthermore, true language has the capacity to discuss displaced objects—those that are not present. True language is also capable of expressing newly created ideas.

The differences and similarities of call systems and true language, together with other evidence, have furnished remarkable insights into the origin of language.

See also Communication

—Frank Salamone, St. John's University

**Campbell, Joseph** (b. 1904). Comparative mythologist best known for his four-volume work *The Masks of God,* in which he discusses Oriental, Occidental, primitive, and American Indian myths. His work is organized around the concept of archetypes, originally propounded by the psychologist Carl Jung.

See also Myth

**Cannibalism.** Also called *anthropophagy,* cannibalism is the eating of human flesh. There is some archaeological evidence that cannibalism occurred in Paleolithic times. Once a widespread custom on all continents, it is practiced today only in the remotest parts of New Guinea and South America. Anthropologists distinguish two forms of cannibalism. *Endocannibalism* refers to the eating of the remains of relatives and other members of one's own group; *exocannibalism* confines the practice to the eating of enemies. Endocannibalism often involves piety and reverence toward one's deceased kinspeople, whereas exocannibalism usually constitutes an act of ritualized vengeance.

The parts of the body eaten and the methods of their preparation for consumption differ widely from society to society. Differences exist also in the degree to which cannibalism is associated with religious or magical beliefs and rituals. In many cases,

*These fancy-dressed warriors of Papua, New Guinea, wear traditional ivory sticks through their noses to indicate that they have killed and eaten a man.*

however, the dominant motive is the consumption of the meat itself. Since very few anthropologists have been able to study this custom by participant observation, the available information on its cultural meaning and function remains very fragmentary. It is possible, however, that some practices of institutionalized cannibalism may relate to a shortage of protein in the diet of a population.

See also Killing, ritual

Consult: Koch, Klaus-Friedrich, "Cannibalistic Revenge in Jalé Warfare," *Natural History,* February 1970.

—Klaus-Friedrich Koch, University of Virginia

**Canoe.** See Watercraft.

**Capacity for Language.** The capacity for language is a common property of all human beings and is qualitatively different from the communication systems of all other species, even those of our closest relatives, the apes. Jan Lancaster has characterized human language as essentially a system of names, governed by grammatical rules and making pre-

dominant use of the vocal-auditory channel. The ability to form associations between words or names and their referents, most often sensory images, depends on the unique evolutionary development of the human cerebral cortex. This ability for environmental reference had great adaptive and survival value for the bipedal, toolmaking, hunting/gathering ancestors of modern humanity.

Nonhuman primates can send complex messages of an expressive, emotional nature; they can communicate information about the motivational state of the signaler, but only limited environmental information. This is reflected in the fact that in nonhuman primates, the relationship between a sound (or other signal) and the emotion it expresses is most often rigidly fixed, while in human beings the words associated with particular referents are largely arbitrary. Indeed, Leslie White considered symbolizing, the ability to arbitrarily bestow meaning, as a unique human capacity at the basis of human language and cultural life in general. Charles Hockett views the use of morphemes and phonemes in speech as unique to language. Phonemes and morphemes allow for "duality of patterning," which enables human language to convey a great variety of messages with a minimum of linguistic conventions.

See also Biological basis of language; Language; Morpheme; Phoneme

Consult: Hockett, C., "Animal 'Languages' and Human Language," in *The Evolution of Man's Capacity for Culture,* ed. J. N. Spuhler (Detroit: Wayne State Press, 1959); Lancaster, J., *Primate Behavior and the Emergence of Human Culture* (New York: Holt, 1975); White, L., *The Science of Culture* (New York: Farrar, Straus, 1949).

—Stan Wilk, Lycoming College

**Capital Punishment.** This term may be defined as the execution of a human being after sentence has been imposed by a competent court or other authority. The institution of capital punishment thus presupposes the existence of some political authority; it is to be distinguished from private revenge, slayings, and other homicides.

Capital punishment still exists in the great majority of countries. It has been abolished in most of Western Europe, in some U.S. states, and in a number of Latin American countries, but it is practiced in all Soviet bloc countries and in all African and Asian states except Nepal. Methods of execution vary widely and include shooting, hanging, electrocution, gassing, garroting, and guillotining.

There is considerable variation in the precise offenses for which capital punishment is considered an appropriate penalty. In 18th-century Europe several hundred crimes, most of them petty offenses involving property, were capital crimes. In most of the states that still have capital punishment, however, the range of offenses has been drastically reduced. In these countries homicide in various degrees is invariably considered a potentially capital offense, and treason or mutinous behavior in the armed forces in wartime may also result in the death penalty. Most states are becoming increasingly reluctant to apply capital punishment, however, even when their laws permit it.

*See also* Sanctions
—*Ian Robertson, Cambridge University*

**Capitalism.** Capitalism is a socioeconomic system characterized by a basic class division between the capitalist class (or *bourgeoisie*), which owns the means of production and controls the productive process for its own private profit, and the working class (or *proletariat*), members of which lack direct access to the productive resources and are therefore compelled to sell their labor power. Important preconditions for the establishment of capitalism include private property, money and markets, and a high degree of development and differentiation of the productive forces of society, including agriculture, metallurgy, and writing.

Although some scholars regard simple societies such as the Kapauku of New Guinea as "primitive capitalists," and although important capitalist elements occur in the precapitalist civilizations of Rome, China, and the Near East, capitalism proper did not occur as a dominant social system until the last few hundred years. In its brief history, capitalism has undergone significant evolutionary changes—from the mercantile capitalism of the 17th century, through the competitive industrial capitalism of the 18th and early 19th centuries, to the monopoly capitalism of the 20th century.

Every Western scholar's view of capitalism is profoundly affected by his or her political ideology and class orientation within the capitalist system. In the Marxian tradition, capitalism is viewed as an exploitative system which generates a variety of social ills (war, depressions, poverty, alienation) but which is transitory. Just as capitalism replaced feudalism, so it will be replaced by socialism as the incompatible interests of the bourgeoisie and the proletariat lead increasingly to class-based clashes and the inherently expansionist economy loses undeveloped acres of the world to exploit. In the tradition of functionalist social science, capitalism is often regarded as a reflection of innate human nature and not, therefore, likely to be replaced by socialism. Within this tradition, liberals tend to see capitalism as having basic faults which must be corrected by governmental action; conservatives tend to see governmental action as the cause of most ills exhibited by the system.

*See also* Communism; Economic systems; Imperialism; Socialism
Consult: Friedman, Milton, *Capitalism and Freedom* (Chicago: University of Chicago Press, 1962) (for a conservative view); Heilbroner, Robert L., *The Making of Economic Society* (Englewood Cliffs, N.J.: Prentice-Hall, 1962) (for a liberal view); Sweezy, Paul M., *The Theory of Capitalist Development* (New York: Monthly Review Press, 1956) (for a Marxist perspective).
—*Eugene E. Ruyle, University of Virginia*

**Capitalism and Protestant Ethic.** *See* Protestant ethic, capitalism and.

**Capitalism, Primitive.** *See* Primitive capitalism.

**Carbon-14 Dating.** *See* Radiocarbon dating.

**Cargo Cults.** These revitalization movements (also designated as revivalist, nativistic, or millenarian) received their name from movements in Melanesia early in this century that were and are characterized by the belief that the millenium will be ushered in by the arrival of great ships loaded with European trade goods (cargo). The goods will be brought by the ancestral spirits and will be distributed to natives who have acted in accordance to the dictates of one of the cults. Sometimes the cult leaders call for the expulsion of all alien elements, the renunciation of all things European on the part of the cult followers, and a return to a traditional way of life. In contrast, other cult leaders promise a future ideal life if followers abandon their traditional ceremonies and way of life in favor of copying European customs.

Cargo cults, like other revitalization movements, develop in situations where there is extreme material and other inequality between societies in contact. Cargo cults attempt to explain and erase the differences in material wealth between natives and Europeans.

*See also* Revitalization movements
—*Edward Green, Catholic University*

**Carpenter, C. R.** (1905–1975). American comparative psychologist who did pioneering field studies on gibbons and howler monkeys and established the Cayo Santiago rhesus colony for long-term studies.

**Carroll, John B.** (b. 1916). American anthropological and psychological linguist noted for his theoretical and empirical work on the relationship between language and thought.

*See also* Language and reality; Language and thought
Consult: Carroll, John B. (ed.), *Language, Thought, and Reality* (Cambridge: M.I.T. Press, 1973).

**Casagrande, Joseph B.** (b. 1915). American anthropologist and linguist whose work has been particularly concerned with the relationship between language and thought and the problems involved in participant observation fieldwork.

**Case Study Method.** This term refers to a technique of recording ethnographic data, a style of reporting them in the form of a story, and a method of analysis. As a biographical record or as an account of political history, a case is the chronological description of a series of events in the life of an individual or a society. Generally, an ethnographer uses the case method to obtain a sample of frequently occurring cultural events, such as life-cycle ceremonies, ritual performances, and economic transactions. In the field of legal anthropology, a case represents the detailed record of a particular dispute and its resolution and constitutes a unit of analysis. By comparing a number of cases collected in the field (or from archives), the anthropologist can discover important correlations between the kind of dispute, relationship between the parties, legal norms, mode of settlement, and outcome. In addition, an ethnographer's collection of actual dispute cases permits other anthropologists to check the analysis and provides the material needed for the comparative study of legal systems.

See also Comparative jurisprudence; Fieldwork methods; Legal systems
Consult: Epstein, A. L., "The Case Method in the Field of Law," in *The Craft of Social Anthropology*, ed. A. L. Epstein (London: Tavistock, 1967).

**Cassirer, Ernst** (1874–1945). A philosopher who stressed the nature of language and studied anthropological data. Cassirer was born in Breslau, Silesia, and was rector of the University of Hamburg when Hitler came to power. As did many other Jews, he left Germany: he went to Oxford (1933–1935), Goteberg in Sweden (1935–1941), Yale (1941–1944), and Columbia (1944–1945). These travels helped spread his influence, which has been formidable.

Cassirer stressed the symbolizing function of the human mind, an approach compatible with much current anthropological thought. He contended that the human mind operates on two separate levels: the mythopoeic, which deals with "internal" reality; and the logical (linear), which deals with "external" reality. On both planes the mind functions to impose structure (order) on a chaotic world. Cassirer was deeply influenced by linguistic thought and developed many of his ideas along linguistic lines. His masterpiece was the *Philosophy of Symbolic Forms* (three volumes, 1923–1929).

See also Linguistics, anthropological

**Caste.** This term refers to a hereditary, endogamous group of people (or a collection of such groups) bearing a common name and having the same traditional occupation. In strict usage, the term applies only to the traditional closed system of social stratification in India, where all status distinctions are ascribed according to circumstances of birth, where the castes are arranged hierarchically, and where the entire system is interwoven with and legitimated by the Hindu religion. The term is sometimes applied, however, to other rigid stratification systems.

See also Social stratification

**Catal Hüyük.** See Cities, development of.

**Caucasoid.** See Race.

**Cave Art.** See Upper Paleolithic art.

**Ceboidea.** This superfamily of New World anthropoids includes New World monkeys (Cebidae) and marmosets (Callitrichidae).

See also Anthropoids; Cercopithecoidea; Primates, evolutionary features of

**Ceramics.** See Pottery and ceramics.

**Cercopithecoidea.** One of the three major superfamilies of anthropoids, the Cerco-

*This spider monkey, a member of the Ceboidea family, carefully protects his prehensile tail as he wades into the water.*

*This Himalayan langur, a member of the superfamily Cercopithecoidea, was photographed in the forests of central Nepal.*

pithecoidea are commonly known as the Old World monkeys, members of which are found from Gibraltar to Japan and throughout the Old World tropics and subtropics. The superfamily consists of one family, the Cercopithecidae, divided into two subfamilies—the Cercopithecinae and the Colobinae. The former includes the baboons, drills, mandrills, macaques, and vervet monkey; the latter includes the leaf-eating langur, colobus, and proboscis monkey.

See also Anthropoids; Ceboidea; Primates, behavior of; Primates, evolutionary features of

**Ceremonial Centers.** These centers, which constitute one form that cities have taken historically, consist almost exclusively of religious structures (temples, ziggurats, sacrificial altars) and buildings to house various religious practitioners and devotees (priests, vestal virgins, temple prostitutes). Thus the population from surrounding areas episodically congregates at the centers and then disperses again, according to their ceremonial calendar. Ceremonial centers usually display major artistic expressions of the society—bas reliefs, wall paintings, sculptures, architectural elaborations. They may often have functioned also as administrative centers of theocratic states—centers for redistributing goods and agricultural produce and centers for foreign policy. Examples include the Mayan Tikal, Cambodian Angkor Wat, and Indian Khajaraho.

*See also* Ritual; Urbanism

**Ceremony.** Ceremonies, rites, or rituals are repetitive and stylized performances of elemental behavioral forms characteristic of a culture and the contextual meanings given those forms by cultural tradition. They are events of high drama and intense symbolic behavior which regulate social life. Many are cyclical and occur at points of the life cycle called life crises: transitions which are a con-

*Catholic pilgrimage to Notre Dame de la Garde in the village of Chanzeaux, Loire Valley, France.*

sequence of change in the physical, biotal, and social environment.

Two kinds of cyclical disturbance universally call forth ritual behavior. The first is a product of change in social status and role of individual members of a group. Birth, initiation into adulthood, marriage, and death are examples. In each case the group must adjust to the change which has transformed a person or category of persons. Ceremonies which regulate these interactional changes are called *rites of passage*. The second cyclical disturbance is a product of fluctuations in the conditions of human life that affect all members of a community at once. The rhythmic change of seasons, the daily solar alteration, and the shift from planting to harvest activities are examples. In each case the entire community must adjust to the new phase of the cycle. Rituals which regulate these interactional changes are called *rites of intensification*.

Both kinds of ceremony reinforce for participants the interaction patterns and symbols which are considered appropriate for the new phase. Through these rites people attempt to regulate interactional change so that it will not be disruptive—so that it will not produce idiosyncratic behaviors or unpredictable adjustments in their lives.

*See also* Ritual

Consult: Partridge, William L., *The Hippie Ghetto: The Natural History of a Subculture* (New York: Holt, 1973); Chapple, Eliot D., *Culture and Biological Man: Exploration in Behavioral Anthropology* (New York: Holt, 1970); Turner, Victor W., *The Ritual Process: Structure and Anti-Structure* (Chicago: Aldine, 1969).
—William L. Partridge, University of Southern California

**Chafe, Wallace L.** (b. 1927). Linguist wellknown for his research on North American Indian languages, especially those of the Iroquoian and Caddoan families. Chafe is the author of *Meaning and the Structure of Language* (1970).

**Chagnon, Napoleon A.** (b. 1938). Cultural anthropologist noted for his study of the Yanomamö Indians of Venezuela and Brazil. Chagnon has also written on field research techniques.

**Chamberlain, Houston Stewart** (1855–1927). Englishman (educated in Germany) who believed in the superiority of the "Teutonic stock" as the creator of modern civilization and in the inferiority of all other races.

*See also* Scientific racism

**Champollion (the Younger), Jean François** (1790–1832). French linguist and Egyptologist whose analysis of the Rosetta Stone and the Obelisk of Philae, demonstrating that Egyptian hieroglyphic writing involved phonetic symbols, provided the key to the decipherment of the Egyptian scripts.

*See also* Hieroglyphic writing; Rosetta Stone; Writing

**Chang, Kwang-Chih** (b. 1932). Chinese archaeologist who has taught at Yale University since 1961 and is the curator of the Peabody Museum there. Chang is the author of *The Archaeology of Ancient China* (1963) and *Rethinking Archaeology* (1967). His area of specialization is E Asian and SE Asian archaeology.

**Change, Cultural.** *See* Cultural change.

**Chapple, Elliot Dismore** (b. 1909). Anthropologist and psychologist whose work deals with rehabilitation, especially of psychopathic and sociopathic adolescents. His published monographs include *Rehabilitation: Dynamic of Change* and *Culture and Biological Man*. He is concerned with the interface of biology and culture as causal factors in human behavior.

**Charisma.** This term refers to the persuasive and personable abilities of a person in a leadership position which enable him or her to attract and maintain a popular following. Often such abilities are attributed to special spiritual powers.

*See also* Leadership

**Chellean Culture.** The term *Chellean* derives from Chelles-sur-Marne (Seine-et-Marne, N France) and was coined by Victore Commont (1906) to refer to then-oldest evidence for hominids in N France. Hand axes with associated fauna were discovered in commercial gravel quarries in river-terrace deposits near St. Acheul, Abbeville (Somme Valley, NW France). The term *Chellean* is often replaced by the terminology developed by the Abbé Henri Breuil in 1939. Approximate equivalents are given below:

| COMMONT | BREUIL |
|---|---|
| Pre-Chellean | Abbevillian |
| – | "Evolved Abbevillian" |
| Chellean | Lower Acheulean |
| Acheulean | Middle Acheulean |
| Upper Acheulean | Upper Acheulean |

The term is sometimes retained to refer to hand-ax-bearing assemblages interposed temporally between developed Oldowan and Lower Acheulean assemblages in E Africa, as described by Mary Leakey.

*See also* Acheulean culture

**Chi-square Test.** A statistical test to determine whether empirically measured fre-

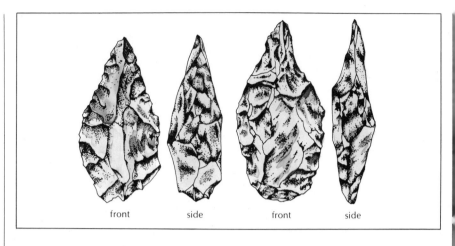

front      side      front      side

AN ABBEVILLIAN (CHELLEAN) HAND AX

*Two early hand axes from Olduvai Gorge, Bed II, front and side views (three-quarters actual size). This tool complex is associated with the remains of* H. erectus, *dating back to 600,000 BP. It is the first stage of the hand-ax tradition.*

quencies (of occurrences) differ significantly (not by chance) from those to be expected from theoretical assumptions.

*See also* Statistical methods

**Chief.** *See* Chiefdom; Headman; Leadership.

**Chiefdom.** Currently this term is used to refer to a society at a level of social integration above that of tribal society in Service's (1971) terminology. While the term *chief* can refer to any person recognized as in some way preeminent in a social group, chiefdom should refer specifically to a social organization which is characterized by a redistributive economic system. This implies a level of complexity which includes an often hereditary, permanent central agency for the coordination of specialization and redistribution—the chieftainship. Service notes that in a chiefdom a chief has the ability to organize and deploy public labor and can also subsidize superior specialists, often at the redistribution center. Such specialists need not be useful in the economic sense, but may serve only to provide the chief with nonessential goods and services. Thus inequality in consumption is coupled with so-

cial inequality. Since, in a chiefdom, there is a single preeminent office, it generally follows that this social inequality stems from the creation of a nobility—in the first instance, members of the chief's immediate family and extending eventually to more distant kinsfolk. Polynesia, the NW Coast of North America, and Scotland provide the best examples of successful chiefdoms.

*See also* Band; Headman; Social organization; Tribe

Consult: Mair, Lucy, *Primitive Government* (London: Penguin, 1962); Service, Elman R., *Primitive Social Organization* (New York: Random House, 1971).

—*Richard L. Stone, California State University, Los Angeles*

**Childe, Vere Gordon** (1892–1957). This anthropologist figures centrally in anthropological thought from about 1930 to 1955, especially in the United States. Unlike most British anthropologists, he combined a fundamentally social science outlook with a chiefly Middle Eastern and European archaeological specialization. His deeply Marxian social science stressed the relationships among means of production, social orders, and ideology, all closely linked to those material remains sustaining archaeological work. His theoretical cogency in synthesizing masses of data in several classics (*Man Makes Himself*, 1936; *What Happened in History*, 1942) has influenced generations of anthropologists interested in evolutionary holistic studies of complex societies and has deeply affected their understanding of ecology.

## Chimpanzees, Social Organization and Behavior of.

Chimpanzee social organization involves a loose grouping of individuals in one locale who interact frequently but may (more rarely) interact with individuals from neighboring locales. Individuals do not always move about together in the manner of a baboon troop. Groups aggregate and disperse in complex ways under a variety of circumstances. One animal may move from group to group or travel alone on any given day. The major groupings include (1) all-male groups, (2) sexual groups composed of males and receptive females, (3) nursery groups of mothers and young, and (4) mixed groups of all ages and both sexes. The only association which is stable over time is the mother-offspring unit. Groups coalesce at highly productive food sources (e.g., ripening fruit trees) and disperse when the food is exhausted. Chimpanzee social organization is ideally suited to exploit food supplies which are dispersed irregularly in space and time. Chimpanzees inhabiting more open terrain (savanna-woodland) tend to coalesce into more readily discernible traveling groups which may migrate as a unit under some conditions.

Among noteworthy features of chimpanzee behavior are the complex communicative repertoire (including begging and reassurance gestures), the use of a variety of tools, small game hunting, and patterned food sharing of game.

*See also* Baboon social organization; Primates, behavior of

Consult: Izawa, K., "Unit Groups of Chimpanzees and Their Nomadism in the Savanna

*The study of chimpanzee social organization and behavior is important because analyses of blood sera have revealed chimpanzees to be our closest living relatives.*

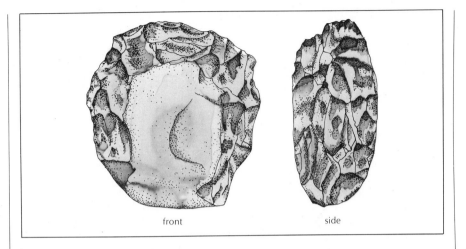

TOOLS OF THE ASIAN CHOPPER TRADITION

*A crude chopping tool from Choukoutien, China, front and side views (one-half actual size).*

Woodland," *Primates* 11:1–46, 1970; Van Lawick-Goodall, J., "The Behavior of Free-living Chimpanzees in the Gombé Stream Reserve," *Animal Behaviour Monographs* 1(3):161–311, 1968.
—*Leanne T. Nash, Arizona State University*

## Chomsky, Noam (b. 1928).

American linguist (currently professor of linguistics at MIT), Chomsky is unquestionably the most influential of all modern linguists. His theories have had considerable impact on both anthropology and psychology.

Chomsky has strongly criticized the behaviorist account of language acquisition, which regards language as being learned through a largely passive conditioning process. Chomsky contends instead that humans have a built-in capacity to acquire language, an innate ability to abstract the basic rules of grammar from the welter of sounds they hear in the early years of childhood. These implicit rules, Chomsky argues, enable us to understand and generate an infinite number of novel sentences—an ability that traditional accounts of language acquisition are hard pressed to explain.

*See also* Behaviorist school of psychology; Linguistics; Transformational linguistics

## Chopper Tools.

These unifacial core tools, sometimes called pebble tools, are found unambiguously associated with *Australopithecus habilis* in Olduvai sequence. They are rounded pebbles with a cutting edge made by knocking off only a few flakes to make a very crude and sinuous surface. The term also refers to generalized chopping tools produced by *Homo erectus* in E and SE Asia as far west as N India.

*See also* Pebble tools

## Choukoutien cave (Dragon Bone Hill).

This series of archaeological, fossil hominid sites is located 27 miles SW of Peking in NE China. The name itself refers to a town adjacent to the limestone hill, which was extensively eroded during the Basal Pleistocene, creating fifteen major fissures subsequently filled with cave sediments, bones, and other external deposits. The major period of deposition was some 400,000 to 500,000 years BP; more than 100,000 quartzite artifacts document an eponymous flake industry (Choukoutienian, of the Chopper/Chopping Tool group). Rich faunal and macrofloral remains document a hunting/gathering adaptation in light to moderately heavy mixed deciduous/coniferous woodland characterized by a cool to seasonally cold, damp paleoclimate. Abundant hominid skeletal material (now lost) originally assigned to *Sinanthropus pekinensis* (Peking man) is now universally regarded as *Homo erectus*. *Homo sapiens sapiens* remains are found in later deposits in association with Upper Paleolithic industry. The lower series exhibits the

*Excavation of Choukoutien Cave.*

earliest recorded use of fire, as well as early evidence for cannibalism.

    *See also* Fire, use by *Homo erectus; Homo erectus*

**Chromosomes.** Each cell contains several chemical chains of genes called chromosomes. Humans have forty-six, other species more or fewer. The number of chromosomes characteristic of a species is not related to the size or complexity of the organism. These genetic chains limit the independent, free assortment of genes, hence reducing variation and providing for stable combinations of genes in the reproductive process. Chromosomal mutation, or the crossing over of genes, is one process which leads to new genetic combinations.

    *See also* Genetics

**Chronology in Archaeology.** *See* Time in archaeology.

**Cicatrization.** *See* Deformation and mutilation.

**Circumcision.** This term refers to the removal of the foreskin of a male or the genital labia of a female. It is not to be confused with other forms of genital mutilation such as subincision and supercision (both involve splitting the penis—the former along the bottom, the latter along the top).

    A number of theses regarding the meaning of male initiation accompanied by genital mutilation have been advanced. John Whiting has offered a psychoanalytic explanation, hypothesizing that it is related to cross-sex identity problems. Others, such as Frank Young, have advanced sociological explanations stressing the need for male solidarity in social systems characterized by polygynous family organization.

    *See also* Ceremony; Rites of passage; Ritual; Subincision

    Consult: Burton, Roger V., and Whiting, John W. M., "The Absent Father and Cross-sex Identity," *Merrill-Palmer Quarterly of Behavior and Development* 7:85–95, 1961; Young, Frank, "The Function of Male Initiation Ceremonies: A Cross-cultural Test of an Alternative Hypothesis," *American Journal of Sociology* 67, 1962.

**Cire-Perdue.** *See* Lost wax technique.

**Cities, Development of.** The term *city* commonly means a site of relatively dense population of considerable size. Cities are a concurrent, parallel aspect of the development of civilization. As such they have much the same attributable complex as civilizations: a densely settled community; a relatively large, concentrated, essentially permanent population; a markedly stratified social structure; a generally differentiated occupational hierarchy; and a political structure similar to, or the same as, the state of which they are part (if, indeed, the city is not the entire thing, as a city-state).

    Cities develop out of earlier settlement patterns typical to the region in which they occur. They tend to grow out of the patterns set by earlier villages or temple centers, and their initial form is usually dictated by these antecedent forms of culturally organized space. At Catal Hüyük in Anatolia, covering a time span from about 6500 to 5700 BC, there are twelve successive building levels representing twelve different cities—each planned as an orderly settlement, each reflecting the previous settlement pattern. This planning is further reflected in the size of bricks; standard plan of houses and shrines; heights of interior panels and doorways; sizes of hearths and ovens; and to a great extent in the size of rooms. This cultural conservatism can be clearly illustrated in later times as well. In Sumer, at the site of Khafajah in the Diyala Valley, there is a series of five consecutively built temples which show a remarkable continuity in architectural style representing a period of time conservatively estimated as at least 500 years.

    The problem of defining whether a city exists at any point in time is one of distin-

*Tenochtitlán, the Aztec name for what is now Mexico City. This scale model is on exhibit at the entrance of the National Museum of Anthropology in Mexico City.*

guishing between such things as cities versus towns and cities versus temple centers. This does not necessarily mean, of course, that all early cities were first villages or temple centers. Cities can be started from scratch. Or the sequence of development through time may be village to city to temple center, or temple center to village to city. The development of trade and trade routes; the exchange of crafts, raw materials, and food (which antedate the growth of civilizations and cities); a minimal population size; an agricultural base sufficient to support this population and its activities; an expansion in the minimum population and its territorial holdings—all are factors which give rise to cities. While one might expect to find cities developing at a point where several trade routes converge (which does in fact occur), trade alone cannot be used as a single-factor explanation. In some cases cities develop as administrative and political centers rather than as reflections of local needs (such as the exchange of goods for raw materials not locally available). Usually it is a combination of these factors that creates cities. Although cities and civilizations develop at much the same time (and place), it would be simplistic to assume that either is the cause of the other's existence. Cities and civilizations seem to be reflections of the same basic needs: how to organize large numbers of people into units which will function efficiently toward the mutual goals of the culture. Thus their growth appears to be primarily a social process. This organization is, for the most part, rather haphazard—an outgrowth of the earlier successful coping mechanisms of the culture.

See also Civilization
Consult: Adams, Robert McC., *The Evolution of Urban Society* (Chicago: Aldine, 1966).
—George R. Mead, Eastern Oregon College

## Civilization.

As a concept, civilization is generally contrasted to the concepts of primitive and folk. Several criteria are used to identify the occurrence of a civilization: the presence of a high level of food production, the development of managerial skills to handle developing institutions (economic, military, social), control of the means of production by ruling classes (regal, theological), professional merchant classes working within a highly developed exchange network radiating outward from the major urban centers, and full-time specialists freed from manual toil (who often are responsible for the development of arithmetic, geometry, astronomy, writing, numerical notation, standards of time, space, and weight). Civilization is also marked by the development of institutions which take over the functions previously handled by extended kinship ties—for example, redistribution of foodstuffs in times of need. The need for organization tends to codify and regularize the value system of the culture involved. At the same time there appears to be an expansion in the aesthetic awareness with a concurrent appearance of tightly organized art styles which are recognizably different from region to region.

See also Agriculture, origins of; Civilization, origins of; Social stratification
—George R. Mead, Eastern Oregon College

## Civilization, Origins of.

Civilization has initially, and more or less independently, appeared in at least six different regions of the world: the Mesopotamian/Near East region (ca. 8000–4000 BC), Egypt (ca. 5000–3000 BC), India/Indus valley (ca. 2600–2400 BC), Northern China (ca. 3000–2000 BC), Mesoamerica (ca. 3000–500 BC), and the Peruvian region (ca. 2500–500 BC).

The development of civilization is a break with the past. This break seems to have two major components: an increase in population density; and changes in subsistence, based on the availability of domestic plants and animals. In the Near East the early villages were based on agriculture, on animal husbandry, or on a combination of both. These beginnings for the most part did not take place where the major urban centers eventually developed, but seem to have been in regions suitable to the agriculture or animal husbandry practiced. It was only later that major centers developed in what appears to be less suitable land—that is, less suitable for the earlier cultural pursuits but more suitable for the large populations that clustered together in cities. These sites were also more suitable for procuring and distributing the resources needed for a large population; for the psychological and physical security a city can offer; for the control of farming and irrigation; and for the centralization of political and theological controls.

By the time large cities appeared, the agricultural base had already been firmly

*This mural depicts the importance of work and cooperation in early Egyptian life.*

established, but the origins of this base are still not all that clear. Although the beginnings in some areas may have been either intensive exploitation of dense stands of food plants, animal husbandry, or a mix of plant and animal domestication, the true basis of the large populations, and hence civilization, was the expansion of agriculture, which became the base of each of the civilizations. Agriculture was practiced in different modes in each of the areas, but in all cases the agricultural product shared a basic attribute: the commodity had to be capable of being produced in large quantities by a small number of individuals (small in comparison to the total population) and be easily stored for lengthy periods of time. It is the combination of large quantities and long storage that is the secret of success. It has been estimated that a family of experienced wheat-gatherers (in the Near East) could, over a three-week period, gather more grain than they could possibly consume in a year. Thus in about 5 percent of their total annual available time they will have guaranteed the basic commodity for their table with some left over. One could arbitrarily double or triple this time commitment and still find large quantities of time left over for activities other than subsistence. The suggestion is, of course, that time not spent in food acquisition is time that can be devoted to finding new solutions to old problems. These new solutions, especially as a reaction to an increasing population, lead to civilization.

Thus the factor of long storage frees people to engage in activities other than food production. A stable food base that can support more people than produce it, coupled with a local increase in population density, leads to organizational stresses which in turn stimulate the development of more effective systems of social control. A local increase in population density is a direct outgrowth of agriculture in terms of the labor required to operate it, store it, redistribute it, and keep track of these activities. This in turn leads to the development of radically new skills in arts, crafts, and bureaucratic organization (necessary to manage large numbers of products and people).

*See also* Agriculture, origins of; Cities, development of; Civilization
Consult: Sabloff, Jeremy A., and Lamberg-Karlovsky, C. C., *The Rise and Fall of Civilizations* (Menlo Park, Calif.: Cummings, 1974); Sanders, William T., and Price, Barbara J.,

*Mesoamerica: The Evolution of a Civilization* (New York: Random House, 1968); Ucko, Peter J., and Dimbleby, G. W., *The Domestication and Exploitation of Plants and Animals* (Chicago: Aldine, 1969).
—*George R. Mead, Eastern Oregon College*

**Clactonian Culture.** This Lower Paleolithic assemblage was defined by Breuil and Warren; the type site is Clacton-on-Sea (Essex). It is poorly dated (Late Mindel–Early Riss) and underlies the Middle Acheulean at Swanscombe (ca. 370,000 to 400,000 BP). Found in SE England and in S and SW France, it is contemporaneous with and interstratified with the Middle Acheulean but lacks bifaces. Retouched, utilized flakes predominate, with choppers made on flint nodules.

**Clan.** A clan is a kinship group whose members trace their descent from a common ancestor. The term is derived from the Gaelic word *clann* and originally referred to the cognatic household descent groups of Scotland. Clan members have collective rights and responsibilities, such as that of mutual support in times of feud or interclan disputes.

The modern use of the term owes much to Lewis Morgan's distinction between clan systems in which descent is traced through females only (matriclan) and those in which it is traced through males (patriclan). Morgan later retermed the patriclan the *gens*, reserving the term *clan* for the matriclan. Many contemporary anthropologists thus use the word to denote unilineal descent groups whose members are recruited through the female line only. Other anthropologists, however, use the term more loosely, as in "totemic clan," to refer to a kin group in which some species of animal or plant is traditionally the symbol of the group or is even ritually considered to be its mythical ancestor.

*See also* Descent; Descent group; Kinship; Lineage; Social structure
Consult: Fox, R., *Kinship and Marriage* (Baltimore: Penguin, 1967); Homans, G. C., *The Human Group* (New York: Harcourt Brace Jovanovich, 1950); Service, Elman R., *Primitive Social Organization: An Evolutionary Perspective* (New York: Random House, 1962).
—*Bruno Pajaczkowski, Cambridge University*

**Clark, John Desmond** (b. 1916). Archaeologist known for his theoretical interests in fossil hominids and human ecology and for his extensive field research on the prehistory of Africa.

**Clark, John Grahame Douglas** (b. 1907). Disney Professor of Archaeology at Cambridge University, Clark is best known for his contributions to the study of the relationships of environment to technology in *Archaeology and Society* (1939) and *Prehistoric Europe: The Economic Basis* (1952).

**Clark, Sir Wilfred Edward Le Gros** (b. 1895). British comparative anatomist and paleontologist noted for his interpretive syntheses of the evolutionary history of the primates, particularly the emergence and development of the hominids (modern humans and their immediate fossil ancestors and relatives). His works include *The Fossil Evidence for Human Evolution* (1964), *Man-Apes or Ape-Men?* (1967), *History of the Primates* (1969), and *The Antecedents of Man* (1971).

**Class.** This term may be defined as a stratum in a hierarchically organized social system. Membership in a class is usually defined by economic criteria, and an individual's class position usually (though not always) correlates closely with his or her *power* and *status* in the society.

Class systems are often distinguished from the *estate* system (such as the feudal stratification of Europe in the Middle Ages) and from the *caste* system (such as that practiced in India for thousands of years). A class system differs from these forms of stratification in that it offers more opportunity for individual mobility and assigns social positions on the grounds of achieved as well as ascriptive characteristics.

Identifiable social classes are virtually unknown in small-scale societies. Classes tend to emerge only in societies that are sufficiently developed technologically to produce a surplus, because this surplus makes possible the accumulation of private wealth. Class divisions are in general most noticeable in advanced agricultural and early industrial societies.

*See also* Caste; Economic systems; Marx, Karl; Mobility, social; Power; Social stratification;

Status; Surplus
—Ian Robertson, Cambridge University

**Classical Archaeology.** This traditional field of archaeology concerns itself with the reconstruction of the way of life in ancient, literate civilizations such as Greece and Rome. In contrast to prehistoric archaeology, classical archaeology covers only the most recent 5,000 years.
*See also* Archaeology; Prehistoric archaeology

**Classical Conditioning.** *See* Behaviorist school of psychology; Conditioning.

**Classification.** *See* Taxonomy.

**Classificatory Kinship Term.** This kin label refers to a category of individuals (rather than to individuals) composed of both lineal and collateral relatives who stand in one specific biological, or putatively biological, relationship to ego. Examples: father and father's brother are called by the same term; siblings and parallel cousins are called by the same term. In American kinship terminology a cousin is classificatory because it includes all the individuals in the category "parents' siblings' children" rather than just one biological relationship such as "mother's brother's child."

Separate labels for each biological link are *descriptive* kinship terms, which distinguish lineal and collateral relatives. Examples: father and father's brother are called by different terms; siblings and cousins (parents' siblings' children, i.e., collaterals) are called by different terms. The distinction between classificatory and descriptive kinship terms is increasingly ignored, since all kinship terms appear to have both descriptive and classificatory elements.
*See also* Kinship; Kinship terminologies

**Clay.** *See* Pottery and ceramics.

**Clifton, James A.** (b. 1927). Trained in cultural anthropology at the University of Oregon, his main work is in applied anthropology and contemporary American Indians. He is former director of the ACTION program and professor of humanism and cul-

tural change at the University of Wisconsin (Green Bay).

**Climate.** *See* Cultural ecology.

**Cline.** This term refers to a gradual series of variations in some characteristic of a population, language, or culture. Expressed geographically, clines are shown as lines on a map which indicate the limits of distribution of some value of the characteristic. Clines are used primarily in physical anthropology and linguistics for population genetics and dialect geography problems.
*See also* Gene flow; Population genetics

**Cliques.** In social science language, clique refers to a self-selective, relatively covert, informal group of persons. The clique's stated or, mostly, unstated purpose (and hence its informality and covertness) is to control some set of resources and protect them against interested outsiders. What is kept covert is the actual relationships among the clique's members as well as their resources. Despite some tendency to confuse cliques with elites, cliques can occur in any stratum of society and in any location within a stratum—not necessarily one of power. Formally, anthropologists have dealt little with cliques or their relationships with strata, elites, and networks.
*See also* Elites; Network, social; Network study

**Clitorectomy.** This term refers to the surgical removal of the external portion of the clitoris—the clitoral glans, clitoral hood, and even a section of the upper surface of the clitoral shaft—usually as part of female initiation rites. Reported from most areas of the world except Native North America, this ritual operation is performed by male religious specialists while women relatives and friends act as sympathetic supporters. In Abyssinia girls as young as six have been subjected to this mutilation, and only women from families or castes that provide prostitutes to the society are exempt. Although this unusually aggressive act is often justified as keeping the women from being too sexy, anthropologists are in disagreement as to function and causality. Correlational factors seem to be economic and psychological. Female initiation rites are found most com-

monly in societies in which women provide the majority of foodstuffs. In addition, such painful rites correlate with structurally induced conditions of sex identity conflict.
*See also* Deformation and mutilation; Rites of passage; Sex roles

**Clothing.** This term has no exact social science meaning and is used interchangeably with the equally imprecise *dress*. Though the meaning of the term seems self-evident, ethnographic data raise interesting problems for the Western social scientist who regards clothing as natural and usually attributes its use, in his own folk theory, to varying climatic rigors. Yet a comparative perspective makes clear that dress, including clothing, is often socioculturally conventional rather than practical. Thus men wearing penis sheathes, women wearing G-strings without hiding their genitals, and (in Western "naturist" camps) well-combed nudists are all appropriately clothed.

Obviously, inclement weather requires some means of maintaining body temperature, but solutions are many and may vary with body hairiness, acclimatization, and basal metabolism (high among the Ona and Yaghan, who wore little in freezing weather). Clearly, being shod in harsh terrain or vegetation helps but, as many unshod peo-

*Clothing is frequently used to communicate social position. These Nuba women are the wives of a chief.*

*Clothing obviously serves more than utilitarian purposes. Culturally prescribed aesthetic notions are of great importance in determining how people dress themselves.*

ples indicate, it is not necessary. Clothing, then, can be regarded as a varyingly weighted interaction among need, convenience, and sociocultural markings of inclusion in the human (as against the animal) world, social roles, status, and rank. Clothing may also signify availability or unavailability (e.g., prostitutes, virgin marriageables), which signals for desired forms of response.

—Anthony Leeds, Boston University

**Clovis Culture.** This mammoth-hunting culture of North America (9500–9000 BC) is characterized by percussion-flaked, fluted points. It is best known from killing and butchering sites in the Southwest.

**Clubs.** See Weapons.

**Coconut.** One of the most useful plants to humans, the coconut palm (*Cocos nucifera*)

is widely distributed throughout the tropics. Native to SE Asia, the coconut was established in the Americas in pre-Columbian times. Whether its introduction there was by human or natural agencies is not yet satisfactorily resolved. Practically all parts of the plant are used—the leaves for thatching, the wood for construction, the flower cluster for a sweet juice, and the growing shoot or heart as a vegetable. Its fruit, however, is of greatest importance. The oily meat (called *copra* when dried) is an excellent food; the fibrous husk (*coir*) is used to make ropes and mats; the hard shell is made into eating and drinking utensils; and the water is drunk as a refreshing beverage.

*See also* Foods and food crops

**Codere, Helen Frances** (b. 1917). Canadian-born cultural anthropologist interested in ethnohistory, primitive art, and economic anthropology. She is best known for her analysis of the NW Coast Indian potlatch.

**Codex.** This written text is found throughout pre-Columbian Mesoamerica. The most important societies producing codices were the Aztec and Mixtec, who used picture writing, and the Maya, who used a more complex logographic system of writing. Various writing surfaces were used, including deerskin, fiber paper, and cotton cloth. The codex was generally made up of a number of pages attached together, side by side, and folded according to style. In pre-Columbian times there were numerous libraries of codices. However, many of these codices were destroyed during the Spanish conquest and only about fifty remain today. The codices dealt primarily with history, astronomy, and astrology.

*See also* Writing

**Coding Materials.** See Fieldwork methods.

**Coe, Michael Douglas** (b. 1929). Specialist on Mesoamerican prehistory, especially Mexico, Guatemala, and Costa Rica. He has written syntheses on Mexican and Mayan prehistory, as well as several books on the Olmec.

*See also* Maya; Olmec culture

**Coe, William R., II** (b. 1926). Archaeologist known for his research on the Classic Period Maya, especially at the Mayan center of Tikal, Guatemala, where he served as project director.

**Cognatic Descent.** See Ambilineal descent.

**Cognition.** The term *cognition* is a broad one that encompasses all the various ways of knowing. It includes, in general usage, perception, judgment, reasoning, remembering, thinking, and imagining.

Much current work in anthropology distinguishes between cognition and other modes of perception, usually considered to be more emotional. Thus cognitive anthropological research emphasizes an intellectual approach to the interpretation of culture, which is usually defined in terms of the categories each society uses to organize its universe and to convey messages among those who share the culture (or enough of it to interact meaningfully with one another). In a cognitive approach to kinship, for example, the focus is on the intellectual meanings that kinship relations have to the informant, rather than on their emotional meaning.

This approach has greatly facilitated our understanding of the way in which prediction within a cultural system takes place. If social relations are indeed based on predictability, then it makes sense to seek a communication model of a cultural system, one that enables investigators to predict behavior of actors within the system.

*See also* Cognitive categories; Cognitive modes; Componential analysis; Ethnoscience; Perception; Thought processes
—Frank A. Salamone, St. John's University

**Cognitive Anthropology.** See New Ethnography, the.

**Cognitive Categories.** This term refers to categories through which groups structure their perception of reality. We cannot assume that each sociocultural group divides the world in the same way. While two groups may have a category labeled kinship, the contents of that category in each group may well be different. The case is even clearer in the domain of color categories, where there is enormous cross-cultural variation and even great variation in the knowledge of categories among members of one culture. The ethnoscientist who wishes to uncover indigenous cognitive categories must constantly be aware of his or her own biases. Ethnoscientists are heavily influenced by models drawn from linguistics. The ultimate aim of eliciting indigenous categories is to facilitate true comparison.

*See also* Cognition; Cognitive modes; Componential analysis; Ethnoscience; Formal semantic analysis

—Frank A. Salamone, St. John's University

## Cognitive Development, Stages of. *See* Piaget, Jean.

## Cognitive Emotional Development. *See* Psychosexual stages of development; Stages of moral development.

## Cognitive Modes. This term refers to the ways in which people know, organize, and process the information they receive. There are a number of ways in which information can be received by humans; these ways include verbal and nonverbal forms. Linguists and psycholinguists, concentrating on speech as a stimulus resulting in cognition, have had a profound influence on anthropology. Recently, however, attention has begun to focus on other modes of communicative cultural information.

Kinesics and proxemics, for example, investigate the use of body motion and space to convey information. Significant advances have been made in these areas, including the beginning of some cross-cultural studies.

Since culture is regarded as a repository of human cognitions, it is only appropriate that anthropologists study the manner in which cognition occurs—hence the renewed interest not only in linguistics, proxemics, and kinesics but also in theories of communication and information processing. Ethnomusicology, ethnopsychology, folklore, and mythology are also being reexamined in this light.

The importance of the human ability to create symbols has received increasing attention, as has the ability to code them, map them, and convert them into cultural messages.

*See also* Cognition; Cognitive categories; Componential analysis; Ethnoscience
Consult: Goodenough, Ward H., "Componential Analysis and the Study of Meaning," *Language* 32:195–216, 1956; Hall, Edward T., *The Silent Language* (Garden City, N.Y.: Doubleday, 1959).

—Frank A. Salamone, St. John's University

## Cohen, Yehudi (b. 1928). Cohen has contributed to the ecological and evolutionary understanding of culture. In his view, culture is the human species' primary means of adaptation. He has incorporated biological and social structural insights into his framework of analysis.

*See also* Culture

## Cohesion, Social. *See* Social integration.

## Colby, Benjamin N. (b. 1931). Social anthropologist concerned with cognitive anthropology, religion, symbolic systems, and culture change, with special interest in ethnic relations in highland Guatemala and Chiapas, Mexico.

## Collaterality. A kin relationship involving at least one sibling link. A man is related by collaterality to his mother's brother's daughter. Two persons related by collaterality are collaterals.

*See also* Kinship

## Collateral Relatives. *See* Collaterality.

## Collecting. *See* Economics and subsistence.

## Collecting Narratives. This is the primary task of folklore studies. The essential ingredient of this task is to record folklore materials as they occur in context. Modern folklore scholars do not accept as sufficient the recording of bare narratives without full description of context and setting of the performance. The style and manner of the narrator, as well as the responses of the audience, are considered to be as important as the tale or myth proper. Contemporary standards require not only recording of narratives (preferably mechanical plus written observations), followed by transcription and translation, but also detailed information on the storyteller, his or her audience, the setting, the functions of the narration, the interactions between narrator and audience, and other relevant materials.

*See also* Ethnography; Fieldwork, ethnographic; Folklore

## Collective Representation. Ideas about physical and biological aspects of the world are called, by Durkheim, individual representations; ideas about social aspects of the world are called collective representations.

*See also* Durkheim, Emile

## Collective Unconscious. This concept, developed by Carl Jung, proposes that in addition to the personal unconscious, hypothesized by Freudian theory, each individual also has a collective unconscious or racial unconscious. The collective unconscious contains ideas, myths, and symbols common to all humanity.

Anthropologists have recognized the existence of unconscious linguistic elements (Boas), unconscious laws of fashion (Kroeber), and unconscious patterning of social behavior (Sapir), but they have either ignored or explicitly rejected James's, Hegel's, and Jung's notion of collective unconscious.

The anthropologist Geza Roheim has asserted that people unconsciously learn collective habits of behavior. Lévi-Strauss proposes a very special notion of collective unconscious: people do not share universal ideas or psychic impulses or collective archetypes (Jung), but fundamental laws or mechanisms through which their mind organizes or imposes structures on the physical and social environment. This, according to Lévi-Strauss, constitutes the specifically human function of symbolizing.

*See also* Archetype; Jung, Carl Gustav
Consult: Jung, C. G., *Analytical Psychology: Its Theory and Practice* (New York: Random House, 1970).

## Colonialism. This term refers to the policy of a nation seeking to acquire, extend, or retain its political authority or its social, economic, and cultural dominance over other peoples or territories.

*British colonial Basil Duke, who designed all of the buildings in Yei, Sudan, speaks with his successors to the council leadership. The French and the British took very different approaches to colonial rule: the former utilized "direct rule," under which all political offices were filled by French people; the British used "indirect rule," under which they appointed members of native populations to enact their policies. Although on the surface the British system appears to be less oppressive, this is inaccurate: the local forms of social and political organization, usually based on kinship networks, became distorted and caused a great deal of confusion and bitterness on both sides. Thus the British were often very disillusioned at the "dishonesty" of their native appointees who insisted on favoring their relatives; and the native groups resented the attaching of formal, political power to what had previously been merely positions of social prestige, and felt betrayed when their politically powerful relatives, under great pressure from the British, tried to resist granting them favors.*

European colonialism began in the 15th century and was the mechanism by which Western civilization was spread to Asia, Africa, and the Americas. Since 1945 more than sixty former colonies have achieved independence—many through formal political processes, and some (Algeria, Vietnam, Angola) through long and bitter wars of independence.

As European empires expanded in the Third World, the subjugated peoples of the various empires were studied and described by missionaries, soldiers, and the colonizers who exploited them economically. The information thus obtained eventually found its way to the libraries of armchair social philosophers, who sought to explain the nature of human society by comparing their European civilization with what they were told about "primitive" groups. The discipline of anthropology was born during the height of the colonial era, and many of its original concepts were biased by an ethnocentric assumption of the natural superiority of Western civilization over all other cultures.

*See also* Colonization; Colonization, internal; Imperialism; Neocolonialism; Racism

Consult: Emerson, Rupert, *From Empire to Nation: The Rise to Self-Assertion of Asian and African Peoples* (Cambridge: Harvard University Press, 1960); Fanon, Frantz, *The Wretched of the Earth* (New York: Grove Press, 1965); Harris, Marvin, *The Rise of Anthropological Theory* (New York: Crowell, 1968); Jalee, Pierre, *The Pillage of the Third World* (New York: Monthly Review Press, 1968); Nyerere, Julius K., *Ujamaa: Essays on Socialism* (Dar es Salaam: Oxford University Press, 1968).

—Phillip Whitten, Harvard University

**Colonization.** Colonization is a process whereby (1) an empty territory is settled by an external polity which sends in settlers as organized groups; (2) such a territory is settled by individuals and small groups and later incorporated into another polity; (3) an already settled area, especially a polity, is incorporated, usually by conquest, into the administrative structure of another polity which is said to own it; or (4) a resettlement of part of the population of a polity to a different area of its territory is effected.

Generally, the colony stands in an exploited relationship to the colonizer, which extracts wealth, labor, or new materials from it to finance its own growth and consumption. Typically, colonization is a means to acquire land, labor, or resources for the benefit of the colonizer.

*See also* Colonization, internal

**Colonization, Internal.** Internal colonization describes a situation in which some part-population—a class, estate, caste, or outcaste—stands to the polity much as an external colony, though both actually occupy the same territory. That is, it is exploited to provide wealth, labor, and raw materials for the rest of the population which controls the polity. American blacks are often said to exemplify internal colonization. That the two populations, unlike colonies, compete for *identical* territory has especially interesting consequences for social movements and conflict.

*See also* Colonization

**Color Blindness.** In all human populations, a small proportion of individuals have color vision defects, ranging from red-green color blindness (which is controlled by genes at two loci on the X chromosome) to total color blindness (most of which is not sex-linked). Because they are X-linked, red-green defects are most prevalent in males, since the male Y-chromosome is not homologous with the X-chromosome.

The frequency of color blindness appears to have increased with the shift in subsistence modes from gathering to agriculture, perhaps as a result of decreased selective pressure for color vision.

*See also* Color vision; Genetics; Sex-linked traits

**Color Vision.** Color vision results from the ability to distinguish mixtures of red, blue, and green; it is particularly characteristic of the higher primates. Together with stereoscopic vision, color vision reflects the shift from a heavy dependence on smell to visual acuity, perhaps related to a diurnal arboreal adaptation and associated with enlargement of the visual areas of the brain.

Color is important in the coats of some primates and for social signaling. In early hominids, color vision may have been a preadaptation for the development of hunting.

*See also* Color blindness; Primates, evolutionary features of; Stereoscopic vision

**Colson, Elizabeth** (b. 1917). Prominent American anthropologist with extensive contributions to African studies in the fields of law and social control, religion, ethnicity, and social change. Her most recent work has been on the consequences of forced resettlement, an African case study.

**Comas, Juan** (b. 1900). Mexican anthropologist who has made important contributions to physical anthropology, applied social anthropology in Mexico, and race relations in Latin America.

**Communes.** In contemporary civilizations, communes are social groups that attempt to bring to realization a social system expressive of a moral order shared by its members. They are voluntarily joined by individuals sharing similar value commitments. Such value commitments differ in kind or intensity from those characteristic of the larger society into which commune members were born and from which they are recruited. Communes are generally small communities: they rarely exceed 1,000 members and often number less than 100. Such small communities generally seek to be self-supporting in order to maximize their independence from the surrounding larger society. However, communes may be as small as seven or eight people, in which case they often approximate an extended family. Irrespective of size, most communes are characterized by mutual ownership and use of resources.

According to Rosabeth Moss Kanter, the history of communes in the United States can be divided into three distinct periods, each characterized by a predominant type of value commitment. The first period, beginning before national independence and lasting until 1845, was characterized by religious and spiritual values. The second, from about 1820 until 1930, was characterized by an emphasis on political and economic utopianism. The third, beginning after World War II and becoming pronounced in the 1960s with the counterculture movement, is characterized by an emphasis on the personal growth of the individual through intimate interpersonal relationships. Contemporary communes attempt to cultivate social relationships which express what Victor Turner has termed *communitas*—undifferentiated, equalitarian, direct, personal relationships.

*See also* Community; Kibbutz

Consult: Kanter, R. M., *Commitment and Community* (Cambridge: Harvard University Press, 1972); Turner, V., *Dramas, Fields, and Metaphors* (Ithaca: Cornell University Press, 1974).
—Stan Wilk, Lycoming College

**Communication.** Virtually all the animal kingdom communicates—that is, transfers messages from a sender to a receiver who may also be a sender. There appears to be an evolutionary trend among animals for increasing frequency of, dependency on, amount of information in, and flexibility of communication. Its importance in one-

*The importance of communication to human groups is attested to by the many ingenious methods they have devised to accomplish it. The inhabitants of St. Kilda, one of the most remote of the New Hebrides Islands which lie off the northwest coast of Scotland, communicated with their neighboring islands by placing messages into a container which was in turn put into a sheep's bladder and attached to a piece of wood. This was then tossed into the sea with the hope that it would wash up on the shore of one of the nearby islands; many, however, were lost.*

celled animals like amoebas is negligible, but it is altogether crucial in *Homo sapiens*, who evolved quite recently. In virtually all sexually reproducing animal species, some form of communication must obviously take place between the sexes, at least for mating.

Within this broad framework, means of animal communication vary drastically: they include chemical (in some insects), taste, touch, visual, olfactory, auditory, and even electrical signals. Generally, all these signals convey messages regarding the sender's location (and, in the case of bats, the receiver's location also), its state of being (sexual preparedness, hunger, fear, playfulness), its relation to territory, and the location of resources (the bees' dance or ants' tactile behavior).

All these means involve irritability of living cells (even the lowly amoeba reacts to touch by withdrawing—a communicatory response). However, this irritability takes different forms in different phyla and their subdivisions. For example, chemical communication seems to be absent or of little importance among primates, and even the olfactory is of reduced significance, espe-

cially among humans. Generally, species are not restricted to a single means but combine several, among which evolutionary selective pressures tend to favor one or more over others. In general, too, it appears that natural selection has, in the long run, favored means which can carry numerous and complex messages. Certainly this is true of physiologically complex animals—perhaps because of their increasingly complicated ecological relationships (such as, in relatively recent evolutionary history, the problem of maintaining body heat among birds and mammals).

Of foremost interest here is communication among the primates, especially *Homo sapiens,* although interesting perspectives arise from a comparative viewpoint—particularly from the social insects and the social mammalian species (whales, porpoises, beavers, wolves) with developed communication systems supporting the social organization and behavior. The higher primates—monkeys, apes, and *Homo sapiens*—are almost always found in various kinds of social groups (though the social structure may change under varying ecological and other conditions). Such sociability is made possible and supported by communication. All the higher primates have, in comparative perspective, a basic set of communicational means which are quite similar: visual signaling, aural-oral message transfers, touch, and smell. (Taste may be disregarded.) Even specific modes of communication are similar. Visual messages are conveyed by movements of eyes, eyebrows, eyelids, mouth, head, hands, and legs; by body postures (e.g., the gorilla's aggressive posture); and by body movements (e.g., the dog's rolling on its back in submission). Aural-oral messages are transmitted by various noises made by the vocal apparatus and also by thumpings (on chest, ground, or tables) or ranting (tearing through the forest or throwing dishes). Furthermore, there are even striking parallels of social situations among many of the species of higher primates. Mother-offspring relations, perhaps governed by relatively long maturation and lactation periods, are often quite similar—and are accompanied by sometimes startling parallels in forms of communications about hunger and other states, the mother's availability to the offspring, offspring-fostering, danger warnings, pure vocal contact ("gootchy-gootch-goo!"), fear, and pain.

Though primate male-female relations vary considerably, these relations among

*Primate Communication. Body contact, holding, looking, maybe making sounds, moving together, all comprise primate patterns of communication inducing learning and conveying messages. These precede and underlie the cultural trappings seen in the photograph.*

*Homo sapiens* have diverged from those of other primates because humans have no estrous cycle. Consequently, men and women are in more or less continuous sexual interaction—i.e., continuous communication occurs between them at least with respect to sexual potentialities. Hence, for adult males and females, social situations tend to display consistent differences from those of the other primates; therefore different communication patterns are required (irrespective of sexual content). Nevertheless, as any experienced person who has watched zoo primates copulating knows, communicatory exchanges during sexual intercourse are rather alike in sounds and acts (e.g., nipping).

There is a parallel between chimpanzees and humans in hunting and game distribution behavior: males hunt, silently, in groups coordinated by *visual* signals; when they re-

turn to the females and children, they distribute the catch with much chatter, or *vocal* signals.

Furthermore, the absence of an estrous cycle and unique male-female relationships engender long-term relationships between human males and children with special communicatory patterns. Still, remnants of generalized primate male-to-child *behaviors* mutedly persist, especially those communicating status differences and authority through vocal and tactile means.

Aside from changes in content and means due to *Homo sapiens*'s peculiar sexuality, the species' communication possibilities are most profoundly altered by the gradual emergence of a form of message transmission—using not signals and signs (though these, too, persist in ancillary fashion) as among other species, but rather symbols: biologically undetermined and arbitrary forms encoding abstracted attributes of "reality" in conventionalized vehicles and meanings. This conventionalization is of supreme importance because it reflects a social process and order which creates conventions and delineates meanings and also because the conventions can be undone or revised, as well as created, with great rapidity, thus giving enormous flexibility of response to changing circumstances. Further, symbols permit responses temporally and spatially separate from stimuli by representing their interrelationships through symbol juxtaposition in the mind, where they are also remembered. Consequently, multisymbol messages can be transmitted over vast distances and times. They can also be encoded to carry multiplex meanings (as in irony) and indefinitely vast information, and they can be manipulated to create new meanings (by implications and innovations). Such means and modes of communication ultimately permit the construction of gigantic—and uniquely human—social systems.

*See also* Communication and culture; Language; Signal systems; Symbol; Symboling ability; Symbolism

Consult: Darwin, Charles, *The Expression of the Emotions in Man and Animals* (Chicago: University of Chicago Press, 1965); Eibl-Eibesfeldt, Irenäus, *Ethology: The Biology of Behavior* (New York: Holt, 1970); Goodall, Jane, "Mother-Offspring Relations in Free-ranging Chimpanzees," in *Primate Ethology,* ed. Desmond Morris (Chicago: Aldine, 1967); Hockett, C. F., *Man's Place in Nature* (New York: McGraw-Hill, 1973); Hockett, C. F., and

Ascher, Robert, "The Human Revolution," *Current Anthropology* 5:135–147, 1964; Lancaster, J. B., "Primate Communication Systems and the Emergence of Human Language," in *Primate Social Behavior,* ed. Phyllis Jay (New York: Holt, 1966).

—Anthony Leeds, Boston University

## Communication and Culture.

Human communication is enormously complex because humans, unlike almost all other animal species, use symbols as well as signs and signals to communicate. It can be cogently argued that all culture, including material objects, insofar as these encode messages from senders (their makers) to receivers (their users or observers), can be subsumed under human communication, though the latter includes messages that are not per se cultural (e.g., blushing).

A *sign* is a token which directly indicates something about the sender, with no indication of other objects, persons, times, or places: a baby rubbing its eyes is a sign of sleepiness; groaning is a sign of pain (but does not indicate *what* pain). The sign calls attention to the sender but is usually ambiguous as to what message is to be received.

A *signal* is a token emitted by a sender to indicate some *other* object, person, or place to a receiver, especially regarding action to be undertaken by the receiver. Pointing is a characteristic signal; the danger call of the gibbon is another. A red light signals attention to some domain of peril to be cognized—but like other signals it cannot specify what kind of danger (cross traffic, railroad, emergency exit, house of prostitution). Signals convey situational, but not referential, meanings.

A *symbol* is a token emitted by a sender which may concurrently indicate not merely other objects, persons, places, or times, but also self and receiver while also indicating a specific referent. Thus symbols can do what signs do—"(You) help me now; my belly aches" not only conveys what the baby's yowl signs but also specifies who is to do what to whom, when, and why. Symbols can also do what signals do—"(You) circle *left* around the antelope"—but unambiguously (one cannot be sure just where a pointing finger points nor if, indeed, one is not supposed to look at the finger itself!). Moreover, the symbol describes relevant abstracted features of the total situation to guide the acts of the receiver in relation to the sender and to objects in their common environments, in jointly understood conventionalized (that is, cultural) forms.

In human communication all these signs, signals, and symbols are often used concurrently or interactively—for instance, as in nonreferential but signaling hand movements accompanying speech sequences.

Symbol use is itself highly complex because many different levels of symbol organization are involved—the morpheme, the word, the phrase, the sentence, and large units made up of sentences. The parts of each level of symbol are connected by various rules composed of symbols, signals, and signs. Levels of meaning may be illustrated by the sequence /go!/, /go to school!/, /go to school and learn!/. All have a root symbolic meaning, /go/, which abstracts conventionally from all possible motions (coming, circling around, climbing, falling) as a special, *culturally* defined sort of motion of persons involving *goals* and *direction away*. In the two latter sentences, the goals are successively more defined by using other conventionalized abstractions. *School* refers to a special class of constructions (not a house or hangar); to a special class of functions (teaching-learning as opposed to warehousing); and to special classes of social relations (staff, student, teacher roles). At still higher linkages, *learn* implies multifarious other meanings: /learn so that you can make more money/, /learn so that you can become wise/, and so forth. All these meanings are themselves abstracted *cultural* conventions set up as culturally valued goals and conveyed as messages from a sender to a receiver, often leaving much understood from linguistic, social, emotional, and other contexts or by allusions in the symbolic vehicle itself.

The preceding discussion delineates three domains of human symbolic communication: *rules* for connecting symbols, the *meanings* of the symbols, and the *relationship* of symbols to senders and receivers. Charles Morris calls these three domains *syntax* (in language it is called grammar), *semantics*, and *pragmatics*, respectively. Together they constitute the field of semiotic, which need not be restricted to language but deals with all systems of signs. Symbols have also been discussed in terms of their *form*, their *content*, and their *meaning*, referred to respectively as the *signifier*, the *signified*, and the *signification*. Take the word *rose* in the phrase "the mystic rose." The signifier is the word *rose;* the signified is the object, a kind of flower. But the signification of the phrase is the Virgin Mary, a signification which occurs in many other uses of the word or idea *rose* with or without the adjective *mystic*—e.g., the rose window of a cathedral; "my love is a rose." The signifier, the signification, and, often, the signified are all *cultural* objects carrying messages between senders and receivers.

Perhaps a certain piquancy appears in the fact that communication about human communication uses tripartite categories: signifier, signified, signification; sign, signal, symbol; syntax, semantics, pragmatics (we forgive Morris his alliterative failure!). Trinities comprise a major folk categorization in the West from Greek times (*triorxos,* meaning "having three testicles," i.e., "vigor in love"; three Muses; three Graces) to the present-day CIA, FBI, FDR, and JFK. It may be doubted that nature always manifests itself in threes; hence the categorizations for discussing communication may be arbitrary and misleading—however culturally proper their tripartite signification.

Limited symbols are embedded in encompassing symbols—in categories, metaphors, rhetorics, ideologies, myths. Threeness is a *cultural* folk category, especially in Western communication: the world does not naturally come in triplet agency names and personal names or wishes. American Indian folk categorization tends to occur in fours and that of Lévi-Strauss in twos. Twoness, threeness, fourness, *n*-ness, and continua emanate from, and articulate with, more inclusive metaphysics and world views, themselves embedded in the central cultural myths of given societies. At each level—myth, metaphysics, metaphor, morpheme—the symbol provides a more or less general vehicle for human communication, to which all normal human beings can refer and from which they draw their models for the interpretation of all events both small and great. In this view, culture itself serves as a mode of human communication—the dominant, but not the exclusive, one.

*See also* Communication; Language; Language and culture; Lévi-Strauss, Claude; Signal systems; Symbol; Symbolism

Consult: Burke, Kenneth, *A Grammar of Motives* (New York: George Braziller, 1955); Cassirer, Ernst, *Language and Myth* (New York: Harper & Row, 1946); Cassirer, Ernst, *Die Philosophie der Symbolischen,* 3 vols. (Berlin: 1923–29); Morris, Charles, "Foundations of the

Theory of Signs," in *International Encyclopedia of Unified Science,* ed. O. Neurath et al. (Chicago: University of Chicago Press, 1938); Lévi-Strauss, Claude, *The Raw and the Cooked* (New York: Harper & Row, 1969); Sapir, Edwin, *Language: An Introduction to the Study of Speech* (New York: Harcourt Brace, 1921); Smith, Alfred G., *Communication and Culture—Readings in the Codes of Human Interaction* (New York: Holt, 1966).
—*Anthony Leeds, Boston University*

**Communication, Nonverbal.** This term refers to the transmission of information without the use of spoken language. In the strict sense of the word, writing is an important form of nonverbal communication, yet it is an outgrowth of speech and follows the same rules of grammar. In animals other than the human species, nonverbal communication takes the form of (1) visual communication, whereby body movements convey information; (2) olfactory communication, in which various smells are used as signs, especially in marking territory; or (3) tactile communication, in which touch is used.

Olfactory and tactile communication play a minor role in human nonverbal communication, whereas visual communication is important. People convey a great deal of information in their facial expressions, gestures, posture, and even in their use of space. Nonverbal communication has sometimes been referred to as the silent language.

The study of gestures and body movements is called *kinesics.* Much of the research in kinesics is directly related to psychiatry: researchers are able to learn some of the problems of patients by concentrating on their nonverbal as well as their verbal communication. The analysis of communication through the ways in which space is used both in public and in private is called *proxemics,* an area of research of increasing interest to architects and urban planners.

*See also* Communication; Communication and culture; Kinesics; Proxemics

Consult: Birdwhistell, Raymond L., *Introduction to Kinesics* (Louisville: University of Louisville Press, 1952); Hall, Edward T., *The Hidden Dimension* (New York: Doubleday, 1966).
—*Michael D. Olien, University of Georgia*

**Communication, Phatic.** Language communicates ideas, but it conveys other messages as well. Language as social pleasantry (e.g., chitchat) communicates a rapport between persons which is the *phatic* message—i.e., that the lines of communication remain open and ready for use.

*See also* Communication

**Communication, Verbal.** *See* Communication; Language; Speech.

**Communism.** In its broadest sense, communism refers to a socioeconomic system marked by egalitarianism and common ownership of the means of production, sometimes including articles of consumption. The

*Two Japanese monks greeting each other. The content of their exchange is being communicated by their careful manipulation of space (the distance between them) and the postures (bowing) they are assuming.*

term also applies to advocacy of or tendencies toward such a system. Within this broad meaning, the term has acquired a variety of connotations for different people at different times and places. Probably no word in the English language is more subject to misunderstanding, controversy, and emotional entanglement than communism, and it is difficult if not impossible to provide a brief, unbiased account. What follows is written from a perspective sympathetic to communism.

Communist ideas hark back to an earlier stage in social evolution, that of primitive communism, which was probably universal until the development of agriculture and the emergence of social classes between 10,000 and 5,000 years ago. Communism as a protest against various systems of class rule is nearly as old as recorded history, and communist ideas were influential in many of the early peasant rebellions against an emerging capitalism in Europe. After capitalism became established, communism, together with socialism and anarchism, became the dominant ideology of protest against the status quo. Marxism, the most important form of communism, holds that capitalism came into being through a violent revolution led by the bourgeoisie, that it is no longer compatible with human material and psychic needs, and that it can and should be replaced with communism through another historic revolution, this time led by the working class. This communist society of the future will be a return, on a higher plane, of the liberty, equality, and fraternity of primitive communism.

**The Development of Modern Communism.** Although the early struggles of the nascent working class were often supported by a communist ideology, and although advocacy of socialism was common among the utopian reformers of the early 19th century, the history of modern communism may properly be said to have begun in 1848 with the publication of the *Communist Manifesto* by Karl Marx and Friedrich Engels. Marx and Engels laid the foundation for scientific socialism, which emphasizes the role of class struggle in historical change, the role of capitalism in changing the face of the world and paving the way for communism, and the central role of the working class in effecting the transition to communism. They called themselves "communists" to distinguish their philosophy from the earlier utopian socialists, but later the terms communism and

socialism came to be used interchangeably by Marxists. Soviet Marxists now use the terms socialism and communism to refer to successive stages in the development of postcapitalist society, but this distinction was not made before 1917 nor do all contemporary Marxists follow this usage.

The subsequent history of communism as an organized political movement may be divided into four phases. (1) The International Workingmen's Association, or First International, was formed in 1864 to spread communism among the workers. It was dissolved in 1874, after the Paris Commune of 1871. (2) The Second, or Socialist, International was formed in 1889 by independent social democratic parties and achieved significant electoral strength in the years before World War I, but it fell apart when its constituent national parties abandoned internationalism and supported their own governments in the war (the American and Italian parties were notable for their continued opposition to the war). (3) The Third, or Communist, International (Comintern) was formed by the Bolsheviks after 1919. This period was marked by the dominance of the Communist Party of the Soviet Union, the only party that held state power. It was during this period that communism became a truly world force, as new communist parties were formed in Asia, Latin America, and Africa. It was dissolved by Stalin as a sop to the Allies in World War II. (4) The present period is one of polycentric communism which developed after the success of communist revolutions in China (1949), Vietnam (1954), and Cuba (1959). It is marked by the continued strength and growth of communist power.

**Communism in Power.** Several phases may be discerned in the history of communism after it attained power in the Soviet Union in 1917. (1) War communism (1917–1923) was marked by terror and the repression of counterrevolutionary forces. (2) The New Economic Policy (1923–1928) was essentially a return to private commodity production. (3) The "Second Russian Revolution," of 1928, was marked by the collectivization of agriculture and the elimination of the rich peasant class. (4) The "Primitive Socialist Accumulation" (1928–1938) was marked by Five-Year Plans and investment in heavy industry, in anticipation of the coming Nazi invasion. (5) During World War II (1939–1945), the Soviet Union suffered terrible losses in helping defeat Nazi Germany.

(6) Since World War II, the expansion of communism into Eastern Europe, Korea, China, Vietnam, and Cuba has been marked by the emergence of a polycentric communism.

The harsh repressive measures which have characterized several phases in communist history have discredited communism in the eyes of many people, but such repression should not be regarded as an inevitable concomitant of communism. Rather, it is better viewed in the context of the extreme poverty and underdevelopment of the Russian economy at the time of the revolution and the continuing threat of intervention from the Western capitalist nations (which became a reality when Hitler's rise was helped materially by Britain's early refusal to take a stand with Russia against his expansionist intents). Adaptation to these conditions led to a strong bureaucratic state organization and to what Trotsky called a "degenerated workers' state" in the Soviet Union. The deformations caused by excessive state power are expected to disappear with the elimination of the material conditions (external threats) that created them.

For the student of anthropology, clarity about the theory, aims, and practice of communism is of the greatest significance, for three reasons. First, about one-third of humanity is living in societies which are consciously communist. Second, communists form the major opposition force not only in most advanced industrial nations but also in the underdeveloped world as well, including most societies studied by anthropologists. Finally, communism claims that it, and not capitalism, represents the social order of the future. The spectacular growth of communism from a few small sects to a major force in human affairs in a little over a century indicates that this claim should be given the most serious consideration.

*See also* Capitalism; Marxism; Primitive communism; Socialism

Consult: Bukharin, N., and Preobrazhensky, E., *The ABC of Communism* (Baltimore: Penguin, 1969) (communist perspective), Cole, G. D. H., *A History of Socialist Thought* (New York: St. Martin's Press, 1953–1958); Huberman, Leo, and Sweezy, Paul M., *Introduction to Socialism* (New York: Monthly Review Press, 1968) (communist perspective); Hunt, R. N. Carew, *The Theory and Practice of Communism,* 5th ed. (New York: Macmillan, 1962) (anticommunist perspective); Marx, Karl, and Engels, Friedrich, *The Communist Manifesto* (New

York: Monthly Review Press, 1964) (communist perspective); Meyer, Alfred G., *Communism*, 2nd ed. (New York: Random House, 1963) (anticommunist perspective).
—*Eugene E. Ruyle, University of Virginia*

**Communism, Primitive.** *See* Primitive communism.

**Community.** The term *community* is used with much freedom by sociologists to characterize a wide range of groups whose members share a sense of identity, specific interest, values, and a role definition with respect to others. In this general sense a village, a neighborhood, a club, a labor union, or a profession can be called a community.

In a more specific sense community refers to the form of social organization characteristic of the small peasant villages of Latin America, parts of Europe, Java, and, less frequently, elsewhere, The "closed corporate community," in Eric Wolf's phrase, is organized according to its own basic principle of social organization as follows.

**Property.** The integrity of the community derives fundamentally from communal ownership of resources. In some cases all land is owned by the community as a corporate entity and its use is allotted to its members. In other instances some land may be individually owned while resources such as pastures or forests are shared. The integrity of community resources may be ensured by rules that encourage endogamy and prevent aliens from buying or inheriting community property. The corporate community is largely a self-contained economic unit, though it will maintain links to outside markets.

**Community Culture.** A corporate community is itself a small cultural system, and members of a community derive their personal identity from their community membership. Communities have distinct territorial boundaries, often marked with a cross or a shrine. These physical boundaries express a social boundedness as well. The homogeneous internal structure of the group depends on a sense of community-centered exclusiveness that divides the world of the community from the world outside. Community members often conform to strict norms in dress, food, and other habits and view any eccentricity or innovation as a threat. Thus small peasant communities tend

to be both culturally distinctive and homogeneous.

**Social Equality.** Inasmuch as a community shares a common economic resource base, equality of wealth is expected and inequality is viewed with fear and suspicion as a threat to the equilibrium of the group. The nuclear family is usually the largest solidary kin group within a community, and each family stands on an equal footing with the others. The household is the basic unit of residence and production.

The norm of equality within the community may be conceptualized as deriving from fear of the malevolent force of envy, which brings sickness and disaster to those whom fortune has favored above others. Similarly, the invidious glance of the evil eye brings trouble to the conspicuously fortunate.

**Religion and Ritual.** All communities have spiritual patrons in the form of spirits, ancestors, or saints. It is the collective duty of the community to participate in the rituals required of their cults. At the same time that the cults objectify the community's unity by demanding universal participation, the costs of feasts, fireworks, liquor, and ceremonial paraphernalia fall most heavily on the wealthiest families of the community, and thus they promote the redistribution of wealth and restore economic equality within the community.

The community and its normal activities are often regarded as being divinely ordained, and it is sometimes believed that the community life is only possible with divine aid. Failure to observe the mandatory rituals of holidays and rites of passage is to invite neglect or punishment by the gods on the whole community.

**The Function of Communities.** The features of the closed community as described above represent an adaptation that protects the independence and traditions of indigenous peasants against the encroachment of outsiders and innovators. Each community is a social, economic, and religious island unto itself. Economic risk is evenly distributed and disruptive outside influences are excluded.

*See also* Limited good, image of; Peasants; Society
Consult: Redfield, Robert, *The Little Community* (Chicago: University of Chicago Press, 1960); Reina, Ruben E., *The Law of the Saints: A Pokoman Pueblo and Its Community Culture* (Indianapolis: Bobbs-Merrill, 1966); Wolf,

Eric R., "Types of Latin American Peasantry: A *pologist* 57 (3):452–472, 1955.
—*Henry F. Schwartz, Ohio State University*

**Community Study.** The community study is both a research method and an ethnographic genre. As a method, it involves intensive, first-hand investigation of relatively small, discrete settlements. All aspects of the settlement—economy, social structure, political organization, customs, life-style, religion, and ideology, as well as the various interrelationships among these phenomena—are by definition the subject of a community study. The community study method has received most attention and elaboration among anthropologists who carry out research in the peasant villages of Asia, Europe, and Latin America. For this reason, as a type of ethnography, the term *community study* usually refers to the thorough description and analysis of life in such peasant settlements. However, the community study method has also been employed effectively in other settings. Some students of sub-Saharan Africa, for example, argue that the study of small sample communities is the only feasible means of investigating populous and dispersed tribal peoples. Sociologists have used the community study method to examine small-town America. The method has even been extended to urban neighborhoods, which are treated, for analytical purposes, as if they were distinct villages. Community studies have recently been the target of controversy. Critics state that the impact of outside political and economic forces on the small community has been neglected, that the communities described in the literature are unrepresentative of the region, city, or nation of which they are a part, and that community studies are too descriptive and lack a problem orientation.

*See also* Fieldwork, ethnographic; Fieldwork methods
Consult: Arensberg, Conrad, *The Irish Countryman* (Garden City, N.Y.: Doubleday, 1968); Redfield, Robert, *The Little Community* (Chicago: University of Chicago Press, 1960).
—*Stanley H. Brandes, University of California, Berkeley*

**Comparative Jurisprudence.** Historically this term has been used by legal scholars to refer to various methods of legal reasoning (positivism, realism, idealism), the relationship between law and morality in various legal systems, the historical development of legal thinking (Greek, Roman, Medieval, Renaissance, Reformation, modern), and the nature and origin of law itself.

Anthropological studies relating to jurisprudence consider the formal structures of a legal system—legal statutes, legal professionals, and legal institutions—in contrast to the ways in which law is actually applied and enforced at the local level. Anthropologists are particularly interested in the low-level (micro-level) perspective because it affords firsthand evidence for comparison of values and ideals within the written or at least formal word of the law, as well as practical application of those values in the daily lives of specific groups of people. Such anthropological studies include ways in which legal concepts and definitions vary between different societies and subcultures, the ways in which rules and law are interpreted and applied differently in various segments of a society, and the consequences of this type of real and ideal structure in legal systems for the management of conflict, change, and development within a society.

Comparison involves not only the study of concepts and practices which differ between whole societies (e.g., American versus Polynesian legal values) but also the analysis of various aspects and levels of one legal system within the same society.

When several legal systems coexist within the same political unit, the situation is called legal pluralism. Legal systems change internally because of the ways people use them, but they can also change when different principles and procedures are introduced from external sources. The application of British rule of law to indigenous African populations during the colonial period is a good example of this type of legal change.

The comparative study of changing legal systems, and the consequences of planned programs of "development" for un-Westernized legal systems, also fall within the comparative scope of cross-cultural jurisprudence in anthropology.

Scholars whose works have become classics in the anthropological study of comparative jurisprudence include Sir Henry Maine (*Ancient Law*, 1861), Montesquieu (*De l'Esprit des Lois*, 1750), and E. A. Hoebel (*The Law of Primitive Man*, 1954).

See also Legal systems
Consult: Hart, H. S. A., "Positivism and the Separation of Law and Morals," *Harvard Law Review* 71:593, 1957–1958; Morris, Clarence (ed.), *Great Legal Philosophers: Selected Readings in Jurisprudence* (Philadelphia: University of Pennsylvania Press, 1959); Nader, Laura, and Yrgvesson, Barbara, "On Studying the Ethnography of Law and Its Consequences," in *Handbook of Social and Cultural Anthropology*, ed. John J. Honigmann (Chicago: Rand McNally, 1973); Pound, Roscoe, *Interpretations of Legal History* (Gloucester, Mass.: Peter Smith, 1923).
—Cathie J. Witty, University of Washington

**Comparative Method.** In a sense all anthropological work is comparative. There are a number of ways in which comparison is conducted. When used without qualification this term refers to the method of earlier evolutionary anthropologists such as E. B. Tylor and Lewis Henry Morgan. They approached comparison by constructing stages through which human societies must pass on the road to civilization. Both compared cultural development with the process of human growth: "primitive" societies were regarded as comparable to the childhood of mankind. In its most extreme form this approach led to a view of the primitive as a child. The theoretical and methodological excesses of this school led to a reaction by Franz Boas against "grand theory" and resulted in his proposal that theorizing be halted until rigorous ethnographic fieldwork has been completed.

**Controlled Comparison.** There are a number of methods of controlled comparison; all attempt to ensure that only comparable things are compared. Culture history, or historical reconstruction, focuses on a specific geographical area and seeks to control the variables operating in that area in order to ensure that proper weight in the analysis is given to each. The work of A. L. Kroeber and his students exemplifies the virtues and faults of this method. A major criticism has been that in its trait approach to culture, each trait is given equal weight in the analysis. Furthermore, some critics fault the method for giving too much attention to what is called material culture (artifacts). Diffusion of traits from other areas is the chief explanation for cultural change.

A structural approach to controlled comparison emphasizes the cross-cultural comparison of relationships rather than items.

Fred Eggan and A. R. Radcliffe-Brown, the leading proponents of this method, urged that one should study such things as kinship relations in a cross-culturally comparative manner. While the goals of controlled comparison are more modest than those of 19th-century evolutionists, they offer a means to go beyond particularism without falling into the excesses of grand theories.

**Cross-cultural Comparison.** The statistical analysis of data from a worldwide sample is what most people mean when they use the term *comparative method*. Its connotation of being similar to that of the 19th-century evolutionists is appropriate, for the statistical cross-culturalist tends to be a cultural evolutionist, although more sophisticated than his 19th-century predecesors. The theoretical work of Leslie White provided an evolutionary framework for contemporary cross-cultural analysis.

The work of George Peter Murdock in organizing the Yale cross-cultural survey of 1937 and its subsequent development into the Human Relations Area Files gave great impetus to the development of sophisticated tools for statistical analysis of ethnographic data. These files, with their detailed coding and attempts at quality control, aided ethnographic hypothesis-testing while pointing out areas in which further research was needed. Murdock's *Ethnographic Atlas*, based on a trait listing and culture area approach to culture, facilitated further statistical work.

Raoul Naroll's methodological work has directly confronted the criticism of the hologeistic (cross-cultural) method. In particular, he and Roy D'Andrade have addressed themselves to Galton's problem—an objection which states that many of the correlations discovered in statistical analysis are merely the artifacts of sampling which allows diffusion to be counted as independent invention because of improper designation of sociocultural units. Naroll developed the concept of the *cultunit* in an effort to eliminate this problem. The cultunit consists of a group of people who speak mutually intelligible dialects, are in at least periodic contact with one another, and belong to the same state if that level of political integration exists.

Other objections have been recognized, and attempts to meet them have led to the use of Guttman scales and correlations in a temporal matrix. Harold Driver's study of kin avoidance is a case in point. However, many anthropologists still make the basic objection that cross-cultural studies have not yet really solved the problem of comparability of their units of analysis.

**French Structuralism.** A major approach to comparison is that associated with Claude Lévi-Strauss and those he has influenced. This approach is sometimes called French structuralism to distinguish it from a social structural approach. The structure that Lévi-Strauss seeks to uncover is that which exists in the human mind and which consequently underlies all social relationships. Principles of logical association are compared, rather than collections of traits. The ultimate aim of the French structural school is to discover the meaning of being human by discovering the possibilities of human action.

Their methods of analysis are based on linguistic procedures. Treating culture as communication, they explore the grammars of cultural systems in much the way that linguists compare the relationships between phonemes, morphemes, and lexemes of different languages. Thus languages and cultures may be very different on their surfaces but exhibit similarities and systematic contrasts at the deeper level of grammatical structure. Eventually cultures can be compared as languages are. Structuralists usually focus on kinship systems, myths, folktales, and rituals for comparative purposes, although Edmund Leach has applied the structural approach to hair as a symbol. It is theoretically possible to use structuralism to analyze any aspect of culture: Lévi-Strauss has analyzed music and cooking by using the methods and techniques of structural anthropology.

**Conclusions.** Anthropologists are in basic agreement that some sort of comparison must mark the advance of anthropology. Whether any of the existing methods of comparison meet the ultimate goal of anthropology remains to be seen. Each has its own adherents and detractors.

*See also* Cross-cultural sampling; Cross-cultural surveys; Ethnology; French structuralism; Galton's problem; HRAF; Lévi-Strauss, Claude; Material culture; Murdock, George Peter Consult: Driver, Harold E., "Geographic-Historical versus Psychological-Functional Explanations of Kin Avoidances," *Current Anthropology* 7:131–148, 1966; Murdock, G. P., *Social Structure* (New York: Macmillan, 1949); Murdock, G. P., *Ethnographic Atlas* (Pittsburgh: University of Pittsburgh Press, 1967); Lévi-Strauss, C., *The Savage Mind* (Chicago:

University of Chicago Press, 1966); Leach, E. R., "Genesis as Myth," in *Myth and Cosmos*, ed. J. Middleton (Garden City, N.Y.: Natural History Press, 1967).
—*Frank A. Salamone, St. John's University*

**Competition.** Competition is a style of organizing the collective activities of a group which involves active rivalries between two or more individuals or subgroups in the system. The rivalries produce a differential allocation of rewards, with more going to the winners of the competition. In some areas of social life, successful competition may itself be a goal (as in games, sports, and some types of warfare). In other kinds of social action, however, competition is an instrumentality—a means of solidifying morale, of intensifying group esteem, of increasing productive efforts, of fixing a sense of group identity. Competition may be prescribed in one area of life (e.g., religion) and proscribed in another (e.g., economics). In some senses, competition is always dysfunctional: where there are winners, there must also be losers. Invariably, by laying the foundation for envy, competition contains the seeds for persistent, disruptive, uncontrolled conflict.

*See also* Cooperation

**Complementary Distribution.** When phones in a given language are distributed in such a manner that each phone never occurs in context in which another phone occurs, those phones are said to be in complementary distribution, and are termed allophones of one phoneme. In English, for example, the sound of *p* in the work *pot* is a highly aspirated bilabial unvoiced stop, indicated with the phonetic symbol [pʰ]; the *p* in *spot* is mildly aspirated, written [p], and the *p* in *stop* is unaspirated, written [p']. There are no utterances in English whose meanings are altered by substituting [p] for [pʰ] or [p']. However, [pʰ] occurs only initially, [p] between other sounds, and [p'] terminally. Being thus distributed in a complementary manner, they are all allophones of the English phoneme /p/.

*See also* Phoneme

**Complementary Filiation.** In a unilineal descent system, this term refers to a child's relationships through the parent who does *not* determine descent. In other words, it is

through complementary filiation that a child is linked to the relatives of the *other parent* in a unilineal system. Complementary filiation can be the principal mechanism involved in the segmentation of patrilineages. Among the Tallensi in W Africa and the Gusii in E Africa, patrilineages are divided into segments by reference to females, on the model of a polygynous family comprising separate matricentral units.

*See also* Descent

**Componential Analysis.** Componential analysis is one of the methodologies (collectively known as *formal semantic analysis*) with which students of the New Ethnography seek to analyze their data. A formal analysis specifies (1) a set of primitive elements and (2) a set of rules for operating on these elements. By such operations a model is generated which is a replica of the original ethnographic data being analyzed. Essentially this amounts to creating a model which will predict back the data in toto, yet require an absolute minimum of special assumptions to account for the data. That is, the model should be both parsimonious ("elegant") and as universally applicable as possible.

The data subjected to formal analysis usually consist of terminologically distinguished (labeled) arrays of objects. More precisely, it is the *terminological system* that distinguishes (and labels) aggregates of objects (by which is meant anything placed in verbal categories—it implies nothing about material concreteness) which is analyzed. An aggregate of objects which is terminologically distinguished is called a *segregate;* the label designating the segregate is a *lexeme.* Many segregates have more than one lexeme; the choice of a lexeme, in such cases, indicates something about the situation and speaker but says nothing distinctive about the objects in the segregate. For example: "something to eat" may be designated by "chow" or by "food."

A *contrast set* is the class of mutually exclusive segregates which are found to occur in the same (as it is culturally defined) context and share exclusively at least one defining feature—i.e., a feature which characterizes the context in which they occur. Alternative responses which occur in the same contexts must, inherently, *contrast* with one another (in the particular culture's terms)—or they would not be perceived as alternatives. A contrast set, then, is a set of segregates which are terminologically contrasted to one another. The *domain* of a contrast set consists of the total range of meaning of its segregates. Thus, for example, a kinship terminological system forms a contrast set; its setting is its use to delineate genealogically reckoned relationships, and its domain consists of all the relationships so reckoned of which it takes account (distinguishes).

No two objects are exactly alike in every respect; thus classifying into sets implies a cultural selection of only a limited number of features as significant for contrasting kinds of objects. *Componential analysis* is based on the assumption that the features which a given culture uses to generate a contrast set occur along a limited number of *dimensions of contrast*. Each such dimension consists, ideally, of two or more *contrasting variables* called *components* or *features*. Thus each segregate of a contrast set can be defined in terms of a bundle of components which distinguish it from every other segregate in the contrast set. This bundle of components specifies the necessary and sufficient conditions under which an object is classified, by a particular culture, as a member of the segregate which the bundle of components defines.

Such a componential definition of a segregate is a precise way of describing what that segregate's lexeme means. Thus the componential definition of a lexeme is called its *significatum*. When all significata of all the members of a contrast set have been componentially defined, the componential analysis of that contrast set is complete.

*See also* Cognitive categories; Formal semantic analysis; Linguistics, anthropological; New Ethnography, the
Consult: Burling, Robbins, "Cognition and Componential Analysis: God's Truth or Hocus-Pocus?," *American Anthropologist* 66(1), 1964; Colby, B. N., "Ethnographic Semantics: A Preliminary Survey," *Current Anthropology* 7(1), 1966; Frake, Charles O., "The Ethnographic Study of Cognitive Systems," in *Anthropology and Human Behavior*, ed. T. Gladwin and W. C. Sturtevant (Washington, D.C.: The Anthropological Society of Washington, 1962); Goodenough, Ward H., "Componential Analysis and the Study of Meaning," *Language* 32:195–216, 1956; Lounsbury, Floyd G., "The Formal Analysis of Crow- and Omaha-type Kinship Terminologies," in *Explorations in Cultural Anthropology*, ed. W. H. Goodenough

(New York: McGraw-Hill, 1964); Sturtevant, William C., "Studies in Ethnoscience," *American Anthropologist* 66(3), part 2, 1964.
—David E. Hunter, *Southern Connecticut State College*

**Composite Family.** *See* Family, the.

**Computer Simulation.** This term refers to a technique for testing a model (say of a social process or system) by using a computer to imitate that process. Variables are calculated and their mutual influences are monitored so that the resulting process is replicated. This is especially useful for stochastic processes, where lengthy calculations are often necessary.

*See also* Deterministic process; Linguistics; Model; Stochastic process; Systems theory

**Comte, Auguste** (1798–1857). This French philosopher and sociologist coined the term *sociology* in his search for underlying, unifying social principles. In his *Cours de Philosophie Positive* (1830–1842) he presented what he believed to be these principles. They involved three stages of psychological and associated social development:

1. The *theological state*, in which the world is perceived as a projection of the self and there is no social differentiation

2. The *metaphysical state*, in which the beginnings of class differentiation produce social groups with enough free time to speculate about the human condition and develop "laws" of nature and other abstractions

3. The *scientific state*, which evolves in industrial society where the scientific method creates a new level of knowledge called *positivism*.

*See also* Sociology

**Conditioning.** Two main types of conditioning—a form of learning by association—are recognized: *classical* conditioning and *operant* conditioning.

Classical conditioning was first investigated by the Russian physiologist Ivan Pavlov; it is still sometimes referred to as Pavlovian conditioning. In this form of learning, a stimulus that evokes an automatic response is paired repeatedly with another stimulus that would not ordinarily evoke the

response. Eventually the subject associates the two stimuli, so that the second stimulus is sufficient to evoke the response. Thus a dog may be conditioned to salivate at the sight of its food dish, which it associates with food.

Operant conditioning has been most fully investigated by the contemporary American psychologist B. F. Skinner. In this type of learning, a random act of the subject is rewarded or punished. The subject associates the act with its consequence and learns to avoid or repeat the behavior. Thus a rat may be conditioned to press a lever if this action is rewarded by food.

The modern behaviorist school of psychology has attempted to elaborate the principles of conditioning into a comprehensive account of human behavior.

*See also* Behaviorist school of psychology
—Ian Robertson, *Cambridge University*

**Conditioning, Classical.** *See* Conditioning.

**Condorcet, Marie Jean Antoine Nicolas Caritat, Marquis de** (1743–1794). Condorcet, a French mathematician, philosopher, and revolutionary, contributed to Diderot's *Encyclopédie* and to probability theory (*Elements of the Calculus of Probabilities and Its Application to Games of Chance, Lotteries, and Human Judgment*, 1804). He also wrote biographies of Turgot and Voltaire, participated in the French Revolution, and designed the subsequent French educational system. Finally, while outlawed, he wrote the *Sketch of a History of the Progress of the Human Spirit* (1793–1794)—his outstanding influence, through Auguste Comte among others, on social science. It deals with human evolution through ten stages (e.g., hunting, pastoralism, agriculture); the tenth stage is a future of ultimate perfection with no inequality.

*See also* Comte, Auguste; Diderot, Denis

**Configurationalism.** This distinctive approach to the study of whole cultural systems developed in the United States in the 1930s. The founders of this school were strongly humanistic: Ruth Benedict was an accomplished poet as well as a cultural anthropologist; Edward Sapir was a composer and culture historian as well as a brilliant linguist and cultural psychologist.

Were a configurationalist to inspect an automobile engine, the isolated parts of the engine would hardly be noted at all. Instead, the questions asked might be "What kind of whole is it? How well integrated is it? In what ways does its configuration distinguish it from other types of engines? What is its meaning? What makes it go?"

Configurational studies focused on the dominant set or theme in a whole culture, and they added entire new dimensions of inquiry, questions about symbolism, meaning, direction, and goal. Benedict, particularly, stressed a typological approach to whole cultures, which she thought had distinctive characters like individuals. She helped psychologize anthropology by viewing cultural systems as introverted or extroverted, paranoid, megalomanic.

The legacy of configurational thinking today is a lasting concern with the cross-cultural study of personality, of value orientations and themes, and of the covert and variant as well as the overt and normative aspects of human social life.

See also Apollonian-Dionysian; Configurations of Culture; Ethos

Consult: Benedict, Ruth, *Patterns of Culture* (Boston: Houghton Mifflin, 1934); Benedict, Ruth, *The Chrysanthemum and the Sword* (New York: NAL, 1967); Mandelbaum, D. G. (ed.), *Selected Writings of Edward Sapir* (Berkeley: University of California Press, 1949).
—James Clifton, University of Wisconsin, Green Bay

## Configurations of Culture.

Although those who belonged to what can loosely be termed the configurationalist school had many differences, they shared a belief in culture as an integrated whole. The more extreme held that no cross-cultural comparison was possible since each culture was unique and unique things cannot be compared.

Edward Sapir was a major influence in the development of the configurational school. It was he who suggested the approach to Ruth Benedict, whose *Patterns of Culture* is probably the best-known work in the genre. In that work she views cultures as being united around one or two dominant characteristics, psychological in nature.

Whether pattern and configuration are synonymous was a matter of disagreement.

Clyde Kluckhohn used pattern to describe what he called overt, or conscious, culture; configuration, he believed, should refer to covert, or hidden, culture. Alfred Kroeber generally did not distinguish between the two in his usage.

See also Benedict, Ruth; Configurationalism; Covert culture; Overt culture

## Conflict.

This term denotes any antagonistic state between two or more parties arising from incompatible interests. The parties may be individuals, social groups, institutions such as churches, or political entities. Their incompatible interests may relate to their competition for the control of territory and other resources or for positions of power; or it may relate to ideological disagreement about values and norms. Conflicts are an inevitable part of social life. They promote as much as they disturb the maintenance of ordered interpersonal and intergroup relations. The conscious management of incompatible interests constitutes a distinct ability of the human species and functions as a main source of sociocultural change. The expression of conflict takes many forms: in witchcraft and verbal abuse, in debates and fights, in strikes and censorship, in litigation, revolutions, and warfare.

Anthropologists have not yet produced a general theory of conflict, possibly because their traditional emphasis on the functional integration of societies has led them to view conflict as the result of irregular, if not pathological, deviations from cultural norms. Recent research, however, has substantially increased our knowledge of conflict behavior. Ethological studies on

free-ranging nonhuman primates have investigated the biological basis of human aggressiveness and patterns of social control (see Montague 1973). Several ecological studies have related the incidence of conflicts to demographic conditions (population pressure on available resources) and to nutritional deficiencies (for example, hypoglycemia). Psychological studies have explained the occurrence and expression of conflict in terms of personality syndromes that derive from socialization practices and discrepancies between the motivation and the available means to achieve certain goals (see Le Vine and Campbell 1972). Finally, structural analyses have linked the form and function of conflict to a society's political organization.

Given the pervasive nature of conflict in interpersonal and intergroup relations, the maintenance of social order requires the institutionalization of methods designed to contain and settle conflicts. One can distinguish six basic processes of conflict management which combine the dimensions of intervention by a third party and outcome in different procedural patterns.

1. In *negotiation* both principals seek a mutually acceptable settlement without the intervention of a third party but often with the aid of supporters.

2. In *mediation* a third party intervenes in a dispute to help the principals achieve an agreement. Three modes of intervention are possible: either principal may solicit the mediator's aid; an administrative agency may appoint the mediator; or the mediator may intervene on his or her own initiative as a party interested in a conciliation of the conflict (and even enforce his or her aim by imposing sanctions on both sides). Regardless of the circumstances that brought the mediator into the conflict, both principals must agree to such intervention.

*PROCESSES OF CONFLICT MANAGEMENT*

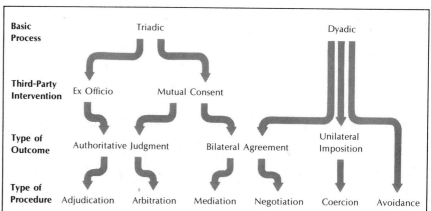

| Basic Process | | Triadic | | | | Dyadic | |
|---|---|---|---|---|---|---|---|
| Third-Party Intervention | Ex Officio | | Mutual Consent | | | | |
| Type of Outcome | Authoritative Judgment | | | Bilateral Agreement | | Unilateral Imposition | |
| Type of Procedure | Adjudication | Arbitration | | Mediation | Negotiation | Coercion | Avoidance |

*In crowded cities, conflict is a fairly common occurrence.*

3. *Adjudication* demands the decision of a third party who has the official authority to render a judgment. The institutionalization of this process tends to formalize the norms of conduct and of judicial procedure and usually requires means to enforce compliance with the decision.

4. In *arbitration* both principals consent to the intervention of the third party, whose judgment they agree to accept beforehand. Industrial disputes, for example, are often settled by this method. Ordeals and divinations represent a special kind of arbitration, one in which the third party is a nonhuman agent.

5. *Avoidance* represents a procedure of indirect confrontation in which one principal takes no action to obtain redress for a wrong or a curtailment of his interests suffered, although his withdrawal tactics may induce his opponent to make amends.

6. Through *coercion* one principal imposes the outcome and alone determines his concession, if any, to the opponent. The threat or use of force often aggravates the conflict and impedes a peaceful settlement. In fact it often leads the parties into warfare.

A typology of this kind can be applied to the exploration of conflict management in relation to other cultural variables. How, for example, do different systems for allocating political power and resources promote, hinder, or eliminate the possibility of settling disputes through negotiation or mediation? What political and economic institutions facilitate or require arbitration or adjudication? Questions such as these can be answered through comparative studies of different societies and different institutions within societies.

*See also* Aggression; Feuding; Functionalism Consult: Curle, Adam, *Making Peace* (London: Tavistock, 1972); Koch, Klaus-Friedrich, *War and Peace in Jalemo: The Management of Conflict in Highland New Guinea* (Cambridge: Harvard University Press, 1974); Le Vine, Robert A., "Anthropology and the Study of Conflict," *Journal of Conflict Resolution* (5) 1:3–15, 1961; Le Vine, Robert A., and Campbell, Donald T., *Ethnocentrism: Theories of Conflict, Ethnic Attitudes and Group Behavior* (New York: Wiley, 1972); Montague, M. F. Ashley (ed.), *Man and Aggression*, 2nd ed. (London: Oxford University Press, 1973).
—*Klaus-Friedrich Koch, University of Virginia*

**Conformity.** Sociologically, to conform is to comply with custom, usage, or practice.

Thus a law-abiding citizen complies with both the prescriptions and the proscriptions of the society. One may refer to the homogeneity of social groups as conformity. The term has always had a faintly pejorative aura, as witnessed by the coupling of genius or artistic talent with nonconformity. However, any social group demands a certain amount of conformity from its members or it dies.

See also Deviance; Normality

Consult: Parsons, Talcott, *Social Structure and Personality* (New York: Free Press, 1964).

**Conjugal Family.** *See* Family, the.

**Conjunctive Definition.** *See* Componential analysis.

**Conklin, Harold Colyer** (b. 1926). Cultural anthropologist who has been a leading figure in the study of folk systems of classification and cultural ecology, especially in SE Asia.

**Conquistador.** This Spanish term for conqueror was applied to 16th-century Spanish explorers in the New World. The two most famous conquistadores were Cortés and Pizarro.

**Consanguineal Relatives.** *See* Consanguinity.

**Consanguinity.** This term refers to a relationship based upon biological descent only. In order to be consanguineal relatives, people must be related by parental ties, sibling ties, or both.

**Conservatism, Cultural.** No sociocultural system is static, however small, simple, and isolated a society may be. The dynamics of sociocultural systems are thus always at least slightly unbalanced in the direction of change. But change is only one facet of this situation: the other is the processes of social stability, the forces of conservatism. Unfortunately, due to the overriding assumption of extreme conservatism among primitive societies long held by anthropologists, the nature of cultural conservatism has been too little studied. Some things are known about

resistance to innovation, others about efforts to restore vitality to moribund cultural systems, and more about such conservative forces as authoritarianism, rigidity in social controls with respect to the handling of deviance, and the influence of enculturation and socialization patterns in producing conformity. But conservatism has been too little studied and too often glossed over to allow many valid insights yet.

See also Conservatism, peasant; Cultural change

**Conservatism, Peasant.** Peasants have long been considered one variety of "traditional society" along with primitives or preliterates. This categorization stresses a supposed high order of cultural conservatism, i.e., resistance to cultural change. Peasants have been viewed as simple folk, lacking the capital and initiative for cultural change, often apathetic, or contented and well adjusted, and accepting of their place in a larger society. Basically, this thinking represents the "consensus model" of peasant life developed by Robert Redfield, Everett Hagan, and others. On the other hand, Oscar Lewis, George Foster, Joseph Lopreatto, and others have argued an alternative position, with good evidence to support it. They regard peasant communities as often characterized by great stress, conflict, social disorder, and the disposition to change their conditions of life, these being frequently expressed by high rates of social and geographic mobility.

See also Conservatism, cultural; Cultural change; Peasants

Consult: Lopreatto, J., *Peasants No More* (San Francisco: Chandler, 1967).

**Continental Glaciations.** *See* Glaciations.

**Contraception and Abortion.** Contraception usually refers to the blocking of fertilization during sexual intercourse. Abortion means ending a pregnancy (usually in an early stage) by causing the fetus to be ejected from the uterus. In cross-cultural perspective, native methods of contraception and abortion (exclusive of *infanticide*) have probably been ineffective forms of population control.

*Cultural prohibitions* on sexual activity are, however, very effective controls since the threat of supernatural sanctions keeps prohibited sexual activities in check. Regulatory marriage rules limit pregnancies by excluding large blocks of kinfolk from being legitimate, potential spouses. Unrestricted sexual activity as a cultural norm either before or after marriage is a rare occurrence in any culture. As an example, societal values praising premarital virginity elevate a powerful control into the realm of morality. Morality, of course, is often given an assist by the size of the brideprice or gift exchange for a virgin, as well as by the nonvirgin's diminished chances of making a desirable marriage. Other sanctions limiting a woman's pregnancy involve the concept of her being unclean during a part of her monthly menstrual cycle or the taboo regarding sex during a long nursing period (up to five or six years). Additional prohibitions may be imposed during extended periods of ritual activity (male initiation/indoctrination periods), planting or harvesting, hunting, and group movements en masse.

*Ecological limitations* also operate as natural contraceptive factors. Anything that is physically debilitating to either sex takes its toll in lowered production of healthy sperm or ova. Disease, parasites, accidents, and infection may limit fertility. Protein (and other) dietary deficiencies have been linked to low fertility rates. Sperm may be less viable, less motile, and fewer in number. Ova may not mature, may have abnormal chromosomal content or, even if fertilized, may not develop. Hormonal cycles may be adversely affected, placing yet another limitation on conception. During the years 1914–1918 many young women in Central Europe, whose diets were severely restricted as food supplies went to the military forces, did not reach menarche until age nineteen or twenty and had menopause begin in their early thirties. Recent studies of both the nomadic !Kung San bushmen of the Kalahari desert in SW Africa (Kolata 1974; Lee and DeVore 1975) and the Yanomamö Indians of S Venezuela and N Brazil (Neel 1970) report a strikingly similar number of children per woman, although the !Kung, unlike the Yanomamö, do not practice contraception or abortion. It has been shown that total body fat must exceed a certain minimum for menarche to occur and menstrual cycles to be maintained. The !Kung are well nourished but thin, and while menarche (and marriage) occurs at an average age of 15.5 years, the women do not bear their first child until about 19.5 years. With easily digestible foods generally unavailable to feed their infants, !Kung women nurse three, four, or even more years. During this time they rarely conceive—notwithstanding warnings from Western obstetricians not to depend upon lactation for contraception. The !Kung woman averages one child every four years so that, assuming menopause in the forties, her child-bearing period lasts a little more than two decades, over which span she may bear five children. This is remarkably close to the figure calculated for the Yanomamö, who, in addition to intercourse taboos and prolonged lactation, also practice infanticide (up to 20 percent of all live births) and abortion. The total number of children per woman that reach adulthood averages fewer than five as additional environmental hazards take their toll.

*Deliberate attempts at contraception* on the part of individuals unassisted by modern medicines and devices seem to have worked no better in small societies than they have in larger ones. Mythical beliefs about how and when a woman is able to conceive are matched in variety only by modern medical data which show that the ovulation period can vary throughout the menstrual cycle, making rhythm methods ineffective. Male techniques such as withdrawal prior to ejaculation or muscular control to retain the semen are likewise lacking in efficacy. Cast-metal cervical caps are reported to have been used thousands of years before their modern analog, the latex diaphragm. But whether or not they were as successful as the modern device (usually used with a spermicidal jelly or foam) is unknown. A method of employing the intrauterine device is said to have been known for some 2,500 years in the Middle East (Reuben 1969), but again there are no reliable data as to how extensive or effective its use may have been.

*Abortion techniques* seem to fare little better. Native medicines, primarily of the alkaloid and metallic poison types (quinine, aloe, arsenic, mercury, lead) have been used to dislodge the placenta by violent muscular contractions. If the woman survives, so, often, does the fetus, now rendered somewhat the worse for the experience. Ergot preparations (from fungi of the genus *Claviceps*) are quite effective in stimulating uterine contractions, but lack of standardized potency in folk medicines and the resultant

possibility of paralyzing overdoses are an ever-present danger to the user. Equally hazardous is the introduction of sharp or pointed objects directly into the uterus, especially when skilled surgical repair and antibiotics are unavailable.

In summation, cultural prohibitions and ecological factors have had far more long-range effect upon population limitation in nonindustrialized societies than deliberate, individual efforts directed toward this end.

*See also* Cultural ecology; Infanticide; Kinship; Marriage

Consult: Kolata, Gina B., "!Kung Hunter-Gatherers: Feminism, Diet and Birth Control," *Science* 185:932–934, 13 September 1974; Lee, R. B., and Devore, I. (eds.), *Kalahari Hunter-Gatherers* (Cambridge: Harvard University Press, 1975); Neel, James V., "Lessons from a Primitive People," *Science* 170:815–821, 20 November 1970; Reuben, David, *Everything You Always Wanted To Know About Sex* (New York: McKay, 1969).

—MaryAnn Foley, *Southern Connecticut State College*

**Contrast Set.** See Formal Semantic Analysis.

**Control, Social.** See Social control.

**Coon, Carlton** (b. 1904). Physical anthropologist noted for his work on the Middle East hominid fossils and human races. He is the author of the controversial book *The Origin of Races*.

**Cooperation.** As a style of organizing the collective activities of a group, cooperation displays these distinguishing features: (1) common effort on the part of many or all members of the group, (2) goal-directed activities, (3) a real or fanciful expectation that the collaboration will result in the achievement of some important satisfactions, and (4) a minimization of rivalrous internal conflicts. On a worldwide basis, cooperation is one of the most consistently and highly valued ways of organizing group activity.

Cooperation may be directed at achieving some social or cultural change in large or small ways, or in maintaining the form and functioning of existing institutions. It is expressed in a wide range of social groups—nuclear families, agricultural work parties,

armies, intertribal and international organizations. Cooperation may be achieved by traditional social norms, in which case it is the outcome of normal socialization processes. Or it may be the result of unconscious and unplanned processes, as in the major types of ecological adaptation.

In complex, stratified, densely populated societies—especially those characterized by a multiplicity of normative standards, a wide variety of roles, and considerable social change—cooperation generally involves specific, conscious contractual agreements. Usually some measure of competition occurs side by side with cooperation—the two do not occur separately. Intercultural differences appear in the amount of value placed on cooperation, the areas of social life where cooperation is the norm, and the degree to which cooperation is practiced rather than simply idealized.

*See also* Competition

Consult: Blau, P., *Bureaucracy in Modern Society* (New York: Random House, 1956); Homans, G. C., *Social Behavior* (New York: Harcourt Brace Jovanovich, 1961); Mead, M. (ed.), *Cooperation and Competition Among Primitive Peoples* (New York: Beacon Press, 1961).

—James Clifton, *University of Wisconsin, Green Bay*

**Copper.** See Metalworking.

**Corporate Descent Groups.** See Descent.

**Correlational Analysis.** In anthropology, correlational analysis refers to the presence of cultural traits that appear cross-culturally in a greater than chance association. Statistical tests are used to discover the probability of the correlation appearing merely by chance. The association can be causal, complementary, parallel, or reciprocal. However, great caution should be exercised in claiming a causal relationship between two variables.

*See also* Statistical methods

**Corroboree.** A six-week (evening) Australian aborigine feast and dance ritual promoting successful activities such as peace or

*A corroboree.*

siblings' children (i.e. cousins in American kinship terminology). Three main characteristics are used to distinguish cousin based kinship terminologies: generation, bifurcation, and lineality.

**Generation.** Generation is distinguished in a system where ego calls his parents' siblings' children by a different set of terms. Generation is not distinguished if he calls the two categories by the same set of terms.

**Bifurcation.** Bifurcation simply means to divide but in kinship studies refers specifically to the division between paternal and maternal cousins. If paternal cousins are called by one term (or set of terms) and maternal cousins by another term (or set of terms), then the terminology is bifurcated. If paternal and maternal cousins are not distinguished terminologically, then the terminology is not bifurcated.

**Lineality.** Lineality is distinguished if ego calls his own siblings by one set of

hunting. The term may refer (inaccurately) to any aborigine ritual-like gathering.

*See also* Dance; Ritual

**Corvée.** This word comes from a Latin phrase meaning works collected *(opera corrogata),* an apt description of corvée. In general, corvée is a tax paid in labor in lieu of money. In Europe it referred to a labor tax, usually on roads, which a vassal owed his lord. In general anthropological usage it refers to any labor required on a regular basis in lieu of taxes. It is usually found in colonial systems, although centralized groups not colonial in type often required corvée labor.

*See also* Feudalism; Taxation

**Cosmetics.** *See* Grooming.

**Cotradition.** This term refers to one of several cultural areas with time depths. The culture area concept was difficult to apply to the archaeological sequence of an area unless it could be shown that a culture area had indeed shown continuity over time. The term *area cotradition* was coined by Ralph Linton to describe a situation in which the archaeological cultures of a particular geo-

graphic region were seen to form culture areas at each successive time period. The area cotradition approach assumes that there has been considerable cultural continuity along with a mutual influence of the component cultures both in space and in time.

*See also* Culture area

**Counterculture.** Group ways of thinking and acting which are in opposition to the prevailing norms and values of the society. Since the mid-1960s the term has come to mean a specific form of youth culture found in all industrialized Western societies.

*See also* Culture

**Courts.** *See* Legal systems.

**Cousin.** *See* Kinship.

**Cousin-Based Kinship Terminologies.** Kinship terminologies categorize relatives in different ways. Some of these ways are not unique to a particular culture but are found in many cultures (although with different linguistic labels for the categories). Anthropologists have categorized the different systems with respect to the ways in which ego categorizes his siblings and his parents'

Figure 1:
DISTINCTIVE FEATURES OF THE SIX KINSHIP TERMINOLOGY TYPES

KEY: 
- G  generation distinguished
- *G*  generation not distinguished
- B  bifurcated
- *B*  not bifurcated
- C  siblings distinguished from collaterals
- *C*  siblings not distinguished from collaterals
- M  cross or parallel cousins merged with siblings

| | GENERATION | BIFURCATION | LINEALITY |
|---|---|---|---|
| **Hawaiian** (generation) | G | *B* | *C* |
| **Eskimo** (lineal) | G | *B* | C |
| **Sudanese** (bifurcate collateral) | G | B | C |
| **Iroquois** (bifurcate merging) | G | B | M |
| **Crow and Omaha** (bifurcate merging sub types) | G | B | M |

terms and his cousins by a different set of terms, i.e., siblings are distinguished from collaterals. It is not distinguished if ego applies the same terms to his siblings and his cousins.

But there are two types of cousins besides paternal and maternal. These are: cross-cousins, where ego is linked to these relatives through two opposite-sexed persons (i.e., mother's brother's children, father's sister's children); and parallel-cousins, where ego is linked to these relatives through two same-sexed persons (i.e., mother's sister's children, father's brother's children). Thus it is possible for siblings to be terminologically distinct from one such type but not differentiated from the other. In this situation the system is described as "merging."

**Types of terminologies.** Figure 1 illustrates the characteristics which define the most commonly found types of cousin-based kinship terminologies.

The descriptive terms (generation, bifurcate collateral, etc.) name the most distinctive characteristics and are quite logical, with the exception of the inconsistency in naming the third variable either lineal or collateral. The cultural terms (Hawaiian, Eskimo, etc.) name a culture which uses a system of terminology with these specific characteristics.

**Bifurcate merging terminology.** Iroquois terminology is often found in conjunction with dual organization (cf. alliance).

If the men of each lineage receive their wives from the opposite lineage and if the solidarity of each lineage is linguistically marked (cf. kinship terminologies), then ego's father and ego's father's brother are

members of the same lineage (therefore they are called by the same term, see Figure 2) and marry women of the opposite lineage (therefore, ego's father's brother is married to ego's mother's sister and ego's mother's brother is married to ego's father's sister). If descent is traced patrilineally, ego is a member of his father's lineage as are his father's brother's children (individuals marked B and Z). If descent is traced matrilineally, ego is a member of his mother's lineage as are his mother's sister's children (again, individuals marked B and Z). In both cases, the children of ego's parents' opposite-sex siblings (cf. cross-cousin) are members of the opposite lineage (individuals marked C) and are the individuals whom ego might marry.

Crow and Omaha terminologies are somewhat more complex. Each is often found in conjunction with matrilateral cross-cousin marriage and therefore with a circulating connubium (cf. alliance). Crow, however, is associated with matrilineal descent and Omaha with patrilineal descent. As in the Iroquois system, terminology often implies a social structure of a particular nature. In the Crow system, ego's

Figure 3:
CROW TERMINOLOGY
(matrilineages shaded)

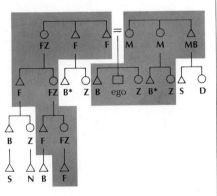

father and father's brother are usually married respectively to ego's mother and mother's sister, thereby making B* the "same" individual. The alliance, however, is asymmetric. Thus a male ego does not marry a woman in his father's lineage nor does ego's FZ marry ego's MB. Rather, a male ego

marries a woman from a third lineage, the male members of which marry women from ego's father's lineage, thereby completing the circle. Schematically over several generations, each man would marry the woman to whom he is joined by an arrow (his mother's brother's daughter, MBD).

Figure 4:
MATRILATERAL CROSS-COUSIN MARRIAGE

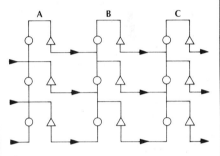

Matrilineages A, B, C—each practice matrilateral prescriptive cross-cousin marriage. This form of social structure is often associated with Crow kinship terminology usage.

Referring again to Fig. 3, it is possible to see that if ego marries his MBD (labeled D) their children will be members of D's matrilineage. Therefore, all three lineages are terminologically distinct.

Omaha terminology is reversed in the sense that it is patrilineages rather than matrilineages which are terminologically distinct, and is associated with patrilateral cross-cousin marriage.

*See also* Alliance; Classificatory Kinship Terms; Cross-Cousin Prescriptive Marriage; Kinship; Kinship and Alliance; Kinship Terminologies; Marriage; Matrilateral Prescriptive Cross-Cousin Marriage; Patrilateral Cross-Cousin Marriage
—*Lilah Pengra, Kenyon College*

**Cousin, Cross.** *See* Cross-cousin prescriptive marriage; Kinship.

**Cousin, Parallel.** *See* Kinship.

**Couvade.** In many societies it is customary for fathers to participate in the period of re-

Figure 2:
IROQUOIS TERMINOLOGY

KEY: △ = male
O = female
M = mother
F = father
B = brother
Z = sister
C = cousin

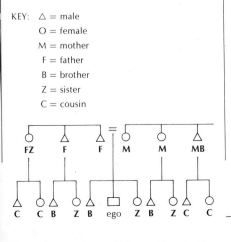

cuperation after their wives give birth. The father's "lying-in" likely marks his new status and expresses that the child is his as well as the mother's. Comparative research suggests that this custom is correlated with strong cross-sex identifications, which may result in psychosomatic ailments in the father during his wife's labor. The couvade has many variations: in one extreme, the mother rises immediately after birth and returns to her normal work while the husband replaces her and simulates the pains of childbirth. In other societies, the couvade consists of various taboos in diet, work, or other activities without the role reversal.

*See also* Sex (gender) identity; Sex roles

**Covert Culture.** This term refers to those aspects of a group's culture which are not amenable to direct observation by the ethnographer. It includes values, beliefs, dreams, and fears.

*See also* Overt culture

**Craftsmen.** *See* Skills and work.

**Cranial Capacity.** *See* Brain size.

**Cranial Index.** The cranial index is one of over twenty indices which express skeletal proportion by ratios of one measurement to another, in this case the maximum breadth of the cranium divided by the maximum length, multiplied by 100.

**Creativity, Cultural.** *See* Cultural creativity.

**Creole.** In the West Indies and Latin America, a Creole is a person born in the region but of European (usually Spanish) ancestry; in Louisiana, the term refers to a person born in the region but of French ancestry. Generally, a Creole is a person born in a region but of foreign ancestry, and hence distinguished from natives and half-breeds. The term may also be used to refer to a language that was formerly a pidgin but which has since become the native language of the group in question.

*See also* Pidgin; Sociolinguistics

**Crime.** A crime is a violation of criminal law for which the offender may be punished through the formal sanctions applied by state authority. Criminal law is often distinguished from civil law, which deals with private disputes between individuals.

The decision to make criminal some acts rather than others is in a sense a political one, since all definitions of crime are culturally relative and are made by the political authority of the time and place in question. Most crimes may be classified into one of three general categories: crimes against property, crimes against the person, and crimes against public safety and morals. In most societies the majority of illegal offenses are crimes against property.

Criminal behavior is usually analyzed as a form of social deviance, but a series of studies over recent years has demonstrated that, in Western societies at least, the great majority of citizens have committed one or more undetected crimes serious enough to carry possible prison sentences. The traditional rigid dichotomy between the criminal and the law-abiding citizen does not seem to accord with the facts.

*See also* Comparative jurisprudence; Deviance; Mores; Sanctions; Social control
Consult: Pospisil, Leopold, *Anthropology of*

*Cro-Magnon man, restoration by Dr. J. H. McGregor.*

*Law: A Comparative Theory* (New York: Harper & Row, 1971); Schafer, Theodore, *Theories in Criminology: Past and Present Philosophies of the Crime Problem* (New York: Random House, 1969); Sellin, Thorsten, *Culture Conflict and Crime* (New York: Social Science Research Council, 1938).
—Ian Robertson, Cambridge University

**Cro-Magnon Fossil Remains.** These skeletal remains of five individuals from Dordogne in SW France were modern in form, and geologists were on hand to verify the age (20,000–30,000 years) and stratigraphy of the site. Cro-Magnon represents the first authoritatively documented modern human fossil remains and indicates that the various Upper Paleolithic tool traditions were the products of people like ourselves.

*See also* Fossil sequence of human evolution; Paleolithic; Upper Paleolithic art

**Cross Cousin.** *See* Kinship.

**Cross-cousin Prescriptive Marriage.** This type of marriage is found in all parts of the world except Europe. Much more frequent than parallel-cousin marriage, it consists of a rule specifying which category of persons one should marry. The category consists of kinfolk—cross cousins—who are the children of the opposite-sexed siblings of one's parents: mother's brother's children and father's sister's children. From the point of view of any individual, if the rule is symmetrical, the available spouses would include the children of the father's sister as well as the mother's brother. This required form of marriage demonstrates that in many societies marriage links social groups in important ways, in this instance by forming and cementing an alliance and by ensuring that one's children will be married to friends and allies.

*See also* Kinship and alliance; Marriage

**Cross-cultural Sampling.** Cross-cultural comparison is one of the many applications of the comparative method. A large, statistically valid sample of societies is examined simultaneously in order to test a given hypothesis, preferably one formulated before the data are gathered. Entire societies are not compared, only certain aspects of them.

If the conclusions reached through cross-cultural analysis are to have applicability beyond the societies investigated, they must be chosen in a way that makes them representative of more than themselves.

A number of procedures have been developed to strengthen the methodology of cross-cultural research. The sample must be chosen in order to represent all parts of the world. Care must be exercised not to overrepresent or underrepresent any area. Before the data are collected, a series of hypotheses to be tested should be clearly formulated. For example, the hypothesis that excessive drinking is related to informal political organizations should be stated before the investigator chooses any societies—frequently from the Human Relations Area Files or the *Ethnographic Atlas*. There are also a number of other sources of coded data. The data are usually placed in a 2 × 2 contingency table. Thus one can test whether one cultural item is associated with another. Furthermore, one can test whether the association is due to chance or is likely to be significant.

A 2 × 2 contingency table has on its vertical axis the cells $A$ present and $\bar{A}$ not present. On its horizontal axis it has the cells $\bar{B}$ not present and $B$ present. The cells intersect thus:

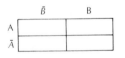

The number of cases fitting in each cell are tabulated, and tests of significance such as the chi-square are used to assess the probability of such a configuration.

There are questions regarding the sampling techniques used in cross-cultural, or hologeistic, research. The most serious concern the validity and comparability of the data themselves. In brief: are comparable items being compared? The intercoder reliability is another serious question. The randomness of the sample is a difficulty that cannot really be answered to everybody's satisfaction. No amount of care can furnish details on unstudied societies or tell us whether there is a systematic bias in the societies anthropologists study. Whether due care has been taken to account for diffusion is another sampling question. Finally, one always wonders how significant the results of such analyses really are.

*See also* Chi-square test; Comparative method; Galton's problem; Probability, social theory and; HRAF; Statistical methods
Consult: Otterbein, Keith, *Comparative Cultural Analysis* (New York: Holt, 1972).
—Frank Salamone, St. John's University

**Cross-cultural Surveys.** These surveys were first used by E. B. Tylor (1889) in a study of marriage and descent. Tylor regarded this approach as a means of investigating the evolution of human institutions. Thus a survey research design of a sample of the world's cultures may be used to seek lawful regularities, that is, recurrent patterns of association between different aspects of social life. But widespread use of cross-cultural surveys had to await (1) the publication of a large body of first-hand ethnographic accounts, (2) refinement of statistical and research procedures, and (3) a mechanism for assembling materials from many ethnographies so that specific information could easily be retrievable.

It was not until the 1940s that all the ingredients needed for extensive cross-cultural surveys were available. That decade saw the preparation of the Human Relations Area Files (HRAF) and the publication of G. P. Murdock's *Social Structure*, the first of numerous large-scale comparative studies based on the HRAF files. These files consist of a classification system for ethnographic data from several hundred of the world's societies. The societies are so selected as to provide a systematic sample of the world's cultures, and random samples can be drawn from the master list. The ethnographic data from each society are precoded and then assembled in a master index. Thus the investigator interested in a particular aspect of culture, say subsistence techniques, need only extract the files for several societies and locate the coded cards containing the data. Originally published in a bulky and expensive format, the HRAF files are now available in inexpensive microformats in numerous university libraries.

Basically, cross-cultural surveys attempt to make firm, valid generalizations about a large number of societies. The investigators may work from the HRAF files (which have many limitations) or from a different sample of original ethnographic accounts. These surveys generally start with several common assumptions. One is the assumption of limited possibilities—that is, universally human problems admit of only a finite number of solutions. Another is the assumption of the psychic unity of humanity—that is, despite cultural variations, human mental processes such as perception and learning are everywhere the same. Beyond such assumptions, the investigator needs a definite body of theoretical ideas about how societies function in order to guide the inquiry. There have been purely descriptive cross-cultural surveys, such as C. Ford and F. Beach's *Patterns of Sexual Behavior* (1951), but these are greatly outnumbered by studies with logico-deductive designs, which attempt to validate theoretical propositions by testing specific hypotheses.

Cross-cultural surveys of many aspects of culture have been done, but the heaviest concentration of such research is in the field of culture and personality. Such studies really involve the antecedents (causes), the consequences, or the correlates of personality traits.

One such study, William Stephens' *The Oedipus Complex* (1962), illustrates this methodology. Stephens sought to reach a firm worldwide test of psychoanalytic generalizations about this psychic conflict. Freud's original propositions about the universality of the Oedipus complex had been contradicted by Malinowski with his data from the Trobriand Islands. Other psychoanalysts rushed to Freud's defense, and other anthropologists marshaled new ethnographic data to the contrary. The result was a protracted, provocative, but unsettled controversy.

Stephens reasoned that here was a place where skillful exploitation of the HRAF files might resolve an important issue. To seek his answer, Stephens had to study a network of intercorrelations between a number of sociocultural variables in a large sample of societies. His sample consisted of ethnographic data from 100 African, Asian, Pacific, and North and South American societies. He decided to test hypotheses related to only one aspect of the Oedipus complex—a boy's sexual attraction to his mother, particularly as it is reflected in customs expressing sexual fears and phobias, inhibitions, avoidance of certain relatives, and the like. He reasoned, for example, that in "diluted marriage" societies, where the father is less involved emotionally with mother and son and there is a long postpartum sex taboo, mothers would behave more seductively toward sons, hence generating Oedipus conflicts since mothers are forbidden sexual objects.

This study illustrates some of the disadvantages of using the HRAF files. In about one-third of the 100 cases, the ethnographer had not reported any information relevant to the variables. In a number of other cases the data were scanty and ambiguous, so that research assistants could not decide on reliable ratings for some variables. In the cases where information was reported, it was often unclear whether the report was of an ideal norm (sons *should* avoid intimate contact with female kin) or actual behavior. Finally, the investigator had to make numerous inferential decisions about the psychological meaning of certain customs.

Nonetheless, Stephens was able to verify most of the hypotheses related to the universal distribution of the Oedipus complex. He concluded that the psychoanalysts were essentially correct, although Oedipus conflicts varied from culture to culture in style and intensity of expression. Cross-cultural surveys of this sort are, of course, not the final word. They could be improved were it possible to obtain systematically relevant psychological data from a sample of individuals in a sample of the world's cultures.

See also Culture and personality; Ethnology; Malinowski, Bronislaw
Consult: Barnouw, V., *Culture and Personality* (Homewood, Ill.: Dorsey Press, 1973); Naroll, R., "What Have We Learned from Cross Cultural Surveys?" *American Anthropologist* 72:1227–1288, 1970.
—*James Clifton, University of Wisconsin, Green Bay*

**Crow Cousin Kinship Terminology.** See Kinship

**Cultivation.** See Economics and subsistence; Food and food crops.

**Cultunit.** As defined by Raoul Naroll (1970), a cultunit consists of "a group of people (1) who speak mutually intelligible dialects; and (2) who belong to the same state" or are in periodic contact with one another. Naroll distinguishes four types of cultunit:

*Hopi type.* People who speak a common distinct language, belong to no state, but are interconnected by successive contact links.

*Flathead type.* People who belong to a state all of whose members speak a common distinct language.

*Aztec type.* People who belong to a state in which there are mutually unintelligible dialects, but who are domestic speakers of a dialect intelligible to speakers of the lingua franca of the state.

*Aymaran type.* People who belong to a state in which there are mutually unintelligible dialects and who are domestic speakers of a dialect not intelligible to speakers of the lingua franca of the state.

See also Comparative method; Culture, a; Culture-bearing unit; Dialect; Ethnos; People
Consult: Naroll, Raoul, "The Culture-Bearing Unit in Cross-Cultural Surveys," in *A Handbook of Method in Cultural Anthropology*, ed. R. Naroll and R. Cohen (New York: Columbia University.Press, 1970).
—*Phillip Whitten, Harvard University*

**Cultural Adaptation.** See Adaptation, cultural.

**Cultural Anthropology.** Cultural anthropology, the study of the cultural diversity of contemporary societies, can be divided into two aspects: ethnography and ethnology. Ethnography is the description of the culture of a specific society or subculture. Ethnology involves cross-cultural comparisons. Every cultural anthropologist is both ethnographer and ethnologist.

The descriptions of specific societies are the empirical statements of fact from which theories are built. The published description of the culture of a society is called a monograph. There are two types of ethnography: rural and urban. Rural ethnography, the more traditional of the two, includes the study of primitive, peasant, and modern rural peoples. In the past, cultural anthropologists emphasized the study of primitive societies, but as these people change or become extinct, anthropologists have turned to the study of other rural peoples, especially peasants. The study of rural peoples has the advantage of dealing with small, homogeneous groups that can be fairly easily defined.

Urban ethnography is rather recent, but it is already popular. The study of urban peoples generally involves a complicated research design, as one must deal with many variables. Urban ethnography often requires

that the traditional field methods of rural ethnography be supplemented with sociological techniques of sampling.

To study a specific group of people, cultural anthropologists must familiarize themselves with published anthropological descriptions of a particular geographical area known as a culture area. The culture area is one in which there is a certain amount of similarity between the cultures of societies that share the same geographical space. Culture areas may be very large, such as Latin America, Africa, or the Middle East, or they may be restricted in size, such as the NW Coast of the United States and Canada or E Africa.

Ethnology involves the theorizing which develops from ethnographical data. It should be kept in mind, however, that the two cannot be easily separated. It is on the basis of ethnographical data that ethnological theory develops, but it is also on the basis of new insights gained from ethnological theory that future fieldwork is planned. Ethnology involves two levels of abstraction: macrotheory and microtheory.

Ethnological macrotheories are broad conceptualizations concerning the general nature of culture and society. The adherents of a particular macrotheory are sometimes thought to represent a school of anthropology. The most important macrotheories are evolutionism, historical particularism, diffusionism, functionalism, and structuralism.

The evolutionists are interested in universal laws of society, culture, and cultural development. The evolutionists of the 19th century, such as Lewis Henry Morgan, thought that all societies pass through the same stages of development in a fixed sequence. The modern evolutionists, such as Leslie White and Julian H. Steward, have developed more complex models of cultural evolution; White emphasizes the harnessing of energy as a measure of cultural development and Steward emphasizes the relationship between societies and their environments.

Historical particularism was influential in the United States during the first half of this century. Franz Boas, the leading proponent, was antievolutionary. He placed great emphasis on ethnography, suggesting that each society is unique, and proposed a moratorium on theorizing until sufficient straightforward ethnography had been completed.

The diffusionists, such as G. Elliot Smith and Wilhelm Schmidt, believed that there were only a few centers of cultural development. In their view, ideas and traits spread from these centers to other societies and resulted in cultural similarity.

The functionalists, such as the British social anthropologists A. R. Radcliffe-Brown and Bronislaw Malinowski, were basically ahistorical. Their concern was not cultural development but the specific functions of various institutions within ongoing societies. Malinowski emphasized psychological and biological functions; Radcliffe-Brown emphasized social functions and is sometimes referred to as a structural-functionalist.

The French anthropologist Claude Lévi-Strauss and other structuralists are concerned with the underlying structure of the mind. Culture is viewed as the surface representation of these underlying universal structures.

Microtheory in ethnology involves an interest in specific topics viewed in cross-cultural perspective. Whereas macrotheory deals with overall patterns of cultural diversity and similarity, microtheory deals with specific patterns. A listing of various microtheories that constitute major subfields of cultural anthropology indicates the range of topics that interest the ethnologist: economic anthropology, which deals with economic organization; anthropology of law, which considers social sanctions and conflict resolution; anthropology of religion; social organization, especially the kinship systems of primitive groups; political anthropology; psychological anthropology, the study of personality in other societies; applied anthropology, in which anthropologists are concerned with introducing changes in other societies, often while working for governmental agencies; peasantry; belief systems, the study of patterns for behavior which is further subdivided into more specialized interests such as ethnobotany and ethnozoology; cultural ecology; complex societies, which includes such interests as urbanism, pluralism, and nationalism; medical anthropology; anthropology of education; demographic (population) anthropology; anthropology of recreation; ethnohistory; ethnomusicology; anthropology of dance, primitive art; folklore; and culture change. Each of these microtheories focuses on one aspect of culture.

See also Boas, Franz; Culture area; Diffusionism; Ethnography; Ethnology; Evolutionism; Functionalism; Lévi-Strauss, Claude; Malinowski, Bronislaw; Morgan, Lewis H.; Radcliffe-Brown, A. R.; Schmidt, Wilhelm; Steward, Julian; Structuralism; Structural-functionalism; White, Leslie
Consult: Bock, Philip K., Modern Cultural Anthropology: An Introduction, 2nd ed. (New York: Knopf, 1974); Clifton, James A. (ed.), Introduction to Cultural Anthropology (Boston: Houghton Mifflin, 1968); Haviland, William A., Cultural Anthropology (New York: Holt, 1975); Keesing, Roger M., and Keesing, Felix M., New Perspectives in Cultural Anthropology (New York: Holt, 1971); Hunter, David E., and Whitten, Phillip, The Study of Anthropology (New York: Harper & Row, 1976).
—Michael D. Olien, University of Georgia

**Cultural Change.** This term refers to modifications in the elements and patterns of a cultural system.

In Korea until the 7th century, when a king died the bodies of some of his noblemen were buried with him. Then it occurred to one nobleman to send not himself but a *statue* of himself. As will be appreciated, this new idea caught on rapidly.

During their first trip to Montreal for trading purposes in 1679, a group of Wisconsin Indians were badly treated by French soldiers there. The soldiers prevented the Indian warriors from entering the council chambers where the Indian leaders were conferring with the governor. Upon returning to Wisconsin, the tribesmen organized their own company of soldiers, elected a captain, mounted sentries, and marched up and down with their war clubs at right shoulder arms. They said their intention was to treat the French in Wisconsin as they had been treated in Montreal, but the Frenchmen were amused by this, not insulted.

In 1974, a major dispute erupted in Charleston, West Virginia. School administrators and teachers, supported by some community members, wanted to introduce a new set of textbooks and readings in the schools. Many others in the community objected to the content, style, and vocabulary of the new books and bitterly resisted their introduction.

These three cases are all examples of cultural change—actual or incipient. That is, they involve actual or potential modifications in the elements and patterns of a cul-

tural system. However, these cases, and others like them, can be fully understood only if further distinctions and specifications are added.

The Korean case shows that significant cultural changes can occur from events within the bounds of one society. Such changes are called *innovations, inventions,* or *discoveries.* In contrast is the Wisconsin Indian case, where the significant events developed in consequence of contact with people from another society and culture. Such changes are called *acculturation.* Finally, the Charleston example suggests that in complex societies with many conflicting institutions and subcultures, the distinction between internal versus external sources of cultural change may be difficult to pinpoint. Nonetheless, it might be useful to think of the school administrators and faculty as representing a larger, outside, external world in contrast to the local, religiously fundamentalist traditionalists who opposed the new textbooks.

The Charleston case also illustrates that cultural change may involve deliberate efforts on the part of one group to alter the beliefs and values of a different group. Deliberate planning was absent, in contrast, in both the Korean and the Wisconsin Indian cases.

Another distinction is crucial—the difference between social change and, in a narrow sense, cultural change proper. In this narrow sense, cultural change involves alterations in ideas and beliefs about how things *might* be done, or values and norms about how things *should* be done. Social change, in contrast, involves changes in the structure of social relationships—that is, changes in social roles and the relations between them, and changes in the relations between groups or institutions. Generally, cultural changes are closely related to and may precede or precipitate social changes, but not necessarily so.

The Korean case illustrates what was first a cultural change in the narrow sense. What was altered was a belief and practice concerning the funerals of kings. But since it also probably symbolized a desire on the part of nobles to reduce the power of the king, it may have contributed to a specific social change in the relative power of these two roles. Similarly, in the Charleston case the introduction of new books (i.e., new ideas) narrowly involved a cultural change. But it was opposed by groups who saw this as a threat to established social relationships —for example, the relations between parents and children, between adults and authority figures, and between local communities and state or national institutions.

Whether the change is externally or internally induced, whether it is deliberately planned or not, and whether or not it involves social and cultural elements, many of the processes are similar. The basis for all changes in sociocultural systems lies in the variations in ideas, values, and beliefs held by individuals. Irrespective of how small a society, how simple its culture, and how strict and disciplined its socialization patterns, the life experiences of each individual are unique.

This salient fact is too often obscured by the theories and concepts of social scientists which ignore individual variation and which stress the duplication and replication of uniformity (e.g., shared norms). Yet without differences between individuals, and without a capacity to conceive new ideas, no society could long endure. The basic fact of cultural systems is dynamic change—adaptations to altered circumstances of life. The most important kind of variation between individuals in this respect is differences in their cognitive maps of the social and physical world they live in, as well as differences in the ways they adjust to their world. Thus all human individuals are potential sources of new ideas about social relationships as well as new ideas about cultural things and ways. Yet such new ideas are like biological mutations in that the great majority of them never spread much beyond the innovator, while some of them may be severely damaging (maladaptive) to a group.

Such permutations and recombinations of older cultural ways into new configurations are called innovations. The Korean nobleman's new idea is an example: he conceived the notion of substituting a sculpted stone image for his own body. Similarly, the Wisconsin Indian warriors identified themselves with the French soldiers (who blocked their entry to the council house) and adopted the same behavior when they returned home by blocking the entry of French soldiers to their council house.

Once conceived, innovative ideas have to be communicated (or diffused) and accepted by others before they become new elements of a cultural pattern. Those which are initially tried may be later discarded. Those which are retained may become radically transformed as they are fitted into an existing pattern. Those which are finally accepted and institutionalized may have little consequence. But some ideas become revolutionary in their impact, radically altering the adaptations of whole societies or dramatically restructuring the nature of a social system.

In the Korean instance, the impact of the new idea, statue = nobleman, was probably negligible by itself. Soon thereafter a deceased king's successor demanded the delivery of statues for a funeral. The basic equilibrium of an older social structure was restored. In the instance of the Wisconsin Indians, the warriors never again imitated the posture of the French soldiers. This novel role was incompatible with their basic social values. The French soldiers had insulted them by blocking the warriors from the council chambers and admitting only their leaders. By their traditions, the warriors belonged inside, participating in deliberations; standing outside as sentries gave them little satisfaction, for the French soldiers were only amused.

The consequences of the Charleston textbook controversy are yet unknown. Were the new textbooks finally accepted? If so, did these new cultural influences affect social relations in the traditional communities? Was the power of the fundamentalist group reduced? Or were they successful in resisting this planned change? Was some compromise reached? Perhaps alternative sets of readings? Or a new book selection committee representing the divergent community interests? What were the consequences of this incipient cultural and social change?

See also Acculturation; Diffusion; Innovation; Revitalization movements
Consult: Barnett, H. G., *Innovations* (New York: McGraw-Hill, 1963); Bee, R. L., *Patterns and Processes* (New York: Free Press, 1974).
—James Clifton, University of Wisconsin, Green Bay

**Cultural Conservatism.** See Conservatism, cultural.

**Cultural Creativity.** In acculturation situations, the cultures receiving new elements frequently modify both the new ways and their own internal organization so as to accommodate them. In Samoa, for example, traditional religious practitioners had been retainers in the families of chiefs. With the advent of Christianity, the family priest became a deacon of the church and he often redirected old rivalries, which once might have led to war, into new channels, such as competitive church building and tithe collecting.

See also Acculturation; Innovation; Syncretism

**Cultural Diffusion.** See Diffusion.

**Cultural Ecology.** Ecology is the study of the relationships between living organisms and physical environment. Cultural ecologists are interested in ascertaining how human adaptation to the physical environment is effected by cultural mechanisms (see Harris 1974) and whether differences among cultures can be significantly explained by the influence of different environments.

There is no agreement among anthropologists on these issues. Some anthropologists argue that the characteristics of the physical environment can explain only the absence of certain cultural traits; for instance, the absence of bodies of water explains the absence of fishing techniques.

*!Kung San collecting ostrich eggs, the contents of which will be eaten by puncturing a small hole in the shell and sucking them out. Whereas western people might discard the shells, the !Kung San ingeniously use them as canteens in their arid environment.*

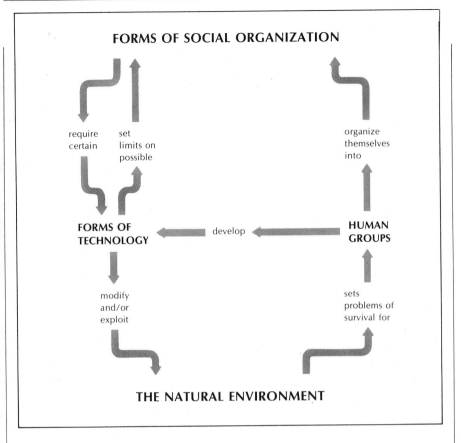

**FORMS OF SOCIAL ORGANIZATION**

require certain — set limits on possible

organize themselves into

**FORMS OF TECHNOLOGY** ← develop ← **HUMAN GROUPS**

modify and/or exploit

sets problems of survival for

**THE NATURAL ENVIRONMENT**

*A schematic representation of the relationship between forms of social organization, the natural environment, and technology. Read any capitalized label and follow any arrow leaving that label. Read the text along that arrow and continue to another capitalized label. This will result in a complete sentence. Each of the sentences you will discover in this manner expresses one aspect of the interaction of social organization, technology, and the environment.*

Other anthropologists, like the diffusionists and *Kulturkreis* scholars, explain the presence of cultural traits only through previous cultural traits and historical processes. Julian Steward, however, pointed out that it is useless to explain cultural phenomena by other cultural phenomena and showed that ecological adaptations produce identifiable cultural traits. It is undeniable that historical, cultural, and ecological factors all influence the origin and functioning of cultures. To explain culture only through direct ecological adaptation, as certain cultural materialists have done, is to reduce it to a mere epiphenomenon of economic relationships (materialism) and to reduce economic relationships to mere adaptive techniques.

Structuralists take an idealist view: they argue that the relationship between culture and the environment is always mediated by societal organization and by symbolic and ideological processes.

> Consult: Harris, Marvin, *Cows, Pigs, Wars, and Witches: Riddles of Culture* (New York: Random House, 1974).
> —*Ino Rossi, St. John's University*

**Cultural Evolution.** Cultural evolution is the oldest attempt to formulate a body of general theory to explain cultural processes, particularly long-term developmental change. As general theory, it has a discontinuous history of wide acceptance.

The early, 19th-century version of evolutionary theory was identified with such pioneer anthropologists as L. H. Morgan, Henry Maine, E. B. Tylor, and J. G. Frazer. Taking their cue from the successes of Darwin's explanation of the causes of variation in the forms of life, they posited unilinear stages of development. But their theorizing was largely armchair speculation, based upon insufficient and inadequate ethnographic facts. Their early formulations of the stages of human cultural evolution—or the evolution of levels of development in institutions such as marriage and the family—were readily discredited by the accumulating, scientifically sound knowledge of particular cultures which began emerging in the early 20th century. At this point, cultural evolutionary theory fell into disuse, to be superseded by historicist, diffusionist, and structural-functional theories.

But the long, complex course of human history in all its local unique varieties lay waiting for someone bold enough to renew an effort to construct an all-inclusive theory of human cultural development. In the phrases of contemporary unilinear evolutionary thinkers such as Elman Service and Leslie White, this requires an attempt to take a bird's-eye view of types of sociocultural systems and a global view of the whole course of cultural history. Here each *type* of culture represented one level of cultural development and might include many local, variant forms.

*Man Makes Himself* was the title of one of V. Gordon Childe's early books. Childe, who was an archaeologist, is the exception to the generalization that evolutionary thinking was for a period superseded. He viewed human cultural growth as consisting of a series of major technological revolutions which increased human capacity to control the environment and to increase the earth's productivity. Childe's *revolutionary stages* of development included the invention of tools, the domestication of plants and animals, the development of urban civilization, and lastly the industrial revolution.

Childe emphasized the importance of environmental factors in cultural evolution. He believed, for example, that the ancient agricultural civilizations of the Near East developed in adaptation to special environmental constraints. There groups of people were constrained to living in densely populated isolated communities by the limited amounts of arable land surrounded by

| CULTURAL EVOLUTION | | BIOLOGICAL EVOLUTION | |
| --- | --- | --- | --- |
| Technology | Economy | Brain Developments | Body Developments |

date (B.P.)

| date (B.P.) | Technology | Economy | Brain Developments | Body Developments |
| --- | --- | --- | --- | --- |
| 10,000 | bow and arrow | food production | | |
| 20,000 | art | | | |
| 40,000 | blade technology | specialized hunting and gathering | modern brain modern speech | |
| | mounted tools | | | |
| | prepared-core flake tools | | | |
| 200,000 | | | premodern speech | reduction of facial skeleton |
| | fire in use | | | |
| 500,000 | hand axes | big game hunting | rapid brain expansion | |
| 2,000,000 | stone tools | hunting and gathering | reorganization of brain and slow expansion | bipedalism perfected |
| | | | | bipedalism begins (?) |
| 10,000,000 | | | | |

ELEMENTS OF HUMAN CULTURAL AND BIOLOGICAL EVOLUTION

*The aspects of human cultural and biological evolution that appear on this table originated at the period indicated by their placement and are assumed to continue until they are either replaced or refined.*

desert. As populations increased, they turned to trade, exchanging with distant communities their products for additional resources. A spurt in population resulted in the growth of urban centers, craft specializations, and writing—the ingredients of civilization. But once invented, the features of urban life diffused to other locales.

*Multilinear evolution* was the name Julian Steward gave his own approach to evolutionary thinking. A cultural anthropologist, Steward was mainly concerned with specific ecological adaptations and the development of different levels of sociopolitical complexity in specific societies. He and his students sought to understand how a given social system was geared to adaptive relations with a given environment. His theoretical ideas, which were strongly empirical and pragmatic, emphasized technology and certain features of culture and social organizations which were directly related to the type of environmental exploitation practiced by the group. The multilinear aspect of his thinking focused on demonstrating that different types of adaptation or exploitation might be found in the same environmental setting, even within a single, complex society. Multilinear evolutionary thought therefore stresses the varieties of cultural adaptations which may be uniquely distinctive and persistent. The essence of this view of cultural adaptation lies in the recognition of multiple solutions to environmental exploitation, with different ethnic groups adapting to and occupying different niches in the same geographical setting.

Contemporary unilinear evolution has become identified with one major figure, Leslie White. Early in his career White set himself square against the dominant historicist-diffusionist school of thought in which he was trained, and identified himself directly with the basic assumptions and positions of E. B. Tylor and other early theoreticians. White and his followers have sparked renewed interest in the evolution of culture and human institutions. They have been responsible for many new ideas, numerous provocative studies, and bold, insightful efforts to reduce the vast domain of historical particulars and cultural distinctiveness to one set of coherent lawful regularities.

Little of White's writings can be appreciated unless his special view of culture is understood. In his theoretical work he never used the word culture in a separatist fashion, to refer to the ways and practices of one society. His reference was all-inclusive: culture was a property of the species *Homo sapiens*. Moreover, it was a distinctive, superorganic property that transcended local differences and variations.

White was, strictly speaking, a cultural determinist. Since culture is a phenomenon which exists on its own plane of reality, it has to be studied, interpreted, and explained in its own terms. His position was strictly antireductionist. There was, for example, no place for consideration of psychological variables in his general scheme. He did accept that special circumstances and local conditions might influence the line of development in one society, but his main interest was in the laws of cultural evolution on a global scale. Thus the work of White and his disciples is strongest and most convincing when they scan past the particulars of specific cultural variations to catch a glimpse of the whole pattern of human evolution. But it is also weakest where it comes to analyzing and understanding the processes of adaptation characteristic of one society, in one historical setting, in one geographical place. The problem with this approach is its attempt to deal with culture as a closed system, a perspective which it is difficult to square with observations of actual groups living under particular circumstances.

Certain of White's students, such as Elman Service and Marshall Sahlins, have tried to soften the rigidities and enrich the perspectives of White's unilinear evolutionary thought. One example of this tendency is their distinction between general evolution and specific evolution. General evolution, they hold, involves the growth of major stages of human cultural evolution. Special evolution, in contrast, involves the multiple lines of development in particular societies, special developments brought about by the accidents of history, local environmental conditions, and the like. In this way, they have attempted to deal with the growing criticism of White's grand theory, which seemed to ignore readily observable facts such as those amply documented by Julian Steward. The point is that general theory must aid in the illumination of particular cases, and when used in this fashion some of White's formulations appear trivial.

In its earlier years unilinear thinking was opposed to historicism and diffusionism as alternative bodies of theory developed to explain cultural phenomena. But in the past decade a new series of theoretical propositions in the area of ecological studies has emerged to confront evolutionary thinking. For, just as White's unilinear scheme of the superorganic culture left no place for individual humans and their psychology, it also excluded from consideration the specifics of environmental adaptation. This is just the place where new approaches growing out of the work of Childe and Steward are the strongest, so that today it is the cultural ecologists who are grappling with the evolutionists in an effort to develop more useful and more powerful theoretical ideas.

In reality, White and other evolutionists never actually excluded human psychology

from consideration. In effect, by reifying culture to the superorganic level and arbitrarily treating it as a closed system, they frequently wrote and spoke of culture in a personified fashion, as if it had wishes, motivations, drives, and perceptions. The psychology was there, but it was amateurish and common-sense psychology. This reflects the risks of rigid, arbitrary boundaries in anthropological—and other—theorizing.

See also Cultural change; Diffusion; Steward, Julian; White, Leslie

Consult: Alland, A., Jr., *Evolution and Human Behavior* (New York: Natural History Press, 1967); Childe, V. G., *Man Makes Himself* (New York: NAL, 1952); Childe, V. G., *Social Evolution* (Gloucester, Mass.: Peter Smith, 1952); Steward, Julian H., *Theory of Culture Change* (Urbana: University of Illinois Press, 1972); White, Leslie, The *Evolution of Culture* (New York: McGraw-Hill, 1959).

—James Clifton, University of Wisconsin, Green Bay

**Cultural License.** See License, cultural.

**Cultural Minorities.** Any discussion of cultural minorities must make clear that the real topic of discussion is differential access to power. Although a cultural minority tends to have fewer people than a majority group, it is not numbers of people that is of account. Potentially a group having a demographic majority could be thought of as a minority group. The Dukawa and Kamberi of Yauri Division, N Nigeria, are considered cultural minorities even though the politically dominant Hausa have fewer members than do these groups. (In many Western societies, including the United States, women constitute a numerical majority but are considered by many to be a minority group.) In brief, there is a distinction between numerical and political concepts of minority.

All other distinctions and their evaluation follow from the unequal access to power. Racial, religious, or ethnic bases for assignment to minority group status result from power relationships in which a group seeks to justify its position in relationship to other groups. In order to do so, means are found for distinguishing group members from nonmembers. Among these means are the attribution of physical and cultural differences (and often inadequacies) to minor-

ity groups. Myths and various forms of religious sanction frequently serve to justify the established order.

The use of various boundary markers to maintain distance and to structure group interaction underlines another important point. Minorities are not the result of *isolation* as some believe. They are the result of *contact.* In fact they are a means for structuring contact. The study of cultural minorities leads inevitably to the study of ascribed status, presentation of self, symbolism, and identity.

Charles Wagley and Marvin Harris (1958) have identified a number of characteristics of minority groups that, used with care, can serve as a general guide to their study. Minority groups are subordinate segments of complex state societies. Their special physical or cultural traits are held in low esteem by the dominant segments of the society, although it does not follow that minorities hold their own traits in low repute. They are self-conscious units held together by special traits. In fact, they may find it advantageous to stay together or they may be prohibited from passing to a higher stratum. Minorities tend to marry within their group and often are bound together through rules of descent.

Not every minority group exhibits all these traits, and their ranking on each of them may vary in degree. In fact, a typology of minority groups could be constructed using Harris and Wagley's criteria. The major point is that their status is an ascribed (imputed) one—not an achieved one. People do, however, pass in and out of the status and sometimes cling to a minority status in order to maintain economic advantages.

Often the empirical situation is more complex than simple models suggest. An individual can be a member of majority and minority groups at the same time. Thus a member of an ethnic group may be a member of a minority group. For example, an American black who identifies himself as a member of Afro-American culture shares a number of cultural traits with other members. While many of these traits may be regarded in a negative fashion by members of the white American majority, he is likely to be a Protestant, which makes him a member of the majority religious faction. In brief, any individual is likely to belong to a number of groups. Some of these may place the individual in a majority situation, others in a minority. The major questions to be asked then are which identity predominates in interaction situations and why is this so. Members of cultural minorities are usually identified in terms of the ascribed and relatively powerless identity of minority group membership regardless of other social identities. A woman in America, for example, is seen as a woman first—then a doctor, teacher, or lawyer. Her identity as woman overrides her other identities.

*See also* Minorities, ethnic
Consult: Wagley, Charles, and Harris, Marvin, *Minorities in the New World* (New York: Columbia University Press, 1958).
—*Frank Salamone, St. John's University*

**Cultural Persistence.** *See* Acculturation; Cultural revitalization; Pluralism; Traditions.

**Cultural Pluralism.** When two or more cultural systems in long continued contact work out a mutual accommodation which allows each to sustain its distinctive way of life, a condition of stabilized cultural pluralism is achieved. Such a situation usually involves asymmetric, symbiotic relationships between the groups involved, with each providing specialized functions. In the Nilgiri Hills in S India, for example, four distinct cultural systems coexist: the Todas are pastoralists, the Bagadas agriculturalists, the Kotas specialized artisans, and the Kurumbas food collectors and sorcerers.

*See also* Acculturation; Assimilation

**Cultural Relativism.** The concept of cultural relativism subsumes two components: an ideological affirmation of the existential uniqueness of every culture and a pragmatic rule of anthropological research, both theoretical and applied. Put simply, cultural relativism is an anthropological dogma which developed in reaction to the blatant ethnocentrism that characterized the reports about "primitive" peoples by European travelers and the naive early ethnographers. Their vision was distorted by a crude 19th-century theory of cultural evolution that equated a society's technology with the people's intellectual capacity and ethical development.

When trained anthropologists began to study tribal customs in their full complexity, they recognized these cultures' inherent logic and functional interdependence.

These insights demanded that native moral and aesthetic ideas must not be evaluated by the norms of the observer's own culture but must instead be understood and appreciated in their cultural context. Carried by this *methodological principle* ethnographic fieldwork became a more objective enterprise. The prejudicial terminology of the older literature is diminishing in the writings of the academic 20th-century anthropologists.

The long residence in a native community which modern field research requires has paradoxical consequences. On the one hand the ethnographer, as a participant observer, becomes personally involved in the life of the native community; on the other hand this partial socialization allows him or her to describe and interpret its culture in a more impersonal manner, detached from the values of the observer's own society. This approach does not deny the possibility of explaining culture-specific patterns of behavior in terms of theories that derive from the observer's traditions of scientific knowledge. On the contrary, our understanding of human behavior must rest on theoretical models that transcend the peculiarities of particular cultures but include those of our own folk beliefs.

The anthropologist constructs such models from a comparative analysis of similar beliefs and institutions in different societies. By this method one can explain, for instance, the universal functions of witchcraft beliefs and initiation ceremonies without distorting their meaning within different cultural contexts. In contemporary anthropological thought this relationship between cultural and universal-scientific meaning has been discussed in terms of etic and emic analyses.

There is no doubt that the idea of cultural relativism represents one of anthropology's most significant epistemological contributions to the other social sciences. However, the idealism that originally fostered relativism as the dogma of a value-free study of cultures has recently come under skeptical scrutiny. Anthropologists now understand that the dogma itself is the product of a particular ideological and historical tradition of Western scholarship. The worldwide political changes created first by the imperialist subjugation of tribal peoples, then by the dissolution of colonial empires, and then by the subsequent neocolonial, economic domination of the new nations in the Third

World have challenged anthropologists to rethink this dogma. Once an expression of empathetic tolerance, today cultural relativism can easily turn into detached indifference toward the needs and aspirations of the developing countries as well as those of ethnic minorities in (post-) industrial societies. But if contemporary cultural relativism means to *relate* a people's way of life to national, regional, or even global historical processes, the same knowledge of human nature and culture that enabled anthropologists to reject racism and demolish vicious myths of ethnic superiority should also allow them to evaluate their observations. This orientation does demand a moral commitment—not one that derives from an ethnocentric ideology but one that emerges from the rational empiricism of the comparative analysis of cultures.

*See also* Emics; Ethnocentrism; Etics, Fieldwork methods; Participant observation
Consult: Bidney, David, "Cultural Relativism," *International Encyclopedia of the Social Sciences*, vol. 3 (New York: Macmillan, 1968); Herskovits, Melville J., *Man and His Works: The Science of Cultural Anthropology* (New York: Knopf, 1948); Horton, Robin, and Finnegan, Ruth (eds.), *Modes of Thought: Essays on Thinking in Western and Non-Western Societies* (London: Faber, 1973).
—*Klaus-Friedrich Koch, University of Virginia*

**Cultural Revitalization.** This term refers to the process through which a society in decline reinterprets symbols from its cultural repertoire and revives its members' will to survive. The new identity is a combination of old and new elements.

*See also* Revitalization movements

**Cultural Selection.** *See* Selection, cultural.

**Cultural Survivals.** *See* Survivals, cultural.

**Cultural Themes.** *See* Themes, cultural.

**Cultural Traits.** *See* Trait, cultural.

**Culture.** One can always start a discussion of what "culture" is by giving the classic definition offered by Tylor (1958) on page 1 of his two-volume work *Primitive Culture:* "Culture or Civilization, taken in its wide ethnographic sense, is that complex whole which includes knowledge, belief, art, morals, law, custom, and any other capabilities and habits acquired by man as a member of society." The problem is that even after the passage of all the years since Tylor, there is yet no single, agreed-upon definition of the term *culture* as it is understood in the anthropological profession. Every anthropologist has, after the years of his or her training and practical experience, a sense of the term which allows colleagues to communicate with each other; but there is no explicit statement of agreement as to what it is.

Thus *culture* is one of the most difficult words in the anthropological vocabulary to define. The difficulty stems from the fact that the concept is used to label various states of awareness occurring at different levels of abstraction. One way of looking at culture is to treat it in terms of these different levels and label them accordingly: $culture_1$, $culture_2$, and $culture_3$. $Culture_1$ is *your* culture, that is, *your* personal, idiosyncratic culture, which is made up of everything you are aware of and have experienced. Obviously this means that no two people have exactly the same $culture_1$. $Culture_2$ is *our* culture. *Our* culture is composed of those aspects of $culture_1$ that are held in common by *us*. *Us* means at least two people at a minimum, but not too large a group as a maximum. "Too large a group" is indefinite, but that too is part of the problem of the definition of culture. The group holding $culture_2$ would often be called a subgroup in anthropological/sociological terms. $Culture_2$ is smaller than national culture, which is $culture_3$, but it is larger than $culture_1$. At the level of $culture_3$ there is still a certain amount of shared aspects of all the individual $cultures_1$, which is why an American audience can share a joke on television that has no meaning for those raised elsewhere (who after all have a different version of $culture_3$, as well as $culture_1$ and $culture_2$). $Culture_2$ is hard to pin down, since it shifts as the groups making it up shift in composition of individuals. One may be an anthropolo-

gist and a teacher and a gardener and a kite flyer. If one belonged to as many groups as one had major interests in, one would have to admit to having a multiplicity of cultures. One can do this because of the underlying $culture_3$, which is shared by everyone regardless of the subgroupings.

In trying to answer the basic question "What is culture?" anthropologists end up working in ever more difficult areas of inquiry. Do chimpanzees have culture? If they do, are they human? If they are not human, what distinguishes human from nonhuman? It was once thought that humans had culture (however defined) and nonhumans did not! It is probably a matter of relative dependence and complexity: we are more dependent on culture and our culture is more complex than theirs. There is one final point to bear in mind: culture is *not* something carried by the genes—that is, one does *not* inherit culture biologically; one inherits culture intellectually. Culture is the patterned behavior learned by each individual from the day of birth as he or she is educated (socialized and enculturated) by parents and peers to become, and remain, a member of the particular group into which he or she was born or joined.

See also Counterculture; Covert culture; Culture, a; Overt culture
Consult: Bidney, David, *Theoretical Anthropology*, esp. pp. 23–33 (New York: Columbia University Press, 1953); Tylor, E. B., *Primitive Culture*, 2 vols. (New York: Harper & Row, 1958).
—*George R. Mead, Eastern Oregon College*

**Culture, A.** The term *a culture*, in anthropological usage, has several meanings, often used concomitantly with considerable ambiguity. One usage refers to any particular *system* of mental or ideational elements and orders (such as values, ideas, rules, norms, world views, theologies, cognitive mappings)—as in the phrase "American culture." Another usage refers to what is usually both internally and externally delimited as an autonomous total society defined by more or

less distinctive cultural characteristics—as in the phrases "the Nuer" or "the Tiv." A third, more infrequent, usage refers to any clearly separate societal subsegment, cross-cut by most major societal institutions, which is distinguished by its own cultural characteristics—as in the phrase "black culture in America." A fourth usage refers to a congeries of traits which may be ordered in various ways but are distributed over a number of delimitable societies—as in the phrase "Western culture." Generally, whichever meaning is used, boundaries of the unit are simply taken for granted rather than taken as in themselves theoretical research problems requiring analysis and rules of evidence.
See also Culture; Culture-bearing unit
—*Anthony Leeds, Boston University*

**Culture and Personality.** Anthropologists have used the notion of personality to refer to characteristic behaviors and ways of thinking and feeling; they have used the notion of culture to indicate life-styles, ideas, and values which influence the behavior and mental life of people.

In the past, anthropologists believed that a typical personality is prevalent among the people living in a given society because of the culture they share; anthropologists also believed that differences among culture correspond to differences in the personalities presumed to be typical or prevalent in those cultures. The typical personality has been conceptualized alternatively as configurational personality, character structure, basic or modal personality, and national character.

Ruth Benedict pioneered culture and personality studies with the book *Patterns of Culture* (1934). She believed that each culture is organized around a central ethos and is consequently an integrated configuration or totality. Through the internalization of the same cultural ethos people will come to share certain basic psychological structures; that is, they will have a configurational or dominant personality in common. For instance, the Zuni, who live in a culture permeated by an Appollonian world view, grow up with an Appollonian personality type—that is, a noncompetitive, nonindividualistic, and non-excess-prone type of personality. On the contrary, people born among the Kwakiutl Indians grow up with a Dionysian personality which tends toward great expressiveness and individualism. According to the configurational perspective, culture can be described in terms of psychological attributes or types of individuals; in other words, culture can be studied through psychological analysis.

Margaret Mead, who was Benedict's first graduate student, followed a similar trend of thought. In *Coming of Age in Samoa* (1928) she showed that certain childrearing practices produce typical character structures among adults. For instance, sexual freedom during childrearing explains why Samoan girls do not experience crises and frustrations during adolescence. In *Growing Up in New Guinea,* Mead found that the Manus, who emphasize hard work and financial success, are trained to be individualistic and independent in their childrearing practices.

Abram Kardiner in *The Individual and His Society* (1939) stated that social experience in the family (especially during childrearing) and in subsistence techniques (primary institutions) gives rise to a basic personality structure common to the majority of the members of the society. Then, through social interaction, the characteristics of the basic personality are projected into secondary institutions such as religion, ideology, and politics. Ralph Linton in *The Cultural Background of Personality* (1945) supported the same view, and so did Cora DuBois in *The People of Alor* (1944). DuBois used the term *modal personality* to indicate that the basic personality is expressed in the most frequent type of patterned individual behavior observed in a society.

The notion that culture gives rise to a common personality was extended to the notion that national groups possess national characters. Geoffrey Gorer maintained that in Japan severe toilet training gave rise to a compulsive character which found its outlet in warfare; Weston LaBarre independently proposed a similar theory. The validity of this theory was later questioned because toilet training was found to be no more severe in Japan than in the United States. With more plausibility, Douglas Haring suggested that the compulsiveness of the Japanese character could be attributed to the close supervision practiced by a police state for three centuries. In another study Gorer suggested that the custom of tightly binding (swaddling) the child for nine months explains why Russian people are prone to manic depression and guilt feelings. However, other scholars believe that the relationship between these behavioral patterns and swaddling is far from established. Even the general assump-

tion of Gorer and LaBarre that the experience of the first five or six years of life has a crucial influence on personality (derived from the strong influence of Freudian psychoanalysis on these anthropologists) seems to be questionable because the experiences of later life may modify the psychological effects of earlier socialization.

All these various ways of understanding the relationship between culture and personality were criticized by other anthropologists for being based on inadequate data and questionable concepts. The early anthropologists seemed to assume that culture is something different from the psychological experience of the individual, while in reality culture is perpetuated and modified by conscious and unconscious human cognitions, affects, and ideals. To a certain extent, culture and personality are merely different ways of looking at the same reality. We do not observe culture on one side and personality on the other: we observe people who think, feel, and act in certain ways (personality structure) under the influence of values and customs prevalent in a given society (culture). Modern anthropologists admit that people do learn certain patterns of behavior, but they do not accept the notion that even the deep structure of human personalities is standardized. To begin with, biological processes seem to have an important influence on the formation of personality; secondly, individuals are exposed to different life situations and, consequently, they internalize different aspects of culture. Moreover, a variety of cognitive and motivational structures is not incompatible with a set of organized mutual expectations and interactions, which is indispensable for social life.

Both Freudian and learning psychologies have been used in culture and personality studies, and J. Whiting and I. Child have tried a synthesis of both approaches. The application of thematic apperception tests has permitted researchers to study personality without using cultural elements so as to avoid the circularity of the early culture and personality studies.

Presently, there are under way a variety of rigorous experimental and comparative studies on all aspects of normal and abnormal psychic processes, such as the cross-cultural study of cognitive and moral development, mental health and deviance, the effect of cultural change on personality formation, and so on.

The old assumption that each person carries a miniature version of his or her culture in his or her psyche is no longer followed. This view, characterized as the replication-of-uniformity perspective, has been supplanted by scholars influenced by Anthony F. C. Wallace, who views culture as a mechanism which organizes individual diversity into viable social matrices.

*See also* Basic personality; Benedict, Ruth; Configurations of culture; Mead, Margaret; Modal personality; National character; Pattern, culture; Personality, cultural determinants of

Consult: Barnouw, V., *Culture and Personality* (Homewood, Ill.: Dorsey Press, 1973); Benedict, Ruth, *Patterns of Culture* (Boston: Houghton Mifflin, 1959); DuBois, Cora, *The People of Alor: A Social-Psychological Study of an East Indian Island* (Cambridge: Harvard University Press, 1960); Gorer, Geoffrey, *The American People* (New York: Norton, 1964); Mead, Margaret, *Coming of Age in Samoa* (New York: Morrow, 1961).

—Ino Rossi, St. John's University

**Culture Area.** This term refers to a part of the world in which the inhabitants share most of the elements of culture, such as related languages, similar ecological conditions, economic systems, social systems, and ideological systems. The separate groups within the area may or may not all be members of the same breeding population.

It seems likely that ancestral groups migrating into an inhospitable area would scatter themselves widely as limited resources became exhausted. It is equally likely that other groups coming into more favorable zones would increase in size and spread into the surrounding terrain. In either case, the dispersing populations would carry their parent culture with them (modifying details as adaptation demanded), thus producing culture areas. However, although ecological conditions may limit the boundaries or choices of cultural systems, they neither explain cultural variation and elaboration nor determine the direction of cultural development.

*See also* Cultural ecology; Culture areas of the world; Language families of the world.

—MaryAnn Foley, Southern Connecticut State College

**Culture Areas of the World.** There are two major problems that must be resolved in order to define related groups of cultures throughout the world. One concerns which of several criteria to choose as the basis for cultural relationships; the other concerns a choice among the variety of *ethnographic presents* available for consideration. Since space limitations prevent the use of all criteria and time periods, decisions resolving problems of choice must (in large part) be arbitrary.

**Theory.** The point of view governing these decisions defines culture as an adaptive mechanism which allows people who live together to solve the problems posed by the environment in which they find themselves.

**Definition.** As the result of this stance, a *culture area* is a part of the earth's surface on which more or less related groups of people, over many millenia, worked out a variety of adaptive mechanisms for survival, beginning with a common heritage: similar ecological conditions, similar economic, social, and ideological systems, and related languages.

**Limitations.** The reader should exercise caution in interpreting the maps, for indigenous peoples hardly think of territories as straight-line boundaries on paper. The boundaries should be used, therefore, as conventions which indicate approximations of interfaces between groups of people whose lifeways differ enough from center to center to be culturally significant. The sociocultural complexities resulting from increased mobility and industrialization over the last five centuries will not be dealt with here. For further explication of details the reader is referred to the many excellent sources available on the topic.

### Major Culture Areas

Middle East
Europe
Africa
North Asia
South Asia
Oceania
North America
South America

**Geographical Boundaries.** The *Middle East* is bounded on the north by the Mediterranean and Aegean seas (with a loop to the east to exclude Cyprus) through the Bosporus and along the southern shores of the Black and Caspian seas. It continues east of the Caspian to include the extremity of SW Asia almost to the Indus River. Crossing the Arabian Sea southwestward, it encloses the Arabian peninsula and the E African Horn. Proceeding northwest, the southern boundary runs south of the Ethiopian highlands, changes direction following the massifs that roughly divide the central desert from north to south, and on west to just north of Cape Verde. The enclosure is completed by running northward off the coast, including the Canaries, to Gibraltar.

*Europe* shares the northern boundary of the Middle East to the Caspian Sea, excludes the western edge of the Eurasian Steppes, and runs north along the western slopes of the Ural Mountains. A sharp turn to the northwest and the line crosses the White Sea, cuts off the Kola and the northern part of the Scandinavian peninsulas, extends into the N Atlantic to include Iceland, then returns south to the Iberian peninsula and Gibraltar.

*Africa* as a culture area comprises the rest of the continent south of the mid-desert boundary with the Middle East.

*North Asia* includes much of the Scandinavian peninsula north of the Arctic Circle, runs east to the Urals, then south, taking in the vast Eurasian Steppes. Turning eastward beyond the steppes, the boundary runs north of the Tien Shan but south of the Altai Mountains and the Gobi Desert. A northward jog takes it along the Khingan range, then sharply east just to the south of Sakhalin and the Kuril Islands. It proceeds through the N Pacific and the Bering Sea, across the eastern tip of the Chukchi peninsula, and out into the Arctic Ocean.

*South Asia* encompasses the rest of the continent of Asia, together with Japan, the Philippines, and Indonesia (and including Madagascar off the coast of Africa).

*Oceania* is bounded by Australia and New Zealand on the south, Easter Island in the eastern S Pacific, and Hawaii and the Marianas to the north. Turning south, the edge of the area runs between the Moluccas and New Guinea, through the Timor Sea, and back down to the Indian Ocean off Australia.

*North America* includes the entire continent south to the Panamanian isthmus. The Aleutians to the west and Greenland to the east are the longitudinal limits, and the Arctic archipelago in the Arctic Ocean is its northern limit.

*South America* incorporates the islands of the Caribbean, the continent of South America, and the Fuegian Islands south to Cape Horn.

### MIDDLE EAST

The domestication of food plants and animals around 10,000 BP in extreme SW Asia exerted a major, irreversible influence upon the aboriginal peoples of Europe, Africa, and Asia.

As the small, scattered populations of early villagers quickly used up the resources of the semiarid highlands by deforestation and overgrazing, two more specialized lifestyles emerged. The agriculturalists were forced into retrenchment along the river valleys and oases, while the pastoralists adapted their activities to tending cattle. When both technologies spread outward from the central region with expanding populations resulting from the more efficient and interdependent use of resources, localized adjustments were made. Horses and camels were added to the system, and throughout the area trading eventually became a third major economic alternative.

Persisting in much of the Middle East today are varying combinations of these interrelated economic systems. All three are observed in their most specialized forms in the SW Asia subarea: the agriculturalists of Anatolia and Egypt, the traders of the Levant, and the Bedouin nomads of the deserts of Arabia and Iraq.

The Mediterranean littoral encouraged trading, with a base of agriculture and small-scale herding as is common today in Algeria and Morocco. The Berber tribes of N Africa might better be described as transhumant than nomadic (over long distances). [Rif, Kabyle, Shluh, Senussi]

The camel nomads of the N Sahara in symbiosis with the oasis villagers have dominated caravan routes across the great desert from ancient times. [Tuareg tribes]

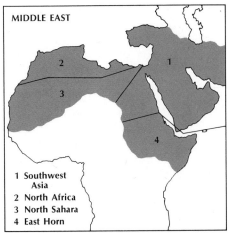

**MIDDLE EAST**

1 Southwest Asia
2 North Africa
3 North Sahara
4 East Horn

The agriculture and cattle cultures of the E Horn share linguistic, ideological, technological, and sociopolitical traditions with SW Asia peoples rather than with the rest of Africa to the west and south. [Somali, Amhara, Galla, Abyssinians]

## EUROPE

For this area the ethnographic present is the point at which conditions existed incipient to or at the point of change from tribal to civil society. Around 5000 BP the expansion of Neolithic peoples from their homelands (see Middle East, above) brought them to Europe by two routes: north of the Black Sea into eastern and northern areas, and along the Mediterranean coast into southern regions. As the Mediterranean littoral became drier and more and more deforested by both climatic change and human land use, prehistoric tribes depended more and more heavily upon the sea, and many became seafaring traders. A thin band of this culture spread over the coast of N Africa and, together with S Europe peoples, is considered by some to have been a single culture area until the Islamic conquest in the 8th century AD. Ideas from the early civilizations of the E Mediterranean spread westward, and in adapting to each set of local conditions there developed a succession of small civil states, each with its own unique flavor. [Crete, Mycenae, Etruria]

Around 4000 BC, W and N Europe Mesolithic societies were displaced by or interbred with several waves of Neolithic migrants from the steppes and SW Asia. There is also evidence of migration from the Iberian peninsula. [Beaker Folk, Battle Axe People]

Climatic conditions became colder and wetter around 2400 BP, forest species gave way to grassland species, and winter-hardy cereal growing for winter fodder gave rise to the haying industry that supported dairying—an economic adaptation which still exists in pockets of the continent today. As the zone of cultivation contracted, some tribes moved south and southeast. [Teutons, Goths]

About 1700 BP a further change in climate drove still more of the northern populations southward and the Steppe and Slavic tribes westward. [Huns, Old Saxons, Angles, Danes]

Within a few centuries the British Isles, Scandinavia, and Europe were virtually

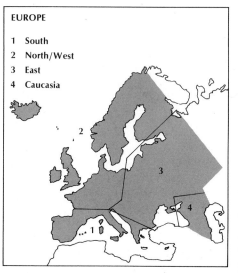

EUROPE
1 South
2 North/West
3 East
4 Caucasia

crowded with small, independent tribal units. Constant conflict over territory and human labor ensued and laid the foundation for the development of the feudal states of the Middle Ages. [Vikings, Gauls, Celts, Vandals, Lombards, Burgundians, Jutes, Picts]

The population unrest in Eurasia during the period 2500–1000 BP is said to have been due to nomads. However, it was probably an agriculture-based population increase together with changing climatic conditions which sent them on their wandering ways. Many waves of migrants passed east, west, north, and south in E Europe and settled when and where they could for as long as they could before they were once again driven on by groups with superior force or technology. The Slavs moved east and northeast from the Carpathian Mountains into what is today W Russia, and the Huns were migrating westward through roughly the same area. At the point at which civil societies arose in E Europe there was a diversity of groups similar in condition to those further west, though perhaps not so crowded. [Russ, Lithuanian, Finn, Latvian (Lett), Estonian, Hungarian, Ukrainian]

In the mountainous region of the Caucasus between the Black and Caspian seas there remain today a number of populations with linguistic and other culture traits traceable to ancestral pre-Indo-European–speaking cattle culture migrants (ca. 4000 BP) as well as to early horse culture migrants (ca. 3000 BP). [Abkhasian, Armenian, Azerbaydzhan]

## AFRICA

Paleolithic hunters populated Africa until the SW Asia Neolithic reached Egypt around 7000 BP. Whether or not the W Sudan (upper Niger region) was the center of an independent agricultural development, there is evidence that Sudanic cultigens had reached Nubia and Ethiopia by 5000 BP, thereby allowing intermingling of the two traditions.

What is today the arid S Sahara and Sahel at one time had more abundant moisture. On the basis of shifting agriculture the Sudanic savanna region supported large populations organized into complex states: kingdoms of Ghana, Mali, Songhai, Segou, and Kaarta (1600–300 BP). Since European contact, the area is best described as transitional. Continuing climatic change and overuse of land in various ways has caused the Sahara to encroach southward at an alarming rate, driving its peoples closer and closer to the coast. Cattle pastorialism in the savanna gradually becomes mixed with, and finally becomes secondary in importance to, hoe grain-farming in the southern and eastern Sudan. [Fulani, Songhai, Hausa, Kanuri, Fur, Maba, Masa]

The coastal forested regions of W Africa along the Guinea Coast seem to have been influenced by the early Sudanic farmers and herders only in minor ways. Crops suited to the drier upland plateau did poorly in the seasonal wet/dry and rain forest areas, and the tsetse fly prevented cattle herding. Around 2000 BP the Malaysian agricultural complex suited to wet, tropical regions was introduced by way of East Africa: it wrought

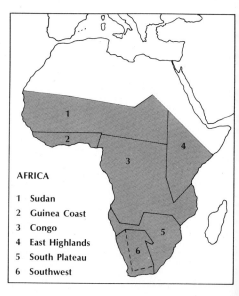

AFRICA
1 Sudan
2 Guinea Coast
3 Congo
4 East Highlands
5 South Plateau
6 Southwest

an immediate transformation in the economic systems of the coastal lowlands. New World plants from the West Indies and Brazil introduced shortly after the discovery of America added to the productivity of the region. In less than three centuries the expanded populations were organized into complex states headed by absolute monarchs, with a three-class social structure, a widespread market system, standing armies, and codified laws. [Yoruba, Ibo, Fon, Ewe, Ashanti]

Until ca. 2000 BP most of the equatorial and southern savanna regions were occupied by hunting groups, some of which survive today throughout the area, though greatly reduced in number. [Mbuti, Twa]

The expansion of the Bantu-speakers with the new tropical agriculture complex from the highland Cameroon area into the Congo began in this period. Primarily swidden farmers, they also depended on fishing, hunting, pigs, plant-gathering, and cattle, in order of decreasing importance. Political organization and trade in the central Congo were more localized than in the lake area to the east coast, where sizable kingdoms existed from 1000 BP until the 20th century AD. [Fang, Bacongo, Lunda, Bemba, Luguru, Zigula]

The pastoralists of the East Highlands are linked with the eastern Sudanic and Abyssinian cultures primarily by languages and cattle pastoralism. Cereal grains are the main crops where climate permits; other animals including camels, sheep, and goats are kept; hunting, gathering, and fishing are practiced where available. Complex political organizations do not exist. Some tribes are fully nomadic. [Masai, Samburu] Others are seasonally transhumant. [Nuer, Dinka, Luo, Turkana, Jie, Tussi, Nyoro, Ganda]

South of the central Congo in the higher South Plateau are further extensions of Bantu-speaking peoples with mixed agriculture-cattle economy. Absence of the tsetse fly allows dairy cattle to thrive, and a combination of Sudanic and American grains, supplemented by other, lesser, crops, are grown. Fishing and hunting also are present. Organized states similar to those of the Congo are found. [Ambo, Herero, Mbundu (west), Thonga, Shona, Xhosa, Swazi, Zulu, Sotho]

By 1000 BP the farmer-herders had caused the hunting peoples of the south to retreat to the inhospitable southwest desert regions. The Khoisan-speaking Bergdama and

Koroca seem to be physically related to the Bantu, but in culture they are akin to the hunting and foraging Bushmen of the Kalahari. The Hottentots diverged from the proto-"Bushmen"-Hottentot stock when they learned cattle pastoralism from the Bantu migrants.

## NORTH ASIA

The single most pervasive characteristic of the peoples of the N Asia culture area is the nomadic life-style which has been retained through many millennia of inhabitation. The groups living in areas adjacent to the Arctic Ocean exhibit typical circumpolar cultural adaptations. The hunting of polar land and sea mammals, together with a heavy dependence upon fishing, forms the basis of subsistence in most of the Paleosiberian subarea. [Chukchi, Yukaghir, Ainu]

To this basic circumpolar technology is added reindeer herding in the rest of N Siberia. Further south, horses, sheep, and a few other herding animals are kept. [Samek (Lapp), Tungus, Yakut]

In the Steppes/Plateau area there were once two distinct cultures. The W Steppe is relatively well watered for grassland, and it supported a mixed dairying–grain-farming economy, clearly derivative of the SW Asia

Neolithic cattle culture. [Uzbek, Kirghiz, Kazak, Hun] The higher, drier Mongolian Plateau, however, offered only sufficient pasturage for sheep, camels, and horses. This eastern horse complex has been interpreted as having been based on the northern Mesolithic of Siberia with a later, pastoral superimposition. [Mongols, early Manchus]

## SOUTH ASIA

Bearers of the peripatetic SW Asia Neolithic complex were well established in the Indus valley by 6000 BP. Once again, the combination of climate change, overuse of land, and aggressive migrants from the north seems to have brought down the high civilization with centers at Mohenjo-Daro and Harappa based on this complex. A brisk maritime trade between the people of the west coast of India and the Middle East was maintained as long ago as the fourth millennium BP. The cultural variations observed on the Indian subcontinent bear testimony to the frequent conquests from the north and west. Many small villages still subsist today on the basis of local agriculture and a unique approach to dairying.

East and south of the Vindhya Mountains which divide the drier north from the tropical south of India, the agricultural com-

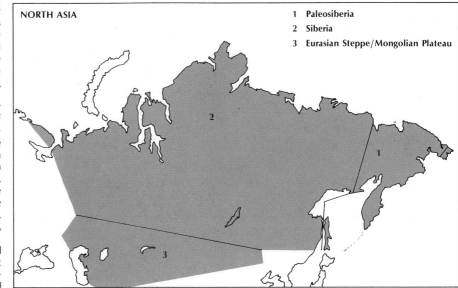

NORTH ASIA

1  Paleosiberia

2  Siberia

3  Eurasian Steppe/Mongolian Plateau

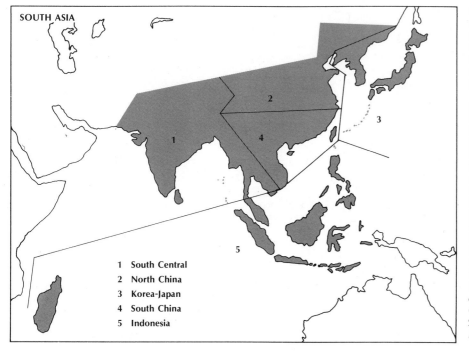

SOUTH ASIA

1 South Central
2 North China
3 Korea-Japan
4 South China
5 Indonesia

main food base of this complex. The plants were especially well suited to moist, tropical areas, and their manner of cultivation in small garden patches required little land-clearing. The S China mainland societies were eventually incorporated into the powerful states to the north.

The vigorous coastal, peninsular, and island peoples refined seamanship and boatmaking to high arts. Their South Asia horticultural pattern was so successful that it enabled its bearers to establish themselves in the next 6,000 years in the tropics and sub-tropics from Madagascar off the east coast of Africa to Easter Island off the coast of Chile. Its influence penetrated deep into the heart of Africa, where the Congo was populated by hunter/gatherers until the rain forest was made to support larger, garden-based societies. The difficulty of clearing land in the jungles made large populations untenable, and the small settlements were fairly independent. This type of loose political structure is also characteristic of much of the Indonesia-influenced regions of Oceania. [Ifugao, Tagalog, Dusun, Dyak, Semang, Jakun, Semai, Alor, Bali, Java, Malagasy]

plexes brought from China predominated. Some of the highland fringe populations of India, Sri Lanka (Ceylon), and the Andaman Islands still exhibit some characteristics of non-Middle East origin, although hunting/gathering has been replaced by agriculture. [Toda, Kota, Badaga, Vedda, Sinhalese, Nayar, Santal]

High-altitude plants (mostly of the N China complex) and pastoralism based on yaks have supported the rather limited populations of the Himalayan and Tibetan plateau region. [Sikkim, Nepal, Tibet]

Deep in NC China near the confluence of the Wei and Yellow rivers, in an area not unlike those which gave rise to the SW Asia and Mesoamerican agricultural patterns, another center of domestication appeared about 8000 BP. Named the Yang Shao culture, the earliest domesticants were millet and pigs (and the ubiquitous dog), but only later, as the complex spread east and south into monsoon and swamp country, rice. In Shantung Province of NE China about 5000 BP another complex, known as the Lung Shan, arose. Building upon a Yang Shao base, they raised grains and animals which could only

have come all the way from SW Asia. The soybean is believed to have originated in this area. The Lung Shan was the base of the earliest known of the great N China dynasties, the Shang, which arose in 3700 BP.

By 10,000 BP Korea and Japan had been settled by Paleosiberian groups with circumpolar technology (see North Asia and North America). Then, as today, the people were heavily dependent upon marine foods, although small game, birds, and plants also were eaten. Rice and taro were both well suited to the wet climate and reached the islands with proto-Malays about four millennia ago, but pastoralism of any sort never took hold. In the third millennium BP migrants from the Korean peninsula with superior agricultural technology spread throughout the southern islands, conquering and interbreeding with the earlier Indonesian inhabitants and displacing the Ainu further north.

A South Asia group of autochthonous cultigens appeared ca. 8000 BP in S China and the Malay peninsula. The yam, taro, citrus fruits, possibly coconut, plus pigs and rice (where feasible) from N China formed the

### OCEANIA

The earliest migrations into the S Pacific from the Malay peninsula are dated before 30,000 BP. Australia, Tasmania, and New Guinea were joined as one landmass, and successive waves of nomads found their way into the remotest corners. As sea level rose with the end of the Würm glaciation, contact with the mainland of SE Asia was cut off and what was by now the island of Tasmania and Australia was effectively isolated until European explorations in the 17th century AD.

There was no domestication of plants or animals among the Australian aborigines. Family bands foraged and hunted through well-defined territories, permanently bound to their lands by remembered and totemic ancestors. Even before recent geological, archaeological, and linguistic evidence established the probability of an early relationship with Melanesia, the elaboration of kinship categories, initiation rites, amorphous political organization, and art was considered strongly indicative of such long-ago common ancestry. [Arunta, Murngin, Walbiri, Tiwi, Tasmanians]

Between 10,000 and 4000 BP the nonagricultural ancient Papuans were almost completely absorbed, eaten, or otherwise replaced by Neolithic wanderers from island Indonesia. At this point Melanesian peoples had taro, yams, bananas, pigs, chickens, the outrigger, and Malayo-Polynesian languages. Some of the backcountry of highland New Guinea seems to have been used only intermittently for horticulture until the introduction of the sweet potato (which will grow at high altitudes) from South America, a little over a century ago. Although the small egalitarian hamlets characteristic of Melanesia were interdependent upon each other for locally unique products (manufactured, grown, caught, or collected), deaths attributed to sorcery led to frequent warfare between them, and headhunting and cannibalism were common. Apocalyptic cargo cults were especially numerous in Melanesia in the last century. [New Guinea (Papua); Bismarck, Solomon, and New Hebrides islands]

Throughout Oceania, volcanic islands support far more agriculture than the limestone soils of coral atolls. Therefore societies on the latter have been more dependent on the bounty of the sea, trade, and therefore seamanship. Micronesia and Polynesia were not populated by small groups on floating logs or rafts, as was probably the original Australian island. Migrants in oceangoing outrigger canoes from Melanesia (and later possibly from the Philippines or Borneo) settled Micronesia. Where they could, they farmed; where it was difficult, they adapted to the sea by becoming increasingly skilled sailors, often losing much of their horticultural technology in the process. Sometimes the land was so bountiful that they remained in self-sufficient contact only with members of nearby islands. Local variations are so numerous that it is difficult to generalize about much of the far-flung northern and eastern stretches of the Pacific, but Micronesian societies are more recent than Melanesians and more closely akin to Polynesians. [Palau, Truk, Yap, Marianas, Marshalls, Carolines]

In much of Polynesia, early migrants from Melanesia and Micronesia using the taro/pig complex were overcome by a group of exceptionally skilled ocean navigators who arose somewhere in the Formosa/Philippines/Celebes area. Originally descended from two China mainland groups, they developed sophisticated political organizational techniques, which together with their seamanship enabled them incrementally to organize the by-now-native islanders into stratified theocracies with centralized power. Only logistic problems seem to have limited political organization short of true states. [Hawaii, Marquesas, Tonga, Samoa, Tahiti, Maori, Easter Island]

### NORTH AMERICA

The same conditions prevailing in the Würm glaciation that joined much of the S Pacific area into Oceania (see Oceania, above) also joined NE Siberia to Alaska. The earliest proto-Paleosiberian migrations into North America are placed around 30,000 BP, although some as yet unconfirmed dates would place them thousands of years earlier. This migration route was subsequently frozen over from 22,000 to 11,000 BP, and polar nomads remained in the Arctic littoral, isolated for millennia from the previous arrivals south of the ice sheet.

The Eskimos and Aleuts diverged from a proto-Eskimo-Aleut stock about 4000 BP. They formed a narrow population ring around the northern coast from S Alaska all the way east to Greenland and the maritime provinces of Canada. The cyclical movements of the Alaskan Eskimos covered somewhat shorter distances than those of groups further east and north, which were coordinated to meet the caribou or musk-ox migrations. Seasonal fish-runs were significant over most of the area. Winter camps were often near or on the frozen Arctic Ocean in order to be close to the seamammal hunting areas. The reconstructed precontact Aleut culture seems to have been intermediate between the Eskimo and NW Coast Indians, with villages crowded together on the Aleutian Islands and with permanent communal houses, but with circumpolar maritime hunting and fishing technology.

The subarctic Indian hunters show a gradual transition from the tundra caribou complex (which shares many technological elements with the Eskimos) to the more southerly woodland complex where deer, elk, moose, and many kinds of plants and smaller game are available. Populations

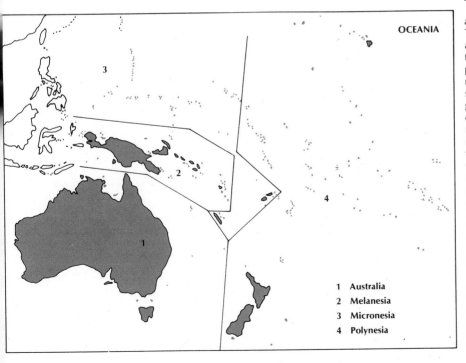

OCEANIA

1 Australia
2 Melanesia
3 Micronesia
4 Polynesia

**NORTH AMERICA**

1 Arctic
2 Subarctic
3 Northwest Coast
4 Plateau/Basin/California
5 Southwest
6 Plains
7 Eastern
8 Mesoamerica

maize, beans, and squash. Their adobe dwellings are called *pueblos,* and the term is often extended in meaning to cover the people who build and use them. [Havasupai, Hopi, Zuni, Yaqui, Tarahumara]

The Navajo and Apache were late migrants into the area from the east and north. They became semipastoral sheepherders with small scattered garden patches.

There is archaeological evidence that some of the bison hunters of the Great Plains were semisedentary horticulturalists when horses, introduced into Mexico by the Spaniards, suddenly entered their area from the south. A rapid cultural adaptation increased mobility, hunting efficiency, and population size. [Blackfoot, Cheyenne, Crow, Arapaho, Comanche, Dakota]

The tribes east of the Mississippi from the St. Lawrence River south to the Gulf of Mexico were mainly farmers, but hunting contributed significantly to their protein intake throughout the area. Many independent tribes populated the northeast, and due to slash-and-burn farming techniques, they were forced to clear new lands every decade or so. Some of the Iroquois groups were beginning to form larger confederations when the European settlers appeared. [Illinois, Seneca, Tuscarora, Mohawk]

The more favorable climate of the southeast provided a plentiful annual harvest that supported palisaded villages organized into theocratic states. Freshwater and marine animals as well as many varieties of land game, plants, and fruits supplemented the farming complex that had reached them from Mexico. [Creek, Choctaw, Natchez, Cherokee]

There is every indication that maize was domesticated in the highlands of Mexico about 6000 BP, and with the addition of beans and squash (and some lesser plants) this balanced diet under duress was independent of a source of animal protein. Supplemented by hunting and gathering, this farming complex supported large populations of theocratic states with politico-religious centers in Yucatan and the central valley of Mexico. [Toltec, Aztec, Maya, Tarascan, Huichol]

**SOUTH AMERICA**

The earliest cultures to be submerged by European conquest were in the Antilles and the north central part of the continent. They were linked to their neighbors of the south

grow larger toward the southern limits of the region, and social and political organization becomes fairly complex. [Kaska, Han, Yellow Knife, Ojibwa, Menomini, Chippewa, Naskapi]

The NW Coast tribes are unusual among nonagricultural hunter/gatherers in that the natural resources of the region—especially the annual salmon runs—were used so skillfully that they supported a large population of settled villages. They had relatively complex social institutions (slavery, potlatch) and sufficient leisure to develop a skilled art form in wood for both ritual and utilitarian purposes. [Tlingit, Haida, Kwakiutl, Nootka, Bella Coola, Salish]

The forager/hunters of the Plateau/ Basin roamed a territory from the Rockies to the NW Coast area in the north and from the Sierras to the Pacific in the south. The main root and tuber food supply of the northernmost Plateau Indians was substantially augmented by abundant and reliable fishing. [Kutenai, Spokane, Klikitat]

The more arid region further south was occupied by two different kinds of native cultures: the desert gatherers of the Basin and the farmers of the Southwest. Where there was not enough moisture to support agriculture a sparse population was sustained by reliance upon acorns or pine nuts as staples, augmented by other seeds, berries, roots, and small game. [Shoshone, Paiute, Washoe]

The California Indians claimed the most favorable territory of this subarea. The mild seasonal wet/dry coastal climate provided a wide variety of edible-nut trees, many kinds of plants, and land and marine animals. [Modoc, Maidu, Yana, Pomo]

South of the Great Basin where a combination of geologic and meteorologic conditions permitted, there were many settled villages supported by the flood farming of

by languages, their manioc and hunting technologies, and ritual artifacts. [Carib, Arawak]

In the northwestern part of the area were combined the agricultural technologies of the maize/beans/squash complex of Mesoamerica and the manioc/potato of the south. [Chibcha]

Based on advanced agricultural technology, a relatively dense population organized into states extended from central Mexico and Yucatan down the western highlands into the southern part of the Andean region by 1000 AD. These states underwent rapid disintegration after their rich mineral resources were discovered by the Spaniards. [Inca, Aymara, Arauca, Manacicos]

Tropical rain forests and grasslands supported less native agriculture than the highlands. In the Amazon and Chaco regions light crops were combined with greater reliance on hunting and gathering. Interspersed among the states in the north, but becoming the rule further south, were many small, loosely organized local societies. Competing for the limited resources, neighboring groups were in frequent conflict. [Pilaga, Auca, Tupinamba, Jivaro, Yanomamö]

Agriculture was more important among the societies of the Brazilian highlands than among the Amazonians. Their languages, social organization, rituals, and other traits were related to the Amazon and Carib culture areas, so evidently agriculture was an adaptation which Carib-related hunting peoples made in the more favorable highland area. [Guarani, Caraja]

The pampas supported hunting and gathering and occasional gardening. The major game animals in the Chaco—guanaco and rhea—were displaced by horses and cattle after European colonization. In lower Patagonia the coastal peoples added to their food supply by harvesting the sea. [Chono, Tehuelche]

The hardy nomadic Fuegians fished the deep waters off Cape Horn and supplemented their diet with shellfish, some gathering, and minimal gardening when feasible. [Ona, Yaghan]

See also Cultunit; Culture; Culture, a; Culture area; Culture history; Language families of the world; Pattern, culture; Religions of the world

Consult: Bellwood, Peter, "The Prehistory of Oceania," Current Anthropology 16:1, March 1975; Forde, C. Daryll, Habitat, Economy and Society (New York: Dutton, 1934); Graburn, Nelson H. H., and Strong, B. Stephen, Circumpolar Peoples: An Anthropological Perspective (Pacific Palisades: Goodyear, 1973); Hockett, C. F., Man's Place in Nature (New York: McGraw-Hill, 1973); Linton, Ralph, The Tree of Culture (New York: Knopf, 1955); Murdock, G. Peter, Africa: Its Peoples and Their Culture History (New York: McGraw-Hill, 1959); Murdock, G. Peter, Outline of World Cultures, 4th ed. (New Haven: Human Relations Area Files, 1972); Newcomb, William W., Jr., North American Indians: An Anthropological Perspective (Pacific Palisades: Goodyear, 1974); Spencer, Robert F., and Johnson, Elden, Atlas for Anthropology, 2nd ed. (Dubuque: Brown, 1960); Thompson, Laura, The Secret of Culture (New York: Random House, 1969); Wagley, Charles, and Harris, Marvin, "A Typology of Latin American Subcultures," American Anthropologist 57, 1955.

—MaryAnn Foley, Southern Connecticut State College

**Culture-bearing Unit.** This term refers to any society or *socially* delimited grouping of people which bears a culture.

See also Cultunit; Culture, a

**Culture Contact.** This term refers to internal changes in a society caused by happenings outside it. Basically the term is a British phrasing for the processes covered by acculturation studies.

**Culture Disintegration.** In culture contact situations where one group defines itself as superior, takes a dominant position, and uses its power to delete or modify objectionable elements in the subordinate culture, extensive dysfunctional and disintegrative consequences may result. The subordinate group may become so weakened, incapable of developing and synthesizing new ways of adapting, and demoralized that a whole series of pathological behaviors will follow, including extensive debilitating alcoholism, psychosocial dependency, and uncontrolled in-group violence.

See also Acculturation; Cultural creativity; Cultural pluralism

**Culture History.** In a generic sense culture history refers to the specific historical experiences and developments in one society or a number of societies. In the development of anthropological theory, however, it has a more specific reference. In the early 20th century, as opposition grew to the speculations of the pioneers in cultural evolution, some European and American anthropologists embarked on the task of reconstructing the long-range history of cultures. The key problem of course was the absence of historical (i.e., documentary) information on the earlier histories of many societies. One group of scholars (Father W. Schmidt, Fritz Graebner) became known as the *Kulturkreis* (culture circle) school. They believed that small primitive bands living isolated from one another had devel-

SOUTH AMERICA

1 Carib
2 Chibcha
3 Inca
4 Amazon/Brazilian Highlands
5 Chaco
6 Araucan
7 Patagonia
8 Fuegian

*Amahoucans from the jungles of Peru looking at U.S. magazines.*

oped distinctive cultural patterns, but that travel and contact had diffused these patterns outward like the ripples from a stone thrown into a pond. These patterns then became blended in later history. The task of the culture historian, therefore, was to identify the "strata" of which a particular culture was composed. Early culture historians saw humankind as fundamentally uninventive, and they often classified together in the same "stratum" (i.e., bow cultures) cultural traits which, although similar in form and in function, represented independent inventions. Interest in historical reconstruction continues today but with more rigorous methods and more kinds of data—archaeological, linguistic, and the like.

> *See also* Cultural evolution; Diffusion
> —*James Clifton, University of Wisconsin, Green Bay*

**Culture of Childhood.** This term refers to the child's-eye view of society and culture or children's perceptions of the world in which they live. The usual study of children is done from the point of view of the adult or the academic discipline of which the adult is a member. Every culture, including the Western scientific community, has beliefs or definitions of what children are and are not, of what they are capable of and what they are not, of how they think and how they do not. Some of these ideas coincide with children's reality, but frequently they do not. As early as 1932 Margaret Mead published a study contesting the prevalent notion that children are less literal-minded and less able to deal with abstractions than adults. This was followed by her famous studies on adolescence which showed that the "storm and stress" of these years in Western society is not a cultural universal. Nonetheless, many misconceptions about children persist, probably in most cultures, and they form the rationalizing basis for childrearing practices.

Two such assumptions in American thinking are discussed by Mary Ellen Goodman in her 1970 posthumous work, *The Culture of Childhood.* Using cross-cultural data she demonstrated the fallacy of age/stage linkages and the underestimation fallacy which underlies the inability of many adults to understand children's actual capabilities. From this point of view, children's perceptions and understandings and how they handle emotions and problems do indeed differ qualitatively and quantitatively from those of adults. Lesser verbal ability and shorter life experience reduce these abilities compared with adults.

*See also* Culture and personality; Education in cross-cultural perspective; Enculturation; Goodman, Mary Ellen Hoheisal

**Culture of Poverty.** *See* Poverty, culture of.

**Culture Pattern.** *See* Pattern, culture.

**Culture Shock.** A common psychological response to exposure to an unfamiliar culture, culture shock is characterized by disorientation, heightened anxiety, and, more rarely, by depressed or paranoid behavior.

**Cuneiform Script.** At the Oriental Institute of the University of Chicago an enormous figure of a winged bull stands with a curious set of wedge-shaped inscriptions. These inscriptions, unreadable for almost 2,000 years, were finally deciphered during the 19th century. They were used for 3,000 years until the beginning of the Christian Era.

*Sumerian clay tablet with impressed cuneiform writing, about 4,000 years old.*

Cuneiform (as these inscriptions are known) originated in Iraq (Sumeria) and spread into nearby Iran, Syria, and possibly Armenia and Turkey. It was chiefly made by the impression of a stylus or pen on a wet clay tablet which was subsequently baked dry in an oven or put out to dry in the sun. Originally hieroglyphic in character, it took on straight lines due to the instruments and materials used. From the time of Hammurabi (1750 BC) to that of Alexander the Great, the laws and records of the Babylonians, Assyrians, and Persians were stamped permanently on these tablets, immutable for all time.

The cuneiform episode in writing systems has been called second only to that of the alphabet as a mode of recording human achievements. The first libraries in the world were cuneiform tablet collections at Nineveh, the capital of Assyria.

*See also* Hieroglyphic Writing; Writing
Consult: Chiera, Edward, *They Wrote on Clay,* ed. G. C. Cameron (Chicago: University of Chicago Press, 1938); Pederson, Holgar, *The Discovery of Language* (Bloomington: Indiana University Press, 1961).

—*William H. Gilbert, U.S. Library of Congress (ret.)*

**Curle, Adam** (b. 1916). This British anthropologist and peace researcher received his D.Phil. at Oxford University. Formerly professor of education and development at Harvard, Curle is now professor of peace studies at Bradford University, England. His most important books are *Making Peace* (1971) and *Education for Liberation* (1974).

**Custom.** This term refers to the totality of socially acquired behavior patterns which are supported by tradition and generally exhibited by members of a society. A custom of only short duration is called a fashion. Customs are distinguished from habits, which are an individual's idiosyncratic behaviors. Whereas society is believed to be the source of customary behavior, habits are believed to grow out of the unique biographical experiences of individuals. When applied to behavior in our own society, the term *custom* is usually restricted to relatively unimportant behavior patterns which are not highly formalized, such as hanging mistletoe at Christmas. Custom was a term taken over from popular usage by anthropologists and by now has largely been replaced by the more precise and objective terms *culture* and *tradition.*

One area of anthropology in which the term *custom* still has a currency is the comparative analysis of legal and political systems, in which it is distinguished from the term *law.* Whereas custom is supported only by psychological constraints which operate within the individual and by the social disapproval which deviation from custom is likely to precipitate, laws have the additional coercive support of specific individuals or groups who have an institutionally vested charge to enforce conformity though formalized procedures often involving the application of negative sanctions. Thus some scholars believe that state-organized societies may be characterized as exhibiting the "rule of law" while stateless societies may be described as being ordered largely through the authority of custom.

*See also* Culture; Folkways; Government; Legal systems; Mores; Norm and normative; Political systems; Traditions
Consult: Diamond, S., "The Rule of Law Versus the Order of Custom," in *In Search of the Primitive,* ed. Stanley Diamond New Brunswick: Transaction Books, 1974); Malinowski, B., *Crime and Custom in Savage Society* (Totowa, N.J.: Littlefield, 1969); Sumner, W. G., *Folkways* (New York: Mentor Books, 1940).

—*Stanley Wilk, Lycoming College*

**Cybernetics.** Cybernetics is a scientific paradigm derived from electronic engineering and now widely applied to the analysis of biological and social systems. As contrasted with the conventional "reductionist" analysis which reduces systems to their component parts, cybernetics studies the structure of self-stabilizing whole systems.

The key principles of cybernetics are (1) that any system has one or more goals or conditions that it strives to maintain and (2) that the components of the system are linked through feedback mechanisms so that a change in one component will produce compensating changes in the others that will maintain the total system in its goal condition.

Consult: Bateson, Gregory, "Cybernetic Explanation," *American Behavioral Scientist* (10)8, 1967; Parsegian, V. L., *This Cybernetic*

*World of Men, Machines, and Earth Systems* (Garden City, N.Y.: Doubleday, 1972).

**Dalton, George** (b. 1926). An economic anthropologist and follower of Karl Polanyi, Dalton is a "substantivist" opposed to the rigid application of formal economic theories to the study of nonmarket societies and an advocate of concentrated cross-cultural studies of different exchange systems. His books include *Tribal and Peasant Economies* (1967).

**Dance.** Dance is a cultural form that results from creative processes which manipulate human bodies in time and space. The movement created is usually performed in conjunction with music and often in conjunction with poetry, giving a visual dimension to these rhythmically based audio phenomena. Dance may be performed for oneself, for a human audience, or for the gods, but it is usually oriented either toward participation or toward presentation. For example, European folk dance is oriented mainly toward participation (although there may be spectators) whereas ballet is oriented to an audience. For comparable examples from the non-Western world, dance of the Maring of New Guinea is preeminently participatory, while dance in Tonga is oriented toward an audience. Audiences may be human, such as for Japanese *buyo,* or supernatural, such as for Japanese *mi-kagura.*

As social behavior dance is interwoven with social organization, art, perception,

*A group of Yanomamö dancers parading around the village, carrying hallucinogens while in an ecstatic state of drug intoxication.*

psychology, and religion, varying from society to society by form and function. From all the physiological possibilities, each dance tradition employs a constellation of movements, positions, and dynamics put together in such a way that the resulting structure is specific to that tradition. Dance is not a "universal language" that can be understood cross-culturally without reference to the total sociocultural context any more than social structure or language can be. Dance is simply one of the surface manifestations of the underlying metastructure of a society. Although dance is often said to be universal, at least one society has no concept of dance (the Tasaday of the Philippines). From an anthropological point of view, one must begin without a priori assumptions that a cultural form which creatively manipulates human bodies in space and time exists or is perceived as such by a society. If such a category is recognized, the essential structure and social functions can be delineated. Movements can be notated with Labanotation (a kinetic system analogous to a phonetic alphabet) or by using other systems such as Benesh or Eshkol.

The varied functions of dance in human societies suggest that dance is not simply an aesthetic activity. Dance may be part of ritual or recreation. It may promote inner calm or be used to induce altered states of consciousness. Social functions range from social criticism to a validation of social distinctions; from supplicating the gods to honoring them. An adequate description of a society should ideally place the same emphasis on dance as that given it by the members of that society. For some societies an analysis of dance may be equally as important as an analysis of social structure, for the one may not be fully comprehensible without the other.

When confronted with dance data, anthropologists are sometimes tempted to use theoretically outdated frameworks such as that presented by Curt Sachs in 1933 (translated in 1937 as *World History of the Dance*) although they have discarded *Kulturkreise* doctrine and simple-to-complex evolutionary sequences for other cultural materials. Unfortunately, even more recent frameworks—such as Alan Lomax's choreometrics (the "measure of dance," or dance as a measure of culture") —do little to advance the study of dance but employ simple-to-complex evolutionary

*!Kung San girls engaging in improvisational dance near their encampment. Such dances later evolve into the serious all-night trance dances that San use in curing ceremonies.*

sequences and promote generalizations and correlations (in this case mainly with modes of subsistence) based on inadequate data and method. If one must argue by authority, one would do better to use Boas, whose orientation offers scope for analyzing dance as culture rather than using dance data to fit theories or generalizations. But for the future, analyses of internal structure, functions, and aesthetic qualities promise to be more productive for an understanding of dance as human behavior.

See also Art

Consult: Kaeppler, Adrienne L., "Method and Theory in Analyzing Dance Structure with an Analysis of Tongan Dance," *Ethnomusicology* 16 (2):173–217, 1972; Kealiinohomoku, Joanne W., "An Anthropologist Looks at Ballet as a Form of Ethnic Dance," *Impulse*, pp. 24–33, 1970; Kurath, Gertrude, "Panorama of Dance Ethnology," *Current Anthropology* 1(3): 233–254, 1960; Royce, Anya Peterson, "Choreology Today: A Review of the Field," in *New Dimensions in Dance Research: Anthropology and Dance—The American Indian,* ed. Tamara Comstock (New York: Committee on Research in Dance, 1974).

—Adrienne L. Kaeppler, Bernice P. Bishop Museum

**D'Andrade, Roy Goodwin** (b. 1931). Cultural anthropologist who has made important theoretical contributions to cognitive and mathematical anthropology and has done fieldwork in the United States, Mexico, and Africa.

**Dark, Philip John Crosskey** (b. 1918). English-born cultural anthropologist best known for his work on primitive art in Africa, in New Guinea, and among the Bush Negroes of Guyana.

**Dart, Raymond** (b. 1893). South African paleoanthropologist who recognized and identified the first australopithecine fossil at Taung in 1924 and later made further discoveries of australopithecines at Makapansgat. He is also responsible for postulating the concept of an osteodentokeratic (bone, tooth, horn) culture for the australopithecines.

**Darwin, Sir Charles Robert** (1809–1882). Deeply influenced by the biologist Henslow and the geologist Charles Lyell, Darwin developed the biological theory of natural selection, which he presented in 1858 (with A. R. Wallace) and published in 1859. *On the Origin of Species by Means of Natural Selection* is based on massive data including his own observation during his trip on the *Beagle (Zoology of the Voyage of the Beagle,* 1840). After considerable resistance and distortion, including Darwin's own later partial backtracking, the theory gained wide acceptance—especially after his equally influential *The Descent of Man*

*Charles Darwin.*

(1871). Darwin also published *The Expression of Emotions* among many other books on specifically biological subjects.

*See also* Darwinism; Wallace, Alfred Russel

**Darwin, Erasmus** (1731–1802). Grandfather of Charles Darwin. In 1794 he published *Zoonomia,* which argued for common descent of all life and suggested a struggle for existence.

**Darwinism.** This term denotes the theoretical approach to biological evolution that Charles Darwin and Alfred Russel Wallace first presented in 1858. The central concept of the theory is *natural selection,* which refers to the greater probability of survival and reproduction of those individuals of a species having "improved" adaptive characteristics for a given environment—usually produced by variations both spontaneous and deliberately fostered (as in stock breeding). Wallace and Darwin discovered a "natural tendency" of populations to vary, although the true explanation of variation appeared only later with the discovery of genes and mutation. Understanding of genetic processes, combined with the concept of natural selection, created the neo-Darwinian theory of evolution. Darwin developed the notion of "pangenesis" to account for variation and heredity, but this concept has not survived.

The cumulative selection of adaptive variations—through sexual reproduction passed down by their possessors, because of their greater probability of survival, to proportionally more members of the species—over generations leads to speciation: the differentiation of aggregates of individuals from other aggregates sufficient to prevent interbreeding under any normal circumstances.

The Darwinian doctrine had several major effects on Western thought. First, it destroyed the universally held notion of the fixity of species—that is, that species never changed or (in late-18th-century evolutionary conceptions) changed only in ways programmed in their essences or "germs." These conceptions were rooted in Judeo-Christian ontogeny: God's creation of *all* (immutable) species is continuously created naturally in a chance and unprogrammed process. No God is *needed,* although Darwinism does not assert the impossibility that a god originally created the whole process.

Second, Darwinism (based on Charles Lyell's geological conceptions, presented in 1832) extended earthly time immeasurably beyond Bishop Ussher's standardly accepted calculation of 4004 BC as the date of God's creation.

Third, Darwinism undercut the controversy regarding the various human races' descent from a common ancestor (monogenism) or from different ancestral lines (polygenism), since the natural selection model comprehended both possibilities. This controversy was linked with racialist theories of human differences and with what are now known as Social Darwinist (better Social Spencerian) doctrines. Generally, these doctrines misuse Darwin's theory and hold that different classes in society have achieved their status—high or low—by natural selection; the rich and powerful achieve theirs by virtue of advantageous variations ("survival of the fittest"—Herbert Spencer's term, later adopted by Darwin) and the poor and the weak ("the miserable" of Thomas Malthus, another major source of Darwin's inspiration) by virtue of deleterious variations. Proof of these propositions lay not in discovering the relevant variations but in the fact that the rich were rich and the poor poor—an exercise in circular reasoning still widely used to account for poverty today.

Fourth, Darwinism helped destroy the Western teleological view of a world moving toward a Final End—perfection, millennium, last judgment—by establishing a mechanism of change resting entirely on secular, material, and chance processes.

Together, these effects elicited fierce religiously based reactions still continuing today—especially in the United States, where fundamentalist groups attack textbooks that refer to the "hypothesis" of evolution, fundamentalist scientists attempt to assimilate geological time to Bishop Ussher's schedule, and some media still attack scientific organizations for "supporting" Darwin. It is striking that the Lamarckian theory of evolution in which species were, from Creation, programmed for change that was brought about by "use and disuse of organs" under given environmental conditions (a doctrine Darwin included in his theory) never elicited violent response: the theory did not destroy God, teleology, or established theological doctrines of species.

All elements of Darwin's theory had been thought of beforehand by Carolus

Linnaeus, Georges Buffon, Jean-Baptiste Lamarck, Erasmus Darwin, Charles Lyell, and others; Darwin's single innovation was their synthesis into a unified theory whose elements were linked by the process of natural selection.

See also Darwin, Charles; Evolution, genetic mechanisms of; Evolutionism; Linnaeus, Carolus; Lyell, Charles; Malthus, Thomas; Spencer, Herbert; Wallace, Alfred Russel

Consult: Darwin, Charles, *The Origin of Species by Means of Natural Selection* (New York: Macmillan, 1962); Eiseley, Loren, *Darwin's Century: Evolution and the Men Who Discovered it* (Garden City, N.Y.: Doubleday, 1958); Glick, Thomas F., *The Comparative Reception of Darwinism* (Austin: University of Texas Press, 1974); Greene, John C., *The Death of Adam: Evolution and Its Impact on Western Thought* (Ames: Iowa State University Press, 1959).

—Anthony Leeds, Boston University

## Darwinism, Social.

**Darwinism, Social.** See Social Darwinism.

## Dating, Absolute.

**Dating, Absolute.** Absolute time is measured by calendars based on cyclical celestial events, usually the rotation of the earth on its axis about the sun. Occasionally it has been possible to date archaeological cultures, for which written records remain, with their own calendars. Absolute (or chronometric) dating methods which measure progressive natural changes have provided the estimates of the ages of prehistoric cultures.

*Dendrochronology* and *varve analysis* are thus far the only absolute dating methods based on predictable cycles, which in both cases are annual. Under ideal conditions these methods are capable of providing dates which are reliable to the nearest year. A second group of absolute dating methods (e.g., *radiocarbon* and the other radioactive decay methods) is based on noncyclical natural changes which occur at a predictable rate. A third group (e.g., *archaeomagnetism*) is based on progressive changes whose rate is not predictable, although it has sometimes been possible to establish a time scale for these methods by using samples of known age.

Absolute dating methods which are not based on predictable cycles are affected by both random and systematic errors. Random errors due primarily to natural variation of datable material in the samples, measurement error, and probabilistic nature of the change being measured affect the precision or repeatability of the result. Random errors are responsible for the familiar ± figure following most reported radiocarbon results. Systematic errors which affect the accuracy of the result may be due to a variety of causes usually related to the validity of the basic assumptions of the method. Even when one or more of the basic assumptions are not true, it is sometimes possible to allow for this and obtain reasonably accurate estimates of a sample's true age. For example, variations in the radiocarbon time scale, due primarily to variation in atmospheric carbon-14 percentage in the past, has been detected with dendrochronologically dated bristlecone pine samples for the past 7,500 years, and extensive tables have been prepared to correct reported radiocarbon dates. Dendrochronologically calibrated radiocarbon dates can now be used to establish obsidian hydration, archaeomagnetic, and other time scales in areas where dendrochronology has not been applied.

At this time it is not possible to check the results obtained on samples older than 7,500 years using dendrochronology or any other technique of such high reliability. However, consistent dating of deposits and material older than 7,500 years using two or more methods based on different assumptions increases the credibility of the results. Consistent independent potassium-argon and fission track results on deposits at Olduvai Gorge were instrumental in convincing many anthropologists that 1.75 million years was a reasonably correct estimate for the age of the *Zinjanthropus* (*Australopithecus robustus*) fossils. In the future, further multiple dating of archaeological material will improve the reliability of results.

Another source of error is the lack of contemporaneity of some samples with the deposits in which they are found. Radiocarbon and tree-ring dates which are apparently too old have been obtained on wooden construction material which was reused in later buildings or for fuel. Fortunately some of the newer dating methods (e.g., alpha-recoil tracks, thermoluminescence, and obsidian hydration) now make it possible to directly date culturally diagnostic material.

Although there is considerable overlap in the time ranges that may be dated by the various methods, they effectively complement one another so that it is now possible to obtain results on material dating from a few to more than 4 billion years.

See also Dating, relative; Dendrochonology; Obsidian hydration; Paleomagnetism and archaeomagnetism; Physical-chemical methods of dating; Radiocarbon dating; Thermoluminescence; Varve analysis

Consult: Michels, J. W., *Dating Methods in Archaeology* (New York: Seminar Press, 1973); Smiley, T. L. (ed.), "Geochronology, with Special Reference to Southwestern United States," *University of Arizona Bulletin* 26(2), 1955.

—Daniel Wolfman, Arkansas Archaeological Survey

## Dating, Relative.

**Dating, Relative.** Archaeology is a historical discipline—time is its most crucial dimension. A chronological framework is the first requirement for even the most straightforward aspects of archaeology, such as the cataloging of prehistoric events. In fact, time is an essential element of archaeological context and must be specified as part of every archaeological definition or description. The larger goals of archaeology—the reconstruction and interpretation of culture history and the investigation of cultural processes and cultural evolution—rely even more heavily on control of the dimension of time. An enormous amount of archaeological research is directed toward measuring and classifying time by perfecting and elaborating dating techniques and constructing chronologies.

It is convenient to distinguish two types of dating: absolute and relative. An absolute date involves discrete, measurable time intervals and is normally expressed in solar years, correlated with our own calendar system. Relative dating refers to the determination of the sequence of events; a relative date specifies that one thing is older or younger than another. Most archaeological dating is relative. The techniques of relative dating are applicable to a much wider variety of archaeological situations and problems than absolute dating methods, which depend on the availability of special types of evidence and which often require complex laboratory equipment. Most absolute dating—radiocarbon and obsidian hydration dating, for example—actually involves the calibration of relative dates to provide an approximation of absolute dates.

In the early 19th century, Scandinavian archaeologists developed a three-part subdivision of prehistoric time—into Stone, Bronze, and Iron Ages—as a means of ordering collections of prehistoric artifacts. The basic validity of this sequence of technological stages was subsequently verified in many parts of the Old World by stratigraphic observation. The usefulness of this three-age system as a framework for placing prehistoric artifacts in a chronological context made it the first widely used relative chronology. The principles involved—stratigraphy and dating by placement in an evolutionary sequence of artifact types—are fundamental to archaeological chronology.

Stratigraphic observation is the most important single technique for reconstructing temporal relationships in archaeology; it is basic to the study of archaeological sites. The underlying principle of stratigraphy is the *law of superposition,* which states that the accumulation of archaeological deposits—the material traces produced by human occupation—is progressive. In normal circumstances lower levels accumulated before, and are older than, layers above them. In practice, stratigraphy is often not straightforward. A variety of complicating factors and special situations must be taken into account, but careful stratigraphic observation usually permits the reconstruction of sequences of events at archaeological sites. Relative chronologies can often be extended to cover long time spans and large geographical areas by the correlation of stratigraphic sequences from separate sites—most often on the basis of similarities among assemblages of artifacts.

When artifacts in an archaeological deposit indicate links with a neighboring region in which chronological control is better, cross-dating may provide an indication of relative or absolute dating. Similarly, geochronology, paleontology, and palynology sometimes permit relative (or even absolute) dating when archaeological deposits can be correlated with established geological, climatic, faunal, or floral sequences.

Seriation—the construction of developmental sequences of cultural traits (stylistic change or change in types or features of artifacts)—is another basic technique of relative dating. Sir Flinders Petrie's "sequence dating" of predynastic Egyptian grave goods at the beginning of the 20th century was one of the earliest examples of the use of changes in artifacts for chronological ordering. Seriation rests on the assumption that traits appear, reach a maximum in popularity, then

decrease in frequency and disappear, never to reappear in identical form. Observation of the presence, absence, and relative abundance of a series of traits can therefore be used to order archaeological assemblages and the deposits in which they occur, although additional evidence such as stratigraphy may be necessary to determine the direction of the sequence.

In many situations, progressive changes in natural phenomena can be measured to provide a relative date for objects associated with archaeological deposits. Buried bones and teeth, for example, gradually absorb fluorine from groundwater, while the nitrogen content of buried bone progressively decreases. The relative fluorine or nitrogen content of bones buried under the same conditions indicates their relative ages. The rates of these processes, however, vary greatly with local conditions (such as the fluorine content of groundwater), so that these measurements provide reliable relative ages only within single sites or very localized areas. Processes subject to less variation—such as the disintegration of carbon 14 in organic matter and the accumulation of a hydrated layer on the exposed surfaces of obsidian—can be calibrated to provide absolute dates of varying accuracy and reliability.

*See also* Dating, absolute; Lithic ages; Prehistoric archaeology; Sequence dating; Stratigraphy; Superposition, law of
Consult: Fagan, Brian M., *In the Beginning: An Introduction to Archaeology,* 2nd ed. (Boston: Little, Brown, 1975); Hole, Frank, and Heizer, Robert F., *An Introduction to Prehistoric Archaeology,* 3rd ed. (New York: Holt, 1973); Michael, H. N., and Ralph, E. K., *Dating Techniques for the Archaeologist* (Cambridge, Mass.: M.I.T. Press, 1971); Michels, J. W., *Dating Methods in Archaeology* (New York: Seminar Press, 1973).
—*John S. Henderson, Cornell University*

**Death.** *See* Burial.

**Decoys and Lures.** *See* Fishing; Hunting.

**Deep Structure of Language.** This term refers to a level of analysis in transformational grammar which is contrasted with *surface* structure (level of actual pronunciation). At the surface level syntactic and semantic structure is not always apparent in

the ordering of sentence elements. Relationships such as those between subject and object of verb phrases are dealt with in the deep structure of transformational-generative grammar. The following sentences illustrate the distinction:
1. John is eager to please.
2. John is easy to please.
At the surface level both sentences are identical syntactically. But in sentence 1 John does the pleasing and is the subject while in sentence 2 John is the one who is pleased. In sentence 2, then, John is actually the object and only superficially the subject.

In a technical sense, deep structure can be defined as phrase-makers generated by the phrase structure rules of a grammar. These rules contain all the information necessary to enable a speaker to comprehend and interpret the meanings of a sentence. A grammar of a language must account for differences of structure of the kind seen in sentences 1 and 2 and thus uses a deep structure level with a series of other rules, called transformational rules, which apply before a sentence reaches the surface level.

Another group of linguists, known as the generative semanticists, use the term *deep structure* slightly differently. For them, deep structure is not just syntactic but is really semantic. Semantic rules rather than syntactic ones account for the fact that speakers recognize the differences between sentences 1 and 2.

*See also* Chomsky, Noam; Grammar; Linguistics; Phrase structure; Surface structure of language; Transformational linguistics
Consult: Chomsky, Noam, *Language and Mind,* 2nd ed. (New York: Harcourt Brace Jovanovich, 1972); Fromkin, Victoria, and Rodman, Robert, *An Introduction to Language* (New York: Holt, 1974); Thomas, Owen, and Kintgen, Eugene R., *Transformational Grammar and the Teacher of English* (New York: Holt, 1974).
—*Elizabeth A. Brandt, Arizona State University*

**Deetz, James John Fanto** (b. 1930). Archaeologist best known for his pioneering work, based on extensive mathematical analyses, on the relationship between residence patterns, ceramics, and social organization among the Arikara.

**Defense Mechanisms.** In Freudian theory, this term refers to a series of psychological strategies that one may adopt, usually unconsciously, to avoid confronting unpleasant or unacceptable facts—usually about oneself.

Freud believed that there is an inherent tension between individual and society. He argued that there would always be a conflict between the instinctual drives of the individual and the prohibitions that civilized society must necessarily impose. Many potential human behaviors and desires are socially unacceptable, and those who find that they have transgressed or wish to transgress the relevant norms may experience feelings of intense anxiety and guilt. These feelings are reduced by the defense mechanisms—which, for example, may permit the repression of a forbidden sexual urge into the unconscious, its projection onto another person, its sublimation into artistic pursuits, or its displacement into harmless dreams.

All normal humans probably have some resort to defense mechanisms, but excessive reliance on these unconscious strategies is regarded in Freudian theory as an indication of neurosis.

*See also* Displacement; Fixation; Freud, Sigmund; Projection; Reaction formation; Repression; Sublimation
—Ian Robertson, Cambridge University

**Deformation and Mutilation.** The ways in which humans have chosen to deform or mutilate themselves seemingly are endless. The ethnographic record is infinite in its variety of ways to incise, mark, and reshape almost every part of the human body. These range from various genital mutilations (circumcision, subincision, clitorectomy) to changing the shape of a baby's head (making it rounder or longer) or the shape of a woman's foot. They include various kinds of tattooing, cutting off fingers, knocking out teeth, inserting lip and ear plugs, filing teeth, and wearing scars (such as Prussian dueling scars or those earned by Fulani youths at the *soro* initiation). The kinds of mutilation can be divided roughly into two categories: those involved in rites of passage and those regarded as personal adornment.

**Rites of Passage.** As first defined by A. E. Van Gennep and then redefined by Turner, Biedleman, and others, rites of passage are processes which lead to change in the social identity of those undergoing the rituals. The most usual occasions of rites of passage are birth, puberty, marriage, and death. These

*Sara-Kaba woman from the vicinity of Lake Chad, shown with lip plates that have been inserted for reasons of beauty and prestige.*

rites mark events which are social as well as biological, an important factor in understanding them. Each rite of passage has three phases: separation, a liminal phase, and reintegration. The initiate passes from one stage through a kind of ritual death, lives in a state of limbo out of society, and then is symbolically reborn to a new social position. Frequently, a physical sign marks that new position.

Perhaps the most spectacular of these new signs are the various forms of genital mutilation. Among these circumcision is by far the most frequent. It is simply the removal of the foreskin of the penis. Certainly it was performed for reasons other than hygiene throughout the world. The widespread occurrence of the practice precludes simple diffusion as an explanation. Although variations in the circumcision ceremony are many, the essential meaning transcends these variations. In each case, circumcision is a prerequisite for full adult status. No uncircumcised male can marry in those societies in which it forms part of a rite of passage.

The following descriptions of circumcision are presented to stress the regularities that underlie them. Circumcision has long been a distinguishing characteristic of Jews. It is a sign of their covenant with God. So much is circumcision regarded as a sign of their identity that Hadrian's attempt to ban it led to open revolt. Recent scholarship holds that his purposes in banning the practice about AD 130 were humane: he considered circumcision and castration to be equal to murder; in fact, he opposed any kind of mutilation. What Hadrian failed to understand was that his humanely intended actions struck at a symbolic means of expressing self-identity among those he purposed to help.

Whereas Jews circumcise males on the eighth day after their birth and do so in a public fashion, they are almost unique in circumcising males so early in life. In Turkey, for example, males are circumcised at about the age of puberty. Fortitude is expected of the initiate at the time of circumcision. Future prestige depends on his calm demeanor during the operation. The same circumstances prevail in other places, such as in Dahomey among the Fon and among the Masai of E Africa.

Many Australian aboriginal groups practice subincision along with circumcision and other types of deformation. Subincision is an incisure of the urethra along the bottom of the penis. Bruno Bettelheim has suggested that female imitation is at the root of these practices. Yehudi Cohen has suggested that Bettelheim may be right regarding subincision but wrong regarding circumcision. In any case, the aborigines seem to lead the world in various kinds of mutilation. In addition to circumcision and subincision, diverse groups also practice piercing of the nasal septum, tooth pulling, various blood rites (opening of an arm vein or penis incisure or both), hair removal, cicatrization (scarification), the tearing out of fingernails, and the gashing open of their own heads by mourners at funerals. Some aboriginal groups also circumcise girls, which involves cutting the sheath covering the clitoris. Also, many groups cut girls' hymens. Among the aborigines at Groote Eylandt, the labia majora are removed. No woman who has not undergone these deformations can be married, for it is believed that any child she might have would surely be born dead.

While not as prevalent as circumcision, clitoridectomy, the removal of the clitoris, is found in a number of human societies. It occurs in New Guinea, Australia, parts of Africa (especially Ethiopia, Egypt, E Africa), the Malay archipelago, S Europe, parts of South America, W Asia, and India.

**Personal Adornment.** Deformation can take place as a way of decorating or adorning the body. On closer examination, however, it is often the case that such decorations are in fact elements of rites of passage. For example, binding the feet of wealthy Chinese women marked their status as clearly as circumcision marked the status of the Masai. Filing a Dukawa's teeth marked him as a group member. Even "purely" decorative markings serve as markers of one kind of status or another: age, sex, ethnic, class, political. Typical markings and deformations in our own society include tattooing, piercing ears, inserting diamonds in incisor teeth, plastic surgery ("nose jobs," face lifts, silicone inflation of breasts), and circumcision. Increasingly, women are asking to have the sheath covering the clitoris removed. Perhaps sex-change operations should also be considered under this rubric.

**The Meaning of Deformation.** Without denying the possible truth of various psychoanalytic explanations, it is equally true that they are inadequate to an anthropological understanding of deformation when such deformation is culturally determined. Subincision may involve an element of "vaginal envy," for instance, but it must also be regarded as the symbolic expression of group membership. Subincision is a sign of changed status. It is necessary to participation in adult roles. Deformation distinguishes people clearly and reduces any ambiguity regarding their status.

*See also* Adornment; Circumcision; Clitorectomy; Rites of passage; Ritual; Subincision
Consult: Bettelheim, Bruno, *Symbolic Wounds, Puberty Rites, and the Envious Male* (Glencoe, Ill.: Free Press, 1954); Cohen, Yehudi, *Transition from Childhood to Adolescence* (Chicago: Aldine, 1964).
—*Frank A. Salamone, St. John's University*

**Democracy.** This term refers to a system of government in which the power to decide upon major public policies rests, theoretically, with the entire people. Thus the power to govern is vested either in the people themselves or in their elected representatives. Small, homogeneous societies often make democratic decisions by reaching group consensus. In larger societies decisions may be made by voting. In such societies democracy is usually held to involve the free choice of elected representatives and freedom of speech, of the press, and of political association. The U.S. Bill of Rights has been considered a classic statement of democratic principles.

*See also* Communism; Fascism; Government; Political Anthropology; Power; Social control; Socialism; Totalitarianism
Consult: Dahl, Robert A. (ed.), *Political Oppositions in Western Democracies* (New Haven: Yale University Press, 1969); Niebuhr, Reinhold, and Sigmund, Paul E., *The Democratic Experience: Past and Present* (New York: Praeger, 1969).

**Demography.** Demography is the quantitative analysis of human populations. Major concerns of demographers include the distribution of populations over space, their composition, and their growth and decline over time. Basic to the study of demography is the collection of data on population size, age and sex distributions, marital status, and birthrates and deathrates. These data are gathered from government censuses, historical records, and direct interviews. Demography often functions as a bridge between various disciplines, providing the basic materials for the analysis of social, economic, and political change.

The works of Thomas Malthus (1766–1834) have been of particular importance to demographers. Malthus (who had fourteen children) held that populations tend to increase more rapidly than their food supplies. Though many of his ideas have been refuted, Malthus did call attention to the social aspects of population pressure and the relationship between economic and demographic variables.

Anthropological demographers are particularly interested in the social, biological, and cultural contexts of population change, as well as in the ways social, cultural, and demographic variables act upon one another. They are concerned, for example, with the effect of ethnic conflict, disease, and modernization on migration patterns and general population structure. In turn, they are also interested in the impact of demographic processes on socioeconomic change, particularly in the developing nations.

Specialists in the field of demography include paleodemographers and population geneticists. Paleodemographers, often working closely with archaeologists, are concerned with the reconstruction of demographic variables in early human populations (see Cook 1972). Population geneticists study the ways in which variables such as inbreeding and migration affect the structure of the gene pool.

*See also* Malthus, Thomas; Population genetics
Consult: Baker, Paul T., and Sanders, William, "Demographic Studies in Anthropology," in *Annual Review of Anthropology*, ed. Bernard Siegel (Palo Alto, Calif.: Stanford Univ. Press, 1972); Cook, S. F., *Prehistoric Demography* (Reading, Mass.: Addison-Wesley, 1972); Malthus, T., Huxley, Julian, and Osborn, Frederick, *On Population* (New York: New American Library, 1960); Wrong, Dennis H., *Population and Society* (New York: Random House, 1961).
—*Phillip S. Katz, State University of New York, Brockport*

**Dendrochronology.** Also known as treering dating, dendrochronology is an absolute dating method based on the covariation of one climatic variable (often rainfall) with annual growth of ring thickness in some tree species. Regional master charts of variation of ring width for individual tree species are established by comparing temporally overlapping sequences of ring widths in living trees with wood and charcoal samples from historic and prehistoric sites. Wood and charcoal samples of unknown age can be dated by comparing their patterns of ring thickness with a regional master chart. The method has had its greatest application in the arid SW United States, where master charts covering up to 2,000 years have been developed.

*See also* Dating, absolute

**Denial.** See Defense mechanisms.

**Denial of Oedipus Complex as Universal.** *See* Oedipus complex.

**Denotation.** Denotative kinship terms must include three criteria: gender, generation, and genealogical connection (e.g., "brother"). Classificatory systems require

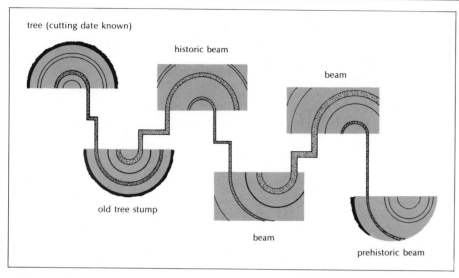

tree (cutting date known)

historic beam

beam

old tree stump

beam

prehistoric beam

*Schematic diagram showing how tree-ring dates can be traced back through wood samples from different, but overlapping, ages (adapted from Zeuner).*

two or more criteria, making denotation a specialized classificatory system.

*See also* Kinship; Kinship terminologies

## Dental Formulas of Primates.

A dental formula is an expression of the number of teeth of each kind in one-half of the upper and lower tooth rows. Multiplication of the formula by two yields the total dental arrangement for a species. Among the primates some variation exists—from thirty-eight teeth in the tree shrews to thirty-two teeth in humans, apes, and the Old World monkeys. The prosimians exhibit more variability in the number and arrangement of their teeth than the anthropoids. A knowledge of dental formulas is especially useful in differentiating fossil finds that consist of only dentofacial fragments and in tracing possible phylogenetic relationships.

The key is illustrated below with the hominoid formula:

$$\begin{array}{c|cccc} & I & C & PM & M \\ U = & 2 & 1 & 2 & 3 \\ L = & 2 & 1 & 2 & 3 \end{array} \times 2 = 32$$

In this formula I = incisors, C = canines, PM = premolars, M = molars, U = upper jaw, and L = lower jaw.

The following is a phylogenetic outline of the various primate dental formulas:

1. *Tupaiiformes*
   $$\frac{2133}{3133} \times 2 = 38$$

2. *Tarsiiformes*
   $$\frac{2133}{1133} \times 2 = 34$$

3. *Lorisiformes*
   $$\frac{2133}{2133} \times 2 = 36$$

4. *Lemuriformes*
   *Lemuridae*
   $$\frac{2133}{2133} \times 2 = 36$$

   *Indriidae*
   $$\frac{2123}{1123} \times 2 = 30$$

   *Daubenthonidea*
   $$\frac{1013}{1003} \times 2 = 18$$

5. *Ceboidea*
   *Cebidae*
   $$\frac{2133}{2133} \times 2 = 36$$

   *Callithricidae*
   $$\frac{2132}{2132} \times 2 = 32$$

6. *Cercopithecoidea*
   $$\frac{2132}{2123} \times 2 = 32$$

7. *Hominoidea*
   $$\frac{2123}{2123} \times 2 = 32$$

*See also* Dentition of fossils; Primates, evolutionary features of
Consult: LeGros Clark, W. E., *The Antecedents of Man* (Chicago: University of Chicago Press, 1971); Napier, J., and Napier, P., *Handbook of Living Primates* (New York: Academic Press, 1968).
—*James F. Metress, University of Toledo*

## Dentition of Fossils.

The shapes of various teeth, their cusp patterns, wear patterns, relative sizes, and position in the jaw are perhaps the primary diagnostic features of fossils. The great taxonomic significance of the dentition stems from several factors: the excellent preservation of dentition compared to other parts of the body; the hereditary nature of dentition; and the fact that the teeth reflect the diet of a fossil, thereby also allowing some inferences about adaptation, life-style, and paleoecology. Our knowledge and classification of the earliest known hominids, the ramapithecines, is based solely on the evidence of jaws and teeth.

*See also* Adaptation, biological; Dental formulas of primates; Hominids; Pongids; *Ramapithecus*

## Deoxyribonucleic Acid (DNA).

This substance is the hereditary material of the cell, capable of self-replication and of coding the production of proteins carrying on metabolic functions. Together with a protein coat, DNA composes most of the chromosome. Genes are segments of the chromosomal DNA molecules, which are made up of smaller units called nucleotides that consist of a sugar (deoxyribose), phosphate, and four nitrogenous bases—adenine, thymine, cytosine, and guanine. Variation in genetic coding results from the sequence in which the bases are arranged within the gene segments of the molecule. This model for DNA was proposed in 1953 by J. D. Watson and F. Crick.

## Descent.

Descent is the principle by which successive parent-child (lineal) links are organized. Every individual has two possible ascending lineal links (one to his/her mother, one to his/her father) and two descending lineal links (one to his/her daughter, one to his/her son). Of these possible lineal links, certain links are stressed and others ignored in a given system of descent.

The most common choice of organization is to stress links to individuals of one sex and to ignore links to individuals of the opposite sex. This is called *unilineal* descent since one line is stressed. Clearly, links to males could be stressed (patrilineal) or links to females (matrilineal). Societies which use both unilineal descent principles, each for a different purpose, are said to have double unilineal descent.

Nonunilineal descent is more complicated, and there is less general agreement on the terms to be used to describe each possible combination of lineal links. Although the terms *bilateral descent* and *cognatic descent* are used as synonyms by some authors, they are beginning to be distinguished. Cognatic descent is described from the point of view of an apical ancestor to whom a number of individuals are linked by any combination of male and female links. Bilateral descent (the principle of descent used in the United States) is described from the point of view of an individual who traces all of his/her ascending lineal relatives through all possible combinations of male and female links.

Bilineal descent is different from either bilateral or double unilineal descent. It is used to describe the Australian section systems where the patrilineal and matrilineal principles intersect. The two remaining possibilities are utilized by a small number of societies. In one system females trace descent through females and males through males. In the other, male and female links alternate so that a female is descended from her father, her father's mother, her father's mother's father, and so forth.

The approximate frequency of the use of each type of descent is summarized in the following chart (adapted from Keesing 1975: 26):

| DESCENT TYPE | NUMBER OF CULTURES | % |
|---|---|---|
| Patrilineal | 248 | 44 |
| Matrilineal | 84 | 15 |
| Double unilineal and bilineal | 28 | 5 |
| Bilateral and others | 205 | 36 |

**Descent Groups.** Descent is often used as the principle by which individuals are recruited to a social group. The existence of a descent principle, however, does not necessarily imply that there will also be descent groups. If descent is used as a recruitment principle, the resulting groups are called descent groups. The use of a particular type of descent principle for recruitment produces a particular kind of descent group. Therefore, use of patrilineality produces patrilineages or patriclans, matrilineality produces matrilineages or matriclans, cognatic descent produces ramages.

**Descent, Inheritance, Succession.** Descent is a concept separate from inheritance and succession. Confusion arises for the be-

### PATRILINEAGES, PATRICLANS, PHRATRY

*A lineage is a kin group whose members can actually trace their descent through either a line of males (patrilineage) or a line of females (matrilineage). Shown here are six skeletal patrilineages (A, B, C, D, E, F); females are omitted for simplicity.*

*A clan is a kin group composed of two or more lineages, all of which believe they can trace their descent from a common ancestor but need not actually demonstrate their ability to do so. A clan composed of patrilineages is a patriclan; of matrilineages, a matriclan. Shown here are two patriclans (I, II).*

*A phratry consists of two or more clans that believe they can trace their descent from a common ancestor but need not actually demonstrate their ability to do so. The largest kin group shown here (included within the dashed line) is such a phratry.*

ginning student since the descent principle is often the principle used for inheritance or succession. However, the three concepts are distinct and have been consistently distinguished since W. H. R. Rivers (1924). *Inheritance* is the transmission of property. *Succession* is the transmission of office. For Rivers, *descent* means the right to membership in a group.

**Descent Theory.** It is on Rivers' interpretation of descent that descent theory rests. Currently, however, a distinction is made between a descent principle and the use of a descent principle as the basis for recruitment to a social group. Descent is merely the filiation of children. Although descent may also be used for determining inheritance, succession, and group membership, this distinction does not invalidate descent theory.

*See also* Alliance; Descent group; Descent rules; Kinship

Consult: Keesing, Roger, *Kin Groups and Social Structure* (New York: Holt, 1975); Rivers, W. H. R., *Social Organization* (London: Keegan Paul, 1924).

—Lilah Pengra, Kenyon College

**Descent Group.** A descent group is a kin group whose members are recruited by one

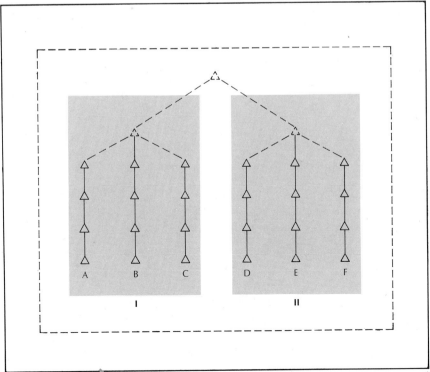

of the principles of descent (matrilineal, patrilineal, cognatic). A descent group whose members are related through known links to an ancestor is a *lineage*. A descent group whose members *say* they are related to the same ancestor but cannot trace the specific links is called a *clan* or, less commonly, a *sib*. A local descent group also has the membership requirement that members live in the same area. Descent groups, particularly lineages, are often corporate groups; that is, members share rights and responsibilities in an estate (e.g., land, women).

*See also* Clan; Descent; Descent rule; Kinship and descent; Lineage

**Descent Rule.** The principle used to trace lineal kin links from generation to generation. A child is filiated to both its parents, but the descent rule stresses one link or the other.

*See also* Descent; Descent group; Kinship and descent

**Descriptive Linguistics (structural linguistics).** The goal of descriptive linguistics is to formulate a theory and methodology for describing objectively the grammars of human languages. *Synchronic* linguistics is the description of a language at a specific point in time, past or present. *Diachronic* (historical) linguistics is the description of a language or group of related languages at different points in time and an account of the changes in them across time. Descriptive linguistics is concerned above all else with describing accurately and objectively how language is actually spoken rather than how someone thinks it should be spoken (Bloomfield 1933).

**Synchronic Description.** The structural levels of language are phonology, morphology, and syntax. Each level consists of *forms* and *constructions*. Forms are the elements that occur at a particular level; constructions are the patterns or combinations of forms that can occur at that level. Another term for forms and constructions is *immediate constituents* (Hockett 1958). An immediate constituent is a grammatical construction at one level which consists of a sequence of forms (immediate constituents) from the next lower level of structure.

**Phonology.** The phonology of a language consists of phonetics and phonemics. Pho-

netics is the description of all the speech sounds (*phones*) and their modes of articulation; phonemics is the description of how the phones are organized into contrastive sets. A phoneme is a set of phones which contrasts with all other phonemes in the language; the phones which constitute a phoneme are called allophones. For example, the English phoneme symbolized by the letter *p* consists of three phonetically similar allophones none of which occurs in exactly the same contexts as the others: the aspirated allophone [pʰ] occurs at the beginning of words and medially (e.g., *pot*); the unaspirated allophone [p] occurs after initial *s* (e.g., *spot*); and the unreleased, unaspirated allophone [p] occurs at the end of a word (e.g., *top*). The phonology also indicates all the possible sequences of phonemes in the language—*str*- is a possible initial combination of phonemes in English (as in *strike*), but *stw*- is not (although it is in other languages).

**Morphology.** The morphology of a language is a description of morphemes and morphophonemics. A morpheme, made up of a sequence of phonemes, is the smallest unit of language that has meaning. Some morphemes have more than one phonemic form; these variant forms of a morpheme are known as *allomorphs*. The prefix in the words *impossible*, *insane*, *irregular*, and *illegal* is an example of a single morpheme with various allomorphs (symbolized by the letters *im-*, *in-*, *ir-*, *il-*), each one occurring in a different context from any of the other allomorphs. Morphophonemics is the description of the phonemic composition of allomorphs according to the contexts in which each allomorph occurs. For example, the allomorph is *im-* when the following sound in the word is a *bilabial* phone (as in *im*possible, *im*mutable), *il-* when the following sound in the word is a *lateral* phone (as in *il*legal, *il*legible), and so on. The morphology also indicates all the possible combinations of morphemes in the language. Thus even though the English prefixes *in-* and *un-* share the same meaning, each occurs only with certain other morphemes to form words—*in-* (but not *un-*) occurs in the words *in*sane and *in*vincible; *un-* (but not *in-*) occurs in the words *un*necessary and *un*do.

**Syntax.** The syntax of a language is the sequential patterning of words within phrases and the patterning of phrases within sentences. Each distinct pattern is a construc-

tion, and the elements within a construction are the *forms* (immediate constituents) of the construction. Forms which occupy the same position within a construction constitute a *formclass*. Syntax is a description of all the constructions and formclasses within phrases and sentences. Syntax also encompasses relations of *government* and *concord* among the constituents of a construction. In the sentence *Homer speaks Latin*, the verb *speaks* requires (governs) that the subject of the sentence be *human*; and the fact that the form of the verb is *speaks* (rather than *speak*) indicates concord between the verb and the subject, *Homer*.

**Historical Linguistics.** The goals of historical linguistics are to reconstruct and describe the grammars of ancient, unrecorded languages (or earlier, unrecorded grammars of recent languages) and to determine whether languages are genetically related (descendants of a common parent language). *Comparative reconstruction* examines the grammars of related languages at successive time periods to determine what changes—innovations or losses—have occurred in each language in order to reconstruct the grammar of the parent language. *Internal reconstruction* examines successive stages of one language—in the absence of any record of related languages—in order to determine the earlier, unrecorded form of the language. The reconstruction of unrecorded, parent languages makes it possible to determine the nature of relationships among groups of languages distantly separated in space and time. This is the basis for language classification—for determining language families. For example, Indo-European is a widely dispersed family of genetically related languages which are descended from a common parent language (Proto-Indo-European) which probably evolved on the plains to the north of the Caucasus Mountains some time before 3000 BC. Historical reconstruction also enables linguists to determine which languages are not genetically related to each other and to state whether similar elements found in two languages are due to genetic inheritance, to borrowing, or merely to chance.

**Language Variation.** Another goal of descriptive linguistics is to describe the range of regional and social linguistic variation among speakers of the same language and to determine, in communities where people are bilingual or speak more than one variety (dialect) of the same language, what factors influence the choice of one language or dialect over the others in particular situations (sociolinguistics).

See also Generative grammar; Linguistics
Consult: Bloomfield, Leonard, *Language* (New York: Holt, 1933); Hockett, Charles, *A Course in Modern Linguistics* (New York: Macmillan, 1958); Joos, Martin (ed.), *Readings in Linguistics: I* (Chicago: University of Chicago Press, 1957).
—*Charles T. Snow, California State University, Chico*

**Descriptive Statistics.** See Statistical methods.

**Despotism.** Despotism is a form of absolute rule whereby virtually total power for social control is lodged in the hands of some centralized governmental institutions. As such, despotism is confined to societies characterized by an explicit, formal, centralized, complex, and powerful institution for governance—that is to say, a state. For this reason, despotic rule is rare and of short duration in the diffuse, informal, egalitarian systems of governance found in bands and tribes. Despotic power can be applied both within the boundaries of the society and also for external purposes such as war and conquest.

See also Oriental despotism; State; State, development of the

**Determinism.** Determinists argue that scientists should study causes of cultures and their changes rather than simply describe diversities. Social phenomena, like natural ones, obey orderly laws, it is argued. Cultural evolution or seemingly bizarre human activities have discoverable *basic* causes—among them economic, racial, environmental, psychological, and religious factors.

Disagreement over which factor determined the others (or whether any did), combined with political and moral issues raised by 19th-century racial and economic theories, caused Boasian anthropologists to reject determinism. Functionalists treated culture as a closed system; factors caused each other. Freudians reintroduced psychological determinism, and Marxists kept economic determinism alive.

Today many anthropologists have returned to determinist theories, especially in concepts of materialism and ecology developed by Julian Steward, Leslie White, Marvin Harris, and their students, but disagreement remains. Structuralists propose idealist, psychological causation in new form, in contrast with materialist theories based on "technoenvironmental" data. Modern theory is *probabilistic* rather than mechanically programmatic. Although many people still object to determinism as fatalistic or dehumanizing, proper use of the concept is a natural outgrowth of the anthropological search for cultural regularities and principles.

See also Cultural ecology; Marx, Karl; Marxism; Structuralism
Consult: Harris, Marvin, *The Rise of Anthropological Theory* (New York: Crowell, 1968); White, Leslie, *The Science of Culture* (New York: Farrar, Straus & Giroux, 1969).
—*John R. Cole, Ithaca College*

**Determinism, Economic.** See Economic determinism.

**Deterministic Process.** A deterministic process, in contrast to a stochastic process, is an event in which the outcome is not influenced by chance. Rather, it is strictly determined by initial conditions, knowledge of which enables prediction of the outcome.

See also Markov chain; Stochastic process; Systems theory

**Deutero Learning.** This term (literally, secondary learning) refers to incidental learning—learning that results not from any conscious effort but as a result of learning something else. For example, a learner may be asked to learn the order of the numbers on a set of cards. The numbers may also be color coded. The learner may recall the correct association between number and color without having been told to concentrate on it. Such learning contrasts with goal-directed activity. It is operationalized and tested in memory experiments in which the learner is tested on recall of items she or he was not asked to learn. The concept of deutero learning has become important to psychological anthropologists, who use it to show the subtle yet powerful consequences of language acquisition and other aspects of enculturation. Not only is the person learning what is explicitly taught, he or she is also absorbing norms, values, and learning styles—all of which are not conscious, yet nevertheless are crucial elements determining a person's behavior and subsequent learning experiences.

**Development, Economic.** In a general sense, this term refers both to an end state and also to an evolutionary sequence in which a society's subsistence patterns change. Economic development viewed as a process of change is the most frequent conceptualization. It generally involves the transition from one subsistence mode to another—e.g., from shifting cultivation to sedentary agriculture or from a predominantly agrarian society to one whose population is employed primarily in industry. The affected population may be aware of or oblivious to the change, which may be planned and encouraged by leadership. Those experiencing economic development may look upon its consequences in the social, political, and ritual spheres of their lifestyles as desirable or undesirable.

A society's economic characteristics often were the basis for classical evolutionists' construction of stages. Each stage was thought to be accompanied by certain political, ritual, and social attributes. Frequently the apex of this evolutionary scale was the economic system and attendant institutions of the investigator's society. The evolutionary perspective continues today in highly qualified and modified form. Stages, if postulated, are void of the moralistic connotations of the past.

Studies of acculturation and culture contact have sensitized anthropologists to the inadequacies of past theory. It was World War II, and the consequent emergence of new nation-states, which prompted scholars to turn their attention to studies of development. Cooperation with economists, psychologists, sociologists, political scientists, and leaders of new nations resulted in the use of conceptual tools and expertise. Fruition of this collaboration has yielded the general consensus that economic development is a process which encourages a cultural ethos and social relations akin to the Weberian concept of "rationality"—salient characteristics of which are the prevalence of the market principle and the law of supply and demand, the predominance of general-purpose money as a means of exchange, the tendency for labor and land to become commodities, and structural complexity indicating greater interdependence between economic entities in addition to occupational specialization. Urbanization and industrialization are generally thought to be key elements in the process; the importance of each is a moot point.

The contemporary anthropological investigation of economic development continues to be influenced by Karl Marx's materialistic conception of history as well as Max Weber's conception of the role of ideas and religion in economic pursuits, Talcott Parsons' pattern variables, and David McClelland's notion of need achievement.

Neoevolutionary interpretations of economic development are coming under increasing criticism for being manifestations of ethnocentrism and intellectual justifications for Western capitalism.

Consult: Brode, John, *The Process of Modernization: An Annotated Bibliography on the Sociocultural Aspects of Development* (Cambridge: Harvard University Press, 1969); Hagen, Everett, *On the Theory of Social Change: How Economic Growth Begins* (Homewood, Ill.: Dorsey Press, 1962); Levy, Marion J., Jr., *Modernization and the Structure of Societies* (Princeton, N.J.: Princeton University Press, 1966); Marx, Karl, *Selected Writings in Sociology and Social Philosophy* (New York: McGraw-Hill, 1956); Marx, Karl, *Early Writings* (New York: McGraw-Hill, 1963); McClelland, David C., *The Achieving Society* (Princeton, N.J.: Van Nostrand, 1961); McClelland, David C., "The Achievement Motive in Economic Growth," in *Industrialization and Society,* ed. B. Hoselitz and W. Moore (Atlantic Highlands, N.J.: Humanities Press, 1963); Parsons, Talcott, and Smelser, Neil, *Economy and Society* (New York: Free Press, 1956); Weber, Max, *The Protestant Ethic and the Spirit of Capitalism* (New York: Scribner, 1958); UNESCO, "Development Studies," *International Social Science Journal* 24(1), November 1972.

—*Paul C. Winther, Eastern Kentucky University*

## Developmental School of Psychology.

This modern school of psychology works in the tradition established by the Swiss psychologist and philosopher Jean Piaget. Adherents of the school take the view that human development passes through a series of qualitatively different stages in which the individual actively constructs his or her understanding of the world. This view is an implicit critique of the dominant behaviorist school in psychology, which regards human development as a cumulative process in which the individual is passively conditioned through the positive and negative reinforcements offered by the environment.

The school focuses primarily on cognitive development, the area of psychology concerned with the various modes and aspects of knowing, perceiving, recognizing, imagining, conceptualizing, and reasoning. Unlike the behaviorists, who contend that hypothetical internal psychic processes cannot be the subject matter of psychology, the developmentalists place particular emphasis on the internal mediating systems by which the individual processes, organizes, interprets, and responds to external stimuli. Anthropologists, who are especially interested in thought processes involving imagery, symbolism, language, and the organization of information, have been profoundly influenced by this aspect of developmental psychology.

Piaget has devoted most of his attention to the developmental nature of the reasoning process. Children, he notes, reason by methods unlike those of adults; and their notions of such concepts as weight, speed, volume, and causation appear to be radically different. Piaget believes that humans in all cultures proceed through an invariant developmental sequence of cognitive stages. In the young infant, intelligence is primarily a *sensorimotor* phenomenon and the child's thought is virtually inseparable from his or her acts. From the ages of about two to seven, the child's thought is *preoperational;* it is simple, egocentric, nonconceptual, and almost exclusively related to the child's subjective experience. From the ages of about seven to eleven, the child is at the stage of *concrete operations;* he or she begins to apply logical thinking and simple abstractions to the concrete world. Finally, at about the age of eleven, the child enters the period of *formal operations;* he or she is able for the first time to engage in hypothetical or logico-deductive thought. Each stage in this hierarchy is built upon and subsumes the previous stages.

Psychologists working in this tradition, notably Lawrence Kohlberg, have applied the principles of cognitive development to other fields. Kohlberg has argued that the acquisition of both moral reasoning and sex roles is not dependent on conditioning processes but is the product of cognitive interpretations and definitions on the part of the individual concerned.

The developmental school of psychology is closely linked with the new Chomskyan linguistics; both theoretical systems conceptualize development as the product of an interaction between innate organizational capacities of the human mind and a particular environmental milieu. The structuralist school in anthropology also owes some of its inspiration to cognitive developmental psychology.

*See also* Behaviorist school of psychology; Piaget, Jean; Psychoanalytic school of psychology; Transformational school of linguistics

—*Ian Robertson, Cambridge University*

## Developmental Stages: Psychosexual Stages. *See* Psychosexual stages of development.

## Devereux, George (b. 1908). A specialist in the study of culture and personality, Devereux has made major contributions to the analysis of dreams and mental disorders among American Indians.

## Deviance. This term refers to any behavior that violates the standards of conduct and expectations of a particular community. As popularly used, the term *deviant* usually implies some moral condemnation on the part of those who are in a position to apply the label, and indeed social scientists earlier in this century often took the view that deviants were psychologically maladjusted. It is now generally recognized by social scientists, however, that deviance is a relative notion: everyone deviates from someone else's norms, and the determination of who is a deviant depends very much on the viewpoint of the observer.

Several explanations of the phenomenon of deviance have been proposed. Some theorists believe that deviance stems from *inadequate socialization:* the deviant is one who has failed to internalize or who has rejected salient norms. Others believe that deviance is not so much a characteristic of individuals as a social process of *labeling:* the deviant is one to whom the label of "deviant" has been successfully applied by those who have the social power to make

*Burial of a Hun. Members of the Boston motorcycle gang called the Huns showered the casket in which one of their deceased leaders was being buried with beer and liquor, then threw the "empties" into the grave. Though by the standards of the wider society such behavior is clearly deviant, it is legitimized within the group which counterposes itself to the dominant society in terms of its beliefs, values, and internal sanctions, all of which control members' behavior.*

such definitions. A third view is that deviance stems from *anomie,* a state of normlessness that may exist when there is a discrepancy between culturally approved goals and the culturally approved means of achieving them: the deviant is one who seeks legitimate goals by illegitimate methods.

Some measure of deviance seems to exist in every culture, although it is more common, and more tolerated, in large-scale heterogeneous societies. The French social scientist Emile Durkheim suggested, in fact, that deviance serves a vital function in every culture. The presence of some degree of deviance contributes to social solidarity among the conforming majority: the deviants serve as moral boundary markers to the community, and the stigma that attaches to them serves to restrain widespread deviance among others. Another important function of deviance is that it provides a source of cultural change.

*See also* Norm and normative; Normality
Consult: Clinard, Marshall B., *Sociology of De-*viant Behavior, 3rd ed. (New York: Holt, 1968).
—Ian Robertson, Cambridge University

**DeVore, Irven** (b. 1934). Harvard ethnographer and primatologist best known for his seminal studies of the !Kung San (Bushmen) and for his field study of baboons in E and S Africa.

**Diachronic.** Diachronic studies of culture involve the dimension of time and may involve specific historical or broad evolutionary processes.
*See also* Synchronic

**Diachronic Linguistics.** *See* Historical linguistics; Linguistics.

**Dialect.** This term refers to a specific variety of a language showing sufficient peculiarities of pronunciation, grammar, and vocabulary to be considered a distinct entity, yet not sufficiently distinct from other dialects to constitute a separate language. In fact, the difference between a language and a dialect is often not clearly demarcated: it is one of degree, not of kind; the practical test is intelligibility. One rule of thumb, by no means authoritative, is the degree of variation from the standard: Canadian French is a dialect of French, but Haitian French is a separate language. Even

when a group develops a standardized written language, this standard is itself but a selected and regularized dialect.
*See also* Language; Linguistics; Speech; Symbol
Consult: Cofer, Charles N., et al., "Language," in *International Encyclopedia of the Social Sciences* (New York: Macmillan, 1968); Hertzler, Joyce O., *A Sociology of Language* (New York: Random House, 1965); Labov, William, *Sociolinguistic Patterns* (Philadelphia: University of Pennsylvania Press, 1973).

**Diamond, Stanley** (b. 1922). American cultural anthropologist concerned with understanding primitive society and with the political and ethical implications of anthropological research. He has done extensive field work (in E and W Africa and among Native Americans) and is the author of numerous books and articles.
Consult: Diamond, Stanley, "Primitive Society in Its Many Dimensions," in *The Critical Spirit: Essays in Honor of Herbert Marcuse,* ed. Kurt Wolff and Barrington Moore (Boston: Beacon Press, 1967); Diamond, Stanley, "Anthropology in Question," in *Reinventing Anthropology,* ed. Dell Hymes (New York: Vintage, 1974).

**Dictatorship.** Complex political systems ruled absolutely—often ruthlessly—by one or a few people are dictatorships. Unlike monarchs or aristocrats, dictators lack roots in traditional social structures.
*See also* Political systems; Totalitarianism

**Diderot, Denis** (1713–1784). Diderot, a French philosopher, created the *Encyclopédie . . . des Sciences, des Arts et des Métiers* (1751–1772), perhaps the most important work ushering in modern times. It exalted technology, science, the common person, speculative freedom, and tolerance. Implied fundamental criticism of church and state led to suppression of the encyclopedia.

Diderot's *Encyclopédie* and other works broadened the scope and influence of materialism in understanding human experience, an approach that was later elaborated by writers like Karl Marx and Friedrich Engels. Diderot inquired into the nature of matter, issues of evolution, societal structure, and religion. Through the *Encyclopédie* and other works, he exercised a profound influence on Western thought.

See also Condorcet, Marquis de; Marx, Karl

**Diet.** See Economics and subsistence; Food and food crops; Preparation and preservation of food.

**Diffusion.** When representatives of different cultures come into contact, whether directly or indirectly, there is an inevitable transfer of some elements from one to the other. Diffusion thus represents the worldwide tendency of human populations to share and pool creative efforts which are in origin locally known and used. All aspects of cultural systems—linguistic, technological, social, artistic—are potentially transferable from one community to another. But with respect to any particular item—a social role, an alphabet, a domestic animal, a pottery style—the transfer is neither automatic nor mechanically imitative. All cultures exercise selectivity in what they accept, and thus those elements which are transferred may be seen as a kind of inventory of what one community defines as important in another. In early contacts between Native

*One of the most dramatic examples of the diffusion of a cultural trait was the spread of tobacco across the world from the Americas, and the great importance it took on in many societies. Depicted here is a pottery statue from Trujillo, Venezuela, showing a smoking man.*

Americans and Europeans, the native communities were very interested in obtaining European technology, particularly iron implements, but they were much less interested in European social forms or religious practices. Moreover, the process of accepting an element from another society generally involves changes in its meaning, form, use, and function. Thus in 1667 a recent convert to Catholicism, queried about the state of his faith, said: "Yes, Father, I am a good Christian. I throw tobacco into the fire every day in honor of your Great Spirit." Here Christian beliefs were transformed into Native American meanings and practices. It is important to note that the processes of diffusion operate in the modern world at a much accelerated rate, due to the development of rapid mass communication and transportation systems. Hence the rejection of birth control techniques by some societies and the widespread acceptance of rock music by others can be interpreted in terms of knowledge about diffusion processes.

See also Acculturation; Cultural change; Innovation; Stimulus diffusion; Syncretism
Consult: Rogers, E. M., and Shoemaker, F. F., *Communication of Innovations* (New York: Free Press, 1971).

—James Clifton, University of Wisconsin, Green Bay

**Diffusion, Cultural.** See Diffusion.

**Diffusionism.** Diffusionism is the belief held by some European cultural anthropologists of the early 20th century that all culture began in one or a few areas of the world and then spread outward. The most extreme form of diffusionism was advocated by several British anthropologists, especially G. Elliot Smith and William J. Perry, who claimed that civilization originated only in Egypt and was then spread worldwide by the Egyptians. A less extreme point of view was held by some of the German anthropologists (such as Wilhelm Schmidt), who claimed that culture originated in several areas of the world which they termed *Kulturkreise* ("culture circles").

See also *Kulturkreise*; Perry, William; Schmidt, Wilhelm; Smith, G. Elliot

**Digging Instruments.** American archaeologists prefer to dig with shovel, trowel,

and screen. The shovel is used for such rough work as stripping the plow zone, moving back dirt, and sometimes excavating stratigraphic levels. The trowel is employed when greater care is necessary—to follow natural stratigraphy, to make careful exposures of features, and to begin cleaning burials. Both shovel and trowel are often used with a screen (usually $\frac{1}{4}$-inch mesh) through which excavated dirt is sifted to recover small artifacts. For really fine work paint-brushes, dental picks, knives, and bellows (for blowing away soil) may be employed.

Many archaeologists have found that *watersorting* (flotation) is an efficient way of recovering very small artifacts and carbonized remains from a midden (shell mound). This method operates on the principle that the fine particles of clay will be washed out of the seine while charcoal will float and small artifacts will sink to the bottom of the seine.

Bulldozers are sometimes used to clear large areas of overburden. A good operator can strip large areas of alluvium or plow zone in 2- or 3-inch layers so that the outlines of ancient villages can be mapped and excavated easily and quickly while most of the information is preserved.

See also Excavation of a site
Consult: Heizer, Robert F., and Graham, John A., *A Guide to Field Methods in Archaeology* (Palo Alto, Calif.: National Press, 1967).

—Thomas P. Myers, University of Nebraska

**Digging Stick.** The digging stick—typically a sharpened and fire-hardened wooden stave—is a multipurpose implement used extensively by both food gatherers and simple horticulturalists. Where the soil is particularly hard, the stick may be weighted with a perforated stone. Food gatherers employ the digging stick to obtain roots and tubers, to excavate animal burrows, and as a carrying yoke. Among preindustrial horticulturalists who lack the metal hoe, the digging stick is used to break clods and serves as the basic planting tool.

See also Economics and subsistence; Gathering

**Dionysian.** See Appollonian-Dionysian.

**Discovery and Invention.** For many years some anthropologists made much

*Sherente Amazon Indians pause on their way to their gardens with sharpened digging sticks.*

of a distinction between discovery and invention. Discovery in this sense means invention by accident, whereas invention proper supposedly involves more deliberate problem-solving efforts or perhaps attempts which involve multiple, complex steps in a definite sequence.

This distinction had some limited utility in contrasting the learning activities of the anthropoids with those of humans, for example, or in seeking plausible explanations for certain very ancient inventions of wide distribution. Thus chimpanzees were thought capable of learning via discovery, if not by deliberate design (i.e., invention). And very old cultural traits such as the various friction devices for making fire (fire drill, fire plow, fire saw), which are not very reliable in even the most skilled hands, were regarded as perhaps having been created by accident, as a by-product of some other activity such as boring a hole.

The contrast between discovery and invention, based on the common-sense distinction between unintentional and intentional, has little current value. More sophisticated psychological thinking (especially in cognitive and perceptual fields) and advances in primate studies have passed the dichotomy by.

*See also* Cultural change; Innovation
—*James Clifton, University of Wisconsin, Green Bay*

**Disintegration, Cultural.** *See* Cultural Disintegration.

**Dislocative Migration.** *See* Migration.

**Displacement.** In Freudian psychology, displacement is the process by which sexual, aggressive, or other energies are diverted into outlets, such as work or sports. When these outlets are in conformity with prevailing cultural patterns, the displacement is given a positive connotation and is termed *sublimation.*

*See also* Defense mechanisms; Freud, Sigmund

**Distinctive Features.** This term refers to the ultimate units into which speech sounds can be resolved; they are the basis for distinguishing one speech sound from all others and are the fundamental units of generative phonology.

**Origin.** The concept of distinctive features of sounds originated with linguists of the Prague School in the 1930s who observed that the neutralization of phonemic oppositions often involves the change of only a single feature of the speech sounds.

**Generative Phonology.** The theory of generative phonology assumes that all human speech sounds can be reduced to a set of articulatory, prosodic, and acoustic features—the distinctive features—which distinguish one speech sound from all others. The most comprehensive work on generative phonology (Chomsky and Halle 1968) tentatively indentifies about thirty-three different features necessary to describe the differences among the speech sounds of a particular language; of this universal set of thirty-three features, only about thirteen apply to the speech sounds of American English.

Every morpheme of a language is represented in the lexicon as a two-dimensional matrix in which the columns are the sequence of speech sounds of the morpheme and the rows are the distinctive features of each sound in the morpheme. Furthermore, each feature represents a binary opposition; i.e., it has either a positive or a negative value for each sound. For example, the English sounds represented by the phonological symbols *m, b,* and *p* are consonants articulated by closing the lips—they are bilabial. Being consonants, they are (−vocalic, +consonantal)—they each have a negative value for the feature *vocalic* and a positive value for the feature *consonantal;* they also share the same values for some of the other thirteen features. However, the sounds *m* and *b* are *voiced* consonants and *p* is *voiceless*. And whereas *m* is a *nasal* consonant, *b* and *p* are nonnasals. Thus the phonological differences which distinguish each of these sounds from the other two can be represented in terms of minimal distinctive features (see table). For a morpheme represented in the lexicon of English, a positive/negative value is indicated for each of the thirteen distinctive features for each of the successive sounds in the morpheme.

| Dimensions of Opposition | Sounds | | |
|---|---|---|---|
| | /m/ | /b/ | /p/ |
| Vocalic | − | − | − |
| Consonantal | + | + | + |
| Voice | + | + | − |
| Nasal | + | − | − |

Thus, although any two distinct speech sounds may share the same values for some of the features, they have opposite values for at least one of the other features; and it is exactly this difference in values that provides the basis for phonological oppositions (either phonetic contrasts or phonemic contrasts) in language.

The phonological rules of a language account for the sound changes that morphemes undergo when they occur in specific contexts in words and sentences. Although some of these changes may mean the substitution of one phoneme for another in the morpheme (e.g., *sing, sang, sung*), most changes merely mean a switch in the value of one or more distinctive features of some sound in the morpheme. For example, the plural suffix *-s* is voiceless in the word *bets* but is voiced in the word *beds*. The sole difference in the pronunciation of the suffix is that plural *-s* has opposite values for one distinctive feature: in *bets* the suffix is (−voice); in *beds* it is (+voice). The treatment of such phenomena in generative phonology differs considerably from other linguistic theories. In descriptive linguistics the difference between the plural suffix in *bets* and *beds* is considered a substitution of one phoneme for another. But in generative phonology the plural suffix is said to have only one underlying form, which is unspecified in the lexicon for the feature *voice;* and the value for this feature is assigned—according to the context in which the suffix occurs—by phonological rule.

**Markedness and Naturalness of Sounds.** Comparative analysis of the sound systems of many of the world's languages reveals that some sounds and sound changes are objectively more natural than others. That is, for some distinctive features, the positive value is more natural (unmarked) than the negative value, which is less natural (marked), and vice versa. For example, *voiceless* obstruents but never *voiced* obstruents occur as the final sound of a word in Modern High German. This (and similar phenomena from many other languages) suggests that in the case of obstruent sounds, the value (−voice) is more natural. Similarly, very few languages have voiceless vowel sounds but all languages have voiced vowels, which suggests that (+voice) is the more natural value for this class of sounds.

Similar phenomena occur in terms of historical sound changes within languages. That is, sounds that have more marked values for some features are more subject to change than those with fewer marked values; and changes in the features of sounds are generally from marked to unmarked values. Markedness theory also holds much promise for the study of first-language acquisition; the order in which infants learn the sounds of language is inextricably related to the features of those sounds.

See also Linguistics; Phonetics; Phonology Consult: Chomsky, Noam, and Halle, Morris, *The Sound Pattern of English* (New York: Harper & Row, 1968); Postal, Paul, *Aspects of Phonological Theory* (New York: Harper & Row, 1968); Trubetzkoy, N., *Principles of Phonology* (Berkeley: University of California Press, 1969).

—*Charles T. Snow, California State University, Chico*

**Divination.** This term refers to any practice aimed at obtaining factual knowledge by means which have no empirical connection to the information being sought. The information sought may concern future events, lost or stolen property, hidden

*Divination: the use of magic to predict the future. Takahashi Sanshiro, 80, of the Japanese village of Takatoya, demonstrates the use of divining sticks to discover the location of a lost object. He is the last "mountain ascetic" (yamabushi); his art combines elements of Shinto, Buddhism, and native folk practices.*

resources, or the identity of a culprit. Means employed may include the interpretation of natural phenomena, such as the flight of birds, or the interpretation of the reactions of artifacts or natural objects to manipulation, as in the formation of cracks in animal bones caused by heating them over a fire. Although the information gained by divination has by definition only a synchronistic relation to the information being sought, it may be of real use by freeing the diviners or their clients from indecision and thus enabling them to act.

See also Religion

**Diviner.** See Divination.

**Division of Labor.** This term refers to the separation of work into distinct elements, each of which is performed by a specified individual or category of individuals. The division of labor is a universal economic feature, although it reaches its most highly developed form in the occupational specialization that is characteristic of the modern industrial state.

Every human society has norms governing the allocation of work according to the criteria of sex and age. In most foraging societies, for example, the division of labor requires men to hunt and women to gather. Within these parameters, however, the precise tasks that are allocated to each sex vary considerably between cultures—carrying heavy weights, for example, is a woman's work in many cultures but emphatically a man's in others. The specific duties allocated to the sexes depend very much on the local environment and on the traditions that have been evolved to deal with it.

Similarly, all cultures exhibit a division of labor along age lines: since the very young and the very old are physically incapable of performing many adult tasks, they have their own age-related duties. The children, for example, may be required to engage in light domestic work while the old become the repository of the myths, stories, and legends of the community.

Apart from specialization based on age and sex, there is relatively little division of labor in cultures with simple technologies. The knowledge and skills of the community are shared by virtually all its adult members. The growing ability to produce a surplus separates increasing numbers of individuals

| Activity | Number of Societies in Which Activity is Performed by: | | | | |
|---|---|---|---|---|---|
| | Men Always | Men Usually | Either Sex Equally | Women Usually | Women Always |
| Metalworking | 78 | 0 | 0 | 0 | 0 |
| Weapon making | 121 | 1 | 0 | 0 | 0 |
| Boat building | 91 | 4 | 4 | 0 | 1 |
| Making musical instruments | 45 | 2 | 0 | 0 | 1 |
| Work in wood and bark | 113 | 9 | 5 | 1 | 1 |
| Work in stone | 68 | 3 | 2 | 0 | 1 |
| Work in bone, horn, shell | 67 | 4 | 3 | 0 | 2 |
| Making ceremonial objects | 37 | 1 | 13 | 0 | 1 |
| House building | 86 | 32 | 25 | 3 | 14 |
| Net making | 44 | 6 | 4 | 2 | 11 |
| Making ornaments | 24 | 3 | 40 | 6 | 18 |
| Making leather products | 29 | 3 | 9 | 3 | 32 |
| Hide preparation | 31 | 2 | 4 | 4 | 49 |
| Making nontextile fabrics | 14 | 0 | 9 | 2 | 32 |
| Making thread and cordage | 23 | 2 | 11 | 10 | 73 |
| Basket making | 25 | 3 | 10 | 6 | 82 |
| Hat making | 16 | 2 | 6 | 4 | 61 |
| Weaving | 19 | 2 | 2 | 6 | 67 |
| Pottery making | 13 | 2 | 6 | 8 | 77 |
| Making and repairing clothing | 12 | 3 | 8 | 9 | 95 |

The division of labor by sex in every society is arbitrary; nevertheless, when studied cross-culturally certain patterns emerge (adapted from Murdock).

from subsistence activities, however, and allows greater specialization. Such specialization often involves greater productive efficiency and may be associated with notable increments in population size and economic development. Karl Marx and other writers have suggested that this increase in specialization may actually constrict the abilities of the individual, who, they charge, becomes progressively more alienated from the community and the environment; and they have drawn attention to the immense potential for conflict that may be generated when a specialized division of labor takes place along the lines of social class.

See also Civilization, origins of; Economics and subsistence; Gathering; Skills and work
—Ian Robertson, Cambridge University

**Division of Labor According to Sex.** See Skills and work.

**DNA.** See Deoxyribonucleic acid.

**Dobzhansky, Theodosius** (b. 1900). Russian-born geneticist known for his work on the genetics of Drosophila (fruitfly) and for his research in population genetics and biological evolution.

**Dollard, John** (b. 1900). Social psychologist who analyzed the effects of long-established patterns of discrimination on blacks and whites in a small Mississippi town in the 1930s.

**Domestic Animals.** See Domestication of plants and animals.

**Domestic Cycle.** This cycle indicates, for any given society, the standard patterns of change in household behaviors as household compositions change through births, deaths, marriages, and aging of members; the concept deals with the household as such rather than with individuals. These patterns vary drastically from society to society; in some cases generations move continuously through a permanent, delimitable household corporation, while in others (as in the United States) we find a continuous spawning of entirely new domestic groups paralleled by the demise of old ones.

In all societies, the unit is constantly changing in either personnel, their ages, or both. Thus the basic (especially economic and housing) requirements of the household evolve and the strategies for managing these evolving requirements must change too. In some societies, changed requirements are marked by drastic shifts in the status of the domestic unit and its relationship to society. For example, the household may not emerge as a discrete unit until a couple's first child is born. Among the Fulani (Nigeria), the discrete household does not appear until the children develop enough to do simple subsistence tasks, even though the married partners both own property.

Any new domestic unit must always be located somewhere—determined, effectively, by residence rules for one or both partners. Residence rules are important because all household members may be potential heirs of property held by the households which begat the spouses, although exclusion principles (e.g., that women cannot inherit) may limit heirship. Household location, then, may be a function of the major kinds of property in the society, as well as the society's legal forms, kinship structures, geographical conditions, and subsistence economy. In American society, for example, property rights are held in perpetuity through kin ties, regardless of sex or location. Thus households can locate anywhere while maintaining property rights continuously; members need not be present to retain rights. Household changes of state may involve great changes in residence patterns, as in the case of the Tallensi and the Ashanti, where residence may vary among viri-, uxori-, patri-, matri-, and other forms of locality depending on household conditions and the domestic cycle. Such residence changes reflect the household's changing economic role and property relationship with other usually progenitor households (and often with the total economy as well).

In other societies, such changes of state are not so neatly determined but reflect the making of choices where the set of alternatives may be evolving or the household's perception of the set is changing. Such strategic choices are characteristic of Western societies, which rarely define household options jurally; locational changes are also common there.

Marriage of younger household members, death of significant household producers, and aging processes govern the later household trajectory and, usually, lead to its ultimate extinction. Decisive, in most societies, is the household's declining labor capacity, which liquidates it as a self-sustaining corporation and may raise the problem of how the aged are to be maintained. The Eskimo evolved the ultimate solution to the problem by encouraging self-immolation by the unproductive aged. Other solutions vary from American ambivalencies about maintaining near-useless elders in their children's households or keeping them in retirement homes to more socially integrative solutions of actively including them as leaders and advisors, often having them live with descendants and participate in the daily household activities.

In sum, studying domestic units and their patterned trajectories in a society often uncovers major institutional arrangements, illustrates basic human adaptations to geographical and societal environments, gives insight into the society's mechanisms of continuity and variation, and permits concomitant dealing with different levels of the social organization.

See also Family, the; Family cycle; Life cycle
Consult: Fortes, Meyer, "Time and Social Structure," in Social Structure: Studies Presented to A. R. Radcliffe-Brown (Oxford: Oxford University Press, 1949); Goody, Jack (ed.), The Developmental Cycle in Domestic Groups (Cambridge: Cambridge University Press, 1958); Leeds, Anthony, "Housing-Settlement Types, Arrangements for Living, Proletarianization, and the Social Structure of the City," in Latin American Urban Research: Vol. 4, ed. W. Cornelius and F. Trueblood (Beverly Hills, Calif.: Sage, 1974).
—Anthony Leeds, Boston University

## Domestication of Plants and Animals.

Bringing plants and animals into close association with humans led to their changing so that often these organisms could no longer reproduce under natural conditions. Thus domestication implies breeding under human control. Some of the changes in animals involve bone structure, loss of horns, development of wool, and increase in milk production or egg laying as well as changes in behavior. Changes frequently observed in plants are increase in size of fruits or seeds, loss of natural means of dispersal, elimination of toxic substances, and rapid and uniform germination of seeds. With continued selection, domesticated animals and plants became much more variable than their wild ancestors, generally showing the greatest variation in the character for which they are cultivated.

All our major food plants and animals, and most of the minor ones as well, were domesticated in the prehistoric period. The dog is generally considered to be the earliest domesticated animal, but that is not yet proved by archaeology. The earliest clear evidence of domestication comes from the Near East, where about 9,000 years ago people were raising sheep and goats and cultivating wheat and barley. Other animals (pigs and cattle) and plants (lentils and peas) were shortly to become domesticated in the Near East or Europe. In SE Asia, the water buffalo, chickens, and rice were eventually domesticated. In the Americas there were early centers of domestication in both Mexico and Peru, where beans and squash (and slightly later, corn or maize) were among the first plants to be domesticated. Only a few animals were ever domesticated in the Americas; the most important were the llama in the Andes and the turkey in Mexico.

Although the American geographer Carl O. Sauer and others have suggested that the vegetative propagation of plants from tubers, root parts, or stem cuttings preceded seed planting, the archaeological record indicates that cultivation of seed plants was earlier than that of vegetatively cultivated plants such as potatoes, yams, manioc, and the banana. The archaeological record, however, might be expected to be more complete for seeds than for vegetative parts of plants, which are more perishable.

The exact circumstances that led people to domesticate plants and animals are not known with certainty. Why should people have practiced domestication when they could obtain enough food from hunting and gathering? Some, including the American anthropologist Lewis R. Binford, have suggested that population growth leading to a reduction of the wild food supply may have been the stimulus for domestication. Since domesticated plants and animals, however,

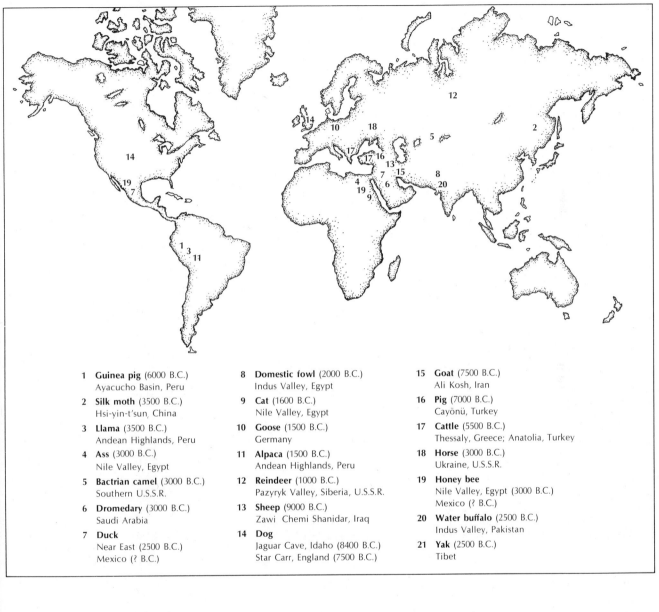

| 1 | **Guinea pig** (6000 B.C.)<br>Ayacucho Basin, Peru | 8 | **Domestic fowl** (2000 B.C.)<br>Indus Valley, Egypt | 15 | **Goat** (7500 B.C.)<br>Ali Kosh, Iran |
|---|---|---|---|---|---|
| 2 | **Silk moth** (3500 B.C.)<br>Hsi-yin-t'sun, China | 9 | **Cat** (1600 B.C.)<br>Nile Valley, Egypt | 16 | **Pig** (7000 B.C.)<br>Cayönü, Turkey |
| 3 | **Llama** (3500 B.C.)<br>Andean Highlands, Peru | 10 | **Goose** (1500 B.C.)<br>Germany | 17 | **Cattle** (5500 B.C.)<br>Thessaly, Greece; Anatolia, Turkey |
| 4 | **Ass** (3000 B.C.)<br>Nile Valley, Egypt | 11 | **Alpaca** (1500 B.C.)<br>Andean Highlands, Peru | 18 | **Horse** (3000 B.C.)<br>Ukraine, U.S.S.R. |
| 5 | **Bactrian camel** (3000 B.C.)<br>Southern U.S.S.R. | 12 | **Reindeer** (1000 B.C.)<br>Pazyryk Valley, Siberia, U.S.S.R. | 19 | **Honey bee**<br>Nile Valley, Egypt (3000 B.C.)<br>Mexico (? B.C.) |
| 6 | **Dromedary** (3000 B.C.)<br>Saudi Arabia | 13 | **Sheep** (9000 B.C.)<br>Zawi Chemi Shanidar, Iraq | 20 | **Water buffalo** (2500 B.C.)<br>Indus Valley, Pakistan |
| 7 | **Duck**<br>Near East (2500 B.C.)<br>Mexico (? B.C.) | 14 | **Dog**<br>Jaguar Cave, Idaho (8400 B.C.)<br>Star Carr, England (7500 B.C.) | 21 | **Yak** (2500 B.C.)<br>Tibet |

could at first offer only a meager supplement to wild food, it is unlikely that they could have greatly eased population pressure. Sauer has pointed out that the domestication of plants, in particular, would require a people who were sedentary most of the year and also had leisure time for experimentation. He has postulated an origin of domestication among fishermen, who could have had a dependable food supply as well as being sedentary. The archaeological record so far, however, provides little support for Sauer's hypothesis.

It has also been postulated that domestication may have originated for other than utilitarian reasons. Eduard Hahn, a German geographer in the 19th century, suggested that cattle may have been domesticated in order to have the animals available for sacrifice in connection with fertility rituals. It is now known that goats, sheep, and pigs were domesticated before cattle; whether a religious motive can be held responsible for their domestication is problematical. People have also attached religious significance to plants. Possibly religious rites were responsible for the first planting of seeds. The questions remain, however, whether domestication was a direct attempt to increase the food supply or whether it was a by-product of some other activity, as well as why it arose so late in our prehistoric period.

Although it is possible that there was but a single origin of plant and animal domestication followed by the diffusion of the idea with new plants and animals being brought into domestication in other places, it is more likely that the idea of domesticating plants and animals developed independently in many different places. Most authorities are inclined to believe that there were at least two separate origins in the Old and New World.

*See also* Agriculture; Food and food crops
Consult: Frazer, J. G., *New Golden Bough*, ed. T. H. Gaster (New York: Mentor, 1964); Heiser, Charles B., Jr., *Seed to Civilization: The Story of Man's Food* (San Francisco: Freeman, 1973); Sauer, Carl O., *Seeds, Spades, Hearths, and Herbs: The Domestication of Animals and Foodstuffs* (Cambridge, Mass.: M.I.T. Press, 1969); Ucko, Peter J., and Dimbleby, J. W., *The Domestication and Exploitation of Plants and Animals* (Chicago: Aldine, 1969); Zeuner, Frederic E., *A History of Domesticated Animals* (London: Hutchinson, 1963).
—*Charles B. Heiser, Jr., Indiana University*

**Dominance and Aggression.** Dominance has been defined as priority of access to desired objects which results from the outcome of aggressive encounters. Dominance (priority) has frequently been interpreted to be a motivating factor in aggression. However, in a common test of dominance where a piece of food is thrown between two animals and the one taking it is scored as dominant, the animal dominant in aggressive situations might not be the one to take the food. Field studies have also pointed out that the male who has priority of access to receptive females may not be the most dominant in terms of aggressive encounters. Consequently, the animals occupying the positions in a hierarchy are variable according to the behavior being observed.

Frequency of aggression is not always correlated with rank. The animal dominant over all others in the group may be the least frequently involved in aggressive episodes. One of the best indicators of dominance is the action of subordinate animals in avoiding or directing submissive gestures toward a higher-ranking animal (Rowell 1966). This, rather than actual aggression, appears to be the most frequent expression of dominance.

That dominance is based solely on aggression has been disproved by long-term studies of macaque populations where maternal kinship relationships are known. The infant of the dominant mother will develop into a dominant individual among its peers. This happens because the mother, dominant among her peers, will support her infant when it becomes involved in agonistic interactions with others. Hence aggression is related to the achievement of status, but in complex ways.

The functions of aggression in primate societies have been debated. Recent studies of the conditions which elicit aggressive behavior in monkeys (Bernstein and Gordon 1974) suggest that aggression may actually integrate social groups. When strangers are put together for the first time, a high frequency of aggression usually ensues, but serious wounding is rare. This suggests that aggression is being inhibited since males possess large, sharp, potentially lethal canine teeth. Further, a set of dominant/subordinate relationships quickly develops, primarily indicated by the behavior of lower-ranking animals. As the hierarchy becomes apparent, the frequency and severity of aggression decrease. Hence, though dominance appears to depend on aggression as an ultimate sanction, the frequency of aggression is often lowest when the hierarchy is well defined.

That an already integrated group will attack a stranger suggests that aggression may serve to protect the established social order. The stranger may be perceived as a threat to that order. This also explains why aggression seems to occur most often between individuals of adjacent rank, whereas a juvenile may threaten an adult male with impunity. Hall (1964) has suggested that a potent elicitor of aggression in primates appears to be a perceived violation of a social code. A young animal is unlikely to be perceived by an adult male as a threat to that male's position. On the other hand, a male of closely equivalent rank who violates the social norm (i.e., threatens the higher-ranked male) might well be perceived as a threat to the established order.

The studies mentioned above have been conducted on baboons and macaques, which tend to have highly structured rank relationships and also to be quite aggressive. In other primate species the relationship between rank and aggression may not be so clear-cut (Jolly 1972).

*See also* Aggression; Dominance hierarchies; Ethology
Consult: Bernstein, I. S., and Gordon, T. P., "The Function of Aggression in Primate Societies," *American Scientist* 62:304–311, 1974; Hall, K. R. L., "Aggression in Monkey and Ape Societies," in *The Natural History of Aggression*, ed. J. D. Carthy and F. J. Ebling (New York: Academic Press, 1964); Jolly, A., *The Evolution of Primate Behavior* (New York: Macmillan, 1972); Rowell, T. E. "Hierarchy in the Organization of a Captive Baboon Group, *Animal Behavior* 14:430–443, 1966.
—*Leanne T. Nash, Arizona State University*

**Dominance Hierarchies.** Dominance is a concept derived from the notion of a hierarchical pecking-order in birds: A, the most dominant, can peck all others; B is pecked by A but pecks all others; and so on. Among nonhuman primates, a dominance hierarchy is often defined by reference to priority of access to some desirable item (food, receptive females); priority of access ultimately rests on the ability of the higher-ranking animal to win aggressive encounters. The concept is generally restricted in scope to animals within the same social group. In some species, however, groups as a whole may also be arranged in order for access to particularly favored locales (water holes, rich food sources).

A common error of circular reasoning holds that dominance *gives* a priority of access, whereas dominance is in fact *defined* by priority of access. Other definitions of dominance have introduced other roles—group protection, leadership of group movement, policing aggression within the group. Such behavioral correlates may or may not occur, however, depending on the species and circumstances. Consequently, dominance is used without operational precision and therefore without much meaning.

*See also* Aggression; Dominance and Aggression
Consult: Gartlan, J. S., "Structure and Function in Primate Society," *Folia Primat* 8:89–120, 1968.
—*Leanne T. Nash, Arizona State University*

**Dominant Gene.** *See* Gene; Genetics.

**Double Bind.** This term refers to a situation in which a person receives simultaneous but contradictory injunctions from one or more other people with whom he or she is emotionally involved. Some social scientists believe that persistent exposure to double binds may contribute to an individual's succumbing to schizophrenia.

*See also* Communication; Schizophrenia

**Douglas, Mary** (b. 1921). Douglas, who conducted her fieldwork in W Africa, is best known for her perceptive studies of symbolic systems and has gained in influence with the publication of *Natural Symbols* (1970).

**Dozier, Edward P.** (1916–1971). A native of Santa Clara Pueblo, New Mexico, Dozier specialized in Pueblo ethnography and linguistics with an insider's view; he also studied the mountain people of N Luzon, Philippines.

Consult: Dozier, Edward P., *The Pueblo Indians of North America* (New York: Holt, 1970); Eggan, Fred, and Basso, Keith, "Obituary of Edward P. Dozier (1916–1971)," *American Anthropologist* 74:740–746, 1972.

**Drama.** In primitive society, drama refers to ceremonies focused on crises and transitions of individuals or groups. Whereas in

*This is a performance of a type of drama called Ram Lila, by a troupe of Brahmans in North India. All of the actors are male. The deities Ram and Sita are being portrayed by the actors in the center of the stage. The performances are underwritten by a wealthier land-owning family, who thereby gain prestige and religious merit. Head scarves are evident in the audience due to the chilly weather of the winter season.*

*Accompanied by the clacking and jangling instruments his musicians are playing, a female impersonator entertains villagers he hopes will make small donations. Such impersonators are generally part-time specialists and heterosexual. Because of the restrictions of parda, a complex of institutions which results in the seclusion of women from public life, most female roles in dancing and drama are played by men or boys. (North India near Varanasi.)*

modern civilization drama is a specialized institution generally set off in the theater and bounded by restrictive conventions, in primitive societies drama is intimately bound up with religion, art, and daily life. Ritual dramas emphasizing participation and performed "on a stage as wide as society itself" are an important component in the expressive systems of primitive cultures. They have a therapeutic, equilibratory, and creative potential in attempting to resolve individual ambivalences and clarify or renew cultural meanings. Such ritual dramas survive in attenuated form in the civilized drama. Recently anthropologists have begun to use the concept of drama systematically as a tool for cultural analysis. E. A. Hoebel has focused on the "trouble case" in the area of legal anthropology and Victor Turner is involved in a continuing analysis of social relations in terms of his concept of "social drama."

*See also* Art; Ceremony; Expressive systems; Religion; Ritual

Consult: Diamond, Stanley, "Plato and the Definition of the Primitive," in *In Search of the Primitive*, ed. Stanley Diamond (New Bruns-

wick, N.J.: Transaction, 1974); Turner, V., *Dramas, Fields, and Metaphors* (Ithaca: Cornell University Press, 1974).
—*Stan Wilk, Lycoming College*

**Draw-A-Person Test (DAP).** The DAP is widely used in cross-cultural research on personality, especially with children. The subject is given a soft pencil and a piece of blank paper and asked to draw a person. The instructions are ambiguous as to sex, and the subject may draw a figure clothed or nude, same sex or other sex, large or small. The results suggest that children are likely to draw a portrait of their real body image, a portrait of their ideal self, or a significant person in their lives. Black children, for example, tend to draw whites; Middle American Indians often draw Ladinos in western clothing. Used with subsequent interviewing, the DAP can reveal information about the body image aspect of self or identity in the sociocultural environment.

*See also* Projective tests

Consult: Barnouw, V., *Culture and Personality*, 2nd ed. (Homewood, Ill.: Dorsey Press, 1973).

**Dream Dance Religion.** This cultural revitalization movement is also known as the Drum Cult or the Sioux Dance, but it is not the same and should not be confused with the Ghost Dance of the Plains. The Dream Dance originated in 1878 when the Sante Dakota prophetess Wananikwe received a visit from Christ in a vision. The period was one of great cultural stress in the Great Lakes region, for by this time most of the Indian populations in the area had been removed west of the Mississippi and the remaining populations were facing a grave cultural crisis. The Dream Dance in the beginning had a strongly magical and revivalist bent to it. Adherents believed that conducting appropriate rituals would cause Catholic Indians (who were regarded as renegades and threats) and whites to fall paralyzed on the earth. In later years, as the tenets of the movement were altered and the rituals became institutionalized, it became known as one of the principal traditional religions of the Algonquian tribes of the Great Lakes region. It still flourishes among a few such groups, the Mesquakie Fox of Iowa and the Potawatomie and Kickapoo in Kansas. Among the Menomini, the Dream Dance became known as the powwow, but this term usually refers to a largely secular and social meeting.

See also Cultural revitalization; Revitalization movements

—James Clifton, University of Wisconsin, Green Bay

## Dreams, Cultural Uses of.

In all cultures people recognize the panhuman phenomenon of dreams, express some interest in them, and make some effort to understand them. But there is much variation in the amount of interest and in the degree to which dreaming is given significance. In some cultures there is no culturally systematized form of explanation and interpretation, while in others—North American Indian societies, for example—interest is great and dreams are thought to be of vital significance in people's lives. Young Plains Indian men could escape the stringent requirements of the warrior's role and assume the role of berdache (enacting all behavior expected of women) if they had appropriate dreams of the moon (a female deity) or a hermaphrodite buffalo. In many tribes, young men obtained their personal spirit helpers through dreams; in others, the interpretation of dreams was used as a basis for making important decisions—individual and tribal. Finally, the Iroquoian tribes of New York in the 17th century had a highly developed theory of dreams and their interpretation, which they assumed expressed the wishes of the soul. This theory anticipated and was essentially similar to that of 20th-century psychoanalysis.

See also Dreams, psychological functions of; Personality, cultural determinants of

—James Clifton, University of Wisconsin, Green Bay

## Dreams, Psychological Functions of.

Dreams consist of emotions, images, thoughts, sensations, and events experienced during sleep. They are aptly called the guardians of sleep, for they protect the individual from both internal, unconscious conflicts and external, disturbing stimuli. Thus private nighttime fantasies work off disturbing influences in a person's experience. Freudians believe that dreams express in disguised, symbolic form deeply repressed, forbidden impulses and wishes. Dreams also have a problem-solving function, but the solutions are generally cryptic and unintelligible (without use of some culturally standardized guides for interpretation). Moreover, dreams reduce some of the tensions of the day by providing symbolic satisfaction. Thus the three functions served by dreams include the preservation of sleep, a means of expressing unconscious wishes in acceptable fashion, and the safety valve function of discharging tension.

See also Dreams, cultural uses of

## Drink.

To an English speaker the word drink—when given special emphasis—refers to alcohol. Such a meaning is appropriate, for comparative studies have shown that wherever alcohol is known it is never neglected. Each culture gives alcohol its own symbolic meaning beyond the physiological factors involved in the drinking of alcohol. How people react to alcohol, for that matter, is in large part conditioned by the meaning alcohol has in their culture. If people are culturally conditioned to feel intoxicated on a small amount of alcohol, then they will feel and act "high" on much less alcohol than will people who have expectations of drinking a lot and yet maintaining their psychological and physical coordination at acceptable levels.

Drinking has a diacritical function—it marks off one type of behavior from another. Frequently, it serves to mark the sacred from the profane. Its precise meaning, however, must be sought within each sociocultural system. A number of cross-cultural studies have only served to strengthen that conviction. It is certain that changes in drinking patterns correlate with other sociocultural changes.

Consult: Field, Peter B., "A New Cross-cultural Study of Drunkenness," in Society, Culture and Drinking Patterns, ed. D. J. Pittman and C. R. Snyder (New York: Wiley, 1962); Horton, Donald, "The Functions of Alcohol in Primitive Societies: A Cross-cultural Study," Quarterly Journal of Studies on Alcohol 4, 1943; Mandelbaum, D. G., "Alcohol and Culture," Current Anthropology 6: 281–293, 1965.

—Frank Salamone, St. John's University

## Driver, Harold (b. 1907).

Cultural anthropologist, retired from Indiana University, well known for his statistical approaches to anthropological theory and his major work Indians of North America.

## Drives, Innate.

See Instincts.

## Drucker, Philip (b. 1911).

American anthropologist known for his detailed descriptive work on NW Coast Indians and his theoretical work on the potlatch.

See also Potlatch

## Drugs.

Drugs are chemical substances which produce a change in the body. These changes may be physical, psychological, or both; they may be curative, maintaining, or degenerative in their effect.

How a drug is culturally regarded depends in large part on the technical understanding of its effects and the purposes for which it is employed. Physiological dependency is not even an issue with the daily medicinal use of penicillin, digitalis in one of its several forms, or insulin, because these compounds are defined as life-saving. Morphine and codeine are salubrious pain relievers when used for short periods (usually three days) after major surgery. Even heroin, today considered a killer, was once believed harmless and was prescribed for addicts as a therapeutic substitute for morphine. In recent years Western M.D.'s have used heroin and LSD as well as other miracles of

Sādhū. A North Indian religious ascetic who lives on alms is shown in an exalted condition after smoking cannabis indica. In this religious context the drug is said to have the effect of inducing the great or universal soul in the worshipper's consciousness.

*Two Yanomamö men are shown blowing ebene, a hallucinogenic snuff, into each other's noses through a tube.*

modern chemistry to relieve pain in terminal patients; but legal and popular reservations against their use have limited them for experimentation in thanatology.

Physiological and psychological effects of drugs are experienced in different ways by different persons. Supernatural explanations for this unpredictability are incorporated into folk medicine. Overreactions and underreactions are often blamed on violation of taboos or on improperly performed rituals. When the same thing happens to an M.D., he checks to make sure his malpractice insurance is paid up.

Wine, mead, beer, and kava are a few of the fermented beverages integral to rituals through the centuries. Their consumption has been symbolic in and of themselves (wine = blood) or a prerequisite for the ritual practitioner to achieve an *altered state of consciousness* necessary to attain the use of supernatural intermediary curing, divining, or visionary powers. Similarly, mescaline (peyote cactus) (Furst 1973) and psilocybin (the "magic mushroom") (Castaneda 1968) have been considered sacred foods

not unlike the unleavened wafers (matzos, hosts) in Jewish and Christian rituals.

The annual peyote hunt of the Huichol Indians of Mexico is a pilgrimage of rebirth to the source of life. The importance of the role this substance assumes in their lives is demonstrated by its symbolic identification with deer and maize. The two latter support the life of the body and peyote supports the life of the soul, without which they would surely die.

Characteristic behavior while under the influence of a drug also varies by culture. The "proper" way of drinking and getting drunk in various Western societies effectively demonstrates this fact (Snyder 1958). Most experimenters with alcohol, marijuana, and other drugs will remember their first experiences vis-à-vis their uncertainties whether or not they were "feeling anything" and their dependence on those who were giving them their first "guided trip" to explain their sensations and reassure them. Socially accepted learning of this sort is nowhere better illustrated than the occasion of the Seder dinner in Judaism. The young boy's typically eager, curious overindulgence in wine is viewed with great amusement, bordering on ridicule, by the sanctioning adults present. From this attitude, he learns that it is childish to lose control and mature to be moderate and disciplined.

History records that various drugs have been used in many cultures as relaxants, stimulants, and social lubricants at gatherings. Royalty and commoners have served them on simple, family occasions and to celebrate great events. The Aymara of the Lake Titicaca region (Peru, Brazil) have chewed coca leaves as an adaptation to surviving the oppressive conditions of high-altitude mining to which they were subjected during the Spanish colonial period. Deliberate addiction to derivatives of the opium poppy is known from 19th-century China and 20th-century America. Such abuses of an inherently neutral, natural product have generated value-laden attitudes which may preclude their humanitarian use in modern medicine.

*See also* Altered states of consciousness; Hallucinations and shamanism; Medicine; Medicine, primitive; Peyote; Possession; Ritual; Trance

Consult: Barnouw, Victor, "The Aymara Indians," in *Culture and Personality* (Homewood, Ill.: Dorsey Press, 1973); Castaneda, Carlos, *The Teachings of Don Juan* (New York: Balantine, 1968); Furst, Peter T., "An Indian Journey to Life's Source," *Natural History*, April 1973; Offir, Carole Wade, "Are We Pushers for Our Own Children?", *Psychology Today*, December 1974; Snyder, Charles, *Alcohol and The Jews* (Glencoe, Ill.: Free Press, 1958).
—*Mary Ann Foley, Southern Connecticut State College*

**Drugs, Hallucinogenic.** *See* Drugs.

**Drum Cult.** *See* Dream dance religion.

**Dryopithecines.** The subfamily Dryopithecinae includes a number of species of the genus *Dryopithecus*, first discovered in France in 1865, as well as the genus *Proconsul* when classified separately. Dryopithecines inhabited tropical forests and perhaps woodland savannas of the Miocene in E Africa some 20 million years BP and persisted into the Pliocene of Eurasia until approximately 10 million BP.

Although the dryopithecines were once considered to be ancestral to the hominids, current scholarship holds them to be ancestral to modern apes, particularly chimpanzees and gorillas. As ancestral forms they were less specialized (and hence were not brachiators), had smaller brains, showed dental differences, and were smaller in size than these contemporary pongids.

**Dual Division.** *See* Moiety.

**DuBois, Cora Alice** (b. 1903). A cultural anthropologist interested in culture and personality, DuBois is best known for her study of the people of Alor, in which she used the concept of modal personality.

**DuBois, Eugène** (1858–1941). Dutch anatomist who, in 1891, in Java, found the first remains of *Homo erectus,* which he called *Pithecanthropus erectus.*
　　*See also* Homo erectus

**Dunder, Alan** (b. 1934). Cultural anthropologist who has specialized in the study of folklore, symbolism (especially North American Indian), and world view.

**Durkheim, Émile** (1858–1917). Durkheim, a French student of society, is regarded as one of the founders of modern social science. His theories have had a profound influence on anthropology, sociology, and social psychology. Durkheim's most important impact on anthropology resulted from his early development of a *functionalist* approach: he argued forcefully that social phenomena could most usefully be analyzed in terms of the functions they serve in maintaining the social system as a whole. A generation of anthropologists, including Bronislaw Malinowski and A. R. Radcliffe-Brown, was deeply influenced by this theoretical perspective.

Durkheim's most significant application of his functionalist approach was his study of religion (*The Elementary Forms of the Religious Life,* 1917). Religious beliefs and rituals, he contended, serve an important social function in enhancing the solidarity of group members, transmitting their culture from generation to generation, and integrating individuals into a normative structure. Durkheim believed that a shared belief system—a religion or some functional equivalent—was essential for social integration. Without such a system, social order would tend to disintegrate, leading to a situation

of societal and individual anomie, or norm-lessness. Other major works include *Division of Labor in Society* (1897). In the former he developed his concepts of *Organic* and *Mechanical* social integration, in the latter the concept of Anomie.
　　*See also* Anomie; Function; Functionalism; Suicide
　　Consult: Lukes, Stephen, *Emile Durkheim: His Life and Works* (New York: Harper & Row, 1973).
　　*—Ian Robertson, Cambridge University*

**Dyad.** *See* Network, social.

**Dysfunction.** This term is often used to explain how a society is held together. Dysfunction, the opposite of eufunction, lessens the adaptation of a unit to its setting, thus encouraging the change or dissolution of the unit. In less abstract terms, a dysfunctional entity is one which fosters the change or dissolution of a society and its institutions or hinders the realization of goals. For example, personal poverty is

*Émile Durkheim*

dysfunctional to being elected to high political office in contemporary America. The most explicit formulation of this notion is found in writings based on general equilibrium theory and the concept of homeostasis (uniform state)—for example, functionalist theory.
　　*See also* Function; Functionalism
　　Consult: Levy, Marion J., "Structural-Functional Analysis," in *International Encyclopedia of the Social Sciences* (New York: Macmillan, 1968).

**Early Humans.** *See* Fossil sequence of human evolution.

**Ecological Niches.** The concept of ecological niches, borrowed from biology, is important to the theory of cultural ecology. It notes that the total environment can be divided into a number of areas within which live different forms of life and different social groups. One studies the relationship between a social group and its microenvironment and also that between groups occupying one niche and those occupying another. Thus although several social groups may live and subsist in the same geographical area, in fact they may occupy quite different niches and have very different methods of subsistence. When two such groups depend on each other for the exchange of subsistence goods, another term borrowed from biology—symbiosis—is used to describe the situation.

Julian Steward's concept of multilineal evolution has made significant use of the notion of ecological niche. He has carefully operationalized the concept of adaptation by urging a step-by-step analysis of the way a specific group adapts to a specific ecological niche; only then can carefully controlled comparisons with other groups in similar niches be made. The ecological relationships of human groups include not only the relations between the group and its specific physical habitat but also those with other groups and those within itself—that is, with its own sociocultural institutions.
　　*See also* Cultural ecology; Evolutionism
　　Consult: Barth, Fredrik, "Ecological Relations of Ethnic Groups in Swat, North Pakistan," *American Anthropologist* 58: 1079–1089, 1956.
　　*—Frank A. Salamone, St. John's University*

**Ecology.** The science of the interrelationship between living organisms and their natural environments.

*See also* Cultural ecology

**Ecology, Cultural.** *See* Cultural ecology.

**Economic Anthropology.** This major subfield of social anthropology deals with the way groups of people obtain a living from nature and with the factors affecting the organization of those engaged in such activities. It also deals with distribution of goods and services in society and attempts to explain who gets what and why.

Economic anthropology is different from economics because it deals primarily with primitive and peasant societies in which the economy is organized significantly differently than it is in industrialized societies, whether capitalist or socialist. Thus economic anthropologists have had to reexamine the fundamental notions which economists take for granted. To take three important examples, the concepts of labor, property, and value in nonmonetary economics have been the source of major theoretical arguments on the part of such writers as R. Firth, M. Herskovits, R. Salisbury, K. Polanyi, and many others.

Economic anthropologists have been forced to examine such fundamentals because of the "embedded" nature of primitive economics: while in industrialized societies economic relations and activities are regarded as "economic," in primitive societies they are part of kinship, political, or religious relations. In these societies people will work for each other because they are kinsfolk or subjects, not because of notions of exchanging or employing labor. Similarly most transactions take the form of bridewealth or tribute or gifts to cement a peace pact, not exchanges for material gain. In such circumstances the assumption that economic relations and transactions are simply motivated by the desire to obtain the maximum profit cannot be made—the interplay between social and material consideration must be examined.

Another difference between economic anthropology and classical economics is that while the latter is normally concerned with problems of distribution, because these dominate in industrialized economies,

anthropologists studying primitive and peasant societies are forced to pay more attention to small-scale production since, because of a simpler division of labor, this is much more important than distribution. Production for consumption is typically organized on a domestic level. It is inextricably linked to familial concerns and is at the same time extremely complex. As a result, this type of production has resisted theoretical analysis until the recent attempt by M. Sahlins.

Economic anthropology not only deals with the inner dynamics of primitive and peasant societies but also explores the involvement of these societies in national or world economies. Often it attempts to explain the success or failure of primitive societies in the wider economy. Studies of this type by anthropologists are often linked with evaluating or even guiding community development projects. Recently, however, the emphasis has turned from stressing the modernizing effect of contact with wider economies to concern with impoverishment, which seems to follow the involvement of marginal societies with the wider economy.

Although concern with economics characterized the work of many early anthropologists such as L. H. Morgan, economic anthropology as such first emerged in the work of B. Malinowski and his pupils, especially R. Firth and A. I. Richards. They produced thorough economic anthropological ethnographies, and their work has been a model for all subsequent studies. In the United States the subject really came into existence with the work of M. Herskovits and S. Tax. In the 1960s a controversy arising from the work of the economic historian K. Polanyi dominated the subject. Polanyi accused earlier writers such as Herskovits and Firth of having incorporated too readily the theories of neoclassical economics for the study of primitive and peasant societies. Polanyi and his followers argued that because primitive economies were different in kind from industrialized economies, two different types of economic theory were needed. This controversy is still continuing. Although Polanyi's charge that anthropologists had imputed capitalist notions where they did not belong seems justified, it is difficult to maintain his rigid contrasts between the two types of economies. Moreover, it is now being realized that the theories which Polanyi rejected for primitive economies

are also insufficient for understanding industrialized economies.

Consult: Firth, R. (ed.), *Themes in Economic Anthropology* (London: Tavistock, 1967); Sahlins, M., *Stone Age Economics* (Chicago: Aldine, 1972).
—Maurice Bloch, London School of Economics

**Economic Determinism.** This theory holds that all historical and sociocultural phenomena have economic causes. The theory is criticized by both Marxian and orthodox social scientists. The latter, who erroneously associate economic determinism with Marxism, concede that economics is important but argue that other factors must also be taken into account. Marxists, on the other hand, are careful to distinguish between economic determinism and their own theory of historical materialism, which holds that economics, although clearly important, does not form a separate sphere of human activity and that it is necessary to look at social relationships, especially class relationships, in their totality in order to understand historical and sociocultural phenomena.

*See also* Functionalism

**Economic Development.** *See* Development, economic.

**Economic Systems.** Because varied definitions of the term *economic* exist, there are different conceptions of economic systems. Generally, economic systems are conceived to involve the production, distribution, and consumption of the goods and services needed and wanted by a population delimited as a societal unit—nation-state, tribe, chiefdom—subdivisions of which are not conceived as having separate economic systems but as being part of the whole system. The system aspect refers to the interlocking of production, consumption, needs, and wants in long-term arrangements, even though each may vary continuously within certain limits. As variables of economic systems, they may, in principle, be measured as may also the limits of variation or their total interaction (e.g., gross national product).

In most known societies, the purely economic aspects have been tightly interlaced with most other institutions, as in so-called primitive societies, or with the state, whether secular or theocratic, as in archaic states and medieval societies. Thus, analyzing a separate economy is often difficult or meaningless. Virtually the only societies in which the economic systems can be described as separate subsystems are the historically recent mercantilist-capitalist ("modern") nations. The asserted discreteness is more a perception arising from applying classical (formalist) economic theory, which developed within, and as a special theory for, those societies, than an actuality —as the study of nonmarket influences on the economy (like cartels and advertising) shows. Still more recently, socialist, neo-colonial capitalist, and semicapitalist/semi-socialist societies have consistently shown the reemergence of close integration between state and economy: significantly, these economies are political organizations, politically conceived, while the polities are economic organizations, economically conceived.

Much recent political economic thought has led to the recognition that the conception of economy and society as coterminous is highly misleading, at least for all recent large-scale societies—and even perhaps for primitive societies in today's world—since foreign exchange, trade balances, and monetary systems have linked virtually all societies in varied economic systems.

See also Capitalism; Economic systems, primitive; Economics and subsistence; Primitive capitalism; Primitive communism; Socialism; Units of study, sociocultural

Consult: Dalton, George (ed.), *Primitive, Archaic, and Modern Economies: Essays of Karl Polanyi* (Boston: Beacon Press, 1968); Frank, Andre Gunder, "On Dalton's Theoretical Issues in Economic Anthropology," *Current Anthropology* 11(1):67–70, 1970.

—Anthony Leeds, Boston University

**Economic Systems, Primitive.** This term refers to the economies of peoples labeled primitive (a dubious category). Such economies are generally categorized as "embedded" (Karl Polanyi) in other societal institutions which determine their form. Kin groups and age grades are units of production; kin networks are systems of distribution; ritual regulates production and consumption. The "rationality" of the West's mythic Economic Man is absent. Primitive "rationality" balances many values: only

some, strictly speaking, are economic; others (e.g., solidarity or aesthetics) are equally weighted.

See also Economic anthropology; Economic systems

**Economics and Subsistence.** Both these terms have ambiguous usages in social science and anthropology. Generally, the term *economics* includes phenomena usually labeled subsistence. However, economics denotes a social science which, in most Western countries, significantly separates

*Generalized reciprocity: A Yaruro Indian villager divides up butchered parts of a pig for equivalent distribution among all seven households in his village.*

production from the other parts of the economy: distribution, exchange, consumption. Production (and especially the distribution of wealth or the means of production) in such economics is taken for granted. Production is regarded as the aggregate of raw materials and goods (and sometimes services) generated in response to demand, not as a fundamental social process governing the forms of exchange and consumption. By this view, all controls over production—such as monopoly, ownership of means of production, organizational constraints on production such as those exercised by unions, government policy structuring production—are effectively omitted from descriptions of the economy or treated as peripheral. Classical economic descriptions, then, represent economies as significantly disembodied from all the institutional networks of the societies in which they occur.

The term *subsistence* often refers to several different ideas and sometimes mixes them together. In the first place, subsistence has often been conceived as a form of production ("means of subsistence") such as hunting, gathering, fishing, horticulture, agriculture. Second, it has also been used to mean merely the wherewithal for eating ("they get their subsistence from . . ."). Third, it has referred to a threshold below which persons cannot survive, as in the phrase "living below subsistence" (nonsensical, since if they were really below subsistence, they would starve to death). Here the first meaning alone will be discussed; the second is better referred to as "food supply"; the third should be eliminated.

The notion of subsistence as forms of production, along with a classification of these forms, stems from the 19th century, which also produced universal evolutionary schemes that tried to establish the order of succession of hunting, gathering, pastoralism, domestication, and so on. Though that particular form of discussion has generally disappeared, its unilinear assumptions still pervade the literature implicitly.

Subsistence or production systems have received considerable attention from anthropologists with ecological orientations. Their treatments often give some technological detail (though never a comprehensive description of the technology, largely because it is so often identified with tools alone), a broad and detailed description of the relationships among the major products or source(s) of products, the geographical conditions, and some aspects of the social order, especially those dealing with work and, in part only, those dealing with distribution.

Two things characterize these descriptions. First, they almost uniformly select one of the 19th-century categories of subsistence *types* to impose on the economy under description. Thus the economy is molded into an example of the type. The Sirionó are described as hunters and gatherers though, at the time of description, they practiced a horticulture which had apparently shrunk as they were pushed into more horticulturally peripheral areas. Some of the Plains Indians have been described as hunters though, at least until they got horses and guns, they had been partly horticulturalists. More problematic, however, is that most economies do not fit a type at all but have much more complex subsistence

components. The Venezuelan Yaruro hunt, gather, fish, garden, and presently herd pigs. A great many South American lowland peoples display similar combinations (e.g., the Shavante, Tapirape, Kwuikuru, Cubeo). The Warrau of the Orinoco Delta fish, gather, harvest a pithpalm (*moriche*) and a starchy root (*ocumo*), and do some hunting. The Ndembu of Rhodesia hunt, garden, and do some fishing. And so on. Even those societies which, for ecological reasons, have a dominant subsistence mode usually have several subsidiary modes—e.g., Northwest Coast Indians hunted and gathered in addition to their predominant fishing; the Chukchi of NE Asia gathered, hunted, and fished, in addition to their reindeer herding. This is no mere quibble, because such activities also require labor power and organization for work and have space and time coordinates. All these strongly affect social organization, transactions, and exchange: they help shape the economy.

Second, what has usually been left out in the ecologists' treatment of subsistence, or form of production, has been the formal social relations of exchange—namely, distribution and consumption. These are the very aspects of the society dealt with by formalist classical economics. This appears to be because a clear logic relating the two domains has yet to be developed. Treating them from the beginning as being in separate spheres of discourse has no doubt made this development unlikely. Given the axioms of classical economics, the construction of such a logic cannot be carried out within it. Nor can it be done in the substantivist economics of Karl Polanyi, despite his treatment of economic institutions as being embedded in sociopolitical spheres, because he still defines economies in terms of distribution. This is seen in all his key concepts and concerns: equivalencies; reciprocal, redistributive, and market systems; special and all-purpose money; ports of trade. He gives us no prolonged theoretical or substantive discussion of production, which, in Western thought, is generally conceived in purely technological, rather than distributional or social organizational, terms.

The Marxian approach to the problem may yield better solutions. Marxists regard means of production—including tools and apparatuses, land, capital—as being distributed in a population; in all stratified societies they are *inequitably* distributed. Legal and

ideological means as well as coercion and various forms of manipulation reinforce this inequity. Furthermore, inequitable distribution is not just a single event in the past but a *continuous* process such that a relatively constant set of social relations becomes established in respect of this distribution process: the *social relations of production.* These, together with the *means of production,* constitute the *modes of production,* a conception which is intended to designate the entire sociocultural structure of society, including its subsistence forms and their *productive* distributional modalities which together provide the organizing principles of every society. The means of production are used in the production of the aggregate social product of society, including replacement (reproduction) and new means of production which must again be distributed through the society in a pattern now determined by the relations of production (the distribution of wealth as social organization). The rest of the social product ultimately is used by consumers whose consumption is itself conceived of as production in that it produces the capacity to work (that is, the maintenance and replacement of society's producers). Thus production, distribution, and consumption are not merely linked (they are considered linked but *separate* in classical economics) but are different aspects of the *identical* process —production itself is a form of production. All these relations are in a continuous flow that is sometimes, as in all recent societies; complicated by the intermediacy of money. All these relations also involve transfers and exchanges—phenomena which, along with consumption (seen in classical economics, contrary to the Marxist view, as the *generator of production*), constitute the domains of classical and substantivist economics. Sophisticated descriptions of medieval and modern complex economies in Marxian terms have been carried out, but none exists for primitive societies. Many ecology-oriented studies have a Marxian cast to them because of their emphasis on production or "subsistence" but are not systematically linked into Marxian theory.

Returning, then, to subsistence types, it has been shown with increasing cogency that these reified types generally help very little in understanding *actual* economies because, on the basis of a single abstracted attribute (e.g., that a people "hunt"), they classify into a single homogeneous entity situations so vastly different that they are often incomparable. Thus Australian tribes are classified together with Plains Indians as "hunters and gatherers"—disregarding differences in density/area of animals hunted or materials gathered so vast that the biomass of food supply (measured in calories, proteins, and other food values) made possible much higher human carrying capacities on the Plains than in the Australian deserts. This had very significant consequences for social organization and settlement forms. Also, large herds and their behavior on the Plains had quite different effects on social organization than did the dispersed resources of the Australians. In important ways, whether the food supply is gotten by hunting, fishing, gathering, or horticulture is for many consequences almost irrelevant. Much more important is how production, through technological organization, land exploitation, water use, and the like (which can have cross-type similarities), governs labor organization and behavior patterns through time and in space, because these basic dimensions also lay out the frameworks of exchanges and distributions as well as of settlement.

For example, the major source of food among Northwest Coast Indians was salmon caught during the spring spawning runs. Major production was thus concentrated along certain parts of rivers and during a relatively brief season of the year. Such production required organization and coordination as well as a system to handle off-season distribution of food resources to maintain both the productive and the future productive populations. That is, work and food exchanges took place—e.g., rights to fish on a riverbank controlled by one person in exchange for labor, goods, or produce. The coordination and control of resource production areas engendered a hierarchy—the typical Northwest Coast ranking system—which was linked to the labor and food resource distribution and exchanges. Labor, of course, contributed to accumulation of social product in good times, an accumulation that also facilitated the accumulation of prestige by means of the ritual giveaway feast called the potlatch. But prestige itself was also exchangeable—for food, labor, rights, and goods which could in turn be exchanged, often as part of the distribution of the means of production. The exchange system was intimately locked into the production system and both involved complex distributions and redistributions of wealth in a constantly readjusting hierarchic system—made possible by the great seasonal productivity of the rivers.

In contrast, the Yaruro of Venezuela have no single overwhelmingly predominant harvest but a number of different crops, riverine products, game sources, and gathered goods, all dispersed temporally and spatially. The carrying capacity for any one of these sources is low. Moreover, their joint carrying capacity is also low, so that human settlements must either be very small or very distant or some compromise between the two. No coordination is needed, since no major tool or resource concentration exists, no yield is great at any moment, and the co-occurrence of harvests in small scale disperses the small labor force. All members, whether male or female, tend to produce roughly similar amounts throughout the year. Thus no centralized distribution of the means of production either spatially or temporally occurs. Rather, a constant state of their distributedness exists, accompanied by continuous smallish exchanges of daily multiple products from different places and different people, flowing through the entire community. The egalitarian exchange system is the logical ordering of the distribution of the means of production in time, in space, and in the community.

Both the Northwest Coast and the Yaruro patterns are often conceived to be anomalous in terms of the received classification of subsistence types: fishers are supposed to be egalitarian, horticulturists stratified. But this is nonsense derived from reified ideal types which thoroughly disregard such matters as carrying capacity, population density, productivities, seasonality of production, resource location, and their interaction. The point of the examples is not to show exceptions but to point out the irrelevancy of the whole inherited typology—since simply talking about subsistence *types* avoids all the crucial dimensions of the economy (the translatability of production, distribution, and exchange). If a typology is needed, it must be based on criteria much more useful than those used heretofore.

Concentration on subsistence types has led to little fruitful consideration of the orders of social existence beyond the economy and its immediate political linkages. That approach has told us little about the state, its variants, its emergence; little about warfare (e.g., "hunter" warfare versus "horticulturalist" warfare); little or nothing about associations; little or nothing about ideological realms, especially religion.

Finally, the correlations between the inherited types—and various societal features—have consistently been weak and in any case not clearly attributable to the subsistence type itself (e.g., chiefs among the Warrau and the Northwest Coast Indians cannot be attributed to fishing per se in any clear way). Analysis of productivity, labor concentration, seasonal labor organization, and carrying capacity can lead to successful correlational studies, although this endeavor has barely begun.

The current trend in the study of subsistence and economy appears, via the twin roads of a more sophisticated ecological analysis and a revived interest in the Marxian approach, to eliminate the inherited categorical boundaries reflected in the title of this article. The trend is to regard these subjects, as well as many aspects of the social and ideological domains of the society, as parts of a single well-articulated system and to delineate even more exactly and quantitatively the nature of the interaction of the elements of the system as a whole, including its production, distribution, and exchange aspects.

*See also* Economic systems; Economic systems, primitive; Technology; Tools and evolution

Consult: Dalton, George (ed.), *Tribal and Peasant Economies: Readings in Economic Anthropology* (Garden City, N.Y.: Natural History Press, 1967); Leclair, Edward E., and Schneider, Harold K. (eds.), *Economic Anthropology: Readings in Theory and Analysis* (New York: Holt, 1968); Marx, Karl, *The Grundrisse*, ed. and trans. D. McLellan (New York: Harper & Row, 1971); Polanyi, Karl, Arensberg, Conrad M., and Pearson, Harry W. (eds.), *Trade and Markets in the Ancient Empires* (Glencoe, Ill.: Free Press, 1957); Sahlins, Marshall D., *Stone Age Economics* (Chicago, Aldine, 1972). —Anthony Leeds, Boston University

**Ecosystem.** *See* Cultural ecology

**Education in Cross-Cultural Perspective.** The term *education* refers to the process of learning within formally structured social institutions, usually schools of some sort. Education is often distinguished from

*A teacher reads an English lesson to his uniformed students in a public high school near Takatoya, Japan. English is the required second language for middle school and high school students in Japan.*

informal learning accomplished within the family or peer group.

As societies grow larger and more complex, it becomes necessary to prepare people to assume the specialized roles necessitated by an ever-increasing division of labor. The family becomes less and less able to fulfill this function as more (and more specific) factual data need to be learned before a person can participate in the socioeconomic systems of modern societies. Each culture must develop ways to sort its members into certain groupings. From these categories are then drawn the recruits to fill the positions which support the society. Thus educational institutions select and prepare people to fulfill social roles for which they are suited by capabilities, interests, and background. These institutions increase people's technical knowledge and offer practice in the skills for which someday, optimistically, they will be sought.

Conflicts at all levels of education exist universally today because of inability to de-fine both the explicit and the implicit functions of education in the modern world. To prepare people to take their place in a technological system based on scientific principles it is necessary to begin indoctrinating them into a scientific mode of thinking at an early age. It often occurs that in educational institutions people learn alternative explanations for natural phenomena which are at variance with, or even contradict, the explanations from the cosmology of the family or local group. In turn, this frequently leads to a rejection of the value system into which a person was enculturated. The results are twofold: ambivalence within the individual and a thinking gap between the educated and the partially educated or noneducated.

The concept of free education for all as a birthright in the modern world has caused a significant shift in the emphasis of educational institutions from the days when formal education was a privilege of members of the upper class in training for the manipulation of power—political, religious, and military. The professionalization of certain activities—curing, counseling (legal and other), running a business, teaching, inventing products, developing processes, growing food—has forced learning institutions into the business of job-training. Formerly, these institutions were charged with producing Educated Persons, humanistic generalists who learned the specific skills necessary to their positions only after they embarked upon their life's work. Today a liberal education (in the liberal arts and sciences) is widely considered a nonproductive luxury; job-training is thought to be the proper business of higher education. Not even all educators, let alone the general public, can see the basic interrelationship between the two.

When it is stated that learning takes place by imitation, instruction, and inference (Bock 1974), there is a corollary that not everyone will be exposed equally to ideal role models, omniscient instructors, and complete (internally sufficient) sets of reasoning rules. Not everyone will be able to do every job. Therefore the problems of who is selected for what positions, how they are selected, and what characteristics are sought must be recognized and resolved. How these problems are defined and resolved varies by culture. The United States and the People's Republic of China may be contrasted vis-à-vis their approach to one aspect of this selection problem. In the United States the emphasis is on individualism and competition; in China the individual is subordinated to society and cooperation is emphasized (Hsu 1972). This is not to say that these orientations are mutually exclusive and absolute in either culture but that explicit recognition and implemented emphasis are greater on the one pair of ideas than the other in each case.

Therefore, in the United States a majority of those who complete a professional education tend to have certain characteristics; ability to draw on financial resources for long periods of time, thus freeing them of the necessity to divide their interests and time between academic and monetary pursuits; ability to compete without guilt as individuals, often attaining success at the expense of others' defeats; a strong sense of identity and self-satisfaction in terms of the goal thus achieved.

In China, many candidates for the coveted positions in universities and the military are chosen by their peers. After the universal, basic education is completed, youths join some kind of collective work project. At the end of the several years necessary to qualify for candidacy, nominations are made by the work group and recommended by the supervisors. Thus the individuals chosen for free professional training have already proved themselves to be cooperative workers and to have productive work habits and an integrated, practical understanding of political ideology and societal values and goals. All further training, therefore, is acquired in the context of contribution to society as a whole, as opposed to (or in addition to) individual choice and gratification.

As a consequence of cultural definitions of social responsibility and self-fulfillment, people learn to be responsible and fulfilled within the context and limits of their own social institutions.

*See also* Enculturation; Needs, human; Primary institutions; Role; Role recruitment criteria
Consult: Bock, Philip K., *Modern Cultural Anthropology* (New York: Knopf, 1974); Curle, Adam, *Education for Liberation* (London: Tavistock, 1974); Goetz, Judith P., and Hansen, Judith F., "The Cultural Analysis of Schooling," *CAE Quarterly*, Washington, 1974; Hsu, Francis L. K., *Psychological Anthropology* (Cambridge, Mass.: Schenkman, 1972).
—*MaryAnn Foley, Southern Connecticut State College*

**Eggan, Fred R.** (b. 1906). An American social anthropologist greatly influenced by A. R. Radcliffe-Brown, Eggan has combined structure-function theory with historical analysis (using his method of "controlled comparison") in studies of social organization and social change among North American Indian cultures.

**Ego.** Freud's "self," the part of the psyche which interprets reality and outside experience, also acts as referee between id and superego.

*See also* Freud, Sigmund; Id; Superego

**Eiseley, Loren C.** (b. 1907). A physical anthropologist who has been interested in early population in the Western United States, Eiseley has also analyzed the history of science, especially Darwin's theory of evolution, which he has endeavored to teach to a wide audience through a platform of books and articles in the popular media.

**Eliade, Mircea** (b. 1907). A scholar whose major work is in the fields of comparative religion and folklore and whose research deals with the fundamental categories of thought. His books include *Zalmoxis: The Vanishing God, Comparative Studies in the Religion and Folklore of Dacia and Eastern Europe,* and *Myth and Reality.*

**Elites.** The concept of an elite refers ambiguously to all members of an upper class, to its especially powerful members, or to powerful members of any class. The ambiguity arises from inadequate analysis of structural aspects of societal power distribution and indecision whether such structural analysis or class analysis is fundamental. Actually, the latter can be subsumed under the former by viewing elites as involving *kinds* of key positions and resources varying with class but regarding *all* the society's elites as hierarchically arrayed according to *total amounts* of power they control. Structure, rather than cultural norms, delineates the social loci called elites—they are composed of aggregates of positions and social networks, rather than roles or statuses.

*See also* Network, social

**Embellishment.** *See* Adornment.

**Embroidery.** This term refers to any decorative needlework applied to fabric or leather. Embroidery may be done by hand or machine; often contrasting colored yarns, metallic threads, and other materials are used.

**Emics.** Emics refers to a variety of theoretical field approaches in anthropology concerned with the inside or native (folk) view of a culture. The concept is based on the formulation of Kenneth Pike (1954), who proposed that a model for studying nonlinguistic behavior be devised analogous to the phonetic and phonemic approaches in linguistic theory—hence "emic" and "etic." The formulation is sufficiently ambiguous to allow for a variety of interpretations. However, the main idea is that the subjects one is studying have their own (folk) categories (cognitive categories), assumptions about these categories, taxonomies and part-whole systems in terms of which they logically relate these categories to each other, as well as values concerning items classified according to these categories. To understand the behavior of subjects, then, it is crucial that the field researcher identify the cognitive properties of these emic categories; otherwise interpretations of behavior cannot claim to reflect units of behavior which are meaningful to the people studied.

*See also* Cognitive categories; Cultural relativism; Etics; New Ethnography, the
Consult: Pike, Kenneth, *Language in Relation to a Unified Theory of the Structure of Human Behavior*, vol. 1 (Glendale, Calif.: Summer Institute of Linguistics, 1954).
—*Richard L. Stone, California State University, Los Angeles*

**Emotions, Cultural Basis of.** This term refers to the learned aspects of emotions which result from membership in a culture. Hildred Geertz, focusing on an assumed universal human potential for emotional experience, maintains that a fundamental and often ignored aspect of the enculturation (socialization) process is the set of expectations and demands of adults regarding the child's emotions. Each culture emphasizes certain emotions and deemphasizes others, simultaneously setting rules for the proper manner of their expression. Such considerations are vital for understanding the development of personality in culture.

Opinion is varied regarding the extent of cultural influence on emotional life, although few would deny it considerable influence. Weston LaBarre has championed a strongly relative cultural deterministic perspective, arguing that there is no natural or cross-culturally shared language of emotional gesture. He notes, for example, the cross-cultural diversity in manifestation and meaning of laughter. Paul Ekman, in contrast, has studied facial expression of emotion. He notes that while cultural factors may influence the inducing stimuli, the manner and extent of display, and behavioral consequences of emotional expression, there are universal elements in the facial expression of emotion that do not vary cross-culturally.

*See also* Communication, nonverbal; Culture and personality; Expressive systems
Consult: Ekman, P., "Universal Facial Expressions of Emotion," *California Mental Health Digest*, 1970; Geertz, H., "The Vocabulary of Emotion: A Study of Javanese Socialization Processes," *Psychiatry* 22:225–237, 1959; LaBarre, W., "The Cultural Basis of Emotions and Gestures," *Journal of Personality* 16:49–68, 1947.
—*Stan Wilk, Lycoming College*

**Empire.** *See* Imperialism.

**Enculturation.** This term, which refers to the process of learning one's culture, is often (but by no means universally) distinguished from *socialization,* which means the general process of learning culture. Enculturation is most often applied to childhood learning.

In anthropological usage, enculturation is not limited to childhood but is a life-long process. Each time a novel situation is encountered in which the content and rules of new roles must be learned, it may be said that enculturation is taking place. One has to learn how to become an acceptable patient in a hospital, how to think and act like a professional, how to interact as a spouse, parent, grandparent, or in-law. We must all learn how to grow old and prepare to die, each within the acceptable limits of behavior and within the context of our own culture.

Whether in the context of formally structured, institutionalized learning or in the informal mode usually understood as the enculturation process, humans learn by imitation, instruction, and inference. Through the interaction of these three processes, the members of every society learn the general patterns of their culture—i.e., what one must or must not believe and do. In addition they learn the social norms (what one should or should not do) as well as allowed variations (what one may or may not do). When people have these understandings internalized, they may be in a position to refine the concepts to the extent of imposing personal behavior and personal interpretations on them.

*See also* Culture and personality

Consult: Hunter, David E., and Whitten, Phillip, *The Study of Anthropology* (New York: Harper & Row, 1976); Redfield, Robert, *Peasant Society and Culture* (Chicago: University of Chicago Press, 1956).

—*MaryAnn Foley, Southern Connecticut State College*

**Endogamy.** Endogamy is a rule defining the largest group from which a person may choose a marriage partner. In most societies one is expected to choose someone from the same tribe, caste, race, religion, social class, or ethnic group.

*See also* Exogamy; Kinship; Marriage

**Energy Sources.** Most human energy sources, until recently, were derived ultimately from plant photosynthesis of carbon dioxide and water in sunlight. Photosynthesis converts these components into various plant substances, such as carbohydrates and cellulose, that are often immediately exploitable by humans for food and other energy uses. Directly or indirectly, these substances can, in turn, be converted into food or energy sources by animals and humans. For humans one major energy conversion is into animal tissue, especially through tame and domestic animal pastoralism. Animals store usable energy in the forms of fats, oils, proteins, and the like—all convertible into calories. Animals cost more, in terms of energy, than plants because their efficiency in converting plant energy into animal tissue is relatively low. That is, plants provide humans more energy from the same biomass and area than animals—if the area can yield usable crops and adequate nutrition, especially proteins. Animals often make accessible areas and plant energy otherwise not usable by humans, thus expanding the adaptive range of human populations into, for instance, tundra and desert areas (e.g., the Siberian Chukchi and Arabian Bedouin, respectively). Animals, including humans, derive energy used for basal metabolism and all activity from plants and other animals.

Plants or plant derivatives (peat, coal, oil) also provide energy when directly burned as fuels. The heat generated can in turn produce chemical conversions in other substances (as in cooking) and can be converted into mechanical energy (for use in machines). Animal products, especially dung, fats, and oils, are also used as fuels for heating and for converting other substances. All these uses parallel those in the human body: for heat, for chemical conversion of substances, and for mechanical action of the body as tool or machine. From the point of view of energy sources and uses, all culturally produced chemical and mechanical conversions may be considered extensions of the bodily ones, created through the human capacity for symbolic communication.

The fact that animal bodies can convert energy into mechanical action has been widely utilized by humans to extend their own body-as-tool use by making animals work, thereby exploiting their energy-transforming capacities. Thus cattle, for example, have a dual energy source role for humans—as food and as draft animals used to produce more plant energy sources.

Besides plant and animal energy sources in immediate or fossilized forms, humans also discovered nonorganic sources. The earliest sources utilized were wind and water, both applied to various machines or mechanical devices, like waterwheels and windmills, which could transform inorganic energy into work useful to humans such as grinding indigestible hard grains into flour. Some machines permitted transforming the inorganic energy (ultimately deriving its energy from the sun) into other forms more useful to humans. Chancy flows of water or wind may operate hydraulic rams, with relatively low energy loss, to fill reservoirs with controlled flows. Quite recently, the conversion of flows into electricity by dynamos (as well as thermally) has produced a virtually global revolution in energy distribution and use. Other recently discovered inorganic energy sources, such as combustible gases, are usually derivative from major natural sources that do not themselves occur freely.

*Ladakhi baby, India. Every normal infant human being is apparently born biologically programmed to learn language, and capable of learning any human language. The culture of the group into which he or she is born sets limits on what the child will learn (including which language) but within those limits makes possible a full range of creative and expressive behaviors.*

Most recently, developments in physical chemistry, microphysics, and electricity have initiated exploitation of the ultimate energy sources—free energy and the atomic and subatomic particles that make up all matter in the universe. To be used, some of this energy must be released from its bound forms in matter on earth to produce atomic energy. Some, however, comes as radiant energy from the sun (the only stellar body sufficiently close to constitute a significant free energy source). But conversion of solar radiation into useful work has only begun.

See also Domestication of plants and animals; Technology

Consult: Cottrell, Fred, *Energy and Society* (New York: McGraw-Hill, 1955).

—Anthony Leeds, Boston University

**Engels, Friedrich** (1820–1895). Born in Germany, Engels spent most of his life in England (see his *Condition of the Working Class in England,* 1845). For nearly forty years, Karl Marx and he built a monumental new synthesis of societal analysis and philosophy. They wrote *The German Ideology* (1845), whose five premises of human existence correspond to those made implicitly by all anthropologists. Engels explored areas

*Friedrich Engels*

that interested Marx less, e.g., Engels' *Dialectics of Nature* (1872). His *Origin of the Family, Private Property and the State* (1884), drawing from Lewis Henry Morgan's work, is central to Marxist, but not to non-Marxist, anthropology.

See also Marx, Karl

**English School of Linguistics.** *See* Firth, J. R.

**Entry into Fieldwork Situation.** *See* Fieldwork, ethnographic.

**Environment.** *See* Cultural ecology.

**Epicanthic Fold.** This fold of skin on the nasal side of the eyelid partially covers the inside corner of the eye. It is characteristic of many Mongolian peoples, including some North American Indians and Eskimos.

See also Race

**Episememe.** The meaning of a tagmeme (which is the smallest meaningful unit of grammatical form).

Consult: Bloomfield, Leonard, *Language* (New York: Holt, 1933).

**Epistemology.** Epistemology concerns the means of knowing anything. Observation underlies all scientific knowledge, whatever the constructs, logical terms, and axioms used. All scientific epistemology must confront the nature of observation, nonobservational elements of scientific discourse, and their relationship. Observation, selecting only some attributes from reality, involves bias, inference, and interpretation—the latter based partly on explicit theory, partly on implicit folk theory. Thus no ultimate, unalterable facts exist. Although some are more durably established than others, even these change with changes in axioms or the perceiving instrument (humans). Epistemic questions entail assumptions about reality (ontology). Since ontological inquiry about culture scarcely exists, anthropological epistemic inquiry, especially of cultural knowledge, is undeveloped.

Consult: Osgood, Cornelius, "Culture: Its Empirical and Non-Empirical Character," *South-*

*western Journal of Anthropology* 7(2):202–214, 1951.

**Epstein, Arnold Leonard** (b. 1924). A social anthropologist who is a leading figure in the study of complex societies, Epstein has been primarily interested in African urbanization.

**Equivalencies.** "They owe us a dinner" expresses the concept of equivalencies. All peoples have calculi for assessing equivalent value for quite different *kinds* of things entering into exchange—e.g., social prestations (like giving a dinner for someone) for prestige (to the honored donor) or gifts for favors, although standard measures like money may also be involved. In some societies equivalencies constitute the only measures of value—e.g., where money is absent. Because the values entering into exchange have no common measure, such equivalencies are extremely difficult to measure objectively, though everyone (including all our Christmas givers and getters) is quite clear, subjectively, when the exchange is unsatisfactory.

Consult: Dalton, George (ed.), *Primitive, Archaic, and Modern Economies: Essays of Karl Polanyi* (Boston: Beacon Press, 1968).

**Erikson, Erik** (b. 1902). The main contribution of this modern psychoanalytic theorist has been to supplement the Freudian theory of psycho*sexual* development with a new account of psycho*social* development. Erikson believes that individuals move through eight psychosocial stages during the life cycle. At any given stage, the integrity of the personality depends largely on the successful adjustment to the previous stages. Erikson contests the Freudian view that most neuroses are primarily sexual in origin; many people, he contends, suffer rather from problems of "identity confusions." His major work is *Childhood and Society* (1950; 1963 rev.).

**Eros.** In Freudian psychology, eros is the sexual or life instinct; it is often opposed to thanatos, the aggressive or death instinct. Eros was the Greek god of sexual (i.e., erotic) love.

*Erik Erikson*

*See also* Freud, Sigmund; Instincts; Psychoanalytic school of psychology; Thanatos

**Estrous Cycle.** The reproductive cycle of the female primate is characterized by a period of sexual receptivity (estrus). The cycle involves changes, mediated by hormones, in the tissues of the reproductive organs. The peak of behavioral sexual receptivity usually corresponds to ovulation, which is the point at which conception is most likely to occur. In the higher primates (monkeys and apes), the cycle recurs at approximately monthly intervals, though some species may cease to cycle at certain periods of the year. Prosimians are clearly seasonal breeders, but may go through more than one estrous cycle if fertilization does not occur. In several species of Old World monkeys and in chimpanzees a pronounced swelling of the external genitalia accompanies the cycle.

**Ethics and Social Research.** In 1919 Franz Boas publicly denounced spying under the guise of scholarship and raised for the first time in professional anthropology the question of ethics and responsibility in social research.

As remote, unwesternized populations disappear from the earth, as imperialism becomes a worldwide phenomenon, and as colonial interests give way to self-government, anthropologists are unable to deal unanimously with the pressing questions of responsibility to informants, the public, the profession, themselves, their students, funding institutions, and national governments. Because the questions are as many and as varied as the research possibilities, there has developed since 1967 a vast literature on ethics and social research.

The history of anthropological involvement with American Indians and other native peoples throughout the world—and the harm which has befallen their cultures—provoked a series of statements from members of the American Anthropological Association during the years 1946–1952. Widespread concern with the state of the professional enterprise, however, did not surface in the association until the Vietnam War, counterinsurgency research in Thailand and Latin America, and the subsequent political ramifications:

> As anthropologists we recognize that mankind . . . is now threatened with the possibility of extinction. . . . It is urgently necessary that the full resources of our science . . . be brought to bear on the easing of the immediate crisis and development of social institutions which will enable all peoples to live and work, however great their differences.

Thus read one resolution passed by the American Anthropological Association in 1967. In fact, the association has produced two statements on the problems of anthropological research and professional ethics (1967, 1971). In the association's preamble (1971) anthropologists were urged to recognize professional responsibility:

> Anthropologists work in many parts of the world in close personal association with peoples and the situations they study. . . . In a field of such complex involvements, misunderstandings, conflicts and the necessity to make choices among conflicting values are bound to arise and to generate ethical dilemmas. It is a prime responsibility of anthropologists to anticipate these and to plan to resolve them in such a way as to do damage neither to those whom they study nor, insofar as possible, to their scholarly community. Where these conditions cannot be met, the anthropologists would be well-advised not to pursue the particular piece of research.

While these statements were being debated in the AAA, members of the SAA (Society for Applied Anthropology) were discussing the dilemmas involved in applying the results of social research to practical problems and the type of direct intervention this necessitates. Subsequently, the SAA revised its 1963 statement on ethics. The AAA and SAA as professional organizations are not enforcement bodies, however, and the implementation of their formally enacted principles is still largely a matter of personal conscience. This means that many problems directly associated with changing people's lives, changing cultural systems, or bringing informants to harm or disgrace still

*Advertisement placed by the Navy in the August 1968 issue of the* American Anthropologist. *This ad touched off a great controversy: should the official organ of the internationally respected American Anthropological Association tacitly give support to anthropologists' engaging in counterinsurgency fieldwork by publishing this kind of ad? Current editorial policy is to refuse such ads.*

remain to be solved on a person-to-person basis in the field.

Professional pressure has provided internal monitoring and practical guidelines for people considering social research either in this country or abroad. Among those most active in redefining professional goals are anthropologists whose communities have been the traditional focus for anthropological research. Furthermore, the Department of Health, Education, and Welfare has implemented restrictive guidelines for the use and protection of human subjects by all research scientists. Besides the increased awareness that such efforts have fostered in the public, the government, and the profession, debates on professional responsibility have made it clear that many social scientists no longer consider themselves separate from the consequences of their research or uninvolved with the problems of humankind.

Consult: Beals, Ralph, *Politics of Social Research* (Chicago: Aldine, 1969); Beals, Ralph, "Resolutions of the Executive Board of the American Anthropological Association," *American Anthropologist* 54(2), 1952; Beals, Ralph, "Resolutions of the Executive Board of the American Anthropological Association," *American Anthropologist* 69(3-4), 1967; Beals, Ralph, "Statement on Ethics" (principles of professional responsibility adopted by the Council of the American Anthropological Association, Washington, May 1971); Beals, Ralph, "Social Responsibilities Symposium," *Current Anthropology*, December 1968; Beals, Ralph, "Toward an Ethics for Anthropologists," *Current Anthropology*, June 1971; Beals, Ralph, "Statement on Ethics," *Human Organization* 22:237, 1963; Beals, Ralph, "Report for the Committee on Ethics," *Human Organization* 10:32, 1949.

—Cathie J. Witty, University of Washington

**Ethnic Character.** See Culture and personality; Minorities, ethnic; National character; Secondary institutions.

**Ethnic Group.** This term refers to any group of people within a larger cultural unit who identify themselves as a distinct entity, separate from the rest of that culture. Along with this element of self-identification, this group usually has a number of other characteristics which show its distinctiveness and put social distance between itself and others. These characteristics may include a separate language (or dialect), distinctive traditions and social customs, distinctive dress, foods, and mode of life, and a circumscribed land base. In some stratified societies ethnic groups may be identical to social classes or castes. In the modern world, ethnic groups are present in many societies for two major reasons: migration of peoples from their original homelands to other countries; and incorporation of several small, separate cultural units into one large nation-state.

*See also* Minorities, ethnic

**Ethnic Minorities.** See Minorities, ethnic.

**Ethnobotany.** The subdivision of ethnoscience which deals with the way a society classifies the plant world of its ecosystem.

*See also* Ethnoscience; New Ethnography, the

**Ethnocentrism.** This term refers to the tendency to use the norms and values of one's own culture or subculture as a basis for judging others. The concept of ethnocentrism is often contrasted with that of cultural relativism—the perception that the norms and values of each culture have their own validity and cannot be used as a standard for evaluating other cultures.

The tendency to ethnocentrism is universal: all humans are born and raised in a culture which is usually the only one accessible to them. Exposed to no other cultural perspectives, they inevitably tend to take their own for granted. This ethnocentrism may serve the positive function of encouraging group solidarity, for it discourages assimilation into other groups and legitimates the existing culture. But ethnocentrism may also contribute to irrational prejudice and severe conflict in intergroup relations, for it may encourage hostility and contempt toward outsiders.

The anthropologists and particularly ethnographers of the 19th and early 20th centuries were often guilty of gross ethnocentrism. Modern anthropologists are well aware of the dangers of cultural bias in their work. They recognize that the investigator must be constantly on guard against the intrusion of unconscious ethnocentrism into his or her research.

*See also* Cultural relativism; Emics; Etics; Xenophobia
—*Ian Robertson, Cambridge University*

**Ethnogenesis.** This term refers to the creation of a new group—or tribal—identity. The development of a new tribe with its own distinctive culture and language generally involves the splitting of one society—for example, the development of Apache and Navajo groups—or scattered groups of refugees from several tribes may coalesce to form a distinctly new society.

Consult: Sturtevant, W. C., "Creek into Seminole," in *North American Indians in Historical Perspective*, ed. E. B. Leacock and N. O. Lurie (New York: Random House, 1971).

**Ethnographic Analogy.** This method of archaeological interpretation consists of interpreting the nonobservable behavior of the ancient inhabitants of an archaeological site (or ancient culture) based on the similarity of their artifacts to those used by living peoples. Archaeologists use ethnographic analogy in two ways: as a direct historical approach in which the modern peoples must be historical descendants of the ancient ones; and as a nonhistorical (or comparative) approach in which the ancient and modern peoples need not be historically connected but must manipulate similar environments in similar ways.

*See also* Archaeology; Artifact; Ethnography

**Ethnographic Fieldwork.** *See* Fieldwork, ethnographic.

**Ethnographic Inference.** *See* Ethnographic analogy.

**Ethnographic Semantics.** *See* Formal semantic analysis; New Ethnography, the

**Ethnography.** Ethnography literally means "a portrait of a people." Currently, it refers both to a special strategy of anthropological research and also to its products. This brief definition raises important questions about ethnographic studies. Why is the research done? Who does it and how? What kinds of information are obtained? Whose viewpoints are reflected in the final portrait—those of the ethnographer or those of the subject?

**Ethnographic Strategy.** Anthropology started as a science by assuming responsibility for the study of small, preliterate, pre-industrial societies—what was known as the primitive (as opposed to the civilized) world. Since the rise of anthropology coincided with the rise of worldwide colonial empires with a consequent high rate of social and cultural change among the small societies studied, one persistent assumption developed early: that the subject matter of the science was disappearing rapidly. This gave to early ethnographic studies the semblance and the haste of salvage operations.

This assumption led to a special bias, one which favored both the past of the people studied—how they lived before disruptive culture contacts with imperialist societies—and a preference for viewing the culture in a static, timeless fashion. For many years the ethnographic product (a book or series of essays describing one culture) consisted of a reconstruction of primitive cultures as they had existed some decades or even centuries earlier. Such monographs were often written in the present tense, and the phrase "ethnographic present" was used to caution readers that the culture, as described, no longer existed.

Such historical ethnographies are now accepted as but one possible approach to the study of cultures, for anthropologists have grown more concerned with the quite difficult problems of studying rapidly changing cultural systems. Thus the exclusive preoccupation with the past has weakened; anthropologists have learned, as A. F. C. Wallace first observed, that ethnographic research is like weather reporting—it has to be repeated at intervals if we wish to learn about the dynamics of cultural systems.

A second major bias developed very early. This was the ideal of first-hand field research, a study conducted for a long period of time by an ethnographer living directly among the people who were subjects of the inquiry.

**Case Studies and Comparisons.** The basic style of ethnography developed out of this stress on field study. Ethnographic research thus came to consist of a case study of one social unit, usually a small-scale society—a foraging band, a pastoral tribe, horticultural chiefdom. The intent of the ethnographer was to obtain detailed, first-hand, systematically collected facts about the culture being studied. The earliest ethnographic reports generally consisted of lengthy descriptive accounts organized under a variety of topical headings. The reports frequently contained lengthy transcriptions of dictated texts, folklore, medicinal practices, ritual spells, and the like. Often such reports, although loaded with content, provided little insight into how the culture actually worked. But as anthropological interest in systems and the dynamics of social life developed, ethnographers more and more attempted to understand the functioning of a society as well as merely describing the contents of belief and custom.

By researching other cultures in this fashion, anthropologists were applying what in other sciences is called the natural history method. Natural history, too, emphasizes fieldwork and case study, but the heart of the approach is comparison (not necessarily history). The strategy of ethnography—like that of natural history—is to approach general knowledge by building up a large series of case studies which can then, inductively, be compared and contrasted with one another. This was the main rationale for doing ethnographic research: it was a means of achieving general knowledge of the varieties of human cultures.

There are other senses in which ethnographic research is comparative. No anthropologist approaches a different culture free of all the biases of his or her own. Moreover, the anthropologist carries into the field specialized training, experience, and theoretical preconceptions. Ethnocentric biases are always a danger, and every anthropologist must learn to identify and control for his or her tendency to prejudge and categorize. However, making *explicit* comparisons—perhaps with similar cultures or settings—is often a fruitful way of generating new hypotheses which can lead to verified insights. This process involves the careful, deliberate use of professional experience and scientific ideas in order to learn new things. It is a very different cognitive process from the ethnocentric prejudgments which may be made by other visitors. This is another reason for doing ethnographic research: it is a better way of achieving systematic, sympathetic understanding of other cultures.

In yet another way ethnographic research may be comparative. Often the ethnographer treats the community studied as a special sample of a larger universe. This larger universe may be other communities in the same tribe or nation; or it may consist of communities with special (e.g., peasant) characteristics. The ethnographer may try to check out a generalization (e.g., whether the Oedipus complex is a human universal) or to develop a new set of insights and hypotheses which can later be checked against other studies. The point is that ethnographers do not wait until all the case studies are in before starting the process of generalization.

**Methods and Tactics.** Anthropologists come to alien communities as strangers. Approaching a culturally different community for the first time, the ethnographer first has to arrange for his or her own life support. The ideal is to subsist and learn directly in the midst of the people being studied, a strategy of research known as participant observation. The next essential task is to become something more than stranger: one must soon establish the beginnings of a social role in the community, a role which is meaningful and acceptable to the local people yet allows the ethnographer to observe, to question, and to learn.

Whatever the ethnographer's own self-concept may be, the subjects of the inquiry will fix the ethnographer in social space in terms of the familiar categories of their own experience. One anthropologist entering a Native American community in the 1950s was initially perceived as "an FBI man." Then, because he did not wear a hat and was too poor, they decided he more likely was a communist. Later they decided he was a psychiatrist, and the beginnings of a workable role emerged. In other places ethnographers have been regarded as government officials, census takers, or even as supernatural figures—a long-awaited messiah. Obviously, such perceptions profoundly influence how a group will respond to the ethnographer until an acceptable, workable set of understandings develops which allows inquiry to proceed.

Ethnographers in effect teach people about a new kind of social role. They have to be in a position where they can freely move around to observe behavior and happenings as they occur naturally in their institutional context. Of critical importance is the need to develop rapport—mutually satisfactory relationships of give-and-take, relationships of a very personal nature—particularly with key informants. Key informants are local people with extensive specialized knowledge in one or more aspects of a culture. Essentially, the relationship between an ethnographer and a key informant is that between a student and teacher or an apprentice and master. The ethnographers present themselves as novices to be socialized or enculturated anew, and the informant agrees to provide systematic instruction and guidance. Sometimes the lay public has been curious, even doubtful, that anthropologists were able to obtain so much valid, comprehensive information and insight about Native American religious practices. The doubt arises due to the erroneous belief that religious practices are closely guarded, private, esoteric matters. In fact, much religious ritual was very public, and much more was regarded as private or group property. As property, the spells, charms, rituals, curing rites, and the like could be given (or taught) to others who displayed the proper interest and attitude and were willing to pay the proper fee or deliver in exchange an appropriate gift.

Developing numerous such relationships enables the ethnographer to participate regularly and meaningfully in the lives of the people studied. Such intensive involvement is known, as has been indicated, as participant observation. As participant observer, the ethnographer sometimes attends to the doings of others, but sometimes the subject observed is his or her own self. In this way the ethnographer is rather like the pharmacologist who tries out a new chemical personally, noting the subjective reactions. Thus an ethnographer might well undergo fasting in search of visionary experiences or participate in a night-long ritual with others. A young woman researcher may be adopted as granddaughter and sister, or she may become actively involved in the food gathering or horticultural work of local women.

This involvement facilitates observation and inquiry, but it also has risks. One risk is overinvolvement with too narrow a range of persons or in too narrow a range of activities. The young woman in our example also needs to learn—from the perspective of adult males—about hunting activities or the ritual and technological preparations for a retaliatory raid. Another risk is that of identity transformation. Sometimes, more than just casually or temporarily, the ethnographer changes personal and group identifications. At minimum, many ethnographers become very defensive or possessive about "their people," wishing to safeguard them from the probing eyes of others, or to protect them from harmful influences. In this way, ethnographers find that entering a community as stranger is a lesser problem than that of leaving it as friend.

Ethnographers employ a wide variety of specialized research techniques and devices. But their basic tools are their own senses and sensitivities and their skills in communication. Communication requires some mastery of the language used. Even in studying an institution or a subculture in one's own country, this means mastery of a specialized vocabulary or set of ideas or class dialect. The results of inquiry have to be recorded for later analysis, and this means extensive note taking, transcription, translation, tape recording, photographing, and so forth. More specialized methods include census taking, genealogical inquiry, geographic and sociometric mapping, and collecting sample cases—of marriage arrangements, conflict resolutions, property exchanges, and the like.

**Units of Study.** Not much attention has been given to the strict definition of the maximal unit studied by ethnographers. A variety of criteria are used in different combinations for different purposes. Thus the culture-bearing unit may be defined as a group which speaks a common language or dialect, one which is a single, autonomous political-administrative entity, or one whose outer boundaries are defined by the people themselves. A territorial criterion may be used, or a distinctive type of ecological adaptation, or demographic features. Often the unit may be defined in terms of a shared identity and a belief in a common history and heritage. Whatever the criteria, the ethnographer invariably specifies some kind of a social grouping whose culture is being studied.

Anthropologists no longer restrict themselves to the study of small, primitive societies. Increasingly, the same approaches and methods perfected in other cultures are being used for the study of communities, institutions, and groupings in complex nation-states. Thus the social unit defined may now be an urban ghetto, an institution such as the U.S. Congress, or Hollywood.

**Ethnography: Old and New.** From the beginning one ideal in ethnographic research was to discover and describe the meanings and distinctions used by the people of other cultures and to avoid leading questions fashioned out of the categories of the ethnographer's own culture. Descriptions of this ideal kind are called *emic statements*, based on an analogy with the phonemes and morphemes of linguistics. But the ideal of achieving such a valid, internal, subjective view of other cultures has been illusive. Most ethnographic reports actually consist of a mixture of emic descriptions and etic descriptions. The latter, by and large, consist of verifiable, objective facts. But ethnographic inquiry and reporting also proceed with the use of a professionally specialized jargon of categories and concepts: such phrases as bilateral kindred, totem, sib, and shaman have specialized meanings and uses peculiar to anthropology. Moreover, when an ethnographic report carves the whole life of a people into subject headings such as Warfare, Descent Groups, or the Supernatural World, we can be certain they

do not correspond to categories meaningful to the people whose lives are so described.

In recent years a minority of anthropologists have tried to develop rigorous methods which may lead to realization of the ideal of tapping and describing the meanings of other cultures. The successes of descriptive linguistics in the 1940s and 1950s prompted this development, which is called the New Ethnography or formal ethnography. Most recently a whole new subfield called cognitive anthropology has opened up that incorporates this approach and links it to the disciplines of psychology and linguistics. Because it has promised more rigorous methods, better control over the ethnographer's biases, and an approach to certainty, the New Ethnography has had widespread appeal. But it also has many detractors—those who claim that little new is added, those who are convinced the results are too few for the labor involved, and others who believe the whole idea is hocus-pocus. However, because the New Ethnography is so recently developed, its final contributions have yet to be properly weighed. Since the methods of inquiry are relatively simple and readily teachable, the student might well try them out and gauge their value in understanding other cultures (see Spradley and McCurdy 1972).

*See also* Cross-cultural surveys; Ethnology; New Ethnography, the

Consult: Berreman, G. D., "Ethnography; Method and Product," in *Introduction to Cultural Anthropology*, ed. J. Clifton (Boston: Houghton Mifflin, 1968); Spradley, J. D., and McCurdy, D. W., *The Cultural Experience: Ethnography in Complex Society* (Chicago: Science Research, 1972).

—*James Clifton, University of Wisconsin, Green Bay*

**Ethnohistory.** This subfield of cultural anthropology is devoted to reconstructing the history of primitive and ethnic groups. Because many of these groups are preliterate, materials other than written documents are utilized by ethnohistorians, such as oral traditions, archaeological remains, and linguistic data. Since 1953, *Ethnohistory*, a journal published by the American Society for Ethnohistory, has been devoted exclusively to publishing the results of this type of research. The term *ethnohistory* has also been used to mean a group's folk explanation of

their past. Ethnohistory in this sense is used interchangeably with folk history.

*See also* Time, cultural orientation toward

**Ethnology.** This term has been defined by anthropologists in several different ways. It is sometimes used broadly as a synonym for cultural anthropology, and in the past it has also been employed to refer to the historical approach to the study of cultures. In recent years, however, a more systematic meaning has emerged which identifies ethnology with a general strategy in the search for knowledge about cultures. In this now widely accepted sense ethnology is the comparative study of cultures.

**The Strategy.** Sometimes the anthropologist engaged in a comparative study may work with data obtained personally from several different societies. Or the facts used for comparison and contrast may come from ethnographic monographs and reports that have been produced by others. This is necessarily true of large-scale comparative studies where data from fifty or more cultures may be used. In this sense, then, ethnographic reports (which reveal truths about single cultures) become the raw material for ethnological study, comparison, correlation, hypothesis-testing, and generalization.

Thus ethnology represents an anthropological expression of the nomothetic or generalizing phase of science. Here the anthropologist abstracts, generalizes, and correlates, in the search for general laws, propositions that are true of many cultures. Generally, when anthropologists make formal comparisons, especially with large samples of cultures, they use an etic approach; that is, the analysis proceeds with a scheme of classification that is drawn up prior to the study. Thus the etic units which are compared represent an external set of categories which may not represent the emic units by which the members of a society categorize their experience. For example, the anthropologist may set up a dimension of "relative permissiveness–harshness" in child-training practices and attempt to correlate it with customary beliefs about the benevolence or arbitrariness of gods.

In comparing and contrasting the aspects of a culture, so long as the societies in the sample meet the criteria for inclusion in a study and are sufficiently well described that the right kind of facts are available about them, the historic period and geographic region in which the culture occurred may be ignored. If the aim is to make generalizations about humankind, then the culture studied constitutes a small sample of the world's societies, past and present. Or the object may be to generalize about societies of a specific kind (e.g., peasants) or to deduce the sequence of cultural processes and developments in one region in the world, in which case only cultures from that area may be studied.

**Small-scale Studies.** These studies involve qualitative analysis and comparison of a few societies to reveal relations between sociocultural variables. In terms of research tactics, small-scale studies often are not far from ethnography in the methods and the variety of information used. Indeed the ethnologist and the ethnographer are often, in this case, one and the same person. Small-scale comparative studies involve the manipulation of detailed, qualitative, particularistic, concrete, unquantified facts about several cultural systems.

A favored approach in small-scale comparisons is to contrast several societies which are historically related and substantially similar in many ways, but which differ in important respects. Then the investigator can try to discover functional or causal relationships which explain the differences between the societies. In two neighboring Pacific island communities which are similar in many respects, why does one have a classic clan type of totemism while the other practices, instead, a personal medicine animal complex? Why did one of these societies willingly accept the efforts of German colonial officials to disarm them, while the other refused and went to war?

One classic example of a small-scale ethnological study is S. F. Nadel's work on witchcraft in four African societies (1952). Nadel examined "concomitant variations" in two pairs of societies: the Nupe and Gwari of Nigeria and the Korongo and Mesakin of the Sudan. The societies in each pair were quite similar in culture and social structure, except that the Mesakin were witchcraft ridden while the Korongo had no witchcraft (their rich mythology explained disease and disaster). That witchcraft beliefs expressed specific anxieties and stresses is suggested by a second paired comparison, for witchcraft accusations arise out of stressful marriage relations in Nupe

but in relations between mother's brothers and sister's sons in Mesakin. In this study, Nadel concluded that there were probably only a few limited types of witchcraft, one involving the deceased enemies of a society's ideals and a second involving persons who were unable to live up to a society's ideals (i.e., the victims). He concluded generally that witchcraft accusations serve to uphold the desired, utopian state of a society.

**Large-scale Comparisons.** Conclusions like those of Nadel have to be taken as tentative and suggestive. They point to broad, insightful generalizations, but they need to be tested systematically against a large sample of cultures. One way of accomplishing this is to test such hypotheses in successive ethnographic studies. If the conclusions are valid, then they should be repeatedly confirmed. But a more powerful approach is to test such hypotheses against a large sample of the world's cultures which have already been studied ethnographically.

Large-scale comparisons were originally suggested by Edward Tylor as one method in the study of cultural evolution. However, his suggestions were made before many cultures had been studied first hand and described by anthropologists. When ethnographic studies accumulated, they did so in a professional atmosphere highly suspicious of evolutionary thinking with respect to cultural and social systems. For this reason, much large-scale comparative research consisted of synchronic, functionalist studies of covariation in the inner workings of the parts of cultural systems. More recently, however, some evolutionary thinkers too have returned to Tylor's suggestion in order to study long-term evolutionary processes in culture.

For many conceivable problems, large-scale comparisons are not possible—the data available are limited by the questions the original ethnographers asked and the materials they published. This approach requires the investigators to start with a firm theoretical perspective. Further, they must decide what type of comparative study to conduct and what model and methods to use. Some comparisons may be aimed at simply increasing general understanding. Here broad, descriptive generalizations may be appropriate. Others may employ sophisticated models with derived hypotheses, in which case a quantitative analysis and statistical design are appropriate.

Numerous cross-cultural comparisons have made use of Yale University's Human Relations Area Files (HRAF). These files consist of excerpts from published ethnographies which are transcribed, coded, and filed under subject headings according to the classification scheme in *Outline of Cultural Materials* (Murdock 1950). The ethnographic materials are filed by code number, with each culture filed separately. Thus research in HRAF files may start by simply going to the filing cabinets and reading through the materials filed under one category. Since 1962 the journal *Ethnology* has regularly published an Ethnographic Atlas which consists of coded cultural materials on a sample of the world's societies. From this atlas, which can be readily transposed for computer analysis, one might readily survey and run intercorrelations on several aspects of the cultures of a sample of 50 or 100 of the world's societies.

The limitations of this atlas and of the materials found in the HRAF files are several. The investigator using them is dependent on the skill and reliability of anonymous coders. The information he or she seeks may have been missed; it may have been miscoded; or it might not occur at all in a large enough part of the HRAF sample. But the HRAF files do contain rich veins of information, even though they are not yet adequately mined.

See also Ethnography; Etics; Statistical methods

Consult: Brown, J., "A Cross-cultural Study of Female Initiation Rites," *American Anthropologist* 65:837-853, 1963; Clifton, J. A. (ed.), *Introduction to Cultural Anthropology* (Boston: Houghton Mifflin, 1968); Ford, C., and Beach, F., *Patterns of Sexual Behavior* (New York: Harper & Row, 1951); Murdock, G. D. (ed.), *Outline of Cultural Materials* (New Haven: HRAF Press, 1950).

—*James Clifton, University of Wisconsin, Green Bay*

**Ethnomathematics.** *See* Numbering, systems of.

**Ethnomusicology.** *See* Music and chants.

**Ethnos.** This term is used by Soviet and some European ethnologists to refer to basic cultural groupings. Soviet ethnologists are critical of what they regard as a general tendency in Anglo-American anthropology to treat racial groups and classes as actual or potential ethnic groups. They insist on a strict separation of "ethnic" from "social" processes.

*See also* Cultunit; Ethnic group

**Ethnoscience.** Ethnoscience, the study of classification systems used by societies, includes such subdivisions as ethnobotany and ethnozoology. It is sometimes a synonym for ethnosemantics.

*See also* New Ethnography, the

**Ethnosemantics.** Ethnosemantics is the study of the ranges of meaning attached to specific terms and classes or terms by members of a group. The prefix *ethno* refers to the fact that a study of a segment of reality from the perspective of the people being studied is being undertaken. The suffix *semantics* refers to meaning. Thus ethnosemantics concentrates on the meaning of categories of reality—folk taxonomies—to the people who use them as their basis for action. The underlying assumption of ethnosemantics is that the categories designated by a language adequately reflect the entire range of things important to a people within a sociocultural system using that language to encode reality. This assumption is far from universally accepted.

*See also* Componential analysis

**Ethology.** Ethology is the scientific study of animal behavior, especially in its natural environments. It developed out of zoological research in the 1930s and is prominently associated with the works of N. Tinbergen and K. Lorenz.

Early research focused on identifying *instincts,* which (though variously defined) are generally agreed to be (1) genetically inherited (innate) determiners which (2) respond to particular environmental stimuli by (3) calling into function specific neural, glandular, and muscular mechanisms that (4) underlie or generate specified behavior patterns (possibly including psychological states). As long as this research focused on the lower animals such as fish and birds, it won scientific approval and wide public acceptance. Recently, however, critics have come to doubt the utility of applying the concept of instincts even to lower species (see Cook 1970; Lehman 1953).

*Konrad Lorenz, one of the founders of ethology, is shown feeding his geese and ducks.*

In the early 1960s a wave of ethologically oriented books hit the popular marketplace. These studies attempted to demonstrate the instinctive and adaptive bases of aggressive and territorial behavior among many animals—ranging from stickleback fish through geese to monkeys and apes. Books like Konrad Lorenz's *On Aggression* (1966), Robert Ardrey's *African Genesis* (1961), *The Territorial Imperative* (1966), and *The Social Contract* (1970), and Desmond Morris's *The Naked Ape* (1967) presented popularized accounts of ethological research—and drew startling conclusions. Human behavior, they claimed, though apparently governed by rational choice and culturally structured priorities, ultimately is determined by the animal nature of the human species. Cultural solutions to aggressiveness and territoriality might at best hope to channel these "instincts" into constructive areas . . . at worst, prove inadequate to ensure the survival of civilization.

Although many anthropologists have reacted with heated alarm to these claims—criticizing them as simplistic and reductionistic to the extreme (see Montagu 1973)—nevertheless a gradual synthesis has emerged which builds on the careful field research of ethologists such as Jane Goodall (1971), George B. Schaller (1963, 1964), and Irven DeVore (1965), among others, who have concentrated their efforts primarily on primate social groups.

Human beings are, indeed, animals. They are less different from apes, for instance, than social scientists had previously supposed. However, it is a dangerous fallacy to fail to realize that human beings—though animals—are very special animals. Although human beings are genetically programmed, the program is for far greater flexibility than in any other animal. Human beings are programmed to be superb learners; and in fact each human learns an awesome amount as he or she masters the language and role behaviors, world view, and motor techniques each culture makes available and promotes. The range of behavioral patterns on the palette of human culture is vast and as varied as the colors of a rainbow. Every culture instructs each person on which patterns to select and how to engage in the art of living.

See also Culture; Instincts; Primates, behavior of

Consult: Ardrey, Robert, African Genesis (New York: Atheneum, 1961); Ardrey, Robert, The Territorial Imperative (New York: Atheneum, 1966); Ardrey, Robert, The Social Contract (New York: Atheneum, 1970); Cook, J. H. (ed.), Social Behavior in Birds and Mammals (New York: Academic Press, 1970); DeVore, Irven (ed.), Primate Behavior: Field Studies of Monkeys and Apes (New York: Holt, 1965); Lehman, D. S., "A Critique of Konrad Lorenz's Theory of Instinctive Behavior," Quarterly Review of Biology 28:237–263, 1953; Lorenz, Konrad, On Aggression (New York: Harcourt Brace Jovanovich, 1966); Montagu, Ashley (ed.), Man and Aggression, 2nd ed. (New York: Oxford University Press, 1973); Morris, Desmond, The Naked Ape (London: Cape, 1967); Schaller, George B., The Mountain Gorilla: Ecology and Behavior (Chicago: University of Chicago Press, 1963); Schaller, George B., The Year of the Gorilla (Chicago: University of Chicago Press, 1964); Van Lawick-Goodall, Jane, In the Shadow of Man (Boston: Houghton Mifflin, 1971).

—David E. Hunter, Southern Connecticut State College

**Ethos.** This concept is used to deal with the problem of integration in whole cultural and social systems. When an analyst wants to put together the details of many observations in a community or nation, questions may be raised about the kind and quality of overall organization, the congruence of separate institutions, and the consistency between different aspects of living.

The concept ethos is used to create such an order by noting and synthesizing the distinguishing affective qualities which are expressed in different institutional contexts, in various kinds of social behavior, or in different cultural products. The aim of this approach is to describe the central or dominant emotional aspects of consciousness which color and give quality to different behaviors observed in a community. Other approaches to the study of cultural integration emphasize cognitive sets, social structure, semantic processes, or historical processes.

The idea of ethos traces to the sociologist W. G. Sumner and his concern with the "dominant set" or the "directions of a culture" and to earlier efforts of philosophers and historians who wrote of the "soul" or "genius" of nations and races. This approach is best exemplified in the work of Ruth Benedict, G. Gorer, and others concerned with national character.

Consult: Gorer, G., The American People (New York: Norton, 1948).

See also Appollonian-Dionysian; National character; Themes, cultural

—James Clifton, University of Wisconsin, Green Bay

**Etics.** Etics is a label for a variety of theoretical approaches in anthropology concerned with the outsider's view of the culture. Etics involves the careful specification of the categories, the logical relations between categories (e.g., taxonomic, part-whole), and assumptions underlying the uses of these categories by social scientists. One can never assume that the researcher's etic categories (e.g., kinship) reflect a perceived reality for an informant, who has his or her own emic categories. It is very easy—especially when engaged in the task of cross-cultural comparative research—to reify one's own etic categories and assume they are the emic categories of the peoples one is studying. Some scholars note that etic categories are the emic categories of Western social science.

See also Cognitive categories; Cross-cultural surveys; Cultural relativism; Emics; New Ethnography, the

**Etiquette.** Etiquette consists of the formal and informal rules for proper behavior to all categories of persons in a society, including prescribed interpersonal rituals of courtesy, deference, superordination, and the like.

See also Manners

**Euthanasia.** This term means mercy-killing. Life-supportive measures may be withdrawn or a painless, quick-acting, lethal drug may be administered for a terminally ill or comatose patient.

**Evans, Sir Arthur** (1851–1941). Excavated Knossos on the island of Crete beginning in 1900, and coined the term "Minoan" to refer to the Bronze Age Civilization he found there. Evans also helped refine the Three Age (Stone, Bronze, and Iron) system of prehistoric taxonomy by noting the contributions made by such Iron Age migrants to Britain as the Belgae, and thus underlined the existence of cultural diversity within each of three stages.

**Evans, Sir John** (1823–1908). A British antiquary and numismatist of the second half of the 19th century, Evans conducted notable research on pre-Roman coinage and the stone and bronze tools of ancient Britain. He was involved in two of the most important archaeological controversies of his time—whether hand axes and eoliths were natural phenomena or were made by early humans. He was the father of Sir Arthur Evans, who is best known for his excavations on the island of Crete.

See also Evans, Sir Arthur

**Evans-Pritchard, Sir Edward** (1902–1974). Professor of social anthropology at Oxford University (1946–1970) and one of the founders of the British school of social anthropology, Pritchard conducted fieldwork in E Africa in the 1920s and 1930s among the Nuer and Azande tribes. Out of this research he developed theories that owe more to Emile Durkheim and his school than to Bronislaw Malinowski's functionalism, to which he remained hostile. Perhaps stimulated by his own experience of conversion to Catholicism, Evans-Pritchard developed a strong interest in cognitive systems.

**Evolution, Biological.** Biological evolution is the change in the hereditary structure of organisms, populations, and species over time. It is usually assumed that this evolution increasingly adapts organisms to their environment through competition within and among species for scarce resources and through shifting environmental challenges. The overall effect is generally a divergence of populations or species as each evolves in accordance with its own environment and life-style. The complexity of organisms and their adaptation have also commonly increased with time. Although the results are often cumulative, evolutionary trends such as larger size are reversible and may change as the environment or adaptation alters.

Physical anthropologists divide human evolution into two branches. *Macroevolution*, concerned with long-range biological changes in the structure and morphology of hominids, is the province of human paleontologists. *Microevolution*, the ongoing evolution of modern human populations, is studied by population geneticists. In both branches, the relation of cultural factors to biological changes is crucial, since culture affects technology, the structure of mating systems, and many other facets of human behavior related to our evolution and adaptation.

*See also* Adaptation, biological; Evolution, genetic mechanisms of
—*Catherine E. Read-Martin, California State University, Los Angeles*

**Evolution, Cultural.** *See* Cultural evolution.

**Evolution, General.** Although the word *evolution* is widely used as a synonym for development, or even more loosely for historical change, its original meaning in biology is more precise and limited. Evolution is the process through which a population of organisms modifies its form, or internal structure, by interaction with its environment. Through reproduction, and thus over

a length of time, organisms are seen to change. From this restricted biological meaning, the term *general evolution* has come to wider use in the social as well as the natural sciences—most notably in history and in cultural anthropology. For as long as our species has been the animal that reflects and is capable of symbolic thought, we have speculated on our origins and our fate. Myths and stories taken from ancient, extinct cultures and contemporary small-scale societies alike represent such evolutionary theories. From the writings of the ancient Greeks onward, there have been debates as to whether heredity or environment is the factor determining change in organisms.

**Foundations of Evolutionary Theory.** We owe the foundations of modern evolutionary theory to Charles Darwin and Alfred Russel Wallace, but it would be a mistake to ignore earlier contributions to the dispute on the origins of life, notably the work of the natural historians Georges Buffon (1707–1788) and Jean Baptiste Lamarck (1744–1829) —both "environmentalists"—and the naturalist Carolus Linnaeus (1707–1778), who made the first classification of plants and animals by species. Darwin's own theoretical position was opposed to that of Lamarck and was based on more thorough research. Darwin postulated three principles to explain the mechanisms of evolution in organic life: first, the "principle of individual variation," that is, individual members of a species show slight differences in morphology (structure); second, these different traits are inherited from generation to generation; third, the "principle of natural selection," that is, that the slight individual differences noted in the first principle give different individuals in the species advantages or disadvantages in their natural life. This third principle is the environmental factor, which explains how species changed, or became extinct, as selective pressures on them varied. As it stands in *On the Origin of Species* (1859), Darwin's theory contains both the heredity and the environment factors, but as the theory gained wider acceptance with the development of geology and archaeology, Darwinism was transformed from a biological theory into a social philosophy through the writings of Herbert Spencer (1820–1903) and others, who profoundly misunderstood both its scientific and philosophical premises.

**Influence of Darwin and Spencer.** The

influence exerted by Darwin and Spencer on their contemporaries was immense; it is reflected in the search for the origins of human culture that pervades most early anthropological writings. Thus Lewis Henry Morgan in his *Ancient Society* (1877) sought to classify the cultural evolution of human into three stages: savagery, barbarism, and civilization. Morgan in turn influenced Karl Marx and Friedrich Engels, who sought to explain the part played by labor in cultural evolution. E. B. Tylor (*Primitive Culture*, 1871) and Emile Durkheim (*Elementary Forms of The Religious Life*, 1917) tried to explain the evolution of religious and scientific thought from what they regarded as the most primitive of contemporary social groups, the Australian aborigines. Common to all these writers was the assumption that the society to which they belonged, that of industrial Europe or America, was superior and in some sense more advanced than the societies which, as ethnologists, they studied. Their concept of general evolution was of fixed stages through which all societies had to pass if they were to evolve at all. This is the doctrine of unilineal evolution, which was usually deterministic and occasionally racist in its application.

Contemporary theories of a general evolution of human culture no longer equate evolution with progress toward some inevitable goal—few of us are that optimistic or positivist. Arising out of a critique of the evolutionary culture theories of Leslie A. White and his pupils, notably Marshall Sahlins and Elman Service, a nonunilinear theory of social evolution has emerged in the work of such writers as Marvin Harris, Andrew Vayda, and Roy Rappaport, among others. These theorists have reasserted the importance of environmental or ecological factors in influencing the changes in societies. Combining the old biological analogy with elaborate uses of cybernetics, they use the characteristic of adaptiveness to explain both short-term (functional) and long-term (general evolutionary) changes through which societies maintain a balance with their natural and cultural environment. This balance, called *homeostasis*, is considered to be temporary and fragile, so that certain social institutions act as safety-valves to keep society from becoming maladapted to the environment in which it functions.

**The Outlook.** The discussion on general evolution continues unabated. Even though we now know more about heredity (through modern genetic theory and molecular biology), about the history and prehistory of life on earth (through geology and archaeology), and about energy (through modern physics), controversy continues in the natural and social sciences. Anthropology is just one of the battlegrounds disputed by evolutionists and environmentalists and others. It may appear overly skeptical to say that the problem may remain unresolved, but the question of human origins and human destiny has long been, and will no doubt remain, at the center of the human predicament.

*See also* Cultural evolution; Darwin, Charles; Darwinism; Evolution, biological; Evolution, genetic mechanisms of; Evolution, human; Social Darwinism; Wallace, Alfred Russel
Consult: Harris, Marvin, *The Rise of Anthropological Theory* (New York: Columbia University Press, 1968); Hunter, David, and Whitten, Phillip, *The Study of Anthropology*, chaps. 1, 2 and 3 (New York: Harper & Row, 1976); Sahlins, Marshall, and Service, Elman (eds), *Evolution and Culture* (Ann Arbor: University of Michigan Press, 1960); White, Leslie, *The Science of Culture* (New York: Grove Press, 1949).

—*Bruno Pajaczkowski, Cambridge University*

**Evolution, Genetic Mechanisms of.** A species consists of a breeding population characterized by internal genetic variations. These variations involve both a potential for constancy—the capacity of the species to sustain an adaptation to a particular environment—and a potential for new adaptations to changed environmental circumstances. Both the capacity for hereditary constancy and the capacity for evolutionary change must be understood together, for the genetic mechanisms in evolution are intertwined in complex ways. Natural selection pressures operate only on the phenotype, not the genotype. Thus some genetic mechanisms which suppress the phenotypic expression of genotypic traits may contribute to a potential for changed adaptations and the development of new varieties in a population.

Certain of these genetic mechanisms involve no basic change in the chemical structure of the genetic materials; hence they affect only the expression and the frequency of phenotypic traits. In *codominance*, for example, the paired alleles produce an $F_1$ generation with characteristics different from either parent. There is no chemical change in the genes, for the parental traits reappear in the $F_1$ generation. *Polygenes* also give the appearance of "blended inheritance." Here several genes on different loci or even on different chromosomes affect one another's phenotypic expression. *Epistasis,* or gene modification, is a variant of the polygenetic effect. Here a gene at one locus suppresses the effect of a gene at a different locus. Gene modification is responsible for albinism in humans.

All these mechanisms ensure the continuity of the basic genetic materials. For example, by suppressing the phenotypic expression of certain genes, which may be less adaptive than those which do appear, the suppressed genes are sheltered from the effects of selection pressures; thus evolutionary elbow room is gained for later adaptations and further speciation.

As the genetic materials from different parents are recombined in the process of gamete formation, the reduction and division (meiosis) of the parental chromosomes provide additional possibilities for genetic variation. One such process is *crossing-over,* where parts of one chromosome wind up in two different gametes (i.e., the crossover). Again, chemical changes in the hereditary materials have not occurred. Variation here involves a reshuffling of existing genetic materials. Other chromosomal variations include *deletion* and *inversion,* where part of a chromosome strand breaks and one part becomes lost (deleted) or else rejoins inverted. These processes are generally harmful if not fatal to the organism; but if not, they will affect the genotypes of succeeding generations. One example of this is Mongoloid idiocy (Down's syndrome), which is caused by a form of chromosomal aberration.

New genetic materials are added to the process of evolution only by *mutation,* which involves an alteration in the structure of the protein molecule and changes in the basic DNA code. Mutations are often reversed by back mutations, with the opposing mutations sometimes reaching a condition of equilibrium. Via mutation, entirely new genetic materials may be added to the gene pool of a breeding population. Generally, mutant genes produce harmful phenotypic results, and this reflects the balance between heredity and the environmental adaptation of a breeding population. However, the action and adaptive value of a mutant gene are often complex, as in the gene which causes sickle-cell anemia. Nonetheless, selection pressures for a mutant gene can act only on the phenotype. If a gene is completely recessive, selection will occur only when it occurs paired as a homozygote, since only then will the recessive trait be expressed phenotypically.

*Genetic drift* consists of sampling accidents, such as when a small population becomes isolated from its parental breeding population. Here the frequency of some genes may be affected significantly, so as to produce important differences in succeeding generations. Since during much of human history the breeding populations were very small, genetic drift has likely been responsible for much hereditary variation between human groups. However, the effects of isolation and sampling accidents are countered by the human capacity for mobility and the predilection for interbreeding.

*Interbreeding* is a process which develops and sustains *gene flow* between formerly isolated and genetically distinct populations. *Inbreeding,* on the other hand, is both promoted and limited among human groups by cultural rules and pressures, especially the ubiquitous incest prohibitions which set limits to inbreeding. The result of such culturally conditioned breeding rules is to reduce the rate of homozygosity for potentially damaging genes.

*See also* Evolution, biological; Mendelian genetics; Selection, natural
Consult: Alland, A., *Evolution and Human Behavior* (New York: Anchor Books, 1973); Wright, S., *Evolution and the Genetics of Populations* (Chicago: University of Chicago Press, 1968).

—*James Clifton, University of Wisconsin, Green Bay*

**Evolution, Human.** The partial Neanderthal skeleton discovered in 1856 was the first to achieve wide recognition as an extinct ancient variety of human. In 1863, Thomas Henry Huxley picked up the challenge offered in Charles Darwin's *On the Origin of Species* with the publication of *Man's Place in Nature.* In that volume, Huxley masterfully used the available evidence on comparative anatomy, the behavior and morphology of the apes, and the very slim hominid fossil record to demonstrate the biological affinities of human beings with the rest of earth's organisms.

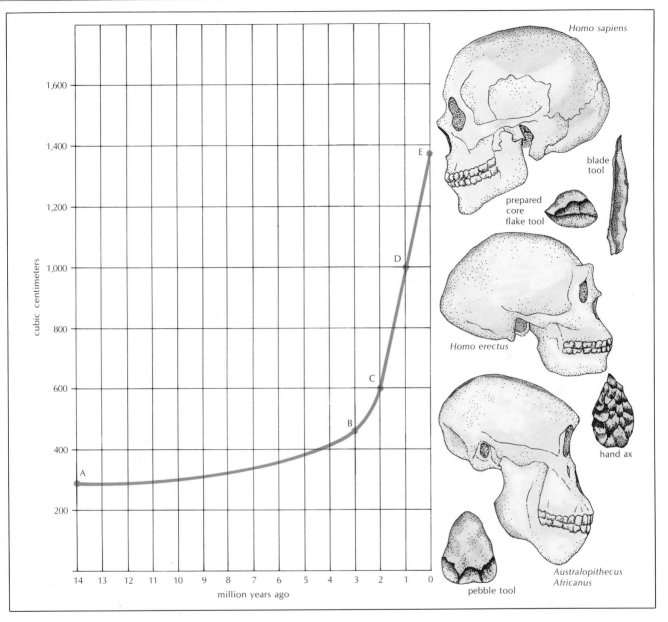

HOMINID BIOLOGICAL AND CULTURAL
EVOLUTION

A = Ramapithecus (300 cc)
B = Australopithecus africanus (450 cc)
C = Australopithecus habilis (600 cc)
D = Homo erectus (1,000 cc)
E = Homo sapiens (1,375 cc)

In the more than 110 years intervening, a flood of anatomical-biochemical details, studies of nonhuman primates in field and laboratory, and works on fossil finds have poured from the presses. The issue to which Huxley addressed himself—the recognition of Homo sapiens as a product of a natural process and not of a special creation—no longer exists. Attention has now been focused on the manner in which evolution has produced the human species.

The fossil evidence for human evolution has been diligently pursued since the middle of the 19th century, with spectacular finds being made in 1892, 1924, 1959, and in the decade 1965–1975. Numerous Neanderthal discoveries have demonstrated conclusively that creatures less modern than ourselves once existed. Discovery of the first "Pithe-canthropus" (or *Homo erectus*) in 1892 added a lower rung to the ladder of human evolution, and the 1924 *Australopithecus* find added a still lower step. Continuing discovery of individuals classifiable in each of those categories continues to this day. In recent years, an additional step has been added and attention has turned from description to an attempt to work out the ecological context of which these hominids were a part and to understand the forces impinging upon the gene pools to bring about biological change.

**Ramapithecus.** It is generally agreed that the first hominid form—that is, the first fossil that can be located in the taxonomic family of which *H. sapiens* is a part—is *Ramapithecus*. Evidence for these forms is scattered between two major locations in Africa and India and has been dated between 10 and 14 million years BP. So far, only fragments of teeth and jaws can be unequivocally attributed to *Ramapithecus*. Yet the general features of those fragments are so typically hominid (small canine teeth; no diastema between the teeth as in apes; jaw rounded in front; low crowded chewing teeth) that *Ramapithecus* must presently be considered as the earliest hominid. As material accumulates, and more variety becomes evident, opinion will possibly alter.

**Australopithecus.** The second hominid group is usually referred to as australopithecine. Much better known than *Ramapithecus*, abundant remains of these highly variable forms derive from numerous sites, principally in Africa but possibly also in the Middle East, China, and Java. These hominids probably varied between about 4 feet to a bit over 5 feet in stature. The remains of pelvic and leg bones indicate a fairly human style of bipedal locomotion. The legs may have been slightly shorter in proportion and the arms slightly longer, but the greatest differences with modern forms were in the skull. The brains averaged not much more than 500 cc in volume, no larger than those of living gorillas. Attached to these small braincases were quite large and heavy faces, set off by noses with low, almost apelike bridges. Set perhaps incongruously in this unique face was a large, but very humanlike dentition. There are, of course, detail differences between the teeth of *Australopithecus* and those of modern *Homo sapiens*, but their shape and the

smoothly curved gapless tooth placement are typically human.

The australopithecine group has been divided into a number of categories, variously representing different species, genera, and adaptations. The most basic distinction appears to be one of size—particularly evident in the skull and dental apparatus. The slightly larger, heavier forms are identified by various investigators as *Paranthropus*, as *Australopithecus robustus*, or simply as robust australopithecines. In the first two cases they are seen as forming separate populations, occupying a different ecological niche, and consequently separated from the gene pool leading to *Homo sapiens*. The smaller, lighter, more gracile forms may also be divided into at least two populations: *Australopithecus africanus* and *Australopithecus (Homo?) habilis*. At least some of the earlier forms of the *A. africanus* population are believed to be ancestral to *A. habilis*, who has been associated with crude chopping or pebble tools; some of the later ones may have shared the extinction imputed to the robust forms.

A third hominid line has also been suggested as a result of recent discoveries in Tanzania. This skull (skull 1470) has been reconstructed, from fragments, with an exceptionally large cranial capacity (800 cc). It predates other australopithecine skulls, which have smaller cranial capacities.

Despite the great variability, some researchers view all these forms as part of a single evolving lineage, attributing the differences among them to time, geographic dispersion, and sex differences (sexual dimorphism). Time is an important factor, since the range for the australopithecines is between about 5.5 million and 1.5 million BP.

**Homo erectus.** The next stage, *Homo erectus*, was more widespread geographically but more constricted temporally. Fossils recovered from Africa, Europe, China, and Java are between about 1 million and 300,000 years old. At sites where no skeletons have been found, tantalizing traces—footprints, indications of structures, and numerous distinctive stone tools—mark their existence. These forms are regarded as the earliest human beings. From the neck down, they seem to be different from us only in insignificant ways. The heads, however, offer considerable contrast. The skull accommodates a brain ranging from about 775 cc for the earlier forms to about 1,225 cc

for the later ones. This results in a sharply sloping forehead, marked by generally heavy supraorbital ridges, a marked postorbital construction, and a large prognathous (forward-jutting) face. The teeth are larger than in most modern populations, and the chin recedes.

They were accomplished hunters, apparently lived in groups, and sought shelter in caves and in structures made of boughs. They produced a variety of stone tools including choppers, hand axes, and crude flake tools, and in later phases they had learned to control fire and used it for light, warmth, and probably for cooking. The bases are missing from some of their skulls—pried off, it is thought, to allow the brain to be extracted and eaten. Cannibalism, however lacking in the social graces, suggests belief systems, for ceremonial significance surrounds nearly all documented contemporary cannibalism.

**Neanderthal.** The next step up the human ladder is taken by Neanderthal in the period from about 300,000 to about 40,000 BP. Most investigators today regard them as variants of our own species—as *Homo sapiens neanderthalensis*. These forms tended to be short and stocky, heavily muscled, and large featured. The skull is large, rounded, and often marked with an occipital "bun" on the rear. The cranial capacity of the earlier forms is over 1,200 cc and exceeds 1,500 cc in the later ones—larger than modern averages. Most are characterized by large brow ridges and prognathous faces. The teeth are within the range of modern size, and the chin recedes slightly.

The latest Neanderthals, notably those from Mt. Carmel, show a mix of characteristics variously interpreted as the result of interbreeding with modern forms, a population "in the throes of evolutionary change," or simply as normal genetic variability. The 100-year debate about the inclusion of Neanderthal in our direct ancestry is not likely to be settled to everyone's satisfaction for some time yet.

These people appear to have been successful and skilled hunters of big game. They used numerous types of stone tools: hand axes, scrapers, flakes, etc. From the evidence of "altars" of bear skulls, deliberate interment and decoration of the dead, and perhaps some cannibalism, Neanderthal is credited with fairly complex belief systems. Speculation by nonanthropologists has often presented a gruesome picture of

Neanderthal life, replete with child abandonment and marginal communication through grunts or ESP—an existence that was "nasty, brutish, and short," as philosopher Thomas Hobbes said about life in the state of nature. We can never really know what life in Neanderthal times was like, but there is an increasing tendency to accept them as more human in all respects as data continue to accumulate. Ralph Solecki has even found evidence in Shanidar Cave (N Iraq) that Neanderthals were capable of simple surgery (limb amputation) and cared for geriatric group members who could not survive on their own.

**Dating the Fossil Records.** Dates given in the foregoing paragraphs derive largely from the revolution in dating accompanying the then-astonishing date of 1.75 million BP given for the "Zinjanthropus" form discovered at Olduvai Gorge by the Leakeys. The potassium-argon (K-Ar) method used there has since been applied to other fossils, multiplying the time attributed to human evolution tenfold. Most paleoanthropologists find these older dates compatible with their views of the time required to effect biological change. However, an alternative view, developed out of biochemical dating techniques, places the divergence of the hominid (human) and pongid (ape) stocks at only 3 million years ago. If this view is found to be correct, substantial revision of many of the opinions widely held today will be necessary. Proponents of biochemical dating have yet to convince many of their colleagues of the validity of their views, but investigations of dating—obviously a critical matter—are continuing.

**Survival and Extinction.** A basic dichotomy exists in the analysis of human evolution. The alternatives are referred to as "lumping" and "splitting." Lumpers prefer to concentrate on the similarities between fossils and groups of fossils. Splitters emphasize the differences between them. The proponents of lumping wish to deal with a minimum number of coexisting hominid ecological niches (usually one at any given time) and a minimum of evolving lineages or lines of descent. The splitters, on the contrary, wish to deal with a larger number of ecological niches and a similarly large number of evolving lineages, only one of which can feed directly into the modern *Homo sapiens* gene pool. The result is that the lumpers recognize few categories (taxa) and those in sequence, with a lower taxon evolv-

ing into a higher. Splitters recognize more taxa, often several simultaneously, which means that some groups of fossils achieve extinction without contributing to the gene pool of more advanced hominids. An excessive amount of splitting during the earlier phases of the discovery of fossils, and perhaps still continuing in some quarters, has begun to be corrected in the last twenty years. A continuing reexamination of the fossils has taken cognizance of variability and has thus sharply reduced the number of names employed as taxonomic (classification) devices.

**Current Directions.** The fossil record also contains two fascinating parallel lineages: *Gigantopithecus*, a huge Pliocene-Pleistocene hominoid sharing many dental features with hominids; and *Oreopithecus*, a Miocene swamp ape once thought to be the ancestral hominid. These are useful in demonstrating the adaptive radiation of primates through environments contrasting with the forest habitat of most types and toward the open woodland and then savanna occupied so successfully first by *Ramapithecus* and then *Australopithecus*.

Most of the "primate characteristics"—stereoscopic and color vision, prehensile five-digited hands and feet, enlargement of the brain, and a reduction in the length of the muzzle and the sense of smell—are the result of an early arboreal (tree-dwelling) adaptation. The process of human evolution has further developed and refined many of these characteristics. In addition, the modification of the anatomical structure to facilitate ground-dwelling bipedality led to other important musculoskeletal, neurological, and behavioral changes. Field studies of modern nonhuman primates have added an important new dimension to the reconstruction of probable early hominid behavior. In the middle 1970s, human evolution is moving toward a more synthetic view of the evolutionary process in which a morphological analysis of the fossils is combined with behavioral aspects—hence a more complete, interrelated view is possible. As the biological basis for behavior becomes better understood, we shall be better able to appreciate not only the fossil record of human evolution but also our present condition.

As more expeditions enter the field, discoveries will increase, variability within each area will increase, and a more complete picture of the human evolutionary

process will emerge. With the number of fossils which have been recovered to date, the general picture presented here is not likely to be greatly altered in the coming years. However, many of the details and interpretations will. The future promises to be exciting, with further and perhaps far-reaching discoveries about our place in nature.

*See also* Australopithecines; Bipedalism; Brain size; Color vision; Dart, Raymond; Darwin, Charles; Dating, absolute; Dating, relative; Dentition of fossils; DuBois, Eugene; Fossil sequence of human evolution; *Homo erectus; Homo sapiens;* Leakey, L. S. B.; Leakey, Mary; Leakey, Richard; Neanderthal man; Olduvai Gorge; Potassium-argon method of dating; Radiocarbon dating; *Ramapithecus;* Shanidar Cave; Skull 1470; Stereoscopic vision; Taxonomy

Consult: Campbell, Bernard G., *Human Evolution: An Introduction to Man's Adaptations,* 2nd ed. (Chicago: Aldine, 1974); Hewes, Gordon W., *The Origin of Man* (Minneapolis: Burgess, 1973); Howells, William, *Evolution of the Genus Homo* (Menlo Park, Calif.: Addison-Wesley, 1973); Pilbeam, David, *The Ascent of Man: An Introduction to Human Evolution* (New York: Macmillan, 1972).
—*Stanley Rhine, University of New Mexico*

**Evolution, Specific.** *See* Cultural evolution.

**Evolution and Genetics.** Human biological evolution can be divided into two branches: *microevolution,* the ongoing changes within modern human populations; and *macroevolution,* large-scale morphological and structural alterations characteristic of the evolutionary development of the hominids. Because macroevolutionary studies depend for their information mostly on bone fragments, genetics is not directly useful. It is assumed, however, that morphological changes express genetic alterations. Population genetics also indicates the mechanisms responsible for evolution and their mode of operation; moreover, it emphasizes that variability is an integral part of present populations and was undoubtedly important in the past.

For microevolutionary studies, genetics and population genetics have been cornerstones. Microevolution is defined as any change in gene or allele frequency in a breeding population. The gene pool of a population and the distribution and frequency of these genes are thus the main data. Blood groups have been particularly useful, since many follow a simple, known inheritance pattern and are found in several forms within human populations as well as varying among populations. Other valuable traits include certain enzymes, abnormal hemoglobins, and metabolic blockages and diseases.

The forces of evolution can best be understood from microevolutionary investigations. Mutations—changes in the structure of a gene—can only be studied from the standpoint of genetics, and they provide the variability essential for evolution to take place. Through analysis of family pedigrees and of populations, it can be shown that many harmful traits reappear in populations through recurrent mutation and are kept at a low frequency by natural selective pressures operating to eliminate them. The classic selection model treats situations where an equilibrium is eventually reached in which mutation replaces genes at the same rate selection removes them.

Studies of the fruit fly, *Drosophila*, have added greatly to our knowledge of mutations—their causes, effects, and location on the chromosomes—and natural selection, since fruit flies reproduce rapidly, are easily kept in a laboratory, and raise few ethical questions when used in experiments. Many of these results can apparently be generalized to humans. It was thus found that heterozygosity characterizes many of the genetic loci of an organism and that many traits occur in more than one form in populations. These polymorphisms are most often maintained by natural selection favoring the heterozygote. The Hardy-Weinberg equilibrium model, which predicts stability in gene frequencies and their distributions in populations under conditions of no evolution, acts as a useful point of departure for measuring ongoing evolution.

Microevolutionary studies focusing on genetic attributes and of particular significance to an understanding of human evolution have included analyses of the extent and effects of inbreeding in small populations, consequences of atomic radiation on mutations in populations, examples of natural selection and genetic drift, and the relation of cultural factors, such as polygyny, hygiene, and medical treatment and counseling, to biological evolution. The impor-

tance of cultural changes to genetic ones is well illustrated by the correlation of sickle-cell anemia with the prevalence of certain forms of malaria, which in turn followed a shift from hunting and gathering to cultivation in the tropical forests of Africa.

The development of genetics has thus been essential to the investigation of the processes involved in human evolution in the past as well as the present.

*See also* Balanced polymorphism; Evolution, human; Genetics; Hardy-Weinberg principle; Population genetics

Consult: Dobzhansky, T., *Genetics of the Evolutionary Process* (New York: Columbia University Press, 1970); Morris, L. N. (ed.), *Human Populations, Genetic Variation, and Evolution* (San Francisco: Chandler, 1971). —Catherine E. Read-Martin, California State University, Los Angeles

**Evolutionary Humanism.** This philosophy is based on integrating knowledge of the origins, nature, and consequences of human evolution. Many anthropologists share this point of view and use it as part of their professional methodology.

*See also* Cultural evolution; Evolutionism; Needs, human

**Evolutionary Mechanism.** *See* Evolution, genetic mechanisms of.

**Evolutionism.** This term refers to doctrines concerning the evolution of anything—the universe, chemical forms, biological forms, society, culture. The latter two domains are often closely intertwined in evolutionary models.

All contemporary scientific evolutionary doctrines and propositions concerning present and past life are uniquely Western—products of our civilization's peculiar history of ideas and, perhaps more indirectly, products of its actual sociocultural history. Thus evolutionary models may be ethnocentric derivatives of a peculiar world view. Lovejoy's classic, *The Great Chain of Being*, traces the development of these ideas, especially the introduction of linear time as central to Western ontology, which is the basis for all contemporary evolutionism.

A major difficulty in research on evolution is establishing patterns of succession;

a crucial question is what time scale one can use given the accessibility of various kinds of data. Thus it is not immediately apparent how one determines whether an observed series A-B-C is cyclically repetitive (A-B-C, A-B-C, A-  ·  ·  · ), merely part of a larger cycle (A-B-C-D-E, A-  ·  ·  · ), or purely accidental without any necessary or repeatable probabilistic connections. Distinguishing chance from necessity, simple transformation from cumulation or from "progress," irreversibility from reversibility (A-B-C, C-B-A)—all present extreme difficulties. Empirical evidence often gives little grounds for deciding among these. Consequently, many interpretations—many evolutionary models—have appeared since temporalized world views have dominated the West. Only slowly has the effect of the empirical evidence on theory produced selection among these models, eliminating all but two major evolutionary paradigms and one pseudoevolutionary one.

The latter, in various versions, retains Christian creationism by temporalizing it. Instead of the Judeo-Christian God's having —in his omnipotence—created all beings at once, this form of Christian creationism postulates a series of creations and destructions (like the Noachian Flood). The great paleontologist and animal taxonomist Baron Cuvier (1769–1832) held this position, which still reappears in Christian fundamentalist scientific circles—though Cuvier was its last major scientific defender. This notion seemed plausible, given contemporary geological and biological knowledge, since the sharp discontinuities ("unconformities" and "disconformities") which characterize observed geological and fossil sequences fit the conception of an omnipotent (and therefore *continuously* productive) God eliminating some species and creating new ones by engendering catastrophes like the Flood. This theory is called catastrophism.

Research eventually proved that the unconformities were local; elsewhere, continuous sequences bridged these gaps—indicating *processual*, not creative, extinction of old species and origins of new ones. Extinction presented a dilemma for Christian theology since it contradicted the medieval conception of eternal species, based on theological doctrines concerning God's attributes. Cuvier's traditionalist solution made omnipotent God himself the agent of extinction. But increasingly, evidence proved it a natural process.

Roughly fifty years before Cuvier's work, the foundations of today's two major paradigms of sequences were elaborated. Georges Buffon (1707–1788) mentioned most of the elements of Darwin's theory of evolution explicitly—but lacked the central concept of natural selection through sexual reproduction. Buffon conceptualized extinction, variation, adaptation, time series, and descent. Carolus Linnaeus (1707–1778) essentially founded modern taxonomy, which implies the evolutionary relatedness (against the medieval aboriginal discreteness) of species. Both thinkers made critical contributions in the development of Darwinism.

A third major figure was Jean Baptiste Lamarck (1744–1829), whose theory of biological changes in species not only dominated biological evolutionism but still dominates sociocultural evolutionism as well. Lamarck's model preserves important aspects of Christian doctrine while accounting for changes in species by a naturalistic mechanism: the use and disuse of organs. Lamarck believed that a species' sequence of changes is immanent in the species—implanted by God in the original "germ" —and unfolds in foreordained stages. Ecological and behavioral aspects of a species are regarded as critical in its development from stage to stage, since they condition the use and disuse of organs. Finally, Lamarck's perspective permitted preserving the teleological conception of moving toward perfection, which reappears in the 19th-century notion of progress. It also underlies current economic and political development models as well as such conceptions as underdevelopment and modernization.

The other major evolutionary model is Darwinism, which in effect destroyed essences, immanences, teleologies, long-term discrete continuities, and stages—by its thorough materialism and its dependence on random occurrences. It is precisely its total destruction of teleologies and its dependence on random processes, as well as its use of the *individual* of the species as the evolutionary unit, which have made the model so difficult to apply to human populations which do display partial teleologies, long-term bounded continuities, and group organization. Furthermore, the diffusibility of culture in ways *not* bounded by individuals has no parallels among biological traits—which *must* pass to descendants whereas culture traits can pass laterally and to ascendants and even to totally nonrelated individuals. The model of natural selection through sexual selection cannot, of course, apply under these circumstances. Nevertheless, periodic attempts are made to apply Darwinian evolutionary models to sociocultural phenomena. Plainly an appropriate model for sociocultural evolution should select and modify appropriate insights from Lamarckian evolutionism divested of its underlying theology; from Darwinian evolutionism divested of its reductionist individualism and emphasis on random processes; and from any useful new approach.

*See also* Darwin, Charles; Evolution, general; Wallace, Alfred Russel

Consult: Burrow, J. W., *Evolution and Society: A Study in Victorian Social Theory* (Cambridge: Cambridge University Press, 1966); Bury, J. B., *The Idea of Progress* (London: Macmillan, 1920); Leeds, Anthony, "Darwin and Darwinian Evolutionism in the Study of Society and Culture," in *The Comparative Reception of Darwinism*, ed. Thomas Glick (Austin: University of Texas Press, 1974); Lovejoy, Arthur O., *The Great Chain of Being* (Cambridge, Mass.: Harvard University Press, 1937); Stocking, George W., Jr., *Race, Culture, and Evolution: Essays in the History of Anthropology* (New York: Free Press, 1968).

—Anthony Leeds, Boston University

**Excavation of a Site.** An archaeological site is a locus of past human activity. The unexcavated site preserves information about both cultural and natural events. Cultural events may include diverse activities conducted at the site and multiple occupations of the site. Natural events may include deposition and erosion of material before, after, and during the occupation of the site. Since the archaeologist must be able to describe the cultural and natural events which took place there, records of both the natural and the cultural context of recovered artifacts must be preserved. When a site is excavated, contextual information is destroyed. For this reason, many countries have enacted legislation to prevent untrained and unauthorized personnel from destroying archaeological sites. For this reason, too, it is incumbent upon the archaeologist to maintain accurate and detailed records during excavation of a site. A field notebook, often with carbon copies, is requisite for recording the plan of excavation, observation about the stratigraphy of the site, and deployment of labor in excavation.

Before excavation, archaeologists prepare a map of the site showing vertical contour intervals and any noticeable surface features. This map is accompanied by notes about the vegetation cover, drainage, and other important details. The archaeologist then establishes a *datum point* which will serve as a control point and is the referent for all measurements. The datum point should, if possible, be tied into some permanent feature such as a benchmark. All artifacts and features recovered will be located both horizontally and vertically with respect to datum. If a site is very large, several sub-datum points will be located and mapped. A *grid system* of two sets of parallel lines intersecting at right angles is generally staked out in string across the site and mapped on the site map. The size of the grid units is determined by the nature of the site and the excavation strategy. Excavation units are located on the site map with reference to the grid system and datum; their nature and number depend on the research strategy. Generally *test pits,* grid units, and trenches are employed.

The tools of excavation are diverse and again are determined by the research strategy. A transit, measuring tapes, spirit levels, compass, plumb bob, and string are considered essential for mapping horizontal and vertical features. The removal of earth is accomplished with a variety of tools. Picks and spading forks may be used to loosen compacted material. Shovels are generally used for removing large amounts of material. Mason's trowels are commonly used for finer work, and paintbrushes and dental tools may be used for very delicate operations.

Excavation may proceed by natural or arbitrary levels, depending on the site. Natural levels are observed strata of different soil and/or cultural deposits. Arbitrary levels, usually of 6 inches, are used if the soil appears to be homogeneous. When a feature, such as a room or pit, is encountered, it may be excavated as a unit. Earth from each level is commonly sifted through $1/4$-inch steel mesh to facilitate recovery of small items which might otherwise be missed. Flotation may be used to recover vegetal material. During excavation, records are kept on the nature of the soil, artifacts recovered, and features encountered. Photographs supplement written descrip-

*The horizontal excavation of an Iron Age site at Maiden Castle, England, conducted by Sir Mortimer Wheeler, using a grid-style excavation technique that retains evidence of the site stratigraphy. This technique allows the pinpointing of the locations of site contents with regard to stratigraphic provenance.*

tions. Throughout excavation various samples are taken for pollen, soil, and other types of analysis. There are several manuals of field archaeology available, including Atkinson (1953), Gorenstein (1965), Heizer and Graham (1967), Meighan (1961), and Robbins and Irving (1965).

See also Archaeology; Site
Consult: Atkinson, R. J. C., *Field Archaeology*, 2nd ed. (London: Methuen, 1953); Gorenstein, S., *Introduction to Archaeology* (New York: Basic Books, 1965); Heizer, R. F., and Graham, J. A., *A Guide to Field Methods in Archaeology: Approaches to the Anthropology of the Dead* (Palo Alto, Calif.: National Press, 1967); Meighan, C. W., *The Archaeologist's Note Book* (San Francisco: Chandler, 1961); Robbins, M., and Irving, M. B., *The Amateur Archaeologist's Handbook* (New York: Crowell, 1965).
—*Linda S. Cordell, University of New Mexico*

**Exchange.** This term refers to processes through which obligations between parties—whether individuals, groups, or institutions—are met. People in specific settings exchange all sorts of things, including subtle eye contacts, compliments, gifts, insults, blows, or worse. Such exchanges between actors, which forge dyads, ramify to other actors and form networks. Exchange theory is fundamental to such specialities as economic anthropology (Schneider 1974), social organization (Barth 1966), social structure (Lévi-Strauss 1957), network analysis (Whitten and Wolfe 1974), symbolic interaction (Goffman 1969), ethnicity (Whitten 1974), and the analysis of power (Blau 1964).

The concept of *reciprocity* is basic to the idea of exchange. Marshall Sahlins (1965: 147–148) provides a splendid review of this concept from the early work of Bronislaw Malinowski and Marcel Mauss through that of Raymond Firth to Alvin Gouldner. Sahlins sets out a continuum from "generalized reciprocity" through "balanced reciprocity" to "negative reciprocity":

> *"Generalized reciprocity" refers to transactions that are putatively altruistic, transactions on the line of assistance given and, if possible and necessary, assistance returned. The ideal type is Malinowski's "pure gift." "Balanced reci-*

procity" refers to direct exchange and "negative reciprocity" is the attempt to get something for nothing with impunity.*

See also Network, social; Trade
Consult: Barth, Fredrik, *Models of Social Organization*, Occasional Paper 23, Royal Anthropological Institute of Great Britain and Ireland, Glasgow, 1966; Blau, Peter M., *Exchange and Power in Social Life* (New York: Wiley, 1964); Goffman, Erving, *Strategic Interaction* (Philadelphia: University of Pennsylvania Press, 1969); Lévi-Strauss, Claude, "The Principle of Reciprocity," in *Sociological Theory*, ed. L. Coser and B. Rosenberg (New York: Macmillan, 1957); Sahlins, Marshall D., "On the Sociology of Primitive Exchange," in *The Relevance of Models for Social Anthropology*, ed. M. Banton (London: Tavistock, 1965); Schneider, Harold K., *Economic Man: The Anthropology of Economics* (New York: Free Press, 1974); Whitten, Norman E., Jr., *Black Frontiersmen: A South American Case* (New York: Wiley, 1974); Whitten, Norman E., Jr., and Wolfe, Alvin W., "Network Analysis," in *Handbook of Social and Cultural Anthropology*, ed. J. Honigmann (Chicago: Rand McNally, 1974).
—*Norman E. Whitten, Jr., University of Illinois*

**Existential Psychiatry.** This modern school of psychiatry is highly critical of conventional psychiatric theory and practice, particularly the notions that mental disorders are an illness and that the role of the practitioner is to readjust the patient to "sanity" or "normality." Leading proponents of the school are R. D. Laing, who insists on the empathetic understanding of the schizophrenic experience (which he believes may be a valuable healing process for the alienated individual), and Thomas Szasz, who draws attention to the infringement of the civil liberties of mental patients and to the alleged role of psychiatrists as agents of social control over individuals who deviate from norms of "reality."

See also Culture and personality

**Exogamy.** Marriage rule based on the *incest* prohibition that defines the group of relatives not available to a person as marriage or sex partners.

See also Endogamy; Incest; Incest avoidance (taboo); Kinship; Marriage

**Exploitation.** Exploitation is the forcible appropriation of a portion of the total product of the labor of direct producers by a class of nonproducers. As such, it is a distinctive feature of all historical (i.e., class-ruled) societies. Although the idea that some individuals, groups, or classes benefit unfairly from the labor of others occurs in all periods of Western thought, the scientific concept of exploitation was developed by Karl Marx, whose book, *Das Kapital,* presents the theory of the exploitative process under capitalism. He argues that capitalist exploitation is made possible by the existence of a margin between the socially established subsistence needs of workers and their total product. Workers not only produce enough to reproduce their own wages *(v)* but also produce surplus value *(s)* which belongs to the capitalist. The measure of exploitation in capitalism, or the rate of surplus value, is given by the ratio *s/v.* The use of the term *exploitation* to apply to noncapitalist systems of political economy (e.g., in speaking of the exploitation of slaves, serfs, or peasants) is derived from the Marxian concept and refers to the fact that the exploited producers are universally forced by some means to produce over and above what is needed to reproduce their own existence.

See also Capitalism; Class; Imperialism; Surplus

—Eugene E. Ruyle, University of Virginia

**Exploration of a Site.** Archaeological sites are usually buried, at least partially, but complete excavation is only one means of exploring them. *Field archaeology* entails observation, recording, and interpretation of surface evidence such as walls, mounds, artifact distributions, and subtle soil and vegetation anomalies. *Surface collecting* is similar but requires disturbing the site when samples are removed. *Test pits* can provide random or arbitrary samples of a site's extent and contents. *Electrical resistivity and magnetometry* occasionally can map major underground features. Actual excavation usually covers only parts of sites—gridded areas determined by preliminary exploration to be of interest to archaeologists.

See also Archaeology; Excavation of a site; Site; Test pit

**Expressive Systems.** This term refers to those aspects of total cultural systems concerned with the organized creation, expression, and utilization of affective states among its human constituents. Expressive systems are usefully conceptualized in a somewhat narrow sense as involving deep emotion; they focus on the cultural dimensions of the emotional life of human groups. So conceived, expressive systems are found in diverse areas of cultural life ranging from the political to the economic, but they are often most pronounced in the arts and religion.

**The Arts and the Sacred.** The creation and expression of feelings are primary aspects of art, music, dance, and folklore cross-culturally. While some of the arts approach being cultural universals, their particular forms and styles vary between cultures. As Carol and Melvin Ember point out, expressive activities have a substantial cultural component in that they depend on learned and shared patterns of behavior, belief, and feeling. For this reason it often takes time and effort for a person to develop an appreciation of the artistic creations of an alien cultural group.

The arts are intimately united with the sacred in primitive societies. As the arts involve the creation and expression of strong emotion, and as the sacred may be the domain that most potently strikes the responsive chords of the panhuman emotional repertoire, such an association is not surprising. Indeed the significance of emotion in understanding the sacred has long been appreciated in the anthropology of religion. Both Sigmund Freud and Emile Durkheim, for example, saw the wellsprings of religion in deeply experienced emotional states. Moreover, for Durkheim religion maintained the sentiments necessary for orderly social life. Bronislaw Malinowski saw the origin and perpetuation of magic in the powerful human emotional reactions precipitated by thwarted efforts to ensure achievement of desired ends. Clifford Geertz views religion as a cultural system of symbols which create powerful, long-lasting moods and motivations. Such a process is clearly exhibited by the Bambuti pygmies of Africa who, by means of a ceremony known as the *molimo,* bring into consciousness, largely through song, a strongly felt sacred presence that permeates and symbolizes their environment while giving meaning to their existence.

**Method of Study.** Recent advances in a field which is becoming known as symbolic anthropology promise to increase our ability to study expressive systems. While all language may be viewed as expressive behavior, it is the role of symbols and other elements of communicative systems in creating, maintaining, and shaping human emotional states that is of primary interest. James Fernandez, for example, has examined the various uses of metaphor for bringing about "affective movement" in human beings. He views religious ritual as acted out metaphor which can achieve affective transformations in the participants.

**Significance of Expressive Systems.** Expressive systems function to some degree as a means of communication. Of greater importance is their functioning to allow the release of emotional tensions, thus providing relief to the individual. This is particularly true in primitive societies with their well-developed collective expressive ritual life (in contrast to modern civilizations). Stanley Diamond believes that this difference accounts for a low incidence of mental maladies among primitive peoples and a high incidence of mental illness in contemporary civilizations. In addition, expressive systems provide experiences which create, clarify, and reinforce the cultural reality, including the accepted meanings of human existence. The Huichol Indians of northern Mexico conceive of their religious rituals as a way of "finding their lives" and experiencing what it is to be Huichol.

An appreciation of the significance of expressive systems among primitive peoples may help anthropologists to abandon the residues of condescension and ethnocentrism in their approach to the primitive by creating an awareness of the sophistication and wisdom displayed in primitive cultures in terms of the concern for, and manipulation of, the affective, subjective aspects of human existence. Although anthropologists agree that all peoples act in a logical manner given their accepted cultural premises, the study of expressive systems will increase our understanding of how and why these cultural premises originate and are maintained—thus broadening our perspective on rationality and enabling us to learn from the people we study.

See also Art; Drama; Emotions, cultural basis of; Primitive peoples; Religion; Symbol

Consult: Fernandez, J., "The Mission of Metaphor in Expressive Culture," *Current Anthropology* 15(2):119–145, 1974; Geertz, C., "Religion as a Cultural System," in *Anthropological*

*Approaches to the Study of Religion*, ed. M. Banton (London: Tavistock, 1965); Otten, C. M., *Anthropology and Art* (Garden City, New York: Natural History Press, 1971). —*Stan Wilk, Lycoming College*

**Extended Family.** A composite family consisting of two or more nuclear families linked by consanguineal ties. It is produced by joining three or more generations.

*See also* Family, the

**Extended Migration.** *See* Migration.

**Extinction of Minorities.** This term refers to the disappearance of a subculture within a larger society. The extinction of minorities occurs in a variety of ways; sometimes it is deliberately planned by members of the larger society.

**Genocide.** The most extreme form of the planned extinction of minorities is genocide, the systematic killing off of an entire subculture. A dramatic incident of attempted genocide occurred in Germany during World War II when the Nazis embarked on a program to exterminate all the world's Jews. Although the German army's invasion of Soviet Russia in 1941 resulted in the massacre of 450,000 Jews, the world was not convinced of the Nazis' intention until 30 January 1942, when Adolf Hitler formally declared the genocide of Jews as his state policy in a speech given to the National Socialist Party. Throughout Germany and the countries conquered by the German army, the Nazi program of systematically killing off Jews proceeded. The plan centered around the deportation of Jews from various European countries to concentration and forced labor camps in Poland and in Nazi-occupied Soviet territory. Jews were shot, stabbed, hanged, burned, gassed, starved, exposed to epidemic diseases, buried alive, and tortured. The electric crematoria at Birkenau first gassed, then burned, 6,000 Jews daily.

During the war, approximately 6 million Jews were murdered. Yet the Nazi attempt at genocide was unsuccessful for several reasons. First, the Jewish minority was dispersed throughout the world; but the Nazis were able to conquer only parts of Europe, Russia, and North Africa. Second, even in the countries occupied by the Nazis, many Jews were able to survive through the help of

non-Jews and by joining underground resistance movements. Third, the Jews were generally indistinguishable from non-Jews; therefore the Nazis often had great difficulty learning who was or was not a Jew.

Attempts at the extinction of minorities through genocide have succeeded primarily when the minority involved was small in number, technologically inferior, and set apart from the rest of the population by their physical appearance. Thus genocide has been practiced most successfully on primitive groups.

A well-known example of genocide aimed at primitive peoples was the extermination of the Tasmanian aboriginal population by the English in the 19th century. Of the several thousand aborigines who once lived in Tasmania, only forty-four survived by 1847. The rest had fallen victim to planned killing by the English. Settlers were encouraged to hunt and shoot aborigines as they did game. Slaying a pregnant woman was considered especially commendable. Poisoned food was left where it would be found and eaten by the aborigines. The policy of outright murder changed after 1847, but disease and alcoholism continued to reduce the number of Tasmanian aborigines until the last remaining aborigine died in 1888. The attempt at genocide by the English was successful because the aborigine minority was small in number, lacked firearms, and was easily distinguishable physically. The English pursued a similar colonial policy in Australia as well, but they were unable to bring about the extinction of the Australian aborigines because of their large number to begin with and because they were dispersed over a much larger territory. Nevertheless the English were able to reduce the population from an estimated 300,000 at initial contact to 60,000 in 1939.

These examples of genocide suggest that racial and cultural prejudice and intolerance have been strong motives for genocide. Genocide continues today, and along with intolerance, economic factors provide especially strong motivation.

In Brazil, where highways are being pushed into the interior and land has become valuable, land speculators and others have attempted a policy of genocide to exterminate Indian groups who inhabit the area. Thousands of Indians have been killed during the past twenty years and at least a dozen tribes are on the verge of extinction. Attempts at genocide have taken the forms

of machine gunning and napalming by air force planes, groups being injected with smallpox virus, poisoning from gifts of sugar mixed with arsenic, and Indians being encouraged to eliminate one another after they have been given whiskey and firearms. Other groups have been taken from their traditional land and relocated, supposedly for purposes of national security, in areas where they will have a hard time surviving. Still others have been enslaved and forced into prostitution or sold to planters and mining firms.

The history of the United States is likewise filled with numerous cases in which Indian groups have become extinct as a result of genocide on the part of the whites. In California, the gold rush brought prospectors and settlers to the Yahi Indians' traditional hunting and fishing territory. Because the Indians hunted some of the ranchers' sheep and cattle, soldiers and vigilante groups embarked on a program to hunt and massacre the Yahis until their number dwindled from 3,000 to just 12 in 1872. The Yahi Indians became extinct in 1916 when their last remaining member, Ishi, died.

**Other Forms of Physical Extinction.** Disease has played a major role in the unplanned extinction of numerous groups during the era of Western expansion. Prior to the Age of Discovery, diseases tended to be endemic rather than epidemic. However, during the first hundred years of contact between the American Indians and the Europeans and Africans, the Indian population was ravaged by epidemic diseases, especially smallpox, which resulted in the deaths of millions and the extinction of many smaller groups. The first New World Indians encountered by Columbus, the Arawak, became extinct as a result of contact with Old World diseases for which they had no immunity, as well as from brutal enslavement by the Spanish.

Some minorities suffered a rapid decline in their birthrate because of the shock of conquest and were unable to reproduce in sufficient numbers to survive. This phenomenon is well documented for some of the Polynesian islanders. It is unclear to what extent these populations consciously refused to reproduce.

**Ethnocide.** Not all extinction of minorities involves the biological extermination of the group. In some cases the minority becomes extinct because it loses the unique way of life that sets its members apart from

The human cost of modernization. This woman is the last surviving member of the Yaghan tribe who lived in Tierra del Fuego, the southernmost tip of South America. This group of Native Americans was decimated by contact with Europeans and the new states they created. Measles killed a good many of them; but also they were pushed out of their lands by the expanding societies of Argentina and Chile, which occupied the territory for the purposes of sheep farming, gold mining, and (more recently) oil drilling.

the larger society. Sometimes, this loss of culture is planned; in other cases it is not. Ethnocide is the systematic destruction of a culture or way of life. In many cases ethnocide has resulted from attempts by missionaries to change a minority's religious beliefs. As missionaries attempted to spread the religions of Western civilization to the rest of the world, they did not realize that native religious beliefs were intimately related to most other aspects of native culture. In many ways the Western religions play a role in only a limited number of sectors of Western life. Native religions of nonliterate societies are generally more pervasive. The missionaries identified many customs they considered heathen and felt obligated to change. Thus, as native minorities were forced to change their religious beliefs and practices, these changes actually affected all aspects of their culture—bringing about the collapse of what had been a well-integrated system of beliefs, values, and practices.

Forced change in educational practices has sometimes also resulted in ethnocide, due to the far-reaching consequences of social policies. Where minorities have controlled the education of their children, the educational system has been able to reinforce traditional values and practices. Increasingly, however, minorities are being denied the right to control the education of their children, and many children are forced to enter the public school system of the municipality or state where they live. Thus they are exposed to new values, those of the dominant majority. Often within a few generations the minorities have been absorbed into the larger society and their separate way of life disappears. In Brazil, for example, German-speaking immigrants began settling in the southern region by the 1820s. They maintained their own schools in which German was the language of instruction. In 1938, the Brazilian government passed a law requiring that all school instruction be in Portuguese. From that time on, the German minority has become more and more integrated into Brazilian society.

**Other Forms of Cultural Extinction.** Perhaps most cultural extinction is unplanned. As a result of a complex of various factors, the minority becomes integrated into the larger society in such a way as to no longer exist as a recognizable subculture. In this process, called assimilation, the minority group is no longer identifiable as a unique group within the larger society. Generally accompanying (and sometimes preceding) assimilation is another process, known as acculturation, in which the minority acquires more and more cultural elements from the dominant society.

Anthropologists have documented many cases of assimilation—such as the acquisition of national languages—that occur only as a result of considerable external pressure from the larger society. In other cases, the acquisition of new cultural elements may be a conscious choice on the part of the minority. Often these acquisitions are a result of new wants or are related to changes in the minority group's prestige structure.

The spread of Western civilization has brought with it urbanization, industrialization, and especially a greater reliance on a money economy. Whereas native societies were often subsistence-based, contact with the Western world necessitated a shift to a cash economy often based on wage labor; this came about because of the forced conversion to cash crops, which made native groups depend on purchase to obtain increasingly larger proportions of their subsistence needs—and newly imported wants such as whiskey and guns. Thus more and more adjustments occurred within the minority societies, adjustments which further integrated them into the larger society. In the most extreme cases, there has been a purposeful rejection of traditional elements by the minority. The Manus in the South Pacific, for example, have purposefully attempted to change their traditional culture and have accepted that of the larger society because of the greater prestige attached to the elements of the larger society since contact during World War II. Societies like the United States until very recently have maintained an ideology that placed great value on the assimilation and acculturation of minorities. This value has been referred to as the melting pot theory. It is a belief that minorities should lose their cultural uniqueness.

In some cases the growth of Third World nationalism represents an example of the extinction of ruling minorities. Where a colonial society was ruled by a minority elite representing a Western power, the end of colonialism has sometimes brought about this minority's demise as a recognizable group—especially in Africa, where the ruling elites were white and the nationalists were black. With the growth of independence, the white minority lost its power base and was either killed off, forced to flee, or obligated to assume a lesser and less visible role in the society. As a ruling colonial minority they have become extinct, although in some cases they may have survived as merely one of several minorities within a black-dominated society.

To a certain extent the process of minority extinction due to genocide, disease, ethnocide, assimilation, and acculturation is being counterbalanced by a growing aware-

ness that in complex societies not all people have to be exactly alike. A certain amount of diversity can in fact enrich the cultural heritage.

*See also* Anti-Semitism; Cultural minorities; Genocide; Minorities, ethnic

Consult: Bodard, Lucien, *Green Hell: Massacre of the Brazilian Indians* (New York: Outerbridge and Dienstfrey, 1972); Bodley, John H., *Victims of Progress* (Menlo Park, Calif.: Cummings, 1975); Jewish Black Book Committee, *The Black Book: The Nazi Crime Against the Jewish People* (New York: Jewish Black Book Committee, 1946); Kroeber, Theodora, *Ishi in Two Worlds: A Biography of the Last Wild Indian in North America* (Berkeley: University of California Press, 1961); Turnbull, Colin M., *The Mountain People* (New York: Simon and Schuster, 1972).

—Michael D. Olien, University of Georgia

**Faction.** A faction is an informal and noncorporate political action group organized for conflict with other factions within some larger unit such as a village or political party. Village factions often act in a pragmatic, opportunistic manner and recruit their members in a variety of ways—through hope for gain, personal allegiance to a leader, or ill will against members of another faction. Nevertheless, factions united by a common goal or ideology do occur. Some anthropologists regard factionalism as a sign of social breakdown; others regard it as a normal part of the social system.

*See also* Clan; Feuding; Lineage; Moiety; Political anthropology; Power

**Factor Analysis.** *See* Statistical methods.

**Fad.** A fad is a temporary style of dress, action, or use of artifact usually adopted only by a subgroup of a society. A fad can also refer to an interest, real or feigned, in a specific subject by many members of a society. The presence of changing fads in a culture suggests that along with the basic stability of that culture there exists also a focus on the acceptance of change.

*See also* Diffusion

**Family, the.** A family is "a married couple or other group of adult kinsfolk who cooperate economically and in the upbringing of

children, and all or most of whom share a common dwelling" (Gough 1971). This anthropological definition provides the basis for a discussion of a related group of cultural universals such as the existence of family, residence rules, sexual/mating behavior, division of labor and other kinds of cooperation in economic affairs, procreation, and primary enculturation of children. It is a statement of those functions, explicit and implicit, which every known human society has found to be an irreducible minimum.

A !Kung San family group. Father smokes a cartridge-shell pipe, baby romps, and mother grooms a young woman's hair for lice. Unlike many nonliterate societies, the !Kung do not have rigid postmarital residence rules. Rather, each group is composed of a core of male and female siblings along with their spouses and children.

An Australian Aborigine family in northern Queensland, c. 1920. The man at right is preparing to roast a kangaroo. Their shelter is obviously not a permanent structure, reflecting the group's commitment to mobility as part of their subsistence strategy.

**Universality.** Time and again it has been recognized that people develop a priority system with respect to primary loyalties and obligations. Ancient Sparta, the USSR, the People's Republic of China, and even Israel (to some extent with its kibbutz system) have attempted to divert the strongest loyalties of their members to the state (or community) at the price of weakening family ties and usurping functions that are traditional family prerogatives. None of these social experiments has been entirely successful, and for whichever of a multiplicity of reasons, a system which successfully substitutes for the family has yet to be invented.

**Origin.** Although it is not at all clear from present evidence, it seems the human family developed incrementally over a long period of time. Its existence is established by archaeological inference by ca. 100,000 BP, but its beginnings must go back several millions of years, as the survival benefits of stable groupings became recognized under varying ecological conditions.

Competing contemporary theories concerning power and prestige within the earliest hominid family groups are moot and dissimulative. Primary evidence of matriarchates versus patriarchates does not exist. Reasoning and extrapolating from secondary sources (archaeology, primate studies, modern hunting/gathering societies) is guesswork at best and subject to interpretations that support the preconceived conclusions of various authors. There is no reason not to hypothesize as well that sometimes a man or men held power, sometimes a woman or women held it, and sometimes the only rule was qualification, regardless of sex. Linton (1936) even reported the case of the Marquesan Islanders in Polynesia, in which the youngest child exerted a certain power over all its elders. From a pragmatic viewpoint there is little reason to believe that the contribution of one sex was valued more highly than that of the other—2 million years ago—when both were indispensable.

**Present Functional Variability.** The major problems that a structured family system solves for human society are the efficient use of economic resources, reproduction and enculturation of the young, and provision for regulated psychosocial (including sexual) interaction.

Both those who live alone and those who are members of communes or cooperatives will attest to the greater efficiency of group use of resources over individual self-suffi-

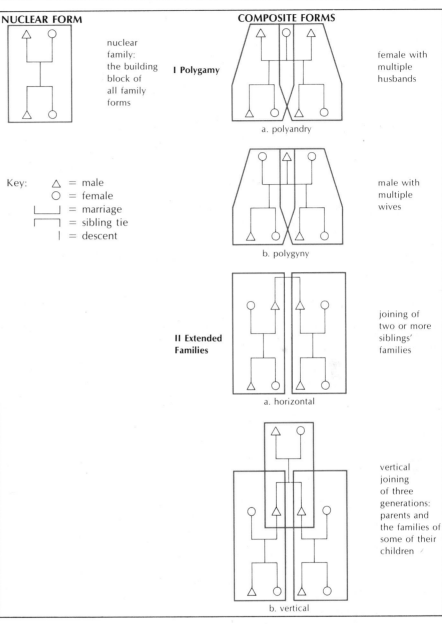

NUCLEAR FORM

nuclear family: the building block of all family forms

Key:
△ = male
○ = female
⌐⌐ = marriage
⌐ = sibling tie
| = descent

COMPOSITE FORMS

**I Polygamy**

a. polyandry

female with multiple husbands

male with multiple wives

b. polygyny

**II Extended Families**

a. horizontal

joining of two or more siblings' families

b. vertical

vertical joining of three generations: parents and the families of some of their children

FORMS OF THE FAMILY

cient independence. The upper limit of efficiency—the point at which further increase in group size reaches the point of diminishing returns—is a function of other factors: ecological resources, religiopolitical system, degree of military activity, and so forth.

Larger populations, decreasing relevancy of the legitimacy of births, declining birthrate, and mass education seem to be lowering the value of legal marriage and the consequent establishment of traditional families in some contemporary cultures. Organized age-group or peer-group activities, changing sexual structures, and the logic of extending egalitarian expectations to members of both sexes also are factors demanding reconsideration of traditional concepts of the family.

**Future of the Family.** What seems clear at the present time is that whatever human requirements demanded of the families of the past, they are not necessarily those which will determine the families of the future. But families in some form will almost certainly continue to exist.

See also Economic systems; Enculturation; Kibbutz, Kinship; Marriage
Consult: Gough, Kathleen, "The Origin of the Family," *Journal of Marriage and the Family,* pp. 760–770, November 1971; Linton, Ralph, *The Study of Man* (New York: Appleton-Century-Crofts, 1936).
—*MaryAnn Foley, Southern Connecticut State University*

**Family Cycle.** This term refers to the series of stages passed through by any family; it is analogous to the individual developmental cycle. The three phases most often cited are *expansion,* from marriage of parents to completion of their family of procreation; *dispersion* or fission, beginning with the first marriage of offspring and ending in the marriage of all children; *replacement,* marked by death of parents and replacement in the social structure by families of offspring. The timing, rites, and roles of various stages differ from culture to culture. As the size and constitution of the domestic group change, so do the rights, duties, and expectations of its members in relation to one another.

See also Domestic cycle; Family, the; Family of orientation; Family of procreation
Consult: Goody, Jack, *The Development Cycle in Domestic Groups* (Cambridge: Cambridge University Press, 1958).

**Family of Orientation.** The nuclear or elementary family (consisting of husband, wife, and offspring) into which ego (the individual) is born and in which he or she is reared and considered a child in relation to the parents.

See also Domestic cycle; Family, the; Family cycle; Family of procreation

**Family of Origin.** See Family of orientation.

**Family of Procreation.** The nuclear or elementary family (consisting of husband, wife, and offspring) formed by marriage of ego (the individual) and in which he or she is a parent.

See also Domestic cycle; Family, the; Family cycle; Family of orientation

**Farming.** See Agriculture.

**Fascism.** Fascism refers to a type of political-economic system similar to that instituted in Italy by Mussolini's Fascist Party in the interwar years. In particular, the term is commonly used to describe Nazi Germany. Fascism involves the development of state capitalism, the rule of a single party, the use of repression against dissidents, the destruction of workers' organizations (such as unions), the adulation of a strong leader, and a totalitarian control over social institutions and private lives. The term is sometimes loosely used to refer abusively to any political system considered to be right wing.

**Fatalism.** This term refers to the belief that one's actions cannot influence the future. It is not, however, necessarily synonymous with despair. It is an adaptive characteristic which enables a person to accept that which is beyond his or her control. The world is in many ways unpredictable, and it is useless to waste one's energy trying to control it completely. Fatalism, often associated with peasant or folk beliefs, is beyond optimism or pessimism. Where and when this belief remains strong, it hinders change and is part of the peasant conservatism noted by many researchers.

See also Conservatism, peasant
Consult: Foster, George, "Peasant Society and the Image of Limited Good," *American Anthropologist* 67:293–315, 1965; Gans, Herbert, *The Urban Villagers* (New York: Free Press, 1962).

**Fauresmith Culture.** This is an archaic term for the Middle Paleolithic Acheulean-derived assemblage characterized by bifacial hand axes, cleavers, and other large cutting tools; it is named for Fauresmith (a town in Orange Free State in South Africa). The

technology represents a grassland/savanna adaptation and is confined to SW Africa dating from approximately 50,000 to 35,000 years BP.

See also Acheulean culture; Middle Paleolithic

**Fayum Culture.** Fayum culture, the earliest Neolithic culture yet discovered in Egypt, is named after the archaeological type site to the west of the lower Nile valley and is thought to have begun around 5000 BC. Tools found at Fayum are of polished stone, and there is evidence of weaving and of the domestication of animals. No pottery has yet been found in the earliest Fayum sites, but some has been discovered in later sites believed to date from around 4500 BC.

**Feast and Redistribution.** In ecological circumstances where human energies can be mobilized to produce periodic food surpluses, while at other times food is in short supply, the feast functions to redistribute surplus food. The potlatch of the Northwest Coast of North America is an example. An abundance of salmon, eulachon oil, halibut, and other foods occurs at certain brief times of the year, and large amounts can be harvested and stored against leaner times. Populous households accumulated food and converted it into potlatch goods such as blankets, slaves, and copper through trading. The potlatch was given at marriages, funerals, and other ceremonies which regulated cyclical changes in social interaction. It entailed assembling large amounts of food and potlatch goods over a period of several years by members of lineally related households and lineages. These items were then given to the invited guests at the potlatch, affinally related members of other households and lineages (who were often trading partners as well). Through such trading relationships and the ceremonial potlatch, great amounts of food and other goods were redistributed and the givers were granted a rank of importance in the society. This brought about a social system in which there were great differences in status or rank but in which many lower-ranking households were saved from famine. Yet the feast does not necessarily save all households from periodic starvation, for myths and stories record numbers of famines in the past. Feast and redistribution increase the probability of survival of a greater number of people, but generally these are affinally and filially related to the most populous and prosperous households.

See also Potlatch

Consult: Oberg, Kalervo, *The Social Economy of the Tlingit Indians* (Seattle: University of Washington Press, 1973); Piddocke, S., "The Potlach System of the Southern Kwakiutl: A New Perspective," *Southwestern Journal of Anthropology* 21:244–264, 1965; Vayda, Andrew P., "A Re-examination of Northwest Coast Economic Systems," *Transactions of the New York Academy of Sciences*, series 2, 23(7): 618–624, 1961.

—*William L. Partridge, University of Southern California*

**Feast and Status.** Anthropologists have investigated a number of traditional societies (notably in the South Pacific, parts of Africa, and North America) in which relatively wealthy individuals are expected to redistribute some of their wealth through periodic feasts to which other members of the community are invited. Attendance at the feast constitutes an implicit recognition of the status of the giver, whose prestige is thus enhanced.

Redistribution of this kind seems to occur primarily in egalitarian societies which are suspicious of or hostile toward the accumulation of individual wealth. The institution of the feast reduces unequal accumulation of wealth, but it offers compensation in the form of status to those who voluntarily share their assets.

See also Feast and redistribution; Prestige

**Feedback.** This term refers to the information a system receives regarding its own operation. There are two types of feedback: *negative feedback* is information which induces a system to adjust its operation toward stability; *positive feedback* is information which induces a system to accentuate its activity. (Positive feedback is also called deviation-amplifying feedback.) Examining feedback as a control mechanism enables us to observe systems in situational change and to identify their adaptation processes.

See also Systems analysis

**Ferguson, Adam** (1723–1816). Scottish professor of moral, natural, and mental philosophy at Edinburgh University who, in a number of works, developed a materialist theory of sociocultural evolution.

**Fetish.** A fetish is an object regarded with awe as having magical qualities or as being the embodiment of some potent spiritual force. The term is also used generally to refer to any object or idea that receives zealous and unquestioning devotion; and it is used by psychologists to designate stimuli which, though normally nonsexual, elicit an erotic response in some individuals.

See also Religion; Ritual; Shamanism

**Feudalism.** This term refers to the social, economic, and political system characteristic of the European Middle Ages. Although there were regional and historical variations in feudal organization, the system had certain characteristic features and was based on the mutual discharge of obligations between distinct social groups: the royal court, the lords or barons, and the serfs or laborers. The monarch granted land rights to the lords in return for their oath of allegiance, or fealty. The lords in their turn granted protection and land rights to the agrarian laborers in return for their economic and military services.

The entire system was characterized by a sharp dichotomy between the manners, mores, rights, and privileges of those who ruled—the monarch and the lords—and those who toiled—the common folk. Feudalism was transformed and superseded by the development of a money economy and the emergence of a rising middle class. Urbanism and growing wealth slowly undermined the feudal society based on personal loyalty and land tenure.

See also Class; Economic systems; Peasants; Peasants and revolution; Social stratification

Consult: Brown, Reginald Allen, *Origins of English Feudalism* (London: Allen & Unwin, 1973); Colburn, Rushton (ed.), *Feudalism in History* (Hamden, Conn.: Archon, 1965); Herlihy, David (ed.), *The History of Feudalism* (New York: Walker, 1971).

—*Bruno Pajaczkowski, Cambridge University*

**Feuding.** Like warfare, feuding indicates the absence, inadequacy, or breakdown of peaceful methods of conflict management. A categorical distinction between warfare and feuding may therefore mask their essential similarities. Nevertheless, anthropologists generally define feuding as a prolonged state of hostility with violence confined to intermittent attacks.

Feuds occur between corporate groups (lineages, clans, villages, etc.) which are distinct segments of a wider political entity. They develop when one party to the original dispute seeks redress for an injury by revenge; subsequent countervengeance exacerbates the conflict, and a cycle of reprisal actions leads to injuries and killings on both sides and may also include mutual seizure or destruction of property and resources. Raiding and ambushing rather than battles are typical feuding operations. The feuding groups always share the obligation to revenge an injury to one of their members, whose corporate liability, in turn, subjects each of them to enemy revenge.

In most societies where feuding has been a common form of conflict management, religions, taboos, and customary laws regulate the accepted range and magnitude of revenge, may stipulate certain times and places of peace, and determine the mode and amount of compensation (like blood money) needed to settle the conflict.

See also Aggression; Conflict; Violence; Warfare

Consult: Koch, Klaus-Friedrich, *The Anthropology of Warfare* (Reading, Mass.: Addison-Wesley, 1974).

—*Klaus-Friedrich Koch, University of Virginia*

**Fieldwork, Ethnographic.** Ethnographic fieldwork is the research carried out by the cultural anthropologist among living peoples in other societies and among subcultures of our own society. It is generally undertaken to collect basic data on a little-known society or subculture or to test a hypothesis. The general model of research is formulated before the fieldwork begins: the ethnographer reads all the available literature about the society. Often this preliminary stage involves the preparation of grant applications for financing the fieldwork.

**Initial Stages.** In many ways the beginning of fieldwork is the most difficult part of the research. Many serious problems can occur during the first few weeks in the field. First there is the problem of the initial impression one creates when first meeting the members of the society or subculture one is studying. The problem is greatest among

*Artist Anne Putnam listening to Cephu, the teller of legends. Among the first to study the Ituri Forest Pygmies, Mrs. Putnam collected many legends and as an artist made valuable contributions to anthropology.*

rural peoples where the social group is small and the stranger is seen as a potential threat to the group.

Entry into the community necessitates the establishment of a role. The role one assumes at the beginning of the fieldwork can affect work during later stages of research. The American Anthropological Association has recognized occurrences of some ethically questionable practices and passed a resolution urging anthropologists neither to collect data while posing as something other than an anthropologist nor to engage in spying while assuming the role of anthropologist.

During the initial stages of fieldwork, ethnographers sometimes experience culture shock—they become disoriented when they realize that the people they are studying operate by a different set of cultural rules. Culture shock usually has only a temporary effect. After a few days of depression the ethnographer is able to return to work.

For the ethnographer who is not fluent in the language of the people being studied, there is an additional difficulty centering around the use of an interpreter. Because the interpreter is bilingual, he or she is often a marginal member of the group. If the group has negative attitudes toward the interpreter, these may be transferred to the ethnographer as well. Also the interpreter serves as a filter through which pass the questions of the ethnographer and the responses of those interviewed. Translations are colored by the interpreter's attitudes toward the group being studied as well as his or her perception of what the anthropologist wants to hear. The ethnographer can only be sure of the interpreter's accuracy by learning the language.

Finally, as the ethnographer attempts to establish rapport with a number of informants, she or he must be cautious of the friendships entered into during the initial stages of research. As research is initiated, the ethnographer is unaware of the social cleavages within the group. For example, the ethnographer may befriend an individual who later turns out to be the town drunk. This can endanger one's entire project if the resentment of the group toward the alcoholic is extended to his friend the ethnographer. Thus caution in the making of early friendships is suggested. Moreover, the ethnographer should make as many initial contacts as possible rather than confining his or her attention to one or two persons or families.

**Collecting the Data.** Information is collected by a variety of means in ethnographic fieldwork, but participant observation and interviewing are the most important methods. Participant observation is a research technique involving the direct, firsthand observation of a group's way of life. Through participant observation, information on the material culture, rituals, and other forms of behavior can be collected while the researcher participates as much as possible in the group's daily affairs. Frequently photography aids in the documentation of these data.

Several types of interviewing are used by the ethnographer, including structured and in-depth interviewing. Structured interviewing, which involves the use of some type of questionnaire, is used more frequently in sociology as a means of collecting data. Informants are often selected on the basis of sampling procedures. Structured interviewing is valuable for quantifying certain types of data.

In-depth interviewing is used more frequently in ethnographic fieldwork because the anthropologist is not familiar with the culture being studied. Sociologists, working in their own society, can make certain implicit assumptions about the responses of their informants: they know what questions are meaningful in their own society. But ethnographers cannot make assumptions about the society they are studying until they become familiar with the culture: they must ask open-ended questions which allow the informants to discuss things they consider important. Eventually, through the extended use of in-depth interviewing, the anthropologist will begin to learn about the society's way of life. At this point, she or he may switch to a more structured interview. In-depth interviewing is often conducted with key informants. Key informants have three important characteristics—they are knowledgeable about their society; they are articulate; and they are the members of the society with whom the ethnographer has been able to establish the best rapport.

*Anthropologist Napoleon Chagnon recording Yanomamö myths. The difficult and time-consuming aspect of much ethnographic fieldwork comes in the transcribing and translating of the taped materials. Finally, they must be analyzed along with other kinds of data—a task that can take many years.*

Besides participant observation and interviewing, cultural data are collected through a number of different means. Photographs are taken of every aspect of the society. Tape recorders are used to collect information on the language of the people and their music. Surveying is carried out to map the area being studied. Projective tests are administered to collect data on personality. Wherever possible archival data are examined in order to view the people being studied from a historical perspective. In some cases census information, newspapers, posters, and other published data can be utilized.

**Processing the Data.** Perhaps the most difficult aspect of fieldwork is the analysis of data, which is done continually by the ethnographer. Each day data are analyzed in a rough manner to discern patterns and to determine what information should be collected the next day. The analysis involves the translation of ideas from one system of beliefs into the categories of another system, that of the anthropologist, without distorting the concepts. Detailed analysis must await the ethnographer's return home.

Anthropologists, because of the uniqueness of fieldwork and the emphasis on qualitative rather than quantitative data, have a difficult time verifying their findings. Most frequently verification occurs through cross-cultural comparisons and by having the results examined by colleagues who have worked in the same culture area.

See also Culture shock; Ethnography; Fieldwork methods; Participant observation; Photography as a research tool

Consult: Chagnon, Napoleon A., *Studying the Yanomamö* (New York: Holt, 1974); Crane, Julia G., and Angrosino, Michael V., *Field Projects in Anthropology: A Student Handbook* (Morristown, N.J.: General Learning Press, 1974); Edgerton, Robert B., and Langness, L. L., *Methods and Styles in the Study of Culture* (San Francisco: Chandler and Sharp, 1974); Wax, Rosalie H., *Doing Fieldwork* (Chicago: University of Chicago Press, 1972).

—*Michael D. Olien, University of Georgia*

**Fieldwork Methods.** Fieldwork is the principal method by which anthropologists gather information. While the idea of "going native" is a professional myth, the technique called *participant observation* has distinct advantages for investigating social behavior in its total cultural context. Ideally a fieldworker should speak (or learn to speak) the local language and actually live among the people whose way of life he or she studies.

Since the beginning of ethnographic research by trained scientists, fieldwork methods have changed in scope and techniques. Nineteenth-century ethnographers conducted mainly area surveys in which they recorded native customs in much the same way as they collected material artifacts for their museums. Their publications are often little more than encyclopedic compilations of assorted beliefs and practices. The work of Bronislaw Malinowski among the Trobriand Islanders set an example for the type of field research that has become known as community studies. In these studies, the ethnographer takes a holistic approach and investigates a society's institutions, belief systems, and behavior patterns in their functional interdependence. Although the community remains the focus of ethnographic research, recent field studies tend to be problem-oriented. These new studies investigate a particular institutional or behavioral complex (economics, politics, socialization, law) within a specific theoretical frame. While this approach limits intensive study to a given theoretically relevant topic, it extends its scope beyond the community to the wider political and economic structure of the society. Even when anthropologists began to explore new areas of research such as public health, education, and city life in complex industrial societies, they continued to gather much of their information through traditional methods of fieldwork. Photography, recording machines, and other technical aids have greatly improved the efficiency of the old-fashioned yet still essential notebook ethnography.

The various places in which anthropologists work and the nature of their theoretical interests require different techniques of ethnographic inquiry. Most fieldworkers collect their data by at least some formal devices in addition to their routine recording of events and impressions in their fieldnotes or diaries and their interview sessions with key informants.

*Mapping* involves the graphic recording of topographic and demographic data of the people's environment. A map may contain the location of important natural resources; garden areas; roads, paths, and ceremonial grounds; territorial boundaries; and building sites. Other maps may detail the layout of a typical house and the occupants' use of its quarters or plot the cultivation patterns of garden land. Still another kind of map can be drawn of social settings in which the physical positions of the participants reflect socially significant relationships.

*Inventories* are lists of material objects, domestic animals, and foods whose manufacture, production, ownership, distribution, use, and consumption need to be compiled in a systematic and often quantitative way. In combination with other data on the people's economy and social organization, these inventories frequently provide valuable insights into patterns of socioeconomic stratification and role specialization.

To collect demographic data a fieldworker makes a *census* of each household or of a representative sample of households, depending on the size of the population. Census sheets usually contain basic biographical data like names, age, sex, kinship links, descent group and caste affiliation, past and present marriages, and residential history as well as information on the educational background, occupation, income, and other economic resources of the household membership. The ethnographer's specific interests may add to this survey questions about rooming arrangements, health prob-

lems, visiting patterns, travels, and other relevant facts and activities. Through a quantitative analysis of such data the anthropologist often detects underlying cultural regularities and obtains statistical measures to support his or her description and explanation of observed social processes.

Other important techniques of fieldwork include the use of precoded *behavior protocols* and specialized *questionnaires* to explore the cognitive structure of semantic domains, *projective tests* and other instruments of psychological research, the collection of *genealogies, kinship terminologies,* and *oral traditions,* the recording of *cases,* and the tracing of *networks.*

In recent years ethnographers have become more conscious of their own role, and many have written about their personal experiences in the field. Moreover, the ethical problems of field research have become as important a topic of professional review as the contents and use of manuals.

*See also* Case study method; Fieldwork, ethnographic; Network study; Reliability of informants

*Yanomamö Indians living in the jungle region between Brazil and Venezuela engaging in a duel, called side-slapping. Full-powered, unblocked blows to the adversary's rib cage are exchanged. This form of dueling is an intermediate level of violence in an explicitly conceived hierarchy along a continuum from competitive shouting to murder and warfare.*

Consult: Chagnon, Napoleon A., *Studying the Yanomamö* (New York: Holt, 1974); Freilich, Morris (ed.), *Marginal Natives: Anthropologists at Work* (New York: Harper & Row, 1970); Pelto, Pertti J., *Anthropological Research: The Structure of Inquiry* (New York: Harper & Row, 1970); Pelto, Pertti J., and Pelto, Gretel H., "Ethnography: The Fieldwork Enterprise," in *Handbook of Social and Cultural Anthropology,* ed. J. Honigmann (Chicago: Rand McNally, 1973); Wax, Rosalie H., *Doing Fieldwork* (Chicago: University of Chicago Press, 1972).
—Klaus-Friedrich Koch, University of Virginia

**Fighting.** Fighting is a means of displaying animosity and demonstrating power. Pertaining to human beings, fighting exists among entities ranging from two individuals to collectivities of persons—for example, nation-states. Fighting may be used to impress or conquer, and the techniques range from silence, verbal accusations, and gossip to the use of physical force involving homicide and genocide. It may be ritualized or spontaneous, a reaction to frustration or part of a cultural pattern.

*See also* Aggression; Dominance and aggression; Dominance hierarchies; Feuding; Warfare

**Film, Ethnographic Research and Report.** The use of motion pictures in cultural anthropology is known as ethnographic

*Stan Washburn, Michael Chalufour, and Ken Nelson (left to right) take time from their careful ethnographic filming in Southern Africa for a bit of humor.*

cinematography. Interest in ethnographic cinematography stems primarily from the early films on native cultures by Robert Flaherty, especially his *Nanook of the North* (1922), a film about Eskimo culture.

While almost every ethnographer records data by means of still photography, only a few have used motion picture film. Cinematography offers obvious advantages over still photography—not only is an added dimension, time, recorded by the film but movements can be recorded as well. However, cinematography presents greater technical problems and considerable expense. Only about one of every ten feet of film is used in the final edited version. Costs in commercial films run as high as $1,000 a minute. Frequently the ethnographer works with a professional cinematographer to ensure a correct representation of the society as well as acceptable film quality. Because of the time dimension in film, cinemato-

graphic data are generally more difficult for the ethnographer to codify.

Although most films of preliterate societies have been made by ethnographers, recently there have been attempts by cinematographers to train members of other societies in the skills of filmmaking, thus, allowing them to produce an inside view of their own culture.

See also Photography as a research tool
Consult: Collier, John, Jr., *Visual Anthropology: Photography as a Research Method* (New York: Holt, 1967); Worth, Sol, and Adair, John, *Through Navajo Eyes: An Exploration in Film Communication and Anthropology* (Bloomington: Indiana University Press, 1972).
—*Michael D. Olien, University of Georgia*

**Fire, Use by Homo Erectus.** *Homo erectus* is the earliest hominid clearly associated with the controlled use of fire, though evidence for fire is much later. Hearths from the cave of L'Escale in S France, over 700,000 years old, were associated with no hominid remains. By 400,000 to 500,000 years ago, fire was widely used in northern latitudes. Choukoutien in China was the first cave site known to contain hearths and charred ani-

mal remains. Fire may have warded off predators competing for the cave, given warmth and light, and allowed food to be cooked (including some specimens of *Homo erectus* as well as other meat). Hearths were also found at Vértesszöllös in Hungary, again associated with human remains, evidence of big-game hunting, and tools. Dating to perhaps 400,000 years ago, hearths were excavated from inside oval huts at Terra Amata in Nice, and fire was used, perhaps to drive game into swamps, at Torralba and Ambrona in Spain.

In addition to use of fire for warmth, light, protection, cooking, and hunting, some authorities have related nighttime use of fire to the development of speech and sociability (sitting around the campfire) and to such anatomical changes as the reduction of the jaw and teeth, which was facilitated through cooking of food.

See also Hominids; Homo erectus
Consult: Time-Life, *The First Men* (Boston: Little, Brown, 1973).
—*Catherine E. Read-Martin, California State University, Los Angeles*

**Firth, John Rupert** (1890–1960). A British linguist whose work dealt with the place of meaning in linguistic analysis, Firth is known for his theory of context of situations and prosodic analysis in phonology.

**Firth, Raymond** (b.1902). British social anthropologist with extensive contributions in the fields of economic anthropology, social change, and anthropological theory (especially social organization). Firth's area of specialization is Oceania (Tipkopia), and he has made major ethnographic contributions to SE Asian and Polynesian studies.

**Fishing.** Viewed broadly, fishing consists of activities and techniques directed toward the exploitation of aquatic animals. From a technological standpoint, however, some of these activities, like the pursuit of sea mammals, are perhaps more appropriately classed as hunting, while others, like the simple collection of shellfish, seem to have more in common with gathering. In essence, it is really the unique qualities of aquatic environments—the physical problems they present as well as their great economic potential—which set fishing apart from the other modes of exploiting wild foods. Adap-

*Australian Aborigine displays remarkable agility and concentration as he attempts to spear deep-water fish.*

tation to these habitats, of course, requires specialized technologies. But it is revealing that many nonagricultural groups dependent primarily on aquatic resources achieved a high degree of cultural complexity, otherwise attainable only with systematic food production. The Northwest Coast Indians are a case in point.

Other than picking fish out of the water by hand, perhaps the simplest means of fishing without special devices consists of herding fish onto stream banks, as once practiced by certain Australian aborigine populations. Weapons of the chase have been modified for use in the aquatic medium. Fish spears designed to transfix the prey include tridents and leisters, as well as more complex devices. The fish bow has been used in parts of Melanesia and Brazil and by the Andamanese. The blowgun has been employed as a fishing weapon in S India. Typically, fishing arrows and darts utilize the distinctive elements of the harpoon, namely, a detachable head and recovery line.

While these weapons may be effective, a more productive strategy involves capturing many fish in either nets, traps, pounds, or weirs. Seines, for example, have been used advantageously by many peoples. These long, weighted and floated nets are cast into the water so as to cut off as large an area as possible and then drawn ashore. Seining is a large-scale undertaking that requires the cooperation of many people to manipulate the net and haul it in. By contrast, dip nets, cast nets, and simple basket traps may be used in shallow water by individuals acting alone. Like fish spears, these devices can be used more efficiently when fish are first driven, confined, or lured as in night-fishing with torches.

The well-known New England lobster pot is an example of one type of movable cage-trap, designed so that the prey is lured into a baited chamber from which it cannot escape. Weirs and dams are built across streams or in tidal zones where they are set below the high-water mark to impound fish attempting to follow the tide out. Weirs are also used to deflect fish into traps. To capture salmon running upstream to spawn, the

Nootka (NW Coast Indians) employed various combinations of convergent weirs and rectangular or conical traps at several points in the river.

Lines and tackle constitute another class of fishing equipment. By the proper combination of line, hook, bait, sinker, or float, the angler can selectively exploit desirable species found near the surface, at the bottom, or at some intermediate depth. Bonito fishing, for example, was highly developed in W and C Polynesia. Pursued from special canoes, bonito were caught with long rods and short lines having distinctive barbless hooks and gleaming pearl shell lures. An unusual type of surface angling, practiced in parts of Indonesia and Melanesia, involves the use of kites manipulated so as to keep the bait or lure skipping across the surface. In the Melanesian version, a tassled spiderweb is used to lure and entangle garfish.

Two other fishing methods deserve special mention. Fish can be stupefied by the addition of toxic substances to still waters and then easily collected. Fish poisons are used more extensively in the Amazon Basin than in any other region. And although fishing with the aid of animals is rare, some attention has been given to the training of cormorants and otters in Asia.

See also Bow and arrow; Economics and subsistence; Harpoon; Spear; Weapons
Consult: Hornell, James, *Fishing in Many Waters* (Cambridge: Cambridge University Press, 1950).
—Seth Schindler, *Southern Illinois University*

**Fission Track Dating.** See Physical-chemical methods of dating.

**Fixation.** In Freudian psychology, this term refers to the arresting of development at a particular developmental stage, usually because the individual in question is emotionally incapable of accepting the responsibilities of the next stage.
See also Defense mechanisms; Freud, Sigmund

**Flake Tools.** These tools are made by taking a flint core and striking it to knock off a flake which may then be further worked to produce the particular tool needed. Thus the flake is basically a blank used for producing other tools. The fragment struck from the core is produced by either a blow or pres-

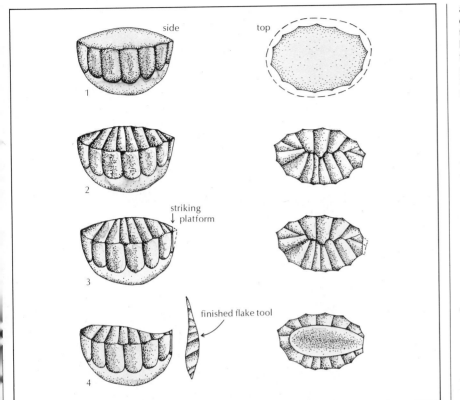

THE TECHNIQUE OF PREPARED-CORE FLAKE TOOL PRODUCTION

*The making of a Levallois core: (1) the edges of a suitable stone are trimmed; (2) then the top surface is trimmed; (3) a striking platform is made, the point where the flake will originate, by trimming to form a straight edge on the side; (4) a flake is struck from the core, and the flake removed. Prepared cores like this one were designed to enable the toolmaker to strike off large flakes of predetermined size.*

sure. This leaves distinctive marks (called the bulb of percussion) on the core, marks which allow its identification as an item of human culture. The finest flake tools were characteristic of the Mousterian culture. A flake industry persists today in England to produce gunflints for black-powder weapons.

*See also* Mousterian culture

**Flannery, Kent V.** (b.1934). An American anthropologist who has combined detailed analysis of archaeological-site faunal remains with ecological reconstruction, Flannery has revolutionized theories of early food production and origins of the state in both the Near East and Mexico.

**Flotation.** *See* Excavation of a site.

**Fluorine and Nitrogen Dating.** *See* Physical-chemical methods of dating.

**Folk Culture.** This ideal type, or model, of a small primitive society was used by Robert Redfield to represent the polar opposite of the typical urban society on his folk-urban continuum. In Redfield's construction a folk culture (or folk society) is small, isolated, and homogeneous; relationships are primary rather than secondary; and it is mainly

a sacred rather than a secular society. Some confusion has surrounded the concept due to the fact that Redfield originally (in his book on Tepoztlán) used the term in a nontechnical sense to refer to nonliterate peoples (especially peasants) with an unwritten tradition of popular folklore, song, and dance.

*See also* Folk-urban continuum; Peasants; Redfield, Robert

**Folklore.** This term, coined in England in 1846 to replace "popular antiquities," refers to a series of genres of cultural material transmitted from person to person (usually orally or by example) and also to the formal study of such materials, though the study is sometimes called *folkloristics.* The genres of folklore include myth, folktale, legend, joke, epic, folksong, folk speech, proverb, riddle, superstition, game, gesture, folk dance, festival, curse, blessing, and many others.

The concept of folklore varies in different countries according to the notion of folk held in those countries. In 19th-century Europe, the folk was defined as the illiterate in a literate society—that is, people who could not read and write in a society which had a written language. Even in the 20th century, some scholars restrict the term *folk* to rural peasant society. The comprehensive study of the total culture of such peasant societies is commonly termed *folklife* rather than folklore. It was also believed that folklore represented survivals carried over from ancient times, survivals doomed to disappear as "peasants" became "civilized." A less ethnocentric and broader definition of folk would be *any group of people who share at least one common factor* (for example, common occupation, religion, or ethnicity). Thus one could speak of lumberjack folklore, Mormon folklore, or Afro-American folklore.

Folklore is autobiographical ethnography that provides a unique picture of a people from the inside-out rather than from the outside-in. In their folk music, folk art, and folk literature, people find a socially sanctioned outlet for anxiety as well as a prized means for expressing feelings of a sense of group identity. Hardly a survival, folklore is a viable functioning part of modern societies, as indicated by the new folklore of computers and of social protest movements. Folklore often provides critical inspirational source material for mass culture (comics, movies, television) and for creative composition in art, music, and literature.

See also Ethnography; Folk culture; Folkways; Oral literature; Myth; Survivals, cultural
Consult: Dorson, Richard M. (ed.), *Folklore and Folklife: An Introduction* (Chicago: University of Chicago Press, 1972); Dundes, Alan (ed.), *The Study of Folklore* (Englewood Cliffs, N.J.: Prentice-Hall, 1965); Hultkrantz, Ake, "Folklore," in *General Ethnological Concepts* (Copenhagen: Rosenkilde and Bagger, 1960).
—Alan Dundes, University of California, Berkeley

**Folkloristics.** See Folklore.

**Folk-Urban Continuum.** This evolutionary scheme was developed by Robert Redfield to explain differences between various communities on the Yucatan peninsula of Mexico. In 1941, Redfield published a summary of a study he conducted with Alfonso Villa Rojas and Asael Hansen a city (Mérida), a town (Dzitas), a peasant village (Chan Kom), and a tribal village (Tusik). Mérida was placed near one end of the continuum and Tusik near the other. Dzitas and Chan Kom were regarded as intermediate types. Redfield found that as one moves along the continuum from folk communities to urban communities there is increasing group size, disorganization, role segregation, individualization, and secularization.

See also Redfield, Robert
Consult: Redfield, Robert, *The Folk Culture of Yucatan* (Chicago: University of Chicago Press, 1941).

**Folkways.** This term refers to the routine patterns and habits of daily social intercourse and behavior. Folkways specify the "proper" ways of doing things in a society, but they involve less compulsion than mores. Folkways are in a real sense the ways of the folk: they arise from the context of interpersonal relationships, they are unwritten and uncodified, and they are transmitted down through the generations. Examples of folkways are such common patterns as social courtesies, customs on street and highway, table manners and food preferences, certain modes of dress, and techniques for using tools and implements.

See also Culture; Folklore; Mores; Social control
Consult: Gillin, John, *The Ways of Men* (New York: Appleton-Century-Crofts, 1948).
—Phillip Whitten, Harvard University

**Folsom Culture.** This North American Paleo-Indian culture is characterized by a distinctive fluted projectile point found in association with extinct large mammals such as *Bison talori.* Dated about 9000–8000 BC, the Folsom culture was centered in the high plains of Canada and the United States.

**Food and Food Crops.** Of the large number of plants and animals that humans have used for food, only relatively few have been domesticated and of these only a small fraction have become of great importance. Human beings obtain all their carbohydrates and nearly three-fourths of their protein from plant sources.

Cereals, which figure prominently among the relatively few species of plants that furnish people with most of their food, belong to the grass family (Gramineae). Wheat, which was domesticated nearly 9,000 years ago in the Near East, is today the world's most widely cultivated plant. Of the several species of wheat domesticated, bread wheat (*Triticum aestivum*) and durum wheat (*T. durum*) are the most important. Rice (*Oryza sativa*), which had its origin in SE Asia, today feeds more people than any other plant. The Americas' only important contribution to the cereals is maize or corn (*Zea mays*). Originally it was the most important food in the Americas, but its chief use today is for livestock. Somewhat less important than those already named is sorghum, which is Africa's major contribution to the cereals. Barley, which was domesticated at the same time as wheat in the Near East, is presently used mainly for livestock feed and malt production. Among other important cereals are rye and oats, both thought to have originally developed as weeds in wheat and barley fields. A number of other grasses, sometimes collectively called the millets, are still grown as cereals in parts of Asia and Africa.

Another grass of great importance is sugarcane (*Saccharum officinarum*), from whose stem a sugary juice is extracted. Sugarcane, which was domesticated in Indonesia or New Guinea, today supplies over 60 percent of the world's sugar. The world's other major source of sugar is the beet of the chenopod family. Although the beet is an old domesticated plant, selection for increased sugar production began only in the early part of the 19th century.

Next in nutritional importance is the legume or bean family (Leguminosae), which supplies foods high in protein content. The soybean (*Glycine max*), originally domesticated in China, now is the world's greatest source of vegetable oil. The common bean (*Phaseolus vulgaris*), one of the first domesticated plants in both Peru and Mexico, has become an important food in many parts of the world. The peanut (*Arachis hypogaea*), apparently domesticated in Bolivia, is also an extremely important food plant as well as a source of oil. Peas and lentils (also legumes) were domesticated in the Near East only shortly after wheat and barley. It was apparently a very early discovery that cereals and legumes in combination produced an excellent diet.

In places where the cereals were poorly adapted, various other plants (chiefly ones with starchy underground parts) were domesticated. These plants, many of which became important world crops, come from a variety of plant families. The white or Irish potato (*Solanum tuberosum*) was domesticated in the Andes and today is one of the most important starch sources in the north temperate zone. The sweet potato (*Ipomoea batatas*) was apparently first domesticated in northern South America. It is the only plant generally considered to have been carried across the ocean by humans in prehistoric times, to certain Pacific Islands where it was found at the time of the first arrival of Europeans. Manioc (*Manihot esculenta*), often called cassava or yuca, was another South American domesticate that has since become widely cultivated in other parts of the world, particularly Africa. Several species of yam (*Dioscorea*), which were domesticated both in the Old World and New World tropics, still serve as the basic food of millions of people. One other important starch source, bananas and plantains (species of *Musa*) grown for their edible fruits, was domesticated in SE Asia and has become one of the most important crops of the New World tropics. Other starchy crops, such as taro and breadfruit, also were early domesticates and continue to be of some significance. Although excellent sources of carbohydrates, the starchy staples are extremely low in protein. Thus when they are eaten largely to the exclusion of other foods, malnutrition often results.

Still another of the major domesticates is the coconut palm *(Cocos nucifera)*, which serves not only for food but in many other ways. Although there has been some controversy in the past concerning the homeland of the coconut, it has now been established as native to SE Asia and the Pacific Island area. Many other plants were domesticated, most of them from the Old World. Beverage plants—coffee from Africa, tea from Asia, and cacao or chocolate from the Americas—were early used for their stimulating effect. Plants used for spices were also domesticated in both hemispheres—for example, black pepper in Asia and chili pepper in the Americas.

Far fewer animals than plants were ever domesticated. Sheep, goats, and pigs were among the first, all apparently having at least one origin in the Near East. Cattle, which were to become our most prized meat source, were domesticated somewhat later, probably in Greece. These animals, along with chickens and the water buffalo (both domesticated in SE Asia), are of great importance today for food. In addition to meat, cattle, goats, sheep, and the water buffalo also furnish milk and are used as draft animals. The chicken, of course, supplies eggs.

The dog, probably the first domesticate, has also served as a source of meat in some cultures. Horses and camels, both domesticates of the Old World, have been and still are used for meat and milk, but they have become more valuable for their other uses.

The New World has furnished far fewer domesticated animals than has the Old World. These include the llama, the alpaca, the guinea pig, and the muscovy duck from South America, and the turkey from Mexico. Only the turkey has ever achieved much importance in other parts of the world.

Fish and other aquatic organisms have always been a source of food, but few have ever been domesticated. It is predicted that the oceans may have to supply an even greater supply of protein in the future.

Although the domesticated meat animals are currently enjoying great popularity and provide an excellent source of protein, their numbers may have to be limited in the future. These animals utilize large amounts of plant food, and as the world's human population continues to grow it may be that much of the food used for livestock (such as cereals and soybeans) will have to be used directly by humans.

See also Agriculture; Domestication of plants and animals
Consult: Bailey, L. H., *Manual of Cultivated Plants,* 2nd ed. (New York: Macmillan, 1949); Cole, H. H., and Ronning, Magnar (eds.), *Animal Agriculture* (San Francisco: Freeman, 1974); Heiser, Charles B., *Seed to Civilization: The Story of Man's Food* (San Francisco: Freeman, 1973); Purseglove, J. W., *Tropical Crops: Dicotyledons* (New York: Wiley, 1968); Purseglove, J. W., *Tropical Crops: Monocotyledons* (New York: Wiley, 1972); Schery, Robert W., *Plants for Man,* 2nd ed. (Englewood Cliffs, N.J.: Prentice-Hall, 1972).
—*Charles B. Heiser, Jr., Indiana University*

**Food Consumption.** *See* Preparation and preservation of food.

**Food Production.** *See* Economics and subsistence.

**Foraging.** *See* Gathering.

**Foramen Magnum.** This term refers to the large opening in the cranium of vertebrates through which the spinal cord passes. With increasing bipedalism, the foramen magnum has moved from the rear to the center of the skull base.

**Ford, Clellan Stearns** (1909–1972). A specialist in human sexuality, Ford was associated with the Human Relations Area Files (HRAF) in New Haven, Connecticut. Among his books is *Patterns of Sexual Behavior* (1951).
*See also* HRAF

**Ford, James Alfred** (1911–1968). Archaeologist who developed a system of dating, known as *seriation,* based on the changes over time in popularity of various types of artifacts, especially ceramics.

**Forde, Daryll** (1902–1973). One of the last of the true generalists in anthropology, Forde is noted for his work in promoting anthropological studies in Africa and especially for the encouragement he gave indigenous scholars. He was employed at the Human Relations Area Files and was director of the African Institute from the end of World War II until his death.

**Forging.** *See* Metalworking.

**Formal Semantic Analysis.** Also known as *componential analysis* or as *ethnographic semantics,* formal semantic analysis aims at making full and explicit accounts of the implicit knowledge people have about cognitive (semantic) domains—i.e., about the knowledge which enables people to organize things in their world into systematic sets including part-whole relationships and hieratically structured taxonomies. Some of the cognitive domains studied extensively (and intensively) are kinship terminology, color terminology, plant and animal taxonomies, food taxonomies, and diagnostic taxonomies of disease and illness.

In describing the cognitive domains of speakers of other languages, some researchers are satisfied with translating terms from one language into those of another in order to explain the meaning of the elements within the domain. But this sort of explanation is invariably inaccurate and inadequate due to the inevitable differences in the ranges of meaning of terms in any two different languages. To avoid the pitfalls of translation, formal semantic analysis uses a system which makes it possible to discover exactly how the native speakers of a given language categorize all the separate elements within their cognitive domains and to describe accurately the native structure of the domain.

**Kinship.** The study of kinship systems illustrates the problems encountered in simple translation and shows the analytical method of formal semantic analysis. Specifically, unilineal descent systems contain features which are very different from all other descent systems, including the bilateral descent system of the English-speaking peoples. In the patrilineal (unilineal) descent system of the Omaha, one calls mother's brother and any of his male lineal descendants *winégi,* and one calls father and father's brother *indádi.* The nearest English term for *winégi,* "uncle," fails not only to indicate clearly and accurately which relatives this term applies to among the

Omaha, but it also suggests that they think of their mothers' brothers' sons and grandsons as uncles. This is just as grossly misleading as the frequent assumption that the Omaha extend the kin term for father to include father's brother. In reality the meaning of the kin term *indádi* includes one's father and his brothers within the same conceptual category, one whose range of meaning is considerably different from that of the English kin term "father." This conceptual category can only be understood fully after a comprehensive formal semantic analysis of all the kin terms within the Omaha system has revealed the full set of relatives to which each kinship term applies and thus the full range of meaning of each term. Formal semantic analysis aims to state the relation between the term and its denotata (semantic elements) as parsimoniously and sufficiently as possible. To this end, it uses two basic procedures: it lists the units to be analyzed, and it eliminates redundant features by specifying reduction rules. These formal rules attempt to reduce the complexity in the terminological system to the underlying logical principles in the system. For an example of the application of formal semantic analysis to the description of an entire kinship system, see Goodenough (1965).

**Semantic Contrast.** The crucial feature of formal semantic analysis which distinguishes it from other systems of description is the emphasis on discovering the dimensions of semantic contrast employed in the semantic domains of native speakers of the language being analyzed, rather than relying on the researcher's preconceived notions about how the system is likely to be structured and what its contrastive dimensions are likely to be. For example, a formal semantic analysis by Conklin (1955) shows how the Philippine Hanunóo employ semantic criteria very different from those of Western peoples to distinguish four primary colors: relative darkness (shade) of the object, relative lightness, relative dryness, and relative wetness of the object. Although parts of the system of color taxonomy employed by the Hanunóo overlap with the systems used by other people, the total range of any term in the Hanunóo system is different from the range of any term in another system—a fact which is made to stand out clearly by the analytical and descriptive methodology of formal semantic analysis.

*See also* Componential analysis; Emics; Ethno-science; Etics; Kinship; Kinship terminologies; New Ethnography, the; Semantics

Consult: Berlin, Brent, and Kay, Paul, *Basic Color Terms* (Berkeley: University of California Press, 1969); Berlin, Brent, Breedlove, Dennis, and Raven, Peter, "Covert Categories and Folk Taxonomies," *American Anthropologist* 70:290–299, 1968; Burling, Robbins, *Man's Many Voices* (New York: Holt, 1970); Conklin, Harold, "Hanunóo Color Categories, "*Southwestern Journal of Anthropology* II:339–344, 1955; Goodenough, Ward, "Yankee Kinship Terminology: A Problem in Componential Analysis," *American Anthropologist* 67(5): 259–287, 1965; Hammel, A. E. (ed.), "Formal Semantic Analysis," *American Anthropologist* Special Publication 67 (no. 2, pt. 5), 1965; Lounsbury, Floyd G., "A Semantic Analysis of the Pawnee Kinship Usage," *Language* 32:158 –194, 1956; Lounsbury, Floyd G., "A Formal Account of the Crow and Omaha Type Kinship Terminologies, " in *Explorations in Cultural Anthropology*, ed. W. H. Goodenough (Philadelphia: University of Pennsylvania Press, 1964); Romney, A. Kimball, and D'Andrade, Roy G., "Cognitive Aspects of English Kin Terms," *American Anthropologist* 66(3): 146–170, 1964.

—Charles T. Snow, California State University, Chico
—Shirley Fiske, University of Southern California

**Formal Universals.** *See* Universals of language.

**Fortes, Meyer** (b. 1906). Fortes, a student of both A. R. Radcliffe-Brown and Bronislaw Malinowski, combined and developed their theories, especially in the field of kinship studies. His work on the Tallensi and the Ashanti of Ghana has served as a model for all subsequent studies of African social organization. Also of great significance is his work on ancestor worship, which combines psychoanalytical insights with the study of its social functions. Fortes chaired the anthropology department of Cambridge University, England, from 1950 to 1973.

**Fortune, Reo Franklin** (b. 1903). British social anthropologist known primarily for his classic study of witchcraft and sorcery among the Dobu Islanders of E New Guinea.

**Fossil Analysis.** The analysis of fossils is painstaking, and the results are often controversial. Locating and excavating fossil remains are problems in themselves, particularly for the scarce and delicate hominid materials. Fossil remains usually consist of fragmented bone parts, particularly teeth and jaws but sometimes skull and long bone fragments. These must be carefully collected, recorded, and cleaned—often with delicate tools like dental picks and brushes —and reassembled as far as possible. Differences of interpretation may enter in even at the stage of reassembly and reconstruction. Because of the necessary relations of various anatomical parts in a functional complex such as the face, and the marks from muscle attachments and behavioral stresses left on the bones, broad inferences about anatomy and behavior can sometimes be made.

A major problem in analyzing fossils is the significance given to variability between specimens. "Splitters" believe that minor variations between forms may be considered evidence of major taxonomic differences; "lumpers" regard variability as normal within a population or species. More research is needed on living populations to determine the type, extent, and importance of variation.

*See also* Dentition of fossils; Hominids; Species; Taxonomy

—Catherine E. Read-Martin, California State University, Los Angeles

**Fossil Sequence of Human Evolution.** Skeletal evidence for fossil humans has been accumulating for more than 120 years. In the century which has elapsed since human antiquity became generally established, a series of attempts has been made to organize hominid fossils into phylogenies which describe or interpret probable relationships among bodies of skeletal data. Although interesting in their own right for historical reasons, these schemes will not be reviewed here (see Tuttle 1974 for a concise synopsis). It should be noted, however, that they have tended in the past to be based strictly on assessments of morphological difference and similarity. In recent years what might be called a functional or functional/morphological approach has emerged (Campbell 1974) which, if used judiciously in conjunction with multivariate statistics (Oxnard 1973), holds considerable promise for resolving (or avoiding) the taxonomic

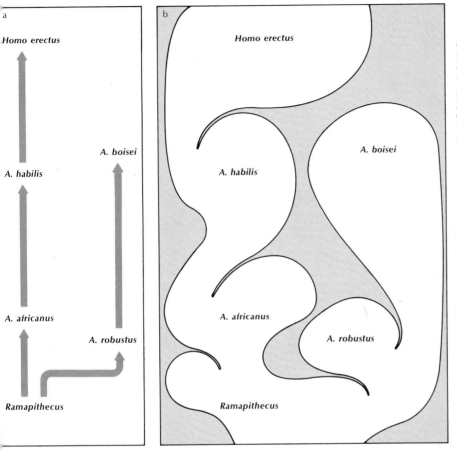

a

Homo erectus

A. boisei

A. habilis

A. africanus

A. robustus

Ramapithecus

b

Homo erectus

A. boisei

A. habilis

A. africanus

A. robustus

Ramapithecus

*Two methods of diagramming phylogenetic (evolutionary) relationships among fossil populations. Style a is easier to read, but it distorts the materials by suggesting sudden beginnings and ends for the existence of fossil populations. Style b is more difficult to read; however, it has the virtue of suggesting gradual evolutionary development from one fossil population to another. It also illustrates how one fossil form can evolve into another, yet later coexist with the new form. This model should be kept in mind through the discussion of hominid evolution.*

conflicts which have plagued human fossil studies since their inception. What follows disregards thorny taxonomic questions as much as possible. Grades in hominid evolution are described which trace the course of human development from a Miocene, forest-dwelling hominoid through the emergence of *Homo sapiens* late in the Middle Pleistocene.

The earliest widely accepted evidence for the existence of hominids dates to Upper Miocene/Lower Pliocene times (14–10 million years ago) and comes from deposits in NW India (Siwalik Hills), Pakistan (Salt Range), and Kenya (Fort Ternan). Because the E African material has been dated from 14.0 to 14.7 million years old and because there is ample evidence for dryopithecines (fossil apes) from Lower Miocene times on, it is inferred that the hominid/pongid split occurred at some point prior to 15 million years ago and that the probable hominid ancestor was one of the geographically widespread and extremely diversified dryopithecines. The ramapithecine fossils consist of twelve to fifteen maxillary and mandibular fragments with dentition; they are assigned to genus *Ramapithecus,* which is usually regarded as bispecific (*punjabicus* refers to the Indian fossils; *wickeri* refers to the E African material). Fossils now assigned to *Ramapithecus* have been known since

about 1910 but were usually regarded as dryopithecines, to which a number of vacuous or preoccupied taxonomic designations were applied (e.g., *Dryopithecus punjabicus, Bramapithecus thorpei, Kenyapithecus wickeri* among many others). As early as 1934, G. E. Lewis recognized certain features of dental morphology now regarded as indicative of hominid status, but the ruling concepts of the day, plus the fact that he was attacked by Professor Aleš Hrdlčka, resulted in his analysis being ignored (this was prior to the general acceptance of *Australopithecus* as a hominid). It was only with E. L. Simons' comprehensive reexamination of the Indian material in the early 1960s that the hominid status of *Ramapithecus* became generally, although by no means universally, accepted.

Evaluation of mammalian faunal assemblages combined with geomorphological analyses have permitted the definition of a series of time/stratigraphic units (e.g., Chinji, Nagri, Dhok Pathan) in India and in E Africa which permit temporal ordering of ramapithecine fossils. Because the Indian material cannot be dated absolutely, the relationship between *R. punjabicus* and *R. wickeri* is not clear. David Pilbeam has suggested that the E African material may be older and that *R. wickeri* may be ancestral to *R. punjabicus.*

The ramapithecine paleoenvironment has been reconstructed by I. Tattersall, K. N. Prasad, and others. In both areas where fossils have been recovered, heavily forested, humid, tropical lowland/open woodland mosaics appear to have been present, although a drying trend and a consequent increase in more open habitats is evident beginning late in the Miocene. Its ecology implies that *Ramapithecus* was a forest-adapted form like the dryopithecines with which it is associated. However, the complete absence of postcranial material precludes informed speculation about posture and mode of locomotion. In sum we can say that *Ramapithecus*—with reduced canines, bicuspid premolars, a shortened, probably parabolic dental arcade, and a comparatively orthognathous face—exhibits facial and dental features presently regarded as indicative of hominid status. There is no evidence that *Ramapithecus* used or manufactured tools of any kind. Throughout most of the latter three-quarters of the Pliocene, a span of some 9 million years, no hominid fossils of any consequence have been recorded anywhere in the world. This gap in the human fossil record is due to the comparative rarity of sediments of Pliocene age. Apparently the Pliocene was a dry period characterized by few of the erosional/depositional cycles which create the massive sedimentary deposits conducive to the preservation of fossils.

The lack of Pliocene sediments is unfortunate because it has been argued that it was during the Pliocene that a protohominid like *Ramapithecus* made the transition from what has been inferred to be a primarily arboreal mode of existence to one characterized by the development of erect posture and bipedal locomotion in a terrestrial environment. Reasons usually cited for the shift in adaptation are the desiccation evident during the Pliocene in Africa and India and the concurrent shrinking of forested habitats in a mosaic pattern. This in turn would have resulted in a multiplication of nutrient-rich, forest margin/savanna environments to which, presumably, one or another form of dryopithecine must already have been adapted. One line of argument asserts that the prerequisites of life on the ground would have selected for the development of erect bipedal posture, given a creature already adapted structurally to arboreal semibrachiation. Habitually erect posture and a bipedal mode of locomotion are the hallmarks of human beings and the morphological criteria most often used to distinguish humans from apes. If the preceding argument is generally accurate, we would expect a hominid more developed than *Ramapithecus,* and later in time, to be characterized by morphological evidence for erect posture and bipedal locomotion. This in fact turns out to be the case.

The australopithecine grade in hominid evolution is distinguished by a mean cranial capacity of about 500 cc, by the parabolic dental arcade characteristic of all later Hominidae, by canines and incisors reduced in size vis-à-vis those of contemporary and fossil pongids, and by a postcranial skeleton which is hominid in morphology, differing only in detail from that of genus *Homo*. Two kinds of australopithecines are commonly recognized on morphological criteria. A widely distributed "robust" variant (mean stature 5 feet 4 inches, weight 100 pounds) occurs in EC and S Africa; a rarer "gracile" form (mean stature 4 feet 9 inches, weight 60+ pounds) appears to be confined to cave cites in S Africa (but see below). The tempo-

ral range of the australopithecines extends from the Late Pliocene (4.5 to 5 million years ago) down to the end of the Lower Pleistocene (less than 1.5 million years ago).

Taxonomic status of many australopithecine fossils is contested due to disagreement about the significance, if any, of the morphological variability observable in collections of hominid fossils from these time ranges. Problems with sampling error, sexual dimorphism, and regional, intergroup, and temporal variation so far defy resolution. Consequently, the role played by australopithecines in various competing phylogenetic schemes is much debated, as is the validity of the gracile/robust dichotomy.

Ignoring taxonomic questions and considering all australopithecines as a group, it is apparent that three significant developments had taken place when these fossils are compared with those of the ramapithecines. First, there is general agreement based on sound morphological evidence (pelvises; limb, ankle, and foot bones) that both forms of australopithecine were characterized by erect posture and were capable of bipedal locomotion. The human mode of progression on the ground, then, appears to have become established very early in the fossil record, certainly by Middle to Late Pliocene times and possibly earlier. Second, a shift in habitat (and by inference adaptation) had taken place since the Miocene. Australopithecine fossils are recovered from contexts which contain fauna indicative of open woodland/savanna habitats—a change in the direction predicted if the Pliocene desiccation model is correct. A savanna adaptation was to characterize early hominids throughout the Basal, Lower, and most of the Middle Pleistocene. Third, the australopithecines were toolmakers. Artifacts assigned to the earliest recognized toolmaking tradition, the Oldowan, occur with australopithecine material at sites in S and EC Africa. The capacity to manufacture standardized stone tools is a consequence of learned behavior, and it is in this sense that the australopithecines are sometimes described as the earliest culture-bearing hominids. Within the corpus of data pertinent to the australopithecine time range, F. C. Howell, Clark, the Leakeys, Tobias, and others believe that they can distinguish evidence for other hominid lines which are morphologically more "advanced"—and therefore better structural ancestors for *Homo erectus*—than the australopithecines.

These fossils, contemporaneous and in some cases associated with *Australopithecus,* are usually assigned to *Homo,* species indeterminate. They are set apart from the australopithecines by cranial capacities on the order of 700–800 cc (argued to lie outside the australopithecine range) and by dental, cranial, and facial characteristics which foreshadow pithecanthropines (*Homo erectus*). Advocates of this point of view argue that these fossils represent the lineage ancestral to *Homo erectus* and that the australopithecines, while clearly hominids, lie outside the line leading to modern *Homo sapiens*. This position cannot be reconciled with that described above; the controversy originates in a failure to understand how to evaluate variability in small samples of hominid skeletal material widely separated in space and time.

Whether its origins lie in a diversified australopithecine population or in that of some more advanced form of hominid, the pithecanthropine (*Homo erectus*) grade in human evolution is recognized by a consensus rarely enjoyed by hominid paleontologists to have emerged by Lower/Middle Pleistocene boundary times possibly as early as 1.5 million years ago. Pithecanthropines are characterized by a mean cranial capacity of 900+ cc; brains housed in platycephalic skulls with variable, often minimal, frontal development (especially the Djetis and Trinil specimens of SC Java); massive supraorbital tori; dentition more robust than that of modern humans; and a thick cranial vault. Most authorities consider the postcranial skeleton indistinguishable from that of *Homo sapiens*. Middle Pleistocene hominids were larger than their australopithecine predecessors (mean stature 5 feet 6 inches), a factor which should be taken into account lest undue stress be laid on the increase in the volume of the braincase.

Pithecanthropines have been known since the 1890s, when the first specimens were recovered from the Djetis and Trinil beds (SC Java) by Eugène Dubois. Since then their remains have turned up in sediments of Middle Pleistocene age (from 1.5 million to 400,000 years BP) in NE and NW China, in N and S Europe, in EC and N Africa, and possibly in S Africa and Israel. Until acceptance of the hominid status of *Australopithecus* became general in the late 1940s, pithecanthropines were regarded as the most ancient form of fossil hominid yet discovered. Although a number of taxonomic designations have been attached to these fossils in the past (e.g., *Pithecanthropus erectus, Sinanthropus pekinensis*), most hominid paleontologists now assign them to a single species in the genus *Homo (Homo erectus)*. It is noteworthy that evidence for multiple hominid lines seems to disappear with the beginning of the Middle Pleistocene. Only *Homo erectus* is present after about 1 million years ago, and few would dispute the conclusion that this form is directly ancestral to modern humans. *Homo erectus* is associated with and assumed responsible for the manufacture of Acheulean, Clactonian, and Tayacian archaeological assemblages in Africa, Europe, and W Eurasia and the chopper/chopping tool industries in NE China (e.g., Choukoutien). The grade in hominid evolution to which modern human beings belong is set apart from that of *Homo erectus* primarily by an increase in cranial capacity (mean 1300+ cc) and by some cranial/facial features which are by-products produced by increased brain size and by a reduction in the role of the masticatory apparatus *vis-à-vis* the pithecanthropine condition. The consensus view is that *Homo sapiens* evolved from *Homo erectus,* the transition occurring during the latter part of the Middle Pleistocene (250,000 to 100,000 years BP). It is important to keep in mind that a continuum is involved and that samples drawn from geographically dispersed early *Homo sapiens* populations should be at least as variable as those of Middle Pleistocene date.

Fossils attributed to *Homo sapiens* can be divided arbitrarily into (1) specimens temporally and morphologically intermediate between *Homo erectus* and Neanderthal man *sensu lato;* (2) specimens representative of Neanderthal and "neanderthaloid" populations, defined on temporal criteria (*Homo sapiens neanderthalensis*); and (3) fossil representatives of morphologically modern humans (*Homo sapiens sapiens*). Membership in the first group is tenuous because fossils are scarce and taxonomic status is debated. This writer believes that these fossils represent morphologically variable populations within a single, polytypic species. They are derived from *Homo erectus* and do not imply the survival of multiple pre-*sapiens* lineages. They are all of probably Middle/Upper Pleistocene boundary date (ca. 250,000 to 100,000 years BP). The second group contains hominid fossils of early/middle Upper Pleistocene age

(less than 100,000 to 40,000 years BP) sometimes classified as Neanderthal on morphological grounds and/or by association with Middle Paleolithic archaeological assemblages (especially Mousterian). The last group comprises fossil representatives of modern human beings; membership is determined by association with Upper Paleolithic archaeological assemblages and/or an age of less than 40,000 years BP.

What constitutes a hominid, and what criteria are selected to partition variability in series of hominid fossils, are paradigm-dependent factors. Some would assert that it is quite pointless to argue the minutiae of taxonomic questions when criteria used in group formation consist of an ill-considered assortment of morphological characters, the evolutionary significance of which is questionable at best. Yet the problem must be reduced to one of evaluating morphological differences and similarities unless still more tenuous dietary and cultural distinctions are introduced. Since about 1968, many hominid paleontologists have adopted a functional approach which is statistically based and population oriented. Although studies in hominid evolution are only a part of this trend and the approach itself is not without problems, advocates would argue that only morphological criteria whose functions are understood in anatomical terms should be regarded as admissible for comparative purposes. Other features might have pragmatic value as gross classificatory criteria but are epiphenomena in functional terms (e.g., brow ridges). One would expect that grades in hominid evolution defined on the basis of functional complexes should reflect major adaptive changes in a hominid direction. Thus, for example, *Ramapithecus* is a "dental man" because his masticatory apparatus indicates the rotary chewing characteristic of all later hominids rather than the vertical motion characteristic of fossil and modern apes. Whether or not he had brow ridges, a sagittal crest, or a cranial capacity outside the dryopithecine range would turn out to be irrelevant.

See also Australopithecines; Dental formulas of primates; Evolution, human; Fossil analysis; Fossils; Hominids; *Homo erectus; Homo sapiens;* Locomotion, primate evolutionary trends of; Neanderthal man; Pongids; *Ramapithecus*

Consult: Buettner-Janusch, J., *Physical Anthropology: A Perspective* (New York: Wiley, 1973); Campbell, B., *Human Evolution,* 2nd ed.

(Chicago: Aldine, 1974); Oxnard, C., *Form and Pattern in Human Evolution* (Chicago: University of Chicago Press, 1973); Pilbeam, D., *The Ascent of Man* (New York: Macmillan, 1972); Tuttle, R., "Darwin's Apes, Dental Apes, and the Descent of Man: Normal Science in Evolutionary Anthropology," *Current Anthropology* 15(4), 1974.

—Geoffrey A. Clark, Arizona State University

**Fossils.** Fossils are the preserved remains of organisms that lived in the past. Most commonly fossils are petrified, but sometimes they occur as molds or prints.

*See also* Fossil analysis

**Foster, George McClelland, Jr.** (b. 1913). A cultural anthropologist interested in the study of peasantry, sociocultural change, and applied anthropology, Foster is best known for his extended research in a Mexican peasant village, Tzintzuntzan.

*See also* Limited good, image of

**Foustel de Coulanges, Numa-Denys** (1830–1889). Foustel de Coulanges is best known for his influence on Emile Durkheim. His study of religion and society, *Ancient City* (1864), was one of the first works to use a functionalist approach.

*See also* Durkheim, Emile; Functionalism

**Frazer, Sir James George** (1854–1941). This Scottish-born anthropologist is best

known for his *The Golden Bough,* a work on the development of the world's religions. Although Frazer taught briefly at the University of Liverpool, most of his life was spent in library research.

Frazer made an important distinction between religion and magic. He viewed religion as the propitiation of supernatural powers and magic as pseudoscience, an attempt to manipulate natural laws. Frazer also distinguished two types of magic: sympathetic, in which like is thought to produce like; and contagious, in which things previously in contact can influence one another at some later time.

*See also* Magic; Religion

**French Sociology.** *See* Durkheim, Emile.

**French Structuralism.** This broad intellectual movement in continental Europe owes much of its inspiration to the Czech linguist Roman Jalcobson and the French anthropologist Claude Lévi-Strauss. The movement embraces scholars from such diverse fields as linguistics, cognitive and developmental psychology, literary criticism, and psychiatry, as well as anthropology.

French structuralism is primarily concerned with the analysis of social behavior and products in such a way as to permit a systematic comparison of all human behavior. Structuralists conceptualize all behavior as communication, whether this behavior is expressed in political, economic, linguistic, literary, kinship,*or other modes. Just as all superficially diverse speech can be explained and systematically compared through explicit reference to the grammatical rules that underlie and structure speech, so, it is hoped, a "grammar of behavior" can be discovered that will permit an analysis of patterns of social behavior. The relationships, or structure, that underlie behavior are believed to be reducible to dichotomous oppositions. They provide the key to an understanding of the ruleful nature of the range of human action.

Lévi-Strauss himself has attempted to analyze expressive culture—mythology, art, ritual—through the structural method in the hope of obtaining universal formulations applicable to all manifestations of culture. Similarly, Jean Piaget has attempted to identify the basic processes of cognitive

functioning while Noam Chomsky, an American linguist influenced by French structuralism, has sought to discover the principles of the "deep structure" of natural languages.

Structuralism is an imaginative and innovative school that draws strength from its holistic approach. It suffers, however, from the considerable distance that still remains between its grand theorizing and the realities of social behavior.

*See also* Lévi-Strauss, Claude; Transformational linguistics

Consult: Lane, Michael (ed.), *Introduction to Structuralism* (New York: Basic Books, 1970); Leach, Edmund, *Claude Lévi-Strauss* (New York: Viking, 1970); Lévi-Strauss, Claude, *Structural Anthropology* (New York: Basic Books, 1963).

—*Ian Robertson, Cambridge University*

**Fresco.** A picture or other decorative pattern painted onto the wet, newly laid plaster of a wall or ceiling.

*See also* Archaeology; Mural; Tomb

**Freud, Sigmund** (1856–1939). This pioneering Austrian psychoanalyst, born in what is now Czechoslovakia, was trained

early in his career in physiology and histology but turned subsequently to researches into various systems of the structure of the human psyche. Freud's work, which explored the mental causes for disease, proceeded on the hypothesis that the infantile life is overwhelmingly influential in the conditioning of the adult.

Freud's *theory of personality* postulated the theoretical division of the human mind into three interacting areas: the id, the ego, and the superego—the balance among which largely determines the health of the individual or lack of it; the conscious, preconscious (forgotten materials), and unconscious (repressed materials)—areas of the psyche complexly related to the former triad. His *theory of psychosexual development* traced the discharge (cathexis) of psychic energy at progressive stages marked by the emergence of various erogenous zones in the body. The source of psychic energy is the polar antagonism between two instincts that underlie all mental phenomena: *eros,* the drive to integrate and reproduce, and *thanatos,* the death instinct that generates aggressive behavior. The specific psychic energy that is either released or inhibited at each stage of psychosexual development is libido—a generalized sexual energy.

Freud's treatment of psychic disorders involved the pioneering use of the "talking cure," in which discursive examination of the patient's recollections of his or her experience yields a key to the alleviation of mental imbalance. The association of free ideas, dream categorization, and analysis supported this technique.

Freud attempted to ascertain the influence of sexuality on the molding of primitive human societies. He posited that recollections of archetypal parricide, guilt, and taboo in the species' prehistory are present in the individual. An early generation of ethnographers undertook to test crossculturally the universal applicability of Freud's hypothesis with regard to the so-called Oedipus conflict.

The corpus of Freud's written and transcribed work is large, among which *The Interpretation of Dreams, Totem and Taboo, Civilization and Its Discontents, The Future of an Illusion,* and *Moses and Monotheism* stand out.

*See also* Ego; Id; Instincts; Oedipus complex; Psychoanalytic school of psychology; Superego

Consult: Roazen, Paul, *Freud and His Followers* (New York: Knopf, 1975).
—*Pell Fender*

**Fried, Morton Herbert** (b. 1923). Cultural anthropologist noted for his contributions to the study of the evolution of sociopolitical forms and his ethnographic research in China, in Taiwan, and among overseas Chinese.

**Friedl, Ernestine** (b. 1920). Cultural anthropologist and former president of the American Anthropological Association noted for her ethnographic research in modern Greece. Her theoretical interests center on peasantry, the process of urbanization, and sex roles.

**Fromm, Erich** (b. 1900). This social psychologist, psychoanalyst, and social philosopher has analyzed the effects of technological society on people, worked with the application of psychoanalysis to the problems of cultural neurosis, studied the effects of childhood environmental factors on adult personality, analyzed the "authoritarian personality," and explored the causes of human cruelty, destructiveness, and aggression. A major thrust of his work has been an exploration of how people can find meaning in life through interpersonal relationships.

Since coming to the United States in 1934, Fromm has written more than twenty books, including *Escape from Freedom* (1941), *The Forgotten Language* (1951), *The Sane Society* (1955), *The Art of Loving* (1956), *The Revolution of Hope* (1968), and *Social Character in a Mexican Village* (1970, with Michael Maccoby).

In *The Anatomy of Human Destructiveness* (1973), Fromm draws on findings in neurophysiology, prehistoric archaeology, ethnography, and ethology to discuss the conditions that elicit defensive aggression and those that cause genuine destructiveness among humans. He presents a global and historical study of human destructiveness and uses anthropological data to argue that "primitive" hunting and gathering societies were the least aggressive human societies and that exploitation and war result from the growth of civilization.
—*Phillip Whitten, Harvard University*

**Function.** This term is used in anthropology and other social sciences with several different meanings. One general definition is a state of affairs or condition of a social system or institution which affects or is affected by some other operations or actions in the system. The idea of function in this general sense is closely associated with the notion of structure, the aspects or patterns of a system or institution that are persistently stable over time. Functional prerequisites consist of some general condition needed to maintain the social system as a going concern. A means of recruiting and socializing new members is one example of a prerequisite.

A secondary meaning of function would more accurately be labeled *eufunction*—for example, processes which contribute to the adjustment or well-being of the system. In contrast is *dysfunction*—processes which contribute to maladjustment and disrepair. *Manifest* functions are those which are recognized and intended by the participants; *latent* functions are those which the participants neither consciously recognize nor intend.

Other meanings of function often encountered are the specific relationships of one part of the society to the whole—that is, the effects of a political system on the functioning of the whole society. Another slightly different one is the contribution one part makes to the maintenance of the whole. Functional explanations generally take the form of a paradigm which incorporates as assumptions the necessary and sufficient conditions for the occurrence of a particular type of social action and a demonstration that—in appropriate cases—the conditions do occur in connection with the consequences.

See also Art and anthropology; Folklore; Functionalism; Myth; Religion; Ritual; Structuralism; Structural-functionalism
Consult: Cancian, F. M., and Levy, M.J., "Functional Analysis," *International Encyclopedia of the Social Sciences* (New York: Macmillan, 1968).
—*James Clifton, University of Wisconsin, Green Bay*

**Functional Prerequisites of Society.** See Society.

**Functionalism.** Functionalism is a mode of analysis, used particularly in the social sciences, which purports to explain social and cultural phenomena in terms of the functions they perform in sociocultural systems. Thus if one were to analyze the Cheyenne Sun Dance ceremony in functionalist terms it could be said that the ceremony, by providing an occasion for the separate residential bands to congregate for a common activity, had the effect of reinforcing tribal solidarity. Thus the ceremony may be said to function as a tribal integrator.

A basic tenet of the functionalist approach is that cultures (or societies) are conceived as systems of mutually interdependent parts, and therefore no single institution can be understood in isolation from the cultural whole. Bronislaw Malinowski, one of the early proponents of functionalism in anthropology, consistently emphasized the interrelatedness of cultural institutions. In his studies of the Trobriand Islanders he attempted to show how the interpretation of any institution (marriage, witchcraft, the *kula*) depends on specifying the connections between that institution and virtually all other aspects of the culture. A consequence of this conception of society is the expectation that any change in one aspect of a culture will lead to further changes throughout the system.

Another element which is central to functionalist theory is the assumption that social systems must meet certain "needs" (Emile Durkheim, Malinowski) or "necessary conditions of existence" (A. R. Radcliffe-Brown) or "functional imperatives" (Talcott Parsons) if the society is to survive. Radcliffe-Brown expresses this proposition by drawing an analogy between biological organisms and social systems. Just as the life of an organism is maintained by the activities of particular cells, fluids, and organs, so the social system is maintained by the proper functioning of its constituent institutions. He therefore defined the function of any institution (or "recurrent social activity") as the part it plays in the maintenance of the larger structural whole. This is his famous organic analogy, a postulate which attributes to social systems an internal integration of parts similar to that found in organisms.

The major sociological contributions to functionalist theory may be found in the writings of Talcott Parsons and Robert Merton. Parsons has elaborated a perspective on society, similar to that of Radcliffe-

Brown, which is often referred to as the equilibrium model. Parsons regards the normal condition of society as one of more or less harmonious balance between the internal parts of the social system. When forces (from outside or within) combine to upset the normal balance, a series of homeostatic adjustments come into play which tend to redress the balance and establish a new equilibrium.

Merton has elucidated the meaning of function by distinguishing between manifest and latent functions. *Manifest functions* are the result of activities which contribute to the adjustment of the system and are both *intended* and *recognized* as such by the participants. The manifest function of the Cheyenne Sun Dance is to renew the natural environment and produce abundance. Its *latent function*, however, is to bring the separate social elements of the tribe together, thereby promoting tribal integration. This latent function is *neither perceived nor intended* by the participants.

Functionalists have often been criticized for creating inordinately static models of society which either fail to allow for social change or treat change as a pathological aberration in an otherwise healthy social order. Closely related is the criticism that functionalism overemphasizes the integrative forces in society and fails to deal with conflictive and dysfunctional elements which, critics point out, are also an integral part of all social life.

See also Society; Structural-functionalism
Consult: Firth, Raymond (ed.), *Man and Culture: An Evaluation of the Work of Bronislaw Malinowski* (New York: Harper & Row, 1964); Martindale, Don (ed.), *Functionalism in the Social Sciences*, Monograph 5, American Academy of Political and Social Science (Philadelphia, 1965); Radcliffe-Brown, A. R., *Structure and Function in Primitive Society* (London: Cohen & West, 1952).
—*Richard A. Barrett, University of New Mexico*

**Functions of Religion.** See Religion.

**Fundamentalism.** A firm or dogmatic belief in certain principles that are held to be basic or fundamental. The term is often used to refer to a belief in the literal truth of the Bible and particularly its account of the origin of the human species.
See also Religion

**Galton, Sir Francis** (1822–1911). A British anthropologist who advocated the planned improvement of humanity by scientific breeding (known as eugenics), Galton also developed statistical methods for studying heredity.
See also Galton's problem

**Galton's Problem.** Sir Francis Galton (1822–1911), after whom the problem is named, offered an objection to Edward B. Tylor's use of adhesions (correlations) in cross-cultural research. He objected that Tylor had presented no means to distinguish correlations due to common origins from those due to diffusion. In short, he argued that Tylor had not taken care that his units were independent. He thus pointed out one of the major problems in the sampling techniques of cross-cultural research. Since the late 19th century, a number of scholars have attempted to offer solutions to Galton's problem. The most tenacious of these has been Raoul Naroll, who has offered a number of techniques to help ensure the independence of cultural units (cultunits).
See also Comparative method; Correlational analysis; Cross-cultural sampling; Galton, Francis; Tylor, Edward B.

**Gambling.** Gambling is wagering on the outcome of contingent or uncertain events, such as games of skill or incidents of pure chance. It is a common pastime among hunting and gathering peoples, who may have a surfeit of free time during seasons when the environment yields an abundant subsistence.

**Game Theory.** This term refers to a technique for determining the optimum strategy for an individual (player) who is a protagonist involved in competition with one or more other individuals for some economic reward or status. The reward is called a payoff and depends on the sets of strategies selected by each player. Each player is assumed to have available a set of strategies and chooses one without knowledge of or control over the strategies chosen by the other players. In a zero-sum game the payoff to one player is taken from the resources of another so that each time the game is played the sum of the payoffs to all the players is zero and the game is thus strictly competitive. A nonzero-sum game may result in all players sharing the proceeds or losses and thus may involve cooperative strategies. In a two-person zero-sum game one player tries to maximize his or her own payoff. Thus the optimum choice will be to select that strategy which gives the largest payoff corresponding to the opponent's selection which gives the first player the smallest payoff (the so-called maximum principle).
Consult: Von Neumann, J., and Morgenstern, O., *Theory of Games and Economic Behavior* (Princeton, N.J.: Princeton University Press, 1947).
—*John R. Lombardi, Boston University*

**Games.** Games are recreational activities, usually competitive, characterized by play organized around an agreed-upon set of rules. Games are important means of socialization; they are often the means used to teach the skills required for gaining a living, as well as inculcating the roles considered correct for an adult in society. In a broad sense, games provide individuals with models or simulations of cultural activities.

In a general study, Caillois (1961) relates various types of games and their functions in society—games of competition give a sense of personal merit, games of chance allow one to feel favored by fate, games involving simulation or mimicry allow one to step into another's position, games involving vertigo alter one's perceptions.

Roberts et al. (1959) classify games according to their relative stress on physical skill (races, boxing), on chance (roulette), or on strategy (chess). Roberts infers that games of strategy are most prevalent in class-structured societies with high levels of political integration, while games of chance are correlated with religious activities and a society's belief in reasonably benevolent gods. Roberts and Sutton-Smith correlate games, social complexity, and childrearing practices cross-culturally. They believe that games of strategy correlate with child training which stresses obedience (assuming that complex social and political structures require obedience), that games of chance are related to a stress on responsibility and achievement, and that games of skill correlate with a stress on self-reliance.

*See also* Play; Sport

Consult: Caillois, Roger, *Man, Play, and Games* (New York: Free Press, 1961); Culin, S., *Games of the North American Indians,* Twenty-fourth Annual Report, Bureau of American Ethnology (Washington: Government Printing Office, 1902–1903, 1907); Roberts, J. J., Arth, M. J., and Bush, R. R., "Child Training and Game-Involvement," *Ethnology* 1:166–185, 1959); Woody, Thomas, *Life and Education in Early Societies* (New York: Hafner, 1970).

—*Phillip S. Katz, State University of New York, Brockport*

## Gamio, Manuel (1883–1960).

Considered the father of modern Mexican anthropology, Gamio introduced the stratigraphic method into Mexican archaeological research. As early as 1916, Gamio attempted to demonstrate to governments the importance of anthropology in aiding culturally different peoples, an approach that today might be considered applied anthropology. Between 1918 and 1924, he directed his most famous research, a multidisciplinary study of the Teotihuacan valley through time. This work served as his Ph.D. dissertation under Franz Boas at Columbia University. In 1925, he studied Mexican immigration to the United States. From 1942 until his death, he served as director of the *Instituto Indigenista Interamericano.*

## Gandhi, Mohandas K. (Mahatma)

(1869–1948). Gandhi, who was born in Sudamapuri, India, elaborated and practiced techniques of nonviolence. His theory of power and conflict (*satyagraha*) was based on the principle that "government of the people is possible only so long as they consent either consciously or unconsciously to be governed" (Gandhi 1967:35). Gandhi and his followers suggested and illustrated that acts of civil disobedience and noncooperation could influence rulers and change government policy. Gandhi was instrumental in helping to end British rule in India, thereby demonstrating that nonviolence is effective in undermining entire political systems. He was assassinated by a fanatic Muslim countryman on 25 January 1948.

*See also* Imperialism; Nonviolence

Consult: Fischer, Louis (ed.), *The Essential Gandhi: His Life, Work, and Ideas* (New York: Vintage, 1962); Gandhi, M. K., *Non-Violent Resistance* (New York: Schocken, 1967).

## Gathering.

The collection of wild plant foods, shellfish, insects, eggs, and slow-moving animals has, in recent times, been the chief subsistence mode among most nonagriculturalists inhabiting the warmer environments of the world. In these societies, gathering is typically the task of women.

Wild foods may either be consumed as they are gathered (that is, foraged) or collected and transported back to camp. The development of burden baskets, net bags, and similar containers allowed the gatherer to collect and carry a larger quantity of foods. With such tools as digging sticks, seed beaters, and milling stones, a greater variety of foods could be exploited more efficiently. An emphasis on seed collecting led to experiments culminating in the development of agriculture.

*See also* Basketry; Digging stick; Economics and subsistence; Skills and work

*Xavante women and girls preparing to leave their village to gather food.*

Consult: Bicchieri, M., *Hunters and Gatherers Today* (New York: Holt, 1972).

## Geertz, Clifford (b. 1926).

Cultural anthropologist noted for his extensive ethnographic research in Indonesia. His theoretical interests include religion, economic change, cultural ecology, and culture as a symbolic system.

## Gemeinschaft und Gesellschaft.

This phrase comes from the title of a classic work published in 1887 by the German sociologist Ferdinand Tönnies. *Gemeinschaft* ("community") and *Gesellschaft* ("society") were the terms Tönnies used to describe the shift from a society whose members were bound by ties of kinship to a more individualistic society where political and economic interests supersede blood ties. *Gemeinschaft* relationships are primary, intimate, and based on tradition; *Gesellschaft* relationships are secondary relationships which are impersonal. In this work, Tönnies introduced the ideal type formulations which in part formed the bases of Robert Redfield's folk-urban continuum.

*See also* Folk-urban continuum; Tönnies, Ferdinand

**Gene.** A basic hereditary unit with a fixed location on a chromosome that influences some phenotypic characteristic and is capable of mutation.

*See also* Chromosomes; Genetics

**Gene Distributions.** Genes, the units of heredity, are transmitted from parents to offspring in a manner first discovered by Gregor Mendel in 1865. Since the rediscovery of Mendel's laws in the early 1900s, tracing family pedigrees in order to determine the mode of inheritance of various traits has been a major concern of genetics. More complex polygenic traits, governed by genes at more than one locus, are investigated primarily by the analysis and comparison of fraternal and identical twins. The distribution of genes within and among human populations has more recently become a major concern of biology and physical anthropology under the rubric of population genetics.

Population genetics was initiated in 1908 with the formulation of the Hardy-Weinberg law for predicting the frequencies of genes and of their combinations in individual genotypes within populations. Although population genetics had played an important role in biology for some time, it was only in the 1950s that physical anthropologists began concentrating on this type of analysis for dealing with human variability.

**Variability within Populations.** A main concern of population genetics is the distribution of genes within breeding populations. Variability among organisms *within* a population is stressed. This reflects a major shift from the earlier typological concepts, which regarded populations or groups of humans as relatively homogeneous as compared to others and stressed the differences *between* populations. Each population was considered to represent a particular race characterized by certain typical features. Research therefore concentrated on examining and measuring only a small number of individuals, since others were expected to fall into the same pattern. Variability was explained as the result of hybridization with other populations. The history of populations could be traced by plotting the distributions of these "racial" characteristics among the populations of the world. The movements and relationships of each race were unraveled with reference to these "marker" traits, thought to be of no adaptive value and therefore unchanging over time.

With the shift in emphasis in the 1950s from continuous, polygenic characteristics (such as skin color) to simple genetic attributes (such as blood group), it became apparent that populations were not internally homogeneous but simultaneously contained a number of genes (alleles) for a given trait at a single genetic locus on the chromosomes. Attempts were still made to classify "races" on the basis of genetic traits, until it became obvious that the variation within a population was in many instances greater than that among populations. Physical anthropologists then became interested in the significance and explanation of this internal variability. The blood groups, in particular, became the focus of these investigations. Human populations, as well as those of other primates, are characterized by blood group polymorphisms—the presence at each genetic locus of two or more genes or alleles in high frequencies. The three alleles for the ABO system, those for the MNSs, and many others are present in most human populations. In fact, it was shown that the frequencies of the ABO blood group alleles do not fluctuate widely, even among populations, but follow a fairly tight pattern, indicating a widespread and strong selective force operating to maintain these alleles within a certain range of frequencies.

Population genetics provides several alternative equilibrium models for dealing with gene frequencies and the distribution of these genes within populations. The principle model is the Hardy-Weinberg law. This states that more than one gene can remain in a population in stable frequencies when no evolutionary forces are operating. The condition of no ongoing evolution is not a very realistic one, but the model does provide a base point from which to determine the directionality and magnitude of changes which might be occurring. More realistic are the classic selection model and the balanced polymorphism model, both of which allow for the operation of some evolutionary mechanisms. The classic selection model treats the case of a harmful gene replaced by mutation at the same rate it is eliminated by natural selection. Examples are the many deleterious recessive traits, such as albinism. The balanced polymorphism model allows for a relatively great selective differential among individuals exhibiting different gene combinations, where not only the homozygous recessive genotype is at a selective

disadvantage. Where several alleles are maintained in high frequencies in a population over time, this generally results from an advantage in terms of natural selection favoring the heterozygote. Examples are the alleles for abnormal hemoglobins conferring resistance to malaria, such as sickle-cell hemoglobin, and some of the blood groups and enzymes.

As the classic and the balanced polymorphism models indicate, natural selection is considered a major force in influencing the variability and distribution of genes within human populations.

**Variability among Populations.** Historically, the major concern of physical anthropologists has been the study of variability among different human populations. The attempt to divide populations into specific types or races has been the main approach for dealing with population differences. Classifications were based on anthropometric or quantitative traits such as skin color, hair form, stature, or head shape (cephalic index). In addition to their complex genetic transmission, however, these characteristics are influenced by environment, a fact shown in 1911 even for the popularly used cephalic index but generally ignored for a number of years. Certain anthropometric measurements, or combinations of these in the form of indexes, were thought to typify each "race" and were regarded as unchanging. Arguments arose over just how fine the breakdown of human groups should be and over the number of "races." The change to characteristics of known simple genetic inheritance made typologies less subjective, although initially the assumption of adaptive neutrality was maintained.

With the recognition of the tremendous variability present within populations, a shift toward dealing with human variation in terms of differences in gene frequencies among populations occurred. But since all populations are unique in their gene frequencies, and yet overlap with other populations in the genes present, the problem of establishing "races" was not solved. Many physical anthropologists decided to discard the concept of *race* altogether, as it appeared misleading and of small utility for analyzing human variation.

The concept of *clines* then came for many to replace that of race. A cline is a geographical gradient in the frequency of certain genes or traits in adjacent populations. For example, the steady increase in the fre-

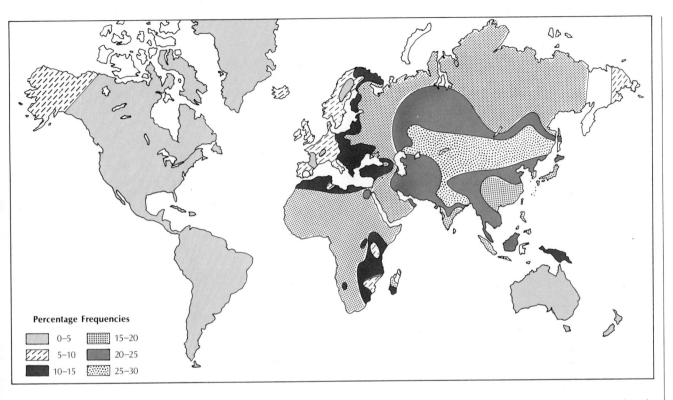

*Distribution of Allele B of the ABO blood type system among the world's aboriginal populations (adapted from Pearson).*

**Percentage Frequencies**

| | | | |
|---|---|---|---|
| 0–5 | | 15–20 | |
| 5–10 | | 20–25 | |
| 10–15 | | 25–30 | |

quency of the gene or allele for type B blood in the ABO system in approaching Central Asia from Europe is clinal, as is the decrease in blondism going southward from the Baltic or the enhanced pigmentation of the skin when moving toward the equator. The term *cline* is less emotionally charged than "race"—*and allows for independence in the variation of the traits.* A shift in the frequency of type B blood does not necessarily indicate changes in the relative proportions of blonds or even in the MN blood group system. The extent to which traits covary, which would make "racial" classifications more useful than the analysis of variability in terms of clines, is still under debate.

Other anthropologists want only to use the concept of the breeding population and to compare populations directly, without use of the racial or clinal approach or by defining "races" as breeding populations or groups of contiguous breeding populations. Whatever type of analysis is used, the variability within populations, as well as among them, must be kept in mind. This method of dealing with populations is known as the analytical or populational, as opposed to the traditional typological, approach.

**Evolutionary and Adaptive Implications.** Traits vary considerably in their distributions within and among human populations. Asian populations are characterized by a high frequency of the gene for type B blood in the ABO system, while this gene is almost absent among Australian aborigines and American Indians. Most populations of the world are principally Rh positive, but the Basques show a very high percentage of Rh negative individuals. Among the abnormal hemoglobins conferring resistance to malaria, HbC is found in equatorial W Africa; HbS in high frequencies in parts of Africa, around the Mediterranean Sea, and in areas of Asia; thalassemia principally in the Mediterranean region; and HbE in SE Asia. Color blindness is most common in populations that have practiced agriculture the longest.

The ability to taste the substance phenylthiocarbamide (PTC) ranges from 63 percent among Arabs to 98 percent in American Indians. Aside from these simple genetic characterics, there is obvious variation in anthropometric traits such as stature, build, hair color, eye color, and nose shape.

The frequency distributions of genetic characteristics within and among populations can give insights into not only the composition of populations but also the evolutionary mechanisms involved in establishing these traits and the changes taking place in living populations. Within a given breeding unit, equilibrium models (such as the Hardy-Weinberg law) predict distributions of genes among organisms in a given generation and in future generations. If these predictions do not hold, it can be assumed that evolution is taking place, that the breeding population was not well defined, or that the population sample was poorly selected. If, for instance, there are more heterozygotes than expected, natural selection could be operating to favor the heterozygote or perhaps genes were introduced from another population. In populations with too many homozygotes, there might be breeding isolates (a preferential mating system favoring inbreeding or perhaps assortative mating of persons of like genotype)—such as the Amish.

Distributions of genes among populations can also allow inferences regarding the evolutionary mechanisms responsible for establishing and maintaining certain traits. A shift in the frequency of a gene which correlates with geographic, climatic, or adaptive variations may suggest natural selection as an important force in regulating this distribution. An example is the decrease in the frequency of the gene for sickle-cell hemoglobin with increasing elevation, which provides evidence to support the malarial hypothesis since malaria also becomes less prevalent at greater altitudes. Sudden, erratic changes in the frequency of a gene in small populations may indicate the operation of genetic drift. The high frequency of the gene for type A blood among the Blood and Blackfeet Indians of North America may be an example. Gradual shifts, as in the frequency of the gene for type B blood in Australia when moving southward from the northern tip, may reflect contact with other populations.

**Climatic Adaptation.** Perhaps the major attempt to deal with human variations in terms of adaptive differences among traits is found in climatic adaptation studies. These focus on explaining a number of variable attributes generally anthropometric in nature—pigmentation of the skin (Gloger's rule), body shape and size (Bergmann's rule), nose form (Thomson's rule), distribution of fat deposits (Rensch's rule), and length of extremities (Allen's rule)—in relation to climatic variables such as the amount of ultraviolet radiation penetrating a habitat from the sun, the temperature, or the humidity of various regions. Studies by Baker have concentrated especially on high-altitude adaptations of the Quechua Indians of South America, who live in conditions of low oxygen as well as cold temperatures.

**Conclusion.** Generally, what is known of human genetics depends on the observation of variation among individuals within a breeding unit and among different populations. Genetic traits which vary in their distribution are both more noticeable and more interesting to physical anthropologists —particularly those concerned with microevolutionary studies and population ge-

netics—than are characteristics typical of all humans. Human paleontologists stressing macroevolutionary analyses of the history of the human species place more emphasis on features held in common by all persons, but the understanding of the extent and significance of variability within populations is important to the investigation of fossil hominids as well as to the study of ongoing human populations.

See also Balanced polymorphism; Blood groups; Cline; Evolution, human; Hardy-Weinberg principle; Human variation, significance of; Pigmentation; Population genetics; Race; Racial classification; Skin color

Consult: Bejema, C. J. (ed.), *Natural Selection in Human Populations* (New York: Wiley, 1971); Montagu, A. (ed.), *The Concept of Race* (New York: Macmillan, 1969); Morris, L. N. (ed.), *Human Populations, Genetic Variation, and Evolution* (San Francisco: Chandler, 1971); Roberts, D. F., *Climate and Human Variability* (Reading, Mass.: Addison-Wesley, 1973).

—*Catherine E. Read-Martin, California State University, Los Angeles*

**Gene Flow.** This term refers to the movement of genes across the cultural, ecological, or geographical barriers which mark the boundaries of a gene pool. Gene flow is caused by interbreeding among previously isolated populations.

See also Evolution, genetic mechanisms of; Gene pool

**Gene Frequency.** See Bergmann's rule.

**Gene Pool.** Any species which lives in a restricted area and consists of a single breeding population shares a common gene pool.

See also Population genetics

**Genealogical Connections.** See Descent.

**General Evolution.** See Evolution, general.

**Generation.** See Kinship.

**Generative Grammar.** When used to refer to a specific language (a transformational

grammar), generative grammar is a theory about that language which accounts in a formal manner for all the possible (permitted) strings of elements of that language and also for the structural relationships among the elements constituting such strings. In a broader sense, generative grammar refers to a metatheory of language—i.e., a theory about the formal nature of language grammars.

See also Grammar; Transformational Linguistics

Consult: Bach, Emmon, *An Introduction to Transformational Grammars* (New York: Holt, 1964); Lyons, John, *Noam Chomsky* (New York: Viking, 1970).

**Generative Semantics.** See Transformational linguistics.

**Genetic Basis of Language.** See Biological basis of language.

**Genetic Drift.** Genetic drift is the consequence of genetic sampling errors which come from the migration of small subpopulations away from the parent group or from natural disasters which wipe out a large part of a population. If the migrant population is very small, it is likely not to carry away a random sample of the genes in the parent stock. Some genes may not be represented at all, others only in frequencies very different from those of the parent population. Thus it is possible for genes to be significantly raised or lowered in frequency. Genetic drift thus contributes to evolutionary divergence in populations.

See also Endogamy; Evolution, genetic mechanisms of; Exogamy; Genetics; Inbreeding

**Genetic Traits.** See Genotype.

**Genetics.** The science of genetics is concerned with the mechanisms for heredity and variation. Since the beginning of this century, the field of genetics has seen a rapid proliferation of knowledge and specialization. One area of specialization, *human genetics*, is further subdivided into the areas of medical genetics, biochemical genetics, cytogenetics, somatic cell genetics, immunogenetics, mathematical genetics, and population genetics. It is population genetics that is probably most involved with the study of human evolution. In reality, however, these areas of human genetics do not have definitive borders and are closely interrelated.

The new physical anthropology relies heavily on population genetics. Instead of focusing primarily on the description and classification of subspecific groups of *Homo sapiens*, the new physical anthropology is concerned with processes, the formulation and testing of hypotheses, and the application of evolutionary theory to the human species. The various aspects of human evolution are studied within the framework

## CHROMOSOMES, GENES, ALLELES

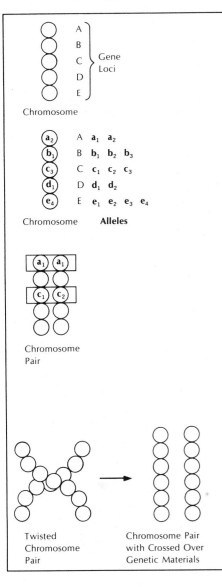

Chromosome

Chromosome    **Alleles**

Chromosome Pair

Twisted Chromosome Pair

Chromosome Pair with Crossed Over Genetic Materials

Chromosomes are strings of genes. Each gene—A, B, C, D, E—has its correct position (locus) on a particular chromosome.

Each gene may have several versions. For example, gene A may have versions $a_1$ and $a_2$. These versions of a gene are called *alleles*. Thus a chromosome really consists of a random selection of each of its genes' alleles.

In somatic cells chromosomes come in pairs. Ideally, the pairs line up next to each other gene by gene. When this happens they are said to be *homologous*. Thus every gene appears twice—or to put it more accurately, each gene is represented by two alleles. If the two alleles are the same (as for gene A), we say the genotype is *homozygous* for that gene. If the two alleles are different (as for gene C), we say the genotype is *heterozygous* for that gene.

Chromosomes often twist around each other. When this happens, they sometimes "trade" genetic materials; this is called *crossing over*. The farther apart two genes are on a chromosome, the more likely they are to become separated due to crossing over.

Crossing over helps to ensure that genes are passed on to the next generation randomly.

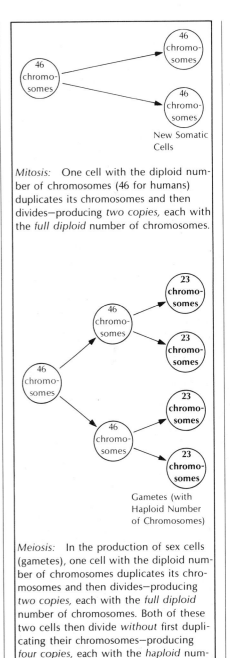

New Somatic Cells

*Mitosis:* One cell with the diploid number of chromosomes (46 for humans) duplicates its chromosomes and then divides—producing *two copies*, each with the *full diploid* number of chromosomes.

Gametes (with Haploid Number of Chromosomes)

*Meiosis:* In the production of sex cells (gametes), one cell with the diploid number of chromosomes duplicates its chromosomes and then divides—producing *two copies*, each with the *full diploid* number of chromosomes. Both of these two cells then divide *without* first duplicating their chromosomes—producing *four copies*, each with the *haploid* number of chromosomes (23 for humans).

CELL DIVISION: MITOSIS AND MEIOSIS

of population genetics. Genetics is essential to the understanding of change seen in fossil species and living populations today. Evolution can occur only in the presence of heredity, which provides for genetic continuity between generations. Evolution, then, can be defined as the change in the *genetic* composition of a population through time.

See also Evolution, genetic mechanisms of
Consult: Lerner, I. M., *Heredity, Evolution and Society* (San Francisco: Freeman, 1968); Morris, L. N., *Human Populations, Genetic Variation and Evolution* (San Francisco: Chandler, 1971); Stern, C., *Principles of Human Genetics* (San Francisco: Freeman, 1973).
—*Mary Jane Moore, San Diego State University*

**Genetics and Behavior.** The relationship between genetics and behavior is fundamental to the overall relation between biology and behavior—that is, if "biology" is understood as the manifestation of a developing organism's genetic potential interacting with its environment. Given this understanding, the genetic control of such diverse traits as red blood cell antigens, eye color, specific enzymes or hormones, tongue curling, or the degree of sensitivity to phenylthiocarbamide in humans is readily accepted by most people. Even certain basic behaviors like movement away from or toward light (phototaxis) in fruit flies or the speed with which individual mice negotiate mazes have been shown to be affected by genetic differences between individual organisms.

To demonstrate the innate basis of such mundane behavioral patterns in simple organisms like fruit flies and mice is one thing; to demonstrate the same genetic basis in more complex organisms is quite another. For, generally speaking, the more of its behavior an animal must acquire in order to survive into adulthood and function viably in its social and environmental context, the less likely it is thought that there is any direct genetic control over its specific behavior patterns, since the patterns themselves are complex and must be learned.

That there is genetic control over the growth and development of those organic structures necessary for learning (the brain and central nervous system) as well as those fundamental to any activity or movement (muscles, autonomic nervous system, endocrine glands) is manifest. But what is contentious and philosophically unsettling to many people is that there is (or might be) a much more direct and immediate connection between specific genes and specific behavior in more complex animals like mammals, primates, and even humans.

Certainly part of the reluctance to accept (or even investigate further) the possibility that an intimate relationship might exist between specific genes and specific behaviors stems from a basic misunderstanding of the nature of genetic mechanisms. Robert Ardrey's dramatic description of a Pliocene-bred mutant gene conferring upon humans a virtually inevitable carnivorous subsistence pattern complete with aggressiveness and predatory tendencies reveals a profound ignorance of genetic processes and mechanisms. Since the biochemical products of gene activity are polypeptide chains which combine to form enzymes and proteins, the assertion that a single gene confers aggressive behavior on an organism is tantamount to claiming that the presence or absence of a particular string of peptides determines whether an organism is aggressive or not. Such biological reductionism is extreme to the point of absurdity. There are no more single genes controlling for behaviors like aggression, intelligence, or territoriality in humans or other animals than there are for aesthetic sensibility, patriotism, or vulgarity.

Nonetheless, it must be recognized that the very existence of humans in the world today is due to the selection and preservation of genetically based organic foundations of behavior which were reproductively advantageous to our evolutionary ancestors. It is true that complex and successful behavior patterns—especially those involving extensive use of symbols—relating to human group organization, food-getting, rearing of the young, and so forth had to be learned and passed on from one generation to the next. But without the simultaneous inheritance of the genetic bases for developing a uniquely complex biological system capable of engaging in and improving on such behavior patterns, they would have been neither possible nor perpetuated. It is equally true that we have no compelling evidence for the existence of specific genes controlling and determining specific human behavior patterns. But so long as we continue to operate within an evolutionary model for explaining human origins, we have no choice but to accept the existence of an underlying genetic basis for *all* human behavioral capacity. It is the staggering intricacy and complexity of the human genetic system *in toto* that confounds our present attempts to explain the ultimate organic foundations of the behavior of *Homo sapiens*.

The crucial concept of behavioral genetics research is *heritability*—an index of the relative contribution of genetic differences (genotypes) causing observed individual variations (phenotypes) in a given population. Central to a proper understanding of this concept is an awareness of what it does *not* entail: "Heritability is not a measure of the extent to which a trait is determined by genetic factors. Rather, it is a measure of the proportion of the total phenotypic variance which is attributable to genetic differences between individuals" (Gregg and Sanday 1971:59). The complexity of actually determining a reliable index of the hereditary component of behavioral (or morphological) variation in a population is inextricably rooted in the difficulty of successfully partitioning the relative amounts of variation attributable to genetic and environmental factors.

There is no artificial dichotomy here between "nature and nurture." The problem is not conceived in terms of either one or the other being more important—since both are indispensable—but rather in what fashion and to what extent both heredity and environment interact to determine the resulting behavioral (or morphological) product. It is the acute awareness that there is an undeniable and critical interaction between genetic and environmental components that underscores the investigator's difficulty in ascertaining the relative contribution of each to the development of a trait.

The fundamental approach of the behavioral geneticist's efforts to investigate the relationship between genetics and behavior is to experimentally control—as nearly as one possibly can—the genetic similarity of study organisms. In this design, the investigator is then free to manipulate the environmental context in which the organisms develop and can, theoretically at least, measure the extent to which a given behavior (pattern) is expressed in different organisms under their varying environmental conditions.

Large groups of carefully bred strains of mice and other nonhuman animals with rigidly controlled pedigrees are available for laboratory experimentation; such is clearly not the case for humans. For research into human behavioral genetics, an investigator ideally attempts to study monozygotic (MZ) twins—i.e., siblings with identical genetic constitutions due to their development from a single fertilized egg. The use of such genetically identical organisms permits the greatest possible control over the hereditary component of the heredity-environment interaction.

There are, however, two drawbacks to conducting any such twin research with humans. First, the number of MZ twins available for study is quite small, a fact which can seriously hinder sound statistical analysis of the findings in a study and, subsequently, the evaluation of the results. Second, there is virtually no opportunity to manipulate the environmental context in which human twins are reared—either separately or together—which means that such twin studies often involve subjective assessment of environmental influences well after they have already affected the development of the individuals being considered.

In any event, whether the study organisms are humans or other animals, the idea is that the more environmental conditions of two developing organisms resemble one another, the more any behavioral differences between them are genetically based. (A comprehensive treatment of the theoretical aspects underlying behavioral genetics research, as well as the statistical computation and evaluation of experimental findings, can be found in McClearn and DeFries 1973.)

Consult: Ardrey, Robert, *African Genesis* (New York: Atheneum, 1961); Ehrman, Lee, Omenn, G. S., and Caspari, E., *Genetics, Environment, and Behavior* (New York: Academic Press, 1972); Gregg, Thomas G., and Sanday, P. R., "Genetic and Environmental Components of Differential Intelligence," in *Race and Intelligence*, ed. C. Loring Brace, G. R. Gamble, and J. T. Bond (Washington: American Anthropological Association, 1971); McClearn, G. E., and DeFries, *Introduction to Behavioral Genetics* (San Francisco: Freeman, 1973); Mazur, Allan, and Robertson, L. S., *Biology and Social Behavior* (New York: Free Press, 1972).

—*Martin K. Nickels, Illinois State University*

## Genetics and Intelligence.

Perhaps the single most hotly debated issue in psychology over the last hundred years has been the issue of nature versus nurture: Is human intelligence (or behavioral capacity in general) primarily determined by the innate, genetically given characteristics of the individual or by the environment in which the individual lives and develops? This question has profound implications not only for the human sciences but also for practical social policy. The position that people's intelligence is largely determined by their fixed genetic endowments leads to the conclusion that not much can be done to improve the performance of those who have difficulty with academic tasks. In particular, it leads one to expect that a certain number of people will always do badly in school and not to criticize the educational system for its failure to educate a considerable fraction of the population.

One reason for the duration and intensity of the nature-nurture debate has been that psychologists actually know so little about either the nature of intelligence or the relationship between genes and behavior that almost any theory can attract adherents. Some psychometricians (psychologists interested in measuring and analyzing human intelligence), however, have claimed to be able to overcome the current primitive state of psychological understanding by adapting statistical tools developed in the more advanced sciences of animal and plant genetics to the analysis of the genetic factor in intelligence (see Jensen 1973a, 1973b). The most important tool borrowed from genetics by the psychometricians is one called *heritability analysis*. In genetics the techniques of heritability analysis are used to calculate the percentage of variation in a physical character (height, weight, etc.) in a given animal or plant population that is due to variation among the genetic constitutions of the organisms. A high heritability number indicates that the variation is mainly genetic in origin; a low one signifies that environmental factors are mainly responsible. The psychometricians hope to analyze intelligence in the human population with these same techniques.

The first step in applying heritability analysis to human intelligence is to devise a quantitative measure of it. For this measure the psychometricians have used scores on standard IQ tests. Next it is necessary to find a population for which the amount of genetic and environmental variation among individuals is known. By comparing the variation in IQ scores of the members of such a population with the known components of genetic and environmental variation, it should theoretically be possible to calculate the heritability of intelligence for it and similar populations.

In the most prominent studies of this sort, IQ tests were administered to pairs of identical twins who had been reared apart from one another due to family difficulties of various sorts (Burt 1966; Shields 1962). The scores of these twins were then compared with one another. Since the twins were genetically identical, any difference in IQ scores had to be due to environmental factors. It was theorized that if the average difference in their scores turned out to be much smaller than the average difference in the IQ scores of unrelated people, it would show that intelligence was highly heritable. Indeed, it turned out that while IQ tests are designed so that the average difference in score between two random people will be 15 points (one standard deviation), the average difference among the twins was only about 5 points. From this result the heritability of IQ could be calculated as being about 0.8. In other words, 80 percent of the variation in IQ in the white population of the United States seemed to be due to genetic variation.

Not all psychologists by far have accepted the results of the heritability studies. At least two striking criticisms of them have been made. The first of these is that IQ tests, universally used in the heritability studies, are not good measures of intelligence. There is a substantial body of research showing that IQ test scores do not reflect intelligence but rather other factors like class background, attitude toward school, and motivation (see Gartner et al. 1974). The second criticism is that the twin studies and related research projects have been improperly conducted. Indeed, a careful review of this research by psychologist Leon Kamin (1974) has greatly weakened the case for the high heritability of IQ. Kamin's most telling of several arguments is that in the twin studies the twins reared apart were not raised in randomly different environments as are the random individuals whose IQ is compared to set the average IQ difference in the population. In fact, in the majority of cases for which information is available, one twin was raised by the mother and the other by a relative or close friend. Thus the twins were not only genetically identical but also environmentally close to one another. The studies, therefore, cannot tell us whether the close correlation between the IQ's of the twins was due to genetic or to environmental factors. Hence no estimate of heritability can be made.

Besides these criticisms of the heritability studies, scholars have also criticized the social policy implications that have been drawn from them. To take one example, "highly heritable" has commonly been taken to mean "genetically fixed." And, as mentioned earlier, the position that intelligence is genetically determined leads to the conclusion that not much can be done to improve the performance of those who do poorly on academic tasks (see Jensen 1973a). Geneticists (e.g., Lewontin 1970, 1974), however, have pointed out that a trait with high heritability is not genetically fixed in the sense of being resistant to environmental influence. Thus height is known to be highly heritable, but it is still greatly affected by environmental factors like diet.

Finally, there has been much criticism of the use of the heritability studies by some psychologists to argue that minority groups and the lower social classes are genetically less intelligent than the social elite. This position, associated in the United States with the names of Arthur Jensen, Richard Herrnstein, and William Shockley, has been widely disseminated, and most critics of the heritability studies have been concerned to refute it.

See also Intelligence; Intelligence quotient
Consult: Burt, C., "The Genetic Determination of Differences in Intelligence: A Study of Monozygotic Twins Reared Together and Apart," *British Journal of Psychology* 57:137, 1966); Gartner, A., Greer, C., and Reissman, F., *The New Assault on Equality: I.Q. and Social Stratification* (New York: Harper & Row, 1974); Jensen, Arthur, *Genetics and Education* (New York: Harper & Row, 1973a); Jensen, Arthur, *Educability and Group Differences* (New York: Harper & Row, 1973b); Kamin, L., *The Science and Politics of I.Q.* (Potomac, Md.: Erlbaum Associates, 1974); Lewontin, R., "Race and Intelligence," *Bulletin of Atomic Scientists* 26:2, 1970; Lewontin, R., "The Analysis of Variance and the Analysis of Causes," *American Journal of Human Genetics* 26:400, 1974; Shields, J., *Monozygotic Twins Brought Up Apart and Brought Up Together* (London: Oxford University Press, 1962); Whitten, P., and Kagan, J., "Jensen's Dangerous Half Truths," *Psychology Today*, August 1969.

—Anthony Kroch, Temple University

## Genetics, Mendelian. See Mendelian genetics.

## Genetrix.
The genetrix—the biological mother of a child—is distinguished from the sociological mother or *mater* through whom the child is socially linked to other kin. Both may be, and in fact generally are, the same person.

See also Sociological parents

## Genitor.
The genitor—the male parent believed to be the biological father of a child—is distinguished from the sociological father or *pater* through whom the child is socially linked to other kin. Both may be, and in fact often are, the same person.

See also Sociological parents

## Gennep, Arnold Van (1873–1957).
An ethnographer and folklorist, Van Gennep was the first to provide a conceptual framework for understanding the importance of ceremonies (*rites de passage*) marking transitions of individuals or groups from one social position to another within a society.

See also Rites of passage

## Genocide.
This term refers to the systematic extermination of a group of people—usually a racial or ethnic group—defined by the exterminators as undesirable. A new term in international law, it was coined in 1945, by the War Crimes Commission at the Nuremberg trials, to cover the "Final Solution" policy of Nazism, which had resulted in the deliberate destruction of millions of Jews and others in gas chambers.

Consult: Drost, Peter N., *The Crime of State: Penal Protection for Fundamental Freedoms of Persons and Peoples* (Leyden: Sijthoff, 1959); Woetzel, Robert K., *The Nuremberg Trials in International Law* (New York: Praeger, 1960).

## Genocide, Cultural. See Acculturation; Assimilation; Extinction of minorities.

## Genotype.
This term refers to the genetic constitution of an organism (not the physical manifestation, called *phenotype*), which may be affected by environmental and other factors. The genotype of an organism thus consists of its *hereditary potential*, which acts in concert with the environment to produce the phenotype. The genotype may

| Genotype | Phenotype | Relationship Between Alleles |
|----------|-----------|------------------------------|
| AO | A | **A** is **dominant** over O; **O** is **recessive** to A |
| BO | B | **B** is **dominant** over O; **O** is **recessive** to A |
| AB | AB | **A** and **B** are **codominant** |
| OO | O | **O** alleles are **recessive** to the other alleles of the **ABO** gene; the only way they can be expressed in the **phenotype** is if the **genotype** is **homozygous** for O |

Dominance, recessiveness, and codominance among alleles as expressed in the ABO blood system. A **dominant** allele masks out the expression of a recessive homologous allele in the phenotype of an organism. A **recessive** allele is prevented from affecting the phenotype of an organism by a homologous dominant allele. Thus recessive alleles can affect the phenotype of an organism only if the genotype of that organism is homozygous for that recessive allele. **Codominant** alleles express themselves equally in the phenotype of an organism when they are homologous.

contain potentials which remain unexpressed physically because of other genetic factors, as in the masking of a recessive by a dominant gene. Or the genotypic potential may be reduced or unexpressed due to environmental factors such as diet, climate, or life experiences.

See also Genetics; Phenotype

## Geochronology.
Dating based on regularized, naturally occurring phenomena in the earth such as radiometric changes, stratigraphic and eustatic correlations; means of research include ocean coring and paleoclimatology.

See also Dating, absolute; Dating, relative; Time in archaeology

## German School of Ethnology. See Kulturkreis.

**Gesture (Body Movement).** *See* Kinesics.

**Ghost Dance Religion.** This new religion was the first cultural revitalization or nativistic movement ever to be studied systematically; this was accomplished by the anthropologist James Mooney. The religion started among the Paviotso led by a Paiute prophet Wovoka, also known as Jack Wilson. Wovoka had already developed a reputation as a spiritual figure and healer when in 1888 he became seriously ill. During his illness an eclipse caused great anxiety among the local Indian communities, and he underwent a profound religious experience of the kind now described as mazeway resynthesis. Wovoka believed he had died and been transported to the spirit world, where he received direct revelations from the Great Spirit. These revelations promised a restoration of the traditional life of the Indians and a return of dead friends and relatives. Wovoka soon became the center of great attention and attracted many disciples who preached this new faith widely. Soon many tribes were participating in the Ghost Dance rituals. The atmosphere of emotionalism and excitement which accompanied the rapid diffusion of this religion greatly disturbed American authorities, and it contributed to the Sioux outbreak of 1891, which led to the Wounded Knee battle. The Ghost Dance stressed revival of old values and ways, the coming of a millennium, and a restoration of the old strength and autonomy of Indian tribes.

*See also* Nativistic movements; Revitalization movements
—*James Clifton, University of Wisconsin, Green Bay*

**Gift Giving.** *See* Exchange.

**Glacial Stages.** *See* Glaciations.

**Glaciations.** Glaciation is the process by which part of the earth's surface is covered and altered by glacier ice. Glaciation alters the landscape by both erosional and depositional processes, producing a variety of distinctive landforms. These landforms provide geologists with information about the age and extent of former glaciations and about past changes in climate. The climatic changes which accompanied large-scale glaciation in the past also affected regions far beyond where the ice front extended. Average temperatures were lowered over much of the earth's surface. Storm tracks were altered, which in turn changed the distribution and amount of precipitation and cloud cover. These climatic changes affected the location, extent, and character of the earth's soil and vegetation zones and the animal life, including human, adapted to these zones.

**Development of Glaciers.** Glaciers tend to develop in cold-dominated regions where the rate of accumulation of snow exceeds the rate of wastage (ablation) by melting and evaporation. Snow falling in the zone of accumulation is converted into small granules of ice (*firn*) by thawing, compacting, and refreezing snowflakes. As the firn becomes buried under additional snow, compaction and recrystallization transform the individual granules into a solid mass of tightly interlocking crystals of ice (glacier ice).

Glacier ice deforms under its own weight and flows downslope. Two principal mechanisms are involved in glacier movement: basal sliding of the ice mass over its floor and internal plastic flow. The mechanism of internal flow is complex. The acceleration of gravity on a slope and the weight of the ice give rise to shear stresses which cause the ice crystals to glide along crystallographic planes parallel to their bases. Gliding is accompanied by progressive recrystallization of the deformed ice crystals. The front of the glacier will flow downslope to the point where the ice melts as fast as it is replenished by flowage. If the rate of accumulation exceeds that of ablation over a period of years, the mass of the glacier will increase and the ice front will advance. Similarly, if ablation outstrips accumulation, the glacier will become thinner and the ice front will recede.

The form of a glacier is determined largely by the terrain over which it flows. Ice streams flowing down narrow mountain valleys are called *valley glaciers.* Several tributary glaciers may merge to form a single large valley system. Valley glaciers may expand into the lowlands beyond the mountains and spread into lobe-shaped *piedmont glaciers.* Further expansion, thickening, and merging of valley and piedmont glacier systems give

*Hubbard Glacier at Disenchantment Bay, Yakutat Bay District, Alaska, in August of 1969. The terminal cliff of the glacier is more than 5 kilometers (almost 3 miles) long and rocky debris marks the line of contact between the main glacier and a tributary.*

rise to *ice sheets,* such as those found today in Greenland and Antarctica. Glacier ice today covers about 10 percent of the land and contains nearly 2 percent of the earth's water. During periods of maximum glaciation in the past, glacier ice covered nearly three times the land area covered today, and a far greater proportion of the earth's water was locked up in the form of ice. Sea level may have been more than 328 feet (100 meters) below its present level.

**Glacial Erosion.** Glaciers often originate at high elevations in cold, mountainous regions. Snow and firn accumulate in natural depressions in the rocky slopes. During the summer, repeated thawing and freezing wedge loose fragments of rock, enlarging the depression and steepening its walls. Gradually the depression takes on a semicircular shape (like a bowl), open on the downslope side. Such basins are called cirques. As ice forms and flows out of a cirque into a mountain valley, the base of the moving glacier scrapes, drags, and quarries rock fragments from the walls and bedrock floor of the valley. The valley is deepened and widened, gradually being transformed from a preglacial V-shaped profile into a glacial U-shaped form. Debris incorporated in the base of the glacier polishes, striates, and grooves the underlying bedrock. The rock floor may also be modified into a series of small, streamlined hillocks with rounded backs or crests called *whalebacks.* The long axis of each whaleback tends to be oriented more or less parallel to the direction of ice flow. Piedmont glaciers and ice sheets, which have expanded beyond the mountains into areas of low relief, strip away softer sediments and abrade the underlying bedrock. Preglacial river valleys may be enlarged and deepened, much like glaciated mountain valleys. In some areas, softer sediments may be molded by the ice into a series of streamlined hills, similar to whalebacks but often larger, called *drumlins.* Maps of the orientation of striations, grooves, whalebacks, and drumlins can be used to determine the direction of flow of glaciers in the past.

**Glacial Deposition.** The rock debris transported and deposited by glacier ice or by glacial meltwater is called *drift.* Drift which shows little or no evidence of stratification is called *till.* Rock fragments in drift which are foreign to the area where they are found (erratics) are useful indicators of the direction of ice flow. Drift carried along

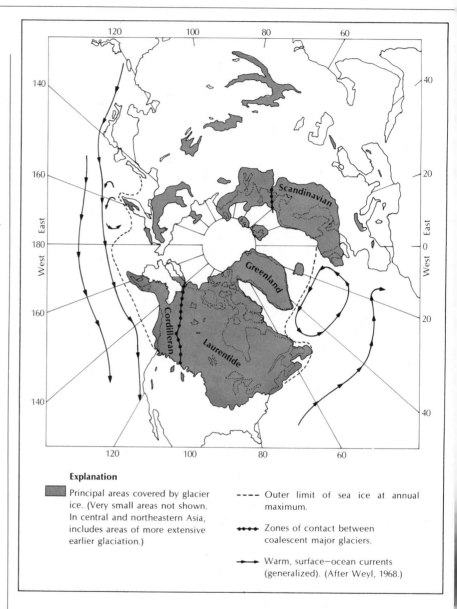

**Explanation**

▨ Principal areas covered by glacier ice. (Very small areas not shown. In central and northeastern Asia, includes areas of more extensive earlier glaciation.)

- - - - Outer limit of sea ice at annual maximum.

◆◆◆◆ Zones of contact between coalescent major glaciers.

→ Warm, surface-ocean currents (generalized). (After Weyl, 1968.)

*Part of northern hemisphere during a glacial age, showing large glaciers, sea ice, and storm tracks (adapted from Flint).*

the margins of a valley glacier forms ridgelike deposits known as *lateral moraines.* Debris incorporated within the ice is carried by flow toward the downstream end or *terminus* of the glacier, where it is reexposed by melting of the ice front. If the front advances or retreats rapidly, the debris is spread uniformly over a wide area as *ground moraine.* When the front is stationary for a long period of time, drift tends to accumulate in a thicker, more ridgelike *terminal moraine.* Terminal moraines which have not been destroyed by more recent advances of the ice provide important evidence of the extent of former glaciations.

**Periglacial Processes.** Glacial meltwater, especially in summer, transports large quantities of debris (glacial outwash) away from the ice front. Silt is picked up by the wind from exposed outwash and till and is carried far beyond the ice front, where it is redeposited as *loess*. Sheets of loess many meters in thickness blanket large areas of central North America and eastern Europe. For a considerable distance beyond the front of an ice sheet, the ground may be perenially frozen (permafrost). Today in the northern latitudes nearly 4 percent of the land surface is permanently frozen. During the summer, only the uppermost layer of sediment thaws. Rock fragments incorporated in this upper layer are gradually broken apart by intense frost action (frost wedging). Saturated with meltwater, this layer gradually flows downslope (solifluction). The intense cold in permafrost areas may cause the sediments below the thaw zone to contract, producing vertical cracks which gradually fill with ice (ice wedges). When climatic conditions eventually improve in the region, the wedges melt and the cracks become filled with sediments (ice wedge casts). In stratified deposits, the casts may be clearly visible. After a thaw, a sudden drop in temperature below freezing converts moisture into ice crystals. The crystals expand, pushing the soil and rock fragments upward (frost heaving). Frost heaving can distort and mix strata, producing *involutions* in the sediments which resemble a series of small, compact folds. Frost heaving may also produce stripes, circles, polygons, and other geometric patterns of rubble on the surface (patterned ground). The distribution of ice wedge casts, involuted sediments, and patterned ground can be mapped to determine the extent of permafrost during a former period of glaciation.

**History of Glaciation.** The earth has experienced at least three major periods of glaciation. The first period occurred late in Precambrian times (ca. 600 million years ago). A second Ice Age took place during the Permian period (ca. 225 million to 270 million years ago). The last Ice Age, and the one with which we are concerned here, began with marked climatic deterioration during the Cenozoic era (Miocene epoch) more than 10 million years ago and culminated with several advances and retreats of massive, continental ice sheets during the Quaternary period. The date for the lower boundary of the Quaternary is subject to considerable debate. Some geologists place the boundary about 3 million years

ago; others place it as recent as 1.7 million years ago. The Quaternary is divided into two epochs: the Pleistocene (from the beginning of the Quaternary to 10,000 years ago) and the Holocene, Recent, or Postglacial (10,000 years ago to the present).

Detailed studies of Quaternary glaciation began in Europe in the first half of the 19th century. Careful examination of drift deposits, erratics, and other features in the Alps and in northern Europe led a German (Bernhardi) and several Swiss (Venetz, de Charpentier, Agassiz) to postulate the existence of former widespread glaciation. By the 1870s, several workers had reported occurrences of two or more superimposed layers of drift, separated by deposits indicative of warmer climatic conditions. It thus became clear that glaciers had advanced and retreated more than once. By the turn of the century, the extent of the former ice sheets had been mapped in considerable detail in both Europe and North America. Studies by Penck and Brückner (1909) in the Alpine region revealed four major glacial advances. From earliest to most recent, these are the Günz (from approximately 1.4 million to 700,000 years BP), Mindel (from approximately 640,000 to 300,000 years BP), Riss (from approximately 265,000 to 125,000 years BP), and Würm (from approximately 110,000 to 10,000 years BP). These major glacial advances were separated by three warmer periods (interglacials) during which the glaciers retreated (often abbreviated G/M, M/R, R/W). Subsequent research indicates that there may have been at least two additional earlier glacial periods—Biber and Donau—although their nature, extent, and correlation to comparable events in other parts of the world remain highly controversial.

Drift deposits in northern Europe provided a sequence (Eburon-Menap, Elster, Saale-Warthe, Weichsel) similar to that in the Alpine region, with three intervening interglacials (Cromer, Holstein, Eem). Four major glacial advances were also recognized in North America (Nebraskan, Kansan, Illinoian, Wisconsin), again separated by three interglacials (Aftonian, Yarmouth, Sangamon). With the exception of the last glacial, the correlation between the European and North American glaciations is subject to considerable debate.

During each glacial maximum, ice covered much of northern North America and northern Eurasia. In North America, two

major ice sheets developed, the Laurentide and the Cordilleran. The Laurentide ice sheet originated in the Labrador-Ungava region. As the ice sheet expanded, it coalesced to the north with extensive glaciers on Ellesmere and Baffin islands. The Ellesmere-Baffin complex in turn may have coalesced to the east with the Greenland ice sheet. The Laurentide ice sheet spread southward over New England and the Great Lakes area and westward almost to the eastern flanks of the Rocky Mountains in western Canada. The Cordilleran ice sheet developed in the Coast Ranges and Rocky Mountains in British Columbia. At its maximum, the Cordilleran ice sheet extended from the Aleutian Islands southward almost to the Columbia River in Washington. In Eurasia, a major ice sheet developed in the mountainous regions of Scandinavia. The Scandinavian ice sheet expanded across the Baltic Sea, spreading southward into Germany and eastward toward the Urals. Smaller ice sheets also developed on the British Isles, the Alps, the Pyrenees, the Urals, and the Caucasus.

Although the fourfold glacial sequence (Günz, Mindel, Riss, Würm) is today firmly embedded in the geological and archaeological literature, ongoing studies of terrestrial and deep-sea sediments are revealing a far more detailed and complex record of climatic change in the Quaternary. These studies have been aided immeasurably by modern techniques of radiometric dating (e.g., radiocarbon and potassium-argon), paleomagnetic dating (reversals of the earth's magnetic field), and paleotemperature analysis of deep-sea sediments (fluctuations in the ratio of oxygen 18/oxygen 16 in marine carbonates). The last major reversal of the magnetic field occurred about 700,000 years ago. The period preceding the reversal is known as the *Matuyama Reversed Epoch*. The period from 700,000 years ago to the present is known as the *Brunhes Normal Epoch*. In deep-sea sediments, paleotemperature analyses have revealed at least eight full glacial cycles above the Brunhes/Matuyama boundary. Eight glacial cycles postdating the last reversal have also been identified in thick loess sediments in Czechoslovakia. Recent studies in northern Europe have placed the beginning of the Brunhes within the interglacial between the Günz and Mindel glaciations. These investigations make it clear that the traditional fourfold glacial sequence is inadequate.

Detailed studies of deep-sea sediments reveal that each glacial period lasts about 90,000 years, followed by an interglacial which lasts only about 10,000 years. A typical glacial cycle appears to follow a somewhat sawtooth pattern. Early in the cycle, climatic conditions are relatively warm and wet. Then temperatures begin to decline. Sea level drops as water becomes locked up in growing snowfields and glaciers. The climate becomes progressively colder and drier. Over tens of thousands of years, the ice sheets build up in the northern latitudes, advancing and retreating (stadials and interstadials) in a series of waves of increasing magnitude and extent. But it is not until comparatively late in the glacial cycle that massive, continental ice sheets advance into the midlatitudes. Then temperatures begin to rise rapidly, marking the onset of an interglacial. Within a few thousand years, temperatures reach a maximum (hypsithermal); then they begin to decline gradually as the next glacial approaches. Many geologists consider the Holocene to be an interglacial. The hypsithermal of the Holocene was passed nearly 6,000 to 7,000 years ago. Systematic comparisons of the climatic record of the last 10,000 years with that of earlier interglacials have led many geologists to conclude that the onset of the next glacial period may be expected within the next few millennia.

See also Dating, absolute; Dating, relative; Physical-chemical methods of dating; Pleistocene
Consult: Butzer, Karl W., *Environment and Archeology*, 2nd ed. (Chicago: Aldine-Atherton, 1971); Cornwall, Ian, *Ice Ages: Their Nature and Effects* (London: John Baker Ltd., 1970); Flint, Richard Foster, *Glacial and Quaternary Geology* (New York: Wiley, 1971).
—*John D. Speth, Hunter College*

**Glass.** The possibilities of glass as a material for containers and artifacts (about 4000 BC in Egypt and Mesopotamia) must have occurred to people after molten silica left pieces of glasslike substances under certain fire sites, possibly those of pottery firings or metal smelting. The presence of glass, rather than unaffected sand and soil, must have led to the eventual discovery that only certain chemical compounds will produce glass under the fusion of heat. These compounds are abundant in nature: silica (sand) or silicon dioxide; soda or sodium dioxide; and lime or calcium oxide.

The first small containers of glass were formed by dipping a hard clay model of the desired form into molten glass, twirling it to keep the thickness even as it cooled and hardened. The modeled clay form was then laboriously dug out of the container's mouth to leave it hollow and translucent. Beads were made by melting glass onto drilled stones, and a faience technique was developed in Egypt—a paste of ground quartz was applied to a finished glass or stone form in designs and a vitreous paste was put over that; then the whole was melted so that it took on a glasslike sheen.

The Phoenicians borrowed glass techniques from the Egyptians and Mesopotamians. But they also invented a form of glassblowing with a long metal tube so that a molten glass blob could be picked up by the end of the hollow tube and blown into a two-piece mold, which was removed and reused when the form cooled. They had seen the possibilities of the new material as a commodity for trade to peoples in the western Mediterranean, and their glass techniques made possible rapid, multiple reproductions of a single design.
—*Justine M. Cordwell, Chicago City Colleges/ Malcolm X*

**Gleason, Henry Allen, Jr.** (b. 1917). Linguist of the American structuralist school who is best known for his textbooks on descriptive linguistics and English grammar.

**Glosseme.** A glosseme is the smallest meaningful unit of linguistic signaling. On the lexical level it is represented by a morpheme, on the grammatical level by a tagmeme.

See also Morpheme; Tagmeme
Consult: Bloomfield, Leonard, *Language* (New York: Holt, 1933).

**Glottochronology.** Also known as lexicostatistics, glottochronology is mathematical method for dating language change. It assumes that a culture-free vocabulary (body parts, kin terms, natural phenomena) does not change as rapidly as other vocabulary items. The rate of change has been determined at 80–81 percent every thousand years. By analogy with carbon-14 dating, this percentage will be retained from the basic 100–200-word core vocabulary. In the second thousand years, 81 percent of the original 81 percent will be retained. By comparing two word lists in languages thought to be related, their date of separation from the parent or protolanguage can be determined with the formula $t = \log C/2 \log$, where $t$ = time in years, $r$ = rate of retention, and $C$ = percentage of cognates (words similar in sound and meaning) between the two word lists.

The method is considered problematic by many linguists because a culture-free vocabulary does not really exist and because the rate of change in language is not constant. As a result, the method gives questionable dates. At present, there is no satisfactory method for absolute dating of language.

See also Historical linguistics; Lexicostatistics
Consult: Gudschinsky, Sarah, "The ABC's of Lexicostatistics (Glottochronology)," in *Language in Culture and Society*, ed. Dell Hymes (New York: Harper & Row, 1964).

**Gluckman, Max** (1911–1975). A British social anthropologist who contributed to studies of rebellion and legal systems, Gluckman argued that Roman legal categories and concepts can be utilized in the study of all legal systems—a position hotly contested by the relativistic wings of the profession.

**Goffman, Erving** (b. 1922). Student of interaction who has stressed the importance of understanding the use of symbols in the rituals of everyday life, as well as identifying the rules which govern people's interactions in social systems.

**Goldenweiser, Alexander Alexandrovich** (1880–1940). American anthropologist who was the first to introduce and elaborate the principle of limited possibilities.

See also Limited possibilities, principles of

**Goodall, Jane** (b. 1934). Presently scientific director of the Gombé Stream Research Center, Tanzania, and head of a research project on animal behavior at Stanford University, Goodall is only the eighth person in the history of Cambridge University to have earned a Ph.D. without a previous B.A. Beginning as a protégée of Louis and Mary Leakey, she has devoted herself to intensive, long-term observations of chimpanzees, baboons, canids (wild dogs), and other wild species in EC Africa. By following the daily activities of animal societies, Goodall has made significant contributions to the knowledge of individual variations in animal behavior. Her work has been instrumental in the modification of notions of instinct and infrahuman learning. Observations that chimpanzees are not totally vegetarians and that they devise tools for the provision of food and water has led to a reconsideration of primate, pongid, and prehominid intellectual capacities. Her major publications include *My Friends, the Wild Chimpanzees* (1967), *Innocent Killers* (with Hugo van Lawick, 1970), and *In the Shadow of Man* (1971).

> *See also* Chimpanzees, social organization and behavior of; Ethology; Leakey, Louis S. B.
> —*MaryAnn Foley, Southern Connecticut State College*

**Goode, William J.** (b. 1917). Sociologist whose research on social organization and social structure includes work on systems of social control, the family, religion, and work.

**Goodenough, Ward Hunt** (b. 1919). Cultural anthropologist famous for his role in the development of the componential analysis of kinship systems and his ethnographic research in Truk.

**Goodman, Mary Ellen Hoheisal** (1911–1969). Goodman, a psychological anthropologist, was a professor at Rice University at the time of her death. Her transcultural studies on childhood values, attitudes, aspirations, and awareness helped to illuminate and modify deterministic developmental theories and cultural stereotypes about children's intellectual capabilities. Her seminal work, *The Culture of Childhood* (1970), was published posthumously.

> *See also* Culture and personality; Enculturation

**Gorer, Geoffrey** (b. 1905). British anthropologist best known for his interests in na-

tional character studies and in developing techniques for the study of culture at a distance.

**Gorilla, Behavior of.** *See* Ethology; Primates, behavior of.

**Gossip.** Gossip is talk, often critical or malicious, about other people's affairs. Anthropologists regard gossip as a means of maintaining social control and preserving group boundaries or as a weapon in factional disputes.

> *See also* Sanctions; Social control

**Gough, Kathleen** (b. 1925). A cultural anthropologist known for her research on matrilineal descent and on the Nayar of India, Gough has questioned the universality of the family. She has also been active as a radical critic of the political ideology and consequences of established anthropological practice.

**Government.** This term may be defined as a series of interrelated statuses whose associated roles are primarily concerned with creating and administering the public policy of a social group usually defined on a territorial basis. Governments function through the exercise of public power—power applicable to the entire social group. A government consists of public officials with varying amounts of public power. Often public power is allocated according to a set of rules which stipulate the proper means of attaining public office and the rights and duties associated with various political statuses. These rules, if widely accepted, provide a basis for legitimacy, that is, governmental support derived from shared values and expectations. The other major source of governmental support is coercion, particularly force. Traditionally anthropologists have emphasized this aspect of governmental dynamics to the exclusion of other factors. Thus A. R. Radcliffe-Brown conceptualized political organization in terms of the maintenance of social order by the exercise of coercive authority backed by physical force. Contemporary political anthropologists have corrected this overemphasis by noting that force is often an inefficient and costly instrument of governance. Moreover they

point out that coercion has its limits—government and force itself depend on at least some interpersonal relations not based on coercion.

> *See also* Legal systems; Power; State, the Consult: Easton, D., "Political Anthropology," in *Biennial Review of Anthropology*, ed. B. Siegel (Palo Alto, Calif.: Stanford University Press, 1959); Fortes, M., and Evans-Pritchard, E. E. (eds.), *African Political Systems* (New York: Oxford University Press, 1940); Swartz, M., Turner, V., and Tuden, A. (eds.), *Political Anthropology* (Chicago: Aldine, 1966).
> —*Stan Wilk, Lycoming College*

**Graebner, Fritz** (1877–1934). German ethnologist (culture historian) who developed the theory of *Kulturkreise*—culture circles, or cluster of diffusing cultural traits—to explain cultural similarities and differences.

**Grammar.** In traditional Bloomfieldian usage, grammar refers to "the meaningful arrangements of forms in a language" (Bloomfield 1933:163). It thus includes syntactic arrangements (arrangements of free forms) and morphemic arrangements (arrangements of bound forms). To restate this notion in slightly more modern terms, there are two elements constituting a grammar of a language: its morphemes and the permissible arrangements in which these morphemes may occur in actual speech.

The approach taken in these definitions is inherently a static one—i.e., it regards grammar as consisting of *items* and their *arrangements*. The modern trend, arising with the school of transformational linguistics, is to conceptualize grammar much more dynamically by discussing it in terms of items and the *processes* by which they are arranged.

> *See also* Generative grammar; Immediate Constituents; Phrase structure; Surface Structure of language; Syntax; Transformational grammar; Transformational linguistics
> Consult: Bloomfield, Leonard, *Language* (New York: Holt, 1933); Hockett, Charles F., *A Course in Modern Linguistics* (New York: Macmillan, 1958).
> —*Phillip Whitten, Harvard University*

**Gravettian Culture.** This tradition of the European Upper Paleolithic flourished about

25,000 years ago. It is associated with Cro-Magnon people and is characterized by special points, figurines (so-called Venus figures), and other forms of art.

See also Cro-Magnon fossil remains; Paleolithic; Upper Paleolithic art

**Great Apes.** See Apes.

**Great Tradition.** This term refers to the formal, literate tradition of a civilization, which is maintained by the elite of the society and is most important in urban areas. The Great Tradition contrasts with the culture of the rural people of the same civilization (the Little Tradition). These concepts were popularized by Robert Redfield in *Peasant Society and Culture* (1956). Most of the discussion of Great Tradition has focused on the civilizations of the Near East and Asia, especially India, but Redfield also applied the concept to the Maya, whose conquest by the Spanish he viewed as the removal of a Great Tradition.

See also Civilization; Little Tradition

**Greenberg, Joseph Harold** (b. 1915). Leading figure in anthropological linguistics who is best known for his work on linguistic theory and language classification, especially the languages of Africa.

**Grimm, Jakob Ludwig** (1785–1863). German linguist known for his collection of Germanic fairy tales and for *Grimm's law*, which showed systematic phonetic changes in Indo-European language development.

**Grinnell, George Bird** (1849–1938). Both a naturalist and an ethnographer, Grinnell was an observer and chronicler of Plains Indian life. He is best known for his detailed descriptive study of Cheyenne culture, *The Cheyenne Indians* (1923).

Consult: Grinnell, George B., *The Cheyenne Indians* (New York: Cooper Square Publishers, 1962).

**Grooming.** Mutual grooming is a common primate trait and is found in a very wide range of primate social interactions, ranging from dominance to affection. The behavior

*Female baboon grooms adult male.*

is clearly much more than an attempt to remove parasites; it is a gesture of amicability that serves to relieve tension at moments of threatened aggression or to enhance solidarity and cohesion at other times. Grooming is especially prevalent in primate societies in which there are significant dominant roles, such as baboons or chimpanzees; the behavior is much less frequent and thorough among gorillas. Some theorists have attempted to analyze certain human "grooming"—such as the reciprocal touching behavior of a mother and her infant—as an expression of the general primate tendency to use grooming for the establishment of close bonds.

See also Primates, behavior of; Toilet

**Group Marriage.** This term refers to a marriage rule which allows a number of men and women to share sexual rights and economic responsibilities. Malinowski (1930), Murdock (1949), and Bohannan (1963) all agree

that this variety of polygamy probably never existed in any human society as the most common and preferred type of marriage. One study reveals that 8 percent of marriages among the Kaingang Indians of Brazil are of this type. Good cross-cultural data are lacking.

See also Polygamy

Consult: Bohannan, Paul, *Social Anthropology* (New York: Holt, 1963); Malinowski, Bronislaw, "Kinship," *Man* 30:2, 1930; Murdock, George Peter, *Social Structure* (New York: Macmillan, 1949).

**Growth.** See Development, economic.

**Günz Glaciation.** See Glaciations.

**Gypsies.** A nomadic people in many lands, Gypsies carry a specific language of Hindu origin called Romany. The name comes from the English word *Egyptians*.

See also Marginal peoples

Consult: Kenrick, Donald, *The Destiny of Europe's Gypsies* (New York: Basic Books, 1972); Yoors, Jan, *The Gypsies* (New York: Simon and Schuster, 1967).

**Haas, Mary Rosamond** (b. 1910). A leading specialist on North American Indian languages, especially those of California and SE United States, Haas is also interested in the prehistory of languages.

**Hacienda.** A privately owned, landed estate of colonial and early republican highland Latin America. The hacienda was organized for both subsistence and the production of cash crops.

**Hair.** See Hair, functions and shapes of.

**Hair, Functions and Shapes of.** There is no society in which the care and styling of hair to convey cultural messages is not found. Styles may differ from one society to another and meanings may vary, but hair is always a component of cultural communication. A change in hairstyles, for example, is often an indication of a change in social status. The public nature of hair is a prime reason for its being so universally used as a symbol for communication.

The most penetrating analysis of hair was written by Edmund Leach. In his study, Leach (1958) surveys a number of hair shapes used to convey meaning: the Trobrianders' shaving of hair for mourning, the Cavaliers' long hair and the Roundheads' short hair. Tonsure, the ritual cutting of a pregnant woman's hair by her husband in South India, is considered along with various other hair shaping practices.

Leach concludes that the public nature of social rituals must be distinguished from their private meanings. Thus they must be seen as social statements, not as private ones. Persons displaying grief, for example, may or may not feel it. For Leach, hair is a public phallic symbol and is used to make a public statement. There is nothing unconscious about its symbolism at all—quite the contrary, in fact. That which is separated, the hair, is sacred and has power in itself. The phallicism in the ritual is conscious and seeks to prevent, not cause, the development of emotional repression.

See also Function; Leach, Edmund; Ritual
Consult: Leach, Edmund, "Magical Hair," *Journal of the Royal Anthropological Institute* 88: 147–164, 1958.
—Frank A. Salamone, St. John's University

**Hall, Edward T.** (b. 1914). A cultural anthropologist interested in intercultural communication, Hall has focused attention on cultural differences in the use of space, the study of which is called proxemics.

See also Proxemics

**Hallowell, Alfred Irving** (b. 1892). A leading cultural anthropologist who has specialized in studying culture and personality, Hallowell introduced Rorschach testing into anthropological research with his fieldwork among the Ojibwa.

**Hallucinations and Shamanism.** The relationship between so-called hallucinations and shamanism is an intimate one. Mircea Eliade has demonstrated that the selection of the shaman, the initiatory experience, the subsequent acquisition and employment of shamanic powers, and the stabilization and use of the temporary "election" experience all involve what can be described as hallucinatory experiences. Eliade maintains that the extreme importance of such experiences in shamanic initiation derives from the fact that they are taken as a sure sign that one has attained a spiritual condition. Although hallucinations are popularly associated with the sense of vision, hallucinations of taste as well as olfactory, tactile, and kinesthetic hallucinations are reported to varying degrees in the literature. Indeed synesthesia, whereby one mode of sensory experience is translated into another, such as seeing sounds, is also reported.

**Derivation and Nature.** Hallucinatory experiences can be spontaneous, as in the case of the Sioux shaman Black Elk, or consciously sought by fasting, torture, sensory deprivation, or frequently by ingesting psychoactive plant substances called hallucinogens. Hallucinatory experiences are not confined to shamanic institutions but are pursued in many primitive cultures as a vital aspect of self-development—as, for example, in the vision quests of the Plains Indians of North America or the Jivaro of the Amazon rain forest. The hallucinatory experiences reported by shamans show interesting similarities. Such elements as a journey (often involving flight), ascent to the sky and encountering spirits (or descent to an underworld), dismemberment, and renewal or resurrection of the body are recurring themes in the shamanic literature. Moreover specific regional

uniformities in shamanic hallucinatory experiences have also been reported—such as visions of snakes and jaguars among certain geographically proximate Indian cultures in South America. Ethnographic and experimental studies leave little doubt that such experiences are heavily influenced in form, content, and impact by the cultural background of the individual undergoing the experience. Some investigators maintain that these cross-cultural uniformities of theme and image may be produced by the biochemical effects of the hallucinogen on the human body. Claudio Naranjo, for example, claims that certain shamanic conceptions are to be understood as the expression of universal experiences rather than as a result of enculturation to local cultural traditions. Other scholars view similarities in shamanic hallucinatory experiences as evidence of the antiquity of shamanism and the derivation of existent shamanic complexes from a somewhat homogeneous Mesolithic or even Paleolithic baseline.

**Cultural Realities.** How one evaluates hallucinatory experience will significantly affect one's appreciation of shamanism: it may determine, for instance, whether one views shamans as mentally ill individuals with personally fortunate cultural adjustments or as spiritual masters possessed of great wisdom and capabilities. Are hallucinations perceptions of objects with no reality? Or are they manifestations to the senses of things immaterial in our ordinary wakeful consciousness? Such questions revolve around cultural definitions of reality, and many primitive peoples exist in realities that are culturally influenced in ways quite different from our own. Michael Harner says of the Jivaro that they consider normal waking life as an illusion, that reality is to be experienced only with the aid of hallucinogens. Black Elk had a similar conception of ordinary wakeful consciousness, as do many primitive cultures and many of the Asian religions. Don Juan, a Yaqui shaman, speaks convincingly of reality as a description, the world as a feeling. William James characterized religion as the belief in an unseen order and the conviction that our fundamental well-being rests on adjusting to it. Shamanism directly seeks to confront this other reality or realities, and it is not surprising that Weston LaBarre and others trace all religions back to the inspired revelations of shamans.

Unquestionably hallucinations have an experiential reality of a quite convincing nature. Moreover there appear to be transcultural techniques for dealing with these experiences taught to the apprentice by his or her shamanic guide, such as not reacting with fear. It is the relationship of these personally experienced happenings, i.e., hallucinations, to "external" or "objective" reality that is at the heart of the problem. In this regard Carl Jung's concept of synchronicity, the Zen concept of correspondences, and the functioning of shamans themselves may be helpful. Shamans frequently recognize a clear distinction between their hallucinatory experiences and those of ordinary wakeful consciousness. As Emile Durkheim maintained, the division of the world into two domains, the sacred and the profane, is the distinctive trait of religions—and the shaman, in Eliade's apt phrase, is the "technician of the sacred."

See also Possession; Religion; Shamanism; Spiritualism

Consult: Castaneda, C., Journey to Ixtlan (New York: Simon and Schuster, 1972); Eliade, M., Shamanism: Archaic Techniques of Ecstasy (Princeton, N.J.: Princeton University Press, 1964); Handleman, D., "The Development of a Washo Shaman," Ethnology 6:444–461, 1967; Harner, M. J. (ed.), Hallucinogens and Shamanism (New York: Oxford University Press, 1973).
—Stan Wilk, Lycoming College

## Hallucinogens. See Drugs.

## Hand Ax.
This artifact is an unspecialized flint tool primarily characteristic of the Lower and Middle Paleolithic. Earlier, Abbevillian hand axes were rough biface core tools; later, Acheulean ones were smaller and more carefully made.

See also Acheulean culture; Chellean culture; Paleolithic

## Handsome Lake Religion.
Following the American conquest of the Northwest Territory, the league of the Iroquois tribe foundered and the six formerly confederated tribes split. Thereafter the Seneca tribe fell into a sharp decline, ending in extreme political-social disintegration and cultural demoralization. Out of the shambles of Seneca social life emerged a visionary, Handsome Lake, whose first apocalyptic vision started in 1799. Beginning in 1801,

and until his death in 1815, this Seneca prophet created and preached a new gospel which promised a revitalized, more satisfying life for the Seneca. As they became widely accepted, Handsome Lake's teachings focused on the themes of sobriety, peacefulness, retention of landholdings, accommodation to American culture, and strict morality in domestic life—themes that became the evangelical core of a renaissance of Seneca culture.

A. F. C. Wallace's early studies of Handsome Lake and his impact on Seneca life led him to develop a systematic, general theory of cultural revitalization movements. Thus the Handsome Lake religion—itself a major development in the lives of a culturally demoralized tribe—was the spur to the creation of one of the firmest and most sophisticated bodies of theory in the study of cultural change. The Handsome Lake religion persists in the present day as a highly influential Seneca church organization.

See also Acculturation; Ghost Dance religion; Revitalization movements

Consult: Wallace, A. F. C., The Death and Rebirth of the Seneca (New York: Knopf, 1970).
—James Clifton, University of Wisconsin, Green Bay

## Hardy-Weinberg Principle.
Developed independently in 1908 by G. H. Hardy, an English mathematician, and G. Weinberg, a German physician, to disprove the common assumption that a dominant gene would automatically spread in a population to displace a recessive one, the Hardy-Weinberg law forms the basis of population genetics. The principle states that in large breeding populations under conditions of random mating, and where natural selection is not operating, the frequencies of genes and alleles will remain constant from one generation to the next. In addition, the Hardy-Weinberg law allows for the calculation of gene frequencies from the relative proportions of genotypes and sometimes of phenotypes, and vice versa. Genotype frequencies also remain constant over time.

If the Hardy-Weinberg conditions are upset and then reestablished, after only one generation of random mating the distribution of genes among the various individuals in the population will again fit Hardy-Weinberg expectations. Although the assumption of no natural selection is unrealistic for most traits, the Hardy-Weinberg equilibrium pro-

vides a useful base point from which deviations due to evolutionary forces can be measured, their directionality determined, and the forces involved isolated.

More realistic equilibrium models in population genetics include the classic selection model and the balanced polymorphism model.

See also Balanced polymorphism; Population genetics
—Catherine E. Read-Martin, California State University, Los Angeles

## Harlow, Harry
(b. 1905). Psychologist at the University of Wisconsin Primate Center whose experiments with monkeys have demonstrated the extreme importance of social interaction and learning in primate behavior.

## Harpoon.
The barbed, detachable head was first developed by Paleolithic people to retain a projectile point in an animal's flesh.

*Drawing of an Eskimo toggle-headed harpoon (adapted from Coon).*

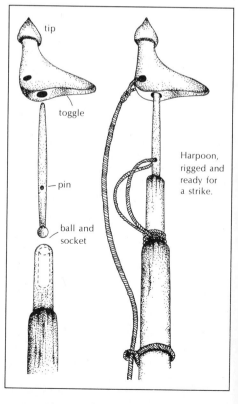

tip

toggle

pin

ball and socket

Harpoon, rigged and ready for a strike.

Harpoon arrows, blowgun darts, and jave-lins with detachable heads are designed for use with poison. In aquatic hunting, where the recovery of an animal poses special problems, the head of the harpoon proper is attached to a line which may be paid out by the harpooner or connected to a float.

*See also* Fishing; Hunting; Spear; Weapons

## Harris, Marvin (b. 1927).
Major cultural theorist noted for his writings on etic eth-nography, cultural ecology, economic an-thropology, the history of anthropological theory, and race relations in Brazil.

## Harris, Zellig Sabbettai (b. 1909).
Lin-guist noted for his *Structural Linguistics* (1960), which attempts to outline a pro-cedure of analysis based on formal struc-tural distinctions rather than on meaning.

## Hart, C. W. M. (b. 1905).
Australian-born social anthropologist best known for his re-search among the Tiwi of N Australia in the 1920s and for his work in applied anthro-pology.

## Hawaiian Form of Social Stratification.
The Hawaiian form of social stratification is characterized by two interesting features: redistribution along royal loyalty lines, and class endogamy for nobility. The supreme chief (*moi*) had title to all the land in his do-main. Upon taking power he would redis-tribute the land of his rivals among his own followers, providing through this spoils sys-tem a means of social mobility. Beneath the *moi* were the chiefs (*arii*), the landed gentry (*raatira*), the landless (*manahune*), and an outcaste group (*kauwa*). Birth order further subdivided the strata. The higher classes practiced class endogamy, giving a castelike characteristic to the highest strata. This ar-rangement was designed to preserve and multiply the mana believed to reside in the royal line. In fact, the *moi* often married his own sisters to add to his mana and hence father heirs even more powerful than him-self. There was some provision for social mobility, however, through personal ability and one's backing the winning party in a power struggle.

*See also* Endogamy; Mana; Mobility, social; Social stratification

Consult: Goldman, Irving, "Status Rivalry and Cultural Evolution in Polynesia," in *Compara-tive Political Systems*, ed. R. Cohen and J. Mid-dleton (New York: Doubleday, 1967).

## Headdress. *See* Masks.

## Headman.
The headman, a local leader of a peasant or tribal community, is distin-guished from a chief by the smaller size of the headman's domain and the more limited authority he exercises within it. The power of headmen within a chiefdom or state de-pends in large part on the strength of the political hierarchy and how much authority it delegates to them. In uncentralized tribal societies, on the other hand, the indepen-dent headmen derive what little power they typically have from within their own com-munities.

*See also* Chiefdom; Leadership

## Health, Cross-cultural Concepts of.
Although the literature of anthropology contains much information about theories of illness, disease, and death and the pro-cesses of curing and healing, the positive or normal state of being, health, is mentioned only infrequently. *Mens sana in corpore sano*—a healthy mind in a healthy body—is a dictum that has been around for millennia in Western culture, but just exactly what *is* a healthy mind or a healthy body? The Latin phrase implies that it is impossible to have one without the other. Both are necessary, and modern medical teachings seem to sup-port that point of view.

Understandings and expectations con-cerning health vary widely by culture. That a person seventy or eighty years of age or all eight of a mother's children are alive at all is worthy of remark in some societies, but not in others, irrespective of the state of health in which they might exist. In other words, standards of health are a function of technological progress and scientific ad-vancement. In the Third World political, military, and religious leaders are often in their thirties and forties; in Europe, Russia, China, and America they tend to be in their fifties, sixties, or even seventies. Population control by means of contraception or sterili-zation tends to be more successful in coun-tries where parents can be reasonably cer-tain that all the children they produce will

*Awiitigaaj, Kapauku Papuan village headman, making a political speech.*

survive to adulthood. It may take several generations to establish the demonstrable effects of better medical help in the value and behavior systems of a culture, only to have the progress in this area undermined by periodic famines or wars.

In any case, the study of what one must and must not do to maintain bodily health is a fascinating one. Does the belief system define that one's state of health is control-lable? Do spirits or other humans do the controlling, or is it up to oneself, or perhaps a combination of all of these? If malevolent spirits cause illness or disease, the healthy person is one who has not been bothered by, managed not to antagonize, or managed to steer clear of such spirits. Therefore this person is a "good" person—defined as care-ful, clever, dutiful, self-effacing, or what-ever the qualities culture defines as neces-sary to control the behavior of malevolents. If health is considered a matter of luck, one's personal qualities may matter very little in *avoiding* illness, and cultural attention may be concentrated on healing and curing.

It is widely accepted throughout Mela-nesia that all deaths are the result of sorcery —i.e., there are no deaths due to what West-ern physicians would call natural causes.

The healthy (or good) people, therefore, are first of all alive, for the dead are dangerous. In addition, they have aroused no one's enmity to the point at which a sorcerer would be hired to harm them, so they would be assumed to be skilled in interpersonal relations, or dutiful to their responsibilities and commitments. This is, indeed, a formidable method of social control.

Some practitioners of Western medicine, on the other hand, now reject old age as a cause for death, thereby removing the last, solacing attempt to resignation in the face of the inevitable. They believe senility is not a disease of old age but a condition resulting from a combination of hereditary factors and physiological and psychological deprivations. This view supports Cora DuBois' discussion (1955) of basic premises of the American middle class—one of which asserts that humans are in control of a mechanistic universe. It would also seem conjunctive with the avoidance of death and the refusal to accept human mortality that many authors regard as American characteristics. So in one society aging is rejected and youthfulness is revered, while in another age is revered and death is welcomed as an old friend.

Slim, even thin, people are thought attractive in segments of Western culture, but in much of Asia, Polynesia, and Renaissance Europe, plumpness to the point of obesity by American medical standards was (and in some cases, still is) a sign of wealth and health. "A fat baby is a healthy baby" is still a widely held belief, but recent medical findings indicate that making a baby fat merely results in poor dietary habits and a tendency toward obesity in adulthood.

One concludes, therefore, that health is a value, just as are beauty and truth. As a value, it is learned. And so it should come as no surprise that ideas about health are as variable as any other cultural concept.

See also Health: culture and environment; Medicine; Mental health; Mental illness and culture
Consult: Dubois, Cora, "The Dominant Value Profile of American Culture," American Anthropologist 57:1233, 1955.
—MaryAnn Foley, Southern Connecticut State College

**Health: Culture and Environment.** Health is a positive state of being in which all functions of the body are performing normally enough that a person is able to do everything necessary for making a living and staying alive. Threats to health vary by culture and by environment. Arctic peoples are especially vulnerable to respiratory diseases, and by their fourth decade of life they tend to be plagued by arthritis and failing eyesight. Accidents and infected wounds, famine, and infectious diseases of the skin and gut are health problems in the tropics. Cardiovascular diseases and cancer are the major causes of death in developed countries, irrespective of geographic location.

To their surprise, health workers have found that as countries become industrialized and assume more and more of the Western life-style, instead of reaping the combined benefits of Western medicine and low incidence of "Western diseases," their illnesses change in the direction of Western patterns. Since World War II, for example, Japan's health problems increasingly parallel those of the United States. A combination of factors—diet, stress, chemical pollutants, and mutagens (including radioactivity)—are believed responsible for the worldwide rising incidence of Western diseases.

This generalization holds for functional as well as organic diseases. As culture change subjects people's bodies to more and more of the same conditions and stresses, the body's physiology responds more and more in the same ways. The omnivorous diet characteristic of the 5 to 10 million years of later hominid evolution consisted of raw, rough, and bulky foods. The energy expenditure necessary to acquire foodstuffs was great and seems to have been pretty equally balanced by their caloric and nutritional yield. As the exigencies of urban life restrict the availability of natural hominid foods in favor of processed foods (which tend to be higher in calories and chemical additives but lower in nutritional value) and the average daily energy neccessary for making a living declines, the body is subjected to conditions quite unlike those that prevailed during hominid development. Since the evolutionary process of adaptive selection, which brings the organism and external conditions into convergence, requires a vast time span, there has developed a disjunction between the two, apparently affecting most seriously those countries in which the standard of living is rising or already high. The general status of health in smaller, isolated societies, in which (by choice or by chance) population and ecological factors are left to balance themselves, tends to remain viably stable—but the number of such societies is steadily diminishing.

Immunological differences as a factor in general level of health vary from one gene pool to another. Populations of Polynesians and Eskimos alike have been decimated by viral colds and influenza which caused only slight discomfort to the explorers and missionaries who carried them. Lest the impression be given, however, that contagion has been a unidirectional matter, it should be observed that a measure of balance was established when syphilis raged as a plague throughout the Mediterranean area in the decades following Columbus's contact with the Caribs, among whom it seems to have been but a minor nuisance.

Even the rate of healing of wounds seems to vary as the result of imperfectly understood cultural/environmental factors. Margaret Mead reports that among the Iatmul of New Guinea wounds close slowly, but among the Balinese the process is quite rapid. Williams (1972) notes that in the United States wounds are supposed to heal in seven to fourteen days whereas the Dusun of N Borneo "believe wounds should be healed by the last 'lucky day' before the end of an eight-day period."

It has been remarked, not entirely facetiously, that if one is lucky enough to survive the health dangers of youth and middle age, one will most assuredly die of heart trouble or cancer in old age, for those are the conditions which develop as the result of an increasingly lesser ability of the body to compensate for the accumulation of cell and chromosomal damage through the years.

See also Health, cross-cultural concepts of; Mental health; Mental illness and culture
Consult: Williams, Thomas R., Introduction to Socialization: Human Culture Transmitted (St. Louis: Mosby, 1972).
—MaryAnn Foley, Southern Connecticut State College

**Heine-Geldern, Freiherr Robert von** (1885–1968). An Austrian ethnologist whose work focused on the culture history of Asia and the Pacific, Heine-Geldern has been most noted as a proponent of the thesis of pre-Columbian transpacific diffusion of Asian culture traits to the Americas. His thesis rests on evidence of metallurgy, ceramic forms and techniques, iconography, wheeled toys, and other complex parallels between contemporaneous early Asian and American cultures. Though Heine-Geldern once stood by his convictions almost alone in the face of general professional skepticism, the evidence that has accumulated in recent years makes it increasingly probable that he was at least partially correct.

Consult: Grottanelli, Vinigi L., "Robert Heine-Geldern's Contribution to Historical Ethnology," *Current Anthropology* 10(4):374–376, 1969; Heine-Geldern, Robert, "The Problem of Transpacific Influences in Mesoamerica," in *Handbook of Middle-American Indians*, ed. Robert Wauchope, vol. 4 (Austin: University of Texas Press, 1966).

**Heizer, Robert Fleming** (b. 1915). Archaeologist well known for his fieldwork on the prehistory of California and Nevada, as well as for his interests in archaeological methodology and theory.

**Heliocentrism.** This concept was proposed by two English diffusion theorists, Grafton Eliot Smith and W. J. Perry. They suggested that virtually all past and contemporary civilized culture in the world originated in Egypt approximately 6,000 years ago.

Consult: Perry, W. J., *The Children of the Sun* (London: Methuen, 1923).

**Henry, Jules** (1904–1969). An American anthropologist, Henry published on the Kaingang and the Pilagá. He also published increasingly bitter attacks on American culture and offered acute perceptions regarding interactions among institutions such as schools and the family, culture, and individual personality.

**Heredity.** This term refers to the set of genes or biological makeup transmitted to an organism from its parents. Heredity and environment interact to influence development, physiology, appearance (morphology), and behavior.

See also Gene; Mendelian genetics

**Heritability.** The proportion of the measurable variation in a given trait in a spe-

cified population estimated to result from hereditary rather than environmental factors.

See also Genetics and intelligence; Heredity

**Herskovits, Melville Jean** (1895–1963). Considered the founder of scientific Afro-American studies and the first Africanist in the United States, Herskovits received his Ph.D. from Columbia University in 1923, having studied under Franz Boas. Throughout his career, he was closely associated with Northwestern University, where he taught from 1927 until his death. Besides his role in black studies, he was a major theorist of his time and made important contributions to the study of primitive economic organizations and culture change—especially his discussion of the concept of acculturation. Herskovits was closely identified with the study of "africanisms," i.e., African survivals in the New World.

Consult: Simpson, George Eaton, *Melville Herskovits* (New York: Columbia University Press, 1973).

**Heterozygote.** When the sperm and egg contain different alleles of the same gene, the new cell formed is called a heterozygote.

See also Chromosomes; Gene; Genetics; Homozygote

**Hierarchical Inclusion.** See Taxonomy.

**Hierarchy.** See Dominance and aggression; Leadership; Social stratification

**Hieroglyphic Writing.** The writing system of the ancient Egyptian language was called hieroglyphic ("sacred carving") because it was used by the priests. The pictorial symbols denoted ideas, words, and speech sounds. Pictorial symbols of similar use found elsewhere in the Near East, India, and Meso-America have also been termed hieroglyphic.

Hieroglyphic writing began about 6,000 years ago in Egypt and continued to about the beginning of the Christian Era. During its long existence two simplified or cursive forms were derived from it, the *hieratic* and the *demotic*. It has been asserted that the

*Egyptian hieroglyphic writing—a combination of phonetic and ideographic representations.*

original alphabet, the Phoenician, was a still further simplification of some twenty-four consonant sound symbols of hieroglyphic.

A French engineer found the Rosetta Stone in 1799 at the mouth of the Nile and this discovery enabled J. F. Champollion to decipher in 1822 the hieroglyphic and demotic versions through the Greek language translation inscribed on the same stone.

Hieroglyphic writing was also done with reed pen on papyrus using ink made from soot and water. The Egyptian Book of the Dead was a hieroglyphic treatise on religion.

See also Alphabet; Champollion, Jean François; Writing

Consult: Budge, E. A. W., *Egyptian Language* (New York: Dover, 1958); Diringer, David, *The Alphabet* (New York: Funk & Wagnalls, 1948); Pedersen, Holger, *The Discovery of Language* (Bloomington: Indiana University Press, 1962).

—William H. Gilbert, U. S. Library of Congress (ret.)

**Hill, James Newlin** (b. 1934). An archaeologist whose primary geographical interest focuses on the American Southwest, Hill was responsible for the excavation at Broken K Pueblo in eastern Arizona.

**Hinterlands.** This term refers to any territory displaying denser interactions with a city respecting exchange, population mobility, and transportation and communication networks than with any other area. Most writers apparently think a city has only *one* hinterland. Case analysis, however, suggests that different domains—manufacturing, commerce, the arts, social networks—map different hinterlands. Any urban nucleation thus has a multiplicity of hinterlands. In some extreme cases, the focal point of a domain is not in the central city (e.g., political control in certain cattle ranching areas). Moreover, some territorial areas may relate to two or more central places or cities.

*See also* Urban anthropology

**Historical Analogy in Archaeology.** A historical analogy may be used to interpret prehistoric remains through comparison with the usages of a society which is known to history. This procedure is particularly useful because many modern societies have been modified greatly by recent contacts with the West. Historical analogy may be done with information gathered before the society was destroyed. In some cases it is possible to document the decline and destruction of a native society under European influence. However, it is always necessary to weigh the biases of the historian since many European observers have been contemptuous of native societies.

Like any analogy, the more detailed the historical analogy, the more likely it is to be useful and interesting. Thus historical analogy is limited by the fact that most of the details subject to archaeological observation are not likely to have been recorded by historians. However, if the archaeologist can excavate a site that has been described historically, she or he can discover the ways in which the distribution of cultural remains reflects the historical situation. This information can be used to account for similar distributions at other sites.

The *direct historical analogy* attempts to tie the archaeologically known culture with its historical descendant. Thus interpretations of classic Mexican culture on the basis of 16th-century observations are direct historical analogies. The accuracy of the analogy is presumed because the historical culture is the "lineal descendant" of the prehistoric culture. In the *indirect historical analogy*, the principles of the historic situation are applied to archaeological circumstances which may or may not be historically related but which appear similar in one or more ways.

*See also* Archaeology

—*Thomas P. Meyers, University of Nebraska*

**Historical Archaeology.** *See* Archaeology.

**Historical Linguistics.** Sometimes called comparative linguistics, historical linguistics has as its goal the discovery of universal principles of change operating in all languages.

**Basic Premises.** Basic premises shared by historical linguists include the view that all languages are constantly changing in a systematic fashion, that these language changes are most clearly seen in the sound system (phonology) of a language, and that changes in the vocabulary also follow a systematic pattern. Comparison of the changes among a number of languages may lead to the discovery of evolutionary relationships between them and to a reconstruction of the steps involved in their splitting off from a protolanguage.

**Comparison.** Genetic comparison seeks to prove and establish evolutionary relationships between languages—i.e., that languages have derived or developed from the same (earlier) language and thus are related. The original language is called a protolanguage.

Before stating that two or more languages are related, the linguist must compare them very carefully to ensure that similarities between them are not merely the result of chance. Further care must be taken to investigate to what extent borrowing or diffusion is responsible for observed similarities. Thus, for example, there are a number of American Indian words in English (canoe, moccasin, tobacco), but English is not genetically related to any American Indian language. Similarly, Japanese has borrowed many words from Western languages. These words say a great deal about Japanese culture contacts—but do not prove a genetic relationship.

In establishing a genetic relationship, the structure of the languages must be taken into account. If the underlying structures are similar, then similarities in vocabulary, sound systems, and so forth are given more weight. Although genetic comparison is easier when written records exist, it is not impossible in nonliterate areas. Numerous anthropological reconstructions of languages in Africa, North America, and elsewhere have demonstrated the value of genetic reconstruction.

The usual pattern of language diversification is for regional variations to develop. If there is no counteracting tendency, these regional variations become *dialects*—regionally patterned, distinctly different versions of a language which are thus recognized by speakers. Eventually, these dialects may become separate languages; this is said to occur when they become mutually unintelligible. The techniques of classical historical linguistics were developed by William Jones (1746–1794) in his study of the Indo-European language family.

Morris Swadesh developed a technique to measure the amount of chronological distance between languages belonging to the same language family, again using Indo-European. He called the technique *glottochronology*, although it is sometimes called lexicostatistics. In brief, he proposed that the "core" words of a language be compared with those of another language in a search for cognates. Core words—consisting of terms specifying body parts, numbers, and other very concrete items which occur cross-culturally—are presumed to change at a fixed rate. The differences between two languages' core words are a measure of their chronological distance (the time over which they have developed away from one another). Although the technique has been modified and the absolute chronology it promised has been acknowledged to be problematical, it still offers a *relative* chronology useful in conjunction with other techniques for establishing historical and evolutionary relationships between languages.

**Role in the Study of Change.** There are at least two ways in which historical linguistics may aid in the study of culture change. The first is to provide a kind of model for change. The second is to help provide evidence for change. In the former, processes seen to operate in linguistic change are seen to be analogously at work in other types of sociocultural change. For example, certain linguistic changes are responses to internal pressures and tensions. The changes which result are simply adjustments, or adaptations, serving to relieve tensions or end ambiguities. Other changes are the result of drift, or chance. Where free variation is linguistically permissible, one form may come to predominate. The reasons it may come to predominate may range from identification with a socially dominant group to mere convenience. Accidental changes may bring about change. Outside pressures and factors —conquest, trade, religious conversion— play a role in some changes.

In addition to serving as a model for culture change, language can help in the reconstruction of changes. Thus genetic relationship between languages is itself an important historical fact, pointing to previous times when peoples might have been members of the same cultural grouping or had other significant connections. The spread of crops such as corn, beans, and tobacco from the New World to the Old is traceable through linguistic factors even if other data (such as historical descriptions) were to be lost. Migrations of peoples, trade, and other kinds of culture contact have linguistic correlates, and a number of historical, ethnohistorical, and culture historical studies have relied on data furnished by historical linguistics.

There is still a great deal of work to be done in the field of historical linguistics. The current emphasis on synchronic, structural, "new linguistic" approaches does not obviate the importance of a diachronic (historical) development approach to language. The advances of structural linguistics are to be welcomed and incorporated into any approach seeking to establish linguistic relationships and regulation of process through time.

Finally, proving a relationship is but the beginning of the task of historical linguistics. Figuring out the *meaning* of the relationship and all its ramifications is a much more difficult undertaking. People are still working on the Indo-European language family, on American Indian languages first described fifty years ago, and on other language groups in which proof of relationship was accepted long ago. Thus historical linguistics acquires its special usefulness when it is applied to problems—and in-

formed by the research of other disciplines such as archaeology. It has a crucial contribution to make to our reconstruction of the prehistory of the cultures of the world.

See also Glottochronology; Lexicostatistics; Linguistics; Semantics
Consult: Allen, W. S., "Relationship in Comparative Linguistics," *Transactions of the Philological Society*, pp. 52–108, London, 1953; Hoijer, Harry, "Linguistics and Cultural Change," in *Language in Culture and Society*, ed. Dell Hymes (New York: Harper & Row, 1964).
—Frank Salamone, St. John's University

**Historical Method.** In anthropology, this term refers to the diachronic study of human culture. The historical method is sometimes combined with a comparative method in the hope of yielding generalized explanations of human cultural evolution and variation.

See also Comparative method; Diachronic

**Historicism.** This term refers to a school of theory which dominated American anthropology through the 1930s. The key names associated with historicism were Franz Boas, Clark Wissler, Alfred Kroeber, and Robert Lowie. Had these men been studying the internal combustion engine, they might have asked questions like these: "What are its basic parts (culture traits)? How do these parts fit together into larger units (complexes)? What are the specifics of the invention and diffusion of the parts, the complexes, and the whole? What is its geographic distribution?" Thus historicism regards a culture as an array of parts.

Historicism involved a preferred strategy for studying and explaining cultural systems. Detailed, first-hand field research was strongly emphasized, and the cultural facts collected were arrayed in chronological and spatial order. The stress was on learning the details of cultural things and events. This led to an emphasis on the uniqueness of varying cultural systems, and thus the doctrine of cultural relativity is especially associated with historicist thinkers.

The emphasis on geographic distribution involved first an effort to study the histories of cultures which had no written histories. However, through the depiction of trait complexes distributed in culture areas, it led

to a systematic concern with ecological relationships and environmental adaptations.

See also Configurationalism; Evolutionism; Functionalism
Consult: Boas, F., *Primitive Art* (New York: Dover, 1955); Kroeber, A. L., *Anthropology* (New York: Harcourt Brace, 1947); Wissler, C., *The Relation of Man to Nature in Aboriginal North America* (New York: Appleton, 1926).
—James Clifton, University of Wisconsin, Green Bay

**Hjelmslev, Louis** (b. 1899). This Danish linguist employs a glossematic approach to the study of Baltic languages. His work uses concepts developed by Ferdinand de Saussure.

**Hockett, Charles Francis** (b. 1916). Linguist noted for his basic text on linguistics, his work on North American Indian languages, and his theories on the evolution of language, which he differentiates from other communication systems in terms of its "design features."
Consult: Hockett, Charles F., "The Origin of Speech," *Scientific American*, September 1960.

**Hoe.** See Economics and subsistence; Horticulture.

**Hogbin, Herbert Ian** (b. 1904). A social anthropologist who has focused his research on social change and law in Oceania, Hogbin has conducted fieldwork in Polynesia and New Guinea.

**Holandric Traits.** See Sex-linked traits.

**Hole, Frank** (b. 1931). An archaeologist who is best known for his work on archaeological method and theory, Hole has undertaken research in SW Iran, Mexico, and Texas.

**Holistic Approach.** This term refers to the inclusive nature of anthropology's study of humanity. By means of physical and cultural anthropology, archaeology, and linguistics, anthropologists attempt to understand human beings as physical, social, and cultural entities, through time and space. As such, anthropology studies many problems that arise at the interfaces of various other disciplines—which led Alfred Kroeber to characterize anthropology as a "coordinating science."

Within cultural anthropology itself the holistic approach is quite pronounced. Robert Redfield noted that in studying a small community, whether in terms of social structure, world view, or as an ecological system, the effort is to understand the community "in its entirety, as a whole." This holistic approach is reflected in the use of the term *integration* to describe the consistency displayed by cultures, which is taken by anthropologists to be the most important aspect of a culture's wholeness. Consistency may be conceptualized at different levels in terms of a logical, affective, or aesthetic consistency; as a congruence of expectations and behaviors, and as being exemplified by the functional interdependence of the various major cultural modalities such as religious, political, and economic life. Ruth Benedict in particular viewed each culture as a unique whole with characteristic patterns (configurations). She believed that cultures could be understood not by reducing them to their components but by studying the "unique arrangement and interrelation of the parts, which brings about a new entity."

See also Configurations of culture; Culture; Functionalism; Pattern, culture

Consult: Benedict, Ruth, *Patterns of Culture* (Boston: Houghton Mifflin, 1934); Redfield, Robert, *The Little Community and Peasant Society and Culture* (Chicago: University of Chicago Press, 1961).

—Stan Wilk, Lycoming College

**Holloway, Ralph L., Jr.** (b. 1917). A physical anthropologist who studies the evolution of the human brain and behavior, Holloway also has done research on comparative primate neuroanatomy, primate aggression and social evolution, and fossil humans.

**Holocene.** The Holocene is the last geological epoch of the Cenozoic Era, although some scientists include it with the Pleistocene epoch. It is commonly referred to as the Recent epoch and began approximately 10,000 years ago with the retreat of the last glaciers.

See also Glaciations; Pleistocene

**Homeostasis.** This term describes the tendency of natural systems to maintain certain critical factors (body temperature, population density) within a narrowly limited range of variation.

See also Cybernetics; Systems analysis

**Homicide.** See Murder.

**Hominid Fossil Sequence.** See Fossil sequence of human evolution.

**Hominids.** Hominids is the common name for those hominoids referred to as the taxonomic family Hominidae (modern humans and their nearest evolutionary predecessors). The only living representatives of the Hominidae are all members of the single genus and species *Homo sapiens* ("wise man"). The essence of the overall adaptive pattern of the hominids is often characterized as being sociocultural or extrasomatic adaptation but, of course, the framework of this pattern is deeply rooted in hominid biology. Adoption of a fully erect posture with bipedal locomotion, coupled with enhanced manipulation by the digits of the hand, remodeling of the dentition plus associated jaw and facial structures, and the development of an elaborate and complex brain—these constitute the principal morphological evolutionary transformations of hominids.

The most commonly accepted modern taxonomic designations for fossil hominids are *Homo sapiens neanderthalensis, Homo erectus, Australopithecus africanus, Australopithecus habilis, Australopithecus robustus, Australopithecus boisei,* and, probably, *Ramapithecus.* The earliest of these, evolutionary speaking, is *Ramapithecus*—if its paleontological basis is accepted—dated to approximately 14 million years ago. However, recent research into the biochemical relationships between humans and other anthropoids is contrary to this paleontological evidence and suggests that the earliest hominids appeared only 5 to 10 million years ago. The controversy surrounding the incompatibility of these dates is, as yet, unresolved.

See also Anthropoids; Australopithecines; Fossil sequence of human evolution; Hominoids; *Homo erectus; Homo sapiens;* Neanderthal man; Primates, evolutionary features of; *Ramapithecus*

Consult: Campbell, Bernard G., *Human Evolution,* 2nd ed. (Chicago: Aldine, 1974); Harrison, Richard J., and Montaga, William, *Man,* 2nd ed. (New York: Appleton Century Crofts, 1973); Rosen, S. I., *Introduction to the Primates* (Englewood Cliffs, N.J.: Prentice-Hall, 1974).

—Martin K. Nickels, Illinois State University

**Hominoids.** Hominoids is the common name for those anthropoids classified within the taxonomic superfamily Hominoidea (all living and extinct apes and humans). The living hominoids are frequently divided into three taxonomic families: gibbons and siamangs (Hylobatidae); orangutans, gorillas, and chimpanzees (Pongidae); and humans (Hominidae). The most notable distinguishing anatomical features of the hominoids include the absence of any external tail, forelimbs quite long in relation to the trunk, a trunk which is relatively wider than it is deep, and scapulas rotated to the back of the trunk. These anatomical similarities between hominoids are often explained in terms of a common ancestral evolutionary adaptation for brachiation—a mode of arboreal locomotion in which the body swings hand over hand from one perch to another—even though the gibbon and siamang are the only hominoids that regularly engage in brachiation as adults.

Gibbons and siamangs have a diploid chromosomal count of 44; orangutans, gorillas, and chimpanzees 48; and humans 46. Consideration of all the biological and behavioral evidence together indicates that the gorillas, chimpanzees, and humans are most closely related to one another while the gibbons and siamangs are most biologically and evolutionarily distinct. The earliest recognized hominoid forms date from the Old World Oligocene.

See also Anthropoids; Hominids; Primates, evolutionary features of

Consult: Napier, J. R., and Napier, P. H., *A Handbook of Living Primates* (New York: Academic Press, 1967); Rosen, S. I., *Introduction to the Primates* (Englewood Cliffs, N.J.: Prentice-Hall, 1974); Schultz, Adolph H., *The*

Life of Primates (New York: Universe Books, 1969).
—Martin K. Nickels, Illinois State University

**Homo Erectus.** This grade in hominid evolution is characterized by a mean cranial capacity of 900+ cc (range 775–1,225 cc). It exhibits platycephalic calvaria with variable, often minimal frontal development. Massive supraorbital tori (brow ridges, especially in the Java and E African specimens) and postorbital constriction are typical. Variable, usually small mastoid process, a thick cranial vault, massive mandible (vis-à-vis *Homo sapiens*), maxillary diastemata (some Djetis specimens), a mean stature of 5 feet 7 inches (estimate), an estimated weight of 100–140 pounds, and a postcranial skeleton closely resembling that of modern *Homo sapiens*—these are the characteristic features which were originally defined by Dutch anatomist Eugene Dubois (SC Java, 1891, "Pithecanthropus erectus").

The temporal span of *Homo erectus* probably ranges from some 1.5 million years to less than Pleistocene. Its geographical distribution ranges over E and N Africa ("Atlanthropus mauritanicus"), S Africa, E and W Europe ("Homo heidelbergensis"), SC Java ("Pithecanthropus erectus," "P. dubius," "P. robustus," "H. modjokertensis"), NE and NW China ("Sinanthropus pekinensis," "S. lantianensis"), and Israel. Former species designations are sometimes appended to the term to indicate geographically localized, subspecifically differentiated populations (e.g., *H. erectus pekinensis*). Some 87 to 100 individuals of all ages and both sexes were known as of 1974.

This fossil grade is associated with Acheulean archaeological assemblages (E and N Africa; e.g., Olduvai Gorge, Peninj) and is generally assumed responsible for their fabrication (Africa, Europe, W Eurasia). It is also associated with the northern variant chopper/chopping tool complex (e.g., Choukoutien) and is generally assumed responsible for their fabrication (E Asia, India). Similarly *Homo erectus* is the manufacturer of the Clactonian (S England) and Tayacian (S France) assemblages. Typically, *Homo erectus* groups were fire-using, unspecialized hunter/gatherers (e.g., Choukoutien, Torralba/Ambrona) whose hypothetical minimal social unit is the extended family band numbering fifteen to twenty-five individuals. This grade is a single, widely

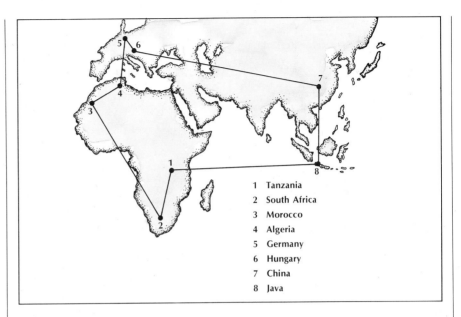

1 Tanzania
2 South Africa
3 Morocco
4 Algeria
5 Germany
6 Hungary
7 China
8 Java

*The more advanced culture of* Homo erectus *enabled some of these groups to inhabit far colder climates than had any previous australopithecine populations. Not surprisingly, it was* H. erectus *who first controlled fire in Europe and China.*

distributed polytypic species assumed ancestral to *H. sapiens* (?after ca. 250,000 BP).
*See also* Fire, use by *Homo erectus;* Fossil sequence of human evolution
Consult: Birdsell, J. B., *Human Evolution* (Chicago: Rand McNally, 1972); Pilbeam, D. R., *The Ascent of Man* (New York: Macmillan, 1972).
—Geoffrey A. Clark, Arizona State University

**Homo Habilis.** *See* Australopithecines.

**Homo Sapiens.** This grade in hominid evolution is distinguished primarily by a mean cranial capacity of about 1,300 cc. Most other characteristics are very variable defined by comparison with *Homo erectus*. For example, reduced maxillary prognathism is linked with reduction in the use of masticatory apparatus; supraorbital tori are also variable but less pronounced than *Homo erectus;* the canines are reduced and molar dentition is smaller; postorbital constriction is reduced and is entirely absent in contemporary pop-

ulations; inflated, rounded frontal, occipital aspects coincide with increased brain volume, especially among modern populations.

Fossil remains attributed to *Homo sapiens* can be trichotomized arbitrarily into (1) specimens temporally and morphologically intermediate between *Homo erectus sensu lato* and Neanderthal man *sensu lato;* (2) Neanderthal and "Neanderthaloid" populations, defined by consensus and on temporal criteria (*H. sapiens neanderthalensis*); and (3) fossil representatives of morphologically modern humans (*H. sapiens sapiens*). It is important to bear in mind that a continuum is involved—the categories are not discontinuous with sharp breaks between them. Membership in the first group is most controversial because its taxonomic status is tenuous and hotly debated. Major fossils include the Swanscombe (SE England) and Steinheim (N Germany) crania; "pre-Neanderthal" specimens from Caune de l'Arago, Le Lazaret, and Fontéchevade (S and SC France); the morphologically primitive (*H. erectus*-like) but comparatively late (early Upper Pleistocene) series from the Ngandong Beds (Solo man, SC Java); the Vérteszöllös and Broken Hill remains (Hungary, Zambia) and Omo crania I and II (Ethiopia). These fossils represent morphologically variable populations within a single, polytypic species. They do not imply (as has sometimes been argued) the survival of multiple pre-*sapiens* lines. They are all of probable Middle/Upper Pleistocene boundary date (approximately 250,000 to 100,000 years BP). The second group contains hominid fossils of early/middle Upper Pleistocene age dating from before 100,000 to 40,000 BP; it is generally referred to as Neanderthal or Neanderthaloid. Usually included are crania and postcranial remains from Neanderthal (which is the type site) and other sites in Germany; from Greece, France, Belgium, Gibraltar, Italy, Israel, Uzbekistan, Iraq, and E Africa; and from various locales along the N African coast. Early descriptions of European material led to a false expectation of morphological homogeneity and a dichotomy between "classic" (*H. erectus*-like) and "progressive/generalized" (*sapiens*-like) groups no longer maintained by most hominid paleontologists. The last group comprises fossil representatives of morphologically modern humans. Membership is determined by association with Upper Paleolithic archaeological assemblages and/or an age of less than 40,000 years BP. Included are skeletal remains from Paviland (S England); Brno and Predmost (Czechoslovakia); Chancelade, Combe-Capelle, Cromagnon, Laugerie-Basse, Solutré (France); Oberkassel (Germany); Grottes des Enfants (Italy); Belt, Hotu Caves (Iran); Choukoutien (Upper Cave) (China); Wadjak (Java); and various sites in Australia, North and South America, and N, E, and W Africa.

See also Fossil sequence of human evolution; Neanderthal man

Consult: Birdsell, J. B., *Human Evolution* (Chicago: Rand McNally, 1972); Buettner-Janusch, J., *Physical Anthropology: A Perspective* (New York: Wiley, 1973).

—Geoffrey A. Clark, Arizona State University

**Homo Sapiens Neanderthalensis.** See Neanderthal man.

**Homosexuality.** Homosexuality—sexual desire or behavior directed toward a person or persons of one's own sex—has traditionally been strongly stigmatized in American society, and most Americans regard the behavior as somehow unnatural. Anthropological and psychological research does not support this view, however. It is clear that humans are not biologically programmed toward heterosexuality or indeed any other form of sexual outlet. The human species appears to have an innate sexual impulse, but this drive is initially undirected and is channeled toward approved objectives through learning experiences whose content is unique to each culture. In consequence, the incidence of and attitudes toward homosexual behavior vary widely from culture to culture.

There are many cultures in which homosexual behavior is, for various categories of people and under various conditions, either tolerated, approved, or even required. Asiatic shamanism, for example, often has a homosexual component, as do the periodic religious ceremonies of some South American Indian tribes. Among the Keraki of New Guinea and the Aranda of Australia, the initiation ceremony for male adolescents requires them to take a passive role in anal intercourse for a full year; thereafter they take the active role until their heterosexual marriage. There are a substantial number of societies in which bisexual behavior is viewed with indifference or even approval. In addition, there exist a very few societies—such as the Etero and the Marind-anim of New Guinea—which are primarily homosexual, but these cultures have some difficulty in maintaining their population numbers. In a study of cross-cultural evidence from 190 small-scale societies, Clellan S. Ford and Frank A. Beach found that in 64 percent of the cultures for which information was available homosexuality was acceptable—sometimes for all members of the community at certain times, but sometimes for only specified individuals or categories of individuals. In many other cultures, however, homosexual behavior was found to be punishable by ridicule, beatings, or even death.

Evidence from these and other studies has done a great deal to modify the highly ethnocentric attitudes toward homosexuality displayed in Western cultures in general and in the United States in particular.

See also Sex (gender) identity; Sex roles; Sexuality, human

Consult: Devereux, George, "Homosexuality Among the Mohave Indians," *Human Biology* 9:498–597, 1937; Martin, M. Kay, and Voorhies, Barbara, *Female of the Species* (New York: Columbia University Press, 1975); Mead, Margaret, *Sex and Temperament in Three Primitive Societies* (New York: Morrow, 1963).

—Ian Robertson, Cambridge University

**Homozygote.** When the sperm and egg contain the same allele of a particular gene, the new cell formed is called a homozygote.

See also Chromosomes; Gene; Genetics; Heterozygote

**Honigmann, John Joseph** (b. 1914). Cultural anthropologist whose research has centered on cultural theory, ethnographic methods, psychological anthropology, and the societies of North America, Pakistan, and W Europe.

**Hooten, Ernest Albert** (1887–1954). Physical anthropologist noted for his interest in the relationship of *Homo sapiens* to the other primates; his racial classification of the human species is now discredited.

**Horizon, Archaeological.** This term refers to the similarity in a series of cultural elements covering a large geographical area during a restricted time span. A horizon may be marked by a variety of archaeological evidence indicating the widespread distribution of distinctive features at approximately the same time level—particularly a recognizable art style (horizon style). Horizons are used in culture-historical reconstruction as indicators of significant cultural unity or at least culture contact over wide areas. Ideally, the recognition of a horizon is based on independent evidence that its elements are coeval, although the distinctiveness of widespread traits is sometimes taken as evidence of their approximate contemporaneity and rapid spread. The inverse of the horizon concept is that of *tradition*—cultural similarity which is restricted in space but has substantial persistence through time. Both concepts were first developed by students of Andean culture history and later came into general use in New World prehistory.

Horizon is sometimes used in an entirely different sense: as a synonym for level or layer in a stratigraphic context.

See also Dating, relative; Time in archaeology; Tradition, archaeological

Consult: Willey, Gordon R., and Phillips, Philip, *Method and Theory in American Archaeology* (Chicago: University of Chicago Press, 1958).

—John S. Henderson, Cornell University

**Horizontal Excavation.** *See* Excavation of a site.

**Hormones.** Hormones are chemical substances produced by certain organs (ductless or endocrine glands) in an animal's body to regulate its metabolic activities. The term is derived from a Greek word meaning to excite. These chemical messengers are secreted in extremely minute amounts into the bloodstream and are transported throughout the body to specific target tissues. The structural composition of hormones includes complex amino acids, steroids, polypeptides, and proteins. The principal endocrine glands are the anterior and posterior pituitary (hypophysis), thyroid, parathyroid, adrenals, pancreas, and the testes or ovaries. The major function of the pituitary seems to be the activation of the other endocrine glands, but the pituitary itself is controlled by a part of the brain known as the hypothalamus.

The potency of hormones is staggering to ponder when one realizes that effective amounts are often measured in terms of micrograms ($\frac{1}{1000}$ milligram) and even nanograms ($\frac{1}{1000}$ microgram). The actual physiological mechanisms by which hormones exert their influence are poorly understood, but they are thought to affect DNA activity and protein synthesis, modify enzyme activities, and affect the transport of materials through cellular membranes. Hormonal activity works in a feedback fashion: the induced function eventually affects the initial hormone secretion.

Consult: Brown, J. H. U., and Barker, S. B., *Basic Endocrinology*, 2nd ed. (Philadelphia: Davis, 1966); Sawin, Clark T., *The Hormones* (Boston: Little, Brown, 1969).

—*Martin K. Nickels, Illinois State University*

**Horse.** *See* Nomadism; Pastoralism.

**Horticulture.** This term refers to shallow cultivation depending on minimally amplified human muscle power. Horticulturalists use either the hoe or the digging stick to turn the topsoil. Introduction of the plow marks the appearance of agriculture.

*See also* Agriculture; Economics and subsistence; Technology and subsistence

*Senegalese hoe horticulturalists. Horticulture refers to plant food production with a technology limited to the use of a digging stick or hoe to turn the topsoil. Thus a major source of work energy is human muscle power only minimally amplified by tools.*

**Housing and Shelter.** Houses have been built for at least 300,000 years, possibly even by precursors of *Homo sapiens*. This most ubiquitous form of built environment has various purposes—to shelter people, their activities, and their possessions from climate, from human and animal enemies, and from supernatural powers; to establish place; to stress social identity and indicate status; and for symbolic reasons.

Shelter is thus not the only function of housing. House form and climate obviously are related, but climate does not *determine* form. In cold climates which make stringent demands for shelter and protection, one finds great variability—ranging from minimal shelter in Tierra del Fuego, through fairly low levels of protection among Amerindian dwellings in Wisconsin and Minnesota, to the highly developed shelter of the Eskimo.

How much shelter do people need? For what purposes do they use shelter? How do they provide themselves with shelter? Such decisions often seem to be made on the basis of nonclimatic and nonphysiological criteria, and one thus finds extraordinary variability in heating, lighting, acoustic, and other standards—even among technologically advanced modern cultures. In the case of traditional dwellings and settlements it is frequently their sacred character which is essential so that they form a humanized, safe space in a profane and potentially dangerous environment. They become humanized by imposing an order using rituals and sacred orientations and, frequently, by becoming cosmological symbols.

The rich variety of house forms is best understood if sociocultural factors are considered to be more important than climate, technology, materials, and economy. In any situation, it is the interplay of all these factors which best explains the form of dwelling people build. No single explanation will suffice. A house is more than a material object or structure—it is an institution created by a complex set of forces, a cultural phenomenon.

**Housing and Anthropology.** Given the primacy of sociocultural factors and the view of housing as a cultural phenomenon, it is rather surprising to find that, by and

*Cave dwellings in Guadix, Spain. Note the chimneys built directly out of the caves. The house fronts are to cave entrances. Some unused cave entrances can be seen just under the brow of the hill. Television antennae also can be seen. Caves are perhaps among the most ancient forms of shelter, though here clearly modified to modern facilities.*

large, anthropology has neglected the study of the built environment and its most common manifestation—the dwelling and the settlement of which it is part. Due to the intimate relationship between built form and culture, the study of dwellings, how they are used, and how they relate to larger settlement systems would be useful for anthropological theory. An anthropological approach would also seem essential to any multidisciplinary study of man-environment interactions, while a consideration of the role and significance of dwellings and settlements should be an important part of applied anthropology. Yet this exciting area of study—the relation of anthropology to the study of built environments—has been overlooked.

**Existing Studies.** In addition to the lack of significant studies there is also a surprising lack of data. In the recent past, even descriptions have been lacking from most ethnographies. Earlier ethnographies, some very recent work, and studies by non-English language scholars contain more information. However, not only is the information scattered, but descriptions tend to be verbal or at best include a few photographs. Missing are such essential elements as details of spatial organization; ways of building (technical and social); inventories of possessions and their location; the way different individuals and groups use dwellings; the relation of dwellings to activities; their relation to values, ideals, cosmologies; how dwellings relate to social organization, privacy, and social interaction; and how dwelling form and culture change affect one another.

Some work has been done on classifying house types (largely in terms of plan shapes, roof shapes, and other morphological criteria) and also some work in cross-cultural studies and culture and personality attempting to find correlations between dwelling shape and various aspects of childrearing,

*A beehive hut of the Yaruro of Venezuela made of palm fronds on a pole frame. The materials are essentially in natural form. Though the shape is notably conventionalized, the structure seems a quite ancient type technically. It is well adapted to allowing breezes to sweep out biting insects while protecting from seasonal rains, just as the caves are cool in the hot summers of Spain and well protected against sharp winters.*

*Improvised squatter housing in Rio de Janeiro, effectively roofed against rain, but relatively breezy for tropical weather. Materials are mostly quite changed from natural form (e.g., boards, tin sheets). The residents' urban outlook is reflected in the "street" sign—"Juscelino Kubitschek Street," named after the then president of Brazil.*

personality development, practices such as circumcision, and so forth.

**Meaning of Dwelling.** None of these approaches considers which human characteristics result in specific housing forms, what effects dwelling forms and changes have on people, and what mechanisms link people and their dwellings. When these questions are considered, however, it soon appears that a crucial factor is the meaning that dwellings have for people.

The specific way of living, interacting with, and avoiding others, the specific nature and form of activities—all affect the dwelling and all have significance through the meanings they have for particular groups. The dwelling can be seen as resulting from a series of choices among the various alternatives which even the most constraining context still makes possible. These choices express ideals and world views, act as symbols of identity, and express status—i.e., the result reflects people's cognitive schemata.

**Dwelling and Settlement.** It is almost impossible to consider the dwelling in isolation from its larger context—the settlement. Considering systems of activities and uses, social interaction and avoidance, one

*Quite clearly, housing forms are very arbitrary and reflect historical contexts, cultural traditions, aesthetic notions, patterns of use, availability of materials, and life style preferences. It is not possible to account for house forms merely as a response to environmental stresses.*

finds that many activities are enacted beyond the confines of the dwelling: in fields, woods, barns, stables, streets, shops, courtyards, men's houses, and other special places. Since the definition of dwelling depends on the activities being considered, it is far from self-evident what constitutes a dwelling. In comparing houses cross-culturally it is thus important to define carefully what is being included or excluded and to examine these matters in terms of cultural specifics. It is interesting to note what a house means to a family, to women (for whom, in most cultures, the dwelling has the most significance), and to children and how the issue of privacy is defined. In some societies eating, for instance, is a private act whereas copulating is not.

**Conclusion.** The dwelling is intimately and intricately related to the rest of culture.

It often acts as a symbol of identity. It is culture-specific and must be considered at the emic level before it can be studied at the etic level. In any case a house is much more than shelter—it reflects the most profound ideals and feelings and is thus a complex entity which may play a central role in interactions among people and between them and their habitat.

See also Architecture; Cultural ecology; Ethnoscience; New Ethnography, the
Consult: Oliver, Paul (ed.), *Shelter and Society* (London: Barrie and Rockliffe, 1969); Rapoport, Amos, *House Form and Culture* (Englewood Cliffs, N.J.: Prentice-Hall, 1969); Rapoport, Amos (ed.), *The Mutual Interaction of People and Their Built Environment: A Cross-Cultural Perspective* (The Hague: Mouton, 1975).
—Amos Rapoport, University of Wisconsin, Milwaukee

encouragement of private industry, or private entrepreneurial speculation. Since construction and replacement of dwellings absorbs much labor and strongly stimulates basic industrial production, controlling the housing market becomes politically and socially important. In capitalist societies, housing construction is also immensely profitable. Therefore, developments like squatter settlements which decrease capitalist profits by creating secondary or informal housing markets often elicit class conflict expressed in political, juridical, and ideological struggles.

**Howell, F. Clark** (b. 1925). A paleoanthropologist from the University of California at Berkeley, Howell is well known for his interpretive research on Neanderthaloids and the australopithecines.

**Housing Market.** At least in most recently formed or reorganized societies—capitalist, socialist, or their variants—housing figures prominently in the national economy whether through state allocations, state

**Howells, William** (b. 1908). Physical anthropologist from Harvard University known for his writings in paleoanthropology and his application of quantitative methods to the study of human populations.

*Bali. As part of a people's culture, housing and settlement patterns encode fundamental cultural themes. Here discrete household units are clearly emphasized.*

**HRAF.** Human Relations Area Files, Inc., is a nonprofit research organization sponsored and controlled by twenty-four major universities. Hundreds more institutions, worldwide, participate in the use of HRAF. Originally conceived by an interdisciplinary group of social scientists at Yale University in the 1930s and known then as the Cross-cultural Survey, the files began to take form with the publication of *Outline of Cultural Materials* (Murdock et al. 1937, revised 1969). The information is indexed both by subject, as listed in the *Outline of Cultural Materials,* and by culture, as listed in the *Outline of World Cultures* (Murdock 1969).

The purpose of HRAF is to make available cross-cultural comparative studies and to lessen scholars' work in sorting through vast amounts of information. Descriptive data on almost 300 cultures (comprising about 10 percent of the world's total) organized into 79 topic headings with 712 categories of information are available on both paper file cards and microfiche. Descriptive data on non-Western, nonliterate cultures predominate. The files are being computerized at the present time to facilitate data retrieval. For further information write: HRAF, Box 2054 Y.S., New Haven, CT 06520.

Consult: Lagacé, Robert O., *Nature and Use of the HRAF Files* (New Haven: HRAF Press, 1974), Murdock, G. P., et al., *Outline of Cultural Materials* (New Haven: HRAF Press, 1969); Murdock, G. P., *Outline of World Cultures* (New Haven: HRAF Press, 1969).

—*Mary Ann Foley, Southern Connecticut State College*

**Hrdlicka, Ales** (1860–1943). Czechoslovakian-born American physical anthropologist who claimed that Indian aboriginal groups came to America over Alaska and the Aleutians and who did much to disprove Nazi race dogma.

**Hsu, Francis** (b. 1909). A Chinese-American anthropologist, Hsu was educated in London and has taught for many years at Northwestern. He is best known for his comparative analysis of Chinese, Indian, and American culture; for his methodological contributions to the study of literate civilizations; and for his "kinship and culture" hypothesis, in which he proposes a functional relationship between attributes associated with those dyadic relationships that tend to be dominant in any kinship system and such diverse areas of culture as values, personality, cognition, political organization, and religion. He has also pointed out the inherent ethnocentrism which continues to characterize American anthropology.

**Hulse, Frederick Seymour** (b. 1906). Physical anthropologist who is interested in the genetic and cultural factors that influence human biological diversity; his best-known work is *The Human Species* (1971).

**Human Evolution.** *See* Evolution, human.

**Human Paleontology.** Subdivision of physical anthropology that deals with the discovery, reconstruction, and interpretation of human and hominid fossil remains.

*See also* Fossil sequence of human evolution; Physical anthropology

**Human Plasticity.** *See* Plasticity, human.

**Human Relations Area Files.** *See* HRAF.

**Human Senses.** The five classic human senses are taste, touch, hearing, smell, and sight, although none is simply defined or independent of other senses. Animal senses may be more acute, but human intelligence and culture compensate for sensory shortcomings.

Sensitivity to pressure, temperature, radiation, equilibrium, internal pain, and even perception of depth, distance, and time are senses to varying degrees. Conscious or unconscious reactions to stimuli are evidence of sensing, by definition, so "extrasensory perception," aside from being unproved, is self-contradictory. Because human nervous systems, psychologies, and cultures filter or translate sensory inputs, perceptions must be tested experimentally to be proved "accurate."

*See also* Cognition; Emics; Etics

**Human Sexuality.** *See* Sexuality, human.

**Human Variation, Significance of.** To understand the extent and significance of the human diversity found in the world today it is imperative to view humanity as the product of evolution. Of particular importance is the fact that human beings, in contrast to other organic forms, are simultaneously involved in two kinds of evolutionary development: biological and cultural. Human evolution and thus human diversity should be analyzed in terms of the interaction of these two processes.

Viewed at any given point in time, human diversity results from differences in each person's inherited genetic endowment and differences in the environments in which people are raised. Human diversity is largely the result of the interaction of these two primary factors. The outcome of the process of interaction between a person's genetic endowment *(genotype)* and his or her environment (cultural aspects of the environment are extremely important) is known as the *phenotype*—i.e., the individual with his or her developed characteristics. However, to understand the nature of these two primary factors in human phenotypic development it is necessary to look at human evolution over time.

Human genotypic diversity arises in evolution as a result of mutation and natural selection. As C. Loring Brace has noted, the most important aspect of the analysis of human physical variation is the investigation of the selective pressures which have operated in human adaptation to environments. In this way we can come to understand the range of variation in human genotypes and phenotypic traits such as skin color and body build. Hypotheses have been put forward to account for the evolutionary development of various aspects of human diversity. C. Coon, S. Garn, and J. B. Birdsell have suggested that tall, thin people have an adaptive advantage in hot climates because such a body type facilitates loss of excess body heat. On the other hand a short, stocky individual is a good conserver of body heat and thus should be found in cold climates. In a similar fashion it has been suggested that light skin color is found in environments characterized by cloud covers and cool temperatures so that those parts of the body exposed to what sun there is will absorb a maximum amount to produce vitamin D. Such hypotheses, as well as others which simultaneously take account of a variety of environmental factors, while not universally accepted by anthropologists, indicate a useful research strategy for understanding the occurrence and significance of phenotypic variation among human populations. Anthropologists must be keenly aware of the cultural elements which may affect the selective pressures exerted by the noncultural environment on the human genetic endowment. Brace, for example, argues that the wearing of clothing, a cultural trait, could be responsible for some human populations exhibiting a lighter skin coloration by eliminating the adaptive advantage of dark skin.

An evolutionary approach to human diversity will thus aid us in understanding the type, degree, and significance of variation exhibited by contemporary humanity. Theodosius Dobzhansky (a population geneticist) emphasizes that heredity determines developmental processes rather than fixed traits; he also notes that, as a rule, those processes whose consequences are essential for survival and reproduction are buffered against environmental and genetic disturbances (canalization). Thus the genetic endowment of almost all human beings leads to the development of two eyes, a four-chambered heart, a sucking instinct in the infant, a sexual drive in the adult, and so on. This observation is important when considering that aspect of human variation which is considered of greatest significance in our culture—differences in mental capacity between human groups. In recent years a number of researchers have maintained that significant differences in genetically determined potential for intellectual activity exist between human groups. Using the results of so-called intelligence or IQ tests, these investigators claim that some human groups are intellectually inferior to others. Leaving aside the substantial problems involved in delineating the human groups to be used for such comparisons, such assertions can be shown to be unsupported by the data presently available. Two philosophers, N. J. Block and Gerald Dworkin, indicate that IQ tests are not based on a substantial theory of intelligence. As a result, assertions based on the data provided by IQ tests must be quite limited and are often unjustified. Specifically the tests may not measure what is ordinarily conceived of as intelligence in our culture. Moreover the correlations between test performance and success in various sociocultural pursuits such as economic activity are wholly inconclusive as regards their signifi-

cance. In addition, it has been shown that performance on IQ tests is influenced by the personality, motivation, and sociocultural background of the person taking the test as well as by the manner of its administration. Such considerations have led Alexander Alland (an anthropologist) to state that it is impossible to make judgments about group differences in intelligence on the basis of published IQ studies.

By returning to an evolutionary perspective, however, we can make some strong inferences regarding the diversity in intellectual abilities between human populations. Alland notes that *Homo sapiens* is characterized by "extraordinary genetic homogeneity." The rich history of human migrations with resultant interbreeding, and gene flow through intermediate populations, have been major factors in the homogeneity that has characterized human evolutionary development. In addition, culture has been a buffer between human beings and the natural environment. This has undoubtedly tended to reduce genetic differentiation between human groups. In their evolutionary development human populations have adapted to various environments primarily by changes in their culture. Human beings pursue different lives not by changing their genes but principally due to different training and enculturation. Thus with the elaboration of cultural evolution and cultural variation, the genetic variation among humans produced by biological evolution has been seriously inhibited.

Of particular importance is the conclusion of L. C. Dunn and Dobzhansky that since culture is the primary human adaptive mechanism, selective pressure in human evolution has been for cultural capacities—for symboling abilities and for educability (the ability to learn from experience and adjust one's behavior to the needs and circumstances that may prevail). They maintain that the movement from genetic specialization and fixity of behavior toward educability is the most important aspect of human evolution. Indeed, unless there has been a continuous, long-term, differential selection for intelligence in some human groups as opposed to others in their evolutionary development, we should not expect to find significant intergroup differences in human mental abilities (even without taking constant interbreeding into account)—and such conditions have not existed. In fact human cultures were substantially uniform up until

about 70,000 years ago. To summarize the reasoning pursued here: If all human beings need two eyes and a four-chambered heart to survive, it is not surprising that evolutionary developments have produced such phenotypic traits in all human populations; if all human beings need culture to survive and thus need substantially the same intellectual or cultural capacities, then we should expect to find these as uniform aspects of all human populations. Such an inference of a uniform human cultural capacity is supported by research showing all cultures to have cognitively and semantically complex and abstract domains.

See also Cultural relativism; Evolution, genetic mechanisms of; Gene distribution; Race

Consult: Alland, A., *Human Diversity* (Garden City: Anchor, 1973); Baker, P. T., "Human Biological Diversity as an Adaptive Response to the Environment," in *The Biological and Social Meaning of Race*, ed. Richard Osborne (San Francisco: Freeman, 1971); Block, N. J., and Dworkin, G., "I.Q.: Heritability and Inequality, Part 1," *Philosophy and Public Affairs* 3(4), 1974; Block, N. J., and Dworkin, G., "I.Q.: Heritability and Inequality, Part 2," *Philosophy and Public Affairs* 4(1), 1974; Brace, C. L., "A Nonracial Approach Towards the Understanding of Human Diversity," in *The Concept of Race*, ed. Ashley Montagu (New York: Free Press, 1964); Brace, C. L., *The Stages of Human Evolution* (Englewood Cliffs, N.J.: Prentice-Hall, 1967); Dobzhansky, T., and Dunn, L. C., *Heredity, Race and Society* (New York: Mentor, 1952).

—Stan Wilk, Lycoming College

**Humboldt, Friedrich Heinrich Alexander, Baron von** (1769–1859). German naturalist who virtually created physical geography and meteorology while also making major contributions to geology, botany, and ethnography (of South America), including collecting important linguistic materials.

**Humboldt, Karl Wilhelm von** (1767–1835). German philosopher and linguist who used Basque, Javanese, South American, and other languages to formulate basic issues of linguistic philosophy still current today and who made major contributions to comparative philology.

**Hunting.** Hunting is usually defined as the pursuit of game, whether land animals or sea

Hunting is a multipurpose human activity. Not only is it a means for obtaining food, but it frequently is a recreational sport. Pictured here in a bas-relief from the seventh century BC is the Assyrian King Assurbanipal.

mammals. But hunting is much more than a means of procuring meat and other valued animal products. Hunting furnishes a unique set of social, psychological, and intellectual rewards, and its impact on myth, ritual, and social relations often transcends its economic importance. Although hunting is rarely the primary subsistence mode in modern nonagricultural societies, a hunting world view is so pervasive in many of these groups that the people see themselves as hunters and are labeled as such by anthropologists. A similar world view contradicting economic reality persists even among some simple horticulturalists.

The actual pursuit of game represents only one phase of one of many hunting strategies. Where game is to be sought in the open field, as in the Kalahari and Australian deserts, the hunter first gathers information on current conditions. Early sightings of fresh spoor as well as dreams and divination techniques may give the hunt its initial direction. The hunter then proceeds to track, stalk, kill or immobilize, and recover his prey. Each hunt, of course, has a character all its own. Disguises may be used to make a close approach, or animals may be lured by means of a call produced with or without some instrument.

Given the limitations of most primitive weapons, the hunter must make as close an approach as possible. Even then, primitive hunters rarely kill game outright, and the success rate for hunting is rather low. The pursuit of large and highly mobile game is an arduous, protracted, and unpredictable activity. The nature of the chase dictates that the young hunter be trained to be an astute observer of wildlife. Proficiency in the fabrication and use of hunting equipment is of little value unless it is coupled with an intimate knowledge of local habitat and the subtleties of animal behavior. The importance of the intellectual component of the chase cannot be overemphasized, particularly in light of its importance in human evolution.

Not all hunting strategies are as complex and as mentally and physically demanding as Nootka whaling, Eskimo kayak hunting, or open-field hunting with the spear or bow and arrow. Preindustrial peoples have relied heavily on simple tactics and basic hand weapons to exploit species which, under certain conditions, are especially accessible or vulnerable. The immature or lame of various species of large game, for example, may be run down on foot and easily dispatched with a club or spear. Other animals are often taken in their burrows, or while asleep or hibernating. Scavenging, though more a form of gathering than hunting, is no doubt the simplest means of obtaining meat.

In some types of hunting physical participation is minimized. The use of a trained hawk or packs of dogs in hunting certainly reduces the hunter's work. However, training an animal requires a considerable investment of the hunter's time and energy. Relying on the element of surprise and his knowledge of animal habits, the hunter constructs blinds near water, close to salt licks, or along game runs. The concealed, stationary hunter may also use a prepared bait or decoy to lure game to within firing range or into some trap which he operates. In most hunting/gathering societies, trapping is a secondary hunting technique. Still, the great variety of snares, deadfalls, cage traps, and other devices designed to act in the hunter's absence bears witness to the inventiveness of the primitive hunter.

The game drive, the most productive hunting tactic, combines elements of the chase with trapping or ambush. The object is to drive many animals, by fire or by beaters, into nets, pits, or pounds or toward a concealed hunting party. To drive or surround game successfully, the participants must coordinate their actions properly.

Prestige is a significant factor in primitive hunting, and the social status of an individual is indicated by the type of hunting task he or she is delegated. Big game hunting, as practiced by solitary individuals or organized groups, brings the most prestige and is typically the task of adult men. Trapping is not valued so highly as those tactics emphasizing pursuit, and thus it is often assigned to boys, girls, and the elderly. In some groups, the hunting of small game is the socially recognized task of women. Participation in nonindividualistic hunting activities like the game drive is not ordinarily limited to any one sex or age group.

See also Atlatl; Bow and arrow; Economics and subsistence; Fishing; Gathering; Harpoon; Skins; Spear; Weapons

Consult: Lee, R., and DeVore, I., Man the Hunter (Chicago: Aldine, 1968).

## Hunting and Gathering. See Gathering.

## Hybrid Vigor. The tendency for organisms produced by parents of different types or populations to show greater size and/or biological fitness than those of more homogeneous parent populations.

See also Evolution, genetic mechanisms of; Gene flow

## Hybridization. See Evolution, genetic mechanisms of.

## Hylobatids. See Apes.

## Hymes, Dell H. (b. 1927). A linguist and anthropologist whose research concerns the relation between language and social life, Hymes is a principal proponent of the emergent field of sociolinguistics. He argues that linguistics should be based on a conception of language as a social phenomenon, spoken in heterogeneous speech communities by speakers in varying social situations and for various social purposes. He urges comparative studies, "ethnographies of communication," that view speech as part of a broad cultural system of communicative action. Hymes has also written on American Indian linguistics (especially Chinookan), problems of language reconstruction, and the history of linguistics and anthropology, among other topics.

## Id. According to Freud, the id is one of the unconscious parts of the mind and reservoir of the instincts—Eros (sex instinct) and Thanatos (death instinct, the basis of aggression).

See also Ego; Freud, Sigmund; Superego

## Ideology. An ideology is a belief system linked to and legitimating the political and economic interests of the group that subscribes to it. The modern concept of ideology was developed by Karl Marx, who argued that the content of belief systems stems from the material conditions of the group that generates them. The dominant ideology in society would inevitably be that of the ruling class, and the content of this ideology would serve to legitimate its interests. Such an ideology may be expressed in law, religion, political or economic philosophy, literature, or folk theories; the religious doctrine of the divine right of kings, for example, legitimated the feudal system, while the economic philosophy of laissez-faire legitimated the emerging capitalist system. The subordinate group in society tends to have its own, more radical ideology, but this ideology can never become the dominant one unless the group that holds it becomes dominant itself.

Many social scientists reject Marx's unilinear view of the relationship between the ideological and the material elements in human culture. They believe that the relationship and interactions between belief systems and their material base may be more complicated and subtle than Marx envisaged. The problem of whether ideologies merely reflect social reality, or whether they can exert an independent influence on culture and social action, remains an important and unresolved issue in social science.

—Ian Robertson, Cambridge University

## Image of Limited Good. See Limited good, image of.

## Immediate Constituents. An immediate constituent is part of a construction. Constructions are combinations of linguistic elements which, though they are expressed in a sequence, have a hierarchical relationship to each other. For example, the sentence

*Mary saw the tree*

reads as a sequence of four words. Yet there are obviously differences in the relationships of the words to each other (among each other) which cannot be represented horizontally (i.e., as a part of the sequence) but rather must be represented vertically (i.e., hierarchically):

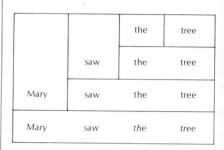

Thus the immediate constituents of the whole sentence are (1) *Mary*; (2) *saw the tree*. The immediate constituents of the verb phrase *saw the tree* are (1) *saw*; (2) *the tree*. The immediate constituents of the noun phrase *the tree* are (1) *the*; (2) *tree*.

See also Descriptive linguistics; Grammar; Surface structure of language; Syntax

## Imperialism. In its broad sense, imperialism refers to any form of domination and exploitation of one people by another. In this sense, imperialism is not unique to capitalism. The more narrow, precise meaning of the term is that developed by V. I. Lenin referring to a special form of international exploitation that occurs only in the capitalist phase of human history. The Leninist theory of imperialism includes the following elements: (1) capitalism has entered its monopoly phase, characterized by the importance of finance capital; (2) in addition to their role as sources of raw mate-

rials and markets for finished goods, colonies become important areas for capital investment; and (3) the world's surface becomes almost completely partitioned into colonies, resulting in struggles between imperialist powers attempting to maintain or expand their empires (as in World War II). Such imperialism, according to Lenin, played an important role in retarding the development of working class revolutions in the imperialist nations, since the colonies acted as a safety valve for surplus population. Further, with the superprofits gained by colonial exploitation, the capitalists were able to buy off the leading elements of their own working class. Others have argued that imperialism tends to deform the social structures of the colonies.

See also Capitalism; Colonialism; Communism; Neocolonialism; Socialism

Consult: Boulding, Kenneth E., and Mukerjee, Tappan (eds.), *Economic Imperialism: A Book of Readings* (Ann Arbor: University of Michigan Press, 1972); Frank, Andrew Gunder, "The Development of Underdevelopment," in *Latin America: Underdevelopment or Revolution* (New York: Monthly Review Press, 1969); Magdoff, Harry, *The Age of Imperialism* (New York: Monthly Review Press, 1969).

—*Eugene E. Ruyle, University of Virginia*

**Imprinting.** Imprinting is the process discovered by ethologists Konrad Lorenz and Eckard Hess by which infant attachment to a maternal figure (real or substitute) is formed. This process represents a blend of learning and innate predisposition inasmuch as imprinting takes place during an early "critical period" and is unlikely to occur before or after that time. Although derived from experiments investigating maternal attachment, imprinting is generally used to describe any such process occurring early in an organism's life. Imprinting is not very evident among higher animals and, to date, few "critical periods" have been identified for human infants.

See also Ethology; Instincts

**Inbreeding.** Inbreeding consists of extreme nonrandom mating and is one means of affecting the frequency of distribution of genes in a population.

See also Evolution, genetic mechanisms of; Genetic drift

**Incas.** This pre-Columbian civilization of the Andes had its capital at Cuzco, Peru. The beginning of the Inca Empire dates from Emperor Pachacuti, who was crowned in 1438. From his reign until the Spanish conquest, the borders of the empire were pushed northward into Ecuador and southward into Chile. At its height, the empire covered more than one-third of a million square miles.

The society was stratified with the emperor, an absolute ruler with divine right, at the pinnacle. Relatives of the emperor held the most important offices in the Incan political structure. The small nobility was made up of the higher-ranking descendants of previous emperors and the lower-ranking *curacas*, who were chiefs of groups that had been conquered by the Inca. The major-

*Machu Picchu, mountain city of the Incan civilization in Peru. The site was abandoned after the arrival of the conquistadors, and was not rediscovered until 1912.*

ity of the population formed the commoner class, which was basically rural. These commoners provided the labor which supported the noble class. They farmed public land and land owned by kin groups, were drafted for public works projects, served in the armies, and worked as servants in noble households. The success of the Incas centered around their ability to make efficient use of the available manpower and varied resources of their empire.

Consult: Brundage, Burr Cartwright, *Empire of the Inca* (Norman: University of Oklahoma Press, 1963); Mason, J. Alden, *The Ancient Civilization of Peru* (Baltimore, Penguin, 1968); Rowe, John H., "Inca Culture at the Time of the Spanish Conquest," in *Handbook of South American Indians*, ed. Julian H. Steward, Smithsonian Institution, Bureau of American Ethnology, Bulletin 143, vol. 2, pp. 183–330, Washington, 1946.

—*Michael D. Olien, University of Georgia*

**Incest.** Minimally this term refers to mating between father and daughter, mother and son, brother and sister. In various societies it is extended to include larger numbers of consanguineal relatives, especially if the society is organized along the principle of lineages and clans.

See also Inbreeding; Incest avoidance (taboo); Marriage

**Incest Avoidance (Taboo).** Sexual intercourse between family members is prohibited almost universally. The limits of incest vary from culture to culture and depend directly on the society's kinship system and forms of social organization. Numerous theories have attempted to explain the taboo—some involve genetic damage due to inbreeding as the explanation; others invoke ethological or social arguments. Most popular is the explanation which views the incest taboo as a cultural invention promoting group exogamy (outmarriage) and thus ensuring alliances between otherwise unrelated human groups.

See also Incest; Marriage

**Indigenous Peoples.** Persons who are born in, reared in, and inhabit a specific country are called indigenous (in contradistinction to immigrants and temporary sojourners). Indigenous people are defined in terms of the laws of individual countries.

Consult: *Indigenous Peoples: Living and Working Conditions of Aboriginal Populations in Independent Countries* (Geneva: International Labour Office, 1963).

## Industrial Archaeology. *See* Archaeology.

## Industrialization.
This term refers to a process involving the growth of manufacturing industries in a hitherto predominantly agrarian or hunting/gathering society. Industrialization is characterized by standardized mass production techniques aimed at maximizing efficiency and monetary profit, predominant use of general-purpose money, the use of scientific technology in exploiting the environment, and the construction of ostensibly permanent buildings to house manufacturing enterprises. Variations of the Weberian concept of rationality have been used to describe the cultural ethos and many of the social relations of the society experiencing industrialization.

Industrialization often is thought to precipitate, or at least accompany, changes of varying degrees of magnitude in the ritual, social, and political life of the indigenous society. Sex roles may be altered, for example, or the bases for status assignment may change from primarily ascription to that of achievement.

Progress, modernity, and industrialization have, in the past, often been used interchangeably. Many studies of industrialization have been cast with an implicit or explicit evolutionary perspective. Frequently found also is the idea that industrialization is a necessary, albeit frequently insufficient, means for a society to achieve economic development. The concept of industrialization, and the theories of development which employ the term, are currently being criticized as neoevolutionary examples of Western ethnocentrism.

*See also* Development, economic; Modernization

Consult: Moore, Wilbert E., *The Impact of Industry* (Englewood Cliffs, N.J.: Prentice-Hall, 1965).

—*Paul C. Winther, Eastern Kentucky University*

## Infanticide.
The practice of killing a baby soon after birth has been reported from every continent and in both technologically simple and complex societies. Some of the reasons for putting infants to death have been eugenic (as in ancient Sparta), lack of desire for the child (especially females, as in old China), inability to provide support (ubiquitous), and psychological disturbance on the part of parents (child abuse).

*See also* Contraception and abortion

## Infantism. *See* Neoteny.

## Inference, Ethnographic. *See* Ethnographic analogy.

*Initiation into adulthood is celebrated with this "maturity dance" performed in traditional grass costume in Zululand, South Africa.*

## Inferential Statistics. *See* Statistical methods.

## Informants, Reliability of. *See* Reliability of informants.

## Initiation.
Ceremonies of initiation occur in all societies. The group conferring membership to a novice may be as diverse as a student fraternity in the United States, a men's house in New Guinea, an age grade in an African tribe, or a monastic order in Europe. In many societies initiation rites represent a ceremonial recognition of an individual's physical maturity and may involve genital mutilation, scarification, and similar modification of the body as well as changes in the initiate's dress and ornaments. Often the initiation requires a change of residence and the observation of certain temporary or permanent taboos.

Several cross-cultural studies on the sociological and psychological functions of initiation ceremonies have produced some of the soundest theories in cultural anthropology. These studies show that initiation ceremonies serve as an integrative ritual that reinforces the solidarity of a particular group and also as an adaptive psychological experience that dramatizes an individual's change of social status.

See also Rites of passage; Ritual
Consult: Koch, Klaus-Friedrich, "Sociogenic and Psychogenic Models in Anthropology: The Functions of Jalé Initiation," *Man* 9(4), 1974.

**Inkeles, Alex** (b. 1920). American sociologist who has analyzed social change and development, social psychology, and social aspects of economic development; his primary geographical area of interest is Soviet Russia.

**Innovation.** The psychological and social processes of creating new ideas and things are fundamental to all cultural change. Three basic positions on these innovative processes can be discerned. First is the popular view which considers only those innovations (inventions and discoveries) that become public and have a major impact on human life. Second is a normative view which defines innovation as desirable changes in belief and practice and asks why some communities reject them (Rogers and Shoemaker 1971). Third is a broad theoretical view which defines innovation as any idea, overt behavior, or concrete thing or practice which one or more individuals perceive as novel. This view incorporates the former two without the culture-bound assumption of the desirability of any or all novel things (Barnett 1953).

In origin every innovation is at first a complex, private, mental event. Thus much private thought and fantasy is innovative: it involves an analysis of existing ideas (prototypes), a recombination of their elements, and the creation of novel notions. As such, the capacity for innovativeness is a universal characteristic of all individuals. There is no special category of an inventive elite, although a wide range of individual differences is obvious, and some cultures encourage the public sharing of innovations.

The private innovative process may be so fleeting that an individual is quite unaware of it; or it may be a deliberate and conscious effort. It is when an individual, conscious of a new idea, communicates it to others that the possibility of cultural and social change occurs. The processes of communication, sharing, acceptance or rejection, modification, and institutionalization are themselves creative, innovative processes which often transform the original novel idea greatly.

See also Cultural change; Diffusion
Consult: Barnett, H. G., *Innovations: The Basis for Cultural Change* (New York: McGraw-Hill, 1963); Rogers, E. M., and Shoemaker, F. F., *Communication of Innovations* (New York: Free Press, 1971); Wallace, A. F. C., *Culture and Personality*, 2nd ed. (New York: Random House, 1971).

—James Clifton, University of Wisconsin, Green Bay

**Instincts.** This term, broadly used, refers to unlearned behavior occuring in all normal members of a species under identical conditions. In the past, the word *instinct* has been so widely applied to so many different aspects of animal and human behavior —ranging from the simple reflex to the sexual drive—that scientists have been obliged to refine their use of the concept. In general it may be said that the following minimal criteria must be met if a pattern of behavior is to be considered instinctive: (1) an instinct is genetically encoded, born into the organism and into all members of the same species, and cannot be unlearned; (2) unlike a simple reflex, an instinct is a complex bundle of behaviors which appears fully developed when first elicited (although an instinct may not be mature at birth); (3) an instinct is elicited by specific and unvarying stimuli; (4) instincts are goal-directed, typically toward the reduction of internal tension.

Although Sigmund Freud and some other psychologists have attributed various instincts to human beings, most social scientists do not find the term useful in the analysis of human behavior. The notion of instinct has little currency among anthropologists today.

See also Ethology; Genetics and behavior; Species-characteristic behavior; Territoriality
Consult: Beach, F. A., "The Descent of Instinct," *Psychological Review* 62:401–410, 1955.

—Ian Robertson, Cambridge University

**Institutions.** All known human societies have standard ways of doing things which consist of three major components: *norms* serving as goals and as guidelines for behavior, *roles* constituted by norms, and *patterned behavior* attached to the norms and roles. Behavior which is standardized in this manner is called institutionalized behavior, and the whole system of standardization of a behaviorial pattern is called an institution. These concepts appear to require that multiplicities of persons be engaged in the standard ways of doing things; that the actions involved be determined by interdependent norms, linked together and embedded in roles; and that there occur *different* roles or role sets in complementary relationships. Taxpaying may be cited as an institution exemplifying all these conditions. It is standardized, normative, behavioral. It involves, minimally, the role set taxpayer–tax collector and probably other roles such as tax beneficiary–treasurer. Moreover, there are multiplicities of persons widely dispersed territorially, there is action determined by norms in roles, and there is a common adherence (sometimes by coercion) to the polity even though the interests in paying and receiving taxes may be diverse.

There are, however, a number of ambiguities in the use of the term. First, not all behavior patterns are institutions, even if they are normatively governed (though this is hard to decide sometimes). Morning getting-up-bathroom-toothbrushing sequences are usually quite patterned for individuals and, maybe, similar for multiplicities of people; but they are scarcely thought of as institutions, because the role aspect is missing or attenuated.

Second, the term is often applied to an association such as the Smithsonian Institution (Washington D.C.) or an asylum, the usage appearing to refer to chartered organizations or even their physical plants such as buildings. (Driving past a cluster of large, commonly designed buildings, one often says "that looks like an institution"—e.g., an asylum.) The ambiguity, here, is that an association is an organization, but *doing things* by means of associating into organizations is an institution. Most actions performed by associations (once chartered) are institutions. Thus a group of people may found a corporation which, to fund itself, issues stock and sells a product in the market to make profit on which it pays taxes and dividends and with which it reinvests. Issuing stock, selling in the market, earning profit, paying taxes, paying dividends, and reinvesting are all institutions. In strict social science usage, the term *institution* should not be used to refer to associations, much less to physical plant.

Third, many behavior patterns which seem quite normative are not ordinarily considered institutions. Customs are the prime example. Though customs like hand-shaking and sweet sixteen parties all have normative guidelines and most involve some aspect of role relations, several limitations appear to be involved. The customs are mapped on very limited role sets; the customary actions occur for any given actor either only once or else sporadically and are not, per se, clearly linked to other normative or role-designated behaviors. Having shaken hands, the relationship stalls; if it develops, it does so not in terms of the handshake but of emerging role relations. A matter of scale also seems involved in customary matters—not enough actors, roles, repetition, or continuity to be called institutions.

Generally, then, the central notions of institution involve action attached to and controlled by the norms entailed in complex role sets and applying to multiplicities of persons over extended territory, since roles themselves are complexly constituted by both customary and jural aspects, unlike customs by themselves. However one defines law, the more or less explicitly formulated (written or unwritten) or formulable principles and codes which all societies seem to have shape the allowed and desired modes of action—that is, institutions—and provide guidelines for assessing the appropriateness of actions.

Many have attempted to classify institutions. Bronislaw Malinowski lists seven institutions which mostly revolve about basic human *biological needs* (e.g., the need for getting food produces the "commissariat"). Constantine Panunzio lists seven or eight institutions which apparently revolve about basic *sociocultural needs*. He does not attempt Malinowski's biological reductionism, which has been almost universally abandoned since diverse social orders and actions can be adapted to each of Malinowski's postulated needs: that is, there is no causal connection or isomorphy between sociocultural forms and biological needs. Categories of institutions are useful only if they relate to a theory of human society and culture—and specifically a theory of sociocultural function.

See also Pattern, behavior; Role; Role set; Units of study, sociocultural

Consult: Leeds, Anthony, "Some Problems in the Study of Class and the Social Order," in *Social Structure, Social Stratification and Mobility*, ed. A. Leeds (Washington: Pan American Union, 1967); MacIver, Robert M., and Page, Charles H., *Society: An Introductory Analysis* (New York: Rinehart, 1949); Malinowski, Bronislaw, *A Scientific Theory of Culture and Other Essays* (Chapel Hill: University of North Carolina Press, 1944); Panunzio, Constantine, *Major Social Institutions: An Introduction* (New York: Macmillan, 1939).

—Anthony Leeds, Boston University

**Integrative Function.** *See* Religion.

**Intelligence.** In everyday use this term denotes the ability of human beings and other higher animals to learn from experience and to solve problems presented by a changing environment.

Many psychologists, working in the psychometric tradition of Alfred Binet, Lewis Terman, and others, have claimed that intelligence can be measured scientifically by means of standard tests of scholastic aptitude (IQ tests). Such tests are designed so that scores will correlate with school achievement, and the psychometricians argue that school achievement must depend heavily on intelligence as we ordinarily conceive it. Therefore, they say, IQ test scores must also depend on, or at least correlate with, intelligence (see Herrnstein 1973).

This line of reasoning has been challenged by other researchers who argue that IQ tests do not measure intelligence at all. They claim instead that much of the variation in IQ scores reflects unequal treatment given by the schools to children from different social class backgrounds (see Gartner et al. 1974), not any differences in the children's mental abilities.

See also Genetics and intelligence; Intelligence quotient

Consult: Gartner, A., Greer, C., and Reissman, F., *The New Assault on Equality: I.Q. and Social Stratification* (New York: Harper & Row, 1974); Herrnstein, R. J., *I.Q. in the Meritocracy* (Boston: Little, Brown, 1973).

—Anthony Kroch, Temple University

**Intelligence Quotient (IQ).** This term designates the score received by a person on a standardized test of mental ability such as the Wechsler Intelligence Scale for Children or the Stanford-Binet test. These tests are designed to predict scholastic achievement. They do so adequately for the population as a whole but are much less reliable in individual cases.

There has been for some time a lively dispute among academics as to what psychological qualities are measured by IQ tests. Some psychologists claim that IQ tests are successful predictors of scholastic achievement because they measure native intelligence; others argue that the tests are successful predictors because the same social values are required for someone to do well on the test and in school.

See also Genetics and intelligence; Intelligence

**Internal Migration.** *See* Migration.

**International Phonetic Alphabet (IPA).** The International Phonetic Alphabet is a phonetic alphabet specifically designed to represent any human speech sound with a special symbol. A phonetic alphabet utilizes the principle of one sound to one symbol. Phonetic alphabets are used by linguists, educators, and people in speech to record notationally the way sound is actually produced. Many writing systems or orthographies do not accurately represent all the sounds of a language. Orthographies sometimes use the same symbol to represent several sounds or write letters that are not pronounced, such as the *k* in English *knife* or the *b* in *dumb*. Any student of French knows the difficulty of trying to read or write a language that is pronounced quite differently from the way it is written. If a language does not have a writing system, a linguist must have a way of writing down the sounds of that language and words in that language before she or he can begin to analyze it. Linguists may also use a phonetic alphabet to record differing pronunciations of the same word in different dialects, and speech pathologists may use it to record the pronunciations of individuals with speech difficulties. The process of recording sounds by using a phonetic alphabet is called *transcription*.

The IPA is one of several phonetic alphabets in use. It is used primarily by British

| | | | Bilabial | Labiodental | Dental | Alveolar | Alveopalatal | Dorsovelar | Uvular | Glottal |
|---|---|---|---|---|---|---|---|---|---|---|
| STOPS | Plain | vl. | p | | | t | tʸ | k | q | ʔ |
| | | vd. | b | | | d | dʸ | g | | |
| | Aspirated | vl. | pʰ | | | tʰ | | kʰ | | |
| | | vd. | | | | | | | | |
| | Affricated | vl. | | | | tˢ | tˢ̌ | | | |
| | | vd. | | | | dᶻ | dᶻ̌ | | | |
| | Laterally affricated | vl. | | | | tˡ | | | | |
| | | vd. | | | | dˡ | | | | |
| | Glottalized | vl. | p' | | | t' | | k' | | |
| | | vd. | | | | | | | | |
| | Labialized | vl. | pʷ | | | tʷ | | kʷ | | |
| | | vd. | bʷ | | | dʷ | | gʷ | | |
| FRICATIVES | Slit | vl. | | f | θ | | | x | | h |
| | | vd. | | v | δ | | | γ | | |
| | Grooved | vl. | | | | s | š | | | |
| | | vd. | | | | z | ž | | | |
| LATERALS | | vl. | | | | ḷ | | | | |
| | | vd. | | | | l | | | | |
| NASALS | | vl. | m̥ | | | n̥ | ñ̥ | ŋ | | |
| | | vd. | m | | | n | ñ | ŋ | | |
| RETROFLEX | | vl. | | | | | | | | |
| | | vd. | | | | γ | | | | |
| FLAP | | vl. | | | | | | | | |
| | | vd. | | | | ř | | | | |
| TRILLS | | vl. | | | | ř̥ | | | | |
| | | vd. | | | | ř | | | R | |

## MODIFIED INTERNATIONAL PHONETIC ALPHABET SYMBOLS FOR CONTOIDS

*The points of articulation shown in Fig. 7-5 are indicated along the top of this diagram. Along the lefthand side the categories of action performed by the articulatory apparatus are indicated.*

**Stop**—*stopping the air flow at the point of articulation. Plain stops are unmodified. Aspirated stops (h) allow air to escape forcefully after the release of the stopped air flow. Affricated stops (s, z) allow air to escape forcefully through the narrow slit made between the tongue and point of articulation after the release of the stopped air flow. Glottalized stops (') involve closing off the pharynx simultaneously with stopping the air flow at the point of articulation. Labialized stops involve "puckering" or rounding the lips as the air flow is released after the stop.*

**Fricative**—*confining the channel of air flow and thus producing a "rushing" sound due to air friction against the passage walls at the point of articulation. Slit fricatives are formed in a tight, horizontal slit between the tongue and the point of articulation (the tongue is kept quite flat). Grooved fricatives are formed by pushing up the edges of the tongue (pulling down the center line of the tongue) and forcing air through the groove that results at the point of articulation.*

**Lateral**—*articulating with the center of the tongue, directing the air flow laterally around the edges.*

**Nasal**—*closing off the mouth with the tongue and directing the air flow through the nasal passage exclusively.*

**Retroflex**—*articulating with the curled back tip of the tongue.*

**Flap**—*in a retroflex position, allowing the tip of the tongue to "slap" against the point of articulation.*

**Trill**—*allowing the tongue to vibrate as the air flow passes between it and the point of articulation.*

*All contoids may be either voiced (**vd.**) or voiceless (**vl.**)*

and European linguists, educators, and speech scientists. Many American linguists use a slightly different system known as the Americanist system, which was originally developed by the American linguist Edward Sapir. Both systems use characters drawn from the Roman alphabet and some special symbols. Diacritic symbols are used when necessary to modify the basic symbols.

The IPA has had a long process of development, beginning in 1886 with the founding of the International Phonetic Association in France. The association publishes a journal, *Le Mètre Phonétique,* which often includes discussions of new symbols that must be voted on by the membership before they are accepted. The primary purpose of the association was to develop a phonetic alphabet which would be accepted by all workers in language and which would provide one symbol for each sound that might occur in any human language. Prior to this time, people transcribed in a variety of conflicting ways, which meant that other readers often did not know which sound a character represented. The IPA systematized all transcriptions and cut through the chaos. But because the development of the IPA preceded contact with a lot of exotic languages spoken in different parts of the world, some new symbols did need to be developed over the years. The system is complete at the present time and provides a way of writing any speech sound that might be encountered in any of the world's languages. Anyone knowing the IPA can read something transcribed in it exactly as the word is pronounced.

Each symbol is tied to the method of production of the sound it represents. Thus the symbol [p]—written in brackets to indicate that it is a phonetic symbol rather than ordinary writing—always represents a sound that is made by closure of the two lips (bilabial), is made without vibration of the vocal cords (voiceless), and involves complete stoppage of the airstream coming through the vocal passages (stop). Methods of sound production are studied in a field known as articulatory phonetics. Vowels are classified by three main characteristics: tongue height (position of the tongue in a vertical dimension), tongue position (front to back), and lip rounding (or its absence). Consonants are classified by two dimensions: manner of articulation (how a sound is made) and point of articulation (front to back, position where the greatest constriction or stoppage of the airstream occurs).

The basic vowel dimensions can be combined with symbols to yield the cardinal vowel system. This represents eight cardinal vowels in terms of the dimensions discussed above. Each point on the chart is equidistant from every other vowel. Thus [i] is the highest front vowel, [u] is the highest back vowel, and [a] is the lowest front vowel.

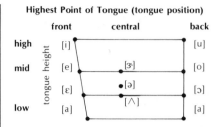

**Highest Point of Tongue (tongue position)**

Additional vowel symbols intermediate in height and position can be inserted between each set of cardinal vowels. The full chart would then look like this, with a key English word in which it is used:

[i] eat [it]                                    [u] tool [tul]

[3ʳ] fur [f3ʳ]

[I] bit [bIt]                                   [U] took [tUk]

[ə] soda [soUdə]

[ɛ] met [mɛt]                                  [o] note [not]

[ʌ] up [ʌp]

[æ] mat [mæt]

[a] palm [pam]                                 [ɔ] law [lɔ]

[ɑ] palm [pɑm]

Sometimes sounds are classified according to the degree of muscular tension involved in producing them. This distinction is known as tense versus lax, and certain pairs of English vowels may be differentiated on this basis: [i] tense and [I] lax, [u] tense and [U] lax.

A number of languages including English have diphthongs, or sequences of two vowels. These can be transcribed by using the symbols for each of the vowels: *how* [aU], high [aI], pail [eI].

The preceding IPA chart for consonants represents only the more common ones found in the world's languages. Many of the symbols have their ordinary English values, such as [b, p, k, f, v, m, n]. The symbol [s] represents the initial sound in *she* [si]; [e] is normally spelled *th* and is the first sound in *thing,* while the symbol [ð], also spelled *th,* occurs in *though.*

*See also* Alphabet; Phonetics

Consult: Abercrombie, David, *Elements of General Phonetics* (Chicago, Aldine, 1967); Fromkin, Victoria, and Rodman, Robert, *An Introduction to Language* (New York: Holt, 1974); Jones, Caniel, *An Outline of English Phonetics,* 8th ed. (Cambridge; Heffer, 1956).

—*Elizabeth A. Brandt, Arizona State University*

**Involuntary Migration.** See Migration.

**IQ.** *See* Intelligence quotient.

**Iron.** *See* Metal working.

**Irrigation.** The artificial use of water for agriculture by means of human technology when naturally available moisture (rainfall or seasonal flooding) is insufficient to sustain desired crop production.

*See also* Agriculture; Economics and subsistence; Technology

**Ivory.** Although this term is properly applied only to the tusks of Old World elephants, it has also been commonly employed in referring to the teeth of the walrus, seal, and killer whale of the Pacific. The material has not been widely used in the

*Terraced rice agriculture in Java. Very often agricultural food production requires large-scale irrigation, terracing, or drainage. These projects are frequently beyond the capacity of any one household to achieve; hence they necessitate some form of centralized planning, as well as a centrally organized work force to execute the plans. It is hardly surprising, then, that it is with the advent of agriculture that the state emerged.*

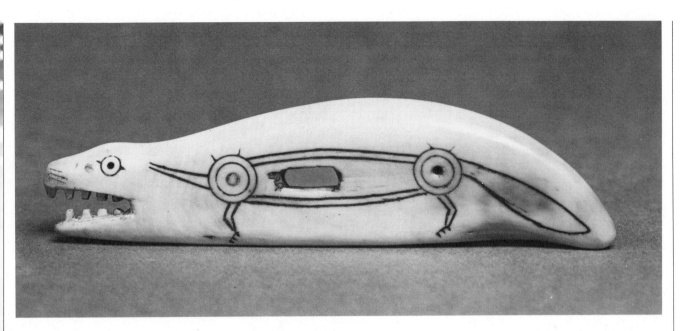

Above, Alaskan Eskimo carved ivory toggle in the shape of a seal with an incised design.

Below, Eskimo human figure made of ivory inlaid with beads, from Banks Island, Canada (c. 1825 AD).

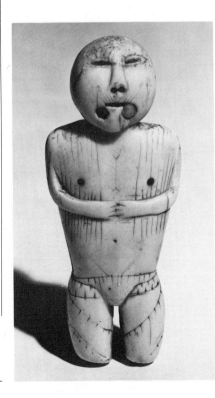

Americas, due to the northerly range of these creatures. Since prehistoric times, ivory ornaments, charms, and decorations have been produced in the Northwest, and this remains today as a major Eskimo craft. Ivory is less frequently worked in contemporary Northwest Coast Indian tribal art, although a few modern Indian artists use it for inlay. Wherever found, ivory (as a basic material) and objects made from it have always been regarded as extremely valuable.

Pendants, ornaments, charms, fetishes, and religious or power objects were all carved from ivory, pierced for suspension, and employed as body or costume decoration. Designs range from zoomorphic and anthropomorphic outline forms to simple or abstract linear gravings. Carvings are usually shallow cut, on thin sheets, with pierced cutouts; they are usually emphasized with linear designs.

The most notable examples of Amerindian ivory art are the shaman's charms and ornaments found among the Northwest Coast tribes—particularly the Tlingit, Niska,

Tsimshian, and Haida peoples—and the tremendous variety of toggles, ornaments, charms, realistic animal forms, and walrus tusk carvings so common among the Alaskan Eskimo. In Greenland, the *tupilak* carvings of the Eskimo are a popular creation for tourists, not unlike the *billiken* of Alaska. An occasional example of ivory carving is to be found in prehistoric Taino sites in the Caribbean area, particularly in Puerto Rico and Hispaniola.

See also Art of the Northwest Coast of North America

Consult: Dockstader, Frederick J., *Indian Art in America* (New York: New York Graphic Society, 1960); Hoffman, W. J., "The Graphic Art of the Eskimo," *U.S. National Museum Annual Report*, 739–968, 1895; Inverarity, R. Bruce, *Art of the Northwest Coast Indians* (Berkeley: University of California Press, 1950).

—Frederick J. Dockstader, Museum of the American Indian

**Jajmani System.** The hereditary functional interrelation of castes in a Hindu Village is called the jajmani system. The priest, bard, accountant, and goldsmith castes are served by the other castes and are considered their

*A social organization, such as the Hindu caste system, which gives each occupational group a fixed standing within the community, must of necessity have certain patterns of behavior which enable each caste to maintain its own status and satisfactorily engage in relationships with others. Among these behavior patterns are marriage, social intercourse in matters of eating, drinking, and smoking, conventions of untouchability and unapproachability, and service interrelationships, with which we are concerned in this study. We find, therefore, that in the service interrelationships, except where social disabilities arise, as in the cases of the lower castes and non-Hindus such as Muslims, each caste renders service within the range noted in the following table, limited or unlimited, to each of the other castes. (This is adapted from W. H. Weber: The Hindu Jajmani System, Lucknow Publishing House, Lucknow, 1936.)*

jajmans or clients. In reciprocity the above castes perform services for the others.

See also Caste; Social stratification

Consult: Wiser, William Henricks, *The Hindu Jajmani System* (Lucknow, India: Lucknow Publishing House, 1936).

**Jakobson, Roman** (b. 1896). Jakobson was a leader, along with Nikolas S. Troubetzkoy (1890–1938), in the Prague school of linguistics. This school believes that the structure of a language cannot be described merely by constructing a catalog of its sounds; rather, it is the (contrastive) relationships between the sounds that are important. These relationships are not, however, conscious in the minds of the speakers.

See also Prague school of linguistics

**Jarmo.** *See* Qalat Jarmo.

**Java Man.** *See* Homo erectus.

**Jay Dolhinow, Phyllis** (b. 1933). American primatologist whose major work includes field studies in Asia and Africa, primarily on North Indian langurs, and research on socialization and play.

**Jennings, Jesse David** (b. 1909). Archaeologist who has made important contribu-

table 1

## LIST OF CASTES, KARIMPUR

| | | |
|---|---|---|
| 1. Brahman | priest and teacher | Brahman and related |
| 2. Bhat | family bard and genealogist | Kshatriya and related |
| 3. Kyasth | accountant | Sudra |
| 4. Sunar | goldsmith | |
| 5. Mali | florist | |
| 6. Kachhi | vegetable grower | |
| 7. Lodha | rice grower | |
| 8. Barhai | carpenter (one family does iron smithy work and is called Lohar-iron worker, although not of that caste) | |
| 9. Nai | barber | |
| 10. Kahar | water-bearer | |
| 11. Gadariya | shepherd | |
| 12. Bharbhunja | grain parcher | |
| 13. Darzi | seamster | |
| 14. Kumhar | potter | |
| 15. Mahajan | tradesman | |
| 16. Teli | oil presser | |
| 17. Dhobi | washerman | Outcaste |
| 18. Dhanuk | mat maker | |
| 19. Chamar | leather worker | |
| 20. Bhangi | sweeper and cesspool cleaner | |
| 21. Faqir | hereditary Muslim beggar | |
| 22. Manihar | Muslim glass-bangle seller | |
| 23. Dhuna | Muslim cotton carder | |
| 24. Tawaif | Muslim dancing girl | |

table 2

## OCCUPATIONS AND SERVICING

| Occupation | Is served by castes | Serves castes |
|---|---|---|
| 1. Priest and teacher | 1–24 | 1–19 |
| 2. Bard and genealogist | 1–24 | 1–19 |
| 3. Accountant | 1–24 | 1–24* |
| 4. Goldsmith | 1–24 | 1–24 |
| 5. Florist | 1–24 | 1–24 |
| 6. Vegetable grower | 1–24 | 1–24 |
| 7. Rice grower | 1–24 | 1–24 |
| 8. Carpenter | 1–24 | 1–24 |
| 9. Barber | 1–24 | 1–15, 22, 23 |
| 10. Water-bearer | 1–24 | 1–19 |
| 11. Shepherd | 1–24 | 1–24 |
| 12. Grain parcher | 1–24 | 1–24 |
| 13. Seamster | 1–24 | 1–24 |
| 14. Potter | 1–24 | 1–24 |
| 15. Tradesman | 1–24 | 1–24 |
| 16. Oil presser | 1–24 | 1–24 |
| 17. Washerman | 1–24 | 1–19, 21–24 |
| 18. Mat maker | 1–24 | 1–24 |
| 19. Leather worker | 1–24 | 1–24 |
| 20. Sweeper and cesspool cleaner | 4–8, 11–16, 18–24 | 1–24 |
| 21. Muslim beggar | 4–24 | 1–16, 21–24 |
| 22. Muslim glass-bangle seller | 4–24 | 1–24 |
| 23. Muslim cotton carder | 4–24 | 1–24 |
| 24. Muslim dancing girl | 4–24 | 1–16, 21–24 |

*As the servant of government

JAJMANI SYSTEM, TABLE 2

*These service relationships in Table 2 reveal that the priest, bard, accountant, goldsmith, florist, vegetable grower, etc., are served by all of the other castes. They are the jajmans of these other castes. In turn, each of these castes has a form of service to perform for the others. Each in turn is master. Each in turn is servant. Each has its own clientele comprising members of different castes, which is its "jajmani" or "birt." This system of interrelatedness in service within the Hindu community is called the Hindu "Jajmani system." (Adapted from W. H. Weber:* The Hindu Jajmani System, *Lucknow Publishing House, Lucknow, 1936.)*

tions to the understanding of North American prehistory through research in the eastern Great Basin, the Southwest, and Guatemala.

**Jensen, Arthur R.** (b. 1923). Educational psychologist Arthur Jensen is a member of the faculty of the Institute of Learning at the University of California at Berkeley. He is best known as an advocate of the theory that people's intelligence is largely determined by their genetic inheritance and that blacks are on the average less intelligent than whites. His first explicit public statement of this view came in 1969 in an article in the *Harvard Educational Review* entitled "How Much Can We Boost I.Q. and Scholastic Achievement?" The article has provoked a torrent of criticism by geneticists, psychologists, and anthropologists who are skeptical of his scholarship and concerned over what they regard as the social dangers inherent in his racial views.

*See also* Genetics and intelligence; Scientific racism

**Jericho.** This tell site, located by a spring in the Jordan valley, was excavated by Sellin and Watzinger (1906–1909), Garstang (1930–1936), and Kathleen Kenyon (1952–1958) among others. It contains the following periods of occupation: Mesolithic (Natufian, 9000 BC), prepottery Neolithic, pottery Neolithic, Chalcolithic, and Bronze Age (early, middle, late). The site is important for two major reasons. First, the proto-Neolithic levels document transition from a nomadic to a settled way of life thought (by Kenyon) to be coincident with the adoption or development of agriculture (although there is no

*Aerial view of excavations at Jericho, Jordan.*

proof of this). Second, the prepottery Neolithic occupations (7825–6770 BC) are noteworthy for a permanent settlement covering some 10 acres with a massive defensive system comprising a 12-foot-high wall, towers, and a rock-cut ditch. The defensive structures and the town itself together imply a considerable labor force directed by some form of central authority; this and the probable accumulation of wealth (surplus goods) by the inhabitants are indications of a degree of social complexity not previously suspected at this early time range. Prepottery Neolithic inhabitants practiced a mixed herding-farming/hunting/gathering economy with primary evidence for domestic emmer wheat, two-row barley, and dog (prepottery Neolithic), as well as einkorn wheat, goats, and possibly sheep (late prepottery Neolithic). Cattle (pottery Neolithic) are present. Wild boar, gazelle, canids, and felids were hunted throughout.

See also Cities, development of; Domestication of plants and animals; Neolithic
Consult: Singh, P., *Neolithic Cultures of Western Asia* (New York: Seminar Press, 1974).

**Jespersen, Jens Otto Harry** (1860–1943). A Danish linguist whose research dealt with the close connection between linguistic form and contents and the idea of progress in language, Jespersen wrote *Language: Its Nature, Development and Origin* (1922).

**Jewelry.** *See* Adornment.

**Joint Family.** A family composed of two or more married brothers or sisters and their families—that is, an extended family composed of families linked together by sibling ties.

See also Family, the

**Joking Relationships.** Joking relationships, which are most often associated with the prescribed and proscribed etiquette of kinship relations, are especially characteristic of many North American Indian tribes. These involved prescribed joking between relations—particularly in-laws. The joking takes the form of sharp teasing, obscene references, and derogatory allusions. Generally the kinfolk involved are those of the opposite sex who are potential mates. Thus in a society encouraging sororal polygyny, a man has a joking relation with his wife's

sisters. However, whole clans and phratries might also be obligated to abuse and belittle one another in a suggestive and obscene fashion.

See also Joking, ritualized; Social organization; Social structure

**Joking, Ritualized.** This term refers to a situation in which some categories of people are allowed privileged behavior with people belonging to another category who are enjoined from taking offense. In many societies, for example, a person is allowed to take the greatest liberties with his or her grandparents—teasing them, calling them by familiar names, pretending to steal from them, and so on.

A. R. Radcliffe-Brown regarded joking relations as primarily a mechanism to maintain distance, but recent work has criticized this approach. Many of these criticisms are summarized in Richard Howell's *Teasing Relationships* (1973). Recent scholars have emphasized the promotion of closeness as an integral part of the joking. Some have preferred to refer to the relationship as one of licensed or privileged familiarity, following the lead of Robert Lowie's earlier work.

See also Kinship; License, cultural

**Jones, Sir William** (1746–1794). Orientalist and jurist who essentially initiated comparative linguistics by recognizing the existence of the Indo-European languages (through identifying affinities among Sanskrit, Greek, Latin, etc.), and their descent from common ancestry—an evolutionary conception.

**Joos, Martin George** (b. 1907). A linguist and Germanist who retired from the University of Toronto in 1972, Joos has done lexicography, linguistic theory, and the history of linguistics in North America.

**Jung, Carl Gustav** (1875–1961). Jung, a Swiss psychiatrist, founded the school of analytical psychology, which stressed individuation, a process whereby an individual's psyche can reach its full maturity. He believed that religious development was a necessary part of this process. Jung is also known for his concept of the collective unconscious and his theory of psychological types, in which he defined extroverted and introverted orientation. He was also a leader in the psychotherapeutic approach in treating schizophrenia. It was Jung who coined the term *complexes* and developed a word association test. Like Sigmund Freud, with whom he collaborated from 1907 until 1913, he was interested in the symbolic meaning of dreams, but he disagreed with many of Freud's theories in other areas. Although primarily interested in the human psyche, Jung had a wide range of interests that embraced archaeology, zoology, mythology, mysticism, and alchemy.

*See also* Collective unconscious

**Junod, Henri Alexandre** (1863–1934). Protestant missionary and ethnographer who wrote about many African tribes, including the Thonga; his *Life of a South African Tribe* (1913) is a functionalist account of a people.

**Jurisprudence, Comparative.** See Comparative jurisprudence.

**Kardiner, Abram** (b. 1891). A psychiatrist and psychoanalyst who studied under Sigmund Freud, Kardiner is known for his psychodynamic approach to the study of group character based on the concept of basic personality.

*See also* Basic personality

**Katz, Jerrold J.** (b. 1932). An American transformational linguist who teaches at M.I.T., Katz has investigated the philosophy and structure of language and developed an integrated theory of linguistic description.

**Kay, Paul** (b. 1934). Linguist noted for his work on ethnosemantics and mathematical anthropology, especially for his research on the evolution of basic color terms.

**Kenyon, Kathleen Mary** (b. 1906). A British archaeologist known for her excavations at Jericho and Jerusalem, Kenyon has been concerned with the origin of plant and animal domestication in the Near East.

**Kibbutz.** This Hebrew term (plural: kibbutzim), "gathering" or "company," refers to a socialist, collective settlement in Israel with strong emphasis on communal life and values. The kibbutz is but one form of cooperative agricultural village in Israel (others are the *moshav ovdim* and *moshav shittufi*); it is collective in the organization of work, ownership of all resources, and living arrangements.

Most kibbutzim emphasize certain values. Among these work, especially physical work, is paramount: no hired help is allowed, although outsiders may join communal life temporarily in some communities. Other values regarded highly are public ownership of all resources, social and economic equality with some consideration for individual needs, and individual liberty combined with the moral value of the group. The kibbutz "strives for complete harmony of the individual and the group in every sphere of life" (Spiro 1971:10).

Seeking political and ideological conformity, kibbutzim deemphasize all but the formal and necessary functions of the family. All the community's children live and eat together and visit their parents for only a few hours a day. The family is not a unit of production, consumption, or education.

Politically socialist leaning, the kibbutz may be either pro-Marxist or anti-Marxist, pro-Soviet or anti-Soviet. Some of the original kibbutzim were natural social adaptations to the unusual natural, social, and political environment of Palestine (Israel) whereas later ones were organized on the basis of preconceived ideals, not unlike utopian communities.

Consult: Spiro, Melford, *Kibbutz: Venture in Utopia* (New York: Schocken Books, 1971).
—Suzanne Griffin, Catholic University

**Kidder, Alfred Vincent** (1885–1963). Kidder is one of the scholars most responsible for the development of American archaeology as a scientific discipline. His early work in the American Southwest pioneered in the analysis of pottery sequences for historical reconstruction. From 1915 to 1929 he directed a major excavation at Pecos Pueblo, New Mexico, on the basis of which he definitively established the main outlines of Southwest prehistory. In 1929, Kidder was appointed director of the Carnegie Institution's research on the Maya of Mexico and Guatemala, and for twenty-one years he

*Kibbutz Ein Geddi on the Dead Sea, Israel.*

guided an important interdisciplinary program of Maya archaeology.

Consult: Woodbury, Richard B., *Alfred V. Kidder* (New York: Columbia University Press, 1973).

**Killing.** *See* Murder.

**Killing, Ritual.** In its most classic definition, ritual killing concerns itself with the intentional death of a human or animal in the course of a ceremony or ritual in honor of a god in order to satisfy a particular need of a people. Theological philosophy and specific symbolic meaning vary from society to society, yet the basic concept of reciprocity between humans and the gods appears to be a common factor.

During the course of cultural evolution, people's relationship to gods and the spirit forces of the universe was often reaffirmed or brought under control by an act of ritual sacrifice. Ritual killing takes many forms, however, and it is not always related to the taking of life, human or animal. In some societies a mock ritual killing is enacted, complete with burial, in which the symbolism of death substitutes for the taking of life. Quite often, too, objects imbued with special importance are thought to have power and life, and destruction of such objects can be subsumed under an extended notion of ritual killing in certain instances.

*—Art Einhorn, Jefferson Community College*

**Kindred.** This extended category of kin found in bilateral societies consists of consanguineal relatives in both ascending and descending generations. The kindred membership differs for every sibling set, since it is an ego-centered social element.

*See also* Kinship

**Kinesics.** Kinesics is the study of how body motion (sometimes also called *body language*) is used to communicate cultural messages as part of nonverbal communication. Ray Birdwhistell pioneered the scientific study of body posture and gesture. He developed a model derived from linguistic theory to describe the basic units involved. The minimal unit is a *kine*. Kines are organized into classes known as *kinemes*. Groups of kinemes form longer units known as

*kinemorphs.* The use of these units and their combinations enables a kinesicist to use a minimal number of basic units to record all the thousands of body movements possible and to begin to determine their meanings. Physiologists estimate that there are over 20,000 different possible facial expressions, but Birdwhistell (1970:99) has been able to isolate thirty-two significant kinemes in the head and face area. There are three kinemes of head nod—the one nod, the two nod, and the three nod—each of which has a different function. One nod encourages a speaker in America. Three nods may make him hesitate or change the subject. As research continues, kinesics is attempting to correlate body motion, speech, and paralanguage or tone-of-voice phenomena.

The field of kinesics has provided a number of insights and corrected many misconceptions about body communication. Each society in a sense selects and uses a minimal number of significant motions. These motions are learned, and children acquire the capacity to use and read them very early. Birdwhistell (1970:8) estimates that fewer than a hundred symbols are needed to record any kinesic subject. Research has determined that there are no universal body motions, facial expressions, or gestures which provoke the same response (Birdwhistell 1970:34). Even smiling, which does occur in a physical sense worldwide, is used to convey a variety of meanings—such as embarrassment, friendliness, or a warning. Nor do gestures or expressions always indicate a physical or emotional state. People are frequently unaware of their own gestures. Kinesic markers function in speech to stop and start interactions and also to indicate whether a speaker is serious, joking, or means the opposite of the spoken message.

Kinesics is an extremely new field which promises to help us understand how we communicate.

*See also* Birdwhistell, Ray L.; Communication, nonverbal

Consult: Birdwhistell, Ray L., *Kinesics and Context* (Philadelphia: University of Pennsylvania Press, 1970).

*—Elizabeth Brandt, Arizona State University*

**Kinship.** This term refers to a social relationship linking people through genealogical lines. The links connect parent to child in a chain that extends back to ancestors and

forward to descendants. Kin relationships are also called consanguineal or blood relations because kinsfolk frequently are thought, in some mystical sense, to share the same blood or vital essence.

In a more general sense the anthropological study of kinship systems is concerned with the social systems that are built up with consanguineal ties as well as ties of marriage and the relations of affinity (in-law relationships) that marriages create. Though kinship is conceptualized in "natural" biological terms, kin systems are cultural systems and their structure varies widely throughout the world.

**Importance of Kinship.** The study of kinship has long been one of the central concerns of anthropology because all societies recognize kinship relations of some kind. Even the most industrialized societies retain an important core of kinship and family organizations. And most small societies are organized largely or entirely on the basis of kinship. In these societies virtually everyone may be considered kin and be treated as such even if the exact genealogical relationship cannot be established. The rights and obligations of kinship may underlie all social, economic, and political relationships so that study of any aspect of such a society must entail an understanding of the system of kinship.

**Descent.** All societies recognize that there are lasting ties between parents and their legitimate children. This principle of descent is frequently elaborated into a set of cultural rules that is used to organize a society into groups. Rules of descent may be defined in various ways. When descent is traced only from fathers to their children, and not from mothers, it is called *patrilineal* descent. In the United States family names are inherited patrilineally. In other societies members of a patrilineage may be collective owners of property or bound to obligations of mutual defense or economic cooperation.

Just as groups of descendants from a male ancestor may constitute a patrilineage, in matrilineal societies groups are defined by virtue of descent traced through females. The potential members of a matrilineage are all people, male and female, who have descended through the female line from a female founding ancestor.

In yet other societies people may trace descent through both male and female ancestors and each person may elect to join

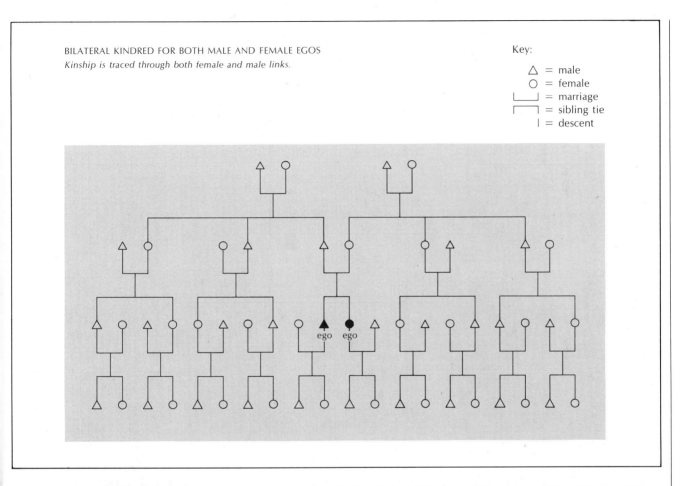

BILATERAL KINDRED FOR BOTH MALE AND FEMALE EGOS
*Kinship is traced through both female and male links.*

Key:

△ = male
○ = female
└─┘ = marriage
┌─┐ = sibling tie
│ = descent

the descent group of either their mother or that of their father. The members of a *cognatic* descent group are descended from an ancestor (or ancestress) through any combination of male or female links.

A few societies have a rule of *double descent* in which people claim membership in patrilineages for some purposes and for others claim membership in their matrilineages. Both lineages coexist but are relevant to different circumstances.

Finally, some societies, like our own, have a rule of *bilateral descent* which holds that one descends from father and mother alike. A rule of bilateral descent does not produce a descent group which is traced downward from a founding ancestor but rather a *kindred* which is traced bilaterally upward from each set of siblings.

**Complementary Filiation.** Where unilineal descent prevails, its principal rule of descent is complemented with other corollary and contingent rules which make its actual application vary according to circumstances. Even under a strict rule of patrilineal descent a person will have kinship ties to his or her mother's kin. The ties that balance or complement the primary rule of patrilineal descent are called ties of *complementary filiation* and are found, *mutatis mutandis,* in some matrilineal societies as well.

**Kinship as Cultural Rules.** At this point it should be stressed that rules of kinship do not necessarily predict what people will actually do. Rules of kinship are not inviolable commandments or mechanical templates for a society. They are, rather, a conceptualization of how people relate to one another

and how they ought to relate. The relationship between the cultural concepts of a social system and actual social behavior is always problematical. The concepts may be used to determine behavior in some cases, to rationalize it retrospectively in others, or be ignored in yet others.

One must also carefully avoid confusing the biology of bisexual reproduction with kinship as a system of social status and role definitions. Kinship is thought of in ostensibly biological terms, and most people hold their rules of kinship to be natural and proper for human beings. But when, for example, a society considers a woman or perhaps a spirit to be a child's father it is not a statement of biological fact. It is the social role of father that is being considered, not the biological father.

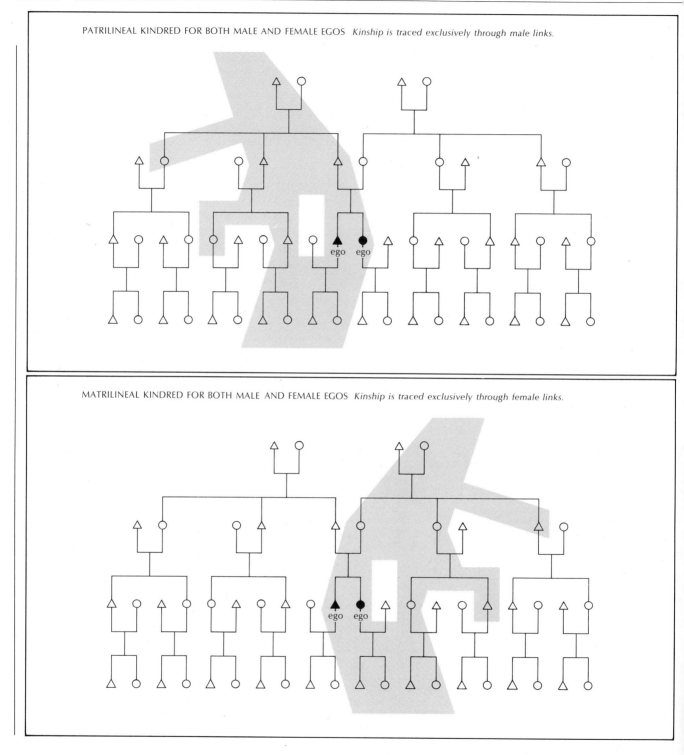

PATRILINEAL KINDRED FOR BOTH MALE AND FEMALE EGOS *Kinship is traced exclusively through male links.*

MATRILINEAL KINDRED FOR BOTH MALE AND FEMALE EGOS *Kinship is traced exclusively through female links.*

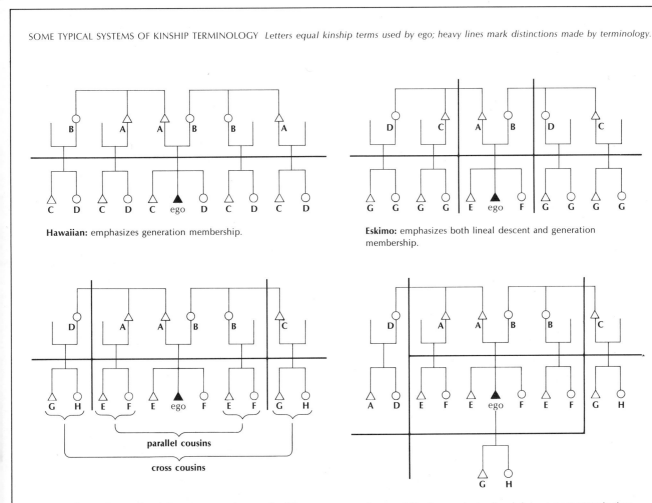

SOME TYPICAL SYSTEMS OF KINSHIP TERMINOLOGY *Letters equal kinship terms used by ego; heavy lines mark distinctions made by terminology.*

**Hawaiian:** emphasizes generation membership.

**Eskimo:** emphasizes both lineal descent and generation membership.

**Iroquois:** emphasizes lineal descent, generation membership, and the distinction between cross and parallel cousins (and thus also cross and parallel aunts and uncles).

**Crow and Omaha:** emphasize lineal descent more strongly than generation membership; maintain distinction between cross and parallel cousins. These two systems of terminology are mirror images of each other: **Crow** is matrilineal, **Omaha** patrilineal. Illustrated here is the **Crow** terminology as used by a male ego.

As a general rule a society will designate kinspeople by terms that reflect the salient social characteristics of different types of people. People with common social characteristics will be classified together. Thus it is common in societies organized in lineages that a person's father and father's brothers ("uncles" in our terminology) will be terminologically classified together as coequal members of their lineage and will be distinguished from mother's brothers who are not. The terms of kinship classification may serve as a rough guide to social structure.

**Kinship and Adaptation.** Organizations do not exist for their own sake, but organize people for a purpose. Kinship systems are an aspect of a society's general adaptation to the physical and social environment, and they change as a people adjusts to a changed adaptation of a certain society.

**Fictive Kinship.** Many societies elaborate their kinship systems with the addition of formalized relations modeled on kin relations. Fictive kin ties such as blood brotherhood, godparenthood, or coparenthood (e.g., the *compadrazco* of Spain and Spanish America) allow people to supplement their kin relations with additional kinlike ties.

*See also* Clan; Complementary filiation; Family, the; Kinship and alliance; Kinship and descent; Kinship terminologies; Lineage; Social organization

Consult: Fox, Robin, *Kinship and Marriage*

(Baltimore: Penguin, 1967); Graburn, Nelson H. H., *Readings in Kinship and Social Structure* (New York: Harper & Row, 1971); Keesing, Roger M., *Kin Groups and Social Structure* (New York: Holt, 1949).

—Henry F. Schwarz, Ohio State University

**Kinship and Alliance.** In recent years, the focus of kinship studies has been broadened to include alliance theory as well as descent theory. Alliance theory is based on the belief that exogamy should be regarded as a positive marriage rule which governs the exchange of women between descent groups. Such exchange provides for the articulation of segments of the society with women as links between them. While descent theory centers on the ways in which people are incorporated into descent groups, alliance theory is concerned with the organic solidarity of the society—with the affiliation of groups through marriage.

See also Kinship; Kinship and descent; Marriage

Consult: Scheffler, Harold W., "Kinship and Alliance," in *Handbook of Social and Cultural Anthropology*, ed. J. Honigmann (Chicago: Rand McNally, 1973).

—*Richard L. Stone, California State University, Los Angeles*

**Kinship and Descent.** Kinship is not the result of or synonomous with descent. Kinship is a *relationship* based on one or more parent-child links (filiation), marriage links (affinity), or a combination of the two. Descent is a *principle* guiding or arising out of a series of parent-child links. It has been argued, however, that since descent entitles one to membership in a social group (e.g., descent group), kinship terminological systems can be described as the result of the solidarity of the group. That is, classificatory kinship terms can be viewed as labels which apply to a category of kin by virtue of the fact that those kin would all be members of the same descent group. Descent theory postulates that descent is the independent variable which generates the organization of the kinship system, specifically the terminological system.

See also Descent

Consult: Buchler, Ira R., and Selby, Henry A., *Kinship and Social Organization* (New York: Macmillan, 1968).

—*Lilah Pengra, Kenyon College*

**Kinship Relationships.** See Kinship.

**Kinship Terminologies.** Although every known society has a kinship terminology, not every society uses the same system: different systems group together under one label different sets of relatives. Yet no kinship terminological system is entirely unique. There are a limited number of general patterns which occur in widely separated parts of the world. Thus it is not possible to explain the similarities in terms of historical borrowing; rather, kinship terminologies seem to be very closely tied to forms of social structure.

The primary goal in studying kin terminology is to explain the existence of structurally similar or equivalent systems. Since every system is slightly different in various particulars, the first step in the explanation is to develop a general typology of terminological systems.

Lewis Henry Morgan developed the distinction between *classificatory* and *descriptive* systems. Although this broad typology instigated the analytic study of kinship, it is too general to be of any explanatory value. The distinction between classificatory and descriptive (i.e., between merging or distinguishing lineals and collaterals) has been retained but only as one of several other factors.

Terminological systems are now also classified with respect to whether they distinguish, for instance, among generations, between sexes, and between cross and parallel cousins. The most well known and widely used typology of kinship terminologies is cousin-based.

Creating typologies is not, however, the end of the study of kinship but merely the means by which other, and perhaps explanatory, variables can be isolated. If, for example, all the societies using one type of kin terminological system also live in similar climates, practice similar technologies, or have similar marriage or postmarital residence rules, then perhaps associated traits explain the similarities among the kin terminological systems of unrelated societies.

There are currently three main theories, two of which (descent theory and alliance theory) have been widely, and sometimes wildly, debated. All too often the two theories have been assumed to be in opposition. They are not, however, mutually exclusive explanations. A moderate view of the topic is that all three theories are correct in some respects. Therefore the future of kinship studies will probably tend toward a theory which incorporates elements of all three contemporary approaches.

The first theory is broadly *neoevolutionary*. Specifically, it approaches the explanation of similarities among kinship terminological systems from the point of view of cultural ecology. Quite simply, the hypothesis is that people who live together and work together will tend to be terminologically grouped together. This hypothesis seems to be particularly alluring when applied to herding technologies where solidarity among males who herd cattle together would be more efficient than atomization of the work group.

The second theory, *descent theory*, hypothesizes that descent, and by extension descent groups, explain the variation in terminological systems since kin terms would categorize relatives of shared descent. The third theory, *alliance theory*, contends that marriage rules, particularly rules which by their operation link two or more social groups (usually descent groups), explain the variation in terminological systems since kin terms would categorize marriageable relatives.

The element common to all three theories is the assumption that relatives called by the same term have something in common—either in terms of activities (work parties), rights and responsibilities (corporate descent groups), or expected behavior (prospective spouses). This assumption is a generalization of the well-accepted correlation between kin terms and behavior. People whom ego calls by the same terms are behaved toward in similar ways. It is not unusual for an anthropologist to find this theory clearly recognized and formulated by the people he or she is studying (see Chagnon 1968).

In addition to the contemporary theories regarding the explanation of patterns in kinship terminologies, a great deal of work has been accomplished in understanding the semantic organization of specific terminological systems. The early, and still common, method for studying a specific kin terminology is to draw a genealogical grid with all the logically possible combinations of sex (male and female individuals), generation (parent-child links), and affinity (marriage links). Kin terms are then applied to each logically possible individual on the chart from the point of view of a single individual (traditionally labeled "ego"). This method is inadequate and sometimes distorting, since not all of the logically possible genealogical positions are considered to be filled by kin in a society.

The recent thrust in the study of kin terminologies is away from the purely descriptive and toward a more analytic approach—componential analysis. Componential analysts (e.g., Tyler 1969) attempt to diagram the *relationships* among kin terms rather than simply identifying the bits of meaning, or sememes, of each term. In American kin terminology, for example, the following table would apply (the third column is extremely simplified for the sake of clarity).

| | Sex* | Collaterality† | Generation |
|---|---|---|---|
| Mother | F | L | 1 |
| Father | M | L | 1 |
| Sister | F | L | 2 |
| Brother | M | L | 2 |
| Aunt | F | C | 1 |
| Uncle | M | C | 1 |
| Cousin | F/M | C | 2 |
| Daughter | F | L | 3 |
| Son | M | L | 3 |

*M = male; F = female.
†L = lineal; C = collateral.

Each term is uniquely defined by its particular combination of features, yet each term shares one or more features with one or more other terms. Componential analysis has not yet progressed beyond specific systems or limited comparisons. It is possible, however, that componential analysis will provide a new typology which will lead to the explanations for the similarities as well as the differences among terminological systems.

*See also* Classificatory kinship term; Componential analysis; Kinship; Kinship and alliance; Kinship and descent; Morgan, Lewis Henry
Consult: Chagnon, Napoleon, *Yanomamö: The Fierce People* (New York: Holt, 1968); Tyler, Stephen (ed.), *Cognitive Anthropology*, part 3 (New York: Holt, 1969).
—*Lilah Pengra, Kenyon College*

**Kinship Terms.** *See* Kinship terminologies.

*Clyde Kluckhohn*

**Kluckhohn, Clyde Kay Maben** (1905–1960). Major figure in American anthropology who made important contributions to the field of culture and personality, Navajo studies, and the concept of culture.

**Kluckhohn, Florence Rockwood** (b. 1905). A sociologist and widow of the late Clyde Kluckhohn, she has coauthored research with him, especially on value orientations and the Navajo Indians.

**Kohlberg, Lawrence** (b. 1927). Harvard psychologist noted for his application of cognitive developmental theory to various areas of psychology, notably sex role acquisition and moral development.

*See also* Developmental school of psychology; Moral development; Stages of moral development

**Kraal.** A stockaded village and an enclosure for the safekeeping of cattle characteristic of a number of South African tribes.

**Krader, Lawrence** (b. 1919). Cultural anthropologist who has contributed theoretical insights on the formation of the early state and ethnographic data on the societies of Central Asia.

**Krieger, Alex Donny** (b. 1911). An archaeologist interested in early peoples in the New World, Krieger has hypothesized an early pre-Columbian "preprojectile" stage which predates the knowledge of pressure flaking.

**Kroeber, Alfred L.** (1876–1960). Cultural anthropologist, ethnohistorian, and linguist, Kroeber has often been considered the dean of American anthropologists. He was probably the last anthropologist whose interests and contributions extended over the entire range of anthropological subjects, including cultural ecology, folklore, kinship, and prehistory. He helped stimulate the development of academic anthropology and its emergence as a professional field of scholarly investigation. His most influential book, *Anthropology* (1923), was a major source from which scholars in other fields as well as the general public learned about anthropology.

*See also* Anthropology; Ethnography; Ethnology; Linguistics
Consult: Beals, Ralph, "Kroeber, Alfred L.," in *Encyclopedia of the Social Sciences* (New York: Macmillan, 1968); Kardiner, Abram, and Preble, Edward, *They Studied Man* (New York: New American Library, 1961).

**Ku Klux Klan.** An American version of the worldwide phenomenon of secret societies, the Klan developed after the Civil War in order to deprive blacks of their rights and to restore, insofar as possible, the power of the old southern establishment. After the original objectives had been achieved by 1880, the Klan ended its existence.

In 1915 a second Klan was organized with headquarters in Atlanta, Georgia. The purpose of this organization was to assert "native American" values against the new immigration of eastern and southern Europeans and the increasing desire of blacks for equality. The Klan became a powerful political force in the 1920s with branches throughout the Midwest, West, and parts of the East, as well as in the South. It continues to attack Amerindian groups, Catholics, and Jews as well as American blacks.

**Kula Ring.** The Kula institution, a trade route established among the island groups immediately to the east and north of New Guinea, was first discovered, described, and analyzed by Bronislaw Malinowski as a result of his fieldwork on the Trobriand Islands. The reciprocal exchange of *soulava* (necklaces) for *mwali* (white cowrie shell armbands) operates in a circle comprising all the islands. *Soulava* travels in a clockwise direction, *mwali* counterclockwise, between participating island populations. Extended sailing expeditions last for weeks and include trading, ritual feasts, and ceremonies where myths and legends about the origins of Kula are recounted.

Additional trade and barter for items other than *soulava* and *mwali* take place between a man and his Kula trading partners on other islands. He also trades for non-Kula items with other persons. Malinowski believed the Kula Ring served two functions: the trading, feasting, and ceremonial activities reinforced trading alliances (and were sometimes stronger than those between kinspeople) and also provided a mechanism for display of prestige. The Kula Ring persists today, despite European influence and substitution of a cash economy, illustrating the socially binding properties of this system of reciprocity.

See also Exchange; Functionalism; Malinowski, Bronislaw

Consult: Malinowski, Bronislaw, *Argonauts of the Western Pacific* (New York: Dutton, 1922).

**Kulak.** Kulak is Russian for the rich peasant farmers who emerged as a class in the late 19th and early 20th centuries. By using other peasants as a labor force, the kulaks were able to produce substantial surpluses and thus farmed on a market-exchange rather than subsistence basis. The kulaks were destroyed as a class by Stalin's collectivization policies (1929–1932), although there is evidence that private enterprise is still discreetly practiced in Soviet agriculture.

**Kulturkreise.** This German term means "culture circles," a key idea in the German diffusionist school of culture history. A culture circle is a cluster of associated traits representing one stratum in the diffusion of culture complexes. *Kulturkreislehre* ("culture circle school") refers to the German diffusionist school prominent in anthropology until the 1930s. The approach was geographic-historical, and it tried to trace the diffusion of clusters or complexes of basic cultural elements over space and time. One aim was to identify the most ancient culture complexes via careful study and analysis of

*Routes for the reciprocal exchange of* soulava *and* mwali *in the Kula exchange system described by Malinowski.*

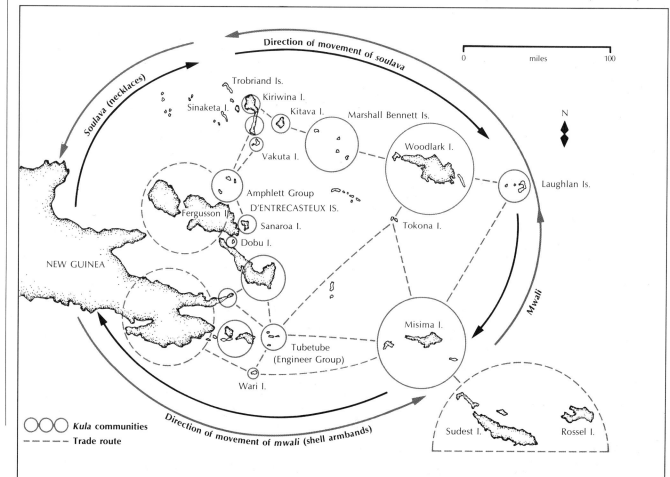

the most primitive cultures then existing. The leading figure in the school, Father Wilhelm Schmidt, believed that nine major culture circles had been identified. The *Kulturkreislehre* did not survive criticism of its assumptions and methods by structural-functionalists.

**Kulturkreislehre.** *See Kulturkreise.*

**LaBarre, Weston** (b. 1911). A cultural anthropologist interested in the application of psychoanalytic theory to anthropological research, LaBarre has worked among American Indians and the snake-handling cult of the American South.

**Labor.** Labor is productive activity, both physical and mental. In its fully elaborated form, the labor process includes not only conscious, purposeful expenditure of energy to transform nature into culturally determined form but also the use of tools or the means of production, cooperation in production, spatial and temporal separation between production and consumption, and distribution of the product among different members of society. Labor, then, is a *social* activity and is found only in human societies. Forms of human social development are often classified according to the dominant kind of labor activity supporting society: hunting and gathering, fishing, horticulture, plow agriculture, herding, and industrial labor activities support different kinds of societies.

All human societies divide labor, at least in terms of age and sex. Adults perform different tasks than children, and there is a sexual division of labor in which household and childrearing labor is performed by women and hunting, herding, or industrial labor is performed by men. Labor is also organized along kinship lines, through voluntary work organizations, and sometimes by various means of coercion (forced labor, peonage, serfdom, slavery). Complex societies are also characterized by a division of labor between different spheres of productive activity, agriculture, mining, metallurgy, handicrafts, and so on.

*See also* Colonialism; Corvée; Economics and subsistence; Labor market; Labor market, informal

Consult: Marx, Karl, "The Labour Process or the Production of Use-Values," in *Capital*, chap. 7, vol. 1 (New York: International Publishers, 1966).

—Eugene E. Ruyle, University of Virginia

**Labor, Division of.** *See* Division of labor.

**Labor Market.** This conception applies to societies in which labor is detachable from locality and from social contexts and is allocated among several alternative labor uses by a variety of mechanisms. The mechanism most familiar to us is the price-making market, partially controlled by supply and demand, in which people sell their work power or skills as commodities, ostensibly to the highest bidder. Strictly speaking, primitive societies have no labor markets, though, of course, they do have labor. Also, in societies where labor is bound to the production units, as in the case of serfs, a labor market, properly speaking, does not exist or exists only incipiently (as, for example, migrant labor in 13th-century England).

In classical economics, the labor market is regarded as an independent market parallel to the capital and commodity markets. Marxist economics makes no such distinction: all these markets are viewed as aspects of a single system—the political economy erected on the control of the means of production. By separating labor from the rest, classical economics fails to deal, both in analysis and as major policy formulator of our times, with labor in relation to the distribution (i.e., control/ownership) of the very means of production themselves. That is, a given distribution, like the capitalist mode of production, structures both the relationship of labor to the means of production and the kinds of rewards it gets. The capitalist mode of production is expressed in the market and its *sociological* manipulations by those who control the means of production.

Nevertheless, for many problems in anthropology and related sciences an analysis of the labor market is absolutely central since most members of societies having such markets articulate with them. Labor markets vary according to regions, subdivisions of regions and even of cities and towns, production and other sectors of the economy, seasonal pay ranges, and discrimination by class, race, ethnicity, caste, sex, and so forth. Together these dimensions, very often deliberately manipulated by societal elites, limit possibilities for persons in the labor market such that their strategic choices, based on their needs and current situations, are constrained in specific ways. These complex relations permit hypothesizing characteristic forms and incidences of behavior of individuals, households, and groups in given labor markets—including, for example, probable forms of marriage selection, incidences of matrifocal, patrifocal, and bifocal households, and likely forms of transfer along social networks.

Strategic choices by persons and groups in relation to labor markets also underlie most phenomena labeled migration. Labor markets—specific demands for types and amounts of skills—vary as resource allocations, capital, plant, and transport and communication networks in the society as a whole vary under different calculations of costs, benefits, and political necessities. Differential improvements of labor absorption in one area and declines in another area, as the societal controllers of basic labor-absorbing resources shift them about, tend to create flows of skills—that is, migrations of people—from the latter area to the former.

Multiple forms of discrimination appear to function in two ways. First, discrimination allows interested parties to maintain their own access to certain jobs by excluding others (e.g., men excluding women from executive jobs). Second, they create a mass of unemployed and underemployed seeking better articulation with the job market, competing with those already employed. This mass—Marx's "reserve army of the unemployed"—functions to depress wages and maximize profits. Much of the reserve army is created deliberately by the policies of those who control resources and hiring in the labor markets, thus undercutting the simple supply-demand relationship that supposedly exists and also nullifying differential bids to prospective workers.

*See also* Labor; Labor market, informal

—Anthony Leeds, Boston University

**Labor Market, Informal.** Socioeconomic theory has increasingly recognized at least a two-part division of labor markets—the formal as against the informal, secondary, or marginal labor markets. The former is defined by the institutionalized, jural relation of worker to job. In Brazil, this means an officially signed, Ministry of Labor work card which serves as identification and inscribes its carrier into the social welfare and electoral system. In Britain, it means membership in a trade union and attachment to the social welfare system.

In contrast, the informal labor market involves a variety of relationships to earning through work, none of which has jural recognition. Much of the theoretical literature discusses these relations under the rubrics "underemployment" and "self-employment" (conceived as underemployment)—usually defined by such attributes as instability of jobs, low earnings, odd-jobbing, marginal forms of work, and the like. However, descriptive data now accumulating from many sources (Brazil, England, Ghana, Kenya, Peru) indicate that each of these relations involves quite different articulations with labor markets even in a single country—and, more important perhaps, cannot be understood in the same way in different countries. This is especially true when one is comparing advanced and "developing" capitalist countries.

Further, contradicting a spate of new theoretical literature, empirical evidence indicates that evolving monopoly capitalism gradually absorbs the informal sector, leaving in it primarily those areas of work which are difficult to organize (in terms of intensive capital) on a continuous (e.g., assembly-line) basis. Such areas especially include work that operates well with a shape-up system, as in construction and dock work, or, more markedly, the services—especially household services (painting, repairs, grounds care) and nonhousehold repair and petty sales services. In other words, the growth of monopoly capitalism tends to organize the labor market formally, leaving less organizable sectors to the informal labor markets and perhaps to serve as a buffer between the formal labor market and the "reserve army of the unemployed."

Also contradicting claims in the current theoretical literature, ethnographic work has increasingly shown that the worker's choice of the informal labor market, in a majority of cases, presents real advantages. First, a significant number of work relationships in the informal sector are full-time, permanent jobs entered through clientelistic contracts with an employer—to the advantage of both parties, since many of the employer's *costs* of employment (e.g., social service payments) decline while he *pays* more to the informal worker than he

would to one formally employed. A second category of informal market workers manipulate networks to keep job contracts producing a relatively steady flow of cash, often higher than the formal market salaries scheduled by a national ministry. A third category combines formal or permanent informal work arrangements with odd jobs. Only a remnant of the informal market personnel perform really peripheral jobs such as watching cars or selling gum. Notably, however, these are usually boys; like boys in the United States with paper routes, they are adding to the family income while learning something of the ways of the city, of money transactions, and of manipulating relationships. Contracts and odd jobs often serve also as vehicles for apprenticing older children for whom no other job training medium exists. Careful cost accounting of household budgets and individual earnings shows that the calculations made by a large number of workers electing to operate in the informal labor market are correct and produce rational and wise decisions about work.

*See also* Labor market; Underemployment; Unemployment
Consult: U.N. Inter-Agency Team, *Employment, Incomes, and Equality* (Geneva: International Labor Office, 1972); Uzzell, J. Douglas, *Bound for Places I'm Not Known To: Adaptation of Migrants and Residence in Four Irregular Settlements in Lima, Peru* (Ann Arbor, Mich.: University Microfilms, 1972).
—Anthony Leeds, Boston University

**Labov, William** (b. 1927). Sociolinguist whose research has concerned urban dialectology, Black English, the social motivation of sound change, and the development of grammars incorporating linguistic variation and social features.

*See also* Sociolinguistics

**Ladino.** This term, which is used in parts of Latin America (especially Guatemala), refers to persons classified elsewhere in Latin America as mestizos or mixed Indian-white offspring.

*See also* Mestizo; Métis

**Laguna, Frederica Annis de** (b. 1906). Cultural anthropologist, archaeologist, and former president of the American

Anthropological Association noted for her work on the Indians of the Northwest Coast.

**Lamarck, Jean Baptiste de** (1744–1829). This French zoologist was a precursor of Charles Darwin and Alfred Russel Wallace. Fifty years before the publication of Charles Darwin's *Origin of Species* Lamarck (1809) put forth the notion of evolutionary change: "Go from the simplest to the most complex and you will have the true thread that connects all the productions of nature; you will have an accurate idea of her progression; you will be convinced that the simplest living things have given rise to all others." Lamarck, however, believed that *acquired characteristics* could be inherited. Thus, for example, the long necks of giraffes might be explained as the result of successive generations of giraffes straining to reach the high leaves on trees. Lamarck's views generally were ignored by his contemporaries, although they were shared by Erasmus Darwin (1731–1802), grandfather of Charles.

Lamarck's views were revived in the 20th century by the Russian scientist T. D. Lysenko, who was allowed absolute control over Soviet biological research and practical agriculture by Stalin with far-reaching and destructive results to the Russian economy.

*See also* Darwin, Charles; Evolution, genetic mechanisms of; Selection, natural; Wallace, Alfred Russel
Consult: Lamarck, Jean Baptiste de, *Philosophie Zoologique* (New York: Hafner, 1960); Medvedev, Zhores A., *The Rise and Fall of T. D. Lysenko* (New York: Doubleday, 1971).

**Land Ownership.** Land ownership consists of the sum of rights which people have over the use of land. In most societies, land is the most desirable form of property. Forms of ownership vary from society to society, depending on the level of complexity and the nature and availability of land. Among nomadic societies where there is a large amount of land available for either foraging or pasturage, there is generally little need for parceling out individual plots. But even among technologically simple societies, the range of ownership behavior varies greatly. Among the Ingalik Eskimo, for example, neither land nor water was considered either individual or group property. However, when the fur trade began in the 19th century, family trapping territories became sharply delineated—a result of the introduction of a commercial trading element into the local economy. The Australian aborigines, with a similar level of technology, held inalienable land rights under the control of local descent groups (clans).

In Melanesia, similarly, real property was vested in the kinship group. Among the Trobrianders, landholding was vested in matrilineal clans. The head of the subclan —the eldest male of the eldest lineage in the subclan—held title of ownership. All members of a subclan had a share in joint ownership and worked as much of the land as they needed or could use. Members were able to pass on plots to heirs, but they had no right to dispose of them outside the subclan.

Communal or clan ownership of land continued in some form even in Europe until the Enclosure Acts, beginning in the 15th century in England and continuing through the 19th century on the Continent. Lands were enclosed first to increase the efficiency of pasturage and eventually for agricultural efficiency. Vestiges of communal ownership still exist in Europe in the forms of village ownership of wooded areas and grazing lands. Widespread individual ownership of land is a recent phenomenon and is tied to more technologically complex agricultural systems, notably those which operate within capitalist economic systems. Allocation of land rights, whether individual or group, cannot be understood in narrow legal terms but must always be viewed in their relationships with the wider social structure.

See also Colonialism; Economic anthropology; Feudalism; Land tenure; Peasants

Consult: Herskovits, M., *Economic Anthropology* (New York: Knopf, 1952); Thurnwald, R., *Economics in Primitive Communities* (New York: Humanities Press, 1965).

—*Richard L. Stone, California State University, Los Angeles*

**Land Tenure.** This term refers to the rightful holding of land by some party—that is, holding rights for its use. Land tenure may or may not involve ownership, however. It may refer to limited use, rights, or normative expectations. Land tenure ambiguities arise from contradictory legal stipulations, conflicting legal domains, or absence of legal definitions of situation. Tenure may take

the form of private ownership and of contracts such as sharecropping and rental arrangements. It may also take such forms as squatting, communal holdings, and public ownership. Each form makes available some tract of land to a party, in general for some use, though all tracts which are held are not necessarily used; e.g., land is sometimes held for speculation. Land tenure is a fundamental form of wealth distribution in society and underlies many basic social relations.

**Land Transport.** In most of human history, land transport was carried out by human beings—carrying things on the head, shoulder, back, hip, and rump, hanging items from the arms, and holding them in one's hands. People themselves were vehicles, a situation which persists today even in highly technological societies (as any backpacker or carrier of supermarket grocery bags can attest). Perhaps the earliest major subsequent development was the use of humans as traction animals pushing or pulling sleds, sledges, travois, or simply objects on the ground. People were no longer supporting items as in carrying but rather used their energy more efficiently simply to move things.

With animal domestication, pulling and carrying was transferred to four-legged creatures. Dogs, oxen, horses, caribou, and elephants pull sleds and travois. Adding the wheel, of course, enhanced the mechanical advantage of haulage immensely and became the basis for almost all land transport vehicles except, under special environmental conditions, the persisting sleds and sledges. Only recently has the conversion of fossil fuels replaced animal power. All civilizations must transport materials on land, regardless of other modes of transport that have been devised. It is fair to say that modes of land transportation are fundamental to the continued functioning of society.

See also Watercraft

—*Anthony Leeds, Boston University*

**Landes, Ruth** (b. 1908). An American anthropologist, Landes is most widely known for her culture and personality research among American Indians (Ojibwa, Sioux, Potawatomi) although she has also studied blacks, Mexican-Americans,

women, and the impact of culture on the educational process.

**Lang, Andrew** (1844–1912). A prolific writer of poetry, children's books and fairy tales, history and biography, fiction, essays, and a translator of Homer, Lang is best known, perhaps, for his twelve-volume collection of fairy tales, which began with *The Blue Fairy Book* in 1889. He is more important to anthropology for his work in the theory of folklore. Lang believed that folklore was not a remnant of a former literary mythology of a people but rather the seed from which mythology later developed. Some of his works in this field are *Myth, Ritual, and Religion* (1887), *The Making of Religion* (1898), *Custom and Myth* (1884), and *Magic and Religion* (1901).

**Language.** In the narrow sense (of transformational linguistics), language refers to the possible sentences generated by a grammar; this is opposed to corpus, which is the body of actual sentences spoken by a speaker in specific circumstances. The former is a *structural* concept, the latter statistical.

However, both among laypersons and anthropologists the term *language* is generally used more broadly to refer to a mode of communication practiced by all human beings. Hockett (1960) has described thirteen "design features" which, in their combination, set language (speech) off from all other modes of communication:

1. *Vocal-auditory channel.* Language is produced through the mouth (and nose) and received through the ears.

2. *Broadcast transmission and directional reception.* Speakers' signals can be heard in all directions, yet receivers (hearers) can perceive the direction from which the utterance was broadcast.

3. *Rapid fading.* The actual signs of speech are sound sequences which last only a very short time before dissipating.

4. *Interchangeability.* Every speaker can reproduce the signals he or she has received. Thus all speakers of a language can participate in any speech event.

5. *Total feedback.* Every (normal) speaker can monitor his or her output and hence "correct" any mistakes in transmission.

6. *Specialization.* Speaking serves no other purpose than communicating. It is not

| Design Features | Bee Dancing | Stickleback Fish Courtship | Gibbon Calls | Language |
|---|---|---|---|---|
| Vocal-Auditory Channel | no | no | yes | yes |
| Broadcast Transmission and Directional Reception | yes | yes | yes | yes |
| Rapid Fading | ? | ? | yes | yes |
| Interchangeability | limited | no | yes | yes |
| Total Feedback | ? | no | yes | yes |
| Specialization | ? | in part | yes | yes |
| Semanticity | yes | no | yes | yes |
| Arbitrariness | no | ? | yes | yes |
| Discreteness | no | ? | yes | yes |
| Displacement | yes | ? | no | yes |
| Productivity | yes | no | no | yes |
| Traditional Transmission | somewhat | no? | ? | yes |
| Duality of Patterning | no | ? | no | yes |

is vast, every language utilizes only a small and discretely bounded set of such sounds to encode its entire semantic range. The advantage is that every speaker of a language must learn only a very limited sound repertoire, but if a speaker deviates from this limited set his or her attempts at communication will quickly become incomprehensible.

10. *Displacement.* People can talk about events far removed from the setting in which they are communicating, including the discussion of imaginary events.

11. *Productivity.* Speakers regularly say things (produce sentences) which are new in the sense that they never before have been uttered in exactly that manner.

12. *Traditional transmission.* Although the human capacity to learn language is genetically encoded and inherited, each person acquires his or her language competence through the process of enculturation—i.e., learns and is taught it.

13. *Duality of patterning.* Two levels of patterning compose every utterance. On the phonological level, each utterance is a patterned sequence (string) of sound units which in themselves are meaningless (*phonemes*). On the grammatical level, each utterance is a patterned sequence of units of meaning (*morphemes*) represented by specific sound sequences.

These thirteen design features result in a communication system unique to human beings—an extremely elegant system which is virtually limitless in its flexibility yet is parsimonious in its primitive elements and rules for their combination.

*See also* Biological basis of language; Communication; Communication, nonverbal; Linguistics; Morpheme; Phoneme

Consult: Hockett, Charles D., "The Origin of Speech," *Scientific American*, September 1960.

—*David E. Hunter, Southern Connecticut State College*

## LANGUAGE COMPARED TO OTHER COMMUNICATION SYSTEMS

*Although the communication systems of other species have some of the design features of language, none has all the design features that, in combination, characterize language. (Adapted from Hockett 1960:8–9.)*

embedded in other activities and can be carried on while other activities are engaged in.

7. *Semanticity.* Messages "mean" something—i.e., there are quite regular associations between message elements and recurring features of the natural and cultural environment.

8. *Arbitrariness.* The connections between language signs and what they refer to (stand for) is entirely arbitrary. This means they have to be learned but have the consequent advantage of permitting communication about anything.

9. *Discreteness.* Although the range of sounds producible by the human vocal tract

**Language and Culture.** This subfield within social and cultural anthropology is concerned with the relationships, both specific and general, between language and culture. Language is generally thought to reflect culture. A great deal of cultural behavior, especially the learning of cultural systems, is carried out through language.

Recently a new field, known as sociolinguistics, has developed which includes topics previously dealt with in language and culture. Sociolinguistics has its primary focus on the study of speech variation, which is conditioned by social factors such as age, sex, ethnicity, identity, and social status of speaker.

The study of language and culture has dealt with a variety of topics—the classification of language relationships, the relationships between language and thought, ethnoscience studies, use of language varieties such as slang, sacred languages, pidgins and creoles, bilingualism, shift from one language to another, maintenance of a native language, men's and women's speech, and speech and personality. This list is not exhaustive.

Language is considered as a model for culture in some of these studies, and models developed in linguistics have been applied to cultural systems. This approach views language as observable behavior that reveals the structuring of cognitive categories such as kinship, color categories, and ethnobotanies that are not easily discovered by other techniques. The idea that language structures cognition and much unconscious behavior in a culture goes back to Franz Boas, but it was explicitly formulated by Edward Sapir and Benjamin Lee Whorf in the 1920s and 1930s. This notion, now called the Sapir-Whorf hypothesis, states that the obligatory grammatical and semantic categories in a language may structure a speaker's thought into habitual patterns which organize thought and thus influence behavior. This idea is frequently misinterpreted to state that there is a deterministic relationship between language and thought, but Whorf held that only habitual patterns were structured this way and believed that language did not constrain thought totally. Whorf's early studies on the Hopi language attempted to show that Hopi was much better suited to discussions of certain phenomena than English and accounted for some differences in world view between speakers of Hopi and speakers of English. These ideas stimulated a lot of research in the 1950s on various cultures and indirectly gave rise to componential analysis, ethnoscience, and the structural analysis of Claude Lévi-Strauss current today. All these research methods analyze vocabularies of speakers and the contrasts between lexical items in order to determine how phenomena are categorized. This general approach views language as essentially separate from (though representing) culture.

Another approach, often called "language in society" (Hymes 1964; Blount 1974), deals with language as part of the social system and examines social relationships as they are expressed in language. Although this approach has always been part of language and culture studies, it is now receiving a great deal of attention in sociolinguistics. Anthropologists want to know why a given language or language variety is used in one situation and not another. What does it tell us about the speakers? How are sex roles reinforced by language? Why do some societies retain a native language after they have acquired a national one, whereas others lose their own language?

Anthropologists are also concerned with "the ethnography of speaking," a term coined by Dell Hymes to deal with the whole question of how speech functions in social interaction, what sorts of speech events are found in different societies and contexts, and how children acquire competence in communication. The range of topics currently being researched is enormous, and the whole field of concern has now expanded beyond anthropology and involves input from fields like psychology, sociology, and speech. The term *language and culture* is being replaced by sociolinguistics as the field expands.

*See also* Componential analysis; Ethnoscience; Ethnosemantics; Language and reality; Language and thought; Sociolinguistics
Consult: Blount, Ben, *Language, Culture, and Society* (Cambridge, Mass.: Winthrop, 1974); Hymes, Dell (ed.), *Language in Culture and Society* (New York: Harper & Row, 1964).
—*Elizabeth Brandt, Arizona State University*

**Language and Reality.** Although perception depends on the reception of stimuli originating from outside the person, these have no meaning for the person until he or she categorizes them. Categorization is the process whereby differing stimuli are identified by a person as being the same, i.e., belonging to the same class. The classes one uses to organize perceptions are called *cognitive categories;* the organizing process is called *cognition.*

The cognitive categories at a person's disposal do not generate themselves spontaneously in his or her mind: they are acquired through the process of *enculturation* —the process through which a person masters a culture and learns to speak a particular language. The so-called Sapir-Whorf hypothesis holds that the vocabulary of a language is an encoding of that culture's cognitive categories; also, that the grammatical constructions of the language impose logical relations between those categories. Thus the act of learning a language simultaneously entails the internalizing of the cognitive categories and logical relations that are the basis for organizing one's experience of the universe, one's perception of reality. In this view the concept of a transcendent Reality has no meaning: reality is a sociocultural product and hence relative.

*See also* Cognition; Enculturation; Language and culture; Language and thought
Consult: Carroll, John B. (ed.), *Language, Thought, and Reality: Selected Writings of Benjamin Lee Whorf* (Cambridge, Mass.: M.I.T. Press, 1956); Tyler, Stephen A. (ed., *Cognitive Anthropology* (New York: Holt, 1969).
—*David E. Hunter, Southern Connecticut State College*

**Language and Thought.** In their effort to explicate the nature of human thought, Jerome S. Bruner, Jacqueline J. Goodnow, and George A. Austin (1956) end their treatise with a discussion of *categorization,* which is defined as the mental process whereby a variety of stimuli are identified by a person as being "forms of the same thing." In other words, perceptibly different stimuli are lumped together into sets or categories. These categories are not generated independently and spontaneously in people's minds. Rather, they are learned in the context of the enculturation process, the process through which a person learns a language and internalizes the culture of the group into which she or he is born. In the view of Bruner et al., these *cognitive categories,* which each person acquires from his or her culture, are embedded in language and constitute the irreducible elements that lie at the base of human thought. Similarly, Michael Cole and Sylvia Scribner in their book, *Culture and Thought* (1974), emphasize the concept of *cognition,* the processes performed by people using the cognitive categories they have learned.

It is clear that thought involves the sorting out of perceptions; that the sorting is done in terms of cognitive categories; that both these categories, and the relationships people conceive to obtain among them (taxonomic relations, part-whole relations), are learned or acquired from the culture and especially the language of one's group(s); that the *formation* of ideas is organized by such categories; that the *manipulation* of ideas is organized by the formal relations that are conceived to obtain among these categories; and that thinking is the dynamic expression of these categories.

Although the research by developmental psychologists such as Jean Piaget clearly demonstrates that thought processes develop through describable and predictable stages as each person matures, it is nevertheless irrefutable that the thought of mature persons is organized in terms of content and process by the culture and language through which they have been enculturated and which they have learned.

*See also* Cognition; Enculturation; Language and culture; Language and reality
Consult: Bruner, Jerome S., Goodnow, Jacqueline J., and Austin, George A., *A Study of Thinking* (New York: Wiley, 1956); Cole, Michael, and Scribner, Sylvia, *Culture and Thought* (New York: Wiley, 1974); Ginsburg, Herbert, and Opper, Sylvia, *Piaget's Theory of Intellectual Development* (Englewood Cliffs, N.J.: Prentice-Hall, 1969).
—*David E. Hunter, Southern Connecticut State College*

## Language as a Model for Understanding Culture.

Language has served as a model for understanding culture in a number of ways. Primary among them has been the conception of culture as a system of symbols patterned as rules which structure actual behavior. The distinction is modeled on that of Saussarian linguistics which distinguishes between *langue* (roughly, language) and *parole* (roughly, speech). Culture is thus a system of rules (*langue*) structuring and limiting the choices manifested through actual behavior. These categories of behavior are really categories for meaningful action (*parole*).

The meaning of a bit of behavior can be arrived at in ways analogous to those in which linguists arrive at the discovery of phonemes, morphemes, and their rules for grammatical combination. A number of methods, usually found under the rubric "ethnoscience," have sought to use linguistic-based methods for other areas of culture. Also, the school of French structuralism is consciously patterned on linguistic methodology; it attempts to elucidate the grammars which underlie all systems of behavior.

*See also* French structuralism; Language; New Ethnography, the; Structuralism

## Language Families of the World.

A group of languages showing descent from a common ancestral source is referred to as a family or stock of languages. The terms for father, mother, brother, and sister in English show similarity with the German terms *Vater, Mutter, Bruder,* and *Schwester* and thus are cognates, illustrating a relationship.

In 1786 William Jones observed that the ancient sacred language of India, Sanskrit, had many similarities in word forms to both Latin and Greek and other languages of Europe. This relationship of languages in Europe and India was termed "Indo-European" by Dr. Thomas Young in 1814. In this way the concept of language family was born.

Some of the languages in Europe did not conform to the rest, notably Hungarian and Finnish. These came to be classed in a language family of their own: Finno-Ugric, later called Uralic. Likewise some of the languages of South India were also found to lack the Indo-European words of the rest of that country, notably Tamil and Telugu, and these came to be called the Dravidian family from the Sanskrit word for south.

The native Indian languages of North and South America did not conform to the Indo-European pattern and had to be classed in terms of their own similarities into separate families.

### North American Native Language Families.

Study of the language families of North America has been historically associated with ethnology. In 1836 Albert Gallatin published a synopsis of Indian tribes of the United States and shortly later founded the American Ethnological Society in 1842. Near the close of the century, in 1891, John Wesley Powell published his *Indian Linguistic Families North of Mexico* while organizing the Bureau of American Ethnology in the Smithsonian Institution.

Powell's list, which comprised some fifty-six families, was considered by some as too unwieldy. The desire for a consolidation of these families grew. As a result Edward Sapir proposed in 1929 a grouping into six superfamilies: Algonquian-Wakashan; Hokan-Siouan; Penutian-Sahaptan; Nadéné; Aztec-Tanoan; and Eskimo-Aleut. With subsequent modifications of Sapir's system in 1964 about nine of Powell's families remain unclassified.

Mexico and Central America (Mesoamerica) comprise some twenty-one linguistic groupings variously styled families, isolates, complexes, stocks, and branches. Extending from Nicaragua through Costa Rica and Panama are tribes now classed with Macro-Chibcha, a South American language family. The Nahuan group of the Uto-Aztecan family along with the Mayan family were distinguished by languages in possession of systems of hieroglyphic writing and calendars.

### South American Indian Language Families.

Reading and writing were introduced into South America by Europeans, missionaries and others. Tropical lowland conditions apparently did not favor the survival of literate groups or individuals. Accordingly, advances in the study of native language have been uneven and the formulation of evidence for language families leaves much to be desired.

Two divisions can be recognized: the Andean division consisting of the Chibchan group and the Quechua-Aymará group; the Lowlands division comprehending the Arawakan, Cariban, and Tupian. The road system of the Incas outlined routes of travel for the first division, the inland and coastal waterway routes of canoe travel for the second.

The Chibchan-speaking peoples were responsible for the highly developed culture of prehistoric Colombia—the Muysca and its legend of El Dorado, "the gilded one." The Gold Museum in Bogotá makes this culture live for us today. The Quechua-Aymará—speaking people were responsible for the civilization of Peru with its architecture, pottery, and social organization.

The Arawakan group was the earliest contacted by the Spaniards with Columbus in the Antilles, and their speech was the first to be recorded. The Cariban-speakers were canoe makers and warriors. The Tupian language was first recorded by Magellan's expedition.

### African Language Families.

The natural features of Africa—its rivers (the Nile, Congo, Niger, and Zambezi); its deserts (the Sahara and the Kalahari); its equatorial forest; its savannas; its lakes (Chad, Victoria, Tanganyika, Nyassa); its mountains and highlands; and lastly, its fauna—have all

## THE PRINCIPAL LANGUAGES OF THE WORLD

| Language | Millions | Language | Millions | Language | Millions | Language | Millions |
|---|---|---|---|---|---|---|---|
| Afrikaans (S. Africa) | 5 | Georgian (USSR) | 3 | Luri (Iran) | 1 | Santali (India) | 4 |
| Albanian | 3 | German | 120 | Macedonian (Yugoslavia) | 1 | Sepedi (see Sotho, Northern) | |
| Amharic (Ethiopia) | 9 | Gilaki (Iran) | 1 | Madurese (Indonesia) | 7 | Serbo-Croatian (Yugoslavia) | 18 |
| Annamese (see Vietnamese) | | Gondi (India) | 2 | Makua (S.E. Africa) | 2 | Shan (Burma) | 1 |
| Arabic | 125 | Greek | 10 | Malagasy (Madagascar) | 8 | Shona (S.E. Africa) | 4 |
| Armenian | 4 | Guarani (mainly Paraguay) | 3 | Malay-Indonesian | 95 | Siamese (see Thai) | |
| Assamese (1) (India) | 13 | Gujarati (1) (India) | 30 | Malayalam (1) (India) | 24 | Sindhi (India; Pakistan) | 9 |
| Azerbaijani (USSR; Iran) | 8 | Hakka (China) | 21 | Malinke-Bambara-Dyula (Africa) | 5 | Sinhalese (Sri Lanka) | 10 |
| Bahase (See Malay-Indonesian) | | Hausa (W. and Central Africa) | 18 | Mandarin (China) | 650 | Slovak | 4 |
| Balinese | 3 | Hebrew | 3 | Mazandarani (Iran) | 1 | Slovene (Yugoslavia) | 2 |
| Baluchi (Pakistan; Iran) | 3 | Hindi (1) (4) | 209 | Marathi (1) (India) | 51 | Somali (E. Africa) | 4 |
| Bashkir (USSR) | 1 | Hindustani (4) | | Mbundu (Umbundu group) | | Sotho, Northern (S. Africa) | 2 |
| Batak (Indonesia) | 2 | Hungarian (or Magyar) | 13 | (S. Angola) | 2 | Sotho, Southern (S. Africa) | 2 |
| Bemba (S. Central Africa) | 1 | Ibibio (see Efik) | | Mbundu (Kimbundu group) | | Spanish | 213 |
| Bengali (1) (Bangladesh; India) | 123 | Ibo (or Igbo) (W. Africa) | 10 | (Angola) | 1 | Sudanese (Indonesia) | 15 |
| Berber (2) (N. Africa) | | Ijaw (W. Africa) | 1 | Mende (Sierra Leone) | 1 | Swahili (E. Africa) | 20 |
| Bhili (India) | 4 | Ilocano (Philippines) | 4 | Min (China) | 39 | Swedish | 10 |
| Bihari (India) | 22 | Iloko (see Ilocano) | | Moldavian (incl. w/Rumanian) | ...... | Tagalog (Philippines) | 21 |
| Bikol (Philippines) | 2 | Indonesian | | Mongolian (see Khalkha) | | Tajiki (USSR) | 3 |
| Bisaya (see Cebuano, Panay- | | (see Malay-Indonesian) | ...... | Mordvin (USSR) | 1 | Tamil (1) (India; Sri Lanka) | 53 |
| Hiligaynon, and Samar-Leyte) | | Italian | 60 | More (see Mossi) | | Tatar (or Kazan-Turkic) (USSR) | 6 |
| Bugi (Indonesia) | 2 | Japanese | 110 | Mossi (W. Africa) | 3 | Telugu (1) (India) | 53 |
| Bulgarian | 9 | Javanese | 44 | Ndongo (see Mbundu-Kimbundu) | | Thai (5) | 30 |
| Burmese | 23 | Kamba (E. Africa) | 1 | Nepali (Nepal; India) | 10 | Tibetan | 7 |
| Byelorussian (mainly USSR) | 10 | Kanarese (see Kannada) | | Netherlandish (Dutch and Flem.) | 20 | Tigrinya (Ethiopia) | 4 |
| Cambodian (Cambodia, Asia) | 7 | Kannada (1) (India) | 28 | Ngala (or Lingala) (Africa) | 4 | Tiv (E. Central Nigeria) | 1 |
| Canarese (see Kannada) | | Kanuri (W. and Cent. Africa) | 2 | Norwegian | 4 | Tswana (S. Africa) | 2 |
| Cantonese (China) | 47 | Kashmiri (1) | 3 | Nyamwezi-Sukuma (S.E. Africa) | 1 | Tulu (India) | 1 |
| Catalan (Spain; France; Andorra) | 6 | Kazakh (USSR) | 5 | Nyanja (S.E. Africa) | 2 | Turkish | 39 |
| Cebuano (Philippines) | 8 | Khalkha (Mongolia) | 1 | Oraon (see Kurukh) | | Turkoman (USSR) | 2 |
| Chinese (3) | | Kikongo (see Kongo) | | Oriya (1) (India) | 23 | Twi-Fante (or Akan) (W. Africa) | 4 |
| Chuang (7) (China) | | Kikuyu (or Gekoyo) (Kenya) | 2 | Panay-Hiligaynon (Philippines) | 4 | Uighur-(Sinkiang, China) | 4 |
| Czech | 11 | Kimbundu (see Mbundu-Kim.) | | Panjabi (see Punjabi) | | Ukrainian (mainly USSR) | 42 |
| Danish | 5 | Kirghiz (USSR) | 2 | Pashto (see Pushtu) | 2 | Umbundu | |
| Dayak (Borneo) | 1 | Kituba (Congo River) | 2 | Pedi (see Sotho, Northern) | | (see Mbundu-Umbundu) | |
| Dutch (see Netherlandish) | | Kongo (Congo River) | 1 | Persian | 24 | Urdu (1) (Pakistan; India) | 57 |
| Edo (W. Africa) | 1 | Konkani (India) | 2 | Polish | 35 | Uzbek (USSR) | 9 |
| Efik | 2 | Korean | 52 | Portuguese | 124 | Vietnamese | 37 |
| English | 358 | Kumauni (India) | 1 | Provencal (Southern France) | 6 | Visayan (see Cebuano, Panay- | |
| Esperanto | 1 | Kurdish (S. W. of Caspian Sea) | 7 | Punjabi (1) (India; Pakistan) | 55 | Hiligaynon, and Samar-Leyte) | |
| Estonian | 1 | Kurukh (or Oraon) (India) | 1 | Pushto (mainly Afghanistan) | 15 | White Russian (see Byelorussian) | |
| Ewe (W. Africa) | 2 | Lao (5) (Laos, Asia) | 3 | Quechua (S. America) | 3 | Wolof (W. Africa) | 2 |
| Finnish | 5 | Latvian (or Lettish) | 2 | Rajasthani (India) | 21 | Wu (China) | 42 |
| Flemish (see Netherlandish) | | Lingala (see Ngala) | | Romanian | 22 | Xhosa (S. Africa) | 4 |
| French | 90 | Lithuanian | 3 | Rundi (S. Central Africa) | 3 | Yi (China) | 3 |
| Fula (W. Africa) | 7 | Luba-Lulua (Zaire) | 3 | Russian (Great Russian only) | 233 | Yiddish (6) | |
| Galician (Spain) | 2 | Luganda (see Ganda) | | Rwanda (S. Central Africa) | 6 | Yoruba (W. Africa) | 12 |
| Galla (Ethiopia) | 7 | Luhya (or Luhia) (Kenya) | 1 | Samar-Leyte (Philippines) | 1 | Zhuang (7) (China) | |
| Ganda (or Luganda) (E. Africa) | 3 | Luo (Kenya) | 1 | Sango (Central Africa) | 1 | Zulu (S. Africa) | 4 |

(1.) One of the fourteen languages of the Constitution of India. (2.) Here considered a group of dialects. (3.) See Mandarin, Cantonese, Wu, Min, and Hakka. The "national language" (Guoyu) is a standardized form of Mandarin as spoken in the area of Peking. (4.) Hindi and Urdu are essentially the same language, Hindustani. As the official language of India it is written in the Devanagari script and called Hindi. As the official language of Pakistan it is written in a modified Arabic script and called Urdu. (5.) Thai includes Central, Southwestern, Northern, and Northeastern Thai. The distinction between Northeastern Thai and Lao is political rather than linguistic. (6.) Yiddish is usually considered a variant of German, though it has its own standard grammar, dictionaries, a highly developed literature, and is written in Hebrew characters. Speakers number about 3,000,000. (7.) A group of Thai-like dialects with about 9 million speakers.

## LANGUAGE FAMILIES OF THE WORLD

### NORTH AMERICA

1. Eskimo-Aleut
   - A. Aleutian
   - B. Eskimoan
2. Nadéné
   - A. Eyak, Tlingit, Haida
   - B. Athabascan (Athapaskan)
3. Algonquian
   - A. Wakashan (incl. Nootka, Kwakiutl, Bella Bella, etc.)
   - B. Salishan (incl. Flathead, Bella Coola, etc.)
   - C. Algonquian
   - D. California Algonquian (Yurok and Wiyot)
4. Aztec-Tanoan
   - A. Uto-Aztecan
   - B. Tanoan
   - C. Zunian
   - D. Kiowan
5. Hokan-Siouan
   - A. Siouan (incl. Winnebago, Catawba-Tutelo, etc.)
   - B. Caddoan (incl. Arikara and Pawnee)
   - C. Muskogean
   - D. Iroquoian (incl. Tuscarora)
   - E. Yuman
   - F. Californian (incl. Shasta, Yana, Yuki, Pomo, Salinan, Chumash, etc.)
   - G. Keresan
6. Penutian (Classification questionable)
   - A. Sahaptan (incl. Klamath-Modoc, Takelma, Chinook, etc.)
   - B. Californian (incl. Wintu, Maidu, Yokuts, Costanoan, Miwok, etc. They may be unaffiliated.)
   - C. Tsimshian
7. Coahuiltecan
8. Mayan

### SOUTH AMERICAN

9. Chibchan-Paezan
   - A. Chibchan
   - B. Paezan
10. Andean-Equatorial
    - A. Andean (incl. Araucanian, Ona-Yahgan, etc.)
    - B. Huelche
    - C. Quechua-Aymará
    - D. Jivaro
    - E. Tucano
    - F. Arawakan
11. Gê-Pano-Cariban
    - A. Gê
    - B. Bororó
    - C. Carajá
    - D. Pano
    - E. Huarpe
    - F. Nambicuara
    - G. Cariban

### AFRICA

12. Hamito-Semitic (Afro-Asiatic)
    - A. Hamitic
    - B. Semitic
    - C. Chad (Chado-Hamitic)
13. Niger-Congo
    - A. Nigritic
    - B. Bantu
14. Central Saharan
15. Eastern Sudanic
16. Central Sudanic
17. Songhai (Songhaic)
18. Bushman-Hottentot (Khoisan or Click Languages)

### EURASIA

19. Indo-European
    - A. Indo-Iranian
    - B. Slavic
    - C. Hellenic
    - D. Romance

| | | |
|---|---|---|
| E. Germanic | 23. Annamese | |
| F. Celtic | 24. Sinitic (Chinese) | 30. Korean |
| G. Albanian-Illyrian | 25. Dravidian | 31. Paleo-Asiatic (probably two to three |
| 20. Ural-Altaic | 26. Munda-Kol (Kolarian)—in area 19A | language families, including |
| A. Finno-Ugric | 27. Mon-Khmer | Yukaghir) |
| B. Turko-Tartar (Turkish) | A. Khmer (Cambodian) | 32. Caucasic (probably two language |
| C. Mongolic | B. Mon (Talaing) | families) |
| D. Tungus-Manchu | C. Nicobarese | 33. Basque—in area 19D |
| 21. Tibeto-Burman | 28. Malayo-Polynesian | 34. Andamanese |
| 22. Shan-Siamese | 29. Japanese | ?—Linguistic Affiliations Unknown |

exerted their influence on the language families, together with the movements of its peoples.

Four major groups of languages may be said to characterize the continent: Niger-Congo (including the Bantu); Nilo-Saharan; Khoisan or Hottentot-Bushman; and Afro-Asiatic or Hamito-Semitic.

The Niger-Congo group of languages, made up of Western Sudanic plus Bantu, is characterized by certain phonological or sound features such as tone or pitch, grammatical agglutination, and prefixes. The Bantu family has been recognized for a long period.

The Nilo-Saharan group in the Eastern Sudan is much in dispute as a recognized linguistic unit.

Khoisan-speaking peoples appear to have inhabited the great area south of the equator prior to the coming of Bantu-speaking peoples. Clicks are characteristic of this group and in the case of certain East African tribes—Sandawe, Hadza, Sanye—may represented survivals.

The Afro-Asiatic or Hamito-Semitic is characterized below under Asiatic groups.

**Language Families of Australia, Papua, Austronesia.** As the mammals of Australia and New Guinea stand apart from those of nearby SE Asia and its islands, so we find the language families of Australia and New Guinea standing apart from the Austronesian (literally South Sea Islander) language family of the rest of Oceania.

The Australian Institute of Aboriginal Studies in Canberra has carried on research on Australian aboriginal languages since 1960 in the same way John Wesley Powell's Bureau of American Ethnology did for American indigenous languages at an earlier time (1890).

Some twenty-eight language families have been recognized in Australia as opposed to Powell's fifty-six families in North America. In Australia, however, the basic unity of all the native language families has been stressed to a greater degree. In the case of Australia also, twenty-seven of the families occupy one-eighth of the continent on the north and northwest shores.

Research on the language families of New Guinea is still in a very embryonic stage. Most of the languages studied are in the highlands of Central New Guinea and these are classified into some twenty-one phyla or superfamilies.

The Austronesian language family has an immense distribution around the world—from Madagascar on the west (just off the east coast of Africa) to Easter Island on the extreme east (not too distant from the west coast of South America). Malayo-Polynesian, the older name of this family, helps us differentiate Western Austronesia—Madagascar, Indonesia, the Philippines, Taiwan, and Guam (Malay)—from Eastern Austronesia, which includes Micronesia, Melanesia, Polynesia, and the islands contained within the triangle of New Zealand, the Hawaiian Islands, and Easter Island.

The unity of this vast language family was first pointed out by in 1706 by a Dutch investigator, Hadrian Reland. Subsequent work in determining the extent of this language family was done by Wilhelm von Humboldt in Java (1836–1839) and H. C. von der Gabelentz in 1861–1873.

**Language Families of Asia and Europe.** Much of the huge continent of Asia takes the form of great peninsulas—Asia Minor, India, SE Asia, Arabia, Korea, Kamchatka—which constitute the homes of particular language developments. (Europe itself is a peninsular continent which constitutes the homeland, along with India and Iran, of the Indo-European language family.) The great rivers of Asia—Hoang Ho, Indus, Ganges, Brahmaputra, Mekong, Irawaddy, Obi, Yenesei, Lena, Amur, Tigris-Euphrates—have also been determinants of language development.

The Sino-Tibetan family of East Asia comprises several literate languages of long-standing development: Chinese, Tibetan, Burmese, and Thai. This group is characterized by monosyllabic roots, isolating syntax, and high tonality, although some in the Himalayas and North Burma are highly agglutinating and consequently toneless. This family, which contains some 300 languages and major dialects, stands next to Indo-European in the extent of its population.

North of China proper is the Altaic family, whose central homeland lies in the Altai Mountains of Central Asia. There are three major subdivisions of this group: Turkic, Mongolian, and Manchu-Tungus. The Altaic family shares many features with Uralic to the west, so that some consider the two together as a phylum, the Ural-Altaic. The Turkic languages are widespread from the Lena valley of Yakutsk in the north-

east to Central Asia and Turkestan in Central Asia and still farther westward in Transcaucasia and Asia Minor. Mongolian speech reaches westward to Afghanistan and the west of Central Asia. Manchu gave its name to Manchuria; Tungus constitutes the major language of eastern Siberia.

Paleo-Asiatic languages, except for the Yenesei group, consist of four unrelated language families located in the far eastern section of Siberia. The Luorawetlan group consists of Chukchi, Koryak, and Kamchadal, the first and last of which give names to peninsulas in eastern Siberia. The Yukaghir group is located in Yakutsk near the mouth of the Indigirka and on the bend of the Kolyma. The Gilyak live at the mouth of the Amur River and in northern Sakhalin.

The Japanese and the Korean tongues are more or less isolated but show some traces of affiliation with the Altaic family.

The Uralic language family occupies the northwest section of Siberia, including the northern sections of the Yenesei and Obi valleys. They reach into the northeastern parts of Europe, including the Finns, Lapps, and Estonians there and the Hungarians of the Balkans. The Samoyeds are a branch located along the Arctic Ocean and are separate from the Finno-Ugric branch. This language family is named after the Ural Mountains, which are thought to have been their original home. Linguistic and cultural research on this group has been done by Finnish and Hungarian linguists.

The languages of the Caucasus fall into two main families, North Caucasus and South Caucasus, the latter containing the Georgian language. The Ossetes are Iranian and there are also Turkic groups. The Georgian language has a literary tradition which reaches back to the 5th century.

The Arabic language in Asia occupies an immense area that includes much of the Tigris-Euphrates valley and Arabia with adjoining parts of Africa reaching westward to the Atlantic Ocean. This tongue is the major representative of the Hamito-Semitic language family at the present time. The Hamitic group comprehends the Ancient Egyptian, Berbers, Cushites, and Chadic.

The peninsula of India includes representatives of at least four linguistic families: Indo-European, Sino-Tibetan, Dravidian, and Austro-Asiatic.

The Austro-Asiatic family is represented by the Munda groups in eastern India, who are linked with the Mons of Burma, the Khmers of Cambodia, and similar groups in Vietnam. The languages have a system of prefixes, infixes, and suffixes in building words.

The Dravidian family is represented by four literary languages: Tamil, Telugu, Kanarese, and Malayalam. Members of this speech group have spread overseas to Ceylon, South Africa, and elsewhere. Agglutination by suffixes is a prevailing characteristic.

The Indo-European languages in India are represented by Indo-Aryan tongues which are part of the Indo-Iranian branch of Indo-European. The oldest Indo-Aryan in India is represented by the Vedic Sanskrit which preceded Classical Sanskrit. Later came the Prakrit languages and Pali, the tongue of Buddhist texts. Finally in modern times appeared the new Indo-Aryan tongues known as the vernaculars: Assamese, Bengali, Oriya, Panjabi, Sindhi, Marathi, Sinhalese, and others. These tongues have been made official for the various states of India.

Intermediate between the Indo-European tongues of India and those of Europe are the Indo-Iranian languages of Iran and adjoining areas. The Iranian languages went through a development similar to the Indo-Aryan of India from an earlier sacred language, Avestan, the speech of the Zoroastrian texts, through Pahlavi to modern Persian or Parsi. Allied tongues are spoken in Afghanistan (Pashto) and in Soviet Central Asia (Tadzhik). In addition there are Kurdish and Baluchi, spoken in Kurdistan and Baluchistan (Pakistan) respectively. Armenian constitutes a separate branch of the Indo-European family.

On the European scene three major groups of Indo-European tongues prevail: Romance, derived from Latin (French, Italian, Spanish, Portuguese, Rumanian); Germanic or Teutonic (German, English, Dutch, Danish, Swedish, Norwegian, Icelandic); and Slavic (Russian, Polish, Czech, Slovak, Slovene, Serbo-Croatian, Bulgarian). Other groups are the Celtic (Welsh, Irish, Scotch Gaelic, Breton), Albanian, Greek, and Baltic (Latvian, Lithuanian).

**The Diffusion of Language Families.** Reviewing the language families of the world is like walking with giants. One's mind is forced to take giant strides across the continents in the comparison of types and genetic relations. When the Portuguese, Spanish, Dutch, French, and English began to sail across oceans in the manner of the Austronesians, they became aware of the unity of the Indo-European family. This knowledge, in turn, suggested the unity between languages of other, non-European continents.

North American native language families, in most probability of Asiatic origin, invite comparison with language families of that continent. As examples we may cite the comparison of the tonal Athapascan family with the Sino-Tibetan family, or of the inflective Macro-Penutian family with the Indo-European family.

The progress in technology of communication and travel between continents facilitates new approaches to the problem of genetic relationships of languages. This should make it possible for many isolate tongues of today to assimilate into the world genetic picture of language development.

*See also* Culture areas of the world
Consult: Graff, Willem L., *Language and Languages* (New York: Russell, 1964); Hughes, John P., *The Science of Language* (New York: Random House, 1962); Pedersen, Holgar, *The Discovery of Language: Linguistic Science in the 19th Century*, trans. J. W. Spargo (Bloomington: Indiana University Press, 1962).
—*William H. Gilbert, U.S. Library of Congress (ret.)*

**Language, Genetic Basis of.** See Biological basis of language.

**Language Types.** A language is classified by type according to its vocabulary (words) and syntax (the way it places words together to form sentences). At present there is insufficient knowledge of the frames of reference in language types to attempt a worldwide typological classification. The history of genetic descent of languages is, however, a matter of some interest. Two modes of classification are often employed.

**Analytic-Synthetic.** An entirely analytic language such as Modern Chinese uses few bound forms and each word consists of one-syllable morphemes or compounds of such units. By contrast a synthetic language, like Eskimo, ties together long strings of bound forms into single words. These distinctions are, however, relative since languages may be synthetic in some respects and analytic in others.

**Isolating- Agglutinative- Polysynthetic-Inflecting.** An isolating language such as Chinese or Vietnamese employs few bound forms. A language like Turkish, which combines bound forms into a single word, is called agglutinative. A polysynthetic language such as the Eskimo is one in which semantically important elements are expressed by means of bound forms, e.g., a composite word centering in the verb. Latin is an example of an inflecting language: semantically distinct features are merged into either a single bound form or closely tied bound forms. In this system, too, actual languages (with some exceptions) are difficult to classify.

*See also* Language families of the world
Consult: Bloomfield, Leonard, *Language* (New York: Holt, 1933); Greenberg, Joseph, *Language Typology: A Historical and Analytic Overview* (The Hague: Mouton, 1974); Horne, Kibbey M., *Language Typology: Nineteenth and Twentieth Century Views* (Washington: Georgetown University Press, 1966); Pei, Mario, and Gaynor, Frank, *Dictionary of Linguistics* (New York: Philosophical Library, 1954).
—*William H. Gilbert, U.S. Library of Congress (ret.)*

**Lanning, Edward Putnam** (b. 1930). Archaeologist best known for his research on the development of agriculture, ceramic analysis, and the origins of ancient civilizations, especially in Peru.

**Latifundia.** This Latin term (singular: latifundium) means "large estates." It refers, generally, to any large agrarian holding organized as a productive system with some form of managerial hierarchy and a separate labor supply which might consist of slaves, rural proletariats, or various forms of bound labor (in the colonial Americas, indenture and *encomienda*). All latifundia, then, involve a class structure of production comprising two basic classes—labor and those who control land and other capital through ownership, trust, stewardship, or usufruct. In a rather indefinite third class the managerial hierarchy is separate from both other classes, as in modern plantations or some agribusinesses. Basically, latifundia represent a kind of industrial system organizing many people as machines—an organization originating, at latest, in Hellenic Egypt whence it diffused to the Roman Mediterranean and later, in varying forms, throughout Europe and thence to Europe's Old and New World colonies. Some usages of latifundium exclude agribusinesses or plantations because they use modern machinery and rationalize production.

See also Minifundia; Plantations
Consult: Grier, Elizabeth, *Accounting in the Zenon Papyri* (New York: Columbia University Press, 1934); Grier, Elizabeth, *Plantation Systems of the New World* (Washington: Pan American Union, 1959).
—Anthony Leeds, Boston University

**Laughlin, William S.** (b. 1919). A physical anthropologist at the University of Connecticut, Laughlin is known for his research on the physical anthropology of the arctic and human biobehavioral adaptability. In 1966, he published a paper in the *Eugenics Quarterly* on the relationship between social class/ethnicity and intelligence, in which he argued that differences in capabilities are created by the mechanism of assortative mating and that through this mechanism certain social groups or classes have a higher percentage of intellectually capable people than others.

**Law.** *See* Comparative jurisprudence; Legal systems; Traditions.

**Lawick-Goodall, Jane van.** *See* Goodall, Jane.

**Leach, Edmund R.** (b. 1910). One of the formost social anthropologists in the world, Leach, who teaches at Cambridge University in England, has pioneered in analyzing culture as communication. His work on culture as a system of symbols has been extremely influential.

**Leadership.** This term is often used colloquially to refer to personal, charismatic qualities in leaders. In contemporary anthropological usage, however, leadership is regarded not in terms of personal attributes but rather in terms of role behavior

within a social context. Thus leadership is a process of interaction between the leader and other members of the group. Generally, the leader occupies a position in the social structure which is the focal point of group decision-making. Leadership is thus viewed in the context of group or collective action. Leaders in one social situation may not be leaders in another.

An important distinction is made between actual leadership and *titular authorities*. Frequently the latter may be individuals with ceremonial authority who have little actual leadership attached to their status; most constitutional monarchies may be seen in this light. Another titular authority is the Samoan "talking chief," who himself has no power to make political decisions but publicly represents decisions made by the *matai* (elected family head). Leadership may also be confused with demagoguery and agitation—both forms of influence which are primarily emotional in appeal and without inherent political legitimacy.

See also Chiefdom; Headman; Power; Status
Consult: Lasswell, H. D., and Kaplan, A., *Power and Society* (New Haven: Yale University Press, 1950); Whyte, W. F., *Street Corner Society* (Chicago: University of Chicago Press, 1943).
—Richard L. Stone, California State University, Los Angeles

**Leakey, Louis Seymour Bazatt** (1903–1972). A paleontologist and archaeologist, Leakey is best known for his work in Tanzania's Olduvai Gorge. There, in 1959, he and his wife Mary found a 1,750,000-year-old fossil skull of an australopithecine, which he named *Zinjanthropus*. In 1960, the husband and wife team unearthed another group of skull fragments which they called *Homo habilis* and claimed as the earliest member of the genus of modern humans. Leakey's own research inspired many people to explore early humans and the living primates. Two of the better known are Jane Goodall, who studies chimpanzees in their natural environment, and Diane Fossey, who studies the mountain gorilla.

See also Fossil sequence of human evolution; Olduvai Gorge

**Leakey, Mary Douglas Nicol** (b. 1913). This renowned archaeologist has worked in East Africa for more than thirty years. It

was she who first discovered *Zinjanthropus* in Tanzania's Olduvai Gorge in 1959, although her late husband, L. S. B. Leakey, is usually credited with the find.

See also Australopithecines; Fossils sequence of human evolution; Olduvai Gorge

**Leakey, Richard E.** (b. 1940). Kenyan archaeologist, administrative director of the National Museums of Kenya, and son of Louis and Mary Leakey, since 1968 he has found the remains of more than 100 separate hominids and their tools in Kenya's Lake Rudolph region—more than all the rest of the world's fossil sites have yielded in the past fifty years.

In 1972 Leakey unearthed more than thirty fragments of a single skull belonging to a hominid different from any previous known form of early humans. Known now as Skull 1470, it has a cranial capacity of about 800 cc and was dated at almost 3 million years old. The discovery of Skull 1470—as well as more recent discoveries in Ethiopia's Omo and Afar valleys—has prompted a reexamination of the sequence of human evolution.

See also Australopithecines; Fossil sequence of human evolution; Leakey, Louis S. B.; Skull 1470

**Lee, Dorothy Demetracopoulou** (1905–1975). Greek-born American cultural anthropologist well known for her research on the conceptual implications of language-induced change and the value of primitive culture.

**Lee, Richard Borshoi** (b. 1937). Cultural anthropologist known for field research on the ecology and the settlement and subsistence patterns of the !Kung San (Bushman) people of southern Africa's Kalahari Desert.

**Leeds, Anthony** (b. 1925). This cultural anthropologist, known for his research on cultural ecology, social organization, and urbanization, has conducted his major fieldwork in Venezuela and Brazil.

**Legal Systems.** Every society contains several legal systems inasmuch as all social groupings or societal segments that have

*The Babylonian Code of Hammurabi (c. 1800 BC) is the earliest recorded fully developed legal system in the world. Among other things, it provides women with legal rights independent of their husbands' statuses.*

some permanence (a family, a kinship group, a local community, a professional association, or an administrative division) must deal with the same problems: (1) defining the norms regulating social interaction in terms of right/duty relationships, (2) establishing procedures to manage disputes arising from conflicting interests, and (3) creating institutions to facilitate the legislation, application, and enforcement of norms. The anthropological study of law explores how members of a group regulate their conduct and deal with breaches of rules and incompatible interests. The systematic exploration of these questions often relies on the case method as an important research technique. One can distinguish between dyadic and triadic patterns of dispute management. Dyadic patterns involve procedures of negotiation and coercion. Triadic patterns require the intervention of third parties—a go-between, a headman, a neighborhood council, a government court—and may involve procedures of mediation, arbitration, and adjudication.

The comparative analysis of legal systems both within a society and in different societies aims at discovering the ideologies and the political and economic conditions that determine the various uses of these patterns.

See also Case study method; Conflict
Consult: Koch, Klaus-Friedrich, "The Anthropology of Law and Order," in *Horizons of Anthropology*, ed. Sol Tax and Leslie G. Freeman (Chicago: Aldine, 1975); Pospisil, Leopold, *Anthropology of Law: A Comparative Theory* (New York: Harper & Row, 1971).
—Klaus-Friedrich Koch, University of Virginia

### Leighton, Dorothea Cross (b. 1908).

Psychiatrist with interests in anthropology and medicine who is especially known for her work with Clyde Kluckhohn on the Navajo Indians.

### Lenin, Vladimir Ilich Ulyanov (1870–1920).

Lenin, the founder of the Russian Communist Party, greatly expanded on the social philosophy of Karl Marx while claiming to be an orthodox Marxist. As a major leader of the 1917 Bolshevik revolution in Russia which led to the formation of the

*A group of Bakhtiari tribesmen conducting a trial. The accused is alleged to have employed a professional thief to steal for him. Many anthropologists who study legal systems collect such cases for their data. Some argue that cases extending far beyond the trial itself must be collected if we are to come to a complete understanding of how society channels and controls behavior.*

Soviet Union, Lenin had first to promote the possibility of a socialist revolution in Russia, at that time one of the least industrialized nations in Europe. Then, after the fact, he had to defend its viability. Thus Lenin had to forge a theoretical link between Marxist revolutionary theory—which stressed the working classes of the industrialized nations as the inevitable source of socialist revolution—and the objective conditions in prerevolutionary Russia. He accomplished this in his major theoretical work *Imperialism: The Highest Stage of Capitalism* (1917), where he argued that the reason the European industrial working classes were not committed to socialist revolution was because their leaders had been bought off by the ruling classes. Even more importantly, the problems (contradictions) of industrial capitalism were being exported to the emerging nations of the colonized Third World. Thus revolutionary socialist struggle must in fact be anticipated and promoted in the relatively less industrially developed nations. Because he was a Marxist theorist as well as a major activist, Lenin's legitimization of socialist revolution in underdeveloped nations was a great source of inspiration to such Third World revolutionary leaders as Mao Tse-tung and Fidel Castro. His writings are important to anthropologists because they provide a well-elaborated theory about imperialism which can be tested in the light of our data. Moreover, they must be understood by any anthropologist who wishes to do research on Third World revolutionary movements, since revolutionary leaders act in terms of them. Because anthropology itself is in many ways the child of imperialism, we need to understand the historical context of our emerging discipline.

Consult: Lenin, V. I., *Imperialism, The Highest Stage of Capitalism* (Moscow: Progress Publishers, 1970); Connors, James E. (ed.), *Lenin in Politics and Revolution* (Indianapolis: Pegasus, 1968); Wilson, Edmund O., *To the Finland Station* (Garden City, New York: Anchor Books, 1953).
—David E. Hunter, Southern Connecticut State College

### Lenneberg, Eric Heinz (1921–1975).

An American psychologist best known for his research in the biology and psychology of language, Lenneberg also did work in the philosophy of language and mathematics.

**Leroi-Gourhan, André** (b. 1911). French archaeologist whose research deals with Upper Paleolithic cave art and the tool industries of prehistoric people.

See also Upper Paleolithic art

**Lesbianism.** See Homosexuality.

**Levallois Technique.** The Levallois technique entails preparation of stone "tortoise cores" from which flakes are struck. Resulting tool forms are predetermined by the core preparation.

See also Levalloisean tradition; Stonework

**Levalloisean Tradition.** Levallois, often called Levallois-Mousterian, is an Old World tradition characterized by flake tools such as triangular projectile points made by the Levallois technique dating to the Riss-Würm interglacial in European and African Acheulean and Mousterian cultures. It continues into the Upper Paleolithic in the Levant.

See also Levallois technique; Middle Paleolithic; Mousterian culture; Neanderthal man; Stonework

**Level of Contrast.** See Taxonomy.

**Leveling Mechanism.** This term refers to a cultural device which reduces wealth differentials between individuals—often by inducing the wealthy to sponsor feasts or to destroy or give away surplus in return for increased prestige.

See also Exchange; Potlatch

**Levirate.** According to this marriage custom, a woman is expected to marry her deceased husband's brother. A rather widespread custom, levirate has been practiced by many patrilineal groups including the ancient Hebrews.

See also Marriage; Sororate

**Lévi-Strauss, Claude** (b. 1908). Claude Lévi-Strauss was born in Brussels of French parents and spent his childhood and youth in Paris. He first studied law and philosophy but found his real vocation in anthropology. During his Brazilian sojourn, he made various expeditions among the aborigines which he described in his literary and anthropological masterpiece, *Tristes Tropiques* (1959). In his first major theoretical work, *The Elementary Structures of Kinship* (1949), he showed that many marriage rules can be understood on the basis of the principles of reciprocity and exchange and thus can be reduced to variations of a few basic marriage types. In *Structural Anthropology* (1958) he explained his structural method, which he applied later to the study of primitive thought. In *Totemism* (1962) he showed that animal and natural objects are chosen as symbols of clans or families because they are useful as linguistic and classificatory devices to conceptualize and organize social relationships and groups. In *The Savage Mind* (1962) he systematically demonstrated that primitives have a logical, although concrete, mode of thought (concrete logic). His four volumes of *Mythologiques* (1964, 1966, 1968, 1972) offer an impressive, although at times controversial, analysis of a large body of myths, which are shown to be not explanations of natural phenomena but resolutions, in concrete language, of basic categorical paradoxes concerning human existence and the organization of society.

See also French structuralism

—Ino Rossi, St. John's University

**Lévy-Bruhl, Lucien** (1857–1939). This French philosopher, sociologist, and ethnologist was particularly interested in the mental processes of primitive peoples and introduced the idea of prelogical thought (also called "primitive mentality"), a concept he later abandoned and which is now discredited.

See also Primitive mentality

Consult: Lévi-Strauss, Claude, *The Savage Mind* (Chicago: University of Chicago Press, 1966).

**Lewis, Ioan Myrddin** (b. 1930). British social anthropologist noted for his structural and historical research on African peoples, especially among the native peoples of Somaliland.

**Lewis, Oscar** (1914–1970). This American anthropologist is best known for his contention, based on his cross-cultural studies, that there is a distinctive "culture of poverty" common to the poor in many parts of

*Claude Lévi-Strauss*

the world. Lewis argued that the poor tend to display such cultural characteristics as present-time orientation, fatalism, a suspicion of major social institutions, machismo among the males, and a high frequency of consensual unions rather than formal marriages. The children of this culture, Lewis contends, are effectively trapped within it because they are socialized into attitudes and values that impede their social mobility. Critics have suggested, however, that these cultural characteristics may be a response to, and not a cause of, continuing poverty.

*See also* Poverty, culture of
Consult: Lewis, Oscar, *La Vida* (New York: Random House, 1966).

**Lexeme.** A lexeme is a unit of meaning which cannot be inferred from anything else in the language. By definition single morphs are lexemes. Composite forms such as *farmers* are single lexemes.

**Lexicostatistics.** This term refers to a method for investigating the historical relationship between languages. It aims to find whether two or more languages show more forms in common than chance alone could explain. If they do, then there must be some historical connection between them. For languages that have a genetic relationship (i.e., are derived from a common ancestral language), lexicostatistics gives a measure of how far they have diverged from one another over time.

The method is based on a comparison of vocabulary by using a standard list of common words that one might expect to find in any language and that do not suggest any particular kind of culture or geographical environment—parts of the body, for instance. Because the association of certain sounds with certain meanings is quite arbitrary in every language, the chance of two unrelated languages choosing the same sounds to represent the same meaning is small. The percentage of cognate forms in two languages' core vocabulary lists then shows how closely the languages are related. For example, two languages that have cognate forms in 60 percent of the list are said to be more closely related than languages with only 20 percent cognates; less than 4 percent cognates is generally thought too few to say whether the languages are related or not.

Criticisms of this method focus on its tendency to assume that languages are related *genetically* when other kinds of historical relationship, such as diffusion and reintegration, should be more carefully considered. In addition, the existence of a core vocabulary, relatively culture-free and resistant to borrowing, has never really been substantiated.

*See also* Glottochronology; Historical linguistics; Linguistic reconstruction
Consult: Hymes, Dell, "Lexicostatistics So Far," *Current Anthropology* 1:3–44, 1960; Swadesh, Morris, "Linguistics as an Instrument of Prehistory," *Southwestern Journal of Anthropology* 15:20–35, 1959.
—*Judith T. Irvine, Brandeis University*

**Libby, Willard** (b. 1908). American scientist who won the Nobel Prize in chemistry in 1960 for developing the radiocarbon dating method.

*See also* Radiocarbon dating

**License, Cultural.** Certain categories of people in a society may have a license to act familiarly with categories of other people. These people may or may not be kin. The purpose of the behavior seems to be to stress the privileged relationship between the two groups, for in other contexts the behavior subsumed under the cultural license may lead to intense hostility. The behavior may range from verbal insults to the stealing of personal possessions from one another—it may even involve joking at the funeral of a member of the other social category. The license may be symmetrical or asymmetrical; that is, there may be an equal or unequal flow of culturally licensed behavior.

*See also* Joking, ritualized

**Liebow, Elliot** (b. 1925). Liebow, an American anthropologist, argues that ghetto blacks are committed to American middle-class aims and values but are prevented from achieving them by patterns in the social and economic systems of the wider society over which they have no control.

**Life Cycle.** This term refers to the orderly progression of individuals through a series of different stages in life from birth to death. Life-cycle studies focus attention on the individual's roles and social positions in these life stages and also on the transitions from stage to stage (the *rites de passage*). Since all people in all cultures go through such series of stages (birth, childhood, puberty, marriage/mature adulthood, old age, death), life-cycle studies are convenient mechanisms for examining the similarities and differences among and between cultures. In turn, such studies provide basic materials for theoretical constructs formulated to account for the nature and variety of cultures.

**Pregnancy and Birth.** Although members of all cultures realize that birth is the outcome of a woman's pregnancy, cross-culturally there are differing beliefs as to what in fact causes pregnancy. The Hidatsa (North America) believe that spirits impregnate women, whereas the Dobu Islanders (South Pacific) believe that semen entering the uterus causes the woman's menstrual blood to coagulate, forming the fetus. Often a pregnant woman is subject to a variety of taboos, food taboos being the most common. In addition, rituals may be performed to promote proper growth of the fetus and easy childbirth. After childbirth, mother and child are usually secluded for a period of time. In some societies, during or immediately after birth, the father retires to bed and seclusion, imitating the hardships of childbirth and postpartum exhaustion, a practice known as the *couvade*. After the first few days or weeks of birth, many societies hold naming ceremonies that symbolize the recognition of a new group member.

**Childhood.** Childhood is the period of life in which people learn both the ways of providing for their physical needs and also the traditions and social customs of their culture. This latter process is known as *socialization* or *enculturation*. Methods of childrearing vary enormously from culture to culture. Fascinated by this variety of childrearing mechanisms, some anthropologists have attempted to correlate certain childrearing practices with specific adult personality traits, an approach known as culture and personality.

**Puberty.** Puberty marks the physical maturation of individuals, and in most cultures it is correlated with the social recognition of adulthood status. Since puberty is such a critical transitional period of life, a time when an individual ceases to be a child and

*Tables such as this one attempt to synthesize what is known about human developmental processes. However, their attempt to equate developmental stages with specific ages is far too arbitrary, static, and culture-bound to be of great usefulness (adapted from Gordon).*

| Life-Cycle Stage | Approximate Ages | Most Significant Others | Major Dilemmas |
|---|---|---|---|
| infancy | 0–12 months | mother | affective gratification/ sensorimotor experiencing |
| early childhood | 1–2 years | mother, father | compliance/ self-control |
| Oedipal period | 3–5 years | father, mother, siblings, playmates | expressivity/ instrumentality |
| later childhood | 6–11 years | parents, same-sex peers, teachers | peer relation-ships/evaluated abilities |
| early adolescence | 12–15 years | parents, same-sex peers, opposite-sex peers, teachers | acceptance/ achievement |
| later adolescence | 16–20 years | same-sex peers, opposite-sex peers, parents, teachers, loved one, wife or husband | intimacy/ autonomy |
| young adulthood | 21–29 years | loved one, husband, or wife, children, employers, friends | connection/self-determination |
| early maturity | 30–44 years | wife or husband, children, superiors, colleagues, friends, parents | stability/ accomplishment |
| full maturity | 45 to retirement age | wife or husband, children, colleagues, friends, younger associates | dignity/control |
| old age | retirement to age of death | remaining family, long-term friends, neighbors | meaningful integration/ autonomy |

takes on the responsibilities of the adult world, it is often associated with elaborate rituals. Puberty rites for women take place at the time of the first menses and often involve seclusion of the pubescent girl in a special menstrual hut with special prescriptions and proscriptions. Among some peoples such as the Bambuti Pygmies of Africa, this seclusion period is also a time for learning adult women's roles, appropriate sexual conduct, and tribal rituals. After these rites, the girls emerge as women, ready for marriage and childbearing. Their marriageability status may be marked by the wearing of certain ornaments, a particular hairstyle or dress, or some form of body scarification. In certain cultures these rites are incorporated into a period of seclusion at which time the young men are taught the cultural traditions and initiated into the ways of manhood. In most societies, adolescence as it is known in America is not marked by internal tensions and alienation of the young from adults. Instead, the time between the onset of puberty and marriage is a time of happiness, filled with expectations of assuming the full responsibilities of adulthood upon marriage.

**Marriage/Mature Adulthood.** In most societies marriage follows soon after the formal recognition of adult status for men and women. Frequently marriage partners are chosen by older family members with the intent of forming or increasing alliance bonds between two kinship groups. Prior to a formal marriage ceremony, there may be a gift of valuables from the groom's kinfolk to the bride's kinfolk. This gift is known as the *brideprice* (or bridewealth or progeny price). With the advent of marriage young men and women take on the full responsibilities of adulthood with all its roles and statuses.

**Old Age.** Old age heralds a time of relaxation of adult responsibilities for both men and women. In many cultures these elders command much respect and prestige from the rest of the community and are often thought to be endowed with special spiritual powers. They are eagerly sought after for their advice and wisdom. However, in a few societies (such as our own) old age is regarded as debilitating and old people are not accorded special attention. In fact, in cultures such as the Eskimos', where there is sometimes a scarcity of food, old people may commit suicide or be left to die so that the young may survive.

**Death.** Death, being the cessation of life as we know it on earth, is a time of special religious significance observed by family and community ceremonies. Death rites not only mark the passing of a group member into another world or condition but also serve as a renewal ceremony for the living whereby the values and essence of the culture are reaffirmed.

See also Adulthood; Culture and personality; Enculturation; Marriage

Consult: Ford, Clellan S., *A Comparative Study of Human Reproduction*, Yale University Publications in Anthropology, no. 32, 1945; Mead, Margaret, *Coming of Age in Samoa* (New York: New American Library, 1949); Whiting, B. B. (ed.), *Six Cultures: Studies of Child Rearing* (New York: Wiley, 1963); Young, Frank, *Initiation Ceremonies: A Cross-cultural Study of Status Dramatization* (Indianapolis: Bobbs-Merrill, 1965).

—Beatrice A. Bigony, University of Wisconsin, Stout

## Life History Approach.

The close study of a single human biography is frequently used both for the study of one personality in a specific cultural setting or as a means of studying a whole culture. Life history materials may be autobiographical (unsolicited) or biographical (encouraged by the questions of an anthropologist). The materials may be presented verbatum as narrated by the individual, or they may be heavily edited, rearranged, and carefully analyzed for psychodynamic factors. The subject may be a contemporary or a historical figure. One serious bias has been a tendency to collect biographies from maladjusted individuals who are most prone to talk about their lives. A special application of the biographical approach is to the study of small primary groups, as in Oscar Lewis's *La Vida* and *The Children of Sanchez*.

Consult: Langness, L. L., *Life History in Anthropological Science* (New York: Holt, 1965).

## Limited Good, Image of.

According to this concept which is associated with George Foster, peasants view their total universe as one in which all desired things in life exist in finite quantity. Hence gains in one area are assumed to involve losses in another. This notion results in resistance to economic development.

See also Foster, George; Peasants

## Limited Possibilities, Principle of.

A concept first introduced and elaborated upon by Alexander Goldenweiser, who pro-

pounded it in order to explain parallels in technological traits (in diverse cultures) that were not caused by diffusion. Simply stated, the principle notes that the (principally environmental) within which people act set limits on the range of possibilities of their actions (and the forms of their cultural traits). Others, notably George P. Murdock, have expanded on the application of the principle to a wide spectrum of cultural domains—including forms of kinship.

See also Comparative method; Ethnology; Goldenweiser, Alexander

## Lineage.

This term refers to the consanguineal members of a descent group (which may include their spouses) who are able to trace their descent to known forebears. Unilineal descent means that kin relationship is traced through one line. Patrilineages trace descent through males, matrilineages through females. Often property as well as group membership and titles are passed from generation to generation along these lineage lines.

See also Clan; Kinship

Consult: Murdock, George P., *Social Structure* (New York: Free Press, 1949).

## Lineal Relatives.

See Descent; Kinship.

## Lines and Rope, Knots and Splices.

Lines are thin but strong cord; ropes thicker, stronger, corded fibers for use in securing or hauling heavy objects. Lines or cords are made of twisted fibers or multiples of twisted fibers again twisted on themselves. The materials have ranged from single twisted strips of rawhide used by the Plains Indians to four-strand cords wrapped shroudlike around a strong core as used in Bronze Age Europe. These latter types of cord were made of a bast from nettle fiber and hair (protowool) of early sheep or lime bark and hair. They were used as pottery slings during the Mesolithic. Nets made of corded line were known in the later Paleolithic and perhaps even earlier. In the Mediterranean reeds and esparto grass were used for baskets and cords, while further north the stem of hair moss, nettle fiber, fiber, lime bark, bast, and even horsehair were used. Fibers of cotton plants and hemp

ranged from India to North Africa. In the Far East, even grass was utilized in great, heavy hawsers.

Splicing is a technique used to lengthen and join lines and ropes. In this way fibers can be continuously added and twisted into existing bundles of fine fiber as the cord or rope is being made. Two lengths are spliced together by raveling the cut ends anywhere from a few inches in cord to a foot and a half in rope, intermingling fibers of matched bundles, then retwisting the bundles again in the same directions as originally started.

Knotting, as a means of joining two or more lengths of line, is of very ancient origin. Both knotted and unknotted netting seem to have a late Paleolithic origin. The elaboration of knotting has had two principal lines of development: one is in marine technology with netting, attachment of fishhooks, boat lines, and boat rigging for sails; the other has resulted in knotting connected with textile production and ranges from pile fabrics (as in Bushongo grass cloths, Benin robes, Coptic shawls, Persian carpets) to Scandinavian *rya* rugs. Present-day fashions in macramé knotting developed out of the original purpose of finishing off the warp threads or cut fringe of rugs. This fashion spread from North Africa into Spain and was exported to Mexico in the New World; in the 16th century in Italy it was used for making fashionable lace.

—Justine M. Cordwell, Chicago City Colleges/ Malcolm X

## Linguistic Reconstruction.

The aim of linguistic reconstruction is to discover the relationships among a number of languages and to reconstruct a common ancestor for them. The usual method is called the comparative method. Its model is the reconstruction of proto-Indo-European. (A protolanguage is an extinct original one that is ancestral to a number of now separate but related languages.)

The usual manner of linguistic reconstruction is to move from the present to earlier stages of a language family. A comparison is made of *cognates* (words with similar phonological and semantic properties) in related languages. These are usually arranged in a tabular form and systematically assigned a value in the protolanguage. The general rule is that the more commonly a form is found in a language family, the older the form is. Furthermore, unanalyzable forms are regarded as older than all others (proper care must be taken to eliminate from consideration borrowed forms which are usually nonanalyzable into smaller forms in the language which borrowed them).

Linguistic reconstruction has implications for a number of other areas of anthropology. It is useful for understanding kinship, material culture, culture contact, migrations, the relative ages for cultural traits, and other problems involved in understanding the evolution of cultural systems. Its role in the study of culture change has only begun to be appreciated.

*See also* Historical linguistics; Lexicostatistics
*—Frank A. Salamone, St. John's University*

## Linguistic Relativity, Theory of. *See* Language and culture.

## Linguistics. Linguistics is the study of language. The academic discipline is often divided into two large categories. *Historical linguistics* is concerned with the evolution of languages and language groups through time and with reconstructing extinct protolanguages from which historically known languages differentiated. *Descriptive linguistics* focuses attention on recording, transcribing, and analyzing the structures of languages distributed across the world today.

*See also* Descriptive linguistics; Historical linguistics; Language; Language and culture; Language and reality; Language and thought; Lexicostatistics; Semantics; Sociolinguistics; Stratificational school of linguistics; Syntax; Transformation linguistics
Consult: Hockett, Charles F., *A Course in Modern Linguistics* (New York: Macmillan, 1958); Waterman, John T., *Perspectives in Linguistics*, 2nd ed. (Chicago: University of Chicago Press, 1970).

## Linguistics, Anthropological. The two primary concerns of anthropological linguistics are to establish the evolutionary relationships between human language and systems of animal communication and to understand the multiple social functions of human linguistic behavior.

**Human Language and Animal Communication.** Although the origin of language no longer holds the interest it formerly did (due to the lack of reliable information), there is abundant interest in the evolutionary development of human speech, especially with regard to the communication systems of the primates more closely related to humans. Comparative structural and functional analysis of human and animal communication systems holds much promise for revealing how each system has evolved and perhaps for some insight into their ultimate origins.

**Language Universals.** The search for language universals aims at discovering what characteristics are common to all languages. There are some universal features which all languages share: either specific forms (e.g., nasal phonemes), kinds of grammatical operations (e.g., pronominalization), or types of changes (e.g., a less natural sound shifts to a more natural sound). Furthermore, some linguistic features are more nearly universal than others—they occur more frequently in a given language or are present in more languages. Tabulation of the comparative frequencies of such features yields hierarchies ("implicational universals") that indicate which ones are more or less likely to be found in most languages.

**Language and World View.** The Sapir-Whorf *linguistic relativity hypothesis* assumes that the structure and forms of a language determine to some extent the perceptual reality (world view) of its speakers. The *semantic differential*, developed by Charles Osgood, is a more objective method for evaluating people's perceptions (and values) on the basis of how they rate a series of words and concepts along scales of opposite polarities. Carroll (1964) summarizes both methods.

**Language Classification.** The classification of groups of languages into different families enables anthropologists to learn much about the prehistory of their speakers. The geographical distribution of the dialects of a language or language family often reveals previous migratory routes. The presence of borrowed elements in a linguistic system indicates previous cross-cultural contacts. Lexicostatistics (glottochronology) is a method used for determining linguistic relationships and for establishing approximate dates of splits of parent languages into distinct offspring languages.

**Writing Systems.** The study of systems of writing throughout history aims at discovering the various origins of the diverse writing systems of the world, at tracing the spread of writing throughout different regions, and at deciphering written messages of ancient civilizations in order to supplement the archaeological evidence for those societies.

**Language in Society.** The study of trade languages (pidgins) aims at revealing the sociopolitical climates in which they arise, at discovering regular patterns in the formative stages of pidgins, and at understanding the forces that transform some pidgins into people's native languages (creoles).

In nations where many different languages or dialects are in use, social scientists work to resolve problems of communication among ethnic groups by applying anthropological linguistic methods to plan language standardization policy and to design flexible educational programs compatible with the language differences of different ethnic groups.

*See also* Distinctive features; Formal semantic analysis; Linguistics
Consult: Carroll, John, *Language and Thought* (Englewood Cliffs, N.J.: Prentice-Hall, 1964); Greenberg, Joseph, *Language Universals* (The Hague: Mouton, 1966); Hymes, Dell (ed.), *Language in Culture and Society* (New York: Harper & Row, 1964).
*—Charles T. Snow, California State University, Chico*

## Linguistics, Descriptive. *See* Descriptive linguistics.

## Linguistics, Structural. *See* Descriptive linguistics.

## Linnaeus, Carolus (Carl von Linné) (1707–1778). Swedish naturalist who devised binomial nomenclature (genus and species) to classify plants and animals in his *Systema Naturae* (1735).

## Linton, Ralph (1893–1953). An internationally known anthropologist, Linton began his training as an archaeologist and was sent by the Bishop Museum in Hawaii to the Marquesa Islands in 1920–1922. While there he became interested in the living peoples of the islands and switched to cultural anthropology. From then on his primary anthropological interests centered on personality, social structure, cultural process, and material culture. He is probably best remembered for his abilities at synthesizing diverse anthropological data, and for his formally

*Ralph Linton*

introducing the concepts of *status* and *role* (1936). He published a number of important works including *The Study of Man* (1936), *The Cultural Background of Personality* (1945), and *The Tree of Culture* (1955).

## Literature, Oral. *See* Oral literature.

## Literature, Written.
There are two ways in which anthropologists use written literature: ethnohistorical reconstruction, and the synchronic study of literate civilizations. For the former, old documents provide important data on everything from shipping inventories to myths; for the latter, they provide data on the grand scope of the society—a background against which ethnographically obtained data can be put into a meaningful context.

*See also* Ethnohistory; Oral literature

## Lithic Ages.
The earliest attempts to divide prehistory into a succession of ages dates to classical antiquity. In the 1st century BC, the Roman philosopher/poet Lucretius, drawing upon still earlier Greek sources, posited the existence of successive ages of stone, bronze, and iron through which all humankind was to pass. Similar assertions continued to be made throughout the Middle Ages and especially during the Renaissance, a period characterized by renewed interest in classical literature and archaeology (see Clarke 1968:3–11 for a concise review). However ramified these schemes became, it is important to note that they remained philosophical speculations down to the latter part of the 18th century. They were never utilized to organize the masses of archaeological data which had been accumulating in European museums since the Renaissance, and so had little pragmatic value. In regions favored with a long written history, prehistoric archaeological remains were classified in terms of the descriptions of primitive peoples (barbarians, in the Greek sense) which abound in classical literature. It is perhaps not coincidental, then, that the earliest data-based schemes for classifying prehistoric remains developed in Scandinavia, outside the sphere of Graeco-Roman influence.

During the latter part of the 18th century, the wave of antiquarian interest which had crested earlier in Italy, France, and the British Isles also swept through Scandinavia (especially Denmark and Sweden). As elsewhere in Europe, it resulted in a proliferation of more or less carefully controlled excavations and the consequent accumulation of still more prehistoric artifacts. By about 1800, Danish antiquaries had acquired so much artifactual material that the government commissioned the librarian at the University of Copenhagen, one Rasmus Nyerup, to organize and care for the collections. What would be regarded as a comparatively simple assignment today was a formidable undertaking in 1800, since Denmark was bereft of a long historical record and no widely accepted scheme existed in terms of which the artifacts could be classified. In 1807 Nyerup was named secretary to the newly formed Royal Commission for the Preservation of Antiquities; in 1808 funds were allocated for the construction of a national museum.

Although three-age theories had appeared from time to time during the earlier part of the 18th century, the first to gain acceptance in Scandinavia was a general prehistory of Sweden, published by Vedel Simonsen in 1813. His three-age system, modeled on the classical formula, consisted of an age of stone/wood, an age of copper/bronze, and an iron age, which, while held to be unilineal and universal, overlapped in time from region to region. Simonsen's book was widely circulated in Scandinavia; more important, it advocated the use of a three-age scheme as a general classificatory device for ordering archaeological material.

Perhaps the most influential figure in the emergence of a paradigm for classification is another Dane, Christian Jørgensen Thomsen, who assumed directorship of the Danish National Museum in 1816, succeeding Nyerup, and who ran the museum for almost fifty years. Thomsen is noteworthy because he attempted (1816–1819) what Simonsen had advocated: the first systematic classification of a large body of artifacts (Nyerup's collections), sorting them on the basis of raw material, form, and method of manufacture. His ages, established for the purposes of museum display, corresponded to and were derived from those of Simonsen, but his classification was more rigorous and dealt in specifics. In 1836, Thomsen published his "Guide to Nordic Antiquities," which set forth the details of his system, illustrating each age with examples and pointing out the chronological relationship inherent in his classification and the stratigraphic evidence on which it was based. The latter are particularly important because, as Clarke (1968) has pointed out, they increase the information content of archaeological data. Whereas the antiquary was confronted with piles of artifacts meaningless in cultural or technological terms, Thomsen created the basis for the typological method and what might be called the technological approach to prehistory.

It took about thirty years before Thomsen's system diffused over Western Europe and the British Isles. It reached England during the 1850s and by 1865 we have Sir John Lubbock referring to a stone age divided into two parts—an early stage characterized by implements of flaked stone, called the paleolithic, and a later stage in which tools were fashioned by grinding and polishing, called the neolithic. In 1858, in the tenth edition of his *Principles of Geology*, Sir Charles Lyell uses these terms as part of the four-stage system still widely employed today.

*See also* Prehistoric archaeology; Prehistory
Consult: Clarke, D., *Analytical Archaeology* (London: Methuen, 1968); Daniel, G., *The Idea of Prehistory* (New York: World, 1963).
—*Geoffrey A. Clark, Arizona State University*

**Little Tradition.** This term refers to the culture of the rural villager living within a civilization. The Little Tradition contrasts with the Great Tradition, which is the formal tradition of the civilization. Robert Redfield is identified with these concepts. Elements of the Little Tradition are continually incorporated into the Great Tradition through a process of universalization. Likewise elements of the Great Tradition filter down to the village level, but in the process of parochialization the elements are transformed, modified, or reinterpreted to fit the rural, peasant tradition. The concept of Little Tradition does not apply to primitive peoples, whose culture is thought to be autonomous.

See also Great Tradition; Redfield, Robert
Consult: Redfield, Robert, *Peasant Society and Culture* (Chicago: University of Chicago Press, 1956).

**Livingstone, Frank** (b. 1928). Physical anthropologist at the University of Michigan well known for his biocultural correlation of the sickle-cell gene with the spread of farming in malarious areas of W Africa. He has been a leader of the movement to discredit *race* as a scientifically useful concept.

**Llano Culture.** Fluted, lanceolate points and other hunting tools of the Clovis and Folsom Llano complex, found throughout most of North America, are the earliest *undisputed* paleo-Indian evidence of the peopling of the New World. This culture dates ca. 12,000–10,000 years BP and is associated with extinct fauna.

See also Plano culture

**Locality.** See Marriage.

**Locomotion, Primate Evolutionary Trends of.** The primate order is generally characterized by the speed, flexibility, and agility adaptive in arboreal life. Possession of freely mobile digits and of pads and nails rather than claws on fingers and toes aids in clinging and climbing. Locomotor patterns vary with age, activity, and time of day. However, the different grades within the order exhibit varying locomotor tendencies, and from an analysis of the bone morphology of extinct primates—particularly the intermembral index based on the ratio of arm to leg length, the structure of the shoulder girdle, and the shape of the hand and foot bones—it would appear that modern locomotor differences can be projected into the past as evolutionary trends.

Some living prosimians move by vertical clinging and leaping. Other prosimians and the Old and New World monkeys are quadrupedal. The apes show the morphological attributes of brachiation, adapted for locomotion and suspension by means of the arms. Today only the gibbons and siamangs are true brachiators; the heavy orangutan uses modified brachiation, while chimpanzees and gorillas spend much time knuckle-walking on the ground. Bipedalism, involving fully erect posture while standing, striding, or running, is an important recent hominid adaptation to terrestrial living.

See also Primates, evolutionary features of
Consult: Jolly, Alison, *The Evolution of Primate Behavior* (New York: Macmillan, 1972); Simons, Elwyn L., *Primate Evolution* (New York: Macmillan, 1972).
—Catherine E. Read-Martin, California State University, Los Angeles

**Loess.** See Glaciations.

**Lomax, Alan** (b. 1915). An authority on folk music and its cultural context, Lomax is the codeveloper of a method for the cross-cultural comparison of song performance called cantometrics.

**Lombroso, Cesare** (1835–1909). This Italian professor of psychiatry believed that potential criminals could be identified by certain physical characteristics and that these people represented survivals of a more primitive stage of human evolution. His *L'uomo delinquente* (The Criminal Man) appeared in 1876.

**Longacre, William** (b. 1937). A pioneer of the New Archaeology, Longacre combined hypothesis with statistical techniques to infer the ancient kinship and residence patterns at the Carter Ranch Site, Arizona.

See also Kinship; New Archaeology, the; Statistical methods

**Loom.** The rigid or semirigid framework for weaving was invented prehistorically in both the Old and the New Worlds. The loom appears throughout the world in diverse forms ranging from simple mobile backstrap loom to complex industrial looms.

See also Textiles

**Lorenz, Konrad** (b. 1903). An Austrian zoologist born in Vienna, Lorenz received his M.D. (1928) and a Ph.D. in zoology (1933) from the University of Vienna. In 1973 he shared a Nobel prize in physiology/medicine with Niko Tinbergen and Karl von Frisch. His "discoveries concerning organization and elicitation of individual and social behavior patterns" (Nobel citation)—for decades at the Max Planck Institute in Germany, presently at the Institute for Behavior Research in Greunau, Austria—led to his writings on what he believes to be innate forms of aggression and the problem of its restraint in humans. Lorenz is best known for *On Aggression* (1966) and the two-volume *Studies in Animal and Human Behavior* (1970–1971).

See also Aggression; Ethology; Imprinting; Instincts; Species-characteristic behavior; Tinbergen, Niko

**Lost Wax Technique.** With this technique, modeled wax covered with clay or plaster produces molds for molten metal. Firing melts away the wax, making possible intricate castings such as many Shang, Ur, Colima, and Inca specimens. This technique is also known as *cire perdue.*

See also Metalworking

**Lounsbury, Floyd Glenn** (b. 1914). Linguistic anthropologist who has made important contributions to the study of the formal semantic analysis of kinship terminological systems.

**Lower Paleolithic.** This division of the Paleolithic prehistoric age is generally dated from 3 million years BP to 200,000 years BP—from the time of the earliest pebble tools to the appearance of specialized flake tools.

See also Lithic ages; Paleolithic; Pebble tools

**Lowie, Robert H.** (1883–1957). One of the foremost American anthropologists of the 20th century, Lowie received his Ph.D. in

1908 from Columbia under the direction of Franz Boas. He worked under Clark Wissler at the American Museum of Natural History from 1907 to 1917, concentrating his efforts on fieldwork among northern Plains Indian groups. Although his publications on Indian culture were numerous, he is best known for his meticulous and comprehensive ethnographic/linguistic research on the Crow (*The Crow Indians*, 1935). In 1917 Lowie joined the anthropological staff at the University of California, Berkeley, where he remained for the rest of his professional career. As a theorist, he promulgated the tradition of the Boasian historical school, insisting that diffusion was of primary importance in reconstructing cultural history and that ethnology could only become a science when facts undergirded theoretical frameworks. Of all his works, *Primitive Society* (1920), which had a major impact on social organization theory, and *History of Ethnological Theory* (1937) perhaps best illustrate his views on the essence and nature of anthropology.

*See also* Boas, Franz

**Lubbock, Sir John** (1834–1913). English prehistorian, biologist, and popular writer. A neighbor, protégé, and ardent supporter of Charles Darwin, Lubbock helped evolutionism gain its general acceptance. In his *Pre-Historic Times, as Illustrated by Ancient Remains and the Manners and Customs of Modern Savages* (1865), he expanded the three-age system of C. J. Thomsen and proposed that the Stone Age be divided into Old and New Stages, resulting in the following four stages: Paleolithic, Neolithic, Bronze Age, Iron Age.

*See also* Lithic ages

**Lyell, Charles** (1797–1875). This British geologist established the modern science of geology with his *Principles of Geology*. He destroyed catastrophism by propounding the theory of uniformitarianism—all geological changes, both ancient and modern, happen because of uniform processes rather than special catastrophes. He accumulated information from many sources that was used by Charles Darwin, Alfred Russel Wallace, and others. Moreover, he pushed back the time span available for evolution to take place and actually had all the ideas and material to write the *Origin of Species* but

*Charles Lyell*

was unable to pull them together. He did, however, influence and encourage Darwin in his magnum opus.

*See also* Uniformitarianism

**Lynching.** This form of punishment involves the killing (generally by hanging) of a person accused of a crime. The guilt or innocence of the victim may not have been determined by trial in a formal court of law. The accused is judged by a segment of the population, often a mob, and guilt may be established by the moral outrage of the people without the presence of valid, incriminating evidence.

Lynching also may be perpetrated if citizens do not agree with the verdict of a court and proceed to "take justice into their own hands." The act is most often associated with the southern United States in previous decades and with the former frontier regions of the country.

*See also* Murder

**Machines.** *See* Technology.

**MacNeish, R. S.** (b. 1918). MacNeish's archaeological research in Mexico has contributed much toward understanding the development of agriculture (especially maize) from hunting/gathering societies to food-producing villages.

**Macrobehavior.** *See* Proxemics.

**Macroevolution.** *See* Evolution and genetics.

**Mafia.** Mafia is the name given to a form of retainership and patronage found in Sicily and Calabria, Italy. It was characterized by an attitude of varying degrees of hostility toward outside authorities, for example the state. Allegiance or cooperation with the state was a violation of the code of *omertà* (manliness). The Mafia was not a highly centralized phenomenon but rather local gangs sharing similar values and norms. This continues to be the predominant pattern today.

Similar attitudes were apparently brought to the United States by immigrants from Italy. Primarily in cities, the bonds of brotherhood and *omertà* proved helpful in achieving upward economic and social mobility. The American example of Mafia has been associated with organized crime, its spheres of operations extending far beyond the confines of the country.

*See also* Protective associations
Consult: Bell, Daniel, "Crime as an American Way of Life," *Antioch Review*, Summer 1953; Dolci, Danilo, *Outlaws* (N.Y.: Orion, 1961); Dolci, Danilo, *The Man Who Plays Alone* (Garden City, N.Y.: Doubleday, 1970); Hobsbawm, Eric J., *Primitive Rebels: Studies in Archaic Forms of Social Movement in the 19th and 20th Centuries* (New York: Norton, 1959).

**Magdalenian Culture.** This term refers to an Upper Paleolithic assemblage whose type site is La Madeleine (SW France); it is dated 17,000–10,000 BP. Frequently this sequence is divided into a lower stage characterized by *raclettes,* multiple borers, and beveled-base antler points (e.g., Laugerie Haute) and an upper stage characterized by uniserial and biserial harpoons (e.g., La Madeleine). The people lived in typical steppe/tundra–adapted hunting societies. The large open sites (e.g., Solvieux, Pincevent) imply social aggregates of more than 100 persons. This assemblage is best known in N and SW France and N Spain.

*See also* Upper Paleolithic

**Magic.** *See* Magic and science; Magic and social controls; Magic and witchcraft.

**Magic and Science.** The relationship between magic and science is a conceptual issue that has traditionally concerned anthropologists. Sir James Frazer in *The Golden Bough* developed the idea of universal stages of human intellectual development. According to Frazer, humanity must everywhere pass through three stages: from magic and superstition to religion and thence to science and rationality. Nevertheless Frazer, following Edward Tylor, thought that magic and science have a pronounced similarity; indeed he conceptualized magic as false or bastard science. Both were attempts to control events, both had a strong faith in the order and uniformity of nature, both believed in invariable natural laws. Religion in contrast postulated a world in which events depend on the whim of spirits. To Frazer magic and science were identical in conception. But the underlying laws of magic—*similarity* (like produces like) and *contagion* (things once in contact continue to act on each other)—were erroneous correlations of cause and effect, conceptualized (following Tylor) as the misapplication of the association of ideas.

Bronislaw Malinowski deviated from this conceptual tradition by denying that magic was false science. He viewed magic as expressive symbolism which is cathartic and functions to relieve anxiety. People do not engage in magic in the absence of science; rather, they are as scientific as their technology allows. They resort to magic to deal with issues beyond their technological capacity. Many contemporary anthropologists do not regard magic as pseudoscience but, following Malinowski's lead, approach it as expressive behavior although possibly of a more subtle nature than Malinowski envisioned. Others have conceived of magic as the expression of a different but not inferior world view than that current in our own culture.

*See also* Expressive systems; Frazer, James George; Malinowski, Bronislaw; Religion

Consult: Frazer, J., *The New Golden Bough*, ed. T. H. Gaster (Garden City, N.Y.: Anchor, 1961); Malinowski, B., *Magic, Science and Religion* (Garden City, N.Y.: Doubleday, 1948); Wax, M., and Wax, R., "The Notion of Magic," *Current Anthropology* 4(5):495–518, 1963; Winch, P., "Understanding a Primitive Society," *American Philosophical Quarterly* 1(4): 307–324, 1964.

—Stan Wilk, Lycoming College

**Magic and Social Control.** Social control is behavior designed to ensure that individuals departing from established standards of behavior will return to such standards. Magic, the (usually ritualized) attempt to manipulate supernatural powers, is often employed toward this end. Witchcraft and sorcery are perhaps the most frequently used forms. Among the Trobrianders, for example, ranking individuals in the community used sorcerers to punish lower-ranked individuals who attempted to behave in an unbefitting manner—getting too rich, failing to pay proper respect, or violating cross-rank sexual taboos. The errant individual, on learning of the sorcery directed toward him, came to conform with the socially demanded standards.

In Polynesia, mana (impersonal supernatural power) coupled with taboos exerted powerful influences on community behavior. A Polynesian chief with strong mana would control the behavior of others. However, social control can also be achieved by *accusing* "deviants" of supernatural practices rather than by employing such practices. In some places, notably the Philippines and parts of Africa, people who behaved in a deviant manner were labeled as witches. Since witchcraft was regarded as antisocial behavior and few wanted to be thought of as witches, this was a powerful influence for social control. Thus it can be the fear of magic practiced against one, or the fear of being accused of practicing magic, which motivates one to avoid antisocial behavior. Hence order in the society is promoted.

*See also* Legal systems; Magic and witchcraft; Mana; Mores; Power; Sanctions; Social control; Taboo

Consult: Hoebel, E. A., *The Law of Primitive Man* (Cambridge, Mass.: Harvard University Press, 1954); Malinowski, B., *Crime and Cus-*

*tom in Savage Society* (London: Kegan Paul, 1926).

—*Richard L. Stone, California State University, Los Angeles*

**Magic and Witchcraft.** Magic supposes a set of beliefs and techniques designed to control the supernatural or natural environments for specific purposes. The element of control helps analytically to distinguish it from religion (more propitiatory) and the empirically untested belief in magic distinguishes it from science, but the frontiers dividing the three are not always clear. Ethnocentric bias ("We have miracles, you have magic") clouds the term. Modern anthropological analysis discards invidious comparison and opens up the concept to wider and more variable interpretation. The emphasis for Edmund Leach (1964) is on the expressive symbolism of magic rather than its falsity (James Frazer's "bastard science") or secrecy (Bronislaw Malinowski's "esoteric speciality"). Spells and incantations in set formulas are common aspects of protective magic for good or evil, for public or private purposes, to relieve anxiety or to provide decisions. Magical techniques are used in many kinds of divination for forecasting or for discovery/detection (criminal guilt, witchcraft). Magic has nothing to do with much of the contemporary occult, which should be studied in terms of psychic phenomena and parapsychology.

Witchcraft is a general term that traditionally refers to acts purported to cause evil to others. Thus it includes sorcery, black magic, and even unconsciously caused evil consequences (e.g., by the Evil Eye). Most societies do not manifest the distinction so clearly made by E. E. Evans-Pritchard (1937)—i.e., that sorcery is performed by learned techniques whereas witchcraft (despite the suffix) is an inherited power. Witches are often thought to be capable of transforming and translocating themselves at will. Some modern witches claim the legitimacy of a pre-Christian Dianic cult/religion which was forced underground. Sorcery has been used legitimately by constituted authorities (premissionary Hawaiian kings, the Roman Catholic Church's anathema, or certain African municipalities today). Otherwise, witchcraft was deemed antisocial and illegal (e.g., a heretical alliance with the devil or demons against the Christian establishment). Anthropologists analyze witchcraft accusations in terms of scapegoatism or tension—indicators of close but disrupted social relationships.

See also Magic and social control; Religion; Supernatural, concept of
Consult: Evans-Pritchard, E. E., Witchcraft, Oracles and Magic Among the Azande (Oxford; Clarendon Press, 1937); Leach, Edmund R., "Magic," in Dictionary of the Social Sciences, ed. J. Gould and W. L. Kolb (New York: Free Press, 1964).
—Michael Kenny, University of Mexico

## Maine, Sir Henry Sumner (1822–1888).
Maine, a student of comparative jurisprudence, formulated the ideal type concepts of status-based and contract-based societies. The former are small, homogeneous groups in which social positions are ascribed; the latter are larger and more differentiated societies in which social positions are achieved.

See also Legal systems; Role; Status and contract
Consult: Flaver, George, From Status to Contract: A Biography of Sir Henry Maine (New York: Humanities Press, 1970); Hoebel, E. Adamson, "Maine, Henry," International Encyclopedia of the Social Sciences (New York: Macmillan, 1968).

## Maladaptive Traits. See Adaptation, biological; Adaptation, cultural; Evolution; Genetics.

## Malinowski, Bronislaw (1884–1942).
This Polish-born anthropologist became interested in the discipline after reading interested in the discipline after reading Sir James Frazer's The Golden Bough in 1910. He traveled to Britain to study the subject in 1913 and became a major influence on the development of modern anthropology.

Malinowski spent several years in the Trobriand Islands of the SW Pacific (Melanesia), where he made close observations of Trobriand culture. His intensive fieldwork methods had great influence on the next generation of British and American anthropologists, and the older tradition of armchair anthropology gave way to a new insistence on rigorous empirical research and fieldwork.

Malinowski was a founder of the functionalist school; he insisted that the task of anthropology was to discover how each so-

cial institution fulfills a specific function in maintaining human needs. He stressed the importance of physiological needs in determining cultural forms and was one of the first anthropologists to apply psychoanalytic theory to cultural studies (though he vigorously argued against the cross-cultural universality of the Oedipus complex in its pure form).

Consult: Kardiner, Abram, and Preble, Edward, They Studied Man (New York: New American Library, 1961); Métraux, Rhoda, "Malinowski, Bronislaw," in Encyclopedia of the Social Sciences (New York: Macmillan, 1968); Richards, Audrey, "Bronislaw Malinowski," in The Founding Fathers of Social Science, ed. Timothy Raison (Baltimore: Penguin, 1969); Wax, Murray L., "Tenting with Malinowski," American Sociological Review 37(1):1–13, February 1972.
—Bruno Pajaczkowski, Cambridge University

## Malthus, Thomas (1766–1834).
This British economic and demographic theorist is best known for his Essay on the Principle of Population as it Affects the Future Improvement of Society (1798), in which he argued that while human population increases geometrically, food supplies can only increase arithmetically. Thus he predicted that increasing pressures on resources would result in massive food shortages if population increases were not checked.

## Mana.
A diffuse force recognized in various parts of the world but especially well known in Polynesia and Melanesia, mana is not a religion or a divinity but an energylike entity which suffuses through various objects, places, and even people.

## Manners.
This term refers to the correct ways of behaving in culturally defined, situationally specific interactions. Manners differ from true politeness in that personal commitment to the behavior is not necessarily implied in the definition of manners, whereas it seems to be in most definitions of politeness.

See also Etiquette

## Mannheim, Karl (1893–1947).
A Hungarian-born German sociologist best known for

his work in the sociology of knowledge, Mannheim was influenced by historicism and by Karl Marx's ideas of society. He believed that social cleavages went deeper than the class conflict described by Marx; he contended that these class cleavages were also caused by differences in modes of thought. Mannheim later moved to England, where his research dealt more with the structure of contemporary society. His best-known work is Ideology and Utopia (1936).

## Mao Tse-tung (b. 1893).
This Chinese Marxist theorist and former soldier is chairman of the Chinese Communist Party. After defeating Chiang Kai-shek's Kuomintang forces in the Chinese Civil War—as well as the invading Japanese army during the period 1927 to 1949—he established the People's Republic of China. Mao adapted the ideology of Karl Marx and V. I. Lenin to the situation in China. Whereas Lenin wrote for the Russian worker, Mao modified his doctrines to fit the needs of an agrarian-based peasant society. In the 1960s, Mao moved China away from the Russian Communist policies of Nikita Khrushchev and repudiated Russia's leadership of the Communist world.

Mao's theory of revolutionary war emphasizes a three-stage process: an organizational stage; a guerrilla warfare stage; and, finally, a conventional war stage. It also stresses the institution of popular social and economic reforms. Many of Mao's concepts have been adapted by revolutionaries in agrarian countries in the Third World.

The cult of Mao is still very strong in China, even after Mao's Red Guards violently proclaimed his "cultural revolution" by attacking many peasants, workers, and party leaders in the mid-1960s.

See also Marxism; Peasants and revolution; Revolution; State and revolution

## Maranda, Pierre (b. 1930).
Social anthropologist and ethnologist whose research deals with social structure and with the use of computers in semantic analysis.

## Marett, Robert Ranulph (1866–1943).
A student of E. B. Tylor, Marett was especially interested in religion and folklore and believed that supernaturalism should include both magic and religion. He coined

the term *animatism* to describe the person-ification of inanimate things.

See also Magic; Religion; Tylor, Edward Burnett

**Marginal Peoples.** In the building of civilizations there have always been casual-ties or marginal peoples, those who have fallen by the wayside in the onward march of the majority. Examples are afforded by the following groups among many others. In Europe: Tinkers (Ireland, Scotland, England, Holland), Cagots (France and Spain), Kjeltringer (Denmark), Fanter (Norway), Inorodtzy (USSR), and Gypsies generally. In Asia: Pariahs and Untouchables (India), Eta (Japan), Solubba and others (Arabia), and Paekchung (Korea). In Africa: blacksmiths, minstrels, leatherworkers, hunters, fisher-men, potters, carpenters, storytellers, and pygmies. In Oceania: Kauwa (Hawaiian Islands) and Mangatchang (Guam and Marianas Islands). In the Americas: Bogenahs (Guaymi Indians of Panama) and Yana-cuna (Inca empire).

See also Acculturation; Imperialism; Pluralism
Consult: De Vos, George, and Wagatsuma, H., *Japan's Invisible Race* (Berkeley: University of California Press, 1967); Ninomiya, Shigeake, "An Inquiry Concerning the Origin, Develop-ment and Present Situation of the Eta in Rela-tion to the History of Social Classes in Japan," *Transactions of the Asiatic Society of Japan* 10:47–154, 1933.

**Market Systems.** This term refers to sys-tems of exchange of multiplicities of goods and services using all-purpose money as a standard measure of relative value. Early market systems are characterized by market-places (bazaars). Usually such market-based societies lack mechanisms to coordinate supply, demand, price, location, and times *among* the various marketplaces: local marketplaces display considerable auton-omy, often enhanced by bureaucratic ad-ministration of prices. Bazaar exchange, then, is characterized either by bureaucratic direction or by arbitrary pricing by sellers who expect bargaining to achieve personal contractual sale agreements. Bazaar mar-kets, especially outside major cities, are often cyclical, moving among a fixed set of localities, each having its specified market days. Merchants circulate with the market, collecting and distributing locally differ-

*Kikuyu market north of Nairobi, Kenya. It is a weekly affair, with both local food producers and importers of foreign trade items congregating to bargain, barter, and exchange their goods.*

entiated products, but redistributive central places are absent or rudimentary.

The historically recent "price-making" or "self-regulatory" market directly links supply crowds and demand crowds by prices attached to a profit system which stimulates production. It coordinates all aspects of economies that formerly operated semiautonomously, including labor—now treated as a *commodity* in a separate labor market. Further, its very self-regulation (changes of production rates responding to price changes responding to demand fluc-

tuations) significantly reduces the political organization's role respecting interventions such as price administration. Further still, the price-making market also coordinates not only local, regional, national, and ulti-mately international levels of economic activity but also coordinates quite diverse *times* of production and consumption —allowing very long gaps between the two. These developments gradually increased the scale of the economies concerned—ulti-mately producing today's vast and inte-grated world economic system.

See also Economic systems; Exchange; Redis-tribution; Surplus; Trade
Consult: Dalton, George (ed.), *Primitive, Archaic, and Modern Economies: Essays of Karl Polanyi* (Boston: Beacon, 1971); Polanyi, Karl, *The Great Transformation* (New York: Rinehart, 1944).

—*Anthony Leeds, Boston University*

A contemporary maroon. A Matawai curer from Surinam listens to his client's complaints before determining which medicinal plants he will use.

### Markov Chain.

The Markov chain, a mathematical technique to describe social change when the probability of transition may be shown to be independent of previous changes, has been applied most successfully to social mobility.

See also Stochastic process

Consult: Blau, P. M., and Duncan, O. D., The American Occupational Structure (New York: Wiley, 1967).

### Maroon Societies.

The word maroon derives from the Spanish cimarron, which originally referred to domestic cattle which had reverted to a wild state. The term came to refer to Afro-American slaves who ran away from their plantations and were considered (at least for a time) rebel outlaws by the governments of their respective colonial societies. Runaways often banded together, both for protection against patrols sent to retrieve or kill them and also in order to organize raiding parties against plantations. Plantations were raided to obtain tools, weapons, cloth, and often slave women

as well. With these necessities Maroons were often able to establish and defend independent and viable communities, some of which lasted less than a year, while others lasted much longer.

Throughout the history of slavery in the Americas, Maroon communities could be found in virtually every area where slaves were kept: in the Spanish Americas, Brazil, the French Caribbean, the Guianas, Jamaica, and southeastern United States. Communities located in inhospitable, inaccessible areas such as swamps (in America) rugged mountains (in Jamaica), or dense rain forests (in Surinam) had the best chance of survival because of the difficulties these environments presented to pursuing troops or vigilantes.

Some Maroon communities grew quite strong, and their cost to colonies such as Surinam and Jamaica became so great that the colonial government entered into treaties with Maroon groups and granted them freedom and considerable independence in return for peace.

Surinam and French Guiana deserve special mention because Maroon tribes still flourish there today as virtual states within states. Melville Herskovits expressed great interest in Guiana Maroon cultures and believed them to be the most African of Afro-American cultures because of their relative isolation from European influences.

See also Slavery

Consult: Price, R., Maroon Societies (New York: Anchor, 1970).

—Edward Green, Catholic University

### Marriage.

Marriage may be defined as a publicly recognized and culturally sanctioned union between a male and female which is intended to be enduring, to give primary (but not necesssarily exclusive) sexual rights in each other to the couple, and to fulfill further social functions. Definitions of marriage that depend on a specific social function such as the legitimation of children cannot hold universally, because for any given function at least a few societies can be found that do not include it in marriage. On the other hand, a limited number of ends, including childrearing, economic partnership between husband and wife, and the formation of alliances between kin groups, are characteristic of marriage in a great many societies.

The words male and female refer here not to physical gender so much as the socially assigned sex role each partner takes in marriage—a qualification necessary because a few societies allow someone to marry a member of his or her own sex or even a ghost or spirit. To make the definition fit other rare forms of marriage, "male" and "female" would also have to include several people of one sex acting as an individual. Probably no definition, however it is stretched and qualified, can encompass all societies and all the relationships that have been called marriage.

**Plural and Single Marriage.** Most societies allow at least some people to take more than one spouse at a time, though even in those societies most people have just one husband or wife at a time. If a man and woman are married only to each other, their marriage is monogamous. If one of the pair also has another spouse or spouses, he or she is polygamous. Of the two possible forms of polygamy, the marriage of one man to two or more women, called polygyny, oc-

The garlanded, crowned groom is treated like a raja ("king") in this North Indian wedding ceremony. His crown is reminiscent of a Christmas tree, adorned as it is with ornaments, some merely decorative, some explicitly symbolic.

curs much more frequently than *polyandry*, the marriage of one woman to more than one man. Polygynous men marry each of their wives separately, but in some forms of polyandry a group of brothers may collectively marry a woman. A very few societies allow *group marriage* between several men and several women. *Serial monogamy* and *serial polygamy* are variant terms for the same system, one in which plural marriage is forbidden but divorce and remarriage are frequent.

**Marriage Rules.** Sexual relations and marriage between siblings or parents and children are almost universally avoided or forbidden. Many cultures also maintain marriage rules that direct one's choice of spouse toward or away from certain people, such as close kin or members of one's own kin group. A kin group is *exogamous* if its members regularly marry outside it, *endogamous* if they marry within it, and *agamous* if they lack a rule or clear tendency concerning in- and out-marriage. Some societies forbid marriage not only within one's own kin group but also with members of certain other groups to which a parent, grandparent, or other relative belongs. Conversely, marriage rules may require or encourage one to find a spouse within a particular group or set of groups or within a certain class of kinsfolk. Such *positive marriage rules* are often one aspect of a system of continuing alliance and exchange of women between kin groups. Some Arab societies favor marriage with a *parallel cousin*, though rules of *preferential* and *prescriptive cross-cousin marriage* are much more common. A widowed person is often expected to marry a sibling of his or her late spouse: in the *sororate* a widower marries his deceased wife's sister; in the *levirate* a widow is taken by her deceased husband's brother.

**Marital Exchanges.** Many societies treat marriage as an exchange between individuals or groups. To receive a wife often puts one in debt to her parents or kinfolk. However, in societies characterized by *hypergamy*, the practice of marrying women to men of higher status, the prestige the husband brings to a marriage puts her kinsfolk in debt. In a common institution known as *brother-sister exchange*, a man gives in marriage a sister or female relative in return for the wife he receives.

Marriage exchanges often include the transfer of goods and services as well as of women and prestige. Gifts from the husband's kin to the wife's kin are called *bridewealth* or *brideprice;* wealth bestowed on the bride or the couple by her parents is called *dowry*. If a husband compensates his wife's parents in the form of labor, he engages in *bride service*. Anthropology lacks precise terms for many other kinds of marriage transaction, such as reciprocal exchanges between both kin groups.

**Postmarital Residence.** Anthropologists have developed an elaborate terminology to describe where and with whom a couple takes up residence after marrying. (They have not been consistent in their use of these terms, however, and readers should not assume that every author follows the definitions given here.) A couple resides *patrilocally* or *virilocally* if they live with or near the husband's parents, *matrilocally* or *uxorilocally* if they move in with the wife's parents. If they live with the husband's mother's brother, as is common in some matrilineal societies, their residence is *avunculocal*. And if they set up an independent household away from kinsfolk, they reside *neolocally*. If all or most of the members of a society follow the same residence pattern, residence is unilocal.

*See also* Alliance; Bridewealth; Brother-sister exchange; Cross-cousin prescriptive marriage; Endogamy; Exogamy; Family, the; Group marriage; Incest avoidance (taboo); Kinship; Kinship and alliance; Levirate; Matrilocality; Monogamy; Neolocality; Patrilocality; Polyandry; Polygamy; Polygyny; Sex roles; Sororate; Women, exchange of

Consult: Bohannan, Paul, and Middleton, John (eds.), *Kinship and Social Organization* (Garden City, N.Y.: Natural History Press, 1968); Fox, Robin, *Kinship and Marriage: An Anthropological Perspective* (Baltimore: Penguin, 1967); Mair, Lucy, *Marriage* (Baltimore: Penguin, 1971); Murdock, George Peter, *Social Structure* (New York: Free Press, 1949); Radcliffe-Brown, A. R., and Forde, Daryll (eds.), *African Systems of Kinship and Marriage* (London: Oxford University Press, 1950).

—*James Howe, Massachusetts Institute of Technology*

**Marriage Prescriptive Rules.** *See* Marriage.

**Marriage Residency Practices.** *See* Marriage.

**Marriage Rules.** *See* Marriage.

**Marriage Types.** *See* Marriage.

**Marx, Karl Heinrich** (1818–1883). Karl Marx was born in 1818 in the Rhine Province of Prussia; he died in London in 1883. Together with Friedrich Engels, Marx was founder of the school of social and economic thought which bears his name. His most important theoretical work is *Das Kapital*, a three-volume analysis which relates the dislocations of the modern period to a single historical process: the development and spread of industrial capitalism. Although his thinking was influenced by Hegelian philosophy and classical economics, he was a seminal thinker, one of the most important minds of modern times.

During his lifetime Marx was known as a political activist and journalist as well as a theoretician. Marx and Engels' best-known work, *The Communist Manifesto*, was written in 1848 as a political program for the Communist League. In 1850, after a period of involvement in the revolutions of 1848 and their aftermath, Marx moved to England

*Karl Marx*

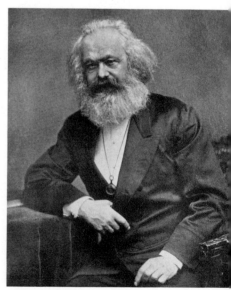

and spent the next fourteen years in historical research and writing. The first volume of *Capital* appeared in 1867.

In 1864 he returned to Europe and to activism as an organizer of the First International; in 1870 he became the most important spokesman in support of the radical Paris Commune. Factionalism developed in the International and, in 1872, Marx returned to England to complete the last two volumes of *Capital,* which were finished by Engels and published after Marx's death.

See also Marxism

Consult: McLellan, David, *Karl Marx: His Life and Thought* (New York: Harper & Row, 1974); McLellan, David (ed.), *Selected Works of Marx and Engels* (New York: International, 1968).

—Regina Holloman, Roosevelt University

**Marxism.** As a theoretical term, Marxism refers to the growing body of writings based on the work of Karl Marx and Friedrich Engels. As a political term, Marxism refers to the concept of the revolutionary struggle by workers (the proletariat) to overthrow and replace capitalist control of society. Marxism should be approached as a major *image* of how human society is and ought to be (a world view), as a *body of theory* regarding the nature of society, and as a *method* for analysis and societal transformation.

Marx addressed himself to one of the principal realities of the modern world: the development and spread of industrial capitalism. His theoretical work can be viewed as comprising a theory of capitalism (presented in the three volumes of *Das Kapital*) and a general paradigm for the analysis of social structures.

**Theoretical Framework.** To understand and use Marxist thought it is necessary to master a basic conceptual framework and vocabulary. Marxism states that social systems develop in accordance with laws. Unlike other animals, human beings can produce what they need to survive (their means of subsistence). Through the division of labor the amount which can be produced is greatly increased, and a struggle develops over power to command and channel the surplus. Generally, the group which can monopolize access to strategic resources (the *means of production*) becomes the *ruling class*. Other classes are shaped by their relationship to the means of production. These *relations of production* are generalized throughout the society and give it its characteristics. This is the "materialist conception of history," which makes the nature of the productive system central to an understanding of the political and cultural aspects (superstructure) of the social system. Marx used the term *political economy* to characterize his general approach; in his view political power ultimately rests on control over the means of production—for example, power in an agricultural society follows control of land.

Marx outlined a progression of socioeconomic stages which he believed summarized the history of civilization: ancient, feudal, and capitalistic. (He also identified an Oriental mode, typical of the ancient Asian empires.) Because his own work did not extend to economically primitive societies, he borrowed from the anthropology of his day the theory of social evolution most compatible with his own—the stage theory of Lewis Henry Morgan, which has matriarchy regularly preceding patriarchy. (This combination of Morgan and Marx is no longer used by Marxist anthropologists, with the exception of those in the USSR and politically allied nations.)

Marx contended that the dominant cultural images of a society reflect and support the economic system. (It is no accident that a consumption psychology is found in all classes in a capitalist society.) Self-image and self-esteem are similarly linked to the economy. Marx traced the roots of alienation to the relations of production under capitalism (e.g., the nature of assembly-line production).

Like the philosophers of the Enlightenment, Marx believed that the development of human society is progressive and in the direction of human freedom. Under capitalism, for example, society is closer to realizing its potential for freedom than under serfdom. But human progress is neither smooth nor peaceful: it takes place in quantum jumps amidst violent struggle. Over time, the material basis of production (rooted in technology) continues to develop, but the system of power relations tends to remain static. New groups develop in relation to changes in production, but they are not represented in the system of power relations until they revolt and overthrow the existing order. This general process is the *dialectical* movement of history, on the basis of which Marx predicted the transformation, through revolution, of capitalist society into a classless society based on socialism.

**Recent Developments.** The success of Marxism as a political doctrine has produced theoretical variations in the body of Marxist writings. At least five major positions can be distinguished. *Marxism/Leninism* (which some groups characterize as Stalinism) is the official version of Marxism in the USSR. *Trotskyism,* developed by Leon Trotsky (who claimed to be the heir of "real" Marxism/Leninism), is a critique of the regime of Joseph Stalin in the USSR. *Social democracy* (as promoted by Edward Bernstein) is the view that the working class can come to power peacefully and gradually through the use of parliamentary tactics. *Maoism,* developed by Mao Tse-tung, reflects Chinese experience in organizing a communist state on a peasant agrarian base. *Neo-Marxism* is a diverse body of writings (many of them by anthropologists) dealing with current problems of Third World and developed nations.

Marx denied that peasants as a group have potential for revolutionary leadership. He predicted that socialist revolutions would be fought and won by the urban proletariat. However, Marxist revolutions have been most successful in underdeveloped nations, where they have depended heavily on peasant support. As a result, much contemporary Marxist work is focused on peasantries.

Marx's work also gave slight attention to nationalism and ethnicity, since he expected the rapid development of class identification across national boundaries. However, the postwar world has seen a resurgence of nationalism and the emergence of so-called new ethnics (e.g., a composite American Indian movement in the United States). The obvious relationship of both factors to competition over resources has stimulated neo-Marxist reconsiderations of both topics.

Finally, Marx's theories in their original form do little to explain the viability and increased prosperity of the industrially advanced nations after World War II. Neo-Marxist theory emphasizes the importance of vertical structuring of relationships between rich and poor nations. Third World nations are increasingly viewed as misdeveloped (rather than underdeveloped) appendages of the economies of developed nations.

In the past, Marxism has not received the general attention in American (as opposed to European) social science which it has merited as a major theoretical position. But events—the increase in disorder and conflict within and between societies and the changing nature of political/economic processes internationally—have stimulated broader interest in the classic issues dealt with by Marxists.

See also Capitalism; Colonialism; Communism; Economic anthropology; Engels, Friedrich; Imperialism; Marx, Karl; Neocolonialism; Peasants and revolution; Revolution; Socialism

Consult: Bottomore, T. B., and Rubel, Maximilian, Karl Marx: Selected Writings in Sociology and Social Philosophy (London: Watts, 1961); Lefebvre, Henri, The Sociology of Marx (New York: Random House, 1968); Mills, C. Wright, The Marxists (New York: Dell, 1962); Wolf, Eric, Peasant Wars of the Twentieth Century (New York: Harper & Row, 1969).

—Regina Holloman, Roosevelt University

## Masks.

In forms such as the visor or gas mask, masks are used for protection, but because the word conjures up primarily the idea of concealment and disguise anthropologists tend to associate masks with various cults devoted to such things as witch-hunting and initiation. In many societies masqueraders are regarded as actually being the spirits of the masks they wear. In West Africa, masked societies such as the poro, using a great variety of wooden masks, perform functions of social control; one type of mask among the Senufo was used to chase away ghosts and evil spirits from the village; Yoruba secret societies are famous for their finely carved masks, such as the gelede and epa. In New Guinea, in the Huon Gulf, tago masqueraders in masks of cane covered with painted coconut bast appeared at initiation; in the Papuan Gulf, the Elema constructed huge masks 15 or more feet high, representing the hevehe (sea spirits), in an elaborate drama performed as part of a cycle of ceremonies lasting some twenty years; the Asaro wear masks of mud in a ceremony commemorative of a victory.

Masking is widespread and there are many forms in the world—death masks cast in memory of the dead, masks of the theater (some worn, others held in front of the face), masks of sacking worn at yuletide in western England, the masks of southern Germany

Masks are made from the most diverse materials. Shown here are a Cara Grande mask from the Tapirape of Brazil, constructed of feathers and wood with shell ornaments; and a wooden deer mask retrieved from the Spiro Mound in Oklahoma, with shell-inlaid eyes and mouth, dating c. 1200–1500 AD.

and Switzerland brought out at an annual festival, our own masks of Halloween, the double masks or masks within masks of the Kwakiutl Indians of British Columbia. Both the variety of mask forms and the uses to which masks are put are for practical purposes almost infinite. Only by examining each cultural setting for its use can the meaning of a mask be determined.

See also Art; Art, primitive; Religion; Ritual

—Philip J. C. Dark, Southern Illinois University

## Mass Culture.

According to some social scientists, industrialization, bureaucratization, urbanization, and geographical mobility have undermined the importance of primary groups or close relationships among people. As a consequence, society tends to be a mass of atomized, undifferentiated, and shapeless individuals. Mass society generates mass culture. Because of the influence of mass media, people tend to share the same feelings and ideas. However, since they are not firmly attached to meaningful groups, they are easily influenced by fashions and fads. At the same time, the ruling elite responds to immediate pressures and fails to encourage the production of "high culture."

See also Culture

## Material Culture.

Material culture is the tangible expression of changes produced by humans in adapting to, and exercising control over, their biosocial environment. If human existence were merely a matter of survival and satisfying basic biological needs, then material culture would consist simply of the tools and equipment of general subsistence and the weapons of warfare and defense against aggression. But human needs are varied and complex, and the material culture of even the simplest human society reflects other interests and emphases. A representative sample of the material manifestations of culture would have to include works of art, ornaments, musical instruments, ritual paraphernalia, and exchange currencies, as well as shelter, clothing, and the means of procuring or producing food and transporting people and goods.

Every item of a culture's material inventory represents the concretization of an idea or sequence of ideas. These ideas, along with the acquired skills and learned tech-

*This man of the Kohar ("potter") caste is making teacups which will be used in a relative's wedding. The cups are baked in the sun. They are used once, then, having become polluted, are thrown away.*

niques for manufacturing and using goods in patterned activities, constitute a technological system. The relationship between technological capability and the nature and extent of a society's material inventory may seem rather obvious, but technology also shapes a group's social structure and establishes limits on its size and its cultural development.

See also Technology
Consult: Bock, Philip, "Technological Systems," in *Modern Cultural Anthropology*, ed. P. Bock (New York: Knopf, 1969).
—*Seth Schindler, Southern Illinois University*

**Materialism.** *See* Cultural ecology; Marxism.

**Materialist Method.** *See* Marxism.

**Materialist School.** *See* Cultural ecology; Marxism.

**Matriarchy.** This term refers to the domination of domestic life or society by women. Beginning in 1861 with the Swiss jurist J. Bachofen, a number of important 19th-century social theorists, including J. F. McLennon, L. H. Morgan, and Friedrich Engels, developed the idea that matriarchy was common among primitive societies and had preceded patriarchy as a stage in human evolution. These authors generally conceived of matriarchy as a special form—

women held many or most positions of authority in public life, religion centered around the cult of a mother goddess, and descent was traced exclusively through the female line. An opposing school of thought, represented by H. Maine and E. A. Westermarck, held that patriarchy was the original state of humanity.

Most modern anthropologists reject both theories. One 20th-century author, R. Briffault, has elaborated on the matriarchal theory and feminists have incorporated it into their ideology, but reliable fieldwork has yet to confirm the existence of even one true matriarchal society. The concept of matriarchy itself consists in large part of a misunderstanding of matrilineal descent and matrilocal residence.

See also Descent; Engels, Friedrich; Marriage; *Mutterrecht, Das*; Patriarchy
Consult: Bachofen, J. J., *Myth, Religion and Mother Right*, trans. Ralph Mannheim (Princeton, N.J.: Princeton University Press, 1967); Bamberger, Joan, "The Myth of Matriarchy: Why Men Rule in Primitive Society," in *Woman, Culture and Society*, ed. Michelle Zimbalist Rosaldo and Louise Lamphere (Palo Alto: Stanford University Press, 1974).
—*James Howe, Massachusetts Institute of Technology*

**Matrifocality.** This concept refers both to the phenomenon of a universal nuclear family unit as made up of mother-child bonds and also to household and/or family organizations which give particular weight to the mother-child bonds. Since, in the latter case, all sorts of data ranging from statistical patterns of residence to social psychological roles of women or power structure of household or kinship network systems have been randomly mixed by dozens of scholars, much matrifocal literature is confusing and confused. For a clear article discussing the issues and clarifying the most productive perspectives, see Gonzalez (1970).

See also Matrilocality; Nuclear family
Consult: Gonzalez, Nancie L., "Toward a Definition of Matrifocality," in *Afro-American Anthropology: Contemporary Perspectives*, ed. Norman E. Whitten, Jr., and John F. Szwed (New York: Free Press, 1970).

**Matrilateral Prescriptive Cross-cousin Marriage.** This rule, by which a man must choose his spouse from among his mother's brothers' daughters, is often found in conjunction with Crow or Omaha kinship terminology and a system of asymmetric alliance.

*See also* Alliance; Kinship and alliance; Marriage

**Matrilineage.** A kinship group made up of people all of whom trace relationships to one another through female links and are descended from a known female ancestor.

*See also* Descent group; Kinship and descent; Patrilineage

**Matrilineal Descent.** The principle by which lineal kin links are traced through females—i.e., a child is descended from his or her mother, mother's mother, etc.

*See also* Descent rule; Kinship and descent; Patrilineal descent

**Matrilocality.** This term refers to postmarital residence that locates the married pair in the vicinity of the wife's mother. Sisters and daughters remain in their mother's domestic unit, brothers and sons are exported, husbands are imported. The husband's status in this home is weakened by the fact that his wife's brothers and other maternal kinsfolk have important roles in authority and decision-making.

*See also* Marriage; Neolocality; Patrilocality
Consult: Murdock, George P., *Social Structure* (New York: Macmillan, 1949); Schneider, David M., and Gough, Kathleen (eds.), *Matrilineal Kinship* (Berkeley: University of California Press, 1961).

**Maturity.** This term from developmental psychology is popularly used synonymously with adulthood. Usage is based on a premise of discontinuity in intellectual development between childhood (immaturity) and adulthood (maturity). Such ideas are only as good as the role definitions on which judgmental observations are made. Imprecision and lack of agreement among different theoretical schools restrict the utility of the concept.

*See also* Adulthood; Culture of childhood

**Mauss, Marcel** (1872–1950). Mauss was a leading figure in French sociology and cofounder of *Année Sociologique*. His most famous work, *The Gift* (1925), dealt with the function of exchange in archaic societies.

**Maya.** This pre-Columbian civilization of southern Mexico, Guatemala, and Honduras was influenced by Central Mexican societies during the period AD 300 to 600, as many of the ceremonial centers were being constructed. The period AD 600 to 900 represents a decline in outside influences and the emergence of uniquely Mayan art styles. About AD 900 there was a period of tremendous change and an abandonment and destruction of many centers for reasons still unclear. After AD 900, the Maya were once again very heavily influenced by the Central Mexican peoples. The Maya developed an elaborate calendrical system and an advanced form of hieroglyphic writing.

Consult: Coe, Michael D., *The Maya* (New York: Praeger, 1966).

*One of the numerous pyramids built by the Maya at the ceremonial center of Tikal (Yucatan Peninsula, Guatemala). This site includes the highest architectural structure (over 300 feet) built in pre-Columbian New World civilizations. This temple dates from the Late Classic period, c. 700 AD.*

**Maybury-Lewis, David H. P.** (b. 1929). British-trained cultural anthropologist, born in Pakistan, whose publications have centered on the Indians of the Amazon, including an account of fieldwork, *The Savage and the Innocent* (1968).

**Mazeway.** This term represents a radically new idea in anthropological thinking, one designed to aid the search for better answers to very specific kinds of questions. One such question is "How do groups of very different individuals organize themselves into orderly, adaptive, changing, expanding societies?" Many social scientists do not consider this question at all. They even deny the relevance of considering individual differences. Others approach the issue with the assumption that socialization practices produce substantial uniformity in each new cadre of members for a society, and they also ignore the manifest fact of individual differences. Recently, with the growing emphasis on cognitive processes and on individual differences in cross-cultural studies, some have begun to address the question directly. Such thinkers as A. F. C. Wallace, for example, argue that we must study directly the cognitive processes of many individuals. They are concerned with individual diversity, with conflicts and

divisiveness between subgroups, and with the fact of continuous change in a culture's policies, tactics, styles, and content. They regard culture as a set of policies agreed on in a kind of implicit contract between individuals who are not homogeneous in values or motivation, but whose values, views, and techniques are only partially equivalent or shared.

Wallace thus defines mazeway as the complete set of cognitive maps of both positive and negative goals which characterize one individual at one point in time. In any society at any time, therefore, it is recognized that the mazeways of its members will be different from one another, although there must be partial equivalences. Similarly, as the situation of an individual alters and new experience is accumulated, the mazeway will change.

The content of a mazeway consists of desirable or undesirable end states or goals, but it also includes images of the body, of self, of other persons, of groups, of objects, and of imagined beings (e.g., supernatural creatures). It also includes images about proper and improper relationships between self and other persons and between self and objects (e.g., a tool). And it includes images about ways and means, tactics and techniques for achieving desirable goals or for avoiding undesirable relationships.

The individual's mazeway has other attributes as well. It may, for example, be more or less well integrated, and in whole or part it may quite disintegrate. Moreover, it may be characterized as more or less effective or adaptive in producing optimum levels of satisfaction and growth or dissatisfaction and stagnation.

The uses of a concept like mazeway are multiple. With this idea we can readily appreciate what went wrong with the configurational approach to the study of whole cultures. Students of Ruth Benedict would look at the world of a whole tribe only through the eyes, say, of a witch, whose views, values, tactics, and beliefs had been studied in great detail. Thus what was characteristic of one (very evil) person would be attributed to a whole group.

Another salient application of the concept is in situations where a group customarily and deliberately sets out drastically to alter the mazeways of a subgroup. This is what happens essentially in rites of passage, when individual identities are deliberately transformed, as in a Chippewa vision quest or a U.S. Marine Corps boot camp. In situations of very rapid cultural change, when individual despair and dissatisfaction mount, a person will often experience the total disintegration of a mazeway and the resynthesis of a new set of goals, values, tactics, and relationships. Such experiences are the basis of cultural revitalization movements.

Consult: Wallace, A. F. C., *Culture and Personality*, 2nd ed. (New York: Random House, 1971).

—James Clifton, University of Wisconsin, Green Bay

**McLennan, J. F.** (1827–1888). An early ethnologist primarily interested in matrilineal descent and the ritual of bride capture, McLennan coined the terms *endogamy* and *exogamy*.

*See also* Marriage; Matriarchy

**Mead, Margaret** (b. 1901). Mead is perhaps the best-known living anthropologist, for her efforts to bring the results of anthropological research to the general public have made her books best-sellers. She writes articles in popular magazines and appears on radio and television. To many she is the embodiment of anthropology.

While her interests are manifold she has consistently focused on culture as learned behavior and has especially studied institutions of cultural transmission across generations. Among the contributions she has made on this score is her demonstration that cultural transmission—especially in complex societies—flows in two directions: from parent generation to children, but also vice versa. In her early career she studied groups on New Guinea, Samoa, and Manus; over the last thirty years she has turned her attention to complex societies, especially the United States. She has written extensively on American educational institutions and on means for improving them. In fact, she was an early advocate for schools that were better integrated into the entire community —full-service institutions that educated people throughout their lives rather than from ages five to twenty-two.

Mead's basic position is that of a cultural relativist who insists that each culture must be understood on its own terms and that each culture forms a unique whole. This has especially characterized her work on male and female gender identity. However, she

*Margaret Mead*

has also shown an interest in general processes of culture change. She has consistently encouraged younger anthropologists to develop new theories, methods, and techniques and has thus provided anthropology with a constant source of creative energy. Among her most important books are *Coming of Age in Samoa* (1949), *Male and Female* (1956), *New Lives for Old* (1956), and *Culture and Commitment* (1970).

*See also* Culture; Culture and Personality; Sex roles; Sexuality, human

—Frank A. Salamone, St. John's University

**Meaning, the Problem of.** The meaning of a cultural trait refers to the interpretation that people place on it. This meaning, however, is usually an ethnocentric one and is inevitably culturally relative. The anthropologist is therefore confronted with a major problem in the analysis of meanings in another culture—how can one establish these meanings or propose valid analyses of them?

Anthropologists have attempted to resolve this problem by distinguishing between the *emic* understanding of culture by the participant in that culture and the *etic* understanding of the anthropological investigator who is interested in cross-culturally valid explanations. Each interpretation is held to have its own validity, but there are strong arguments for the view that only the etic analysis provides a truly scientific explanation. The French structuralists in particular have argued that conscious meaning is simply a surface manifestation of the real meaning which is to be found in the deep structures underlying observable phenomena. These structures are not imposed by the anthropologist but are found in biological, cultural, and psychological phenomena universal to the species.

*See also* Emics; Etics; Language and culture; Language and reality; Language and thought
—*Ino Rossi, St. John's University*

**Measurement Scales.** Measurement consists of assigning numerical values to observations in such a way as to facilitate analysis by operations permissible under given mathematical models. The objective of analysis is to reveal properties of the phenomena observed which were not before apparent. The relationship between the things observed and the numbers assigned to the observations may be direct and self-evident, as in the case of physics and some of the natural sciences; or it may be abstract, complex, and at times obscure, as in the case of many variables measured by social scientists. Different kinds of measurement are possible, depending on the nature of the phenomena observed, which imposes certain limitations. But, more important, measurement depends on the observational technique of the investigator, which in turn is conditioned by the objectives—what he or she intends to do with the data obtained. It might be added that data do not exist *sui generis* but are only created with the act of measurement. The types of measurement are usually called measurement scales; the operations permissible on a given set of observations are determined by the level of measurement achieved (Siegel 1956:21,22).

**The Nominal Scale.** The weakest level of measurement is called the nominal, categorical, or classificatory scale. Here numbers (or other symbols) are used arbitrarily to designate categories; they serve as category names into which observations on phenomena can be assorted. Examples are commonplace. In elementary probability, the outcome of a coin toss might be scored 1 in the case of a head or 0 in the case of a tail. State

license plates classified numerically (or alphabetically) by county are nominally scaled categories, as are many responses on the technician's checklist or the sociologist's questionnaire. The point is that a symbol is arbitrarily assigned to designate a category. The only relation involved is that of equivalence (=); in other words, the numbers used as category names can be replaced by other numbers so long as the categories themselves are not altered. The *mode* is the measure of central tendency most often associated with nominal scaling; nonparametric statistics based on frequency counts are appropriate (e.g., chi square).

**The Ordinal Scale.** An ordinal scale of measurement is achieved when rank ordering of classes is possible. Ordering may be complete (an ordinal scale) or partial (a partially ordered scale). The relation "greater than" (>) is incorporated along with that of equivalence. According to Conover (1971: 66), "the numerical value of the measurement is used only [to arrange] elements being measured in order." Perhaps the most familiar example of an ordinal scale is the system of military grades used by armies throughout the world (sergeant > corporal > private). Many score systems used on questionnaires eliciting preference responses (e.g., best/better/good) result in ranked data (generally x > y > z). The *median* (rather than the mean) is the measure of central tendency most appropriate for use with ordinal data. A large number of nonparametric statistics have been developed to analyze information of this kind (e.g., Kolmogorov-Smirnov tests), prompting Siegel (1956) to observe that most social science data attain at best this level of scaling and in many cases are not amenable to analysis by more powerful, but more demanding, parametric techniques.

**Internal and Ratio Scales.** Measurement on an internal scale is considerably stronger than measurement of ranked data, but it is more difficult to achieve. It occurs when not only the relative order of the measurements is known, as is the case with ordinal scaling, but also the size of the interval between measurements. The concept of unit distance is therefore involved; that is, the distance between any two measurements must be expressed as some number of real but arbitrary units. The zero point is also arbitrary (Conover 1971). The classic example of an interval scale is that used to measure temperature. The unit involved (degrees) refers

to volumetric changes of mercury in a thermometer. The zero point is arbitrary and variable, depending on whether a Fahrenheit or a Celsius scale is used. However, the ratio of any two differences is independent of the unit of measure and the zero point. The measure of central tendency appropriate for analysis of interval data is the *mean* ($\bar{x}$); the measure of dispersion is the standard deviation ($\sigma$). Parametric statistics are thus most appropriate for analyzing intervally scaled (truly quantitative) data.

Ratio scaling is the strongest form of measurement attainable. It differs from the interval scale only by possessing a "true" or "natural" zero point. Weights, mass, heights, and distances are measured on a ratio scale. Any statistical test is appropriate when ratio measurement has been attained.

*See also* Statistical methods
Consult: Conover, W., *Practical Nonparametric Statistics* (New York: Wiley, 1971); Siegel, S., *Nonparametric Statistics for the Behavioral Sciences* (New York: McGraw-Hill, 1956).
—*Geoffrey A. Clark, Arizona State University*

**Mechanical Solidarity.** *See* Solidarity.

**Medicine.** In Anglo-American culture, medicine is something you take when you are sick. The most pervasive medicines are pills, taken orally, but the category extends to other substances: shots, X rays, even fresh air. The territory of meaning occupied by medicine can be grasped by thinking how medicines differ from foods, poisons, drugs, and so forth.

On a more abstract level medicine means the theory and practice of treating sickness—here it is no longer the name of a substance introduced into the body but that of a whole profession or body of knowledge.

There is another, very peculiar meaning of the English word *medicine*. In the history of English colonization of North America (and nowhere else in the world), medicine came to mean nearly the whole of native religion—hence words like *medicine man* and *medicine wheel*. It was a matter of taking the English word and extending it to a vast array of things in an exotic culture. Why this happened has not been satisfactorily explained. It is clearly something that developed between the English and the Indians, not something Indians invented for them-

*This medicine man of Nigeria, backed by his assistants, is wearing cowry shells and other supernatural charms.*

selves or something the colonists would take to heart for themselves. It is a special topic in primitive medicine.

See also Medicine, primitive
Consult: Vogel, V., *American Indian Medicine* (Norman: University of Oklahoma Press, 1970).
—Don Bahr, Arizona State University

**Medicine Man.** *See* Shaman.

**Medicine, Primitive.** Primitive medicine can be defined as medicine in a primarily spoken, not written, tradition. Its study takes two directions—one toward what non-Western cultures know about sickness and healing, the other toward popular medicine wherever it is found. The first would compare theories made by specialists ("medicine men"); the second would focus on the layperson's experience, not as it is supposed to be but as it is actually lived.

Western medicine has affected every primitive system in that no people is wholly beyond the reach of our doctors. Every native or popular system must orient itself to modern science, either as an alternative or as a backwash. The interaction between primitive and modern medicine would seem more interesting to study than the primitive varieties viewed in isolation. So far the best studies along these lines have been on the history of medicine in Europe.

A major interest in primitive medicine has been to "see whether they have anything"—e.g., a good drug or technique. Ethnobotanists have pursued this course to some extent. Clearly, if we are to learn what primitive medicine has to offer, it will necessitate our withholding prejudgments in an area which is especially important to, and elaborated within, our civilization.

See also Medicine
Consult: Ackerknecht, E., *A Short History of Medicine* (New York: Ronald Press, 1968); Ackerknecht, E., *Medicine and Ethnology* (Baltimore: Johns Hopkins, 1971); Bahr, D., et al., *Piman Shamanism and Staying Sickness (Ka: cim Mumkidag)* (Tucson: University of Arizona Press, 1974); Kiev, A., *Magic, Faith, and Healing* (New York: Free Press, 1964).
—Don Bahr, Arizona State University

**Meditation.** Sometimes called passive attention and often associated with spiritual discipline, meditation is a technique for focusing the mind. It is present in some form in many cultures and is particularly well articulated in Eastern religious traditions.

See also Altered states of consciousness

**Megalith.** Tomb or sanctuary made of huge blocks of stone which is characteristic of late Neolithic and Bronze Age European cultures.

**Meganthropus Paleojavanicus.** This term refers to three massive hominid mandible fragments with PM1 (first premolar), PM2, and M1–M3 in place. They were recovered (1941–1953) in the Djetis Beds of Sangiran in SC Java: Their probable age is greater than 1.5 million years, and their taxonomic status is uncertain but probably transitional between Basal Pleistocene *Australopithecus* of indeterminable species and *Homo erectus*. Robinson has argued that

they be included in *Paranthropus* (*Australopithecus robustus*).

See also Australopithecines; Dental formulas of primates

**Meggers, Betty J.** (b. 1921). An archaeologist noted for her extensive field research in South America, especially on the cultures of the lowlands, Meggers has been particularly interested in cultural ecology and prehistoric trans-Pacific contact.

See also Cultural ecology

**Meggitt, Mervyn John** (b. 1924). A social anthropologist who studies the social organization of Australian aborigines and Melanesian people, Meggitt has written *The Lineage System of the Mae Enga of New Guinea* (1965).

**Melanin.** This brownish pigment, which is found in varying amounts in the hair, eyes, and skin of all humans except albinos, is necessary for tanning and protection from sunlight.

See also Skin color

**Menarche.** *See* Menstruation.

**Mendel, Gregor Johann** (1822–1884). Austrian botanist whose experiments with pea plants in the second half of the 19th century formed the basis of the scientific study of genetic heredity.

See also Genetics; Mendelian genetics

**Mendelian Genetics.** In the 1860s the Abbé Gregor Mendel conducted a series of controlled experiments on the processes involved in selective breeding to enable him to predict the outcome of particular crosses. The results of his brilliant research were published in 1866 but were unknown or ignored by other scientists until after 1900. His work added a significant new body of well-demonstrated theory to the evolutionary thinking of his era. This consisted of an explanation of the actual mechanisms of continuity and variation across the generations of a species, a theory which was sound and powerful enough to allow accurate prediction.

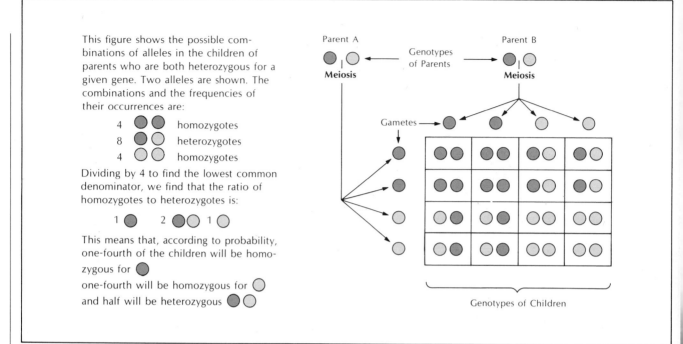

This figure shows the possible combinations of alleles in the children of parents who are both heterozygous for a given gene. Two alleles are shown. The combinations and the frequencies of their occurrences are:

4 ⬤⬤ homozygotes
8 ⬤◯ heterozygotes
4 ◯◯ homozygotes

Dividing by 4 to find the lowest common denominator, we find that the ratio of homozygotes to heterozygotes is:

1 ⬤    2 ⬤◯    1 ◯

This means that, according to probability, one-fourth of the children will be homozygous for ⬤

one-fourth will be homozygous for ◯

and half will be heterozygous ⬤◯

Parent A          Parent B
Genotypes of Parents
Meiosis                    Meiosis

Gametes →

Genotypes of Children

---

MENDELIAN INHERITANCE

Unlike the natural history approach of Charles Darwin, Mendel added the weight of laboratory research via replicable and verifiable controlled experiment to the study of evolutionary processes. His classic experiment involved the common garden pea. He used only plants of pure strain, which bred true for seven distinct traits. Each trait had two easily observable variant forms (e.g., tall versus short, green versus yellow). From these cross-breeding experiments, Mendel developed via skillful deduction many of the key concepts of modern genetics: the principle of segregation, dominance-submissiveness, independent assortment of genes, and genotype versus phenotype.

*See also* Deoxyribonucleic acid; Evolution, genetic mechanisms of; Gene; Genetics; Mendel, Gregor; Population genetics; Selection, natural

Consult: Alland, A., Jr., *Evolution and Human Behavior* (New York: Anchor, 1973); Peters, J. A., *Classic Papers in Genetics* (Englewood Cliffs, N.J.: Prentice-Hall, 1959).

—*James Clifton, University of Wisconsin, Green Bay*

**Mendel's Laws of Heredity.** *See* Mendelian genetics.

**Menstruation.** This term refers to the periodic discharge of the membranous lining (endometrium) of the uterus of some anthropoids following failure to fertilize after ovulation. Menstruation is merely one phase in a complex, hormonally regulated physiological cycle common to female mammals. The modification essentially consists of the manifest expulsion of the endometrium and, usually, some slight bleeding associated with the destruction of this glandular membrane. The length of the estrous or ovarian cycle in mammals varies from species to species. The entire menstrual cycle of human females ranges from 21 to 34 days with an average length of 28 days (34 to 35 days in chimpanzees); the actual period of menstruation ranges from 2 to 8 days with an average of 5 days. The initial menstruation of human females is termed menarche and occurs at approximately 13 ± 2 years of age. The cessation of ovulation is termed menopause and occurs at approximately 45–50 years of age.

An interesting aspect of the human menstrual cycle is that menarche in Euro-American societies has occurred at successively earlier ages for at least the last century, probably because of enhanced nutrition.

*See also* Rites of passage

Consult: Avers, Charlotte J., *Biology of Sex* (New York: Wiley, 1974); Katchadourian, Herant A., and Lunde, Donald T., *Fundamentals of Human Sexuality* (New York: Holt, 1972).

—*Martin K. Nickels, Illinois State University*

**Mental Health.** This term, vaguely defined and variously conceived of, refers to the absence of mental illness; equilibrium in a sociocultural context; and the ability to make and maintain emotional and affective relationships. Commonly it refers also to the absence of functional psychosis or severe neurosis—functional aspects of the opposed concept of psychiatric disorders. Anthropological concern, beginning with the culture and personality theorists of the 1920s and 1930s, has focused on the conflicts between cultural prescriptions and individual cognition and/or emotional dilemmas demonstrated in behavior. Anthropology has contributed to a broader definition of mental health by using cross-cultural data to indicate interplay between the individual, culture, and society. Anthropologically, mental health may be defined as a person's capacity to function (perceptually, cognitively, and affectively) in his or her own society with specific cultural, subcultural, or class norms and expectations for behavior.

*See also* Health, cross-cultural concepts of; Mental illness and culture; Neurosis; Normality; Psychosis

## Mental Illness and Culture.

The relationship between culture and mental illness has interested a significant number of anthropologists for a long period of time. The relationship, in fact, can be viewed in a number of ways. One approach is to view culture or a set of cultural institutions as causing certain types of behavioral disorders. This leads to the study of associations between certain cultural patterns and certain types of mental disorders.

This approach is difficult, however, for there is no agreement on the cross-cultural definition of behavioral disorders. What is considered mental illness or a behavioral impairment in one society is not so considered in another. Thus comparison of any significance is not easy. Nevertheless, there is widespread agreement that at least the content of mental disorders, whatever their definition may be, is culturally influenced. It would be impossible for someone who had never heard of Jesus to have delusions about being him. But cultures apparently pattern disorders in more subtle ways. As Marvin K. Opler's study of Italian and Irish schizophrenics in New York has clearly shown, the *way* a person becomes mentally ill is influenced by his or her culture, and mental illness within a sociocultural system is an exaggeration of "normal" behavior within that system.

There is also evidence that all communities need individuals with behavioral problems—since these deviants become, in effect, cultural or moral boundary markers.

Better data collecting through the use of more sophisticated hypotheses and statistical techniques will no doubt lead to a better understanding of these issues in the future.

*See also* Cross-cultural surveys; Culture and personality; Deviance; Health, cross-cultural concepts of; Mental health; Normality
Consult: Opler, M. K., *Culture and Mental Health: Cross-cultural Studies* (New York: Macmillan, 1959).
—*Frank A. Salamone, St. John's University*

## Mercantilism.

System of economic absolutism common in Europe from the 16th to 18th centuries whereby governments controlled economies to augment state power at the expense of rival nations.

*See also* Colonialism

## Merton, Robert H.

(b. 1910). A prominent American sociologist whose principal contributions have been in social action theory and functionalism, Merton is best known among anthropologists for his concept of dysfunction and his distinctions between manifest and latent functions. His ideas on functionalism have been greatly influenced by the work of anthropologists B. Malinowski, A. R. Radcliffe-Brown, and Clyde Kluckhohn.

*See also* Dysfunction; Function; Functionalism

## Mesolithic.

This stage concept, coined by Torell (1874) and formerly thought to have universal currency, now designates assemblages of post-Pleistocene age (i.e., since 10,000 BP) which predate the local appearance of domesticated plants and animals. It is best documented in N, NW, and NC Europe, where the term entails an adaptive shift away from the exploitation of steppe/tundra–dwelling megafauna (mammoth, horse, woolly rhinoceros) toward the exploitation of small/medium–sized, forest-dwelling ungulates (red deer, roe deer, wild boar) and also aquatic resources (especially shellfish). Elsewhere (i.e., in more southerly latitudes) no break in continuity with late Pleistocene hunting/gathering adaptations is implied. Dogs appear to have been domesticated in Mesolithic contexts, probably to assist in tracking wounded animals. Cultures of Europe commonly included in this stage are the Maglemøsian and Ertebølle (N Europe), the Tardenoisian/Sauvetterian (W France, W Portugal), and the Asturian (N Spain).

*See also* Holocene

## Messianic Movements.

*See* Millenarian movements; Nativistic movements; Revitalization movements.

## Mestizo.

Originally this term denoted half-breeds with one Spanish parent, although it is now more widely used of people with mixed Spanish or Portuguese and Amerindian ancestry. Intermarriage in Central and South America has been extensive, and mestizos can no longer be regarded as an ethnic minority.

*See also* Métis

## Metallurgy.

*See* Metalworking.

## Metalworking.

Metalworking in its most primitive form—treating native ore as a stone that could be shaped by pounding (*cold hammering*)—is widespread and very ancient. The principal drawback of this method is that after a while the piece produced in this manner will become very brittle. This defect can be remedied by alternating hammering with heating (*annealing*) until the piece reaches the desired shape. All the native North American metalworking traditions—Old Copper, Hopewell, Eskimo—were characterized by these two techniques. Native copper could be pounded into finished artifacts or thin

*Cast gold effigy from Quimbaya, Colombia, that was produced by means of the lost wax technique.*

sheets to be cut into intricate shapes or rolled into beads. However, these techniques did not necessarily lead to the development of *smelting,* the extraction of metal from its ores, which is the hallmark of *metallurgy.* A temperature of 1085°C is required to melt copper. Since the only primitive furnace reaching this temperature is a pottery kiln used to fire superb ceramics, ceramic technology may have provided the expertise necessary for the development of metallurgy.

**Copper.** Smelted copper trinkets first appear at Çatal Hüyük (Anatolia) about the middle of the 7th millennium BC. The next step in the development of metallurgy is indicated by the appearance of *open molds,* demonstrating that people had learned that the bubbly mass at the bottom of the furnace could be liquefied by reheating and then poured rather than hammered into shape. By 3000 BC, the invention of the *two-piece mold* permitted the casting of objects that were shaped on both sides so that only final trimming was required to attain the desired shape. As Near Eastern smiths became more experienced, they learned to use multiple-piece molds to cast even more complex objects. The most intricate pieces were shaped by *lost wax casting* whereby the desired shape was first carved out of wax and then encased in clay. The wax was melted by the fire hardening of the clay and the molten metal was poured in its place, acquiring all the intricacies of the wax model. To remove the metal the clay cast had to be broken; thus every object cast by the lost wax method was unique. Early metallurgy was limited by the fact that large quantities of metal could not be melted at the same time, thus restricting the size of the object that could be cast.

The new calibration of radiocarbon dating reopens the case for an independent invention of metallurgy in the Balkans prior to 4000 BC. In eastern Yugoslavia mines reached a depth of 20–25 meters. There are tools of smelted copper from western Russia by 4000 BC and the earliest open molds from Bulgaria and Yugoslavia have about the same date.

In both Europe and the Near East most early copper artifacts are either trinkets or weapons, notably daggers. Stone continued to be the basic raw material until the spread of bronze.

**Bronze.** A superior quality tin-bronze, rigorously controlled for its tin content by mixing precise quantities of copper and tin, appears to have been invented in southern Russia around 3000 BC. From there it spread rapidly into eastern Europe, the Near East, and northern India by 2500 BC—a spread which has been associated with the Aryan invasions of India by some authors. The earliest appearance of bronze in the Far East (at Non Nok Tha, Thailand) is sufficiently late to imply that bronze was invented only once, in Eurasia, even though the elaboration of bronze casting in the Shang Dynasty (China) must be regarded as the product of Chinese innovations.

The great advantage of bronze is that although it becomes molten at lower temperatures than copper, it is more easily cast and also provides a more durable working edge. Warriors with bronze weapons had the advantage over enemies armed only with copper or stone. Since bronze could be cast into more intricate shapes than copper, the smith's art improved markedly. But so valuable was bronze for weapons and art that it took several centuries for the advantages of the new metal to diffuse from the upper classes to farmers and carpenters. The invention of the *bellows* (about 2000 BC) permitted the maintenance of higher furnace temperatures. Enough bronze to permit its use for tools as well as for weapons was obtained through vast mining projects. Stone tools were gradually replaced by bronze in western Asia and parts of Europe, but in China bronze remained the prerogative of the rich and powerful. Since the raw materials for bronze had to be traded, commerce became a necessity rather than a luxury. The balance of power shifted toward those who could control the trade routes.

**Iron.** Ironworking differs from working softer metals in that primitive furnaces could not attain sufficiently high temperatures to liquefy iron so that it could be cast. Instead, the spongy lump produced by the furnaces had to be heated until red hot and then beaten into shape, a process called *forging.* Although some iron objects from the Near East date as early as the 3rd millennium BC (among the Hittites of Anatolia), the working edge of this kind of iron was inferior to that of a bronze tool until the process of *carburizing* (steeling) was invented sometime around 1500 BC. This important technique probably was invented in the vicinity of the Caucasus Mountains, not far from the area most likely for the invention of bronze. In forging a bar of wrought iron, constant reheating was necessary. If the smith reheated the bar by thrusting it into the heart of a charcoal fire, and if the heat was sufficient, the outer surface of the bar would become carburized to a depth proportionate to the length of the treatment and the heat of the fire, thus giving the bar a steel case hardening which greatly increased its efficiency. This remained a hit or miss process for several centuries so that traders sometimes seem to have had difficulty in fulfilling their obligations. The Hittites controlled the flow of iron to the Near East during most of the latter half of the 2nd millennium BC. Only about 1200 BC did iron begin to replace bronze for agricultural purposes in the Near East, and it took another thousand years for iron tools to become widespread in China. Truly effective ironworking technology did not reach Egypt until the 7th century BC, resulting in the rise of the Meroe Kingdom shortly before the birth of Christ. Then the technology spread across the southern Sahara to West Africa by about 500 BC.

**Metallurgy in the New World.** The New World metallurgical tradition is entirely independent of the one which developed in Eurasia. Although New World smiths knew the use of copper and bronze as well as gold, archaeological interpretations have emphasized the artistic aspects of metallurgy rather than the instrumental ones. Goldworking probably originated somewhere in the northern Andes of Colombia or Ecuador about 1500 BC. *Soldering* and *welding* were invented by 1200 BC, but there is no evidence of *casting* until about 700 BC, associated with copper metallurgy.

Copper metallurgy was invented in southern Peru or northern Chile before 1000 BC, but the earliest copper spearheads and digging-stick tips do not appear until about the time of Christ. Tin-bronze appears earliest in Argentina, about AD 400.

The finest creations of American smiths come from the area of northern Colombia and lower Central America. Some of their work has been retrieved in the form of offerings in Chichen Itza (Yucatan) about AD 700, but metallurgy did not appear in Mesoamerica until about AD 900, arising simultaneously in the southern Maya area and also on the west coast. The techniques spread quickly toward the Valley of Mexico and a few odd pieces even reached the SW United States. The Mixtec were the finest

Mexican smiths. At the time of the Spanish conquest they were making tools for agriculture and war as well as exquisite jewelry.

Consult: Hodges, Henry, *Technology in the Ancient World* (London: Allen Lane, 1970); Renfrew, Colin, *Before Civilization* (New York: Knopf, 1973); Spier, R. F. G., *From the Hand of Man: Primitive and Preindustrial Technologies* (Boston: Houghton Mifflin, 1970); Wooley, Sir Leonard, *The Beginnings of Civilization* (New York: Mentor Books, 1965). —*Thomas P. Myers, University of Nebraska*

**Methods of Fieldwork.** *See* Fieldwork methods.

**Métis.** The offspring of French and American Indian parents are called métis in Canada, particularly in Manitoba and Saskatchewan. Métis is a term related to a corresponding Spanish word, mestizo, defined as the offspring of Spanish and Indian parentage.

*See also* Mestizo.

Consult: Slobodin, Richard, *Métis of the Mackenzie District* (Ottawa: Canadian Research Center for Anthropology, St. Paul University, 1966).

**Métraux, Alfred** (1902–1963). Swissborn cultural anthropologist who did extensive fieldwork among a number of South American Indians, the peasants of Haiti, and the inhabitants of Easter Island.

**Microbehavior.** *See* Kinesics.

**Microevolution.** *See* Evolution, biological; Evolution and genetics.

**Microlith.** Small stone tools made from fragments of blade tools are associated with the Mesolithic period approximately 13,000–6000 BC. They were hafted in bone and antler handles to make composite tools.

*See also* Mesolithic

Consult: Bordes, Jacques, *Tools of the Old and the New Stone Age* (New York: Natural History Press, 1968).

**Midden.** This term refers to a mass of poorly stratified shell, bone, carbon, ash, lithic, and other cultural debris accumulated by human activity and combined with geologically deposited fine sediments (e.g., silts). Middens were widespread in W Europe during the early Holocene (i.e., since the end of the Pleistocene ca. 10,000 BP). The Danish *køkkenmøddingen* (kitchen middens) refers to such sites.

*See also* Excavation of a site; Site

**Middle Paleolithic.** The age of *Homo sapiens neanderthalensis* and Mousteroid culture is dated 70,000–35,000 BP. Diagnostic points and scrapers made of prepared-core flakes, which were often trimmings for woodworking and skin preparation, are almost universal in Middle Paleolithic sites from Europe, Asia, and Africa. Regional specialization in human cultures became marked in the Middle Paleolithic. Neanderthal peoples on the Russian tundras were roving hunters of mammoth and bison whereas French Neanderthals occupied rock shelters throughout the year. Other groups adapted to life in the dense rain forests. Concern with the afterlife is evidenced by careful burials and occasional grave goods. Cult activities are suggested by concentrations of bear bones in some caves.

*See also* Paleolithic

**Migration.** There are basically two definitions of human migration used in anthropology. The one which will be called *dislocative migration* for purposes of the present discussion is defined as a permanent or semipermanent change of residence by a group. Spatial movement is assumed, of course, in this definition, but the distance can range anywhere from a hop from one town to the next all the way up to intercontinental odysseys.

The second way in which the term *migration* is used is simply to mean a spatial movement of people. Here it is understood that the new residence resulting from the move is generally quite transitory, in contrast to the first definition, and, in fact, movement itself is an integral part of the group's life-style. Such is the case with nomadic and transhuman bands or tribes; thus we may refer to this as *nomadic migration.*

**Related Definitions.** *Internal migration* is dislocative migration within specified political boundaries—usually a nation-state.

*External migration* is dislocative migration that takes place across political boundaries. *Immigration* refers to dislocative migration into an area (usually delimited by a political boundary) and *emigration* is dislocative migration out of an area. *Involuntary (dislocative) migration* is the term usually used to designate a forced migration resulting from social factors (e.g., political upheavals and persecution) or natural ones (e.g., volcanic eruptions). *Voluntary (dislocative) migration* comes about by the migrants' willing decision to relocate.

**Complexity of Migration Studies.** Somewhat ironically, scholars interested in dislocative migration are only peripherally interested in the actual trek of the migrants. They are generally more concerned with such questions as (1) the reasons for the move (social, political, economic, psychological); (2) the characteristics (ethnic, psychological, economic and social status, age, family size) of the migrants which separate them from the persons who remain stationary; (3) the patterns or problems of assimilation and acculturation of the migrants in their new setting; and (4) if the migration takes place in large numbers, the social, political, and economic impact of the migration on the places of origin and destination.

Because dislocative migration includes demographic, economic, political, psychological, sociological, and cultural aspects, there have been few attempts at constructing a general theory even though it is a worldwide phenomenon as old as the human species itself. The best-known attempt at a general theory was made in 1885 by E. G. Ravenstein of England. Ravenstein's "laws of migration" are seven statements which relate demographic and economic factors with characteristics of migrants and migrations. Over the years Ravenstein's theory has been severely criticized. It has been realized that dislocative migration, caused and influenced as it is by such varied circumstances and historical events, is not amenable to laws parallel to those the chemist strives for in describing our physical world. Nonetheless, Ravenstein's work has been the point of departure for practically all dislocative migration theory which has appeared since his time.

**The Push-Pull Model.** Today, efforts at migration theory are much narrower in scope and less ambitious than works such as Ravenstein's. The emphasis is on expressing empirically testable hypotheses which deal

An Eskimo community, photographed in 1915 by Diamond Jenness, migrating to a new winter location in the vicinity of Coronation Gulf in northern central Canada. Such highly mobile hunting and gathering groups tend to have the most egalitarian forms of political organization.

with limited aspects of migration and which take into consideration social, cultural, political, and economic conditions. The most successful approach so far in dealing with migration in these terms is what has come to be known as the push-pull model: In all dislocative migrations there are both factors which push the migrants from their habitat (e.g., persecution) and factors which pull them to a new destination (e.g., occupational opportunities). Depending on the situation, the pushes might greatly outweigh the pulls; the reverse might be the case; or the pushes and pulls might be quite evenly influential. An elaboration of the push-pull model of particular worth is that offered by Lee (1969). Lee divides migration into four distinct parts: factors which hold people in a habitat and also attract people to it; factors which repel people from a habitat; the difficulties of the journey as seen by the prospective migrants; and personal factors. Also included are factors which are neutral to the staying or going decision. Lee realizes that what is a push for one person might be a pull or a neutral factor for another, but he maintains that often in migration situations large numbers of people will be attracted or repulsed by similar social, political, or geographical factors. The advantages which Lee's model offers over the basic push-pull model are twofold: he includes the intervening obstacles, such as distance and dangerous travel, which enter into the migration decision in many cases; moreover, he contends that people are not only pushed to leave one place and pulled toward another but are also constrained to stay put. This aids in understanding why some people leave while others remain.

**International Involuntary Migration: Refugees.** Involuntary migrations in our century have had enormous impact on transforming the ethnic, linguistic, social, and cultural makeup of entire nations. It is estimated that some 100 million or more people in the world were victims of involuntary migration in the time span from 1912 to 1967. It is overwhelming, indeed, to realize that the number of people who were ousted from one country to another in the decade after World War II approximates the entire overseas migration from Europe in the 19th century and the first decade of the 20th.

**Seminomadic Migration.** Between nomadic migration and dislocative migration we can identify a kind of migration with characteristics of both. We may call it seminomadic. This is a phenomenon quite familiar to Americans. Approximately 40 million Americans move to a new residence at least once each year, and over a third of these migrations are across county or state boundaries.

William Watson coined the term *spiralism* to describe the activity of persons moving from one residence to another as they climb for a higher occupational status which requires either a company transfer or a change of employer. Spiralism accounts for a large portion of the seminomadic migration in the United States and other highly industrialized nations.

See also Acculturation; Nomadism; Transhumance

Consult: Beijer, G., "Modern Patterns of International Migratory Movements," in *Migration*, ed. J. A. Jackson (London: Cambridge University Press, 1969); *International Migration Review* (a journal published quarterly by the Center for Migration, Staten Island, N.Y.); Lee, Everett S., "A Theory of Migration," in *Migration*, ed. J. A. Jackson (London: Cambridge University Press, 1969); Packard, Vance, *A Nation of Strangers* (New York: McKay, 1972); Watson, William, "Social Mobility and Social Class in Industrial Communities," in *Closed Systems and Open Minds*, ed. Max Gluckman (Chicago: Aldine, 1964).

—James N. Bellis, University of Oregon

**Millar, John** (1735–1801). A Scottish moral philosopher, Millar developed a materialist theory of social stratification based on economic considerations and on the nature of social institutions.

**Millenarian Movements.** These movements are one variety of cultural revitalization and nativistic movements. They involve deeply held beliefs that radical and supernatural changes in the structure of a society and its culture are about to happen. This expectation is accompanied by profound emotional commitment and identity transformations. A group organizes and works with great enthusiasm to prepare for the millennium. Sometimes the millennium is expected momentarily, here and now, on earth. Often the coming is in the indefinite future, or the expectation may be for only minor changes and improvements on earth—with radical change and true bliss reserved for heaven and the afterlife.

Millenarian movements have been very common in the Pacific Islands, Africa, Eurasia, and the Americas. Even subgroups in complex, modern societies become involved. Indeed, new millenarian movements occur annually in industrialized nation-states. However, the best-known millenarian movements have been the so-called cargo cults of the Melanesian cultures in the Pacific.

In these cargo cults new social organizations are created to make preparations for the millennium. Docks or airstrips are constructed to await the coming of ships and planes loaded with the wealth of the industrialized world; warehouses and stores are built to store and dispense the cargo. The adherents often abandon their traditional subsistence activities, fishing and agriculture. Sometimes they destroy their tools, houses, and livestock to clear the way for the new goods.

These movements are particularly prevalent where there is great social distance between native peoples and outsiders, divisions marked by racial, caste, or class barriers. Hence millenarian movements tend to be a characteristic of plural societies and function as one means of reducing the strains of life in societies marked by profound inequalities. They are probably most often associated with the earlier stages of colonial development, and they are often readily displaced by political-economic movements which lack the magical supernatural emphasis of millenarianism. Millenarian movements tend to break down older tribal and cultural loyalties and distinctions, for example, with the consequent development of pantribal solidarity and organization.

See also Cargo cults; Nativistic movements; Revitalization movements
Consult: Mead, M., New Lives for Old (New York: Morrow, 1956); Worsley, P. W., Millenarian Movements in Melanesia (Indianapolis: Bobbs-Merrill, 1957); Worsley, P. W., The

Trumpet Shall Sound (New York: Schocken, 1968).
—James Clifton, University of Wisconsin, Green Bay

**Mind.** This term refers to the collective attributes and contents of consciousness, such as cognition, emotion, memory, or perception. Behaviorist psychologists have been highly critical of the concept of mind on the grounds that it is a vague abstraction inaccessible to scientific investigation. Cognitive psychologists, however, have emphasized intrapsychic processes of the mind as being the determinants of behavior. This view has found more favor with anthropologists, who are attempting to discover general principles in terms of which the mind orders reality.

See also Language and thought

**Minifundia.** This Latin term (singular: minifundium) refers to tiny, often fragmented, agrarian production units held under various tenure contracts. Holders, as decision-makers, run them primarily with their own or their household's labor. Larger tracts are fragmented by various inheritance patterns or enforced modes of tenancy. Minifundia often produce only marginally for household subsistence or markets.

See also Land tenure; Latifundia; Tenancy

**Mining.** See Metalworking.

**Minorities, Cultural.** See Cultural minorities.

**Minorities, Ethnic.** Ethnic minorities are social groups that are distinguished from the larger society of which they form a part by certain traits such as language, national origin, religion, race, values, or customs. Often subjected to discrimination or even outright repression by the dominant group in their society, they may respond either by seeking to blur the distinctions between themselves and others or by emphasizing these distinctions and demanding recognition and tolerance for their own group.

The presence of ethnic minorities has posed a political problem in many parts of the world, particularly in former colonial

territories (such as India, Nigeria, Pakistan, Chad, Sudan, and Iraq) where arbitrarily defined national boundaries have included diverse and sometimes mutually antagonistic ethnic groups. In the United States, there has been a recent resurgence of ethnicity, with individuals taking renewed pride in the traditions and social cohesiveness of their ethnic minority and deriving personal identification from their group membership.

See also Colonialism; Cultural minorities; Ethnocentrism; Extinction of minorities; Genocide; Pluralism
Consult: Brown, Francis J., and Roucek, Joseph S. (eds.), One America (Westport, Conn.: Negro University Press, 1970); "Ethnic Groups in American Life," Daedalus 90(2), Spring 1961; Hunt, Chester L., and Walker, Lewis, Ethnic Dynamics (Homewood, Ill.: Dorsey Press, 1974); Makielski, S. J., Jr., Beleaguered Minorities (San Francisco: Freeman, 1973); TeSelle, Sallie (ed.), The Rediscovery of Ethnicity (New York: Harper & Row, 1974).
—Ian Robertson, Cambridge University

**Mintz, Sidney Wilfrid** (b. 1922). Social anthropologist who has specialized in comparative race relations as well as social and economic organization in the Caribbean (especially Puerto Rico), particularly in peasantry and plantation systems.

**Missionaries, Research of.** Missionaries, in the ecclesiastical sense, are people sent out by religious organizations who have authority to preach and administer the sacraments. Research in native languages and regional ethnographies has been accepted as a crucial ingredient in successful missionary work.

An example of missionary research is afforded by the Summer Institute of Linguistics of the University of Oklahoma. In its courses of language analysis, students are taught to recognize and reproduce phonetically the speech sounds of a specific language and create a workable alphabet for writing words and sentences. Following up their mastery of the phonology they are instructed in how to develop a dictionary and work up a grammar. The construction of primers and texts for teaching illiterates to read their own native speech concludes the process. Fieldwork with a native language, hitherto unwritten, is then undertaken.

The activities of the students in the field, in conjunction with Wycliffe Bible Translators, Inc., began in the 1940s in Mexico and has gradually extended to Indian languages of Colombia, Ecuador, Peru, Bolivia, and Brazil, making use of air transport and pontoon landings in jungle areas. In the Eastern Hemisphere work has been undertaken in Australia and New Guinea, the Philippines, and Nepal.

Consult: Harner, Michael J., *The Jivaro: People of the Sacred Waterfalls* (New York: American Museum of Natural History, 1972); Huxley, Matthew, and Capa, Cornell, *Farewell to Eden* (New York: Harper & Row, 1964); Wallis, E. E., and Bennett, M. A., *Two Thousand Tongues To Go—the Story of the Wycliffe Bible Translators* (New York: Harper & Row, 1959).
—*William H. Gilbert, U.S. Library of Congress (ret.)*

**Mixed Blood.** *See* Mestizo; Métis; Race.

**Mobility, Social.** The study of social mobility is the study of the ability of people to change their social position. While people, or groups, can be downwardly or horizontally mobile, most studies have concentrated on upward mobility. Greater attention to people who change jobs but within the same social ranking or who fail to progress in social ranking above their father and fall below him in ranking would add to our knowledge of the process of social mobility.

Most studies of social mobility have compared the occupation of sons with fathers, thus biasing the sample and not taking into account men who have no sons (married or not); also, the study of women has, for the most part, been neglected. Studies indicate that there has been less mobility in the United States than previously thought true. Future studies are likely to move beyond the construction of mobility scales and begin to explore the causes of differential rates of mobility.
*See also* Status
—*Frank A. Salamone, St. John's University*

**Modal Personality.** This term refers to the statistically most frequent pattern of personality attributes found in a sample of psychological test materials. It is essentially a methodological device conceived by Cora DuBois and developed by A. F. C. Wallace to cope with a flaw in the theory of basic personality as developed by Abram Kardiner. This defect involved the lack of a systematic, objective means of determining the typical configuration of personality traits in a society. The statistical mode was selected as the appropriate measure of central tendency.
*See also* Basic personality; Measurement scales; Projective tests
Consult: Spindler, L., and Spindler, G. D., "A Modal Personality Technique in the Study of Menomini Acculturation," in *Studying Personality Cross-Culturally*, ed. B. Kaplan (Evanston: Northwestern University Press, 1961).

**Mode of Artifact.** *See* Types and modes of artifacts.

**Model.** This term, though used in somewhat different ways, has a core of commonly shared meaning. A model involves an abstract, generalized representation of the relationships among a set of variables which is so stated that it predicts (1) the various known empirical cases of specific relationships among the variables designated, (2) possible other cases as yet unknown, (3) the form the model would take if the abstract relationships among the variables were changed, and thereby (4) other known and unknown empirical cases which would be subsumed under the variant model. Models are intermediaries between abstract theory and empirical observation—serving as a form of low-level generalization (about a limited set of possible cases) which generates discovery of new empirical cases. These either confirm the theory or broaden known facts requiring modification of either the model or the theory. Models are extremely useful for guiding research on a day-to-day basis because it is difficult to jump from the level of grand theory to empirical observation (or vice versa).
—*Anthony Leeds, Boston University*

**Modernization.** This is a recently coined synonym for such older terms as civilization, westernization, and industrialization. The usage comes primarily from United States government agencies concerned with the restructuring and development of Third World societies. It refers to the development in these societies of national-level institutions characteristic of Western or industrialized (i.e., modern) nations—such as bureaucracies, mass education systems,

*Modernization is not an all-or-nothing process. Here a Kikuyu tribesman in Nairobi, Kenya, retains vestiges of traditional dress while riding in a modern bus.*

national police forces, and similar structures. The specific content of "modernity" varies with the ideology of the nation sponsoring the modernization project. Because of such built-in ideological biases, modernization does not constitute a distinct, legitimate field of scientific inquiry. The problems and issues covered in modernization studies are more systematically handled by such approaches as innovation theory or forced acculturation studies.
*See also* Acculturation; Cultural evolution; Innovation; Social change

**Moiety.** This term refers to a group which is one of two units of a larger group—e.g., each clan of a society composed of two clans is a moiety.
*See also* Clan; Kinship

**Money.** Money is a token or item which symbolizes command over goods or services. It may function as a means of storing wealth, as a common measure of value, as a medium of exchange, and as a standard of deferred payment. It may also serve ornamental or religious purposes. Money may be of limited purpose and therefore be restricted in exchange for only one or a few items; or money may be all-purpose and therefore in principle exchanged for all items which may be transferred in a society. Items as diverse as 12-foot-diameter stones, bird feathers, tobacco, dead rats, and shells have been used as money.

Due to the diversity of kinds as well as functions of money, there has been considerable controversy among anthropologists as to an acceptable definition. The definition offered here is perhaps one of the more general.

See also Exchange; Money systems; Shell money

Consult: Armstrong, W. E., "Rossel Island Money," The Economic Journal 34:423–429, 1924; Bohannan, Paul, "Some Principles of Exchange and Investment Among the Tiv," American Anthropologist 57:60–70, 1955; Bohannan, Paul, "The Impact of Money on an African Subsistence Economy," Journal of Economic History, pp. 491–503, 1959; Codere, H., "Money Exchange Systems and a Theory of Money," Man, pp. 557–577, 1968; Dalton, George, "Primitive Money," American Anthropologist 67:44–65, 1965; Einzig, P., Primitive Money (London: Eyre and Spottiswoode, 1949); Herskovits, M. J., Economic Anthropology (New York: Norton, 1940); Jevons, W. S., Money and the Mechanisms of Exchange (New York: Appleton, 1920); Quiggens, A. H., A Survey of Primitive Money (New York: Barnes & Noble, 1949).

—John R. Lombardi, Boston University

**Money Systems.** Money may be classified according to the degree to which it has been integrated with the other symbolic systems of a society. In particular we refer to systems of numeration, weights and measures, and writing. On the lowest level, money is simply a token which may be exchanged for a certain good or service. If a system of numeration is used, two or more tokens may be exchanged. In other words tokens may be counted, in contrast to the lowest level in which they must be used individually. If a system of weights and measures is used for the goods exchanged, this enables complete exchangeability of money for all combinations of goods and allows money to assume full power as a medium of exchange. Incorporation of a writing system allows denominations to be issued. (For example, a five-dollar bill is worth five one-dollar bills. This is not true, say, of shell money, for which each shell is a unit and worth only one shell.) This issuance usually implies the existence of a state and allows this state to control the supply of money and therefore the price of all goods and services of the society.

See also Economic anthropology; Market systems; Money; Numbering, systems of; Shell money

Consult: Codere, H., "Money Exchange Systems and a Theory of Money," Man, pp. 557–577, 1968.

—John R. Lombardi, Boston University

**Mongoloid Spot.** Among many peoples of East Asia, and also Native Americans, infants are born with a purplish-blue spot at the base of the spine. Quite often the spot disappears with maturity, though not entirely in some individuals, where it may concentrate into a small birthmark-size spot. The trait is not exclusive to Asians but occasionally occurs among a small percentage of black Africans.

**Monogamy.** This marriage rule permits both the man and the woman only one spouse at a time. It may or may not rule out divorce and remarriage (serial monogamy).

See also Marriage

**Monogenesis.** Monogenesis is the doctrine that human races descended from a single original stock or even, more theologically, an original human pair. Nineteenth-century monogenists, by explicitly or implicitly defending Christian cosmogony, also had to consider human history as unitary and brief. Monogenesis supposed that rapid racial differentiation resulted from climate and other environmental causes. However, it was observed that migrational redistributions of races produced little noticeable rapid phenotypic changes; thus this view became untenable. Ultimately, monogenesis was subsumed under Darwinian-Mendelian evolutionism. Today's view generally is that selection took place among aboriginal stock variants which dispersed around the world, with subsequent local "racial" specialization during great time periods.

See also Polygenesis

**Monotheistic Religions.** The conceptualization and development of monetheism is a problem that has engaged many students of religion, including leading anthropologists. If we mean by monotheistic religions those that postulate the existence of only one spiritual being, then Judaism, Christianity, and Islam would not qualify as monotheistic religions. For these religions recognize other spiritual beings besides their primary deity. According to Guy Swanson (1960), however, they are monotheistic religions in that they stipulate their primary deity as the first cause of all effects and the necessary and sufficient condition for reality's continued existence. Swanson notes that a few primitive and early civilized cultures have a similar conception of such a god. In addition he provides the basis for a broader definition of monotheism by defining what he terms "high gods"—deities that are considered ultimately responsible for all events, either as history's creator, director, or both. Defined in terms of high gods, monotheistic religions are quite prevalent. In a cross-cultural survey Bourguignon and Greenbaum found that a belief in a high god is present in the majority of societies of Africa, the Mediterranean area, and South America. In aboriginal North America and the insular Pacific the majority of societies do not exhibit such a belief. They further noted that only in the Mediterranean area is the belief in a high god generally connected with morality, and there 88 percent of the societies surveyed have a belief in a high god concerned with the moral life of human beings.

Edward Tylor, the 19th-century English anthropologist, viewed the development of monotheistic religions from an evolutionary perspective. Starting with a postulation of the earliest religion as a belief in spiritual entities (animism), he traced a conjectural evolutionary development of religious beliefs through ancestor worship, polytheism, and eventually to monotheism. Tylor conceived of spirits as personified causes and suggested that monotheistic religions might have developed from the postulation of a "first cause" realized in the conception of a supreme deity. Thus Tylor saw an orderly and logical development from animism to monotheism. Paul Radin takes a similar intellectualistic approach to monotheism but sees the development of such beliefs as limited to the shamans and priests rather than the general population of societies. He contends that monotheistic beliefs in a supreme deity are the expression of people of a certain temperament in all societies and that the postulated deities are not meant to be worshipped. Indeed, when they are made the focus of religious institutions their original character is distorted. Radin holds that monotheism as the acknowledged religion of the whole community is not found in primitive society.

Raffaele Pettazzoni takes sharp exception to Tylor's theory of the gradual and logical development from animism through polytheism to monotheism. Tylor saw one possible development of a belief in a supreme deity as the fusion of the attributes of the great polytheistic deities into a more or less common personality who combines all the explanatory potential of the previously-believed-in polytheistic deities. Pettazzoni conceives of monotheism as the negation of polytheism—a revolutionary divergence rather than a gradual and logical emergence from polytheism. As such he would limit the occurrence of monotheism to certain religions such as Judaism, Christianity, and Islam while denying its existence in primitive societies. His divergence from Tylor, however, is more superficial than substantial in that Tylor might indeed have regarded Pettazzoni's religious revolution as a logical outgrowth of the philosophical thought of earlier evolutionary stages.

Swanson, following Durkheim's emphasis on social causation, undertook a cross-cultural survey of the occurrence of belief in a high god. He found such beliefs to be associated with a certain degree of societal complexity. Specifically, he found that such a belief was positively related to the presence of a hierarchy of three or more groups (sovereign groups) having original and independent jurisdiction over some sphere of life. His finding does not necessarily contradict Tylor, who held that "man being the type of deity, human society and government become the model on which divine society and government were shaped." Thus Tylor maintained that animistic spiritual beings, polytheistic deities, and monotheistic deities differed in rank rather than in basic nature.

See also Animism; Religion; Religions of the world; Tylor, E. B.
Consult: Pettazzoni, R., *Essays on the History of Religion* (London: Brill, 1954); Radin, P., *Monotheism Among Primitive Peoples* (London: Allen and Unwin, 1924); Swanson, G., *The Birth of the Gods* (Ann Arbor: University of Michigan Press, 1960); Tylor, E., *Primitive Culture* (New York: Gordon Press).
—*Stan Wilk, Lycoming College*

**Montagu, Ashley** (b. 1905). Free-lance anthropologist well known as a popularizer of anthropology; noted for his attacks on the race concept and his consideration of a variety of biosocial problems.

**Montesquieu, Charles Louis de Secondat, Baron de la Brède et de** (1680–1755). This French philosopher and historian wrote *Lettres Persanes* (1721), a satire on French sociopolitical and cultural institutions. It opened the Philosophe Movement, which led to the *Encyclopédie* and to basic institutional analyses making use of a perspective later characterizing anthropology. From his history of Rome (1734) and wide European travel, he evolved the *Esprit des lois* (1748), essentially a general theory of society treating the relationship of law to government and to customs, manners, religion, and economics, including considerable thought on climatic determinism. It fundamentally influenced all subsequent sociopolitical and cultural analytic thought.

**Moral Development.** This term refers to the process by which individuals internalize the moral norms of their society. There are three main theories of moral development. *Freudian* theory postulates the existence of a superego or conscience, which represents the internalized authority of the parents. The superego is said to develop around the age of seven. *Behaviorist* theory holds that moral rules and attitudes are cumulatively learned as a result of conditioning processes, in which morally appropriate responses are socially rewarded while inappropriate ones are punished. *Cognitive-developmental* theory, as outlined by Jean Piaget and Lawrence Kohlberg, regards moral development as a sequence of cognitive growth through progressively more elaborate

stages; each stage is said to employ a qualitatively different mode of reasoning.

See also Stages of moral development

**Mores.** Mores are important norms of a society deeply rooted in its belief system. They are involved with moral and ethical conduct, and violation can lead to severe punishment such as social isolation. As contrasted with *folkways,* mores have compelling social and emotional connotations and represent values of particular significance to a society.

See also Culture; Custom; Folkways; Social control; Traditions
Consult: Loomis, Charles P., *Social Systems: Essays on Their Persistence and Change* (Princeton, N.J.: Van Nostrand, 1960); Williams, Robin M., Jr., *American Society* (New York: Knopf, 1960).

**Morgan, Lewis Henry** (1818–1881). Morgan's *League of the Iroquois* (1851) is thought to be the first complete ethnography of a non-Western people. His *Systems of Consanguinity and Affinity of the Human Family* (1871) established kinship as a central topic of research in anthropology. In it he developed the distinction between descriptive and classificatory kinship terminologies. In his last major work, *Ancient Society* (1877), Morgan argued that societies progressed from savagery through barbarism to civilization—one of the many unilineal theories of evolution developed in the 19th century.

**Morpheme.** In traditional descriptive linguistics, a morpheme is the smallest unit of meaning in a language. It may be a word or part of a word. In either case, it has a complete meaning. The word *birds,* for example, has two morphemes—*bird* and the plural morpheme *s.*

See also Lexeme; Morphemes and words; Phoneme

**Morphemes and Words.** Although a morpheme (for example, *dog*) may be a word, words may be composed of more than one morpheme (for example, *dogs*) and some morphemes are never words (for example, the *s* that is one of the signs of plurality in English). The linguist is concerned with the morpheme and its combination with other such linguistic units to form complex verbal forms including words, phrases, and sentences. This branch of linguistics is called morphology. Morphology is concerned with the way phonemes combine to form morphemes and in turn with the way morphemes combine into more complex forms. There are a finite number of morphemes in every language and a limited number of ways they can be combined. Some morphemes are roots of words, others affixes (prefixes and suffixes), yet others infixes (found in the middle of a word).

*See also* Lexeme; Morpheme; Phoneme

## Morphology.
In the study of languages morphology consists of the internal grammar of words, in contrast to syntax or the grammar of sentences. That is, morphology consists of a study and description of the systematic ways that words are formed from lesser units. It consists, then, of paradigms of the principal parts of speech in a language, an examination of inflectional systems and allomorphs, and an analysis of the way stems are formed and also of words that are not inflected.

*See also* Language; Linguistics; Morpheme; Morphemes and words

## Morphophonemics.
Morphophonemics is the study of the structure of language in terms of the phonological patterning of morphemes, particularly allomorphic variations, including the substitution, addition, or loss of phonemes. Morphophonemic analysis proceeds by selecting a base allomorph and then describing the conditions that determine which other allomorphs will occur in particular contexts. For example, if the English noun plural allomorph /-s/ is taken as the base form, the /-s/ becomes /-z/ after a voiced sound, except that after /s z c j/ a vowel /-i-/ is inserted to make it /iz/.

*See also* Language; Linguistics; Morpheme; Morphology; Phoneme

## Morris, Charles William
(b. 1901). A philosopher who works in the field of semiotic (the theory of signs), Morris has clarified three major concepts: *semantics* is the relationship of signs to what they represent;

*syntax* is the relationship of signs to each other; *pragmatics* is the effects signs have on their users.

*See also* Semiotic

## Morris, Desmond
(b. 1928). British zoologist responsible for the popularization of human ethology through his controversial books *The Naked Ape* (1968) and *The Human Zoo* (1969).

## Mortuary Practices.
Customs for the disposal of deceased kinfolk and friends are at least as old as the Mousterian period. Up to a certain level of cultural development, the elaborateness of mortuary practices increases; thereafter, only a diminishing percentage of a culture's wealth is invested in burials. Customs for handling and disposing of the body vary widely. It may be buried in the ground in extended, flexed, seated, or squatting position. The body may be completely interred or left with the head aboveground. The body may be abandoned or left in caves, cairns, or caches. It may be cremated or left exposed on a platform.

*See also* Burial

## Mosaic.
This ancient art involved the fashioning of precut materials into a design mounted on a base. The art was widely distributed throughout the New World and was most highly developed in the SW United States, Mexico, and Peru. The base material was usually wood, although bone and shell are also known to have been used. The primary ornamentation applied in mosaic technique was turquoise, followed by shell, bone, lignite, and feathers; some mother-of-pearl was also known. Designs were usually geometric or an occasional realistic form worked into semiangular design. In such instances, tiny bits of material were carefully fashioned to fit precisely into patterns and then sometimes further carved or cut to enhance the effectiveness of the detail—especially where hands, feet, eyes, or other anatomical details are depicted.

In North America, the primary area of mosaic artistry was the Pueblo Southwest, where early artists left numerous examples of turquoise, shell, and jet designs overlaid on wood and shell. The Chumash Indians of California applied shell and bone in mosaic

patterns to the surface of bone, shell, and steatite objects, using asphalt as an adhesive. Indians in the Eastern United States practiced a certain amount of quasi-mosaic work involving wampum beads applied to wooden ceremonial objects in geometric designs. Today the Zuni, Hopi, and Rio Grande Pueblo people are noted for their skill in continuing this art.

In Central America, probably the most skillful exponents of mosaic art were the Mixtec peoples living in the Oaxaca region of Mexico. Their mastery of the art, as evidenced by numerous examples of inlaid wooden masks, shields, and similar ceremonial objects, is well known and was highly prized. Some mosaic work is also known from Guatemala and Honduras, but in fewer numbers.

West Indian mosaic work was highly developed, as is demonstrated by the rare but effective examples of Taino artistry using shell and bone, primarily applied to wood.

South American mosaic art seems to have been most commonly practiced in Peru, where turquoise, lapis, bone, shell, and other materials were inlaid on wood, bone, and shell bases. The Nazca, Chimú, and Inca peoples refined this art significantly.

In sum, it can be said that mosaic art was well represented throughout the New World in ancient times, equaling anything found in the Old World for technical and aesthetic qualities. Wherever found, mosaic objects were highly valued as extremely fragile reflections of a beautiful art form, intended primarily for wealthy or religiously important personages. The ability to skillfully fashion tiny bits of precut materials into intricate designs gave it an importance it retains to this day.

Consult: Burnett, Edwin K., "Inlaid Stone and Bone Artifacts from Southern California," *Contributions from the Museum of the American Indian*, vol. 13, 1944; Heye, George G., *Certain Aboriginal Artifacts from San Miguel Island, California*, Museum of the American Indian Monographs, vol 7, no. 4, 1921; Hodge, Frederick W., *Turquois Work of Hawikuh, New Mexico*, Leaflet 2, Museum of the American Indian, 1921; Saville, Marshall H., "Turquois Mosaic Art in Ancient Mexico," *Contributions from the Museum of the American Indian*, vol. 6, 1922.

—*Frederick Dockstader, Museum of the American Indian*

**Mother-in-Law Taboo.** This taboo is one of a number of avoidances found in many societies throughout the world. One function of such avoidance is to preclude problems in a society in which mothers and sons-in-law are in structural opposition to each other. Thus they may be enjoined from speaking, looking at, or even referring to one another. Mother-in-law avoidance is often found in societies in which a man goes to live with his wife and descent is through the female line (matrilineal-matrilocal societies). While the woman remains with her kin and with women of her work team, the man is a stranger and has little structural control over his children, who belong to his mother-in-law's lineage or clan. A milder form of this taboo is found in our own white middle- and working-class society and is given wide recognition in jokes.

*See also* Joking, ritualized; Kinship

*Polychrome* incensario *fashioned in a jaguar motif, typical of many of the pre-Columbian Meso- and South American civilizations.*

**Motif.** A motif is a regularly recurrent thematic element in a body of art or folklore. Motifs are basically creative design elements which give style unity and predictability to a culture's art and folklore.

*See also* Art; Folklore

**Motion Pictures.** *See* Film, ethnographic research and report.

**Mousterian Culture.** This group of Middle Paleolithic assemblages equates with a level of technological development characterized by flake tools (especially sidescrapers and denticulates). The type site is LeMoustier (Dordogne, France), dated from somewhat more than 80,000 to less than 44,000 years BP. This culture derived from the Acheulean and perhaps also the Clactonian. *Homo sapiens neanderthalensis* fossils are associated with these assemblages (W Europe, Iraq), which are best known from SW France and N Spain but also W and C Europe, N Africa, and the Near East. The incidence of Levallois prepared-core technique is variable and nondiagnostic. There are regionally variable adaptations. Some groups have left remains of the first or earliest evidence for intentional burial (e.g., La Ferrassie).

*See also* Middle Paleolithic

**Movius, Halam Leonard, Jr.** (b. 1907). An archaeologist interested in the Paleolithic of Europe and Asia, Movius is especially known for his work on the Périgordian and Aurignacian cultures in France.

**Müller, Friedrich Maximilian** (1823–1900). A linguist and philologist specializing in Sanskrit literature, Max Müller was one of the first to study religion on a comparative basis. Although he originated the phrase "science of religion," his methods were primarily linguistic. He believed that all European myths and folklore could be traced back to Sanskrit sources and that sun worship was the unifying factor in all mythology and folklore. He coined the term *Aryan* and often used it in his writings when referring to race, although he said that he did not believe in equating language with race. He was also well known as a translator of Far Eastern texts.

**Multilineal Evolutionism.** *See* Evolutionism.

**Multivariate Analysis.** This term refers to the statistical study of relationships among more than two variables. It includes, among others, such techniques as partial and multiple correlation, multiple regression analysis, path analysis, and factor analysis.

A typical (and relatively simple) question considered by multivariate analysts is the extent to which an observed bivariate correlation must be explained by the joint and independent effects of one or more other variables. Partial correlation and path analysis, in particular, are used to explore this kind of question.

Another purpose of multivariate analysis is the discovery of clusters of specialized relationships among large numbers of variables. Most frequently, factor analysis has been applied to this purpose.

*See also* Statistical methods
Consult: Erickson, Edwin E., "Other Cultural Dimensions," *Behavior Science Notes* 7:95–

156, 1972; Overall, John E., and Klett, C. James, *Applied Multivariate Analysis* (New York: McGraw-Hill, 1972).

**Mural.** A picture, design, or similar artwork affixed to or covering a wall.

*See also* Fresco

**Murder.** The killing of one person by another, often with premeditation and malicious intent, is construed as violating custom or law. But what is considered murder in one society is not necessarily identical in another. Human beings may not be considered "people" until they have undergone a rite of passage such as a name-giving ceremony. The conferral of a name gives an individual social presence and hence makes her or him a person having rights and obligations. There is a time lag between biological birth and social birth, and extinction of life in this period is not murder—in fact, little or no significance may be attached to the act. Other societies may make no distinction; biological birth, even conception, automatically confers the status of person. Killing an individual in this society therefore constitutes murder.

When killing is construed to be appropriate to circumstances—as by soldiers at war—although the act may have been both malicious and premeditated it is not considered murder.

*See also* Fighting; Killing, ritual; Legal systems; Warfare

—*Paul C. Winther, Eastern Kentucky University*

**Murdock, George Peter** (b. 1897). Murdock began the cross-cultural survey of human relations at Yale that has since become the Human Relations Area Files. He has also supervised the compilation of the Ethnographic Atlas and done significant work in African ethnology. His *Social Organizations* (1949), a comparative study of kinship organization, is one of the most influential works in anthropology.

*See also* HRAF

**Murra, John Victor** (b. 1916). A Russian-born ethnohistorian, Murra is an authority on the economic and political organization

*George Peter Murdock*

of early states, especially those of the Andean region.

**Museums.** Museums are buildings to house collections of material objects: minerals, vegetables, animals, human cultural objects; frequently these are displayed in their settings and culturally appropriate arrangements. Only cultural or ethnographic museums are considered here. Museum curators arrange collections in ways current scholarship believes to be significant, but these ways are themselves products of cultural preconceptions and phases of scientific thought. Thus Oxford's Pitt-Rivers Museum—virtually the last remaining example of 19th-century museology—is itself a historical monument (to be preserved!) to a concept of culture as constituted by traits and reified trait categories (Boats, Weapons, Baskets) which duly governed the organization of the museum displays by category.

At the American Museum of Natural History in New York, Franz Boas initiated a major change in museum organization. Though still perceiving culture as traits, he saw a certain patterned or functional unity among trait complexes which he believed should form the basis of ethnographic exhibits and collections. Most museums are not organized in this manner. Even Amsterdam's Tropics Museum, organizing displays around mostly economic activities, nevertheless indicates the sociocultural unit including them.

Museums, aside from their intrinsic appeal to human interest in diverse cultural solutions to universal problems, are useful pedagogically and are excellent study centers for understanding the material foundations of human existence.

*See also* Museums as research tools

—*Anthony Leeds, Boston University*

**Museums as Research Tools.** Anthropological collections from around the world are stored in museums. Usually only a small percentage of the entire collection is on display, leaving the bulk available for study. The content and nature of anthropological collections range from random examples of material culture—collected at any time, in any place, by anyone—to specific assemblages of artifacts collected by one or more people, at one place, and at one time.

**Other Resources.** Aside from the collections of artifacts available for study, museums also provide for scholars a catalog to the collections, a library, albums of photographic prints which can sometimes be ordered, and archival materials which may include original fieldnotes and unpublished manuscripts relating to museum collections. Some museums also have color slides of artifacts in the collections, but this is rare, as is the availability of tape recordings.

The major use of museum resources by anthropologists currently involves the study of variability among assemblages of artifacts. Some museums have access to computers to facilitate such research, but most do not. Museums usually provide scholars with a guide to the collections in storage and will help in moving artifacts to where they can be photographed and examined. Sometimes specific places for study and photography are available, but not always. Photographic equipment is rarely on hand. All resources are available to scholars by written request and appointment only. Today museums are incredibly busy and staff is occupied with cataloging, photographing, filing, answering questions in the mail and on the phone, preparing exhibits, consulting on educational materials, and conducting research.

**Identifying Artifacts.** Some scholars and collectors believe that museum personnel should also identify artifacts. This has become a touchy situation in the last few years because of the increased traffic in smuggled antiquities. Many American museums have taken a stand against this business by adopting antiquity policies which prohibit museum personnel from accepting as gifts, authenticating, or purchasing any artifacts not proved to have been legally exported from their country of origin. Exceptions are made for artifacts known to have been in private collections before an antiquity policy was adopted. Scholars should obtain legal export papers when collecting artifacts in foreign countries. This practice not only enables museum scholars to aid in identifying artifacts but also permits scholars and collectors to donate important anthropological materials to museums.

**Interdisciplinary Research.** A major advantage at a large natural history museum is the interdisciplinary research that is possible due to the availability of curators in other departments besides anthropology: botany, zoology, and geology. This kind of contact is especially important when one is trying to fit anthropological data into a general systems framework.

**Future Research.** Museums will continue to be important centers for research as more artifacts are added to the collections and as more money is allocated for research by staff and for auxiliary staff to help visiting scholars. Due to the rising costs of anthropological art, and decreasing financial resources for museums, there will be an increasing tendency for museums not to purchase artifacts but to rely on scholars to donate their artifacts once research is completed and for collectors to donate their art. The more fully documented these artifacts are, the more useful they can be to a museum—for comparative research, for possible use in exhibits, and for information for education materials.

*See also* Museums
—*Maude Southwell Wahlman, Field Museum*

**Music and Chants.** Music is a culturally meaningful, entoned, and rhythmized pattern of sounds. Chant is a repetitious vocal music of limited melodic range. Every known society has music, and one of its important uses in every society is to communicate with the supernatural.

Ethnomusicology, the study of non-Western music, began in Western Europe in the late 19th century when musicologists became fascinated with the music of American Indians. Like some present-day ethnomusicologists, they were concerned more with the style (structure) of the music than with its social significance. Such studies

*!Kung San playing a musical bow, altering its tone pitch by changing the size and shape of the oral cavity, and causing the string to vibrate by rubbing the bow with a stick.*

have allowed us to conclude, for example, that scales with five tones are most common among preliterate groups.

Some of these "exotic" musical systems are indeed intrinsically interesting. Among the Tuvin of the USSR an individual can sing two melodies simultaneously; the Ba-Benzele Pygmies of Central Africa produce music which rivals Bach's in its interweaving and polyphonic textures.

Other ethnomusicological studies, usually framed in some kind of anthropological theory, have analyzed music as an aspect of culture. Curt Sachs, for example, tried to demonstrate the evolution of melody. Frances Densmore notated American Indian music and described its rituals, but without attempting to explain it with reference to other aspects of culture (exemplifying the particularistic, antitheoretical approach of her era). A. R. Radcliffe-Brown, a British social anthropologist, posited the persuasive but difficult to prove functionalist hypothesis that participatory music reenergizes and harmonizes the operation of society.

Perhaps the most fascinating problem is to demonstrate that the formal, structural aspects of music are influenced by nonmu-

sical aspects of culture or express deep mental structures which are culturally transmitted. As yet there have been no definitive solutions of this problem, although there have been some encouraging attempts. For instance, in *Folk Song Style and Culture* Alan Lomax advances the theories that a society's technoeconomic arrangements influence certain dimensions of the structure of music

*This jogī lives on alms. He walks from village to village, then goes from door to door singing devotional songs, which set an appropriate mood for donations. Givers gain religious merit. The instrument is a sarangi, which has three (sometimes four) bowed strings and seven sympathetic strings. (Northern India near Varanasi.)*

and that other dimensions (e.g., the melodic range of a society's music) are related to institutionalized early childhood traumas such as circumcision.

Although there is no certainty that we can understand another society's music as do the individuals of that society, it does give us a valuable impression of the ethos of the group. Song lyrics are especially valuable data, for in every culture they reveal some of the most deep-seated values and concerns of the society. Moreover, they sometimes disclose beliefs, sentiments, attitudes, or values not expressed in any other mode of communication.

*See also* Art; Dance

Consult: *Ethnomusicology* (the journal of the Society for Ethnomusicology); Keil, Charles, *Urban Blues* (Chicago: University of Chicago Press, 1966); Merriam, Alan P., *The Anthropology of Music* (Evanston: Northwestern University Press, 1964); Nettl, Bruno, *Music in Primitive Culture* (Cambridge, Mass.: Harvard University Press, 1956).

—*Edward O. Henry, San Diego State University*

**Mutation.** *See* Evolution, genetic mechanisms of.

**Mutilation.** *See* Adornment; Deformation and mutilation.

**Mutterrecht, Das.** "Mother-right" (1859) was written by Bachofen as an evolutionary history of the family (largely derived from Greek and Roman classics) which suggested that matriarchy (mother-right) preceded patriarchy (father-right).

**Myrdal, Jan** (b. 1927). Swedish anthropologist and novelist best known for his *Report from a Chinese Village* (1966), the result of his interviews with and living among Chinese peasants in Liu Ling in northern Shensi province.

**Myrdal, (Karl) Gunnar** (b. 1898). Swedish sociologist and economist whose most famous research has been a study of race relations in the United States in the late 1930s and, more recently, an encyclopedic study of SE Asia.

**Mysticism.** This term refers to a process of seeking union with a transcendent being or force. In general, the mystic uses intuition as the key faculty in seeking this union. Whatever the mystical doctrine or method she or he is following, the mystic believes in a reality beyond reality—or at least beyond any reality knowable through intellect or perception. Spiritual exercises are not ends in themselves but only ways to go beyond normal modes of knowing in order to effect a mystical union with true reality. Deep meditation and trances are thus only ways to bring about union with the source of all being. Since the being is beyond normal ways of knowing, the language used to describe it is usually metaphorical and highly poetic. The mystic is not opposed to intellection per se, but only to positing intellect as the ultimate manner of knowing.

*See also* Religion; Spiritualism

**Myth.** Myth is a sacred narrative explaining how the world and people came to be in their present form. Typically myths involve creations and origins. In cultures throughout the world one finds different mythic accounts of the creation of the earth, the creation of man and woman, the origin of death, and the acquisition of such essentials as food. The main actor in myths is a god or culture hero who successfully brings to humanity some necessity such as the sun or fire.

Rarely in myth is there creation *ex nihilo*, creation from nothing. For it is evidently hard for the human mind to conceive of absolute nothingness. Rather the divine creator takes material already in existence and shapes the earth or people from it—e.g., the creation of earth from mud, the creation of humans from dust. Similarly, such crucial items as fire are stated as given in the beginning of the myth. Usually the needed item is being hoarded by gods, monsters, or some other beings, and it is the task of the culture hero to make the item readily available to humanity at large.

Although the term *myth* is virtually a synonym for error or fallacy as used loosely by many social scientists, myth in the narrow technical sense refers to a narrative or story believed to be true by the people who tell it. The time of myth is set in the remote past, any time up to the moment of creation. In this respect, myth differs from legend, another form of prose narrative. Legend, also

believed to be true by the people who tell it, is set in the real world any time *after* the moment of creation, right up to the present and on into the future. (Legends tell of ghosts who continue to haunt.) Both myth and legend may be contrasted with folktale insofar as folktale is normally considered to be fiction—that is, folktales are not believed to be accounts of historical events. However, the standard European categories of myth, legend, and folktale are not always easily applied to native narrative systems from other cultures which might, for example, distinguish only two categories: stories which are true and stories which are fictional.

One important characteristic of myth is its social rather than individual aspect. If in a story a man steals fire from a neighbor because his own fire has gone out, it would be a folktale. If a culture hero or trickster steals fire and gives it to all people, it would be a myth.

The study of myth is called mythology (though the term is also used to refer to the entire sacred narrative system of a people). The more closely related two different peoples are, the more myths they are likely to have in common. Some mythologists are concerned primarily with Indo-European mythology while others are interested in tracing parallels between Asian and American Indian mythologies. Although the comparative method of studying myth is mostly concerned with historical reconstruction (either of the original form of a myth or of the relationship presumed to have existed between two or more peoples), there have been other trends in mythological scholarship. The functionalist approach was championed by anthropologist Bronislaw Malinowski, who observed that myth provided a sociological charter for belief. That is, people point to myth as the ultimate rationale for their behavior or mores. The interrelationship of myth and ritual has occupied many students of myth. Some claim that rituals simply reenact older myths; others contend that myths are merely the spoken counterpart of rites, with the rites being primary. Anthropologist Clyde Kluckhohn wisely noted that the facts do not permit any universal generalizations as to ritual being the cause of myth or vice versa.

Most anthropologists tend to study myths in a literal way as reflections of the culture from which they have been collected. Franz Boas and many of his students

*Painting of Adam and Eve by Lucas Cranach. One interpretation of the story of Genesis is that it is a creation myth in which the paradox of the human condition is explored. The obvious accomplishments of human sociocultural evolution (as represented by the acquisition of the forbidden fruit of knowledge) are accompanied by a loss of innocence and security (the expulsion from the Garden of Eden). Many scholars believe that the myths of all peoples are similarly projections of panhuman universals.*

regarded myths as repositories of ethnographic information. In the Boasian "culture reflector" approach, one simply picked out facts about social organization, hunting techniques, and the like from a corpus of myths. Boas's *Tsimshian Mythology* (1916) or *Kwakiutl Culture as Reflected in Mythology* (1935) are examples of this anthropological approach to myth. Later, partly influenced by the psychoanalytic theory of Sigmund Freud, anthropologists began to

look at myth as a symbolic form. Melville Jacobs in *The Content and Style of an Oral Literature* (1959) demonstrated how myths and folktales of the Clackamas Chinook provided an outlet for expressions of sibling rivalry and male-female tensions among other themes.

It should be stressed that the historical-literal and the psychological-symbolic approaches to myth are not mutually exclusive. The widespread flood myth denoted in Thompson (1955) as Motif A1010, *Deluge*, may reflect an actual historical flood and at the same time its popularity may stem from an imagined similarity to human birth—in which the newborn baby is delivered from a flood of amniotic fluid. According to Freudian theory, myths may represent cosmogonic projections of basic human events. This does not mean that there was an actual flood or that the flood myth is a cosmogonic projection of human birth. It means only that one approach does not rule out the other. Incidentally, the *Motif-Index* suggests that few, if any, myths are universal. The vast majority of myths have very definite limited areas of geographical provenience. For example, the common African myth of the origin of death in which human immortality is lost through a misdelivered message from the gods is not found in Polynesia and aboriginal North America, though these areas have their own myths of the origin of death (cf. Motif A1335, *Origin of Death*).

In addition to the comparative, functionalist, myth-ritual, culture reflector, and psychoanalytic approaches to myth, there is also the structuralist approach. Structuralists are concerned with describing the basic organizing patterns of myth. French anthropologist Claude Lévi-Strauss, among others, has sought to demonstrate that myths are crucial cultural means of resolving or mediating critical binary oppositions such as life-death, matrilineal-patrilineal, nature-culture. In his four-volume *Mythologiques* (1964–1971) devoted to an extended exegesis of South and North American Indian myths, Lévi-Strauss cites different versions of numerous myths in presenting his elaborate binary model. Perhaps the most useful introduction to Lévi-Strauss's unique method of explicating the semantic content of myth is his analysis of Asdiwal, a Tsimshian narrative collected originally by Boas.

The anthropology student should be aware of the variety of approaches to myth and should realize that no approach all by itself is completely satisfactory. From Malinowski's notion of myth as primordial charter, one moves to structural and psychological notions of myth as model (e.g., a patterned projection in fantasy of ideal and actual social and interpersonal relationships). Most importantly, the student should appreciate the fact that anthropologists do not study myth texts as literary fossils but rather as dynamic and eloquent articulations of human perception of our place vis-à-vis our fellow humans, the gods, and the universe.

See also Folklore; Lévi-Strauss, Claude; Mythopoesis; Oral literature; Religion; Ritual
Consult: Bascom, William, "The Forms of Folklore: Prose Narratives," Journal of American Folklore 78:3–20, 1965; Cohen, Percy S., "Theories of Myth," Man 4:337–353, 1969; Fischer, J. L., "The Sociopsychological Analysis of Folktales," Current Anthropology 4: 235–295, 1963; Lévi-Strauss, Claude, "The Story of Asdiwal," in The Structural Study of Myth and Totemism, ed. E. Leach (London: Tavistock, 1967); Thompson, Stith, Motif-Index of Folk Literature (Bloomington: University of Indiana Press, 1955–1958).
—Alan Dundes, University of California, Berkeley

**Mythopoesis.** The process of myth generation, regarded by some as an innate property of the human mind and by others as merely a mode of composition.

See also Myth; Thought processes

**Nadel, S. F.** (1903–1956). A student of B. Malinowski, Nadel is generally considered one of the more brilliant anthropological theoreticians. He has contributed especially to the study of witchcraft and the nature of status and role in human behavior. His studies of the Nupe of Nigeria and the Nuba of the Sudan have become classics.

See also Role; Status; Witchcraft

**Nader, Laura** (b. 1930). A social anthropologist associated with the study of law, conflict resolution, and social organization, Nader has done ethnographic research in S Mexico and among Muslims in Lebanon.

**Names, Personal.** Personal names, in contrast to place names, designate or identify individuals in a society. Family names, clan names, and tribal names identify the individual's group affiliations.

As the irreducible unit in a society, each person has a name beyond the kinship terms or other titles designating his or her social positions. Personal names may be linked with the concept of mana or supernatural power appertaining to individuals and are sometimes subject to various taboos. Personal names can play an important part in magical formulas. The personal names of ancestors may be referred to as lineage emblems and can govern by myth and ritual the behavior of clan members.

See also Joking, ritualized; Mana; Taboo
Consult: Chagnon, Napoleon A., Yanomamö: The Fierce People (New York: Holt, 1968); Clodd, Edward, Magic in Names (Detroit: Singing Tree Press, 1968).

**Nash, June C.** (b. 1927). A cultural anthropologist who has worked in Mexico, Guatemala, Bolivia, and Burma, Nash has focused her recent work on Mayan modernization and Bolivian mining communities.

**Nash, Manning** (b. 1924). A cultural anthropologist interested in the comparative study of primitive and peasant economic systems, Nash has conducted field research in Mexico, Guatemala, and Burma.

**National Character.** Studies of national character are one of the earliest approaches to the study of other cultures. Indeed, some of the very earliest historical writings involve efforts to exemplify the distinctive characteristics of other groups. Thus in Exodus, the Histories of Herodotus, and the Germania of Tacitus the authors try to set down the essential traits of the people of Sodom, of Scythia, and of Germania. Basically these are stereotyped, self-serving group portraits which mix together racial, psychological, cultural, and social factors with results that are of doubtful reliability and questionable validity.

Yet the tradition of national character portrayals continues to this day; during the past forty years a number of anthropologists, psychologists, sociologists, and political scientists have tried to infuse scientific discipline into the study of the personality structure of people who are members of

culturally complex nation-states. Generally the basic ideas and approaches of the culture and personality field are used—basic personality structure, modal personality, cultural character—except that the problems of adequate sampling and sound generalization are recognized to be greater. As in culture and personality studies generally, two basic approaches are used: one is through the psychological testing and study of a sample of individuals; the other is through the analysis of a sample of expressive cultural materials, such as art or religion, which are regarded as projecting group wishes, conflicts, and needs.

See also Basic personality; Configurationalism; Modal personality
Consult: Barnouw, V., Culture and Personality (Homewood, Ill.: Dorsey Press, 1973); Duijker, H. C. J., and Frijda, N. H., National Character and National Stereotypes (Amsterdam: North Holland, 1960).
—James Clifton, University of Wisconsin, Green Bay

**National Culture.** See National character.

**Nationalism.** This term refers to the acceptance of the state—rather than group, community, region, colonial power, or other form of organization—as the ultimate arbiter of human affairs. The term is also used to refer to unquestioning allegiance to a specific political group.

**Nativistic Movements.** Ralph Linton defined nativistic movements as involving a "conscious, organized attempt on the part of a society's members to revive or perpetuate selected aspects of its culture." Nativistic movements, in turn, are one variety of cultural revitalization movements.

The conscious efforts involved are different from the work of cultural perpetuation, which is part of normal social life. Here it involves a conviction of serious threat to the existence of a culture, usually coming from other societies. Moreover, in nativistic movements the society selects and focuses on specific elements of its traditional culture for revival or perpetuation. The advocates of the movement may in fact encourage others to discard many other traditional ways and practices. Indeed, the advocates of a nativistic movement generally believe that in many ways the traditional culture was inferior to and incompatible with present circumstances.

Linton also distinguished two polarized pairs of characteristics which he used to identify four distinct types of nativistic movement. One dimension distinguished *revivalistic* from *perpetuative* nativism. The other contrasted *magical* with *rational* nativism. Revivalistic nativism emphasizes the restoration of a former cultural state whereas the perpetuative variety aims at the continuity of a current selection of cultural elements. Magical nativism stresses the use or interference of supernatural agencies. Magical nativism generally is a spectacular collective process which may be very disturbing to outsiders because it seems to involve a kind of mass hysteria—as in the messianic and millenarian movements which frequently erupt throughout the world. In contrast, nativistic movements employing rational means generally seek to reestablish old symbols of group worth and self-respect which are to be the new focus of a group identity.

These polar types do not, of course, represent absolute or mutually exclusive categories; moreover, a nativistic movement with one set of characteristics through time is likely to alter and take on quite a different set of attributes.

In 1882, for example, a group of Western Chippewa and Potawatomi Indians appeared on the Menomini reservation in Wisconsin. They were attempting to persuade the Menomini to accept the promises and practices of a new faith. The promise was that if all Indians would beat a new, sacred drum and sing certain songs for four days, then suddenly a Great Drum in the sky would sound and all the Catholic Indians and white men would fall paralyzed on the ground. These visitors were the disciples of a prophetess who had created a religious movement which tried to use magical devices to solve a serious social problem.

The Chippewa-Potawatomi nativistic movement was widely accepted by a number of reservation communities, where it became known as the Dream (or Drum) Dance religion. When it started in 1878, it clearly involved magical efforts to restore and revive a past cultural state. By about 1925, however, the adherents of this movement had changed its thrust to stress the

perpetuation of current practices and current identity through rational devices.

When Ralph Linton first prepared an outline of general ideas about nativistic movements, he tried to emphasize that they arise in complex societies in a position of strength and dominance as well as in small, weak societies. Unfortunately, his suggestions have rarely been followed up with systematic research. The result has been a misidentification of nativistic movements as exclusively the religion of the oppressed. Linton tried to point out that oppressive societies also have nativistic movements, particularly of the rational-perpetuative type. The example he had in mind was Nazi Germany. There are, of course, others.

See also Millenarian movements; Revitalization movements

Consult: Linton, R., "Nativistic Movements," *American Anthropologist* 45:230–240, 1943.

—*James Clifton, University of Wisconsin, Green Bay*

**Natufian.** This archaeological assemblage is of terminal Pleistocene date (ca. 11,000 BP); the type site is Wadi Natuf (Israel). The Natufian assemblage has a distribution across the Palestine littoral and Judean desert. It exhibits a hunting/gathering (especially cereal grasses) economy in productive areas which permitted the establishment of permanent villages (e.g., Ain Mallaha) without evidence for domesticated plants or animals. It was first documented from cave sites (e.g., El Wad, Kebara, Erq el Ahmar) and more recently from open sites (e.g., Basal Jericho, Beidha, Ain Mallaha, Nahal Oren).

See also Mesolithic

**Natural Selection.** See Selection, natural.

**Nautical Archaeology.** See Archaeology.

**Nayar.** See Polyandry.

**Neanderthal Man.** This subspecies of humans, called *Homo sapiens neanderthalensis,* is thought to have descended from an earlier hominid called *Homo erectus.* Neanderthal man was first identified from the valley of Neander in Germany in 1856; since

then over one hundred Neanderthaloid individuals have been found in widespread sites in N and E Africa, Europe, SW Asia, the Far East, and Indonesia. Evidently they had adapted successfully to various climatic regimes and environments—tundra, forested mountains, seashore, savanna. The Neanderthals lived between about 120,000 years to about 35,000 years ago. They averaged about 5 feet 6 inches tall and were power-

*Above, Neanderthal skull discovered by Ralph Solecki in Shanidar Cave, Iraq, dating from 48,000 years BP. Below, the first scientific reconstruction of the Neanderthal.*

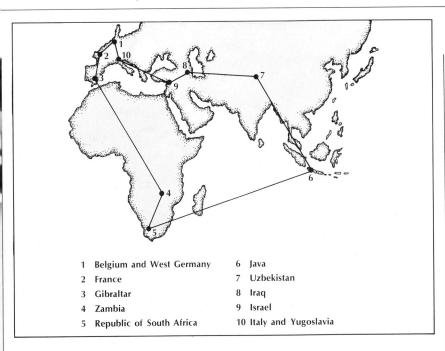

| 1 | Belgium and West Germany | 6 | Java |
| 2 | France | 7 | Uzbekistan |
| 3 | Gibraltar | 8 | Iraq |
| 4 | Zambia | 9 | Israel |
| 5 | Republic of South Africa | 10 | Italy and Yugoslavia |

*Neanderthal groups in Europe inhabited greater extremes of environment than had any previous hominid form, living as far north as the ice sheets of the Würm glaciation would allow, in arctic tundra environments. They were able to do this because they had developed a sufficiently complex and versatile technology.*

fully built and barrel-chested. Neanderthals are believed to have possessed language, a sense of community and social organization, and a belief in religion (as revealed in their burials). They collected vegetable foods and hunted mainly the herbivores, including the mammoths. They knew how to make fire and had a flint-knapping technique, called Levalloiso-Mousterian, which surpassed in excellence the stone craft of some modern primitives. Two varieties of Neanderthals are generally recognized—the "classic" or "cold-adapted" Neanderthals and the "progressive" or more modern-appearing Neanderthals. Most investigators believe *Homo sapiens sapiens* or modern humans evolved from the latter.

See also Middle Paleolithic

Consult: Clark, F., *Early Man* (New York: Time-Life, 1974); Constable, George, *The Neanderthals* (New York: Time-Life, 1973); Solecki, Ralph S., "Neanderthal Is Not an Epithet But a Worthy Ancestor," in *Anthropology: Contemporary Perspectives,* ed. David E. Hunter and Phillip Whitten (Boston: Little, Brown, 1975).

—Ralph Solecki, Columbia University

**Needham, Rodney** (b. 1923). This British social anthropologist is best known for his writings on kinship (especially prescriptive marriage systems), left-hand and right-hand symbolism, and the philosophy of belief.

**Needs, Human.** This term refers to the minimum physiological and psychosocial requirements without the satisfaction of which individuals or societies cannot survive. Much of the seeming confusion about this topic—which has resulted in conflicting and even bizarre statements—could be clarified by recognizing whether the discussion concerns individuals or societies. Not too many years ago, under the influence of Freudian concepts about infantile sexuality, lecturers were defending the idea that newborn infants' "sexual needs" (defined variously) must be met—or else. Today it is more acceptable to state that there is a societal requirement for reproduction, but not an individual one.

**Individual Needs.** Oxygen, water in some form, carbohydrates, vitamins, and minerals (including trace elements) will keep the body functioning. Most native diets succeed in maintaining the proper pH of body fluids, incorporating enough indigestible bulk foods to keep the plumbing operating, and providing the necessary chemical components for energy, growth, and cell replacement. The immediate consequence of providing for these needs is the necessity for the elimination and sanitary disposal of body wastes—the toxic solid, liquid, and gaseous by-products of human metabolism.

Sufficient manipulation of the environment so that the body can maintain itself at a more or less constant temperature is almost as important in hot regions as it is in cold. And a diurnal cycle that allows for sequenced periods of restful sleep and alert activity avoids the debilitating effects of psychobiological deprivation.

It is generally accepted evolutionary theory today that not only have the physical organisms changed through time from the simpler to the more complex but intellectual abilities and social behavior also followed such a route. Therefore, it is reasonable to assert that social interdependency and intellectual activity are as necessary for the individual human being as is physical exercise, popular feral myths notwithstanding. (Of course, we are considering conditions for average health of normal humans, not those produced by the heroic measures for keeping a body alive artificially of which Western medicine is capable.)

**Societal Needs.** Every cultural system must provide patterned ways by means of which the individual needs listed above can be met. It must provide for the protection and socialization of its youngest members. No human society has been discovered that lacks at least a minimal social structure to facilitate ordered, necessary cooperative activities. And it must provide its members with a way of coping with those questions for which there are no objective answers founded on empirical evidence.

Some authors go so far as to state that it is not enough to provide for all these needs. A society must end up with individuals who will not merely know how to survive but who will actively *want* to participate in the system as adults. This implies a choice of whether or not to join the social organization. This view, however, seems to be the product of thinking from within a pluralistic society in which there are alternative choices—a condition which need not prevail in less complex societies, such as the recently discovered Tasaday in the Philippines.

**Canalization.** Besides the individual/societal distinctions, confusion over the synonymous usage of such terms as needs, wants, drives, and tensions has led to a further clouding of the issues surrounding minimal human requirements. The significance of specific cultural input into the resolution of need problems has been frequently overlooked. Murphy's (1947) concept of canalization is of distinct value here. All (normal) infants are born with identical requirements which are nonspecific vis-à-vis the nature of their fulfillment. It is through the process of meeting these requirements in specific ways unique to each society's resources and beliefs (canalization) that these needs become particular wants, possibly even to the involuntary exclusion of all other potential choices.

Thus the need of aboriginal Australians for fat and minerals in their diet was partially met by the periodic consumption of witchety grubs, which they considered a delicacy. Most Americans, however, would undoubtedly prefer a dietary deficiency to eating grubs—but will happily eat ice cream, which also provides both these food elements. It is no overstatement to say that these needs may become so specific in their satisfaction after a few years that an actual physical revulsion to the point of gagging would prevent many people from satisfying them when confronted with items culturally defined as nonfood.

Dire necessity may overcome strong cultural restrictions. In the recent case of the plane downed in the Andes, those who lived through the crash turned to cannibalism in order to survive. But the reverse has also been recorded. A group of arctic Eskimos was suffering from severe starvation when found, because aberrant weather conditions prevented the caribou from migrating all the way north that year. Although seals were basking in plain sight near the shore and could have been taken easily, a taboo restricted the killing of marine mammals in the summer. The Eskimos were more terrified of the consequences of violating the taboo than of starving to death.

**Summary.** Some interpretations of human needs are restrictive—they refer only to the metabolic and social contact requirements of infants. Other interpretations are broad—they include the canalized wants and societal demands on adults.

Not too many years ago the social/behavioral sciences were both too rich and too poor with respect to definitions of human being and human behavior. *Homo sapiens* was at the apex of the evolutionary pyramid, and academics and nonprofessionals alike took vast homocentric pride in listing all the ways that humans are superior to all other creatures.

In recent decades there has been an integration of knowledge about the living world, and ideas about our place in it have changed considerably. As a result of this holistic point of view, some of the issues involving biological needs and cultural wants have been clarified. However, it is still difficult to distinguish factors that are so closely interwoven as societal, psychological, and biological dependency needs.

*See also* Instincts; Species-characteristic behavior

Consult: Lee, Dorothy, "Cultural Factors in Dietary Choice," *Freedom and Culture,* ed. D. Lee (Englewood Cliffs, N.J.: Spectrum, 1959); Murphy, Gardner, *Personality* (New York: Harper, 1947); Williams, Thomas R., "Organic Bridgeheads to Socialization," in *Introduction to Socialization: Human Culture Transmitted,* ed. T. R. Williams (St. Louis: Mosby, 1972).

—*MaryAnn Foley, Southern Connecticut State College*

**Negation.** In hypothesis-testing, negation is disproof. In dialectical materialism or structuralism, it is opposition/antithesis. In linguistics, it is meaning reversal with morphemes such as *non-*. In psychology, it is the denial of a person's validity.

*See also* Communication

**Negroes.** *See* Ethnic groups; Gene distributions; Race.

**Neocolonialism.** Continuation of a former colony's dependency on, and control by, an external polity which was once an imperialist or colonizing country is called neocolonialism. Though such colonies became sovereign states, their sovereignty was weakened because they needed capital, research results, technology, and often even military resources. The former colonizers supply all of these to the ex-colonies, thus subjugating the latter by indebtedness and restricting their ability to choose strategies

of development, independent foreign policies, and internal political ordering. For colonies to win real sovereignty they must absorb all costs of government (formerly footed by the metropoles); to the extent that they cannot accomplish this, neocolonial indebtedness continues to keep them subjugated.

*See also* Colonialism; Colonization; Imperialism

**Neolithic.** This stage in cultural evolution is generally marked by the appearance of ground stone tools but primarily by the domestication of plants and animals. Such domestication is accomplished by people's interference in the breeding processes of plants and animals by selecting for traits they deem useful. In some cases, such as corn, the domesticated plant cannot naturally reproduce itself because domesticators have selected for husks which will not open when the corn ripens; thus the seed cannot disperse without human action. In other cases, people have selected for a heavier coat, as in sheep, or larger eggs, as in chickens.

V. Gordon Childe wrote of the Neolithic as a revolution. Since his time archaeologists have recognized that the Neolithic was an evolutionary process which took many thousands of years—but it was revolutionary in its effects. The stability of the food supply encouraged population growth and eventually made it possible for people to form permanent settlements. The time of the Neolithic period varies. A date of ca. 6000 BC is accepted for parts of SW Asia. Europe is supposed to have entered the Neolithic some 2,000 years later. For the New World the Neolithic is dated as beginning about 5,000 BC in the Valley of Mexico. Wilhelm Solheim gives a date of about 20,000 years ago for the inception of the Neolithic in SE Asia.

*See also* Lithic ages

Consult: Childe, V. G., *The Dawn of European Civilization* (New York: Knopf, 1925); MacNeish, Richard, "Prehistory of Tehuacan Valley," in *Environment and Subsistence,* vol. 1, ed. Douglas Byers (Austin: University of Texas Press, 1967); Solheim, Wilhelm, "The Earlier Agricultural Revolution," *Scientific American,* April 1972.

—*Evelyn S. Kessler, University of South Florida*

**Neolocality.** This term refers to the custom for a newly married couple to set up a separate home, living with neither the husband's nor the wife's parents or relatives. This marriage residency rule is consistent with bilateral emphasis in kinship systems and with traditions of individualism, romantic love, and individual choice in the selection of a mate. It permits much geographical mobility and is typical of white middle-class American society.

*See also* Family, the; Marriage; Mobility, social

Consult: Fox, Robin, *Kinship and Marriage: An Anthropological Perspective* (Baltimore: Penguin, 1967); Murdock, George, *Social Structure* (New York: Macmillan, 1949).

## Neoteny.

Neoteny is a phenomenon in which more generalized and earlier ontogenetic states of development are retained in adulthood. In evolutionary perspective this results in less specialized adult features, a significant element in human morphology.

## Nets and Netting.

Nets are usually made of string tied together where strands cross, producing a mesh fabric. Alternative techniques, similar to crocheting, employ complex looping of a single strand into an open mesh without knots. Netting and twining were probably the earliest weaving techniques. Nets are pliable, unlike other meshlike artifacts such as sieves, baskets, fish weirs, and even tennis rackets.

There are various kinds of fish nets. Dip nets, stitched to hoops with handles, are used to land fish hooked by or visible to fishermen. Casting seines, usually several meters in diameter, have edge weights (and often, floats) to spread the net when thrown and cause its margins to sink, trapping fish to be hauled in by shoreline or small-boat fishermen. Gill nets (often with floats) have wide meshes which trap fish—especially salmon—behind the gills after they thrust partially through the net. Baglike trawler or drag nets, pulled behind moving boats, are used mostly in commercial fishing.

Nets have other uses, such as clothing, hair covers, and especially bags for carrying and storage. Outside the United States most people carry net bags for marketing. Hammocks, hangers for large pots, and animal traps are among the nonmaritime uses of netting.

*See also* Basketry; Fishing; Hunting; Lines and rope, knots and splices; Textiles; Twining; Weapons

Consult: Davidson, D. S., "Knotless Netting in America and Oceania," *American Anthropologist* 37(1):117–134, 1935; O'Neal, Lila, "Weaving," in *Handbook of South American Indians*, vol. 5, ed. J. Steward (New York: Cooper Square, 1957).

—*John R. Cole, Ithaca College*

## Network Analysis. *See* Network study.

## Network, Social.

Networks are arrangements of elements fastened together in some manner to make up a pattern. Human interaction forever generates interpersonal linkages called *dyads*. A dyad is an interpersonal relationship between two actors in which each actor is indebted to the other. Dyads are maintained by systems of exchange. Strings or chains of dyads constitute *social networks*. Anthropologists have always analyzed social networks, but explicit attention to the ramifying nature of interpersonal dyads was introduced by J. A. Barnes only twenty years ago (Barnes 1954). Subsequent pivotal work was undertaken by Barnes himself, Elizabeth Bott, Jeremy Boissevain, P. H. Gulliver, Adrian Mayer, John Mitchell, Norman Whitten, Alvin Wolfe, and Eric Wolf, among many others. Recent reviews of the literature by Bott (1971), Barnes (1972), Whitten and Wolfe (1974), and Mitchell (1974) offer extensive summaries of social networks.

Some scholars think of all social structure as constituting a network of relationships. Others have conceived of social networks as those aspects of social life which remain after an analysis of definable social groups and social institutions has been teased out. When applying the former reasoning, establishment of network segments into specified sets and arrangements is important. In the latter reasoning, social networks may be regarded as a sort of residue of the functioning of tangible social units. Some scholars delimit networks in terms of one or two institutional criteria. In such cases one may speak of a genealogical network, a political network, an economic network, or a friendship network.

Much current network analysis, however, seeks to bypass such approaches and regards social networks as a "relevant series of linkages existing between individuals which may form a basis for the mobilization of people for specific purposes, under specific conditions" (Whitten and Wolfe 1974:720). This conceptualization of a social network allows application of relevant concepts to the construction of network theory and network models which cut across specific domains such as the genealogical, economic, political, or bureaucratic. Indeed, the application of such a concept of network as a "relevant series of linkages" allows for the study of such formal organizations as a bank or military bureaucracy by the same techniques and criteria used to understand a community of scholars or even a dispersed set of people linked together through their mutual interests in illegally purchasing pre-Columbian pottery.

Social networks provide the basis for understanding the flow of information and emotional tone, as well as goods and services, across cultural, ethnic, national, and international boundaries, no matter how the boundaries are conceptualized. When analyzing a social network it is up to the investigator to make the rationale explicit. One could identify a social network (or segment thereof) anywhere, under any circumstances. "Discovery" or mere identification of networks is a scientifically worthless exercise, one comparable to continuously discovering that blood circulates in a living body. Problem orientation and a clear sense of hindrances to direct communication are essential to the productive analysis of social networks. For example, suppose it is well known that the president of bank A will not communicate directly with the president of bank B because of a deep animosity arising from sharp ethnic conflict between their respective spouses' families. Yet much social action in their town revolves around covert exchanges, through intermediaries, between the two presidents. By addressing oneself to the linkages, criteria, exchanges, and consequences of covert communication between the presidents, a dynamic model of a societal segment can be built up by social network analysis and applied to the interpenetrating results of other such analyses.

Social networks exist not only as actual sets of transacting individuals—individuals forever forging and breaking dyadic ties—but also as sets of conceptualizations constructed by interacting individuals. People who feel bound together because of a tie such as that established by the construct "Jesus loves me" or "What's in it for Uncle Sam?" also constitute a relevant problem for social network analysis, even if a field investigator cannot definitely state the nature of the exchanges involved in the maintenance of such a network. Indeed, people may *think* of themselves as tied into certain groupings whether or not such groupings can be confirmed by the investigator. Social networks exist overtly and covertly in observable and stereotypic dimensions. They are conceptualized not only by the person studying them but also by every individual interacting in multiple contexts in every conceivable social arena.

*See also* Exchange; Network study
Consult: Barnes, John A., "Class and Committees in a Norwegian Island Parish," *Human Relations* 7:307–312, 1954; Barnes, John A., *Social Networks* (Reading, Mass.: Addison-Wesley, 1972); Bott, Elizabeth, *Family and Social Network*, 2nd ed. (New York: Free Press, 1971); Mitchell, J. Clyde, "Social Networks," *Annual Review of Anthropology* 3:279–299, 1974; Whitten, Norman E., Jr., *Black Frontiersmen: A South American Case* (New York: Wiley, 1974); Whitten, Norman E., Jr., and Wolfe, Alvin W., "Network Analysis," in *Handbook of Social and Cultural Anthropology*, ed. John J. Honigmann (Chicago: Rand McNally, 1974).
—*Norman E. Whitten, Jr., University of Illinois*

**Network Study.** Network study, the analysis of interpersonal relations, usually focuses on a specific individual (ego) and examines the interactions between ego and others. Such interaction is visualized as links forming a network of real or potential ties between individuals.

Network study developed as one alternative to structural-functional analysis. By focusing on specific individuals the observer is able to trace the *choices* involved in activating certain relationships or sets of relationships in specific situations. Network analysis is the methodological means by which we can systematically study *personal behavior*. If the content of the interaction between individuals can be adequately measured, quantitative methods can be used in the analysis of networks. Network study has proved particularly useful in urban studies, legal and political ethnography, studies of family behavior, and the investigation of social change.

*See also* Fieldwork methods; Network, social
Consult: Bott, Elizabeth, *Family and Social Network*, 2nd ed. (New York: Free Press, 1971); Mitchell, C. (ed.), *Social Networks in Urban Situations* (Manchester: Manchester University Press, 1969).

**Neurosis.** This term usually refers to a category of functional psychological disorders. The limits of the category are not well defined, but the disorders involved are considered less severe than psychoses. A specific neurosis may have somatic involvement, either as cause or symptom. In Western cultures a variety of neurotic complaints are often identified—hysterias, obsessions, fugues, phobias, anxiety. Increasingly, however, less attention is given to nosological categories and more to the study and treatment of the whole individual's unique problems of living. Anxiety is the most common symptom of neurosis. The basic syndrome consists of a persistent, mildly debilitating, intensive, subjective feeling of distress which the individual does not understand and from which relief is sought.

*See also* Culture and personality; Mental illness and culture; Normality; Psychosis

**New Archaeology, the.** This (primarily American) development began in the early 1960s, largely through the efforts of Lewis Binford and his students (Binford 1972; Binford and Binford 1968). Concerned with the lack of theory and explanation in archaeology, the new archaeologists work toward developing both. Viewing culture as the human species' extrasomatic means of adaptation (White 1959:8) allows one to take a systemic view of archaeological data. This is accompanied by rigorous, often statistical, treatment of archaeological material within a deductive logical framework. Among other things, the New Archaeologists have dealt with prehistoric social organization, prehistoric demography, cultural ecology, functional variability in artifact types, and a systemic explanation for the origins of agriculture.

*See also* Archaeology; Prehistoric archaeology
Consult: Binford, Lewis R., *An Archaeological Perspective* (New York: Seminar Press, 1972); Binford, Sally R., and Binford, Lewis R. (eds.), *New Perspectives in Archaeology* (Chicago: Aldine, 1968); White, Leslie A., *The Evolution of Culture: The Development of Civilization to the Fall of Rome* (New York: McGraw-Hill, 1959).

**New Ethnography, the.** Now more appropriately defined as cognitive anthropology, the New Ethnography consists of a series of principles, approaches, and data-collecting procedures which share the assumption that culture consists of the knowledge one must know or believe in order to behave appropriately in a culture. It has a concern for the categories, plans, rules, and organizing principles of behavior that a person has in his or her mind as a member of culture. Generally, the New Ethnography (also known as ethnoscience) includes topics such as the emic/etic distinction, folk taxonomies, ethnosemantics, componential analysis, and color terminology. This discussion will focus on the similarities of all these perspectives with special emphasis on the discovery procedures or data-collecting techniques.

The New Ethnography approaches a culture from the perspective of a member of that culture. This point of view is not new and goes back to the early years of anthropology. Several important differences, however, distinguish the new from the old ethnography. First of all, the new ethnographers use the native language itself as the *data* of the description rather than as just a tool to obtain the data. Secondly, with their preoccupation with language as a data source, they tend to exclude the anthropologist's categorizations of the nonverbal behavior in the culture and use only the informant's description of such behavior as data. Thirdly, the New Ethnographers are concerned about obtaining an accurate record of the process of gathering the data. They view the old ethnographies as sets of answers to unrecorded questions which have been organized under standard headings such as religion, social organization, and technology. In order to be accurate, they believe that the anthropologist should record not only the response but also the stimulus or question which produced it. Fourthly, some New Ethnographers assume that the question-response pair constitutes the basic unit of the informant's cognitive structure. In totality, then, this structure consists of all the questions the informant addresses to the world and the answers to those questions. The fifth difference between the New Ethnography and the old variety rests on the systematic approach to data collecting, which proceeds in a definite sequence. First the ethnographer asks the informant to formulate an appropriate question about a topic; then the informant is asked to answer that question. For example, an ethnographer studying American culture may ask the informant:

Q: What is an appropriate question I can ask about cars?

R: What kinds of cars are there?

The ethnographer then asks the informant:

Q: What other appropriate questions can I ask about cars?

The informant responds with a series of acceptable questions. Beginning with the first response of the informant, the ethnographer then asks:

Q: What kinds of cars are there?

R: There are foreign cars and American cars.

The ethnographer then proceeds by using the basic framework of the informant's properly formulated question (R) but substituting "American cars" for "cars":

Q: What kinds of American cars are there?

R: There are Chevys, Fords, Cadillacs, Chryslers, Plymouths, Dodges, Oldsmobiles . . .

Repeating the same question but substituting "Plymouth" for "American cars," the ethnographer can continue to elicit kinds of Plymouths. By substituting "foreign cars" for "cars" in the original question, the ethnographer can move along a different sequence of questioning and exhaust the different kinds of cars.

The advantage of this systematic approach to ethnography is twofold: other anthropologists working in the same culture can theoretically reproduce the data, if they desire, by using the same techniques; moreover, the data from several informants can easily be stored and organized by computers for analysis later. Reproducibility constitutes an important tenet of scientific research, and computer processing makes data organization easier and faster. Thus with accuracy, reproducibility, and computer processing the New Ethnographers consider their approach more scientific than the old method.

*See also* Cognition; Componential analysis; Emics; Ethnography; Ethnoscience; Ethnosemantics; Etics; Language and culture; Language and reality; Language and thought
Consult: Frake, Charles O., "Notes on Queries in Ethnography," *American Anthropologist* 66(3):132–145, 1964; Sturtevant, William C., "Studies in Ethnoscience," *American Anthropologist* 66(3):99–131, 1964.
—*Dean E. Arnold, Wheaton College*

**Nida, Eugene** (b. 1914). Missionary and linguist who has been concerned with mor-

phological theory and also the application of linguistics to the achievement of practical ends such as Bible translation.

**Niebuhr, Barthold Georg** (1776–1831). German historian who was one of the founders of the modern historical method and the relativist conception—both of which influenced Franz Boas and his formulation of historicist concepts in cultural anthropology.

**Nomadic Migration.** *See* Migration.

**Nomadism.** This term comes from the Greek *nemo*, meaning "to pasture." In its present usage in anthropological literature, nomadism refers to a characteristic trait as-

*A Mutayr Bedouin encampment. The Mutayr are a nomadic pastoralist group. Their society is organized around male-centered kinship groups. Among the Arab Bedouin nomads the great concentrations of livestock and people occur during the hot dry season—unlike, for instance, among the Fulani nomads of Africa, where cattle and people concentrate during the cool wet season. Bedouin summer camps are located near permanent wells. The camels are brought to camp in the afternoon, watered (about 35 gals. per adult camel), then taken to the edge of the camp to rest for the night. They are watered again in the morning (about 15 gals.), then led to pasture. At the height of the summer this process is repeated every third or fourth day. This picture shows the edge of a Mutayr summer camp. Their black tents are in the background; in the foreground a Mutayr tribesman is coaxing his camels to settle down for the evening.*

sociated with a number of ecologically adaptive systems in which continuing residential mobility is necessary for the subsistence of the group, resulting in a lack of a permanent abode. These adaptive systems are hunting and gathering; slash-and-burn shifting agriculture; herding or pastoralism. Transhumance—adaptation which calls for limited spatial mobility (often seasonal) with a relatively permanent settlement base—is often considered seminomadic. Some groups with nomadic life-styles are Tungus reindeer herders, Bedouins and other desert herders, many Alpine transhumant peasant communities, !Kung San (Bushmen) and other marginal peoples such as unassimilated Australian Aborigines, the many groups of Asian and European Gypsies and, to some extent, the present-day migrant farmworkers of the industrialized world.

*See also* Pastoralism
Consult: Irons, William B., and Dyson-Hudson, Neville (eds.), *Perspectives on Nomadism* (Leiden: Brill, 1972).
—*M. Nazif Shahrani, University of Washington*

**Nonverbal Communication.** *See* Communication, nonverbal.

**Nonviolence.** This term refers to techniques used to control or lessen, with maximum effectiveness, the power of an opponent without resorting to killing, demolishing, or terrorizing. Instances of nonviolent action have been recorded in Roman times, and documentation in many Western and non-Western societies is ample. A wide variety of nonviolent techniques exist. They may be spontaneous and unplanned, or they may be premeditated

and part of a general strategy. The direction of nonviolent action may be in support of an establishment—e.g., defense of a government against attack. But nonviolence is most commonly associated with antiestablishment tactics that may aim to achieve limited objectives, general reforms, or even the destruction of a regime. Mahatma Gandhi used one form of nonviolence (civil disobedience) in his strategic and tactical plans to end British rule of India—e.g., the Salt March of 1930–1931. In the United States, nonviolence is associated with the civil rights movement under Dr. Martin Luther King's leadership.

See also Violence

Consult: Sharp, Gene, *The Politics of Nonviolent Action* (Boston: Sargent, 1973).

—*Paul C. Winther, Eastern Kentucky University*

**Norbeck, Edward** (b. 1915). Canadian-born cultural anthropologist well known for his ethnographic research on Japan and his theoretical work on religion, social and cultural change, and personality.

**Norm and Normative.** In one sense, a norm is simply a shared standard of a social group to which members are expected to conform. In another sense, norm may mean the modal or average behavior, attitude, or opinion found in a social group. Homans (1950) defines norm as "an idea in the minds of members of a group, an idea that can be put in the form of a statement specifying what the members or other men should do, ought to do, are expected to do under given circumstances." These norms are not the same as what is actually done in a given situation or even what members of the group believe is done. They are simply standards to which people are expected to conform, probably because they are believed beneficial for the group. The moral norm, such as "Thou shalt not commit adultery," is the most distinct type, but rules of logic and mathematics also are examples. Sherif and Sherif (1948) suggest that there is a process of norm formation. Faced with an ambiguous situation, a group of individuals initially will have widely divergent opinions, but then the opinions gradually converge, thus giving rise to normative behavior.

See also Folkways; Mores

Consult: Homans, George C., *The Human Group* (New York: Harcourt Brace, 1950);

Sherif, M., and Sherif, C. W., *An Outline of Social Psychology* (New York: Harper & Row, 1948).

—*Richard L. Stone, California State University, Los Angeles*

**Normality.** Until anthropologists pointed out that each culture defines for itself what is normal behavior, both lay and scientific notions of normality were confined to definitions which had, fundamentally, moral and ethical prejudices. In Victorian culture, for instance, infantile sex play was considered sick and disgusting, and myths about the woeful outcome of continued masturbation, both physical and emotional, frightened many adolescents. There are three definitions of normality which are applied, often interchangeably, by laypeople, medical personnel, and social scientists alike.

**Normal Distribution.** Ruth Benedict demonstrated that what was considered abnormal or even pathological behavior in one society might be normal and even valued in another. Each culture, through socialization processes based on traditional values, produces a certain personality type. The distribution of personality types within a culture may be illustrated by the bell-shaped curve. The dominant personality type is the most frequently encountered (represented by the peak of the curve), though virtually the entire range of possible behavior will be found to some degree in every culture. The Kwakiutl chief poses an example: obsessive about shaming other chiefs with lavish gifts of wealth, and paranoid about his own social decline through a similar process, he might be hospitalized in Western society; in his own he is an example of what every boy should aspire to.

If (as Ruth Benedict illustrates for personality and Margaret Mead demonstrates for sex roles) personality is distributed normally and each culture's dominant personality type differs from that of other cultures, a universal definition of what is normal behavior is impossible.

**Normal As Coping.** The medical model of normality, deriving from Freudian tradition, was developed from the study of mental patients: normal behavior is regarded as the process of coping with average amounts of stress while meeting ordinary obligations and responsibilities. This definition attempts to avoid a universal statement about the qualities of normal human behavior while

recognizing that in every culture there are individuals who become antisocial, destructive, or withdrawn (termed mentally ill or deviant). Like the previous definition, this one is relative—it describes how people do behave rather than how they might behave if conditions were optimal.

**Normal As Fulfilled.** A third definition derives, to some extent, from Freud and, more recently, from existential psychology: normal behavior is defined as that which fulfills the "human potential."

Sigmund Freud wrote that the normal condition of humanity is, to some degree, neurotic (and the previous definition is built on that assumption). Socialization, which Freud viewed as a process of taming instinctual (and antisocial) urges, produces psychic scars. One can transcend these barriers to fulfillment by overcoming neurotic traits and living maximally in a full, loving manner.

Existential psychologists, dissatisfied with concepts of normal behavior that fail to meet the changing needs of the 20th century and that emphasize the negative and destructive features in human personality, began to search for universal variables which define the person who is "becoming" (Gordon Allport), "individuating" (Carl Jung), or "self-actualizing" (Abraham Maslow)—processes and conditions describing an individual who, regardless of occupation or status, makes the most of talents and interests.

See also Benedict, Ruth; Culture and personality; Deviance; Existential psychiatry; Freud, Sigmund; Mead, Margaret; Mental illness and culture

Consult: Allport, Gordon W., *Becoming: Basic Considerations for a Psychology of Personality* (New Haven: Yale University Press, 1955); Benedict, Ruth, *Patterns of Culture* (New York: Mentor Books, 1934); Maslow, Abraham, *Toward a Psychology of Being* (Princeton: Van Nostrand, 1962); Mead, Margaret, *Sex and Temperament in Three Primitive Societies* (New York: Morrow, 1963); Turnbull, Colin, *The Mountain People* (New York: Simon and Schuster, 1972).

—*Pell Fender, Columbia College*

**Novelty, Cultural.** See Innovation.

**Nuclear Family.** Small social unit consisting of a husband and wife and their children.

See also Family, the

**Numbering, Systems of.** Virtually every society has some system of counting, though some only need words for 1 and 2 while Hindi, for example, has words for numbers as large as $10^{421}$. The most striking feature of a number system is its base—the number (or set of numbers) from which other numbers may be built. The base of our own number system is 10, and we express 20 (two 10s), 30 (three 10s), and so forth as multiples of 10. The number 100 (10 times 10) is a new word. The simplest possible base is 2, but few examples of this base exist. The bushmen of Botswana have the words o (1) and oa (2). Higher numbers are expressed oa o (3), oa oa (4), oa oa o (5), and so on. Modern digital computers also use the base 2.

There are many languages in which the numeration is based on some combination of 5 and/or 20. The ancient Mayans are a classic example; moreover, quite a few African languages, including almost all the Bantu, express numbers as multiples of 20. Usually the number 400 (20 times 20) is a new word. The word for 20 in many of these languages is "whole man" or "complete man," while the word for 5 is often "hand."

The only other base used to any extent is 6 (or equivalently 12 or 60). The major advantage of such a system is that, say, the number 12 is divisible by 2, 3, 4, and 6 whereas 10 is divisible only by 2 and 5. Consequently, in situations where division is important, such as with weights and measures, one might expect to find at least vestiges of a base 6. The ancient Sumerians used 60 as a base, and it is from them that we obtained our temporal divisions as well as 360 degrees to the compass. Their money was powdered silver and barley necessitating division in economic transactions. The Bram, Mankanye, Bolan, and Balante of West Africa utilize a base 6. We also find in our English system of weights and measures base 12: 12 inches to a foot, a dozen eggs, 144 (12 times 12) sheets of paper to a ream.

Another important feature of a numbering system is its mode of expression. The four modes are spoken, written, gesture, and what we may call physical. The previous paragraphs refer mainly to spoken modes. But spoken and written do not always correspond. Compare, for example, the way we say "three hundred and four" but write 304. In the absence of writing, gestures are often used. In Africa a wide variety of finger combinations and arm positions denote numbers. In medieval Europe a similar gesture system was in widespread use prior to the introduction of Arabic numerals. Gestures are especially useful between groups which trade but do not speak a common language.

Physical modes include such items as tally sticks, abacus, bead counters, medieval counting boards, and notched sticks (as well as electronic calculators). These often enable a permanent or semi-permanent record to be kept in the absence of a written language, as well as serve as an aid in computation.

It is also useful to examine the extent to which a number system applies the principles of ordering, grouping, and gradation. Ordering is simply the collection of identical symbols to represent a number. Thus the Egyptians and early Romans used I, II, III, and so on. Grouping is the combination of several ordered sets by using a new symbol, such as the Roman V (= IIIII) or X (= VV). Gradation is the stepwise division of a symbol into distinct digits such as 1,2,3, . . . ,8,9. Note that gradation, combined with positional ordering, results in the easiest and most powerful computational system.

Consult: Menninger, K., *Number Words and Number Symbols* (Cambridge, Mass.: MIT Press, 1969); Zaslavsky, C., *Africa Counts* (Boston: Prindle, Weber & Schmidt, 1973).
—*John R. Lombardi, Boston University*

**Numbers, Ritual.** Ritual numbers are used by many different societies as a basis for structuring the repetition of ritual acts and episodes, incidents in myths and folktales, the number of days in a ceremony, the length of a period of mourning, the number of actors required for a ritual, and a great many other features of expressive culture and social organization. Sometimes, but not often, a myth specifically explains why one number is favored; more often, the hero in a cycle of myths merely repeats significant acts a certain number of times. In North America, the ritual number most often used is 4, then 3. The number 7 was never used, and few tribes used 5, 6, or 10. Some tribes had several ritual numbers, but many used a base number and some permutations of it—such as 4 with its permutations 8, 12, 48.

*See also* Ritual

**Oakley, Kenneth Page** (b. 1911). British paleoanthropologist who developed a means of dating fossil remains through fluorine tests—which he applied to the Piltdown skull, proving it a hoax.

**Objectification.** This term refers to treatment of data and actions which exist in reality, outside the mind, and the psychological perception or categorization of confirmable phenomena. In popular psychological usage it refers to the process whereby one person manipulatively interacts with another in such a way as to limit that person's choices—i.e., treating that person like an object.

*See also* Defense mechanisms

**Observation of Behavior.** See Fieldwork methods.

**Obsidian Hydration.** Obsidian, a volcanic glass, absorbs moisture during a process called hydration. An absolute dating method is being developed that is based on the depth of hydration (which is proportional to time) from chipped obsidian artifact surfaces. There are problems, however, because past temperature and chemical composition of obsidian are significant variables and there are conflicting data on hydration rates.

*See also* Dating, absolute; Physical-chemical methods of dating

**Oedipus Complex.** This Freudian psychological term has to do with the supposed origin of the incest taboo in the human species and certain corresponding patterns of psychoneurotic development in individuals.

The shame and ruin of King Oedipus of ancient Greek lore were said to have been occasioned by his unintentional murder of his father and equally unintentional sexual liaison with his mother. According to Freud, the Oedipus complex is manifest in the male infant's hostility toward its father and jealousy of its mother's attentions to her mate. Guilt over this feeling supports a strict moral taboo against incest. A parallel theory for females, the Elektra complex, also derives its paradigm from Freud's reading of Hellenic myths.

See also Freud, Sigmund; Incest avoidance (taboo);

Consult: Malinowski, Bronislaw, *Sex and Repression in Savage Society* (Cleveland: Meridian, 1955; orig. 1927).

**Old Age.** See Life cycle.

**Oldowan Culture.** The type site of this oldest recognized Lower Paleolithic assemblage is Olduvai Gorge (Tanzania). It dates from more than 2.2–1 million years BP and comprises core tools (choppers/chopping tools, polyhedrals, spheroids, discoids, proto-bifaces) and crudely retouched, utilized flakes. This culture is best known in NC/NW E Africa and also in S Africa, the Near East, and W Europe. It is associated with australopithecine (*habilis*) remains. (Some scholars assign the *habilis* remains to genus *Homo*.)

See also Australopithecines; Olduvai Gorge; Pebble tools

**Olduvai Gorge.** This gorge in Tanzania revolutionized anthropology and established Africa as the birthplace of the human species. In 1959 Louis and Mary Leakey found *Zinjanthropus,* a hominid fossil associated with tools and a potassium-argon date of 1.76 ± 0.25 million years BP—nearly tripling known human antiquity. Bed I then yielded *Homo habilis* remains, which L. Leakey called the true human antecedents, although others group the Olduvai finds as varieties of *Australopithecus.* Bed II produced *Homo erectus* remains.

A Bed I stone circle may be the earliest known "architecture." Olduvai's stratified cultural sequence—Oldowan, Developed Oldowan, Acheulean, and Middle and Later Stone Age—is longer than any other known, although earlier sites have since been found.

See also Australopithecines; Fossil sequence of human evolution; Fossils; *Homo erectus;* Leakey, Louis S. B.; Leakey, Mary; Oldowan culture

**Olmec Culture.** This culture is the earliest protocivilization of pre-Columbian Mesoamerica. The heartland of the Olmec was centered in the lowlands of the Caribbean coast of Mexico. Here there were at least

*Olduvai Gorge, Tanzania, the site where the Leakeys found many of the crucial hominid fossil remains of the australopithecine and* Homo erectus *grades of human evolutionary development. Historical note: a German exploratory team had previously investigated Olduvai Gorge and found it to be devoid of significant archaeological remains.*

three major ceremonial centers: San Lorenzo de Tenochtitlan (1200–900 BC), La Venta (1000–600 BC), and Tres Zapotes (1000–100 BC). Olmec art represents the first great art style of Mesoamerica. It included colossal stone heads up to 9 feet in height and weighing 4 tons, as well as excellent jade work. Writing, the calendar, and dot and bar numerals used for counting, once thought to have originated with the Maya, are all found in the earlier Olmec culture.

Consult: Coe, Michael D., *America's First Civilization* (New York: American Heritage, 1968).

**Operant Conditioning.** See Behaviorist school of psychology; Conditioning; Skinner, B. F.

**Opler, Marvin Kaufmann** (b. 1914). Opler is known for his interest in the relationship between culture and mental dis-

orders and for his fieldwork among various ethnic groups, including the Ute Indians.

**Opler, Morris E.** (b. 1907). Opler's primary ethnographic interests are the Apachean-speaking peoples of the American Southwest and Southern Plains in addition to South Asia. To date, his major theoretical contribution has been the concept of cultural themes.

**Oracle.** Any device, thing, or person used magically as a means of forecasting future events, usually as a means of reaching a decision or uncovering a disputed truth.

See also Divination

**Oral Literature.** Simply defined, oral literature is any body of tradition, history, myth, folklore, fables, and tales which are orally recounted in fixed or informal form and passed on from generation to generation.

Although great libraries throughout the world house the embodiment of the accumulated knowledge of our species, such written works have only existed since the invention of writing within the last eight thousand years. For untold millennia before then, and to a great extent since then, vast bodies of knowledge and tradition were memorized and passed on by word of mouth from one generation to the next. Strange as it may seem, oral tradition is not exclusive to preliterate societies but is very much a part of sophisticated civilizations with a long history of written tradition. In American society, for example, there are folk stories about Santa Claus, George Washington, Paul Bunyan, Railroad Bill, Pecos Bill, Stagger Lee, and Johnny Appleseed. Even though they have been written down for some time, these stories continue to be passed on in oral form in varying versions.

More often, however, oral literature is associated with preliterate societies. Such verbal art takes a number of forms which serve various purposes among the peoples who practice it. Generally, there are works classified as *fiction* and *nonfiction* and told in a prose or poetic style. Added to this is *drama,* which is merely the bodily enactment of events as narrated by a storyteller or as expressed by the participant actors themselves. Puppet shows are also used in some societies to dramatize oral tradition.

Also, stories may be encompassed in musical form and recounted or chanted.

The purposes oral literature has served include moral teaching, religious instruction, entertainment, medical cure (in curing rituals), the facilitating of social and judicial procedure, perpetuation of the memory of major historical events, and explaining the natural world and its unseen forces. For many societies such oral literature was committed to memory by individuals delegated the responsibility or by members of a clan or family whose traditional duty it had always been. In some instances memory aids, or mnemonic devices, were employed to help the individual recall the various parts of a story and the prescribed sequence. One example of this is the ritual Roll Call of Iroquois Chiefs, wherein a speaker recounts the founding of the Iroquois League and names the fifty chiefs during the "condolence ceremony." In this eulogy for the dead chiefs and the naming of a new one, memory aids are often employed since the ritual is lengthy and complicated and must be recited without error. Many societies also have traditional storytellers who entertain or individuals who memorize and recapitulate historical events and genealogies.

*Creation myths* constitute a major element in the oral literature of most peoples. These stories, like the biblical Genesis, attempt to explain how the earth and people came into being; they also build a universal order which forms the basis for their cognitive system of the natural world (cosmology). Many groups share identical themes, plots, or elements in such creation myths. A well-known example of this correspondence is the creation myths grouped under the heading of Earth Diver stories. Widely distributed among native American Indian groups, the story also has its counterpart in Asia. Naturally, on a regional basis there are other examples of shared stories to be found the world over. However, many scholars believe that such sharing of themes and elements suggests psychic human unity rather than simply the diffusion of themes.

The basic difference between a myth and folklore stems largely from a strong emphasis on the supernatural in myth, with its attendant religious connotations. Folklore, however, most often treats with the secular realm and usually concerns folk heroes, famous events, or imaginary characters. Clever twists in plot are frequent.

A good example of American folklore is Johnny Appleseed; the epic sagas of the Icelandic Norsemen are a European example. Folklore often has its roots in historical fact, and sometimes it is difficult to separate the factual content from later embellishments added by storytellers. Quite often, too, it is hard to distinguish between myth and folklore, since the latter may ultimately take on a sacred flavor with the passage of time—as in the case of the Mexican folk hero Quetzalcoatl, who became a god in subsequent centuries. This is also the case with stories about St. Patrick, who brought Christianity to Ireland.

*Fables* constitute another form of oral literature, the most famous in Western tradition being Aesop's fables. Stories of like content are found the world over and generally utilize animals as characters while teaching some moral lesson. Some Native American "Coyote" tales from California fall into the fable category, as do some Chippewa tales of the trickster hero called Nanabozo.

*Tales* usually concentrate on creatures such as the Irish leprechauns or the "little people," as they are generally called in most societies. Such elfin creatures are imbued with magical powers and are the supposed source of many unusual circumstances in the lives of humans. Other tales concern animals and attempt to explain natural phenomena, such as the Mohawk story of why the bear lost his tail. Still others concern themselves with gods who transmute into human form and mingle with people to achieve some purpose, or who mate with a human during their visitation.

It is easy to see that the various categories of oral literature are not mutually exclusive but tend to blend at the edges—and that some types of oral literature might be categorized in several ways.

Oral literature has been a mainstay of all human groups since the acquisition of language. It has connected past to present and has provided explanations of natural phenomena, rules for social behavior, and educational entertainment. It has also provided a foundation for each cultural cognitive system during the early years of enculturative training. Recently civilization has added writing and science to our cultural baggage, but in essence our needs are not far removed from the purposes which gave rise to all the forms of oral literature so long ago.

*See also* Dance; Drama; Folklore; Literature, written; Music and chants; Myth; Religion; Ritual

—*Art Einhorn, Jefferson Community College*

**Orangutan.** *See* Apes.

**Ordeal.** An ordeal is a painful and life-threatening test inflicted on someone suspected of guilt. The results are accepted as involving a supernatural judgment.

*See also* Rites of passage

**Organic Solidarity.** *See* Solidarity.

**Organization, Social.** *See* Social organization.

**Oriental Despotism.** This key idea in the thinking of Karl A. Wittvogel concerns the interactions between certain environmental adaptations and the development of certain social institutions. Wittvogel was convinced that Oriental civilizations developed as distinctive, major types of societies notable for an especially despotic variety of bureaucratic-governmental rule. He called these *hydraulic civilizations,* since they developed in consequence of an emphasis on building and supervising the operation of huge irrigation systems. Despotism, then, is the political form which evolved with the hydraulic adaptation in these Oriental cultures.

*See also* Cultural evolution; Despotism

**Ornamentation.** *See* Adornment.

**Ornaments.** *See* Adornment.

**Osgood, Cornelius** (b. 1905). A cultural anthropologist best known for his extensive ethnographic coverage of the Athapaskan-speaking Ingalik, the Koreans, and a massive study of Hong Kong, Osgood has also contributed to the epistemology of the concept of culture.

**Ossification.** *See* Bone.

**Ostracism.** Social control mechanism most formally developed in certain village societies in which deviant or offending individuals are systematically denied virtually all forms of social contact.

*See also* Social control

**Overt Culture.** This term refers to actions and artifacts of a people which can be directly perceived by the ethnographer—such as house types, clothing, gestures, speech.

*See also* Covert culture

**Paleolithic.** The Paleolithic (Old Stone Age) is the period of time during which chipped stone tools, but not ground stone tools, were made. Tools of the Paleolithic include a wide range of artifacts—from the crude percussion-flaked choppers and bifaces of the Lower Paleolithic to fine pressure-flaked knives and projectile points of the Upper Paleolithic. The Paleolithic is one subdivision of the Lithic (Stone) Age of the three-age system (Stone, Bronze, Iron) developed by Christian Jurgenson Thomsen in 1836. The first (Lower) Paleolithic tools were identified by Jacques Boucher Crèvecour de Perthes, who found the flint tools in the gravels of the Somme River (France). The Middle Paleolithic is associated with *Homo sapiens neanderthalensis,* the Upper Paleolithic with *Homo sapiens sapiens.*

*See also* Lithic ages

**Paleolithic Art.** *See* Upper Paleolithic art.

**Paleomagnetism (Archaeomagnetism).** Temporal variations of the direction and intensity of the geomagnetic field provide the basis for two absolute dating methods. Fired clay and volcanic rock are magnetized parallel to the direction and proportional to the intensity of the magnetic field in which they are cooled. The regional history for both these variables can be established from samples of known age which then allows the dating of samples of unknown age. Although dates may be determined from either intensity or direction measurements, those based on the latter are more reliable. The periodic nature of geomagnetic variation limits the effective time range of these methods.

*See also* Dating, absolute; Physical-chemical methods of dating

**Paleontology.** *See* Fossil analysis.

**Paleontology, Human.** *See* Human Paleontology.

**Palynology.** Palynology is the study of fossil pollen. Identification of a plant species through preserved pollen (which is relatively indestructible) allows reconstruction of past environments.

*See also* Physical-chemical methods of dating; Soils and archaeology
Consult: Gray, Jane, and Smith, Watson, "Fossil Pollen and Archaeology," *Archaeology* 15(1):16–26, 1962.

**Pan-Africanism.** In some ways this term is the English equivalent of the French *négritude.* It is a more political concept than Leopold Senghor's *négritude,* which stressed the existence of unconscious archetypes shared by all black Africans. While Kwame Nkrumah added a mystical dimension to the concept of Pan-Africanism, it is significant that he did so at the time that Pan-Africanism had all but died as a potent force in the world. Independence did not bring with it a supranational government, and the Organization of African Unity (OAU), created in 1963, has yet to become the nucleus of one. The newly independent African states found that there were a number of national tribal interests which demanded their immediate attention and that many of these interests conflicted with those of their immediate neighbors.

However, the freeing of Africa from European colonialism that was the goal of the first Pan-African Congress in 1900 in London has been all but achieved. The dreams of W. E. B. DuBois and H. S. Williams have in large measure come to pass. By 1945, when leadership of the organization passed from non-Africans to indigenous Africans at the Fifth Pan-African Congress in Manchester, England, it was clear that the emancipation of Africa was near.

Perhaps the 1975 Pan-African Congress in East Africa, the first to be held there, may rekindle the dreams of Pan-African unity held by Nkrumah and DuBois, a unity that would be spiritual and continent-wide without regard to national or tribal membership.

*See also* Colonialism; Imperialism; Neocolonialism

*—Frank A. Salamone, St. John's University*

**Pan-Indianism.** This phrase is dignified by frequent use, rarely by clear definition. The prefix *pan* is actually redundant, since the word *Indian* by itself has always been used in a collective sense to refer to all the peoples native to the American continents and to their—presumably—shared characteristics. For this reason, Pan-Indian is something of a misnomer: pantribal is a more accurate way of referring to the experiences and processes by which different American tribal societies have come to share common cultural elements, social forms, values, language, and a growing sense of identity.

There has been very little systematic research on these processes or their results. The exceptions are a few scattered studies of reactions in a single reservation community to an element or institution in process of diffusion (e.g., acceptance of the Native American Church) or a study of the spread of a culture complex over an area (e.g., Plains-style clothing and headdress). Most other descriptions of the content of pantribalisms are largely anecdotal and highly impressionistic. They consist mainly of generalizations drawn from limited experience with one group of Indians in one area, or one type of Indian in a special cultural setting (e.g., professional leaders in national organizations). Much too often such descriptions strongly reflect the personal biases of the observer or are bent by the observer's role involvement with the Indian group.

These cautions are important because the labels Indian or Pan-Indian have been so long and so often used that everyone expects them to have sound specific meaning. Unfortunately, because the generalizations available are too often racial and national stereotypes, they are very compelling. This is so because stereotypes meet two important needs—to simplify and make comprehensible matters inherently complex and to form a simple image compatible with the needs of the user.

These wants are common to Euramericans as well as to many, but not all, individuals categorized as Indian. One prime source of pantribalisms is thus in the identity needs of people who are believed to be or who believe they are Indians. This is especially true of those who have not been socialized in a specific tribal tradition, those who have been raised in a highly acculturated community, and those who have become alienated from the customs of a particular Indian community. Such persons actively seek out appropriate symbols, styles of dress, ways of believing, music, and other "Indian" cultural elements out of which they can form a satisfying self-image.

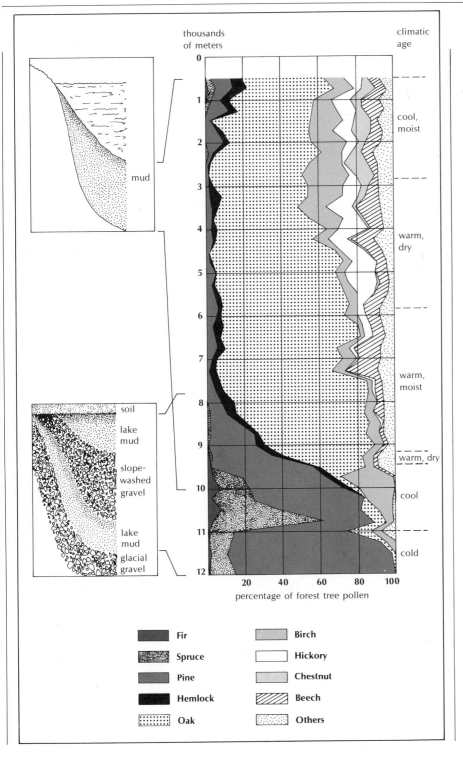

thousands
of meters

climatic
age

percentage of forest tree pollen

| | |
|---|---|
| Fir | Birch |
| Spruce | Hickory |
| Pine | Chestnut |
| Hemlock | Beech |
| Oak | Others |

*Pollen analysis is a method of dating which, together with other methods, can be used to test the validity of radiocarbon dates; the principles of this method are outlined in this illustration. If mud is taken from the bottom of a lake (upper left), it will be found to contain the pollen of various plants. If a vertical sample is taken from several layers, however, the relative amount of pollen from each species at each level of the mud will vary (diagram at right). From the kinds of pollen that predominate at any one level the pollen analyst can infer the vegetation, and hence the climate, when the pollen drifted down from the surface of the lake. To extend the usefulness of the method backward in time, the same kind of analysis can be applied to the bed of an extinct lake (lower left). Adapted from Scientific American.*

They also seek identification with groups and organizations on which they can hinge a social identity. Such materials and reference groups are increasingly available in the mass media, from specialized commercial firms, in colleges and universities, and from reservation communities and national Indian organizations and periodicals.

Another major source of pantribalisms is the current wave of protest advocating the union of all local reservation groups into one political body, a cohesive interest group. A number of different regional and national organizations have developed, and their well-staged and much publicized activities have drawn the attention of a great many people. These activities have increased group identification and the rate of interaction, which contribute to the pooling of common beliefs and practices to such a degree that a definite ideology is emerging. Similarly influential are the many local organizations which grew out of the War on Poverty. Most of these are little publicized (e.g., Indian Community Action Programs) but are yet viable and influential. New ones, in fact, are forming every day (e.g., The Institute of Indian Religion). These organizations promote innumerable conferences, workshops, institutes, training sessions, and social affairs which regularly draw together people of different tribal backgrounds.

In general, the sources of belief and practice which make up Pan-Indianism or pantribalism, and the process by which they spread and become accepted, have to be the same as those which characterize all cultural change. These sources merit special discussion.

Above all, it should be recognized that certain elements which are held to represent the continuity of Indian cultural traits were widespread but certainly not universal when Europeans first arrived. One example might be consensus-seeking as a preferred mode of group decision-making. Such an element was not exactly the same in all Indian bands, tribes, and chiefdoms, however, and today it generally lacks the magical controls and supernatural sanctions which formerly validated group decisions.

Moreover, some elements are clearly European in origin—for example, "fry bread" or "Indian bread," which is made of milled wheat flour, sugar, salt, with yeast or soda for leavening, and which is deep fried in lard. Today this bread is thought to be distinctively Indian although neither the ingredients nor the product is Indian in origin.

Finally, some pantribalisms are innovative responses to contact with Europeans and are neither European nor Indian in origin. One example might be contemporary Indian humor, especially jokes.

Whatever their source, the need to fix the content and form of an Indian identity is so profound that origins are ignored. However, the processes of cultural and social change which make up Pan-Indianism or pantribalism are neither adequately studied nor well understood.

See also Acculturation; Assimilation; Cultural change; Diffusion

Consult: Leacock, E. B., and Lurie, N. O., North American Indians in Historical Perspective (New York: Random House, 1971).

—James Clifton, University of Wisconsin, Green Bay

**Panini** (4th century BC). Indian grammarian whose work *Sutras* (Instructions), a detailed analysis of Classical Sanskrit, is the first known formal grammar of any language.

**Pantribalism.** See Pan-Africanism; Pan-Indianism.

**Paradigm.** This term refers to an arrangement in which units are not ordered by inclusion, as in a taxonomy, but are members of a given *domain* (kinship, sports,

etc.) and differ from other members by one or more features. The arrangement is multiple and intersecting. In the American kinship system, for example, it is enough to know that a lineal relative is of the first ascending generation and male to know that he is termed "father"; "mother" is in the same domain and differs only in terms of the component female (instead of male).

See also Componential analysis; Formal semantic analysis

**Paradigm, Scientific.** This concept was introduced by Thomas Kuhn in *The Structure of Scientific Revolutions* (1962). In this work Kuhn argues that the growth of a science is not only through a slow accumulation of data and theories: science starts with fundamental assumptions about the phenomena studied. The paradigm is the orthodox doctrine of the science, as well as the training exercises with which new scientists are enculturated, and the normal pursuit of scientists is to elucidate the paradigm with new supporting data and ancillary theories. Science grows by accretion until a residue of anomalous data forces the overthrow of the old and the establishment of a new paradigm.

**Paralinguistic Communication.** Paralinguistic communication involves human noises such as tone-of-voice phenomena. Humans make a variety of noises—coughs, sneezes, hesitations (uh-huhs), sniffles, belches, snickers, groans—which involve sounds that are not part of ordinary language. These sounds convey messages about the speaker's emotional state or culturally defined messages (in our culture, clearing the throat is a message). In addition to these examples, people also communicate paralinguistically by manipulating their tone of voice, raising or lowering pitch, prolonging syllables, drawling, clipping their words, and so on. Paralanguage accompanies language and may have the effect of letting the hearer know the speaker's subjective stance toward what he or she is saying.

See also Communication; Linguistics

Consult: Pittenger, Robert E., and Smith, Henry, Jr., *The First Five Minutes: A Sample of Microscopic Interview Analysis* (Ithaca: Martineau, 1957); Trager, George L., "Taos II: Paralanguage," *Anthropological Linguistics*

2(2):24–30, 1960; Trager, George L., "The Typology of Paralanguage," *Anthropological Linguistics* 3(1):17–21, 1961; Trager, George L., "Paralanguage: A First Approximation," in *Language in Culture and Society*, ed. Dell Hymes (New York: Harper & Row, 1964).

**Parallel Cousin.** A cousin traced through a same-sex sibling link—e.g., ego's mother's sister's child is ego's parallel cousin.

See also Kinship

**Parallel Cousin Marriage.** See Marriage.

**Paranthropus.** See Australopithecines.

**Parapithecus.** This name was assigned to a broken mandible found in the Egyptian Fayum but is now supplemented with other specimens. The form is clearly an Oligocene monkey.

**Parricide.** This term refers to the act of killing one's father. According to Freudian psychoanalytic theory, the most ancient form of human social organization was dominated by a fierce patriarch who had sexual relations with his wives and daughters but did not allow his sons sexual access to these women. Eventually the sons killed their father, ate him, and copulated with their mothers and sisters. Because of a lingering fear of their dead father, however, they could not enjoy these sexual relations. They chose mates from women of neighboring groups and instituted a taboo against relations with their mothers or sisters. According to Freud, these primal events were stored in the human psyche as a racial memory that continues to affect all individuals' development.

See also Incest; Incest avoidance (taboo); Murder; Oedipus complex; Patricide; Psychoanalytic school of psychology; Psychosexual stages of development

**Parsons, Elsie Clews** (1875–1941). An American anthropologist who did fieldwork in the American Southwest, Mexico, and Ecuador, Parsons is best known for her breadth and depth of research on the Pueblo Indians, which has never been equaled.

**Parsons, Talcott** (b. 1902). A Harvard sociologist whose social theories were very influential in the 1940s and 1950s, Parsons evolved a grand theory of society, which he analyzed from a functionalist perspective.

*See also* Functionalism

**Participant Observation.** It was Bronislaw Malinowski who originated this field method whereby the ethnographer is immersed in the day-to-day activities of the community being studied. It is believed that the ethnographer becomes a more effective observer if he or she is able to internalize the language and the routine of the resident group. The objective of this method is to minimize the presence of the fieldworker as a factor affecting the responses of the people and to provide a record of observed behavior under varying conditions. It is important to recognize that all observations are made within the context of a theoretical frame of reference or bias, and one must examine the relationship between what the ethnographer observes and how the people themselves view the observed event.

This passive process of data collection is rarely an end in itself. It provides the basis for the formulation of hypotheses which suggest the use of more manipulative procedures such as interviews and tests. The investigation can be structured to elicit responses which elucidate the fundamental cognitive patterns of an informant and in so doing yield information about the manner in which members of a group relate events and ideas.

See also Fieldwork methods
Consult: Malinowski, Bronislaw, *Argonauts of the Western Pacific* (New York: Dutton, 1961); Pelto, Pertti J., *Anthropological Research: The Structure of Inquiry* (New York: Harper & Row, 1970).
—*Patricia Eyring Brown, Arizona State University*

**Passage, Rites of.** *See* Rites of passage; Ritual.

**Pastoralism.** This type of ecological adaptation is found principally in the geographically marginal areas (the arid and semiarid zones) of Asia and Africa where natural resources cannot support agriculture and hence the people are entirely devoted to the

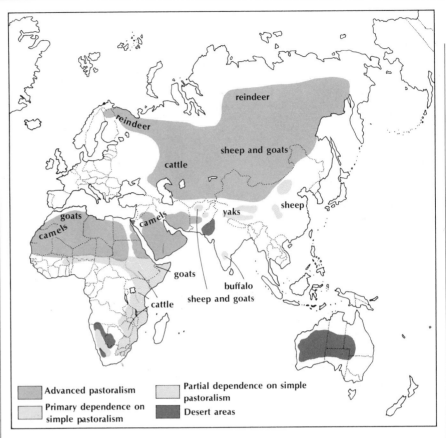

WORLD DISTRIBUTION OF PASTORALISM

*(Adapted from Pearson)*

Legend:
- Advanced pastoralism
- Primary dependence on simple pastoralism
- Partial dependence on simple pastoralism
- Desert areas

care and herding of animals. Their total reliance on livestock breeding and their nomadic way of life are mutually interdependent, and they entertain a strong socioeconomic (and not infrequently predatory) relationship with neighboring sedentary agriculturalists.

See also Economics and subsistence; Nomadism
Consult: Spooner, Brian, *The Cultural Ecology of Pastoral Nomads* (Reading, Mass.: Addison-Wesley, 1973).

**Patination.** Patination is the chemical alteration (by local conditions) through time of the textures and colors of stone artifact surfaces. Fresh or faked modifications may appear as patination anomalies. The term also refers to the oxidized crust formed on

*Below, Masai herdsman in Kenya. Cattle are a source of wealth, prestige, and nourishment for the Masai, who drink both the milk and the blood of the animals.*

the surfaces of metal artifacts—especially bronze and copper.

*See also* Physical-chemical methods of dating

**Patriarchy.** A form of social organization characterized by the domination of domestic life and/or the administration of public policy-making by men. Friedrich Engels' *The Origin of the Family, Private Property and the State* (1884)—derived from the unilineal evolutionary theories of Lewis Henry Morgan—posits the orthodox Marxian view that patriarchy arose from pre-existing matriarchal society and is associated with the creation of private property and the emergence of the family.

*See also* Matriarchy

**Patricide.** The murder of one's own father, universally regarded as a particularly heinous offense.

*See also* Murder; Parricide

**Patriclans.** *See* Clan.

**Patrilateral Cross-Cousin Marriage.** Marriage between a man and his father's sister's daughter, often found in conjunction with Crow kinship terminology.

*See also* Kinship; Kinship terminologies; Marriage

**Patrilineage.** This term refers to an exogamous descent group based on relationship to a known male ancestor. Members of patrilineages often share residences or localities.

*See also* Descent; Exogamy; Lineage; Matrilineage

**Patrilineal Descent.** The principle by which lineal kin links are traced through males—i.e., a child is descended from his or her father, father's father, and so on.

*See also* Descent rule; Kinship and descent; Matrilineal descent

**Patrilocality.** According to this postmarital residence rule, a newly wed couple takes up permanent residence with or near the

*All cultures pattern peoples' behavior systematically. A careful examination of this photograph reveals patterning of behavior in terms of both age and sex.*

parents of the groom. As with matrilocality, this rule of residence favors the development of extended families.

In some instances, the couple may reside temporarily with or near the bride's parents before going to live with the groom's parents. This pattern is commonly associated with *bride service,* a custom whereby the groom "pays" for his bride by working for her family for a specified period of time.

*See also* Marriage; Matrilocality; Neolocality
Consult: Murdock, G. P., *Social Structure* (New York: Macmillan, 1949); Nimkoff, Meyer F. (ed.), *Comparative Family Systems* (Boston: Houghton Mifflin, 1965).

**Pattern, Behavior.** Clyde Kluckhohn referred to a conventionalized sequence or set of behaviors (for instance, a tea ceremony or an obsessive cleansing ritual) as a behavior pattern. More widely the term refers to all culturally conventionalized or personally repeated ways of behaving. The term does *not* refer to the behavior of an agency or institution. In other words, the conception refers to *culturally* standardized behaviors rather than role- or institution-

determined behaviors. The conception is useful as a shorthand but is not very productive scientifically.

*See also* Pattern, culture

**Pattern, Culture.** The concept of culture pattern has several different meanings. Most important is that of Ruth Benedict, who argued that various domains of sociocultural existence which are quite different in origin, constitution, societal process, and material foundations nevertheless produce *formal* attributes of organization common to all (e.g., a central *style*). She called the common formal attributes a pattern and often labeled it with a single metaphoric term such as "Dionysian" or "paranoid." These terms were not necessary to the pattern idea, nor were they intrinsically psychologistic (as is often alleged).

In this perspective, social organization, cognitive maps, technical orders—each phenomenally distinct—may have common ordering characteristics. This concept of pattern suggests a sociopsychological process of human ordering and is also useful in fieldwork for discovery purposes.

Another pattern concept, such as that used by Kluckhohn, refers to *ordered sequences* of behaviors such as formulaic rituals or greeting patterns. Still another (Kroeber's) refers to the *systemic pattern*—that is, to a cluster of culture traits which stick together as the cluster diffuses across cultural boundaries. Examples of this concept are the phonetic alphabet and its internal sequence, or plow-with-animal-traction agriculture. Systemic patterns are mainly interesting for purposes of historical reconstruction.

See also Pattern, behavior
—Anthony Leeds, Boston University

**Pattern Maintenance.** See Social Integration.

**Pavlov, Ivan** (1849–1936). This Russian physiologist was awarded a Nobel prize in 1914 for his work on digestive systems. Pavlov is best remembered, however, for his research into the conditioned reflex, a phenomenon now often referred to as Pavlovian conditioning.

See also Conditioning

**Pavlovian Conditioning.** See Conditioning.

**Peasant Conservatism.** See Conservatism, peasant.

**Peasants.** Peasants comprise the lowest rural stratum of the great, complex, preindustrial, and (usually) literate civilizations. They are primary producers, extracting their living directly from the environment, whether as farmers, artisans, or fishermen. Though they produce largely for their own subsistence, they are intimately involved in market relations with urban centers, to which they are also bound politically and administratively. Peasants always have some degree of immediate control over production resources; in this respect, they differ from landless laborers such as plantation workers or migrant farmhands. Among peasants, too, the household is the main unit of economic activity: all household members are coordinated to fulfill most of the household's own labor needs. This feature distinguishes them, for example, from rural people in collectives such as the Israeli kibbutz or Chinese commune.

Peasants are identifiable by social and cultural criteria as well. They almost always reside in small communities, which in many respects become the focus and boundary of their world. Each peasant community is characterized by a basic moral unity—that is, by essential agreement over what is good or bad, right or wrong. It also maintains distinctive customs and traditions, which are frequently only minor variants of those found in the wider society but which assume a magnified importance in the peasant's eyes. With industrialization, the moral unity and cultural distinctiveness of small rural communities disappear and we can no longer speak of a peasantry. The main peasant areas of the globe today are Asia, the Mediterranean world, and Latin America. Many scholars consider black sharecroppers of the southern United States and rural whites of Appalachia and the Ozarks to be peasants. The status of sub-Saharan Africans has been the subject of considerable debate in the anthropological literature.

See also Colonialism; Feudalism; Limited good, image of; Neocolonialism; Peasants and revolution
Consult: Potter, Jack, Diaz, May, and Foster, George (eds.), Peasant Society: A Reader

Peasant in the Loire Valley region of France harvesting grapes—his major cash crop.

(Boston: Little, Brown, 1967); Wolf, Eric, *Peasants* (Englewood Cliffs, N.J.: Prentice-Hall, 1966).
—*Stanley H. Brandes, University of California, Berkeley*

**Peasants and Revolution.** Despite the much-discussed conservatism of peasants, sporadic uprisings and even sustained armed movements have not been unknown in the history of peasantry. The exploited nature of peasantry, whether in Manchu China or medieval Europe, has led to revolt. Thus while Karl Marx and Friedrich Engels viewed peasantry as a stronghold of reaction, an obstacle to the achievement of their revolutionary aims, it was Mao Tse-tung who realized the distorted perspective of his mentors and successfully based his Chinese communist revolution on the rural peasant masses. Indeed the 20th century has witnessed numerous political upheavals from Algeria to Cuba in which peasants have been the major protagonists.

The contemporary anthropological analysis of peasantry has recently become interested in the role of peasants in revolutionary movements. Eric Wolf has carefully worked out a preliminary analysis of the stages of peasant involvement in 20th-century revolutions and has emphasized that it is precisely the peasants' attempt to remain traditional that has ultimately caused them to become revolutionaries. Modern peasant rebellions aimed at redressing wrongs have been transformed, with the help of outside leadership, into revolutions attempting to overthrow the entire social order.

*See also* Lenin, V. I.; Marx, Karl; Peasants; Revolution; Social change
Consult: Hobsbawm, E. J., *Primitive Rebels: Studies in Archaic Forms of Social Movement in the 19th and 20th Centuries* (New York: Praeger, 1963); Wolf, E. R., *Peasant Wars of the Twentieth Century* (New York: Harper & Row, 1969).
—*Stan Wilk, Lycoming College*

**Pebble Tools.** These implements form the earliest tool tradition of the Lower Paleolithic. These unifacial core tools are all-purpose chopper tools produced by removing a few flakes from a pebble.

*See also* Chopper tools; Oldowan culture

**Pedology.** *See* Soils and archaeology.

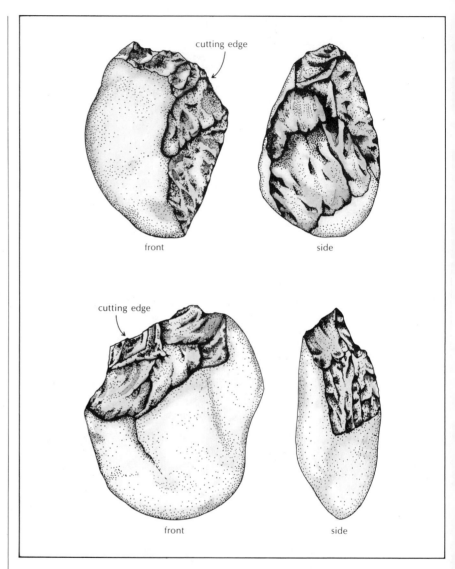

OLDOWAN PEBBLE TOOLS (OR CHOPPERS)
*Two Oldowan chopping tools (front and side views) made by removing a few flakes from lava lumps to form jagged working edges, indicated by arrows (four-fifths actual size).*

**Peking Man.** *See Homo erectus.*

**Pelvis.** *See* Bipedalism; Locomotion, primate evolutionary trends of.

**People, a.** Any group of human beings characterized by a unity of sentiment, beliefs, culture, geographical location, and other traits may be called a people. In a classified library catalog the term may be interchangeable with tribe or nation and sometimes a culture.

*See also* Culture, a; Culture areas of the world; Ethnic group

**Perception.** *See* thought processes.

**Perigordian Culture.** This Upper Paleolithic assemblage is named for Périgord (SW France). It developed from Mousterian culture around 33,000 years BP and lasted some 13,000 years. It is divided into three stages: Lower (I = Chatelperronian), Evolved Lower (e.g., Les Cottés), and Upper (IV = La Gravette). The Perigordian culture is found in SW France and Cantabrian Spain: it is characterized by Châtelperron, La Gravette, and Font Robert points, truncated elements, and Noailles burins.

**Permafrost.** *See* Glaciations.

**Perry, William James** (1889–1949). A British anthropologist who was an expert on Malaysia, Perry became associated with G. Elliot Smith as a leader of the British diffusionist school.

> *See also* Diffusionism

**Personality.** This term refers to the enduring, distinctive patterns of psychological traits characteristic of one individual, including those which are unique and those which are shared with others in a group.

> *See also* Culture and personality; Personality, cultural determinants of

**Personality, Cultural Determinants of.** In discussing the impact of culture on personality, two key conceptual problems must be kept in mind. The first is that Culture and Personality are both abstractions: the former designates the repetitively patterned strivings and actions of a group, the latter the repetitively patterned strivings and actions of an individual. The second problem is that in this context, culture has a larger and more inclusive meaning than is often the case. Specifically, in this discussion culture includes the social organizational components of human living and how they affect the development and functioning of personality. But it also includes the value and belief systems of a group—expressive culture.

More than a little thought has gone into demonstrating—and much evidence accumulated in support of—the position that social organizational factors are more influential in the formation of basic personality characteristics than are expressive cultural factors. Culture, in this narrow sense, seems to be conditioned heavily by the kinds of personalities which characterize a society. This does not imply that each personality is a culture in microcosm. Every person has inborn, temperamental characteristics which in themselves create individual differences. Moreover, every individual during the period of socialization and enculturation has direct experiences with only a portion of the available sociocultural spectrum. Thus we should think of personality (on the individual level) not as a system separate and autonomous, but as one linked to and overlapping with, if not merged into, the sociocultural system.

The impact of culture on personality begins before birth with respect to the mother's nutritional state and its effects on the developing fetus. It continues—through the culturally shaped life stages of infancy, childhood, adolescence, and young adulthood—to leave lasting marks on the structure, content, and style of personality functioning. But cultural experiences also continue to shape personality throughout life—for example, in specifying the behavioral content of roles such as shaman or mother.

Specific social and cultural systems affect all areas of personality functioning, conscious and unconscious, motivational, emotional, perceptual, and cognitive. They affect levels of psychobiological functioning through nutrition, levels of energy expenditure required, and the mind-altering chemicals permitted or encouraged. They have impacts on the form and content of the self system by defining and then rewarding or punishing for appropriate role behavior. They define what is valued, good, and proper and may (or may not) influence the formation of a strong superego (internalized conscience), which serves as a self-regulating mechanism through the mechanism of guilt. Alternatively, a society may rely on external controls of behavior through public shaming, gossip, and ridicule, producing personalities which are strongly other-oriented.

Sociocultural patterning touches all levels of personality functioning, even the prevalence and nature of mental disorders. All cultures provide the individual with some (but by no means all) of the attitudes and skills needed to cope with the stresses of living. But at the same time, all cultures generate many of the most important stresses which puzzle and perturb people's minds. The specific psychological stresses created in, and characteristic of, a culture are never precisely the same as those of any other. But there are communalities in all cultures, derived from the fundamental nature of *Homo sapiens*—e.g., a long infantile dependency period. In the 17th century the Indians of the eastern woodlands of the United States dreamed fearful dreams of being captured, tortured, burned alive, and eaten by their enemies. Dreaming is part of the universal nature of humankind, but not this particular kind of dream. Indeed, three centuries later the descendants of these Indians are no longer obsessed with these fears, for the stresses and conflicts which disturb them have altered as their cultures—and their social environments—have changed.

> *See also* Basic personality; Culture and personality; Enculturation; Mental illness and culture
> Consult: Endleman, R., *Personality and Social Life* (New York: Random House, 1967); Honigman, J. J., *Personality in Culture* (New York: Harper & Row, 1967).
> —James Clifton, University of Wisconsin, Green Bay

**Petrie, Sir William Matthew Flinders** (1853–1942). This British archaeologist pioneered the development of Egyptian archaeology. His study of burials led to his developing sequence dating, which is a form of seriation.

**Petroglyph.** Designs pecked, scratched, carved, or otherwise engraved into a stone surface.

**Peyote.** This stimulant drug comes from a small cactus (*Lophophora williamsii*) which is native to Mexico and the American Southwest. Of Nahuatl origin, the term *peyotl* refers to the fresh or dried plant; *mexcalli* refers to the drug or derivative drink.

After harvesting, the plant is divided into segments which are sliced and dried. The dried slices are known as mescal buttons. The buttons are chewed or macerated in water to extract the active ingredient, mescaline, an alkaloid stimulant and antispasmodic. In refined form, mescaline is a white powder in widespread use in drug experiments.

Physical symptoms which frequently accompany its use, and which are similar to those of other alkaloid poisons, are vomiting and headaches. Psychological effects are euphoria and, if taken in sufficient quantity, hallucinations. Its ritual use as a hallucinogenic intoxicant seems to have been an integral part of certain Native American cosmologies and ceremonies since preconquest times, and usage has been reported from Mesoamerica to as far north as Wisconsin and Minnesota.

Peyotism was legalized in the United States in the late 1960s with the restriction that official sanction applied only to formal ceremonies of the Native American Church. The constitutional right to freedom of religion was cited as the basis of the court's decision.

*See also* Drugs
—*MaryAnn Foley, Southern Connecticut State College*

**Phatic Communication.** *See* Communication, phatic.

**Phoneme.** The phoneme is the basic unit of significant but meaningless sound in a language. Phonemes differentiate meanings. In English, the initial sounds of *pit, bit, kit* and the vowel sounds of *cat, kit, cut* distinguish these words from one another. Each form in these series differs by only one sound. Although without meaning, the sound in question is significant and can be called a phoneme. There are also sounds in a language which are nonsignificant and do not differentiate words. In English, the first sound of *pit* always has a puff of breath after it [ph]; in *spin,* the *p* has no puff of breath and sounds like a *b;* and in *dip,* the sound may or may not have a puff of breath. Each one of these variants is considered a *p* by speakers of English, and each occurs only in its specified position. If a speaker were to put a puff of breath after the *p* in *spin,* it would not change the meaning of the word, but it would be poorly spoken English. These are all variants or allophones of the phoneme /p/. Phonemes are always symbolically represented between slash lines. In every language, the hundreds of individual sound variants can be reduced to a small number of phonemes.

*See also* Linguistics; Morphophonemics; Phonemic analysis; Phonetics

**Phonemic Analysis.** This method is used by linguists to determine the significant sounds of a language. The simplest way to find phonemes is to use minimal pairs (words which differ in meaning, phonolog-

ically, and by only one sound). The data must be transcribed phonetically. The words *pit* and *pet* differ by only the vowel sound and mean different things. A hearer or speaker must discriminate these two words on the basis of the vowel. Thus *i* and *e* contrast with one another and the difference between the two is significant. The sounds /i/ and /e/ are vowel phonemes of English.

If enough minimal pairs are not available, the linguist must look at each sound's distribution (position or environment) in a word. Sounds which belong to different phonemes will contrast; that is, they can occur in the same position in a word. Sounds which do not contrast, and are thus allophones (versions) of a phoneme, will never occur in the same position in a word or in the same sound environments. The following example from Spanish (Gleason 1964) illustrates the process:

| | | | |
|---|---|---|---|
| [avana] | Havana | [uva] | grape |
| [bala] | ball | [pero] | but |
| [buřo] | burro | [gosař] | to enjoy |
| [dever] | to owe | [pero] | dog |

Consider [b] and [v]. Are these the same phoneme or different phonemes? We list the positions where each occurs:

| Phoneme | Initial | Medial |
|---|---|---|
| [b] | 2 | |
| [v] | | 3 |

Note that [b] does not occur in the middle of a word and [v] does not occur at the beginning. Each is restricted to one position. We can say they are allophones of a single phoneme symbolized as /b/ (or equally logically as /v/).

If we consider the status of [ř] and [v], what do we find?

| Phoneme | Medial | Final |
|---|---|---|
| [ř] | 1 | 2 |
| [ř] | 1 | |

Here both can occur in the middle of a word. Since they overlap in their distribution, they are in *contrast* and hence are separate

phonemes /ř/ and /ř/. To a speaker of Spanish, these two varieties of [r] are different sounds whereas [v] and [b] are the same sound—[v] is the variety of /b/ that is always found in the middle of the word. A full analysis of a language would use many more data than this, but the principles would be the same.

*See also* Complementary distribution; Phoneme; Phonetics; Phonology
Consult: Gleason, Henry A., *An Introduction to Descriptive Linguistics* (New York: Holt, 1964).
—*Elizabeth Brandt, Arizona State University*

**Phonetic Features.** *See* Distinctive features.

**Phonetics.** This branch of linguistics deals with actual sounds produced by humans. It is usually contrasted with phonemics, the study of *significant* sounds. Phonetics is not concerned with whether people in a speech community are producing significant sounds (sounds which distinguish meaning). Phonetics is concerned with the way sounds are produced. It is concerned, for example, with whether a sound is voiced or unvoiced, a labial or a dental, and so on. It is concerned with how to describe, measure, and represent sounds and how they are produced and reproduced. It is concerned with representing sounds through written symbols. Phonetics is thus the attempt to describe carefully and represent symbolically all the sounds produced by speakers of a language.

*See also* Distinctive features; Linguistics; Morphophonemics; Phonology

**Phonological System.** A phonological system is the arrangement of speech sounds of a language and the interrelationship that underlies a given arrangement. It consists of phonemes (the significant sounds of a language) and morphemes (minimal units of meaning); it also involves determining the rules by which phonemes are combined to form morphemes.

*See also* Linguistics; Morpheme; Phoneme; Phonology

**Phonology.** Phonology is the science of speech sounds and their interrelationships. There are two major areas of phonological

Comparison of speech apparatus of *H. sapiens,*
*H. erectus,* and modern human infant

**Homo sapiens.** When we compare the
vocal apparatus and brain power of a
modern baby and adult with reconstructions of early men, we can assess
the speaking ability of *Homo sapiens
neanderthalensis.* Like *Homo sapiens* he
had a larynx to generate sounds, but to
form words with these sounds he would
have had to modulate them with spaces
above the larynx. In modern man, the
nasal cavity, mouth, and pharynx are used
for this purpose. In the mouth and
pharynx the tongue movements vary the
size and shape of these spaces to produce
the sounds needed for modern speech.

**Homo sapiens neanderthalensis.** H.S.N. is
believed to have possessed a vocal tract
similar to the one shown here. The larynx
sits higher up in the throat, thus limiting
the size of the pharynx. The tongue
was relatively long and rested almost
entirely in the mouth rather than in the
throat. Therefore, it could be used only
to vary the size and shape of the mouth
alone, and not the pharynx. This single-
cavity system restricted *H.S.N.* to slow,
clumsy speech. Note the right angle
formed in the modern adult's tract, the
short, round tongue and mouth cavity
versus *H.S.N*'s oblique angle and long,
flat tongue and mouth cavity.

**Modern baby.** The fact that the vocal
tract of a newborn modern baby resembles that of *H.S.N.* has caused many to
assume that the sounds the baby is
capable of making resemble those that
*H.S.N.* could make. Although the baby's
sounds are limited, they could have been
formed into words by an adult brain.

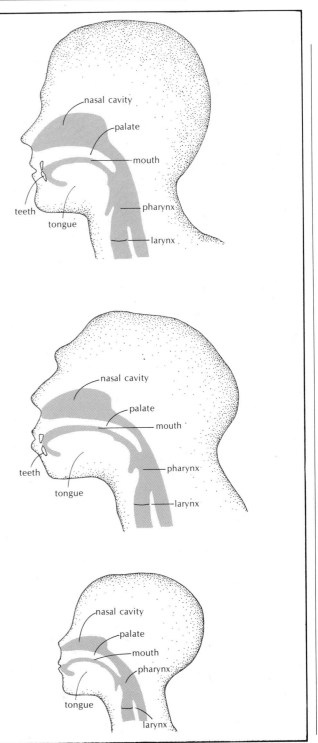

investigation: *articulatory phonetics,* the study of how humans produce verbal sounds through their speech apparatus, and *phonemics,* the study of how sounds are clustered together into significant groupings (phonemes) in all languages.

Phonology distinguishes between sounds (phones) and significant sounds (phonemes). A phoneme may comprise a number of phones, called allophones. For example, [f] and [p] are different phones. In English they are also different phonemes but in Hausa they are allophones of the same phoneme—that is, they are in complementary (rather than contrastive) distribution.

Each language has a phonological system that provides rules, or structure, for the sounds that compose it. It patterns sounds chosen from among the almost infinite range of possible human sounds and it limits the manner in which categories of sounds may be combined. These categories determine the sounds a member of a speech community must learn in order to communicate with other members.

*See also* Allophones; Complementary distribution; Phoneme; Phonemic analysis; Phonetics; Phonological system; Speech community

## Photography as a Research Tool. 

Photography is rapidly becoming an integral aspect of anthropological research—visual anthropology. In fact, the Society for the Anthropology of Visual Communication (SAVC) was formed in 1972.

Generally three types of photographic equipment are used in anthropological research: 35-mm still cameras, $2\frac{1}{4} \times 2\frac{1}{4}$ inch still cameras, the 16-mm movie cameras. The 35-mm camera is especially important in all phases of anthropological research. Its negative size is large enough for quality prints; moreover, the film is inexpensive and thus large quantities of pictures can be taken. Serious work in 35-mm photography requires the use of cameras with interchangeable lenses. Some anthropologists prefer the rangefinder type of 35-mm camera. The Leica is the only camera of this type still being manufactured which has interchangeable lenses. The rangefinder camera has the advantages of being compact, lightweight, quiet, easy focusing with wide-

angle lenses, and fast focusing in dim light. The rangefinder type is especially useful as a quick-shooting action camera. Perhaps more anthropologists prefer the single-lens reflex (SLR) type of 35-mm camera, such as the Nikon or Pentax. While it is generally heavier and bulkier than the rangefinder type, it is more versatile and easier to use for closeup and telephoto photography. The SLR system of focusing shows the depth of field of the picture being taken.

The $2\frac{1}{4} \times 2\frac{1}{4}$ inch format of such cameras as the Hasselblad and Rolleiflex are generally preferred by the archaeologist over the 35-mm cameras because of the larger negative. The 35-mm camera's advantage of rapid picture-taking is of little value to the archaeologist, whose subjects are generally motionless. Since the archaeologist works with a tripod, the added weight and bulk of the $2\frac{1}{4} \times 2\frac{1}{4}$ inch camera create no problems.

The use of 16-mm movie cameras has increased in recent years as a number of excellent movies on various human societies and on primate behavior have been produced. To be successful, a 16-mm movie requires considerable financing and promotion. Many of the better new movies have resulted from the combined efforts of an ethnographer familiar with the culture of the society being filmed and a professional cinematographer who handles the technical aspects of filmmaking.

Finally, photography can be used to record spatial relationships. This aspect of photography is of importance to both the archaeologist and the ethnographer. In archaeology, aerial photography is used for mapping and locating sites. Also, at the sites themselves skeletal material and artifacts are photographed *in situ* to record stratigraphic and spatial relationships. In ethnographic research, although mapping is sometimes accomplished with aerial photography, generally cameras are used to record ground-level spatial relationships.

*See also* Fieldwork, ethnographic; Fieldwork methods; Film, ethnographic research and report.

Consult: Bateson, Gregory, and Mead, Margaret, *Balinese Character: A Photographic Analysis* (New York, New York Academy of Sciences, 1942); Byers, Paul, "Still Photography in the Systematic Recording and Analysis of Behavioral Data," *Human Organization* 23: 78–84, 1964; Collier, John, Jr., *Visual Anthro-*

pology: *Photography As a Research Method* (New York: Holt, 1967); Hitchcock, John T., and Hitchcock, Patricia J., "Some Considerations for the Prospective Ethnographic Cinematographer," *American Anthropologist* 62: 656–674, 1960.

—Michael D. Olien, University of Georgia

**Phrase Structure.** This term is employed by the transformational school of linguistics to refer to immediate constituent structure. In the transformational approach, the *process* which generates a phrase structure is critical, rather than a description of the structure itself. The phrase structure of a construction (generally a sentence) is conceptualized as being generated through the application of an ordered set of *phrase structure rules,* the first set of rules in a transformational grammar. Phrase structure rules are followed by *transformational rules* which give the elements generated by the phrase structure rules their desired order and add and delete elements as well. Finally, *morphophonemic rules* generate the actual utterance sound segments.

The phrase structure of a sentence is represented by a tree showing the hierarchical relationships among the elements. Let us use a simple sentence to illustrate such a phrase structure tree. The phrase structure of the sentence:

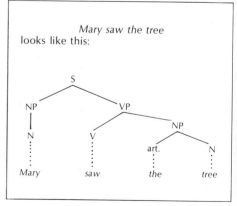

*Mary saw the tree* looks like this:

It is generated by the following phrase structure rules:

1. S → NP + VP
2. VP → V + (NP)
3. NP → (art.) + N

Key: S = sentence
NP = noun phrase
VP = verb phrase
N = noun
V = verb
art. = article
(X) = X is optional
X → Y = X is to be replaced by Y

*See also* Immediate constituents; Transformational grammar; Transformational linguistics Consult: Bach, Emmon, *An Introduction to Transformational Grammars* (New York: Holt, 1964).
—*David E. Hunter, Southern Connecticut State College*

**Phrases.** *See* Grammar; Linguistics; Words.

**Phratry.** Kinship group composed of two or more clans that recognize a common unilinear bond—that is, all members of the group claim a common mythological ancestor.
*See also* Clan; Lineage; Moiety

**Phylogeny.** Phylogeny, tracing the evolution or history of a life form's development, shows relationship and ancestry in a lineage. Phylogeny is often illustrated with branching tree diagrams.
*See also* Taxonomy

**Physical Anthropology.** This discipline is sometimes called biological anthropology or, with a slightly different emphasis, human biology. The physical anthropologist attempts to amalgamate the data of human biological variability, past and present, with the matrix of behavior. This field shares with the rest of anthropology a dedication to the understanding of *Homo sapiens* as a cultural animal. The beginnings of physical anthropology as a self-conscious discipline have been traced to the publication of Charles Darwin's *On the Origin of Species* and to the researches of Paul Broca and Francis Galton. Using instruments designed mostly by Broca, physical anthropology quickly became synonymous with *anthropometry,* the measurement of the body and its parts.

With the rapid accumulation and discoveries of fossilized hominid remains beginning in the latter half of the 20th century, physical anthropologists have spearheaded the search for the beginnings of humankind. Interest in the nature of human variability has characterize the field from its inception, and with the rise of a genetical basis for evolutionary explanation, statistical treatments have become common. A quickening of interest in the nonhuman primates has led to studies of comparative behavior and anatomy, both in the field and in the laboratory.

The field may be divided into two complementary portions: *human evolution* and *human variation.* But the concerns of physical anthropology range across a wide spectrum of interests, approaches, materials, and methods in biological science. Any catalog of research specialities among those identifying themselves as physical anthropologists would surely include evolutionary theory, primate evolution, genetics, demography, primate behavior, anatomy, adaptation, growth, disease, and osteology. As a consequence of this diversity, some schools have physical anthropologists in departments of anatomy, genetics, and biology, in addition to anthropology.

**Human Evolution.** In the slightly more than a hundred years since the first widely reported fossil discovery, human paleontologists, as researchers in human evolution are frequently termed, have uncovered fossil hominids and their predecessors from all the continents of the Old World. Although it was once fashionable to talk of "missing links," the proliferation of fossil finds has produced representatives of all the major forms in the long sequence from generalized ancestral ape to human. As discoveries accumulate, however, so do the grounds for disagreement about the specific details of the evolutionary process. Consequently, many beginning students find the larger picture obscured by the fog of detail surrounding the controversies over specific finds. This picture of human evolution can be briefly painted as one in which selection for bipedality enhanced opportunities for manipulation of the environment. This ultimately led to the use of tools to alter the environment and acted to change the social context. All these factors combined to promote an increase in brain size. Hence the hominid fossil record (those forms directly in human ancestry) consists of a series of groups of

animals that, by about 5 million years ago, had become capable bipeds. Subsequent refinement in bodies, hands, face, and teeth, combined with the increase in brain size, resulted about 40,000 years ago in forms indistinguishable from contemporary ones.

**Human Variation.** Like early studies in human evolution, those in human variation initially emphasized classification. Beginning with a strictly anthropometric-anthroposcopic (measuring-observing) approach, studies of "race" aimed at discovering better means of classifying living humans into neat, orderly "racial" groups. Decades of little real progress in the endeavor—and a burgeoning quantity and variety of information on the nature of genetic variability—caused attention to swing toward the description of populations in terms of gene frequencies. With this change, the goal of "racial" classification was gradually abandoned. At the same time, emphasis on understanding population differences increased. At the present time, then, differences in rates of disease susceptibility, various blood types, and other genetic population markers are being explored for their selective advantage and their ability to elucidate the process of the evolution of variability.

**Skeletal Biology.** A third major area of concern to physical anthropologists is that of human skeletal biology. Because only bones and teeth undergo fossilization, a familiarity with skeletal anatomy is necessary for every paleontologist (student of fossil remains). Using the traditional methods of measurement and observation, a great deal of information has been gleaned from even incomplete skeletons recovered in the last hundred years. The identity of an individual (in terms of age, sex, and even some personal idiosyncracies), cause of death, and something of the life-style may also be deduced if the preservation is adequate. Thus the osteologist may be called on to aid law enforcement officials or to provide a description of a population that has been recovered from an archaeological excavation.

In each of these disciplines the specialist generally begins with data from an individual, moves to a number of individuals, and ends by making statements about the population of which the individual is a part. Studies of teeth, bones, growth, biochemical genetics, ecology, population genetics, and nonhuman primates all combine as physical anthropology to illuminate humanity's oldest and most fascinating problem: What are we, and how did we become what we are?

See also Anthropometry; Blood groups; Evolution, human; Genetics; Human variation, significance of; Primates, evolutionary features of; Race

Consult: Kelso, A. J., *Physical Anthropology: An Introduction*, 2nd ed. (Philadelphia: Lippincott, 1974); Lasker, Gabriel Ward, *Physical Anthropology* (New York: Holt, 1973).

—Stanley Rhine, University of New Mexico

## Physical-Chemical Methods of Dating.

A variety of physical and chemical changes over a period of time have provided the bases for archaeological dating methods.

**Radioactive Decay.** Radioactive decay processes in which the nuclei of radioactive isotopes change their structure by giving off subatomic alpha and beta particles or adding an electron have provided the bases for more dating methods than any other type of change. Dating is based on radioactive decay, which occurs at a regular rate in such a way that half the atoms in any mass of a radioactive isotope will decay, within certain statistical limits, after a fixed time—the half-life of the isotope. If the relative amounts of a radioactive isotope and its daughter products in a sample and the half-life of the isotope are known, the approximate age of the sample can be determined. The great range of half-lives of different radioactive isotopes has led to the development of dating methods with applications in archaeology and other disciplines. These methods provide age determinations ranging from a few years to several billion. Radiocarbon, potassium-argon, and thermoluminescent dating are the radioactive decay methods most commonly used in archaeology.

**Spontaneous Fission and Fission Track Dating.** Spontaneous fission, a process similar to radioactive decay during which some radioactive isotopes break into two or more pieces, provides the basis for fission track dating. Uranium 238, which has a fission half-life of $10^{16}$ years, is present in small quantities in most material; and when it fissions in electrically nonconducting solids, two fragments break apart with sufficient force to form a short tube called a fission track. Fission tracks in crystals and glass can be enlarged by etching with a variety of

solvents. Since tracks are erased when the material is heated sufficiently, determination of the number of tracks per unit area on a surface and the uranium 238 concentration in the material allows estimation of the time elapsed since the sample was last heated, which may be the time it was formed. Because the uranium content of minerals likely to be found in archaeological contexts is low, this method has had its greatest applicability in dating material older than 10,000 years. The fission track dating of volcanic glass in deposits at Olduvai Gorge helped establish the age of early hominid fossils in that area. A similar method based on alpha-recoil tracks left in mica by radioactively decaying uranium and thorium atoms is being developed. Since radioactive decay is much more frequent than spontaneous fission this method, which is being applied to mica inclusions in ceramics, holds great promise for dating young samples.

**Chemical Changes.** Dating methods based on progressive chemical changes have not yet met with great success. Obsidian hydration has been the most widely used of these methods, but a number of problems still need to be solved. A dating method based on chemical changes in bone would be of great utility because of the abundance of this material in most archaeological sites. It has been shown that fluorine is absorbed by bone and chemically combines with some of its constituents in ever-increasing amounts. However, the great number of variables such as soil chemistry, moisture and temperature which affect the rate of fluorine absorption has limited this method to the relative dating of bones from the same deposit. One interesting application of the method was in proving the Piltdown find a fraud by demonstrating that the jaw and calvarium could not have been contemporaneous if they came from the same deposit. Recently there has been a great deal of interest in the progressive chemical changes which take place in amino acids in bone. Although soil chemistry, temperature, and moisture are important variables, it is possible that the different effects of each variable in the several reactions on the nearly twenty amino acids in bone may allow an absolute dating method to be developed.

**Geomagnetic Changes.** Changes in the direction and intensity of the geomagnetic field which are recorded in fired clay and volcanic rocks have provided scientists with

the bases for a group of dating methods.

**Sources of Error.** The dates obtained from the physical-chemical methods of dating are approximate because of a variety of random and systematic errors. The random errors, manifested as variable results from multiple specimens taken from the same sample, affect the *precision* of the result. Such variation may be due to the probabilistic nature of the change being measured (particularly important in the radioactive decay methods), natural variation of datable material in the sample, or laboratory measurement error. Random errors give rise to the familiar ± factor which follows most reported radiocarbon results.

Systematic errors, often related to the basic assumptions of a method and potentially a more serious problem, affect the *accuracy* of the results. In radiocarbon dating, for example, the assumption is made that the percentage of carbon 14 in the atmosphere, which is the source of this isotope in organic material, has been constant in the past. It is also assumed that all plants absorb carbon 14 and carbon 12 in a fixed ratio. Recent studies have shown that both these assumptions are false. Thus most radiocarbon dates differ, sometimes considerably, from the correct value. Radiocarbon dates continue to be reported without allowing for these variables, but corrections and sometimes further analyses are made to obtain an estimate closer to the true age.

Many physical and chemical dating methods are still in a developmental stage. Currently only radiocarbon, potassium-argon, and obsidian hydration dates are routinely reported. Several other methods hold great promise, and there is reason to believe that those based on thermoluminescence, archaeomagnetism, and alpha-recoil tracks will soon be providing consistently useful data.

See also Dating, absolute; Obsidian hydration; Paleomagnetism and archaeomagnetism; Potassium-argon method of dating; Radiocarbon dating; Thermoluminescence

Consult: Faul, H., *Nuclear Clocks*, rev. ed. (Oak Ridge, Tenn.: U.S. Atomic Energy Commission, Division of Technical Information, 1968); Michael, H. N., and Ralph, E. K. (eds.), *Dating Techniques for the Archaeologist* (Cambridge, Mass.: M.I.T. Press, 1971); Michels, J. W., *Dating Methods in Archaeology* (New York: Seminar Press, 1973).

—Daniel Wolfman, Arkansas Archeological Survey

**Physiology of Speech.** Humans produce speech by forcing air through the vocal chambers, thus changing the shapes of these chambers to produce noises with varying acoustic and perceptual characteristics. In speaking, air is generally exhaled—though inhaled for ingressive/implosive sounds in some languages—with the subglottal organs (the lungs and respiratory muscles) controlling the rate of breathing.

**Modifying the Airstream and Vocal Chambers.** The nature of the sounds (phones) produced in speaking depends on *phonation* and *articulation*. Phonation means making different types of sounds (e.g., voiced, voiceless, aspirated) by changing the tension and vibration of the vocal cords to obstruct the airstream. Articulation refers to obstructing the airstream by changing the shapes of the supraglottal vocal chambers—the oral, nasal, and pharyngeal cavities. As air passes through these cavities, they become resonating chambers; and changes in their shapes produce sounds with different resonances.

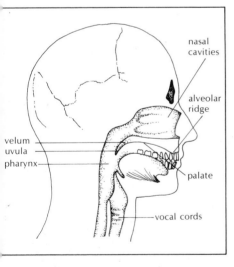

nasal cavities

alveolar ridge

velum
uvula
pharynx

palate

vocal cords

**Articulation.** If the uvula is lowered, air flows through the nasal cavities rather than through the oral cavity, producing *nasal* sounds (the initial sound of *meet* and *neat*). Partially lowering the uvula results in *nasalized* sounds (the vowel sound of *man*).

The shape of the pharyngeal cavity (pharynx) is changed by drawing back the root of the tongue or by contracting the

pharyngeal muscles and constricting the cavity to produce *pharyngeal* sounds. But most articulation occurs in the oral cavity, which contains articulatory organs that can be moved (tongue, lips, uvula) and others that are stationary (teeth, alveolar ridge, palate, velum). The shape of the oral cavity is altered (constricted) by moving one or more of the movable organs until it is opposite one of the stationary organs.

**Classes of Speech Sounds.** Different manners of articulation and degrees of constriction separate the major classes of speech sounds—*consonants* (contoids) and *vowels* (vocoids). Of the consonants, *stops* are produced by complete closure, *obstruents* (fricatives, affricates) by about 90 percent closure, and *resonants* (flaps, trills, laterals, nasals, semivowels) by momentary closure or by constriction less than that of obstruents. Vowels are articulated with the least amount of oral constriction. Speech sounds can be further modified by *secondary articulation,* which means that a secondary articulator (e.g., labialization by puckering the lips) constricts the oral chamber at the same time a primary articulator constricts it in another region.

**Syllables.** Although the physiological and acoustic bases of syllables are still relatively unclear, speech sounds occur in sequences of syllables, each of which has a peak of energy (usually a vowel) which can be preceded and followed by one or more consonants within the same syllable.

**Prosodic Features.** In addition to the segmental features of speech sounds described above, all sounds have prosodic (suprasegmental) features: the amount of *stress* (intensity) of each syllable; the *tone* (pitch) of each syllable, varied by tensing or relaxing the vocal cords; and the relative *duration* of each separate phone.

See also Biological basis of language
Consult: Abercrombie, David, *Elements of General Phonetics* (Chicago: Aldine, 1967); Heffner, R.-M. S., *General Phonetics* (Madison: University of Wisconsin Press, 1950); Hockett, Charles F., *A Manual of Phonology* (Baltimore: Waverly Press, 1955); Ladefoged, Peter, *Preliminaries to Linguistic Phonetics* (Chicago: University of Chicago Press, 1971); Malmberg, Bertil, *Phonetics* (New York: Dover, 1963); Peterson, Gordon, and Shoup, June, "A Physiological Theory of Phonetics," *Journal of Speech and Hearing Research* 9(1):6–67, 1966.
—Charles T. Snow, California State University, Chico

**Piacular Rites.** This term was used by the sociologist Emile Durkheim to describe religious rituals that serve to comfort both individual and community in times of crisis, such as funeral services or remembrance ceremonies.

See also Durkheim, Emile; Ritual

**Piaget, Jean** (b. 1896). A Swiss biologist, philosopher, and psychologist, Piaget is best known for his theories of cognitive development, which have been of great interest to anthropologists, psychologists, and educators. Piaget believes that cognitive growth proceeds through an invariant sequence of progressively more elaborate stages, and his model places a particular emphasis on the individual's active construction of and judgments about reality. For this reason, Piaget's theories are often regarded as an important critique of the cumulative, passive-conditioning model of cognitive growth offered by the behaviorist school.

See also Developmental school of psychology

**Pictograph.** A pictograph is a design painted on stone. The term is also used to mean a design made on natural desert pavements by removing darker surface material to expose lighter material underneath.

**Pidgin.** This term refers to a language originating from attempts by speakers of two different languages to communicate with one another. A pidgin language is essentially a simplified form of one of the two languages, usually that of the dominant group.

See also Sociolinguistics

**Piggott, Stuart H.** (b. 1910). This British archaeologist is noted for his work on Europe and India. His major research has been on the Neolithic and Bronze Age of Great Britain.

**Pigmentation.** Coloration of the skin, eyes, and hair is related both to processes of natural selection and sociocultural factors affecting the amount of pigment found in these tissues.

The color of human skin is due largely to the amount and distribution of melanin in the epidermis, though other pigments (carotene and hemoglobin) are present. The amount of melanin found in the skin may have adaptive value in various environments. Though not conclusive, studies indicate that dark skin may offer protection against solar (ultraviolet) radiation which, in large doses, may cause burning, circulatory collapse, and skin cancer. Natural selection would thus favor large amounts of melanin in the skin of peoples in sunny and unshaded areas. A correlation between skin color and intensity of solar radiation does appear to exist, for skin color lightens as one moves away from the equator (see Brace 1964). Light skin may also be adaptive, since decreased amounts of melanin facilitate the production of vitamin D from stimulation by the sun in areas of great cloud cover. Alternatively, light skin may have developed in W Eurasia due to mutation, genetic drift, and a simple lack of selective pressure for dark skin that previously had kept dark the populations that were evolving in the tropics.

Human hair color varies from black to blond according to the amount of melanin present. Red hair has some melanin, high iron content, and the pigment trichosederin.

Eye color is due to the amount of melanin in the iris. Eye coloration may have adaptive value in that melanin reduces the amount of light entering the pupil, thus offering some protection to the retina against ultraviolet radiation.

Whatever biologically selective advantages various forms of pigmentation offer, cultural, social, and economic factors play an increasingly important role in shaping their distribution. Hulse (1955) argues that the development of village life and food production reduced the adaptive significance of high or low pigmentation. Also, Hulse considers important the rise of colonial powers and overseas trade in the spread of certain physical traits such as the light skin and hair of northern Europeans.

See also Gene distributions; Hair, functions and shapes of; Human variation, significance of; Melanin; Race
Consult: Brace, Loring, "A Nonracial Approach Towards the Understanding of Human Diversity," in The Concept of Race, ed. A. Montagu (New York: Free Press, 1964); Garn, S. M., Human Races (Springfield, Ill.: Charles C Thomas, 1971); Hulse, F. S., "Technological Advance and Major Racial Stocks," Human Biology 27:184 ff., 1955; Hulse, F. S., The Human

Species (New York: Random House, 1971).
—Phillip S. Katz, State University of New York, Brockport

**Pike, Kenneth L.** (b. 1912). Linguist who coined the terms *etic* and *emic* from the comparable words *phonetic* and *phonemic* in linguistics and applied them to the study of human behavior.

See also Emic; Etic

**Pilbeam, David Roger** (b. 1940). An English-born physical anthropologist interested in human evolution and the primates, Pilbeam is best known for his research on early hominid fossils in Africa.

**Pilot Study.** Short-term field research undertaken to collect preliminary data for the formulation of hypotheses to be tested later by a full-scale project.

See also Fieldwork methods

**Pithecanthropus.** See Homo erectus.

**Pitt-Rivers, General Augustus Lane-Fox** (1827–1900). One of the most scientific of the early archaeologists, Pitt-Rivers insisted on absolute precision in every aspect of excavation and the recording of finds. He was also perhaps the first to arrange collected ethnological specimens by use rather than by provenience.

**Pitt-Rivers, Julian Alfred Lane-Fox** (b. 1919). British social anthropologist best known for his pioneering study of the social structure of a Spanish peasant community in Andalusia.

**Plano Culture.** Scottsbluff, Plano, Angostura, Plainview, and other Plano complexes succeeded Llano culture on the American Plains some 10,000 to 6,300 years BP (later in Canada) with nonfluted lanceolate projectile points and greater cultural diversity.

See also Llano culture

**Plantations.** These large landholdings devoted to cash crops are found primarily in

the tropical regions of the world. The plantation is usually geared to the production of a single crop such as banana or rubber. Modern plantation organization is characterized by a wage labor force and impersonal ties between labor and management. These plantations are often part of an international corporation whose major decisions about the plantation are made by corporate officials living in other countries. Because of their heavy capital investment in foreign countries, plantation corporations are often intimately involved in the politics of those countries.

See also Colonialism; Hacienda; Latifundia

**Plasticity, Human.** Plasticity makes possible the adaptive nature of human beings. People are born with no real instincts but only with needs that can be satisfied in a large number of ways. Though humans must eat to satisfy their hunger, whether they eat, say, steak or fish is a matter of cultural preference.

This lack of rigid genetic programming is important to the development of culture. It enables humans to adapt through learning rather than through biological changes and has accounted for the ability of human beings to live successfully in many different ecological zones.

**Play.** This term refers to both individual and group behavior which is frequently highly patterned (there are rules) and generally of a somewhat frivolous nature. The concept

*Play. Games children play often express salient sociocultural themes. In this photograph from western France, a boy shows his sister how to operate a wind-up doll she has received.*

*!Kung San women playing melon toss game, in which a melon is tossed back and forth in rhythm with prescribed songs and dance steps.*

is never applied to behavior which meets individual or group survival needs.

Psychologists are interested in individual play as behavior which reveals the person's cognitive and motor-skill development. Play is also regarded as a projective medium in which the person displays deeply patterned affects and conflicts.

Both psychologists and anthropologists are interested in peer group play as a major context of the individual's enculturation; games are regarded as microcosms of future role expectations (playing house) and also as contexts in which socially appropriate goals and values (teamwork, self-assertion, willingness to play by the rules) are taught.

Claude Lévi-Strauss has pointed out that, in structural terms, competitive games are mechanisms which impose the condition of nonequality on previously equal parties (there must be a winner and a loser—nobody likes a tie).

Human beings are perhaps unique in the animal kingdom in that they continue a high degree of playful behavior far into maturity.

*See also* Games; Joking, ritualized

**Pleasure Principle.** This term refers to the id's "primary process" or drive—energy directed toward the immediate release of tension (cathexis), according to Sigmund Freud. Nonlogical and maladaptive, it is indirectly satisfied through fantasy.

*See also* Freud, Sigmund; Reality principle

**Pleistocene.** This epoch is the earlier of two (Pleistocene, Holocene) which together comprise the Quaternary period. The Pleistocene lasted from perhaps 3.3 million to 10,000 years BP. Customarily, it is divided into basal (Villafranchian faunal stage), lower, middle, and upper time/stratigraphic

| Temperature Lower  Higher | | Date (BP) | Periods | Epochs | European Mammal Ages | European Glacials/Interglacials | North American Glacials/Interglacials | Prehistory |
|---|---|---|---|---|---|---|---|---|
| | C-14 dating | 10,000- | | Holocene | Holocene | Holocene | Holocene | Cities, Agriculture |
| | | | | | Upper Pleistocene | Weichsel | Wisconsin | Settlement of New World Hunters and gatherers |
| | | 75,000- | | | | | | |
| | Indirect dating | ?130,000- | | | | Eem | Sangamon | |
| | | ?200,000- | | | | Saale | Illinoian | Homo sapiens |
| | Fission track dating? | | | Pleistocene | Middle Pleistocene | | | |
| | | ?400,000- | Quaternary | | | Holstein | Yarmouth | |
| | | | | | | Elster | Kansan | Homo erectus |
| | | ?850,000- | | | | | | |
| | Potassium argon dating | | | | Lower Pleistocene (Villafranchian) | Uncertain sequence of geological events | Uncertain sequence of geological events | Early hominids and Australopithecus africanus |
| Uncertain climatic sequence | | ?5,000,000- | | | | | | |
| Present climate | | | Tertiary | Pliocene | | | | |

*Highly simplified chart showing climatic characteristics, geological features, and two glacial chronologies of the Pleistocene, with relationship to selected events in human evolutionary history (adapted from Flint).*

units. The Pleistocene is distinguished generally from the Upper Pliocene (Astian faunal stage) by (1) evidence for increased tectonic activity; (2) the appearance of a new and more cold-tolerant fauna in which the southern elephant (*Archidiskodon*), true cattle (*Leptobos*), true (i.e., one-toed) horse (*Equus*), and camel (*Camelus*) are diagnostic; and (3) the first (Cenozoic) evidence for major climatic deterioration (i.e., montane and continental glaciation) vis-à-vis the normal climate of geological time.

The Pleistocene is defined regionally on variable combinations of these criteria. It is best documented stratigraphically from continental sediments in NW and C Europe and littoral sediments (fossil beach deposits) in NW Africa (especially Morocco). Rarer macrofloral and pollen data are known from NW Europe. Twelve to sixteen warm/cool/cold climatic shifts have been docu-

mented in NW Europe (W German plain, Holland, Scandinavia) from glaciofluvial sediments, flora, and fauna. The partially analogous glaciofluvial sequence from S Germany/Alps (Donau, Günz, Mindel, Riss, Würm) is commonly cited but requires redefinition. Littoral/fluvial sequences of variable reliability have also been defined in E and S Africa; in W India and N Burma; in C and SC China and SC Java; and in E and SE North America. The Pleistocene/Holocene boundary is defined regionally on variable criteria (e.g., draining of the Baltic Ice Lake = 10,200 BP), but dates cluster around 10,000 BP.

*See also* Villafranchian period

Consult: Butzer, K. W., *Environment and Archaeology: An Ecological Approach to Prehistory*, 2nd ed. (Chicago: Aldine, 1971); Kurtén, B., *Pleistocene Mammals of Europe* (Chicago: Aldine, 1968).

—*Geoffrey A. Clark, Arizona State University*

**Pliocene.** During the Pliocene epoch (10–3 million years ago) major landmasses were approximately modern in shape; the climate was markedly cooler and drier than the Mio-

cene, foreshadowing the glacial climates of the Pleistocene. Considerable mountain building took place, as well as the culmination of mammalian specialization and major anthropoid radiation during late Miocene and Pliocene times. Four principal hominid genera appear. *Gigantopithecus* was a huge, specialized pongid line which died out in the Middle Pleistocene. *Oreopithecus* was a bipedal primate which became extinct during the Pliocene; in spite of the parallel evolution toward a bipedal niche, its evolutionary history was quite distinct from the hominid line since the Oligocene. *Dryopithecus* evolved into modern apes. *Ramapithecus* signifies the beginning of the hominid line which leads to modern *Homo sapiens sapiens*.

**Plow.** This agricultural tool, which generally requires animal power, is used to loosen, aerate, and invert the soil so as to cover weeds, expose a large area of soil to weathering, and prepare a seedbed. In the course of human history, plows represent a great advance over human-powered horticulture, which has generally been too inefficient an investment of energy to produce much more than the consumption needs of the worker. Plows were first used in Mesopotamia about 3600 BC and appeared in Egypt about 3000 BC. This early type—the ass- or ox-driven *ard* (or scratch plow)—lacked a moldboard to turn over the soil. The ard was adaptive in arid areas with light soil but was useless in the heavy clay soil of N Europe, where the moldboard plow came into use before 300 BC. The earliest plows were entirely of wood; later ones were tipped with metal.

*See also* Economics and subsistence

**Pluralism.** This characteristic of many societies is marked by the presence of several subsocieties or subcultures which coexist within a single, common political and economic system. Generally these subsocieties are made interdependent by a complex set of social and cultural bonds. Yet each may exhibit a greater or lesser degree of political autonomy and cultural-linguistic distinctiveness. In this sense, a very large number of the world's nations are pluralistic, including some of the most ancient (China and Iran) as well as some of the youngest (Malaysia and Nigeria). This is evidence of a recent rapid territorial expansion of complex nation-states which grow partly by incorporating formerly autonomous, smaller societies.

*See also* Cultural pluralism

**Pluvial Period.** Pluvials are rainy periods formerly considered direct tropical corollaries of Pleistocene glaciations. This was too simplistic. Now any major climate change rainy period is called pluvial.

*See also* Glaciations; Pleistocene

**Pogrom.** The word *pogrom* comes from two Russian words meaning "like thunder." These words are rather appropriate for the way a pogrom is carried out. A pogrom is an officially endorsed persecution of a minority, usually Jews. While the word derives from Russian sources, its practice was not limited to Russia or even to Eastern Europe. The most fearful and far-reaching pogrom, in fact, was that carried out by Adolph Hitler in Nazi Germany under the cloak of legality given him by the notorious Nuremberg Laws. The element of legality

and official sanction is the distinguishing characteristic in the definition of a pogrom and sets it off from other massacres and persecutions of Jews. By extension the term, like ghetto, has been applied to other minority groups in pluralistic societies.

*See also* Extinction of minorities; Minorities, ethnic; Pluralism

**Polanyi, Karl** (1886–1964). This British economic anthropologist argued that the application of economic theories that were derived from the study of Western, market-dominated economic systems to societies without a market economy was unjustified.

**Political Anthropology.** This field of cultural anthropology deals with the aspect of social behavior known as political organization. Political organization is specifically concerned with the organization and management of the public affairs of a society, whether it be organizing a fishing expedition or managing a military conscription. Political organization may be viewed as the network of social relationships that allows for the coordination and regulation of behavior related to the maintenance of public order. This inevitably involves the problem of how power is distributed and enacted in society. Care should be taken to distinguish political organization from government, which may be defined as an administrative system with specialized personnel. Probably all societies have some form of political organization—but it is not always government.

A basic tenet of political anthropology is that the political organization of a society cannot be studied apart from the rest of the social organization. A political system must be understood in terms of its relationship to the ecological, technological, structural, and ideological aspects of the society.

A variety of approaches have been suggested for the study of political organization. Notable are those of David Easton (1965), who defines politics as activities directed toward authorities; Marc Swartz (1968), who emphasizes the study of processes involved in the determination and implementation of public goals; and Frederick Bailey (1969), who views politics in terms of contest goals and strategies.

*See also* Government; Leadership; Legal systems; Political systems; Power; Social control; Social organization

Consult: Bailey, Frederick G., *Stratagems and Spoils: A Social Anthropology of Politics* (Oxford: Blackwell, 1969); Easton, David, *A Systems Analysis of Political Life* (New York: Wiley, 1965); Swartz, Marc, *Local-Level Politics* (Chicago: Aldine, 1968).
—*Richard L. Stone, California State University, Los Angeles*

**Political Economy.** In Marxist social science, this term refers to the interpenetration of the economy and the system of power and authority in a society.

*See also* Marxism

**Political Repression.** *See* Repression, political.

**Political Systems.** This term refers to those aspects of total social systems which are involved with the articulation and implementation of public policy. They are the means by which groups and individuals achieve and, more precisely, use power.

Political systems may be divided into two major types based on the degree to which they have become functionally specific: there are societies with governing institutions consisting of specifically *political statuses* with their associated roles; there are also societies which lack a differentiated government.

In groups without formal government, the formation and implementation of political decisions is only one aspect of statuses whose associated roles include many other duties. Such groups, for example the Nuer and Tallensi of Africa, are often called stateless societies. They are characterized by the absence of centralized authority and administrative institutions. They typically display a lack of pronounced differences in wealth among their members. The reverse is true of societies which have governments, such as the Bemba and Zulu of Africa, often called primitive states.

The study of stateless societies has demonstrated that anarchy is not the necessary alternative to state organization. Social order can be maintained in societies without governments.

*See also* Government; Legal systems; Political anthropology; Power; State, the
Consult: Easton, D., *The Political System: An Inquiry into the State of Political Science* (New

York: Knopf, 1953); Fortes, M., and Evans-Pritchard, E. E. (eds.), *African Political Systems* (New York: Oxford University Press, 1940); Middleton, J., and Tait, D. (eds.), *Tribes Without Rulers* (London: Routledge & Kegan Paul, 1970); Swartz, M., Turner, V., and Tuden, A. (eds.), *Political Anthropology* (Chicago: Aldine, 1966).

—*Stan Wilk, Lycoming College*

**Pollen Analysis.** *See* Palynology.

**Polyandry.** This marriage rule allows a woman to have more than one husband at the same time. Fraternal polyandry requires that cospouses be brothers (as among the Todas of S India). The other, nonfraternal, form of this rarely found rule has also been reported (as among the Marquesan Islanders).

*See also* Polygamy; Polygyny

*A polygynous Kikuyu family. Shown here are, from left to right: grandmother, 2nd wife with her baby, 2nd son of 1st wife, patriarch, 1st son of 1st wife.*

**Polygamy.** This general term refers to all forms of the marriage rule that allows several spouses at the same time. Social anthropologists often regard polygamy as an adaptive response to changes in a group's way of making a living (Fox 1967) or economic hard times (Linton 1936). Bohannan (1963) disagrees with respect to polygyny. He states that even with equal numbers of men and women, there will always be more marriageable women than men because women mature and marry earlier. Therefore the implicit adaptation lies in devising a way of providing full adult status to as many members of the group as possible.

*See also* Group marriage; Marriage; Polyandry; Polygyny

Consult: Bohannan, Paul, *Social Anthropology* (New York: Holt, 1963); Fox, Robin, *Kinship and Marriage* (Baltimore: Penguin, 1967); Linton, Ralph, *The Study of Man* (New York: Appleton-Century-Crofts, 1936).

—*MaryAnn Foley, Southern Connecticut State College*

**Polygenesis.** Polygenesis is the (anti-Biblical) doctrine that known races of *Homo sapiens* descended from aboriginally different stocks. Various combinations of polygenist thought and monogenist ideas exist in anthropology today. Perhaps the best-known contemporary exponent of the polygenist perspective is Carlton Coon (1962).

*See also* Monogenesis

Consult: Coon, Carleton, *The Origin of Races* (New York: Knopf, 1962).

**Polygyny.** This marriage rule allows a man to have more than one wife at the same time. It is the most common form of polygamy. *Sororal* polygyny requires cospouses to be sisters.

*See also* Polyandry; Polygamy

**Polysemy.** Polysemy refers to different meanings of what appears to be a single morpheme but is in reality multiple morphemes which are phonemically identical. The morpheme *bank* (side of a river) is phonemically identical to *bank* (for savings), but the meanings are different.

*See also* Morpheme; Phoneme

**Pongids.** This is the common term for the members of the Pongidae family. The pongids include the three great apes—the orangutan (*Pongo*), the gorilla (*Gorilla*), and the chimpanzee (*Pan*). One of the more important fossil pongid groups is the dryopithecines, among which possibly the first exclusive ancestor of the great apes may be found.

*See also* Apes; Dryopithecines

**Population Genetics.** This field of study is concerned with the mechanisms of genetic change in populations. As individuals, we inherit our genetic makeup from parents who are part of a larger *breeding population*. The probability that we will inherit certain genetic traits varies from one set of parents to the next, from family to family, and from one breeding population to another. Population geneticists attempt to understand the variability within and between populations caused by evolutionary mechanisms.

Fundamental to an understanding of population genetics is the *Hardy-Weinberg theorem*, which predicts the distribution of genes in infinitely large, randomly mating populations experiencing no evolutionary change. This theorem predicts that under such conditions the gene frequencies of our generation would not be different from our parents' generation and that their frequencies would not be different from our grandparents' generation and so on. In fact, we know that frequencies commonly do vary from one generation to the next and that these changes are the result of the mechanisms of evolution.

The field of human population genetics studies genetic change in human populations both theoretically and empirically. Two primary concerns for anthropology are the *macroevolutionary* trends that led from early hominids to modern *Homo sapiens* and the *microevolutionary* trends that account for contemporary genetic variation within the species.

See also Evolution, genetic mechanisms of; Gene flow; Genetic drift; Genetics; Hardy-Weinberg principle; Populations, breeding; Selection, natural

Consult: Kelso, A. J., *Physical Anthropology: An Introduction*, 2nd ed. (Philadelphia: Lippincott, 1974); Mettler, L. E., and Gregg, T. G., *Population Genetics and Evolution* (Englewood Cliffs, N.J.: Prentice-Hall, 1969); Williams, B. J., *Evolution and Human Origins* (New York: Harper & Row, 1973).

—Alan C. Swedlund, University of Massachusetts

**Populations.** See Demography; Populations, breeding.

**Populations, Breeding.** A breeding population is a group of organisms (individuals) interbreeding and sharing a common gene pool. In experimental situations individuals in a breeding population may exclusively interbreed within the group. In natural situations, however, breeding populations are seldom entirely isolated, and some exchange of mates (and genes) usually occurs between populations. Breeding populations also are referred to as *demes* or *Mendelian populations*. Since species are defined as noninterbreeding taxonomic units, demes must exist within a species. Depending on the amount of *gene flow*, a deme might be defined as one of a series of semi-isolated populations, a geographic "race," or the entire species.

In empirical studies human demes often correspond to levels of sociopolitical organization—that is, villages, towns, bands, tribes, cities. When considering early human evolution it is usually thought that our ancestors lived in semi-isolated bands with limited amounts of gene flow between groups. As population density and mobility increased, it is logical to assume that gene flow also increased. Today human populations demonstrate various types of social organization including bands, tribes, and villages, and some types may be representative of prehistoric patterns. One of the more interesting and perplexing problems in human genetics is the identification of breeding populations within this variety of contemporary structures. It should be clear from this discussion that both cultural and biological factors are influential in determining the nature of human breeding populations.

See also Demography; Evolution, genetic mechanisms of; Gene; Gene flow; Population genetics

Consult: Kelso, A. J., *Physical Anthropology: An Introduction*, 2nd ed. (Philadelphia: Lippincott, 1974); Mettler, L. E., and Gregg, T. G., *Population Genetics and Evolution* (Englewood Cliffs, N.J.: Prentice-Hall, 1969); Williams, B. J., *Evolution and Human Origins* (New York: Harper & Row, 1973).

—Alan C. Swedlund and Roy Rosenblatt, University of Massachusetts, Amherst

**Positive Reinforcement.** See Reinforcement.

*Potlatch held in Victoria, Vancouver Island, Canada, around 1875.*

**Pospíšil, Leopold Jaroslav** (b. 1923). This Czechoslovakian-born lawyer and anthropologist has specialized in comparative primitive law, primitive economics, and social organization, and has published extensively on the Kapauka Papuans.

**Possession.** This trance state is based on the culturally supported belief that curative or malevolent spirits may displace people's personalities and use their bodies for temporary residence.

See also Altered states of consciousness; Culture and personality; Hallucinations and shamanism; Ritual; Shamanism

**Post and Lintel.** See Architecture.

**Potassium-Argon (K-A) Method of Dating.** The decay of radioactive potassium, which has a half-life of 1.3 billion ± 40 million years, to inert argon allows the approximate "absolute" dating of volcanic rocks and ash falling in the time range of 10,000 to more than 4 billion years ago.

See also Dating, absolute; Physical-chemical methods of dating

**Potlatch.** This ceremonial feast accompanied by the giving of gifts to guests according to rank was practiced by the Indians of the Northwest Coast of Canada. The potlatch was given to announce an event of social significance for a kin group, such as the validation of a title by a new title holder. At the turn of the century, due to increasing acculturation and economic stress, a new type

of potlatch appeared in which great quantities of gifts were destroyed, often by fire, on behalf of the guest to humiliate rivals competing for the same title. In 1880, the potlatch was made illegal.

*See also* Exchange; Prestige

**Pottery and Ceramics.** *Ceramics* may be defined as (1) objects made from moist clay, most of which are later heated to a durable state, and (2) the techniques used in making such objects. *Pottery* usually refers to containers, especially pots for food and water, but ceramics in the broadest sense includes a larger range of objects modified by cultural behavior: granaries, buildings (houses, mosques, shrines), kilns, ovens, portable stoves, molds for making pots, containers, toys. Ceramics may be portable or stationary, utilitarian or ceremonial, plain or decorative.

**Technologies.** Ceramics may be made with or without a wheel, with or without the addition of a tempering material to the clay, and may be fired with heat or sunbaked. Ceramics may be fired in a pit, a clamp or half kiln, or in a kiln, a partly or fully enclosed structure.

Some ceramic techniques suggest development from preceramic techniques, especially in regard to containers such as baskets

*Detail of a molded ceramic decoration on a housefront in Kano, Nigeria.*

*Cholula Indian (Mexico) modeled clay vase, painted to represent Chicomecóatl.*

and calabashes. The Navajos, for example, coat their pottery with pitch, a technique more suitable for waterproofing baskets. Archaeologists have noted the dimple in the bottom of some pots, similar to the indentation found in the bottom of a calabash or gourd (Robinson 1961).

Ceramics may be decorated by incising, impressing, stamping, painting, slipping, burnishing, resin painting, glazing, and basting (done after firing), and by adding materials such as mica to the clay, which causes a shiny surface. Mastery of ceramic techniques is also prerequisite to the lost wax method of metal casting.

**Cultural Change.** Ceramics break easily but the shards are durable. Thus archaeologists can study changes in pottery style through time and use this information in relating sites, levels, and cultures (Deetz 1965). Even absolute dates can be obtained from ceramics.

The study of contemporary ceramics affords one the opportunity to observe changes taking place. Traditional ceramics are suited to traditional needs. Low-fired ceramics are porous and thus resistant to thermal shock when used for cooking over an open fire; they are also good for keeping water cool because seepage evaporates from the sides. But aluminum, plastic, and factory china all compete with utilitarian local pottery, and as traditional life-styles change, demand for locally made decorated pottery diminishes.

Some potters, however, such as those at the Abuja pottery training center in Nigeria, have adapted stoneware clays, high-firing techniques, and glazes to their traditional techniques and designs in order to produce dinnerware that is traditional in character

*Statue of a Chinese warrior, believed to represent Chin Shih-huang, founding emperor of the Chin dynasty, 221–107 BC. This statue was one of about six thousand life-sized pottery figures of warriors and horses discovered in 1975 near Sian, in northwest China, constituting one of the rarest finds anywhere in the world.*

and style but suited to new social needs (Cardew 1969). In other areas, nearly extinct ceramic techniques have been revived to meet the demands of a growing tourist industry (Marriott 1948).

**Theoretical Approaches.** Most of the preceding information relates to a *formal* theoretical approach to the study of ceramics—an approach concerned with chemical and physical attributes of ceramics, style, style change, relations between ceramic style and social units, and the cross-cultural study of regularities and similarities in formal ceramic properties.

There are other theoretical approaches to the study of ceramics and pottery. A *social* approach analyzes the relationships between ceramic variation and social structure (Longacre 1964) with or without reference to style. An e*cological* approach analyzes the relationships between ceramic variation and environmental resources. A *geographical* approach analyzes the spatial distribution of ceramics in cultural contexts—households, shrines, villages, sites—and between such contexts. An e*thnoscience* approach involves a linguistic analysis of words for types of pots, categories of ceramics, or verbal plans for making ceramics. A *temporal* approach involves the study of stability and change in ceramic traditions over time. This approach is often used by archaeologists looking at long-range patterns of behavior.

*Information theory* analyzes the ways in which cultural information is encoded in ceramics, as well as redundancy, relative information, and relative organization as evidenced by ceramic attributes (Whallon 1972). *General systems theory* attempts to relate information about ceramics to social systems by analyzing the inherent integration between social behavior, ideas and meanings, technology (ceramics, other artifacts, technical processes), and energy. Variation in ceramics is analyzed to see which aspects can be accounted for by random factors, functional factors, environmental factors, and cultural factors.

*See also* Material culture; Metalworking; Physical-chemical methods of dating; Pre-Columbian art; Thermoluminescence; Tourist art
Consult: Cardew, Michael, *Pioneer Pottery* (London: Longmans, 1969); Deetz, James, *The Dynamics of Stylistic Change in Arikara Ceramics* (Urbana: University of Illinois Press, 1965); Longacre, William, "Sociological Implications of Ceramic Analysis," *Fieldiana: Anthropology* 55:155–169, 1964; Marriott, Alice,

*Maria: The Potters of San Ildefonso* (Norman: University of Oklahoma Press, 1948); Matson, Frederick (ed.), *Ceramics and Man* (Chicago: Aldine, 1965); Robinson, K. R., "A Note on Hollow Based Pottery from Southern Rhodesia," *Man* 61:86–88, 1961; Shepard, Anna, *Ceramics for the Archaeologist* (Washington: Carnegie Institute, 1968); Wahlman, Maude, *Contemporary African Arts* (Chicago: Field Museum of Natural History, 1974); Whallon, Robert, "A New Approach to Pottery Typology," *American Antiquity* 37(1):13–33, 1972.
—*Maude Southwell Wahlman, Field Museum*

**Poverty.** This word has several different but related meanings, but it is always defined relative to the socioeconomic conditions of a society. Poverty involves economic and social inequality—an unequal distribution of what a society defines as the good things of life, including power. Hence poverty implies some measure of social stratification, with certain of the strata in a position of dependence, subordination, and exploitation.

In this sense, poverty is a condition of stratified societies where the several strata are directly related to one another by reciprocal ties and obligations (e.g., peasants and urbanites, socioeconomic classes). Or it may involve relationships between different societies which have lasting economic ties (e.g., nomadic herdsmen and town-dwellers). A condition of poverty within a society means that the capacity to make authoritative decisions goes primarily to the wealthy strata, much less so to the impoverished ones. With the rise of complex, modern industrialized nation-states, poverty becomes associated as well with the class system, particularly the working class and more so those unable to enter industrial or other stable work (e.g., dispossessed tenant farmers).

With the growth of an interdependent world economy, whole ethnic and racial groups and sometimes even nations become—relative to the power and wealth of other nations and groups—poor. For administrative purposes within one nation, some arbitrary, absolute criterion may be specified to define "impoverished people." Usually this is accomplished in terms of income level. Generally, poverty includes lack of wealth and access to wealth (material poverty), the biosocial consequences of this lack (inadequate nutrition, poor health, alienation), and the lack of social power and influence.

*Two Quechua women selling their homemade bread in the village of Pisac, Peru. Although their income from this endeavor is negligible, their opportunity cost—the income they could earn by investing the same amount of time in other endeavors—is so small that it pays them to try to make whatever money they can in this manner.*

Although there has been great faith in the efficacy of wise governmental planning aimed at eliminating poverty through development, the evidence indicates that "successful" economic development very often breeds further poverty, in both the absolute and the relative sense.

*See also* Poverty, culture of; Social stratification
Consult: Valentine, Charles, *Culture and Poverty* (Chicago: University of Chicago Press, 1968).

—*James Clifton, University of Wisconsin, Green Bay*

**Poverty, Culture of.** This phrase refers to a way of life among the lower sectors of capitalist countries that allows them to adapt to and survive in their environment. The concept was advanced by Oscar Lewis as a result of fieldwork in Mexico, India, Puerto Rico, and New York. According to him, this way of life represents the lower sector's efforts to cope with the despair that results from their realization that they will not be able to achieve success in terms of the larger society's prevailing values and goals. Lewis contended that by the time slum children are six or seven, they have absorbed the basic attitudes and values of the culture of poverty. He suggested four basic characteristics of that culture: lack of effective participation in the major institutions of the larger society, a minimum of organization beyond the family level, the absence of childhood as a prolonged and protected stage in the life cycle, and feelings of helplessness, fatalism, dependence, and inferiority. Lewis hypothesized that the culture of poverty does not exist in socialist countries because the poor are highly organized and are integrated into the larger society to a much greater degree than is the case in capitalist countries. For representative criticism of this concept consult Leacock (1971); Valentine (1968).

Consult: Leacock, Eleanor Burke (ed.), *The Culture of Poverty: A Critique* (New York: Simon and Schuster, 1971); Lewis, Oscar, "The Culture of Poverty," *Scientific American* 215: 19–25, 1966; Valentine, Charles, *Culture and Poverty* (Chicago: University of Chicago Press, 1968).
—*Michael D. Olien, University of Georgia*

**Power.** As have scholars in other disciplines, anthropologists have regarded power as a social process: as an attribute of social systems. They have used it sometimes distinct from, and at other times synonymously with, one or more of the following: influence, authority, office, coercion, politics, social control, rights, esteem, prestige, ad infinitum.

There is a fragile consensus that power refers to the ability—or the process by which such ability is implemented by one individual or group—to control the behavior of others or produce a desired reaction in them. This inclusive definition yields different kinds of power—economic, political, religious—all suggesting that power is an attribute of various spheres of life. Some students focus on sources of power, attributing the creation of power-based relationships to control of modes of production in a society or an ability to manipulate rituals dealing with the supernatural. Still others regard authority (ability to control others by virtue of office) and influence (ability to control without benefit of office) as the components of power. This traditional problem of defining

power in political philosophy is reflected in the wide range of usages in anthropology.

See also Headman; Political anthropology; Political systems; Revolution; Social stratification; State and Revolution

Consult: Bierstedt, Robert, "An Analysis of Social Power," *American Sociological Review* 15:730–738, 1950; Olsen, Marvine (ed.), *Power in Societies* (New York: Macmillan, 1970).
—*Paul C. Winther, Eastern Kentucky University*

**Power, Distribution of.** See Headman; Political anthropology; Political systems; Revolution; Social stratification; State and Revolution.

**Prague School of Linguistics.** This group of linguists, organized in Prague in 1926, is best known for its structural approach to phonology and its concept of the phoneme as a bundle of distinctive features. Nikolas S. Troubetzkoy (1890–1938) gave this group its initial direction; Roman Jakobson (b. 1896) has popularized it and extended the scope of its inquiries.

**Prayer.** Prayer is communication, usually verbal, addressed by humans to superhuman beings. This communication may be undertaken by groups, by individuals in solitude, or indirectly by devices such as the Buddhist prayer wheel. Although prayer typically is verbal, it may also be silent or written. It is part of a continuum of forms of communication which includes nonlinguistic acts such as offering gifts of food, flowers, and so forth. Although there is no intrinsic limit to the substantive content of prayer, it often includes either a request or thanks for the fulfillment of a request. Both the content and the form of prayer, in comparison to the range of usual communications between humans, are highly stereotyped and limited.

See also Religion; Ritual

**Pre-Columbian Art.** The art created by indigenous Indians of the New World (North and South America) prior to the Spanish conquest is known as pre-Columbian. The term is used primarily for the art of the people of Mesoamerica (Mexico, Guatemala, Honduras), Central America, and parts of South America. These art forms are ex-

pressed in many media, but most are linked with ritual and religion.

**Stonework.** Both Mesoamerica and South America produced outstanding stone carving. Most of these carvings are found at ceremonial centers, complexes built specifically for religious purposes which usually contain pyramids, mounds, temples, and a number of other buildings. Buildings in such centers are often decorated by elaborate friezes, while some have finely carved facades. Ceremonial centers also contain freestanding stone art.

La Venta, in Mexico, is a ceremonial center built ca. 1200 BC. This site has colossal portrait heads, altars, and stellae (upright carved stones) as well as two mosaics made of serpentine in the form of jaguar masks. Stellae at La Venta and at later Mayan centers are covered with glyphs, some of which are calendrical in nature. Others have not yet been deciphered.

Jade was a precious stone in Mesoamerica analogous to gold in Europe. Many figurines and axes carved of jade are found buried both in ceremonial centers and in graves. Beads, pendants, and masks of jade and serpentine are also found. In Mexico, from Olmec times on, dignitaries are shown wearing round, finely ground and polished hematite mirrors, the use of which is unknown.

*Mixtec (Mexico) wooden shield, decorated with an intricate mosaic design in turquoise and shell.*

*Chibcha Indian human pottery head representing the goddess Bachue, with incised decoration on headdress (c. 1400 AD.)*

**Metallurgy.** Gold was seldom used in Mexico except by the Mixtecs, who made gold ornaments during the postclassic period (about AD 700–1100). The Cocle culture of Panama, and areas in South and Central America, used gold, silver, and copper for ornaments at least 200 years earlier. Peru used gold for ornate masks and other objects as early as 1000 BC. Bronze and iron were not worked in the New World.

**Murals.** Temple walls are decorated by brightly colored murals both in Mesoamerica and in Peru. Most of these are portrayals of gods. The Maya site of Bonampak has yielded outstanding murals of wars and conquests, chiefs and prisoners.

**Textiles.** Peru is distinguished by early weaving of highly decorative cotton cloth. Some is known from Huaca Prieta, 2500–1000 BC. Designs are both geometric and naturalistic—portraying birds, humans, and animals. Bodies wrapped in such textiles are found preserved in the necropolises of Peru.

**Pottery.** The art most prevalent and highly developed in the New World was the making of pottery. The potter's wheel was unknown, so pottery was made either by coiling or by use of the paddle and anvil technique.

The origin of New World pottery is still obscure; however, the earliest dates seem to be from Colombia and Ecuador, which have pottery dating back to 2800 BC. Each region in the New World had a distinctive form of decorating its pottery. Each period brought distinctive stylistic changes. Thus pottery can be used as cultural markers by archaeologists seeking to place a culture in time. During the classic period in Mexico (100 BC to AD 600) and also during the middle horizon in Peru (AD 600–1000), each locality specialized in highly distinctive pottery. Pottery was used for bowls, pitchers, jars, plates, graters, figurines, dishes. Decoration included incising, molding, clay slips, painting, and negative painting. Both in Nayarit (N Mexico) and in the Moche culture (N Peru) pottery jugs were made which portrayed everyday people in their usual activities. Houses were represented, as were people suffering from various diseases and afflictions. Other areas, such as Yucatan, Oaxaca, and the Gulf Coast, also produced highly stylized pottery easily identifiable wherever found.

Consult: Anton, Ferdinand, *The Art of Ancient Peru* (New York: Putnam, 1972); Anton, Ferdinand, *Ancient Mexican Art* (New York: Putnam, 1969); Bernal, Ignacio, *Ancient Mexico in Color* (New York: McGraw-Hill, 1968); Coe, Michael D., *America's First Civilization* (New York: American Heritage, 1968); Covarrubias, Miguel, *Indian Art of Mexico and Central America* (New York: Knopf, 1957); Keleman, Pal, *Art of the Americas* (New York: Crowell, 1969); Sawyer, Alan R., *Ancient Peruvian Ceramics* (New York: Metropolitan Museum of Art, 1966).

—*Evelyn Kessler, University of South Florida*

**Prehensility.** This term refers to the ability of the hand, foot, or tail to wrap around an object to grip it firmly. Prehensility of the hand is combined in most primates with the opposable thumb.

See also Primates, evolutionary features of

*New World monkeys, such as the Howler monkey pictured here, are the only monkeys that developed prehensile tails.*

**Prehistoric Archaeology.** Archaeology is the study of the past through the surviving material traces produced by human activities. Prehistoric archaeology is the use of this approach to investigate prehistory—the non-literate phases of human history. As a field of study, prehistoric archaeology, or prehistory, embraces more than 99 percent of human history; writing first appeared only about 5,000 years ago in the Near East and the first written records in most other parts of the world are considerably more recent. Prehistoric archaeology has created a proper chronological perspective for human history—a crucial contribution to human knowledge.

Prehistoric archaeology has its roots in the antiquarianism of the 16th, 17th, and 18th centuries. It emerged as a discipline only in the 19th century, after the acceptance of the concept of uniformitarian geology—that the earth had been shaped by continuous natural geological processes, not by catastrophes—set the stage for the recognition of the antiquity of humankind. The actual demonstration that human history was vastly longer than the 6,000 years envisioned by the traditional scriptural chronology was an achievement of prehistoric archaeology, which revealed many examples of human artifacts in association with the remains of extinct animals.

Prehistoric archaeology emphasizes the careful collection, recording, and analysis of data—through excavation, classification and description of artifacts, and particularly the chronological ordering of data.

Time is the most crucial dimension of prehistoric archaeology. Since it is concerned with periods for which historical dates are unavailable, prehistoric archaeology has been heavily oriented toward the measurement and classification of time—the construction of chronologies and the perfection and elaboration of dating techniques. In this sense, it is seen in Europe as basically a historical discipline. Chronology is not, however, an end in itself. It is a necessary tool for the reconstruction and interpretation of culture history.

In the United States, where prehistoric archaeology is considered part of anthropology, it has emphasized the concept of culture and the attempt to reconstruct complete ways of life—whole cultural systems. The material remains which constitute archaeological evidence—structures, tools, food remains—reflect technology and economy fairly directly. A wide variety of techniques have been developed for reconstructing prehistoric systems of subsistence and resource exploitation, settlement patterns, and trade and economic networks. Paleoecology—the investigation of the relationships between prehistoric cultures and their environments—has become extremely elaborate and sophisticated.

Other aspects of culture—social organization, for example—do not leave obvious material traces. Investigation of these aspects of prehistoric cultures requires a broad perspective and a recognition that cultures are integrated systems which are more than mechanisms by which human groups adapt to their physical environments. Recent research in prehistoric archaeology focusing on the patterning of the material traces of human activity as a reflection of culturally patterned behavior has clarified such prehistoric cultural features as patterns of descent, marriage, and residence.

Many of these trends are part of what is sometimes called the New Archaeology, along with an increased use of scientific method and greater attention to the investigation of cultural processes. Renewed interest in cultural evolution stresses the attempt to explain culture change, particularly through emphasis on problem-oriented research—the collection of archaeological data suitable for testing explicitly formulated hypotheses.

*See also* Archaeology; Prehistory
Consult: Deetz, James, *Invitation to Archaeology* (Garden City, N.Y.: Natural History Press, 1967); Fagan, Brian M., *In the Beginning: An Introduction to Archaeology*, 2nd ed. (Boston: Little, Brown, 1975); Hole, Frank, and Heizer, Robert F., *An Introduction to Prehistoric Archaeology*, 3rd ed. (New York: Holt, 1973).
—*John S. Henderson, Cornell University*

**Prehistoric Reconstruction.** See Archaeology; Dating, absolute; Dating, relative; Prehistoric archaeology

**Prehistory.** This term refers to the nonliterate periods of human history. In this sense it is often used in contrast with history in its narrow meaning. As a field of study, prehistory embraces more than 99 percent of all human history, since writing first appeared only about 5,000 years ago in the Near East and the first written records in most other parts of the world are still more recent.

Prehistory is commonly employed as a synonym for prehistoric archaeology: the reconstruction of the past from the surviving material traces produced by human activities. In this sense, prehistory is a branch of archaeology, which also includes the same approach to the reconstruction of historical cultures. In the United States, prehistory or prehistoric archaeology is considered part of anthropology and emphasizes the reconstruction of whole cultural systems, the interpretation of culture history, and the investigation of cultural processes—in addition to the more traditional archaeological goals of classifying and describing artifacts and placing them in a chronological context.

Occasionally, archaeology and prehistory are treated as separate disciplines—archaeology referring to the excavation, classification, and description of the material remains of human activities and prehistory referring to the reconstruction of preliterate human history primarily (but not exclusively) on the basis of such material traces. Few prehistorians, however, in practice actually restrict themselves to synthetic and interpretive activities.

*See also* Archaeology; Prehistoric archaeology
Consult: Fagan, Brian M., *In the Beginning: An Introduction to Archaeology*, 2nd ed. (Boston: Little, Brown, 1975); Hole, Frank, and Heizer, Robert F., *An Introduction to Prehistoric Archaeology*, 3rd ed. (New York: Holt, 1973); Rouse, Irving, *Introduction to Prehistory: A Systematic Approach* (New York: McGraw-Hill, 1972).
—*John S. Henderson, Cornell University*

**Preparation and Preservation of Food.** Foods are prepared and preserved through the use of relatively few techniques which are, however, modified in innumerable ways. Preparation and preservation should be examined with regard to each culture's patterns of food distribution and consumption. Geography and climate may determine availability of foods, but spiritual values and taboos have prescribed processes of slaughter, preservation, and preparation.

Foods are eaten raw or cooked. Cooking—defined as food preparation through action of heat—was employed by hunters,

*This young woman of the grain parcher caste in a North Indian village has just winnowed garbanzo beans. The beans had been parched in her family's oven, and then husked in the concave surface of the petrified stump beside her with one of the pestles in the foreground. The polychromatic basket on the right was woven in the village by a nonspecialist.*

fishers, and gatherers long before the rise of agriculture. Principal methods include boiling, simmering, and steaming with water as the main cooking medium; broiling, baking, and roasting with air as the chief medium; and frying and braising with fat as the medium.

Since foods in natural states remain edible only a short time, preservation has long been critical in satisfying biological needs. Hunters, fishers, and gatherers discovered that dry nuts and berries keep well and that meat and fish—if dried (nature's main means of preservation), salted, or frozen—can be stored for long periods without spoiling. Preindustrial agriculturists have preserved fruits and vegetables by drying, cereals by parching, milk as cheeses and fermented products, and fruit juices as ciders and wines. Increased urbanization and penetration into diverse climatic zones have both stimulated and necessitated refinement of preservation techniques.

*See also* Agriculture; Domestication of plants and animals; Food and food crops

Consult: Lévi-Strauss, Claude, *The Raw and the Cooked* (New York: Harper & Row, 1964); Simoons, Frederick, *Eat Not This Flesh: Food Avoidances in the Old World* (Madison: University of Wisconsin Press, 1961).

—Barbara L. K. Pillsbury, San Diego State University

## Preservation of Artifacts, Methods of.

Environment plays a major role in the conservation of artifacts. Changes in the temperature and relative humidity are particularly important. When objects are buried for a long time, they tend to come into equilibrium with their environment. When they are introduced to new conditions as a result of excavation, that equilibrium is upset and dimensional changes may be caused by the addition or withdrawal of moisture. These changes may cause the artifact to swell, shrink, or warp—which will result in severe damage. A good general rule is this: If perishable goods are recovered from an archaeological excavation, they should be kept in the same kind of environment until they reach a conservation laboratory to be treated by a specialist. This dictum holds for any organic material which is liable to deterioration.

Objects buried in salty ground are subject to additional deterioration from dissolved salts. When the object is dried and the salt crystallizes, the object is weakened and the surface may become disrupted. If salt-free water is available, the salts should be washed out before crystallization takes place. This problem can affect pottery as well as organic materials.

**Wood.** Wood normally decays under combined biological and chemical attack when buried in the ground, but it may be preserved under conditions of extreme dryness or extreme wetness. However, there is a great difference in the kind of preservation. Worked timbers from extremely dry Early Dynastic tombs of Egypt may still be sound and fresh whereas wood preserved in peat bogs may have suffered profound changes in its chemical composition and microstructure. When encountered by the field archaeologist, waterlogged wood should be lifted on a rigid support and kept thoroughly wet during its transport to the conservation laboratory. In the laboratory the object should be transferred to a water bath where it can be cleaned, examined, measured, and photographed. If the object is allowed to dry out without special treatment, the weakened cellular structure may collapse and the specimen may be damaged beyond recovery. The shape of the artifact may be maintained either by filling the pores with a liquid (such as alum) which will solidify and make contraction impossible or by fixing the tissue so rigidly that it will not collapse after the water is removed.

**Bone and ivory.** Bone and ivory are easily warped from exposure to heat or damp. They may be decomposed also by water, but before destruction is complete they will pass through a spongelike stage similar to waterlogged wood. Waterlogged bone is a much easier conservation problem, however, since it can be strengthened directly in the field by impregnation with polyvinyl acetate, especially when the bones are very wet and soft.

**Metals.** In nature, metals are rarely found in a free or uncombined state. Instead they are combined with nonmetallic minerals from which metals are won through smelting. Especially when buried in the ground for long periods of time, metals tend to revert to their natural state. Ordinarily, the more easily a metal is won from its ore, the more stable it is. Thus gold is a relatively stable metal whereas iron is relatively unstable. The rate of corrosion of buried metals is accentuated according to the degree of acidity in the soil, its porosity, and the presence of soluble salts—all of which promote the flow of electricity in the presence of water. Essentially, the corrosion of metals is an electrochemical phenomenon. Although metals corrode in the ground, they may eventually attain a state of equilibrium with their environment so that corrosion will stop. Upon being exposed to a new environment through excavation, corrosion may begin again as the artifacts adapt to new conditions. To stop deterioration, the microenvironment surrounding the piece must be stabilized by the removal of accumulated salts and possibly the addition of an inert coating which can be removed if necessary.

**Care in Storage.** In museums or private collections artifacts stand a good chance of being preserved even though they are liable to destruction by heat, light, moisture, mold, and insects. Providing the specimens are kept clean and dry, insects are the greatest danger. Moths may attack furs, feathers, felt hats, or woolen textiles which can be destroyed within a short period of time. A handful of mothballs, regularly checked and replenished, will go a long way to retard this kind of depredation.

Wood or basketry is liable to damage by noxious creatures such as post beetles which may eat their way through a collection. Particularly if the specimen is from a tropical clime, there may be a telltale sprinkle of fine sawdust beneath the object. The piece should be isolated in an airtight container in the presence of insect killers such as DDT or thymol crystals.

The most tragic event is the destruction of artifacts by the very means that were meant to preserve them. The use of varnish on baskets and bones has ruined many fine specimens.

See also Archaeology; Metalworking
Consult: Plenderleith, H. J., *The Conservation of Antiquities and Works of Art: Treatment, Repair, and Restoration* (London: Oxford University Press, 1956).
—Thomas P. Myers, University of Nebraska

**Prestige.** This term refers to the ability to command admiration and esteem from others in one's community. Prestige is closely linked to social status and is usually, though not always, determined by the individual's access to resources of power and wealth. These resources may be the result of personal achievement, or they may attach to one's ascriptive role in the community. Differences in prestige are usually accompanied by differences in opportunities, rights, and obligations. Prestige in the community may often serve as a social reward in circumstances in which other forms of reward are unavailable or inappropriate.

See also Status

**Priesthood.** In anthropology, the most basic distinction between religious specialists is that between shamans and priests. In contrast to a shaman, a priest is formally trained for the office and performs rituals on a regular (often full-time) basis for a congregation. A priest is a specialist whose office is often hereditary. The priest's authority derives not from personal charisma but from the institution of priesthood (i.e., the priestly office) and it often extends into the secular political sphere. The shaman type of religious specialist is found more often in simple, nonliterate, stateless societies; priests are commonly found in complex, literate societies.

See also Power; Religion; Shamanism

**Primary Institutions.** This term refers to those social structures which are most influential in determining the basic personality of a society's members. The emphasis is on institutions which directly impact on socialization practices and childhood experiences, since early learning experiences are assumed to be most influential in creating basic personality. Hence deciding which institutions are primary in a society is an empirically open question. In one society, the subsistence patterns may cause maternal deprivation or they may encourage intensive childcare behavior; in another society, the subsistence patterns may have little influence on socialization, so they would not be considered primary institutions.

See also Basic Personality; Secondary Institutions
Consult: Kardiner, A., *The Psychological Frontiers of Society* (New York: Columbia University Press, 1945).

**Primary Process Thought.** This style of thinking expresses deep-seated instinctual (id) wishes. In primary process thinking, reality is not distinguished from fantasy and imaginary things may substitute for objective relations and real rewards. Such means of drive reduction are only temporary and have little lasting satisfaction. Primary process thought is characteristic of infants and small children, adults in diminished or altered states of consciousness, and schizophrenics. Known mainly from the study of dreams, the primary process is nonlogical, does not stress cause and effect, and has some unique features of its own—such as *condensation,* the representation of more than one unconscious element in a single manifest form, and *displacement,* where, for example, an emotion is transferred from an improper or forbidden object to a more acceptable one symbolizing the former.

See also Altered states of consciousness; Dreams, psychological functions of; Drugs

**Primate City.** In urban hierarchies, primate cities are politically dominant central places and population centers which are usually many times larger than the next largest cities. They concentrate, like Paris, the society's wealth and functions.

See also Urban hierarchy

**Primates.** See Primates, behavior of; Primates, evolutionary features of.

*A female spider monkey with her clinging baby. Among infra-human primates it is common for young offspring to hold themselves onto adults, behavior of great survival value because it enables the mature individuals to use all four limbs for locomotion.*

**Primates, Behavior of.** Behavior refers to any action an animal performs; primate can refer to the order including humans, the apes, monkeys, and prosimians. In this discussion, however, primates will mean nonhuman primates and behavior will refer to certain classes of activity which have been of greatest interest to anthropologists. These activities might be labeled *maintenance* (nonsocial) *behavior* and *social behavior*, though these categories may overlap and interact.

Maintenance behaviors comprise feeding and foraging (including predation), locomotor and postural patterns, choice of sleeping locales, object use, and predator avoidance—i.e., behaviors by which the individual animal interacts with its ecology. Obviously, it is important to study maintenance behaviors in the environments to which they are adapted—i.e., field studies are required for a full understanding of the

behaviors and their anatomical correlates. Limb structure (bone form, muscle form, attachments) will vary with differing modes of locomotion (brachiation versus quadrupedalism versus bipedalism). The form of the dentition will vary with diet. To the extent that correspondences are found between anatomy and behavior, the behavior of extinct primates may be inferred from the anatomy of fossils and their probable ecology.

Social behavior is primarily concerned with interactions among individuals of the same species. Primates are highly social animals; most species show grouping patterns which involve animals of all ages and both sexes and persist the year round. Their sociability is expressed through complex communication systems involving visual, vocal, and tactile signals. Among these signals, social grooming is one of the most pervasive indicators of interanimal bonds throughout the order.

A wide variety of social organizations (grouping patterns) are known among primates (one-male groups, multimale troops, mated pairs). The type of organization a species exhibits is related to its ecology. The variation with habitat of organization type and other behaviors such as territoriality

(defense of the group's range from conspecifics) within species indicates that these behaviors are not genetically determined in a precise way. Correspondences between the ecology and social behavior of extant forms will help in the construction of models for social organization in extinct primates if their ecology can be reconstructed. As the ecology/behavior interaction becomes better understood, it becomes possible to determine the selective pressures influencing social behavior and discover how social behavior might influence selection.

Primate sociability appears related to the importance of learning in primate adaptation. Most of the behavior necessary for physical and social survival must be learned. Though the form of communicative signals may be unlearned, their proper use appears to be learned. Even appropriate sexual and maternal behaviors must be learned. Primates show a prolonged developmental period in which learning can occur, and this learning must take place in a social setting. The social group provides this setting—a protected environment in which the young animal can learn what it must to survive. This ability to learn allows primate species a range of flexibility in adapting to widely and rapidly varying conditions. In turn, the very complexity of the social group may have selected for individuals capable of integrating a wide variety of information in order to function within the group. Hence learning capabilities and complex social life are probably in a positive feedback relationship with one another.

See also Primates, evolutionary features of
Consult: Crook, J. H., "The Socio-ecology of Primates," in *Social Behavior in Birds and Mammals*, ed. J. H. Crook (London: Academic Press, 1970); Jolly, A., *The Evolution of Primate Behavior* (New York: Macmillan 1972); Tuttle, R. (ed.), *The Functional and Evolutionary Biology of Primates* (Chicago: Aldine, 1972).
—Leanne T. Nash, Arizona State University

**Primates, Evolutionary Features of.** Among mammals, the primates are unusual in that the living forms fall into grades reflecting the major evolutionary features of the order as revealed by the fossil record. The features of the primitive primates (prosimians) which distinguish them from their mammalian forerunners (insectivores) include (1) enhancement of grasping capabilities (retention of five digits, mobile digits

| Suborders | Infraorders | Subfamilies | Families | Examples |
|---|---|---|---|---|
| Prosimii | Lemuriforms | | | lemurs indris sifakas |
| | Lorisiforms | | | lorises bushbabies |
| | Tarsiiforms | | | tarsiers |
| Anthropoidea | Platyrrhini | | | New World monkeys |
| | Catarrhini | Cercopithecoidea | | Old World monkeys |
| | | Hominoidea | Hylobatidae | lesser apes |
| | | | Pongidae | great apes |
| | | | Hominidae | humans |

TAXONOMY OF THE ORDER OF PRIMATES

*The taxonomy, increasingly differentiated as we approach humans, shows phylogenetic (evolutionary) relationships as well as how categories are included in each other. Thus, for example, the great apes (chimpanzee, gorilla, orangutan) are our closest living relatives, with the lesser apes (gibbon, siamang) next. Humans and apes (Hominoidea) are more closely related to Old World monkeys (Cercopithecoidea) than to New World monkeys, which belong to a different infraorder, the Platyrrhini.*

with flat nails, and associated tactile pads rather than claws) and (2) an increased reliance on vision as the primary sense with a concomitant reduction in dependence on smell. Consequently, the snout becomes abbreviated, the portions of the brain involving vision increase, those involved with smell decrease, and color vision and binocular depth perception both develop. A recent theory (Cartmill 1972) suggests that these features relate to life in an arboreal habitat characterized by small-diameter branches and visually directed predation. These trends continue in the monkeys and apes, especially the increasing dominance of vision over smell.

Another set of interrelated features which can explain the success of primates involves increasingly efficient reproduction through more efficient placental mechanisms, an extended period of development and increased parental care (including social groups), and increased brain size and learning capabilities.

See also Primates, behavior of
Consult: Cartmill, M., "Arboreal Adaptations and the Origin of the Order Primates," in *The Functional and Evolutionary Biology of Primates,* ed. R. Tuttle (Chicago: Aldine, 1972); Napier, J. R., and Napier, P. H., *A Handbook of Living Primates* (New York: Academic Press, 1967).
—*Leanne T. Nash, Arizona State University*

**Primitive Art.** *See* Art, primitive; Expressive systems.

**Primitive Astronomy.** *See* Astronomy, primitive.

**Primitive Capitalism.** In its most general sense, capitalism is an economic system based on the class ownership of strategic resources. Such a system is a relatively common one in the modern world, and some anthropologists have sought to apply the concept of capitalism to certain primitive societies as well. Most anthropologists, however, take the view that this analogy is an invalid one: although there are some small-scale societies in which individuals attempt to accumulate surplus wealth, the similarity with capitalism is essentially superficial. So-called primitive capitalism generally lacks many of the distinguishing features of true capitalism—notably a highly rationalized system of accounting, a systematic reinvestment of profits into the enterprise, a work ethic which depreciates instant gratification, and an organized exploitation of the labor of one group by another group that dominates access to capital or other scarce resources, as well as the distributive system, resulting in a highly stratified class-divided society.

*See also* Capitalism; Economic systems; Exchange; Primitive communism

**Primitive Communism.** In Marxian evolutionary typologies, primitive communism refers to the stage in social evolution which preceded the development of class societies. Primitive communism is presumed to have been marked by a rough social equality and an absence of private property in land and other strategic resources. The term is not used by most anthropologists—and such societies, usually hunting and gathering societies, are referred to as egalitarian.

*See also* Communism; Economic systems; Primitive capitalism

**Primitive Culture.** *See* Primitive peoples.

**Primitive Economic System.** *See* Economic systems, primitive.

**Primitive Medicine.** *See* Medicine, primitive.

**Primitive Mentality.** The idea that "primitive" peoples think in a way that is qualitatively different from the thought processes of "advanced" peoples was common in the anthropology of the late 19th and even the early 20th centuries. The most sophisticated exposition of this view was that of Lucien Lévy-Bruhl, as expressed in his *Primitive Mentality* (1923).

Lévy-Bruhl contended that primitive peoples use a prelogical thought process; he held that the form, style, and content of their thought differs from our own in kind and not simply in degree. Primitives, he argued, think in terms of mystical collective representations, and their reasoning is distorted by their belief in nonempirical forces.

Under criticism from Émile Durkheim, Bronislaw Malinowski, and E. Evans-Pritchard, Lévy-Bruhl later recanted this position. Claude Lévi-Strauss and other modern theorists take the view that primitive peoples are endowed with the same capacity for logical and abstract thought as modern peoples, although the environment may pose different intellectual demands on each.

*See also* Culture and personality; Lévi-Strauss, Claude; Lévy-Bruhl, Lucien

*—Ino Rossi, St. John's University*

**Primitive Mind.** *See* Mind; Primitive mentality.

**Primitive Peoples.** Anthropologists presumably study "primitive peoples," yet there is considerable controversy over use of the term. The term *savages,* long since discarded by anthropologists, was once used to refer to people who were not considered civilized. The latter term, deriving from the Latin *civitas* (city-state), refers to cultural traits associated with urban life. If urban life is to be the criterion for civilization, then there were no civilized people in the world before about 3000 BC.

Primitive peoples came to replace savages in the parlance of anthropologists who felt the need for a generic term to refer to all those cultures that fall beyond the scope of civilization, however defined. The term was intended to denote cultures that lacked domesticated plants and animals; that lived by hunting, fishing, and gathering; that had no permanent dwellings; and that lacked writing, weaving, pottery, and similar technological capabilities.

Even if scientific use of the term in this sense is justified, many anthropologists prefer not to use the term *primitive* at all, since in its popular usage it has derogatory connotations. And since the term implies earliest and original (coming as it does from the Latin *primitivus,* meaning earliest or oldest), the use of *primitive* to denote contemporary peoples carries the unfortunate connotation that these peoples accurately represent the earliest stages of cultural development—which anthropologists know is not the case. Anthropologists have not agreed on a substitute term for *primitive peoples,* although *nonliterate peoples* is often encountered today.

Consult: Diamond, Stanley, *In Search of the Primitive* (New Brunswick, N.J.: Transaction Books, 1974).

*—Edward C. Green, Catholic University*

**Primitive Society.** *See* Primitive peoples; Society.

**Primitive Thinking.** *See* Primary process thought.

**Probability, Social Theory and.** Implicitly or explicitly, the notion of probability has always been integral to social theory. Exceptions to predictive generalizations are especially numerous in the social sciences, and they necessitate some way of reckoning the likelihood of predicted events under uncertainty or under a complex set of contingencies. Informally, such probabilities are often expressed in intuitive terms: "If A happens, then B very likely will follow." More formally, attempts have been made to apply mathematical probability to the construction of social theory.

Such attempts can be grouped in two classes: (1) the application of statistics to tests of hypotheses in probability samples and (2) the modeling of sociocultural processes by probability processes. The first set of approaches, dating from the pioneering work of Edward Tylor and Sir Francis Galton, is amply discussed in this encyclopedia. The second group of approaches has been used more rarely in anthropology.

Typical of the latter approaches are attempts to apply *game theory* to the understanding of choice behavior (Davenport 1960; Buchler and Nutini 1969). As another example, attempts have been made (though seldom by anthropologists) to apply *Markov processes* to the understanding of social change. In these examples and others, the common elements are (1) the hypothesis that a given probability process will predict real social outcomes; (2) the input of observational data to the mathematical model; and (3) a demonstration of goodness of fit.

*See also* Game theory; Markov chain; Statistical methods

Consult: Buchler, I. R., and Nutini, H. (eds.), *Game Theory in the Behavioral Sciences* (Pittsburgh: University of Pittsburgh Press, 1969); Coleman, James, *Introduction to Mathematical Sociology* (Glencoe, Ill.: Free Press, 1964); Davenport, William, "Jamaican Fishing: A Game Theory Analysis," New Haven: *Yale University Publication in Anthropology* 59:3–11, 1960; Kemeny, J., and Snell, L., *Mathematical Models in the Social Sciences* (Boston: Ginn, 1962).

*—Edwin E. Erickson, University of Virginia*

**Probability, Statistical.** *See* Statistical methods.

**Procreation, Beliefs Regarding.** Nearly all cultures recognize the relationship between sexual intercourse and procreation. In many cultures, however, two or more systems of explanation of procreation may exist simultaneously.

All societies have folktales about procreation which are told to children; our own baby-bringing stork is but one of many such tales in our own culture. Many societies further have religious beliefs which account for the birth of children in ways unrelated to genital sexual intercourse; the spirits of the ancestors, for example, may be presumed to be responsible. Finally, many societies also have, in addition to these folk explanations, a system of explanation that we believe to be scientifically correct.

A scientific system of explanation, however, says nothing about the *meaning* of life and reproduction. Thus it is not in direct competition with the other two systems, which do provide such meaning. For this reason all systems can, and frequently do, coexist.

See also Contraception and abortion; Infanticide; Myth

—Frank A. Salamone, St John's University

**Production, Methods of.** See Economics and subsistence; Technology; Technology and subsistence; Tools and evolution.

**Profane.** What is profane is ordinary, or not sacred. According to Émile Durkheim, all religions divide the universe into two opposed realms, sacred and profane, and establish rules distinguishing and protecting the former from the latter.

See also Durkheim, Émile; Religion; Sacred

**Progress and Cultural Evolution.** See Cultural evolution.

**Projection.** In Freudian psychology, projection is the act of attributing to some other person an emotion or attitude that is in reality one's own but which one is reluctant to recognize as such.

See also Defense mechanisms; Freud, Sigmund; Projective tests

**Projective Tests.** These tests are psychological devices used to obtain insights about the nature and functioning of a personality. Sigmund Freud first defined projection as one of several intrapsychic defensive mechanisms, but he later recognized that projection is a much more widespread psychological process and that more was involved than an effort to defend the self against awareness of unacceptable feelings and impulses.

Projection in everyday life consists of an actual misperception and a misbelief: an impulse which is subjective and internal is attributed to an external source—another person or thing. In the narrower sense of a defensive maneuver, projection in real life involves (1) an actual misperception, (2) a genuine conviction that an internal tendency is externally caused, (3) a tendency which is an important part of the subject's personality, and (4) a tendency which is unacceptable to the self, shameful, or guilt-producing. All four of these characteristics are not always present when a subject is asked to respond to a Rorschach inkblot, to

draw a person, or to engage in a role-playing episode.

The reason why they may not be present is that psychological testing situations are not real life: they involve a kind of stylized make believe. Both Subject and Analyst recognize this. The subject is not dealing with a normal, everyday situation. Instead she or he is asked to cooperate in a situation where the task is to reveal something of the inner self, consciously or otherwise. The subject is asked to respond imaginatively, to produce revealing fantasies, to express the inner self. Once the subject has produced creative fantasies at some length—say powerfully negative images about authority figures or fantasies indicating a sense of inadequacy in peer relations—the analyst's critical task is to determine which aspects of the responses actually reveal important attributes of the subject's personality.

Projective tests came into use by anthropologists in the 1930s as part of the surge of interest in cross-cultural studies of personality. They achieved much popularity for a time because of the conviction that the tests were free of cultural biases and because they could be easily used with little training or experience. Unfortunately, some did not recognize that achieving rich, valid, and substantial results with projective tests depended a great deal on the clinical skills, experience, sophistication, and training of the analyst.

For this reason a considerable amount of cross-cultural use of projective tests involved what clinical psychologists call cookbook interpretations. That is, the test protocols (the subject's responses) were categorized and scored, and the scores were interpreted by reading out results from a test handbook. This defect was particularly evident in studies using such concepts as modal personality: the protocols from a sample of individuals were lumped together in a single statistical, modal profile which supposedly expressed what was most typical of the group studied. This approach involves the least effective use of this type of psychodiagnostic test, which is most valid when employed as part of an in-depth study of an individual in combination with other approaches such as life histories, extensive interviewing, and observations.

The most extensively used projective tests have been the Rorschach inkblot, the Thematic Apperception Test, the Draw-a-

Person Test, the house-tree-person test, word association, and sentence completion. Also used are doll play, painting, and role playing.

Although anthropologists no longer use projective testing as often as in the 1950s, sophistication in the choice and application of tests has grown, as have skill and caution in their interpretation. There is still much promise in their application.

See also Draw-A-Person Test; Rorschach test; Thematic Apperception Test

Consult: Anderson, H. H., and Anderson, G. L., An Introduction to Projective Testing (Englewood Cliffs, N.J.: Prentice-Hall, 1951); Barnouw, V., Culture and Personality (Homewood, Ill.: Dorsey Press, 1973); Lindzey, G., Projective Techniques and Cross-Cultural Research (New York: Irvington, 1961).

—James Clifton, University of Wisconsin, Green Bay

**Property.** In most legal, social, and scientific usages, the term property refers to rights of ownership or possession of something. In the broadest sense, it means any right or interest which has value and may be considered as a source of wealth. In many usages rights are conceived as exclusive to the rightholder and include his or her right to enjoy, dispose of, or alienate the property at will. Thus property has a dual aspect—things and some person's rights to the things. Things to which no rights are attached are not property. In our society they are difficult to find; indeed, even airspace has become marketable property.

However, property rights are never untrammeled—even in societies, like ours, which most emphasize private or personal exclusionary rights to, and alienability of, property. Rights are always restricted in some degree and are often hedged about by specific obligations and duties whose nonobservance may generate legal claims, litigation, and redress. In Texas law, property acquired by married couples is joint and cannot be alienated by one spouse alone. Moreover, family residence, legally designated "the homestead," cannot be sold for or taken in payment of debt—a law created during frontier times to protect mothers and children from errant husbands' gambling debts. Until recently, a Texas wife could not own business property without her husband's legal consent and signature.

PROTESTANT ETHIC, CAPITALISM AND

Everywhere, inheritance laws limit property rights both for the devisor and the heirs, especially in cases of estates in trust wherein the decedent's will may establish restricted forms of access (rights) and also duties and obligations. Another restriction concerns societal definitions of the public interest as a restriction on private property (e.g., "national seashores," the national trust which preserves historical monuments for public enjoyment), nationalized utilities, and nationalized basic resource of production of any sort (as in socialist countries). Restrictions, by limiting exclusiveness of rights, specifying duties and obligations, and defining the scope of alienability, sometimes virtually eliminate private rights to property altogether. Finally, most societies seem to consider a person's life a right—in this case inalienable.

Exclusionary rights in property are one of the major bases of differential power in society, especially where they give certain persons control over the society's strategic resources and basic means of production. Since such rights are neither genetic nor inherent in nature, social means for maintaining such unequal distributions develop—e.g., coercion by force or by law and ideological suasion, both closely linked with the state.

In primitive societies, especially where strategic resources and means of production are concerned, corporate groups, rather than individuals, usually hold property. Even then "ownership" is often restricted by still wider social obligations to other corporate groups. In effect, the entire local, or even tribal, population has access to property because everyone has rights in it. In this sense, the property is communal. Further, rights in the product of property are usually widely distributed in primitive societies—the foundation of their relative egalitarianism and relative absence of social conflict concerning property.

See also Capitalism; Communism; Economic anthropology; Economic systems; Land tenure; Socialism

—Anthony Leeds, Boston University

**Propliopithecus.** A fossil ape found (1908) in the Egyptian Fayum, probably dating from the Oligocene, with some gibbonoid features but having stronger overall affinities with the dryopithecines.

**Prosimians.** Prosimians, one of the two suborders of primates, represent the earliest grade of primate evolution. They originated from the Insectivora in the Paleocene period, 70 to 58 million years ago. Primate paleontologists are unsure about what kind of prosimian or prosimians gave rise to the higher primates or anthropoids. The suborder today includes four infraorders, the Tupaiiformes or tree shrews, the Tarsieriformes or tarsiers, the Lemuriformes or lemurs, and the Lorisiformes or lorises. Some taxonomists, however, consider the tree shrews to be insectivores, not primates. Although the suborder's distribution is somewhat limited today, the fossil record indicates a more widespread geographic distribution in the Paleocene.

See also Primates, evolutionary features of

**Prostitution.** This word commonly refers to women's (less frequently, men's) use of their bodies as instruments for earning money by granting sexual access to paying customers. Researchers disagree basically on what leads women into prostitution—hypotheses range from psychological to economic reasons. Rare actual field observations on prostitution compound the difficulty. In a given society, widely varying pay-for-intercourse exchanges occur, including convenience and arranged marriages; moreover, attitudes toward paid intercourse differ vastly, ranging from condemnation (as in the United States) to acceptance as a wholesome matter of course. In short, the concept of prostitution does not illuminate social science analysis of sexual behavior.

**Protective Associations.** In a very general sense, protective associations refer to reactions by groups of varying size and composition to changes they perceive in the values and norms of their society. These collective responses may involve violence or nonviolence. They may be unsuccessful in voicing their consternation, or they may evolve highly organized methods for protecting the values, norms, and life-styles they sense are threatened. Numerous and diverse examples exist throughout the world and history—some of the more obvious are the Ku Klux Klan, the Black Panthers, the John Birch Society, the Minutemen, many Chinese secret societies, and several phenomena classified under the rubric of revitalization movements.

The term *protective association* is increasingly being used in a more restricted sense. Their origins suggest that they are similar to the groups cited above—essentially inward-looking, seeking to protect a valued life-style—and that behavior attendant upon such goals placed them at odds with custom or written rules. Thus they have had a varying legal status in society. Kinship ties, actual or fictive, have been an important element in their structure and organization in the past, and these elements remain today. Conformity is induced through the idiom of kinship; the notion of brotherhood is salient. The rights and obligations attendant upon brotherhood are binding, and penalties for disobedience are severe. Mutual aid is extended to brothers and their families. Outsiders are viewed with suspicion or are to be exploited. It is the tactics and attitudes engendered by these ideas that make them distinct. They survive, even prosper, in society by using tactics imbued with negative, unethical, criminal connotations. Homicide, extortion, kidnapping, bribery—these are some of the acts associated with protective associations. Commonly construed as criminal and indicative of the presence of organized crime, such behavior is perceived by participants as a necessary, even legitimate, means to protect traditions in a changing socioeconomic milieu. Examples of these groups are the Cosa Nostra of the United States and varieties of dacoit (robber) gangs of India.

See also Mafia; Nativistic movements; Revitalization movements

Consult: Hobsbawm, Eric, *Primitive Rebels: Studies in Archaic Forms of Social Movement in the 19th and 20th Centuries* (New York: Norton, 1959); Hobsbawm, Eric, *Bandits* (New York: Delacorte Press, 1969).

—*Paul C. Winther, Eastern Kentucky University*

**Protestant Ethic, Capitalism and.** This phrase refers to a set of values, originally associated with the rise and spread of Protestantism in Europe, which celebrate the virtues of self-discipline, hard work, initiative, acquisitiveness, and thrift. It has been hypothesized, principally by the German sociologist Max Weber, that these religiously inspired values (as embodied particularly in the Calvinism of the 17th century) created a favorable moral environment for the rise of European and American capitalism. The Calvinist doctrine of predestination maintained that only God's small group of elect could gain salvation and that those not so chosen were damned. The faithful also believed that the state of grace was manifested in personal traits such as systematic self-control, diligence, and avoidance of luxury and worldly vice. The effect of these beliefs was to impel Calvinists to scrutinize their personal behavior continually for signs of grace. Those who were to be saved were persons who served God by means of earnest dedication to a worldly occupation or calling, since work was considered the primary ascetic discipline. These values encouraged dedication to hard work, reinvestment of capital, and thrift—characteristics which promoted successful entrepreneurial activity.

See also Religion; Weber, Max
Consult: Weber, Max, The Protestant Ethic and the Spirit of Capitalism (New York: Scribners, 1958).
—Richard A. Barrett, University of New Mexico

## Proxemics.
Proxemics is the study of the cultural meaning of space. Until recently the cultural use of space by people was

*People communicate nonverbally using gestures (kinesics) and the manipulation of space (proxemics). Which of these western French peasant women is dominating the discussion?*

taken for granted. The systematic investigation of the meanings given to space by social groups, pioneered by Edward T. Hall and others, has led to a growing body of knowledge of theoretical and practical significance. The communicative aspects of the cultural patterning of space have been given most attention. Efforts toward comparative studies are being made as the methodology of proxemic studies becomes increasingly sophisticated.

See also Communication, nonverbal; Hall, Edward T.; Pattern, culture

## Psychic Unity of Human Species.
See Archetype; Collective unconscious; Culture and personality; Jung, Carl G.; Lévi-Strauss, Claude.

## Psychoanalysis.
See Freud, Sigmund.

## Psychoanalytic School of Psychology.
This psychological tradition was founded by Sigmund Freud (1856–1939) and subsequently modified by a number of writers whose main ideas derive from Freud's work.

Freud believed that most human behavior is unconsciously motivated and that neuroses have their origins in early childhood memories or wishes that have subsequently been repressed. He placed particular emphasis on the sexual drive, which he believed is present even in infancy and which, because it is so malleable, imperious, and subject to social regulation, becomes the source of many subsequent psychological disorders. It is fundamental to Freudian theory that the workings of the unconscious mind can be made manifest by various methods, including hypnosis, free association, prolonged personal interviews, and the analysis of dreams. Psychoanalysis consists of this process of seeking out the unconscious origins of behavior.

Subsequent writers have often accepted some of Freud's basic postulates, such as the notion of psychic determinism or the concept of psychological development as an arena of conflict between the basic biological impulses of the individual and the prohibitions and demands of society. But many neo-Freudians have rejected important elements in the original theory, notably the preeminent role assigned to sexuality. Alfred Adler, for example, assigned more

importance to a hypothesized drive to dominate, while Erik Erikson believes that many neuroses stem from a crisis of identity rather than from sexual repression.

The psychoanalytic school still has many practitioners and adherents, but it remains vulnerable to the charge that most of its theories are pure speculation, unverified or unverifiable by scientific investigation.

See also Culture and personality; Defense mechanisms; Ego; Erikson, Erik; Id; Repression; Superego
Consult: Hall, Calvin S., A Primer of Freudian Psychology (New York: New American Library, 1954).
—Ian Robertson, Cambridge University

## Psychological Anthropology.
See Culture and personality.

## Psychosexual Stages of Development.
The concept of psychosexual stages of development was developed by Sigmund Freud as he evolved the theoretical structure of psychoanalysis. Freud distinguished four major stages: oral, anal, Oedipal, and genital. A fifth possible stage was the interim period between the Oedipal and genital which he called "latency." Freud's conception was that human beings develop in a fixed progression determined in significant part biologically, including degrees of awareness—either conscious or unconscious—of their own biological maturation. All this takes place in a sociocultural and psychological environment which determines the content and form taken at each stage of the fixed progression.

The earliest focal interests of the neonate continue as primary interests for some time. The significant ones remain for life and are oral: eating, sucking, mouthing, teething, spitting—all giving pleasure. Older babies and small children discover defecation as satisfaction and become concerned with the whole process of anality: retention, evacuation, release, pleasure.

During the next two or three years, until about six years of age, the child begins to develop perceptions of male/female role differentiation through affective relations with others who are role models. In Western culture, mothers and fathers purportedly provide the prevailing behavioral paradigms, although it is not socioculturally necessary that they do so—uncles, aunts, teachers, and nannies could serve as models, too. The parental paradigm familiar to Freud led him to designate this affective-cognitive development the Oedipus complex. After the initial structural and affective aspects of male and female roles are learned, children supposedly enter a period of latency in which further development of sexual role recognition stagnates.

At puberty, the child's maturation re-initiates the sexual role development in the context of biological sexuality—and the person enters the genital stage with its attendant pleasure. In the fully developed adult, all four stages persist, with some dominance of the genital stage over the others. (The importance of this, for Freud, is connected with his idea of sublimation of sexual energy into all forms of activity, especially creativity.) If a person is traumatized at some point in his or her development, he or she may "fixate" at an earlier stage and never mature properly, hence displaying neuroses of various sorts (e.g., obsessions, fixations).

One need not be committed to Freud's specific set of stages to see the fundamental importance of his argument—to appreciate that for all human beings there is a progressive, transformational, cumulative development that is rooted in human biology and *biological* maturation. It is interesting to note, in passing, that in rejecting the universality of the *specific* (parental) Oedipal paradigm, one cannot reject the paradigmatic proposition Freud intended by it—enculturation of all children in all societies into male/female roles.

Freud's view is a complex understanding of structures (personalities) in historical transformation—a genetic view based on biological givens interacting with environmental givens and accidents to create a developmental psychic system which reflects its own history. It is worth noting that Freud's conception of development is intrinsically attached to the conception of pleasure and trauma—notions again rooted in the biology of the organism.

See also Culture and personality; Freud, Sigmund; Oedipus complex

Consult: Freud, Sigmund, "Three Essays on the Theory of Sexuality," in *The Standard Edition of the Complete Psychological Works of Sigmund Freud,* vol. 7 (London Hogarth, 1953); Freud, Sigmund, *New Introductory Lectures on Psychoanalysis* (New York: Norton, 1965).
—Anthony Leeds, Boston University

**Psychosis.** This term refers to a major, inclusive category of mental disorders which are so damaging and debilitating that they interfere severely with the usual work and activities of a person's life. Two broad categories of psychoses are identified by Western psychiatrists: those involving organic brain syndromes (e.g., senile dementia) and functional disorders without organic brain impairment (e.g., melancholia). A diagnosis of psychosis is not made unless the mental functioning of the individual is so grossly impaired that he or she cannot cope with the presses of everyday life. This may involve total distortion of the capacity to distinguish reality from private fantasy (hallucinations and delusions), sharp and profound alterations of mood which impair appropriate social behavior, or severe defects of memory and language. Cross-culturally, a number of psychoses have been distinguished which are quite different from those known to the Western world, while others such as schizophrenia may have radically different forms, expressions, and prognosis. *Windigo* (a North American Indian obsessive craving for human flesh) and *latah* (compulsive imitating and sexual delusions in the Philippines and Indonesia) are two of the psychoses identified in other cultures.

See also Culture and personality; Deviance; Mental illness and culture; Neurosis; Normality

**Puberty Rites.** A kind of *rite de passage,* these rituals of transition mark a change in the social identity of a person or group from child to adult. Girls' puberty rites generally coincide with the first menses, boys' with some evidence of the achievement of physiological (and perhaps social) maturity. These rituals are known worldwide, but they tend to decline in importance and intensity as societies become more complex. Indeed, in some highly developed and complex societies such as the United States, well-marked intensive puberty rites are nearly absent.

Native American puberty rites for boys generally took the form of an individual vision quest, although small groups of boys were sometimes sent off to fast and seek contact with a spirit helper. In some tribes, there were formal, collective initiation rituals marking the transition to adult status. For girls, group puberty rites might involve elaborate and lengthy public ceremonies;

although in other tribes an individual girl would—at first menstruation—go into temporary seclusion under the supervision of an older woman who would instruct her.

See also Enculturation; Rites of passage; Ritual

**Public Opinion.** This term refers to the attitude of members of a social aggregate toward a particular issue at a particular time. The sources of influence on public opinion are difficult to isolate, but public opinion itself may be assessed through such methods as opinion polls, elections, referenda, plebiscites, and statements of group consensus at meetings.

See also Gossip; Sanctions

**Punishment.** See Reinforcement; Sanctions.

**Qalat Jarmo.** This early village farming site is located in the Zagros Mountains of Iraqi Kurdistan. It was excavated by R. Braidwood between 1948 and 1955 and typifies his "era of primary village farming efficiency," defined by evidence for an economy in which domesticated plants and animals permit the establishment of permanent villages. The site consists of a low (7 meters) tell 90 × 140 meters in area (an artificially created stratified hill built up by successive periods of occupation). For the most part, Jarmo has no pottery. Architecture consists of clusters of multiroomed, rectilineal, *tauf* buildings scattered around courtyards. The estimated population is about 150 and the estimated duration of occupation 250+ years. The practice of long-distance trade is evident from the high incidence (about 40 percent) of obsidian, whose probable source areas are Lakes Van and Aksaray (250 and 650 miles N and NW of the site, respectively). Domesticated grains include emmer and einkorn wheat and two-row barley; the goat and possibly the pig are associated with remains of wild-harvested plants (pistachio, acorns) and dead game animals (boar, gazelle, sheep). This suggests a mixed economy. The dating is controversial (3300–9300 BC), with the best date for the (aceramic) primary village farming phase placed at 6750 BC.

See also Domestication of plants and animals; Neolithic

Consult: Singh, P., *Neolithic Cultures of Western Asia* (New York: Seminar Press, 1974).

**Quadrupedal Locomotion.** *See* Locomotion, primate evolutionary trends of.

**Quaternary Period.** *See* Glaciations.

**Quételet, Lambert Adolphe Jacques** (1796–1873). Belgian astronomer, meteorologist, and statistician who developed the concept of the *homme moyen* ("average man"), coined the term *social physics,* and developed the Gaussian curve.

**Quine, Willard van Orman** (b. 1908). Professor of philosophy at Harvard whose major research contributions are in logic, set theory, semantics, and ontology.

**Race.** This folk category of the English language refers to discrete groups of human beings who are categorically separated from one another on the basis of arbitrarily selected *phenotypic* traits. Historically, three "diagnostic" traits have been used to divide the human species into races: skin color, hair form, and various combinations of nose, face, and lip shapes.

Increasingly, physical anthropologists and biologists are reassessing the concept of race and finding it of no scientific use whatever. There are both empirical and theoretical reasons for this rejection of the concept. Empirically, as research on population *genotypes* accumulates, it is becoming increasingly clear that the growing number of known gene frequencies do not cluster together into polar groupings: although any two or three specific genes might have high correlations of cooccurrence, other gene distributions will fall into widely varying patterns. Thus as we learn more and more about human gene distributions, it becomes less and less possible to divide the species into discrete, genetically defined groups (races).

On the theoretical level the concept of race raises problems because it treats as "explained" questions that are not. Moreover, it causes us to neglect problems that need solving and also obfuscates the distinction between genotype and phenotype. Finally, it treats as static ("pure races") the biological aspects of human groups which evolutionary theory tells us must be viewed dynamically. Even when applied by "experts," the notion of race results in wildly differing categorizations of the "races of the human species."

Current research on population genetics focuses increasingly on the *worldwide distributions of specific genes* (rather than on the genetic compositions of breeding populations); the intent is to account for such genetic clines by showing the *adaptive function* a specific gene plays in relationship to specific environmental stresses. This approach allows for a dynamic, evolutionary perspective.

*See also* Adaptation, biological; Cline; Evolution, genetic mechanisms of; Gene distributions; Genotype; Racial classification; Racism; Scientific racism

Consult: Montagu, Ashley (ed.), *The Concept of Race* (New York: Macmillan, 1964).

—*David E. Hunter, Southern Connecticut State College*

**Race and Intelligence.** *See* Intelligence; Intelligence quotient; Jensen, Arthur; Race; Racism; Scientific racism.

**Races.** *See* Gene distributions.

**Racial Classification.** Racial taxonomy, or racial classification, is the attempt to place the various populations of the world into an organized set of categories. Racial classifications have occupied anthropologists since the days of Johannes Blumenbach, the father of physical anthropology. But in spite of the great amount of time and effort in this area, scientists still cannot agree on any set number of human races. In fact, the various schemes of classification show a range from three to over two hundred races.

All human beings today belong to a single polytypic species, *Homo sapiens,* that occupies a very large geographical area. Any species with such an extended range should be expected to subdivide into groups called races. The size of human racial groups varies from large geographical races such as the African race to small breeding isolates such as the Pitcairn Islanders. Systems of racial taxonomy must take into account these different levels of population integration.

Any system of racial classification has a number of built-in weaknesses. All individuals or groups do not neatly fit into definite racial categories. Often the differences between individuals within a race or within a population are greater than the average differences between groups defined as races or breeding populations.

Actually much of human variation grades from one population to another, so racial classifications tend to oversimplify the true patterns of human variation. The so-called racial traits are a matter of proportion—that is, the genes are the same in all populations but occur in different frequencies from one population to another. Most racial classifications are based on a statistically abstracted type that obscures the actual range of human variability.

Other problems in racial classification relate to the nature of the inheritance and expression of genes. First, most traits are controlled by multiple genes and are therefore difficult to study. Second, most biological traits are the result of a complex interaction of heredity and environment, thus making it hard to unscramble the contributions of each for purposes of a racial (genetic) analysis. Even the existence of similarities among groups does not necessarily indicate a common ancestry, since it could be a result of evolutionary convergences due to similar environmental pressures.

All these problems related to classification—plus the fact that biologically defined races are of virtually no biological significance today—have led many authorities to question the value of racial classification. This school of thought, associated with C. Loring Brace, Frank Livingstone, and others, suggests that a nonracial or clinal approach to human variation should replace the old racial approaches. Proponents of this view believe that the study of clines—that is, the frequencies of specific genes in different environments—will allow us to relate human variation to selective factors that cross population boundaries and will therefore lead to a better understanding of the processes of human evolution.

*See also* Gene distributions; Race

Consult: Alland, A., *Human Diversity* (New York: Columbia University Press, 1971); Brace, C. L., "A Non-Racial Approach Towards the Understanding of Human Diversity," in *Man in Evolutionary Perspective,* ed. C. L. Brace and J. F. Metress (New York: Wiley, 1964); Coon, C., *The Living Races of Man* (New York: Knopf, 1965); Garn, S., *Human Races* (Springfield, Ill.: Charles C Thomas, 1969); Livingstone, F., "On the Nonexistence of Human

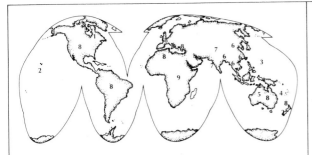

| Type of race: | **Local**—Real breeding populations, significant evolutionary units |
|---|---|

**Races** — **Locations**

1. Amerindian — Alaska to Labrador to tip of South America
2. Polynesian — Pacific islands from Hawaii to Easter Island to New Zealand
3. Micronesian — Small islands east of Japan
4. Melanesian — New Guinea, New Britain, and Solomon Islands
5. Australian — Australia
6. Asiatic — Main continent of Asia, Japan, Taiwan, Philippines Indonesia, Sumatra, Borneo, Java
7. Indian — Himalaya Mountains to Indian Ocean
8. European — Rapidly expanding since 1500, extending from North Africa and Western Asia to New World, Europe, Australia, New Zealand, etc.
9. African — Sub-Saharan Africa

| Type of race: | **Geographical**—Collections of breeding populations, inhabiting geographically defined areas. |
|---|---|

**Races** — **Locations**

1. Northwest European — Scandinavia, North Germany, low countries, British Isles, and their descendants abroad
2. Northeast European — Russia, Poland, Lithuania, Estonia, and their descendants abroad
3. Alpine — Alps and Balkan Mountains
4. Mediterranean — North Africa, Levant, Turkey, Greece and westward through Spain, and their descendants abroad
5. Iranian — Asiatic Turkey through Iran and India
6. East African — East Africa to Sudan
7. Sudanese — North Sudan
8. Forest African — West Africa, Congo
9. Bantu — Southeast Africa
10. Turkic — Central Asia
11. Tibetan — Sikkim, Tibet, Central Mongolia
12. North Chinese — Northern China
13. Extreme Mongoloid — Siberia, Mongolia, to Kamchatka Peninsula
14. Southeast Asiatic — Expanding group in Southwest Asia
15. Hindu — India subcontinent
16. Dravidian — Southern India to Sri Lanka
17. North American Amerindian — Canada and United States
18. Central American Amerindian — Southwestern U.S. to Bolivia
19. South American Amerindian — Peru, Chile, Brazil, etc.
20. Fuegian — Southern end of South America
21. Lapp — Tundra and swamps of west Russia and Northern Scandinavia
22. Pacific "Negrito" — Australia to Philippines
23. African Pygmy — Congo rain forest
24. Eskimo — Circumpolar area
25. Ainu — Yezo Island of Northern Japan
26. Murrayian Australian — Central Australia
27. Carpenterian Australian — Northern Australia
28. Khoisan — Kalahari Australia
29. North American Black — Black population of U.S.A. (forest African plus European mixture)
30. Cape Colored — South Africa (Bantu and Khoisan plus European mixture)
31. Ladino — Central and South America (southern European plus Amerindian mixture)
32. Neo-Hawaiian — Hawaii (European plus Polynesian, Chinese, Japanese, Filipino mixture)

Races," *Current Anthropology* 3:279–381, 1962; Mead, M., et al. (eds.), *Science and the Concept of Race* (New York: Columbia University Press, 1968); Montagu, A. (ed.), *The Concept of Race* (New York: Free Press, 1964).
—*James F. Metress, University of Toledo*

**Racial Distributions.** *See* Gene distributions.

**Racialism.** *See* Racism.

**Racial Traits.** *See* Race.

**Racial Unconscious.** *See* Collective unconscious.

**Raciation.** This term refers to the process of "race" formation. The composition of races is dynamic, not static, but the formation of races is due to the process of natural selection, mutation, genetic recombination, migration, gene flow, and genetic drift. Racial groups have become extinct, changed their composition through evolution, and fused as a result of contact and interbreeding.

    *See also* Gene flow; Migration; Race; Selection, natural; Speciation

**Racism.** In its standard use this term denotes the doctrine that the cultural and intellectual characteristics of a population are linked to its biological racial character, especially the notion that some races are inherently superior to others. The term also denotes a social system in which certain ethnic groups are especially oppressed and exploited with the rationalization that they are racially (biologically) inferior. In an expanded sense of the term, racist doctrine has been applied not only to putative differences between populations that are recognizably distinct in physical characteristics but also to nonbiological groups (religious, national, and ethnic groups and language communities).

    Racism is a pejorative term, implying that the belief in a biologically determined hierarchy of human groups is unfounded. Thus advocates of racism almost always prefer other terms to designate their opinions. Indeed feelings about race are so sensitive in

American society that elaborate linguistic codes have developed to permit the oblique expression of racist views. Ever since the American Revolution politicians have used the slogan Support States' Rights as a code phrase for defending at first slavery and then segregation. Currently popular code expressions for the exclusion of minorities from social equality include Protect Property Values (used to keep minorities out of all-white neighborhoods) and No Busing of Schoolchildren (used to keep school systems segregated).

    **Theories of Racism.** Social scientists and psychologists have proposed numerous theories to explain the extraordinary strength of racism in modern Western societies. These theories have tended to fall into two categories according to whether they stress the psychological force of prejudiced attitudes in individuals or the social forces underlying systematic and institutionalized racial oppression (see Allport 1958). Marxist and radical scholars have held that racism is generated by the need of dominant social classes to justify the subordination of conquered, enslaved, and otherwise oppressed populations and also to prevent exploited and oppressed groups of different ethnic origins from uniting politically (see Cox 1948).

    **Institutional Dynamics of Racism.** In the course of the last two decades anthropologists and sociologists have come to distinguish sharply between individual and institutional racism. The latter form of racism is associated with social forces and the former with prejudiced attitudes acquired by the individual living in a racist society. Attitudes are regarded as the result of social forces acting on individuals. Research by a number of scholars has shown in detail how institutional circumstances generate racism. One striking example of the rise of racism can be found in the reports of European traders who visited the coast of Africa from the 16th to the 19th centuries. The original voyagers were not universally prejudiced against Africans. Indeed, many were impressed by the high level of African culture. However, when the creation of plantations based on slave labor in the New World transformed the African commodity trade into a traffic in human beings, the attitudes of the Europeans underwent a sharp reversal. It was then that the image of the animal-like African savage became dominant (see Davidson 1961; compare Jordan 1968), for

it allowed the Europeans to rationalize the practice of chattel slavery.

    To take another example, students of racism in the United States have remarked that its strength appears to wax and wane with fluctuations in national economic circumstances and policies. Thus the resurgence of racist ideology at the end of the Reconstruction Era after the Civil War coincided with the decision by northern capitalists to abandon social reform in the South and reestablish their antebellum alliance with the plantation owners. A sharp rise in racism against eastern and southern Europeans in the early years of the 20th century is similarly related to the desire of powerful social forces to restrict immigration to the United States (Gossett 1963).

    **Significance of Racism.** Racism is one of the most pressing social problems of the modern world. It has in this century been a major factor in the denial of political and economic justice and also in many political struggles and wars. To see this one need only consider such examples as the role of anti-Semitism in the rise of the Nazi regime in Germany, the role of apartheid and other forms of racism in the conflicts in southern Africa, anti-Asian racism in rationalizing the Vietnam War and the expulsion of Asians from Uganda in 1972, anti-Irish and anti-Catholic feeling in Northern Ireland, as well as the continuing racial oppression and conflict in the United States today. In all these instances racially pejorative stereotypes have been created and perpetuated to justify inhuman treatment.

    *See also* Anti-Semitism; Ethnocentrism; Genocide; Scientific racism

    Consult: Allport, G., *The Nature of Prejudice* (Garden City, N.Y.: Doubleday, 1958); Cox, O., *Caste, Class and Race* (New York: Monthly Review Press, 1948); Davidson, B., *The African Slave Trade* (Boston: Little, Brown, 1961); Gossett, T. F., *Race: The History of an Idea in America* (New York: Schocken Books, 1963); Jordan, W. D., *White Over Black* (Baltimore: Penguin, 1968); Robertson, I., and Whitten, P. (eds.), *Race and Politics in South Africa* (Chicago: Trans-action Books/Aldine Publ. Co.; 1976).

    —*Anthony Kroch, Temple University*

**Racism, Scientific.** *See* Scientific racism.

**Radcliffe-Brown, A. R.** (1881–1955). This major figure in the establishment of contemporary social anthropology was born in England and educated at Cambridge. A dedicated and inspirational teacher, he devoted his life to the development of anthropology as a natural science of society based on the comparative analysis of the social systems of primitive peoples. His goal was the establishment of a mature theoretical discipline capable of discovering valid general laws of human society by means of a vigorous inductive methodology. His many honors included the presidency of the Royal Anthropological Institute.

Radcliffe-Brown conceptualized social life as an adaptive system of interdependent parts whose interconnections should be examined. The ongoing social life or social process of a society is coordinated by accepted rules of conduct (institutions) which lead to the emergence of a social structure—i.e., a continuing arrangement of persons in rule-defined and rule-controlled relationships. The concepts of social process and social structure are bound together through the concept of function. The function of a recurrent social activity is its contribution to the maintenance of the social structure. Thus one understands various aspects of social life such as religious activities or legal procedures by concentrating on their consequences for the social structure—specifically, how they contribute to its maintenance. Among Radcliffe-Brown's most influential books are the following: *The Andaman Islanders* (1948), *A Natural Science of Society* (1957), *Method in Social Anthropology* (1958), and *Structure and Function in Primitive Society* (1965).

*See also* British social anthropology; Functionalism; Kinship; Social structure; Sociocultural system; Structuralism

—*Stan Wilk, Lycoming College*

**Radin, Paul** (1883–1959). A prominent American anthropologist, Radin received his anthropological training under Franz Boas at Columbia, finishing his Ph.D. in 1911. He began ethnographic and linguistic fieldwork among the Winnebago Indians in 1908; in 1923 he published *The Winnebago Tribe*, which still stands as the definitive work on that society. He continued his interests in the Winnebago throughout his life. In studying culture, Radin preferred to concentrate on the individual: he believed that historical universals manifested themselves through studying specific case histories (see his

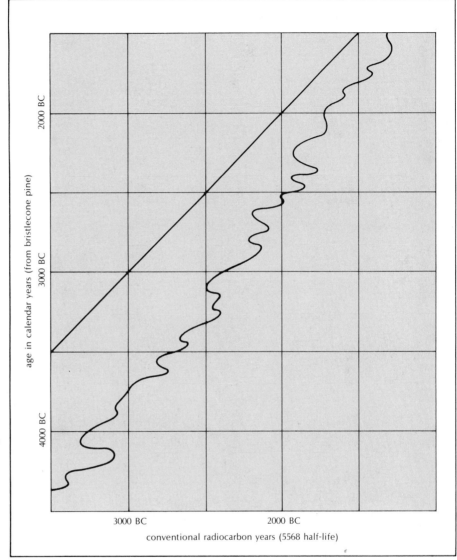

Chart showing the conversion corrections estimated by Colin Renfrew with regard to C-14 dating, as revealed by the careful analysis of bristlecone pine specimens, the ages of which were determined by dendrochronology (adapted from Colin Renfrew).

*Method and Theory of Ethnology*, 1933). As an ethnologist, his primary interests lay in religion and mythology: two of his major works are *Primitive Man As Philosopher* (1927) and *Primitive Religion* (1937). Radin

believed that by reaching an understanding of "primitive man," people of the modern, industrialized world could better comprehend and evaluate themselves.

**Radioactive Methods of Dating.** *See* Dating, absolute; Physical-chemical methods of dating; Radiocarbon dating.

**Radiocarbon Dating.** Radiocarbon (carbon 14 or C-14) dating is the most widely used dating method for time periods up to 50,000 years. Since it was developed almost 30 years ago its use has led to the revision of many ideas about the development of prehistoric cultures. Radioactive carbon, which is present in living plants, diminishes with a half-life of 5,740 ± 40 years. Determination of the percentage of this material in a wood or charcoal sample allows an estimation of the sample's age. Although they are theoretically applicable to other organic material including shell and bone, results on these materials have not been consistent. Recent studies have refined the method and more accurate results are now being obtained.

See also Dating, absolute; Physical-chemical methods of dating

**Ramage.** Nonunilineal descent group composed of individuals who are descended from one ancestor through any combination of male and female links.

See also Kinship and descent

**Ramapithecus.** *Ramapithecus,* one of *Homo sapiens'* earliest-known ancestors, is represented by several fossil fragments from India and Africa. *Ramapithecus brevirostris* ("short-faced") was excavated in the 1930s, by G. E. Lewis of Yale University, from the Siwalik hills of India. Teeth and reconstructed jaw fragments of this early Pliocene creature display a relatively small face, short canines, parabolic dental arcade, and an arched palate—all indicative of hominid status. Unfortunately the importance of Lewis's fossils remained unrecognized until recently.

In 1962, L. S. B. Leakey, digging at Fort Ternan in Kenya, discovered a fossil he called *Kenyapithecus wickeri,* which he described as bipedal and possibly a tool user. Potassium-argon dates of about 14 million years were attached to Leakey's find. Elwyn Simons condensed *Ramapithecus brevirostris, Kenyapithecus wickeri,* and other closely related fossils into a single genus now labeled *Ramapithecus punjabicus,* a forest margin-dwelling hominid whose dentition suggests both a relatively extended infant dependency period and a coarse diet which included seeds, roots, and possibly raw meat.

The Upper Pliocene is largely absent of hominid fossils; a gap of some 9 or 10 million years separates *Ramapithecus* from the first

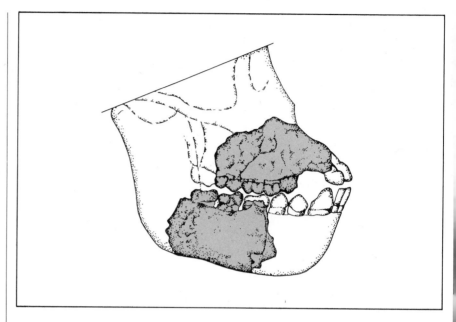

*Reconstruction of the face of* Ramapithecus *derived from mandibular and maxillary fossil remains.*

australopithecines now being excavated primarily in E and S Africa. *Ramapithecus* may well have been their ancestor.

See also Aegyptopithecus
Consult: Simons, Elwyn, "Some Fallacies in the Study of Hominid Phylogeny," *Science* 141: 879–889, 1963.
—Pell Fender, Columbia College

**Rank.** This term refers to the hierarchical evaluation of individuals or groups in a society. All societies have some sort of ranking, even if it is as simple as young/old. More elaborate ranking of groups on an ascriptive level is referred to as *stratification.*

See also Social stratification

**Rates of Chemical Change in Soil.** See Soils and archaeology.

**Ratzel, Friedrich** (1844–1904). German geographer who founded the study of anthropogeography, wrote *Völkerkunde* (Eth-

nology), and made contributions to thought on environment, history, culture seen as traits, and diffusionism—all of which remain fundamental to anthropological thought today.

**Reaction Formation.** In Freudian psychology, this term refers to the defensive process by which a person converts an unacceptable attitude or emotion (such as love for someone who is unattainable) into its opposite (such as hate).

See also Defense mechanisms; Freud, Sigmund

**Reactive Adaptation.** See Acculturation.

**Reasoning Ability.** See Thought processes.

**Recessive Gene.** See Gene; Genetics.

**Reciprocity.** See Exchange; Trade.

**Reconstruction, Linguistic.** See Linguistic reconstruction.

**Reconstruction, Prehistoric.** See Archaeology; Dating, absolute; Dating, relative; Ethnographic analogy; Linguistic reconstruction; Prehistoric archaeology; Prehistory.

**Recording of Behavior.** See Fieldwork Methods.

**Red Power Movement.** In this movement by and for Indian people, Native Americans are strongly affirming their rights to self-determination. They are working toward this goal by raising awareness of Indian identity and needs, redefining institutional policies and programs for Indian peoples, reviving treaty rights grievances, and promoting Indian self-sufficiency. First used nationally in 1964 by Indian youth in speaking out against white America's paternalistic Indian policies, the term Red Power as a symbol of self-determination has spread throughout the United States and Canada. Dynamic expressions of Red Power are seen in the fishing/hunting rights controversies of the past decade, the emergence of the American Indian Movement (1968), the Alcatraz occupation (1969), the Trail of Broken Treaties and resultant Bureau of Indian Affairs sit-in (1972), and the Wounded Knee occupation (1973).

> See also Cultural revitalization; Ethnic group; Nativistic movements; Pan-Indianism

**Redfield, Robert** (1897–1958). A major theorist of the 1940s and 1950s, Redfield was instrumental in widening the scope of American anthropology from an almost exclusive interest in primitive societies and the comparative study of civilizations. He began his professional career as a lawyer, but decided to undertake graduate work in anthropology instead. He received his Ph.D. from the University of Chicago in 1928. Redfield's theoretical orientations reflected the influence of Boasian historical particularism, the Chicago school of sociology, and European evolutionists. His major, and most controversial, theoretical construct was known as the folk-urban continuum.

> See also Folk-urban continuum; Great Tradition; Little Tradition

**Redistribution.** Redistribution is a mechanism whereby a politically or economically powerful individual (or group) collects goods and services from the members of the society and reallocates them among the society's members. The collection as well as the distribution may be based on relative social status, kinship, or a variety of traditional relationships. Examples are the feudal system of medieval Europe and the ancient Mayan economy.

> See also Exchange; Social stratification; Trade

**Regression Analysis.** Method for determining the magnitude of correlation between two or more measured variables.

> See also Statistical methods

**Reichel-Dolmatoff, Gerardo** (b. 1912). Austrian-born, Gerardo Reichel-Dolmatoff is a preeminent Latin American (Colombian) archaeologist and ethnologist who has made major discoveries and contributions in his specialities and in ecological, social organizational, and symbolic theory.

**Reinforcement.** This term refers to the means by which an organism's response is made more likely to recur. Primary reinforcements satisfy survival needs; secondary reinforcements substitute or are exchanged for primary ones.

> See also Behaviorist school of psychology; Conditioning; Extinction; Sanctions; Skinner, B. F.

**Relative Dating.** See Dating, relative.

**Relativism, Cultural.** See Cultural relativism.

**Reliability of Informants.** This term refers to the problem encountered in ethnographic fieldwork of the accuracy of information provided by different informants. For many years ethnographers working in primitive societies collected their information from a single key informant—a man who was knowledgeable about his society. It was assumed that the primitive society was so homogeneous that one person's information would be the same as any other's. As more attention was given to women in primitive societies, it was discovered that their responses were often different from those of male informants. Ethnographers have also learned that there are people who deviate from the norm in every society. Even in primitive societies, some informants will have specialized knowledge which is not shared by most members of the group. When ethnographers study complex societies, the problem of shared knowledge becomes more complicated as knowledge becomes more specialized.

Related to the question of informant reliability is the problem of validity of response. By validity is meant the degree to which scientific observations actually measure what they attempt to measure. In this regard it has become well known that informants' responses to questions about certain aspects of culture may be more truthful than about other areas.

> See also Fieldwork, ethnographic
> Consult: Cancian, Frank, "Informant Error and Native Prestige Ranking in Zinacantan," *American Anthropologist* 65:1068–1075, 1963; Dean, John P., and Whyte, William F., "How Do You Know If the Informant Is Telling the Truth?," *Human Organization* 17(2):34–38, 1958; Young, Frank W., and Young, Ruth C., "Key Informant Reliability in Rural Mexican

*Robert Redfield*

Villages," *Human Organization* 20(3):141–148, 1961.

—*Michael D. Olien, University of Georgia*

**Reliability, Statistical.** In statistics, reliability refers to the quality of data design and collection such that the results can be reproduced statistically by another researcher. It involves the use of statistically testable hypotheses, mutually inclusive and exclusive attribute categories, and statistically valid sampling techniques.

*See also* Statistical methods

**Religion.** No single definition of religion is universally accepted. Value judgments, historical stereotypes, and immense cultural variety cause disagreement about the nature and range of the phenomena involved. Anthropologists have tended to broaden the term—from the minimal definition of Tylor (1874:424–425), "a belief in spiritual beings," to the carefully explicit definition of Geertz (1966:4), "a system of symbols which acts to establish powerful, pervasive and long-lasting moods and motivations in men by formulating conceptions of a general order of existence and clothing these conceptions with an aura of factuality that the moods and motivations seem uniquely realistic."

Most anthropologists stress the institutionalized interaction with superhuman beings or extraordinary powers capable of harming or aiding humans. Religion is firmly regarded as a cultural institution distinguishable from others by its "culturally patterned interaction with culturally postulated superhuman beings" (Spiro 1966:96). Both psychological and sociological factors are required to describe the role and function of a particular religion in the lives of individuals and their society. Beliefs and practices are so organized as to "shape an ethic manifest in the behavior" (Birnbaum 1964:588) and characterize each religious system.

If all religion involves belief in some spiritual beings, then the ordering of these beliefs into a structure and hierarchy differs greatly according to the religious system. So-called revealed or Great Religions such as Islam and Christianity depend on a prophet (Mohammed) or messiah (Jesus) who reveals the Word of a unique Creator (trinitarian godhead for the Christians). Classical Greek and Roman religions packed their pantheons with deified culture heroes.

Many modern religions immortalize their supreme leaders as divinities (the Japanese Emperor, the Tibetan Dalai Lama, the Nilotic Shilluk king, the Ismaili Aga Khan). Monotheistic Christianity and unorthodox Islam both produce saints who act as patrons channeling belief and ritual. Manifestations of gods and holy personages (Jove, the Virgin Mary) focus ritual and cult as do the avatars of polytheistic Hinduism (Vishnu, Shiva). The anthropopsychic conception of spiritual beings is variously capricious, vengeful, and ethical, but all are the source of supernatural power whether personal (grace) or impersonal (mana in Polynesia and its equivalents elsewhere).

Socialization of an orthodoxy in literate societies led to Great Traditions perpetuated by sacred texts (Koran, Bible, Talmud, Sanskritic lore) and formal ritual directed by a public functionary-priesthood. Temple, mosque, and church epitomize the institutionalization of religion. Thus The Church is often synonymous with The Establishment and is at times both evangelistic and ideocentrically imperialistic (witness the holy wars—the Muslim *jihad*, the Christian crusade).

Specific cults (peyotism, cargo cults, mystery cults) and dissenting sects (the Sikhs, Jehovah's Witnesses) may unite under charismatic leaders rather than sacerdotal bureaucrats. Folk and primitive religions (usually defined by an absence of a written tradition) may diffuse ritual responsibility among the group (the civic-religious cargo system in Mesoamerica); or a variety of shamans (especially through trance or spirit possession in the Northern Hemisphere), diviners, and mediums may serve a more private function. Among the Eskimo, private and public functions are combined in the same specialist. In contrast, North American Plains Indians realize their most important religious experience in the highly individualistic vision quest.

Rituals are regarded as the dramatic and socially sanctioned representations of myths. Calendrical rites publicly mark the passage from one season to another (e.g., the first fruits harvest festivals) and are usually performed for the commonweal; critical rites mark the passage from one individual human condition to another (hence *rites de passage* such as initiation rites). The Durkheimian sacred/secular dichotomy, which distinguishes (by the element of mysticism) ritual from ceremony,

masks the fine line between religious and magical acts. For Leach (1954:13) ritual is the symbolically significant aspect of routine. In the modern West, secularization and the declining influence of institutionalized religion have been accompanied by a rise of the occult wherein symbolic behavior and ritual merge the sacred (religious) and profane (technological).

*See also* Cargo cults; Magic; Magic and witchcraft; Mysticism; Profane; Religions of the world; Rites of passage; Ritual; Sacred; Sects; Spiritualism; Symbol; Symbolism

Consult: Birnbaum, N., "Religion," in *A Dictionary of the Social Sciences,* ed. Julius Gould and W. L. Kolb (New York: Free Press, 1964); Geertz, C., "Religion As a Cultural System," in *Anthropological Approaches to the Study of Religion,* ed. Michael Banton (London: Tavistock, 1966); Leach, E. R., *Political Systems of Highland Burma* (London: Bell, 1954); Malinowski, B., *Magic, Science and Religion* (Glencoe, Ill.: Free Press, 1948); Spiro, M. E., "Religion: Problems of Definition and Explanation," in *Anthropological Approaches to the Study of Religion,* ed. Michael Banton (London: Tavistock, 1966); Tylor, E. B., *Primitive Culture* (New York: Gordon Press).

—*Michael Kenny, University of Mexico*

**Religions of the World.** The ethnography of religions can conveniently be considered under typological headings arranged in a culture area framework. The types of religion considered here are *shamanic* (in the circumpolar regions of Eurasia and North America); *communal* or *totemistic* (in North America, Africa, Australia, Oceania); *Olympian* or *polytheistic-fetishistic* (in the state societies of aboriginal America, Central Africa, borderlands of India and China); and *monotheistic* (in the state societies of Eurasia, Europe, the Middle East, India, China). These types are not exclusive. One may find monotheism, for example, appearing in any of the other three types. The time reference is AD 1600, before the great colonizations and migrations of modern times.

**Shamanic Religions.** The Ugro-Finnish, Altaic, paleo-Siberian, northern Athapaskan and Algonquian, and Eskimo linguistic divisions are basic areas of circumpolar shamanism. These societies are characterized by hunting, fishing, and foraging economies along with some domestication of reindeer and dogs.

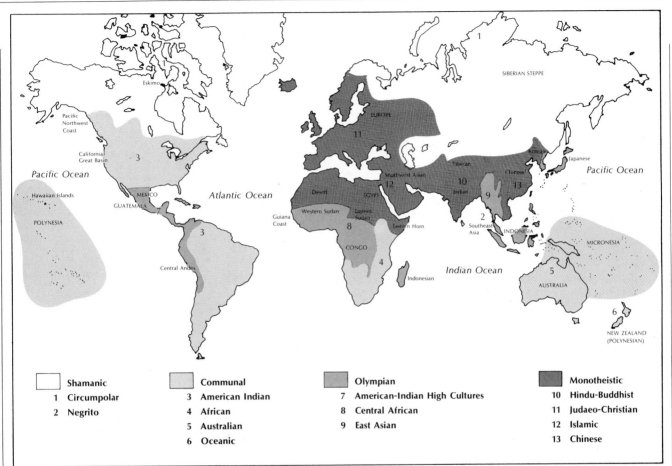

WORLD MAP OF RELIGIOUS CULTURE AREAS, 1600 AD *(adapted from Wallace)*.

**Shamanic**
1  Circumpolar
2  Negrito

**Communal**
3  American Indian
4  African
5  Australian
6  Oceanic

**Olympian**
7  American-Indian High Cultures
8  Central African
9  East Asian

**Monotheistic**
10  Hindu-Buddhist
11  Judaeo-Christian
12  Islamic
13  Chinese

Culturally these religions are characterized by shamans—religious specialists who are believed to communicate with the spirit world and who serve as keepers of the game, especially the bear and sea mammals. Myths of the "magic flight" and the "world tree" are also present. In these societies are found individualistic religious cult institutions involving death rituals and interdictions on behavior, self-administered by individuals without the assistance of shamans. Generally the rituals are responses to crises rather than calendric occurrences.

**Communal Religions.** In the New World this type of religion prevailed in North America between the shamanic area of the Canadian Indians and the Olympian cults of Mexico and Guatemala. It could be said to have involved the major linguistic groupings found in what is now the United States. In South America communal religions characterized all the linguistic groupings except the Chibcha, Aymara, and Quechua.

In the Old World communal cults included the Nilotic, East African Bantu, and the South African Hottentot-Bushmen areas of Africa; similar cults could also be found in the Oceanic cultures of Australia, New Zealand, Polynesia, Melanesia, Papua–New Guinea, and Micronesia.

The variegated nature of the environments was seen to require the support of a pantheon of deities to control the departments of nature. There were numerous rituals related to seasons, individual life cycles, and other events. Accompanying the rich development of rituals was a corresponding complex growth of mythologies.

The totemism of North American communal cults corresponded with a similar development in Australia and in sub-Saharan Africa. The emphasis on subsistence rituals was particularly marked in each of the major areas of totemic practice.

In the temperate zone environments of the Indian societies of North America, an individual's lonely vision quest was accompanied by the rituals of puberty and with the assumption of a new name and a new totemic guardian. In the tropical and semi-tropical African areas, puberty rituals were also stressed for both males and females. Secret societies prevailed in some areas such as West Africa, allied with ritual moralistic functions.

The isolation of aboriginal Australia encouraged a basic common linguistic tie (except in the northwest and extreme north) and was accompanied by the development of puberty rituals and initiation rites. In tropical and nontropical Oceania house structures for deities, mana, and taboo were stressed.

**Olympian Religions.** Religions of a character similar to that of ancient Greece existed in the Nahua, Maya, Chibcha, Aymara, Quechua, and parts of the Arawak language areas of the New World. In Africa the Dahomey, Yoruba, and Ashanti (in the west) and tribal groups in what is now Uganda and Madagascar (in the east) maintained Olympian cults thought by some to have originated in ancient Egypt. In Asia similar cults existed in what is now Burma, Thailand, Cambodia, Malaysia, Indonesia, Korea, and Japan.

The Olympian cults were characterized by a pantheon of gods, temples, highways for processions to shrines, pyramids, ziggurats, fetishes, idols, amulets, and other sacred objects and places. Another characteristic was the high development of a priesthood to maintain the shrines and conduct the worship performed there. The gods were thought to control the rain needed for crops, the seasons (through their manifestations as stellar objects), and the fertility of cultivated plants, domesticated animals, and people.

Writing systems are associated with Olympian cults. Examples are the ideographic systems of the Maya, the hieroglyphics of ancient Egypt, and Sumerian-Chaldean cuneiform.

**Monotheistic Religions.** Religions in which there is one high god are called monotheistic. This form of religion had its birth among the Semitic peoples of western Asia. Typically, monotheistic religions are associated with societies in which there is a high degree of political complexity and which depend on food production rather than food collecting. Judeo-Christian monotheism seems to have arisen from an Olympian cult of the eastern Mediterranean. With the appearance of Christianity, monotheistic beliefs spread first into the western Mediterranean and then throughout Europe. Islam, which originated in western Arabia in the 7th century, spread rapidly westward over North Africa and eastward into Central Asia, India, Southeast Asia, and Indonesia.

See also Culture areas of the world; Language families of the world; Monotheistic religions; Religion

Consult: Faruqi, I. R., and Sopher, D. E., *Historical Atlas of the Religions of the World* (New York: Macmillan, 1974); Lanternari, Vittorio, *The Religions of the Oppressed: A Study of Modern Messianic Cults* (New York: Knopf, 1960); Swanson, Gary, *The Birth of the Gods* (Ann Arbor: University of Michigan Press, 1960); Wallace, Anthony F. C., *Religion: An Anthropological View* (New York: Random House, 1966).

—William H. Gilbert, U.S. Library of Congress (ret.)

**Renfrew, Colin** (b. 1937). Renfrew, who is professor of archaeology at the University of Southampton, has been concerned with the independence of the European Bronze Age from that of the Mediterranean. In *Before Civilization* (1973) he uses the new radiocarbon calibration to support his arguments.

**Rent, Landownership and.** Owners of land or other real estate do not always use it directly for their own needs, especially if they own large or numerous tracts. Property owners have assets from which they may gain by permitting use of the property under specified contractual conditions in return for payment—i.e., rent. Payment may be in kind, labor, money, or transfers of rights. Property owners retain various proprietary rights over their property, often including eviction rights. Under some systems of law wherein the private and public domains are not clearly separated, it is difficult to distinguish among tribute, taxation, and rents. Clearly landownership and rents are quickly becoming universal bases of power and social stratification.

See also Tenancy

**Replicability.** See Scientific method.

**Repression.** In its extreme form, repression is a defense mechanism against anxiety or guilt, but generally it involves selective forgetting—the exclusion from consciousness and memory of specific, unwanted psychological content or activities.

See also Defense mechanisms; Freud, Sigmund

**Repression, Political.** This term refers to the systematic subordination, through use of force, or the threat of force, of one social group by another. The ultimate cause of a repressive response is usually a competition for scarce resources between the groups in question, with the subordinate group challenging the legitimacy of the dominant group's continued control over these resources.

See also Extinction of minorities; Power; Social stratification

**Reproduction, Beliefs Regarding.** See Procreation, beliefs regarding.

**Research Design.** A research design is a methodological tool which organizes and directs anthropological investigation, including the fieldwork, laboratory analysis, and data evaluation phases common to most anthropological research. It is used to resolve a specific set of questions (usually cast into hypothesis form) that are relevant to a specific problem deemed worthy of investigation. The research design consists of the object of investigation (i.e., an explicitly delineated cultural phenomenon), a set of hypotheses or relational statements which are potential solutions to the problem, and a series of test implications and procedures in terms of which data are acquired and analyzed and hypotheses are tested. A research design must be flexible enough to allow for revision based on unexpected results: unexpected results provide the investigator with new ideas for further research and necessitate modification of the research design. The formulation of a research design for an anthropological project permits the investigator to develop a program for information recovery and analysis which is feasible in terms of time, personnel, and funding.

See also Fieldwork methods; Scientific method

—Bettina H. Rosenberg, Arizona State University

**Reservation Indian Culture.** See Pan-Indianism.

**Revenge.** See Feuding.

**Revitalization, Cultural.** See Cultural revitalization.

**Revitalization Movements.** In 1956 Anthony Wallace defined cultural revitalization movements as deliberate, organized attempts by some members of a society to create a more satisfying culture. The key process was a sudden identification and acceptance of a new organized pattern of multiple innovations. In this way, Wallace tried to bring order into the chaos which characterized the study of religious movements—by viewing them as one variety of culture change and one kind of social movement. This means identifying the necessary and sufficient preconditions for the occurrence of revitalization movements, the key social roles involved, and the major processes and stages which characterize this kind of sociocultural change.

The preconditions include extreme social, cultural, and personal disorganization which force a system past the point where an equilibrium can be restored by use of traditional values and practices. Unfortunately, revitalization movements have come to be identified narrowly and solely with damaging, forced acculturation. But there are other sources of cultural dislocation, including natural disasters, rapid climatic change, resource exhaustion, faunal changes, or uncontrolled conflict between interest groups in one society. Such conditions create in a society's members extreme disillusionment, a pervasive sense of unpredictability, and a loss of self-esteem and the capacity to cope. By this point, the culture has moved through several of the sequential stages of a revitalization movement—from a state of equilibrium, to a period of vastly increased stress, to a stage of cultural distortion wherein the attempts to reduce the stress and restore a satisfactory organization are ineffective and, indeed, are themselves adding to the confusion and conflict.

At this juncture, without revitalization, the culture is apt to disintegrate and the population to disperse. Then occurs the most striking feature of the revitalization process. An individual or a small group emerges and creates a totally novel, utopian model for a cultural system. Often the core of this utopian blueprint is the work of one individual who has undergone an experience of hallucinatory revelation (which Wallace calls mazeway resynthesis). Such prophets—Wovoka of the Ghost Dance or Joseph Smith of the Mormon movement—usually become surrounded by disciples who act as public advocates for the new model for living and assume responsibility for communicating it widely and making converts. With the attraction of numerous converts comes the need for organization, and an administrative structure with formal roles emerges. This organization may become authoritarian, doctrinaire, and repressive (e.g., the Nazi Party) or permissive, segmentary, and acephalous (e.g., Human Liberation).

With wide acceptance, organization, and successful efforts at acting out the utopian model, the movement enters into a period of adaptation. Since revitalization movements are revolutionary, the needs of those threatened must be met or accommodated. Then, too, new issues, problems, and ambiguities will arise as the utopian ideal is transformed into effective practice.

When such a movement receives widespread general acceptance in a population, the culture may be transformed. Then, as the new utopia becomes institutionalized and routinized, a new steady state is achieved. As Wallace points out, institutionalized religions generally have their origins in older revitalization movements. Thus mass movements which originate in revolutionary efforts to create a new and more satisfactory culture, once successful, become conservative forces that buttress the new status quo. But not all revitalization movements are successful. The record of incipient, partial, bypassed, and failed movements is a long one.

Wallace's general treatment of revitalization movements, although it has advanced our knowledge substantially, obviously obscures the unique characteristics of specific movements. In 1964, Igor Kopytoff proposed an improved approach to the comparative study of religious movements. Instead of using Wallace's developmental model, he outlined an analytic framework which would treat each movement as a cluster of dimensions. Kopytoff does not regard each movement as one member of a species; rather, he would specify its characteristics in a profile of multiple dimensions. An approach like this should lead to even more systematic and substantial knowledge concerning religious movements and cultural change processes.

See also Cultural change; Mazeway; Millenarian movements; Nativistic movements
Consult: Festinger, L., et al., *When Prophecy Fails* (New York: Harper & Row, 1956); Kopytoff, Igor, "Classification of Religious Movements: Analytic and Synthetic," in *Proceedings of the 1964 Meeting of the American Ethnological Society*, Seattle, 1964; Mead, M., *New Lives for Old* (New York: Morrow, 1966); Wallace, A. F. C., "Revitalization Movements," *American Anthropologist* 58:264–281, 1956; Wallace, A. F. C., *Culture and Personality* (New York: Random House, 1971).
—*James Clifton, University of Wisconsin, Green Bay*

**Revolution.** A revolution is the complete overthrow of a political system and hence the complete transformation of a social order. Revolutions are to be distinguished sociologically from *coups d'état*, in which one political faction replaces another without altering the underlying structure of society. For Marxists, a revolution involves the seizure of state power by one class from another and the use of this state power to effect a transition from one social order to another—i.e., from feudalism to capitalism or from capitalism to socialism. Marxists distinguish, therefore, between *bourgeois revolutions*, in which a rising bourgeoisie wrests state power from a feudal aristocracy, and *proletarian revolutions*, in which a working class seizes state power and begins to build socialism.

In anthropology, the term *revolution* is also used to apply to major transitions in human development, such as V. Gordon Childe's *Neolithic revolution*, which involved the transition from hunting and gathering to food production, and *urban revolution*, involving the rise of cities, social classes, and the state.

See also Lenin, V. I.; Mao Tse-tung; Marx, Karl; Peasants and revolution; State and Revolution
Consult: Childe, V. Gordon, *Man Makes Himself* (London: Watts, 1936); Woddis, Jack, *New Theories of Revolution* (New York: International, 1972).
—*Eugene E. Ruyle, University of Virginia*

**Reward.** See Reinforcement; Sanction.

**Richards, Audrey Isabell** (b. 1899). Social anthropologist known for her extensive ethnographic work in C and E Africa, primarily among the Bemba of N Rhodesia.

**Ridicule.** Ridicule is a stylized form of insulting or demeaning a person or group. It is used as an informal sanction and is a very powerful mechanism of social control.

See also Gossip; Sanctions

**Riss Glaciation.** See Glaciations.

**Rites of Intensification.** See Ceremony.

**Rites of Passage.** This term refers to ceremonies marking changes in status or social position undergone as a person passes through the culturally recognized life phases of his or her society.

Rites marking a person's entry into adulthood are called *puberty rites*. These have received a great deal of attention from anthropologists. Puberty rites may consist merely of formal teaching about adult life, but they are often accompanied by temporary isolation from the rest of the group and by some

Induction into the U.S. Army, a contemporary American rite of passage.

Xavante Amazon elder ritually washes boy during rite of passage into adulthood.

physical operation (e.g., circumcision or scarification). The ceremonies accompanying the entry of novices into the religious orders, pledges into fraternities or sororities, and freemasons into lodges are similar in kind. Christian confirmation rituals and the Jewish bar mitzvah are parallels in our society. Marriage ceremonies and funerals are also rites of passage.

See also Ritual; Secret societies; Social control Consult: Endleman, Robert (ed.), *Personality and Social Life* (New York: Random House, 1967); Gennep, Arnold Van, *The Rites of Passage* (Chicago: University of Chicago Press, 1960); Seligson, Marcia, *The Eternal Bliss Machine: America's Way of Wedding* (New York: Morrow, 1973); Young, Frank W., *Initiation Ceremony: A Cross Cultural Study of Status Dramatization* (Indianapolis: Bobbs-Merrill, 1967).

—Joseph S. Roucek, City University of New York (ret.)

**Rites of Solidarity.** See Solidarity, rites of.

**Ritual.** Ritual implies a category or an aspect of behavior which is stereotyped, predictable, prescribed, communicative, and non-

instrumental. Its stereotypy and predictability mean that the behavior suitable to a given situation, such as that of worshippers at a church service, is of a very limited range and, once begun, follows a nearly invariable sequence. It is prescribed in that its performance does not depend solely on the whim of an individual but is expected by others under specific circumstances and in a specific manner. It is communicative of some fact about the performer, the subject, or the relation between them, to an audience (although the only audience may be the performer). Finally, ritual is noninstrumental in that its performance is not considered to have a direct or mechanical effect on the external world.

Ritual as defined here is an analytic concept, not an independent fact. As such, it covers a range of actual behavior which is continuous with other, nonritual behavior. It is particularly close to ceremony and etiquette and is often distinguished from these terms by limiting its use to a religious context.

Varieties of ritual may be categorized in several ways. Calendrical rites may be contrasted with critical rites according to whether they are performed regularly, as at spring and autumn equinoxes, or occasionally, as for curing an illness. One widely recognized category is that of *rites of passage* which mark social transition, such as the rites concerning birth, initiation, marriage, and death.

*This Australian Aborigine circumcision rite marks the transition to adulthood for males. The circumcision is performed with a sharp stone tool while the boy is held down on top of the body of his sponsor.*

*Funeral ritual: A dead baby is prepared for ritual cremation in eastern Nepal.*

Ritual as a kind of behavior frequently is associated by anthropologists with belief as a kind of thought. In this case the two categories, ritual and belief, are usually regarded as complementary to one another in some way. For example, ritual is said to express or to reinforce belief, or belief is said to form the basis of, or to rationalize, ritual. These assertions remain points of controversy.

*See also* Myth; Religion; Rites of passage
Consult: Goody, J. R., "Religion and Ritual: The Definitional Problem," *British Journal of Sociology* 12:142–164, 1961.

—*Stewart Guthrie, University of Rhode Island*

**Ritual Killing.** *See* Killing, ritual.

**Ritual Numbers.** *See* Numbers, ritual.

**Ritualized Joking.** *See* Joking, ritualized.

**Rivers, William Halse** (1864–1922). A medical doctor and anthropologist who participated in the Cambridge University Torres Strait Expedition to New Guinea and Austra-

lia in 1898, Rivers tested sensory function among the Melanesians and explored the nature of color vision. He not only recorded genealogies and kinship terms but also tried to place them within the context of the entire social organization. In later years, he was a firm advocate of the diffusionist theories of Sir Grafton Elliot Smith and William James Perry. Two of his best-known publications are *The Todas* (1906) and *The History of Melanesian Society* (1914).

*See also* Diffusionism; Perry, William James; Smith, Grafton Elliot

**Robertson-Smith, William** (1846–1894). Author of *The Religion of the Semites* and *Kinship and Marriage in Early Arabia,* Robertson-Smith studied Semitic ritual, tradition, and religion from an anthropological point of view. He believed that religion served a social and practical purpose in society.

**Rock Art.** This term refers to anything carved or painted on rock, especially by prehistoric or contemporary preliterate societies. Rock art is widely distributed from the Old World to the New World; the most spectacular examples are the Upper Paleolithic cave paintings found in SE Europe.

*See also* Upper Paleolithic art

**Róheim, Géza** (1891–1953). A psychoanalyst and anthropologist, Róheim has analyzed culturally patterned behavior such as rituals, pointing out their roots in human psychosexual processes.

*See also* Oedipus complex

**Role.** This term refers to the rules for behavior appropriate to a given status (social position). The classical definition after Linton (1936) has been useful in *functional* analyses within a *synchronic* framework. Difficulties arose, however, when it was found inadequate to deal entirely successfully with social change. Changing the emphasis from behavior patterns to the people who are doing the behaving (or interacting) allows for greater flexibility and understanding of the interrelationships of all parts of dynamic *social systems*. Most roles are *reciprocal* in

nature: parent/child, curer/patient, employer/employee. Therefore, mastery of a role means learning not only the rules for behavior of the person assuming the role but also the rules for those interacting reciprocally with the paired member.

*Role conflict* occurs under conditions of disjunction—i.e., when the interacting members (or groups of members) of a role-pair category have learned different rules and therefore have different expectations. There is conflict also when societal conditions change to the extent that certain expectations are no longer fulfilled or certain behavior becomes dysfunctional. Role conflict is becoming an increasingly frequent phenomenon, as in societies everywhere many traditional roles are being challenged.

*See also* Functionalism; Role recruitment criteria; Sociocultural systems; Status; Synchronic
Consult: Linton, Ralph, *The Study of Man* (New York: Appleton Century, 1936); Nadel, S. F., *The Theory of Social Structure* (New York: Free Press, 1957).

—*MaryAnn Foley, Southern Connecticut State College*

*Prehistoric rock drawings in Libya.*

**Role Recruitment Criteria.** These criteria refer to the characteristics a person needs to become eligible for a particular social role. Two kinds of criteria, ascribed and achieved, were identified by Linton (1936).

*Ascribed* roles usually come by birth. Roles based on age, sex, kinship, caste, and class are ascribed. One need do nothing at all to be assigned to such categories. One is born a Rockefeller or a Smith, a Canadian or a Bantu, a Brahmin or an Untouchable. One becomes (ascribed as) an adult and attains the rights and duties of adulthood simply by living long enough.

Some effort must be exerted to qualify for *achieved* roles. Occupational and leadership roles are frequently (but not always) of this type. In Western cultures one must earn an M.D. degree to become a physician, and in East Africa a Zar cultist spends years attaining a leadership role in health maintenance and curing. Qualifications for political office in the United States require that the candidate be nominated and elected. Artists, scientists, people in business—all must study, practice, and perform their skills in order to assume and maintain those roles.

Many roles combine both kinds of criteria, but all the criteria may not be explicitly acknowledged. An implicit rule in white middle-class American culture carries the expectation that people will marry someone from the same social class who is relatively close in age. Further, it is more acceptable for a man to marry a much younger woman than the other way around and for a woman to marry upward in socioeconomic status rather than downward.

Ascribed roles fare rather poorly in democratic societies because of conflicts with egalitarian ideals, just as the need to achieve role qualifications can be a threat to security in societies organized along more traditional lines. It is no accident, therefore, that most roles in small societies are ascribed and the majority of roles in large, industrialized societies tend to be achieved.

*See also* Caste; Enculturation; Marriage; Role
Consult: Linton, Ralph, *The Study of Man* (New York: Appleton Century, 1936).
—*MaryAnn Foley, Southern Connecticut State College*

**Role Set.** This term is often used to refer to a cluster of closely related role variants revolving about a specified social position (status) or varied interpretations of the social action entailed by the position. The conception leaves obscure how one designates the determinants of the position independently of its role attributes. Thus it is ambiguous what the supposed role set really is. Another usage refers to the fact that the components of any role—rights, duties, obligations, prerogatives—entail minimally one additional complementary role; thus the term *role set* is used to designate the set of roles necessarily implied or usually connected by the components. Hence the role "father" requires the roles "mother" and "child"—all of which constitute the role set "nuclear family."

*See also* Role

**Ropes.** *See* Lines and rope, knots and splices.

**Rorschach Test.** This test, also called the inkblot test, was for many years the most often used projective instrument in cross-cultural studies of personality. However, its use has declined markedly since about 1960. Consisting of ten symmetrical inkblots, five black and white, five partly in color, the test is generally administered to subjects individually in a formal face-to-face interview. The subject's task is to examine each blot in sequence and then describe verbally *what* is perceived there (content) and *how* it was perceived (determinants). Since the blots are highly ambiguous and unstructured, the subject's responses vary widely and constitute personal fantasy products which project important aspects of covert needs, wishes, conflicts, and styles of coping with experience. Culture and personality research tries to account for these personal psychological traits through reference to cultural themes.

*See also* Projective tests
Consult: Barnouw, V., *Culture and Personality*, 2nd ed. (Homewood, Ill.:Dorsey Press, 1973).

**Rosetta Stone.** This small black basalt tablet was discovered in the western Nile delta, near Alexandria, by Napoleon's expedition to Egypt in 1799. It was subsequently confiscated by the British army and sent to the British Museum. On its face are three parallel texts written in Egyptian hieroglyphs, in demotic (a later cursive form of Egyptian script), and in Greek. The Greek text—a priestly decree of 190 BC in honor of Ptolemy V—was easily read, and attempted decipherments of Egyptian hieroglyphs based on the parallel hieroglyphic text proliferated. All were based on the erroneous assumption that the hieroglyphs were exclusively pictographic or ideographic. Jean François Champollion was the first to hypothesize that some of the signs might be phonetic. Noting that the group of hieroglyphs enclosed in an oval cartouche presumably represented Ptolemy's name, he postulated phonetic values for them. This identification and several of the phonetic values were verified by a second Greek-hieroglyphic text on the Obelisk of Philae which contained the names of Ptolemy and Cleopatra. With his extensive knowledge of Oriental languages, particularly Coptic (derived from ancient Egyptian), Champollion went beyond isolated readings and began to analyze the linguistic structure of the writing system. Although his work was not universally accepted for some years, it proved to be the breakthrough which led to a full decipherment of Egyptian hieroglyphic writing.

*See also* Champollion, Jean François; Hieroglyphic writing; Writing
Consult: Diringer, David, *The Alphabet: A Key to the History of Mankind* (London: Hutchinson, 1968).
—*John S. Henderson, Cornell University*

*The Rosetta stone.*

*Hindu law prohibits the killing of cattle, which consequently roam wild through the streets of Indian cities. Many observers have felt this to be a waste of resources in a hunger-ridden country. However, careful analysis by cultural ecologists has shown that the economic benefit derived from free manure and the use of cattle as traction animals—as well as a source of free meat when they die of natural causes—renders these sacred cattle into efficiently utilized economic resources.*

**Rouse, Irving** (b. 1913). A dominant figure in Caribbean and Venezuelan archaeology, Rouse is recognized for theoretical contributions to the solution of various problems of artifact classification and interpretation.

**Rousseau, Jean-Jacques** (1712–1778). This French philosopher made three major contributions to anthropology. The first is his elaboration of the idea of the inherently social nature of the human species (*Social Contract*, 1762). The second is the concept of human moral degeneration with the progress of civilization (*Discours sur les arts et sciènces*, 1750), which played an important role in 19th-century evolutionist thought. The third is his conception of the sociocultural nature of education, concerning which he had many ideas today labeled progressive. The notion of humans as inherently social and culture-bearing underlies later social science developments, especially those descended from Durkheim.

**Rowe, John Howland** (b. 1918). This archaeologist is a leading figure in the study of Andean civilization, especially the Incan society of the pre-Columbian and early conquest periods.

**Ruling Classes.** See Marxism; Social stratification.

**Sacred.** The sacred is a category of things and actions set apart as holy and entitled to reverence. Such a category is often held to represent symbolically the key values of a society.

    *See also* Profane; Religion

**Sacred Cows of India.** Hindu belief in *ahimsa*, the sanctity of life, prohibits slaughter of cattle in India. Cattle roam the city and countryside. Many people, aware of food shortages in India, regard this phenomenon as noneconomic. Marvin Harris refutes this, however, arguing that farmers cultivate small landholdings with cattle-drawn plows and that there are fewer cattle than needed at plowing time but not enough grain to feed them were they kept in stalls. Allowing them to roam and forage preserves them for the next plowing season. Meanwhile, they provide dung (a cheap fuel) and milk.

    *See also* Cultural ecology
    Consult: Harris, Marvin, "The Cultural Ecology of India's Sacred Cattle," *Current Anthropology* 7:51–56, 1966; Harris, Marvin, *Cows, Pigs, Wars and Witches* (New York: Random House, 1974).

**Sacrifice.** This term refers to the ritualized offering of a living creature—human or nonhuman—to a supernatural entity for its consumption. W. R. Smith popularized the term, suggesting that in Semitic societies the deity and the people were brought closer to each other by their common eating of the meal. Later interpretations made consumption by humans an unimportant aspect, and today the infrequent usage of the idea suggests a gift or offering to gods of spirits.

    *See also* Cannibalism; Prayer; Religion; Ritual
    Consult: Benedict, Ruth, "Religion," in *General Anthropology*, ed. F. Boas (Boston: Heath, 1938).

**Sacrifice, Human.** *See* Sacrifice.

*Sacrificed dogs are impaled by the reindeer-herding Koryak of the Kamchatka Peninsula (U.S.S.R.). They are hung with their muzzles pointing up and their bellies pointing east to insure good hunting. Dogs are also sacrificed to the evil spirits (kalau) to protect the people from disaster and to ward off disease. These practices are an expression of beliefs which are very foreign to us, and seem, therefore, to be impractical and even foolish. It has been pointed out that all beliefs are ultimately grounded in one way or another in material conditions. For instance, regarding these sacrificed dogs: the Koryak usually only sacrifice young, disabled, or sick animals—i.e., animals which cannot draw the sleighs which are the people's primary means of transportation. This eliminates the need to feed unproductive animals—a very practical, economically useful device.*

**Sagittal Crest.** This crest, located in the midline of the skull vault, anchors large temporal muscles. It is found in great apes and some fossil hominids.

*See also* Primates, evolutionary features of

**Sahlins, Marshall D.** (b. 1930). American anthropologist who has made major contributions to ecological anthropology and substantivist economic theory, to cultural evolutionary thought, and to Oceanian ethnography.

**Salisbury, Richard Frank** (b. 1926). This British-born cultural anthropologist is best known for his research on technological and social change in Melanesia and on small-group interaction in mental hospitals.

**Salvage Archaeology.** Archaeological sites are an irreplaceable, nonrenewable resource. Once destroyed, they are gone forever. Salvage archaeology is the attempt to recover as much information as possible from sites facing destruction.

Many cultural activities modify the earth's surface, destroying sites. City, road, and reservoir construction and deep plowing in the past century have drastically accelerated destruction which has always occurred through slower, natural erosion. Air pollution decays materials which have survived millennia, and commercial art markets inspire pothunters to loot countless sites.

Salvage work requires special field methods because of time pressures. But rescuing artifacts from bulldozers should be preceded by coherent planning and followed by analysis and publication or it is meaningless. Widescale statistical sampling can quickly assay threatened sites and regions. Compiling site rosters allows selection of more important ones for excavation or further sampling, and it records at least minimal information about what is being destroyed by human or natural agents.

In the United States most states have salvage archaeologists to monitor official construction, and the National Parks Service and Smithsonian River Basin Survey sponsor salvage on federal construction projects. Other countries such as Britain, Canada, and Mexico have similar or larger programs.

During World War I Germany even employed archaeologists to monitor military trenching. Environmental impact statements now required for most American construction take archaeology into account and channel contract funds into salvage. Nevertheless, since prehistoric people tended to live in the same favored locations as modern settlements, the race to study or preserve archaeological sites too often is lost to the expediency of "Progress."

*See also* Archaeology; Exploration of a site; Site; Test pit
Consult: McGimsey, C. R., *Public Archaeology* (New York: Seminar Press, 1972); Meyer, K., *The Plundered Past* (New York: Atheneum, 1973).

—*John R. Cole, Ithaca College*

**Sampling Techniques.** Sampling is the process of drawing inferences from a subset of like objects to the totality of such objects. Most broadly, sampling includes the operation of the ethnographer who takes the experience of a few informants as representing the totality of their culture. In a more technical sense, the term describes the procedures by which a subset of objects is chosen so as to maximize the likelihood that it is representative of the totality—the *population* or *universe*.

In general, sampling techniques are classified in two categories: probability and nonprobability methods. This discussion concentrates on the former category, but since nonprobability methods have been used very often in anthropology, they merit brief mention.

**Nonprobability Sampling.** Traditionally, the most common procedure in anthropological research has been *opportunity sampling*, in which cases are drawn simply because they are easily available. Thus fieldworkers most often have recruited informants and respondents from those willing to serve as such. Also a frequently used technique has been *judgment sampling*. Here cases are chosen for study because they are "interesting" in some a priori theoretical way or because the researcher thinks they are typical of the universe.

Nonprobability sampling renders invalid any statistical analysis based on an assumption of random sampling distributions. Moreover, many writers (e.g., Naroll 1970a,

1970b) have commented on the substantive, as well as the stochastic, pitfalls of such samples.

**Probability Sampling.** A probability sample is one in which all members of the population have a *known probability* of being drawn. Such samples are based on a number of different strategies, the most common of which are described below.

A *simple random sample* is one in which every member of the population has an equal chance ($P = 1/N$, the sample size) of being chosen. Sampling units are drawn at random from a complete roster of the universe. The simple random sample is conceptually and operationally the least complex design. In many cases, however, it is not feasible or it is too costly. For example, a roster of the universe (e.g., all members of a society or all societies of a given type) may not be available. Drawing a random sample from an incomplete population list may introduce serious biases. Moreover, when the sampling units are spread widely in space, the cost of reaching them may be excessive. And when one type of sampling unit is rare in comparison to others, a simple random sample may not include sufficient cases of the type to permit statistical analysis. Alternative techniques have been developed to meet these problems.

A *stratified random sample* is one in which the units of the population are classified according to some relevant criterion (e.g., religion or dominant technology) and then sampled randomly within classes (*strata*). Such samples can be *proportional*, with strata sampled proportionately to their numbers in the population, or *disproportional*, with strata sampled in proportions dictated by cost or other considerations.

A *cluster sample* is one drawn by dividing the population into clusters of cases (e.g., into neighborhoods or regional units on a map) and sampling randomly among such clusters. In the simplest case, *single-stage sampling*, all units in sampled clusters are studied. This design requires clusters of maximum heterogeneity in respect to the variable under study.

*Multistage sampling* is a more complex cluster strategy in which sampling takes place in two or more steps. For instance, one might sample randomly among clusters of villages and then, within clusters, draw a sample of villages stratified according to some criterion.

Cluster sampling has had very little use in anthropology. Indeed, the requirement of heterogeneity would appear to make it unsuitable for cross-cultural analysis, given the well-known homogeneity of culture areas.

*See also* Cross-cultural sampling; Galton's problem; Statistical methods; Stratified sample

Consult: Blalock, Hubert M., *Social Statistics*, 2nd ed. (New York: McGraw-Hill, 1970); Kish, Leslie, *Survey Sampling* (New York: Wiley, 1965); Naroll, Raoul, "What Have We Learned from Cross-Cultural Surveys?," *American Anthropologist* 72:1227–1288, 1970a; Naroll, Raoul, "Cross-Cultural Sampling," in *A Handbook of Method in Cultural Anthropology*, ed. Raoul Naroll and Ronald Cohen (Garden City, N.Y.: Natural History Press, 1970b).

—*Edwin E. Erickson, University of Virginia*

**Sanctions.** This term refers to rewards or penalties that serve to maintain social control over individual members of a community. Sanctions may be positive, as when a socially approved act wins prestige for the person who performs it; or they may be negative, as when fines or ridicule are im-

*The art of sand painting is still taught to some Native American children.*

posed on transgressors. Some sanctions are highly organized and are encoded in law and applied by the appropriate officials; others are informal and diffuse, and their authority rests on a community consensus. The force of public opinion is a potent sanction and a means of ensuring individual conformity to social norms.

*See also* Legal systems; Social control; Taboo

**Sandpainting.** This term is applied to a design representing mythic tales and sacred symbols that is composed of sand and pulverized vegetable or mineral matter. Sandpaintings are drawn on the ground by "singers" (shamans) during curing ceremonies among the Navajo Indians.

**Sapir, Edward** (1884–1934). This American linguist and anthropologist was professor of anthropology at Yale (1927–1939). Sapir had a profound knowledge of Indo-European languages and was inspired by his mentor, Franz Boas, to devote his attention to Native American languages. His resulting work in comparative linguistics has had lasting influence and his *Language* (1921) is still a classic. Sapir always insisted that the study of language should be an integral part of the discipline of anthropology.

With his student and later colleague Benjamin Whorf, Sapir developed the theory of *linguistic relativity* (also known as the

Sapir-Whorf hypothesis). According to this theory, the perception of reality varies in accordance with the language of the speaker.

Never one to avoid controversy, Sapir argued, among other things, for the psychological reality of the phoneme. He also advanced the notion that genuine culture is to be found only in technologically primitive, face-to-face societies (a concept related to Marx's theory of alienation).

*See also* Language and culture; Language and reality

—*Ian Robertson, Cambridge University*

**Saussure, Ferdinand de** (1857–1913). A Swiss linguist who pioneered in the study of structural linguistics, Saussure studied language as an organized system and as a system of signs—semiology. His primary work is *Mémoire sur le système primitif des voyelles dans les langues indo-européennes.*

**Scale Analysis.** This term refers to a body of techniques for discovering and demonstrating the scalar order of variables. Two common approaches (among many others) are *Guttman scaling* and *latent structure analysis.*

*See also* Scales; Statistical methods

**Scales.** A scale can be defined either as the rules for "the assignment of numerals . . . to aspects of objects or events" (Stevens 1951) or as a "set of numerals given to . . . objects by using a certain rule of assignment" (Green 1954). Scaling, then, is the process by which the arrangement, or order, of the states of a variable is defined.

The properties of scale types are important in statistical analysis because given scalar orders have specific implications for permissible mathematical operations. A general classification of scales in terms of metric order has been developed by S. S. Stevens.

Stevens's scale types, or "levels of measurement," fall into a nested hierarchy of four classes distinguished by the amount of metric information they contain. Each class contains all the information of those below plus an additional point of information. The first of Stevens's types is the *nominal* scale, the states of which are distinguished only by mutual exclusivity. Thus the only relationship among states is equivalence/non-

equivalence. The second type is called the *ordinal* scale, whose states are arranged in a rank order. In addition to equivalence/non-equivalence, the relationships "greater than" and "less than" and the rule of transitivity apply. The third type is the *interval* scale, in which the mutually exclusive, rank-ordered states are defined by a standard metric interval (unit of magnitude). Variables at this level can be operated upon mathematically. Finally, there is the *ratio* scale, which in addition to the foregoing qualities has a true zero point. In such scales, the ratio of any two scale values (i.e., magnitudes of states) can be calculated. Stevens's typology has been variously elaborated by other researchers (e.g., Coombs 1953; Torgerson 1958).

In addition to the scales embraced in Stevens's typology and its elaboration, there are others, derived mathematically from various other properties of variable states. In this latter category, among others, are Guttman scales and scales derived from latent structure analysis.

*See also* Scale analysis; Statistical methods
Consult: Coombs, C. H., "Theory and Methods of Social Measurement," in *Research Methods in the Behavioral Sciences*, ed. L. Festinger and D. Katz (New York: Dryden, 1953); Green, B. F., "Attitude Measurement," in *Handbook of Social Psychology*, ed. G. Lindzey (Cambridge, Mass.: Addison-Wesley, 1954); Stevens, S. S. (ed.), *Handbook of Experimental Psychology* (New York: Wiley, 1951); Torgerson, W. S., *Theory and Methods of Scaling* (New York: Wiley, 1958).
—Edwin E. Erickson, University of Virginia

**Scapulimancy.** This form of divination involves forecasting future events by a shaman's reading of the charred cracks in the burnt scapula (shoulder bone) of an animal.

*See also* Divination

**Scarification.** *See* Adornment; Deformation and mutilation.

**Schaller, George B.** (b. 1930). A zoologist known for his ecological and behavioral research on animals, Schaller has done pioneering and monumental work in primate behavior with his detailed ecological study of the mountain gorilla.

**Schapera, Isaac** (b. 1905). This social anthropologist is known for his ethnographic research on the Tswana tribes of S Africa and his editing of David Livingstone's writings on Africa.

**Schizmogenesis.** This term refers to a form of progressive, increasingly tense conflict formation which produces a schism or cleavage in a social group. G. Bateson coined this word to identify a process of differentiation in cultural norms which stem from cumulative interactions between individuals. Bateson saw schizmogenesis as influential in causing culture change processes, particularly the generation of new norms. He later believed that this division-creating process was much involved in all intimate human relations, acculturation situations, and the increasing maladjustment of prepsychotic individuals.

*See also* Cultural change

**Schizophrenia.** Schizophrenia is one of the functional psychoses (i.e., a severe mental disorder lacking any known organic basis). The term is a general category comprising such subtypes as simple schizophrenia, hebephrenia, catatonia, and chronic undifferentiated schizophrenia.

*See also* Culture and personality; Mental illness and culture; Normality; Psychosis; Shamanism

**Schliemann, Heinrich** (1822–1890). After amassing a private fortune in international commerce, Schliemann turned to archaeology, pursuing research based on his faith in the reliability of Greek legendary history. His excavations at Homer's Troy (Hissarlik), Mycenae, Tiryns, and Orchomenos revealed the existence of a spectacular Bronze Age Aegean civilization.

*See also* Troy

**Schmidt, Wilhelm** (1868–1954). Best known as a leading proponent of the *Kulturkreislehre* (culture circle school) of diffusionism, Father Smith proposed a theory of devolution to counterbalance that of cultural evolution. In 1926 he founded the journal *Anthropos*.

*See also* Kulturkreise

**Scientific Method.** This term refers to the logical processes of thought which direct the observation and explanation of empirically perceptible events. These processes differ in the way they relate data (particular events) to generalizations (hypotheses, theories, laws).

There are many factors which determine what are considered data, including the training and experience of the observer, the goals of the investigation, and the current methodology and philosophy of the discipline. The search for regularities and patterns in the data may follow several logical lines.

*Induction,* in the narrow sense, means that through the repetition of certain events one arrives at an empirical generalization about all events of the same nature. In the broad sense, induction is a form of reasoning from premises which support, but do not logically entail, the conclusion. The truth of the conclusion can only be asserted with a certain degree of probability. The direction of inference is from a particular event to a generalization. The end result of inductive reasoning is a descriptive generalization of little explanatory value.

The formulation of causal theories and hypotheses is the function of *abduction* (or *retroduction*). This process is not well understood and is often ignored by logicians. In essence, the origination of a theory is not considered to be a random psychological accident but rather the product of an informed and disciplined mind coupled with accumulated observational experience. When an apparent anomaly is observed, the mind moves to hypothesize a general principle from which the event would logically follow.

*Deductive reasoning* is applied to the testing of hypotheses after they have been advanced. Particular events are subsumed under laws or hypotheses of universal form. Given certain antecedent conditions and general laws, the occurrence of a particular event can be predicted and, by the same process, explained. Deductive inference is logically sound. The truth of the premises entails the truth of the conclusion. Thus deduction is a more powerful explanatory process than induction.

One of the most important aspects of scientific method is how closely these logical concepts approximate the reality of scientific investigation. Scientific method in anthropology is determined more by pragmatic than by logical concerns. A deductive system based on highly probable general laws has no validity in a field where a general law has yet to be identified. However, the deductive principle may still have value as an explanatory tool. A *hypothetico-deductive* approach has come to represent scientific method for many anthropologists. In this model, hypotheses take the place of general laws in the premise. Predictions are based on the hypotheses. Test implications are derived and the predictions are tested against new sets of data. If the fit is good, the probability that the hypotheses are true increases. If the fit is not good, alternative hypotheses must be tested. Such a model can aid the anthropologist in the search for regularities in the data, despite the possibility that general laws may not be forthcoming.

An alternative to the hypothetico-deductive model has been presented by advocates of a *systems approach* to explanation in the social sciences. They argue that social sciences are unable to meet the requirements of a deductive model, that valid statements of universal form are rare, and that all antecedent conditions can seldom be identified. Instead of using a linear, deductive model, systems theorists prefer to base their explanations on the logical structure of systems and their rules of interaction. The explanations are relatively graded according to their completeness and usefulness rather than their logical validity.

Scientific method in anthropology is still in an experimental stage. It is promising that anthropologists are examining the manner in which they arrive at their conclusions. How this will ultimately affect the way they actually conduct their research is uncertain.

Consult: Hanson, Norwood Russell, *Patterns of Discovery* (Cambridge: Cambridge University Press, 1958); Kaplan, David, and Manners, Robert A., *Culture Theory* (Englewood Cliffs, N.J.: Prentice-Hall, 1972); Meehan, Eugene J., *Explanation in Social Science: A System Paradigm* (Homewood, Ill.: Dorsey Press, 1968).

—*Patricia Eyring Brown, Arizona State University*

**Scientific Paradigm.** *See* Paradigm, scientific.

**Scientific Racism.** This term is applied to theories that claim to demonstrate scientifically the inferiority of some "racial" or ethnic groups to others. Such theories generally argue that social inequality results from differences in intelligence between higher and lower status racial, ethnic, and class groups. Their major social implication is that significant inequality is inevitable (see Herrnstein 1973) or at the least that massive therapeutic measures are needed to raise the people at the bottom of the class pyramid to the level of their supposed betters (see Moynihan 1967).

Opponents of scientific racist theory argue that it is not based on scientific evidence but is rather an ideological defense of the social elite. By blaming inequality on those oppressed by it, the ideology is said to rationalize society's biased allocation of power and wealth (see Ryan 1972).

**Current Theories.** Scientific racism in the United States currently appears in two distinct forms—geneticist and environmentalist. On the one hand, a school of hereditarian psychologists led by Arthur Jensen claims on the basis of IQ test results that blacks and certain other oppressed groups are genetically less intelligent than whites (see Jensen 1969, 1973). On the other hand, a number of academics, including such prominent men as Daniel Moynihan and Edward Banfield, have argued that lower-class groups, especially blacks, suffer from psychological and intellectual deficits due not to genetic factors but to disrupted family life and other damaging environmental influences (Moynihan 1967; Banfield 1970).

Both the environmentalist and the geneticist explanations of social inequality have been challenged by the findings of research. For example, the idea that IQ tests can be used to measure differences in intelligence between groups has been extensively criticized. Others (see Billingsley 1968) have argued that Moynihan's theory of the black family (i.e., that the structure of black families causes psychological damage to black children) has no basis in fact. Evidence has also been adduced that mistreatment (including malnutrition), not a weak cultural background or low intelligence, is to blame when poor children fail in school.

Geneticist and environmentalist theories have sometimes been presented by scholars as diametrically opposed explanations of inequality. One school argues that inequality is biologically inevitable while the other argues that compensatory programs may make up for the environmental deprivation suffered by the poor—especially if the programs aim at young children who have not yet been too seriously hurt. This difference has led to acrimonious debate between geneticists and environmentalists over the value of government programs of compensatory education. Dissenting scholars, however, have suggested that the two schools are less different than they appear to be. They point out that both schools rely on the assumption that deficiencies in the poor are the source of their low social position and both schools refuse to locate the source of inequality in the wider society's social structure (see Aronowitz 1974).

**Origins.** The origins of modern scientific racism date from the rise of the science of biology in the 18th and 19th centuries (see Gossett 1963). At that time the development of biology, especially of theories of evolution, undermined then current religious justifications for slavery and for social hierarchy in general. Apologists for inequality looked, therefore, to the new science of biology to support their social views. They first attempted to demonstrate, on the basis of anatomical measures like brain size, that blacks and oppressed immigrant groups were "less evolved" than White Anglo-Saxon Protestants. By the beginning of the 20th century, however, this approach had been proved fallacious, and scientific racist theorists began to use scores on the newly developed IQ test as their major argument for the intellectual inferiority of blacks and immigrants. The environmentalist school came into prominence after World War II because critical scholarship was demonstrating the IQ test to be invalid as a measure of mental functioning. The current rise of "jensenism," therefore, can be seen as an attempt—by those to whom the steady retreat of scientific racism over past years is disturbing—to resurrect previously discarded hereditarian theories (see Kamin 1974).

*See also* Genetics and intelligence; Intelligence; Intelligence quotient; Jensen, Arthur; Racism

Consult: Aronowitz, S., "The Trap of Environmentalism," in *The New Assault on Equality: I.Q. and Social Stratification*, ed. A. Gartner et al. (New York: Harper & Row, 1974); Banfield, E. *The Unheavenly City* (Boston: Little, Brown,

1970); Billingsley, A., *Black Families in White America* (Englewood Cliffs, N.J.: Prentice-Hall, 1968); Gossett, T. F., *Race: The History of an Idea in America* (New York: Schocken, 1963); Herrnstein, R. J., *I.Q. in the Meritocracy* (Boston: Little, Brown, 1973); Jensen, A., "How Much Can We Boost I.Q. and Scholastic Achievement?," *Harvard Educational Review* 39(1), 1969; Jensen, A., *Educability and Group Differences* (New York: Harper & Row, 1973); Kamin, J., *The Science and Politics of I.Q.* (Potomac, Md.: Erlbaum, 1974); Moynihan, D., *The Negro Family: The Case for National Action* (Cambridge, Mass.: M.I.T. Press, 1967); Ryan, W., *Blaming the Victim* (New York: Pantheon, 1972); Whitten, Phillip, and Kagan, Jerome, "Jensen's Dangerous Half-Truths," *Psychology Today*, August 1969.
—Anthony Kroch, Temple University

**Sculpture.** See Art; Art, primitive.

**Sebeok, Thomas Albert** (b. 1920). A student of linguistics, folklore, and Uralic-Altaic studies, Sebeok is also known for his work in computational linguistics, psycholinguistics, and stylistics. He is the editor of *Current Trends in Linguistics*.

**Secondary Institutions.** Also called projective systems, secondary institutions include much of what anthropologists otherwise call belief systems, religion, mythology. These are seen as collective fantasy products or group projections of subjectively shared wishes, needs, and conflicts. A. Kardiner argued that, once formed, the basic personality structure of a society would mold the content and meaning of projected fantasies, such as beliefs about the supernatural. Thus a strongly authoritarian basic personality type should be correlated with projected beliefs about powerful high gods.
See also Basic personality; Primary institutions
Consult: DuBois, Cora, *The People of Alor* (Cambridge, Mass.: Harvard University Press, 1960).

**Secret Societies.** Secret societies are found in a number of areas throughout the world. They differ in what they keep secret from nonmembers. In West Africa membership is generally known to nonmembers but certain religious or ritual knowledge is kept

*The Ku Klux Klan is a secret society that still exists in the U.S.A.*

from them. In other societies membership itself may be kept a secret. This is true, for example, of the "secret" rituals of the Masons, whose general membership is, however, unknown.

No matter what is kept secret, the mere fact that a secret is known only by members limited by some criterion (age, sex, ethnic origin) gives them a certain added mystical quality. These societies often use that quality to strengthen their functioning as adjuncts to political systems—for example, the Muslim Brotherhood in Arab countries and the Bruderbond among Boers in South Africa.

West African societies have been the most studied, and the role of the Poro in Liberia is, perhaps, the best understood. Studies of West African societies indicate that they may well function as a means for facilitating sociocultural change.
Consult: Salamone, Frank A., "Mid-West Igbo Title Societies: An Example of Ethnic Boundary Maintenance," *Anthropos*, 1974.
—Frank A. Salamone, St. John's University

**Sects.** This term refers to groups, usually religious, whose distinctive (perhaps heterodox) beliefs and practices set them apart from similar groups. Sects may arise in protest against established groups.
See also Religion; Revitalization movements

**Segregation.** The institutionalized separation of one category of people from another may be based on differences in such attributes as age, sex, religion, or social class, but the term *segregation* is generally used in reference to enforced social distance between racial groups.

The practice of segregation usually implies a belief that one group is superior to another. The two most extreme examples of segregation are probably the caste system traditionally practiced in India, in which segregation was integrated with racial and religious elements, and the apartheid system currently practiced in South Africa, where the white minority segregates the nonwhite majority in almost every aspect of political, economic, and social life.

In the United States, institutionalized segregation was long a crucial element in intergroup relations between blacks and whites, especially in the South. Segregation was practiced informally before the Civil War, but after Reconstruction a series of "Jim Crow" laws led to its formal, judicially sanctioned application. A series of Supreme Court decisions and federal laws have subsequently made racial segregation illegal in the United States, although informal institutionalized discrimination still persists.

*See also* Apartheid; Caste; Class; Ethnic group; Extinction of minorities; Jajmani system; Minorities, ethnic; Social stratification; Status

Consult: Glazer, Nathan, and Moynihan, Daniel P., *Beyond the Melting Pot: The Negroes, Puerto Ricans, Jews, Italians, and the Irish in New York City* (Cambridge, Mass.: M.I.T. Press, 1963); Gordon, M. M., *Assimilation in American Life: The Role of Race, Reliation, and National Origin* (New York: Oxford University Press, 1964).

—*Ian Robertson, Cambridge University*

## Selection, Cultural.

The selective dimension of culture can be conceptualized in terms of the formation and transformation of a given culture and in terms of the effects of cultural existence in general on the human species. From an evolutionary perspective C. Loring Brace has written that human beings live in a cultural ecological niche. Just as the natural environment (through natural selection) has affected human organic evolution, after the development of culture cultural life may have similarly affected human organic evolution. Thus the physical anthropologist S. L. Washburn speculates that cultural selection may have eliminated the most irascible individuals who could not adapt to the new cultural existence and this may be reflected in changes in the form of the human skull in the evolutionary development of contemporary *Homo sapiens*.

In terms of the formation of culture, Ruth Benedict noted that each culture of necessity must be a limited selection from the arc of human potential. Each culture is only a partial expression of possible human cultural life. She further indicated that each culture is a whole that is greater than the sum of its parts. It is integrated according to characteristic patterns, "the motives and emotions and values that are institutionalized in that culture." The elements it will readily accept from other cultures, and the internally developed innovations it will adopt, depend on how these novel cultural elements accommodate to the dominant

cultural patterns. Moreover, how newly adopted traits will be expressed in the culture is also influenced by the existing cultural patterns. Thus culture, insofar as it is a patterned, organized, and integrated whole, will exert a selective influence on the nature of the transformations it will undergo.

*See also* Benedict, Ruth; Cultural change; Diffusion; Evolution, human; Pattern, culture; Social integration

Consult: Benedict, R., *Patterns of Culture* (Boston: Houghton Mifflin, 1934); Dobzhansky, T., "Evolution—Organic and Superorganic," in *Human Variation*, ed. H. Bleibtreu and J. Downs (Beverly Hills: Glencoe Press, 1971).

—*Stan Wilk, Lycoming College*

## Selection, Natural.

The process whereby some organisms or groups of organisms are reproductively more successful or "fit" than others in a given environmental or ecological setting.

*See also* Adaptation, biological; Darwin, Charles; Evolution, genetic mechanisms of; Wallace, Alfred Russel

## Seligman, Charles Gabriel

(1873–1940). This British ethnologist and instructor of Bronislaw Malinowski is known for his broad studies of cultures in New Guinea and the Sudan. Along with A. C. Haddon and W. H. R. Rivers he took part in the Cambridge Expedition to Torres Straits (1898–1900), one of the first major ethnological field studies. Seligman did important work in psychological anthropology and rejected Lucian Lévy-Bruhl's notion of the "primitive mind."

## Semantic Domains.

*See* Formal semantic analysis.

## Semantics.

Semantics is the study of meaning. In Charles Morris's (1938) formulation of *semiotic* (the study of signs), semantics is the study of the relationships between signs and what they represent ("mean"). Anthropologists concerned with semantics have focused most of their attention on identifying the semantic domains represented by the lexical items (vocabulary) of the languages they have studied. Of particular difficulty has been the problem of delineating the exact nature of the systematic

relationships obtaining among such domains. These efforts are variously identified as the New Ethnography, cognitive anthropology, formal semantic analysis, ethnoscience, and componential analysis, to name but a few.

*See also* Communication; Componential analysis; Culture and personality; Ethnoscience; Formal semantic analysis; Language; Linguistics; New Ethnography, the; Semiotic; Syntax

Consult: Morris, Charles D., "Foundations of the Theory of Signs," *International Encyclopedia of a Unified Science*, vol. 1, no. 2 (Chicago: University of Chicago Press, 1938); Tyler, Stephen A., *Cognitive Anthropology* (New York: Holt, 1969).

—*David E. Hunter, Southern Connecticut State College*

## Sememe.

This word, coined by Leonard Bloomfield (1933), refers to the meaning of a morpheme.

*See also* Morpheme

Consult: Bloomfield, Leonard, *Language* (New York: Holt, 1933).

## Semiotic.

Semiotic is the study of signs and sign-using behavior in general. *Semiosis* is the process whereby something functions as a sign. These concepts were formalized by Charles Morris (1938).

The usual confusion in understanding semiotic results from confounding it with semantics. The two areas are related. However, in normal usage semiotic is the more general of the two disciplines. *Semantics* is usually restricted to the study of the relationships between signs and what they represent; *syntax* is the study of the (ordering) relationships among signs; *pragmatics* is the study of the relationships between signs and the organisms that produce and receive them. For some of its proponents, semiotic encompasses all the disciplines interested in human interaction and holds the promise of uniting all the behavioral sciences under the general banner of semiotic. While that claim may be somewhat premature, there is no doubt that its influence has been felt, and it has led to many interesting interdisciplinary exchanges.

*See also* Communication

Consult: Morris, Charles W., "Foundations of the Theory of Signs," *International Encyclopedia of a Unified Science*, vol. 1, no. 2 (Chicago: University of Chicago Press, 1938).

**Senses, Human.** *See* Human senses.

**Sensory Deprivation.** This term refers to the elimination of most sensory input to an individual. Sensory deprivation may be achieved by placing the subject in a totally dark, soundless room, often with limbs bandaged to limit tactile sensation. Sensory deprivation is a disturbing experience: subjects may respond with acute distress within hours or even minutes, and if deprivation is continued for several days virtually all subjects display temporary symptoms of mental breakdown, particularly visual and auditory hallucinations. Under experimental conditions, the subject readjusts relatively rapidly when deprivation is discontinued, but sensory deprivation may be used as a means of psychological torture or as a technique for "brainwashing," with serious long-term consequences.

**Sentences.** Sentences are utterances consisting of sequences of conjoined phrases arranged in accordance with phrase/constituent-structure rules. Sentences represent a level of structure between phrase structure and, in discourse, paragraph structure. Different sentence types (transitive, equational interrogative, imperative) are distinguished from each other by the kinds of constituents present and their sequential order and by prosodic (e.g., pitch) patterns characteristic of each sentence type. Matrix sentences contain subordinate sentences (clauses) embedded within some constituent of the matrix sentence: in *The man who came to dinner was John*, the constituent *who came to dinner* is the embedded sentence; the remainder is the matrix sentence.

Sentences are transformed by rules of conjoining (yielding compounds like *John and Mary wept*), permutation (e.g., *Are you listening?*, a permutation of *You are listening*), and deletion. Deletion may produce elliptical sentences (*Not today!* and *Ready yet?*), which have the sequential order and intonation patterns of their respective full sentence types but without some constituents of the full underlying form of the sentence.

*See also* Language; Linguistics; Morpheme; Words

**Sequence Dating.** The relative dates of artifacts, or groups of associated artifacts, may be reconstructed by arranging them so that the variation in form or style forms a gradual series which can be inferred to represent a developmental sequence and therefore a chronological order. Sir Flinders Petrie developed sequence dating at the beginning of the 20th century as a means of ordering Predynastic Egyptian grave goods. By concentrating on such features as handles on ceramic vessels, Petrie was able to arrange the grave lots in a series that seemed to reflect gradual, developmental change. The fifty stages of his sequence were assigned numerical "sequence dates," producing a relative chronological framework which was extended over a large portion of the Nile Valley.

Petrie's use of variation in artifacts for chronological ordering was one of the first examples of dating by seriation, which remains a fundamental method of relative dating in archaeology. Seriation rests on the principle that cultural traits—such as types or features of artifacts—appear, reach a maximum in popularity, then decline in frequency and disappear, never to reappear in identical form. The presence, absence, and relative abundance of a series of such traits can therefore be used to order archaeological assemblages and the deposits in which they occur, although additional evidence such as stratigraphy may be necessary to determine the direction in time of the sequence.

*See also* Dating, relative

Consult: Hole, Frank, and Heizer, Robert F., *An Introduction to Prehistoric Archaeology*, 3rd ed. (New York: Holt, 1973); Petrie, W. M. Flinders, *Diospolis Parva*, Egyptian Exploration Fund Memoirs, no. 20, London, 1901.
—*John S. Henderson, Cornell University*

**Seriation.** *See* Sequence dating.

**Service, Elman R.** (b. 1915). Cultural theorist whose classification of the levels of sociopolitical integration has standardized the terminology for various types of societies into band, tribe, chiefdom, and state. He has recently, however, abandoned this terminology because empirical cases have shown the categories to be spuriously precise (especially the term *tribe*).

*See also* Band; Chiefdom; Tribe; State, the

**Settlement Patterns.** This term refers to the ways in which human populations are residentially arranged in a designated territory. The extent of clustering and dispersal of residences is a major dimension in the analysis of settlement patterns; other dimensions include the arrangement, planned or unplanned, of settlements and also the ecological setting. Such dimensions of settlement give considerable information on a society's social structure and patterns of social interaction since these are closely linked with the society's means of production and its mechanisms of distribution. Because settlements usually leave material remains, reconstructing settlement patterns is particularly interesting to archaeologists.

**Settlements, Squatter.** Squatter settlements occur where individuals or collectives invade tracts of land belonging to public or private parties usually unknown to the invading settlers. In this century they are found almost always in cities. Jurally, individual settlers are illegal occupants subject to eviction and the squatter settlement is an illegal place. Three major squatter situations may be noted: the settlements are ultimate refuge places, like the American Hoovervilles during the Depression; they provide temporary bases for persons whose

*Settlement patterns express the systematic relationships between societies and their environments and the strategies that societies use to meet their needs. What can you tell about Dublin, California, by this picture?*

*A squatter settlement (favela) in Rio de Janeiro, 1966. The lack of care taken with regard to the appearance of these structures belies their actual physical stability, for they provide good shelter even in violent rainstorms. Because this favela was constantly threatened with removal by the government, people invested their incomes in movable property instead of attractive housing: many houses are well equipped and comfortable inside.*

main socioeconomic interests lie elsewhere, such as in their tribal agrarian property; they urbanize *progressively* because permanently committed settlers massively invest risk capital in housing and infrastructure—which is developmentally opposite to the process found in slums.

See also Land tenure; Settlement patterns; Urbanism

**Sex (Gender) Identity.** This term refers to the subjective awareness that one is a member of the male or female sex, with the consequence that one conforms to culturally determined expectations of appropriate masculine or feminine behavior. Although the categories of male and female are in most instances biological givens, the content of the identity that attaches to these givens is culturally variable and culturally acquired.

The earliest social scientific account of the acquisition of gender identity was that of Sigmund Freud, who believed that appropriate sex-role behavior followed the successful resolution of the Oedipus complex in the male and the Elektra complex in the female. This view has few adherents today.

A widely held current account of gender acquisition is provided by the behaviorist or social learning model, which regards the identities as the product of a conditioning process: children are selectively rewarded or punished for gender-appropriate or gender-inappropriate behavior and so learn their adult roles.

A more recent explanation is that of the cognitive developmental school of psychology, which regards gender identity as the

*Villagers of the Brahman caste in a North Indian village. Mothers often "beautify" their daughters, who thus learn how to make themselves beautiful. Later, when they are adults, it will seem perfectly "natural" for them to line their eyes, wear saris, and in general behave the way a woman "should." (Black design on the child's forehead is to avert the "evil eye.")*

### GENDER IDENTITY DEVELOPMENT

*The acquisition of an adult gender identity is a long process that starts at conception with the determination of chromosomal sex and proceeds through gonadal and hormonal developments, social identification and reinforcement of a sexual identity, and finally, in adulthood, to the interaction among the person's sexual self-identification, body image, and erotic orientation(s).*

| STAGES OF DEVELOPMENT | | | | |
|---|---|---|---|---|
| **Conception** | **Fetal Development** | **Juvenile Development** | **Pubertal Transition** | **Adult Gender Identity** |
| typical chromosomal sex XX = ♀ XY = ♂  atypical chromosomal sex XO, XXY, XYY, etc. | gonadal development  hormones  external genitals  neural pathways | genital morphology can be ♂ or ♀ or ambiguous  behavior of others reinforces ♂ or ♀ image  individual cognitive development regarding own body image (♂ or ♀)  juvenile gender identity differentiates as ♂, ♀, or ambivalent | pubertal hormonal sex  secondary sexual characteristics  erotic orientation toward ♂ or ♀  psychological or cognitive self-identification as ♂ or ♀ | sexual self-identification (♂ or ♀)  person's image of own body (♂ or ♀)  erotic orientation toward ♂ or ♀ or both |

result of a personal cognitive judgment: the children take their cues from the surrounding culture but actively construct their own sex roles.

*See also* Behaviorist school of psychology; Developmental school of psychology; Freud, Sigmund; Sex roles

Consult: Maccoby, Eleanor E. (ed.), *The Development of Sex Differences* (Stanford: Stanford University Press, 1966); Martin, M. Kay, and Voorhies, Barbara, *The Female of the Species* (New York: Columbia, 1975); Money, John, and Ehrhardt, Anke A., *Man and Woman, Boy and Girl: Differentiation and Dimorphism of Gender Identity from Conception to Maturity* (Baltimore: Johns Hopkins, 1972).

—*Ian Robertson, Cambridge University*

**Sex-linked Traits.** These traits are carried by genes located on the X or Y sex chromosomes. Most X-linked characteristics are recessive in females, which means that unless they are present on both X chromosomes of a female, the trait is carried but not expressed. Males, with only one X chromosome, more commonly exhibit such traits phenotypically. Examples include hemophilia and red-green color blindness. Y-linked traits are also called *holandric* and are manifested only by males. Known examples are rare but probably include the long hairs on the ear rims of some South Indian men.

*See also* Color blindness

**Sex Roles.** Certain patterns of behavior are expected of males and females in a culture. These patterns include personality attributes, relations of dominance and submission, and economic or domestic roles.

Every person is classified at birth on the basis of morphological characteristics into one of two categories, male or female. But all cultures elaborate these basic biological differences between male and female into secondary, nonbiological differences—cultural notions of masculine and feminine. Each society tends to regard these concepts of masculinity and feminity as being also rooted in biology, but this view is rejected by contemporary anthropologists.

The first anthropological research into sex roles in other cultures was conducted by Margaret Mead. In her enthnographic studies in the South Pacific, she found one society with sex roles very much like our own, one society in which these roles are

*Herero boy in Southern Africa has hunted mongooses, taking on expected adult male role behavior.*

reversed, and one society in which male and female sex roles closely overlap. Other anthropological research has confirmed that there is a very wide variation in the content of sex roles in different cultures. Clearly, this variation cannot be ascribed to genetic factors and must be a product of cultural influences. It is now generally accepted that most differences in male and female sex roles are the result of socialization into the norms considered appropriate in each society.

There are, however, certain general cross-cultural patterns in the content of sex roles. Studies of other cultures have consistently shown a fairly clear division of labor between the sexes: women commonly assume responsibility for child care, domestic duties, and those arduous tasks (such as collecting firewood or carrying loads) that require little or no cooperation among individuals; while men tend to become engaged in activities involving more travel from the home, and tasks frequently requiring teamwork (such as hunting large land and sea mammals, and fishing on a large scale). This division of labor is presumably related to inherited differences between the sexes: women bear and suckle children; men are better adapted to short-term feats of endurance such as hunting or fighting.

There are also recurrent differences in the personality attributes of the sexes in different cultures; the general cross-cultural mode is that males are more active and aggressive but less nurturant and emotional than females. The extent of these differences varies considerably from culture to culture, however, and in some cultures the patterns are actually reversed. Family and kinship patterns also reveal a general tendency toward male dominance, but again this is by no means a uniform or universal tendency. For a discussion of the evolutionary and adaptive features of these patterns, consult Martin and Voorhies (1975).

*See also* Culture and personality; Personality, cultural determinants of; Sex (gender) identity

Consult: Maccoby, Eleanor E. (ed.), *The Development of Sex Differences* (Stanford: Stanford University Press, 1966); Martin, M. Kay, and Voorhies, Barbara, *The Female of the Species* (New York: Columbia, 1975); Mead, Margaret, *Sex and Temperament in Three Primitive Societies,* 3rd ed. (New York: Morrow, 1963).

—*Phillip Whitten, Harvard University*
—*Pell Fender*

*BaMbuti men frequently take turns with the women in caring for small children.*

*Sexual Dimorphism. This male baboon is displaying a dramatic aspect of sexual dimorphism among his species: the canine teeth of males are considerably larger than those of females; not surprisingly, male baboons often open their mouths to display their impressive weaponry when making hostile gestures.*

### Sexual Dimorphism, Evolution of.

Sexual dimorphism is a difference between the males and females of a species that is not related directly to reproductive function. The difference may be in physical form or behavior, including differences in size, color, hair patterns, group roles, or possession of special anatomical structures.

Several factors have been postulated in the evolution of sexual dimorphism, but agreement has not been reached as to which are causal. Different ones may be important under different circumstances, or they may interact. *Intrasex competition for mates* leads to the development of features useful in combat with other members of the same sex or in attracting members of the opposite sex. The sex competed for (the limiting factor) is usually the one which spends the greater amount of time rearing the young.

*Ecological pressure* is another factor: males and females of different sizes can exploit different food sources, thus avoiding competition with one another for scarce resources. *Protection from predators* is yet another factor. Males frequently evolve larger body size and better weapons (e.g., large canine teeth) to protect the group from predators. Females may then remain small because the environment can consequently support more of them, a reproductive advantage.

*See also* Evolution, genetic mechanisms of; Primates, evolutionary features of

Consult: Campbell, Bernard (ed.), *Sexual Selection and the Descent of Man: 1871–1971* (Chicago: Aldine, 1972).

—R. Linda Wheeler, Arizona State University

### Sexual Division of Labor.

Much of the work in which people engage can be done by all people, regardless of sex. In fact, however, all societies differentially distribute tasks according to sex. Universally in human society, even in those with advanced technologies where the physical strength of the body as tool has become, for the most part, irrelevant, tasks still are distributed both by age and by sex. The latter distribution is called the sexual division of labor.

This division of tasks is striking in several ways. Though isolated partial exceptions may be found, the following generalizations are still nearly universally true: women care for neonates and little children; men do the extreme heavy work; men do those tasks requiring large, sudden outputs of energy (like running down prey); women do paced tasks like foraging for roots and seeds; men do those tasks requiring coordinated teamwork. Behaviorally one finds that few, if any, tasks are done exclusively by one sex: people pragmatically use their labor resources as they are available. However, these *statistical* distributions of task by sex are represented in each society as *norms* of mutually exclusive behavior. The various physical attributes of males and females strongly suggest the evolutionary adaptiveness of the sexual patterning of the division of labor, especially under primitive conditions. However, it is clear that the continued sexual patterning of work in technologically advanced societies operates on a symbolic level to reinforce sexual differences and repolarize gender identity.

*See also* Economic systems; Sex (gender) identity; Technology and subsistence

—Anthony Leeds, Boston University

### Sexual Reproduction.

Most organisms reproduce sexually: by uniting sperm and egg cells. Human females produce fertile eggs relatively constantly, unlike most species, thus allowing human reproduction to be culturally patterned rather than seasonal.

*See also* Estrous cycle; Genetics

### Sexuality, Human.

*Homo sapiens*, unlike other species, has no estrous cycle. Men and women are, at least potentially, always available for sexual relations and must continually control potentially disruptive behavior caused by that fact. All known cultures declare appropriate and inappropriate times and partners for sex and provide sanctions to keep people behaving appropriately. However, human sexual behavior often defies cultural norms and social sanctions so that "inappropriate" behavior occurs everywhere and continuously. Sociocultural systems respond variously to biological sexuality—trying to repress it, refining it as an art, glorifying it as ultimate symbol of the creative unity of the universe, or defining it ambivalently as desirable, fun, corrupt, and dirty (a prevalent American view). Since cultural systems constrain *total* sexuality, every society evolves unauthorized or countercultural expressions of sexuality—pornography in America, homosexuality in Greece—which develop normative and social contexts of their own (e.g., "skin flick" cinemas or Bacchanales). Also, the ways in which sexual conventions are flaunted by individuals (e.g., adultery) are themselves socioculturally patterned.

Most cultures authorize culturally thematic selected aspects of sexuality, often elevating them to important ritual and religious status—phallic and vaginal worship and ritual wedding defloration in India; ritual defloration of a peasant's bride by the lord in medieval Europe; fertility worship; formal transvestitism like the *berdaches* among the Plains Indians; breast worship in American society. Likewise, all cultures select thematically important sexual aspects for prohibition—masturbation; incest (variously defined) everywhere; various sexual positions; various sexual acts (e.g., anal and oral intercourse); sexual relations with children; male and female homosexuality (still widely illegal in the United States); adultery and fornication.

See also Homosexuality; Sex (gender) identity; Sex roles; Sexual reproduction
Consult: Comfort, Alex (ed.), *The Joy of Sex* (New York: Simon and Schuster, 1972); Ellis, Havelock, *Studies in the Psychology of Sex* (Philadelphia: Davis, 1900–1928); Ford, Cleland S., and Beach, Frank A., *Patterns of Sexual Behavior* (New York: Harper, 1951); Gordon, Chad, and Johnson, Gayle (eds.), *Readings in Human Sexuality: Contemporary Perspectives* (New York: Harper & Row, 1976); Malinowski, Bronislaw, *Sex and Repression in Savage Society* (New York: Humanities Press, 1927); McCary, James L., *Human Sexuality—Physiological and Psychological Factors of Sexual Behavior* (Princeton: Van Nostrand, 1967); Van de Velde, Th. H., *Ideal Marriage: Its Physiology and Technique* (New York: Random House, 1926).
—*Anthony Leeds, Boston University*

**Shaman.** The shaman, a part-time magico-religious specialist adept at trance, divination, and curing, derives magical power directly from a supernatural source, usually through mystic experience. An important

*Two Guere shamans of the Ivory Coast toss a young girl back and forth in the air. The girl is in a deep trance. This ritual and dance are being performed to aid the wife of a chief as she gives birth.*

element of the shaman's work is the performance of public (rather than private) rituals, in which divination and curing are accomplished through trance and also sleight-of-hand tricks.

See also Hallucinations and shamanism; Magic; Shamanism; Taboo
Consult: Radin, P., *Autobiography of a Winnebago Indian* (New York: Dover, 1920).

**Shamanism.** Shamanism means a belief in the power of medicine men, sorcerers, or other specialists in the manipulation of spiritual forces for human ends. The term was coined from a term used in Siberia, where it is applied to traditional beliefs in the powers of native practitioners of magico-religious rites, but it is now used to refer to apparently similar elements that are found in the belief systems of a great many preliterate cultures.

Shamanism has sometimes been regarded as a precursor of more systematized religion; Anthony F. C. Wallace, for example, suggests that shamanism is a rudimentary religious form which is subsumed, at more complex levels of social structure, by communal and finally ecclesiastical forms of religious organization. Shamanism, which is essentially a phenomenon of part-time practitioners, thus gives way to the full-scale ecclesiastical bureaucracy with its systematic theology. Some shamanistic practices may, however, be retained in the more elaborated religious form.

See also Culture and personality; Hallucinations and shamanism; Magic; Religion; Schizophrenia; Shaman; Voodoo; Witchcraft
—*Ian Robertson, Cambridge University*

**Shanidar Cave.** This Paleolithic cave site, excavated by R. Solecki between 1951 and 1960 in N Iraq, yielded the skeletal remains of nine Neanderthal individuals. Pollen analysis indicated that several of them had been buried, some 60,000 years ago, with brightly colored flowers. This represents the earliest known example of ceremonial burial and implies strongly the existence of religious beliefs among Neanderthals. A recent analysis by Solecki indicates that most of the plants buried with the Neanderthal individuals at Shanidar are known to have medicinal properties; thus, he postulates, *Homo Sapiens Neanderthalensis* may also have developed a primitive medicine.

*See also* Burial; Neanderthal man
Consult: Solecki, Ralph S., *Shanidar* (New York: Knopf, 1971).

**Shapiro, Harry** (b. 1902). A physical anthropologist at the American Museum of Natural History, Shapiro is known primarily for his studies on human variation and the Pacific area.

**Sharecropping.** In this form of agrarian land use, a person needing but not owning land receives from a landowner the right to use a designated tract for agricultural purposes. In return the person pays, in effect, a rent consisting of a designated share of the crops that are raised. Often this share ranges as high as 50 percent or more. Sharecropping contracts may vary, depending on whether the landlord supplies seeds, tools, or neither. Generally, sharecropping systems are exploitive and reflect sharply stratified control over the means of production (strategic resources). Often they lead to ecological degradation.

**Sharing.** Although sharing is part of most human societies, and of some infrahuman primate ones as well, it is especially important in those that are based on kinship. It serves as the primary mechanism for social cohesion in these societies, as Marcel Mauss's seminal work, *The Gift*, aptly pointed out. Lévi-Strauss's key work, *The Elementary Structures of Kinship*, focuses on the importance of sharing in the formation of alliances in human societies. Such actions are adaptive, for not only do they reduce jealousy but they also tend to ensure that members receive adequate goods to meet their needs whenever possible. Thus among the !Kung San (Bushmen) of the Kalahari any large animal killed by a hunting team is shared with the community through

*!Kung San children sharing a drink of water. In hunting and gathering societies great cultural importance is given to interpersonal sharing and cooperation. These attitudes are elaborated into systems of reciprocal food sharing that are crucial for survival, given a limited technology and a harsh environment.*

kinship-structured obligations. Such sharing, called generalized reciprocity, is a way all participants can ensure their subsistence needs will be met at future times. Sharing, while diminished in its importance as a crucial survival mechanism, survives as a means for promoting social integration and emotional ties in complex societies.

*See also* Alliance; Economic systems; Exchange; Kinship and alliance; Primitive communism

—Frank A. Salamone, St. John's University

**Shell Money.** Shells had been used as money long before silver and gold coinage came into general use and have probably ranged farther than any form of money since. Starting in China and India, they travelled eastward to the Pacific islands and westward throughout Africa and finally to the New World. Often they serve ornamental purposes as well as a medium of ex-

change. They serve this latter purpose partly because money must be durable, easy to count, and difficult to counterfeit.

*See also* Money; Money systems; Numbering, systems of
Consult: Einzig, P., *Primitive Money* (London: Eyre & Spottiswoode, 1949); Quiggens, A. H., *A Survey of Primitive Money* (New York: Barnes & Noble, 1949).

**Shelter.** *See* Housing and shelter.

**Sib.** This term was proposed by George P. Murdock in place of the less precise *clan* to signify a consanguineal unilineal kin group whose ancestry is too old for all the members of the group to trace all the links.

*See also* Clan; Kinship; Lineage; Unilineal descent

**Sickle-cell Anemia.** This usually fatal disease is caused by a chemical mutation which changes one of the amino acids in normal hemoglobin. The result is a peculiar sickling of the red cells, a pathological condition which affects their oxygen-carrying capacity. The mutant sickle-cell gene is a partial recessive. Heterozygotes show some effects of the disease, but they live long enough to reproduce, passing the gene along to succeeding generations.

This mutant sickle-cell gene occurs in unusually high frequency in parts of Africa and the Arabian Peninsula. The high frequencies in these areas are due to the fact that individuals heterozygotic for the sickle-cell gene thereby also have a special resistance to falciparum malaria, a serious disease endemic in the same areas. The genetic and evolutionary mechanisms are clear-cut. Individuals heterozygotic for the sickling gene are resistant to malaria and have only mild cases of sickle-cell anemia. Individuals homozygotic for the recessive sickling gene get anemia and die. Individuals homozygotic for the dominant nonsickling gene get malaria, and many of them die. Here is an unusual genetic case where the heterozygote is favored over either homozygote, leading to high frequencies of heterozygotes in the breeding population.

*See also* Balanced polymorphism; Evolution, genetic mechanisms of; Heterozygote; Homozygote

—James Clifton, University of Wisconsin, Green Bay

**Signal Systems.** One of the major trends throughout anthropological history has been the search for systems—i.e., organized relationships among phenomena. The success of linguistics inspired the application of a systems approach to other areas of cultural life in a manner comparable to that of the linguistic sciences. Cultural anthropologists began to view culture as a system of communication—or as a series of systems each with signals or symbols strung together in a coherent manner—conveying messages to those who knew the proper code. These systems have been profitably studied in a number of recent works in proxemics and kinetics. The explicit viewing of culture as a signal system has led anthropologists to regard it as a plan for action—an underlying reality that structures behavior.

See also Communication; French structuralism; Kinesics; Language; Proxemics

**Significance, Statistical.** See Statistical significance.

**Silent Trade.** In this form of exchange, there is no face-to-face interaction between the parties involved. Silent trade is often practiced where potential for conflict between groups exists (e.g., between Pygmies and Bantu). Each party simply leaves the trade goods and picks up those left by the other party at an agreed-upon place.

See also Exchange

**Simmel, Georg** (1858–1918). Simmel established the formal or "pure" school of sociology—forms of social interaction in all spheres of human life are analyzed, resulting in a geometry of the structure of association and dissociation.

**Simple Sample.** See Sampling techniques; Statistical methods.

**Simpson, George Gaylord** (b. 1902). This American vertebrate paleontologist is noted for his contributions to evolutionary theory (*The Meaning of Evolution*, 1949) and to the biological classification of mammals (*Principles of Animal Taxonomy*, 1961; *Primate Taxonomy and Recent Studies of Nonhuman Primates*, 1965).

**Sinanthropus Pekinensis (Peking Man).** See *Homo erectus*.

**Sister Exchange.** See Brother-sister exchange.

**Site.** This term generally refers to any evidence of past human activity confined to a geographical area. It may range from an isolated hearth to the remains of an ancient city.

See also Archaeology; Excavation of a site

**Skills and Work.** The concept of skills is not easy to define precisely since both motor and mental phenomena are involved and even work described as "unskilled" often requires high levels of motor ability. Generally skills are thought of as motor dex-

*!Kung San hunter crushes a grub against the shaft of an arrowhead to produce a blood-soluble poison which he hopes will kill large game animals he hunts. The metal arrowhead is detachable from the wooden shaft of the arrow to permit it to lodge in the animal's body. Poison is not put on the sharp arrow tips, to avoid possible accidents with humans.*

terities, manual or other bodily capabilities, physical abilities to manipulate objects, and the like. But usage includes mental capacities and also training and proficiencies intermediate between the motor and the mental. Thus phrases such as "acquiring study skills," "having library skills," "being a skilled debater," clearly indicate not solely motor habits but also mental training and agility. These intermediate skills include competences such as operating a calculator or computer machinery, for which some motor skills are required, but the main skills are the mental mappings which guide the motor skills.

In fact, however, all motor skills require mental mappings of some sort. What is interesting is that much of the mapping, with practice, is transferred to neuromotor responses so that most exercise of skill goes on either just below consciousness or very automatically—like touch typing. Thus the concert pianist does not think about how to place each finger, or how to stretch the hand or flex the wrist, or even about each element of a phrase; rather the pianist plays the phrase automatically as a whole. In short, all skills have some corresponding mental organization. Both physical and purely mental skills increasingly take on a reflex, automatic aspect with practice.

*Division of labor. Although all societies make distinctions between men's and women's work, there is great cross-cultural variety in the nature of the tasks so designated.*

All effective work, then, requires skill in some degree. Failure to develop skill at best peripheralizes a person from effective work and at worst may contribute to disaster: incompetence in hunting may drive away the game, perhaps with dire consequences for a group dependent on it; assembly-line maladroitness may destroy the units being produced (and is sometimes used deliberately in labor conflict). Hence concern for achieving skill is virtually universal in human society.

In technologically primitive societies, most skills are learned by children as part of people's general enculturation. In technologically advanced societies, skills are generated at several different stages: as small children at home; in school while learning reading, writing, arithmetic, and other arts and crafts; and, later, through various highly differentiated channels—represented by vocational schools, apprenticeships, specialized technical schools, academic colleges and universities, self-teaching situations, and on-the-job training. This process enables people to learn specific skills adapted to highly specified work niches called specialties, jobs, or occupations.

Eliciting skills for distribution into the structure of work varies with the type of so-

ciety being considered and clearly evolves with the evolution of specialties and their organization. In societies with little specialization, but varied activities, each person possesses many skills. These are usually acquired by children during observation of, and participation in, their elders' various work activities, often as they work along. Work and skills are themselves directly experienced. So, too, do they usually have direct experience and enjoyment of the product of their work and their craft: so-called unalienated work. Likewise they are able to assess their own skill, judging if it is adequate to the tasks required of them.

In highly complex societies, skill learning, except for on-the-job training, is usually separated from work itself. Under these circumstances, the acquisition of skills must be made official—by certificates, diplomas, degrees, licenses—a phenomenon called *cre-*

*Yaruro Indians in Venezuela shown cutting mortices in roof beams with machetes. Work skills must be understood in the context of communities' work patterns. The Yaruro, like all peoples, divide labor by sex; however, as we see here, people of widely different ages perform the same task.*

*dentialism* and a process which is competitive. A number of interesting social phenomena are connected with credentialism. First, credentialism means that the skill-acquirers are separated from the world of work, which is also the world of "responsibility," remuneration, social security, and even political articulation (as in Brazil, where voting is attached to possession of official work cards). Skill-acquirers are, in short, remanded to a structural and often prolonged adolescence rarely found in technologically less complex societies. Second, credentialism fosters discrimination in the labor market since anyone without formal credentials can be excluded. But even formal credentials can always be questioned ("He doesn't have a very good Ph.D."; "That electronics course is no good") if one wishes to exclude some skilled persons from work—e.g., blacks, women, "dangerous radicals." Third, acquisition of credentials may provide routes of social mobility so that one may try to acquire them by teaching oneself or by getting spurious credentials on a black market.

Related to specialized skill training and credentialism is the conventional classification by census bureaus, academicians, and controllers of labor markets alike into "un-

skilled," "semiskilled," "skilled," "professional." These categories fail to recognize that all labor requires skill, but redefine work operations as if some had no skills, some had only limited skills, and some great skills. This results in a combined ideology and social structure of recruitment to jobs which more strongly discriminates against those workers with supposedly lower skill levels. In turn, this discrimination leads to reduced wages and salaries, peripheralizing portions of the labor force where labor is a commodity in a (capitalist) labor market— and thus creating "reserve armies" of the unemployed and underemployed, including, in times of economic crisis, even those with highly valued mental skills (as in America today). The entire classification lends itself to the exercise of controls over employment by those who regulate access to the labor markets.

*See also* Underemployment; Unemployment
—*Anthony Leeds, Boston University*

## Skin Color.

**Skin Color.** The most important determinant of human skin color variation is the amount of melanin, a light brown to black pigment produced by the melanocytes in the basal layer of the epidermis. Also contributing to skin color are melanoid, a dispersed degradation product of the melanin granules; keratin, a yellow to tan protein found in the upper layer or stratum corneum of the epidermis; carotene, a yellow to orange pigment; and the red color of the hemoglobin of the blood showing through from the dermis.

The number and distribution of melanocytes is similar for all human groups, but skin color differences occur because of the variation in the amount of melanin in the epidermis. Melanin shields the skin from sunburn and prevents too much ultraviolet light from penetrating to epidermal layers of the skin where vitamin D is produced.

**Genetics.** The amount of melanin produced is influenced by nutritional and hormonal factors, by the quantity of ultraviolet light penetrating the skin, and by heredity. The genetics of skin color is poorly understood. Until recently, with the development of the reflectance spectrophotometer, judgments of skin color were highly subjective, based on comparison with colors produced by a spinning color top, color chart, or colored tiles. Skin color is a continuous, quantitative, or polygenic trait involving at least

several genetic loci and two or more alleles at each.

**Adaptive Significance.** Gloger's rule observed in the 19th century that within many species of birds and mammals, pigmentation of feathers and fur increased in warmer, more humid climates. Among humans, before European expansion, pigmentation showed a clinal distribution, appearing heaviest near the equator and diminishing with increasing latitude. Correlations could also be made with altitude, vegetation, and cloud cover.

The best accepted explanation of this distribution of melanin in *Homo sapiens* invokes the amount of ultraviolet radiation to which the skin is exposed in various habitats and climates. Although dark skin picks up a higher heat load than light skin (which reflects some of the sun's rays), heavy pigmentation protects the skin from sunburn and skin cancer, as well as regulating the amount of ultraviolet light penetrating the skin and stimulating the production of vitamin D. Vitamin D or calciferol is essential for the utilization of calcium in the blood, muscles, and bones. A deficiency causes rickets, a softening and malformation of the bones, and adult rickets or osteomalacia. An overproduction of vitamin D produces calcium deposits in the soft tissues which causes the bones to become brittle.

One theory holds that until the Upper Paleolithic, with the first evidence of fishing, human populations obtained much of their vitamin D in the skin in response to ultraviolet penetration. In higher latitudes, light skin allowed maximum penetration of ultraviolet radiation in the winter and tanning acted as a shield in summer. Dark skin near the equator prevented hypervitaminosis D.

**Evolution.** The primates show a phylogenetic trend toward greater epidermal pigmentation (darker skin color) and reduced numbers of hair follicles in hair groups. Production of vitamin D shifts from the body surface to the epidermis. The epidermis of early hominids was probably heavily pigmented to prevent an overdose of vitamin D in the lower latitudes they inhabited. Light skin may have evolved in northern climates, perhaps with *Homo erectus*, as an adaptation to cold, cloudy conditions. Classic Neanderthal, however, showed signs of rickets and may not yet have evolved light skin.

*See also* Adaptation, biological; Cline; Melanin; Race; Raciation

Consult: Ivanhoe, F., "Was Virchow Right About Neanderthal?," *Nature* 227:577–579, 1970; Livingstone, F. B., "Polygenic Models for the Evolution of Human Skin Color Differences," *Human Biology* 4:480–493, 1969; Loomis, F., "Rickets," *Scientific American* 223(6):76–90, 1970.
—*Catherine E. Read-Martin, California State University, Los Angeles*

**Skinner, B. F.** (b. 1904). This Harvard psychologist is a leading exponent of the behaviorist school. Skinner's experimental and theoretical refinements of behaviorism have made him one of the most influential and controversial of contemporary social scientists.

*See also* Behaviorist school of psychology

**Skinner, Elliot Percival** (b. 1924). This cultural anthropologist was United States ambassador to Upper Volta (1966–1969). He is a specialist on the Mossi of Upper Volta and with regard to problems relating to modernization.

*See also* Modernization

**Skins.** The hides of animals have been used by humans for the greater part of our existence as a culture-bearing creature. How long is uncertain, but perhaps as long as half a million years. Skins have served many purposes—as clothing, blanket robes, bedding, shelter cover, bags and containers, hats, cooking containers, wine and milk containers, harnesses and saddles, book covers, shoes, shields, writing parchment, boat covers, seat covers, ad infinitum.

Among the animals whose hides were most commonly used in prehistoric and historic times are the bison, bear, elk, moose, deer, seal, wolf, cow, panther, horse, and antelope.

When animals were killed by hunting peoples, the skins (hides) were almost always taken as a useful and necessary by-product. Processing the skins into leather necessitated a series of steps which varied from one region to another. If a warm blanket was desired, the fur would be retained; otherwise the fur (or hair) was removed by soaking the skin in water. Among some peoples this process was speeded up by the addition of wood ash which contains lye and loosens the hair. The fat, flesh and other organic fibers were completely scraped from

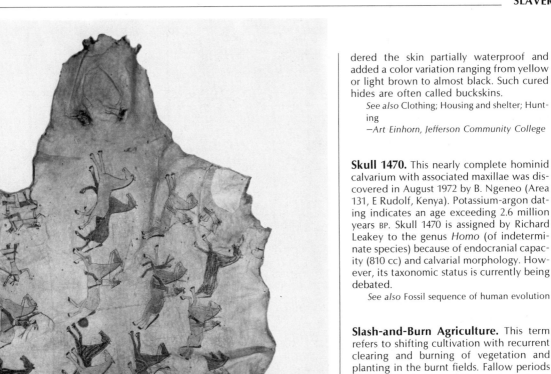

*Cheyenne painted buffalo skin robe (c. 1850–1875).*

dered the skin partially waterproof and added a color variation ranging from yellow or light brown to almost black. Such cured hides are often called buckskins.

*See also* Clothing; Housing and shelter; Hunting

—*Art Einhorn, Jefferson Community College*

**Skull 1470.** This nearly complete hominid calvarium with associated maxillae was discovered in August 1972 by B. Ngeneo (Area 131, E Rudolf, Kenya). Potassium-argon dating indicates an age exceeding 2.6 million years BP. Skull 1470 is assigned by Richard Leakey to the genus *Homo* (of indeterminate species) because of endocranial capacity (810 cc) and calvarial morphology. However, its taxonomic status is currently being debated.

*See also* Fossil sequence of human evolution

**Slash-and-Burn Agriculture.** This term refers to shifting cultivation with recurrent clearing and burning of vegetation and planting in the burnt fields. Fallow periods for each plot last longer than periods of cultivation. It is sometimes referred to as swidden (or shifting) cultivation.

*See also* Agriculture

**Slavery.** Slavery is an institution whereby individuals are to some extent considered property and are obliged to perform labor or other services for those who hold nearly

*Richard Leakey and wife examine a complete femur and the reassembled 2.7 million-year-old Skull 1470.*

the inner side of the skin. At this point in the process, the skin will shrink and dry, being perfectly preserved for future use. This intermediate condition is correctly called rawhide, a term often misused today when referring to thick leather. As rawhide, the skin had many uses, including shields and saddles. Rawhide has often been called the iron of the Plains Indians.

Processing into leather from the rawhide state took many forms, but all included resoaking, twisting, rubbing (to break down the fibers), and the application of some natural chemical catalyst. Many people used the rotted brains of the animal whose skin they were curing; others used bear fat, fish oil, or urine (in the case of arctic peoples such as the Eskimo). When the skin finally achieved a condition comparable to suede, it would generally be white in color and ready for use. Some peoples (e.g., Algonquian Indians) would add a final stage to the process—that of smoking the skin. Rotted wood from various conifer trees was best suited for this purpose, since it contains a high degree of tar components. The skin would then be held over a smudge fire and the smoke allowed to permeate it. This ren-

total power over them. The distinction has been made between genuine (commercial) slave societies, where slaves are the main dependent labor force, and slave-owning societies, where this is not the case and only the rendering of personal and household services characterizes the institution. Classical Greece and Rome and the southern United States are examples of the former; the ancient Near East, India, China, and parts of Africa are examples of the latter. Some degree of societal complexity seems to be necessary for the development of slavery. Slaves are often outsiders (i.e., of differing racial, ethnic, or religious status) with respect to the slaveholders.

*See also* Property; Social stratification

**Sledge.** *See* Land Transport.

**Slums.** These urban residential areas which have undergone decay form part of the formally organized urban area (with officially recognized streets, buildings, and licensed businesses) which has, for ecological or specific historical reasons, been neglected by local government. Furthermore, slums are inadequately supported by the informal sociopolitical and economic institutions of the society. The decay appears in squalid housing, inadequate facilities, and undesired levels of population density. These are suffered by populations ranging from simply poor to starving. Slums are symptoms of societal processes—especially the inequitable distribution of wealth and the maintenance of class barriers. Slums are different from squatter settlements, which, though often poor, in many ways represent progressive rather than degenerative processes.

*See also* Settlement patterns; Settlements, squatter; Urbanization

**Smelting.** *See* Metalworking.

**Smith, Grafton Elliot** (1871–1937). British anthropologist who proposed that most of the world's civilized cultural inventory developed in Egypt and spread to the rest of the world through diffusion and colonization.

**Social Anthropology.** This discipline involves the comparative study of social systems and how they work. Social systems are the interdependent activities, institutions, and values by which people live. It is the job of the social anthropologist to identify the components of social systems and analyze their interdependence. As a school of thought, social anthropology (also called comparative sociology) developed in England in the 1920s, but its significance must be judged in terms of its antecedents.

**Evolutionary Anthropology.** The prevailing approach to anthropology prior to the development of social anthropology was evolutionary and comparative. Evolutionists started with the premise that society evolved everywhere along roughly similar lines from rudimentary beginnings through stages to its highest manifestation in European industrial civilization. It was the goal of evolutionary anthropology to reconstruct the history of social evolution through the detailed comparison of the customs of simpler and, thus, less evolved societies. Social anthropology was a reaction against this evolutionary tradition.

**Durkheim.** The French sociologist Emile Durkheim (1858–1917) had a decisive influence on the development of social anthropology. His work was based on the premise that social phenomena are autonomous and that their relationships should be studied in their own right without reference to biology, geography, or any other body of data or theory. A society, in Durkheim's view, is a system analogous to a biological organism which is sustained through the ordered interdependent functioning of its parts. It was the relationship between the parts within a society that was the proper study of sociology.

**Radcliffe-Brown.** A. R. Radcliffe-Brown (1881–1955) developed social anthropology in England following the principles of Durkheim. He began his career with training in the evolutionary traditions of anthropology. However, in his first major ethnography, *The Andaman Islanders* (1922), he repudiated the evolutionary approach on two grounds: that historical reconstruction in the absence of historical data is conjectural and unscientific and that the comparative method abstracted institutions from their social context and thus divested them of their meaning. Instead he embraced the organic model of society of Durkheim and explained the social institutions of Andamanese society by identifying their specific functions in maintaining the structure of that society. Because of their concern with the functional integra-

tion of social structures, Radcliffe-Brown and his followers are often called structural-functionalists.

**Malinowski.** The Polish-born and English-trained anthropologist Bronislaw Malinowski (1884–1942) developed a functionalist approach of his own. Malinowski's functionalism was less true to Durkheimian principles than was Radcliffe-Brown's. The functions Malinowski sought to discover related to the biological needs of a society's members: the need to eat, the need to reproduce, the need for shelter, and so forth. Rather than viewing the function of institutions as responsive to the requirements of society he viewed institutions as answering the primary or derived needs of people.

**Later Developments.** All social anthropology derives from the initial work of A. R. Radcliffe-Brown and Bronislaw Malinowski. Though neither one originated the concept of function, both made it the unifying theme of social anthropology.

As a direct consequence of a functionalist approach, which demands that social facts be related to their social context, social anthropologists have maintained the highest standards of field research. Taken too rigorously, however, the functionalist premise is self-limiting because of the logical circularity of explaining a system in terms of itself and because of the implicit suggestion that societies are locked in a functional equilibrium. Later trends have added flexibility and dynamics to the concepts of social structure and function by depicting structure as a series of alternative models of behavior between which people freely choose as it suits their needs.

*See also* Durkheim, Emile; Malinowski, Bronislaw; Radcliffe-Brown, A. R.

Consult: Evans-Pritchard, E. E., *Social Anthropology and Other Essays* (New York: Free Press, 1962); Mair, L., *An Introduction to Social Anthropology* (New York: Oxford University Press, 1965); Malinowski, B., *A Scientific Theory of Culture* (New York: Oxford University Press, 1960); Radcliffe-Brown, A. R., *Structure and Function in Primitive Society* (New York: Free Press, 1965).

—Henry A. Schwarz, Ohio State University

**Social Change.** This term refers to significant variations in the relatively stable relationships that make up a social structure. These relationships are considered to be institutionalized. Therefore studies of social change are concerned with changes in social institutions, norms, values, and the cultural symbols associated with each.

No theory of social or cultural change has yet emerged that has satisfied the majority of social anthropologists. Part of the difficulty resides in the concept of change. Permanence is necessary to any change situation, since the nature of that which changes must be defined before change itself can be dealt with. If change led to an entirely new situation, all change would be inherently disruptive. Since, on the other hand, change of some kind is part of the maintenance of stability and adjustment, it is sometimes difficult to know what is encompassed in change. Furthermore, change can be either large-scale or small-scale. The society undergoing change can be large or small. Changes can result from population growth or decline, lack of correspondence between cultural, ideal, and actual behavior, adaptation to outside pressures, role discrepancies, structural conflicts inherent in the society (such as class stratification), and other factors.

Three major categories of theories to explain change have been put forth: functionalism, Marxism, and cultural evolution.

*See also* Cultural evolution; Functionalism; Marxism

Consult: Moore, Wilbert E., *Social Change* (Englewood Cliffs, N.J.: Prentice-Hall, 1963); Smelser, Neil J., *Theory of Collective Behavior* (New York: Free Press, 1963).

—*Frank A. Salamone, St. John's University*

**Social Class.** *See* Class.

**Social Cohesion.** *See* Social integration.

**Social Control.** Social controls are general (or universal) practices that induce members of a society to conform to the expected behavior patterns of their culture. Through the medium of informal and formal *educational processes* the individual learns one way to act to the virtual exclusion of alternatives.

*Public opinion* and gossip reinforce what is learned by constantly judging the propriety of one's behavior in public. *Supernatural sanctions* exert control through beliefs of right and wrong and what is necessary and what is forbidden. Finally, there is the threat of *physical punishment* (perhaps with the ultimate threat of death) for transgressors who are judged incorrigible or unreachable by any other strategies or appeals.

By supernaturally justifying a certain world view and sanctioning no others, by constantly keeping people under evaluative surveillance, and by threatening them with punishment either here or in the hereafter, most societies get most of their members to conform to most of their rules most of the time.

*See also* Conformity; Education in cross-cultural perspective; Enculturation; Legal systems; Power; Religion; Sanctions; World view

**Social Darwinism.** This term refers to any doctrine which makes use, or misuse, of C. Darwin's biological evolutionary principles to explain or justify existing forms of human social organization. Social Darwinism was actually formulated by Herbert Spencer, whose name it should bear; he and his many successors argued that "natural selection" remands humans "less successful" in "the struggle for existence" to misery or lower-class status. This view not only fails to deal with basic demographic processes (e.g., mortality) in working classes but drastically fails to recognize the ways in which the structures of society's institutions and socially organized coercions generate and perpetuate misery and lower-class status.

*See also* Class; Darwinism; Sociocultural system; Sumner, William Graham

Consult: Banfield, Edward C., *The Unheavenly City: The Nature and Future of Our Urban Crisis* (Boston: Little, Brown, 1968); Hofstader, Richard, *Social Darwinism in American Thought* (Boston: Beacon Press, 1955).

**Social Group.** A social group is a kind of social organization, in contrast to social networks, aggregations, and classes. Social groups are generally small organizations composed of individuals tied together in personal relations who identify with and know one another. This category would include age groups, work teams, and some whole societies, such as small hunting and gathering bands. But it would exclude dispersed corporate organizations, confederacies, social classes, and very large communities. Social groups are most characterized by shared identity, high rates of interaction, and strong interpersonal bonds. Primary groups are those in which interaction rates are particularly high and the relationships especially intense.

*See also* Social organization

Consult: Olson, M. E., *The Process of Social Organization* (New York: Holt, 1968).

**Social Integration (Pattern Maintenance).** This term refers to the tendency for all aspects of a culture to function together as an interrelated whole. Although anthropologists may dismantle a culture for purposes of analysis, the distinctions they make between the religious, economic, political, social, kinship, and other systems are essentially arbitrary. In practice, the various elements of a culture are closely intertwined and complement one another in the maintenance of an overall cultural pattern. Disruption of any one element tends to disrupt the entire pattern and to encourage disintegration in other elements of the system or even in the system as a whole.

*See also* Function; Functionalism

**Social Mobility.** *See* Mobility, social.

**Social Movements.** These movements consist of conscious, organized attempts to bring about changes in an established social system, up to the point of efforts to create entirely new social orders as in utopian or revolutionary movements. Social movements vary widely in the institutional context concerned, the style, methods, and aims of the movement, and in their impact on societies.

The social movements most often studied by anthropologists include cultural revitalization movements (nativism, millenarianism), social revolutions, and nationalistic movements. Since the mid-19th century, the phrase *social movement* has come to be used popularly to refer to the strivings of the new industrial class. However, this is too restricted a meaning for systematic study and theory building.

Some social movements never attract more than a few individuals. But often, in small-scale societies, a cultural revitalization movement may sway and mobilize an entire population. In large nations, multiple mass movements with radically different aims may coexist for years. The most common fate of a newborn social movement in a complex nation-state is to be ignored and unrecognized or to evolve quickly into an interest group.

All social movements have political implications and employ various political techniques to sway and recruit a member-ship as well as to achieve their ends. They may or may not have a formal organization, a coherent ideology, or even a well-defined set of objectives and directions. As action groups, social movements need some minimal organization—leaders, spokespersons, a decision-making process—as well as minimal means for conflict resolution. Some social movements employ direct action (e.g., a strike); others rely on indirect techniques (e.g., propaganda). The history of the world's cultures—that is, the history of sociocultural change—in large part reflects the workings of a great many social movements.

See also Millenarian movements; Nativistic movements; Revitalization movements; Revolution; Social change
Consult: Cantril, H., The Politics of Despair (New York: Macmillan, 1962); Gusfield, J. R., "Social Movements," in International Encyclopedia of the Social Sciences (New York: Macmillan, 1968); Hoffer, E., The True Believer (New York: Harper & Row, 1951); Mannheim, K., Ideology and Utopia (New York: Harcourt Brace, 1954).
—James Clifton, University of Wisconsin, Green Bay

## Social Network. See Network, social.

## Social Organization.

This term is often used as a synonym for social structure. Raymond Firth (1951) distinguished between the two terms: while both structure and organization are aspects of every social system, structure is essentially the static and organization the dynamic aspect. Structure consists of ideals and expectations and provides members of the society with a reliable guide to action (statuses and roles). Social organization refers to the systematic ordering of social relations by acts of choice and decision; these acts are guided by precedents that are provided by the social structure and limited by the range of possible alternatives. Thus observable behavior including change and variation in a social system is accounted for in its social organization. Specifically, the acts of individuals, responding to influences from inside or outside (for Firth, mostly the former) their social systems, lead to fundamental changes in the values, norms, ideals, and expectations of the society. Furthermore, as the term

implies, social organization involves unified, planned, and concerted efforts or actions—that is, groups of individuals cooperating over a period of time.

See also Social structure
Consult: Firth, Raymond, Elements of Social Organization (New York: Philosophical Library, 1951).
—Edward Green, University of Kentucky

## Social Organization, Theories of.

Human social organization is the process that brings about the ordering of social activity as a result of ongoing decision-making by the members of a society. The bisexual nature of the human species, as well as the long period of dependence of human offspring, necessitates the development of an orderly social life. While human beings are not the only social animals, they are the ones whose social life most pervasively depends on a shared, learned cultural tradition.

It is in the attempt to conceptualize and analyze the regularities of human social activity exhibited by members of various societies that the concept of social organization as well as the related concepts of social structure and function have been developed.

**Organization, Structure, Function.** Social organization, structure, and function stem from the attempt to view human social life as an ordered system—a social system. Raymond Firth, whose thinking is reflected in the following discussion, clearly distinguishes these three interrelated concepts. The structural aspects of social relations are the principles, or rules, on which their form depends. An example of structural principles is the set of rules underlying the kinship system such as matrilineal or patrilineal descent, which gives a continuity of form to social systems. The functional aspects of social relations are the ways in which they serve given ends, either individual or collective. Thus far the social system has been conceptualized as an orderly, purposive, and stable system; its purposiveness is conceptualized in terms of function, its stability in terms of structure. But social systems are also dynamic: people adopt different strategies to secure their ends, people succeed one another in desired positions, groups contend with one another. Moreover, while the principles of a social structure may limit the range of alternatives

for social activity, quite often alternatives exist: choice is possible. This dynamic, situationally determined, choice-based social activity is conceptualized in terms of social organization. The organizational aspect of social activity is then the directional activity which maintains forms and serves ends. Social organization is the systematic ordering of social relations by acts of choice and decision. The study of social organization, in that it focuses on the individual actor's evaluation of a situation and the choice among alternative courses of action, is particularly helpful for the study of social change. While the concept of social structure emphasizes the continuities of social life, the concept of social organization emphasizes the variations.

Statistical changes in the pattern of decision-making among recognized legitimate alternative courses of action may lead, for example, to a significant change in the size and position of social units in a society. In this way organizational changes may lead to a change in the nature of the social unit itself and the normative principles underlying it—i.e., to structural change. Indeed Firth's own study of the island society of Tikopia demonstrated how organizational change may lead to structural change. It should be noted, however, that entirely new choices may be made in response, for instance, to a changed environmental situation. The actors' evaluation of the new situation in terms of their own interests may lead to a decision to adopt a novel course of action. Such action, if effective, may influence the decisions of other societal members, causing a new behavior pattern to emerge. Such a changing organizational pattern of decision-making may lead to the formation of new social forms that are justified, reinforced, and perpetuated by new structural principles with normative and therefore coercive force. As F. G. Bailey has pointed out in his investigations of political systems, pragmatic rules, i.e., technical rules, which are repeatedly successful in the political arena may replace older normative rules and themselves acquire a normative or moral strength.

The study of social organization is closer to the empirical facts and more concrete than the study of social structure. As such, it provides a needed complement to structural analysis. While analysis of social structure utilizes mechanical models describing normative behavior, the analysis of social

| Features of Society | Egalitarian Society | Rank Society | Stratified Society | The State | | |
| --- | --- | --- | --- | --- | --- | --- |
| | | | | Feudalism | Capitalism | Socialism |
| Subsistence Activities | hunting and gathering | hunting and gathering; horticulture | horticulture; pastoralism | agriculture; pastoralism | industrialism; agriculture | industrialism; agriculture |
| Distribution System | reciprocity | reciprocity; redistribution | redistribution; reciprocity | market exchange; redistribution; reciprocity | market exchange; redistribution; reciprocity | redistribution; market exchange; reciprocity |
| Classes | none | none | chiefly class; peasants | landed aristocracy; peasants (plus emerging merchant class) | capitalists; workers (plus small business-people) | none (but often bureaucratic elite) |
| Governing Body | whole society: consensus | whole society: but leaders have more influence than others | chiefdom | monarchy | government bureaucracy | people's government bureaucracy |

SOCIOPOLITICAL EVOLUTION

organization should employ statistical models based on actual behavior. As Hugo Nutini has noted, "mechanical and statistical models complement each other in explaining social phenomena."

**Background and Recent Developments.** The concept of social organization presented here has developed over many years of anthropological discourse. It is only in the 20th century that anthropologists have attempted to give precise meaning to the term. Bronislaw Malinowski conceived of the notion as referring to the ways in which members of a society coordinate their activities and organize their material environment to fullfil their needs. Thus he emphasized the purposive dimension of social organization. A. R. Radcliffe-Brown stressed the relationship between social organization and social structure. To him, social structure referred to the prescribed relationships between social positions called statuses. Social organization referred to the arrangement of the activities associated with statuses, activities he called roles. Thus the conceptualization presented here

owes to Radcliffe-Brown the emphasis on an intimate relationship between organization and structure, as well as an emphasis on the processual dynamics of organization. However, Radcliffe-Brown viewed the individual's social behavior as if it were simply determined by the (pre-)existing rules associated with his or her social position. The conceptualization of social organization presented here reflects Raymond Firth's emphasis on social life as presenting choices among alternative modes of action and the individual as a rational, purposive, decision maker. In that it focuses on the goal-oriented activities of human beings rather than on more abstractly postulated societal needs, it is closer to Malinowski's conceptualization than to Radcliffe-Brown's.

Contemporary anthropologists such as F. G. Bailey and Fredrick Barth have attempted to apply aspects of game theory to social inquiry in an effort to attain greater precision in the analysis of decision-making; their hope is to improve our understanding of social organization. If, as Firth stresses, social life confronts the individual with choices between alternatives, and if structural principles provide rules which delimit rather than determine possible decisions,

then game theory with its emphasis on situational evaluation and strategies may aid in the further refinement of our understanding of social organization.

See also Social structure

Consult: Barth, F., *Models of Social Organization,* Royal Anthropological Institute of Great Britain and Ireland, Occasional Papers, no. 23, London, 1966; Firth, R., *Elements of Social Organization* (New York: Philosophical Library, 1951); Firth, R., *Essays on Social Organization and Values,* London School of Economics and Political Science, Monographs on Social Anthropology, no. 28, London, 1964; Fortes, M., *Kinship and the Social Order* (Chicago: Aldine, 1969); Nutini, H., "Some Considerations on the Nature of Social Structure and Model Building: A Critique of Claude Lévi-Strauss and Edmund Leach," *American Anthropologist* 67(3), 1965.

—Stan Wilk, Lycoming College

**Social Stratification.** This term refers to an arrangement of statuses or subgroups within a society into a pattern of socially superior and inferior ranks. The key element in any system of stratification is *inequality:* the various social ranks have differential access to the valued goods and goals (property, means of production, power, privilege, wealth, symbols of prestige) as defined within the society.

Systems of social stratification vary widely in terms of the criteria used to differentiate strata, as well as in the rigidity of the separation between different levels. The gradation of traditional Hindu castes, for example, was based largely on religious grounds: the hierarchy ranged from ritually pure Brahmins to the impure or polluted Untouchables. The castes were also thought to be permanent, endogamous groups; no mobility between them was possible during one's lifetime. Social classes in contemporary American society, on the other hand, are based largely on levels of income, education, and occupational prestige. The classes are not reinforced legally; thus there is the theoretical possibility of upward mobility.

Scholars generally agree that all complex societies may be said to be stratified. In regard to certain simpler societies (hunting and gathering bands, horticultural tribes), however, many writers prefer to say that while there is differentiation of role and status positions, there is no genuine stratification in the sense of a division of society into unequal levels or strata.

See also Caste; Class
Consult: Fried, Morton H., *The Evolution of Political Society* (New York: Random House, 1967); Littlejohn, James, *Social Stratification* (London: Allen & Unwin, 1972).
—Richard A. Barrett, University of New Mexico

**Social Structure.** The total pattern of social organization within a culture serves to maintain orderly relationships among individuals and groups, to regulate the production and distribution of wealth, and to provide a setting for the breeding and socialization of new members of the society. The elements of social structure therefore include, among others, the patterns of kinship, descent, and affiliation, the techno-economic system, and the politico-legal system. There is considerable debate among anthropologists, however, as to whether social structure is a concrete entity consisting of observable social facts or whether the concept refers merely to the principles according to which these social facts are organized.

See also Social Organization
—Ino Rossi, St. John's University

**Socialism.** Socialism refers to a world industrial society in which land and the means of production are socially owned and democratically managed in order to produce for *use* rather than for *profit*. Although private property in the means of production will have been eliminated, personal property in articles of consumption (houses, automobiles, clothing, books) might well continue. The term socialism is often used to refer not only to this future social order but also to advocacy of such a system and, loosely, to tendencies toward or approximations of such a system.

Although the terms socialism and communism are frequently used interchangeably, the latter is usually associated with the policies and practices of communist parties formed under the aegis of the Russian-controlled Third International (Comintern) after the Russian Revolution, whereas socialism is often used to indicate a lack of such affiliation.

There are a variety of socialist forms. The term socialism itself was first used in the 1830s to characterize a future society from which the evils of capitalism would have been eliminated. The earliest form of socialism was what later became known as utopian socialism. Reformers such as Robert Owen, Charles Fourier, and Henri Saint-Simon attempted unsuccessfully to build model communities which would pave the way for the future socialist society.

The dominant form of socialism, both in terms of intellectual prestige and political power, is Marxian (or scientific) socialism. Karl Marx and Friedrich Engels called themselves communists to distinguish themselves from the utopian socialist reformers, and they developed their version of scientific socialism in a dialectical fashion: they participated in the very revolutions their writings helped inspire (especially in 1848) and subjected their failures to rigorous criticism from which new and improved theory emerged.

Other, non-Marxian forms of socialism are also important in various places. In England, Fabian socialism as espoused by G. B. Shaw and Sidney Webb was influential in the formation and later policies of the British Labour Party. In Germany, the evolutionary socialism of Eduard Bernstein was very influential in the social democratic movement. Both these variants are distinguished from Marxian socialism by their rejection of the concept of the inevitability of class struggle.

In the United States, the most important form of socialism has been that of the Socialist Party, which, under the leadership of Eugene V. Debs, became an important political force in the years before World War I. The party's opposition to the war opened the way to governmental repression from which the party never recovered. Other important socialist parties in the United States include the Socialist Labor Party, founded in 1874, which espouses an uncompromising form of Marxian socialism, the Communist Party (formerly affiliated with the Comintern), and the Trotskyist Socialist Workers Party.

Closely related to socialism in their opposition to existing social orders are *anarchism* and *syndicalism*. Anarchism seeks equality and justice in the abolition of the state, which is seen as intrinsically evil. Syndicalism resembles anarchism in its opposition to the state but regards trade unions as the instrument for building an egalitarian society.

Although the use of the term socialism to refer to precapitalist social orders such as the Inca empire is clearly anachronistic, the concept of socialism is very important for the student of anthropology, for socialism is a powerful force in the world today. In addition to the Communist nations of Russia, East Europe, Korea, China, Vietnam, and Cuba and the communist parties throughout the world, the past few decades have seen with the growth of Third World revolutionary struggles—in Vietnam, Cambodia, Angola, Mozambique, and elsewhere—the emergence to political viability of a socialist antiimperialist ideology, which the established international capitalist order is less and less able to contain.

See also Capitalism; Communism; Marxism
Consult: Fried, Albert, and Sanders, Ronald (eds.), *Socialist Thought: A Documentary History* (Garden City, N.Y.: Anchor Books, 1964); Fried, Albert (ed.), *Socialism in America from the Shakers to the Third International: A Documentary History* (Garden City, N.Y.: Anchor Books, 1970); Shaw, G. B., *The Intelligent Woman's Guide to Socialism and Capitalism* (London: Constable, 1928); Sweezy, Paul M., *Socialism* (New York: McGraw-Hill, 1949).
—Eugene E. Ruyle, University of Virginia

**Socialization.** See Enculturation.

**Society.** The term *society*, like many other terms employed by anthropologists, derives from common usage and consequently is variously defined by different anthropologists. Nevertheless, all students of society agree that the term refers to social groupings or collectivities.

In their attempts to define what kind of social groups may usefully be termed societies, anthropologists generally agree that the central features are relatively large size, relative self-sufficiency, and continuity of existence across generations. Thus a social group which can sustain itself more or less independently, recruits most of its members through socializing (enculturating) members' children, has patterned and predictable intergenerational interactions, is larger than a community (few of which manage to be entirely self-sustaining), and is more generalized (less specialized) than an institution (such as a corporation) may legitimately be called a society. It should be noted that societies, unlike nations, do not always have specific political boundaries.

The functional prerequisites of a society have been enumerated by Aberle et al. (1950) in their classic article on the subject: provision for adequate relationship to the environment and for sexual recruitment; role differentiation and role assignment; a communication system; shared cognitive orientations; a shared and articulated set of goals; normative regulation of the means used by members to attain socially appropriate goals; regulation of the expression of affect; socialization (enculturation) mechanisms; and means for effectively controlling disruptive behavior.

In the same article the authors identify four ways in which a society's existence may be terminated: the biological extinction or dispersal of its members; excessive apathy on the part of its members; pervasive anarchy; and its absorption into another society.

There are two major orientations toward the study of society. One school, often called *functionalist* (or equilibrium-model oriented), views society as fundamentally stable with episodic periods of greater or lesser change. The functionalists, typified by Talcott Parsons, analyze society in terms of a homeostatic equilibrium model which suggests that society, like a pendulum, may respond to various influences by swinging in diverse directions but over time consistently seeks the center of its arc. The other school, rooted in Marxist theory, sees *change* as the social constant, generated by the irreconcilable conflicts obtaining between the various groups which constitute a society. These

*conflict theorists,* represented by Morton Fried among others, view times of social stasis as temporary, brought about by the repressive measures of a society's powerful members who seek to perpetuate their political ascendancy. To date, various efforts to synthesize the two approaches into one general theory of society have not been successful.

*See also* Community; Community studies; Functionalism; Marxism

Consult: Aberle, D. F., et al., "The Functional Prerequisites of a Society," *Ethics* 60, January 1950; Parsons, Talcott, *Societies: Evolutionary and Comparative Perspectives* (Englewood Cliffs, N.J.: Prentice-Hall, 1966).

—*Phillip Whitten, Harvard University*

**Sociocultural System.** This label is applied to the perceived systemic context of human behavior which occurs predominantly as social relations (i.e., as a social system) and is guided by cultural norms and values that designate appropriate goals and behavior. The normative and the social so continuously cooccur that even conceiving of either as having meaningful existence separately is difficult. Even individuals isolated by accident, coercion, sleep, or voluntary separation operate in terms not only of inculcated norms, but even in terms of conceptualized social relations (e.g., Crusoe's conversations with himself and God). All standardly enculturated humans employ cognitive maps of sets of social relations and related sets of norms and values (cultural systems). Hence behavior tends constantly to be shaped by sociocultural systems external to the individual—thus reinforcing and maintaining those very systems. Sociocultural systems are also reinforced and maintained by the organization of technology and its environmental constraints. Finally, institutionalization of social relations, especially through formal charters, also tends to reinforce the systemic structure of society and culture.

*See also* Culture, a; Institutions; Norm and normative; Technology; Units of study, sociocultural

—*Anthony Leeds, Boston University*

**Sociolinguistics.** This discipline emerged in the early 1960s when certain anthropologists, linguists, and sociologists found that their interests converged on the social dimension of language. Though not wholly

novel, the focus on language in society differs somewhat from earlier language and culture studies. These studies, in the 1940s and 1950s, generally looked at language as a cognitive system and searched for its similarities to other such systems in a given culture. Sociolinguistics is the field more concerned with language use—with speakers who have social identities and who make their utterances in social situations and for social purposes.

Sociolinguists may still be interested in a cognitive perspective, when (like the Chomsky school) they construct grammars of an individual speaker's competence; but unlike the Chomskyans, they mean by this a broad, communicative competence that includes the speaker's knowledge of appropriate social contexts for particular utterances—as well as his or her knowledge of linguistic structure. Some sociolinguists, however, take as their object of analysis the speech community, not the competence of individual speakers.

A central concern of this field is linguistic variation. Sociolinguistics deals with variation that is systematic in a community and that marks different social groups or functions. For instance, different subgroups in a community (men and women, age groups, social classes) may have special ways of speaking that distinguish them from one another. Such linguistic differences can be a way in which these social boundaries and group identities are marked and maintained. Similarly, there may be special linguistic varieties associated with certain social occasions or places or topics of conversation. Studies of bilingualism in Paraguay, for example, show that speakers switch between Spanish and Guarani depending on the location of the interaction and on the degree of intimacy between interlocutors (Rubin 1968). In Japan, speakers choose among honorific levels (variant lexical and syntactic forms) depending on the social situation and the relationship between speakers (Martin 1964).

The attempt to write grammars incorporating variation has led to some new conceptions about how grammars are to be constructed and what kinds of rules they should include. *Polylectal grammars,* describing at once several linguistic varieties in use in a community, and *variable rules,* where variation in the use of linguistic form is built into the rules of grammar, are among the proposals that have been offered.

Sociolinguistic studies tend to fall into

two groups, according to the research strategy they employ. One type of research starts from the social organization of a community—the frame of groupings, events, and contexts that might control language use—and looks for linguistic correlates. Another type of research takes linguistic varieties as its starting point and investigates social contexts of their use. A third type can perhaps also be discerned, however, that seeks to discover both social organization and linguistic variation through the study of social interaction. This kind of study looks for ways in which language use can define the nature of a situation, as well as how properties of the situation may evoke certain kinds of speech.

Some important topics in sociolinguistic research are multilingualism, urban dialectology, language in social subgroups, language in small-group interaction, social motivations of sound change, pidgins and creoles, the language of special speech acts and events, and language and socialization.

*See also* Language and culture; Linguistics, anthropological; Transformational lingustics
Consult: Fishman, Joshua, *Sociolinguistics* (Rowley, Mass.: Newbury House, 1972); Fishman, Joshua (ed.), *Readings in the Sociology of Language* (The Hague: Mouton, 1968); Gumperz, John, and Hymes, Dell (eds.), *Directions in Sociolinguistics* (New York: Holt, 1972); Martin, Samuel, "Speech Levels in Japan and Korea," in *Language in Culture and Society,* ed. Dell Hymes (New York: Harper & Row, 1964); Rubin, Joan, *National Bilingualism in Paraguay* (The Hague: Mouton, 1968); *Language in Society* (journal published by Cambridge University Press).
—*Judith T. Irvine, Brandeis University*

**Sociological Parents.** This term is applied to those adults labeled *pater* and *mater* who are the socially recognized, but not always the biological, parents of a child. It is through the *pater* and *mater* that a child is linked by kinship with other members of the society.

*See also* Genetrix; Genitor

**Sociology.** Sociology may be defined as the scientific study of human social relationships. This study encompasses the description and analysis of all the following: cultural values, norms, and social controls; socialization processes; patterns of individual and group behaviors; social deviance;

the types, structures, and functions of social organizations and institutions; the nature of social processes (cooperation, competition, conflict); social stratification and social power; human ecology; and patterns and processes of social change. In recent decades a number of subdisciplines have emerged in sociology, including social psychology and "sociologies" of knowledge, law, education, religion, politics, economics, and science.

Sociology as a discipline arose in the 19th century. Its formal beginnings are rooted in August Comte's systematic and codified syntheses of society and in Herbert Spencer's comprehensive social science system formulated on (misapplied) evolutionary laws.

Sociology has addressed itself to a study of human social life with an emphasis on group behavior and social structure, especially in Western societies. In this endeavor, it has been characterized by formal statistical methods of data collection (e.g., sampling populations by using surveys and interview questionnaires). Anthropology, on the other hand, has focused on the entire realm of cultures and embraces such diverse studies as those of material culture traits; traditions, social customs, and beliefs; the prehistory of humankind; human physical and cultural diversity; the evolution of culture; and cross-cultural comparisons. Anthropologists have concentrated their efforts on non-Western societies and generally use the informal participant-observation method of data collection. In recent years, however, methods of data collection and focuses of interest have increasingly overlapped: the result has been a convergence of methodological and theoretical approaches to the study of humanity.

*See also* Anthropology; Fieldwork methods
—*Beatrice A. Bigony, University of Wisconsin, Stout*

**Sodalities.** These secondary groups or associations may be based on voluntary membership (e.g., a ritual/medical association) or on involuntary membership (e.g., an age class). Sodalities are special-purpose groupings which, in different societies, are organized on widely variant principles—among them age, sex, economic role, and personal interest. Similarly, they serve very different functions—among them police, military, medical, initiation, religious, and recreation.

Some sodalities conduct their business in secret, others in public. Membership may be ascribed or it may be obtained via inheritance, purchase, attainment, performance, or contract. Men's sodalities are more numerous and highly organized than women's and, generally, are also more secretive and seclusive in their activities.

Consult: Hsu, F. L. K., *Clan, Caste, and Club* (New York: Van Nostrand Reinhold, 1963).

**Soils and Archaeology.** Pedology, the science of soils, is one of many auxiliary disciplines which aid archaeologists in site interpretation and cultural reconstruction. In recent years, archaeologists have come to realize more fully the possibility and the necessity of total analysis of archaeological sites—including soil interpretations.

Analysis of soils enables an archaeologist to determine how the site was formed, how it may have been disturbed, the environment during its occupation, why preservation of some materials may be poor, and where certain features were located. Soil analysis can even help date the site.

Soil samples are collected both inside and outside the actual site so that comparisons can be made. Samples from the vertical profile of the excavation are taken at regular intervals, but they must also include any features that might be dissected by the excavation. In addition, soil auger samples from below the earliest occupation zone should be obtained (Heizer and Graham 1967:106–108).

Both chemical and physical analyses of soil are necessary. Chemical analysis enables an archaeologist to delineate the soil constituents, some of which relate directly to the preservation of bone, plant remains, pollen, and other organic materials. An example would be the hydrogen ion value (or pH) of the soil. If the pH is above 7.0 (on a scale of 14.0), the soil is alkaline; if it is below 7.0, the soil is acid. While some things such as pollen are better preserved in acid soils, others such as bone are not.

Other soil constituents may be significant in determining the location of sites or features within a site which are not determinable by any other means. For example, a relative increase in elements such as phosphorus, carbon, nitrogen, or calcium, which are indicators of human occupation (Cook and Heizer 1965:1–3), may enable one to locate a site from soil examinations. Also, changes in the relative frequency of these elements may aid in the determination of features or disturbances within a site. Soil analysis may reveal the functional areas of a site and how the inhabitants utilized and modified the area in which they lived. Ralph Solecki (1953:383) thought he could determine burial features at a site in West Virginia due to the higher concentration of phosphate even though the bone had disappeared due to the acid soil.

Physical analysis also enables an archaeologist to learn what the climate was like at the time of occupation and what climatic fluctuations may have occurred since (Movius 1960). The analysis is accomplished through such means as X-ray diffraction, soil color quantification, texture description, and particle size analysis. The chemistry and morphology of soil undergo change through time as climatic shifts occur. This changing climate affects, among other things, the vegetation and thus the soil. The rate of chemical and morphological change in soil is variable, then, but these variations may enable an archaeologist to extract information about the site, especially past climatic conditions (Hole and Heizer 1973:275–276).

The soil, then, reveals a considerable amount of information to the archaeologist about the people who occupied a site and the environmental setting within which they lived and interacted.

See also Archaeology; Dating, relative; Physical-chemical methods of dating; Stratigraphy
Consult: Cook, S. F., and Heizer, Robert F., Studies on the Chemical Analysis of Archaeological Sites, University of California Publications in Anthropology, vol. 2, 1965; Cornwall, I. W., Soils for the Archaeologist (London: Phoenix House, 1958); Heizer, Robert F., and Graham, John A., A Guide to Field Methods in Archaeology (Palo Alto: Mayfield, 1967); Hole, Frank, and Heizer, Robert F., An Introduction to Prehistoric Archaeology (New York: Holt, 1973); Movius, Hallam L., "Radiocarbon Dates and Upper Paleolithic Archaeology," Current Anthropology 1(5–6):355–375, 1960; Solecki, Ralph S., "Exploration of An Adena Mound at Natrium, West Virginia," Bureau of American Ethnology Bulletin 151, Washington, 1953.

—J. Raymond Williams, University of South Florida

**Solecki, Ralph S.** (b. 1917). American archaeologist from Columbia University who excavated the important Neanderthal site at Shanidar Cave in the Zagros Mountains of N Iraq.

**Solheim, Wilhelm Gerhard, II** (b. 1924). An archaeologist who is interested in the prehistory of E and SE Asia and the Pacific, Solheim has attempted to demonstrate the existence of agricultural developments in Thailand before 10,000 BC, making it the earliest site of the agricultural revolution.

**Solidarity.** This term refers to a state of union or community based on the common recognition by the members of their mutual interdependence and shared interests. Feelings of solidarity are an important basis for the maintenance of social order and social integration in any social group.

Solidarity is based on shared beliefs and shared practices. Members of the group tend to adhere to the same attitudes and values, and they perceive other members of the group as sharing their interests. In communal practices, sometimes known as rites of solidarity, group members are able to participate periodically in public rituals that enhance the sense of group identity.

See also Ritual; Solidarity, rites of

**Solidarity, Rites of.** This term refers to various rituals, usually but not necessarily religious, which in addition to their intended purposes also serve to develop and maintain feelings of group solidarity among the participants.

See also Ritual; Solidarity

**Solutrean Culture.** This Upper Paleolithic assemblage is characterized by beautiful foliate, shouldered points which have been delicately pressure-retouched. Its type site is Solutre (Mâcon), but it is best represented at Laugerie-Haute (Dordogne). The Solutrean culture flourished 19,000 to 17,500 years BP in SW/SC and C France in NC/NE and E Spain. Smith defines four stages: Proto, Lower, Middle, and Upper/Final.

**Sorcery.** See Magic and witchcraft; Witchcraft.

**Sororal Polygyny.** See Polygyny.

**Sororate.** This marriage custom requires a man to marry his deceased wife's sister.
See also Levirate; Marriage

**Soul.** Broadly, soul is the principle of life and individuation in living beings. Soul implies contrast to and separability from body. Separation may occur during dreams, trance, or illness, but permanent separation is the cause of, or is equivalent to, death. At death, the soul may travel to another world, be reborn in another body, be amalgamated into a reservoir of souls, dwindle away and disappear, or cease to exist immediately. It may or may not continue to have relations with the living. A person may have more than one soul, in which case each soul has a distinct function such as cognition or emotion.
See also Animism; Religion; Trance

**Southall, Aidan William** (b. 1911). A British social anthropologist interested in the study of urban anthropology and social change in Africa, Southall is a specialist on E Africa and Malagasy.

**Space in Archaeology.** Spatial distances or concentrations are measured horizontally to determine relationships between synchronic (simultaneous) artifacts and sites. Space is also measured vertically in a time-space grid, providing data for diachronic studies (e.g., culture change).
See also Archaeology; Stratigraphy; Superposition, law of; Time in archaeology

**Spear.** The simple spear, a solid wooden stave with a sharpened and fire-hardened point, is probably the most ancient piercing weapon. As people learned to fashion stone and bone points and to haft these to make compound weapons, the spear, as javelin or lance, became increasingly more effective. Particular attention was directed toward specialization of the spearhead. The spear, for example, may be fitted with multiple points to transfix swift and elusive birds and fish. Or it may be provided with a barbed, detachable head as in the harpoon.
See also Atlatl; Fishing; Harpoon; Hunting; Weapons

**Speciation.** This term is applied to the process whereby populations of organisms within a single species become reproductively isolated from one another, leading to the formation of new species. Speciation most commonly results from adaptive radiation: populations spread out into new environments or develop new and divergent

*Herbert Spencer.*

life-styles in a given environment, evolve along separate paths in adaptation to their changed situation, and eventually become distinct breeding units. Reproductive isolation may occur as the result of geographic, ecological, or behavioral differences culminating in morphological and genetic divergence of the populations, until they represent separate and distinct species.

*See also* Species

**Species.** A group of organisms or populations capable of interbreeding and producing fertile offspring but reproductively isolated from other such groups.

**Species-characteristic Behavior.** This ethological concept enjoys somewhat more precision and informational value than the older term *instinct*, which it seeks to replace. Ethologists discovered that almost all the behavior observed in both the wild and the domesticated animals they studied was modifiable to a greater or lesser extent by learning and experience. Every organism has its *ethogram*—its characteristic cluster of behavior patterns. With the exception of humans, most of these behavior patterns are shared by other members of the species. (Humans seem not to be born with large clusters of complex, unlearned behavior as are other animals such as birds and fishes.) Fixed action patterns or inborn skills are "released" by key stimuli which may be biochemical (hormone cycles), social (courtship or appeasement gestures), audible (warning calls), ecological (changes in temperature and length of daylight signal time for bird migrations), and gestural (facial expressions).

*See also* Ethology; Goodall, Jane; Imprinting; Instincts; Lorenz, Konrad; Tinbergen, Niko

**Species-specific Behavior.** *See* Species-characteristic behavior.

**Specific Evolution.** *See* Cultural evolution.

**Speech.** Most linguists, following F. de Saussure, distinguish between speech (*parole*) and language (*langue*). Speech is considered to be actual statistically observable behavior. Language is considered to be the rules for behavior—the structure (grammar) behind reality that presents mental choices manifested in speech behavior.

*See also* Language

**Speech Community.** A speech community is an aggregate of persons who share a set of conventions about how communication is to take place. These persons need not all speak the same language or linguistic variety, although there should be at least one variety they can all interpret. For the *set* of varieties that are used, however, members of the speech community share a knowledge of when, or by whom, the use of a variant is appropriate. The speech community is defined by a repertoire of codes and by shared knowledge of the organization of their use.

*See also* Sociolinguistics

**Spencer, Herbert** (1820–1903). This British philosopher sought to apply the principles of natural selection to human societies and became a leading Social Darwinist. Spencer believed that social change is a natural, evolutionary process that leads inevitably from simple to more complex forms. He regarded society as being comparable to a biological organism—slowly evolving from a simple, undifferentiated, aggregate structure into a complex system of distinct but interrelated parts. Spencer strongly opposed social and economic planning because he believed it would merely interfere with the natural process of social evolution. His philosophy, justifying the exploitation of the poor by the rich classes (the latter are more "fit"), has been rejected by social scientists as a misapplication of evolutionary thought.

*See also* Social Darwinism

**Spengler, Oswald** (1880–1936). A German philosopher of history, Spengler is best known for his *Untergang des Abendlandes* (*The Decline of the West*). He believed that most civilizations must pass through a life cycle and that Western civilization was already in its decline. He also espoused the theory that the spirit of one culture could never be transferred to another.

**Spicer, Edward H.** (b. 1906). This American anthropologist is best known for his work (in N Mexico and SW United States) on ethnology, ethnohistory, and culture change, with special emphasis on Yaqui culture.

**Spier, Leslie** (1893–1961). Known primarily for his research on the origin and development of the Ghost Dance religion of the Northwest Indians, Spier showed its rela-

tionship to the older Prophet Dance religion.

*See also* Ghost Dance religion

**Spinning.** The act of twisting multiple fibers into a thread, yarn, cord, or rope in order to produce a line many times stronger than the individual component fibers.

*See also* Loom; Textiles

**Spiritualism.** This term refers to the belief in the continuance of life after death and the possibility of communication with the dead through mediums. Ghosts are believed to be concerned with affairs of the living.

*See also* Mysticism; Religion

**Spiro, Melford Elliot** (b. 1920). This leading figure in psychological anthropology has worked in Micronesia, Burma, and Israel. Spiro showed, in his study of Ifaluk, that even in societies characterized as having a placid life there are tensions; thus he has questioned some of Margaret Mead's conclusions about the lack of conflict in Samoan society. In a cross-cultural study of the relationship between patterns of early child training and concepts of the supernatural, Spiro was able to provide support for the hypothesis that religions are projective systems. He has also studied a kibbutz to determine the effects of communal childrearing and has questioned the universality of the family as it is generally viewed.

**Spiro Mound.** This mound is the largest of six prehistoric earthworks located in Le-Flore County, Oklahoma, approximately 1 mile southeast of Old Fort Coffee on the Arkansas River. It is one of the most remarkable and culturally rich mound sites in the United States. First reported by Thoburn in 1916, it was not extensively worked until 1933, when impressive artworks began to appear on the commercial relic market; these were so sophisticated in form that they were at first regarded as fraudulent. In 1934, Spiro was pot-hunted for a two-year period by a group of amateur looters operating under the title of the Pocola Mining Company; from this period come most of the objects presently in museums and private collections. The finds included such magnificent examples of prehistoric art as

*A carved stone effigy pipe depicting a warrior decapitating his victim, unearthed in Spiro Mound (c. 1200–1500 AD).*

the famous engraved conch shells, gorgets, pendants, finely worked stone effigies, weapons and implements, textiles, and superb wooden sculpture.

Many of these objects are of unusual importance to archaeological research in view of their realistic portrayal of the life of the people—many of the costume and body adornments shown on the shells and stone carvings have survived. It is this factor of social context with its use that adds so much to the value of Spiro archaeology.

The people who created the Spiro civilization are believed to be ancestors to the present-day Creek Indians; apparently they developed what has come to be known as the Craig Focus sometime around AD 900. Named after the owner of the area, the Craig Mound (also called the Great Temple Mound) was apparently a religious and ceremonial center of the region for some five hundred years. It lost its dominant activity sometime before AD 500 and had been abandoned by the time the first Spanish explorers entered the Texas-Oklahoma area in 1541.

In 1936, the WPA took over much of the excavation at Spiro under the direction of archaeologists of the University of Oklahoma; this work continued until 1938. More recently a group of archaeologists from that same institution undertook a reworking of the entire site in an effort to evaluate the material scientifically.

Spiro remains one of the greatest single sources of prehistoric evidence relating to the aesthetic magnificence of the SE Indian civilizations yet discovered, as well as providing many examples of the so-called Southern Death Cult. It also provides the greatest single archaeological tragedy in the United States: human greed, combined with national indifference, destroyed in two years a five-hundred-year record of one of North America's major civilizations.

See also Excavation of a site

Consult: Burnett, Edwin K., "The Spiro Mound Collection in the Museum," *Contributions from the Museum of the American Indian,* vol. 14, 1945; Hamilton, Henry W., "The Spiro Mound," *The Missouri Archaeologist,* vol. 14, 1952; Orr, Kenneth G., "The Archaeological Situation at Spiro, Oklahoma," *American Antiquity* 11(4):228–256, 1946; Shead, Ralph B., "The Engraved Shells of the Spiro Mound," *Museum of the University of Oklahoma Annual Report 7,* 1951.

—Frederick J. Dockstader, Museum of the American Indian

**Sport.** The study of the sociocultural meaning of sport and games has recently become more prominent, and the founding in 1974 of the Association for the Anthropological Study of Play has ensured continued interest by anthropologists. For many years anthropologists showed a passing interest in the importance of sports as well as the broader category of play, yet very few devoted serious attention to its study. Prominent among those who have is John Roberts.

Sport may be defined as organized athletic competition, and it is of interest to anthropologists both with regard to the needs of the human species as well as to specific sociocultural systems. That sports are found in most if not all known societies and vary in function and form with different social structures and cultural systems suggests that the study of sport will provide another tool for investigating sociocultural systems. For example, the participant/onlooker relationship may vary greatly from society to society, reflecting the function of sport in each.

See also Games

—Frank A. Salamone, St. John's University

**Stages of Moral Development.** Traditionally, moral development has been conceived as a relatively simple process of socialization: the young duly internalize the moral norms of their elders in a manner that is essentially cumulative. Modern cognitive psychologists, notably Jean Piaget and Lawrence Kohlberg, have challenged this assumption. They argue that the moral reasoning of children is qualitatively different from that of adults and is not learned directly from adult example. Instead, moral reasoning is a matter of personal cognitive judgment, and moral development consists of a progression through a series of qualitatively different stages.

Piaget's early work on moral reasoning led him to the view that moral development passes through two distinct stages. The first stage is a *morality of restraint,* in which the child believes that wrong behavior is the behavior that elicits punishment; the stricter the punishment, the more wrong the act is presumed to be. The second stage is a *morality of reciprocity,* in which the young person recognizes the social origins of morality in the need to receive and reciprocate the consideration of others. Right and wrong are judged in terms of the effect of actions on others.

Kohlberg has elaborated Piaget's system into a somewhat more complex one that consists of three fundamentally different developmental levels, each containing two stages. The individual moves through these stages in a fixed sequence, although most people do not proceed beyond the fourth stage. Kohlberg's stages are defined as follows:

*Preconventional level.* Stage 1 is *punishment and obedience orientation:* Right and wrong are judged in terms of the physical consequences of an act. Stage 2 is *instrumental-relativist orientation:* The right action is that which satisfies one's own needs and desires.

*Conventional level.* Stage 3 is "good boy"/"nice girl" *orientation:* Moral behavior is that which is approved by others; immoral behavior is that which others criticize. Stage 4 is *law and order orientation:* Morality is presumed to reside in the established rules, laws, customs, or religious values of one's group.

*Postconventional level.* Stage 5 is *social contract/utilitarian orientation:* There is a clear awareness of moral relativism; moral acts are those which take account of

various viewpoints; the good of society becomes of paramount importance. Stage 6 is *universal ethical principle orientation:* Morality is a decision of conscience based on self-chosen, universally applicable, ethical principles.

Kohlberg's model has attracted a great deal of attention, although some social scientists doubt whether moral development really conforms to such a neat schema. Kohlberg's sixth stage, in particular, has been criticized on the grounds that his belief in absolute ethical principles is philosophically untenable: it is argued that moral principles, like any other belief system, are a cultural product and hence inherently relative.

See also Developmental school of psychology; Kohlberg, Lawrence; Moral development; Piaget, Jean

Consult: Kohlberg, Lawrence, "Stage and Sequence: The Cognitive-Developmental Approach to Socialization," in *Handbook of Socialization Theory and Research,* ed. David A. Goslin (Chicago: Rand McNally, 1969); Kohlberg, Lawrence, and Whitten, Phillip, "Values and Morals: Understanding the Hidden Curriculum," *Learning,* December 1972; Piaget, Jean, *The Moral Judgment of the Child* (New York: Free Press, 1965).

—Ian Robertson, Cambridge University

**Stanford-Binet IQ Test.** See Intelligence quotient.

**State, the.** States organize power on a basis beyond kinship and, empowered with the ultimate sanction of physical force, they enforce their laws and maintain the existing order of stratification.

Definitions of the state used to refer to the will of a group or even to the highest social good. There has been a negative reaction to such apotheosis that has led some contemporary political scientists to favor abandoning the term. To most anthropologists, however, the term denotes a stage of sociopolitical evolution and a characteristic group of institutions, and as such it is useful.

Group decision-making is universal, but not so the state. The functions of the state give rise to certain characteristic institutions that are found only in complex (and usually literate) societies. Simple, nonliterate societies with informal, kinship-based administration and also more complex societies

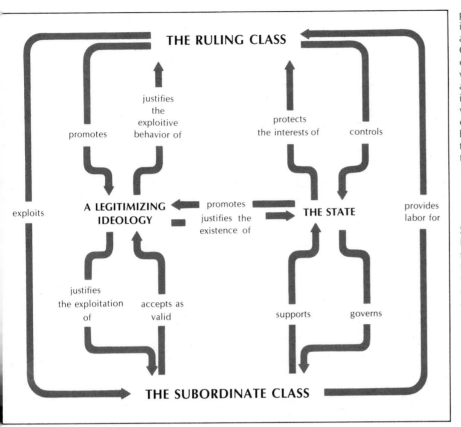

THE RULING CLASS

justifies
the
exploitive
behavior of

promotes

protects
the interests of          controls

exploits

A LEGITIMIZING
IDEOLOGY          promotes
justifies the          THE STATE          provides
existence of          labor for

justifies
the exploitation          accepts as
of          valid          supports          governs

THE SUBORDINATE CLASS

FUNCTIONAL RELATIONSHIPS IN STATE
SOCIETY

*Read any capitalized label. Follow any arrow
leaving that label; read the text along that
arrow. Then read the capitalized label the
arrow leads to. This will result in a sentence
explaining one of the relationships delineated
by this model. This model generates twelve
such statements.*

with multicentric administration or with a
centralized government that lacks the
power to employ physical force can be
called stateless societies (even if they exist
as polities within larger states). The defining
characteristic of the state, then, is the concentration of physical force in a central authority; the primary function of the state,
according to Morton Fried, is the maintenance of an order of social stratification. This
function gives rise to certain characteristic

institutions—laws, taxation, an ideology that
consecrates the state's power, and complex
administrative organization (usually including police and a military organization). To
ensure control over citizens, state societies
also institute census-taking.

> *See also* Government; Power; Social stratifi-
> cation; Society; State and Revolution; State,
> development of the
> Consult: Fried, Morton, *The Evolution of Po-
> litical Society* (New York: Random House,
> 1967).
> —*Edward Green, University of Kentucky*

**State and Revolution.** This is the title of
an important book written by V. I. Lenin in
1917, just before the Bolshevik Revolution.
In this book, Lenin argued that the proletarian revolution must smash the existing state
machinery (the dictatorship of the bourgeoisie) and institute a dictatorship of the

proletariat designed to protect the proletariat from the old exploiting classes and act
as the instrument for building socialism.
Only after class antagonisms have been
eliminated can the state be expected to
wither away. Lenin thus fought both the
anarchists, who were opposed to the state
in any form, as well as the social democrats,
who simply wanted to have more socialists
elected into the existing state structure. This
book exerted a tremendous influence on
the subsequent development of Marxist
thought.

> *See also* Lenin, V. I.; Mao Tse-tung; Peasants
> and revolution; State, the
> —*Eugene E. Ruyle, University of Virginia*

**State, Development of the.** The process
involved in the transition from stateless to
state societies is largely a matter of speculation. Morton Fried maintains that societies
first become stratified (that is, a system
evolves in which members of the same sex
and equivalent age status do not enjoy
equal access to basic resources) and then
state-type institutions soon follow. This
happens when societies produce surpluses
(usually associated with agriculture). When
one subgroup of a society can gain permanent control of the means of subsistence,
classes with inherently opposed interests
emerge. To prevent social rupture along
class lines, the state—a set of specialized
institutions entrusted with maintaining the
ongoing existence of the society—develops.
It protects the society against external and
internal dangers—thus protecting the status
quo and consequently operating in the interest of the ruling classes. Fried argues that
stratification-statehood has developed at
various times in various places due to specific conditions or causes. Causes of "pris-
tine" state formation which Fried, Southall,
and others have noted include climatic
changes, alternation of basic resources,
migration, the impingement of a market
system, shifts in postnuptial residence patterns, warfare, and the development of managerial roles due, for example, to the demands of complex irrigation systems in
"hydraulic societies" (Karl Wittvogel's
term). Whatever the root cause, the process
of state development usually involves an increase in the food supply, population
increase, competition for land or other
basic resources, inequality of access to such
resources, the proliferation of roles, and

greatly increased specialization. The pressures and conflicts that result when inequality becomes institutionalized are formidable and cannot be reconciled by a kin-organized system, Fried argues, and for this reason state-type institutions emerge.

See also Government; Power; Social stratification; State, the; Wittvogel, Karl

Consult: Fried, Morton, *The Evolution of Political Society* (New York: Random House, 1967); Wittvogel, Karl, *Oriental Despotism* (New Haven: Yale University Press, 1957).

—Edward Green, University of Kentucky

## Statistical Methods.

The application of statistical techniques has been extremely useful in the social sciences in several ways: firstly as a descriptive tool to summarize large bodies of measured data in terms of a few, easily comprehensible parameters; secondly as an inferential tool to allow drawing conclusions about the properties of a population on the basis of measured sample results. It is necessary to use statistical techniques because of the great variability obtained when attempts are made to quantify social phenomena. In addition, human behavior often is affected by many influences and an experiment usually cannot be designed to isolate the effects of only one or two at a time. It is therefore necessary to devise techniques to enable causal inferences to be made from data obtained on many variables simultaneously. Let us first look at some of the descriptive variables and then examine some of the inferential techniques.

**Descriptive Statistics.** A distribution is a description of measured data in terms of the frequency of observation of a measured variable as a function of that measured variable. For example, the height of all adult males in a village might be measured. The

Graph 1

**Distribution of Height in Village**

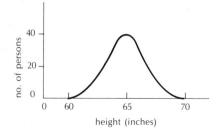

Table 1

**Distribution of Height in Village**

| Height (inches) | No. of persons |
|---|---|
| 60 | 2 |
| 61 | 5 |
| 62 | 13 |
| 63 | 24 |
| 64 | 35 |
| 65 | 40 |
| 66 | 35 |
| 67 | 24 |
| 68 | 13 |
| 69 | 5 |
| 70 | 2 |
| Total | 198 |

Mean: 65 inches
Median: 65 inches
Mode: 65 inches
Range: 10 inches
Variance: 3.81
Standard deviation ($\sigma$): 1.95

observed distribution may be displayed in a table or a graph (see Table 1 and Graph 1). Another measurement of interest on this population might be the monthly income of each adult male. This distribution is displayed in Table 2 and Graph 2.

Note that the first distribution is symmetric and bell-shaped. This is called a *normal distribution* and may be expected when variations are caused by random chance. The income distribution, on the other hand, is very asymmetric and we may conclude that variations here are not purely by chance: other forces may be important. Several descriptive statistics are useful in summarizing and comparing distributions. These fall into two classes—the measure of central tendency and the measure of variability or deviations from central tendency.

**Central Tendency.** The most common measures of central tendency of a distribution are the mean (average), the median, and the mode. The mean is obtained by adding all the measures and dividing by the total number measured. For example, the mean height in the village is 65 inches. The

median is that measure which divides the population so that half have a greater measure and half have a smaller measure. Note that this is the same as the mean only for a symmetric distribution. A large difference between median and mean is often a good indication of asymmetry in a distribution. The mode is that measure which occurs with highest frequency in the population. For a normal distribution this is the same as the mean and median; for the asymmetric distribution it is the same as neither (see Tables 1 and 2).

Graph 2

**Distribution of Income in Village**

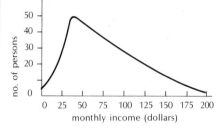

Table 2

**Distribution of Income in Village**

| Income (dollars) | No. of persons |
|---|---|
| 0 | 4 |
| 25 | 28 |
| 50 | 53 |
| 75 | 37 |
| 100 | 27 |
| 125 | 22 |
| 150 | 15 |
| 175 | 10 |
| 200 | 2 |
| Total | 198 |

Mean: $80
Median: $75
Mode: $50
Range: $200
Variance: 196
Standard deviation ($\sigma$): 14.0

**Variability.** These statistics indicate the degree to which measurements deviate from the central tendency. One indicator of variation is the range—the difference between the largest and smallest measure. Much more useful, however, is the variance—the average sum of squares of the difference between the mean and each measurement. Closely related to the variance is the more commonly used standard deviation $(\sigma)$, which is just the square root of the variance. It can be seen that either of these provides a useful measure of the degree of variability in the population. If the standard deviation is large, there are many measurements which deviate considerably from the mean and the bell-shaped curve will be broad and flat. If the standard deviation is small, the curve is narrow and this means that very little variation from the mean is observed (see Graph 3).

Graph 3

**Comparison of Two Distributions with Same Mean but Two Different Standard Deviations**

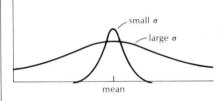

small $\sigma$

large $\sigma$

mean

**Inferential Techniques.** Once an adequate description of variables has been obtained for a population, it may then be desirable to use these and possibly other statistical parameters to test hypotheses concerning the group under study. It may be of interest, for example, to know whether the average height in the village under study differs significantly from the average height in the country in which the village is located. By "significantly" we mean whether an observed difference can be accounted for by chance alone. Numerous techniques have been devised to do this: the most common one is the *chi-square* $(\chi^2)$ *test.* Chi-square is the number obtained by summing the squares of the differences between each measured frequency and the frequency expected if the hypothesis is correct, and then dividing by the expected frequency. If we suspect that the heights of the villagers

Table 3

**Calculation of Chi-Square**

| Height | 2 | 3 | 4 |
|--------|-----|-----|------|
| 60 | 1 | 1 | 1.0 |
| 61 | 2 | 3 | 4.5 |
| 62 | 5 | 8 | 12.8 |
| 63 | 12 | 12 | 12.0 |
| 64 | 24 | 11 | 5.0 |
| 65 | 35 | 5 | 0.7 |
| 66 | 40 | −5 | 0.6 |
| 67 | 35 | −11 | 34.6 |
| 68 | 24 | −11 | 5.0 |
| 69 | 12 | −7 | 4.0 |
| 70 | 5 | −3 | 1.8 |
| 71 | 2 | −2 | 2.0 |
| 72 | 1 | −1 | 1.0 |
| | | Total | 85.0 |

(given in Table 1) do not differ from the heights of people of the country, we may test this hypothesis by examining the distribution from the country and determining the frequency distribution expected for the village if there were no difference. See Table 3 for the calculation. In Table 3, column 2 shows heights expected with no difference. Column 3 shows the difference between observed heights (Table 1, column 2) and expected heights. Column 4 is the square of column 3 divided by column 2. As this table shows, chi-square is 85.0.

Suppose we wish to be confident that the probability of deviation by chance alone is less than one in a thousand. (Values for chi-square at various confidence levels are given in most statistics texts.) Since chi-square (85.0) is greater than this value (32.9) we may conclude that the hypothesis is correct.

It is often quite useful to determine whether several variables are correlated with each other and, if so, to determine the degree of the relationship. One might ask, for example, whether there is a relationship between height and income in our village. Do taller people tend to make more money than short ones? If the villagers were primarily engaged in picking citrus fruits, one might expect such a correlation; if they were

Graph 4

**Citrus Pickers' Height Versus Income ($r^2 = 0.91$)**

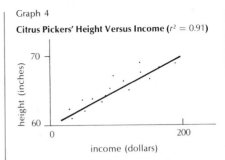

height (inches)

income (dollars)

all accountants, one might not. If for two such villages we plot height versus income we might obtain the results shown in Graph 4 (citrus pickers) and Graph 5 (accountants). By means of a regression analysis we can determine how strong a correlation exists (assuming, for example, a linear relationship) by measuring the correlation coefficient ($r^2$). If $r^2$ is near 1 there is a strong correlation; if it is near zero there is little or no correlation. In addition we obtain the straight line which best fits the data for the village where the correlation is strong. This line is shown in Graph 4.

Graph 5

**Accountants' Height Versus Income ($r^2 = 0.04$)**

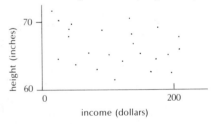

height (inches)

income (dollars)

When many variables are involved, a multivariate regression analysis may be carried out. Computer techniques are commonly used. Correlation coefficients between pairs of variables may be obtained while holding all other variables constant. This enables the social scientist to determine systematically which of the many variables are related to other variables—and, possibly, to construct a model which at least approximately describes the causal workings of the system under study.

*See also* Probability, social theory and
Consult: Blalock, H. M., Jr., *Social Statistics* (New York: McGraw-Hill, 1972).

—*John R. Lombardi, Boston University*

**Statistical Reliability.** *See* Reliability, statistical.

**Statistical Significance.** Statistical significance indicates the likelihood that a measured set of sample results would be obtained if certain assumptions about the population parameters were true. It is usually expressed as a probability (for example, better than one chance in a thousand) that any observed deviations from some other sample could have been obtained by chance alone.

*See also* Statistical methods

**Statistics, Descriptive.** *See* Statistical methods.

**Statistics, Inferential.** *See* Statistical methods.

**Status.** The interrelated positions in a social structure or hierarchy are called statuses. Each status carries certain expectations of behavior (*role*) with respect both to those occupying the status and to those occupying interrelated statuses. More popularly, the term is also used as a synonym for prestige.

*See also* Linton, Ralph; Prestige; Role; Role recruitment criteria; Social structure

**Status and (to) Contract.** This proposition by Sir Henry Maine summarizes a general trend in social evolution. Maine believed that the direction of human evolution has led from societies based on *status* to those based largely on *contract*. Status-based societies (preliterate and ancient societies) are those in which individuals are submerged in kin groups (family, clan, caste) and are represented legally by these groups. Contract-based societies (modern ones) are those in which individuals are released from submergence within kinship groups and are able freely to contract their own legal relationships.

*See also* Maine, Sir Henry

**Steatopygia.** This term refers to the presence of extraordinarily large amounts of adipose tissue in the upper thighs and buttocks

*A young man of southern Africa showing protrusion of the buttocks, known as steatopygia.*

(most commonly in Bushmen-Hottentot females). Its function is unclear.

**Stereoscopic Vision.** Depth perception, or stereoscopic vision, results from overlapping fields of vision when the eyes are located on the front of the skull. Such vision is characteristic of primates (an adaptation to arboreal habitat) and is also found in many carnivores.

*See also* Primates, evolutionary features of

**Stereotype.** The attribution of certain invariable personality or behavioral characteristics to *all* members of a group, most notably those defined by race, religion, sex, nationality, or ethnic origin.

*See also* Anti-Semitism; Cultural minorities; Ethnic group; Minorities, ethnic

**Steward, Julian** (1902–1972). This American evolutionary theorist and cultural ecologist introduced the concept of *levels of sociocultural integration,* which enabled him to discuss evolution in terms of adaptation. The comparison with biological evolution was intended: rather than emphasizing grand stages of evolution, Steward was concerned with the adaptation of specific societies to specific ecological niches. For Steward, technology offered a key to understanding environmental adaptation. He stressed the *multilinear* nature of evolution while accepting that evolutionary levels could be identified: just as biological evolution is measured by increasing control of complexity, so too is cultural evolution.

Steward was enormously influential in the field of cultural ecology, which is concerned with articulating the processes a society uses to adapt to its environment. It differs from other kinds of ecology in that it considers both the interrelationships between a group and its natural environment and also those it has with other social groups. In all his cultural-ecological studies, Steward emphasized the technoenvironmental and technoeconomic interactions, a procedure that is now becoming standard. His fieldwork study on the Mono and Paiute Indians of California—*The Economic and Social Basis of Primitive Bands* (1936)—was a major anthropological landmark because, as Marvin Harris observed, it was "the first coherent statement of how the interaction between culture and environment could be studied in causal terms without reverting to a simple geographical determinism or without lapsing into historical particularism."

Steward was interested in culture change throughout his career and sought to discover universal processes of culture change. In his *Theory of Culture Change* (1957; revised 1973) he argues that cultural change consists of complex, continuing processes rather than isolable acts or events of unitary character. His conviction that anthropology should not be limited to the study of technologically simple societies led to his focusing on technologically complex societies and to his encouraging his students to do likewise.

Steward edited the encyclopedic, six-volume *Handbook of the South American Indians* (1946–1950), the major reference work on the subject.

See also Band; Cultural change; Cultural ecology; Fieldwork methods; Tools and evolution
—Phillip Whitten, Harvard University

**Stimulus Diffusion.** Stimulus diffusion involves the intercultural transfer of a basic idea which is then reinterpreted by the receiving culture. Other elements of the theme or pattern are not picked up.

See also Acculturation

**Stimulus-Response Psychology.** See Behaviorist school of psychology.

**Stochastic Process.** This term is applied to an event in which the outcome depends on some chance element so that only the probability of occurrence can be stated beforehand. Its opposite is the deterministic process.

See also Deterministic process; Markov chain; Statistical methods

**Stocking, George Ward, Jr.** (b. 1928). Cultural anthropologist known for his contributions to the history of anthropology and other social sciences, especially his studies of the work of Franz Boas and on theories of race.

**Stonehenge.** This most spectacular of the British henge monuments is situated on the Salisbury Plain in southern England. The original Neolithic (late 3rd millennium BC) construction included a circular bank and ditch (about 350 feet in diameter) enclosing a ring of pits, some containing cremations. The metalworking Beaker Folk erected the first stones—bluestone transported 150 miles from Wales—and probably laid out the associated avenue. The early Bronze Age Wessex people (mid-2nd millennium BC) added the central circle and horseshoe of huge sarsen uprights capped with lintels, and reset the bluestone megaliths among them. Stonehenge is usually interpreted as ceremonial with some astronomical fea-

tures (its axis is oriented approximately to midsummer sunrise). Hypotheses of more sophisticated astronomical functions (other celestial alignments and eclipse prediction)

*Stonehenge (c. 1800–1400 BC). A Neolithic construction on Salisbury Plain, Wiltshire, England. The large stone in the foreground is typical of the bluestone that was transported to construct this ceremonial site.*

are highly controversial, as is the suggestion of Mycenaean stimulus for the megalithic construction.

See also Astronomy, primitive

Consult: Baity, Elizabeth Chesley, "Archaeoastronomy and Ethnoastronomy So Far," *Current Anthropology* 14(4):389–449, 1973.

## Stonework.

Perhaps as long as 2.5 to 3 million years ago, our antecedents seized upon the common pebble, cracked it for a crude cutting tool, and thereby created the prototype of all subsequent tools devised and developed for scores of purposes over thousands of millennia.

The classic stonework chronology established in the 19th century includes the Paleolithic (old stone age), Mesolithic (middle stone age), and Neolithic (new stone age), representing successive stages in stone tool development. Although the terms generally denote the level of the stone technology in question, they may also have a broader definition in usage which implies the life-style, biological evolution, and social organization of human beings in the period discussed.

Beyond the earliest pebble tools (sometimes referred to as eoliths, or dawn stones, in the earlier literature), our ancestors developed a *percussion flaking* technique for creating a hand-ax tool from siliceous materials, i.e., stones with glasslike properties such as flint, chert, and obsidian. The percussion technique involved the use of a bone or antler wand which was used to strike large flakes from a stone core. As each flake was removed, first on one side, then the other, the form of the tool slowly took shape. In later periods additional techniques were developed which refined stone tools even more. *Pressure flaking* and retouching of the tool edges allowed for smaller tools with a variety of purposes, such as spear points, knives, gravers, blades, scrapers. A few of these stone tools, particularly the blades, were among the sharpest tools ever created; their cutting edge, however, was short lived.

The last major phase of stonework development emerged just prior to the Neolithic period, when metamorphic and igneous rocks were pecked, ground, rubbed, and polished into the desired shape to create adzes, chisels, axes, celts, and gouges. The advantage to this development derived from the tool's suitability to resharpening

when dull, thus paving the way for the metal ages which followed.

See also Lithic ages; Mesolithic; Neolithic; Paleolithic

—*Art Einhorn, Jefferson Community College*

## Storytelling, Drama, Poetry, and Proverbs.

See Expressive systems; Oral literature.

## Strata.

See Stratigraphy.

## Stratification.

See Social stratification.

## Stratificational School of Linguistics.

Stratificational grammar, conceived by Sydney Lamb, assumes a hierarchy of patterned levels (strata) intervening between meaning and articulation. Each level is *represented* by elements from the next lower level, and there are rules (tactics) governing permissible combinations of these elements.

Consult: Lamb, Sydney, *Outline of Stratificational Grammar* (Washington: Georgetown University Press, 1966).

## Stratified Sample.

A stratified sample is a probability sample (i.e., one in which every unit of the population has a known probability of being drawn) whose sampling likelihoods are varied. Such a sample is drawn in two steps. First, the population is divided into classes, or *strata*, according to some criterion (religion, geographic region, language family). Second, cases are drawn randomly within each stratum to fill out the sample.

Stratified sampling is used generally when given types of sampling units are so rare in the population that a simple random sample would not produce enough such cases to allow full statistical analysis. Some cross-cultural surveyists have used this strategy in attempting to achieve balanced interregional comparisons.

See also Cross-cultural sampling; Sampling techniques; Statistical methods

## Stratified Societies.

See Social stratification.

## Stratigraphy.

This term refers to the arrangement of geological or archaeological deposits in superimposed layers or strata. The concept of stratigraphy was developed in the late 18th and early 19th centuries by geologists, who recognized that the rocks of the earth's crust form superimposed, successive layers. The underlying principle of stratigraphic observation is the law of superposition: that the accumulation of deposits is progressive. In normal circumstances, lower levels accumulated before, and are older than, layers above them.

Stratigraphic observation was subsequently applied to the study of archaeological sites; it is the foundation of relative dating in archaeology. Ideally, natural strata are distinguished by differences in physical features such as color and texture, and each is excavated as a unit. Where no physical differences are discernible, excavation proceeds by levels of arbitrary thickness; stratification may be detectable from variation in the cultural content of the arbitrary levels. In practice, archaeological stratigraphy is often not straightforward, and a great many complicating factors and special situations must be taken into account: there may be discontinuities in the sequence of layers; or material may have been removed from its original stratigraphic context by soil movement, burrowing animals, or aboriginal excavation activities. Careful stratigraphic observation usually permits the reconstruction of sequences of events at archaeological sites. Relative chronologies covering long time spans and large geographic areas can often be produced by correlating stratigraphic sequences from sepa-

*Simplified cross-sectional diagram of a cave in southern France, showing four successive cultural layers separated by sterile strata (adapted from Oakley).*

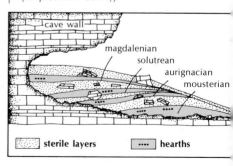

cave wall

magdalenian
solutrean
aurignacian
mousterian

sterile layers    hearths

rate sites. Reliable relative chronologies are essential for the reconstruction and interpretation of culture history and for the investigation of cultural processes.

Some archaeologists distinguish between stratification (referring to the existence of superimposed layers) and stratigraphy (referring to the study and interpretation of the stratified deposits).

*See also* Dating, relative; Superposition, law of

Consult: Adams, R. E. W., "Stratigraphy," in *Field Methods in Archaeology*, ed. T. R. Hester et al., 6th ed. (Palo Alto: Mayfield, 1975); Drucker, Philip, *Stratigraphy in Archaeology: An Introduction* (Reading, Mass.: Addison-Wesley, 1972); Hole, Frank, and Heizer, Robert F., *An Introduction to Prehistoric Archaeology*, 3rd ed. (New York: Holt, 1973).

—*John S. Henderson, Cornell University*

## Structural-Functionalism.

Structural-functional analysis is a doctrine or viewpoint about sociocultural systems which asserts that "structures" that are observed perform "functions" in or for the structure of a larger system. This minimal version of the conception does not list various additions implicitly or explicitly attached by various theorists. For instance, A. R. Radcliffe-Brown thought of structure at two levels: institutions or relationships such as the mother's brother/sister's son relationship and the societal organization globally. Function, for him, was the contribution of the former to the harmonious equilibrium of the latter. This view is not necessarily connected with the structural-functional idea and is useless in confronting conflict and dissolution in society. It is also limited because it does not deal with the problem of alternative solutions to the same functional problem but regards the given solution as the only one; hence it does not deal with process, selection, and, thereby, *history*. Radcliffe-Brown's conception is essentially static and, some would say, defunct.

Other structural-functional conceptions have succeeded in handling conflict by linking conflicting parties to common societal rewards while viewing institutions and relationships rather more dynamically than Radcliffe-Brown in terms of real, fluctuating situations of daily life. Nevertheless, the structural *system* in these views, represented by such theorists as Bronislaw Malinowski, Meyer Fortes, Raymond Firth, E. E.

Evans-Pritchard, Max Gluckman, Victor Turner, and others, remains stable, and structural-functional analysis of this type has not lent itself to coping with historical systemic change—despite dutiful chapters on history in monographs. To summarize: These conceptions deal with process internal to a sociocultural system but not with the system's history, since they still involve implicit equilibrium models.

Another type of structural-functionalism was represented by Kingsley Davis's theory of stratification, which dominated American sociology for twenty years. Davis argued that *stratification*—ranked hierarchies of occupations—was a structure of strata so ranked because of the relative importance of the societal function of the occupations. This conception was systematically attacked from several directions, especially by showing that such differential importance was undemonstrable and untenable and that continuities of organized aggregates of persons— classes—occurred regardless of occupation. Davis subsequently rejected structural-functionalism—an overreaction since the errors in his "functional" interpretation of stratification did not derive from structural-functional assumptions but from erroneous implicit axioms about intrinsic rankability of occupations. Davis's view was also essentially historical.

The present rejection of structural-functionalism stems fundamentally from contemporary concern for the temporal or historical dimension of systems. Though this concern is worthy, even essential, it does not, logically, destroy structural-functionalism since functionality need not be identical with *stable* equilibria nor exclude regular systemic change from structural and functional viewpoints. Probably the major *historically* oriented social science/philosophy —Marxism—is at the same time overwhelmingly the study of structure and function. The concepts are not inherently contradictory or exclusive. Another metatheory—general systems theory—also permits (in a manner somewhat like Marxism) the fusion of structure, function, and temporal change by talking about variables comprising the structure, their motions in the formation of the system ("function"), and their feedback effects on the system ("function in time").

*See also* British social anthropology; Functionalism; Radcliffe-Brown, A. R.; Structuralism

Consult: Firth, Raymond, "Function," in *Current Anthropology*, ed. W. L. Thomas, Jr. (Chicago: University of Chicago Press, 1955). —*Anthony Leeds, Boston University*

## Structural Linguistics. *See* Descriptive linguistics.

## Structuralism.

In its general sense structuralism denotes an analytical approach based on the assumption that observed phenomena are specific instances of an underlying generalized principle of relationship or structure. The structuralist does not analyze the articulation of the observed phenomena themselves but assumes that below the surface of observable appearance there are more profound relationships which give rise to the observable and which, when understood, explain the order of the observed world. In this sense, then, any theorist may be considered a structuralist if she or he posits deep subconscious (and unobservable) realities which give rise to observable realities. But structuralism should not be confused with the terms *social structure* or *structural-functionalism*, which refer to quite different concepts.

In the context of contemporary anthropology, structuralism refers to the work of the French anthropologist Claude Lévi-Strauss and his followers. It is this work that is described below.

**The Premises.** The objective of structuralism is to gain a general understanding of how the human mind works, through the analysis of different cultures. It is assumed that the human species has an innate mental capacity to order and classify the world of experience. The apparent order of the natural world is a product of this mental ordering. Order is a product of mind or, more concretely, the brain. Since all humans have the same kind of brain, the basic mental organization of structure that concerns Lévi-Strauss is the same for all people. It is only the surface expression of the mental structure that varies from one culture to the next.

Structuralists assume that people's ability to create categories involves the creation of binary distinctions: the opposition of a concept with its negation. Thus the idea of *life* necessarily entails the idea of its negation *death*; the idea of *man* stands in conceptual opposition to *woman*; *right* stands conceptually opposed to *left*. These binary pairs are in irreconcilable opposition inasmuch as each term is defined by contrast to its opposite.

Finally, Lévi-Strauss holds that all human social behavior has symbolic meaning—not just at the superficial level of everyday appearance, but at the deep level of underlying structure as well. Village settlement patterns, systems of kinship and marriage, totemic belief, personal names, tattoo designs—all may contain tangible expressions in a particular cultural code of a structure that is reiterated through all the other cultural subsystems of that society. For instance, the sacred, central part of a Trobriand village is where the unmarried men live and where uncooked (raw) food is kept. The profane periphery is where the married women cook food. The distinctions *sacred: profane, central:peripheral, unmarried:married, men:women, raw:cooked* are, according to Lévi-Strauss, coded transformations of the same basic structural dichotomy and illustrate the symbolic nature of culture as a redundant expression of dichotomized categories.

**Myth.** Structural analysis has been most frequently applied to myth. To the structuralist the narrative of the myth is only a vehicle for a much more profound message expressed in code as a set of dialectical (categorical) dilemmas. To many people it is an unwelcome realization that death is the ineluctable consequence of life. But in the code of a myth the life-death contradiction can be magically resolved with a third mediating term. At least on a mythical plane some form of immortality is possible.

Lévi-Strauss has an inspired creative imagination and poetic flair that have earned him recognition as one of the most ingenious and exciting anthropologists of the present time. His fascination stems in part from the delphic quality of his writings, the exact meaning of which is open to a wide variety of interpretations. While he commands an enthusiastic following among some anthropologists, others criticize him sharply for the mystical, nonpredictive, nonreplicable nature of his work, which sometimes can seem more like verbal sleight of hand than science.

See also Jakobson, Roman; Lévi-Strauss, Claude

Consult: Gardner, Howard, *The Quest for Mind: Piaget, Lévi-Strauss and the Structural Movement* (New York: Vintage, 1972); Hays, E. Nelson, and Hayes, Tanya, *Claude Lévi-Strauss: The Anthropologist As Hero* (Cambridge, Mass.: M.I.T. Press, 1970); Leach, Edmund, *Lévi-Strauss* (London: Fontana, 1970); Lévi-Strauss, Claude, *Structural Anthropology* (New York: Basic Books, 1963); Lévi-Strauss, Claude, *The Savage Mind* (Chicago: University of Chicago Press, 1966); Lévi-Strauss, Claude, *The Raw and the Cooked* (New York: Harper & Row, 1969).

—Henry A. Schwarz, Ohio State University

**Structure, Social.** See Social structure.

**Subculture.** This term refers to a group within a society which shares the fundamental values of the society but which also has its own distinctive folkways, mores, values, and life-styles.

See also Ethnic group; Minorities, ethnic

**Subincision.** This form of genital mutilation practiced by certain Australian Aboriginal peoples is performed as part of the male puberty rite. The operation, which may substitute for or accompany circumcision, involves slitting or perforating the uretha along the bottom of the penis.

See also Circumcision; Deformation and mutilation; Rites of passage

**Sublimation.** In Freudian psychology, this is the process by which an instinctual drive (such as sex) is diverted into a culturally valued goal (such as art).

See also Defense mechanisms; Freud, Sigmund

**Submission and Dominance Displays.** These behaviors, found in many species including nonhuman primates, define the relationships of two or more animals within a dominance hierarchy. In some primates, the dominance display includes such acts as ritualized sexual mounting or the baring of teeth whereas the submission display includes presentation of the rump, whimpering, or crouching. These displays minimize overt aggression between members of the animal group in question: a dominant animal will not normally attack a subordinate animal which exhibits a submission display.

See also Dominance hierarchies; Primates, behavior of

SUBSISTENCE STRATEGIES AND SOCIAL FORMS

*This chart is a summary of màjor trends. It oversimplifies the actual complexity of the forms and makes them look much more static and unchanging than they in fact are.*

**Subsistence.** See Economics and subsistence; Technology and subsistence.

**Subsistence Methods.** See Economics and subsistence; Technology and subsistence.

**Subsistence Techniques.** See Economics and subsistence; Technology and subsistence.

**Subspecies.** A population or populations of organisms partially reproductively isolated and taxonomically distinct from others of the same species, sometimes treated as varieties or races.

See also Populations, breeding; Race; Species

*A female baboon, with her baby clinging to her stomach, "presents" herself to a dominant male. Although the position is that which is used for sexual intercourse, in this case it is being used to signal social submissiveness within the group hierarchy. Many of our current conceptions about baboon society, however, are based on observations such as this one which were made in game parks or in crowded conditions which might well distort baboon behavioral patterns. Thus contemporary research is emphasizing the study of baboons and other primates in their uncrowded, natural habitats—far from contact with human beings.*

| Subsistence Strategy | | | Marriage Form | ♀ / ♂ Dominance | Social Organization | Degree of Competition for Resources | Political Form | Work Tasks | |
|---|---|---|---|---|---|---|---|---|---|
| | | | | | | | | ♀ | ♂ |
| hunting and gathering | | | primarily monogamy | social equality | ♂ centered kin groups in small bands* | variable | amorphous* | foraging for vegetable foods and small game; nurturance (child care) | fishing and hunting large animals; community protection |
| horticulture | subsistence farmers | poor environment | frequent polygyny | ♂ dominance | ♂ centered kin groups | high | variable centralization | primary producers: planters, tenders, and harvesters of crops; nurturance | heavy tasks such as land clearing; community protection |
| | | rich environment | primarily monogamy | social equality | ♀ centered kin groups | low | | | |
| | surplus farmers | | frequent polygyny | ♂ dominance | ♂ centered kin groups | high | partiarchal centralization and incipient development of state | | |
| pastoralism | | | monogamy and polygyny | ♂ dominance | ♂ centered kin groups | high | patriarchal clan organization; uncentralized except where under political or economic pressure from neighboring states | some dairying; nurturance | limited cultivation; herding; community protection |
| agriculture | | | primarily monogamy | ♂ dominance | differentiation of non-kin groups | high | state bureaucracy of a feudal nature | processing of raw produce and manufacturing; nurturance | predominate in agricultural sphere; urban wage labor; community protection |
| industrialism | | | monogamy and serial monogamy | ♂ dominance with increasing androgeny | kin groups lose social importance to industrial corporate structures and state institutions | high | state bureaucracy of a bourgeois or workers' state nature | increasing participation in labor force; nurturance | predominate in labor force; community defense |

* The social forms of contemporary hunters and gatherers have been greatly simplified by culture contact. It is likely that they formerly exhibited the same social forms as do subsistence horticulturalists, varying according to ecological niche.

**Substantive Universals.** *See* Universals of language.

**Suicide.** The contexts and significance of suicide vary a great deal across cultures: in some instances, for example, suicide may represent an honorable and culturally esteemed act; in others it may be highly disapproved. The subject of suicide is of considerable interest to social scientists, for it provides a striking demonstration of the potency of culturally acquired choices and responses over the basic biological impulse toward self-preservation.

The study of suicide has been profoundly influenced by Emile Durkheim's pioneering study *Suicide,* first published in 1897. Durkheim insisted that although an individual suicide might be explicable in psychological and biographical terms, the meaning and incidence of suicide in a society as a whole have to be explained in cultural and social terms.

Durkheim distinguished two main types of suicide. *Altruistic suicide,* which is found more commonly among traditional peoples, occurs in response to strong social norms which specify suicide as an appropriate act in certain circumstances. The honorable suicides of ancient Rome or traditional Japan are examples of such acts. *Anomic suicide,* the more common form in the modern world, occurs among individuals who are so poorly integrated into social norms that their behavior is no longer adequately regulated: they are in a state of anomie. The person who commits suicide because "life is meaningless" is an example of this category. (Durkheim also distinguished a third category, *egoistic suicide,* which refers to suicides resulting from an excess of individualism; but modern social scientists usually consider this a form of anomic suicide.)

In summary, suicide can be seen as a function of close integration into specific social norms or as a function of lack of such integration. In either event, a full understanding of this act—perhaps the most personal act of which anyone is capable—must take account of the cultural environment.

*See also* Anomie; Culture and personality
Consult: Alvarez, A., *The Savage God* (New York: Random House, 1972); Durkheim, Emile, *Suicide* (New York: Free Press, 1951, orig. 1897).
—*Ian Robertson, Cambridge University*

**Sumner, William Graham** (1840–1910). A sociologist, economist, and advocate of Social Darwinism, Sumner believed in keeping individual liberty unfettered and in a laissez-faire economic policy. Arguing that people are not created equal, he was the antithesis of a humanitarian. In his book *Folkways,* published in 1909, he expressed his belief that customs and morals result from instinctive responses to stimuli such as fear, sex, or hunger.

*See also* Social Darwinism

**Sun Dance.** The sun dance was a widespread summer ritual among the Plains Indian tribes; however, its content, form, and functions varied widely from tribe to tribe. The dance was conducted with the participants, all males and generally young males, oriented to a central pole in a brush shelter. The dancers fasted, danced fairly continuously, gazed at the sun, and sometimes tortured themselves—all in search of a revelatory vision. The participants acted as individuals, not as a collectivity, and sought personal communion with the supernatural. Banned in the late 19th century by American officials as a pagan rite, the sun dance never really died out. In the past decade it has reappeared among several tribal communities, if in different forms and with different functions and meanings. Today the sun dance often symbolizes defiance of assimilation pressures and acts as a focus of cultural conservatism and tribal identity.

*See also* Religion; Ritual
Consult: Jorgensen, J., *Sun Dance Religion* (Chicago: University of Chicago Press, 1972).

**Superego.** According to S. Freud, the superego contains two aspects: the *conscience,* or ethical system, instilled directly by socializing agents promoting culturally relative values, guides all individual actions requiring moral decision; the *ego ideal* is the set of ideal behavioral absolutes imposed by the superego upon the ego.

*See also* Ego; Freud, Sigmund; Id

**Supernatural, Concept of.** The supernatural is a Western folk category of existence which transcends the natural in being largely beyond human understanding and control. This dichotomy is absent from many non-Western cultures.

*See also* Religion

**Superposition, Law of.** The law of superposition states simply that archaeological deposits—the material traces produced by human occupation—accumulate progressively: in normal circumstances, lower levels accumulated before, and are older than, layers above them. This is the basic principle underlying stratigraphy, which is fundamental to the study of archaeological sites and to relative dating—determining the order or sequence of events. The principles of superposition and stratigraphic observation were developed by geologists in the late 18th and early 19th centuries and were subsequently applied to the interpretation of archaeological deposits.

*See also* Dating, relative; Stratigraphy

**Superstition.** This term refers to a belief in supernatural influences and signs. Superstitions are sometimes distinguished from religious beliefs on the grounds that superstitions are more specific and less systematic.

*See also* Supernatural, concept of

**Supraorbital Ridge.** This ridge is a torus or bony bar surmounting orbital cavities. It is large and continuous in apes, small and divided in *Homo sapiens,* and present to some degree in fossil hominids.

*See also* Evolution, human; Primates, evolutionary features of

**Surface Finishes (Resins, Lacquers, Varnishes).** Natural resins that are secreted from tree wounds (particularly balsams) fall into two categories: *oleoresins* are hard and form the basis of clear varnishes, turpentines, and oils; *gum resins* remain soft. The dissolving of resins to a liquid state for use as a surface finish requires knowledge of boiling and refining, as well as a knowledge of solvents such as alcohol and turpentine—knowledge gained only within the last century and a half in Western culture and not at all by Indians of the Americas. However, the Indians did make extensive use of gums for caulking and for setting of weapon and tool heads. Some resins, such as copal, were burned as incense and for their hallucinogenic properties. Resins were used on postfired pottery, painted on as decoration and, in more useful fashion, to render the insides of baskets and clay pots waterproof (as early as 2000 BC in the Amazon Basin). The famous pre-Columbian lacquer work of Central America and the Andes was done with a resinous substance from the resin lac insect found living on cactus. When the popularity of this art form became more widespread, the insect was deliberately cultivated. Resinous lacquer was perfected in China in the 7th or 8th century and was not introduced into Europe until the 17th. Lacquer in this instance is built up in layers; each layer is polished by fine abrasion before the next layer is applied and dried.

—Justine M. Cordwell, Chicago City Colleges/ Malcolm X

**Surface Structure of Language.** This term refers to the arrangement or organization of the elements of sentences as they are generated in perceptible form by morphophonemic rules. Less technically stated, surface structure means the arrangements of morphemes constituting actual sentences. Such strings of morphemes must be arranged in permissible sequences, and these sequences are the surface structure of a language. Underlying this surface structure is a *deep structure* which expresses the formal, logical relationships obtaining among the elements represented in the surface structure. The deep structure of a sentence is generated by the application of *phrase structure rules* and *transformational rules.*

See also Deep structure of language; Morpheme; Morphophonemics; Phrase structure; Transformational linguistics
Consult: Chomsky, Noam, *Cartesian Linguistics* (New York: Harper & Row, 1966).

**Surplus.** There are two distinct but interrelated meanings of the term *surplus* in social science. In most anthropological writings, surplus refers to *surplus production,* that is, to production over and above the immediate subsistence needs of food producers. Such surpluses may be traded or used to support non-food-producing specialists and are therefore seen as essential for social and cultural development. In Marxian social science, the term is used in a manner related to Marx's concept of *surplus value,* which refers to the labor extracted from workers after they have reproduced the equivalent of their wages. By extension, the *economic surplus* is that portion of the total social product which is neither consumed by the direct producers nor used to reproduce the means of production. This economic surplus is appropriated by a ruling class which uses it for its own consumption, to maintain the state, and for capital investment.

See also Agriculture; Economic systems
Consult: Harris, Marvin, "The Economy Has No Surplus?," *American Anthropologist* 61:185–200, April 1969 (for an anthropological view); Mandel, Ernest, *Marxist Economic Theory,* vol. 1 (New York: Monthly Review Press, 1970) (for a Marxist view).
—Eugene E. Ruyle, University of Virginia

**Surplus Production.** See Surplus.

**Surplus Value.** See Surplus.

*Sherente Amazon Indian medicine man leads his villagers in a dance intended to cure sick children—a cultural survival despite the fact that Sherente contact with industrial civilizations dates back over 100 years.*

**Surveys.** See Fieldwork methods.

**Survivals, Cultural.** Cultural survivals —sometimes called cultural lags—were once considered to be elements of ancient cultures which had carried over into the present with little change in form, meaning, and function. This interpretation was disputed by the structural-functionalists, however, who argued that the long-term persistence of traits in altered social contexts without change in meaning and function was unlikely.

**Swadesh, Morris** (1909–1967). This linguist invented a method for measuring the rate of change in the core vocabularies of historically related languages, a technique known as glottochronology (also called lexicostatistics).

**Swidden Agriculture.** See Slash-and-burn agriculture.

**Syllabary.** An arranged system of written characters representing the syllables of a language constitutes a syllabary. Writing of this type has been rather widely used in the ancient Near East and in modern times elsewhere. The Cherokee Indian syllabary of eighty-five characters, invented by Sequoya about 1821 and cast into type, was used for

printing a Bible in Cherokee and also for publishing a tribal newspaper. Correspondence was carried on, and the medicine men recorded magical formulas in syllabaries for curing some patients (and imposing diseases on others), controlling the weather, finding lost objects, and securing the affections of diffident girls.

*See also* Alphabet; Writing

Consult: Diringer, David, *The Alphabet* (New York: Funk & Wagnalls, 1948); Mooney, James, *Sacred Formulas of the Cherokees,* part 1, 7th Annual Report, Bureau of American Ethnology, 1897–1898; Olbrechts, Frans M., and Mooney, James, "The Swimmer Manuscript," *Bureau of American Ethnology Bulletin* 99, 1932.

**Symbol.** A symbol is anything—object, gesture, word—that stands for or represents some other thing with which it has no intrinsic connection. A flag can represent "the nation," "nationalistic piety," and "allegiance." Symbols may be derived from diverse sources, are often arranged hierarchically, can include other symbols, and frequently take different forms of representation. One symbolic sign may also have numerous meanings.

*See also* Semiotic; Symboling ability; Symbolism; Symbolization

**Symboling Ability.** This term refers to the capacity to create and utilize symbols—signs without a natural or necessary association with their meaning. Leslie White has termed such activity "symboling," the arbitrary bestowal of meaning on a thing or act or appreciating meanings thus bestowed. He maintained that symboling, the most significant example of which is human language, is the primary basis for the development of culture. He believed that this capacity is found only in human beings and is a qualitative distinction between *Homo sapiens* and the rest of the animal world. Recent work with the chimpanzees Washoe, via sign language, and Lana, via a symbol system connected to a computer console, indicates that the appreciation of symbolic meanings as well as the semantic ability to manipulate symbols so as to communicate desires is a capacity our close primate relations share with us to some extent. Nevertheless, to date only human beings have evidenced a capacity to create noncontextual symbols.

Clifford Geertz has pointed out a crucial aspect of human symboling ability through his distinction between models *for* and models *of* reality. Models for reality, blueprints for processes external to themselves, are found throughout nature (for example, genes); but the ability to create models of reality, symbolic structures believed to parallel established nonsymbolic systems (for example, the Watson-Crick DNA model), is unique to human beings. Such humanly created models *of* reality can then serve as models *for*—giving humanity the capacity to shape physical, social, and psychological reality through their symboling ability.

*See also* Culture; Language; Symbol; White, Leslie

Consult: Geertz, C., "Religion As a Cultural System," in *Anthropological Approaches to the Study of Religion,* ed. M. Banton (London: Tavistock, 1966); White, L., *The Science of Culture* (New York: Farrar, Straus, 1949). —Stan Wilk, Lycoming College

**Symbolism.** This term is applied primarily to the phenomenon whereby any set of

*In a funerary rite in Northern India, a man of the Thakur caste offers a ball of cooked (and thereby purified) rice to the spirit of his recently deceased father. He uses only his right (pure) hand; the ball of rice is placed on an altar made of mud which is also pure, having been in contact with water (a primary instrument of purification) in a nearby pond. Thus does the Hindu concept of purity permeate the believer's life.*

meanings is represented through a sign vehicle, as in assigning a word to a concept. It also refers to conventionalized symbolic vehicles—e.g., the Cross to stand for Christianity, resurrection, redemption—whose meanings become recognized in a society almost regardless of context. Thus one can place symbols in unanticipated contexts and create virtually infinite juxtapositions of meaning—the foundation of innovation, wit (the pun), dreams, rhetoric, poesy, montage. Finally, it refers to specific schools of painting or literature which use highly symbolic references to convey other meanings.

*See also* Symbol

**Symbolization.** Symbolization is the process of conferring arbitrary meaning on things. In Leslie White's terminology it is "symboling"—the basic foundation of culture and a process that distinguishes human beings from other animals.

*See also* Semiotic

**Synchronic.** Synchronic studies of culture consist of cross-sectional (and often cross-cultural) studies at one point in time, in contrast to diachronic approaches.

*See also* Diachronic

**Synchronic Linguistics.** *See* Linguistics.

**Syncretism.** This term refers to the reinterpretation and recombination of elements which is part of all cultural change. This process occurs whether change is induced from inside or outside a cultural system. New meanings or new functions can be attached to old elements, as when antique tools that no longer have a useful function acquire a symbolic or prestige value. Or old elements can be attributed to newly introduced cultural elements, as generally occurs in diffusion. When Great Lakes Indians, for example, worshipped the Christian cross and Jesuit chapels by casting tobacco on them, they attached their own meanings to these new elements. M. J. Herskovits originally proposed the concept when he observed the extensive blending of African religious meanings and Christian forms among New World Negro cultures.

*See also* Cultural change; Diffusion; Innovation; Stimulus diffusion

**Syndicalism.** *See* Socialism.

**Synergy.** *See* Benedict, Ruth.

**Syntax.** In a strict sense syntax is the relationship of signs to each other (Morris 1938). In broader usage, syntax means the sequential patternings of morphemes permitted in a language.

> *See also* Communication; Grammar; Language; Linguistics
> Consult: Morris, Charles D., "Foundations of the Theory of Signs," *International Encyclopedia of a Unified Science*, vol. 1, no. 2 (Chicago: University of Chicago Press, 1938).

**Systems Analysis.** Systems analysis concerns the relationships obtaining between elements of a system. Systems especially interesting to anthropologists include kinship systems (in which the elements are genealogically reckoned social positions), political systems (elements are positions with differential access to power), economic systems (elements are strategic and desired resources and positions of differential access to them), belief systems (elements are ideas), symbolic systems (elements are signs, symbols), and cognitive systems (elements are the dimensions and their features which both define and contrast cognitive categories).

**Systems Theory.** This approach to the study of societies rejects the idea that one or another aspect may be studied in isolation from all other aspects; it holds instead that all the relevant variables must be studied simultaneously since they mutually influence one another. It is recognized, for example, that economic changes influence religion (or politics, population size, social stratification, the environment) and vice versa. Thus their mutual influence and simultaneous evolution must be examined.

The collection of all mutually influential variables and their causal relationships is termed a system. Systems theory examines the way the magnitude of each variable influences the rate of change and thus the magnitude of all the other variables in the system. Systems theory was originally developed to explain electrical networks and biological organisms but in recent years has found increasing application in the social sciences, especially economics and human ecology.

> *See also* Cybernetics; Feedback; Systems analysis
> —*John R. Lombardi, Boston University*

**Taboo.** This term refers to an exceptionally powerful prohibitory norm whose violation by individuals usually attracts strong sanctions from the community. The word derives from the Polynesian *tabu* or *tapu*, meaning "sacred."

These prohibitions may be imposed only on specific members of the society (such as priests, kings, or menstruating women) or may be generally applicable to all members (as in the case of the taboo on eating pork in Muslim and Jewish societies). Taboos may be more or less strictly enforced; in some cases the violation of a taboo may attract a death penalty, while in others the violation can be rectified by performance of the appropriate purification ritual. The authority invoked in support of the taboo is almost universally supernatural.

All societies have taboos of some form or another that restrict the food, dress, or conduct of the members, but the only universal taboo so far discovered is that prohibiting incest—a fact that has yet to be explained by anthropologists. Taboos are particularly strong in small-scale, preliterate societies, in which they exist alongside sanctions as important means of social control.

> *See also* Incest avoidance (taboo); Manners; Mores; Mother-in-law taboo; Norm and normative; Religion; Sanctions; Social control
> Consult: Hardin, Garrett, *Stalking the Wild Taboo* (Los Altos, Calif.: Kaufman, 1973); Harris, Marvin, *Culture, Man and Nature* (New York: Crowell, 1971); Lienhardt, Godfrey, *Social Anthropology* (New York: Oxford University Press, 1964); Webster, Hutton, *Taboo: A Sociological Study* (New York: Octagon, 1973).
> —*Bruno Pajaczkowski, Cambridge University*

**Tabula Rasa.** *See* Mind.

**Tagmeme.** The smallest meaningful unit of grammatical form.

> *See also* Taxeme

Consult: Bloomfield, Leonard, *Language* (New York: Holt, 1933).

**Tapa.** *See* Bark cloth.

**TAT.** *See* Thematic Apperception Test.

**Tattooing.** *See* Deformation and mutilation.

**Tawney, R. H.** (1880–1962). English economic historian, Labour Party activist, and social critic who wrote *The Acquisitive Society* and *Religion and the Rise of Capitalism*.

**Tax, Sol** (b. 1907). This cultural anthropologist has encouraged the worldwide exchange of ideas between anthropologists and is the founder of *Current Anthropology*, the international anthropological journal. His field research was undertaken in highland Guatemala.

**Taxation.** The process by which a government or dominant power (e.g., colonial) collects money, goods, or services from persons, groups, or businesses within its domain.

> *See also* Government; Peasants; Redistribution; Rent, landownership and; State, the

**Taxeme.** The smallest unit of grammatical form.

> *See also* Tagmeme
> Consult: Bloomfield, Leonard, *Language* (New York: Holt, 1933).

**Taxon.** *See* Taxonomy.

**Taxonomic Classification.** *See* Taxonomy.

**Taxonomy.** Systematics is the study of the kinds and diversity of objects and of the types of relationships existing among them. Systematics includes *taxonomy*, the theory and method of how classifications are made, and *classification,* the systematic ordering of data in groups or classes according to some set of criteria. Taxonomy is thus the study of the rules and procedures for classifying objects. Objects may be grouped into classes, categories, or taxa and named and ordered according to a system of nomenclature into a schema (which may itself be termed a classification or taxonomy) or into types by typology.

In every science, the systematic ordering of data and the classifying of objects, events, and observations for purposes of analysis and comparison are fundamental. Unfortunately, although classification is basic to all subfields of anthropology, taxonomy usually refers to the scheme for classifying rather than the methods behind the ordering. Taxonomy is necessary because classifications are arbitrary, not natural, entities, which are analytically useful and varying for the same set of objects in the light of different scientific goals. Classifications are not, however, capricious, since they must respond to the scientific problems under consideration. The philosophical position of nominalism holds that only the data being classified are "real"; the larger groupings of data into categories are artificial arrangements to which labels are attached for convenience. Realism, on the other hand, treats categories as natural groupings despite variations for different purposes.

Taxonomy and the reality of classification systems are important in physical anthropology, where the classification of plants and animals according to the Linnaean hierarchical scheme and also the problem of human races are primary focal points. Although Linnaeus did not base his ordering on phylogeny, modifications have since been made to bring the scheme in line with modern evolutionary theory. Controversies occur over the placement of organisms or classes within the scheme, in the reality of species, and in the utility of racial and subspecies classifications in the human species.

In archaeology, the most significant taxonomic concern lies in the classification and typology of artifacts. The reality of types has been an issue. Classification is based on various attributes—material, method of manufacture, function, shape, style, location—depending on the questions asked. Computers have aided in the simultaneous consideration of a number of attributes by multivariate statistical analysis.

Cultural and social anthropologists are concerned with establishing typologies of cultures or societies for analytic and comparative purposes and in the analysis of folk classifications of their own social and cultural categories. Classification depends on the problem under consideration. It can be based, for instance, on political, kinship, religious, or economic systems, on level of sociocultural integration and technological complexity, on supposed level of evolutionary progression, on types of ethos, on adaptation, or on geographical location.

There is thus no ultimate typology or classification, whether for organisms, artifacts, societies, or cultures. Assuming ones the existence of a unique ordering with mutually exclusive categories for all purposes leads only to a very complex classification with a proliferation of classes—of questionable utility for any scientific goal.

*See also* Componential analysis; Formal semantic analysis; Linnaeus, Carolus; Multivariate analysis; New Ethnography, the; Race

Consult: Ford, J. A., "On the Concept of Types," *American Anthropologist* 56:42–54, 1954; Kaplan, D., and Manners, R. A., *Culture Theory* (Englewood Cliffs, N.J.: Prentice-Hall, 1972); Simpson, G. G., *Principles of Animal Taxonomy* (New York: Columbia University Press, 1961).

—*Catherine E. Read-Martin, California State University, Los Angeles*

**Taylor, Walter W.** (b. 1913). Archaeologist known for his critical evaluation of traditional (taxonomic) American archaeology and his call for the use of a conjunctive and processual approach toward archaeological data.

**Techniques of Fieldwork.** *See* Fieldwork methods.

**Technology.** Strangely, despite broad generalizations which assert that technology is a critical part of culture or is the key articulation between humans and environment, anthropologists have given little theoretical attention to technology. Most thought on technology has been the province of economists, historians, and engineers, though anthropologists and archaeologists have made extensive descriptions of material culture and subsistence techniques.

Lacking is some rigorous and generally accepted specification of the elements of technology and some set of principles concerning their organization and logic parallel, say, to kinship theory. Without such a theory, it has been impossible to make interesting and testable propositions concerning the relationship between technology and the social and ideological orders of sociocultural systems.

Generally, anthropological writings on technology·talk mainly of *tools* and *material culture* while nonanthropological ones specify *tools* and *information.* Still other writings include resources and the *tasks, skills,* and *activities* involved in their conversion into values of use to humans. The latter three categories imply labor, but labor as an element of technology is, at best, usually included only in its physical sense (work) and not its organizational sense; the latter is designated social organization, the social order, or relations of production. Anthropology's identification of tools alone as technology greatly limits its view, since many technical activities are carried out without tools proper (e.g., picking berries with the hand used as a tool) while others depend on nontool relations to environment (e.g., cognitions of soil types in agriculture). In what follows, all these elements are considered variables of technology.

Tool refers to any object, including parts of the body or the body as a whole, applied to materials in order to change their form or attributes for purposes of human use. Tools may be simple or complex, ranging from simple machines such as the lever and the inclined plane to complex automated electronic machines. Tools may be multipurpose and generalized like a machete, which can be used as knife, ax, hammer, beater, and digging stick, or single-purpose and specialized like a drill press; they may be producible by almost anyone (hammer stones) or producible only by specialists (micrometers); they may be used directly for conversion of materials or used on other tools. Each of these attributes entails, for a given tool assemblage, *patterns* of work and some aspect of labor organization. As assemblages become more complex, specialized, produced by specialists, and secondary, the organization of work becomes more complex and more highly organized.

*An Ecuadorian Indian youth learns to sharpen an arrow. The technology which every society creates to exploit the environment, and the system of distribution it utilizes to circulate goods among its members, are adaptive mechanisms which solve the problems posed by the environment, make use of the environment's possibilities, and provide the material base upon which each society is organized and because of which its culture can flourish.*

Resources have a dual aspect, usually overlooked by anthropologists. They are both material things in nature and cultural objects of value for use in making things (raw materials, often later converted into semifinished goods—or resources—before ultimate use). They become resources for humans only when cultural value is attached to them; otherwise they are irrelevant to the consideration of—and nonexistent for—a given technology. The locations, temporal availability (e.g., seasonality), and conditions of amassment of resources are crucial since they entail significant effects on labor organization and the societal order (e.g., by property law).

Information or knowledge is obviously critical to an understanding of technology since it defines the utility of a resource and the technical processes for its conversion to some end. Information is an ideational input into technology. Information also includes cognitions of contextual aspects of the tool-resource relationship—e.g., awareness of seasonality governing tool-resource use as in temperate zone agriculture, calendrical sequences, cues respecting animal behavior for hunters and fishers, and the like.

Task refers to a discrete bit of work with tools (including the body) carried out in a conventionalized manner (e.g., "the chores") as part of a sequence leading to some ultimate product whose production is an activity. The sequence may have only one task in it—e.g., pulling ears off cornstalks to produce corn; here the activity is corn harvesting. Sequences of tasks may be extremely complex. The activity of making an automobile may in fact include whole subsystems of activities and tasks while itself being articulated with other systems and subsystems of activities and tasks (e.g., marketing automobiles).

A given activity in a given society may be accomplished with many different tasks (housebuilding, even with a standard style, can be carried out with varying tasks in diverse sequences) and skills, while identical tasks and skills may contribute to very different activities (metal stamping machines may make pieces for diverse objects). The articulation between task and activity is part of the social organization of labor as well as part of technological organization. Tools are also partly independent of activities, as well as of tasks and even skills, since different tools can often be used for any one of them, whereas identical tools may be used for different ends. The same holds true for resources.

The partial independence of tools, resources, skills, tasks, and activities from each other allows for considerable variation in the organization of labor and the patterns of work—both, themselves, influenced by the society's ideology. For example, capitalist ideology values maximizing profits by maximizing money benefits and minimizing money costs regardless of other possible values such as social solidarity among a work group. This ideology defines patterns of work and labor organization purely in terms of technologically defined productivity as measured only by product output versus labor input, but not by any other cultural values.

Despite this partial independence of "parts," insofar as they are closely linked or mutually determining, a certain logic of technology can be described. Given standard cultural inventories of tools, resources, tasks, skills, activities, and knowledge, their location and temporal aspects, and ideological inputs into the work patterns, this logic of the technological system delineates major features of the overall social order, often symbolically reflected in the culture in many ways. The logic of the technological-social order of the United States, for example, is reflected in innumerable folk phrases regarding time ("time is money," "losing time," "buying time," "being on time")—all of which indicate a conception of time as bits, linear, numerable, purchasable, wastable, i.e., subject to sequencing and to cost-benefit analysis maximizing monetary value as in time-motion studies. Other folk phrases correspond: "the timing was off," "we're out of phase," "get your ass in gear," "get the show on the road"—all of which indicate motion, alignment of parts and time, and the like. Moreover, the model of mass production and the assembly line is reflected in such obvious phrases as "he doesn't produce," "she doesn't put out." Other aspects of the American logic of technology are seen in the following: "low man on the totem pole," "at the bottom of the heap," "on the bottom rung" "climbing the ladder to suc-

cess," "the brass," "the front office"—all reflecting hierarchy and stratification, differential decision-making, and perhaps bureaucracy, especially with respect to persons on the production line. None of the metaphoric symbols cited here would be found, say, among the Eskimo or the San (Bushmen), not only because such cultural traits as gears, clocks, and offices are absent but also because the very logic of the technology and social orders are fundamentally different—and their symbolic forms, including art and musical styles, reflect those differences in turn.

A still broader conception of technology not dependent on inclusion of any of the elements listed above may be noted, although it is rarely used in anthropology. This conception depends on a distinction between instrumental and ultimate human ends. Any social or cultural order, such as an agency or a voluntary association, which is used instrumentally toward some goal can be defined as part of the technological order. Since tools, resources, and the like are held by social groups and serve as instrumentalities, they are indirectly linked to the instrumental or technological social order in this conception (presented by the sociologist, Robert M. MacIver). This concept is less useful for anthropology than others focusing more on tools and resources because of anthropology's inclusion of archaeology, which has dealt so much with material items and with relatively unknown societies whose tools and subsistence have had to be described.

See also Economics and subsistence, Technology and subsistence; Tools and evolution
Consult: Leeds, Anthony, "Some Preliminary Considerations Regarding the Analysis of Technologies," *Kroeber Anthropological Society Papers* 2:1–9, Spring 1965; MacIver, Robert M., and Page, Charles H., *Society: An Introductory Analysis* (New York: Rinehart, 1949); Singer, Charles, et al., *A History of Technology* (New York: Oxford University Press, 1958); *Technology and Culture* (a journal).
—Anthony Leeds, Boston University

**Technology and Subsistence.** This phrase refers to the relationship between the technical means by which people extract, transform, and use their basic food supplies, the time and space dimensions of these activities, and the labor organization which accompanies them. Loosely, the basic food supplies are called subsistence. Note

that the same technology may be used for producing resources other than food and transformations other than those of converting raw food resources into edibles. Subsistence, then, as a subdomain of the human technology/environment relationship, is that which provides the material foundations for the production and reproduction of human labor.

Social science literature provides no systematic treatment of theory of technology. Anthropologists, in particular, suffer from a platonic heritage of thought regarding subsistence "types" which mires them in a set of ideal types which do not correspond to observed realities. "Hunters," "pastoralists," "agriculturalists"—usually seen in some unilinear evolutionary sequence—are quite meaningless in two ways, if one is concerned with the *processes* linking a technology and its relevant environmental features.

First, any two populations which might both be classified under one such rubric (e.g., "pastoralists") may be drastically different socioculturally because the techno-environmental content and relationships are virtually noncomparable. Thus the Warrau of the Orinoco delta have been classified as "hunters, fishers, and gatherers," as have the Shoshone of the American Great Basin. This type of subsistence supposedly subtends a very low level of organization characterized by bands. This is true for the Shoshone but not for the Warrau, who were regarded as anomalous because they had villages, headmen, priests, "temples" (shrines), and idols—all features supposedly characteristic of "higher" types of society based on "higher" types of subsistence such as horticulture. This sort of view contains an implicit unilinear evolutionary model linked with platonically reified types considered as actual societies: it fails to examine the techno-environmental relations and their implications for subsistence and for productivity levels. Examination reveals the Warrau's continuous access to two major caloric sources—ocumo, a root densely dispersed over wide areas, and moriche palms, whose pith often supplies several hundred pounds of starchy flour per tree. These may number as many as twenty-five per acre. The Warrau's annually endured protein shortages are ameliorated by fish and by great annual crab runs in the rivers. The Shoshone's virtually desert habitat provides only scattered sources of food, such as piñon nuts and rabbits, which, for most of the year, prevents

| | $E$ | $=$ | $m$ | $\times$ | $t$ | $\times$ | $r$ | $\times$ | $e$ | |
|---|---|---|---|---|---|---|---|---|---|---|

| Society | Annual Calories | Food Producers | Hours Per food Producer | Calories Expended Per hour | Techno-Environmental Efficiency | Subsistence Technology |
|---|---|---|---|---|---|---|
| !Kung San (S. Africa) | 23,000,000 | 20 | 805 | 150 | 9.6 | hunting and gathering |
| Genieri (W. Africa) | 160,000,000 | 334 | 820 | 150 | 11.2 | hoe horticulture |
| Tsembaga* (Highland New Guinea) | 150,000,000 | 146 | 380 | 150 | 18 | slash-and-burn horticulture |
| Luts' un (Yunnan China) | 3,780,000,000 | 418 | 1,129 | 150 | 53.5 | irrigation agriculture |
| U.S.A. | 260 trillion | 5,000,000 | 1,714 | 150 | 210 | industrial agriculture |

\* The data only includes vegetable food production. The formula for pigs is:

$$\underset{18,000,000}{E} = \underset{146}{m} \times \underset{400}{t} \times \underset{150}{r} \times \underset{2.1}{e}$$

Thus meat production is much less efficient.

## COMPARISON OF TECHNOENVIRONMENTAL EFFICIENCY OF FIVE SOCIETIES

*Increasing technoenvironmental efficiency (e) has not meant increased leisure, contrary to popular belief. Rather, with the exception of the remarkably undemanding subsistence technology of slash-and-burn horticulture, increased efficiency has also meant increased work (t) for more people (m), who produced more and more food (E). (Condensed from Harris 1971:203–217.)*

more than a small number of people banding together or maintaining specialized roles and constructions. Thus it is not "gathering" as such that is relevant but the comparative productivities of the resources made available through technology. The "gathering" Warrau's starch production (and storage!) involves considerable technical control and expertise. Finally, note that productivities of one subsistence system, typically labeled lower, may indeed be higher than those of a system labeled higher: measured in caloric and protein intakes, Warrau or Northwest coast ecosystems appear considerably more productive than some horticultures or agricultures based on grain crops.

Second, as the preceding examples indicate, virtually no population corresponds wholly to one type. Although the Chukchi subsist almost entirely by reindeer herding, they also engage in some hunting, fishing, and gathering. Their degree of dependency on a single resource is relatively rare among societies. In short, the fact that almost all *actual* ecosystems and their subsistence subsystems display complex mixtures of the abstracted types makes them analytically useless and highly hazardous or downright erroneous in creating typologies.

These difficulties are compounded, in a nonunilinear evolutionary view which takes account of broad culture-historical events, by the fact that technology, more than any other aspect of culture, displays both systemic and *traitlike* characteristics—i.e., it behaves diffusionally. Elements of technology—*specific* tools, resource uses, techniques, tasks, even activities—diffuse among populations, usually with relative ease. For example, basic production and utilization techniques for tobacco diffused around the world in about fifty years after the New World, where tobacco originated, was discovered by Europeans. The dissemination of steel tools like axes or machetes to the antipodes is another example. Still another is the diffusion of that enormously calorically productive root crop, manioc, from South America to all tropical areas as a major subsistence item. The potato, maize, tomatoes, and other New World crops likewise diffused, transforming the subsistence structures of immense populations and numerous societies.

Such technological diffusion, including the dissemination of subsistence items, leads to continuous major reorganization of subsistence bases of society throughout history and everywhere: that is, a continuous, cumulative, and transformational evolution of both world and local technological-environmental systems and the subsistence subsystems occurs. The evolutionary rates may change greatly as world areas become linked to one another, new modes of transmission are evolved, or as these and other variables governing diffusion remain relatively stable (e.g., continued isolation of a population). Nevertheless, subsistence structures modify continuously because evolutionary processes are continuous, even if rates vary.

Concurrently, long- and short-term environmental changes, cyclical or effectively linear (on human time scales), have also forced technological modifications at given times and places. For example, long-term desiccation increasingly restricts or even eliminates horticulture so that, in an older conceptualization assuming a unilinear subsistence evolution, the society must have "devolved." The perspective emphasized here is that of technoenvironmental oscillatory variation in response to environmental variation, rather than old-fashioned unilinear types.

Two major aspects respecting the last point should be noted: the intended and the unintended modifications of environment through technology. The anthropological and other literatures clearly reify environment into a Thing which *functions* as some kind of systemic whole. Environment is seen as an organized, encompassing ground on which human populations play out their scenarios. This relationship has been viewed as ranging from complete environmental control over sociocultural life (environmental determinism) to degrees of such control (possibilism). In either case, explicitly or implicitly, environment is reified and treated as responsible for sociocultural content and organization.

This view is untenable because technological content is not determined by environment. The presence of any given technological inventory in some geographical locale is historically accidental (by diffusion, migration, or innovation), not environmentally causal. At most one can say that not all known technological inventories are diffusible to all known geographical locales because specific environmental variables are prohibitive; moreover, the form the technology takes locally must adapt, in some degree, to the appropriate local environmental variables. The view is also untenable because technologies—and even "nontechnological" activity of all higher animals—act on environmental variables, constantly modifying their qualitative and quantitative relationships. Thus, in hunting or gathering, many peoples burn savannas, effectively reducing or eliminating tree cover and converting them into grassy plains where reforestation might otherwise have occurred. Environmental variables are not only thus shaped but are also *selected* by animal, especially human, populations as goals of deliberate shaping. In other words, human environments are far from absolutes but are themselves often products of human, chiefly technological, activity so that subsistence forms are continually transformed outcomes of human action through technology. The human species makes itself, its environment, and its subsistence.

See also Economics and subsistence; Technology

Consult: Forde, C. Daryll, *Habitat, Economy and Society: A Geographical Introduction to Ethnology* (New York: Dutton, 1963); Leeds, Anthony, "Some Preliminary Considerations Regarding the Analysis of Technologies," *Kroeber Anthropological Society Papers* 2:1–9, Spring 1965; Vayda, Andrew P. (ed.), *Environment and Cultural Behavior: Ecological Studies in Cultural Anthropology* (Garden City, N.Y.: Natural History Press, 1969).
—Anthony Leeds, Boston University

**Teeth.** *See* Dental formulas of primates.

**Teilhard de Chardin, Pierre** (1881–1955). This French Jesuit paleoanthropologist helped discover *Sinanthropus pekinensis (Homo erectus)*. His increasing interest in biocultural evolution resulted in several rather metaphysical and heavily teleological treatises.

**Teknonymy.** This term refers to the custom of identifying a person with a name which marks him as the parent of a child—i.e., "Father of Bill." This custom requires relatives to view an adult from a child's point of view.

**Telanthropus.** Genus name for fossil material recovered by Broom and Robinson in 1949 from the Swartkrans site in South Africa (later reclassified by Robinson as *Homo erectus*).

See also Homo erectus

**Temple.** A temple is a structure built especially for ritual, ceremonial, or religious activities. Generally, it is not used for habitation, crop storage, practicing a craft, or any other human activity. The existence of ruined temples in the archaeological record implies the presence of non-food-producing specialists such as priests who performed the rituals in the temple; it may also imply

The Parthenon is a much celebrated Doric temple of Athena. It was built on the acropolis at Athens in the 5th century BC.

construction by a group of builder-specialists if the structure was large or elaborate. Thus temples seem to be tightly associated with stratified societies.

See also Cities, development of; Priesthood; Religion; Social stratification

**Tenancy.** A tenant has right of usage over real estate, usually by virtue of renting or leasing. Tenants do not own land but rather acquire such rights through contractual arrangements with proprietors.

See also Land tenure; Rent, landownership and

**Terminologies.** *See* Componential analysis; Formal semantic analysis; Kinship terminologies; New Ethnography, the; Taxonomy.

**Territoriality.** This term refers to the possession and defense of territory against other animals of the same species. Territorial behavior of this kind has been observed in a very large number of species and appears to be to a significant degree biologically inherited. In most of these species, territory is defended by individual males against all other males, and secure possession of territory by a male appears to be a prerequisite for subsequent courting and mating behavior. In some social animals, however, the entire group defends the territory or range against other groups of the same species. Ethologists believe that territorial behavior functions as a spacing mechanism and thus ensures an adequate food supply.

Konrad Lorenz and some other ethologists have put forward the controversial
view that the human species is also innately
territorial. It is true that humans tend to
define and defend territory, but most social
scientists take the view that this behavior is
learned rather than "instinctive" and that
the roots of human territoriality are ideological and symbolic. Although the largely
arboreal Old and New World monkeys
behave quite territorially, the great apes, our
closest phylogenetic relatives, display little
or no territoriality. Evidence from the study
of contemporary hunting and gathering
bands suggests that our ancestors were primarily cooperative (both within and between bands) rather than competitive or territorially aggressive.

*See also* Ethology; Lorenz, Konrad
*—Ian Robertson, Cambridge University*

**Test Pit.** Test pits in archaeological sites
reveal information about buried artifacts
and stratigraphy. They can guide further
excavation or provide quick samples in a
broad survey.

*See also* Excavation of a site

**Textiles.** Textiles appear to have been
made as early as the late Paleolithic period,
when they were made by knotting and
braiding (plaiting) which led much later to
knitting, crocheting (hooking), and weaving
on many forms of looms. It seems that textiles developed out of the needle sewing of
skins and from knotting and looping for the
production of various types of nets. The
evolution of textiles from their earliest
form, such as nets, basketry, mats, belts, and
harnesses, led to the eventual creation of
fabrics to substitute for the animal skins
that had served as human clothing. In time,
there also came into use textiles of
various types (reed mats, felted hair, woven
bast blankets) used as substitutes for skins
to line drafty dwellings and to cover dirt
and stone floors. Textiles also became the
medium for bearing symbols—whether for
nonutilitarian articles of clothing, such as
headgear or stoles that indicated status
and prestige, or for banners bearing the
society's symbols.

Textile experts have demonstrated that
parallel cords (twisted line) could have been
sewn together by needle and thread to
produce flat bands for belts and harnesses.
Reconstruction of such a harness by sewing

*This woman, of a Muslim caste in a North
Indian village near Varanasi, is spinning cotton
thread which will be woven into saris on her
family's loom. The family sells the finished saris
to an agent in a nearby city from whom they
also purchase the raw cotton.*

cords shows that it is a duplicate of bands
produced by tablet weaving, indicating
perhaps that the latter was the predecessor
of the simple backstrap loom and other
types invented in the Neolithic and later
ages.

The development and distribution of
loom types are as important in discussing
textiles as is the discovery in various regions
of specific plant fibers and animal hairs
whose qualities of being both pliable and
strong, as well as soft, were factors in their
selection as basic materials. One of these
very early loom forms consisted of two
vertical uprights with a heavy crossbar between them from which hung weighted
warp threads. The weft threads were then
twined (two horizontal threads at a time)
around the individual warp threads or
cords in a technique borrowed from basketry. In northern Europe an early fabric was
made of a bast made from lime bark and the
hair of an early sheep in a prewool form.
Milkweed fibers were also used, then later a
wool from domesticated sheep. A similar
loom and twining technique used with
shredded cedar bark and goat hair is found
in the Pacific Northwest in the New World
and on these the well-known, beautiful
Chilkat blankets are produced. Increased
efficiency came to weaving with the invention of the continuous warp thread loom,
which seems to have come from an area
east of the Mediterranean. Its introduction
into Egypt gave rise to the production of

large quantities of linen cloth. Flax became
one of the essential crops of Egypt, though
it originated in an area to the east, probably
Mesopotamia.

In the 1st millennium BC historians mention a white fiber from trees—cotton—which
was first used in India from whence its use
spread to the west; some say it was carried
back from Bactria by Alexander's army.
Arabs introduced it to the Middle East and
North Africa. Regarding its eastern spread,
it is difficult to believe it did not enter China
until the 10th century (as is generally accepted), since we know the extent of trade
routes from India to China and their great
antiquity.

The use of silk fiber from several species
of silkworm was known as early as the 27th
century BC in China and was kept a secret
by the Chinese. But there is mention of silk
in India's literature of the 1st millennium
BC, and Japan gained technical knowledge
of it in the 4th century AD. However, at the
time of Alexander the Great in the 4th
century BC silk was introduced into Greece
as a special, valuable textile material and was
added to the inventory of known fibers of
linen and wool.

The Indians of the New World produced
quantities of beautiful and technically
superior textiles on floating, hanging, backstrap looms anchored by the body of the
weaver—the same type of loom that was in
use throughout Southeast Asia, the Indonesian archipelago, and the Philippine Islands.
On the looms of Central America and the
Andes were produced textiles ranging from
the sheerest of cotton gauze and intricate
multicolored patterns of the Central Americans to the llama and alpaca woolen tapestry
of the Andes. Almost every type of weaving
variation known in the Old World was
practiced in the New World, even the addition of metallic threads.

The only other loom types in the New
World beyond those abovementioned were
the hanging warp loom of the Northwest
Coast Indians and the continuous-warp upright loom introduced into the Southwest by
the Spanish along with the wool-bearing
sheep. The famous Navajo and Hopi blankets and saddlecloths are the textiles resulting from acculturation under Spanish rule.

*See also* Loom; Spinning
*—Justine Cordwell, Chicago City Colleges/
Malcolm X*

**Thalassemia.** Hereditary deficiencies in a
hemoglobin chain, distributed around the

Mediterranean and in parts of Africa and Asia, thought to confer resistance to malaria.

*See also* Balanced polymorphism

**Thanatos.** In Freudian psychology, thanatos is the aggressive or "death" instinct, often opposed to eros, the sexual or "life" instinct. In his later life, Freud contended that humanity has an instinct for self-destruction.

*See also* Eros; Freud, Sigmund; Instincts; Psychoanalytic school of psychology

**Thematic Apperception Test (TAT).** The TAT is a projective test second only to the Rorschach in cross-cultural usage. Because the TAT consists of pictures of people in various combinations, the original test materials are culturally biased. Hence in cross-cultural applications they are frequently redrawn to take account of local styles of dress, physical features, and the like. The test is individually administered, and the subject's task is to invent a coherent story about each picture. The pictures vary from very highly structured to quite ambiguous as to activity, and one card is entirely blank. The fantasy products narrated by the subject are analyzed for thematic consistencies and patterns—concerning relations with power figures, for example, or with siblings or cross-sex relations. The TAT differs from and supplements the Rorschach in that it produces more specific content about interpersonal relations, self-concepts, and ego functioning.

*See also* Projective tests

Consult: Henry, W. E., *The Analysis of Fantasy* (New York: Krieger, 1973).

**Themes, Cultural.** In contrast to the search for the dominant motif or pattern in a culture which characterized the configurational approach, some anthropologists argue that cultures can be aptly characterized in terms of a set of multiple cultural themes. Here themes are to cultural systems as a melodic element is to a symphony or the motif to a folklore tradition. They are fundamental postulates which underlie and occur in a number of different behaviors or which recur often to cause the patterning of behaviors in different sorts of social roles. Morris E. Opler, the major proponent of this notion, believes that themes are

"dynamic affirmations" characteristic of a culture, affirmations which actively structure the way people view reality.

An example of one of the numerous (and often conflicting) themes in contemporary American culture is the widespread assumption that there is a probably inexhaustible supply of desirable goods in the world. A theme in traditional Potawatomi Indian culture is the high value placed on the elderly and on old age. Opler has identified eleven major themes in the cultures of North India: divisiveness, hierarchy, right action (Dharma), ritual purity, male ascendancy, familism, harmony, nonviolence, intellectualism, transcendentalism, and cycles of existence. Some of these themes balance or support others, some limit or restrain others, some are in conflict. But together they help us understand the North Indian cultural system.

*See also* Configurationalism; Ethos

Consult: Clifton, J. A. (ed.), *Introduction to Cultural Anthropology* (Boston: Houghton Mifflin, 1968); Opler, M. E., "The Themal Approach in Cultural Anthropology and Its Application to North Indian Data," *Southwestern Journal of Anthropology* 24:215–227, 1968.

—*James Clifton, University of Wisconsin, Green Bay*

**Thermoluminescence.** Fired clay can be dated by measuring the amount of light emitted (the so-called thermoluminescent glow) when it is heated to approximately 300°C. The light emitted is proportional to the length of time since it was last heated.

*See also* Dating, absolute; Physical-chemical methods of dating

**Thinking.** *See* Thought processes.

**Thomas, William Isaac** (1863–1947). This American sociologist and social psychologist studied the interrelation of sociocultural and biological factors in human behavior. His major works include *Sex and Society* (1907), *The Polish Peasant in Europe and America* (1918–1921, five vols., with Florian Znaniecki), and *Primitive Behavior* (1937). Thomas is noted for his "Thomas axiom," which states that "'facts' do not have a uniform existence apart from the persons who observe and interpret them.

Rather, the 'real' facts are the ways in which different people come into and define situations."

**Thompson, Laura** (b. 1905). A cultural and applied anthropologist who does comparative and interdisciplinary research in small communities. Thompson is especially interested in ecology and ethnopsychology.

**Thorndyke, Edward Lee** (1874–1949). This American educator and psychologist developed the first integrated theory of learning. He also was one of the first psychologists to conduct laboratory experiments with animals, extending his findings to human beings. Thorndike is a major influence on contemporary behaviorist psychology.

*See also* Behaviorist school of psychology

**Thought Processes.** "Thought" refers to the representational capacity of the human mind. The belief that there are at least two modes of thought (often called logical and intuitive) is an old one. In anthropology, the study of possible cross-cultural differences in thought processes was first approached through the concept of primitive thinking. Although this term is contaminated by connotations of cultural superiority/inferiority, it is still found in the literature. It usually refers to some or all of the following: lack of separation between observer and object (a participatory, emotion-based approach to experience); *post hoc ergo propter hoc* explanations (if one event follows another, the second was caused by the first); belief in sympathetic magic (imitation of significant attributes of an entity gives control over it); lack of concern for logical consistency; and extensive use of metaphoric identification and classification (as in totemism). Many of these attributes correspond to properties of Jean Piaget's preoperational thought. There is also a partial correspondence with Sigmund Freud's distinction between primary and secondary psychic processes (the former referring to dream and fantasy thought, the latter to analytic/adaptive functioning).

In the 19th century the importance of mythic and magical thinking in simple societies was explained by the stage theory of cultural evolution: as savagery gave way to civilization, mythic thought gave way to reasoning. Émile Durkheim and Marcel Mauss believed that social organization is the model for thought and that lack of structural differentiation is reflected in undifferentiated thought processes.

With the growth of systematic fieldwork it became evident that mythic and logical thought processes coexist in all populations but are given differential emphasis. Paul Radin approached this problem at the level of personality, hypothesizing a difference between "thinkers" and "men of action." Lucien Lévy-Bruhl contended that as the emotional importance of a cultural idea declines it is opened to correction by experience and becomes demythologized. E. E. Evans-Pritchard, following the lead of Bronislaw Malinowski, contended that there is considerably more logic in primitive beliefs than is superficially apparent. He concluded that Azande thinking about witchcraft and magic is internally logical and consistent if the premises of the system are granted.

Benjamin Whorf suggested the possibility that linguistic structure is a conditioner of thought. A considerable amount of current work in linguistics is concerned with the relationship between language and thought (for example, work based on transformational and stratificational grammar). Ethnoscience (a subfield of linguistics) is concerned with the structuring of cultural knowledge, and ethnoscientific analyses of modes of classification and forms of syllogistic reasoning are clearly relevant for an understanding of thought processes. Claude Lévi-Strauss has been interested in the description and analysis of the relationships found in myths. He contends that the mind manipulates the concrete symbols used in primitive thought in the same way it manipulates abstract mathematical symbols: by equivalences, binary oppositions, inversions, and other permutations.

A new direction in the cross-cultural study of thought processes was given by the work of Segall, Campbell, and Herskovits (1966). They established that visual perception is responsive, at a very basic level, to cultural conditioning. Their work spurred interest in further cross-cultural testing of existing theories of intelligence, learning, perception, and problem-solving. In particular, there has been interest in testing Piaget's theory that thought processes evolve in all human beings through the same stages: sensory/motor; preoperational; concrete/operational; and formal/analytic. Concrete operations meet the basic conditions of logic in the sense of "correct reasoning," but the level of abstraction is low (hence the contrast implied by concrete versus formal analytic). In his later work Piaget has raised the possibility that adult thinking in some societies does not regularly proceed beyond the level of concrete operations. The American psychologist Jerome Bruner, who shares many of Piaget's assumptions, has contended that Western-type intellectual training (associated with Western-style schooling) has clear and very basic effects on thought. He suggests that persons who have had Western schooling (regardless of base culture) are cognitively more like persons of the same educational level in the West than like members of their own culture who have not had such schooling. The Soviet psychologists L. S. Vygotsky and Alexander Luria are also interested in the way sociocultural organization (in their case, political economy) affects the nature of thinking (not just the content of thought).

The study of thought has been hampered heretofore by our inability to demonstrate a simple relationship between "mind" (thought as experienced and as known through its products) and "brain" (the physiology and anatomy of the nervous system). Evidence is now accumulating that thought modalities have a physiological basis. Although in most animals the structure of the nervous system is essentially symmetrical, in the human species the two cerebral hemispheres differ greatly in their functions. The left hemisphere plays a dominant role in analytic thinking, especially language and logic. The right hemisphere predominates in pattern synthesis, spatial orientation, body awareness, and musical and artistic capacities. Incompleteness in the hierarchical relationship between cortical and subcortical regions is also involved. Findings of this sort will enrich and perhaps redirect cross-cultural study of thought processes in the future.

*See also* Chomsky, Noam; Cognition; Culture and personality; Dreams, psychological functions of; Durkheim, Emile; Evans-Pritchard, Edward; Freud, Sigmund; Herskovits, Melville J.; Language and culture; Lévi-Strauss, Claude; Lévy-Bruhl, Lucien; Piaget, Jean

Consult: Cole, Michael, and Scribner, Sylvia, *Culture and Thought: A Psychological Introduction* (New York: Wiley, 1974); Eccles, Sir John, *The Understanding of the Brain* (New York: McGraw-Hill, 1973); Gladwin, Thomas, *East Is a Big Bird: Navigation and Logic on Puluwat Atoll* (Cambridge, Mass.: Harvard University Press, 1970); Lévi-Strauss, Claude, *The Savage Mind* (Chicago: University of Chicago Press, 1966); Piaget, Jean, *The Child and Reality: Problems of Genetic Psychology* (New York: Grossman, 1973); Price-Williams, D. R. (ed.), *Cross-Cultural Studies* (Baltimore: Penguin, 1969); Segall, Marshall H., Campbell, D. T., and Herskovits, M. J., *The Influence of Culture on Visual Perception* (Indianapolis: Bobbs-Merrill, 1966).
—Regina Holloman, Roosevelt University

**Three-Age System.** See Lithic ages.

**Thurnwald, Richard** (1869–1954). Perhaps Germany's greatest anthropologist, Thurnwald contributed major works on economics, acculturation, and Melanesian and African ethnography. He combined culture trait and functional approaches in his analyses.

**Time, Cultural Orientation Toward.** Perceptions of time are functions of systems of time-reckoning and are culturally determined. As a result, notions of time vary from society to society. The anthropological interest in cultural orientations toward time leads sometimes to the study of folk history. A people's view of their history is important because it forms part of the thought of living people and hence part of the social life which the anthropologist directly observes.

Some of the pre-Columbian peoples of Mesoamerica, those with calendrical systems, related time to astrology. Each day of the year was thought to have particular qualities. People were thought to have the special characteristics of the day on which they were born. For example, the Aztec sacred calendar book, the *tonalamatl*, recorded the signs under which people were born. These signs determined whether one would have ill fortune or luck the rest of one's life. Mesoamerican religion also emphasized the repetition of time, especially a 52-year cycle. The basis of this cycle was the interlocking of two lesser cycles: a year of 260 days and a solar year of 365 days.

It took 52 years before the same two days of each cycle appeared together again.

See also Culture; Culture and personality; Ethnohistory; Language and reality; Language and thought; Numbering, systems of
Consult: Evans-Pritchard, E. E., "Nuer Time-Reckoning," *Africa* 12(2):189–216, 1939; Hall, Edward T., *The Silent Language* (Garden City, N.Y.: Doubleday, 1959); Hudson, Charles, "Folk History and Ethnohistory," *Ethnohistory* 13(1–2):52–70, 1966.

—*Michael D. Olien, University of Georgia*

**Time in Archaeology.** Time is perhaps the most basic concept in archaeology. The control of temporal variables, relative and absolute, is a major concern in all levels of archaeological research.

A variety of methods based on progressive natural changes have been used to measure approximately the passage of absolute time on material found in archaeological sites. Relative dating, which in many instances is of greater immediate concern than the determination of absolute age, is accomplished by stratigraphic and seriation methods.

Culture-historical syntheses integrate the spatial and temporal variations in archaeological data at the descriptive level. The methodology and definition of basic concepts of this type of synthesis as used in American archaeology are discussed by Willey and Phillips (1958). The *phase*, which is temporally and spatially very limited, is the basic unit of time, and a chronological succession of phases is a *sequence*. Temporal and contemporaneous spatial continuities are called *traditions* and *horizons* respectively.

Recently there has been an increasing interest in examining and attempting to explain the processes of cultural change due to adaptation to environment and other mechanisms. In the more abstract models of change, absolute time is of little importance but relative time or succession of events is crucial.

See also Dating, absolute; Dating, relative; Horizon, archaeological
Consult: Hole, F., and Heizer, R. F., *An Introduction to Prehistoric Archeology*, 3rd ed. (New York: Holt, 1973); Willey, G. R., and Phillips, P., *Method and Theory in American Archaeology* (Chicago: University of Chicago Press, 1958).

—*Daniel Wolfman, Arkansas Archeological Survey*

**Tinbergen, Niko(-laas)** (b. 1907). This Dutch ethologist, presently professor of animal behavior at Oxford University, shared a Nobel prize (1973) in physiology/medicine with Konrad Lorenz and Karl von Frisch. Granted the Ph.D. in 1932 at the University of Leyden, Tinbergen joined Lorenz in animal studies in the late 1930s and 1940s. He extrapolated from his animal studies to the origins of human violence and hypothesized that the development of long-range weapons freed human beings from natural semiotic (symbolic systems of) restraints against killing other humans. Tinbergen's major publication is *The Herring Gull's World* (1960).

See also Aggression; Ethology; Imprinting; Instincts; Lorenz, Konrad; Species-characteristic behavior

**Titiev, Mischa** (b. 1901). Cultural anthropologist noted primarily for his ethnographic research on the Hopi Indians of Old Oraibi and the Araucanian Indians of Chile.

**Tobacco.** Native to the New World (the Americas) and domesticated by Indian peoples, tobacco is the name given to the leafy plant genera (*Nicotiana* sp.) in widespread use by Indian cultures in North and South America prior to the arrival of the Europeans. The word comes from the Spanish *tabaco*, in turn a derivative of the Arawak word for cigar. Utilizing both wild and cultivated species, Indian peoples smoked, snuffed, chewed, ate, drank, and licked tobacco either by itself or in combination with other plants. Tobacco served a variety of purposes: as a sacred item integral to ceremonial rituals, often as an offering to the supernatural; as a medicine to relieve ailments; as the symbolic binder in friendship pacts between Indian groups; as a medium for inducing intoxication either for enjoyment or for religious/medicinal reasons; and for recreation and pleasure.

See also Drugs

**Toilet.** See Grooming.

**Tomb.** A tomb is any structure constructed especially for the bodies of the dead. Tombs may be used for a single individual or for several. They usually consist of an open chamber which contains the body of the

*A tomb in Greece.*

deceased—often along with pottery, food, and other objects which presumably will be used by the deceased in the afterlife. Tombs may be specially constructed buildings such as a pyramid or mausoleum; they may be hewn out of rock or constructed underground with stone or adobe. Because the structure was built for the singular purpose of burial, archaeologists infer that the dead individuals placed in a tomb were of high social status during life. If present in a tomb, objects placed with the body provide important information about religious beliefs of the culture by suggesting the presence of a belief in an afterlife. These objects may also provide essential economic information such as the craft specialities practiced in the ancient culture and the patterns of trade for exotic, luxury, and nonlocal materials.

See also Archaeology; Burial
—*Dean E. Arnold, Wheaton College*

**Tönnies, Ferdinand** (1855–1936). A German sociologist, Tönnies introduced the dichotomous conceptual framework of

*Gemeinschaft* (emphasis on kinship bonds, community) and *Gesellschaft* (emphasis on formal relationships, competition) as ideal types in studying and comparing societies. His work influenced Émile Durkheim's theories of mechanical/organic solidarity and Robert Redfield's theories of the folk-urban continuum.

*See also* Gemeinschaft und Gesellschaft

**Tools.** *See* Technology.

**Tools and Evolution.** It would seem a tenable hypothesis that the evolution of tools, information, information storage, and the human brain go hand in hand. This metaphor is chosen deliberately because the hand itself is a many-faceted tool—the most versatile of the human body, which carries other tools such as teeth, arms, and legs. The hand is the chief manipulator (from the Latin *manus*, "hand") of extrasomatic tools; its touch gives information to the brain; it fashions conventionalized objects (including tools) serving as paradigms, cultural encodings of forms and meanings.

Perspectives from comparative anatomy, primatology, and ethology suggest an ever-increasing information storage capacity (memory) among the primates and especially the genus *Homo*. One may reasonably suppose that forms of communication involving signs, signals, and protosymbols must cumulatively have evolved beyond the communicational means displayed today by gibbons or chimpanzees, but short of the emergence of the systemic, multilayered communicational form we call language. What seems lacking among the former are the multilayeredness (phonemes, morphemes, words), grammars, and symbols. Signs and signals, though conventionalized (perhaps initially genetically), are not linked grammatically. This situation seems paralleled by the tools and technology of very ancient hominids like the australopithecines. Their tools, such as the pebble-derived instruments, are clearly conventionalized. But they entail no necessary sequential relations—that is, they are not "grammatical"—in the sense of the sequential relations between a waterwheel and a millstone or the successive tasks on an assembly line. The conventionalizations suggest *nongenetically* generated forms, also clearly not inherent in the materials.

Hence it suggests a protosymbolic initiation of tradition which is both stored in the organism's memory and conventionalized in the tool, a protocultural encoding. The tool becomes a mnemonic device both of the tradition and of its own use.

One may hypothesize that continuously varying experience, along with accident and possible encounters with other tradition-bearing hominid groups, would increase the stock of conventions and the possible combinations and orders in which tools could be used—with concomitant increasingly complex information storage and the evolution of memory functions and nongenetic abilities for communication.

Though these early developments are highly speculative, the past 5,000 years clearly show the development of interaction of information, communication, meanings, and tool use in a fully developed human brain with fully evolved language. This development is represented by the evolution of communication systems to complement speech and memory—mnemonic devices, hieroglyphic, syllabic, and alphabetic writing, pictorial representation, photography, sound recording, and ultimately electronic communication and storage. The evolution of these systems has involved the evolution of appropriate tools like the typewriter, teletype, and electronic synthesizer. Increasingly, technologies have come to have a systemic—a "grammatical"—character, linking tools in utilization sequences which may be represented by flowcharts. In modern industry, such flowcharts become very complex, increasingly needing the assistance of artificial memory and information-scanning devices—computers.

The progression from simple, conventionalized, disarticulated tools encoding protocultural conceptions to extremely complex, interconnected tool systems encoding highly complex cultural messages and symbols entails a causally parallel evolution of the social structure of work. More complex dimensions of labor, more complex articulations, and ultimately ever greater hierarchies of personnel, including supervising bureaucracies, continuously and cumulatively emerge.

*See also* Evolution, general; Evolutionism; Technology

Consult: Hockett, Charles F., and Ascher, Robert, "The Human Revolution," *Current Anthropology* 5:135–147, June 1964.

—*Anthony Leeds, Boston University*

**Totalitarianism.** As states evolve, public works projects and services partially compensate individuals for their lost absolute equality and freedom, but some degree of coercion is necessary to extract taxes, tribute, and labor from people. As pressures increase on them, rulers usually resort to greater force to maintain their power. Totalitarian systems control people—and basic resources and production—with institutions of brutal repressive force and thought control ranging from magic and religion to propaganda and censorship. State-level societies need not necessarily be totalitarian (although they *are* coercive); totalitarianism can evolve from traditional hierarchical institutions under stress.

*See also* Dictatorship; Fascism; Political anthropology; Political systems; Social stratification

**Totem.** *See* Totemism.

**Totemism.** This term refers to the symbolic association of plants, animals, and objects with individuals or classes of people, especially the association of animal species with exogamous clans as their emblems or mythological ancestors.

The concept of totemism, which was developed during the late 19th century, derived from a recognition that primitive societies often name social groups after animals and that group members frequently observe a special relationship with their group's totem—for instance, by claiming it as their ancestor, refusing to eat its flesh, or carrying out rituals to increase its numbers. More recently, anthropologists have come to believe that too many different kinds of relationships between animals, plants, and humans have been labeled totemism for the term to have much meaning or usefulness. Nevertheless, interest in totemism has focused attention on significant problems. For the foremost modern student of the subject, Claude Lévi-Strauss, the essence of totemism lies in the universal tendency of all cultures to divide up the natural world into separate species and things, and the social world into different groups and classes of people—and to use the differences between the parts of one world to represent differences between the parts of the other.

*See also* Clan; Lévi-Strauss, Claude; Primitive peoples; Religion; Totem pole

Consult: Lévi-Strauss, Claude, *Totemism* (Boston: Beacon Press, 1963).
—*James Howe, Massachusetts Institute of Technology*

## Totem Pole.

A pole or post, carved and painted with animal or bird symbols, before or beside an Indian dwelling on the American Northwest Coast is called a totem pole. These were formerly used by Haida, Kwakiutl, Nootka, Salish Tlingit, and Tsimshian Indians.

*See also* Totemism

*Northwest Coast Indians created the unique art form called totem poles. These carved and painted pillars represent mythical entities that give each clan its unique identity. This totem pole, located near Ketchikan, Alaska, is said to be the tallest in the Northwest. Behind it can be seen the top of the Indian ceremonial house.*

*Pueblo Indian Hemis Kachina doll, carved in 1972 by Marshall Lomakema. The Pueblo and Hopi formerly carved these dolls for their own children; now they are produced primarily for tourists.*

## Tourist Art.

Also known as souvenir art and airport art, the arts made for appreciation by foreigners are important indicators of what travelers and tourists wish to convey about the ethnic group visited and what a people regards as special about themselves. Thus tourist arts stress exotic characteristics and materials as well as a culture's unique features. Examples include black woodcarvings of exaggerated figures and spirit beings in East Africa and the Sepik area of New Guinea; miniature totem poles from the Northwest Coast Indians; bears and salmon among the Ainu. Because these arts need to tell a simple theme repeatedly, they tend toward mass-production methods and may even be made elsewhere—e.g., Eskimo sculptures made in Hong Kong or Southwest Indian jewelry made in Japan. Other tourist arts express a high degree of skill and meaning to the creators themselves, such as Inuit lithographic prints or Seri Indian ironwood carvings, and such arts range right into the traditional and even religious genres in parts of Africa and the Near East.

*See also* Art; Art, primitive
Consult: Dawson, L., Frederickson, V.-M., and Graburn, N. H. H., *Traditions in Transition* (Berkeley: Lowie Museum, 1974).
—*Nelson H. H. Graburn, University of California, Berkeley*

## Towns.

*See* Village settlements.

## Toys.

Any object used for play may be considered a toy; but the activities that are

*Sculpture of an old man, six inches high. Wakamba carvers in Kenya make these for tourist sale.*

considered *play* vary from one culture to the next. So play and toys can only be identified in the context of specific cultures.

All cultures use toys in the process of socializing children. Toys like balls or scaled-down implements provide explicit models for learning adult behavior. Games played with toys like tops or dice frequently develop skills and attitudes in children that carry over to adult life.

See also Games

Consult: Bateson, G., *Steps to an Ecology of Mind* (New York: Ballantine Books, 1972); Hilger, M. Inez, *Field Guide to the Ethnological Study of Child Life* (New Haven: HRAF Press, 1960).

**Trade.** Trade is the exchange of goods between people. The ways in which people trade and the distance over which they trade vary from place to place and time to time. There is strong prehistoric evidence that trade has always taken place between human groups, and the role of trade in the formation of states is important.

See also Economic systems; Exchange

**Tradition, Archaeological.** This term refers to the similarity in cultural elements which persists through a considerable span of time in a relatively restricted geographical area. The tradition concept was originally used with reference to ceramics (pottery traditions). Subsequent usage expanded its inclusiveness from the level of a single technological category to that of entire cultures. It is commonly employed at an intermediate level of generalization to refer to complexes of related traits which persist through time in restricted areas. Traditions are used in culture-historical reconstruction as indicators of significant cultural continuity through time and of genetic relationships between cultures. The inverse of the concept of tradition is that of *horizon*: cultural similarity which is restricted to a narrow time span but which covers a large geographical area. Both concepts were initially developed by students of Andean culture history and later came into general use in New World prehistory.

See also Horizon, archaeological; Time in archaeology

Consult: Willey, Gordon R., and Phillips, Philip, *Method and Theory in American Archaeology* (Chicago: University of Chicago Press, 1958).

—John S. Henderson, Cornell University

**Traditions.** Traditions are values, beliefs, rules, and behavior patterns that are shared by a group and passed on from generation to generation as part of the socialization process. Traditions provide a society's body of daily behavior as well as its concepts of morality: the rules of what it considers right and wrong. A tradition tells members of the society what is correct behavior and also explains why it is correct to do the right thing. Such an explanation is called a world view. It deals with the nature of things and with unanswerable questions about life and death.

In relatively homogeneous societies, tradition often provides the only acceptable way of doing things. Customs and values may seldom be questioned. Traditions are followed because that is what the ancestors did. Hence the tradition acquires a sacred quality. At the same time, the traditions of primitive groups are oral and can be reworked to justify new situations. A tradition need not be completely logical, consistent, or even based on true information. In complex societies, tradition becomes less important as various subgroups perpetuate different traditions and there is a greater tendency to question the validity of a given tradition as the only system of explanation.

See also Great Tradition; Little Tradition; World view

Consult: Griaule, Marcel, *Conversations with Ogotemmeli: An Introduction to Dogon Religious Ideas* (London: Oxford University Press, 1965); Guiteras-Holmes, C., *Perils of the Soul: The World View of a Tzotzil Indian* (New York: Free Press, 1961); Redfield, Robert, *The Primitive World and Its Transformation* (Ithaca: Cornell University Press, 1953).

—Michael D. Olien, University of Georgia

**Trager, George Leonard** (b. 1906). Linguist of the American structuralist school who coauthored (with Bernard Bloch) an important outline of linguistic analysis and an outline of the linguistic structure of English.

Consult: Bloch, Bernard, and Traeger, George L., *Outline of Linguistic Analysis* (Baltimore, Md.: Linguistic Society of America, 1942).

*Uros Indian woman and child returning from the mainland to their artificially constructed floating islands in Lake Titicaca, high in the Andes mountains. These Aymará-speaking people use cut reeds to construct the islands they live on, the huts they live in, and the boats they use for transportation. Although their way of life allows them few options, they have resisted attempts by the Peruvian government to relocate them onto cultivatable plots of land.*

**Trait, Cultural.** Cultural trait refers to material and nonmaterial cultural objects, conceptualized as discrete entities not intrinsically linked to other such objects. Although such traits are sometimes arranged into systematic culture patterns, they have no necessary linkage. Traits (so conceived) are separable from contexts—that is, diffusable. The trait structure of culture is presumed to underlie the process of diffusion, since relationships rarely diffuse and do so only if "objectivized" as separable traits—e.g., primogenitural succession to kingship as *trait* rather than as relationship between king and eldest son. Some quite complex "traits," such as plow agriculture, disarticulate into subsidiary traits—moldboard, plowshare, tongue, traction animals, yoke, row planting—of which none must necessarily be present.

See also Culture areas of the world; Historicism; *Kulturkreis*

**Traits, Biological.** *See* Genetics; Genotype.

**Traits, Genetic.** *See* Genetics.

**Trance.** This altered state of consciousness often involves ritual situations during which an individual may exhibit some combination of the following: trembling, excessive perspiration, hyperventilation, muscular rigidity (catalepsis), vigorous rhythmic or jerky movements, shouting, speaking in tongues (glossolalia), and personality dissociation.

> *See also* Altered states of consciousness; Culture and personality; Hallucinations and shamanism; Shamanism

**Transcendent Symbols.** *See* Religion; Symbol; Symbolism.

**Transcription.** *See* International Phonetic Alphabet.

**Transculturation.** *See* Acculturation.

**Transformation Rules.** *See* Transformational grammar.

**Transformational Grammar.** This term refers to the specific form of generative grammar developed by Noam Chomsky and other members of the school of transformational linguistics. As initially formulated by Chomsky in his revolutionary work *Syntactic Structures* (1957), a transformational grammar links what a speaker wishes to communicate (initial element) with the phonemic representation of sentences via a sequence of three components:

1. *Phrase structure component:* an ordered set of obligatory phrase structure rules which generate the *deep structure* of sentences—i.e., strings of sentences' elements and the hierarchical relationships among them.

2. *Transformational component:* a set of obligatory and optional transformation rules which rearrange, add to, and delete elements of the deep structure of sentences (according to the semantically relevant options) and generate acceptably arranged strings of words and morphemes (the *surface structure* of sentences).

*A shaman of the !Kung San in a trance, serving his people through his ability to establish immediate connections with the supernatural world.*

3. *Morphophonemic component:* a set of obligatory rules which converts the surface structure representations of sentences to their phonological representation as sequences of phonemes.

In 1965 Chomsky published *Aspects of the Theory of Syntax* in which he modified this model substantially. Whereas in the first case he argued that the syntax of a sentence could be analyzed without reference to its meaning (semantics), in the intervening period he was persuaded that semantics and syntax are both crucial elements of grammar. The new model of a transformational grammar retains the *initial element;* however, there are now four components—not three—and *meaning* is generated as well as sound. These components are:

1. *Base component:* essentially the old phrase structure component, but with the addition that phrase structure rules now have taken over from transformation rules the task of accounting for sentences' seman-

tically relevant options, as well as continuing their original task of generating sentences' deep structures. The base component feeds into two other components: the *transformational component* and the *semantic component.*

2. *Transformational component:* transformation rules are now for the most part obligatory and continue to convert deep structures into derived surface structures.

3. *Semantic component:* a new addition to the old model, this component operates on the deep structure generated by the base component and, through rules of semantic interpretation, generates sentences' meanings. A major element of this component is the *lexicon* of a language.

4. *Phonological component:* pretty much the same as the old morphophonemic component, but includes additionally the rules for converting strings of phonemes into actual strings of *sounds.*

In this newer model of transformational grammar, then, the grammar is explicitly designed to generate semantic structure (meaning) as well as syntactic structure and phonological representations (sounds).

> *See also* Generative grammar; Phrase structure; Surface structure of language
>
> Consult: Chomsky, Noam, *Syntactic Structures* (The Hague: Mouton, 1957); Chomsky, Noam, *Aspects of the Theory of Syntax* (Cambridge, Mass.: M.I.T. Press, 1965); Lyons, John, *Noam Chomsky* (New York: Viking, 1970).
>
> —*David E. Hunter, Southern Connecticut State College*

**Transformational Linguistics.** Transformational (generative) grammar, conceived by Noam Chomsky (1957, 1965), attempts to account explicitly for the knowledge and intuitions underlying the human ability to speak and understand language. In opposition to the goal of descriptive (taxonomic) linguistics of developing procedures for discovering grammar, the goal of transformational theory is to develop procedures for selecting from alternative grammars the one that best describes the creativity of language—the human ability to produce and understand novel utterances never before spoken—and the intuitions that enable humans to distinguish between grammatically acceptable and unacceptable sentences. Transformational theory rejects the Bloomfieldian view that the only valid data for analysis are directly observable speech acts, in favor of a more abstract, rationalist approach. Since the aim of transformational grammar is to account for human linguistic *competence* rather than performance, the description of actual speech is secondary to the basic goal.

**Model.** Transformational theory assumes that every sentence has a deep (underlying) structure and a surface (derived) structure —the structure of sentences actually spoken is surface structure—and that a set of transformational rules mediates between the two to derive surface structures from deep structures. The deep structure of a sentence is generated from the *base component* of the grammar—a set of phrase structure rules and a lexicon. The deep structure—represented by a tree with the nodes of the branches labeled to identify the constituents of the sentence—is then subjected to three different operations to produce the surface structure: semantic projections, transformations, and phonological projections (the subject of generative phonology). A meaning is assigned to the sentence by the semantic projection rules, which are part of the *semantic interpretive component* of the grammar. Then the deep structure tree is subjected to the *transformational component,* which is an ordered and obligatory set of rules that operate in a cycle to transform the sentence by rearranging, substituting, deleting, and/or conjoining some of the sentence's constituents to produce a surface structure tree—one with newly labeled branches to identify the derived sentence's constituents. The surface structure tree is then subjected to the rules of the *phonological component,* which indicate how the sentence is pronounced.

Figures 1 and 2 illustrate the derivation of the sentence *Harry seems to enjoy soccer.* Figure 1 shows the underlying tree structure of the sentence (S = sentence, NP = noun phrase, VP = verb phrase, V = verb), generated by the phrase structure rules with words from the lexicon inserted under the labels. The *raising* transformation is then applied to the structure in Figure 1: this raises the constituent *Harry* to replace *it* (which is then deleted) and raises the constituents that came after *Harry* in the tree. Figure 2 is the surface structure tree of the transformed sentence.

The theory assumes that although the specific phrase structure, lexicon, projec-

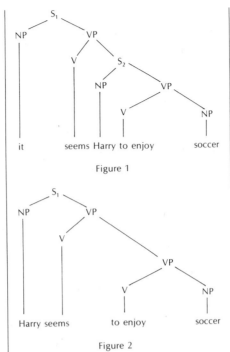

Figure 1

Figure 2

tion, and transformation rules are different for each language, the overall organization and operation of the model is the same for all languages. Whereas descriptive linguistics aims at developing procedures for discovering the grammar of each language, transformational linguistics aims at developing a general model capable of explaining how language operates—but without distorting the different facts of each language.

**Generative Semantics.** An important variety of transformational theory is generative semantics (See Grinder and Elgin 1973), which denies the existence of a semantic interpretive component and equates the underlying semantic representation of a sentence with its deep structure tree, thus simplifying the overall model.

*See also* Chomsky, Noam; Descriptive linguistics; Grammar; Language; Linguistics; Surface structure of language; Transformational grammar

Consult: Chomsky, Noam, *Syntactic Structures* (The Hague: Mouton, 1957); Chomsky, Noam, *Aspects of the Theory of Syntax* (Cambridge, Mass.: MIT Press, 1965); Grinder, John T., and Elgin, Suzette Haden, *Guide to Transfor-*

*mational Grammar: History, Theory, Practice* (New York: Holt, 1973).
—*Charles T. Snow, California State University, Chico*

**Transhumance.** The seasonal migration of domestic livestock and their herders for the purpose of grazing different pastures at different times of the year.

*See also* Migration; Pastoralism
Consult: "Comparative Studies of Nomadism and Pastoralism," *Anthropological Quarterly,* Special Issue, 44(3), 1971.

**Traps.** *See* Fishing; Hunting; Weapons.

**Traumatic Childhood Experiences.** In Freudian psychology, unsatisfying or painful experiences of early childhood decisively affect the adult personality. Critical events include weaning, toilet training, and resolution of the Oedipus complex.

*See also* Defense mechanisms; Oedipus complex; Psychoanalytic school of psychology

**Tree-Ring Dating.** *See* Dendrochronology.

**Tribal Art.** *See* Art, primitive.

**Tribal Society.** *See* Primitive peoples.

**Tribe.** Although this term is widely used in reference to preliterate peoples in many parts of the world, there is no commonly accepted definition of the word.

Originally a tribe was simply a territorially defined social group. The Romans identified *tribua* as political units. Lewis Morgan regarded as tribal those societies that exhibited social institutions but lacked political ones; Henry Maine, on the other hand, saw the distinction in legal terms, with tribal societies basing their laws on status rights rather than contractual rights. Others have seen a common language, or the presence of chieftains, as the defining characteristic.

Modern usage suggests that tribal societies are characteristically small-scale groupings that display some form of cultural unity; the members themselves explicitly recognize some affinity toward one another.

In particular, the tribe is the unit that assembles in the event of warfare.

See also Chiefdom; Clan; Headman; Social Organization

Consult: Gutkin, Peter C. W., The Passing of Tribal Man in Africa (Leiden: Brill, 1970); Moore, Clark D., and Dunbar, Ann (eds.), Africa Yesterday and Today (New York: Bantam, 1968); Thomas, Elizabeth M., Warrior Herdsmen (New York: Vintage, 1972); Turnbull, Colin M., Tradition and Change in African Tribal Life (New York: Avon, 1971).

—Bruno Pajaczkowski, Cambridge University

**Tripod.** See Architecture.

**Trophy Taking.** The custom of capturing trophies, particularly the heads of human victims or other portions of the body, is widespread throughout the Americas as well as other areas of the world. In some instances, the purpose is to appease evil spirits, to extract vengeance for past damages, to alleviate retribution from the deceased, or to satisfy the demands for revenge from one's own ancestors. In others, it is to taunt the enemy or to absorb the strength of the victim by religious osmosis. In only a few in-

Incised shell gorget from Castalian Springs, Tennessee (c. 1200–1600 AD), depicting a warrior carrying a trophy head.

stances does the primary purpose seem to be out-and-out "showing off" similar to the wearing of a medal by a soldier.

Other trophies include portions of animal bodies, such as the jawbone, teeth, or leg bones. The latter are also important trophies from human bodies, particularly the femur. Human fingers are a commonly encountered trophy; often they are strung on thongs as a charm or necklace. The human skull vault is sometimes employed as a gorget or a decorative ornament. These bones often are regarded as powerful medicine and are commonly among the contents of religious or medicine bundles. The use of toes, ears, or the penis is also known, although it is less common.

The shrinking of human heads, as practiced in South America among a variety of tribes, most notably the Jivaro, is not only a technological tour de force which has captured popular fascination but apparently was also an early convenience, since it was manifestly easier to travel or perform ceremonial rites with the reduced scalp and tissue than the complete skull. This may have led to scalp taking, although tribes that took scalps seemingly did not always have a prior practice of decapitation. Scalping itself is certainly a prehistoric custom dating to well before the coming of European explorers.

The custom of retaining complete human heads, as practiced by the Mundurucú of Brazil, for example, is often confused with trophy taking. Here the complete head and skull of an ancestor is carefully preserved as a measure of respect and affection. Such objects are regarded with high regard rather than contempt or insult.

An abundance of prehistoric South American pottery shows the taking of human heads, most notably in Peru, where Nazca pottery often depicts the severing of the head or the carrying of a head in a victory rite. This is equally common in other prehistoric regions of the continent, as well as in Central America and Mexico; the famous Aztec tzompantli structures are among the most dramatic indications of trophy-head-taking in the world, possibly equaled only by the New Guinea skull displays.

See also Cannibalism; Warfare

Consult: Karsten, R., "Blood Revenge, War, and Victory Feasts Among the Jivaro Indians of Eastern Ecuador," Bureau of American Ethnology Bulletin 79, 1923.

—Frederick J. Dockstader, Museum of the American Indian

**Troubetzkoy, Prince Nikolas S.** (1890–1938). Leading member of the Prague linguistic circle who summarized their conception of phonology and distinctive features in his Grundzüge der Phonologie (1939).

See also Prague school of linguistics

**Troy.** The capture of this ancient city in NW Asia Minor is the subject of Homer's Iliad. Troy was rediscovered at Hissarlik and excavated by Heinrich Schliemann in the late 1800s.

See also Schliemann, Heinrich

**Turner, Victor W.** (b. 1920). Turner has adopted a processual approach to the study of symbols and rituals. He uses an intensively ethnographic (case study) method of research.

**Twining.** Twining is the simplest and probably earliest cloth and basketry weaving technique. Double weft strands wrap like continuously twisted figure eights around the warps.

See also Textiles

**Tylor, Sir Edward Burnett** (1832–1917). The focus of this English anthropologist's work was the application of scientific method to the study of human society, the prehistoric past, and the development of culture along a progressive, uniform line. In 1861 he published Anahuac, a travelogue with ethnological observations of a trip taken through Mexico in 1855. In 1865 he published Researchers into the Early History of Mankind, his first systematic ethnological look at the world. The year 1871 marks the major point in his career with the publication of the two-volume work Primitive Culture. This achievement resulted in his election as a Fellow of the Royal Society. Tylor's major assumption, shared by various of his contemporaries, was that civilized society has evolved by natural (rather than supernatural) processes from origins similar to the observable, existing "savagery" reported from other parts of the world. In Primitive Religion he presented the concept that human culture (especially religion) is the product of a natural, regular, continuous, progressive, and law-abiding ("natural law") evolution of the mental capacities of Homo sapiens and that this evolutionary process, as a reflection of the concept of uniformitarianism, is a proper subject of scientific study.

*See also* Uniformitarianism

−*George R. Mead, Eastern Oregon College*

**Type Frequency.** *See* Sequence dating.

**Types and Modes of Artifacts.** Artifacts exhibit various formal attributes such as length, color, and weight. Collections or assemblages of artifacts may be described in terms of diagnostic attribute sets or modes (Rouse 1939:25–28; 1941:30–31; 1972:56–57). For example, rim shards may be classified according to the modes everted, inverted, or straight. Each mode is often thought of as a standard followed by the artisan who produced the artifact. A type is a demonstrable, nonrandom clustering of attributes observed in a class of artifacts (Spaulding 1960:443). If in a collection of projectile points, for example, attributes such as length of 2–3 inches, stems, and corner notches are found to cluster more than would be expected by chance, this clustering defines a type. It can be seen that such clusterings may represent the concepts of the manufacturer, the function of the artifact, the nature of the material used in manufacture, or all of these. There has been a long and fruitless argument among archaeologists as to whether or not types reflect the norms being followed by extinct artisans (Ford 1954a, 1954b). Today it is generally agreed that types are more productively viewed as instruments by which the archaeologist monitors the past.

*See also* Archaeology; Artifact

Consult: Ford, James A., "On the Concept of Types," *American Anthropologist* 56:42–54, 1954a; Ford, James A., "Comment on A. C. Spaulding, 'Statistical Techniques for the Discovery of Artifact Types,'" *American Antiquity* 19:390–391, 1954b; Rouse, Irving J., *Prehistory in Haiti: A Study in Method,* Yale University Publications in Anthropology 21, 1939; Rouse, Irving J., *Culture of the Ft. Liberté Region, Haiti,* Yale University Publications in Anthropology 24, 1941; Rouse, Irving J., *Introduction to Prehistory: A Systematic Approach* (New York: McGraw-Hill, 1972); Spaulding, Albert C., "The Dimensions of Archaeology," in *Essays in the Science of Culture in Honor of Leslie A. White,* ed. Gertrude E. Dole and Robert L. Carneiro (New York: Crowell, 1960).

−*Linda S. Cordell, University of New Mexico*

**Types of Fieldwork.** *See* Fieldwork methods.

**Unconscious, the.** A hypothesized realm of the mind of whose content we are not ordinarily aware. Many psychologists, particularly Freudians, believe that much human activity is unconsciously motivated.

*See also* Collective unconscious; Freud, Sigmund; Id; Psychoanalytic school of psychology; Superego

**Unconscious, Collective.** *See* Collective unconscious.

**Underdevelopment.** *See* Development, economic; Social change.

**Underemployment.** Although the term *underemployment* is part of common parlance, its precise definition proves difficult. Several different characteristics, regarded singly or jointly, may be subsumed under the term: part-time employment where full-time employment is sought; odd-job types of work as the main mode of earning a living; low-wage or underpaid jobs; full-time employment without contract as in certain informal labor markets; any sort of temporary work, part-time or full-time; unpaid work, such as housewifing. The logical links among all these referents are obscure—especially since quite different socioeconomic processes may generate them. They may *not,* as is frequently assumed, necessarily generate incomes lower than those of the fully employed. Much recent literature from both the "underdeveloped" and the "developed" countries shows that at times it is highly rational for workers to opt for odd-jobbing and contractless work in preference to the formal employment markets whose wage scales provide *lower* incomes than can be gleaned from "underemployment." Thus the concept lacks general analytic validity and its general utility in comparative research is dubious.

*See also* Labor market; Labor market, informal; Unemployment

**Unemployment.** This term refers to a situation in which a potential worker has no job. A narrower definition (more common in the neoclassical economics used for labor statistics) considers only a job-seeker who cannot find a job as unemployed, not those who may have given up looking for jobs in depressed labor markets or those such as housewives who never appeared in any officially defined labor market. Usually unemployment depends on the existence of a labor market—a far from universal societal institution but one highly characteristic of price-making (capitalist) market systems. In such contexts, unemployment generates a labor supply outstripping labor absorption, thus depressing wages and maximizing profits.

*See also* Labor market; Labor market, informal; Underemployment

**Uniformitarianism.** This notion was originally (1785) called the Huttonian theory, which proposed that the key to the past geological history of the earth could be found by examining the existing forces at work. Thomas Huxley is credited with giving the name *uniformitarianism* to C. Lyell's formulation (1830s) of the doctrine of uniformity of geological processes: that the geological forces operative today were active in former geologic times, produced the same results, and to them alone—not catastrophes—are due the structural features of the earth. C. Darwin applied the concept to the organic world, although the processes he described were of a different type.

*See also* Darwin, Charles; Lyell, Charles; Tylor, Sir Edward Burnett

**Unilineal Descent.** Descent rule in which kinship is reckoned exclusively either through the female's or the male's line.

*See also* Descent; Kinship; Lineage

**Unilocal Residence.** Postmarital residence established exclusively through either sex—either matrilocality or patrilocality.

*See also* Marriage; Matrilocality; Patrilocality

**Units of Study, Sociocultural.** Anthropologists use various units of study characterized by both societal and cultural dimensions, which coexist almost universally in human behavioral contexts. When dealing with "primitives," anthropologists claim the *tribe* as their holistic unit, although most ethnographers in fact deal only with a small selection of local or domestic groups of the tribal population. In large-scale societies, anthropologists have chosen the *community*—usually ill-defined but identified as a specific locality—as a major unit of study. Tribe and community are territorial units, as are nations, regions, and neighborhoods in cities; these units are also used in anthropology, although the region is primarily a geographer's unit. Anthropologists also use many nonterritorial units for study: kinship networks, age grades, associations, ethnic groups, social classes, agencies. Where these exist in primitive groups, they tend to be coterminous with the tribal or domestic unit. In highly complex, large-scale societies, especially in large urban centers, none of them is coterminous with the city or any of its communities, so that study of such units is atomistic and often divorced from context. All the units listed here have specifiable social relations and social orders, governed by systems of cultural norms.

*See also* Culture, a; Society; Sociocultural system

**Universals in Art.** Those who are concerned with research on the underlying reasons for cross-cultural appreciation of art forms recognize that though the phenomenon exists, neither scientific method on the one hand nor aesthetic analysis in philosophy on the other has been able to produce a hypothesis with which anthropologists can work comfortably. The underlying assumption in many attempts to explain why people enjoy and respond to art forms created in other cultures is that there exists a psychic unity of the human species and humans everywhere recognize beauty as a quality, even in exotic forms alien to their own culture. Anthropologists trained to analyze and measure observable behavior find this difficult to correlate with their comparative material. When dealing with affective response generated by aesthetic appreciation or artistic creativity instead of observable behavior, one soon discovers that methodologies developed in the behavioral sciences are not applicable.

Just as philosophers developed scientific inquiry as a philosophy of science, they have struggled with the intellectual problems of describing human feeling, particularly that feeling with which we are here concerned: aesthetic emotion in either its contemplative or its creative aspects. The field of philosophy concerned with this problem is aesthetics.

It is to aestheticians, or at least some of them, that anthropologists must turn for assistance in dealing with human emotions inherent in the acceptance of a concept of universals in art.

One of the aestheticians whom artists and anthropologists alike regard as successful in developing a means to understanding universals in art is Suzanne Langer (1953). In essence, she is pointing out that we must accept the reality of aesthetic emotion and at the same time not confuse the feelings of the creative and the contemplative by considering them as two sides of the same coin, since the virtual experience in each is completely different. She also maintains that there is a different virtual experience in each of the art forms—sculpture, painting, dance, music, and so on. Through empathy we seem to respond—in visual forms through color, line, and texture—in terms of our own life experiences and that in which we see life as we are familiar with it. It was in this direction that Franz Boas was groping, with his insistence on the basic need of order and rhythm by humans, in his *Primitive Art*. But by using the terminology of Euramerican art historians and critics, he obscured from himself the essential concepts he thought would explain universal feelings in art.

There are a growing number of methodologies concerned with art forms in a cross-cultural context—from structural analysis for museum series to ethnohistory and film. All have been developed to examine some aspect of this phenomenon of human expression and pleasure in aesthetic feeling. But anthropologists and art historians alike must still keep in mind that though humans react with channeled behavior in terms of what they have learned from cultural training and idiosyncratic experience, they have an even more essentially human ability to recreate symbols of life and living that all humans with aesthetic sensitivity feel. The key, then, is in the symbolizing ability of humans and the phenomena of empathy and projection—which, when applied to aesthetic creativity and aesthetic contemplation, produce that nonverbal symbol, the art form.

*See also* Art; Universals of culture; Universals of language

Consult: Boas, Franz, *Primitive Art* (New York: Dover, 1927); Langer, Suzanne, *Feeling and Form* (New York: Scribner, 1953).

—*Justine M. Cordwell, Chicago City Colleges/Malcolm X*

**Universals of Culture.** This phrase refers to two distinct phenomena, one within a culture and one between cultures. Within a culture, a universal, as defined by Ralph Linton, includes all the culture content, ideas, behaviors, and conditioned emotional responses that are common to all normal adult members of the culture—for example, the use of a language or shared ideas in regard to proper behavior.

On an intercultural level the term refers to aspects of culture believed to exist in all human societies—for example, the nuclear family, consisting of father, mother, and children, established by marriage, and exhibiting a division of labor between the sexes among adult members. Other universals often cited include incest prohibitions, funeral rites, modesty in regard to natural functions, and gift giving. Such universals are not genuine uniformities of culture content but of *form,* termed by G. P. Murdock "common denominators" of culture. As Melville Herskovits notes, all cultures exhibit a morality, which is thus a universal, but the specific content of these moralities differs from culture to culture. The cross-cultural similarities that anthropologists have discovered are generally attributed to the basic biological and psychological characteristics of the human species and to the universal environmental conditions which set the context for human existence.

*See also* Cross-cultural surveys; Culture; Pattern, culture

Consult: Bourguignon, E., and Greenbaum, L., *Diversity and Homogeneity in World Societies* (New Haven: HRAF Press, 1973); Kluckhohn, C., "Universal Categories of Culture," in *Anthropology Today*, ed. Sol Tax (Chicago: University of Chicago Press, 1962); Linton, R., *The Study of Man* (New York: Appleton-Century, 1936); Murdock, G. P., "The Common Denominator of Cultures," in *Culture and Society*, ed. G. P. Murdock (Pittsburgh: University of Pittsburgh Press, 1965).

—*Stan Wilk, Lycoming College*

**Universals of Language.** The concern with a universal system of symbolization goes back to Plato, and more recently to medieval philosophers and Leibniz. Using Latin and Greek as their basis, the Port Royal grammarians of 17th-century France attempted to formulate a grammar underlying all grammars. Their concern with linguistic universals has been kept alive by rationalist philosophers interested in universal rational processes and by the followers of Noam Chomsky's school of transformational linguistics. Empiricists tend to be interested in the uniqueness of particular languages, and structural linguists such as Bloomfieldians have downplayed the importance of linguistic universals. While empiricists see language as entirely learned through experience, for rationalists the universal blueprint of language is innate and activated by the individual's enculturation.

There is, however, a substantial agreement among all scholars on the existence of characteristics common to all languages (linguistic universals). Linguists distinguish between *substantive universals,* or elements present in all languages, and *formal universals,* or constraints and limitations on the forms assumed by all languages. Substantive universals can be grouped into phonological, grammatical, and semantic universals. Examples of phonological universals are found on the level of articulatory phonetics: every language has vowels, stops, fricatives, nasals, and so on. On the level of phonemes, all languages exhibit a severely restricted set. Also, we find a universal tendency toward phonological symmetry. Roman Jakobson hypothesizes that the sound patterns of every language contain a limited number of discrete features, which are in binary opposition to each other and resist change. He claims also that it might be possible to build a universal table of distinctive features from which we can reconstruct the system of each language by way of transformations. Other linguists accept the universality of distinctive features but not that of binary oppositions. Jakobson has also hypothesized that all human infants learn a certain set of sounds (phonological features), then add to them and lose some due to aphasia; these initially learned sounds—if this is so—are universals.

Grammatical universals include the use of proper names and deictic elements (personal pronouns, demonstrative pronouns,

and so on), some of which indicate the speaker and others the addressee. In the realm of syntax there are universals such as verbal and nominal phrases, adjective and verbal modifiers, intransitive and transitive forms, and so on. Joseph Greenberg has listed as many as forty-five such grammatical universals.

The realm of semantic universals finds much less agreement among scholars. Some have formulated the hypothesis of a universal phonetic symbolism—that is, the cross-cultural identity of meaning of certain sounds. The technique of semantic differential has revealed the existence of cross-culturally valid synesthetic associations, or the connection of meanings such as happy and sad with the visual dimensions, respectively, of up and down. The same technique has established the existence of universally valid components of affective meanings. B. Berlin and P. Kay claim to have established the existence of semantic universals in the color terminologies of many languages.

Linguists give greater importance to formal than to substantive universals. Among all logically possible syntactical and phonological rules, actual languages exhibit a very delimited set. This tells us that the organization of languages is limited by structural constraints. For instance, every language has a deep structure and a surface structure; every lexical element is a combination of phonological, syntactic, and semantic components. The existence of universal constraints seems strikingly consistent with the notion of innate linguistic structures, verifying the rationalist point of view.

*See also* Language; Linguistics; Transformational linguistics

—Ino Rossi, St. John's University


**Upper Paleolithic.** This subdivision of the Paleolithic prehistoric age is characterized by a large and refined repertory of blade tools and by specialized instruments of ivory and bone. The Upper Paleolithic is dated around 45,000 years BP to 10,000 years BP.

*See also* Blade tools; Lithic ages; Paleolithic; Upper Paleolithic art; Venus figurines


**Upper Paleolithic Art.** Associated with the advent of early modern *Homo sapiens,* the Upper Paleolithic cultural period saw the increased importance of blade tools,

burins or gravers, bone, ivory, and antler tools, and the appearance of a specialized big-game hunting adaptation focusing on reindeer and mammoths. The complexity and diversity of traditions augmented, with art flourishing in many forms from as early as

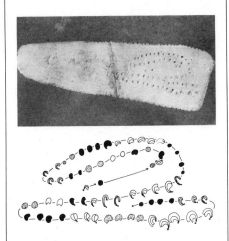

*This carved piece of antler bone is approximately 4 inches long and was found at the site of Blancharde, in the Dordogne region of France. It dates from the Aurignacian culture, some 34,000 years old. Many such objects have been found in Upper Paleolithic sites; their markings have largely been ignored and they have been called anything from "spatulas" to "palettes" or "knives."*

*Recently Professor Alexander Marshack of Harvard has begun reexamining these objects, including the microscopic examination of the details of their manufacture. His accompanying drawing shows some of the details he has noted. The significance of the finds is that these prehistoric people had a notational system; that this system was rather complex; that it was part of an established tradition; and that it expresses complicated cognitive development. It makes sense to further presume that these people would not have taken the trouble to carve these notations unless their belief system told them it was meaningful behavior. Marshack suggests that the 24 changes of point, style of stroke, or pressure used show that the creation of this notation was divided into 24 separated moments, of significance to the maker(s). A computer analysis suggests that this notational system was used to record or predict phases of the moon.*

30,000 BP to the end of the Upper Paleolithic about 10,000 BP. Climaxing particularly in W Europe, aesthetic expression was found in animal and human figurines; engravings, bas-reliefs, and paintings on rocks, rock shelters, and caves; delicately flaked willow and laurel leaf blades of rainbow flint; carving and incising of bone; and bone necklaces, bracelets, and beads. Art in Europe underwent a decline at the end of the Ice Age, but some see continuity in the animal figurines of the arctic Eskimo.

**Art Mobilier and Art Parietal.** Best described from French sites, Upper Paleolithic art is divided into two main types: *art mobilier* (portable art) and *art parietal* (found on permanent surfaces such as cave walls). Portable art includes naturalistic animal figurines of bone, ivory, or fired clay representing antelope, bison, horses, or other large animals. Human "Venus" figurines or females with highly accentuated sexual characteristics—perhaps fertility symbols—were widespread in Europe and are exemplified by the carving from a mammoth tusk from Predmost, Czechoslovakia, the stone Venus of Willendorf, Austria, and the French ivory figure from Lespugue. Carved and perforated bones and teeth were used for personal adornment, and beads were sewn to leather caps and clothing. Flat bone disks, perhaps relics, were perforated and engraved. Bone, ivory, and antler objects were often incised or carved, perhaps as art, status symbols, or for ritual purposes.

Parietal art, the most famous Upper Paleolithic form of aesthetic expression, reaches a climax in the art of the caves and rock shelters of the French Dordogne and Cantabrian Spain at such sites as Lascaux and Altamira. Although discovered in 1879, Altamira remained scientifically unaccepted until a number of French finds were also unearthed. Because of the growth of green algae fostered by human presence in the cave, Lascaux is now generally inaccessible to the public.

Cave painting occurred during most of the Upper Paleolithic, evolving from simple lines and flat washes to elaborate polychromes. Ochre was used for red, yellow, and brown coloring; manganese oxide or charcoal was used for black. These substances were ground into powder and mixed with a lubricant for application. Paintings were often made in inaccessible regions of caves, necessitating the use of lamps. Game animals, such as bison, horses, deer, and reindeer, were commonly depicted; human figures are scarce and highly stylized by comparison. Human figures often had an animal's head, perhaps representing a shaman or sorcerer. Impressions and outlines of human hands, however, and geometric figures of dots and lines were quite prevalent.

**Interpretation.** Interpretations of cave paintings are numerous and speculative, ranging from the hypothesis that leisure time allowed people to create art for its own sake to the assumption of art for magical and religious purposes to increase game animals and ensure hunting success. Still another association made is with totemism and tribal identification. More recently, the French prehistorian Leroi-Gourhan has suggested male and female symbolism as an explanation of varying elements, including geometric designs.

**Distribution.** Although the classic area for defining Upper Paleolithic art is W Europe, figurines extended as far as Asia eventually, and Australian engravings may date to 18,000 BP.

See also Gravettian culture; Leroi-Gourhan, André; Paleolithic; Venus figurines
Consult: Leroi-Gourhan, A., *The Art of Prehistoric Man in Western Europe* (London: Thames & Hudson, 1968); Marshack, Alexander, "Exploring the Mind of Ice Age Man," *National Geographic*, January 1975; Powell, T. G. E., *Prehistoric Art* (New York: Praeger, 1966); Ucko, P. J., and Rosenfeld, A., *Paleolithic Cave Art* (New York: McGraw-Hill, 1967).
—*Catherine E. Read-Martin, California State University, Los Angeles*

**Urban Anthropology.** This discipline involves the application of anthropological research techniques and methods to the study of people living in cities. Urban anthropology is a relatively new field which developed as a consequence of the rapid worldwide transformation of rural groups (including peasant agriculturalists and tribal horticulturalists), the traditional objects of anthropological study, into city dwellers. Studies in urban anthropology tend to focus on five major topics: (1) communities of recently immigrated country folk (urban villagers); (2) the ongoing rural-urban links or networks of interaction; (3) voluntary associations and other institutions which recent immigrants into cities develop (or transpose from their rural homelands) to help them cope with the problems of city life; (4) culture change and the survival of traditional cultural themes in urban contexts; and (5) the problem of developing a cross-culturally useful theory of urban life and a definition of the concept of city that applies usefully in all cases.

The latter concern is far from successful solution. So far, it is clear that the term *urban* refers to much more than a population density. It includes as yet unspecified minimal levels of occupational differentiation, societal segmentation, and (quite high) spatial concentrations of social interactions.

See also Associations; Cities, development of; Network, social; Social stratification; Urbanism; Urbanization
Consult: Southall, Aidan (ed.), *Urban Anthropology: Cross-Cultural Studies of Urbanization* (London: Oxford University Press, 1973).

**Urban Hierarchy.** An urban hierarchy is the size ranking of a society's cities. Concentrations of wealth and centralization of function increase with rank.

**Urbanism.** This term refers to the conditions of city life. A vague concept, urbanism has always been strongly ethnocentric, assuming urban conditions characteristic of the recent West or its two basic urban traditions—Mediterranean and (late) medieval Europe—disregarding other urban organizational forms. It generally refers to population density, personal anonymity, ethnic diversity, and other such characteristics—but in very limited cross-cultural, cross-historical, or contextual perspectives. Urban phenomena have been identified with *cities* rather than with the societal structures generating cities as locational concentrations of social process. Urbanism in the latter perspective looks sharply different because it illuminates processes which may also produce rural population decline, tribalism, community intensification, and homogenization as characteristics of urban development.

See also Urban anthropology

**Urbanization.** In English-speaking countries, this term refers vaguely to a process of urban growth (sometimes of all medium and larger towns) at the expense of rural populations. It thus is mainly a demographic idea that is not very informative respecting societal institutions or their changes. In countries speaking Romance languages, urbanization refers to the creation of infrastructures of streets, sewers, water and lighting systems, transport, and housing appropriate to a city.

*See also* Urban anthropology; Urbanism

**Utopia.** Sir Thomas More (1478–1535), in his book of the same name represented the imaginary island of Utopia as a perfect society. Hence the term refers to any community dedicated to idealized social or ethical principles.

**Uxorilocality.** According to this postmarital residence rule, a couple is expected to live with the wife's family or kin group after marriage.

*See also* Marriage

**Validity of Results.** *See* Scientific method; Statistical methods.

**Value (Economic).** This term refers to the quality of an object, material or nonmaterial, which makes it more, or less, desirable than other objects. A relationship with another human being may have economic value if it enhances the satisfaction of one's physical and emotional needs. A more rigorous interpretation would restrict attachment of economic value to material objects.

*See also* Economic anthropology
Consult: Van der Pas, H. T., *Economic Anthropology, 1940–1972: An Annotated Bibliography* (New York: Humanities Press, 1973).

**Value Hierarchy.** A value hierarchy is a model for ranking cultural values; ideally, such a model should be cross-culturally valid. Values are essentially the meanings attached to categories of experience and as such are culturally relative. The relationships between categories—taxonomic or part-whole—are also culturally relative. Nevertheless, anthropologists have proposed cross-culturally valid value hierarchies. One model contains (1) *value premises* at the top of the hierarchy which define the nature of humanity and society; (2) then *focal*

*values* which specify areas of central importance; (3) then *directives* or rules of behavior; (4) finally, *valued activities,* situations, or objects.

—Ino Rossi, St. John's University

**Value Judgments and Anthropology.** *See* Emics; Ethics and social research; Etics.

**Van Gennep, A.** *See* Gennep, A. Van.

**Van Lawick-Goodall, Jane.** *See* Goodall, Jane.

**Varnishes, Resins, Lacquers, Shellacs.** *See* Surface finishes.

**Varve Analysis.** Varves are annual deposits of sediment consisting of two or more layers. Before radiocarbon dating was developed, the counting of thousands of superimposed varves in glacial lake beds provided some indication of the number of years since the end of the Pleistocene.

*See also* Dating, absolute; Glaciations

**Vayda, Andrew P.** (b. 1931). This Hungarian-born American anthropologist, using general systems theory, has developed a rigorous approach to cultural ecology and the study of warfare. He edits *Human Ecology,* an important ecological journal.

*See also* Cultural ecology

**Veblen, Thorstein B.** (1857–1929). This American political economist is best known today for his *Theory of the Leisure Class* (1899) and *The Theory of Business Enterprise* (1904). Unlike most classical economists, he saw the broader institutional and social aspects which encompass the economy —particularly the price-making economy— and which are, in turn, affected by such economies. Thus, on the one hand, the leisure class is understood in terms of values and social relations which give form to economic activity while, on the other hand, the capitalist economy destroys craftsmanship.

**Vengeance.** *See* Cannibalism; Feuding.

*Four-inch-high limestone "Venus of Willensdorf," from the Gravettian culture of the European Upper Paleolithic.*

**Venus Figurines.** These carvings from the (largely) Central European Gravettian culture (ca. 25,000–18,000 BP) display exaggerated breasts, hips, and pregnantlike bellies suggesting their use as female fertility charms. (Formerly these figurines were considered Aurignacian.) The term is also applied frequently to unrelated Neolithic female figurines found throughout the world.

*See also* Gravettian culture; Upper Paleolithic art

**Verbal Communication.** *See* Communication.

**Villafranchian Period.** This period is a basal Pleistocene faunal stage whose type site is Villafranca d'Asti (NW Italy). It dates from 3.5 million to 1 million years BP. The Villafranchian is characterized in Europe and

*A village settlement of the Yaruro of Venezuela. This village had two parts, of which all but one house of one part is seen in the picture. The building on the right is a drying and storage frame to keep corn and meat safe from vermin and dogs. The three in the back are residences whose doors are visible. These are rainy season houses, more closed to the weather than the open dry season shelters. The new house going up is not of the usual plan but square, more like peasant houses in the region some distance away. It was to be used for ceremonies on rainy nights, but was in fact used as kind of a men's dormitory. The ceremonies (when not danced) were usually held in the open space lying between the new and the old houses. Note the male work group and communal behavior as well as the egalitarianism—the two men working at the moment of photographing are the two shamans of the village of 24 people.*

Africa by the appearance of *Leptobos, Equus,* and *Archidiskodon.* It is divided into an early (Astian-like) stage (starting ca. 3.3 million years ago) marked by the appearance of the large bovid *Leptobos* (e.g., at Étouaires) in a temperate/subtropical forest context; a middle stage (2.6 million BP) associated with the true horse (*Equus*) replacing Late Pliocene *Hipparion* in steppe contexts (e.g., at Roccaneyra Pardines, Villaroya); and a complex upper stage or stages (1.5 million BP) with primitive elephants (*Archidiskodon*) appearing initially in humid, temperate woodland/grassland environments (e.g., at Saint Vallier, Chagny). Terminal Villafranchian faunas document desiccated steppes at Senèze and Chilhac

(Haute-Loire) and a subsequent return to wetter, forested conditions (e.g., at Val d'Arno and Olivola in Tuscany). The appearance of Villafranchian faunal index fossils is a major criterion used to define the Pliocene/Pleistocene boundary.

*See also* Pleistocene

**Village Settlements.** This term is usually used in two contexts: archaeologically, and with reference to primitive stateless ("tribal") societies. In both contexts it indicates small clusters of dwellings situated in surroundings otherwise empty of housing though economically important for subsistence, as in the ancient Near East. The term's redundancy—villages *are* settlements—suggests there are other (e.g., urban) settlements, but neither case cited has urban settlements. When these are present one drops the word "settlements" and speaks only of villages (along with towns and cities). What seems intended is reference to people-land relationships in which total territorial use is spread over some specifiable area but residence, householding, and related economic aspects agglomerate, allowing immediate contact with one another—i.e., they localize. Localization of people, with their physical equipment, creates villages. Thus *village settlement* suggests relatively unstratified societies with territorially broad bases of economic activity and reciprocal and redistributive forms of economy. Though the term *village* is used for very small settlements in large-scale urban societies, their connections with

urban centers and the larger urban society are recognized and in this context the term *settlement* is attached not to them but to the entire territorial population distribution.

*See also* Economic systems; Land tenure
*—Anthony Leeds, Boston University*

**Violence.** Violence is a concept that eludes precise definition because the practice of actions characterized by explosive outbursts, coercion, antagonistic aggression, and the like is so varied and carried out by such diverse parties that commonality among them dissipates and propositions about them evade formulation. It is not a very useful scientific category. In fact, murder by knifing, rape, drunken verbal abuse, police brutality in repressing peaceful demonstrations, jailing of political opponents, committing anti-Establishment protesters to asylums, warfare, feuding, and American ice hockey may all be designated violent: as doing violence to persons or groups. But, obviously, they fundamentally differ culturally and institutionally, involving distinct kinds of "doing violence" to persons with *jurally* diverse redresses (or none). In some cultural contexts, violence is normatively and rhetorically disavowed—as in American society—however much it seems formally and informally institutionalized. In other cultures, it is normatively praised—for example, the violent man among the Chukchi or verbal violence in Brazilian political speeches. In other societies, like the Venezuelan Yaruro, violence is both normatively and behaviorally played down.

*See also* Aggression
*—Anthony Leeds, Boston University*

**Virchow, Rudolf** (1821–1902). Virchow, a German pathologist, specialized in skull pathology and cretinism. He and Adolph Bastian (1826–1905) founded the Museum für Völkerkunde and the German Society for Anthropology.

*See also* Bastian, Adolph

**Virilocality.** *See* Marriage.

**Vision Quest.** This phrase refers to the acquisition of power, protection, or guidance through direct, individual, personal contact with the supernatural. The vision quest is characteristic of the North American Indians and Eskimos.

See also Altered states of consciousness; Religion

**Visual Anthropology.** See Photography as a research tool.

**Vogt, Evon Zartman** (b. 1918). This cultural anthropologist is known professionally for his research in the Southwest and among the Maya of Chiapas, Mexico. His theoretical interests lie in primitive religion and culture change. Vogt is also an extremely successful writer of science fiction (pen name: A. E. Van Vogt).

**Völkerwanderungen.** See Migration.

**Von Rancke, Leopold** (1795–1886). As the originator of modern historiography, Von Rancke essentially formulated the methodological and conceptual principles of Boasian anthropology, including particular and general history, relativism, contextualism, and, partly, a trait ontology.

See also Boas, Franz

**Voodoo.** This popular magico-religious cult of Afro-American populations of the West Indies, Brazil, and the southern United States combines African religious traditions with some Christian elements.

See also Magic; Religion; Ritual

**Wages.** See Economic systems.

**Wagley, Charles W.** (b. 1913). This social anthropologist specializes in Latin America (especially Brazil), race relations, cargo cults, and economic anthropology. He is the co-author of a major typology of Latin American subcultures.

**Wallace, Alfred Russel** (1823–1913). This naturalist, while working in Malaya, formulated the theory of natural selection independently of C. Darwin. Although they were cofounders of the theory, the two later came to differ on its intricacies and variations.

See also Darwin, Charles; Evolution, biological; Evolution, genetic mechanisms of; Selection, natural

**Wallace, Anthony F. C.** (b. 1923). A leading figure in the study of culture and personality, Wallace has focused his research on the Indians of the Northeast, especially the Tuscarora, Iroquois, and Seneca. He introduced the concept of the *mazeway* to refer to cognitive maps. Related to this concept is his important work on revitalization movements. Another significant contribution to culture and personality is his suggestion that certain types of mental illness, such as arctic hysteria, may have a biological base. Wallace is also well known for his interest in the anthropology of religion and has published a major text on the subject, as well as a highly regarded text on culture and personality.

See also Culture and personality; Mazeway

**Warfare.** War may be defined as conflict carried on by hostile groups using armed force. In simple, low-energy-producing societies (such as tribes), warfare may be more in the nature of raids, which are carried out for specific objectives and are of short duration. In complex, high-energy-producing societies (such as modern nation-states), warfare may be carried out over long periods of time and for obscure reasons.

Ethnologists have tried to attribute warfare to innate human aggression. If this were so, then warfare would exist in every society and all warfare would be conducted in a similar mental state. In fact, aggression is common to all animals, but the way that hostility is acted out in human societies depends on the values of the society. The Semai, a tribe in Malaysia, have no warfare, nor do they condone violence of any kind in their society. Eskimos may settle arguments through individual duels, in which one opponent kills another; or the opponent may seek popular support through a song contest in which each adversary tries to discredit his opponent in verse. Neither society practices warfare. The Tiwi of Australia also have a system of settling disputes which involves older men throwing spears at younger men who jump and turn to avoid being hit. If anyone is slightly wounded, the contest is over.

The Tiwi do not know organized warfare.

Warfare, as it is practiced in complex societies, has little to do with hostility or anger. Wars are conducted by impersonal means such as air warfare, missile warfare, and tank warfare which require that the individuals involved be in full command of their intellectual capacities, not at the mercy of emotions. If modern warfare were to be an outlet for innate hostility as some ethnologists would have it, then there would be no need for propaganda, parades, and the promotion of patriotism.

Some anthropologists trace the beginnings of warfare to the beginnings of agriculture, even before irrigation made relatively small areas of land extremely valuable. Before the development of irrigation, fertilizers, and plow agriculture, land became less fertile with each crop and had to be left fallow for a number of years. Tribes who lived by this type of swidden agriculture had constantly to expand into new territory, which made warfare with other groups inevitable. In such cases warfare could be regarded as an adaptive device. The Iban of Borneo lived in a hardwood forest. Rather than laboriously chopping down trees with stone axes, they took to the river in their canoes and followed the sound of others chopping down trees. When the land was cleared, the Iban attacked and attempted to take over the cleared fields.

The Dugum Dani have a ceremonial type of warfare by which they regulate boundaries with neighboring tribes. The Tsembaga Maring also use warfare as means of expansion into new territories. However, there are dangers implicit in the use of warfare as adaptive technique. The Yanomamö are almost constantly at war with some of their neighbors and in tentative alliance with others. They, too, have the need to expand territory, but they also fight to get wives. Hostility among the Yanomamö is at such a high level that they must be said to actively cultivate aggression among males. As a result, the society is constantly on the verge of fission. Some anthropologists have suggested that alternatives to warfare might be found in aggressive sport and games. This implies that warfare channels aggression. It has recently been shown that those societies which practice warfare also encourage violence in sports and entertainment.

See also Aggression; Feuding; Revolution

Consult: Curle, Adam, *Making Peace* (New York: Harper & Row, 1972); Fried, M., Harris,

*Aymará Indian family constructing a reed boat on the shores of Lake Titicaca, Bolivia. The pattern of the boat is several thousand years old and was developed by the Uros Indians, who still live on artificially constructed floating reed islands today.*

M., and Murphy, R., *War* (Garden City, N.Y.: Natural History Press, 1968); Harris, Marvin, *Cows, Pigs, Wars and Witches* (New York: Random House, 1974); Harrison, Robert, *Warfare* (Minneapolis: Burgess, 1973); Sipes, Richard G., "War, Sports and Agression: An Empirical Test of Two Rival Theories," *American Anthropologist* 75(1), 1973.

—*Evelyn S. Kessler, University of South Florida*

## Warner, William Lloyd (1898–1970).

This American social anthropologist is noted for his work on tribal kinship systems in Australia and for his pioneering studies of modern urban communities, in which he especially tried to isolate the components that enter into differentiating social classes.

## Washburn, Sherwood L. (b. 1911).

Washburn has been president of the American Association of Physical Anthropology and the American Anthropological Association. He has made major contributions to the study of human evolution by emphasizing the function of anatomical structures in interpreting fossils and the use of field studies of primate behavior to gain functional understanding of anatomy and to develop models for the behavior of extinct hominid forms. He has also stressed the use of experiments in analyzing behavior and structural-functional complexes of anatomy.

## Watercraft.

Watercraft were surely in use 25,000 years ago when humans crossed the deep-water channel between mainland SE Asia and the island of Australia–New Guinea. For almost 20,000 years there is no archaeological clue to the kinds of watercraft in use, but the appearance of human beings on islands far from the mainland and the bones of deep-water fish found in village sites attest to the effectiveness of the unknown

craft. In Europe, a paddle from Star Carr (Yorkshire) dates back to 7500 BC.

The development of efficient water transportation played an important role in the development of riverine civilizations since boats could move large quantities of goods, including food, with very little expenditure of human labor. In Egypt and Mesopotamia, the boat was probably the single most important means of transport. Such New World civilizations as Tiahuanaco, Teotihuacan, and Tenochtitlan probably used boats to obtain supplies.

**Natural Craft.** The earliest watercraft were possibly nothing more than a large log or a natural raft of wood or rushes that was large enough and solid enough to sit on or hang onto. Once the utility of such natural craft was recognized, improvements could be made by adding wood and lashing it together. Such simple rafts were used by the ancient Egyptians to haul those massive stones from which pyramids were constructed. Rafts are still favored by many peoples to move bulky goods over calm waters.

**Dugout Canoes.** The improvement of the log into a dugout canoe was more difficult because the technology required fire and adze work as well as considerable patience. Nevertheless, this was accomplished by 6400 BC in Europe, and dugout canoes on the Mississippi and Amazon Rivers contributed to the spread of cultures along these waterways. Near Honduras, Christopher Columbus encountered a canoe with twenty-five paddlers transporting cotton goods, obsid-

*New Guinea sailing canoe with outrigger and square-rigged sail, photographed in 1919.*

ian edged swords, and copper ornaments for trade. In the Pacific, dugout canoes were stabilized with single or double *outriggers* which made them safer for ocean travel. With such craft the early Polynesians crossed the Pacific before 1500 BC.

**Reed Boats.** By 3000 BC reed boats were used in Egypt and Sumeria. Such boats were made of bundles of reeds laid horizontally and lashed together terminating in an upturned, pointed bow and stern. Early drawings suggest that square-rigged sails on a bipod as well as paddles and poles were used to propel these boats. In America, reed boats were used on the north coast of Peru by the time of Christ and similar boats are still used on mountain lakes in Ecuador, Peru, and Bolivia. Marsh Arabs also use reed boats which they cover with pitch to keep the reeds from becoming waterlogged. There are severe limitations to the use of reed boats. Boats that are too long or too heavily laden will break their backs in rough water. The virtual absence of freeboard makes them easy to capsize in rough water. Therefore reed boats are generally limited to use on rivers and lakes, although Thor Heyerdahl did prove that one could cross the Atlantic Ocean (with enough help).

**Frame Boats.** Boats with wooden or bone frames covered with skins were used in Europe by 3000 BC as evidenced by their appearance in Norwegian rock art. Frame boats are still favored by the Eskimo, who make two types: the open, flat-bottomed *umiak* for ocean hunting with a crew of six to ten men and the one-man *kayak* with deck covered fore and aft to carry game and for speed on inland waters.

**Plank Boats.** Wooden boats made of planks sewed together edge to edge (rather than overlapped), and without keel or ribs to add strength, were made by the Egyptians by 2500 BC. Initially, the rowers sat on separate stools rather than fixed benches (which would have given them greater mechanical advantage). Within 500 years, Knossos dominated Mediterranean trade with boats 60 to 75 feet long, propelled by rowers on benches and square-rigged sails.

Consult: Driver, Harold E., *Indians of North America* (Chicago: University of Chicago Press, 1961); Hodges, Henry, *Technology in the Ancient World* (London: Allen Lane, 1970); Wooley, Sir Leonard, *History of Mankind: Cultural and Scientific Development*, vol. 1 (New York: Mentor Books, 1965).

—*Thomas P. Myers, University of Nebraska*

**Watersorting.** *See* Digging instruments.

**Watson, James Bennett** (b. 1918). A student of cultural ecology, sociocultural change, and primitive and peasant economic systems, Watson has conducted research in Melanesia and Latin America.

**Weapons.** Weapons are one class of tools aiding human groups in adapting to their environment so as to satisfy diverse biosocial needs. On the one hand, weapons increase the efficiency of the quest for wild foods and related raw materials such as skins. Yet, it must be noted, human ingenuity is also applied to the realm of aggression.

Like other tools, weapons can be classified as to form and function. With regard to form, one basic distinction is that between simple tools and compound tools—the latter have more than one component. This principle of classification, for example, is generally applicable to the bow. The simple self-bow, a solid stave, was used throughout much of the aboriginal world. Notable examples include the Andamanese S-shaped bow and the Siriono longbow attaining a length of over 9 feet. The compound bow, composed of partially overlapping lengths of one or more types of material, was a response to the scarcity of long pieces of elastic material in certain environments, such as the arctic.

Perhaps the best way to understand weapons is in terms of their mode of use and effects as piercers, crushers, and entanglers. These effects can be produced with hand weapons, projectiles, or self-acting devices. Thus the effect of piercing can be produced with a dagger, a blowgun dart, or a (concealed) spike; a crushing blow can be produced with a hand club, a sling stone, or a deadfall trap; an object may be entangled with a hand net, a bola, a lasso, or a staked snare. More than one type of impact or effect may be produced with the same device. A battle-ax can crush as well as cut or pierce. New Guinea "man-catchers," as well as many fish spears and burrow probes, are designed both to surround and to pierce.

*Jivaro Indians from the Peruvian Amazon region carrying their blowguns. Notice the quiver of darts hanging from the boy's neck. Two darts have been prepared for immediate use by adding wadding to their ends. This increases firing pressure by preventing the air that forces the dart through the blowgun from escaping.*

Offensive weapons of war should be distinguished from defensive weapons. The contrast is provided here mainly to draw attention to the special function of defensive devices, since these, unlike many primitive offensive weapons, do not have counterparts in the weaponry of subsistence. Weapons of defense include those which offer protection for the individual and those which furnish cover for several people. For the individual's protection, shields, body armor, and parrying devices are employed. Protection for more than one person is provided by movable screens and large shields and by fixed defenses such as earthworks, pile dwellings, and various other fortifications.

Technological innovations like the barb, the detachable head, and the spear-thrower increased the effectiveness of simple weapons. Modifications of piercers,

*Australian Aborigine about to hurl his handmade, sharp-pointed spear with the aid of a spear-thrower. The tool in effect extends the hunter's reach, thus enabling him to increase velocity but also limiting accuracy to 100 feet.*

crushers, entanglers, and defensive implements have given rise to specialized forms suitable for a particular type of warfare or hunting pursuit. The short and powerful Turkish compound bow was a war weapon adapted to the needs of the horseman. The shaft of a type of parrying shield from the Eastern Solomons was used to deflect javelins while its feather-shaped blade protected the back of the head. The design of the Australian aborigine boomerang, a truly specialized throwing club, allows for a high degree of flight control. Certain Eskimo thrusting harpoons utilize the principle of the ball and socket and that of the toggle. In parts of South America and Melanesia, blunt arrowheads are used to stun birds with valuable plumage. !Kung San (Bushman) arrows and Sakai blowgun darts kill by the action of a poison applied to (or behind) the point, rather than by penetration itself. In colder regions, the development of untended devices receives special attention. Ingenuity and an appreciation of physical principles are reflected in an Eskimo version of a wolf trap in which the animal's own body heat triggers a sharp baleen spring embedded in a piece of frozen meat.

*See also* Atlatl; Bow and arrow; Fishing; Harpoon; Hunting; Spear; Warfare
—*Seth Schindler, Southern Illinois University*

**Weaving.** See Textiles.

**Weber, Max** (1864–1920). This German sociologist is regarded as one of the founders of modern sociology. Weber has had a lasting influence as a result of his theoretical writings and his investigations into the relationship between belief systems and economic development.

Weber strongly contested the Marxist concept of universal economic determinism and contended that belief systems could, under appropriate circumstances, influence the economic order. His exhaustive studies of the world religions led to his famous thesis that the "Protestant ethic" has been an important factor in the development of capitalism in Europe.

To Weber, the key process in the modern world was what he termed "rationalization" —the substitution of calculated, formal rules of procedure for earlier spontaneous, rule-of-thumb methods. The world, Weber argued, was being "disenchanted" by this process and he analyzed bureaucracy as an example of the rationalization of human behavior to meet impersonal goals.

Weber's methodological writings, which emphasized the importance of a value-free stance on the part of the investigator—while recognizing that true objectivity is virtually impossible—have also been extremely influential in Western social science.

*See also* Bureaucracy; Protestant ethic, capitalism and
—*Ian Robertson, Cambridge University*

**Weidenreich, Franz** (1873–1948). An anatomist and physical anthropologist who reconstructed human fossil remains, Weidenreich is known for his descriptive study of Peking man (*Sinanthropus pekinensis*).

*See also* Homo erectus

**Weinreich, Urial** (1926–1967). This Polish-born linguist was educated and taught at Columbia University. His research dealt with the Yiddish language and folklore, semantic theory, and bilingualism.

**Weltanschauung.** *See* World view.

**Westermarck, Edward** (1853–1936). A sociologist, philosopher, and anthropologist who studied marriage customs and the history of morals, Westermarck is best known for *The Origin and Development of Moral Ideas* (1924–1926).

**Wheel.** One of the most important human inventions, the wheel is basically a round device attached to an axle which minimizes friction and transforms rotary to linear motion. Originally of solid wood with fixed axles, the wheel developed in Mesopotamia and Egypt about 3400 BC. There it was at first little used for travel or transporting goods, more so for war. In the New World the wheel was unknown except for a child's pull-along toy in Mesoamerica.

*See also* Land transport

**Wheeler, Sir Mortimer** (b. 1890). A British archaeologist who introduced rigorous field techniques into archaeology, Wheeler is known for his research on the Indus civilization and on Roman sites in Britain.

**White, Leslie Alvin** (1900–1975). It was White who almost single-handedly reintroduced the concept of cultural evolution back into cultural anthropology. He has profoundly influenced the thinking of an important school of anthropology by viewing culture as adaptation and as a system for producing and controlling energy. Furthermore, he has concentrated on the evolution of culture in general as opposed to particular cultures—what his disciples call general as opposed to specific evolution. Among his most influential books is *The Evolution of Culture* (1959).

*See also* Cultural evolution; Evolution, general

**Whiting, John Wesley Mayhew** (b. 1908). A cultural anthropologist who has pioneered research in psychological anthropology, Whiting is the coauthor of a classic cross-cultural study of child training and personality. Moreover, he has directed massive comparative research on child-rearing in six cultures.

**Whorf, Benjamin Lee** (1897–1941). This American anthropological linguist is noted for his theoretical and empirical work on Native American languages.

Although he was originally trained as an engineer, Whorf was profoundly influenced by the linguistic theories of Edward Sapir and devoted most of his professional career to the study of language. With Sapir, he developed the theory of *linguistic relativity* (often known as the Sapir-Whorf hypothesis), which asserts that every language is a representation of the reality of those who speak it. The speakers of different languages are therefore predisposed to perceive reality in different ways in accordance with the different linguistic resources (categories and grammatical relationships) available to them.

Whorf also made major contributions to the classification of Native American languages and was the first investigator to recognize that Mayan hieroglyphs constituted a fully developed system of writing.

*See also* Language and culture; Language and reality

—*Ian Robertson, Cambridge University*

**Whorf-Sapir Hypothesis.** *See* Language and culture.

**Wife-Lending.** This form of hospitality is found among egalitarian band-level societies in which a man would loan his wife to a stranger for the night or to a friend or kinsman for a longer period. This practice, which is found among a number of Eskimo societies, is an example of the great value the Eskimo places on sharing and generosity. If he were asked, a husband would be obligated to give his consent for the occasional sharing of his wife. Wife-lending shades into a form of polyandry, as when two brothers share one woman for a considerable period. Such cases were probably an expedient, when a younger brother had not yet been able to acquire a wife.

Wife-lending practices are generally correlated with a number of other structural conditions. In general, it is found in societies in which there is a great need for the reduction of jealousy among group members in order for the smooth enactment of social relationships to take place. In such societies, a number of goods are shared and circulated, usually before one asks for them. Reciprocity is a general social adhesive. Divorce is usually easy and sex regarded with fewer inhibitions than among Western societies. Contrary to popular beliefs, however, the system does not exist to humiliate women, since women among the Copper Eskimo, for example, are reported to endorse the system as much as the men.

*See also* Etiquette; Polyandry; Sharing

**Wife-Sharing.** *See* Wife-lending.

**Willey, Gordon R.** (b. 1913). Willey is a major figure in New World prehistory and archaeological theory. His primary works have synthesized the cultural development of the entire pre-Columbian New World.

**Wilson, Monica** (b. 1908). Social anthropologist recognized for her extensive research on the rituals and age villages of the Nyakyusa of Central Africa.

**Winkelmann, Johann Joachim** (1717–1768). A Prussian-born historian of classical art, Winkelmann worked with the art of Greece and Rome and believed in using artifacts, as well as written documents, to learn about ancient cultures.

**Wire.** *See* Metalworking.

**Wissler, Clark** (1870–1947). An American anthropologist, Wissler was instrumental in initiating many anthropological fieldwork expeditions as researcher/curator at the American Museum of Natural History; and as a teacher he led the way in promoting and popularizing anthropology as a social science discipline. His best-known work is *The American Indian* (1917), a comprehensive compilation of information for its time which remains a landmark in American anthropology.

**Witchcraft.** This term refers to the human performance of evil by means of transhuman power vested in the performer. It is usually distinguished from sorcery in that the latter may be learned whereas the capacity for witchcraft is intrinsic. Unlike magic, which

*Witchcraft; the use of magic in order to control the behavior of another person or group of persons. Shown here is an Australian Aborigine engaged in "bone pointing," a practice which mobilizes spiritual energy, then channels it in such a way as to inflict damage on an enemy from a distance.*

may be used either for good or for evil, witchcraft is always harmful. In some cases a person may be a witch without knowing it and do harm without intending it. Since accusations of witchcraft are difficult to refute, they are a ready means of finding scapegoats. It has been suggested that witchcraft beliefs indicate stress within a society.

> See also Magic; Magic and witchcraft; Religion; Social control

**Wittfogel, Karl A.** (b. 1896). A German-born economic historian, Wittfogel was originally inspired by Marx's formulation of an "Asiatic mode of production." Wittfogel theorized that the state evolved as a form of social organization in adaptive response to the need for centralized irrigation, especially in Asian agricultural societies. His conceptual work on what he calls "Oriental despotism" has had a pronounced influence on anthropological scholarship dealing with the state level of sociopolitical evolution.

> See also Irrigation; Oriental despotism; State, the

**Wolf, Eric Robert** (b. 1923). This Austrian-born cultural anthropologist is a major theorist—especially on peasant organization and the study of complex societies—and a specialist on Latin America and Europe.

**Wolpoff, Milford** (b. 1942). A physical anthropologist from the University of Michigan and a leading proponent of the single-species hypothesis for the australopithecines, Wolpoff is known for his exacting application of statistics in the interpretation of the fossil record.

**Women, Exchange of.** In certain primitive societies, specified descent groups supply each other with women for marriage and procreation. This exchange takes two forms. The first is direct or symmetrical exchange between two groups (wife-givers and wife-takers)—for example, group A gives women to B, group B gives women to A. The second is indirect or asymmetrical exchange involving at least three groups in which women are given—that is, A → B → C → A.

The exchange of women—as the basis of complex structures of marriage and descent studied extensively in anthropology—is based on the principle of exogamy (outmarriage) by which primitive tribes have chosen to marry their potential enemies rather than kill or be killed by them. Such an arrangement may be viewed as the original form of scarce goods exchange which joins groups in an alliance.

> See also Alliance; Descent; Family, the; Marriage
> Consult: Fox, Robin, *Kinship and Marriage: An Anthropological Perspective* (Baltimore: Penguin, 1967).

**Women, Power of.** The influence, force, or authority vested in women (as contrasted with men) may be related to special position, skills, or influence in kinship structure (such as the female matrilineage head on Truk), in political office (such as Golda Meir or Indira Gandhi), in economic capacity (such as market women of W Africa), in property ownership (such as Hopi women), or in religious role (such as the female shaman of the arctic)—but usually not in a physical sense. Attention is often focused on domestic power (the threat of sexual denial, gossip, verbal power tactics) and relations of women. Usually this power is considered as one aspect of the larger questions related to bio-socio-cultural differences and relations between the sexes and in contrast to male dominance in all spheres of human activity.

Recent studies in anthropology and sociology have focused on three common theses: sex differences (biological, psychological, socialization, cultural); sex role studies; and sexual stratification. In the latter view, women are regarded as occupying minority status (i.e., prejudiced against, segregated) and competing for statuses equal to men in all areas.

In anthropology, interest in the topic was initiated by early evolutionists of the middle and late 19th century, such as Bachofen, Morgan, and Briffault, who argued that matriarchy was the earliest form of kinship structure. Except for a brief resurgence in interest during the women's struggle for suffrage in the United States, only occasional research was reported on this subject until the work of Mead and others rekindled concern in the 1940s and 1950s. The women's liberation movement of the 1970s has also promoted this concern.

*See also* Power

Consult: Rosaldo, M. Z., and Lamphere, Louise (eds.), *Woman, Culture and Society* (Stanford: Stanford University Press, 1974); Stoll, Clarice Stasz, *Female and Male: Socialization, Social Roles and Social Structure* (Dubuque, Iowa: Brown, 1974).

—*Suzanne Reber Griffin, Catholic University*

**Wood.** The earliest manufactured tools probably were made of wood. Even some of our nonhuman relations, the chimpanzees, sometimes modify sticks into ant-catching tools. A yew wood spearpoint recovered near London is the oldest wooden tool yet found: it is more than 200,000 years old. Associated with it were crude stone tools of the Clactonian tradition, including spokeshaves which were probably used for shaping wooden artifacts. In Germany, a wooden spear more than 7 feet (2.1 meters) long, with fire-sharpened wooden point, was

*The Women's movement has gained much support in the past few years. Through organization, women have been able to delegalize some forms of prejudice. Specific strides have been made in the economic situations of women.*

found in the ribcage of an extinct elephant. This German spear was associated with Levalloisian tools. During the Middle Paleolithic people learned to make composite tools by fixing a stone spearpoint into a wooden shaft, probably by fitting it into a slot where it was fixed with resin or beeswax and then bound with leather or bark to give added strength. Bows and arrows have been found in Mesolithic deposits. Pointed stone tools with wooden hafts, such as knives, drills, and scrapers, were common in the Upper Paleolithic. Backed points were also mounted end to end in wooden handles to provide a continuous cutting edge during this period.

Wood is also the fundamental architectural material. Gorillas make sleeping nests by bending boughs together. Early in human history our ancestors learned that the strength and flexibility of poles permitted them to be bent into a series of arches which would support a covering of skin, brush, or bark. Later, post and lintel construction was developed in wood long before it was copied in such megalithic Bronze Age structures as Stonehenge.

Wood is also combustible. With fire, people could modify their environment by producing warmth in the cold. They could frighten animals away with a bright, roaring fire or attract them to investigate the dull, gleaming coals which would bring them close enough for hunters to make an easy kill. They could set brush fires to drive animals over cliffs, into marshes, or into enclosures. Long into the industrial age, wood continued to be the essential fuel.

The properties of wood which make it adaptable to such a wide range of uses are its relatively high tensile and compressive strength and its range of elasticity. Different kinds of wood have a considerable variation in toughness, tensile strength, weight, and permeability. Wood has a natural range of adaptability to various purposes that was not matched by metals until the 19th century. Its sheer size was unique in nature. No other material that could be employed by early groups was so large. When large, open windows became the fashion in Europe during the 16th century, wood was still the material used to provide the span, just as it had been in earlier ages.

Wood was until recently the most shapable of all materials that have been employed in human technology. It could be split into long slabs with tools as simple as a wooden mallet and wedges, and it could be shaped across the grain by simple stone tools. Ordinarily, primitive people approached the manufacture of a wooden tool more directly than their modern counterparts. Rather than starting with a board of standard dimensions, technologically simple groups went into the forest to find a branch or a tree which approximated the shape of the desired product.

To be useful, many pieces of wood must be reduced either by splitting with a *mallet and wedges* or by *sawing*, a technique which did not become common in Europe until the Middle Ages. Shaping into final form could be done with an *ax* for cross-cutting wood, with an *adze* for smoothing and hollowing, with a *chisel* for fine work, or with *fire* for rough shaping accompanied by periodic scraping to expose fresh wood.

Wood was more often bent by primitive artisans than by modern woodworkers. Flexible green wood could be bent into a considerable variety of shapes simply by bending it and keeping the piece in that position until it dried. Dried wood could be soaked to approximate the properties of fresh-cut wood. Many circular boxes and drums were shaped in this manner.

*See also* Architecture; Clactonian culture; Levalloisean tradition; Mesolithic; Middle Paleolithic; Paleolithic

Consult: Hawkes, Jacquetta, *History of Mankind: Cultural and Scientific Development*, vol. 1, pt. 1 (New York: Mentor Books, 1965); Hodges, Henry, *Artifacts: An Introduction to Early Materials and Technology* (London: Baker, 1964); Oakley, Kenneth P., *Man the*

| Earliest Pictographs (3000 BC) | Denotation of Pictographs | Pictographs in Rotated Position | Cuneiform Signs ca. 1900 BC | Basic Logographic Values | | Additional Logographic Values | | Syllabary (Phonetic Values) |
|---|---|---|---|---|---|---|---|---|
| | | | | Reading | Meaning | Reading | Meaning | |
| | Head and body of a man | | | lú<br>lú | man<br>man | | | |
| | head with mouth indicated | | | ka | mouth | kiri₃<br>zú<br>gú<br>dug₄<br>inim | nose<br>teeth<br>voice<br>to speak<br>word | ka<br>zú |
| | bowl of food | | | ninda | food, bread | níg<br>gar | thing<br>to place | |
| | mouth + food | | | kú | to eat | šagar | hunger | |
| | stream of water | | | a | water | duru₅ | moist | a |
| | mouth + water | | | nag | to drink | emmen | thirst | |
| | fish | | | kua | fish | | | ku₆<br>ha |
| | bird | | | mušen | bird | | | hu<br>pag |
| | head of an ass | | | anše | ass | | | |
| | ear of barley | | | še | barley | | | še |

*Evolution of Sumerian writing is outlined in this chart. The earliest pictographs were inscribed vertically on tablets. Around 2800 BC the direction of this writing was changed from vertical to horizontal, with a corresponding rotation of the pictographs. The pictographs were now reduced to collections of linear strokes made by a stylus, which had a triangular point. Some of these cuneiform signs are logographic, i.e., each sign represents a spoken word. Some of the signs represent more than one word; some are syllabic, i.e., they also represent syllables. The accents and subscript numbers on the modern transliteration of the cuneiform signs are used by modern scholars to distinguish between signs having the same pronunciation but different meanings. In the chart at right are 15 cuneiform words, their transliteration, and their English translation (adapted from Scientific American).*

*Tool-Maker* (Chicago: University of Chicago Press, 1959); Spier, R. F. G., *From the Hand of Man: Primitive and Preindustrial Technologies* (Boston: Houghton Mifflin, 1970).
—*Thomas P. Myers, University of Nebraska*

**Words.** This term has several meanings: minimal permutable signs bearing meaning (in Louis Hjelmslev's theory of glossematics); elements in a level of structure (e.g., at the lexicological level of stratificational grammar); or a type of vocabulary item appearing as constituents of phrases and sentences (e.g., in transformational grammar). A simple word consists of and is isomorphic with a root morpheme—e.g., *fair*. A complex word consists of a root morpheme and one or more affixes—e.g., *unfairness*. A compound word consists of at least two root morphemes—e.g., *fallout*. Words are distinguished from other linguistic elements by phonological features (stress, tones, juncture) and by categorical features governing the occurrence of words in phrases and sentences.

*See also* Grammar; Language; Morpheme; Sentences

**Work.** *See* Labor.

**World View (Weltanshauung).** Anthropologists use this term to refer to the corpus of beliefs about the world shared by the members of a society and represented in their myths, lore, ceremonies, social conduct, and general values. The very vastness of the field of study involved in the concept has made anthropological case studies of world views extremely difficult. Redfield attempted such a study in his work with the peasants of the Yucatan in Mexico, but died before completing his research. Mendelson has usefully subdivided the concept of a world view into three aspects: *cognitive systems,* which are the most abstract and are articulated in religion or ideology; *attitude systems,* which refer to behavior and are articulated in codes of conduct; and *action systems,* which provide explanations of social action. The concept remains a nebulous one, however, although the development of cognitive anthropology may lead to a more precise breakdown of its components. It is also necessary to recognize that members of a society may have somewhat different world views according to their position in the network of social relations.

*See also* Culture and personality; Emics; Language and culture

**Writing.** In the broadest sense, writing is communication by means of a system of conventional graphic symbols which may be carved, incised, impressed, painted, drawn, or printed in a wide variety of media. This definition would include many symbol systems not normally thought of as writing—property marks, heraldic devices, astronomical and numerical notations, mnemonic devices, even art styles. True writing is more commonly considered a surrogate for language—a system of graphic signs which conveys the equivalent of spoken communication. While it is useful to investigate the relationships between writing systems and the languages they represent, it is also important to maintain the distinction. The letters of the alphabet, commonly referred to as the basic units of language, are in fact secondary symbols which represent, imperfectly, the basic units of sound. No matter how intimate the relationship, a writing system is secondary and distinct from the primary symbol system—language.

Although large-scale complex cultures have developed without true writing systems—the Inca empire of the Andes is the outstanding example—writing has always been considered the hallmark of civilization. Writing permits the displacement of communication in time and space, transcending some of the limitations on spoken communication. It is enormously important in facilitating such aspects of complex cultures as statecraft, large-scale and long-distance commerce, and particularly the accumulation of many varieties of knowledge. The appearance of writing marks the beginning of history proper and opens new avenues for understanding the past. Beyond the specific information contained in documents, writing systems are rich sources of information about language change in general, about the history of specific languages, and about the structures of past languages. This information may reflect much about aspects of culture, such as conceptual categories and systems of classifying experience, which are difficult or even impossible to reconstruct in other ways.

Writing systems are usually classified according to the predominant type of sign. It is useful to distinguish *pictographic, ideographic, logographic,* and *phonetic* symbolic principles, but they do not represent inevitable stages in the development of writing. Few writing systems are pure types; most utilize several of these principles.

Pictographic signs are recognizable pictorial representations; although they may be highly stylized, there is a clear representational link between the symbol and the meaning. The difficulty in representing abstractions—such as love, honor, truth—pictographically places definite limitations on a purely pictographic writing system. Pictographs represent things, not linguistic forms. If the conventions are understood, they can be read in any language.

Ideographs represent things or ideas, though not necessarily pictorially. Ideographic signs may be pictographic in origin, but they usually have broader ranges of meaning: a circular ideograph might stand for light, heat, day, and a sun deity as well as for the sun itself. Ideographs involve a closer relationship with language than pictographs in that the extensions of meaning assigned to the symbols follow the semantic domains of a language. Ideographs are not always language-specific, however; the largely ideographic Chinese script is used to represent a number of mutually unintelligible dialects.

Logographs represent not ideas but the spoken linguistic forms (words) for them. Logographic symbols have an intimate relationship with a language.

Writing systems which depend heavily or exclusively on any one of these three

| Cuneiform signs | Transliteration | Translation |
|---|---|---|
| | ama-ar-gi₄ | freedom |
| | arḫuš | compassion |
| | dingir | god, goddess |
| | dub-sar | scribe |
| | é-dub-ba | school, academy |
| | ḫé-gál | plenty, prosperity |
| | me | divine laws |
| | nam-lú-lu₇ | humanity, humaneness |
| | nam-lugal | kingship |
| | nam-tar | fate, destiny |
| | níg-ga | property |
| | níg-ge-na | truth |
| | níg-si-sá | justice |
| | sag-gíg | black-headed ones, the Sumerian people |
| | ukkin | assembly |

principles—pictograph, ideograph, logograph—are subject to "overloading": unless the range of information to be represented is narrowly limited, a tremendously large number of signs is required. The phonetic principle removes this limitation. When the graphic signs represent the sounds of linguistic forms rather than the forms themselves, the writing system shows duality of patterning: the signs themselves do not carry meaning—they are combined to represent meaningful sound combinations. This permits economy in the number of signs required, since all languages have many fewer units of sound than units of meaning. A simple application of the phonetic principle is *rebus writing*—a kind of graphic punning in which the sounds of the linguistic forms for objects represented by pictorial signs convey the message. When the graphic symbols represent still smaller units of sound, as in *syllabic* systems, greater economy can be achieved. The common syllables of most languages can be represented by fewer than a hundred signs. *Alphabetic* writing systems, in which the graphic signs represent individual consonant and vowel sounds, are the most economical, requiring no more than thirty signs. Rebus writing is entirely language-specific. Syllabic and alphabetic systems, in which the relationship between symbol and sound is arbitrary, are relatively easily adaptable for the representation of different languages if they have similar sound systems.

Writing appears quite late in human history. The earliest recognizable graphic symbols, which appear in the art and astronomical notation of the Upper Paleolithic period, deal with a relatively narrow range of subject matter and certainly do not constitute a full writing system. True writing first appears in the Near East in the 4th millennium BC. The evidence, although incomplete, suggests a pictographic system. The earliest well-known writing systems—the Mesopotamian cuneiform and Egyptian hieroglyphic scripts, which appear at the end of the 4th millennium BC—are mixed systems utilizing pictographic, ideographic, and phonetic principles. They may have a common origin in the earlier Mesopotamian pictographic writing; certainly the many later scripts of western Asia are ultimately related to them. Syllabic and alphabetic writing systems appear in the Near East in the 2nd millennium BC. The Indus Valley script of the late 3rd and early 2nd millennia BC has not

been deciphered; its nature and relationships are unknown.

The largely ideographic Shang script, which appears in North China in the 2nd millennium BC, in all probability represents an entirely independent development of writing in eastern Asia. It is ancestral to the modern Chinese writing system.

Maya hieroglyphic writing is the only full, general-purpose writing system which developed in the New World. Like the early Near Eastern scripts it is a mixed system with ideographic, logographic, and phonetic signs. Other Mesoamerican peoples had partial writing systems: the Aztecs of central Mexico used a form of rebus writing to represent place names and personal names, and complex systems of calendrical and astrological symbols were in use throughout Mesoamerica.

See also Alphabet; Astronomy, primitive; Champollion, Jean François; Civilization, origins of; Codex; Cuneiform script; Hieroglyphic writing; Language; Language and thought; Maya; Rosetta Stone; Syllabary; Symbol; Upper Paleolithic art
Consult: Diringer, David, *Writing* (London: Thames & Hudson, 1962); Diringer, David, *The Alphabet: A Key to the History of Mankind*, 3rd ed. (London: Hutchinson, 1968); Gelb, I. J., *A Study of Writing*, rev. ed. (Chicago: University of Chicago Press, 1963).
—*John S. Henderson, Cornell University*

**Written Literature.** *See* Literature, written.

**Würm Glaciation.** *See* Glaciations.

**Xenophobia.** This term from the Greek means "fear of the stranger." Its more general use, however, is fear and hatred of the unknown (usually persons or groups of persons). In anthropology, as distinct from psychology, it is thought of as a social-psychological phenomenon rather than a personal neurotic trait. We talk of a certain society, for example, as harboring *xenophobic* tendencies—meaning that members of that society manifest strong suspicion of other societies with which they have had little or no contact. There are, of course, many causes for war, but it is not uncommon for anthropologists to find xenophobia to be among the root causes of out-group hostilities.

**Yeti.** Derived from the Tibetan meaning "foul-smelling snowman," this is the alleged Abominable Snowman of the Himalayas. The majority of the evidence for the yeti's existence consists of eyewitness accounts, mostly by Sherpas living in the region. Very large, humanlike footprints in the snow and even "yeti skins" have also been advanced as evidence. The footprints may be distortions of human or animal footprints caused by melting. And at least two "yeti skins" are from Tibetan bears. *Sasquatch* is a Salish In-

*A yurt being assembled.*

*Ziggurat (terraced temple tower) at Agar Zur in Iraq. Standing in front are, from left, Mr. Sabri Shurri; Dr. Naj al Asil, director general, Iraq's Antiquities; Dr. Samuel Noah Kramer, of the University of Pennsylvania; and Mr. Taha Baqir, curator of the Iraq Museum.*

dian word for the Northwest American version of the yeti who is usually called Bigfoot.

Consult: Napier, John, *Bigfoot* (New York: Dutton, 1972).

—*Martin K. Nickels, Illinois State University*

**Yurt.** Dome-shaped, circular, easily portable tent constructed of heavy felt and used by the nomadic Mongols of Siberia.

*See also* Housing and shelter

**Zero Morpheme.** More properly, this is the zero allomorph, indicated by [∅]. Zero allomorphs are used to indicate that some allomorphs are not marked by any overt phonemic features—as in the difference be-

tween the present and past tenses of English *cut* and *hit*.

*See also* Morpheme

**Ziggurat.** The archaeological remains of ancient Mesopotamian temple towers are called ziggurats. A ziggurat is a terraced pyramid with outside stairways and/or ramps which lead to the top where there is a shrine.

*See also* Cities, development of; Temple

**Zinjanthropus.** *See* Australopithecines.

**Znaniecki, Florian** (1882–1958). A Polish sociologist who contributed to social action theory and functionalism, Znaniecki is also well known for his study of the Polish peasant (*The Polish Peasant in Europe and America*, with W. I. Thomas) in which he traced the changes in, and interrelations between, personality and social structure.

*See also* Culture and personality; Peasants

**Zygote.** *See* Heterozygote; Homozygote.

# Tell us what you think _____

I am   ☐ a student     ☐ an instructor     ☐ other _____

1. Why did you purchase the *Encyclopedia of Anthropology?*

    ☐ It was required for the course.

    ☐ It was recommended for the course.

    ☐ It was required for majors.

    ☐ I saw it in the bookstore and thought it would be useful.

    ☐ Other _____

2. Overall, how do you evaluate the *Encyclopedia of Anthropology?*

    ☐ excellent,     ☐ good,     ☐ fair,     ☐ poor

3. What do you like best about the encyclopedia?

_____

_____

4. How do you feel the book might be improved?

_____

_____

5. What additional articles would you like to see added to the encyclopedia?

_____

_____

6. The graphic material in the encyclopedia consists of photographs, maps, artwork, charts, graphs, diagrams and tables. Do you find this material useful?

    ☐ yes     ☐ no.     How can it be improved? _____

_____

_____

7. General Comments _____

_____

**Personal Information**

    Name _____

    Address _____

    City _____ State _____ Zip _____

    Name of school _____

    City _____ State _____ Zip _____

**If you are a student, please complete the questions below:**

☐ Freshman    ☐ Sophomore    ☐ Junior    ☐ Senior    ☐ Graduate student

Course title for which this book was used _____

Instructor's name _____

What textbook, if any, did you use with the encyclopedia?

    Author(s) _____ Title _____

**Thank you very much.**